# The Content Analysis of Verbal Behavior

## FURTHER STUDIES

**Louis A. Gottschalk, M.D.**
*Department of Psychiatry and Human Behavior*
*College of Medicine*
*University of California*
*Irvine, California*

SP

**SP MEDICAL & SCIENTIFIC BOOKS**
a division of Spectrum Publications, Inc.
New York • London

Distributed by Halsted Press
A Division of John Wiley & Sons

New York Toronto London Sydney

SPECTRUM PUBLICATIONS, INC.
175-20 Wexford Terrace, Jamaica, New York 11432

**Library of Congress Cataloging in Publication Data**

Gottschalk, Louis A.
Content analysis of verbal behavior.

Includes index.

1. Verbal behavior. 2. Content analysis (Communication) 3. Psychopharmacology. 4. Mentally ill—Language. I. Gottschalk, Louis A. [DNLM: 1. Verbal behavior—Collected works. BF455 C761]
BF455.C678 616.8'9'075 7-28623
ISBN 0-89335-047-8

# Contributors


RONALD L. ALKANA, PHARM. D., Ph.D.
Assistant Professor of Pharmacy (Pharmacology)
School of Pharmacy
University of Southern California

WILBERT S. ARONOW, M.D.
Professor of Medicine,
Chief, Cardiovascular Research,
University of California at Irvine
Chief, Cardiovascular Section, and Assistant Chief of Medicine for Research,
Long Beach Veterans Administration Hospital,
Long Beach, California

ROLAND M. ATKINSON, M.D.
Associate Professor of Psychiatry,
University of Oregon School of Medicine;
Staff Psychiatrist, Veterans Administration Hospital,
Portland, Oregon

FRIEDRICH BALCK, M.A.
Department of Psychosomatic Medicine
(Chairman Prof. Dr. Dr. A.-E. Meyer)
II. Med., University of Hamburg, Germany

DANIEL E. BATES, Ph.D
Pyschologist II
Department of Psychiatry and Human Behavior
University of California at Irvine Medical Center
Irvine, California

ANITA I. BELL, M.D.
Practicing Psychoanalyst
New York, New York

ROBERT BIENER, M.D.
Staff Psychiatrist
Canyon General Hospital
Anaheim, California

HERMAN BIRCH, Ph.D.
Assistant Research Psychologist
Department of Psychiatry and Human Behavior
University of California at Irvine
Irvine, California

THOMAS BLASS, Ph.D.
Associate Professor
Department of Psychology
University of Maryland Baltimore County
Baltimore, Maryland

JOHN SEELY BROWN, Ph.D.
Senior Technical Scientist
Bolt Beranek and Newman, Inc.
Cambridge, Massachusetts

CHARLES BUCHWALD, Ph.D.
Assistant Professor
Department of Psychiatry
State University of New York
Downstate Medical Center
Brooklyn, New York

CLAIRE CABLE
Mental Health Worker II
Community Mental Health,
County of Orange
Anaheim, California

JOHN M. CLEGHORN, M.D.
Professor and Chairman
Department of Psychiatry
McMaster University
Hamilton, Ontario, Canada

HARVEY D. COHEN
Senior Biomedical Engineer
Behavioral Science Laboratory Section
Midwest Research Institute
Kansas City, Missouri

LINO COVI, M.D.
Associate Professor of Psychiatry
The Johns Hopkins University School of Medicine
Baltimore, Maryland

EUGENE C. DINOVO, Ph.D.
Chief, Clinical Chemistry
Laboratory Service
Veterans Administration Hospital
Sepulveda, California
Research Consultant
Department of Psychiatry and Human Behavior
University of California at Irvine
Irvine, California

JOHN P. DOCHERTY, M.D.
Director, Psychiatric Research
West Haven V.A. Hospital;
Assistant Professor
Department of Psychiatry
Yale University
New Haven, Connecticut

MANFRED DRUCKE, Dr. MED., DGPPT
Psychotherapist in Private Practice
Heidelberg, Germany

MICHAEL J. ECKARDT, Ph.D.
Research Psychologist
Clinical and Biobehavioral Research Branch
Division of Intramural Research
National Institute on Alcohol Abuse and Alcoholism
Rockville, Maryland

*HENRY W. ELLIOTT, M.D., Ph.D.
Professor and Chairman
Department of Medical Pharmacology and Therapeutics
Lecturer in Anesthesia
University of California at Irvine Medical Center
Orange, California

*DANIEL J. FELDMAN, M.D.
Chief, Alcoholism Treatment Program
Long Beach Veterans Administration Hospital,
Adjunct Professor (Rehabiliatative Medicine)
Department of Psychiatry and Human Behavior
University of California at Irvine
Irvine, California

EUGENE W. FLEMING, Ph. D.
Research Fellow in Ophthalmology
Berman-bund Laboratory
Department of Ophthalmology
Harvard Medical School
Massachusetts Eye and Ear Infirmary
Boston, Massachusetts

RUTH A. FOX, M.D.
Assistant Clinical Professor
Department of Psychiatry and Human Behavior
University of California at Irvine, Medical Center
Orange, California

NORBERT FREEDMAN, Ph.D.
Professor and Director
Clinical Behavior Research Unit
Downstate Medical Center
State University of New York
Brooklyn, New York

GOLDINE C. GLESER, Ph.D.
Professor and Director
Psychology Division
Department of Psychiatry
University of Cincinnati
Cincinnati, Ohio

DONALD R. GOODENOUGH, Ph.D.
Senior Research Psychologist
Division of Psychological Studies
Educational Testing Service
Princeton, New Jersey

LOUIS A. GOTTSCHALK, M.D.
Professor and Chairman
Department of Psychiatry and Human Behavior
University of California at Irvine,
Director, Psychiatric Services
University of California at Irvine Medical Center
Orange, California

STANLEY GRAND, Ph.D.
Clinical Assistant Professor
Associate Director of the Research Training Program in Psychiatry
Downstate Medical Center
Brooklyn, New York

JOHN L. HAER, Ph.D.
Formerly with the Department of Social Relations
Immaculate Heart College
Los Angeles, California
(Present address and affiliation unknown)

CATHERINE HAUSMANN (KATHY MOSS LARKIN)
Computer Scientist
Bolt Beranek and Newman, Inc.
Cambridge, Massachusetts

JON F. HEISER, M.D.
Assistant Adjunct Professor
Department of Psychiatry and Human Behavior
University of California at Irvine, Medical Center
Orange, California

JULIA C. HOIGAARD, B.A.
Staff Research Associate
Communications and Measurement Laboratory
Department of Psychiatry and Human Behavior
University of California at Irvine
Irvine, California

JAMES M. IACONO, Ph.D.
Deputy Assistant Administrator
Agricultural Research Service
U.S. Department of Agriculture
Washington, D.C.

STANLEY KAPLAN, Ph.D.
Associate Director of Biochemistry and Drug Metabolism
Hoffman La-Roche, Inc.
Nutley, New Jersey

FREDERIC T. KAPP, M.D.
Professor of Psychiatry
College of Medicine
University of Cincinnati

ISMET KARACAN, M.D.
Associate Chief of Staff for Research and Education
Veterans Administration Hospital
Houston, Texas,
Professor of Psychiatry
Baylor College of Medicine
Houston, Texas

MARTIN M. KATZ, Ph.D.
Chief, Clinical Research Branch
Division of Extramural Research Programs
National Institute of Mental Health
Rockville, Maryland

JOSEPH G. KEPECS, M.D.
Professor of Psychiatry
University of Wisconsin School of Medicine;
Faculty, Institute for Psychoanalysis
Chicago, Illinois

PETER H. KNAPP, M.D.
Professor and Associate Chairman
Division of Psychiatry
Boston University School of Medicine
Boston, Massachusetts

W. KNAUSS, M.A.
Senior Psychologist
Psychosomatik Clinic, University of Heidelberg
Heidelberg, Germany

UWE KOCH
Department of Psychosomatik Medicine
(Chairman Prof. Dr. Dr. A.-E. Meyer)
II., Med., University of Hamburg, Germany

DAVID KOULACK, Ph.D.
Professor
Department of Psychology
University of Manitoba
Winnipeg, Canada

ROBERT KUNKEL, M.D.
Assistant Clinical Professor of Psychiatry
College of Medicine
University of Cincinnati
Cincinnati, Ohio

F. LAMPRECHT
Dept. of Neurology
Freie Universitat eBerlin
Klinikum Charlottenburg
Germany

HELEN BLOCK LEWIS, Ph.D.
Professor (Adjunct) of Psychology
Yale University
New Haven, Connecticut

F. LOLAS, M.D.
Laboratory of Neuropsychology
Department of Physiology and Biophysics
University of Chile

*ARDIE LUBIN, Ph.D.
Research Psychologist
U.S. Naval Health Research Center
San Diego, California

LESTER LUBORSKY, Ph.D.
Professor of Psychology in Psychiatry
University of Pennsylvania School of Medicine
Philadelphia, Pennsylvania

RONALD W. MANDERSCHEID, M.A.
Research Sociologist
Mental Health Study Center
Naitonal Institute of Mental Health
Rockville, Maryland

REUBEN MARGOLIS, Ph.D.
Director of Psychology
Kings County Hospital Center
Brooklyn, New York;
Associate Professor of Psychiatry
State University of New York
Downstate Medical Center
Brooklyn, New York

ALLAN F. MIRSKY, Ph.D.
Professor of Psychiatry (Neuropsychology) and Neurology
Boston University Medical Center
Boston, Massachusetts

LORENZ K. Y. Ng, M.D.
Research Scientist
National Institute of Mental Health
National Institute on Drug Abuse
Rockville, Maryland

ERNEST P. NOBLE, Ph.D., M.D.
Director, National Institute on Alcohol Abuse and Alcoholism
Rockville, Maryland;
Professor
Department of Psychiatry and Human Behavior
University of California at Irvine (Leave of Absence)
Irvine, California

JAMES E. OLSSON, Ph.D.
Assistant Professor in Clinical Psychology
Institute of Psychiatry & Human Behavior
University of Maryland
Baltimore, Maryland

PATRICIA H. O'NEILL, M.S.N.
Clinical Specialist in Psychiatric Nursing
Mental Health Study Center
National Institute of Mental Health
Rockville, Maryland

ELIZABETH S. PARKER, Ph.D.
Staff Fellow
Clinical and Biobehavioral Branch
Division of Intramural Research
National Institute on Alcohol Abuse and Alcoholism
Rockville, Maryland

JANICE PERLEY, M.S.W.
Formerly with Tufts New England Medical Center
(Present address and affiliation unknown)

CARLOS A. PLACCI, M.D.
Chief of the Outpatient Service
Staff Psychiatrist
Pittsburgh Veterans Administration Hospital;
Pittsburgh, Pennsylvania;
Clinical Assistant Professor of Psychiatry
School of Medicine
University of Pittsburgh Pittsburgh, Pennsylvania

Acting Chief of Cardiology
Associate Professor of Medicine in Cardiology
University of California at Irvine Medical Center
Orange, California

FREDERIC QUITKIN, M.D.
Research Psychiatrist
New York State Psychiatric Institute and College of Physicians and Surgeons

JOSEPH L. RAUH, M.D.
Director, Division of Adolescent Medicine
University of Cincinnati and Children's Hospital Medical Center
Professor of Pediatrics
University of Cincinnati College of Medicine

KARL RICKELS, M.D.
Professor of Human Behavior and Reproduction
Professor of Psychiatry and Pharmacology
University of Pennsylvania, Department of Psychiatry
Philadelphia, Pennsylvania

ARTHUR RIFKIN, M.D.
Director, General Clinical Research Service
New York State Psychiatric Institute;
Faculty, Department of Psychiatry
College of Physicians and Surgeons of Columbia University
New York, New York

EUGENE L. SAENGER, M.D.
Professor of Radiology
Director of the Radioisotope Laboratory
University of Cincinnati
College of Medicine

GERT SCHOFER, M.A.
Department of Psychosomatik Medicine
(Chairman Prof. Dr. Dr. A.-E. Meyer)
II. Med., University of Hamburg, Germany

ROSLYN SELIGMAN, M.D.
Associate Professor of Child and Adolescent Psychiatry
Department of Psychiatry
University of Cincinnati
Cincinnati, Ohio

*A. SHAPIRO, M.D.
Psychiatric Treatment Research Center of the Department of Psychiatry
State University of New York
Downstate Medical Center
Brooklyn, New York

SAM SILBERGELD, Ph.D., M.D.
Senior Research Psychiatrist,
Chief, Biopsychosocial Research Section
Mental Health Study Center
National Institute of Mental Health
Rockville, Maryland

STEVEN STARKER, Ph.D.
Assistant Clinical Professor of Psychology
Yale School of Medicine
New Haven, Connecticut

Gottschalk Contributors Cont.

IRVING STEINGART, Ph.D.
Adjunct Associate Professor
Post-Doctoral Training Program for Specialization in Psychotherapy and Psychoanalysis
New York University
New York, New York

*GORDON E. STOLZOFF, M.D.
Fellow, Child Psychiatry
California College of Medicine
University of California at Irvine
Orange, California

WALTER STONE, M.D.
Professor of Psychiatry
University of Cincinnati College of Medicine
Cincinnati, Ohio

MICHAEL SYBEN, B.A.
Research Assistant
Department of Psychiatry and Human Behavior
University of California at Irvine
Irvine, California

THOMAS C. TODD, Ph.D.
Chief Psychologist & Chief of Service
Putnam Community Services
Harlem Valley Psychiatric Center
Wingdale, New York

ROBERT D. TOLZ, J.D., LL. M.
Practising Attorney
New Jersey

REGINA ULIANA, Ph.D.
Post Graduate Research Psychologist
Communications & Measurement Laboratory
Department of Psychiatry & Human Behavior
University of California at Irvine
Irvine, California

MICHAEL VON RAD, M.D.
DEPUTY CHIEF
Psychosomatic Clinic, University of Heidelberg
Germany

IRENE ELKIN WASKOW, Ph.D.
Research Psychologist
Clinical Research Branch
National Institute of Mental Health
Rockville, Maryland

*EDMUND WEIL, B.A.
Psychology Laboratory and Psychiatric Treatment Research Center
Department of Psychiatry
State University of New York
Downstate Medical Center
Brooklyn, New York

DONALD E. WILBERT, M.D.
Assistant Clinical Professor
Department of Psychiatry and Human Behavior
University of California at Irvine Medical Center
Orange, California

CAROLYN N. WINGET, M.A.
Senior Research Associate
University of Cincinnati Medical Center
College of Medicine
Cincinnati, Ohio

HERMAN A. WITKIN, Ph.D.
Senior Research Psychologist and Chairman,
Personality and Social Behavior Research Group
Educational Testing Service
Princeton, New Jersey

THEODORE H. WOHL, Ph.D.
Director of Psychology
Cincinnati Center for Developmental Disorders
Professor, Department of Psychology,
University of Cincinnati
Cincinnati, Ohio

*Deceased

# Contents

# Introduction

In 1969, two books were published on a method of the measurement of psychological states through the content analysis of verbal behavior (Gottschalk and Gleser, 1969; Gottschalk et al, 1969). One of these books (Gottschalk and Gleser, 1969) gave the rationale, theoretical background, reliability, validity, and applications of this content analysis method, as well as describing further developments of other content analysis scales of a similar type. The other (Gottschalk et al, 1969) was a manual of instructions for using these content analysis scales.

The present collection of papers, some appearing in print for the first time and others previously published, constitute a representative sample of further studies applying this specific method of content analysis, since the publication of those studies reported in the 1969 books. The papers have been classified and arranged according to topical areas, and each such group of papers has been briefly summarized and discussed in introductory sections.

The rationale for organizing such a collection of papers involving

the application of a particular method of content analysis of language is several-fold. Students in the behavioral sciences, social sciences, psychiatry, and other disciplines frequently call or write the author-editor of this book requesting information on further studies using the Gottschalk-Gleser content analysis scales appearing since 1969. The work that has been carried out applying these and related scales have been done in widely disparate fields and, hence, when published have appeared in a wide variety of publications not always readily accessible. Not only students, but also experienced scientists, clinicians, academicians, and individuals from other scholarly fields, have asked to be informed about the details of new or further applications of this content analysis procedure. And people totally unfamiliar with this unique method of measuring psychological states or traits may be desirous of having available for reference an organized collection of selected papers using this method. Finally, these papers deal with subjects that are in the forefront of interest among the behavioral and social sciences, psychiatry, neurology, neuropsychopharmacology, psychosomatic medicine, and other medical sciences. The reader can get an introduction from perusing these papers what the issues are, who is working in the area, what are the methodological problems, what have been the technological and research approaches, what has been learned, where can one find out more about the subject, and what additional studies are needed?

References:

Gottschalk, L.A., and Gleser, G. The Measurement of Psychological States Through the Content Analysis of Verbal Behavior. University of California Press, Berkeley, Los Angeles (1969).

Gottschalk, L.A., Winget, C.N., and Gleser, G.C. Manual of Instructions for Using the Gottschalk-Gleser Content Analysis Scales: Anxiety, Hostility, and Social Alienation-Personal Disorganization. University of California Press, Berkeley, Los Angeles (1969).

The Content Analysis of

# Verbal Behavior

FURTHER STUDIES

# Part I

# The Development of New Content Analysis Scales or Further Validation Studies on Previously Developed Content Analysis Scales

This section, divided in two parts - Adult Studies and Children Studies, gives new reliability and validity studies on a Hope scale, Chapter 1, entitled "A hope scale applicable to verbal samples" (Gottschalk, 1974). It also includes a preliminary report on further validation studies of the Cognitive and Intellectual Impairment scale, in Chapter 2, entitled "Further validation studies of the Cognitive and Intellectual Impairment scale derived from verbal samples" (Gottschalk et al, 1977). Another chapter in this group compares scores obtained with a content analysis method as compared to self report and rating scales and this chapter (3) is entitled "The measurement of psychological states: relationship between Gottschalk-Gleser content analysis scores, and Hamilton Anxiety Rating Scale scores, Physician Questionnaire Rating Scale score and Hopkins Symptom Checklist scores" (Gottschalk et al, 1976).

A subsection of this portion of the book is devoted to a set of two outstanding and original papers, heretofore unpublished, involving the use of the Gottschalk-Gleser content analysis scales by a German group of

investigators from the University of Hamburg, (Schöfer et al, 1977) on large samples of German-speaking subjects. These papers are so unique that special commentaries have been written for each of these chapters. The chapters (4 and 5) in this section contributed by Schöfer and his coworkers are entitled "The Gottschalk-Gleser content analysis of speech: a normative study (the relationship of hostile and anxious affects to sex, sex of the interviewer, socioeconomic class, and age)" and "Test criteria of the Gottschalk-Gleser content analysis of speech: objectivity, reliability, validity in German studies."

# A Hope Scale Applicable to Verbal Samples

Louis A. Gottschalk, MD, Irvine, Calif

**A Hope scale is described, applicable to the content analysis of verbal samples. Percentile Hope scores are provided from a normative sample of children (109), adults (91), and a group of psychiatric outpatients (68).**

**Construct validation studies indicated significant negative correlations between Hope scores and psychiatric ratings from the BPRS Depression and Anergia factor scores, the Hamilton Depression Rating Scale factors of Anxiety-Depression and Sleep Disturbance and, also, with scores from the Jacobs Ego Weakness Scale. Significant positive correlations occurred with scores from the Anant Belongingness Scale.**

**Hope scores were found capable of predicting favorable outcome among patients in a Mental Health Crisis Clinic, survival time in patients with terminal cancer, patients likely to follow treatment recommendations, and improvement in the BPRS Depression factor in acute schizophrenic patients after a single dose of thioridazine.**

The concept of hope has been used widely in the social, behavioral, and medical sciences to denote an optimistic outlook or expectation of a favorable outcome, be it luck in gambling, success in a business venture, improvement in the welfare of a socially deprived subculture, recovery from a serious illness, or the reaching of a spiritual goal.

The converse of hope, namely hopelessness, has been customarily regarded as a symptom of mental depression[1,2] and as a psychological state which is often associated with, if not an etiological factor in, bodily disease.[3-5]

Hope has been viewed as a necessary motivating force in pressuring an individual to overcome inner psychological conflicts and to seek to resolve disabling neurosis or psychosis.[6]

Social workers have noted[7] that the presence of a fair amount of hope (and discomfort) is likely to be associated with a client's following through with a recommendation for social casework or psychiatric therapy. Psychotherapists have observed[8,9] that an attitude of hope or the mobilization of such is often necessary for a successful outcome in psychotherapy.

All these ideas of hope presume or allude to a quantitative dimension. But most of the published works on hope deal primarily with the qualitative aspects of hope rather than provide a means of measuring it.

Preliminary work involving the development of a scale of hope derived from the content analysis of speech was reported by Gottschalk and Gleser.[10] These authors defined their concept of hope (a definition followed in the present report) as follows: A measure of optimism that a favorable outcome is likely to occur, not only in one's personal earthly activities but also in cosmic phenomena and even in spiritual or imaginary events.

## Purpose

The specific purposes of this study were: (1) to examine the interrater reliability in scoring the Gottschalk Hope scale; (2) to obtain some norms for Hope scale scores and intercorrelations with scores for other psychological states; (3) to carry out a preliminary set of construct validation studies using this Hope scale.

## Methods and Procedure

**Subjects.**—For normative groups, both an adult and child sample were obtained. The group of adults was composed of 91 gainfully employed, medically healthy white men and women between the ages of 20 and 50 employed by the Kroger Company, Cincinnati, the characteristics of which sample have been described elsewhere.[11] The group of children was composed of 109 children, white boys and girls from the first through 12th grades, in the Laguna Beach, Calif, school system.

Other subjects were either paid or nonpaid volunteers or psychiatric medical patients from whom five-minute speech samples had been obtained in other studies using the Gottschalk-Gleser[10] method of eliciting and content analyzing speech. These other samples of subjects include: (1) group of medical patients with terminal cancer scheduled to receive radiation treatment[12,13]; (2) a group of psychiatric patients coming to a mental health crisis clinic in Cincinnati,[14] and a similar group coming to such a clinic in Orange, Calif[15]; and (3) a group of male prisoners incarcerated at a penal institution in Patuxent, Md.[16] (4) group of 23 acute schizophrenic patients.[25]

**Method.**—Five-minute speech samples were elicited from the various groups of subjects in response to the following standardized instructions: "This is a study of speaking and conversational habits. I would like you to speak into the microphone of this tape recorder for five minutes about any interesting or dramatic personal life experiences you have ever had. While you are talking I would prefer not to reply to any questions you may have until the five minutes has elapsed. Do you have any questions now? If you have no more questions, you may start speaking now."

These instructions were designed to elicit speech behavior approximating free-association and, at the same time, to minimize the influence of the interviewer's behavior, verbal and nonverbal, in determining the content of the interviewee's speech. The am-

Accepted for publication June 19, 1973.

From the Communication and Measurements Laboratory, Department of Psychiatry and Human Behavior, College of Medicine, University of California, Irvine, Calif.

Reprint requests to the Department of Psychiatry and Human Behavior, College of Medicine, University of California, Irvine, CA 92644 (Dr. Gottschalk).

Table 1.—Percentile Scores for the Hope Scale in a Children's Group by Sex and School Grade

| Per-centile | Sex | | Grades | | | |
|---|---|---|---|---|---|---|
| | Boys | Girls | 0-3 | 4-6 | 7-9 | 10-12 |
| 90 | 1.84 | 1.07 | 1.73 | 0.68 | 1.14 | . . . |
| 75 | 0.61 | 0.56 | 0.73 | 0.37 | 0.34 | . . . |
| 50 | −0.02 | 0.05 | 0.15 | −0.06 | 0.00 | . . . |
| 25 | −0.48 | −0.58 | −0.50 | −0.47 | −0.48 | . . . |
| 10 | −1.81 | −1.29 | −1.37 | −1.26 | −0.91 | |
| Mean | 0.05 | 0.03 | 0.24 | −0.14 | 0.10 | 0.26 |
| SD | 1.38 | 1.17 | 1.44 | 0.93 | 0.98 | 1.93 |
| N | 41 | 68 | 35 | 37 | 20 | 11 |

Table 2.—Percentile Scores for the Hope Scale in a Normative Adult and Mental Health Crisis Clinic Group

| Percentiles | Normative Adult Group | Mental Health Crisis Clinic Group |
|---|---|---|
| | | . . . |
| 95 | 2.63 | . . . |
| 90 | 1.90 | 1.39 |
| 85 | 1.55 | . . . |
| 80 | 1.35 | . . . |
| 75 | 1.19 | 0.16 |
| 70 | 1.08 | . . . |
| 60 | 0.80 | . . . |
| 50 | 0.47 | −0.47 |
| 40 | 0.32 | . . . |
| 30 | 0.16 | . . . |
| 25 | 0.00 | −1.42 |
| 20 | 0.00 | . . . |
| 15 | 0.00 | . . . |
| 10 | −0.16 | −2.21 |
| 5 | −0.54 | . . . |
| | | . . . |
| Mean | 0.73 | −0.45 |
| SD | 1.03 | 1.49 |
| N | 91 | 64 |

biguity of these instructions sets up, to a large extent, a projective test situation to which the speaker reacts in terms of his preferred response-tendencies, both superficial and deep. Moreover, the speaker has no clear understanding what psychological or behavioral states are being assessed by this procedure.[17,18]

The typescripts of these five-minute tape-recorded speech samples were scored for the seven content categories on the Hope scale by content analysis technicians who were uninformed of the sources of the speech samples or the purpose of these studies.

### "Hope" Scale

| *Weights* | *Content Categories and Coding Symbols* |
|---|---|
| +1 H | 1. References to self or others getting or receiving help, advice, support, sustenance, confidence (*a*) from others; (*b*) from self. |
| +1 H | 2. References to feelings of optimism about the present or future (*a*) others; (*b*) self. |
| +1 H | 3. References to being or wanting to be or seeking to be the recipient of good fortune, good luck, God's favor or blessing (*a*) others; (*b*) self. |
| +1 H | 4. References to any kinds of hopes that lead to a constructive outcome, to survival, to longevity, to smooth-going interpersonal relationships (this category can be scored only if the word "hope" or "wish" or a close synonym is used). |
| −1 H | 5. References to not being or not wanting to be or not seeking to be the recipient of good fortune, good luck, God's favor or blessing. |
| −1 H | 6. References to self or others not getting or receiving help, advice, support, sustenance, confidence, esteem (*a*) from others; (*b*) from self. |
| −1 H | 7. References to feelings of hopelessness, losing hope, despair, lack of confidence, lack of ambition, lack of interest; feelings of pessimism, discouragement (*a*) others; (*b*) self. |

All content analysis technicians were trained in their familiarity with the content items in the Hope scale and with the scoring procedures to the point where an interscorer reliability of at least .85 had been obtained.

Table 3.—Intercorrelations* of Hope Scale Scores and Other Psychological Scores in a Children's Group

| | Anxiety | Hostility Out | Hostility In | Ambivalent Hostility† | Social Alienation-Personal Disorganization | Cognitive-Intellectual Impairment | Human Relations | Achievement Strivings |
|---|---|---|---|---|---|---|---|---|
| Hope | −0.46 (N = 109) P <.001 | −0.45 (N = 109) P <.001; Overt −0.35 P <.001; Covert −0.39 P <.001 | −0.36 (N = 109) P <.001 | −0.38 (N = 109) P <.001 | −0.61 (N = 109) P <.0001 | −0.07 (N = 109) | 0.51 (N = 109) P <.001 | 0.55 (N = 109) P <.001 |
| Hope (Girls) | −0.31 (N = 68) P <.01 | −0.55 (N = 68) P <.001; Overt −0.48 (N = 68) P <.001; Covert −0.43 (N = 68) P <.001 | −0.37 (N = 68) P <.01 | −0.41 (N = 68) P <.001 | −0.53 (N = 68) P <.001 | −0.06 (N = 68) | 0.53 (N = 68) P <.001 | 0.48 (N = 68) P <.001 |
| Hope (Boys) | −0.63 (N = 41) P <.001 | −0.32 (N = 41) P <.04; Overt −0.16 (N = 41); Covert −0.33 (N = 41) P <.05 | −0.35 (N = 41) P <.05 | −0.34 (N = 41) P <.05 | −0.71 (N = 40) P <.001 | −0.08 (N = 40) | 0.49 (N = 41) P <.01 | 0.64 (N = 41) P <.001 |

* Pearson Product-Moment correlations.
† References to others disliking or having hostile feelings towards the self.

Table 4.— Intercorrelations* of Hope Scale Scores and Other Psychological States in a Normative Adult Group

| | Anxiety | Hostility Out | | Hostility In | Ambivalent Hostility | Social Alienation-Personal Disorganization |
|---|---|---|---|---|---|---|
| Hope | −0.19 (N = 91) | −0.26† (N = 91) | | −0.14 (N = 91) | −0.22† (N = 91) | −0.30† (N = 91) |
| | | Overt | Covert | | | |
| | | −0.21† (N = 91) | −0.21† (N = 91) | | | |

* Pearson Product-Moment correlations.
† $P < .05$.

Table 5.—Intercorrelations* of Hope Scale Scores and Other Psychological State Scores in Two Adult Patient Groups

| Hope | Social Alienation-Personal Disorganization | Human Relations | Object Relations |
|---|---|---|---|
| Orange County Crisis clinic sample | −0.63 (N = 55) $P < .005$ | +0.68 (N = 54) $P < .005$ | +0.70 (N = 46) $P < .005$ |
| Cincinnati General Hospital medical inpatient samples | −0.75 (N = 36) $P < .005$ | +0.75 (N = 25) $P < .005$ | |

* Spearman Rank Order correlation.

All speech samples were the first verbal sample provided by each individual. Scores for various other psychological dimensions were also obtained by the Gottschalk-Gleser content analysis method,[10] including scores for anxiety, hostility outward, hostility inward, ambivalent hostility, achievement strivings, human relations, object relations, social alienation-personal disorganization, and so forth.

Statistical procedures were carried out to obtain normative frequency distributions of Hope scores according to different age groups and sex. Also obtained were intercorrelations of Hope scores with scores for other psychological states, the relationships of demographic factors to Hope scores, and preliminary construct validation data.[19]

### Results

**Normative Studies and Intercorrelations of Hope Scores With Scores of Other Psychological Variables.**—By providing normative or standardized data for nonpsychiatric and psychiatric subjects, there is no intent to imply that ideal standards for the dimension of hope can be established on a statistical basis. The term normative is not being used here in the sense of ideal or preferred, but rather in the sense of typical or average for a group of people in a similar life situation. Percentile scores are provided to answer the question what is a high or low score for the Hope scale using this content analysis procedure.

Any factor that can affect the central tendency or range of values of a psychological variable, such as hope, can provide a basis for classification for some evaluative purpose. Thus, the distribution of Hope scores might vary as a function of a subject's age, sex, educational level, medical condition, and relationships to the examiner[10] or as a function of any combination of these factors. In the following section, the effect of some of these factors on the central tendency of Hope scores is examined and illustrated.

### Hope and Various Demographic Factors

For the children's sample (N = 109) Hope scores did not correlate with age ($r = .04$) nor education level ($r = -0.10$). The mean Hope scores for boys (N = 41) was 0.05±1.38 and for girls (N = 68) 0.03±1.17.

In the adult sample of subjects (N = 91) Hope scores correlated −0.22 with IQ[20] and −0.19 with educational level. Again, there was no correlation with age ($r = .09$).

In the adult sample, the mean Hope score for men was 0.60±0.97 (N = 46) and for women 0.87±1.07 (N = 45); a $t$-test of the difference between these means was not significant ($t = -1.30$). There was no significant difference between mean Hope scores ($t = 0.81$) of married ($\overline{X} = 0.72 \pm 1.03$, N = 54) and single ($\overline{X} = 0.91 \pm 1.06$, N = 30) adults.

### Normative Scores

For the children's sample, percentile scores for the Hope scale are as follows (N = 109):

| | |
|---|---|
| 95% | 1.90 |
| 90% | 1.37 |
| 85% | 1.04 |
| 80% | 0.83 |
| 75% | 0.61 |
| 70% | 0.40 |
| 60% | 0.19 |
| 50% | 0.01 |
| 40% | 0.07 |
| 30% | −0.38 |
| 25% | −0.50 |
| 20% | −0.67 |
| 15% | −0.95 |
| 10% | −1.38 |
| 5% | −2.30 |
| Mean | 0.04 |
| SD | 1.25 |
| N | 109 |

Table 1 gives percentile scores for the children's group by sex and grade. There were no sexual or age differences to be noted among these children with respect to average Hope scores. The only exception to this finding involved children in the grade four to six group, and this group had a slightly lower mean Hope score which did not reach a convincing level of significance.

For the adult sample, percentile scores on the Hope scale are given in Table 2. The mean Hope score for our children's group (0.04±1.25) was significantly lower ($t = 4.21$; $P < .001$) than for our adult group (0.73±1.03). Table 2 also gives percentile scores on the Hope scale for a group of patients (N = 68) from the Orange County Mental Health Crisis Intervention Clinic.

**Intercorrelations of Hope Scores With Other Psychological Scores Derived From Speech Samples.**—The intercorrelations of Hope scores from the children's normative group with other psychological variables, also derived from the content analysis of verbal behavior, help to es-

Table 6.—Correlations of Hope Scores, Improvement in Psychiatric Morbidity Scores, and Various Ego-Strength Scores in a Group of Mental Crisis Patients

| | Psychiatric Patient Improvement ($PHS_2$-$PMS_1$) (Posttreatment) | Jacobs Ego Weakness (Pretreatment) | Anant Belongingness (Pretreatment) | Barron Ego Strength (Pretreatment) | Jacobs Ego Strength (Pretreatment) |
|---|---|---|---|---|---|
| Hope scores (pretreatment) | +0.26 (N = 55) $P<.05$ | +0.38 (N = 56) $P<.05$ | +0.29 (N = 57) $P<.05$ | +0.21 (N = 58) (NS) | +0.15 (N = 56) (NS) |

tablish the boundaries of the psychological construct measured by this Hope scale. Significant positive correlations were found between Hope scores and Human relations[21] and Achievement strivings[16] scores; significant negative correlations were obtained between Hope scores and Anxiety, Hostility out (overt and covert), Hostility inward, Ambivalent hostility, and Social alienation-personal disorganization scores (Table 3). No correlations were found between Hope scores and Cognitive-intellectual impairment scores.

The intercorrelations of Hope scores and other psychological scores derived from speech samples in a normative adult group are shown in Table 4 and from adult patient groups (Orange County Crisis Clinic Sample and Cincinnati General Hospital Medical Inpatient Sample) are given as Table 5. Again, we see a significant positive correlation between Hope scores and Human relations scores and a negative correlation between Hope scores and Social alienation-personal disorganization scores (Table 4).

**Validation Studies.**—Validation of this Hope scale is at a preliminary stage. The psychological dimension measured by this content analysis scale is considered to be more of a psychological state rather than a psychological trait when the Hope score is derived from a single five-minute speech sample. Even when such a speech sample is elicited in response to standardized instructions "to talk about any interesting or dramatic life experiences," the speaker's feelings of hopefulness, in the sense of this Hope scale, may well be influenced by the situational context in which he is speaking, his immediate and momentary affects and attitudes that have any bearing whatsoever on his hopefulness and his physiological status. Since there are no well-validated independent criterion measures for the psychological state of hope, validation of the Hope scale described here presents problems.

Before reporting the construct validation evidence that has been collected on this Hope scale, it is important to indicate that this scale will provide an approximation of a psychological trait measure if the Hope scores from at least three or more five-minute speech samples are averaged. This average of Hope scores from separate speech samples obtained from one individual will give a central tendency and standard deviation which can serve as the more typical Hope score and, hence, trait measure of any one person. Logically, such a composite score would be the more appropriate score to compare with other measures of hope as a trait.

Aside from face validity of the content categories in the Hope scale, what further evidence is there that this content analysis measure assesses hope as defined here?

**Comparison of Hope Scores From a Normative Group of Patients Coming to Mental Health Crisis Clinic.**—Presumably, adults who are suffering an emotional crisis, while not necessarily giving up their usual degree of hope, might be expected to have undergone at least some erosion of their typical hopefulness. Hence, comparison of the average Hope score of a sample of adult patients coming to a Mental Health Crisis Intervention Clinic with the average Hope score of our normative group of people should indicate whether our Hope scores fluctuate in the expected direction.

The mean Hope scores ($-0.45\pm1.49$) for this Mental Health Crisis Group of patients (N=68) were significantly lower ($t=2.32$; $P<.05$) than the mean Hope scores from our normative children's group ($0.04\pm1.25$) and quite significantly lower than the mean Hope scores ($0.73\pm1.03$) from the normative adult group ($t=5.84$; $P<.001$) (see the childrens' sample, percentile scores in "Normative Scores" and Table 2).

**Correlations of Hope Scores With Independent Measures (Mental Health Crisis Clinic Group).**—Patients coming to a Mental Health Crisis Intervention Clinic, during initial diagnostic evaluative procedures[15] gave five-minute speech samples for obtaining Hope scores and, then, took the Barron Ego Strength test,[22] the Jacobs Ego Strength test,[23] the Jacobs Ego Weakness test,[23] and the Anant Belongingness test.[24] In addition, a measurement of improvement[14] in psychiatric morbidity scores ($PMS_2$-$PMS_1$) following psychiatric treatment was also correlated with pretreatment Hope scores. The intercorrelations are shown in Table 6.

The various ego-strength and ego-weakness measures and the Anant Belongingness measures are, presumably, all varieties of trait measures based on self-report procedures. The Jacobs Ego Weakness scale scores have a significant negative correlation and the Anant Belongingness scale scores have a significant positive correlation with Hope scale scores in this group of psychiatric patients. Though in the expected direction, the correlations of the Barron Ego Strength and Jacobs Ego Strength scores do not reach convincing levels of statistical significance. Relatively low correlations would be expected between a measure of a psychological state, such as a single Hope score, and a psychological trait, such as the self-report criterion measures used in this study. Nevertheless, the Hope scale can be seen to measure a personality characteristic somewhat similar to the "belongingness" assessed by the Anant test and dissimilar to the dimension of ego weakness as assayed by the Jacobs test.

One of the purposes of developing an objective measure of hopefulness is to use it to examine empirically some of the various hypotheses which claim that a hopeful attitude

or motivation influences the course of a medical illness, the resolution of a social or psychological set-back, any kind of vocational or occupational achievement, and the quality of human relationships. The Mental Health Crisis Intervention study was organized, in part, to search for predictors of favorable outcome in response to a brief problem-oriented type of psychotherapy provided to emotionally disturbed people coming to such a clinic. This goal was similar to the use of these Hope scores for the prediction of longer survival time or more hopeful outlook of cancer patients returning home from the hospital after radiation treatment[12] cited in this report.

When pretreatment Hope scores from patients in emotional crises were used to determine to what extent they predicted relative degrees of improvement in psychological, interpersonal, vocational, and somatic malfunctioning (changes in Psychiatric Morbidity scale scores),[14] a low yet statistically significant positive correlation ($r = 0.26$, $N = 55$, $P < .05$) was found between pretreatment Hope scores and psychiatric patient improvement. These findings help validate the construct of hope being measured. Other independent criteria increasing our knowledge of the composition of the psychological dimension measured by the Hope scale are described below.

**Correlations of Hope Scores With Other Independent Measures (Acute Schizophrenic Patient Group).**—Another construct validation study involving the Hope scale was carried out on 23 acute schizophrenic patients at the Orange County Medical Center[25] (L.A. Gottschalk, R. Biener, E.P. Noble, unpublished data). New admissions to the Psychiatric Service, these patients had not received any psychoactive drugs for at least four weeks prior to hospitalization. Before drug administration their mental status was carefully evaluated by means of the Overall-Gorham Brief Psychiatric Rating scale (BPRS), the Hamilton Depression Rating scale, and the Gottschalk content analysis scores derived from five-minute speech samples. The reliability of the psychiatric ratings was tested through independent ratings from video taped interviews of the patients and a measure of agreement, A, was calculated[26] for the rating scales: Overall-Gorham BPRS, 0.82 and Hamilton, 0.80. Factors derived from these rating scales[27] were correlated with Hope scale scores using a Dixon Computer program.[19] Significant negative correlations between Hope scores and psychiatric ratings were found with the BPRS Depression factor ($r = 0.61$; $P < .005$) and the BPRS Anergia factor ($r = -0.45$; $P < .05$) and the Hamilton Sleep Disturbance factor ($r = 0.51$; $P < .01$) and the Hamilton Anxiety/Depression factor ($r = 0.55$; $P < .01$) (Table 7).

Correlating the seven Hope scale content subcategories with Hamilton Depression scale factors revealed significant or nearly significant correlations in the expected directions between the Anxiety/Depression factor and $H_1$ ($r = -0.38$; references to getting help, advice, support, confidence), $H_3$ ($r = -0.47$; references to receiving good fortune, luck, God's favor), $H_4$ ($r = -0.38$; references to constructive outcomes, survival, longevity, good interpersonal relationships), $H_5$ ($r = 0.50$; references to *not* wanting to be the recipient of good luck or God's favor), and $H_7$ ($r = 0.43$; references to feelings of hopelessness, pessimism, discouragement) as well as between the Apathy factor and $H_1$ ($r = -0.35$) and $H_3$ ($r = -0.36$) and Sleep Disturbance factor and $H_6$ ($r = 0.39$; references to *not* getting help, advice, support, confidence).

**Intercorrelations of Hope Scores With Other Psychological State Scores Derived From Content Analysis of Speech.**—Some very definite ideas of the psychological measures of the Hope scale are provided by the intercorrelations of the Hope scores with other psychological state scores, all scores being derived by content analysis of the same five-minute speech samples. Though these data cannot be strictly considered as construct validation data, they serve to indicate how this Hope scale might be expected to interrelate with other psychological variables. Examination of these intercorrelations, (Tables 4 to 6) tells us that this dimension of hope is positively associated with the dimension of achievement strivings and with interest in human relations and object relations; and it is negatively correlated with anxiety, hostility directed outwards, hostility directed inwards, ambivalent hostility (talking about hostile feelings from others directed towards the self), social

Table 7.—Correlations (Pearson Product-Moment) of Hope Scale Scores and Behavioral Rating Scale Scores in Acute Schizophrenic Patients, N = 23

| Behavioral Rating Scales | Hope Scale Scores |
|---|---|
| Brief Psychiatric Rating scale factors (Overall-Gorham) | |
| Depression | −0.61* |
| Thinking disorder | −0.39† |
| Anergia | −0.45‡ |
| Excitement disorientation | −0.35† |
| Hamilton Depression scale factors | |
| Sleep disturbance | −0.51§ |
| Somatization | |
| Anxiety/depression | −0.55§ |
| Apathy | −0.38† |

* P <.005.
† P <.10.
‡ P <.05.
§ P <.01.

Table 8.—Intercorrelations of Psychological State Scores in a Children's Sample, N = 109

| | Hostility Out (Total) | SA-PD | Cognitive Impairment | Human Relations | Achievement Strivings |
|---|---|---|---|---|---|
| 1. Anxiety | 0.46 | 0.37 | −0.27 | −0.30 | −0.61 |
| 2. Hostility out (total) | | 0.25 | −0.30 | −0.41 | −0.50 |
| 3. Social alienation-(SA-PD) personal disorganization | | | 0.25 | −0.58 | −0.42 |
| 4. Cognitive impairment | | | | 0.00 | 0.31 |
| 5. Human relations | | | | | 0.38 |

alienation-personal disorganization (schizophrenic-like orientations). These intercorrelations hold for children and adults and, among adults, in both healthy and sick groups.

Item analysis of the verbal behavior contents composing these different scales indicates that the significant intercorrelations cannot be accounted for by identical content categories being included in different scales. Rather, these psychological states (and, operationally, verbal associations unique for each) tend to polarize around each other, in some instances being positively correlated and in other instances, covarying negatively. Elsewhere, we have indicated that certain ones of our psychological measures of affects derived from content analysis tend to covary and that this covariation is influenced by the nature of the groups of people involved, eg, healthy, neurotic, psychotic, and so forth.[10] In the present report, intercorrelations of the psychological state scores, exclusive of Hope scores, from the children's sample (Table 8) again reveal that certain affects or states are positively correlated with one another (anxiety, hostility out, social alienation-personal disorganization) and some are negatively associated with these states (human relations and achievement strivings) (Table 8).

The Hope scale is an addition to the other psychological measures with positive valence among the content analysis scales that have been developed by our research group. Its intercorrelations with affects and other psychological states of a negative valence, eg, anxiety, hostility, social alienation-personal disorganization, should generally be inverse.

**Validation of the Hope Scale Through Prediction of Outcome.**—Preliminary use of this Hope scale as a predictor of outcome was tried on patients with metastatic cancers of various kinds receiving partial or total body radiation with radioactive cobalt at the Cincinnati General Hospital.[12,28] In a group of 16 patients, a correlation of +.38 was obtained between Hope scores obtained from the first five-minute verbal sample given by the patients in response to standard and purposely ambiguous instructions (to speak for five minutes about any interesting or dramatic personal life experiences one has ever had) and the duration of survival of the patients, in days, after receiving the actual body irradiation. Also, the average Hope score (+5.42) obtained the third day postradiation of 11 cancer patients who returned home was significantly higher (by a Mann-Whitney U test, $P<.01$) than the comparable average Hope scores (+1.9) of a group of 11 patients obliged to remain in the hospital.

Further studies with another 27 patients (making a total of 43) using scores derived from the Hope scale as a predictor of survival time in metastatic cancer patients receiving radiation therapy at the Cincinnati General Hospital, indicate that preradiation Hope scores correlate significantly with duration of survival.[29]

A group of 27 patients seeking psychiatric help in the emergency room of a large general hospital in Pittsburgh gave five-minute speech samples on the occasion of their initial evaluation.[30] Hope scores obtained by content analysis of these verbal samples revealed that patients who follow treatment recommendations have higher Hope scores ($0.61 \pm 0.96$, $N=16$; $\pm=1.76$, $P<.05$) than those who do not follow through on recommended treatment ($-0.19 \pm 1.40$, $N=11$).

Hope scores were used as a predictor of outcome in the short-term treatment of a mental health crisis intervention clinic in Orange, Calif.[15] On this study, walk-in patients were randomly selected for immediate crisis intervention treatment or a six-week wait. Symptomatic and behavioral changes were measured by an objective means (Psychiatric Morbidity Scale[14]) through a tape-recorded standardized interview, assessing relative functional capacity in the psychological, vocational, domestic, interpersonal, and somatic spheres. Pretreatment Hope scores correlated negatively, as expected, with the degree of psychiatric morbidity six to ten weeks later in the group of patients receiving active therapy ($r=-0.23$, $N=35$) and positively ($r=0.20$, $N=23$) in those patients obliged to wait six weeks for their help from the clinic. These findings suggest that hope, as measured by our Hope scale, is related to internalized expectations of satisfying and favorable interpersonal and object relationships (also, supported by the intercorrelations given in Tables 3 to 5), and when individuals with high hopes for a helping human relationship are not immediately realized, as in the group of patients required to wait for treatment, such individuals may be more likely to continue to have their psychiatric dysfunctions. This same study[15] indicates that patients on the waiting list improve as much, as a group, as patients receiving immediate crisis intervention treatment, which suggests that resilience and adaptiveness to life crises certainly involve other personality characteristics than hope.

Hope scale scores improved significantly ($\pm=1.79$, $P<.05$) and total hostility outward ($\pm=-1.73$, $P<.05$), social alienation-personal disorganization scores ($\pm=-2.27$, $P<.025$), and depression scores ($\pm=-1.83$, $P<.05$) decreased significantly, all scores obtained by content analysis of five-minute speech samples, 48 hours after 22 acute schizophrenic patients received thioridazine (4 mg/kg), orally. The greater the plasma thioridazine half-life in these patients on this drug dose, the greater the increase in Hope scores after thioridazine ($r=0.50$, $P<.02$). Moreover, the greater the predrug Hope scores, the greater the decrease in the postdrug depression factor scores of the Brief Psychiatric Rating scale ($r=0.43$, $P<.04$) (L.A. Gottschalk, R. Biener, E.P. Noble, unpublished data).

## Comment

This is a report on a method of measuring the magnitude of immediate hopefulness of individuals through the content analysis of verbal behavior. The theory and rationale of this content analysis procedure have been described in detail elsewhere,[10] and a manual describing how to score similar content analysis scales (anxiety, hostility, social alienation-personal disorganization) is available.[10] The scoring of this Hope scale in the present study was carried out from the typescripts of five-minute speech samples elicited in response to standardized and purposely ambiguous instructions rather than to other instructions

or to written material. Preliminary studies using five- and ten-minute written verbal samples obtained in response to our standardized instructions, have suggested that the affect scores derived from these written verbal samples are in a similar range to affect scores from spoken verbal samples.[10] In studies where the verbal material is obtained in reaction to different methods of eliciting the speech, the percentile scores for children and adults given here may well not be applicable. Different methods of eliciting verbal behavior for content analysis can be used in systematic studies by requiring that the same method of eliciting the verbal behavior be used before, during, and after exposure of the subject to an experimental stimulus, agent, or natural event.

For some types of investigations it may be desirable to obtain from the same speech sample a profile of various psychological scores by means of content analysis, including Hope scores. The range of content analysis scores should, of course, depend on the research goals and design of the study. Repeated speech samples may be obtained, without notable practice effects, hours, days, or weeks apart. For example, in a recent study[16] 14 prisoner volunteers at Patuxent Institution gave a five-minute speech sample in response to instructions to talk about any interesting or dramatic life experiences; then they were administered a placebo by mouth, and two and four hours later they again gave five-minute speech samples. The average Hope score before the placebo was 0.53±1.01, two hours later it was 0.17±1.10, and four hours later it was 0.12±0.73, indicating slight and nonsignific Hope scores over a four-hour period when s placebo. (Another group of 16 prisoner-vol same institution had a slight nonsignifica Hope scores over the same time period when amphetamine (15 mg) immediately after g speech sample.)

The specific content categories in this H being critically examined in their relative use in normative and deviant groups of pe respect to how these content categories are age, sex, and educational level. The weight these categories are also being studied aga vant independent criterion measures that Work along these lines is too preliminary to i this paper. As well as looking into these inte tions, we intend to see what differences are i quality of the dimension of hope when the on some aspect of self-reliance as compared someone else. Moreover, we plan to explore t logical differences in hopefulness extendab decades in the future in contrast to a few mi the time-factor in hope). Once commitments investigate systematically the dimension of *measurement point of view*, these intriguing be tackled with high expectations of getting swers.

Daniel E. Bates, AB, and Claire A. Cable provided tech and Herman Birch, PhD, provided statistical assistance.

**References**


1. Grinker RR Sr, et al: *The Phenomena of Depressions.* New York, Paul B Hoeber Inc, 1962.
2. Lehmann HE: Depression: Categories, mechanisms, and phenomena, in Cole JO, Wittenborn JR (eds): *Pharmacotherapy of Depression.* Springfield, Ill, Charles C Thomas Publisher, 1966.
3. Schmale AH: Relationship of separation and depression to disease. I: A report on a hospitalized medical population. *Psychosom Med* 20:259, 1958.
4. Schmale AH: Needs, gratifications, and the vicissitudes of the self-representation: A development concept of psychic object relationships. *Psychoanal Stud Soc* 2:9-41, 1962.
5. Engel GL: *Psychological Development in Health and Disease.* Philadelphia, WB Saunders Co, 1963.
6. French TM: *The Integration of Behavior.* Chicago, University of Chicago Press, 1952, vol 1.
7. Van Dyke N: Discomfort and hope: Their relationship to outcome of referral. *Smith College Stud Soc Work* 32:205-219, 1962.
8. Frank J: The role of hope in psychotherapy. *Int J Psychiatry* 5:383-395, 1968.
9. Melges FT, Bowlby J: Types of hopelessness in psychopathological process. *Arch Gen Psychiatry* 20:690-699, 1969.
10. Gottschalk LA, Gleser GC: *The Measurement of Psychological States Through the Content Analysis of Verbal Behavior.* Los Angeles, University of California Press, 1969.
11. Gleser GC, Gottschalk LA, John W: The relationship of sex and intelligence to choice of words: A normative study of verbal behavior. *J Clin Psychol* 15:182-191, 1959.
12. Gottschalk LA, et al: Total and half body irradiation: Effect on cognitive and emotional processes. *Arch Gen Psychiatry* 21:574-580, 1969.
13. Winget CN: Effect of total and half body radiation on patients with metastatic cancer, in Saenger EL (ed): *Metabolic Changes in Humans Following Total Body Irradiation.* DASA 1844 Progress Report in Research Project DA-49-146-XZ-315 Defence Atomic Support Agency, Washington, DC, 1971.
14. Gottschalk LA, Mayerson P, Gottlieb A: The prediction and evaluation of outcome in an emergency brief psychotherapy clinic. *J Nerv Ment Dis* 144:77-96, 1967.
15. Gottschalk LA, et al: A study of prediction and outcome in a mental health crisis clinic. *Am J Psychiatry,* 130:26-33, 1973.
16. Gottschalk LA, et al: Effect of amphetamine o zine on achievement strivings scores derived fro analysis of speech. *Compr Psychiatry* 12:420-435, 19
17. Gottschalk LA: Some psychoanalytic research munication of meaning through language: The qualit tude of psychological states. *Br J Med Psychol* 44:1
18. Gottschalk LA: An objective method of meas logical states associated with changes in neural fu *Psychiatry* 4:33-39, 1972.
19. Dixon WJ (ed): *Biomedical Computer Progra* University of California Press, 1968.
20. Wonderlic EF: *Wonderlic Personnel Test Ma* field, Ill, 1945.
21. Gottschalk LA: Some applications of the psycho cept of object relatedness: Preliminary studies on a tions scale applicable to verbal samples. *Compr Psyc* 620, 1968.
22. Barron F: An ego strength scale which predicts psychotherapy. *J Consult Psychol* 17:327-333, 1953.
23. Jacobs MA, Pregatch D, Spilken A: Ego streng weakness. *J Nerv Ment Dis* 147:297-307, 1968.
24. Anant SS: Belongingness, anxiety, and self-suffi *chol Rep* 20:1137-1138, 1967.
25. Gottschalk LA, et al: Thioridazine plasma levels response, to be published.
26. Ronbinson WS: The statistical measure of agre *Soc Rev* 22:17, 1957.
27. Guy W, Bonato RR: *Manual for the ECDEU A Battery,* ed 2. Chevy Chase, Md, National Institute Health, 1970.
28. Kunkel RL, Gottschalk LA: Hope and denial in carcinoma: A preliminary report. *US Med* 2:31, 1966.
29. Saenger, et al: *Radiation Effects in Man: Man and Therapeutic Efforts.* Defense Nuclear Agency D 2599 and 275IT. Contract No. DASA-01-69-C-0131. Pr University of Cincinnati College of Medicine, Cincinna Hospital, Cincinnati, Ohio, April 1971, and October 197
30. Perley J, Winget CN, Placci C: Hope and discomf tors influencing treatment continuance. *Compr Psychiat* 563, 1971.

# 2

# Further Validation Studies of A Cognitive-Intellectual Impairment Scale Applicable to Verbal Samples[1]

Louis A. Gottschalk[2], Michael J. Eckardt[3]
and Daniel J. Feldman[2,4]

The Cognitive-Intellectual Impairment Scale to be described here was initially developed empirically from a comparative study (Gottschalk and Gleser, 1964) of verbal samples from various populations using content categories derived from a Social Alienation-Personal Disorganization scale applicable to verbal samples. This Social Alienation-Personal Disorganization scale can be applied to consecutive grammatical clauses in speech or written language and provides mathematized indices of the relative severity of the schizophrenic syndrome in any patient; detailed reliability and validity studies have been published elsewhere (Gottschalk et al,

---

[1]We acknowledge the technical assistance of Douglas Halpern, Julia Hoigaard, and Michael Syben of the University of California at Irvine, and the statistical assistance of Charles Pautler and Robert Rawlings of ADAMHA. Special recognition is due Michael Syben for developing the breakdown of verbal category III. This research project was supported, in part, by AAA05024 and NIA-76-32(P) from the National Institute on Alcohol Abuse and Alcoholism.

[2]Department of Psychiatry and Human Behavior, College of Medicine, University of California, Irvine, California (92717); [3]National Institute on Alcohol Abuse and Alcoholism; [4]Alcohol Treatment Section, Psychiatry Service, Veterans Administration Hospital, Long Beach, California (90822).

1958, 1961; Gottschalk and Gleser, 1969; Gottschalk, 1977a). In the study by Gottschalk and Gleser in 1964, it was noted that although brain-damaged patients obtained a score distribution on the total scale which was very similar to that of chronic schizophrenia, there were some categories on which they differed considerably. For example, references to interpersonal relationships were used more frequently by the schizophrenics; whereas verbal statements indicating disorientation occurred more often in the speech of brain-damaged patients. These data suggested that it was possible to develop a scale of cognitive and intellectual impairment that could be applied to short samples of speech. It was anticipated that such a scale would be capable of measuring transient and reversible changes in cognitive and intellectual function as well as irreversible changes, all due principally to brain dysfunction and minimally to transient emotional changes in the individual. The usefulness of such a psychological measure, if it could be developed, in basic and applied psychological and psychiatric research is obvious.

Initial Validation Studies. Selection of the Verbal Categories and Associated Weights for the Cognitive and Intellectual Impairment Scale

From the data obtained on the comparative frequency of response to the content categories of the Social Alienation-Personal Disorganization scale given by groups of schizophrenic patients, other psychiatric patients, brain-damaged patients, general medical patients, and normal subjects (Gottschalk and Gleser, 1964), those categories were selected which were used most frequently or most rarely by brain-damaged patients. The categories were weighted initially to maximize the difference between the average score of the brain-damaged patients relative to each of the other groups (Gottschalk and Kunkel, 1966).

The various diagnostic groups listed in Table 1 gave five-minute speech samples which were scored on the Social Alienation-Personal Disorganization scale. These speech samples were recorded on the Cognitive-Intellectual Impairment scale and the mean scores by groups

Table 1.

Distribution of Scores on the Social Alienation-Personal Disorganization Scale by Groups

| Score Interval | Chronic schizophrenic | | Acute schizophrenic | | Brain syndrome | | Psychiatric nonschizophrenic | | General medical | | "Normal" employed | |
|---|---|---|---|---|---|---|---|---|---|---|---|---|
| | Frequency | Cumulative % | Frequency | Cumulative % | Frequency | Cumulative % | Frequency | Cumulative % | Frequency | Cumulative % | Frequency | Cumulative % |
| 18.0 or greater.... | 4 | 100.0 | ...... | ...... | 1 | 100.0 | ...... | ...... | ...... | ...... | ...... | ...... |
| 16.0 to 18.0 .... | 7 | 96.5 | ...... | ...... | 0 | 94.5 | ...... | ...... | ...... | ...... | ...... | ...... |
| 14.0 to 16.0 .... | 1 | 90.3 | ...... | ...... | 0 | 94.5 | ...... | ...... | ...... | ...... | ...... | ...... |
| 12.0 to 14.0 .... | 1 | 89.4 | ...... | ...... | 1 | 94.5 | ...... | ...... | ...... | ...... | ...... | ...... |
| 10.0 to 12.0 .... | 4 | 88.5 | ...... | ...... | 1 | 88.9 | ...... | ...... | 1 | 100.0 | ...... | ...... |
| 8.0 to 10.0 .... | 11 | 85.0 | ...... | ...... | 0 | 83.3 | ...... | ...... | 0 | 97.9 | ...... | ...... |
| 6.0 to 8.0 .... | 9 | 75.2 | 4 | 100.0 | 1 | 83.3 | 1 | 100.0 | 1 | 97.9 | ...... | ...... |
| 4.0 to 6.0 .... | 14 | 67.3 | 2 | 86.2 | 2 | 77.8 | 2 | 96.2 | 2 | 95.8 | ...... | ...... |
| 2.0 to 4.0 .... | 16 | 54.9 | 7 | 79.3 | 6 | 66.7 | 3 | 88.5 | 7 | 91.7 | 1 | 100.0 |
| 0.0 to 2.0 .... | 14 | 40.7 | 6 | 55.2 | 1 | 33.3 | 4 | 76.9 | 6 | 77.1 | 4 | 98.3 |
| -0.1 to -2.0 .... | 15 | 28.3 | 3 | 34.5 | 3 | 27.8 | 5 | 61.5 | 11 | 64.6 | 16 | 91.7 |
| -2.0 to -4.0 .... | 11 | 15.0 | 4 | 24.1 | 0 | 11.1 | 6 | 42.3 | 9 | 41.7 | 19 | 65.0 |
| -4.0 to -6.0 .... | 3 | 5.3 | 0 | 10.3 | 0 | 11.1 | 2 | 19.2 | 7 | 22.9 | 11 | 33.4 |
| -6.0 to -8.0 .... | 1 | 2.7 | 1 | 10.3 | 1 | 11.1 | 2 | 11.5 | 0 | 8.3 | 8 | 15.0 |
| -8.0 to -10.0 .... | 1 | 1.8 | 1 | 6.9 | 0 | 5.6 | 1 | 3.8 | 2 | 8.3 | 0 | 1.7 |
| -10.0 to -12.0 .... | 1 | 0.9 | 1 | 3.4 | 0 | 5.6 | 0 | 0.0 | 1 | 4.2 | 0 | 1.7 |
| -12.0 to -14.0 .... | 0 | 0.0 | 0 | 0.0 | 1 | 5.6 | 0 | 0.0 | 1 | 2.1 | 0 | 1.7 |
| -14.0 to -16.0 .... | 0 | 0.0 | 0 | 0.0 | 0 | 0.0 | 0 | 0.0 | 0 | 0.0 | 1 | 1.7 |
| Total .............. | 113 | | 29 | | 18 | | 26 | | 48 | | 60 | |
| Median.............. | 3.3 | | 1.5 | | 3.0 | | -1.2 | | -1.3 | | -2.9 | |

are given in Table 2. The means indicate a plausible ordering of the groups with respect to cognitive impairment, if it can be assumed that a portion of long hospitalized chronic schizophrenics are, indeed, likely to have some brain damage.

Correlations of Cognitive Impairment Scores with Scores from the Halstead and Trail Making Tests

Five-minute verbal samples were elicited, using standard instructions (Gottschalk and Hambidge, 1955; Gottschalk and Gleser, 1969), from a group of 20 subjects, male and female, ranging in age from 42 to 84. The Halstead Battery (1947) and the Trail Making Test (Reitan, 1955) were administered to the subjects. Sixteen of the subjects were terminal cancer patients, and the other four were patients with miscellaneous ailments at the Cincinnati Veterans Administration Hospital. The verbal cognitive-intellectual impairment scores derived from the speech samples of these patients were correlated with the scores from the Halstead and the Trail Making tests. The initial set of weights for the verbal content categories on the Cognitive Impairment scale yielded correlations of .33 and -.37, respectively. While neither of these correlations was significantly different from zero at the .05 level, they did indicate some possible validity in the proper direction.

The weights associated with the verbal categories in the Cognitive Impairment scale were modified (See Schedule 1) and recalculating the scores resulted in a substantial increase in the correlation of the verbal cognitive-intellectual impairment scores with the Halstead Battery (r=.55) and with the Trail Making Test (r=-.48). The average score for this group on the revised scale was 1.21 with a standard deviation of 2.05. The eight subjects showing the most severe brain damage on the basis of both tests had an average score of 2.90.

Table 2

Mean Scores on the Cognitive Impairment Scale
for Various Diagnostic Groups

| Group | N | Average score |
|---|---|---|
| Brain syndrome . . . . . . . . . . . . . . . . . . . | 18 | 2.72 |
| Chronic schizophrenics . . . . . . . . . . . . . . . | 113 | 2.12 |
| Acute schizophrenics . . . . . . . . . . . . . . . . | 29 | 1.24 |
| General medical. . . . . . . . . . . . . . . . . . . | 48 | .79 |
| Psychiatric (nonschizophrenics). . . . . . . . . . . | 26 | .66 |
| Normal employed. . . . . . . . . . . . . . . . . . . | 60 | .47 |

Changes in Cognitive Impairment Scores Compared to Clinical Changes Observed in Patients with Acute or Chronic Brain Syndromes

To test further the validity of the Cognitive Impairment Scale, verbal samples were obtained from 17 male patients at the Cincinnati Veterans Administration Hospital, ranging in age from 23 to 83, who demonstrated an acute or chronic brain syndrome from a clinical neuro-psychiatric examination. Whenever possible, those patients with acute brain syndrome were tested again when the symptoms had subsided. Altogether, 27 observations were available for analysis. The average score obtained when the patients were rated as moderately to severely impaired clinically was 1.71, as compared to an average of 1.36 when they were rated as mildly impaired and 1.14 when no clinical impairment was evidenced.

SCHEDULE 1

Cognitive and Intellectual Impairment Scale

| Weights | | Content Categories and Scoring Symbols |
|---|---|---|
| | I. | Interpersonal References (including fauna and flora). |
| | | B. To unfriendly, hostile, destructive thoughts, feelings, or actions. |
| $-\frac{1}{2}$ | | 1. Self unfriendly to others. |
| | | C. To congenial and constructive thoughts, feelings, or actions. |
| $-\frac{1}{2}$ | | 1. Others helping, being friendly toward others. |
| $-\frac{1}{2}$ | | 2. Self helping, being friendly toward others. |
| $-\frac{1}{2}$ | | 3. Others helping, being friendly toward self. |
| | II. | Intrapersonal References. |
| +3 | | A. To disorientation-orientation, past, present or future (do not include all references to time, place, or person, but only those in which it is reasonably clear the subject is trying to orient himself or is expressing disorientation with respect to these; also, do not score more than one item per clause under this category). |
| | | B. To self. |
| $-\frac{1}{2}$ | | 1. Injured, ailing, deprived, malfunctioning, getting worse, bad, dangerous, low value or worth, strange. |
| $+\frac{1}{4}$ | | 3. Intact, satisfied, healthy, well. |
| +1 | | 5. To being controlled, feeling controlled, wanting control, asking for control or permission, being obliged or having to do, think or experience something. |
| +1 | | C. Denial of feelings, attitudes, or mental state of the self. |
| | | D. To food. |
| -1 | | 2. Good or neutral |
| | III. | Miscellaneous. |
| | | A. Signs of disorganization. |
| +1 | | 2. Incomplete sentences, clauses, phrases; blocking. |
| | | B. Repetition of ideas in sequence. |
| +1 | | 2. Phrases, clauses (separated only by a phrase or clause). |
| $+\frac{1}{2}$ | IV. | A. Questions Directed to the Interviewer. |

The stability of the revised Cognitive Impairment Scale over a short interval of time was examined in 12 male Veterans Administration patients from each of whom two verbal samples had been obtained in two- to four-week intervals. The intraclass correlation between the two sets of scores was .70. From these data, the standard error of measurement over occasions was estimated to be .57.

Relationship of Verbal Content Categories with the Subjective Drug Effects Questionnaire (SDEQ)

In a study carried out by Atkinson et al (1977) (See also Chapter 17 of this volume), 56 subjects gave five-minute speech samples while intoxicated from inhaling nitrous oxide and about 25 minutes later filled out the SDEQ Subjective Drug Effects Questionnaire (Katz et al, 1968). Seven items from the SDEQ Questionnaire are considered to measure collectively "impaired cognition, time sense, and psychomotor activity." Another twelve items from this questionnaire are said to measure "improved cognition."

Scores from the Impaired Cognition portion of the SDEQ were significantly correlated in a positive manner with the frequency of use of the following content categories:

1. Feeling controlled or wanting control (IIB5) ($r=0.32$, $p<.02$).
2. Sleep good, pleasant or neutral (IIF2) ($r=0.29$, $p<.03$).
3. Repetition of words (separated by no more than a word) (IIIB1) ($r=0.34$, $p<.01$).
4. Questions directed to the interviewer (IVA) ($r=0.28$, $p<.04$).

Scores from the Improved Cognition portion of the SDEQ Questionnaire were significantly correlated in a negative direction with the frequency of occurrence of the following content categories:

1. Not being prepared or able to produce, perform, act, not knowing, not sure (IIB4) ($r=-0.31$, $p<.02$).

2. Feeling controlled or wanting control (IIB5) ($r=-0.26$, $p < .05$).
3. Repetitions of phrases or clauses (separated only by a phrase or clause)(IIIB2) ($r=-0.28$, $p < .04$).

Further Validation Studies of the Specificity of the Speech Patterns Indicative of Cognitive Defects

The verbal categories indicative of cognitive defects in the Social Alienation-Personal Disorganization and Cognitive-Intellectual Impairment scales have undergone further validation studies using a large neuro-psychological battery of criterion measures that are customarily used in the detection and assessment of cerebral organic disorders. The results provide further validation of the specificity of each verbal category of these scales insofar as the dimension of cognitive defect is involved.

Subjects. The sample consisted of 54 male participants in an alcohol treatment program at the Veterans Administration Hospital, Long Beach, California. Subjects were volunteers between the ages of 21-60 and were tested within 7 days of the last drink, but only after it was documented that no psychoactive medication had been taken during the previous 48 hours and no psychiatric disorder was present.

Procedures. Each subject was individually given the 18 tests described below over a two-day period, with the order of tests determined randomly. These neuropsychological tests were selected so as to assess cognitive and intellectual dysfunction. Five-minute verbal samples were obtained at the beginning of either the first or second day of cognitive testing, following the procedures of Gottschalk and Hambidge (1955) and Gottschalk and Gleser (1969).

The typescripts of these tape-recorded speech samples were scored for all the verbal categories, of the Social Alienation-Personal Disorganization and Cognitive-Intellectual Impairment scales. Since all the verbal categories in the latter scale were originally derived from the former scale but were assigned different weights, all verbal categories of the Social Alienation-Personal Disorganization scale were

intercorrelated with the criterion measures. Weights of one for each verbal category as well as original weights (Gottschalk, Winget, and Gleser, 1969) were assigned to the verbal categories.

Neuropsychological Tests (More detailed descriptions of these tests are provided in Appendix 1 of this chapter). These eighteen cognitive tests were compiled on the basis of recent literature reviews that indicated that chronic alcoholics possess specific neuropsychological deficits (Kleinknecht and Goldstein, 1972; Goodwin and Hill, 1975; Grant and Mohns, 1975; Tarter, 1975; Parsons, 1977).

(1) Wechsler Adult Intelligence Scale (WAIS) Subtests: Unscaled scores on Digit Symbol, Digit Span, Block Design, and Object Assembly (Matarazzo, 1972).

(2) Halstead-Reitan Battery: Categories; Tactile Perceptual Test (TPT) - TPT Total Time; TPT Memory; TPT Location; Speech Perception; Finger Tapping, dominant hand; Seashore Rhythms (Reitan, 1966).

(3) Trail Making Test: Parts A and B (Reitan, 1955).

(4) Benton Visual Retention Test: Number of correct, Administration B (Benton, 1974).

(5) Wisconsin Card Sorting Test: Number of completed shifts (Tarter and Parsons, 1971; Parker and Noble, 1977).

(6) Shipley-Hartford Institute of Living Scale: Number of correct responses (Shipley and Burlingame, 1941).

(7) Rod and Frame Test (Witken et al, 1959).

## RESULTS

Performances on the 18 cognitive tests are summarized in Table 3. It is apparent that many of these subjects presented with brain dysfunction, and therefore this sample constitutes an appropriate group with which to test the capability of the content and form of verbal behavior to measure impairment of cognitive performance.

Table 3.

Cognitive Performance Within 7 Days of Last Drink (N=54)

(Asterisks indicate performance which would be consistent with a diagnosis of brain dysfunction.)

| Test | Mean | S.E.M. |
|---|---|---|
| 1. Tactile Performance Test (TPT) | * 21.0 min. | 1.35 |
| 2. TPT-Memory | 7.0 | 0.23 |
| 3. TPT-Location | * 3.1 | 0.34 |
| 4. Tapping | * 44.1 | 0.99 |
| 5. Trails A | * 38.1 sec. | 1.62 |
| 6. Trails B | * 98.9 sec. | 6.75 |
| 7. Categories | *-76.4 | 3.85 |
| 8. Speech Perception | * -9.7 | 0.74 |
| 9. Seashores | -6.0 | 0.44 |
| 10. Wisconsin Card Sorting Test | * 4.2 | 0.30 |
| 11. Digit Symbol | * 41.7 | 1.37 |
| 12. Digit Span | 10.9 | 0.33 |
| 13. Block Design | 29.6 | 1.14 |
| 14. Object Assembly | 28.7 | 1.05 |
| 15. Rod and Frame | $-2.2^{o}$ | 0.21 |
| 16. Benton Visual Retention Test | * 5.0 | 0.26 |
| 17. Shipley-Hartford, Verbal | 28.8 | 0.74 |
| 18. Shipley-Hartford, Abstract | * 9.6 | 0.63 |

A correlational analysis was then conducted to determine whether the frequency of usage of any of the 40 different verbal categories was correlated with performance on any of the 18 cognitive tests. Verbal categories which were found to be correlated above 0.20 with a

particular cognitive test (Table 4) were considered as independent variables in a multiple regression analysis, with the cognitive test being the dependent variable. These regression models and outcomes are depicted in Table 5. An attempt was then made to reduce the number of verbal categories required to explain a significant amount of variance in the cognitive test variable by eliminating all verbal categories which had not explained a significant amount of variance in Table 5. The final regression models are listed in Table 6. These results clearly demonstrate that verbal behavior can predict cognitive dysfunction, with the single exception of the Block Design Test.

Education and age are two variables also known to influence cognitive performance. Therefore, additional analyses were undertaken to discern the relative capabilities of education, age, and verbal behavior to predict cognitive performance. Those verbal categories significantly correlated ($p < 0.05$) with performance on a particular test, with age and education effects partialled out, were included in multiple regression analyses. The independent variables consisted of education, age, verbal categories related to test performance above and beyond age and education effects, and the dependent variable was test performance. The results of these analyses are located in Table 7.

## Discussion

The findings from the successive studies reviewed here indicate that certain organic brain syndromes and various chemical substances, such as, nitrous oxide and chronic exposure to alcohol, produce evidence of cerebral malfunction in the content or form of speech. These manifestations in spoken language are significantly correlated with a wide variety of neuropsychological test scores used as clinical criteria of transient or irreversible brain impairment. Moreover, various combinations of the frequency of use of various verbal categories occurring in natural speech can significantly predict the neuropsychological test scores from 17 out of 18 standardized neuropsychological measures.

Table 4

Correlations Between Verbal Category Scores and Separate Neuropsychological Test Scores (N=54)

| Verbal Item | Test [a] | R | t [b] | P (one-tail) |
|---|---|---|---|---|
| Cognitive Defects | | | | |
| Remarks not understandable by scorer (IIIA1)........ | 1 | -.223 | -1.65 | .10 |
| " | 6 | -.259 | -1.93 | .05 |
| " | 8 | -.284 | -2.13 | .025 |
| " | 9 | -.286 | -2.15 | .025 |
| " | 17 | -.230 | -1.70 | .05 |
| Remarks not understandable by typist (IIIA1x)........ | 3 | .296 | 2.24 | .025 |
| " | 6 | .209 | 1.54 | .10 |
| " | 7 | .224 | 1.65 | .10 |
| Remarks - telegrammatic, incomplete but under-....... standable (IIIA2a) | 1 | .255 | 1.90 | .05 |
| | 10 | .319 | 2.43 | .025 |
| " | 15 | -.357 | -2.76 | .01 |
| Incomplete phrases, clauses, blocking (IIIA2b)....... | 1 | -.229 | -1.70 | .025 |
| " | 2 | -.373 | -2.90 | .005 |
| " | 7 | -.240 | -1.78 | .05 |
| " | 8 | -.311 | -2.36 | .025 |
| " | 13 | -.219 | -1.62 | .10 |
| " | 16 | -.274 | -2.06 | .025 |
| " | 18 | -.316 | -2.40 | .025 |
| Sentence syntactically scrambled and off-hand........ <u>not</u> understandable (IIIA2c) | 16 | -.215 | -1.58 | .10 |
| | 17 | -.285 | -2.15 | .025 |
| " | 18 | -.204 | -1.50 | .10 |
| Illogical or bizarre statements (IIIA3)............. | 3 | .238 | 1.74 | .05 |
| " | 9 | -.272 | -2.04 | .025 |
| " | 10 | .217 | 1.60 | .10 |
| " | 18 | .248 | 1.85 | .05 |
| Repetition of words (intentional) (IIIB1a)........... | 8 | -.314 | -2.38 | .025 |
| " | 9 | -.220 | -1.62 | .10 |
| Repetition of words (without intervening word)(IIIB1b) | 1 | -.347 | -2.67 | .01 |
| " | 2 | -.225 | -1.67 | .10 |
| " | 8 | -.385 | -3.01 | .005 |
| " | 9 | -.209 | -1.54 | .10 |
| " | 10 | -.225 | -1.67 | .10 |
| " | 12 | -.214 | -1.58 | .10 |
| " | 14 | -.282 | -2.12 | .025 |
| Repetition of phrases, clauses (intentional) (IIIB2a) | 10 | -.417 | -3.31 | .005 |
| " | 14 | -.220 | -1.63 | .10 |
| " | 15 | -.307 | -2.33 | .025 |
| Repetition of phrases, clauses (without intervening.. words) (IIIB2b) | 3 | .317 | 2.41 | .025 |
| | 12 | -.291 | -2.20 | .025 |
| " | 17 | -.245 | -1.82 | .05 |
| Repetition of phrases, clauses (all other types)..... | 3 | .306 | 2.32 | .025 |
| " (IIIB2c) | 10 | .274 | 2.05 | .025 |

Table 4, cont.

| Verbal Item | Test [a] | R | t [b] | P (one-tail) |
|---|---|---|---|---|
| **Psychosocial Problems** | | | | |
| Self avoiding others (IA1)........................ | 4 | .308 | 2.33 | .025 |
| Others avoiding the self (IA2).................... | 2 | .285 | 2.15 | .025 |
| Self unfriendly to others (IB1)................... | 15 | -.322 | -2.45 | .01 |
| Others unfriendly to the self (IB2)............... | 4 | -.342 | -2.62 | .01 |
| " | 5 | -.266 | -1.99 | .05 |
| " | 6 | -.460 | -3.74 | .0005 |
| " | 8 | -.221 | -1.63 | .10 |
| Others friendly towards others (IC1).............. | 4 | .232 | 1.72 | .05 |
| Self friendly towards others (IC2)................ | 10 | .258 | 1.93 | .05 |
| Others friendly to the self (IC3)................. | 3 | .274 | 2.05 | .025 |
| " | 12 | -.331 | -2.53 | .01 |
| Others bad, dangerous, ill (ID1).................. | 11 | -.247 | -1.84 | .05 |
| " | 16 | -.253 | -1.55 | .10 |
| Others healthy, well (ID2)........................ | 12 | -.261 | -1.95 | .05 |
| " | 17 | -.253 | -1.88 | .05 |
| Psychological malfunction (IIB1b)................. | 2 | -.385 | -3.00 | .01 |
| " | 3 | -.280 | -2.10 | .025 |
| " | 7 | -.250 | -1.86 | .05 |
| " | 15 | -.275 | -2.06 | .025 |
| " | 16 | -.301 | -2.27 | .025 |
| Indeterminate malfunction (IIB1c)................. | 2 | -.236 | -1.75 | .05 |
| " | 14 | -.402 | -3.16 | .005 |
| " | 16 | -.280 | -2.10 | .025 |
| " | 17 | -.390 | -3.05 | .01 |
| " | 18 | -.278 | -2.09 | .025 |
| Intact, satisfied, well - neutral affect (IIB3b)... | 17 | .247 | 1.84 | .05 |
| Not being able to perform or know (IIB4).......... | 1 | .346 | 2.31 | .01 |
| " | 3 | .223 | 1.65 | .10 |
| " | 10 | .208 | 1.54 | .10 |
| Being, feeling, or wanting control (IIB5)......... | 1 | -.299 | -2.26 | .025 |
| " | 3 | -.249 | -1.85 | .05 |
| " | 5 | -.279 | -2.09 | .025 |
| " | 7 | -.291 | -2.19 | .025 |
| " | 11 | -.356 | -2.75 | .01 |
| " | 18 | -.217 | -1.60 | .10 |
| Denial of feelings, attitudes, etc., of self (IIC). | 2 | .210 | 1.55 | .10 |
| " | 3 | .271 | 2.03 | .025 |
| " | 7 | .260 | 1.94 | .05 |
| " | 12 | .244 | 1.82 | .05 |
| Food bad, etc. (IID1)............................. | 5 | .285 | 2.15 | .025 |
| " | 13 | -.246 | -1.83 | .05 |
| Food good or neutral (IID2)....................... | 1 | -.242 | -1.80 | .05 |
| " | 14 | -.239 | -1.78 | .05 |

Table 4, cont.

| Verbal Item | Test[a] | R | t[b] | P (one-tail) |
|---|---|---|---|---|
| **Psychosocial Problems, contd.** | | | | |
| Weather bad, etc. (IIE1)............................ | 3 | -.260 | -1.94 | .05 |
| " | 11 | -.232 | -1.72 | .05 |
| " | 16 | -.215 | -1.59 | .10 |
| " | 17 | .319 | 2.42 | .025 |
| Sleep bad (IIF1).................................... | 9 | .276 | 2.07 | .025 |
| " | 15 | -.231 | -1.71 | .05 |
| Sleep good or neutral (IIF2)........................ | 12 | -.246 | -1.83 | .05 |
| Questions directed to the interviewer (IVA)......... | 5 | -.206 | -1.52 | .10 |
| " | 10 | .219 | 1.62 | .10 |
| Other references to the interviewer (IVB)........... | 5 | -.217 | -1.60 | .10 |
| " | 10 | .268 | 2.00 | .05 |
| " | 17 | -.222 | -1.64 | .10 |

[a] Key to Neuropsychological Tests:

1. Tactile Performance Test
2. Tactile Performance Test - Memory
3. Tactile Performance Test - Location
4. Tap Preferred Hand
5. Trails A
6. Trails B
7. Categories
8. Speech Perception
9. Seashores
10. Wisconsin Card Sorting
11. Digit Symbol
12. Digit Span (Forward & Reverse)
13. Block Design
14. Object Assembly
15. Rod & Frame - Worst Score
16. Benton Visual Retention Test
17. Shipley Hartford Vocabulary
18. Shipley Hartford Abstracting

Halstead-Reitan Battery (#1,2,3,4,7,8,9)

Reitan's Tests (#5,6)

Wechsler Adult Intelligence Scale Subtests (#11,12,13,14)

[b] Statistical tests were done according to Edwards, 1967, p.246. All tests are one-tail because prior directional hypotheses were made. Negative correlations signify that the neuropsychological test variables and speech variables indicative of cognitive defects (or social alienation) vary in the same direction.

Table 5

Multiple Correlations of Verbal Categories from Cognitive-Intellectual Impairment Scale and Separate Neuropsychological Cognitive Test Scores

| Neuropsychological (cognitive) tests | Squared multiple correlation ($R^2$) | Probability level of overall regression equation | Regression coefficients | Verbal Category | Probability level of separate categories (two-tail) |
|---|---|---|---|---|---|
| 1. Tactile Performance Test - Time | .36 | .004 | 1.21 | IIB4 | n.s. |
| | | | -5.45 | IIB5 | .04 |
| | | | -8.63 | IID2 | n.s. |
| Mean = 30.08 | | | -6.30 | IIIA1 | n.s. |
| | | | 1.46 | IIIA2a | n.s. |
| | | | -1.71 | IIIA2b | n.s. |
| | | | -5.47 | IIIB1b | .02 |
| 2. Tactile Performance Test - Memory | .36 | .003 | 2.10 | IA2 | n.s. |
| | | | -0.51 | IIB1b | .007 |
| | | | -0.92 | IIB1c | n.s. |
| | | | 2.52 | IIC | n.s. |
| Mean = 8.0 | | | 1.55 | IIE1 | n.s. |
| | | | -0.93 | IIIA2b | .07 |
| | | | -0.16 | IIIB1b | n.s. |
| 3. Tactile Performance Test - Location | .56 | .0001 | 0.56 | IC3 | n.s. |
| | | | -0.73 | IIB1b | .006 |
| | | | -1.25 | IIB5 | .02 |
| | | | 6.24 | IIC | .01 |
| Mean = 2.06 | | | -0.35 | IIE1 | n.s. |
| | | | 0.65 | IIIA1x | .04 |
| | | | 3.89 | IIIA3 | .01 |
| | | | 1.61 | IIIB2b | .08 |
| | | | 1.41 | IIIB2c | .01 |
| 4. Tapping Preferred Hand | .25 | .005 | 7.42 | IA1 | .03 |
| | | | -1.18 | IB1 | n.s. |
| Mean = 43.05 | | | -13.41 | IB2 | .01 |
| | | | 10.61 | IC1 | n.s. |
| 5. Trails A | .38 | .002 | -15.60 | IB2 | .05 |
| | | | 72.77 | IIA | .02 |
| Mean = 83.84 | | | 3.02 | IIB3b | .08 |
| | | | -6.92 | IIB5 | .02 |
| | | | 26.11 | IID1 | .04 |
| | | | -0.77 | IVA | n.s. |
| | | | -4.56 | IVB | n.s. |
| 6. Trails B | .29 | .009 | -108.94 | IB2 | .002 |
| | | | -43.73 | IIIA1 | .04 |
| Mean = 274.55 | | | 8.18 | IIIA1x | n.s. |

Table 5, cont.

| Neuropsychological (cognitive) tests | Squared multiple correlation ($R^2$) | Probability level of overall regression equation | Regression coefficients | Verbal category | Probability level of separate categories (two-tail) |
|---|---|---|---|---|---|
| 7. Categories | .28 | .01 | -13.72 | IA1 | n.s. |
| | | | -5.88 | IIB1b | .08 |
| Mean = 145.69 | | | -14.14 | IIB5 | .06 |
| | | | 67.15 | IIC | .06 |
| | | | 5.18 | IIIA1x | n.s. |
| | | | -6.18 | IIIA2b | n.s. |
| 8. Speech | .35 | .005 | 4.30 | IA2 | n.s. |
| | | | -6.50 | IB2 | .07 |
| Mean = 54.64 | | | -0.68 | IIB1c | n.s. |
| | | | -4.43 | IIIA1 | .06 |
| | | | -2.57 | IIIA2b | n.s. |
| | | | -2.54 | IIIB1a | n.s. |
| | | | -2.61 | IIIB1b | .06 |
| 9. Seashores | .22 | .05 | 10.15 | IIF1 | n.s. |
| | | | 6.97 | IIF2 | n.s. |
| Mean = 24.99 | | | -2.12 | IIIA1 | n.s. |
| | | | -2.55 | IIIA1x | n.s. |
| | | | -1.43 | IIIB1a | n.s. |
| | | | -0.73 | IIIB1b | n.s. |
| 10. Wisconsin Card Sorting | .54 | .0002 | 2.18 | IC2 | .005 |
| | | | -0.12 | IIB4 | n.s. |
| | | | 4.25 | IID1 | .06 |
| Mean = 2.49 | | | 0.04 | IIIA2a | n.s. |
| | | | 1.48 | IIIA3 | n.s. |
| | | | -1.10 | IIIB1b | .02 |
| | | | -5.05 | IIIB2a | .003 |
| | | | 1.73 | IIIB2c | .002 |
| | | | -1.14 | IVA | n.s. |
| | | | 1.15 | IVB | .03 |
| 11. Digit Symbol | .24 | .02 | -2.03 | ID1 | n.s. |
| | | | 44.69 | IIA | n.s. |
| Mean = 46.23 | | | -6.51 | IIB5 | .02 |
| | | | -10.13 | IIE1 | n.s. |
| | | | -36.70 | IIE2 | n.s. |
| 12. Digit Span | .26 | .02 | -0.99 | IC3 | n.s. |
| | | | -0.64 | ID2 | n.s. |
| Mean = 11.78 | | | 4.81 | IIC | n.s. |
| | | | -10.23 | IIF2 | .09 |
| | | | -0.94 | IIIB1b | n.s. |
| | | | -0.13 | IIIB2b | n.s. |

Table 5, cont.

| Neuropsychological (cognitive) tests | Squared multiple correlation ($R^2$) | Probability level of overall regression equation | Regression coefficients | Verbal category | Probability level of separate categories (two-tail) |
|---|---|---|---|---|---|
| 13. Block Design | .12 | .09 | -15.59 | IID1 | n.s. |
| | | | 8.99 | IIE1 | n.s. |
| Mean = 31.70 | | | -3.13 | IIIA2b | n.s. |
| 14. Object Assembly | .23 | .01 | -14.79 | IIB1 | .02 |
| | | | -7.43 | IID2 | n.s. |
| Mean = 31.12 | | | -1.09 | IIIB1b | n.s. |
| | | | -5.59 | IIIB2a | n.s. |
| 15. Rod and Frame | .34 | .003 | -1.38 | IB1 | n.s. |
| | | | -0.21 | IIB1b | n.s. |
| Mean = 8.91 | | | -0.87 | IIF1 | n.s. |
| | | | -5.09 | IIF2 | n.s. |
| | | | -0.37 | IIIA2a | .08 |
| | | | -3.53 | IIIB2a | .006 |
| 16. Benton Visual Retention Test | .33 | .007 | 0.29 | ID1 | n.s. |
| | | | -0.20 | IIB1b | n.s. |
| | | | -2.43 | IIB1c | .08 |
| Mean = 6.57 | | | -3.04 | IIB2 | n.s. |
| | | | -4.35 | IIE1 | .009 |
| | | | -1.20 | IIIA2b | .04 |
| | | | -0.72 | IIIA2c | n.s. |
| 17. Shipley Hartford - Verbal | .54 | .0001 | -4.23 | ID2 | .003 |
| | | | -12.60 | IIB1c | .002 |
| | | | 0.96 | IIB3b | n.s. |
| Mean = 32.24 | | | -12.44 | IID1 | .02 |
| | | | 9.55 | IIE1 | .02 |
| | | | -3.19 | IIIA1 | n.s. |
| | | | -4.45 | IIIA2c | .02 |
| | | | 2.60 | IIIB2b | n.s. |
| | | | -1.01 | IVB | n.s. |
| 18. Shipley Hartford - Abstract | .26 | .01 | -3.76 | IIB1c | n.s. |
| | | | -1.49 | IIB5 | n.s. |
| | | | -2.72 | IIIA2b | .06 |
| Mean = 12.64 | | | -3.16 | IIIA2c | .05 |
| | | | 5.76 | IIIA3 | .06 |

Table 6

Regression Models and Outcomes

(Probability levels are two-tail.)

| | | Model | $R^2$ |
|---|---|---|---|
| [a] | 1. | $\text{TPT} = 29.89 - \overset{0.006}{6.87(\text{IIB5})} - \overset{0.003}{6.91(\text{IIIB1b})}$ | .24 |
| | 2. | $\text{TPT-Memory} = 7.73 - \overset{0.004}{0.59(\text{IIB1b})}$ | .15 |
| | 3. | $\text{TPT-Location} = 2.53 - \overset{0.01}{0.69(\text{IIB1b})} - \overset{0.009}{1.46(\text{IIB5})} + \overset{0.03}{5.99(\text{IIC})} + \overset{0.02}{0.79(\text{IIIA1x})} + \overset{0.01}{3.82(\text{IIIA3})} + \overset{0.02}{1.33(\text{IIIB2c})}$ | .46 |
| | 4. | $\text{Tapping} = 43.39 + \overset{0.01}{8.61(\text{IA1})} - \overset{0.007}{13.39(\text{IB2})}$ | .22 |
| [a] | 5. | $\text{Trails A} = 84.67 - \overset{0.04}{16.56(\text{IB2})} + \overset{0.04}{66.82(\text{IIA})} - \overset{0.05}{5.81(\text{IIB5})} + \overset{\text{n.s.}}{24.40(\text{IID1})}$ | .26 |
| [a] | 6. | $\text{Trails B} = 280.23 - \overset{0.0007}{118.46(\text{IB2})} - \overset{0.05}{40.63(\text{IIIA1})}$ | .27 |
| [a] | 7. | $\text{Categories} = 145.69 - \overset{\text{n.s.}}{13.72(\text{IA1})} - \overset{\text{n.s.}}{5.88(\text{IIB1b})} - \overset{\text{n.s.}}{14.14(\text{IIB5})} + \overset{\text{n.s.}}{67.15(\text{IIC})} + \overset{\text{n.s.}}{5.18(\text{IIIA1x})} - \overset{\text{n.s.}}{6.18(\text{IIIA2b})}$ | .28 |
| | 8. | $\text{Speech Perception} = 53.48 - \overset{\text{n.s.}}{6.51(\text{IB2})} - \overset{0.03}{5.12(\text{IIIA1})} - \overset{0.002}{3.82(\text{IIIB1b})}$ | .28 |
| | 9. | $\text{Seashores} = 24.99 + \overset{\text{n.s.}}{10.15(\text{IIF1})} + \overset{\text{n.s.}}{6.97(\text{IIF2})} - \overset{\text{n.s.}}{2.12(\text{IIIA1})} - \overset{\text{n.s.}}{2.55(\text{IIIA1x})} - \overset{\text{n.s.}}{1.43(\text{IIIB1a})} - \overset{\text{n.s.}}{0.73(\text{IIIB1b})}$ | .22 |
| | 10. | $\text{Wisconsin Card Sorting} = 2.77 + \overset{0.005}{2.07(\text{IC2})} - \overset{0.03}{0.98(\text{IIIB1b})} - \overset{0.002}{5.38(\text{IIIB2a})} + \overset{0.001}{1.65(\text{IIIB2c})} + \overset{0.02}{0.97(\text{IVB})}$ | .47 |
| | 11. | $\text{Digit Symbol} = 45.23 - \overset{0.008}{7.07(\text{IIB5})}$ | .13 |

Table 6, cont.

| | | $R^2$ |
|---|---|---|
| 12. | Digit Span $= 11.78 - 0.99(\text{IC3}) - \overset{\text{n.s.}}{0.64(\text{ID2})} + \overset{\text{n.s.}}{4.81(\text{IIC})} - \overset{\text{n.s.}}{10.23(\text{IIF2})}$ | |
| | $- \overset{\text{n.s.}}{0.94(\text{IIIB1b})} - \overset{\text{n.s.}}{0.13(\text{IIIB2b})}$ | .26 |
| 13. | Block Design $= 31.70 - \overset{\text{n.s.}}{15.99(\text{IID1})} + \overset{\text{n.s.}}{8.99(\text{IIE1})} - \overset{\text{n.s.}}{3.13(\text{IIIA2b})}$ | .12 |
| 14. | Object Assembly $= 29.78 - \overset{0.003}{17.68(\text{IIB1c})}$ | .16 |
| [a] 15. | Rod/Frame $= 8.63 - \overset{0.001}{0.57(\text{IIIA2a})} - \overset{0.003}{3.78(\text{IIIB2a})}$ | .27 |
| 16. | Benton Visual Retention Test $= 6.12 - \overset{0.03}{3.59(\text{IIE1})} - \overset{0.01}{1.47(\text{IIIA2b})}$ | .15 |
| 17. | Shipley Hartford-Verbal $= 31.72 - \overset{0.01}{3.31(\text{ID2})} - \overset{0.004}{10.57(\text{IIB1c})} - \overset{0.02}{12.77(\text{IID1})}$ | |
| | $+ \overset{0.02}{9.68(\text{IIE1})} - \overset{0.02}{3.84(\text{IIIA2c})}$ | .42 |
| 18. | Shipley Hartford-Abstract $= 10.20 - \overset{\text{n.s.}}{2.57(\text{IIIA2c})}$ | .04 n.s. |

[a] Values used in our calculations (if different from normal clinical usage):

TPT, 45.0 - TPT total time
Trails A, 120 - time to complete task
Trails B, 360 - time to complete task
Categories, 208 - number incorrect
Rod/Frame, 10.0 - mean deviation from zero, poorest of two sides.

Table 7

Regression Models and Outcome

(Probability levels are two-tail.)

| Model | $R^2$ |
|---|---|
| [a] 1. TPT = 41.85 - 5.70(IIB5) - 5.32(IIIB1b) + 0.71(Educ.) - 0.38(Age)<br>(p: IIB5 0.01; IIIB1b 0.01; Educ. n.s. [b]; Age 0.002) | .39 |
| 2. TPT-Memory = 9.44 + 3.28(IA2) - 0.52(IIB1b) - 1.12(IIIA2b) + 0.13(Educ.) - 0.04(Age)<br>(p: IA2 0.01; IIB1b 0.006; IIIA2b 0.02; Educ. n.s.; Age 0.02) | .40 |
| 3. TPT-Location = 4.97 - 0.66(IIB1b) + 6.25(IIC) + 2.45(IIIB2b) + 1.40(IIIB2c) - 0.03(Educ.) - 0.06(Age)<br>(p: IIB1b 0.01; IIC 0.02; IIIB2b 0.003; IIIB2c 0.02; Educ. n.s.; Age 0.02) | .43 |
| 4. Tapping = 47.90 + 9.31(IA1) - 14.10(IB2) + 0.46(Educ.) - 0.15(Age)<br>(p: IA1 0.01; IB2 0.006; Educ. n.s.; Age n.s.) | .26 |
| [a] 5. Trails A = 102.30 - 16.34(IB2) + 2.56(IIB3b) - 5.64(IVB) - 0.35(Educ.) - 0.42(Age)<br>(p: IB2 0.05; IIB3b n.s.; IVB 0.04; Educ. n.s.; Age 0.005) | .28 |
| [a] 6. Trails B = 312.07 - 132.00(IB2) + 7.33(Educ.) - 1.70(Age)<br>(p: IB2 0.0002; Educ. n.s.; Age 0.004) | .35 |
| [a] 7. Categories = 190.77 - 6.90(IIB1b) + 73.01(IIC) + 0.76(Educ.) - 1.34(Age)<br>(p: IIB1b 0.02; IIC 0.02; Educ. n.s.; Age 0.0002) | .37 |
| 8. Speech perception = 60.64 - 4.84(IIIA1) - 2.40(IIIA2b) - 2.55(IIIB1a) - 2.40(IIIB1b) - 0.07(Educ.) - 0.14(Age)<br>(p: IIIA1 0.04; IIIA2b n.s.; IIIB1a n.s.; IIIB1b n.s.; Educ. n.s.; Age 0.03) | .35 |
| 9. Seashores = 22.19 + 13.79(IIF1) + 0.33(Educ.) + 0.01(Age)<br>(p: IIF1 0.05; Educ. n.s.; Age n.s.) | .09 n.s. |
| 10. Wisconsin Card Sorting = 6.64 + 0.90(IA1) - 5.24(IIIB2a) + 1.14(IIIB2c) + 0.03(Educ.) - 0.07(Age)<br>(p: IA1 n.s.; IIIB2a 0.003; IIIB2c 0.05; Educ. n.s.; Age 0.006) | .38 |

Table 7, cont.

| | Equation (significance levels printed above each term) | $R^2$ |
|---|---|---|
| 11. | Digit Symbol = 55.57 - 4.52(ID1) [n.s.] - 5.21(IIB5) [0.03] + 2.01(Educ.) [0.04] - 0.42(Age) [0.0009] | .37 |
| 12. | Digit Span = 12.46 - 1.08(IC3) [n.s.] - 1.06(IIIB2b) [n.s.] + 0.08(Educ.) [n.s.] - 0.04(Age) [n.s.] | .14 n.s. |
| 13. | Block Design = 29.81 - 19.96(IID1) [0.04] + 1.74(Educ.) [n.s.] - 0.16(Age) [n.s.] | .15 |
| 14. | Object Assembly = 34.10 - 14.53(IIB1c) [0.009] + 1.42(Educ.) [n.s.] - 0.25(Age) [0.008] | .30 |
| [a] 15. | Rod/Frame = 9.50 - 1.79(IB1) [n.s.] - 0.14(IIB1b) [n.s.] - 0.44(IIIA2a) [0.05] - 3.39(IIIB2a) [0.009] + 0.06(Educ.) [n.s.] - 0.02(Age) [n.s.] | .33 |
| 16. | Benton Visual = 7.58 - 0.28(IIB1b) [n.s.] - 2.72(IID1) [n.s.] - 0.20(IIIA2a) [n.s.] + 0.42(Educ.) [0.03] - 0.09(Age) [0.0005] | .36 |
| 17. | Shipley Hartford-Verbal = 18.75 - 3.70(ID2) [0.004] - 7.83(IIB1c) [0.02] + 11.95(IIE1) [0.003] + 2.01(Educ.) [0.0002] + 0.07(Age) [n.s.] | .51 |
| 18. | Shipley Hartford-Abstract = 10.62 - 2.84(IIIA2b) [0.03] + 6.93(IIIA3) [0.03] + 1.23(Educ.) [0.01] - 0.12(Age) [0.03] | .31 |

[a] Values used in our calculations (if different from normal clinical usage):

- TPT, 45.0 - TPT total time
- Trails A, 120 - time to complete task
- Trails B, 360 - time to complete task
- Categories, 208 - number incorrect
- Rod/Frame, 10.0 - mean deviation from zero, poorest of two sides

[b] Key to educational level:

- 1 = some grade school
- 2 = finished grade school
- 3 = some high school
- 4 = finished high school
- 5 = some college
- 6 = finished college
- 7 = attended graduate or professional school after college

Other studies by Gottschalk and his coworkers have demonstrated that the content analysis of natural speech can be applied to the objective detection and assessment of subtle to gross impairment of cognitive and intellectual function and, in so doing, these studies constitute a growing body of evidence of the construct validation of this measurement procedure for assaying temporary or permanent dysfunction and impairment of brain activity.

Most of the same verbal categories (for example, IIB1, IIB5, IIIA1, IIIA2, IIIA3, IIIB1, IIIB2) observed here to vary significantly with disturbances of cognitive function have also been observed to occur more frequently: (1) in the speech of children 6 to 8 and to decrease up to the age of 16 (Gottschalk, 1976); (2) with the withdrawal of phenothiazine pharmacotherapy from chronic schizophrenic patients (Gottschalk et al, 1970); (3) with the short term administration of benzodiazepine derivatives to anxious patients (Gottschalk, 1977b; Gottschalk and Elliott, 1976); (4) and with the inhalation of 40% nitrous oxide by normal subjects (Gottschalk, Introductory Comments to Chapter 17 by Atkinson in this book); (5) with total body irradiation (Gottschalk et al, 1969); (6) with the administration of LSD-25 or Ditran (Gottschalk and Gleser, 1969, pp 232f); (7) with smoking marihuana (Gottschalk et al, 1977). We have located and specified here a set of verbal categories occurring in natural speech whose frequency of use is sensitively influenced by central nervous system malfunction. It is quite likely as indicated in Tables 4, 5, 6, and 7 that different categories measure somewhat different cognitive processes, such as, memory, ability to abstract, attention, general intelligence. Our intention is to replicate further our present findings and the predictor formulas for assaying these different kinds of cognitive functions.

## SUMMARY

A Cognitive-Intellectual Impairment scale, derived from the frequency of use of various verbal categories used in natural speech, has

been developed from a validated Social Alienation-Personal Disorganization (content analysis) scale which is capable of measuring changes in the severity of social withdrawal and cognitive defects in the schizophrenic syndrome. Various construct validation studies have been carried out more precisely designating the verbal categories significantly associated with central nervous system dysfunction and providing bases for weighting the relative importance of each verbal category in assessing cognitive defects. These validation studies include comparisons of the frequency of use of certain verbal categories from known brain-function impaired patients and cognitively normal patients, the assessment of the effects of chemical substances (alcohol, nitrous oxide, and marihuana), psychotomimetic and other drugs and correlations of verbal categories from the Cognitive-Intellectual Impairment scale with criterion measures based on clinical neuropsychological test scores such as, from the Halstead-Reitan Battery, subtests from the Wechsler Adult Intelligence Scale, the Shipley Hartford Intelligence test, the Benton Visual Retention test, the Rod and Frame test, and so forth. Multivariate analyses have provided statistically significant equations using certain verbal categories to predict these neuropsychological test scores.

## References

Atkinson, R.M., Morozumi, P., Green, J.D., and Kramer, J.C. Nitrous oxide intoxication: subjective effects in healthy young men. Unpublished manuscript (1977).

Benton, A.L. Revised Visual Retention Test: Clinical and Experimental Applications. Psychological Corp., New York (1974).

Goodwin, D.W., and Hill, S.Y. Chronic effects of alcohol and other psychoactive drugs on intellect, learning and memory, in Alcohol, Drugs and Brain Damage. J.G. Rankin, ed. Addiction Research Foundation, Toronto (1975).

Gottschalk, L.A. Children's speech as a source of data toward the

measurement of psychological states. J. Youth and Adolescence 5, 11-36 (1976).

Gottschalk, L.A. Cognitive defect in the schizophrenic syndrome as assessed by speech patterns. (Presented at the Symposium on "Cognitive Defects in the Development of Mental Illness." Kittay Scientific Foundation, New York, April 1977). Brunner-Mazel, New York (1977a), in press.

Gottschalk, L.A. Effects of certain benzodiazepine derivatives on disorganization of thought as manifested in speech. Curr. Ther. Res. 21, 192-206 (1977b).

Gottschalk, L.A., Aronow, W.S., and Prakash, R. Effect of marihuana and placebo-marihuana smoking on psychological state and on psychophysiological cardiovascular functioning in anginal patients. Biol. Psychiatry 12, 255-266 (1977).

Gottschalk, L.A., and Elliott, H.W. Effects of triazolam and flurazepam on cognitive function. Res. Commun. Psychology, Psychiatry, and Behavior 1, 575-595 (1976).

Gottschalk, L.A., and Gleser, G.C. Distinguishing characteristics of the verbal communications of schizophrenic patients, in Disorders of Communication of the Association for Research in Nervous and Mental Disease. Williams & Wilkins, Baltimore (1964), pp. 400-413.

Gottschalk, L.A., and Gleser, G.C. The Measurement of Psychological States Through the Content Analysis of Verbal Behavior. University of California Press, Berkeley (1969).

Gottschalk, L.A., Gleser, G.C., Cleghorn, J.M., Stone, W.N., and Winget, C.N. Prediction of changes in severity of the schizophrenic syndrome with discontinuation and administration of phenothiazines in chronic schizophrenic patients: language as a predictor and measure of change in schizophrenia. Compr. Psychiatry 11, 123-140 (1970).

Gottschalk, L.A., Gleser, G.C., Daniels, R.S., and Block, S.L. The speech patterns of schizophrenic patients: A method of assessing

relative degree of personal disorganization and social alienation. J. Nerv. Ment. Dis. 127, 153-166 (1958).

Gottschalk, L.A., Gleser, G.C., Magliocco, E.B., and D'Zmura, T.L. Further studies on the speech patterns of schizophrenic patients. Measuring inter-individual differences in relative degree of personal disorganization and social alienation. J. Nerv. Ment. Dis. 132, 101-113 (1961).

Gottschalk, L.A., and Hambidge, G., Jr. Verbal behavior analysis: A systematic approach to the problem of quantifying psychological processes. J. Projective Techniques 19, 387-409 (1955).

Gottschalk, L.A., and Kunkel, R.L. Changes in emotional and intellectual functioning after total body radiation, in Metabolic Changes in Humans Following Total Body Radiation. E.L. Saenger, B.J. Friedman, J.G. Keriakis, and H. Perry, eds. University of Cincinnati College of Medicine, Cincinnati General Hospital, Cincinnati, Ohio (1966).

Gottschalk, L.A., Kunkel, R.L., Wohl, T., Saenger, E., and Winget, C.N. Total and half-body body irradiation. Effect on cognitive and emotional processes. Arch. Gen. Psychiatry 21, 574-580 (1969).

Gottschalk, L.A., Winget, C.N., and Gleser, G.C. Manual of Instructions for Using the Gottschalk-Gleser Content Analysis Scales: Anxiety, Hostility, and Social Alienation-Personal Disorganization. University of California Press, Berkeley (1969).

Grant, I., and Mohns, L. Chronic cerebral effects of alcohol and drug abuse. Int. J. Addict. 10, 883-920 (1975).

Halstead, W.C. Brain and Intelligence. University of Chicago Press, Chicago (1947).

Katz, M.M., Waskow, I.E., and Olsson, J. Characterizing the psychological state produced by LSD. J. Abnorm. Psychol. 73, 1-14 (1968).

Kleinknecht, R.A., and Goldstein, S.G. Neuropsychological deficits associated with alcoholism. Quart. J. Stud. Alc. 33, 999-1019 (1972).

Matarazzo, J.D. Wechsler's Measurement and Appraisal of Adult Intelli-

gence. Williams and Wilkins Co., Baltimore, Maryland (1972).

Parker, E.S., and Noble, E.P. Alcohol consumption and cognitive functioning in social drinkers. J. Stud. Alc. (in press).

Parsons, O.A. Neuropsychological deficits in alcoholics: Facts and fancies. Alcoholism 1, 51-56 (1977).

Reitan, R.M. The relation of the Trail Making Test to organic brain damage. J. Consult. Psychol. 19, 393-394 (1955).

Reitan, R.M. A research program on the psychological effects of brain lesions in human beings, in International Review of Research in Mental Retardation, Vol. 1 N.R. Ellis, ed. Academic Press, New York (1966).

Shipley, W.C., and Burlingame, C.C. A convenient self-administering scale for measuring intellectual impairment in psychotics. Am. J. Psychiatry 97, 1313-1317 (1941).

Tarter, R.E. Psychological deficit in chronic alcoholics: A review. Int. J. Addict. 10, 327-368 (1975).

Tarter, R.E., and Parsons, O.A. Conceptual shifting in chronic alcoholics. J. Abnorm. Psychol. 77, 71-75 (1971).

Witkin, H., Karp, S., and Goodenough, D. Dependence in alcoholics. Quart. J. Stud. Alc. 20, 493-504 (1959).

Appendix I

Descriptions of the 18 Neuropsychological Tests

1. TPT (Tactile Performance Test):

This test measures the amount of time required to place wooden blocks of different geometric designs in the appropriate "cut-outs" on a wooden board. Time is recorded for the preferred hand, the non-preferred hand, and both hands used simultaneously. This test is performed while the patient is blindfolded and neither the blocks nor the board are ever seen by the subject.

2. Tactile Performance Test - Memory:

After the form board is removed, the blindfold is removed and the subject is asked to reproduce the blocks by drawing them on a sheet of blank white paper. The memory score is the number of blocks correctly remembered and reproduced.

3. Tactile Performance Test - Localization:

This score is the number of blocks correctly localized in the drawing; i.e., the triangle is drawn in the place where it actually is on the board, etc.

The above tests measure (1) tactile form discrimination; (2) kinethesis and its memory; (3) coordination of movements of the upper extremities and manual dexterity; and (4) visualization and reproduction of spatial configurations of space.

4. Tapping Test, Preferred Hand:

The forefinger of the preferred hand taps a counter mounted on a 6 x 6 inch block of wood as rapidly as possible for 10 seconds. The score is the mean number of "taps" determined from at least 5 trials. This test measures motor speed.

5. Trails A:

This test measures the time required to draw a line connecting circles containing numbers in sequence from 1 to 25, placed at random on the test sheet.

6. Trails B:

This test measures the time required to connect circles containing a number and a letter in sequence; i.e. (1) must be connected with (A), then from (A) to (2) to (B) etc. There are 25 circles in Trails B. This test measures (1) recognition of the symbolic significance of numbers and letters; (2) the ability to scan the page continuously to identify the next number or letter in the sequence; (3) flexibility in integrating numerical and alphabetical series.

7. Categories Test:

In this test a slide is projected on a screen setting up a problem. The subject responds by depressing one of four levers mounted on a plate, which will solve the problem. If the solution is correct, a tone is sounded; if incorrect, a buzzer is sounded. Immediately the next slide is presented with a similar or new problem.

This is a complex concept formation test and measures ability: (1) to note similarities and differences in material; (2) to postulate the hypothesis that seems most reasonable. Because of the positive or negative reinforcement accompanying each response, it also becomes a learning experiment. Thus, an essential purpose is to determine ability to profit from both positive and negative experiences as a basis for altering test performance.

8. Speech Perception Test:

The subject is given a printed sheet of paper containing "nonsense" words. These are presented in rows with four words in each row. A tape is played with a speaker pronouncing one of the "nonsense" words in the first row of four. The subject must decide which of the words on the paper corresponds to that given by the speaker on the tape. The next word is given by the speaker and the process is repeated. A 5-second interval elapses between each stimulus word presented on the tape. This test measures: (1) ability to maintain attention through 60 items comprising the test; (2) perceive spoken stimuli; (3) relate perception through vision to the correct configuration of letters on the test form.

9. Seashore Rhythm Test:

This is the Rhythm subtest of the Seashore Test of Musical Talent. It requires the subject to differentiate between 30 pairs of rhythmic beats. Sometimes the beats are the same and sometimes they are different. This test measures (1) alertness; (2) sustained attention; (3) ability to perceive and compare different rhythmic sequences.

10. Wisconsin Card Sorting:

This test measures brain function, primarily frontal lobe. Subjects are presented with four base cards, varying in color, shape, and number. Subject takes a card from a deck and places it below one of the four cards which most resembles it. After 10 consecutive correct sortings (matchings) of either color, shape or number, another criterion for matching is instituted. Correct matchings are shifted until 6 sets are accomplished correctly (or 60 trials without 10 consecutive matchings). There is no time limit and immediate feedback is given after each trial as to correct or incorrect. Scored on basis of number of correctly completed sets.

11. Digit Symbol:

This is a subtest from the Wechsler Adult Intelligence scale. The subject is requested to examine a line of boxes or squares. Each box has a number in the upper part and a symbol in the lower part and every number has a different symbol. The subject is given a chance to practice substituting the proper symbol for the numbers and then is given 90 seconds to substitute as many correct symbols for the numbers appearing in the boxes as possible. The score is the number correctly reproduced. This test measures (1) new learning and a rapid switching of set; (2) visual acuity, motor coordination, and speed.

12. Digit Span:

This test requires the subject to repeat a series of digits pronounced by the examiner at 1-second intervals. The first series must be repeated as given and in the second series the subject must say the numbers backwards. The series of numbers ranges from 3 to 9. This

measures (1) retentiveness; (2) reveals memory defects which helps differentiate organic disease. Reduced performance in memory span is often one of the early indications of mental impairment.

13. Block Design:

This test was originated as a comprehensive measure of non-verbal intelligence. The subject must reproduce a design presented on a small card with "colored wooden blocks."

Patients with mental deterioration and seniles have particular difficulty in managing the tasks and often cannot complete the simplest design. This is also true of many cases of brain disease. The test purports to measure: (1) ability to synthesize and form the necessary abstraction in order to solve the problem; (2) the ability to "shift" to meet the changing designs; (3) ability to attend simultaneously to color and pattern.

14. Object Assembly:

This consists of four different figure formboards consisting of a "mannekin", "human profile", "hand", and an "elephant". The mannekin and profile are essentially the same used by the Pintner-Patterson test. The hand was devised by Wechsler, and the "elephant" added to the WAIS series was also devised by Wechsler. Diagnostic value is found in the manner in which the problem is solved. One can distinguish between the individual who recognizes from the start that a figure is to be put together and does it fairly quickly. The mental defective usually has no idea what is to be assembled and merely fits the pieces together by trial and error. The third method is rapid recognition of the whole but imperfect understanding of the relationship between parts. The other usual method is a beginning of complete failure to take in the total situation but after a certain amount of trial and error, recognition develops and leads to a sudden appreciation of figure. According to Wechsler, the value of this test is that it reveals the subject's mode of perception, the degree to which trial and error is relied on and the manner of reaction to mistakes.

15. Rod and Frame Test:

This procedure is used to measure field dependence and independence which are considered to be perceptual and cognitive functions. Test is presented with frame in a tilted condition and the experimenter manipulates the rod toward vertical position. The subject tells the experimenter when to stop the rod when it is in a perfectly vertical position. Test is performed 10 times consecutively starting either from left or right side, then repeated 10 times in the opposite direction. For scoring, an average score is taken from each direction; poorest score is used and this score measures field dependence.

16. Benton Visual Retention Test:

This test measures cerebral organic deficit. A subject is given a view of a card for 5 seconds, then is asked to immediately reproduce the figures from memory immediately. This test is scored according to correct number of reproductions.

17. and 18. Shipley-Hartford Intelligence Scale:

The Vocabulary and Abstraction tests are the two subtests making up this scale. This is a short, easily administered and simply scored intelligence scale.

# 3

# *The Measurement of Psychological States: Relationships Between Gottschalk-Gleser Content Analysis Scores and Hamilton Anxiety Rating Scale Scores, Physician Questionnaire Rating Scale Scores and Hopkins Symptom Checklist Scores*

L.A. GOTTSCHALK
J.C. HOIGAARD
H. BIRCH
K. RICKELS

This was part of a double-blind, placebo-drug study examining the differences in psychological effects resulting from the oral administration of lorazepam (3 mg/day), diazepam (15 mg/day) or a placebo to a *randomly selected group* of 35 outpatients over a period of 4 weeks. The focus of interest in this report is the interrelationship of scores derived from various psychological measures utilizing quite different means of data collection and analysis to provide assessments of similar or identical psychological/behavioral dimensions.

The assumption is often made by the unsuspecting or naïve clinician that the "anxiety," "depression," "hostility" and other psychological states measured in psychopharmacological, psychophysiological and psychotherapy studies are the same, though quite different methods may be used in assaying these states. Experienced clinicians and researchers are well aware of the measurement problems involved in assessing psycholog-

ical states and traits. They worry about the extent to which different kinds of measurement methods result in similar qualitative as well as quantitative estimates of presumably, at least by name, identical emotions or other psychological conditions.

This report provides a detailed examination of the correlations between the scores obtained pre-drug and post-drug from this group of 35 outpatients using three methods of assessment: rating scales, self-report scales and content analysis scales.

## METHODS

The sample of psychiatric outpatients was obtained from the Symptomatic Volunteer Clinic at Philadelphia General Hospital. These outpatients were suffering from neurotic anxiety and tension of at least moderate degree, with or without somatization and depression.

The measures used to assess psychological dimensions pre- and post-treatment were:

(1) *The Gottschalk-Gleser Content Analysis Scales,*[1,2] which provide scores on a number of psychological states by content analysis of 5-minute speech samples. In this report, the only content analysis scores obtained were total anxiety and 6 anxiety subscales; total hostility outward, composed of overt hostility outward and covert hostility outward; hostility inward; and ambivalent hostility. These scales are given in Schedule I (Anxiety), Schedule II (Hostility Outward), Schedule III (Hostility Inward) and Schedule IV (Ambivalent Hostility).

(2) *The Hopkins Symptom Checklist (HSCL),* a 52-item self-report measure originally developed by Parloff, Kelman and Frank,[3] and further refined by Frank et al.,[4] Mattsson et al.[5] and Derogatis et al.,[6] and factor-analyzed for 5 factors and a total score. (See Schedule V.)

(3) *The Hamilton Anxiety Scale,*[7] a 13-item rating scale which has been cluster-analyzed into an emotional and somatic cluster. (See Schedule VI.)

(4) *The Physician Questionnaire,* a 16-item rating scale[8] consisting of an emotional and somatic cluster. (See Schedule VII.)

The Hamilton Anxiety and Physician Questionnaire rating scales were filled out by the psychiatrist. The Hopkins Symptom Checklist (HSCL) was filled out by the patient and hence constituted a self-report measure. The content analysis scales were scored blindly by content analysis technicians in the Communications and Measurement Laboratory, University of California at Irvine, from 5-minute speech samples obtained by two research assistants from the psychiatric outpatients in Philadelphia, Pennsylvania.

Scores from the rating scales, self-report scales and content analysis

scales, as well as scores from single items, subscales, factors and clusters, were intercorrelated by computer analysis, using the Social Science package of Nie et al.[9]

## RESULTS

In the lengthy and detailed tables shown below, there are included pre-drug (pre-treatment) and post-drug (post-treatment) measures. The pre-drug measures were obtained on patients receiving no medication, and the post-drug measures included patients who were receiving either a placebo, diazepam (15 mg/day) or lorazepam (3 mg/day). Whenever the correlations under either the pre-drug or post-drug condition reached a convincing level of statistical significance, the correlation occurring with the other condition was included, whether or not it was statistically significant. One could reasonably expect that correlations between two different measures should, at least, be in the same direction under the two conditions (pre- and post-drug), but there are conceivably several reasons why the correlations might not be either in the same direction or statistically significant under both conditions:

(1) The reliability and validity error variances of the different measurement procedures might vary widely, especially over different occasions.

(2) The mild tranquilizers, diazepam and lorazepam, might differently affect patient responses as measured by means of self-report, behavioral rating or speech content.

(3) By chance, when running many correlations, a few usually significant ones might appear to be not significant. And some correlations might appear to be significant when they are actually not significant, for example, 5 out of 100 if the criterion selected for statistical significance is a probability at the .05 level of confidence.

On those occasions where apparently significant correlations were found during both pre- and post-drug time periods, we can have some tentative assurance that the two different measurement procedures were assaying similar psychological variables.

I. *Correlations of Anxiety Content Analysis Scale Scores*

A. With the Hamilton Anxiety Rating Scale

1. *Total Anxiety Scale and Anxiety Subscale (Content Analysis) Scores and Cluster Scores of the Hamilton Anxiety Rating Scale*

*Pre-drug correlations* (that is, correlations between *pre-drug* total anxiety content analysis scale scores and *pre-drug* cluster scores of the Hamilton Anxiety Rating Scale): none significant.

*Post-drug correlations* (that is, correlations between the different psychological measures obtained when the patients were under the influence of the psychoactive drug—*after the administration of the drug*): The post-drug total anxiety (content analysis) scale scores correlated positively ($r = .44$, $p < .05$) with the post-drug Emotional cluster of the Hamilton Anxiety Rating Scale (Table I). This correlation was based entirely on the correlation of post-drug shame anxiety subscale scores ($r = .45$, $p < .05$) of the content analysis measure rather than on the correlation with any other content analysis anxiety subscale scores (Table II).

2. *Total Anxiety Scale and Anxiety Subscale (Content Analysis) Scores and Separate Items of the Hamilton Anxiety Rating Scale*

None of the separate items (13) of the Hamilton Anxiety Rating Scale correlated significantly with the total Anxiety (Content Analysis) Scale scores (Table III). But Table IV indicates that *pre-drug* separation anxiety scores correlated significantly positively ($r = .48$, $N = 34$, $p < .005$) with the *pre-drug* anxious mood item (#1) scores of the Hamilton Anxiety Rating Scale, and *post-drug* shame anxiety (content analysis) scores correlated significantly positively ($r = .44$, $N = 21$, $p < .05$) with *post-drug* anxious mood item (#1) scores of the Hamilton Anxiety Rating Scale.

Curiously, the *pre-drug* death anxiety (content analysis) subscale scores correlated significantly *negatively* ($r = -.58$, $p < .005$) with the *pre-drug* tension item (#2) scores from the Hamilton Anxiety Rating Scale (Table IV).

Other correlations of interest from Table IV are as follows:

*Pre-drug correlations:* pre-drug mutilation (content analysis) anxiety scores and pre-drug item #5 (Intellectual) scores—$r = .43$, $p < .01$; pre-drug separation (content analysis) anxiety scores and pre-drug item #11 (Genito-urinary) scores—$r = .40$, $p < .05$.

*Post-drug correlations:* post-drug shame (content analysis) anxiety scores and post-drug item #6 (Depressed mood) scores—$r = .48$, $p < .05$; post-drug mutilation (content analysis) anxiety scores and post-drug item #8 (Cardiovascular) scores—$r = .52$, $p < .05$; post-drug guilt (content analysis) anxiety scores and post-drug item #12 (Autonomic) scores—$r = .46$, $p < .05$.

B. With the Physician Questionnaire Rating Scale

1. *Total Anxiety Scale and Anxiety Subscale (Content Analysis) Scores and Cluster Scores of the Physician Questionnaire Rating Scale*

Neither the total score nor the separate scores of cluster I (Emo-

tional) or cluster II (Somatic) of the Physician Questionnaire correlated with the total (content analysis) anxiety score (Table I).

However, the pre-drug death anxiety (content analysis) scores correlated positively with the pre-drug cluster I (Emotional) scores ($r = .36$, $N = 35$, $p < .05$) and with the pre-drug cluster I plus II (Total) scores ($r = 0.34$, $N = 35$, $p < .05$) of the Physician Questionnaire; also post-drug diffuse anxiety (content analysis) scores correlated positively ($r = 0.44$, $N = 21$, $p < .05$) with post-drug scores from Cluster I (Emotional) (see Table II).

2. *Total Anxiety (Content Analysis) Scale Scores and Items of the Physician Questionnaire Rating Scale*

The post-drug total anxiety (content analysis) scores correlated significantly ($r = .46$, $N = 21$, $p < .05$) with the item #3 (Irritability) and item #15 (Impairment of Interpersonal Relationships) scores ($r = .62$, $N = 21$, $p < .005$) (see Table V).

3. *Anxiety (Content Analysis) Subscale Scores and Items of the Physician Questionnaire Rating Scale*

The death anxiety and mutilation anxiety (content analysis) subscales scores did not correlate significantly with any of the separate item scores of the Physician Questionnaire. However, the separation anxiety (content analysis) scores correlated significantly with pre-drug item #3 (Irritability) scores ($r = .35$, $N = 35$, $p < .05$) and post-drug item #6 (Obsessive-compulsive) scores ($r = .45$, $N = 21$, $p < .05$).

The guilt anxiety (content analysis) scores correlated significantly with post-drug item #4 (Hostility) scores ($r = .54$, $N = 21$, $p < .05$), post-drug item #13 (Psychomotor Retardation)scores ($r = .52$, $N = 21$, $p < .05$) and pre-drug item #7 (Hypochondriasis) scores ($r = .51$, $N = 35$, $p < .005$) of the Physician Questionnaire.

The shame anxiety (content analysis) scores correlated significantly with post-drug item #2 (Depressive Mood) scores ($r = .48$, $N = 21$, $p < .05$), post-drug item #15 (Impairment of Interpersonal Relationships) scores ($r = .52$, $N = 21$, $p < .05$) and item #16 (Degree of Global Psychopathology) scores ($r = .46$, $N = 21$, $p < .05$) of the Physician Questionnaire.

The diffuse anxiety (content analysis) scores correlated significantly with post-drug item #3 (Irritability) scores ($r = .48$, $N = 21$, $p < .05$), post-drug item #6 (Obsessive-compulsive) scores ($r = .45$, $N = 21$, $p < .05$) and post-drug item #15 (Impairment of Interpersonal Relationships) scores ($r = .59$, $N = 21$, $p < .005$) of the Physician Questionnaire.

**Table I. Intercorrelations of Affect Content Analysis Scores with Behavioral Rating Scale and Symptom Checklist Scale Cluster Scores.**

*** $p < .005$
** $p < .01$
* $p < .05$

1 = (correlations of pre-drug scores from both scales)
2 = (correlations of post-drug scores from both scales)

| Behavioral or Psychological Measure | Affect Scales† | | | | | | | | | | | |
|---|---|---|---|---|---|---|---|---|---|---|---|---|
| Hamilton Anxiety Scale | Anx. 1 | Anx. 2 | Host. Out Ov. 1 | Host. Out Ov. 2 | Host. Out Cov. 1 | Host. Out Cov. 2 | Host. Total 1 | Host. Total 2 | Host. In 1 | Host. In 2 | Amb. Host. 1 | Amb. Host. 2 |
| Cluster I (Emotional) | –.08<br>n = 34 | .44*<br>n = 21 | | | | | | | | | | |
| Cluster II (Somatic) | | | | | .35*<br>n = 34 | .33<br>n = 21 | | | | | | |
| Cluster I + II (Total) | | | | | .28<br>n = 34 | .44*<br>n = 21 | | | | | | |
| **Physician Questionnaire** | | | | | | | | | | | | |
| Cluster I (Emotional) | | | .43**<br>n = 35 | .12<br>n = 21 | | | .44**<br>n = 35 | .21<br>n = 21 | .37*<br>n = 35 | .10<br>n = 21 | | |
| Cluster II (Somatic) | | | | | .25<br>n = 35 | .42<br>n = 21 | .19<br>n = 35 | .47*<br>n = 21 | | | | |
| Cluster I + II (Total) | | | | | .31<br>n = 35 | .44*<br>n = 21 | .36*<br>n = 35 | .38<br>n = 21 | | | | |

| Symptom Checklist (SCL) | | | | | | | | | | | | |
|---|---|---|---|---|---|---|---|---|---|---|---|---|
| Factor I (Somatization) | .28 n = 35 | .46* n = 21 | | | | | | | .19 n = 35 | .46* n = 21 | −0.6 n = 35 | .47* n = 21 |
| Factor II (Obsessive-compulsive) | | | .37* n = 35 | .20 n = 21 | | | .31 n = 35 | .22 n = 21 | .43** n = 35 | .50* n = 21 | | |
| Factor III (Inter-personal-sensitivity) | .26 n = 35 | .47* n = 21 | | | | | | | | | | |
| Factor IV (Depression) | .31 n = 35 | .43* n = 21 | | | | | | | .37* n = 35 | .31 n = 21 | | |
| Factor V (Anxiety) | | | | | | | | | | | | |
| **Total SCL Score** | .33* n = 35 | .45* n = 21 | | | | | .35* n = 35 | .28 n = 21 | .36* n = 35 | .47* n = 21 | | |

† = Anxiety, Hostility Out, Hostility In, and Ambivalent Hostility Scales

**Table II. Intercorrelations of Anxiety Subscale Content Analysis Scores with Behavioral Rating Scale and Symptom Checklist Scale Cluster Scores**

***p < .005
**p < .01
*p < .05

1 = Pre-drug (correlations of pre-drug scores from both scales)
2 = Post-drug (correlations of post-drug scores from both scales)

| Behavioral or Psychological Measure | Anxiety Subscales † | | | | | | | | | | | |
|---|---|---|---|---|---|---|---|---|---|---|---|---|
| **Hamilton Anxiety Scale** | **Death 1** | **Death 2** | **Mutil. 1** | **Mutil. 2** | **Separ. 1** | **Separ. 2** | **Guilt 1** | **Guilt 2** | **Shame 1** | **Shame 2** | **Diff. 1** | **Diff. 2** |
| Cluster I (Emotional) | | | | | | | | | –.05<br>n = 34 | .45*<br>n = 21 | | |
| Cluster II (Somatic) | | | | | | | | | | | | |
| Cluster I + II (Total) | | | | | | | | | .15<br>n = 34 | .43<br>n = 21 | | |
| **Physician Questionnaire** | | | | | | | | | | | | |
| Cluster I (Emotional) | .36*<br>n = 35 | –.12<br>n = 21 | | | | | | | | | –.14<br>n = 35 | .44*<br>n = 21 |
| Cluster II (Somatic) | | | | | | | | | | | | |
| Cluster I + II (Total) | .34*<br>n = 35 | –.06<br>n = 21 | | | | | | | | | | |

| Symptom Checklist (SCL) | | | | | | | | | | | | |
|---|---|---|---|---|---|---|---|---|---|---|---|---|
| Factor I (Somatization) | | | | | | | | | .29<br>n = 35 | .55**<br>n = 21 | .03<br>n = 35 | .47*<br>n = 21 |
| Factor II (Obsessive-compulsive) | | | | | | | | | .49***<br>n = 35 | .44*<br>n = 21 | | |
| Factor III (Inter-personal sensitivity) | | | | | | | | | .14<br>n = 35 | .62***<br>n = 21 | | |
| Factor IV (Depression) | | | | | | | | | .34*<br>n = 35 | .51*<br>n = 21 | .09<br>n = 35 | .45*<br>n = 21 |
| Factor V (Anxiety) | | | | | | | | | | | | |
| **Total SCL Score** | | | | | | | | | .40*<br>n = 35 | .57**<br>n = 21 | .08<br>n = 35 | .47*<br>n = 21 |

† = Death, Mutilation, Separation, Guilt, Shame and Diffuse Anxiety Subscales

**Table III. Intercorrelations of Affect Content Analysis Scale Scores with Behavioral Rating Scale Scores and Symptom Checklist**

*** p < .005
** p < .01
* p < .05

1 = Pre-drug (correlations of pre-drug scores from both scales)
2 = Post-drug (correlations of post-drug scores from both scales)

| Behavioral or Psychological Measure | Affect Scales† | | | | | | | | | | | |
|---|---|---|---|---|---|---|---|---|---|---|---|---|
| Hamilton Anxiety Scale | Anx. 1 | Anx. 2 | Host. Out Ov. 1 | Host. Out Ov. 2 | Host. Out Cov. 1 | Host. Out Cov. 2 | Host. Total 1 | Host. Total 2 | Host. In 1 | Host. In 2 | Amb. Host. 1 | Amb. Host. 2 |
| 1. Anxious mood | | | | | | | | | | | | |
| 2. Tension | | | | | | | | | | | | |
| 3. Fears | | | | | | | | | | | | |
| 4. Insomnia | | | | | | | .18<br>n = 34 | .42<br>n = 21 | | | | |
| 5. Intellectual | | | | | | | | | | | | |
| 6. Depressed mood | | | | | | | | | | | | |
| 7. General somatic | | | | | | | | | | | | |
| 8. Cardiovascular | | | | | −.06<br>n = 34 | .53**<br>n = 21 | | | | | | |
| 9. Respiratory | | | | | | | | | | | | |
| 10. Gastrointestinal | | | .13<br>n = 34 | .49*<br>n = 21 | | | .24<br>n = 34 | .48*<br>n = 21 | | | | |
| 11. Genito-urinary | | | | | .20<br>n = 34 | .45*<br>n = 21 | | | | | | |
| 12. Autonomic | | | | | | | | | | | | |
| 13. Behavior at interview | | | | | | | | | −.48***<br>n = 34 | −.02<br>n = 21 | | |

† = Anxiety, Hostility Out, Hostility In, and Ambivalent Hostility

**Table IV. Intercorrelations of Anxiety Subscale Content Analysis Scores with Behavioral Rating Scales and Checklist Scale Scores.**

*** $p < .005$
** $p < .01$
* $p < .05$

1 = Pre-drug (correlations of pre-drug scores from both scales)
2 = Post-drug (correlations of post-drug scores from both scales)

| Behavioral or Psychological Measure | Anxiety Subscales† | | | | | | | | | | | |
|---|---|---|---|---|---|---|---|---|---|---|---|---|
| Hamilton Anxiety Scale | Death 1 | Death 2 | Mutil. 1 | Mutil. 2 | Separ. 1 | Separ. 2 | Guilt 1 | Guilt 2 | Shame 1 | Shame 2 | Diff. 1 | Diff. 2 |
| 1. Anxious mood | | | | | .48***<br>n = 34 | .28<br>n = 21 | −.33<br>n = 34 | −.02<br>n = 21 | .01<br>n = 34 | .44*<br>n = 21 | | |
| 2. Tension | −.58***<br>n = 34 | −.23<br>n = 21 | | | | | | | | | | |
| 3. Fears | | | | | | | | | | | | |
| 4. Insomnia | | | | | | | | | | | | |
| 5. Intellectual | | | .43**<br>n = 34 | −.02<br>n = 21 | | | | | | | | |
| 6. Depressed mood | | | | | | | | | .05<br>n = 34 | .48*<br>n = 21 | | |
| 7. General somatic | | | | | | | | | | | | |
| 8. Cardiovascular | | | −.27<br>n = 34 | .52*<br>n = 21 | | | | | | | | |
| 9. Respiratory | | | | | | | | | | | | |
| 10. Gastrointestinal | | | | | | | | | | | | |
| 11. Genito-urinary | | | | | .40*<br>n = 34 | .30<br>n = 21 | | | | | | |
| 12. Autonomic | | | | | | | .03<br>n = 34 | .46*<br>n = 21 | | | | |
| 13. Behavior at interview | | | | | | | | | | | | |

† = Death, Mutilation, Separation, Guilt, Shame, and Diffuse Anxiety Subscales

**Table V. Intercorrelations of Affect Content Analysis Scale Scores with Behavioral Rating Scale Scores and Symptom Checklist**

*** $p < .005$
** $p < .01$
* $p < .05$

1 = Pre-drug (correlations of pre-drug scores from both scales)
2 = Post-drug (correlations of post-drug scores from both scales)

| Behavioral or Psychological Measure | Affect Scales[†] | | | | | | | | | | | |
|---|---|---|---|---|---|---|---|---|---|---|---|---|
| Physician Questionnaire | Anx. 1 | Anx. 2 | Host. Out Ov. 1 | Host. Out Ov. 2 | Host. Out Cov. 1 | Host. Out Cov. 2 | Host. Total 1 | Host. Total 2 | Host. In 1 | Host. In 2 | Amb. Host. 1 | Amb. Host. 2 |
| 1. Anxiety | | | | | | | | | | | | |
| 2. Depressive mood | | | | | | | | | | | | |
| 3. Irritability | .01 n = 35 | .46* n = 21 | | | | | | | | | | |
| 4. Hostility | | | | | | | | | | | | |
| 5. Phobia | | | | | | | | | | | | |
| 6. Obsession-compulsion | | | | | | | | | | | | |
| 7. Hypochondriasis | | | | | | | | | | | | |
| 8. Somatization–Musculo-skeletal | | | | | | | | | | | | |

| | | | | | | | | | | | | |
|---|---|---|---|---|---|---|---|---|---|---|---|---|
| 9. Somatization–Autonomic | | | | | | | | | | | | |
| 10. Insomnia | | | .18<br>n = 35 | .48*<br>n = 21 | | | .17<br>n = 35 | .53*<br>n = 21 | | | .22<br>n = 35 | .47*<br>n = 21 |
| 11. Appetite disturbance | | | .08<br>n = 35 | .55**<br>n = 21 | | | .17<br>n = 35 | .64***<br>n = 21 | .12<br>n = 35 | .50*<br>n = 21 | −.06<br>n = 35 | .44*<br>n = 21 |
| 12. Headaches | | | | | | | | | | | | |
| 13. Psychomotor retardation | | | | | | | | | | | | |
| 14. Fatigue, tiredness, lethargy | | | | | | | .32<br>n = 35 | .18<br>n = 21 | | | | |
| 15. Impairment of interpersonal relationships | .07<br>n = 34 | .62***<br>n = 21 | .36*<br>n = 34 | .27<br>n = 21 | | | .33<br>n = 34 | .28<br>n = 21 | .25<br>n = 34 | .49*<br>n = 21 | | |
| 16. Degree of global psycho-pathology | | | .42**<br>n = 35 | .12<br>n = 21 | | | | | | | | |

† = Anxiety, Hostility Out, Hostility In, and Ambivalent Hostility Scales

**Table VI. Intercorrelations of Anxiety Subscale Content Analysis Scores with Behavioral Rating Scales and Checklist Scale Scores.**

*** $p < .005$
** $p < .01$
* $p < .05$

1 = Pre-drug (correlations of pre-drug scores from both scales)
2 = Post-drug (correlations of post-drug scores from both scales)

| Behavioral or Psychological Measure | Anxiety Subscales† | | | | | | | | | | | |
|---|---|---|---|---|---|---|---|---|---|---|---|---|
| Physician Questionnaire | Death 1 | Death 2 | Mutil. 1 | Mutil. 2 | Separ. 1 | Separ. 2 | Guilt 1 | Guilt 2 | Shame 1 | Shame 2 | Diff. 1 | Diff. 2 |
| 1. Anxiety | | | | | | | | | | | | |
| 2. Depressive mood | | | | | | | | | .06<br>n = 35 | .48*<br>n = 21 | | |
| 3. Irritability | | | | | .35*<br>n = 35 | .27<br>n = 21 | | | | | −.02<br>n = 35 | .48*<br>n = 21 |
| 4. Hostility | | | | | | | −.16<br>n = 35 | .54**<br>n = 21 | | | | |
| 5. Phobia | | | | | | | | | | | | |
| 6. Obsession-compulsion | | | | | −.25<br>n = 35 | .45*<br>n = 21 | | | | | −.23<br>n = 35 | .45*<br>n = 21 |
| 7. Hypochondriasis | | | | | | | .51***<br>n = 35 | −.13<br>n = 21 | | | | |
| 8. Somatization–Musculo-skeletal | | | | | | | | | | | | |

| | | | | | | | | | | | | |
|---|---|---|---|---|---|---|---|---|---|---|---|---|
| 9. Somatization–Autonomic | | | | | | | | | | | | |
| 10. Insomnia | | | | | | | | | | | | |
| 11. Appetite disturbance | | | | | | | | | | | | |
| 12. Headaches | | | | | | | | | | | | |
| 13. Psychomotor retardation | | | | | | | .24<br>n = 35 | .52*<br>n = 21 | | | | |
| 14. Fatigue, tiredness, lethargy | | | | | | | | | | | | |
| 15. Impairment of interpersonal relationships | | | | | | | | | .03<br>n = 34 | .52*<br>n = 21 | −.16<br>n = 34 | .59***<br>n = 21 |
| 16. Degree of global psychopathology | | | | | | | | | −.05<br>n = 35 | .46*<br>n = 21 | | |

† = Death, Mutilation, Separation, Guilt, Shame and Diffuse Anxiety Subscales

C. With the Symptom Checklist (SCL) Self-report Scale

1. *Total Anxiety Scale (Content Analysis) Scores and SCL Factor Scores*

Several factors from the Symptom Checklist (SCL) correlated significantly with total anxiety (content analysis) scores. These are the post-drug Factor I (Somatization) scores ($r = .46$, $N = 21$, $p < .05$), the post-drug Factor III (Interpersonal Sensitivity) scores ($r = .47$, $N = 21$, $p < .05$), the post-drug Factor IV (Depression) scores ($r = .43$, $N = 21$, $p < .05$) and the post-drug Total SCL Score ($r = .45$, $N = 21$, $p < .05$). Curiously, the Factor V (Anxiety) scores of the SCL did not correlate significantly with the total anxiety (content analysis) scale scores in this sample of patients (Table I).

2. *Anxiety Subscale (Content Analysis) Scores and SCL Factor Scores*

Significant correlations were obtained between post-drug shame anxiety subscale scores ($r = .55$, $N = 21$, $p < .01$) as well as post-drug diffuse anxiety subscale scores ($r = .47$, $N = 21$, $p < .05$) and Factor I (Somatization) scores of the SCL.

Significant correlations occurred between both pre-drug ($r = .49$, $N = 35$, $p < .005$) as well as the post-drug ($r = .44$, $N = 21$, $p < .05$) shame anxiety subscale scores and Factor II (Obsessive-compulsive) scores of the SCL.

The post-drug shame anxiety subscale correlated significantly with Factor III (Interpersonal Sensitivity) scores ($r = .62$, $N = 21$, $p < .005$) of the SCL.

The pre-drug ($r = .34$, $N = 35$, $p < .05$) and post-drug ($r = .51$, $N = 21$, $p < .05$) shame anxiety subscale scores correlated significantly with Factor IV (Depression) scores of the SCL. Also, the post-drug diffuse anxiety subscale scores correlated significantly ($r = .45$, $N = 21$, $p < .05$) with Factor IV (Depression) scores.

The pre-drug ($r = .48$, $N = 35$, $p < .05$) and post-drug ($r = .57$, $N = 21$, $p < .01$) shame anxiety subscale scores correlated significantly with Total SCL score of the SCL. Also, the post-drug diffuse anxiety subscale scores correlated significantly ($r = .47$, $N = 21$, $p < .05$) with the Total SCL score of the SCL (see Table II).

### 3. *Total Anxiety (Content Analysis) Scores and Symptom Checklist (SCL) Items*

The *pre-drug* total anxiety (content analysis) scale scores correlated significantly with the following item scores from the pre-drug Symptom Checklist (SCL) (see Table VII):

| *SCL Item #* | *Description* | |
|---|---|---|
| 17 | Faintness or dizziness | (r = .43, N = 35, $p < .01$) |
| 21 | Constipation | (r = .40, N = 35, $p < .05$) |
| 33 | Trouble concentrating | (r = .37, N = 34, $p < .05$) |
| 39 | Low back pains | (r = .39, N = 35, $p < .05$) |
| 45 | Muscle soreness | (r = .34, N = 35, $p < .05$) |
| 47 | Weakness in parts of body | (r = .36, N = 35, $p < .05$) |
| 50 | Sleepy during day | (r = .33, N = 35, $p < .05$) |

The *post-drug* total anxiety (content analysis) scale scores correlated significantly with the following items from the post-drug Symptom Checklist (SCL):

| *SCL Item #* | *Description* | |
|---|---|---|
| 1 | Sweating | (r = .61, N = 21, $p < .005$) |
| 17 | Faintness or dizziness | (r = .43, N = 21, $p < .05$) |
| 20 | Feelings being easily hurt | (r = .53, N = 21, $p < .01$) |
| 22 | Loss of sexual pleasure | (r = .49, N = 21, $p < .05$) |
| 23 | Feeling easily annoyed | (r = .56, N = 21, $p < .01$) |
| 25 | Difficulty making decisions | (r = .49, N = 20, $p < .05$) |

### 4. *Anxiety Subscale (Content Analysis) Scores and Symptom Checklist (SCL) Items (See Table VIII):*

a. *Death anxiety subscale*

*Pre-drug correlations:*

| | | |
|---|---|---|
| *SCL Item #33* | Trouble concentrating | (r = .38, N = 34, $p < .05$) |

*Post-drug correlations*

| *SCL Item #* | *Description* | |
|---|---|---|
| 1 | Sweating | (r = .43, N = 21, $p < .05$) |
| 7 | Trouble remembering things | (r = .43, N = 21, $p < .05$) |
| 46 | Having to check and double-check | (r = .45, N = 21, $p < .05$) |

b. *Mutilation Anxiety Subscale*

*Pre-drug correlations:*

| *SCL Item #* | *Description* | |
|---|---|---|
| 1 | Sweating | (r = .43, N = 34, $p < .01$) |
| 16 | Heavy feelings in arms or legs | (r = .33, N = 35, $p < .05$) |

*Post-drug correlations:*

| | | |
|---|---|---|
| *SCL Item #7* | Trouble remembering things | ($r = .43$, $N = 21$, $p < .05$) |

c. *Separation Anxiety Subscale*

*Pre-drug correlations:*

| | | |
|---|---|---|
| *SCL Item #11* | Feeling fearful | ($r = -.33$, $N = 35$, $p < .05$) |

*Post-drug correlations:*

| | | |
|---|---|---|
| *SCL Item #35* | Thoughts of ending your life | ($r = -.46$, $N = 21$, $p < .05$) |

d. *Guilt Anxiety Subscale*

*Pre-drug correlations:*

| *SCL Item #* | *Description* | |
|---|---|---|
| 18 | Crying easily | ($r = .40$, $N = 35$, $p < .05$) |
| 45 | Muscle soreness | ($r = .35$, $N = 35$, $p < .05$) |

*Post-drug correlations:*

| | | |
|---|---|---|
| *SCL Item #8* | Hot or cold spells | ($r = .43$, $N = 21$, $p < .05$) |

e. *Shame Anxiety Subscale*

*Pre-drug correlations:*

| *SCL Item #* | *Description* | |
|---|---|---|
| 7 | Trouble remembering things | ($r = .56$, $N = 34$, $p < .005$) |
| 10 | A lump in your throat | ($r = .34$, $N = 35$, $p < .05$) |
| 21 | Constipation | ($r = .43$, $N = 35$, $p < .01$) |
| 33 | Trouble concentrating | ($r = .53$, $N = 34$, $p < .005$) |
| 34 | Mind going blank | ($r = .49$, $N = 34$, $p < .005$) |
| 39 | Low back pains | ($r = .49$, $N = 35$, $p < .005$) |
| 46 | Having to check and double check | ($r = .40$, $N = 35$, $p < .05$) |

*Post-drug correlations:*

| *SCL Item #* | *Description* | |
|---|---|---|
| 2 | Trouble getting your breath | ($r = .47$, $N = 21$, $p < .05$) |
| 5 | Feeling low in energy or slowed down | ($r = .53$, $N = 21$, $p < .01$) |
| 13 | Feeling critical of others | ($r = .45$, $N = 21$, $p < .05$) |
| 15 | Having to do things very slowly | ($r = .50$, $N = 21$, $p < .05$) |
| 20 | Feelings being easily hurt | ($r = .65$, $N = 21$, $p < .005$) |
| 23 | Feeling easily annoyed | ($r = .55$, $N = 21$, $p < .01$) |
| 24 | Poor appetite | ($r = .51$, $N = 20$, $p < .05$) |
| 25 | Difficulty making decisions | ($r = .57$, $N = 20$, $p < .01$) |
| 39 | Low back pains | ($r = .45$, $N = 21$, $p < .05$) |
| 40 | Worrying about things | ($r = .48$, $N = 21$, $p < .05$) |
| 46 | Having to check and double-check | ($r = .44$, $N = 21$, $p < .05$) |
| 47 | Weakness in parts of body | ($r = .46$, $N = 21$, $p < .05$) |
| 48 | Feeling tense | ($r = .49$, $N = 21$, $p < .05$) |
| 49 | Nausea or upset stomach | ($r = .54$, $N = 21$, $p < .05$) |

f. *Diffuse Anxiety Subscale*
*Pre-drug correlations:* none significant.
*Post-drug correlations:*

| *SCL Item #* | *Description* | |
|---|---|---|
| 8 | Hot or cold spells | ($r = .45$, $N = 21$, $p < .05$) |
| 17 | Faintness/dizziness | ($r = .46$, $N = 21$, $p < .05$) |
| 23 | Feeling easily annoyed | ($r = .60$, $N = 21$, $p < .005$) |
| 25 | Difficulty making decisions | ($r = .50$, $N = 20$, $p < .05$) |
| 33 | Trouble concentrating | ($r = .43$, $N = 21$, $p < .05$) |
| 35 | Thoughts of ending your life | ($r = -.47$, $N = 21$, $p < .05$) |
| 39 | Low back pain | ($r = .47$, $N = 21$, $p < .05$) |
| 41 | Feeling no interest | ($r = .43$, $N = 21$, $p < .05$) |

II. *Correlations of Total Hostility Outward Content Analysis Scales*

A. With Hamilton Anxiety Rating Scale

1. *Total Hostility Outward Scale and Hostility Outward Subscale (Content Analysis) Scores with Cluster Scores of the Hamilton Anxiety Rating Scale (Table I)*

a. *Total Hostility Outward (Content Analysis) Scale Scores*
No significant correlations.

b. *Overt Hostility Outward (Content Analysis) Scale Scores*
No significant correlations.

c. *Covert Hostility Outward (Content Analysis) Scale Scores*
*Pre-drug correlations:* Cluster II (somatic) scores correlated significantly with pre-drug covert hostility outward scores ($r = .35$, $N = 34$, $p < .05$).
*Post-drug correlations:* Cluster I plus II (total) scores correlated significantly with post-drug covert hostility outward scores ($r = .44$, $N = 21$, $p < .05$).

2. *Total Hostility Outward Scale and Hostility Outward Subscale (Content Analysis) Scores with Separate Items of Hamilton Anxiety Rating Scale (Table III)*

a. *Total Hostility Outward (Content Analysis) Scale Scores*
Item #10 (Gastrointestinal) scores correlated significantly with post-drug total hostility outward scores ($r = .48$, $N = 21$, $p < .05$).

b. *Overt Hostility Outward (Content Analysis) Scale Scores*
Item #10 (Gastrointestinal) scores correlated significantly with post-drug *overt* hostility outward scores ($r = .49$, $N = 21$, $p < .05$).

c. *Covert Hostility Outward (Content Analysis) Scale Scores*
Item #8 (Cardiovascular) scores correlated significantly with

**Table VII. Intercorrelations of Affect Content Analysis Scale Scores with Behavioral Rating Scale Scores and Symptom Checklist**

*** $p < .005$
** $p < .01$
* $p < .05$

1 = Pre-drug (correlations of pre-drug scores from both scales)
2 = Post-drug (correlations of post-drug scores from both scales)

| Behavioral or Psychological Measure | Affect Scales† | | | | | | | | | | | |
|---|---|---|---|---|---|---|---|---|---|---|---|---|
| Symptom Checklist | Anx. 1 | Anx. 2 | Host. Out Ov. 1 | Host. Out Ov. 2 | Host. Out Cov. 1 | Host. Out Cov. 2 | Host. Total 1 | Host. Total 2 | Host. In 1 | Host. In 2 | Amb. Host. 1 | Amb. Host. 2 |
| 1. Sweating | −.11 n = 34 | .61*** n = 21 | | | | | .01 n = 34 | .44* n = 21 | −.04 n = 34 | .52* n = 21 | | |
| 2. Trouble getting your breath | | | | | | | | | | | | |
| 3. Suddenly scared for no reason | | | | | | | | | | | | |
| 4. Difficulty in speaking when you are excited | | | | | | | | | | | | |
| 5. Feeling low in energy or slowed down | | | | | | | | | | | | |
| 6. Pains in the heart or chest | | | | | | | | | | | | |
| 7. Trouble remembering things | | | | | | | | | .34* n = 34 | .18 n = 21 | | |
| 8. Hot or cold spells | | | | | | | | | | | | |

| | | | | | | | | | | | | |
|---|---|---|---|---|---|---|---|---|---|---|---|---|
| 9. Blaming yourself for things | | | | | | | | | .41*<br>n = 35 | .29<br>n = 21 | | |
| 10. A lump in your throat | | | | | | | .35*<br>n = 35 | −.09<br>n = 21 | | | | |
| 11. Feeling fearful | | | | | .01<br>n = 35 | .43*<br>n = 21 | .05<br>n = 35 | .46*<br>n = 21 | .35*<br>n = 35 | .33<br>n = 21 | | |
| 12. Numbness or tingling in parts of your body | | | | | | | | | .07<br>n = 35 | .43*<br>n = 21 | | |
| 13. Feeling critical of others | | | .04<br>n = 35 | .47*<br>n = 21 | | | | | | | | |
| 14. Having to avoid certain things/ places due to fear | | | | | | | | | | | | |
| 15. Having to do things very slowly to be sure they are right | | | | | | | | | .24<br>n = 35 | .47*<br>n = 21 | | |
| 16. Heavy feeling in your arms or legs | | | | | .33*<br>n = 35 | −.04<br>n = 20 | | | .04<br>n = 35 | .44*<br>n = 20 | | |
| 17. Faintness or dizziness | .43**<br>n = 35 | .43*<br>n = 21 | | | | | | | .29<br>n = 35 | .43*<br>n = 21 | .15<br>n = 35 | .47*<br>n = 21 |
| 18. Crying easily | | | | | | | .22<br>n = 35 | .46*<br>n = 21 | .34*<br>n = 35 | .37<br>n = 21 | | |
| 19. Nervousness or shakiness inside | | | .32<br>n = 35 | .47*<br>n = 21 | | | .37*<br>n = 35 | .52*<br>n = 21 | .19<br>n = 35 | .52*<br>n = 21 | | |
| 20. Your feelings being easily hurt | .27<br>n = 34 | .53**<br>n = 21 | .08<br>n = 34 | .51*<br>n = 21 | | | | | .12<br>n = 34 | .69***<br>n = 21 | | |

**Table VII. Intercorrelations of Affect Content Analysis Scale Scores with Behavioral Rating Scale Scores and Symptom Checklist (contd.)**

| Behavioral or Psychological Measure | Affect Scales† | | | | | | | | | | | |
|---|---|---|---|---|---|---|---|---|---|---|---|---|
| Symptom Checklist | Anx. 1 | Anx. 2 | Host. Out Ov. 1 | Host. Out Ov. 2 | Host. Out Cov. 1 | Host. Out Cov. 2 | Host. Total 1 | Host. Total 2 | Host. In 1 | Host. In 2 | Amb. Host. 1 | Amb. Host. 2 |
| 21. Constipation | .40* n = 35 | .01 n = 21 | | | | | | | | | | |
| 22. Loss of sexual interest or pleasure | .02 n = 35 | .49* n = 21 | | | | | | | | | .03 n = 35 | .50* n = 21 |
| 23. Feeling easily annoyed or irritated | .28 n = 35 | .56** n = 21 | .39* n = 35 | −.01 n = 21 | | | .42** n = 35 | −.01 n = 21 | | | | |
| 24. Poor appetite | | | | | | | | | | | | |
| 25. Difficulty making decisions | .21 n = 35 | .49* n = 20 | | | | | | | .17 n = 35 | .47* n = 20 | | |
| 26. Difficulty in falling or staying asleep | | | .24 n = 35 | .54** n = 21 | | | .19 n = 35 | .60*** n = 21 | | | | |
| 27. Feeling hopeless about the future | | | | | | | | | .36* n = 35 | .26 n = 21 | | |
| 28. Feeling blue | | | | | | | | | | | | |
| 29. Feeling lonely | | | | | | | | | | | | |
| 30. Temper outbursts you could not control | | | | | | | | | | | | |

| | | | | | | | | | | | | |
|---|---|---|---|---|---|---|---|---|---|---|---|---|
| 31. Headaches | | | | | | | | | | | | |
| 32. Heart pounding or racing | | | | | | | | | | | | |
| 33. Trouble concentrating | .37* n = 34 | .27 n = 21 | .43** n = 34 | .31 n = 21 | | | .36* n = 34 | .26 n = 21 | .43** n = 34 | .63*** n = 21 | | |
| 34. Your mind going blank | | | .34* n = 34 | .24 n = 21 | | | | | .34* n = 34 | .43* n = 21 | | |
| 35. Thoughts of ending your life | | | | | | | | | | | | |
| 36. Worried about sloppiness or carelessness | | | .41* n = 35 | .09 n = 21 | | | .37* n = 35 | .18 n = 21 | | | .06 n = 35 | −.44* n = 21 |
| 37. Trembling | | | | | | | | | | | | |
| 38. A feeling of being trapped | | | | | | | | | | | | |
| 39. Low back pains | .35* n = 35 | .40 n = 21 | | | | | | | .38* n = 35 | .46* n = 21 | | |
| 40. Worrying about things | | | | | | | | | | | | |
| 41. Feeling no interest | | | | | | | | | | | | |
| 42. Feeling others are unsym-pathetic | | | .44** n = 35 | .11 n = 21 | | | .46** n = 35 | .20 n = 21 | | | | |
| 43. Feeling people are unfriendly | | | | | | | | | | | | |

**Table VII. Intercorrelation of Affect Content Analysis Scale Scores with Behavioral Rating Scale Scores and Symptom Checklist (contd.)**

| Behavioral or Psychological Measure | Affect Scales† | | | | | | | | | | | |
|---|---|---|---|---|---|---|---|---|---|---|---|---|
| Symptom Checklist | Anx. 1 | Anx. 2 | Host. Out Ov. 1 | Host. Out Ov. 2 | Host. Out Cov. 1 | Host. Out Cov. 2 | Host. Total 1 | Host. Total 2 | Host. In 1 | Host. In 2 | Amb. Host. 1 | Amb. Host. 2 |
| 44. Feeling inferior to others | | | | | | | | | .34* n = 35 | .25 n = 21 | | |
| 45. Muscle soreness | .34* n = 35 | .04 n = 21 | | | | | | | | | | |
| 46. Having to check and double-check | | | | | | | | | .43** n = 35 | .50* n = 21 | | |
| 47. Weakness in parts of the body | .36* n = 35 | .22 n = 21 | | | .37* n = 35 | –.25 n = 21 | .33* n = 35 | .08 n = 21 | | | | |
| 48. Feeling tense | | | .33* n = 35 | .22 n = 21 | | | .40* n = 35 | .24 n = 21 | | | | |
| 49. Nausea or upset stomach | | | | | .38* n = 35 | –.25 n = 21 | | | | | | |
| 50. Sleepy during day | .33* n = 35 | –.15 n = 21 | | | | | | | | | | |
| 51. Dry mouth | | | | | .36* n = 35 | –.33 n = 21 | | | | | | |
| 52. Loose bowel movements | | | | | .39* n = 35 | –.38 n = 21 | | | | | | |

† = Anxiety, Hostility Out, Hostility In, and Ambivalent Hostility Scales

post-drug *covert* hostility outward scores ($r = .53$, $N = 21$, $p < .01$)

Item #11 (Genito-urinary) scores correlated significantly with post-drug *covert* hostility outward scores ($r = .45$, $N = 21$, $p < .05$)

B. With Physician Questionnaire Rating Scale

1. *Total Hostility Outward Scale and Hostility Outward Subscale (Content Analysis) Scores with Cluster Scores of the Physician Questionnaire Rating Scale (Table I)*

a. *Total Hostility Outward Scale Scores*

*Pre-drug correlations:* Cluster I (Emotional) scores correlated significantly with pre-drug total hostility outward (content analysis) scores ($r = .44$, $N = 35$, $p < .01$); Cluster I plus II (Total) scores correlated significantly with pre-drug total hostility outward (content analysis) scores ($r = .36$, $N = 35$, $p < .05$).

*Post-drug correlations:* Cluster II (Somatic) scores correlated significantly with post-drug total hostility outward (content analysis) scores ($r = .47$, $N = 21$, $p < .05$).

b. *Overt Hostility Outward (Content Analysis) Scale Scores*

*Pre-drug correlations:* Cluster I (Emotional) scores correlated significantly with pre-drug *overt* hostility outward scores ($r = .43$, $N = 35$, $p < .01$).

*Post-drug correlations:* no significant correlations with cluster scores of Physician Questionnaire.

*Post-drug correlations:* Cluster I plus II (total) correlated significantly with post-drug *covert* hostility outward scores ($r = .44$, $N = 21$, $p < .05$).

2. *Total Hostility Outward and Hostility Outward Subscale (Content Analysis) Scores with Separate Items from the Physician Questionnaire Rating Scale (Table V)*

a. *Total Hostility Outward (Content Analysis) Scale Scores*

*Pre-drug correlations:* none significant.

*Post-drug correlations:* Item #10 (Insomnia) scores correlated significantly with post-drug total hostility outward scores ($r = .53$, $N = 21$, $p < .05$); Item #11 (Appetite disturbance) scores correlated significantly with post-drug total hostility outward scores ($r = .64$, $N = 21$, $p < .005$).

b. *Overt Hostility Outward (Content Analysis) Scale Scores*

*Pre-drug correlations:* Item #15 (Impairment of interpersonal relationships) scores correlated significantly with pre-drug overt hostility outward scores ($r = .36$, $N = 34$, $p < .05$); Item #16

**Table VIII. Intercorrelations of Anxiety Subscale Content Analysis Scores with Behavioral Rating Scales and Checklist Scale Scores.**

*** $p < .005$
** $p < .01$
* $p < .05$

1 – Pre-drug (correlations of pre-drug scores from both scales)
2 – Post-drug (correlations of post-drug scores from both scales)

| Behavioral or Psychological Measure | Anxiety Subscales† | | | | | | | | | | | |
|---|---|---|---|---|---|---|---|---|---|---|---|---|
| Symptom Checklist | Death 1 | Death 2 | Mutil. 1 | Mutil. 2 | Separ. 1 | Separ. 2 | Guilt 1 | Guilt 2 | Shame 1 | Shame 2 | Diff. 1 | Diff. 2 |
| 1. Sweating | .00 n = 34 | .43* n = 21 | .43** n = 34 | –.10 n = 21 | | | | | | | .03 n = 34 | .42 n = 21 |
| 2. Trouble getting your breath | | | | | | | | | –.04 n = 35 | .47* n = 21 | | |
| 3. Suddenly scared for no reason | | | | | | | | | | | | |
| 4. Difficulty in speaking when you are excited | | | | | | | | | | | | |
| 5. Feeling low in energy or slowed down | | | | | | | | | –.09 n = 35 | .53** n = 21 | | |
| 6. Pains in the heart or chest | | | | | | | | | .22 n = 34 | .42 n = 21 | | |
| 7. Trouble remembering things | .11 n = 34 | .43* n = 21 | –.04 n = 34 | .43* n = 21 | | | | | .56*** n = 34 | .34 n = 21 | | |
| 8. Hot or cold spells | | | | | | | .11 n = 34 | .43* n = 21 | | | –.09 n = 34 | .45* n = 21 |

| | | | | | | | | | | | | |
|---|---|---|---|---|---|---|---|---|---|---|---|---|
| 9. Blaming yourself for things | | | | | | | | | | | | |
| 10. A lump in your throat | | | | | | | | | .34*<br>n = 35 | .01<br>n = 21 | | |
| 11. Feeling fearful | | | | | −.33<br>n = 35 | .19<br>n = 21 | | | | | | |
| 12. Numbness or tingling in parts of your body | | | | | | | | | | | | |
| 13. Feeling critical of others | | | | | −.03<br>n = 35 | .42<br>n = 21 | | | −.01<br>n = 35 | .45*<br>n = 21 | | |
| 14. Having to avoid certain things/places due to fear | | | | | | | | | | | | |
| 15. Having to do things very slowly to be sure they are right | | | | | | | | | .22<br>n = 35 | .50*<br>n = 21 | | |
| 16. Heavy feelings in your arms or legs | | | .33*<br>n = 35 | −.23<br>n = 20 | | | | | | | | |
| 17. Faintness/ Dizziness | | | | | | | | | | | .07<br>n = 35 | .46*<br>n = 21 |
| 18. Crying easily | | | | | | | .40*<br>n = 35 | .23<br>n = 21 | | | | |

Table VIII. Intercorrelations of Anxiety Subscale Content Analysis Scores with Behavioral Rating Scales and Checklist Scale Scores.

| Behavioral or Psychological Measure | Anxiety Subscales† | | | | | | | | | | | |
|---|---|---|---|---|---|---|---|---|---|---|---|---|
| Symptom Checklist | Death 1 | Death 2 | Mutil. 1 | Mutil. 2 | Separ. 1 | Separ. 2 | Guilt 1 | Guilt 2 | Shame 1 | Shame 2 | Diff. 1 | Diff. 2 |
| 19. Nervousness or shakiness inside | | | | | | | | | | | | |
| 20. Your feelings being easily hurt | | | | | | | | | .12 n = 34 | .65*** n = 21 | | |
| 21. Constipation | | | | | | | | | .43** n = 35 | .17 n = 21 | | |
| 22. Loss of sexual interest or pleasure | | | | | | | | | | | | |
| 23. Feeling easily annoyed or irritated | | | | | | | | | .11 n = 35 | .55** n = 21 | .01 n = 35 | .60*** n = 21 |
| 24. Poor appetite | | | | | | | | | .16 n = 35 | .51* n = 20 | | |
| 25. Difficulty making decisions | | | | | | | | | .24 n = 35 | .57** n = 20 | .30 n = 35 | .50* n = 20 |
| 26. Difficulty in falling or staying asleep | | | | | | | | | | | | |

| | | | | | | | | | | | | |
|---|---|---|---|---|---|---|---|---|---|---|---|---|
| 27. Feeling hopeless about the future | | | | | | | | | | | | |
| 28. Feeling blue | | | | | | | | | | | | |
| 29. Feeling lonely | | | | | | | | | | | | |
| 30. Temper outbursts you could not control | | | | | | | | | | | | |
| 31. Headaches | | | | | | | | | | | | |
| 32. Heart pounding or racing | | | | | | | | | | | | |
| 33. Trouble concentrating | .38* n = 34 | .24 n = 21 | | | | | | | .53*** n = 34 | .35 n = 21 | .13 n = 34 | .43* n = 21 |
| 34. Your mind going blank | | | | | | | | | .49*** n = 34 | .14 n = 21 | | |
| 35. Thoughts of ending your life | | | | | −.05 n = 35 | −.46* n = 21 | | | | | −.01 n = 35 | −.47* n = 21 |
| 36. Worried about sloppiness or carelessness | | | | | | | | | | | | |
| 37. Trembling | | | | | | | | | | | | |
| 38. A feeling of being trapped | | | | | | | | | | | | |
| 39. Low back pains | | | | | | | | | .49*** n = 35 | .45* n = 21 | .12 n = 35 | .47* n = 21 |
| 40. Worrying about things | | | | | | | | | .19 n = 35 | .48* n = 21 | | |

Table VIII. Intercorrelations of Anxiety Subscale Content Analysis Scores with Behavioral Rating Scales and Checklist Scale Scores (contd.)

| Behavioral or Psychological Measure | Anxiety Subscales† | | | | | | | | | | | |
|---|---|---|---|---|---|---|---|---|---|---|---|---|
| Symptom Checklist | Death 1 | Death 2 | Mutil. 1 | Mutil. 2 | Separ. 1 | Separ. 2 | Guilt 1 | Guilt 2 | Shame 1 | Shame 2 | Diff. 1 | Diff. 2 |
| 41. Feeling no interest | | | | | | | | | | | .13 n = 35 | .43* n = 21 |
| 43. Feeling people are unfriendly | | | | | | | | | | | | |
| 44. Feeling inferior to others | | | | | | | | | .31 n = 35 | .42 n = 21 | | |
| 45. Muscle soreness | | | | | | | .35* n = 35 | −.18 n = 21 | | | | |
| 46. Having to check and double-check | .11 n = 35 | .45* n = 21 | | | | | | | .40* n = 35 | .44* n = 21 | | |
| 47. Weakness in parts of the body | | | | | | | | | .24 n = 35 | .46* n = 21 | | |
| 48. Feeling tense | | | | | | | | | .17 n = 35 | .49* n = 21 | | |
| 49. Nausea or upset stomach | | | | | | | | | .17 n = 35 | .54** n = 21 | | |
| 50. Sleepy during day | | | | | | | | | | | | |
| 51. Dry mouth | | | | | | | | | | | | |
| 52. Loose bowel movements | | | | | | | | | | | | |

† = Death, Mutilation, Separation, Guilt, Shame, and Diffuse Anxiety Subscales

(Degree of global psychopathology) scores correlated significantly with pre-drug *overt* hostility scores (r = .42, N = 35, $p < .01$)

*Post-drug correlations:* Item #10 (Insomnia) correlated significantly with post-drug *overt* hostility outward scores (r = .48, N = 21, $p < .05$); Item #11 (Appetite disturbance) correlated significantly with post-drug *overt* hostility outward scores (r = .55, N = 21, $p < .01$).

c. *Covert Hostility Outward Scores*

No significant correlations with separate item scores of the Physician Questionnaire.

C. With Symptom Checklist (SCL)

1. *Total Hostility Outward Scale and Hostility Outward Subscale (Content Analysis) Scores and Factor Scores of the Symptom Checklist (SCL) (Table I)*

a. *Total Hostility Outward (Content Analysis) Scale Scores*

*Pre-drug correlations:* Total SCL score correlated significantly with pre-drug total hostility outward scores (r = .35, N = 35, $p < .05$).

*Post-drug correlations:* none significant.

b. *Overt Hostility Outward (Content Analysis) Scale Scores*

*Pre-drug correlations:* Factor II (Obsessive-compulsive) correlated significantly with pre-drug *overt* hostility scores (r = .37, N = 35, $p < .05$).

*Post-drug correlations:* none significant.

c. *Covert Hostility Outward (Content Analysis) Scale Scores*

No significant pre-drug or post-drug correlations.

2. *Total Hostility Outward Scale and Hostility Outward Subscales (Content Analysis) Scores with Separate Items of the Symptom Checklist (SCL) (Table VII)*

a. *Total Hostility Outward (Content Analysis) Scale Scores (Table VII)*

*Pre-drug correlations:*

| *SCL Item #* | *Description* | |
|---|---|---|
| 10 | A lump in your throat | (r = .35, N = 35, $p < .05$) |
| 19 | Nervousness or shakiness inside | (r = .37, N = 35, $p < .05$) |
| 23 | Feeling easily annoyed | (r = .42, N = 35, $p < .01$) |
| 33 | Trouble concentrating | (r = .36, N = 34, $p < .05$) |
| 36 | Worried about sloppiness or carelessness | (r = .37, N = 35, $p < .05$) |
| 42 | Feeling others are unsympathetic | (r = .46, N = 35, $p < .01$) |
| 47 | Weakness in parts of body | (r = .33, N = 35, $p < .05$) |
| 48 | Feeling tense | (r = .40, N = 35, $p < .05$) |

*Post-drug correlations:*

| SCL Item # | Description | |
|---|---|---|
| 1 | Sweating | ($r = .44$, $N = 21$, $p < .05$) |
| 11 | Feeling fearful | ($r = .46$, $N = 21$, $p < .05$) |
| 18 | Crying easily | ($r = .46$, $N = 21$, $p < .05$) |
| 19 | Nervousness or shakiness inside | ($r = .52$, $N = 21$, $p < .05$) |
| 26 | Difficulty in falling asleep or staying asleep | ($r = .60$, $N = 21$, $p < .005$) |

b. *Overt Hostility Outward (Content Analysis) Scale Scores (Table VII)*

*Pre-drug correlations:*

| SCL Item # | Description | |
|---|---|---|
| 23 | Feeling easily annoyed | ($r = .39$, $N = 35$, $p < .05$) |
| 33 | Trouble concentrating | ($r = .31$, $N = 35$, $p < .05$) |
| 34 | Your mind going blank | ($r = .34$, $N = 34$, $p < .05$) |
| 36 | Worried about sloppiness or carelessness | ($r = .41$, $N = 35$, $p < .05$) |
| 42 | Feeling others are unsympathetic | ($r = .44$, $N = 35$, $p < .01$) |

*Post-drug correlations:*

| SCL Item # | Description | |
|---|---|---|
| 13 | Feeling critical of others | ($r = .47$, $N = 21$, $p < .05$) |
| 19 | Nervousness or shakiness inside | ($r = .47$, $N = 21$, $p < .05$) |
| 20 | Your feelings being easily hurt | ($r = .51$, $N = 21$, $p < .05$) |
| 26 | Difficulty in falling or staying asleep | ($r = .54$, $N = 21$, $p < .01$) |

c. *Covert Hostility Outward (Content Analysis) Scale Scores*

*Pre-drug correlations:*

| SCL Item # | Description | |
|---|---|---|
| 16 | Heavy feeling in arms or legs | ($r = .33$, $N = 35$, $p < .05$) |
| 47 | Weakness in parts of body | ($r = .37$, $N = 35$, $p < .05$) |
| 49 | Nausea or upset stomach | ($r = .38$, $N = 35$, $p < .05$) |
| 51 | Dry mouth | ($r = .36$, $N = 35$, $p < .05$) |
| 52 | Loose bowel movements | ($r = .39$, $N = 35$, $p < .05$) |

*Post-drug correlation:*

*SCL Item #11* Feeling fearful ($r = .43$, $N = 21$, $p < .05$)

III. *Correlations of Hostility Inward (Content Analysis) Scale*

A. With Hamilton Anxiety Rating Scale

1. *Relationships to Cluster Scores (Table I)*

No significant correlations, pre-drug or post-drug, with cluster

scores of the Hamilton Anxiety Rating Scale.

2. *Relationships to Separate Items of Hamilton Anxiety Rating Scale (Table III)*

*Pre-drug correlations:* Item #13 (Behavior at interview) correlated significantly negatively with pre-drug hostility inward scores ($r = -.48$, $N = 34$, $p < .005$).
*Post-drug correlations:* none significant.

B. With Physician Questionnaire Rating Scale Scores (Table I)

1. *Hostility Inward (Content Analysis) Scale Scores and Cluster Scores of the Physician Questionnaire*

*Pre-drug correlations:* Cluster I (Emotional) scores correlated significantly with pre-drug hostility inward scores ($r = .37$, $N = 35$, $p < .05$).
*Post-drug correlations:* none significant.

2. *Hostility Inward (Content Analysis) Scale Scores and Separate Items of the Physician Questionnaire*

*Pre-drug correlations:* none significant.
*Post-drug correlations:* Item #11 (Appetite disturbance) scores correlated significantly with post-drug hostility inward scores ($r = .50$, $N = 21$, $p < .05$); Item #15 (Impairment of interpersonal relationships) correlated significantly with post-drug hostility inward scores ($r = .49$, $N = 21$, $p < .05$).

C. With Symptom Checklist (SCL) Self-report Scores

1. *Hostility Inward (Content Analysis) Scale Scores and Factor Scores from the Symptom Checklist (SCL) (Table I)*

*Pre-drug correlations:* Factor II (Obsessive-compulsive) scores correlated significantly with pre-drug hostility inward scores ($r = .43$, $N = 35$, $p < .01$); Factor IV (Depression) scores correlated significantly with pre-drug hostility inward scores ($r = .37$, $N = 35$, $p < .05$); Total SCL Score correlated with pre-drug hostility inward scores ($r = .36$, $N = 35$, $p < .05$).
*Post-drug correlations:* Factor I (Somatization) scores correlated significantly with post-drug hostility inward scores ($r = .46$, $N = 21$, $p < .05$); Factor II (Obsessive-compulsive) scores correlated significantly with post-drug hostility inward scores ($r = .50$, $N = 21$, $p < .05$); Total SCL Score correlated significantly with post-drug hostility inward scores ($r = .47$, $N = 21$, $p < .05$).

2. *Hostility Inward (Content Analysis) Scale Scores and Separate Items from the Symptom Checklist (SCL) (Table VII)*

*Pre-drug correlations:*

| *SCL Item #* | *Description* | |
|---|---|---|
| 7 | Trouble remembering things | (r = .34, N = 34, p < .05) |
| 9 | Blaming yourself for things | (r = .41, N = 35, p < .05) |
| 11 | Feeling fearful | (r = .35, N = 35, p < .05) |
| 18 | Crying easily | (r = .34, N = 35, p < .05) |
| 27 | Feeling hopeless about future | (r = .36, N = 35, p < .05) |
| 33 | Trouble concentrating | (r = .43, N = 34, p < .01) |
| 34 | Mind going blank | (r = .34, N = 34, p < .05) |
| 39 | Low back pains | (r = .38, N = 35, p < .05) |
| 44 | Feeling inferior to others | (r = .34, N = 35, p < .05) |
| 46 | Having to check and double-check | (r = .43, N = 35, p < .01) |

*Post-drug correlations:*

| *SCL Item #* | *Description* | |
|---|---|---|
| 1 | Sweating | (r = .52, N = 21, p < .05) |
| 12 | Numbness or tingling | (r = .43, N = 21, p < .05) |
| 15 | Having to do things slowly | (r = .47, N = 21, p < .05) |
| 16 | Heavy feeling in arms or legs | (r = .44, N = 20, p < .05) |
| 17 | Faintness or dizziness | (r = .43, N = 21, p < .05) |
| 19 | Nervousness or shakiness | (r = .52, N = 21, p < .05) |
| 20 | Feelings easily hurt | (r = .69, N = 21, p < .005) |
| 24 | Poor appetite | (r = .47, N = 20, p < .05) |
| 33 | Trouble concentrating | (r = .63, N = 21, p < .005) |
| 34 | Mind going blank | (r = .43, N = 21, p < .05) |
| 39 | Low back pains | (r = .46, N = 21, p < .05) |
| 46 | Having to check and double-check | (r = .50, N = 21, p < .05) |

IV. *Correlations of Ambivalent Hostility (Content Analysis) Scale Scores*

A. With Hamilton Anxiety Rating Scale Scores

1. *Ambivalent Hostility (Content Analysis) Scale Scores and Cluster Scores from the Hamilton Anxiety Rating Scale (Table I)*

No significant correlations, pre-drug or post-drug, occurred with the cluster scores of the Hamilton Anxiety Rating Scale.

2. *Ambivalent Hostility (Content Analysis) Scale Scores and Separate Items from the Hamilton Rating Scale (Table III)*

No significant correlations.

B. With the Physician Questionnaire Rating Scale (Table I)

1. *Ambivalent Hostility (Content Analysis) Scale Scores and Cluster Scores from the Physician Questionnaire*

No significant correlations.

2. *Ambivalent Hostility (Content Analysis) Scores and Separate Items from the Physician Questionnaire (Table V)*

*Pre-drug correlations:* none significant.

*Post-drug correlations:* Item #10 (Insomnia) correlated significantly with post-drug ambivalent hostility scores ($r = .47, N = 21, p < .05$); Item #11 (Appetite disturbance) correlated significantly with post-drug ambivalent hostility scores ($r = .44, N = 21, p < .05$).

C. With Symptom Checklist (SCL) Self-report Scale Scores

1. *Ambivalent Hostility (Content Analysis) Scale Scores and Factor Scores from the Symptom Checklist (SCL) (Table I)*

*Pre-drug correlations:* none significant.

*Post-drug correlations:* Factor I (Somatization) scores correlated significantly with post-drug ambivalent hostility scores ($r = .47, N = 21, p < .05$).

2. *Ambivalent Hostility (Content Analysis) Scale Scores and Separate Items from the Symptom Checklist (SCL) (Table VII)*

*Pre-drug correlations:* none significant.

*Post-drug correlations:*

| *SCL Item #* | *Description* | |
|---|---|---|
| 17 | Faintness or dizziness | ($r = .47, N = 21, p < .05$) |
| 22 | Loss of sexual pleasure | ($r = .50, N = 21, p < .05$) |
| 36 | Worried about sloppiness or carelessness | ($r = -.44, N = 21, p < .05$) |

## DISCUSSION

IA. *Anxiety (Content Analysis) Scale and Hamilton Anxiety Rating Scale*

The Hamilton Anxiety Rating scale, as adjudged from its total score, measures an anxiety construct much different from that measured by the anxiety (content analysis) scale, for there was no correlation whatsoever between total Hamilton Anxiety Rating scale scores and total anxiety (content analysis) scale scores.

There is some similarity between what is measured by Cluster I (Emotional) of the Hamilton Anxiety Rating scale scores and the total anxiety (content analysis) scale scores, and the significant correlation between these two measures is based entirely on post-drug shame anxiety (content analysis) scale scores. The Somatic Cluster (II) of the Hamilton Anxiety Rating scale has no bearing on what the total Anxiety (content analysis) scale measures.

Specific items of the Hamilton Anxiety Rating scale, while not correlating significantly with the total Anxiety (content analysis) scale scores, did

correlate with various Anxiety Subscale (content analysis) scores. Some moderate reassurance is provided to those who place much weight on face validity as a criterion for construct validation that scores from the Anxious mood item (#1) of the Hamilton Anxiety Rating scale correlated significantly positively at similar time periods (pre or post-drug) with separation (content analysis) anxiety ($p < .005$) and shame (content analysis) anxiety scores ($p < .05$). Of further interest was the finding that the Depressed mood item (#6) scores correlated significantly with shame anxiety (content analysis) scale scores and no significant correlations appeared between this Depressed mood item and guilt anxiety (content analysis) scale scores. Also, the significant correlations between several of the somatic items of the Hamilton scale (Genito-urinary, Cardiovascular, Autonomic) and anxiety subscale (content analysis) scores may provide suggestions for further research.

IB. *Anxiety (Content Analysis) Scale and Physician Questionnaire Rating Scale*

The total scores of the Physician Questionnaire and the scores of Cluster I (Emotional) and Cluster II (Somatic) have no relationship to the total Anxiety (content analysis) scores. Cluster I (Emotional) of the Physician Questionnaire rating scale did give scores, however, that correlated significantly, at comparable pre- or post-drug time periods, with death anxiety and diffuse anxiety subscale scores.

Of some interest is the finding that scores from two other Physician Questionnaire items—Irritability (#3) and Impairment of interpersonal relationships (#15)—correlated significantly with total Anxiety (content analysis) scale scores.

Perusal of those items' scores of the Physician Questionnaire which correlated significantly with Anxiety subscale (content analysis) scores provides additional construct validation of some of the components of these content analysis measures. For example: *Separation anxiety* (content analysis) scores correlated with Irritability item scores and Obsessive-compulsive item scores from the Physician Questionnaire. *Guilt anxiety* (content analysis) scores correlated with Hostility, Psychomotor retardation, and Hypochondriasis item scores. *Shame anxiety* (content analysis) scores correlated with Depressive mood, Impairment of interpersonal relationships, and Degree of global psychopathology item scores. *Diffuse anxiety* (content analysis) scores correlated with Irritability, Obsessive-compulsive, and Impairment of interpersonal relationships item scores from the Physician Questionnaire.

IC. *Anxiety (Content Analysis) Scale and Symptom Checklist (SCL) Self-report Scale*

The total (52-item) SCL scores did correlate significantly (post-drug)

with the total Anxiety (content analysis) scale scores, and several Cluster scores of the SCL (Somatization, Interpersonal sensitivity, and Depression) correlated significantly with total Anxiety (content analysis) scale scores. But these positive findings do not establish that the anxiety measured by these two scales is identical, for Factor V (Anxiety) scores of the SCL did not correlate significantly with total Anxiety (content analysis) scale scores.

Death, mutilation, separation, and guilt anxiety (content analysis) subscale scores did not have any relationship with the 5 factor scale scores of the SCL. However, shame anxiety (content analysis) scores correlated significantly with Factor I (Somatization), Factor II (Obsessive-compulsive), Factor III (Interpersonal sensitivity), Factor IV (Depression), and total SCL score. And diffuse anxiety (content analysis) scale scores correlated significantly with Factor I (Somatization), Factor IV (Depression), and total SCL scores. These findings certainly indicate that the SCL self-report anxiety measure and the content analysis anxiety measure are not equivalent and that the points at which these two kinds of measures assay a similar affect need to be established. Our further dissection of these points here was carried out by determining what specific items of the SCL correlated with total anxiety and subscale anxiety (content analysis) scale scores. The details of these statistical analyses need not be repeated here, but they do prove useful to reveal what items of the SCL measure similar facets of the anxiety content analysis scale and subscale scores.

IIA. *Total Hostility Outward (Content Analysis) Scale and Hamilton Anxiety Rating Scale*

Anxiety rating scale scores would not be expected to correlate highly with a hostility scale, but from the psychodynamic point of view anger, hostility or aggression should correlate with some kinds of apprehension, fear or anxiety. For example, a very angry person in our society might well be expected to be fearful that retaliation will occur if the angry impulses are acted upon.

The total hostility outward scale and overt hostility outward subscale (content analysis) scores had no correlations with the cluster scores of the Hamilton Anxiety Rating scale scores. Covert hostility outward subscale (content analysis) scores correlated with Cluster II (Somatic) and total scores of the Hamilton Anxiety Rating Scale. The items of the rating scale that account for these correlations are the somatic items, including the Gastrointestinal, Cardiovascular and Genito-urinary item scores. The somatic concomitants of hostility outward are revealed by these findings, and other associated variables from other hostility measures will be indicated below.

IIB. *Hostility Outward (Content Analysis) Scale and Physician Questionnaire Rating Scale*

The Physician Questionnaire Rating Scale, as compared to the Hamilton Anxiety Rating Scale, appears to measure more aspects or concomitants of hostility outward that are similar to what the hostility outward (content analysis) scale measures. Not only both cluster scores (Emotional and Somatic) but also the total score of the Physician Questionnaire relate to various aspects of hostility outward as measured by content analysis.

Examples of these intercorrelations that have face validity are the significant correlations of overt hostility outward (content analysis) scale scores and the item scores of Impairment of interpersonal relationships, (#15) Degree of Global psychopathology (#16), Insomnia (#10) and Appetite disturbance (#11).

IIB. *Hostility Outward (Content Analysis) Scale and Symptom Checklist (SCL) Self-report Scale*

SCL scale scores correlated significantly with total hostility outward (content analysis) scale scores, and Factor II (Obsessive-compulsive) scores correlated with overt hostility outward (content analysis) scale scores.

The large variety of SCL item scores that correlate with the hostility outward (content analysis) scale scores provide further construct validation for these content analysis scales and, at the same time, provide a rosetta stone enabling researchers to translate findings from one type of measure and relate them to another type of psychological measure.

III. *Hostility Inward (Content Analysis) Scale and the Rating Scales and Self-report Scale*

The Hamilton Anxiety and the Physician Questionnaire rating scales showed few, if any, correlations with hostility inward (content analysis) scale scores. The Cluster I (Emotional) scores of the Physician Questionnaire correlated significantly with the hostility inward (content analysis) scores, a finding one would expect.

The Symptom Checklist (SCL) Self-report scores had more similarities to the hostility inward (content analysis) scores. Factor I (Somatization), Factor II (Obsessive-compulsive), Factor IV (Depression) and total SCL scores all correlated significantly with hostility inward scores.

The item scores of the SCL that correlated significantly with the hostility inward (content analysis) scores are quite numerous, and they describe very well what the hostility inward content analysis measure has been

previously validated to assay.[1] Certain somatic items of the SCL (Low back pains, Sweating, Numbness or tingling, Heavy feelings in arms or legs, Faintness or dizziness, Poor appetite) correlated with hostility inward (content analysis) scores, and these findings may be useful in psychosomatic and somatopsychic research.

IV. *Ambivalent Hostility (Content Analysis) Scale and the Rating Scales and the Self-report Scale*

Ambivalent hostility scores are derived from verbal statements about hostile ideation or actions from external sources toward the speaker. In previous validation studies, these ambivalent hostility scores have been found to be associated with the expression of anger toward others or depressive mood, depending on the characteristics of the sample of patients studied.[1,10,11]

There were no similar counterparts found from the Hamilton Anxiety and Physician Questionnaire rating scales with the ambivalent hostility (content analysis) scale, except that Item #10 (Insomnia) and Item #11 (Appetite disturbance) scores of the Physician Questionnaire correlated with ambivalent hostility scores.

On the other hand, SCL Factor I (Somatization) scores and a few of the item scores (Faintness or dizziness, Loss of sexual pleasure, and Worried about sloppiness or carelessness) correlated significantly with ambivalent hostility (content analysis) scores.

This thorough dissection of the interrelationships of content analysis scores of anxiety and hostility with behavioral rating scale scores from the Hamilton Anxiety Scale and the Physician Questionnaire and with self-report scores from the SCL should be replicated by other investigators. Such studies indicate in what respects our measurement tools in the behavioral sciences and psychiatry fail to assay similar psychological or behavioral characteristics and in what respects common features of these variables are being evaluated. These different measurement procedures, often claiming to be measuring similar or overlapping psychological variables, actually are not doing so, but often some of their subscales or separate item scales do, indeed, measure associated characteristics. These all need to be more definitely described and defined.

The concept of validity is, of course, more than the concordance occurring between the scores obtained by different measurement procedures (concurrent vs. *construct* validity). Some consideration of the validity of these various measurement approaches in psychopharmacological research has been made elsewhere,[12] but the topic requires much fuller treatment than can be given here.

## SUMMARY

Intercorrelations were obtained of the measurement scores, from 35 patients (pre- and post-drug), of a content analysis scale procedure (Gottschalk-Gleser), two behavioral rating scales (Hamilton Anxiety and Physician Questionnaire rating scales) and a self-report method (Symptom Checklist). The intercorrelations included a correlative dissection of the subscales and item components of these different measurement procedures. This approach served as a means of translating the common meanings measured by these three different kinds of psychological measurement tools, an endeavor metaphorically labeled a "rosetta stone" search.

These different measurement procedures do not uniformly measure similar or overlapping variables, but often some of their subscales or separate item scales do indeed assay associated characteristics.

## REFERENCES

1. Gottschalk, L.A., Gleser, G.C.: *Measurement of Psychological States Through Content Analysis of Verbal Behavior.* Berkeley, Los Angeles, University of California Press, 1969.
2. Gottschalk, L.A., Winget, C.N., Gleser, G.C.: *Manual of Instructions for Using the Gottschalk-Gleser Content Analysis Scales: Anxiety, Hostility, Social Alienation–Personal Disorganization.* Berkeley, Los Angeles, University of California Press, 1969.
3. Parloff, M.B., Kelman, H.C., Frank, J.D.: Comfort, effectiveness, and self-awareness as criteria of improvement in psychotherapy. *Amer. J. Psychiat.* 3:343–51, 1954.
4. Frank, J.D., Gliedman, L.H. Imber, S.D., Nash, E.H., Stone, A.R.: Why patients leave psychotherapy. *AMA Arch. Neurol. Psychiat.* 77:283–99, 1957.
5. Mattsson, N.B., Williams, H.V., Rickels, K., Lipman, R.S., Uhlenhuth, E.H.: Dimensions of symptom distress in anxious neurotic outpatients. *Psychopharm. Bull.* 51:19–32, 1969.
6. Derogatis, L.R., Lipman, R.S., Rickels, K., Uhlenhuth, E.H., Covi, L.: The Hopkins Symptom Checklist (HSCL): a measure of primary symptom dimensions. In *Psychological Measurements in Psychopharmacology Mod. Prob. Pharmacopsychiat,* 7, edited by P. Pichat. Basel, Karger, 1974, pp. 79–110.
7. Hamilton, M.: The assessment of anxiety states by rating. *Br. J. Med. Psychol.* 32:50–55, 1959.
8. Rickels, K., Howard, K.: The Physician Questionnaire: a useful tool in psychiatric drug research. *Psychopharmacologia* 17:338–44, 1970.
9. Nie, N.H., Bent, D.H., Hull, C.H.: *Statistical Package for the Social Sciences.* New York, McGraw-Hill, 1970.
10. Gottschalk, L.A., Gleser, G.C., Springer, K.J.: Three hostility scales applicable to verbal samples. *Arch. Gen. Psychiat.* 9:254–79, 1953.
11. Gottschalk, L.A.: The measurement of hostile aggression through the content analysis of speech: some biological and interpersonal aspects. In *Aggressive Behavior,* edited by S. Garattini, E.B. Sigg. New York, Wiley, 1969.
12. Gottschalk, L.A.: Drug effects in the assessment of affective states in man. In *Current Developments in Psychopharmacology,* edited by Essman and Valzelli. New York, Spectrum, 1975.

## SCHEDULE 1
### Anxiety Scale*

1. Death anxiety–references to death, dying, threat of death, or anxiety about death experienced by or occurring to:
   *a.* self (3).
   *b.* animate others (2).
   *c.* inanimate objects destroyed (1).
   *d.* denial of death anxiety (1).
2. Mutilation (castration) anxiety–references to injury, tissue, or physical damage, or anxiety about injury or threat of such experienced by or occurring to:
   *a.* self (3).
   *b.* animate others (2).
   *c.* inanimate objects (1).
   *d.* denial (1).
3. Separation anxiety–references to desertion, abandonment, loneliness, ostracism, loss of support, falling, loss of love or love object, or threat of such experienced by occurring to:
   *a.* self (3).
   *b.* animate others (2).
   *c.* inanimate objects (1).
   *d.* denial (1).
4. Guilt anxiety–references to adverse criticism, abuse, condemnation, moral disapproval, guilt, or threat of such experienced by:
   *a.* self (3).
   *b.* animate others (2).
   *d.* denial (1).
5. Shame anxiety–references to ridicule, inadequacy, shame, embarrassment, humiliation, over-exposure of deficiencies or private details, or threat of such experienced by:
   *a.* self (3).
   *b.* animate others (2).
   *d.* denial (1).
6. Diffuse or non-specific anxiety–references by word (see pp. 60–61) or in phrases to anxiety and/or fear without distinguishing type or source of anxiety:
   *a.* self (3).
   *b.* animate others (2).
   *d.* denial (1).

* Numbers in parentheses are the weights.

## SCHEDULE 2

### Hostility Directed Outward Scale: Destructive, Injurious, Critical Thoughts and Actions Directed to Others

**I Hostility Outward–Overt**

**Thematic Categories**

*a* 3* Self killing, fighting, injuring other individuals or threatening to do so.

*b* 3 Self robbing or abandoning other individuals, causing suffering or anguish to others, or threatening to do so.

*c* 3 Self adversely criticizing, depreciating, blaming, expressing anger, dislike of other human beings.

*a* 2 Self killing, injuring or destroying domestic animals, pets, or threatening to do so.

*b* 2 Self abandoning, robbing, domestic animals, pets, or threatening to do so.

*c* 2 Self criticizing or depreciating others in a vague or mild manner.

*d* 2 Self depriving or disappointing other human beings.

*a* 1 Self killing, injuring, destroying, robbing wild life, flora, inani-

**II Hostility Outward–Covert**

**Thematic Categories**

*a* 3* Others (human) killing, fighting, injuring other individuals or threatening to do so.

*b* 3 Others (human) robbing, abandoning, causing suffering or anguish to other individuals, or threatening to do so.

*c* 3 Others adversely criticizing, depreciating, blaming, expressing anger, dislike of other human beings.

*a* 2 Others (human) killing, injuring, or destroying domestic animals, pets, or threatening to do so.

*b* 2 Others (human) abandoning, robbing, domestic animals, pets, or threatening to do so.

*c* 2 Others (human) criticizing or depreciating other individuals in a vague or mild manner.

*d* 2 Others (human) depriving or disappointing other human beings.

*e* 2 Others (human or domestic animals) dying or killed violently in death-dealing situation or threatened with such.

*f* 2 Bodies (human or domestic animals) mutilated, depreciated, defiled.

*a* 1 Wild life, flora, inanimate objects, injured, broken, robbed,

mate objects or threatening to do so.

*b* 1 Self adversely criticizing, depreciating, blaming, expressing anger or dislike of subhumans, inanimate objects, places, situations.

*c* 1 Self using hostile words, cursing, mention of anger or rage without referent.

destroyed or threatened with such (with or without mention of agent).

*b* 1 Others (human) adversely criticizing, depreciating, expressing anger or dislike of subhumans, inanimate objects, places, situations.

*c* 1 Others angry, cursing without reference to cause or direction of anger. *Also* instruments of destruction not used threateningly.

*d* 1 Others (human, domestic animals) injured, robbed, dead, abandoned or threatened with such from any source including subhuman and inanimate objects, situations (storms, floods, etc.).

*e* 1 Subhumans killing, fighting, injuring, robbing, destroying each other or threatening to do so.

*f* 1 Denial of anger, dislike, hatred, cruelty, and intent to harm.

* The number serves to give the weight as well as to identify the category. The letter also helps identify the category.

## SCHEDULE 3

### Hostility Directed Inward Scale: Self-Destructive, Self-Critical Thoughts and Actions

### I Hostility Inward

#### Thematic Categories

*a* 4* References to self (speaker) attempting or threatening to kill self, with or without conscious intent.

*b* 4 References to self wanting to die, needing or deserving to die.

*a* 3† References to self injuring, mutilating, disfiguring self or threats to do so, with or without conscious intent.

*b* 3 Self blaming, expressing anger or hatred to self, considering self worthless or of no value, causing oneself grief or trouble, or threatening to do so.

*c* 3 References to feelings of discouragement, giving up hope, despairing, feeling grieved or depressed, having no purpose in life.

*a* 2 References to self needing or deserving punishment, paying for one's sins, needing to atone or do penance.

*b* 2 Self adversely criticizing, depreciating self; references to regretting, being sorry or ashamed for what one says or does; references to self mistaken or in error.

*c* 2 References to feeling of deprivation, disappointment, lonesomeness.

*a* 1 References to feeling disappointed in self; unable to meet expectations of self or others.

*b* 1 Denial of anger, dislike, hatred, blame, destructive impulses from self to self.

*c* 1 References to feeling painfully driven or obliged to meet one's own expectations and standards.

* The number serves to give the weight as well as to identify the category. The letter also helps identify the category.

† This code is reduced to a weight of 2 if the injury is slight. It is then written 1a.

## SCHEDULE 4

### Ambivalent Hostility Scale: Destructive, Injurious, Critical Thoughts and Actions of Others to Self

### II Ambivalent Hostility

#### Thematic Categories

*a* 3* Others (human) killing or threatening to kill self.

*b* 3 Others (human) physically injuring, mutilating, disfiguring self or threatening to do so.

*c* 3 Others (human) adversely criticizing, blaming, expressing anger or dislike toward self or threatening to do so.

*d* 3 Others (human) abandoning, robbing self, causing suffering, anguish, or threatening to do so.

*a* 2 Others (human) depriving, disappointing, misunderstanding self or threatening to do so.

*b* 2 Self threatened with death from subhuman or inanimate object, or death-dealing situation.

*a* 1 Others (subhuman, inanimate, *or situation*), injuring, abandoning, robbing self, causing suffering, anguish.

*b* 1 Denial of blame.

* The number serves to give the weight as well as to identify the category. The letter also helps identify the category.

## Schedule V

### SELF-RATING SYMPTOM CHECK LIST

NAME ________________________

DATE: ________________________

INSTRUCTIONS: Listed below are some symptoms or problems that people sometimes have. Please read each one carefully and decide how much the symptoms bothered or distressed you *during the past week, including today.*

Decide how much the symptom affected you. NOT AT ALL? A LITTLE? QUITE A BIT? EXTREMELY? and place a check in the appropriate column to the right.

HOW MUCH WERE YOU BOTHERED BY THE FOLLOWING SYMPTOMS?
(Do not leave out any items)

| SYMPTOMS | Not at All<br>1 | A Little<br>2 | Quite a Bit<br>3 | Extremely<br>4 |
|---|---|---|---|---|
| 1. Sweating | | | | |
| 2. Trouble getting your breath | | | | |
| 3. Suddenly scared for no reason | | | | |
| 4. Difficulty in speaking when you are excited | | | | |
| 5. Feeling low in energy or slowed down | | | | |
| 6. Pains in the heart or chest | | | | |
| 7. Trouble remembering things | | | | |
| 8. Hot or cold spells | | | | |
| 9. Blaming yourself for things | | | | |
| 10. A lump in your throat | | | | |
| 11. Feeling fearful | | | | |
| 12. Numbness or tingling in parts of your body | | | | |
| 13. Feeling critical of others | | | | |
| 14. Having to avoid certain things, or places or activities because they frighten you | | | | |

| | | | | |
|---|---|---|---|---|
| 15. Having to do things very slowly in order to be sure you are doing them right | | | | |
| 16. Heavy feeling in your arms or legs | | | | |
| 17. Faintness or dizziness | | | | |
| 18. Crying easily | | | | |
| 19. Nervousness or shakiness inside | | | | |
| 20. Your feelings being easily hurt | | | | |
| 21. Constipation | | | | |
| 22. Loss of sexual interest or pleasure | | | | |
| 23. Feeling easily annoyed or irritated | | | | |
| 24. Poor appetite | | | | |
| 25. Difficulty making decisions | | | | |
| 26. Difficulty in falling asleep or staying asleep | | | | |
| 27. Feeling hopeless about the future | | | | |
| 28. Feeling blue | | | | |
| 29. Feeling lonely | | | | |
| 30. Temper outbursts you could not control | | | | |
| 31. Headaches | | | | |
| 32. Heart pounding or racing | | | | |
| 33. Trouble concentrating | | | | |
| 34. Your mind going blank | | | | |
| 35. Thoughts of ending your life | | | | |
| 36. Worried about sloppiness or carelessness | | | | |
| 37. Trembling | | | | |
| 38. A feeling of being trapped or caught | | | | |
| 39. Pains in the lower part of your back | | | | |

## SELF-RATING SYMPTOM CHECK LIST (cont'd.)

| | Not at All | A Little | Quite a Bit | Extremely |
|---|---|---|---|---|
| SYMPTOMS | 1 | 2 | 3 | 4 |
| 40. Worrying or stewing about things | | | | |
| 41. Feeling no interest in things | | | | |
| 42. Feeling others do not understand you or are unsympathetic | | | | |
| 43. Feeling that people are unfriendly or dislike you | | | | |
| 44. Feeling inferior to others | | | | |
| 45. Soreness of your muscles | | | | |
| 46. Having to check and double-check what you do | | | | |
| 47. Weakness in parts of your body | | | | |
| 48. Feeling tense or keyed up | | | | |
| 49. Nausea or upset stomach | | | | |
| 50. Sleepy during the day | | | | |
| 51. Dry mouth | | | | |
| 52. Loose bowel movements | | | | |

## DEROGATIS FACTORS SCL-52
## (Based on SCL-58 and SCL-90)
## AND ADDITIONAL FACTORS

**FACTOR I Somatization (14 items, need 11)**

1. Sweating (*Not used by Derogatis*)
2. Trouble getting your breath.
5. Feeling low in energy or slowed down
6. Pains in heart or chest
8. Hot or cold spells
10. A lump in your throat
12. Numbness or tingling in parts of your body
16. Heavy feeling in your arms and legs
17. Faintness or dizziness
31. Headaches
39. Pains in lower part of your back
45. Soreness of your muscles
47. Weakness in parts of your body
49. Nausea or upset stomach

**FACTOR II Obsessive-Compulsive (7 items, need 5)**

7. Trouble remembering things
15. Having to do things very slowly to insure correctness
25. Difficulty making decisions
33. Trouble concentrating
34. Your mind going blank
36. Worried about sloppiness or carelessness
46. Having to check and double-check

**FACTOR III Interpersonal Sensitivity (7 items, need 5)**

13. Feeling critical of others
20. Your feelings being easily hurt
23. Feeling easily annoyed or irritated
30. Temper outbursts you could not control
42. Feeling others do not understand you
43. Feeling people are unfriendly or dislike you
44. Feeling inferior to others

**FACTOR IV Depression (12 items, need 10)**

9. Blaming yourself for things
18. Crying easily
22. Loss of sexual interest or pleasure
24. Poor appetite
26. Difficulty in falling or staying asleep (*Not used by Derogatis*)
27. Feeling hopeless about the future
28. Feeling blue
29. Feeling lonely
35. Thoughts of ending your life
38. Feeling of being trapped or caught
40. Worrying or stewing about things
41. Feeling no interest in things

**FACTOR IVA Without item no. 26 (11 items, need 9)**

**FACTOR V Anxiety (7 items, need 5)**

3. Suddenly scared for no reason
11. Feeling fearful
14. Having to avoid certain things, places, etc., because they frighten you
19. Nervousness or shakiness inside
32. Heart pounding or racing
37. Trembling
48. Feeling tense or keyed up

**SUBFACTOR IIIA Anger Hostility (2 items, need 2)**

23. Feeling easily annoyed or irritated
30. Temper outbursts you could not control

**SUBFACTOR IIIB Interpersonal Sensitivity (4 items, need 3)**

20. Your feelings being easily hurt
42. Feeling others do not understand you or are unsympathetic
43. Feeling that people are unfriendly or dislike you
44. Feeling inferior to others

**TOTAL** (not including items 50, 51) (50 items, need 40)

Schedule VI

HAMILTON ANXIETY RATING SCALE

| PATIENT | DATE |
|---|---|
| | |

MILD - OCCURS IRREGULARLY AND FOR SHORT PERIODS OF TIME

SEVERE - CONTINUOUS AND DOMINATES PATIENT'S LIFE

MODERATE - OCCURS MORE CONSTANTLY AND OF LONGER DURATION REQUIRING CONSIDERABLE EFFORT ON PART OF PATIENT TO COPE WITH IT.

VERY SEVERE - INCAPACITATING

TO ELIMINATE BIAS PLEASE DO NOT REFER TO THE PRECEDING HAMILTON SCORES.

| | NOT PRESENT | MILD | MODERATE | SEVERE | VERY SEVERE |
|---|---|---|---|---|---|
| | 1 | 2 | 3 | 4 | 5 |
| 1. ANXIOUS MOOD: WORRIES, ANTICIPATION OF THE WORST APPREHENSION (FEARFUL ANTICIPATION), IRRITABILITY. | | | | | |
| 2. TENSION: FEELINGS OF TENSION, FATIGABILITY, INABILITY TO RELAX, STARTLE RESPONSE, MOVED TO TEARS EASILY, TREMBLING, FEELINGS OF RESTLESSNESS. | | | | | |
| 3. FEARS: OF DARK, STRANGERS, BEING LEFT ALONE, LARGE ANIMALS, TRAFFIC, CROWDS, ETC. | | | | | |
| 4. INSOMNIA: DIFFICULTY IN FALLING ASLEEP, BROKEN SLEEP, UNSATISFYING SLEEP AND FATIGUE ON WAKING, DREAMS, NIGHT-MARES, NIGHT TERRORS. | | | | | |
| 5. INTELLECTUAL: (COGNITIVE) DIFFICULTY IN CONCENTRATION, POOR MEMORY. | | | | | |
| 6. DEPRESSED MOOD: LOSS OF INTEREST, LACK OF PLEASURE IN HOBBIES, DEPRESSION, EARLY WAKING, DIURNAL SWING. | | | | | |
| 7. GENERAL SOMATIC: MUSCULAR, MUSCULAR PAINS AND ACHES, MUSCULAR STIFFNESS, MUSCULAR TWITCHINGS, CLONIC JERKS, GRINDING OF TEETH, UNSTEADY VOICE, INCREASED MUSCULAR TONE, SENSORY TINNITUS, BLURRING OF VISION, HOT AND COLD FLASHES, FEELINGS OF WEAKNESS, PRICKING SENSATION. | | | | | |
| 8. CARDIOVASCULAR: TACHYCARDIA, PALPITATIONS, PAIN IN CHEST, THROBBING OF VESSELS, FAINTING FEELINGS, MISSING BEAT. | | | | | |
| 9. RESPIRATORY: PRESSURE OR CONSTRICTION IN CHEST, CHOKING FEELINGS, SIGHINGS, DYSPNEA. | | | | | |
| 10. GASTRO-INTESTINAL: DIFFICULTY IN SWALLOWING, WIND, DYSPEPSIA: PAIN BEFORE AND AFTER MEALS, BURNING SENSATIONS, FULLNESS, NAUSEA, VOMITING, BORBORYGMI, DIARRHEA, WEIGHT LOSS, CONSTIPATION. | | | | | |
| 11. GENITO-URINARY: FREQUENCY OF MICTURITION, URGENCY OF MICTURITION, AMENORRHEA, MENORRHAGIA DEVELOPMENT OF FRIGIDITY, PREMATURE EJACULATION, LOSS OF LIBIDO, IMPOTENCE. | | | | | |
| 12. AUTONOMIC: DRY MOUTH, FLUSHING, PALLOR, TENDENCY TO SWEAT, GIDDINESS, TENSION HEADACHE. | | | | | |
| 13. BEHAVIOR AT INTERVIEW: GENERAL-TENSE NOT RELAXED, FIDGETING: HANDS, PICKING FINGERS, CLENCHING TIES, HANDKER-CHIEF, RESTLESSNESS, PACING, TREMOR OF HANDS, FURROWED BROW, STRAINED FACE, INCREASED MUSCULAR TONE, SIGHING RESPIRATION, FACIAL PALLOR. PHYSIOLOGICAL-SWALLOWING, BELCHING, HIGH RESTING PULSE RATE, RESPIRATION RATE OVER 20 MIN. BRISK TENDON JERKS, TREMOR, DILATED PUPILS, EXOPHTHALMOS, SWEATING, EYE-LID TWITCHING. | | | | | |

Schedule VII

## PHYSICIAN QUESTIONNAIRE

PQ² – Page 1

Visit 2 (Post 2 Wks.)

PATIENT ______________ DATE ________ PATIENT CODE ________

BP ______________

Card No. 1 __1__ 2 __2__

PULSE ______________

| | Not Present | Very Mild | Mild | Moderate | Moderately Severe | Severe | Ext. Severe | Col. |
|---|---|---|---|---|---|---|---|---|
| 1. **Anxiety** (Apprehensive, tense, worried, frightened, anxious, nervous) | 1 | 2 | 3 | 4 | 5 | 6 | 7 | 10 ___ |
| 2. **Depressive Mood** (Feelings of depression, unhappiness; sorrow, pessimism, sadness; hopelessness, tearfulness) | 1 | 2 | 3 | 4 | 5 | 6 | 7 | 11 ___ |
| 3. **Irritability** (Easily annoyed or irritated) | 1 | 2 | 3 | 4 | 5 | 6 | 7 | 12 ___ |
| 4. **Hostility** (Anger, animosity, contempt, belligerence, disdain for other people) | 1 | 2 | 3 | 4 | 5 | 6 | 7 | 13 ___ |
| 5. **Phobia** (Unrealistic fears) | 1 | 2 | 3 | 4 | 5 | 6 | 7 | 14 ___ |
| 6. **Obsession-Compulsion** (Repetitive unwanted thoughts or actions) | 1 | 2 | 3 | 4 | 5 | 6 | 7 | 15 ___ |
| 7. **Hypochondriasis** (Preoccupation with physical health) | 1 | 2 | 3 | 4 | 5 | 6 | 7 | 16 ___ |
| 8. **Somatization—Musculo-Skeletal** (e.g. Backache, muscle ache, heaviness of limbs) | 1 | 2 | 3 | 4 | 5 | 6 | 7 | 17 ___ |
| 9. **Somatization – Autonomic** (e.g. G.I., respiratory, sweating, trembling, heart palpitations | 1 | 2 | 3 | 4 | 5 | 6 | 7 | 18 ___ |
| 10. **Insomnia** | 1 | 2 | 3 | 4 | 5 | 6 | 7 | 19 ___ |
| 11. **Apetite Distrubance** | 1 | 2 | 3 | 4 | 5 | 6 | 7 | 20 ___ |
| 12. **Headaches** (Frequency and intensity) | 1 | 2 | 3 | 4 | 5 | 6 | 7 | 21 ___ |
| 13. **Psychomotor Retardation** (Slowness of thought, speech, motor activity) | 1 | 2 | 3 | 4 | 5 | 6 | 7 | 22 ___ |
| 14. **Fatigue, Tiredness, Lethargy** | 1 | 2 | 3 | 4 | 5 | 6 | 7 | 23 ___ |
| 15. **Impairment of Interpersonal Relationships** (Home, work, social) | 1 | 2 | 3 | 4 | 5 | 6 | 7 | 24 ___ |

| | Not Ill | Very Mild | Mild | Moderate | Moderately Severe | Severe | Extremely Severe | |
|---|---|---|---|---|---|---|---|---|
| 16* **Degree of Global Psychopathology (OJP):** How ill is this patient now, compared to your experience with other neurotic patients? | 1 | 2 | 3 | 4 | 5 | 6 | 7 | 25 ___ |

COMMENTS: ______________

**17. Time spent with patient:** ________ **minutes** 26 ___

**18. How many pills/day are prescribed today?** 27 ___

**19. How did you feel today with the patient?** 28 ___
- Very Comfortable ☐ 1
- Comfortable ☐ 2
- Uncomfortable ☐ 3

5-72 RICKELS

*(OVER)*

PQ2 – Page 2

**20. How much has patient changed:** a)* Since last visit — Col. 29 a

| | |
|---|---|
| Very much better | 1 ☐ |
| Much better | 2 ☐ |
| A little better | 3 ☐ |
| No change | 4 ☐ |
| A little worse | 5 ☐ |
| Much worse | 6 ☐ |
| Very much worse | 7 ☐ |

**21. If better, how many days on drug when improvement first appeared?** ______ 31 ____ 32 ____

**22. Dosage Intake Record**
a) Average number of pills per day taken since last visit: ☐ 33 ____
b) If medication discontinued between visits, how many days did patient take medication? ☐ 34 ____
c) If deviated from Dr. prescribed dosage, reason: 35 ____

| | | | |
|---|---|---|---|
| No deviation | ☐ 0 | Worse or no change | ☐ 3 |
| Side effects only | ☐ 1 | Side effects and felt worse | ☐ 4 |
| Felt Improved | ☐ 2 | Other (specify) ______ | ☐ 5 |

36 ____

***23. Presence of side effects due to study medication.**
Yes ☐ 1 No ☐ 2
If no side effect, skip to #25. 37 ____

**24. If Yes:**
a) How many days on drug when side effects first appeared? ☐ 38 ____
b) Check which side effects occurred since last visit 39 ____

| ADVERSE BEHAVIOR EFFECTS | 1 Mild | 2 Marked | |
|---|---|---|---|
| *Insomnia | | | 40 |
| *Drowsiness | | | 41 |
| *Excitement | | | 42 |
| *Depression | | | 43 |
| *Confusion | | | 44 |
| *Other (Specify) | | | 45 |
| CENTRAL NERVOUS SYSTEM | | | |
| *Rigidity | | | 46 |
| *Tremor | | | 47 |
| *Dystonic symptoms | | | 48 |
| *Akathisia | | | 49 |
| *Other (Specify) | | | 50 |
| AUTONOMIC NERVOUS SYSTEM | | | |
| *Hypotension | | | 51 |
| *Syncope | | | 52 |
| *Tachycardia – Palpitations | | | 53 |
| *Nasal congestion | | | 54 |
| *Dry mouth | | | 55 |
| *Increased salivation | | | 56 |
| *Blurred vision | | | 57 |
| *Nausea or vomiting | | | 58 |
| *Diarrhea | | | 59 |
| *Constipation | | | 60 |
| *Other (Specify) | | | 61 |

| MISCELLANEOUS | 1 Mild | 2 Marked | |
|---|---|---|---|
| *Dermatitis – Allergy | | | 62 |
| *Headache | | | 63 |
| *Light-headedness, dizziness, weakness | | | 64 |
| *Weight gain | | | 65 |
| *Weight loss | | | 66 |
| *Other (Specify) | | | 67 |

**25. a) At this moment, which medication do you believe the patient is receiving?**

Drug ☐ 1
Placebo ☐ 2 — 68 ____

**b) Basis for medication guess:**

Presence or absence of side effects ☐ 1
Improved, worse, no change ☐ 2
Both ☐ 3
Other (Specify) ☐ 4 — 69 ____

**26. External Events:** In your opinion has anything occurred in the patient's life situation (since the time of his last visit) which might affect his treatment response.

NO ☐ 1 — 70 ____
YES, A Good or Favorable Event ☐ 2
YES, A Bad or Unfavorable event ☐ 3
IF YES, Specify: ______ 71 ____
______ 72 ____

**PHYSICIAN OR NURSE:**
Number of Pills Returned ______ — PILL COUNT 73 ____ 74 ____

**COMMENTS:** *(INCLUDE INTERCURRENT MEDICAL ILLNESS AND/OR NON-STUDY MEDICATION)*

6-72 RICKELS

# Introduction to Chapter 4

Introductory Comments by Louis A. Gottschalk

A group of researchers, G. Schofer, U. Koch, and F. Balck, from the Department of Psychosomatic Medicine, University of Hamburg, Germany, has done outstanding studies involving the content analysis of speech. Schofer introduced the Gottschalk-Gleser content analysis procedure to Germany with a German translation in 1974 of a portion of the two 1969 books on the Gottschalk-Gleser content analysis method (Gottschalk and Gleser, 1969; Gottschalk et al, 1969) dealing with the anxiety and hostility scales. In 1975, Schofer spent several weeks at the Communications and Measurement Laboratory, Department of Psychiatry and Human Behavior, University of California at Irvine, consulting with Gottschalk and his coworkers there on the use and applications of these content analysis scales. Michael Syben, a German and English speaking member of Gottschalk's research team, provided some useful and critical suggestions regarding the German translation. One of Schofer's major reasons for using the Gottschalk-Gleser content analysis scales was to apply them to studies of the process and outcome of psychoanalytic and other kinds of psychotherapy. In preparation for doing so and with

commendable thoroughness, Schofer and his collaborators obtained a large group of five minute speech samples, elicited by the standard instructions, from a normative population of subjects. He examined the effect of sex of the speaker, sex of the interviewer, socioeconomic class, and age on the group's anxiety and hostility scores.

Of immediate interest is the observation that the norms obtained for anxiety and hostility and their respective subscale scores from the German group are very similar to the average scores for the normative samples from the United States. This indicates that the method can be used across ethnic and language boundaries, provided the content analysis scores are well-versed in the idiomatic understanding of the language being spoken. This finding also indicates a, perhaps, surprising uniformity in group averages for the affects of anxiety and hostility across national boundaries. The extent of such cross-cultural similarities merits further study. Whether such similarity is limited to American and European cultures or is widespread across more diverse societies and cultures is the question.

The first of the papers from the University of Hamburg group offers some innovative ways of examining the hostility scores derived by the Gottschalk-Gleser method, for example, a reclassification of the scores such that one can look at scores for:

1) others the victim;
2) self the victim;
3) self the agent; and
4) others the agent (of hostility).

This paper is the first reported study demonstrating that social class is definitely related to the magnitude of affect expression and that, in general, the lower social class in West Germany has significantly higher affect scores than the upper social class.

There are many other findings of interest in this paper, for the authors examine a number of important questions, such as, the effect of number of speech samples, sex of speaker, and sex of interviewer, in exquisite detail. At times their findings corroborate those of Gottschalk and others and, on occasions, the German subjects reveal different characteristics or features not yet explored by American investigators.

# 4

# The Gottschalk-Gleser Content Analysis of Speech: A Normative Study (The Relationship of Hostile and Anxious Affects to Sex, Sex of the Interviewer, Socioeconomic Class and Age)*

Gert Schöfer, Uwe Koch, and Friederich Balck**

## Introduction

Problems in establishing norms for the Gottschalk-Gleser content analysis of speech were discussed by Gottschalk and Gleser (1969 , p. 68) in their introduction to the chapter "Normative Study and Intercorrelation of Scores" in their book. It is our opinion, too, that the establishing of norms is problematic, because a certain average score for an affect does not consider the strong fluctuation of affects. But we believe, as Gottschalk and Gleser do, that the influence of such fixed factors as age, sex, socioeconomic status, etc. results in typical behavioral patterns in regard to affective behavior in such individual groups and that these influences, if present, must be recognized in order to be able to interpret the results. This was one reason why we did this assessment. At the same time the assessment intended to check on the test criteria of this instrument, which will be described in the next chapter.

---

* Granted by the German Research Society: Sonderforschungsbereich 115 - Projekt C4

** Department of Psychosomatik Medicine (Chairman Prof.Dr.Dr. A.-E. Meyer) II. Med., University of Hamburg, GFR

A further aspect, which questions the establishment of norms, is that the scores of affects of a speech sample are dependent upon the situation. Since a speech sample is supposed to grasp the presently predominant affects, the influence of situational variables must be taken into consideration. Therefore, we have assessed a large sample of subjects in a specific situation in order to check on the instrument.

One might ask if there is any sense in publishing such an assessment which has been conducted in Germany and in the United States. We can see two reasons for it:

1. In a pilot study (Schöfer, 1977), we could show that the scores themselves as well as the intercorrelations of the hostility scales and the anxiety scales of a sub-sample (N=200) of our total sample are very similar to those which Gottschalk and Gleser have published for a normal population (Kroger-sample) (Gottschalk and Gleser, 1969). The same study also showed that in rating translated original speech samples of Gottschalk our team arrived at the same results as the American raters. There were very few differences between the scores of two of our raters and those given by Gottschalk with respect to 16 identical (translated) texts: correlation coefficients were .88 and .91 respectively. We, therefore, believe that to a certain degree American and German results are comparable.

2. Among other things, our study served to evaluate the content analysis of speech, its test criteria, and also the dependence of speech samples upon certain variables, and we believe that these results are equally as interesting for Americans as for Germans.

## The investigation and description of the samples

In an empirical study about hostility (Koch and Schöfer, 1974), a sample of 406 persons representative of the normal population of Hamburg was assessed by the Gottschalk-Gleser content analysis of speech. After a special training the assessment was carried out by viewers of an demoscopic institute. At the beginning and at the end of the assessment, lasting approximately one hour, a 5-minute speech sample was recorded

after giving the standard instruction. Between the two speech samples several personality inventories were administered and also a short interview, having a specific topic, was conducted. Because of the drop-out quotas described below, we collected from 355 subjects the first and from 346 subjects the second speech sample only, while from 340 subjects we received the first and second speech sample. A break-up of the total group is shown in Table 1. In the first column you find the absolute number of scorable speech samples per group. The second column gives the percentage of scorable speech samples related to the total number of subjects belonging to that group (e.g. 355 out of 406 subjects have rendered a scorable speech sample, that is 87.4% of the total group). We have split up the sample in such a manner that we could analyze the data in respect to differences depending on sex, sex of interviewer, on socioeconomic status, and on age. Differences between the two speech samples were tested with the Wilcoxon pair test. To analyze the differences between the individual groups, the Mann Whitney U-Test was used since parametric tests could not be applied to our sample.*

The scoring of the speech samples was done by two technicians** using a translation of the scales (Schöfer, 1974) which had been authorized by L.A. Gottschalk. Already previous to this study, both raters had interrater agreements of about .85 (correlation coefficient). Such interrater agreements were also achieved for the supervisor with each of those raters. The supervisor had participated in a period of training to score by this content analysis method with L.A. Gottschalk at Irvine, California.

---

*A test of distribution showed that all distributions have a skewness to the left. In addition all hostility scales and the anxiety subscales showed deviations in all criteria from a normal distribution. Only the combination of the hostility scales as well as the total anxiety satisfied the conditions for a normal distribution.

**We wish to express our gratitude to Mrs. Prockl-Pfeiffer and Mrs. Riemann for their enduring and painstaking scoring work of a total of 691 speech samples.

Table 1

| | | 1. Sample | | 2. Sample | | 1. & 2. Sample together | |
|---|---|---|---|---|---|---|---|
| | | N | % | N | % | N | % |
| | Total Group | 355 | 87.4 | 346 | 85.2 | 340 | 83.7 |
| Sex of | male | 184 | 85.5 | 180 | 83.7 | 175 | 81.3 |
| subject | female | 171 | 89.5 | 166 | 86.9 | 165 | 86.3 |
| Sex of | male | 167 | 83.9 | 163 | 81.9 | 160 | 80.4 |
| Interviewer | female | 188 | 90.8 | 183 | 88.4 | 180 | 86.9 |
| Combination sex | I♂ S♂ | 89 | 84.7 | 88 | 83.6 | 86 | 81.9 |
| of interviewer | I♂ S♀ | 78 | 82.9 | 75 | 79.7 | 74 | 78.7 |
| and sex of | I♀ S♂ | 95 | 86.3 | 92 | 83.6 | 89 | 80.9 |
| subject | I♀ S♀ | 93 | 95.8 | 91 | 93.8 | 91 | 93.8 |
| Socio- | high | 57 | 81.4 | 54 | 77.1 | 54 | 77.1 |
| economic | middle | 201 | 89.7 | 197 | 87.9 | 194 | 86.6 |
| class | low | 49 | 89.0 | 47 | 85.4 | 45 | 81.8 |
| Age | 30 | 117 | 92.1 | 114 | 89.7 | 112 | 88.1 |
| | 30-39 | 119 | 84.3 | 115 | 81.5 | 114 | 80.8 |
| | 40-49 | 60 | 88.2 | 60 | 88.2 | 58 | 85.2 |
| | 50 | 56 | 83.5 | 55 | 82.0 | 54 | 80.5 |

Table 1: Absolute (N) and percent frequencies (%, with respect to the number of subjects per sample) for the first and the second speech sample for the total group and the individual subgroups. Third column gives the number of subjects which have given both speech samples. E.g. first row 355 subjects produced a first speech sample equals 78.4% of 406 interviewed persons, 346 produced a second speech sample equals 85.2%, 340 produced both speech samples equals 83.7%.

The first 300 speech samples were scored independently by both raters and the interrater agreements were continuously checked on. Discrepancies in coding were discussed with the supervisor and then a final decision was taken. A checkup on the interrater agreement (N=30) for the scores of the first 100 speech samples showed results

between .85, .96 depending on the scale (further information regarding this matter can be found in the chapter "Test Criteria"). When it was guaranteed that the raters showed a sufficiently high interrater agreement, the remaining speech samples were not scored twice anymore, but each rater scored half of them. The protocols were then scrutinized by the second rater once more and in the end a final coding decided upon.

## Results

Drop-out quotas:

406 subjects gave 388 (95.5%) initial speech samples, which means that 4.4% of subjects refused to do so. In an additional 8.1% of the cases, the transcripts could not be scored, because of the low number of words (below 70 words), so that a total of 355 (87.4%) speech samples could be scored. In the group of subjects who gave a second speech sample, there was a drop-out of 2.2%, so that 346 transcripts could be scored. Looking at the subgroups, one finds different drop-out quotas (see Table 1). The most prominent differences are shown by the combinations of sex of interviewer and sex of subject (interviewer male, subject female 17.1%; interviewer female, subject male 4.2%).

### A. Hostility

The traditional Gottschalk-Gleser scoring was done using the three hostility scales: Hostility-Directed-Outward with two subscales "overt" and "covert", Hostility-Directed-Inward, and Ambivalent Hostility. The combination of the scores of Hostility-Directed-Outward overt and Hostility-Directed-Outward covert into Total-Hostility-Directed-Outward was based mainly on theoretical considerations. Since we saw that besides this combination further combinations were justified by their contents, we decided that on one hand we should use four Hostility-scales, namely:

1. Hostility-Directed-Outward overt (HDOo)
2. Hostility-Directed-Outward covert (HDOc)
3. Hostility-Directed-Inward (HDI)
4. Ambivalent Hostility (AH)

and on the other hand we could form four combinations out of the four scales and in addition combine all scales into a "Total Hostility" scale. Since each scale can be defined through an agent (self or other) and through a victim (self or other), the following combinations could be arrived at (As shown in Table 2).

1. HDOo + HDOc = others victims (OV)
2. HDI + AH = self victim (SV)
3. HDO + HDI = self agent (SA)
4. HDOc + AH = others agents (OA)
5. HDOo + HDOc + HDI + AH = total hostility

The combinations of scores are performed in the same manner as with the Hostility-Directed-Outward total (now meaning OV) by summing up the raw-scores and then transforming them into scores.

We find these five combinations equally as acceptable as the previous Hostility-Directed-Outward total. All of them can be also explained in regard to their contents. Our assumptions leading to those combinations were that an individual has a certain potential of hostility; therefore, total hostility, which according to the psychological structure and the defense mechanism being predominant in an individual will express itself in different forms as being measured by the separate scales. Since each scale contains the two elements "agent" and "victim", one arrives at the described combinations by combining identical elements (See Table 2).

1. <u>Comparison between first and second speech sample</u>

Both speech samples were recorded with an interval of an hour in between, within which other tests and an interview were performed. As can be seen in Table 3, there are no differences in the mean averages between the first and the second speech sample in regard to the hostility scores for the total group. This result suggests a stability over the time interval. The consistently low correlations between both speech samples are showing, though, that within the samples the rank order is changing (for further details see the chapter, "Test Criteria").

Table 2.

| | | VICTIM | | |
|---|---|---|---|---|
| | | OTHERS | SELF | |
| AGENT | SELF | $HDO_o$ | HDI | SELF AGENT SA |
| | OTHERS | $HDO_c$ | AH | OTHERS AGENT OA |
| | | OTHERS VICTIMS OV | SELF VICTIM SV | total Hostility |

Table 2: Diagram illustrating combinations of the traditional hostility scales being combined with respect to agent and victim.

2. Hostility and Sex of Speaker

Gottschalk and Gleser reported a difference in sex (Gottschalk and Gleser, 1969, p. 79/80) in hostility directed outward covert scores (HDOc) and total hostility directed outward scores (HDOt) (corresponding with our others victims scores (OV)). We could not find this difference. Taking the traditional scales, hostility directed inward scores (HDI) showed a difference in the first speech sample in so far as women had a significantly higher score (5% level) than men. The difference could be found in the second speech sample only as tendency. In the second sample, the combined scales showed a difference in self agent scores (SA) at the 5% level. Here also, women had higher scores than men (SA is the combination of HDOo + HDI) (See Table 4).

Table 3.

| Hostility Scales | | 1. Sample | 2. Sample | $d^+$ | Corr. |
|---|---|---|---|---|---|
| HDOo | M | .74 | .76 | - | $.18^{xxx}$ |
| | S | .42 | .46 | | |
| HDOc | M | .78 | .76 | - | .06 |
| | S | .46 | .47 | | |
| HDI | M | .57 | .59 | - | $.15^{xx}$ |
| | S | .35 | .43 | | |
| AH | M | .76 | .72 | - | $.10^{x}$ |
| | S | .50 | .50 | | |
| OV | M | 1.08 | 1.08 | - | $.22^{xxx}$ |
| | S | .50 | .58 | | |
| SV | M | .93 | .90 | - | $.17^{xxx}$ |
| | S | .55 | .61 | | |
| SA | M | .91 | .95 | - | $.27^{xxx}$ |
| | S | .98 | .56 | | |
| OA | M | 1.08 | 1.06 | - | $.13^{xx}$ |
| | S | .58 | .60 | | |
| Total Hostility | M | 1.44 | 1.43 | - | $.25^{xxx}$ |
| | S | .61 | .70 | | |
| N | | 355 | 346 | 340 | 340 |

Table 3: Differences in scores from hostility scales between first and second speech sample tested with Wilcoxon pair test. Average means (M), standard deviation (S). d gives the levels of significance for differences. Next to it one finds the correlation coefficients of the individual scales between the first and the second sample.

x = $p < .05$
xx = $p < .01$
xxx = $p < .001$

Table 4.

| Hostility and sex | | 1. Sample | | | 2. Sample | | |
|---|---|---|---|---|---|---|---|
| | | ♂ | ♀ | d | ♂ | ♀ | d |
| HDI | M | .53 | .63 | .05 | .55 | .64 | .10 |
| | S | .31 | .39 | | .38 | .46 | |
| SA | M | .92 | .91 | - | .90 | 1.00 | .05 |
| | S | .47 | .49 | | .53 | .58 | |
| N | | 184 | 171 | | 180 | 166 | |

Table 4: Differences in sex in scores from hostility scales. Average means (M) and standard deviations(S) in the first and second speech sample. Level of significance for differences in the Mann Whitney U-Test in column d.

3. Hostility and Effect of Sex of Interviewer

Gottschalk pointed out that by recording speech samples the personality and sex of the interviewer can have an influence on the affect scores (Gottschalk, 1973). To investigate further into this matter, we used four male and four female interviewers, who recorded speech samples of 25 men and 25 women each. For the first speech sample, we therefore had a group of 167 subjects (for the second speech sample of 163) with male interviewers and a group of 188 subjects (second speech sample, 183) with female interviewers. Neither for the traditional hostility scales nor for the combinations could a difference be shown which was significant at least on the 5% level. (Only in the second speech sample was there a tendency for female interviewers to elicit higher hostility directed inward scores (HDI) scores than male interviewers).

The combinations of the variables sex of interviewer and sex of subject, resulting in four subgroups, showed significant differences in hostility directed inward scores (HDI). Women in both speech samples

interviewed by men showed higher hostility directed inward scores (HDI) (1% level) than men interviewed by men. In addition to this in the second speech sample, we found a difference at the 5% level: men being interviewed by women showed higher hostility directed inward scores (HDI) than men being interviewed by men.(See Table 5)

4. Hostility and Socioeconomic Class

The categorization of our sample into socioeconomic classes was done with a system frequently used in Germany (Kleining and More, SSE= Social-Self-Esteem, 1968). In accordance with the recommendations by the authors, the nine scale system was combined into a three scale system:

Social class 1 (high): upper class, upper middle class, middle middle class

Social class 2 (middle): lower middle class, upper lower class

Social class 3 (low): Lower lower class, social outcasts

With respect to these three social classes, differences could be detected in all hostility scales and combination of scales. One can observe an almost consistent increase in the individual hostility scores from high social class to low social class (Table 6).

With very few exceptions all differences between high and low social class are significant. At this point one cannot decide, whether members of the low class are more aggressive than members of the high class or whether the difference is due to the fact that hostility is expressed more directly. Our results agree with those of a study (Koch and Probst, 1976) in which the authors analyzed a multidimensional aggression inventory; here, also, an increase of the average scores from the upper class over the middle class to the lower class could be demonstrated consistently for all hostility scales.

5. Hostility and Age

Our sample was categorized in four groups in regard to age: A1:

Table 5.

| Hostility and Sex Combination | | 1. Sample | | | | | | 2. Sample | | | | | |
|---|---|---|---|---|---|---|---|---|---|---|---|---|---|
| | | $I^1$♂ S ♂ | $I^2$♂ S ♀ | $I^3$♀ S ♂ | $I^4$♀ S ♀ | d | | $I^1$♂ S ♂ | $I^2$♂ S ♀ | $I^3$♀ S ♂ | $I^4$♀ S ♀ | d | |
| HDI | M | .50 | .61 | .56 | .64 | 1:2 | .01 | .50 | .65 | .60 | .62 | 1:2 | .01 |
| | S | .31 | .33 | .32 | .43 | | | .36 | .41 | .40 | .50 | 1:3 | .05 |
| N | | 89 | 78 | 95 | 93 | | | 88 | 75 | 92 | 91 | | |

Table 5: Differences in the scores from hostility scales for groups which are arrived at by combining interviewer sex and subject sex (See legend Table 4).

below 30, A2: 30-39, A3: 40-49, A4: above 50. There were differences for HDOc, HDI and AH in both speech samples as well as for OV, SV, OA and Total Hostility in the first speech sample (See Table 7). An increase or decrease in the hostility scales being connected with the increase in age could not be observed though.

For the first speech sample one notices that the differences are brought about by the fact that group A3 (40-49 years) always reaches higher scores than any other of the three groups.* This phenomenon regarding group A3 cannot be detected in the second speech sample (except for AH). In the second speech sample one finds two differences between the youngest and the oldest group: HDOc is higher for the oldest, HDI is higher for the youngest. The combinations of scales show no differences within the second speech sample. We have no hypothesis for the higher scores in the age group 40-49, but obviously for this group for the first speech sample was a stronger stimulus for hostility than for the other groups.

------------------------------

*Because of the differing number of cases sometimes more or less identical differences are significant, sometimes not.

Table 6

| Hostility and socioeconomic class | | 1. Sample S1 high | S2 middle | S3 low | d | | 2. Sample S1 high | S2 middle | S3 low | d | |
|---|---|---|---|---|---|---|---|---|---|---|---|
| HDOo | M | .65 | .75 | .88 | 1:3 | .01 | .72 | .75 | .93 | 1:3 | .05 |
| | S | .31 | .44 | .46 | | | .44 | .46 | .55 | | |
| HDOc | M | .84 | .76 | .84 | | | .73 | .74 | 1.01 | 1:3 | .01 |
| | S | .46 | .46 | .46 | | | .42 | .47 | .53 | | |
| HDI | M | .50 | .58 | .64 | 1:3 | .05 | .65 | .56 | .68 | | |
| | S | .27 | .37 | .36 | | | .62 | .36 | .36 | | |
| AH | M | .68 | .77 | .89 | 1:3 | .01 | .68 | .70 | .92 | 1:3 | .01 |
| | S | .53 | .51 | .53 | | | .43 | .49 | .58 | | |
| OV | M | 1.05 | 1.07 | 1.22 | 2:3 | .01 | 1.00 | 1.04 | 1.39 | 1:3 | .01 |
| | S | .46 | .53 | .50 | | | .55 | .58 | .60 | 2:3 | .01 |
| SV | M | .81 | .94 | 1.08 | 1:3 | .01 | .92 | .85 | 1.10 | 1:3 | .05 |
| | S | .54 | .56 | .55 | 2:3 | .05 | .69 | .55 | .71 | | |
| SA | M | .78 | .92 | 1.08 | 1:3 | .01 | .95 | .90 | 1.14 | 1:3 | .01 |
| | S | .35 | .51 | .47 | 2:3 | .01 | .70 | .52 | .61 | 2:3 | .01 |
| OA | M | 1.10 | 1.08 | 1.21 | 2:3 | .05 | .99 | 1.00 | 1.39 | 1:3 | .01 |
| | S | .59 | .59 | .59 | | | .50 | .59 | .62 | 2:3 | .01 |
| Total Hostility | M | 1.35 | 1.45 | 1.65 | 1:3 | .05 | 1.39 | 1.36 | 1.81 | 1:3 | .01 |
| | S | .58 | .63 | .58 | 2:3 | .01 | .73 | .68 | .73 | 2:3 | .01 |
| N | | 57 | 201 | 49 | | | 54 | 197 | 47 | | |

Table 6: Differences in scores from hostility scales between socioeconomic classes (See legend Table 4)

B. Anxiety

In measuring anxiety we have not gone any further than the traditional scoring by Gottschalk and Gleser. Just as they did, we scored total anxiety as well as the six subscales: "death anxiety," "mutilation anxiety," "separation anxiety," "guilt anxiety," "shame anxiety," "diffuse anxiety." *(see footnote following page)

Table 7: Age differences in scores from hostility scales (see legend Table 4)

| Hostility and age | | 1. Sample A1 | A2 | A3 | A4 | d | | 2. Sample A1 | A2 | A3 | A4 | d | |
|---|---|---|---|---|---|---|---|---|---|---|---|---|---|
| HDOc | M | .70 | .78 | .97 | .74 | 1:2 | .05 | .75 | .81 | .72 | .83 | 1:4 | .05 |
| | S | .41 | .45 | .53 | .38 | 1:3<br>2:3 | .01<br>.05 | .49 | .51 | .42 | .47 | | |
| HDI | M | .57 | .57 | .60 | .57 | - | | .67 | .54 | .60 | .51 | 1:4 | .05 |
| | S | .32 | .36 | .37 | .33 | | | .54 | .33 | .36 | .39 | | |
| AH | M | .76 | .70 | .92 | .71 | 1:3 | .05 | .72 | .69 | .81 | .71 | 2:3 | .05 |
| | S | .50 | .48 | .61 | .40 | 2:3 | .01 | .48 | .50 | .52 | .50 | | |
| OV | M | 1.04 | 1.05 | 1.24 | 1.02 | 2:3 | .01 | 1.06 | 1.14 | 1.01 | 1.03 | - | |
| | S | .48 | .51 | .55 | .55 | | | .59 | .58 | .62 | .45 | | |
| SV | M | .92 | .87 | 1.10 | .88 | 2:3 | .05 | .94 | .85 | .97 | .84 | - | |
| | S | .54 | .54 | .63 | .48 | | | .68 | .54 | .59 | .59 | | |
| OA | M | 1.02 | 1.04 | 1.37 | 1.05 | 2:3 | .01 | 1.03 | 1.07 | 1.05 | 1.10 | - | |
| | S | .57 | .58 | .68 | .41 | | | .59 | .62 | .60 | .54 | | |
| Total Hostility | M | 1.40 | 1.38 | 1.69 | 1.37 | 2:3 | .01 | 1.44 | 1.44 | 1.43 | 1.36 | - | |
| | S | .59 | .61 | .69 | .46 | | | .77 | .66 | .70 | .60 | | |
| N | | 117 | 119 | 60 | 56 | | | 114 | 115 | 60 | 55 | | |

Footnote:

Anxiety subscale scores were calculated by adding 0.5 to the total weighted anxiety subscale score, multiplying by one hundred, dividing by the number of words in the speech sample, and taking the square root of the result. Namely, the corrected anxiety subscale score = $\sqrt{\frac{100(\mathcal{E}\, fxwx + 0.5)}{\text{Number of words}}}$,

where $\mathcal{E}$ fxwx represents the sum of all weighted scores on the anxiety subscale in the speech sample. This method of arriving at the corrected anxiety subscale scores has been recommended and used by Gottschalk recently (1976), though it is not the same as the procedure used earlier by Gottschalk and Gleser (1969, pp 74-78).

Table 8: Differences in anxiety scale scores and number of words between first and second speech sample calculated with the Wilcoxon pair test (See Legend Table 3)

| | | 1. Sample | 2. Sample | d | Corr. |
|---|---|---|---|---|---|
| Death | M | .60 | .55 | .01 | -.03 |
| | S | .44 | .44 | | |
| Mutilation | M | .58 | .49 | .01 | .07 |
| | S | .45 | .39 | | |
| Separation | M | .67 | .70 | - | .01 |
| | S | .43 | .51 | | |
| Guilt | M | .48 | .51 | - | $.18^{xxx}$ |
| | S | .32 | .38 | | |
| Shame | M | .65 | .67 | - | $.22^{xxx}$ |
| | S | .48 | .53 | | |
| Diffuse Anxiety | M | .75 | .80 | - | $.20^{xxx}$ |
| | S | .53 | .60 | | |
| Total Anxiety | M | 1.55 | 1.55 | - | $.09^{x}$ |
| | S | .73 | .85 | | |
| Number of words | M | 488.60 | 499.08 | - | $.54^{xxx}$ |
| | S | 194.49 | 220.31 | | |
| N | | 355 | 346 | 340 | 340 |

1. Comparison between first and second speech sample

Comparing both speech samples with the Wilcoxon-pair-test, we found two differences at the 1% level of significance: in the first speech sample "death anxiety" and "mutilation anxiety" were higher than in the second speech sample. In absolute figures, the differences were small. Here also the correlations between the two speech samples showed low significant and nonsignificant results (See Table 8).

2. Anxiety and Sex of Speaker

Gottschalk and Gleser reported three differences in regard to sex:

Table 9: Sex differences in anxiety scale scores and number of words (See legend Table 4)

| Anxiety and sex | | 1. Sample | | | 2. Sample | | |
|---|---|---|---|---|---|---|---|
| | | ♂ | ♀ | d | ♂ | ♀ | d |
| Separation | M | .63 | .73 | .05 | .62 | .81 | .08 |
| | S | .41 | .45 | | .38 | .60 | |
| Diffuse Anxiety | M | .70 | .88 | .06 | .67 | .95 | .01 |
| | S | .50 | .58 | | .51 | .65 | |
| Total Anxiety | M | 1.54 | 1.60 | - | 1.44 | 1.70 | .01 |
| | S | .75 | .72 | | .77 | .88 | |
| Number of words | M | 464.29 | 513.51 | .05 | 470.99 | 529.55 | .05 |
| | S | 180.92 | 205.20 | | 191.03 | 226.04 | |
| N | | 184 | 171 | | 180 | 166 | |

death anxiety (men > women), separation anxiety (women > men) and shame anxiety (women > men). In our study we found a similar difference in separation anxiety: women scored higher than men. The difference was significant at the 5% level in the first speech sample; in the second speech sample it could be noticed as a tendency. In addition, in the second speech sample we found a difference significant at the 1% level in diffuse anxiety (women > men) and in total anxiety (women > men). As a tendency the difference in diffuse anxiety was also detectable in the first speech sample (See Table 9).

3. Anxiety and Effect of Sex of Interviewer

On dividing the groups in regard to sex of interviewers, in the second speech sample differences were seen in death anxiety and mutilation anxiety scores at the 5% level: subjects with male interviewers show higher scores than those with female interviewers. The difference in death anxiety could also be detected in the first speech sample as a tendency (See Table 10).

Table 10: Differences based on sex of interviewer in anxiety scale scores and in number of words (See legend Table 4)

| Anxiety and Sex of Interviewer | | 1. Sample | | | 2. Sample | | |
|---|---|---|---|---|---|---|---|
| | | I ♂ | I ♀ | d | I ♂ | I ♀ | d |
| Death | M | .67 | .55 | .06 | .59 | .53 | .05 |
| | S | .49 | .38 | | .47 | .41 | |
| Mutilation | M | .61 | .56 | - | .56 | .46 | .05 |
| | S | .49 | .42 | | .39 | .28 | |
| Number of words | M | 464.79 | 508.62 | .05 | 473.82 | 521.54 | .05 |
| | S | 192.25 | 194.66 | | 201.38 | 216.02 | |
| N | | 167 | 188 | | 163 | 183 | |

By looking at the groups which result from a combination of sex of interviewers and sex of subject, differences could be seen in all scales. For both speech samples, women with female interviewers had the lowest death anxiety and mutilation anxiety scores. The differences in regard to the other groups were partly significant, especially within the second speech sample. With respect to separation anxiety, women both with female and male interviewers had high scores, the differences being partly significant on the 5% level. With regard to guilt anxiety, women with male interviewers showed significantly higher scores than those with female interviewers in the first speech sample. With regard to shame anxiety, one difference occurred (first speech sample, 1% level); women with male interviewers had higher shame anxiety scores than those with female interviewers. With respect to diffuse anxiety scores as well as with respect to separation anxiety scores a difference between men and women was shown, but could not be explained by a specific combination with sex of interviewer. The same was true for total anxiety. In contrast to these findings, a definite influence of difference in sex of the interviewer and subject could be found with regard to death anxiety and mutilation anxiety (See Table 11).

Table 11: Differences in anxiety scale scores and number of words in the groups which were arrived at by combining interviewer sex and subject sex (See legend Table 4)

| Anxiety and Sex Combined | | 1. Sample | | | | | 2. Sample | | | | |
|---|---|---|---|---|---|---|---|---|---|---|---|
| | | I ♂ Vp ♂ | I ♂ Vp ♀ | I ♀ Vp ♂ | I ♀ Vp ♀ | d | I ♂ Vp ♂ | I ♂ Vp ♀ | I ♀ Vp ♂ | I ♀ Vp ♀ | d |
| Death | M | .67 | .67 | .59 | .51 | 2:4 .10 | .58 | .60 | .58 | .48 | 1:4 .01 |
| | S | .47 | .50 | .43 | .32 | | .45 | .49 | .44 | .37 | 3:4 .01 |
| Mutilation | M | .63 | .58 | .58 | .55 | | .56 | .55 | .47 | .44 | 1:4 .05 |
| | S | .55 | .43 | .45 | .39 | | .40 | .39 | .28 | .28 | |
| Separation | M | .62 | .75 | .65 | .72 | 1:2 .05 | .57 | .84 | .67 | .78 | 1:2 .05 |
| | S | .41 | .45 | .40 | .45 | 1:4 .05 | .36 | .62 | .40 | .59 | 1:3 .10<br>1:4 .10 |
| Guilt | M | .50 | .48 | .51 | .42 | 2:4 .05 | .55 | .52 | .54 | .48 | |
| | S | .37 | .27 | .36 | .23 | | .44 | .36 | .40 | .28 | |
| Shame | M | .58 | .70 | .72 | .66 | 1:2 .01 | .61 | .69 | .72 | .68 | 1:2 .06 |
| | S | .45 | .43 | .56 | .48 | | .43 | .44 | .58 | .61 | |
| Diffuse Anxiety | M | .71 | .83 | .69 | .83 | 3:4 .10 | .64 | .99 | .69 | .92 | 1:2 .01 |
| | S | .47 | .60 | .53 | .57 | | .41 | .74 | .59 | .57 | 1:4 .01<br>2:3 .01<br>3:4 .01 |
| Total Anxiety | M | 1.55 | 1.66 | 1.53 | 1.55 | | 1.39 | 1.75 | 1.49 | 1.65 | 1:2 .05 |
| | S | .73 | .76 | .77 | .69 | | .72 | .95 | .81 | .82 | 1:4 .06<br>2:3 .10 |
| Number of Words | | 461.83 | 468.17 | 466.60 | 551.54 | 1:4 .01 | 483.59 | 462.35 | 458.93 | 584.93 | 1:4 .01 |
| | | 177.20 | 209.22 | 185.24 | 195.63 | 2:4 .01<br>3:4 .01 | 192.19 | 212.37 | 190.18 | 222.99 | 2:4 .01<br>3:4 .01 |
| N | | 89 | 78 | 95 | 93 | | 88 | 75 | 92 | 91 | |

4. Anxiety and Socioeconomic Class

The relationships observed between hostility scores and socioeconomic class were, also, observed between anxiety scores and the three social groups. Differences were found associated with social class in total anxiety scores and in all anxiety subscale scores. The differences in mutilation anxiety, in separation anxiety, and in guilt anxiety scores

were significant in both speech samples (See Table 12). While in the first speech sample, there were no differences in death anxiety scores, in the second sample the low class had the highest score and showed a significant difference in comparison to both other classes (1% level). The low class had significantly higher mutilation anxiety scores than the middle class in both speech samples. In the second speech sample, separation anxiety scores from the members of the low class again were significantly higher than the scores of the middle and high class, which were practically identical. The low class, also, had significantly higher guilt anxiety and shame anxiety scores in comparison to both other groups. In contrast to these findings, the high class had by far the highest diffuse anxiety scores and showed a signficant difference to both other groups in the first speech sample. In regard to total anxiety scores, as one might expect, the low class scored highest, and there was a significant difference on the 1% level in comparison with both other groups. In contrast to hostility scores, anxiety scores showed no general increase with decreasing socioeconomic class. With anxiety scores the high and the middle classes showed about the same scores, while the scores of the low class were definitely higher, with one exception: the findings for diffuse anxiety were exactly the other way around.

5. Anxiety and Age

Like Gottschalk and Gleser, we also found the plausible phenomenon that death anxiety increased with increasing age (Gottschalk and Gleser, 1969, p 75 ff). In addition, we also found differences with age for shame anxiety, diffuse anxiety, and total anxiety scores. There was no consistent increase or decrease with increasing age. Shame anxiety scores were, however, higher in two younger age groups than in two older ones (at the 1% level significance in the second speech sample, and in the first speech sample, this was observable as a tendency). Again, the age group A3 (40-49) stood out with particularly high scores in diffuse

Table 12: Differences in anxiety scale scores between three socioeconomic classes (See legend Table 4)

| Anxiety and socioeconomic class | | 1. Sample | | | | | 2. Sample | | | | |
|---|---|---|---|---|---|---|---|---|---|---|---|
| | | S1 | S2 | S3 | d | | S1 | S2 | S3 | d | |
| Death | M | .61 | .65 | .53 | | | .57 | .53 | .74 | 1:3 | .01 |
| | S | .47 | .47 | .34 | | | .53 | .37 | .55 | 2:3 | .01 |
| Mutilation | M | .69 | .57 | .61 | 2:3 | .05 | .49 | .50 | .54 | 1:3 | .01 |
| | S | .59 | .44 | .36 | | | .37 | .34 | .31 | 2:3 | .01 |
| Separation | M | .66 | .67 | .81 | 1:3 | .07 | .66 | .67 | .95 | 1:3 | .01 |
| | S | .41 | .43 | .50 | 2:3 | .05 | .56 | .44 | .69 | 2:3 | .05 |
| Guilt | M | .44 | .47 | .61 | 1:3 | .01 | .45 | .51 | .64 | 1:3 | .05 |
| | S | .24 | .33 | .39 | 2:3 | .01 | .24 | .38 | .43 | 2:3 | .05 |
| Shame | M | .57 | .66 | .74 | 1:3 | .10 | .75 | .65 | .71 | | |
| | S | .36 | .51 | .54 | 2:3 | .05 | .65 | .51 | .55 | | |
| Diffuse Anxiety | M | .97 | .74 | .68 | 1:2 | .05 | .87 | .76 | .87 | 2:3 | .10 |
| | S | .61 | .52 | .56 | 1:3 | .05 | .85 | .52 | .57 | | |
| Total Anxiety | M | 1.68 | 1.57 | 1.67 | | | 1.62 | 1.46 | 1.90 | 1:3 | .01 |
| | S | .79 | .74 | .65 | | | 1.08 | .76 | .83 | 2:3 | .01 |
| N | | 57 | 201 | 49 | | | 54 | 197 | 47 | | |

anxiety and total anxiety. In the first speech sample, this difference was significant in both forms of anxiety; in the second speech sample, only in diffuse anxiety scores (See Table 13).

C. Number of Words

Even though the number of words per speech sample is probably no measure of affects and, because of the transformation after the formula for deriving the magnitude of a psychological state, is related to 100 words, we have analyzed the number of words in different groups (the scores can be found in the Tables for the anxiety scales.) For the total

Table 13: Age differences in anxiety scale scores (See legend Table 4)

| Anxiety | | 1. Sample | | | | | | 2. Sample | | | | | |
|---|---|---|---|---|---|---|---|---|---|---|---|---|---|
| and Age | | A1 | A2 | A3 | A4 | d | | A1 | A2 | A3 | A4 | d | |
| Death | M | .52 | .60 | .74 | .67 | 1:4 | .01 | .47 | .54 | .62 | .71 | 1:2 | .05 |
| | S | .33 | .44 | .60 | .41 | 2:4 | .05 | .38 | .40 | .42 | .60 | 1:3<br>1:4 | .01<br>.01 |
| Shame | M | .69 | .66 | .61 | .58 | | | .81 | .66 | .64 | .50 | 1:4 | .01 |
| | S | .46 | .53 | .46 | .40 | | | .65 | .42 | .53 | .37 | 2:4 | .01 |
| Diffuse Anxiety | M | .74 | .76 | .92 | .65 | 1:3 | .05 | .78 | .80 | .91 | .75 | 1:3 | .06 |
| | S | .56 | .52 | .62 | .46 | | | .59 | .63 | .63 | .49 | 2:3 | .05 |
| Total Anxiety | M | 1.50 | 1.55 | 1.83 | 1.45 | 1:3 | .05 | 1.57 | 1.55 | 1.65 | 1.50 | | |
| | S | .74 | .73 | .80 | .58 | 2:3<br>3:4 | .01<br>.05 | .93 | .79 | .84 | .71 | | |
| N | | 117 | 119 | 60 | 56 | | | 114 | 115 | 60 | 55 | | |

sample, the average number of words in both speech samples was identical. Women in both speech samples showed a significantly higher number of words than men (5% level). Looking at the effect of sex of interviewer, in the first speech sample we found a significantly higher number of words (5% level of significance) for female interviewers; in the second speech sample, the difference was only existent as a tendency. Therefore, in combining sex of interviewer and sex of subject, differences must be found: they were very distinct between the combinations male interviewer with male subject and female interviewer with female subject (significant on the 1% level for both samples). With respect to socioeconomic class and age group, no differences in the number of words could be shown.

## Summary and Discussion

In this study, 406 subjects were assessed with the Gottschalk-Gleser verbal behavior content analysis scales of hostility and anxiety. We endeavored an answer to the question what influence sex, sex of interviewers, socioeconomic status, and age would have on affective reactions in two speech samples. In this study, we had a drop-out quota of 12.6% (first

speech sample) and 16.3% (second speech sample). Using an instrument such as the Gottschalk-Gleser and having a research setting of the kind used in our study, a certain percentage of drop-outs must be expected. A comparison between the first and the second speech sample showed that the total group of samples did not reveal any differences in affect scores except for death anxiety and mutilation anxiety scores. At the same time, it could be clearly seen that the correlations between the same scores in the first and the second speech sample were significant, but rather low. The scoring of hostility was modified by us to a certain extent. We applied four hostility scales: Hostility-Directed-Outward overt (HDOo), Hostility-Directed-Outward covert (HDOc), Hostility-Directed-Inward (HDI) and Ambivalent Hostility (AH). In addition, we formed four combinations, which resulted from the elements agent and victim, which are contained in each scale: others victims (OV), in Gottschalk Gleser: Hostility-Directed-Outward total), self victim (SV), self agent (SA), others agents (OA). Finally, we combined all hostility scales into one total hostility. In almost all groups, we could find differences in the individual scales as well as in the combinations. The scoring of anxiety was done by the traditional mode. Here also differences in all groups could be shown. For both hostility and anxiety, we could demonstrate that, especially, the socioeconomic status is an important factor. An increase in expression of affects goes along with a decrease in socioeconomic class.

In addition to the subject variables, sex, socioeconomic status, and age, we also analyzed the influence of the interviewer variable, sex of the interviewer. We found, that especially in regard to anxiety, through the combination of sex of interviewer and sex of subject, specific situations are created, which can be distinguished from situations with other combinations.

It can be concluded from our results that, as was postulated already by Gottschalk and Gleser, a standardization of the interview situation should be aimed at and furthermore, that variables, such as, age, sex, and particularly socioeconomic status should be controlled. The necessary

research on the test criteria of the Gottschalk-Gleser content analysis is presented in the next chapter.

## References


Gottschalk, L.A. Childrens speech as a source of data toward the measurement of psychological states. J. of Youth and Adolescence 5, 11-36 (1976).

Gottschalk, L.A. Some psychoanalytic research into the communication of meaning through language: the quality and magnitude of psychological states. Br. J. Med. Psychol. 44, 131-147 (1971).

Gottschalk, L.A., and Gleser, G.C. The Measurement of Psychological States Through the Content Analysis of Verbal Behavior. University of California Press, Berkeley, Los Angeles (1969).

Gottschalk, L.A., Winget, C.N., and Gleser, G.C. Manual of Instructions for Using the Gottschalk-Gleser Content Analysis Scales: Anxiety, Hostility, and Social Alienation-Personal Disorganization. University of California Press, Berkeley, Los Angeles (1969).

Kleining, G., u. Moore, H. Soziale Selbsteinschätzung SSE Ein Instrument zur Messung sozialer Schichten. Kölner Z. Soziol. Sozialpsychol., 3 (1968).

Koch, U., u Schöfer, G. Arbeitsbericht des Cl-Projektes des SFB 115 Hamburg, unpublished (1974).

Koch, U., u. Probst, P. Der Freiburger Aggressionsfragebogen (FAF) in Abhängigkeit von der sozialen Schicht. Diagnostica (1977), in press.

Schöfer, G. (Hrg.) Die Gottschalk-Gleser-Inhaltsanalyse: Die Messung von Aggressivität und Angst in Sprachproben. Auszugsweise Übersetzung aus Gottschalk und Gleser (1969) und Gottschalk, Winget, Gleser (1969). unpublished (1974).

Schöfer, G. Das Gottschalk-Gleser-Verfahren: Eine Sprachinhaltsanalyse zur Erfassung und Quantifizierung von aggressiven und ängstlichen Affekten. 2. Psychosomat. Med. Psychoanal. 23, 1 (1977).

# Introduction to Chapter 5

Introductory Comments by L.A. Gottschalk

In this chapter Schöfer and his coworkers systematically examine to what extent the Gottschalk-Gleser content analysis method satisfies various criteria for an effective test and measurement procedure. They focus particularly on the criteria of objectivity, reliability, and validity. These criteria are defined in terms similar to those used by American authors.

The authors describe some of the special problems encountered in assessing the Gottschalk-Gleser content analysis measures of affects when criteria are applied that are more applicable to the measurement of intelligence, performance, or personality traits. The issues of internal consistency of test items and stability of affect scores over time are not found to be quite relevant to the measurement of affects by content analysis of speech, primarily because of their rapid change. Moreover, the finding that anxiety and hostility scores from their German normative samples did not distribute themselves normally, but tended to be skewed to the left (in the direction of low affect scores), has led them to prefer the use of

non-parametric statistics in data analysis involving these scores.

Reliability studies revealed satisfactory interrater and intrarater coefficients of reliability. Stability of the affect scores taken an hour apart was low, though guilt, shame, and diffuse anxiety as well as overt hostility outward and hostility inward scores showed a significant correlation over this time period. When speech samples were split in half according to the odd-even method, such that even numbered and odd numbered clauses were separately grouped together, and the halved samples were scored for affects, the average correlations between the two text halves was .50, which was higher than the congruence between the two speech samples an hour apart.

Factor analytic studies by the principal component model were carried out on two speech samples from 340 subjects. From the 10 affect variables factor analyzed (overt hostility outward, covert hostility inward, ambivalent hostility, and the six anxiety subscales) four factors were extracted from each of the speech samples; the characteristics of these factors are described. The association of guilt anxiety with hostility outward and shame anxiety with hostility inward confirms the findings of Witkin et al (1968) and Gottschalk and Gleser (1969) as well as the observations of Lewis in Chapter 47 of this book.

The authors conclude this chapter with a report of validity studies of these affect scales using as external criterion measures a questionnaire, a mood adjective check test, and a rating scale. The discussion of their findings is astute and penetrating. Chapter 3 in this book, by Gottschalk et al, should be consulted in connection with these validation studies.

Reference

Witkin, HA, Lewis, HB, and Weil, E. Affective reactions and patient-therapist interactions among more differentiated and less differentiated patients early in therapy. J Nerv Ment Dis 145:193-208, 1968.

# 5

# Test Criteria of the Gottschalk-Gleser Content Analysis of Speech: Objectivity, Reliability, Validity in German Studies

G. Schofer, U. Koch, F. Balck

In the previous chapter, group differences (depending on sex of speaker, sex of interviewer, socioeconomic status, age) relating to hostile and anxious affects were investigated. In this chapter, we shall discuss to what extent the American findings in respect to the test criteria of the Gottschalk-Gleser content analysis of speech can be reproduced in German studies. We shall present data on the objectivity, reliability, and validity of this method collected by the Hamburg team between 1974 and 1976. The results stem from the standard population described in the previous chapter.

Before presenting the results, the test criteria shall be discussed in regard to their importance for the Gottschalk-Gleser content analysis.

------------------------

* Granted by the German Research Society, Sonderforschungsbereich 115, Projekt C4

**Department of Psychosomatic Medicine (Chairman Prof.Dr.Dr.A.-E. Meyer), II. Med., University of Hamburg, GFR

This seems to be necessary, since terms as internal consistency, stability, and validity raise special problems, when applied to content analysis in general and to the Gottschalk-Gleser method in particular.

Discussion of the test-criteria

Content analytic methods are defined by Berelson and Lazarsfeld (1952) as techniques of investigation, which serve to describe objectively, systematically, and quantitatively the overt content of messages of all forms. Content analytic methods vary from procedures roughly classifying whole texts into categories of content to special procedures such as the Gottschalk-Gleser method, which measures affects and other psychological states. Like the authors mentioned above, Gottschalk and Gleser also view their method as a measuring instrument. The stage of development of a method can be evaluated by asking to what extent it fulfills certain test criteria, Lienert (1965) mentions objectivity, reliability, and validity as well as utility, economy, comparability and standardization as being the essential criteria. Here the first three criteria shall be discussed in more detail.

Objectivity

Objectivity can be defined as the degree to which the results of content-analytic categorizations are independent of the investigator, that is the amount of agreement among different investigators. Lienert distinguishes between objectivity of administering, scoring, and interpreting a test. Objectivity of administering deals with the question, whether the results are independent of the individuals having administered the test. The problem of the Gottschalk-Gleser data being dependent upon the interviewer's personality traits or sex were discussed in the previous chapter. Here we are mainly concerned with the question of the objectivity of evaluation: to what extent are the scores for the various scales independent of the raters? Occasionally in publications the term "interrater reliability" is used instead of the term "objectivity of evaluation." Another approach to examining the accuracy of the rating

procedure is to have the same rater assess the same text at two different times. In this case one speaks of "intrarater reliability," although this is also aiming at the same type of objectivity as above. The objectivity of evaluation depends upon the accuracy with which the specific categories are defined and on how correctly the raters carry out the procedure of categorization. The latter depends on a thorough training of the raters. The objectivity of evaluation can be increased, on the one hand, by computing the average of the scores of several raters so that individual errors are cancelled out statistically and, on the other hand, by instructing the raters to discuss differences and to come to a mutual agreement.

The objectivity of interpretation is concerned with the question to what extent different investigators, on the basis of identical results, arrive at identical statements about the subjects. So far little attention was paid to this aspect in connection with the Gottschalk-Gleser method. We too shall not enter into discussing this question here.

Reliability

Reliability is generally defined as the degree of accuracy with which a test does its measuring, i.e. the extent up to which measurements can be reproduced. In this respect, two aspects must be differentiated: stability and internal consistency. Stability refers to what extent measurements obtained from the same subject at different times lead to corresponding results. It has been empirically found that the congruence of the results depends on the time interval between both measurements.

This aspect of reliability obviously raises many problems in relation to the Gottschalk-Gleser method, for the Gottschalk-Gleser method aims at assessing spontaneously occurring affects, rapid change over time being one of their fundamental characteristics. As a rule, high stability over time cannot be expected with the Gottschalk-Gleser method of measuring

affects because of this nature of affects. In psychometric tests, the internal consistency refers to the extent the items of an instrument are measuring the same aspects. With respect to the Gottschalk-Gleser method, it is impossible to speak about internal consistency, if one has not first of all answered the question which element of the content analysis represents an equivalent to the test item? The different verbal categories of the content analytic scales have another function than test items. Items are expected to represent approximately the same aspect of a variable. Transferring this requirement to content analytic categories would mean that content analytic categories should overlap as much as possible. But this would be a contradiction to the aim of categorical systems. As an alternative, the coding unit - the grammatical sentence - could be considered as being equivalent to a test item. This approach raises problems, too, for the sentence is not part of the measuring instrument, but rather the unit to which the measuring instrument is applied.

The classical methods to establish the internal consistency, therefore, could not be used for this instrument. Investigating the stability over time by repeated measurements raises problems, too, due to the rapid change of the variable under consideration. In our study we have compared the affect scores obtained from the same individuals at two different times with one hour in between. In addition, for the Gottschalk-Gleser method, it seemed to be more appropriate to us to apply a method roughly corresponding to a split half procedure. Several strategies could have been considered (here we only refer to a split half of the speech samples and not to a split half of the categories). For example, the text samples could have been split chronologically into a first and a second half. But since affects can change systematically during a five minute speech sample, we choose a different splitting technique. In analogy to the so called odd-even-method, the sentences were numbered and then grouped according to being either odd or even

into two text halves. The affect scores of the two parts of the text sample were then correlated.

Validity

Validity is defined as the degree of accuracy with which an instrument measures what it intends to measure. With respect to the Gottschalk-Gleser content analytic scales, thus, the question is raised whether the obtained scores actually measure the defined affects. Here, only the criterion validity and the construct validity shall be discussed.

To establish the criterion validity the test results are compared with an external criterion. Frequently there is a problem in finding objective and reliable external criteria. This happens to be true for the affects measured by the Gottschalk-Gleser method. For a number of years, Gottschalk carried out a multitude of studies in which the verbal affect scores were compared with those of other methods attempting to objectify affects (by means of psychological, physiological, and biochemical procedures). In the present article, we shall refer to several correlations between affect scores derived from the Gottschalk-Gleser procedure and psychological test findings and external psychological ratings.

The definition of construct validity states that theoretical assumptions are derived from a defined concept and are subsequently tested empirically. Testing construct validity requires an extensive process of investigation during which several testing strategies may be applied. For instance, psychological experiments or group comparisons might be carried out in order to clarify the construct. Factor analytic studies may be used likewise. In doing so, two aspects might be considered: 1. Is the empirically found structure (relations between scales) congruent with the theoretical assumptions (scales being largely independent)? 2. Can this structure be reproduced at different times?

Empirical testing of the criteria of the Gottschalk-Gleser method

Distributions

Before describing the results in regard to the criteria mentioned above, we shall briefly refer to the distributions of test scores of the scales. Gottschalk and Gleser were aware of the fact that the scores of the different scales did not follow a normal distribution, and this led them to introduce a constant by adding 0.5 to the raw score and to transform the scores by taking the square root. Testing for existence of normal distributions led to the following results:

- in general the scores computed on the basis of the root function show no normal distribution
- no further uniform mode of transformation for all scales could be found in order to produce a normal distribution
- the sum scores* showed the closest approximation to the normal distribution; in general the distributions turned out to be left-skewed, i.e. the deviations from a normal distribution were due to the over representation of particularly low affect-scores (affects being frequently completely absent).

We have not yet come to a final conclusion about how to deal with the statistical problems involved in this lack of a normal distribution of affect scores by this method. Our own approach to this problem, since the use of parametric statistical methods ordinarily requires a normal distribution, was not to use parametric statistics. Thus, for further computing, nonparametric methods were applied.

Studies on objectivity

As mentioned above, in connection with objectivity, inter- and intrarater congruence was tested. Two studies on interrater congruence were carried out (N=30, N=45). Both speech samples are random samples drawn from the standard population described in the preceeding chapter.

---

*(OV, SV, SA, OA, total hostility, total anxiety)

Table 1: Interrater congruence of two raters in two studies.

| | 1. Study N=30 | 2. Study N=45 | Average Corr.* |
|---|---|---|---|
| HDOo | .88 | .84 | .86 |
| HDOc | .85 | .80 | .82 |
| HDOt | .87 | .84 | .85 |
| HDI | .89 | .76 | .83 |
| AH | .94 | .83 | .89 |
| Anxiety | .96 | .93 | .94 |
| Average Corr.* | .91 | .84 | .87 |

* by Fischer's z-transformation

Raters were two psychological technicians. The results are demonstrated in Table 1.

The average correlations (computed by Fischer's z-transformation) for all scales are above .80. They, thus, come up to a level corresponding to the coefficients found by Gottschalk and Gleser. The results of the first study are in general slightly higher than those of the second. In both studies a maximum of congruence was found in the anxiety scale. Our conclusion is that with well trained raters a sufficiently high interrater congruence can be achieved.

In order to test the intrarater congruence, 25 records (again as random samples) were selected from the same population in order to find out how stable a rater's judgment remains over time. The time interval between the first and the second rating of the speech samples was one year. As for the interpretation of the results (Table 2), the following should be noted: for the first rating the raters had to agree to a joint score. With those joint scores the individual scores of the raters in the second rating were correlated. The results permit the following conclusions:

- the coefficients of congruence for rater 2 are generally higher than those for rater 1 with the exception of scale AH.
- The coefficients of congruence are lowest for both raters with the Hostility Inward Scale; this scale had been also the one with a relatively low interrater congruence, since coming to an agreement on it at the same time of the first rating was most difficult.
- The values of the intrarater congruence are approximately corresponding to those of the interrater congruence. Apart from the Hostility Directed Inward Scale, they as a whole can be considered satisfactory.

Studies on reliability

In our theoretical discussion on reliability, we pointed out the problem which arises from the fact that affects are by definition rapidly changing entities. We carried out two studies on the question of reliability:

The scores for the different scales, belonging to time $t_1$ and $t_2$ (with an interval of an hour in between) were compared. As described in the preceeding chapter, two Gottschalk-Gleser speech samples were obtained under standard conditions with one hour in between interviews. During the time interval various questionnaires and a short interview were administered to the subject. The results of the study on stability are shown in Table 3. The total number of the speech samples included in this study is 340. The results can be interpreted as follows:

- Table 3 shows clearly that the stability over one hour is very low. Although there are some significant coefficients, they are hardly striking. The total anxiety score is not significantly stable. While the magnitude of specific anxieties of guilt and shame as well as diffuse anxiety is somewhat continuous over time, this is not the case for death, mutilation, and separation anxiety scores.
- The coefficients of stability over time of the new combinations (see preceeding chapter) "others victims" (OV), "self victim" (SV), "self agent" (SA) and "others agents" (OA) as well as total hostility are all significant, but the correlations are very low.

Table 2: Intrarater congruence of two raters

| | 1. Rater | 2. Rater | Average Corr.* |
|---|---|---|---|
| HDOo | .81 | .84 | .82 |
| HDOc | .86 | .92 | .89 |
| HDOt | .83 | .92 | .88 |
| HDI | .59 | .80 | .71 |
| AH | .89 | .88 | .88 |
| Anxiety | .86 | .92 | .89 |
| Average Corr.* | .82 | .88 | .85 |

* by Fischer's z-transformation

- The most stable factor in regard to time is the number of spoken words per speech sample (r=.54), i.e. the amount of verbal output can be regarded as being fairly constant.

In the second study, the congruence of the affect scores was tested after splitting the speech samples according to the odd-even-method. The reasons for doing so and the technique, itself, have already been described above. The sentences were attributed to either the first or to the second half of the speech sample according to their position in the sequence. A total of 48 speech samples were drawn randomly from the total population of samples and congruences for the affect scores between the two halves were computed. Table 4 shows the following results:

- The average correlation between the two text halves amounts to .50. Even though this is significant, we had expected a somewhat higher congruence.
- The congruence coefficients of the scores computed on the basis of split records are nevertheless higher than the congruence between the two speech samples with a time difference. This finding confirms the assumption that with affects we are dealing with rapidly changing variables.

Table 3: Stability over time of affect scores given an interval of 1 hour apart (Hostility, Table 3a; Anxiety and number of words, Table 3b) N=340

Table 3a:

| Scale | Corr. |
|---|---|
| HDOo | .18*** |
| HDOc | .06 |
| HDI | .15** |
| AH | .10* |
| OV | .22*** |
| SV | .17*** |
| SA | .27*** |
| OA | .13** |
| total hostility | .25*** |

Table 3b:

| Scale | Corr. |
|---|---|
| Death | -.03 |
| Mutilation | .07 |
| Separation | .01 |
| Guilt | .18*** |
| Shame | .22*** |
| diff. anx. | .20*** |
| total anxiety | .09 |
| Number of words | .54 |

* p $<$.05

** p $<$.01

*** p $<$.001

- Like in the preceeding studies here too hostility directed inward is the most unstable variable. Hostility directed inward values are the lowest of all scale values and deviate clearly from the others. This might be due to the fact that, as a whole, sentences with hostility directed inward score occur rather seldomly. The high frequency of low scores results in a decrease in variance and therefore reduction of the correlation.
- The scores of the combined hostility scales do not lead to an increase in "internal consistency"; however, the values of the two combinations, "self victim" and "self agent" which both contain hostility directed inward scores, do now reach the same height as the other combinations.

Table 4: Congruence of affect scores (correlation) after splitting the speech samples according to the odd-even-method.
(Hostility, Table 4a; Anxiety, Table 4b) N=48

Table 4a:

| Scale | Corr. |
|---|---|
| HDOo | .45 |
| HDOc | .52 |
| HDI | .25 |
| AH | .63 |
| OV | .51 |
| SV | .49 |
| SA | .53 |
| OA | .45 |
| total hostility | .56 |

Table 4b:

| Scale | Corr. |
|---|---|
| Death | .67 |
| Mutilation | .72 |
| Separation | .37 |
| Guilt | .56 |
| Shame | .62 |
| Diff. anx. | .59 |
| total anxiety | .63 |

- Anxiety turns out to be relatively consistent over time. Looking at the specific forms of anxiety, one can see that, in particular, death anxiety and mutilation anxiety contribute to this consistency, whereas separation anxiety ranks lowest.

Studies on validity

Factor-analytic investigations based on the affect scores were carried out within each speech sample. Furthermore, the invariance of the obtained factorial structure in respect to both speech samples was examined. In addition, correlations with other instruments measuring affects were investigated.

a) Factor-analytic studies:

The data from the first and second interview were factor-analyzed separately. The number of subjects included in the two studies was N=340 each. Since some of the variables are not independent from each other, not all of the affect scores could be analyzed. The following 10 variables were computed: hostility directed outward overt (HDOo), hostility directed outward covert (HDOc), hostility directed inward (HDI), ambivalent hostility (AH), and the 6 specific anxieties. The intercorrelation matrix was factor-analyzed according to the principal component model. Based on the criterion of Eigen values $\geq 1$, four factors in each of the analyses were extracted and then a varimax rotation was carried out. Table 5 shows the results of the varimax rotation of the first speech sample.

Using a matrix transformation method by Fischer-Roppert (1964) we tried to approximate the similarity of the factorial solution for the second speech sample as closely as possible to the factor structure of the first one. The resulting factor structure of the second speech sample is also shown in Table 5. With the four-factor-solution 64.8% of the total variance of the first speech sample and 64.2% of the second speech sample can be explained. A comparison of the two factor matrices with the similarity transformation by Fischer-Roppert results in a coefficient of congruence (Tucker, 1951) of .91. This value can be interpreted as suggesting that the structures of the obtained factors vary relatively little over the time interval. Congruence is particularly high in factor 3 (.96) and in factor 1 (.93). It is lower in factor 2 (.79) and factor 4 (.77). Another result shall be mentioned briefly in this context. In a further factor analysis the 10 variables of the two speech samples were analyzed together (i.e. a total of 20 variables). This resulted in separate factors for both speech samples. Two factors each could be grouped together, since they were characterized by high loadings of the same variables. The relations between the variables are constant. The fact that two factors each have the same structure of variables appears to support the assumption that the variance over time is high. This result corresponds with our findings

Table 5: Factor-analytic results for the 4 hostility scales and the 6 anxiety subscales (N=340)

| | | F1 | | F2 | | F3 | | F4 | |
|---|---|---|---|---|---|---|---|---|---|
| | | 1. Sample | 2. Sample | 1. Sample | 2. Sample | 1. Sample | 2. Sample | 1. Sample | 2. Sample |
| HOSTILITY | HDOo | .71 | .71 | -.09 | .11 | .18 | .14 | -.15 | -.07 |
| | HDOc | .14 | .29 | .76 | .74 | -.25 | -.13 | .05 | .01 |
| | HDI | .03 | .07 | -.05 | .02 | .85 | .87 | .17 | .20 |
| | AH | .49 | .48 | .25 | .19 | .14 | .17 | .67 | .60 |
| ANXIETY | Death | -.12 | -.15 | .55 | .64 | -.14 | -.07 | .40 | .41 |
| | Mutilation | .07 | .05 | .77 | .58 | .20 | .03 | -.19 | .29 |
| | Separation | -.03 | .31 | .03 | -.22 | .03 | .16 | .86 | .68 |
| | Guilt | .81 | .79 | .05 | .16 | -.02 | .13 | .20 | .09 |
| | Shame | .13 | .02 | .02 | .10 | .83 | .91 | -.08 | -.13 |
| | Diff. Anx. | -.27 | -.12 | .50 | -.04 | .12 | .18 | .28 | .73 |

concerning stability (See over time Table 3).

In the following paragraph the meaning of the four factors shall be described briefly. We put them into order according to the four hostility scales. With the exception of ambivalent hostility (AH) (factor 1 and 4), each hostility scale has a high load in one particular factor. Moreover each form of hostility is related to one or two specific anxieties.

Factor 1: Is characterized by hostility directed outward overt (HDOo) with guilt anxiety loading in the same direction. Moreover AH is represented on this factor with medium high loading.

Factor 2: Here the loading of hostility directed outward covert (HDOc) is high and shows the same direction as death and mutilation anxiety.

Factor 3: Is characterized by hostility directed inward (HDI) and shame anxiety having high loadings in the same direction.

Factor 4: Here ambivalent hostility (AH) is loading as well as death and

separation anxiety. The factor structure described above applies to the total population. It will not be investigated here in detail to what extent this structure depends upon the specific sample of subjects. Nevertheless, the correlation analyses of the subsamples* support the assumption that the structure depends to a certain extent on the specific sample.

b) Correlations with other instruments:

Here the relationship of the Gottschalk-Gleser scales to other instruments measuring hostility were investigated. Table 6 shows the correlations between the hostility-scales, combined scales, and total anxiety on one hand and the dimensions of an aggression-questionnaire, a mood adjective check list, and an interviewer rating on the other hand. The standardized aggression-questionnaire SAF (Koch and Schöfer, 1974) intends to measure the following aspects of aggression as personality traits in 5 dimensions: irritability, instrumental aggressiveness (intentionally putting up with aggressions in order to achieve one's own aims), aggressivenes directed inward, competition, and inhibition of aggressiveness. The mood adjective check list, which was originally developed by Mertesdorf and Hecheltjen, was administered in an abridged version by Koch (Koch and Schöfer, 1974) consisting of the following scales: depression, activity, anger, and anxiety. In order to rate the momentary aggressiveness of the subject, the interviewer used a so-called "thermometer of aggression." Table 6 lists the correlations of the first as well as of the second speech sample and the following conclusions may be drawn:

- The correlations are consistently very low. In regard to the aggression-questionnaire, this finding corresponds with our expectation, since the Gottschalk-Gleser method deals with momentary affects, while the questionnaire aims at personality traits. The weak relationship between the Gottschalk-Gleser scores and the scores of the mood adjective check

-------------------------------

* (sex of speaker, sex of interviewer, socioeconomic class, age)

Table 6: Significant correlations (.11: 5%-level of significance; .14: 1%-level of significance) between hostility scales, combined scales and total anxiety scale on one hand and aggression-questionnaire (SAF), mood adjective check list (EWL), and external rating (Th) on the other hand.

| | | SAF | | | | | EWL | | | | Th |
|---|---|---|---|---|---|---|---|---|---|---|---|
| | | 1 | 2 | 3 | 4 | 5 | 1 | 2 | 3 | 4 | |
| HDOo | a | | .14 | | | | .16 | | | .11 | .14 |
| | b | .12 | | | | | | | .11 | | |
| HDOc | a | | | | | | | | | | |
| | b | | .15 | | | | | | | | |
| HDI | a | | | .20 | | | .22 | | | .14 | |
| | b | .12 | | .20 | | | .19 | -.13 | | .12 | |
| AH | a | | | | | | | | | | |
| | b | | | .13 | | | .12 | | | | |
| OV | a | .11 | .09 | | | | | | | | |
| | b | .13 | .11 | .14 | .12 | | .11 | | .09 | | |
| SV | a | | | .15 | | | .16 | | | .12 | -.10 |
| | b | .11 | | .18 | | | .16 | | | .12 | |
| SA | a | | | .18 | | | .22 | | | .14 | .15 |
| | b | .16 | | .20 | | | .16 | | | .12 | |
| OA | a | | | | | | | | | | |
| | b | .10 | .15 | .15 | | | .12 | | | | |
| Total Hostility | a | .09 | | .11 | | | .12 | | | | .13 |
| | b | .16 | | .21 | | | .16 | | | .10 | |
| Total Anxiety | a | .11 | | .12 | | | | | | | |
| | b | | | | | | .12 | | | | |

SAF 1: irritability
2: instrumental aggressiveness
3: aggressiveness directed inward
4: competition
5: inhibition of aggressiveness

EWL 1: depression
2: activity
3: anger
4. anxiety

Th : thermometer of aggression

a = 1. speech sample
b = 2. speech sample

list, however, was a disappointment. We can give two explanations for the latter finding:

a) The mood adjective check list may be measuring traits, after all, rather than states.

b) Even if the mood adjective check list should in fact measure states, the aspects which are measured here do not correspond at what the Gottschalk-Gleser scales aim. Moreover, there was a time interval of at least 10 minutes between recording the Gottschalk-Gleser interview and administering the mood adjective check list. The problem of affects changing over time has been previously pointed out.

It is noticeable as a general tendency that, whenever a significant relationship between the first speech sample and the other instruments exists, this is very frequently true for the second speech sample, too, i.e. the correlations seem to have a certain stability despite being low.

The existing correlations are definitely meaningful. Only a few of them shall be mentioned here: the hostility directed inward scale as well as "self victim" and "self agent" correlate with aggressiveness directed inward (SAF) and with depression and anxiety (mood adjective checklist). "Others victims" correlates with irritability (SAF). As for the subsample (sex, sex of interviewer, socioeconomic class and age) the correlations in certain cases differ and are sometimes clearly higher.

Utility and economy

Since so far there are hardly any reliable and valid instruments to measure affects, the Gottschalk-Gleser method meets a definite need. This is especially true, since it can also be applied to "natural" materials (interview, psychotherapy-transcripts, etc.). The economy of a method refers to the amount of time and material which is needed to administer it. One should always evaluate economy in connection with utility. Contrary to initial fears, we have realized by experience that the scoring procedures for a written text when using the standard instruction takes approximately 15 minutes for the hostility and anxiety scales. From our point of view this amount of time is acceptable.

Summary

In this chapter the meaning of test criteria was discussed as these relate to the Gottschalk-Gleser content analysis. The terms "objectivity," "reliability," and "validity" were defined in respect to this method. On the basis of empirical studies of inter- and intrarater congruence on stability and on the congruence of scores, when applying a split half technique to the speech samples, aspects of objectivity and reliability were investigated. It was found that it is possible to rate the Gottschalk-Gleser scores objectively. Furthermore, it was shown that the recorded affects are of a transitory character. There is hardly a significant correlation between the measurements taken with an hour between. The correlations are distinctly higher when the text is split according to the odd-even-method.

Factor analytic studies of affect scores (hostility and anxiety) from the two speech samples revealed a construct consisting of four factors. A comparison of the similarity between the factor structures of the two speech samples obtained with a time interval between them showed that the structures depend upon the particular speech samples. Nevertheless these structures could be related to each other without difficulties.

The studies on correlations resulted a number of weak but significant and meaningful correlations between Gottschalk-Gleser scores, and other methods (aggression-questionnaire, mood adjective check list, external ratings). Because of the findings of this and the other chapters, we believe that the Gottschalk-Gleser method has been investigated to such an extent that by now it can be applied in clinical studies more effectively.

References

Berelson, B., u. Lazarsfeld, P. Die bedeutung von Kommunikationsmaterialien, in Praktische Sozialforschung 1. R. König, ed. Band,(1952)

Fischer, G., u. Roppert, J. Bemerkungen zu einem Verfahren der Transformationsanalyse. Arch. Ges. Psychol. 116, 98 (1964)

Koch, U., Witte, H. u. Witte, E.H. Die Inhaltsanalyse als Messinstrument. Publizistik, 19, 2 (1974)

Koch, U., u. Schöfer, G. Arbeitsbericht des C1-Projektes des SFB 115. Hamburg (1974) unpublished

Lienert, G.A. Textaufbau und Textanalyse. Meisenheim, Beltz-Verlad (1969)

Tucker, L.R. A method for synthesis of factor analysis studies. Personal Research Section Report, No. 984, Washington, Department of the Army (1951)

# B.
# Children's Studies

Several chapters are devoted to studies on these content analysis procedures applied to children. The first chapter (6) of this series is entitled "Children's speech as a source of data toward the measurement of psychological states" (Gottschalk, 1976). A second chapter (7) in this series of children's studies is entitled "Measurement of black children's affective states and the effect of interviewer's race on affective states as measured through language behavior" (Uliana, 1977), and since this chapter has not been previously published, a special commentary precedes it. A third chapter (8) details findings in a study of adolescents (Gleser et al).

It is instructive to compare, at this point, the average affect scores, obtained by this content analysis method, for the sample of white and black children described in Chapters 6 and 7 respectively. Both groups were located in Orange County, California, and speech samples from both groups were elicited by young women. But white women obtained the speech samples from the white children, and both white and black women obtained the speech samples from the black children. So, some of the

differences that might be seen between these groups could be a result of an interviewer effect. Somewhat higher anxiety scores (due mostly to shame anxiety scores) were obtained from black children by white women than black women interviewers in Uliana's study (Chapter 7). Otherwise, no significant differences were noted with respect to interviewer effects on the affect scores of black children.

In any event, Uliana (1976) has kindly supplied the following Tables indicating differences in mean affect scores between the two Southern California groups of children.

Table 1

Mean Differences Between Affect Scores of Black and White Children[a]

| Subjects | Anxiety Total | Hostility outward Overt | Hostility outward Covert | Hostility outward Total | Hostility inward | Ambivalent hostility |
|---|---|---|---|---|---|---|
| Black Children (N=276) | | | | | | |
| Mean | 1.82 | 0.83 | 1.07 | 1.35 | 0.63 | 0.76 |
| s.d. | 0.89 | 0.44 | 0.69 | 0.74 | 0.37 | 0.52 |
| White Children (N=109) | | | | | | |
| Mean | 2.04 | 0.79 | 0.85 | 1.14 | 0.73 | 0.67 |
| s.d. | 0.89 | 0.48 | 0.48 | 0.58 | 0.53 | 0.38 |
| T - Test | -2.20* | 0.80 | 2.95** | 3.57*** | -1.76 | 1.88 |

[a]For F-tests that were significant, a t-test estimate formula for unequal variances was applied. Variances were pooled when F-tests were not found to be significant.

* = $p<.05$
** = $p<.005$
*** = $p<.001$

Table 2

Mean Differences Between Anxiety Subscale Scores of Black and White Children

| Subjects | Death | Mutilation | Separation | Guilt | Shame | Diffuse |
|---|---|---|---|---|---|---|
| Black Children (N=276) | | | | | | |
| Mean | 0.56 | 0.59 | 0.76 | 0.74 | 1.10 | 0.56 |
| s.d. | 0.35 | 0.40 | 0.40 | 0.51 | 0.83 | 0.31 |
| White Children (N=109) | | | | | | |
| Mean | 0.62 | 0.86 | 1.14 | 0.41 | 0.85 | 0.63 |
| s.d. | 0.43 | 0.66 | 0.66 | 0.29 | 0.63 | 0.40 |
| T-Test | -1.31 | -4.02** | -5.67** | 8.01** | 3.20* | -1.65 |

* = p<.005
** = 0<.001

Table 3

Mean Differences Between Affect Scores of Black Male and White Male Children

| Subjects | Anxiety Total | Hostility outward | | | Hostility inward | Ambivalent hostility |
|---|---|---|---|---|---|---|
| | | Overt | Covert | Total | | |
| Black Males (N=137) | | | | | | |
| Mean | 1.80 | 0.81 | 1.04 | 1.32 | 0.65 | 0.74 |
| s.d. | 0.80 | 0.46 | 0.70 | 0.74 | 0.39 | 0.48 |
| White Males (N=41) | | | | | | |
| Mean | 1.97 | 0.76 | 0.84 | 1.10 | 0.81 | 0.71 |
| s.d. | 1.03 | 0.46 | 0.50 | 0.58 | 0.64 | 0.39 |
| T-Test | -0.97 | 0.61 | 2.04* | 1.99* | -1.52 | 0.37 |

* = $p < .05$

Table 4

Mean Differences Between Affect Scores of Black Female and White Female Children

| Subjects | Anxiety Total | Hostility outward | | | Hostility inward | Ambivalent hostility |
|---|---|---|---|---|---|---|
| | | Overt | Covert | Total | | |
| Black Females (N=139) | | | | | | |
| Mean | 1.84 | 0.85 | 1.10 | 1.38 | 0.61 | 0.79 |
| s.d. | 0.96 | 0.42 | 0.69 | 0.73 | 0.34 | 0.56 |
| White Females (N=68) | | | | | | |
| Mean | 2.07 | 0.82 | 0.85 | 1.16 | 0.69 | 0.64 |
| s.d. | 0.80 | 0.49 | 0.47 | 0.59 | 0.46 | 0.38 |
| T-Test | -1.82 | 0.46 | 3.08** | 2.33* | -1.28 | 2.29* |

* = $p<.025$
** = $p<.005$

Table 5

Mean Differences Between Anxiety Subscale Scores of Black Male and White Male Children

| Subjects | Death | Mutilation | Separation | Guilt | Shame | Diffuse |
|---|---|---|---|---|---|---|
| Black Males (N=137) | | | | | | |
| Mean | 0.53 | 0.63 | 0.77 | 0.74 | 1.01 | 0.52 |
| s.d. | 0.34 | 0.46 | 0.38 | 0.55 | 0.76 | 0.27 |
| White Males (N=41) | | | | | | |
| Mean | 0.64 | 0.78 | 1.17 | 0.40 | 0.94 | 0.54 |
| s.d. | 0.45 | 0.63 | 0.78 | 0.22 | 0.69 | 0.27 |
| T - Test | -1.46 | -1.42 | -3.17* | 5.84** | 0.53 | -0.50 |

* = p<.005
** = 0<.001

Table 6

Mean Differences Between Anxiety Subscale Scores of Black Female and White Female Children

| Subjects | Death | Mutilation | Separation | Guilt | Shame | Diffuse |
|---|---|---|---|---|---|---|
| Black Females (N=139) | | | | | | |
| Mean | 0.59 | 0.55 | 0.75 | 0.73 | 1.18 | 0.59 |
| s.d. | 0.36 | 0.35 | 0.42 | 0.48 | 0.90 | 0.34 |
| White Females (N=68) | | | | | | |
| Mean | 0.62 | 0.91 | 1.12 | 0.42 | 0.79 | 0.68 |
| s.d. | 0.42 | 0.67 | 0.58 | 0.32 | 0.59 | 0.45 |
| T - Test | -0.54 | -4.19* | -4.70* | 5.58* | 3.74* | -1.46 |

* = $p<.001$

# B. Children Studies

6

## Children's Speech as a Source of Data Toward the Measurement of Psychological States[1]

Louis A. Gottschalk[2]

*Received September 16, 1975*

*A measurement of psychological states, based on the objective content analysis of small samples of speech, has undergone thorough reliability and construct-validation studies for individuals in the age range 17-70. The present report is a first step in the extension of this method to children ages 6-16. It has involved a descriptive analysis of the frequency of use of various verbal content categories of 109 schoolchildren, roughly stratified for grade. Percentile scores have been obtained for such content analysis scales as anxiety, hostility outward, hostility inward, ambivalent hostility, social alienation personal disorganization, cognitive impairment, human relations, hope, and achievement strivings. Comparisons are made between these children's scores on such measures and similar scores obtained from adults. Sex differences and developmental trends are examined.*

[1] See NAPS document No. 02760 for 22 pages of supplementary material. Order from ASIS/NAPS, c/o Microfiche Publications, 440 Park Avenue South, New York, New York 10016. Remit in advance for each NAPS accession number. Make checks payable to "Microfiche Publications." Photocopies are $5.50. Microfiche are $3.00. Outside of the U.S. and Canada, postage is $2.00 for a photocopy or $1.00 for a fiche.

[2] Professor and Chairman, Department of Psychiatry and Human Behavior, California College of Medicine, University of California at Irvine, Irvine, California, and Director, Psychiatric Services, Orange County Medical Center, Orange, California. Received his medical degree at Washington University School of Medicine, St. Louis. Interned in straight medicine at Barnes and McMillian Hospitals, St. Louis, and also spent 2½ years as a psychiatric resident there. Had additional psychiatric residency training (Adult and Child) at the U.S. Public Health Service Hospital, Fort Worth, Texas, and Michael Reese Hospital, Chicago. Had psychoanalytic training (Adult and Child) at the Chicago Institute for Psychoanalysis and the Washington, D.C. Psychoanalytic Institute. Had a Research Career Award, National Institute of Mental Health, for 7½ years (1960-1967). Current research interests include the development of measurement methods in mental health and research in psychotherapy, psychosomatic medicine, psychopharmacology, and pharmacokinetics.

## INTRODUCTION

The measurement of transient psychological states, sensitively and with specificity, precision, and objectivity, has always posed serious and unsolved obstacles. Many of these measurement problems have been recently solved for the assessment of such states in adults through the content analysis of speech by Gottschalk and his collaborators (Gottschalk and Hambidge, 1955; Gottschalk, 1971, 1972, 1974a,b, 1975; Gottschalk and Gleser, 1969; Gottschalk *et al.*, 1969a,b, 1972a,b, 1973, 1974). Since these studies with adults are being used as a paradigm and as guidelines for the development of a similar measurement method with children, a survey of the content analysis method of Gottschalk and coworkers is appropriate.

The method uses a function that is uniquely human, namely, verbal behavior and its content or semantic aspect. Small samples of speech ranging in duration from 2 to 5 min (Gottschalk and Gleser, 1969; Luborsky *et al.*, 1975) have been found sufficient to provide objective measures of various psychological states, such as anxiety, hostility outward, hostility inward, social alienation personal disorganization (schizophrenic syndrome), human relations, hope, achievement strivings, and so forth.

The development of this method has involved a long series of steps. It has required that (1) the psychological dimension to be measured (for example, anxiety or hostility) be carefully defined; (2) the unit of communication, the grammatical clause, be specified; (3) the content, i.e., the lexical cues, be spelled out from which a receiver of the verbal message infers the occurrence of the psychological state; (4) the linguistic, principally syntactical, cues conveying intensity also be specified; (5) the differential weights signifying relative intensity be assigned for semantic and linguistic cues whenever appropriate; (6) a systematic means be arrived at of correcting for the number of words spoken per unit time so that one individual can be compared to others or to himself on different occasions with respect to the magnitude of a particular psychological state as derived from the content of verbal behavior; (7) a formal scale of weighted content categories be specified for each psychological dimension to be measured; (8) content analysis technicians be trained to apply these to typescripts of human speech (much as biochemical technicians are trained to run various complex chemical determinations by following prescribed procedures); (9) the interscorer reliability of any two trained content technicians using the same scale be 0.85 or above (a modest but respectable level of consensus in the psychological sciences for these kinds of measurements); (10) a set of construct validation studies be carried out to establish exactly what this content analysis procedure is measuring — these validation studies have included the use of four kinds of criterion measures: (a) psychological, (b) psychophysiological, (c) psychopharmacological, and (d) psychobiochemical; (11) on the basis of these construct validation studies, changes be routinely made in the content categories and their associated weights in certain specific scales (anxiety, hostility, and social alienation–per-

sonal disorganization) in the direction of maximizing the correlations between the content analysis scores and these various criterion measures.

Construct validation is a step-by-step process that requires repeated reexamination and retesting, in new situations, of the constructs being evaluated. After initial validation studies were completed in adults (ages 17-70) for verbal behavior measures of the psychological constructs of anxiety, hostility out, hostility in, ambivalent hostility, and social alienation–personal disorganization (the schizophrenic syndrome), a large variety of additional investigations were carried out using these verbal behavior measures. These investigations have provided considerable data on the ways in which such verbal behavior scores relate to other relevant measurable phenomena. These data have afforded evidence as to how the construct measured by these verbal behavior measures "fit" with other empirical data (Gottschalk *et al.*, 1958, 1960, 1961a,b, 1963, 1964, 1965a,b, 1969a,b, 1970, 1971, 1972a,b, 1973, 1974; Gottschalk and Gleser, 1964, 1969; Gleser *et al.*, 1961, 1965).

The formulation of these psychological states has been deeply influenced by the position that they have biological roots. Both the definition of each separate state and the selection of the specific verbal content items used as cues for inferring each state were influenced by the decision that – whatever psychological state was measured by this content analysis approach – it should whenever possible be associated with some biological characteristic of the individual in addition to some psychological aspect or some social situation. Hence not only psychological but also physiological, biochemical, and pharmacological criterion measures have all provided further construct validation.

These long-term studies with adults have provided a series of empirically derived steps for measuring the magnitude of psychological states in adults. These steps will be summarized below.

## EMPIRICALLY DERIVED STEPS FOR MEASURING THE MAGNITUDE OF PSYCHOLOGICAL STATES[3]

A. The relative magnitude of a psychological state can be validly estimated from the typescript of 2-5 min of speech of an individual, using solely content variables and not including any paralanguage variables. In other words, the major part of the variance in an immediate psychological state of an individual can be accounted for by variations in the content of verbal communications (Gottschalk *et al.*, 1958, 1961a,b, 1963; Gleser *et al.*, 1961; Gottschalk and Frank, 1967; Gottschalk and Gleser, 1969; Gottschalk and Kaplan, 1958).

[3] This material has been excerpted, with some minor alterations, from pp. 15-18, Gottschalk, L. A., and Gleser, G. C., *The Measurement of Psychological States Through the Content Analysis of Verbal Behavior*, Los Angeles, Berkeley: University of California Press, 1969.

B. On the basis of verbal content alone, the type and magnitude of any one psychological state at any one period of time are directly proportional to three primary factors: (1) the frequency of occurrence of categories of thematic statements; (2) the degree to which the verbal expression directly represents or is pertinent to the psychological activation of the specific state (for example, to say that one is killing or injuring another person or wants to do so is regarded as a more direct representation of hostile aggression than to say that one simply disapproves of another person); (3) the degree of personal involvement attributed by the speaker to the emotionally relevant idea, feeling, action, or event.

C. The degree of direct representation can be represented mathematically by a weighting factor. Higher weights have tended to be assigned to scorable verbal statements which communicate feelings that, by inference, are more likely to be strongly experienced by the speaker. Completely unconscious or repressed feelings of any kind are not, by this method of weighting, considered to signify states of high magnitude, but rather to amount to zero or no feelings. This numerical weight, which is assigned to each thematic category, designates roughly the relative probability that the thematic category is associated with the construct of the psychological state. Initially, weights have been assigned deductively on the basis of common sense (as in the example of B2 above) or from clinical judgment (as in D below). Subsequently, the weights have been modified and revised whenever further empirical evidence has been sufficient to warrant such a change (Gottschalk *et al.*, 1961a, 1963; Gottschalk and Gleser, 1964).

D. The occurrence of suppressed and repressed feelings can be inferred from the content of verbal behavior by noting the appearance of a variety of defensive and adaptive mechanisms. Also, the immediate magnitude of a psychological state is considered to be approximately the same, whether the affectively toned verbal thematic reference is expressed in the past tense, present tense, or future tense, as an intention, as a conditional probability, or as a wish. Some of the defensive and adaptive mechanisms signalizing the presence of suppressed and repressed feelings in language are (1) the psychological state or its associated ideation or behavior attributed to other human beings; (2) the psychological state or its associated ideation or behavior occurring in subhuman animals or in inanimate objects; (3) the psychological state and its equivalents repudiated or denied; (4) the psychological state and its equivalents acknowledged but reported to be present in attenuated form.

E. The product of the frequency of use of relevant categories of verbal statements and the numerical weights assigned to each thematic category are used as an ordinal measure of the magnitude of the psychological state.

In other words, the greater the specific kind of feeling state of a speaker over a given unit of time, the more verbal references will be made, as compared to thematic statements of all types, to experiences or events of the types that have been classified in relevant categories with varying weights. Thus multiplying the weight for the category by the number of references in the verbal sample

classified in that category and then summing up all the content categories pertinent to the specified state gives an ordinal index of the intensity of the feeling state.

F. Individuals differ considerably in the rate of speech, and the same individual may vary in rate of speech from one unit of time to another. Since numerical indices of magnitude of emotion can vary with the number of words spoken per unit time, the numerical score derived from one verbal sample may be compared to the score derived from another verbal sample composed of a different number of words by using a correction factor which expresses the score of the feeling state of the speakers in terms of a common denominator, namely the score per 100 words.

Initially this correction was made by dividing the total raw score by the number of words spoken and multiplying by 100. It was decided later, for use with the anxiety and hostility scales, that the best method to take into consideration rate of speech was by adding 0.5 to the raw score, multiplying by 100, and dividing by the number of words spoken. This method avoids the discontinuity occurring whenever no scorable items have occurred in some verbal samples. It also provides a uniform transformation over all samples and, with rare exceptions, reduces the correlation between the score of the psychological state and the number of words produced essentially to zero.

A further transformation is made to obtain the final score, using the square root of the corrected score. This transformation is intended to reduce the skewness of the score distributions, thus making the measure more amenable to parametric statistical treatment. This square-root transformation tends to make the ordinal scale approximate the characteristics of an interval scale.

The above section outlines the assumptions and methods for measuring the magnitude of psychological states from samples of speech with adults. What follows is a review of research studies undertaken to determine whether this same method can be reliably and validly applied to children's speech.

## METHODS AND PROCEDURES

Several steps were involved in extending the content analysis of speech, now available as a measurement method of psychological states in adults, to a method equally applicable to children. These steps may be enumerated:

1. Obtaining speech samples from children under such circumstances that there are minimal effects of the means of, context of, or person eliciting the speech and so that the major variance in the psychological scores derived from the content analysis of the speech originates from the speaker.
2. Establishing a satisfactory level of scoring reliability (0.85 or above) from the content analysis technicians.

3. Obtaining a cross-sectional set of speech samples from a stratified sample of normative children in terms of sex and educational level (Kindergarten and grades 1-12).
4. Obtaining another set of speech samples, a longitudinal series, following a group of normative children from the first through the twelfth grade.
5. Scoring all speech samples according to the scales previously developed for adults and calculating preliminary norms, including percentile scores, for sex and grade level for each psychological dimension.
6. Determining to what extent, if any, there are quantitative differences in affect and other psychological scores according to sex and age.
7. Initiating new validation studies for each of the content analysis scales.

## Procedure for Eliciting Speech Samples from Children

The goal with children was, as it was with adults, to develop a measurement procedure for psychological states that was highly sensitive both to rapid phasic fluctuations in emotions and to the more gradual and slow changes in the magnitude of psychological responses customarily called traits. Obviously, the means of eliciting the speech sample and the personal characteristics of the individual evoking speech, as well as the situational context in which the speech is brought forth, are quite capable of influencing the kind and quantity of the psychological responses, especially of a very sensitive psychological measure. But since the major goal of such a measurement tool is that it reflect primarily a process going on in the speaker, namely a psychobiological process, either innate or acquired and in any event internalized, an attempt is made to standardize or otherwise control these external variables and stimuli so that the major portion of the variance in the content analysis scores originates in the speaker. Once a reliable and validated psychological measure has been developed for children, the effect of varying one at a time these external factors (for example, the means of eliciting the speech, the interviewer, and the situational context) can be investigated; in fact, such studies can provide further construct validation of the measure.

## Laguna Beach School District Study

An initial cross-sectional study was done of 109 Caucasian children, categorized by sex and grade, from the Laguna Beach, California, School District. Actually, 133 children were interviewed, but only 109 children (82%) produced speech samples of enough words (70 words or more) to be acceptable for this study. In studies of adults, it has been generally assumed that the smaller the number of words in a verbal sample the less the adequacy or reliability of the sample as a true measure of any psychological variable. Evidence for this has been based on the observation that short speech samples (for example, less than 45 words) tend to give content analysis scores that are either relatively high or, rarely, quite

low when compared to mean scores. The whole issue as to how many words per speech sample constitute a reliable and valid one for purposes of assessment of posychological states should be studied further. Interestingly, studies of adults involving content analysis, using the Gottschalk-Gleser scales, of very short speech samples (5-45 words) of schizophrenic patients (Gottschalk and Gleser, 1969, pp. 208-210) and epileptics (Luborsky *et al.*, 1975) have provided surprisingly definitive scientific data. But for the present investigation, until more specific information is available, it was felt advisable to follow a conservative approach to this matter and require an arbitrary limit of 70 words or more for acceptable speech samples from these children.

In the present study, as was done in adult studies (Gottschalk and Hambidge, 1955; Gottschalk and Kaplan, 1958; Gottschalk and Gleser, 1969), standardized procedures were used for eliciting verbal behavior. These instructions, it can be seen, are purposely ambiguous and nondirective, so that they aim, like projective test stimuli, to catalyze the speaker to reveal the self without being aware of so doing. Borrowing directly from our procedure with adults (Gottschalk and Hambidge, 1955; Gottschalk *et al.*, 1969b), research team members eliciting speech samples from children first repeated the standardized instructions used with adults.

"I have a tape recorder here and here is a microphone. I would like you to speak into this microphone, please."

"This is a study of speaking and conversational habits. Upon a signal from me, I would like you to speak for five minutes about any interesting or dramatic life experiences you may have had. Once you have started I will be here listening to you, but I would prefer not to reply to any questions you may feel like asking me until the five minute period is over. Do you have any questions you would like to ask me now before we start? Well, then you may begin."

If the child was unable to respond, the following instructions were tried: "I'll tell you what to do; try telling me any stories you like about yourself."

If the child did not respond after about 1 min, the instructions were further modified. "Try telling me any stories about any one you know." (Pause) "Or try telling me about any television program you have recently seen."

Following the elicitation of a speech sample, other data were obtained from each child if time allowed. A factor limiting what could be obtained was that the informed consent of the children's parents had been secured for this study, and this consent was limited to investigation of speech patterns and examination of the children's school records.

## The Minnesota Percepto-Diagnostic Test

The Minnesota Percepto-Diagnostic (MPD) Test (Fuller, 1969) is a clinical and research instrument designed to assess visual perception and visual motor abilities. It consists of six gestalt designs which the subject copies. The repro-

duced designs are scored for degrees of rotation, separation, and distortion. The author states that the MPD test provides a rapid and objective method which (a) classifies the etiology of reading and learning disorders among children into primary, secondary, or organic retardation; (b) classifies children who have behavioral problems as having normal, emotionally disturbed, or schizophrenic perception; (c) measures the maturational level of normal and retarded children with IQ adjustment in the visual perceptual gestalt and their reproductions; (d) classifies adults as having organic brain damage, personality disturbances, or being normal in their perceptions.

## Psychological Questionnaires

Direct questions, pertaining to various psychological dimensions (anxiety, hostility, etc.), were presented in standardized form and order to each child by the interviewer.

Demographic data, school grades, and IQ test and other test scores were also obtained from the principal's office of the collaborating school to the extent that these data were available.

## Loban (Berkeley School District) Study

To complete a longitudinal study of verbal behavior of children as they develop and mature from kindergarten through 12 grades of school would take at least 13 years. Rather than collecting such a time-consuming sample, it was decided to borrow a longitudinal series of speech samples of exactly this sort collected by Walter Loban and his coworkers (Loban, 1963, 1966a,b) for a quite different investigation of language behavior in children.

These speech samples were elicited from the children by showing them certain selected pictures from the Thematic Apperception Test (Murray, 1943) or from other sources. The children were instructed: "Tell me a story about this picture and how everything will come out." Unfortunately for the purposes of the present study, but apparently necessary for Loban's research goals, some of the pictures used in this longitudinal study were changed every few years. Only one picture was used annually throughout the 13 years of schooling; all the rest were changed every 2 or 3 years. The actual schedule of pictures used is given in Table I. This aspect of the means of elicitation of speech in the Loban study is one source of variation in the means of evoking speech that could not, obviously, be avoided. The fact that at least one picture (B) was used throughout the Loban study did allow comparison of the findings based on a set of varying pictures with the findings based on one constant picture.

Although Loban actually collected his longitudinal set of speech samples from *a total of* 338 children, we selected only 20 children from this study to follow, 12 boys and eight girls.

**Table I.** Pictures Used to Elicit Speech Samples in Loban Study[a]

| Grade | Order picture presented | | | | | |
|---|---|---|---|---|---|---|
| | 1 | 2 | 3 | 4 | 5 | 6 |
| K | A | B | C | D | E | |
| 1 | A | B | C | D | E | |
| 2 | F | B | A | C | D | E |
| 3 | F | B | A | C | D | E |
| 4 | G | H | B | I | J | K |
| 5 | G | H | B | I | J | K |
| 6 | G | H | B | I | J | K |
| 7 | L | M | B | N | O | |
| 8 | L | M | B | N | O | |
| 9 | L | M | B | N | O | |
| 10 | P | Q | B | R | S | |
| 11 | P | Q | B | R | S | |
| 12 | P | Q | B | R | S | |

[a]Key: A, Chinese girls; B, clowns; C, dogsled; D, boy crying; E, girl and rabbit; F, fixing pan; G, operation; H, cabin; I, girl on bridge; J, man grabbed; K, girl on stairs; L, bicycles; M, diver; N, colts; O, sharks; P, plowing; Q, factory; R, girl hiding; S, man on ladder.

Content analysis technicians thoroughly familiar with the Gottschalk-Gleser content analysis scales and having an interscorer reliability of 0.85 or above on these content analysis scales scored the speech samples for anxiety, hostility outward, hostility inward, ambivalent hostility, social alienation–personal disorganization, cognitive impairment, hope, human relations, and achievement strivings. The specific content categories and other details of each of these content analysis scales have been described elsewhere (Gottschalk and Gleser, 1969; Gottschalk *et al.*, 1969b).

In addition to the scores on the content analysis scales applied to their speech samples, other data were available from each of these subjects: (1) demographic data; (2) school grades; (3) IQ, health records, and other tests from school records; (4) a large group of variables derived from the speech samples by Loban (1963, 1966a,b). These variables were the number of phonological units, number of communication units, number of mazes (hesitations, false starts, meaningless repetitions), a classification of conventional syntactical and grammatical usage, and vocabulary diversity such as the amount of subordination.

## RESULTS

In the present article, primarily average and percentile scores will be reported for this normative sample of children on the content analysis measures of anxiety and anxiety subscales, hostility outward, hostility inward, ambivalent hostility, social alienation–personal disorganization, cognitive impairment, hope, human relations, and achievement strivings. Intercorrelations of content analysis scores, comparisons with scores from the longitudinal (Loban) sample, and some developmental trends and sex differences in speech content will also be reported here. In a later article will be reported the relationships of these content analysis scores to the Percepto-Diagnostic scores, the self-report psychological questionnaires, and other findings of interest.

As with all testing procedures – whether involving clinical laboratory procedures (blood chemistries, hematological measures, urinalysis, radiological chest screening), opinion surveys, intelligence estimates, performance measures – many variables may influence the normal range of variation of these measures. These variables include biological, psychological, and social factors, which in turn may be associated with geographical, meteorological, ethnic, dietary, and other variables. Hence the generalizability of psychological scores from a Southern California sample of schoolchildren may be limited. But this sample provides a starting point to answer a number of crucial questions: (1) Do the psychological scores of this sample of children differ from comparable scores of a group of adults? (2) Do the scores of boys and girls differ? (3) Do these scores distribute themselves normally? (4) Are there differences in scores over age groups? (5) What do percentile scores for these psychological states look like?

### Anxiety Scores of Children vs. Anxiety Scores of Adults

Total anxiety scores from the Laguna Beach sample of children average $1.97 \pm 1.03$ for boys and $2.07 \pm 0.80$ for girls (Table IIA), with combined scores averaging $2.04 \pm 0.89$ (Table IIIA). These scores appear significantly higher ($t = 6.10$, $p < 0.001$, two-tailed) than the average score ($1.46 \pm 0.71$) of a normative group of adults ($N = 282$), ages 17-65 (see Gottschalk and Gleser, 1969, p. 70).

Are these apparently lower anxiety scores in adults as compared to children ranging in age from 6-16 due to a gradual decrease beginning during childhood? A look at Table IIA, which gives a breakdown of mean psychological scores for children in grades 0-3, 4-6, 7-9, 10-12, suggests that there is no stepwise decrease in anxiety scores with increasing chronological age during the ages 6-16, for average anxiety scores range between 1.90 and 2.11 from the Laguna Beach sample of children, which is a cross-sectional group of schoolchildren.

Looking at the Loban sample of children ($N = 20$), which constitutes a longitudinal sample of the same children followed over 13 grades of schooling,

**Table IIA.** Mean Psychological Scores from Assorted Subgroups of Laguna Beach Children[a]

| Subgroups | N | Anxiety | Hostility outward | | | Hostility inward | Ambivalent hostility |
|---|---|---|---|---|---|---|---|
| | | | Overt | Covert | Total | | |
| All children | | | | | | | |
| Grades 0-3 | 35 | 1.94 (0.88) | 0.72 (0.35) | 0.83 (0.40) | 1.03 (0.48) | 0.65 (0.41) | 0.59 (0.35) |
| Grades 4-6 | 37 | 2.11 (0.85) | 0.70 (0.45) | 0.93 (0.58) | 1.18 (0.60) | 0.82 (0.60) | 0.71 (0.39) |
| Grades 7-9 | 20 | 1.90 (0.84) | 0.76 (0.32) | 0.70 (0.26) | 1.02 (0.35) | 0.58 (0.38) | 0.68 (0.43) |
| Grades 10-12 | 11 | 2.11 (0.94) | 1.21 (0.75) | 0.90 (0.67) | 1.49 (0.93) | 0.73 (0.39) | 0.67 (0.44) |
| Males | 41 | 1.97 (1.03) | 0.76 (0.46) | 0.84 (0.50) | 1.10 (0.58) | 0.81 (0.64) | 0.71 (0.39) |
| Females | 68 | 2.07 (0.80) | 0.82 (0.49) | 0.85 (0.47) | 1.16 (0.59) | 0.69 (0.46) | 0.64 (0.38) |

[a] Standard deviations given in parentheses.

**Table IIB.** Mean Psychological Scores from Assorted Subgroups of Laguna Beach Children[a]

| Subgroups | Achievement strivings | Hope | Human relations | Social alienation–personal disorganization | Cognitive impairment |
|---|---|---|---|---|---|
| All children | | | | | |
| Grades 0-3 | 1.47 (2.18) | 0.24 (1.44) | 2.31 (1.91) | −1.88 (5.89) | 2.88 (2.52) |
| Grades 4-6 | 1.29 (2.48) | −0.14 (0.93) | 1.77 (1.08) | −0.92 (2.32) | 2.57 (1.30) |
| Grades 7-9 | 1.54 (2.09) | 0.10 (0.98) | 1.74 (0.82) | −0.94 (2.88) | 2.04 (1.13) |
| Grades 10-12 | 1.16 (2.57) | 0.26 (1.93) | 0.78 (1.45) | −1.24 (3.04) | 1.72 (1.28) |
| Males | 1.62 (2.52) | 0.05 (1.38) | 1.74 (1.45) | −0.69 (5.83) | 2.74 (2.17) |
| Females | 1.27 (2.08) | 0.03 (1.17) | 1.89 (1.47) | −1.40 (2.94) | 2.35 (1.57) |

[a] Standard deviations given in parentheses.

**Table IIIA.** Percentile Scores on Assorted Psychological Scales of All Children in the Laguna Beach Study ($N$ = 109)

| Percentile | Anxiety | Hostility outward | | | Hostility inward | Ambivalent hostility |
|---|---|---|---|---|---|---|
| | | Overt | Covert | Total | | |
| 95 | 3.51 | 1.69 | 1.77 | 2.23 | 1.95 | 1.50 |
| 90 | 3.31 | 1.34 | 1.47 | 1.83 | 1.50 | 1.28 |
| 85 | 3.01 | 1.25 | 1.31 | 1.67 | 1.10 | 1.01 |
| 80 | 2.80 | 1.03 | 1.19 | 1.57 | 0.93 | 0.82 |
| 75 | 2.55 | 0.94 | 1.09 | 1.48 | 0.82 | 0.72 |
| 70 | 2.48 | 0.88 | 0.94 | 1.38 | 0.79 | 0.71 |
| 60 | 2.26 | 0.75 | 0.81 | 1.20 | 0.65 | 0.61 |
| 50 | 1.99 | 0.64 | 0.74 | 1.04 | 0.56 | 0.55 |
| 40 | 1.74 | 0.56 | 0.64 | 0.88 | 0.48 | 0.48 |
| 30 | 1.55 | 0.49 | 0.55 | 0.74 | 0.40 | 0.41 |
| 25 | 1.35 | 0.47 | 0.51 | 0.67 | 0.37 | 0.38 |
| 20 | 1.19 | 0.42 | 0.43 | 0.61 | 0.35 | 0.37 |
| 15 | 1.04 | 0.39 | 0.37 | 0.55 | 0.31 | 0.35 |
| 10 | 0.86 | 0.35 | 0.33 | 0.51 | 0.28 | 0.32 |
| 5 | 0.65 | 0.32 | 0.30 | 0.41 | 0.26 | 0.30 |
| Mean | 2.04 | 0.79 | 0.85 | 1.14 | 0.73 | 0.67 |
| S.D. | 0.89 | 0.48 | 0.48 | 0.58 | 0.54 | 0.38 |

may give us some information on the question of a possible stepwise decrease in anxiety scores for children from kindergarten through high school (see Table IV). The anxiety scores derived from stories told in reaction to groups of Thematic Apperception Test and other pictures show only minor variations from kindergarten through grade 9 (2.05-2.38), and then dip somewhat for grades 10, 11, and 12 (1.78, 1.77, and 1.87, respectively). The average score for these 20

**Table IIIB.** Percentile Scores on Assorted Psychological Scales of All Children in the Laguna Beach Study ($N$ = 109)

| Percentile | Achievement strivings | Hope | Human relations | Social alienation–personal disorganization | Cognitive impairment |
|---|---|---|---|---|---|
| 95 | 5.53 | 1.90 | 3.60 | 4.38 | 5.40 |
| 90 | 4.31 | 1.37 | 3.22 | 2.74 | 4.62 |
| 85 | 3.90 | 1.04 | 2.94 | 1.94 | 4.23 |
| 80 | 3.26 | 0.83 | 2.75 | 1.30 | 3.67 |
| 75 | 2.65 | 0.61 | 2.57 | 0.79 | 3.51 |
| 70 | 2.12 | 0.40 | 2.42 | 0.61 | 3.18 |
| 60 | 1.75 | 0.19 | 2.06 | 0.04 | 2.76 |
| 50 | 1.22 | 0.01 | 1.78 | −0.52 | 2.27 |
| 40 | 0.95 | −0.07 | 1.50 | −1.27 | 1.93 |
| 30 | −0.04 | −0.38 | 1.13 | −2.53 | 1.56 |
| 25 | −0.25 | −0.50 | 1.01 | −2.86 | 1.37 |
| 20 | −0.44 | −0.67 | 0.82 | −3.56 | 1.17 |
| 15 | −0.84 | −0.95 | 0.45 | −4.90 | 0.89 |
| 10 | −1.37 | −1.38 | 0.11 | −5.89 | 0.69 |
| 5 | −1.99 | −2.30 | −0.39 | −7.13 | 0.22 |
| Mean | 1.40 | 0.04 | 1.83 | −1.14 | 2.50 |
| S.D. | 2.25 | 1.25 | 1.46 | 4.24 | 1.81 |

**Table IV.** Affect Scores Derived from Speech Samples over a 13-Year Period from 20 Children in Response to Pictures (Loban Sample)

| Grade | | 0 | 1 | 2 | 3 | 4 | 5 | 6 | 7 | 8 | 9 | 10 | 11 | 12 | T |
|---|---|---|---|---|---|---|---|---|---|---|---|---|---|---|---|
| Scores derived from all pictures | | | | | | | | | | | | | | | |
| Anxiety | Mean | 2.18 | 2.32 | 2.18 | 2.14 | 2.21 | 2.15 | 2.38 | 2.06 | 2.05 | 2.23 | 1.78 | 1.77 | 1.87 | 2.10 |
| | S.D. | 0.81 | 1.10 | 0.62 | 0.55 | 0.65 | 0.62 | 0.49 | 0.61 | 0.51 | 0.47 | 0.50 | 0.65 | 0.55 | 0.62 |
| Hostility out, overt | Mean | 0.71 | 0.88 | 0.70 | 0.85 | 0.61 | 0.68 | 0.73 | 0.46 | 0.47 | 0.77 | 0.77 | 0.86 | 1.11 | 0.73 |
| | S.D. | 0.36 | 0.39 | 0.39 | 0.51 | 0.28 | 0.38 | 0.47 | 0.18 | 0.25 | 0.67 | 0.44 | 0.45 | 0.51 | 0.44 |
| Hostility out, covert | Mean | 1.44 | 1.40 | 1.33 | 1.49 | 1.77 | 1.85 | 1.99 | 1.50 | 1.65 | 1.56 | 1.36 | 1.47 | 1.53 | 1.58 |
| | S.D. | 0.59 | 0.30 | 0.41 | 0.33 | 0.42 | 0.56 | 0.60 | 0.37 | 0.44 | 0.31 | 0.41 | 0.48 | 0.58 | 0.49 |
| Hostility out, total | Mean | 1.57 | 1.62 | 1.49 | 1.71 | 1.85 | 1.96 | 2.14 | 1.55 | 1.70 | 1.71 | 1.59 | 1.69 | 1.95 | 1.74 |
| | S.D. | 0.62 | 0.23 | 0.47 | 0.48 | 0.41 | 0.63 | 0.63 | 0.34 | 0.44 | 0.33 | 0.47 | 0.59 | 0.52 | 0.52 |
| Hostility in | Mean | 0.42 | 0.47 | 0.41 | 0.38 | 0.45 | 0.46 | 0.40 | 0.39 | 0.36 | 0.38 | 0.39 | 0.40 | 0.37 | 0.40 |
| | S.D. | 0.13 | 0.20 | 0.22 | 0.09 | 0.29 | 0.28 | 0.20 | 0.18 | 0.16 | 0.18 | 0.18 | 0.21 | 0.17 | 0.20 |
| Ambivalent hostility | Mean | 0.45 | 0.47 | 0.38 | 0.37 | 0.41 | 0.36 | 0.33 | 0.33 | 0.34 | 0.33 | 0.40 | 0.34 | 0.35 | 0.37 |
| | S.D. | 0.16 | 0.20 | 0.10 | 0.08 | 0.15 | 0.08 | 0.07 | 0.09 | 0.08 | 0.09 | 0.26 | 0.08 | 0.13 | 0.13 |
| Scores derived only from picture B | | | | | | | | | | | | | | | |
| Anxiety | Mean | 1.75 | 1.21 | 1.54 | 1.18 | 1.13 | 1.03 | 1.64 | 1.37 | 1.25 | 1.16 | 1.44 | 1.53 | 1.31 | 1.36 |
| | S.D. | 1.31 | 0.45 | 0.94 | 0.71 | 0.55 | 0.64 | 0.92 | 0.63 | 0.65 | 0.46 | 0.65 | 0.85 | 0.64 | 0.78 |
| Hostility out, overt | Mean | 0.99 | 1.29 | 1.03 | 1.08 | 0.98 | 0.90 | 0.93 | 0.94 | 0.91 | 1.01 | 0.90 | 1.30 | 1.38 | 1.03 |
| | S.D. | 0.37 | 0.36 | 0.50 | 0.49 | 0.28 | 0.27 | 0.29 | 0.29 | 0.29 | 0.29 | 0.29 | 0.48 | 0.69 | 0.41 |
| Hostility out, covert | Mean | 0.95 | 1.21 | 0.93 | 0.89 | 1.09 | 0.89 | 1.18 | 1.19 | 1.17 | 0.97 | 0.95 | 1.07 | 1.05 | 1.03 |
| | S.D. | 0.30 | 0.45 | 0.39 | 0.20 | 0.59 | 0.31 | 0.71 | 0.57 | 0.40 | 0.38 | 0.28 | 0.27 | 0.27 | 0.43 |
| Hostility out, total | Mean | 1.01 | 1.29 | 1.06 | 1.08 | 1.11 | 0.98 | 1.26 | 1.25 | 1.20 | 1.11 | 1.06 | 1.35 | 1.38 | 1.16 |
| | S.D. | 0.37 | 0.36 | 0.60 | 0.49 | 0.58 | 0.39 | 0.73 | 0.55 | 0.43 | 0.39 | 0.40 | 0.49 | 0.69 | 0.52 |
| Hostility in | Mean | 0.92 | 1.21 | 0.88 | 0.89 | 0.96 | 0.79 | 0.94 | 0.86 | 0.87 | 0.85 | 0.84 | 1.01 | 1.13 | 0.92 |
| | S.D. | 0.29 | 0.45 | 0.29 | 0.20 | 0.30 | 0.23 | 0.45 | 0.32 | 0.28 | 0.30 | 0.23 | 0.29 | 0.54 | 0.33 |
| Ambivalent hostility | Mean | 0.96 | 1.21 | 0.88 | 0.89 | 0.96 | 0.79 | 0.82 | 0.86 | 0.87 | 0.85 | 0.84 | 1.01 | 1.08 | 0.91 |
| | S.D. | 0.38 | 0.45 | 0.29 | 0.20 | 0.30 | 0.23 | 0.21 | 0.32 | 0.28 | 0.30 | 0.23 | 0.29 | 0.36 | 0.30 |

children is 2.10. Although this decrease in total anxiety scores for older children from the Loban sample suggests a decreasing trend in anxiety, one cannot be certain of this conclusion, for sets of pictures used to elicit speech were changed every 2 or 3 years on these children (see Table I), and the possibility cannot be discounted that a new set of pictures used at grade 10 might have facilitated such a decrement in anxiety scores. Furthermore, if one looks at the anxiety scores generated from these children by the only one picture (B) presented over all these years of schooling, the average anxiety score is noted to be 1.36, but the range of variations of these anxiety scores from grade to grade is rather high (1.03-1.75), peaking at kindergarten and again at sixth grade and showing no definite slope. Unfortunately, even though this one picture was used uniformly as a stimulus to elicit speech throughout the 13 grades of school, it was surrounded by different pictures every 2 or 3 years, and this varying context of other pictures as stimuli to elicit speech could conceivably have carryover or halo effects on the stimulus valence of the one picture consistently used throughout the 13 years.

So, final answers to these questions must await more data.

### *Anxiety Subscale Scores*

Table V gives mean anxiety subscale scores for all 109 children in the Laguna Beach sample, as well as percentile anxiety subscale scores.[4] Tables VI and VII show the average anxiety subscale scores for, respectively, boys and girls, broken down into percentiles. There appear to be no marked sex differences in these average scores, except that the mutilation and diffuse anxiety scores are slightly higher (nonsignificant) for girls than for boys and the shame anxiety scores are higher for boys. When these subscale anxiety scores are contrasted with similar average subscale scores for adults (ranging in age from 17 to 70), the adults again appear to have lower scores than children for both men and women. Separation anxiety scores were significantly higher for both male ($t = 5.64, p < 0.005$) and female ($t = 5.81, p < 0.005$) children when compared with adult males and females. In addition, male children had significantly higher shame anxiety ($t = 1.93, p < 0.05$) than adult males.

### *Percentile Scores for Anxiety*

Percentiles for total anxiety scores derived by content analysis from 5-min speech samples elicited from the 109 Laguna Beach schoolchildren are given in

[4] The anxiety subscale scores were obtained by taking the raw subscale score (for instance, for death anxiety or separation anxiety), adding 0.5 to this raw score, and dividing by the number of words spoken during the 5-min period of speech, the square root of the quotient being the corrected score; this is the identical procedure used in obtained corrected total anxiety from raw total anxiety scores, the rationale for which is given in Gottschalk and Gleser (1969, pp. 17-18).

**Table V.** Percentile Scores for the Anxiety Subscales of All Children in the Laguna Beach Study ($N$ = 109)

| Percentile | Death | Mutilation | Separation | Guilt | Shame | Diffuse |
|---|---|---|---|---|---|---|
| 95 | 1.59 | 2.13 | 2.22 | 0.94 | 2.01 | 1.42 |
| 90 | 1.21 | 1.87 | 1.95 | 0.85 | 1.58 | 1.14 |
| 75 | 0.80 | 1.15 | 1.57 | 0.52 | 1.20 | 0.83 |
| 50 | 0.49 | 0.58 | 1.06 | 0.26 | 0.70 | 0.56 |
| 25 | 0.26 | 0.38 | 0.59 | 0.22 | 0.29 | 0.28 |
| 10 | 0.21 | 0.24 | 0.29 | 0.20 | 0.22 | 0.23 |
| 5 | 0.19 | 0.19 | 0.23 | 0.19 | 0.20 | 0.20 |
| Mean | 0.62 | 0.86 | 1.14 | 0.41 | 0.85 | 0.63 |
| S.D. | 0.43 | 0.66 | 0.66 | 0.29 | 0.63 | 0.40 |

**Table VI.** Percentile Scores for the Anxiety Subscales of Male Children in the Laguna Beach Study ($N$ = 41)

| Percentile | Death | Mutilation | Separation | Guilt | Shame | Diffuse |
|---|---|---|---|---|---|---|
| 95 | 1.71 | 1.95 | 2.34 | 0.87 | 2.44 | 1.00 |
| 90 | 1.20 | 1.86 | 2.16 | 0.65 | 1.71 | 0.87 |
| 75 | 0.74 | 0.93 | 1.66 | 0.56 | 1.22 | 0.70 |
| 50 | 0.52 | 0.54 | 1.03 | 0.28 | 0.78 | 0.50 |
| 25 | 0.29 | 0.30 | 0.48 | 0.24 | 0.39 | 0.28 |
| 10 | 0.23 | 0.24 | 0.25 | 0.21 | 0.24 | 0.23 |
| 5 | 0.22 | 0.22 | 0.22 | 0.19 | 0.22 | 0.21 |
| Mean | 0.64 | 0.78 | 1.17 | 0.40 | 0.94 | 0.54 |
| S.D. | 0.45 | 0.63 | 0.78 | 0.22 | 0.69 | 0.27 |

Table IIIA, and this table includes percentiles for various types of hostility scores obtained from the same speech samples.

Percentiles from the six anxiety subscale scores which go to make up the total anxiety scale scores are listed in Table V. These anxiety subscale scores include percentiles for death anxiety, mutilation anxiety, separation anxiety, guilt anxiety, shame anxiety, and diffuse anxiety. Tables VI and VII give a breakdown of the percentiles for these anxiety subscale scores for boys (Table VI) and girls (Table VII).

**Table VII.** Percentile Scores for the Anxiety Subscales of Female Children in the Laguna Beach Study ($N$ = 68)

| Percentile | Death | Mutilation | Separation | Guilt | Shame | Diffuse |
|---|---|---|---|---|---|---|
| 95 | 1.55 | 2.30 | 2.01 | 1.00 | 1.79 | 1.51 |
| 90 | 1.20 | 1.82 | 1.84 | 0.89 | 1.43 | 1.31 |
| 75 | 0.85 | 1.16 | 1.48 | 0.47 | 1.08 | 0.91 |
| 50 | 0.49 | 0.74 | 1.05 | 0.26 | 0.63 | 0.57 |
| 25 | 0.24 | 0.41 | 0.68 | 0.22 | 0.26 | 0.28 |
| 10 | 0.20 | 0.22 | 0.26 | 0.19 | 0.21 | 0.21 |
| 5 | 0.19 | 0.19 | 0.23 | 0.19 | 0.19 | 0.19 |
| Mean | 0.62 | 0.91 | 1.12 | 0.42 | 0.79 | 0.68 |
| S.D. | 0.42 | 0.67 | 0.58 | 0.32 | 0.59 | 0.45 |

At this stage of development and validation of these speech content scales of various psychological states in children, these percentiles cannot be generalized extensively beyond the Laguna Beach sample of children. The percentiles are provided, at this time, as a basis for comparison of the same kind of speech content analysis scores obtained from other children from different geographical locations, from different ethnic, racial, socioeconomic backgrounds, from groups with a different health status, or from any different kinds of groups. There is not currently available any psychological or personality test for children which gives percentile or standardized scores on affects or other psychological dimensions. The present study is a first step in this direction, providing information that is expected to be subject to modification and enlargement as more data are collected which can be compared to the present findings and incorporated into a growing body of knowledge with respect to the quantitative aspects of these psychological responses in children.

A preliminary example of the possible use of these percentiles can be appropriately mentioned at this point. In a recent study from the Childrens Outpatient Psychiatric Service, Orange County Medical Center, four withdrawn, inhibited, disturbed 10- to 12-year-old boys gave 5-min speech samples in response to the standardized and purposely ambiguous instructions to talk for 5 min about any interesting or dramatic personal life experiences (Jacobson *et al.*, 1973). The average total social alienation--personal disorganization score from the initial 5-min speech sample given by each boy was 4.70, which is in the 99th percentile for children in the Laguna Beach study (Table IIIB). This finding is certainly in the expected direction, for one would expect that such children attending a psychiatric outpatient clinic would have higher average social alienation--personal disorganization scores on these psychological dimensions as compared to the average scores from a group of normative schoolchildren. The percentiles for the anxiety scale and hostility scales of these young psychiatric patients, using Table IIIA, are also illustrative of the possible usefulness of these percentiles for a normative sample of children: anxiety, 1.45 (28th percentile); total hostility outward, 1.29 (65th percentile); overt hostility outward, 0.85 (68th percentile); covert hostility outward, 0.92 (69th percentile); hostility inward, 0.43 (34th percentile); and ambivalent hostility, 0.44 (35th percentile).

## Hostility Scores of Children vs. Hostility Scores of Adults

### *Total Hostility Outward, Hostility Inward, and Ambivalent Hostility Scores*

*Total hostility outward* scores from the Laguna Beach sample of children average $1.10 \pm 0.58$ for boys and $1.16 \pm 0.59$ for girls (Table IIA), with com-

bined scores averaging 1.14 ± 0.58. These scores may be compared to the average total hostility scores (0.96 ± 0.50) of a group of nonpsychiatric adult subjects ($N$ = 322) (see Gottschalk and Gleser, 1969, p. 79) and also to male and female scores on hostility outward in normative adult samples (Gottschalk and Gleser, 1969, p. 80).

Male adults have significantly higher hostility outward scores, as assessed by our content analysis method, than female adults. The mean score on hostility outward for a sample of employed men (0.92) was higher than that for a group of employed women (0.79) at the 0.03 level of significance. The mean hostility outward score for male college students was slightly higher than that for female students, and likewise for male and female patients, although these differences did not reach statistically significant levels. No significant differences have been found between the adult sexes in the means or medians for hostility inward or ambivalent hostility in any of our studies. Hostility inward scores increase with age and more in adult females than adult males. For adults no other definite relationships have been found between the three hostility scales described here and such variables as age, educational level, and intelligence. How children's speech varies with respect to sex and other variables will be discussed more fully later, but there are no significant sex differences with respect to children from the Laguna Beach sample in total hostility outward scores.

Total hostility outward scores on this content analysis scale are made up of overt and covert hostility subscales, the overt hostility outward scores being derived from verbal statements about adversely critical, angry, assaultive, asocial impulses of the self toward objects outside oneself and covert hostility outward scores being assessed from verbal statements concerning *other people or non-self forces* initiating or carrying out hostile or destructive activities toward objects external to the self. Means, standard deviations, and percentiles are given in Table IIIA and stepwise scores for grade levels and sex differences are given in Table IIA. An increase in total hostility outward scores appears in the grades 10-12, accounted for primarily in overt hostility outward scores. It is plausible that adolescents may make more hostile, aggressive statements than younger children — at least this is consistent with the notion of adolescent rebellion — but since there were only ten subjects from the Laguna Beach sample in this group, much more data are needed for substantiation of this trend. The high total hostility outward scores and overt hostility outward subscale scores during grades 11 and 12 from the Loban longitudinal sample of 20 children, especially the responses to picture B, would appear to support this trend (Table III).

*Hostility inward scores* from the Laguna Beach sample of children average 0.81 ± 0.64 for boys and 0.69 ± 0.46 for girls, with combined scores averaging 0.73 ± 0.54 (Tables IIA and IIIA). Adult hostility inward scores ($N$ = 322) average somewhat lower ($t = 4.52, p < 0.001$), 0.59 ± 0.35.

*Ambivalent hostility scores* are derived from verbal statements regarding destructive, injurious, critical thoughts and actions of others to the self. Ambivalent hostility scores from the Laguna Beach sample average 0.71 ± 0.39 for boys and 0.64 ± 0.38 for girls, with combined scores of 0.67 ± 0.38 (Tables IIA and IIIA). Adult ambivalent hostility scores (0.61 ± 0.39) are not different from the children's scores. The absolute values of the scores from the Loban sample of children cannot be directly compared to those from the Laguna Beach sample since the former scores were obtained from verbal samples elicited by pictures rather than by instructions to talk about interesting life experiences.

### *Percentiles for Hostility Scores*

Percentiles for hostility outward scores (total, overt, and covert), hostility inward, and ambivalent hostility are given for the 109 children in Table IIIA.

## Other Psychological State Scores in Children

Table IIB gives mean psychological scores for schoolchildren of the Laguna Beach sample and also provides male and female means for the content analyses scales of achievement strivings, hope, human relations, social alienation–personal disorganization, and cognitive impairment. Developmental trends on these psychological scales and the affect scales will be discussed below.

Table IIIB provides percentile scores for children on the achievement strivings, hope, human relations, social alienation–personal disorganization, and cognitive impairment scales. Comparisons of these percentiles can be made with similar percentile scores from adults (see Social Alienation–Personal Disorganization Percentile Scores – Adults; Cognitive Impairment Scale Percentile Scores – Adults; Hope Scale Percentile Scores – Adults).[5]

## Intercorrelations of Psychological State Scores

Table VIII gives the intercorrelations of these content analysis measures for children. Anxiety, hostility, and social alienation–personal disorganization scores, as with adults, correlate positively with one another and negatively with achievement strivings, hope, and human relations scores. The latter three scale scores correlate positively. These intercorrelations cannot be accounted for on the basis that there might be a similarity of content categories scored. For the

[5] Copies of these tables as well as copies of the content analysis scales used in this study are available from the National Auxiliary Publications Service of the American Society for Information Science – Microfiche Publications, 1155 16th Street, N.W., Washington, D.C. 20036.

**Table VIII.** Intercorrelations of Psychological Scores of Children ($N$ = 107)

| | Age | Number of words | Grade | Hostility outward | | | Hostility inward | Ambivalent hostility | Achievement strivings | Hope | Human relations | Social alienation personal disorganization | Cognitive impairment |
|---|---|---|---|---|---|---|---|---|---|---|---|---|---|
| | | | | Overt | Covert | Total | | | | | | | |
| Anxiety | | | | 0.22[a] | 0.47[c] | 0.46[c] | 0.62[d] | 0.47[c] | −0.61[d] | −0.46[c] | −0.30[b] | 0.37[c] | 0.27[b] |
| Hostility outward | | | | | | | | | | | | | |
| Overt | | | 0.25[a] | | 0.12 | 0.70[c] | 0.20[a] | 0.30[b] | −0.26[b] | −0.35[c] | −0.36[c] | 0.29[b] | 0.16 |
| Covert | | | | | | 0.75[c] | 0.07 | 0.22[a] | −0.45[c] | −0.39[c] | −0.24[a] | 0.08 | −0.28[b] |
| Total | | | | | | | 0.16 | 0.32[c] | −0.50[c] | −0.45[c] | −0.41[c] | 0.25[a] | 0.30[b] |
| Hostility inward | −0.19 | −0.26[b] | | | | | | | −0.26[b] | −0.36[c] | −0.19[a] | −0.37[c] | 0.07 |
| Ambivalent hostility | | | | | | | | | −0.44[c] | −0.38[c] | −0.25[b] | 0.23[a] | 0.18 |
| Achievement strivings | | | | | | | | | | 0.55[c] | 0.38[c] | −0.42[c] | 0.31[b] |
| Hope | | | | | | | | | | | 0.51[c] | −0.61[d] | 0.07 |
| Human relations | −0.22[a] | | −0.29[a] | | | | | | | | | −0.58[c] | 0.00 |
| Social alienation–personal disorganization | | | | | | | | | | | | | 0.25[b] |
| Cognitive impairment | −0.22[a] | | −0.22[a] | | | | | | | | | | |

[a] $p < 0.05$.
[b] $p < 0.01$.
[c] $p < 0.001$.
[d] $p < 0.0001$.

most part, these different scales do not include identical, scorable content categories, and when they do, for example, in the instances of the social alienation–personal disorganization and cognitive impairment scales, the weights applicable to the content items differ. When these positive intercorrelations reach a convincing level of significance, we assume that the psychological dimensions are associated variables, whether or not on a cause-effect basis.

The low negative correlation ($r = -0.26$) between hostility inward scores and number of words spoken per verbal sample (Table VIII) is, perhaps, in the expected direction; that is, the more one is self-critical or hostile to the self, the less one talks.

## Developmental Differences of Children in Content of Speech

Table VIII indicates, from the Laguna Beach children, low negative correlations between age and hostility inward scores ($r = -0.19$), human relations scores ($r = -0.22$, $p < 0.05$), and cognitive impairment scores ($r = -0.22$, $p < 0.05$). There is, also, a low positive correlation between school grade and overt hostility outward scores ($r = +0.25$, $p < 0.01$) and a low negative correlation between school grade and human relations scores ($r = -0.29$, $p < 0.01$). These findings, based on cross-sectional data, would suggest that the children from this sample tend to outgrow talking about disliking the self and overtly being interested in other people. As they grow older, they speak more coherently and in a less disorganized fashion. Also, as they develop they more openly express hostility to others.

Scores from individual content categories or subscales from each psychological scale could uniformly change with development when the scores from a total scale might not do so with age. This possibility has been examined, and many interesting trends with growth and development in the relative frequency of various verbal themata or contents uttered in the speech of children have been detected. The large number of relationships looked at could result, however, in a number of significant or near significant correlations by chance, and hence the trends reported here must be regarded as preliminary observations requiring further corroboration. Correlations at a probability level of less than 0.10 (based on two-tailed tests) are included to provide hypotheses to replicate in future studies. As previously indicated, cross-sectional studies while providing clues for noting developmental and maturational changes require longitudinal studies to pin down such changes convincingly. At any rate, the results of such correlations are given below under the name of each scale.

*Anxiety Scale.* No significant trends with age or grade were noted for the anxiety scale.

*Overt Hostility Outward Scale.* Overt hostility outward scores *increased* with age ($r = 0.25$, $N = 103$, $p < 0.01$), especially after the eighth grade.

*Achievement Strivings Scale.* References to vocational, occupational, educational activities (I) *increased* with age ($r = 0.20$, $N = 103$, $p < 0.05$).

References to deterrents to achievement (IV) *increased* with age ($r = 0.16$, $N = 104$, $p < 0.10$). These include references to the following: (A) External danger or problems of fear of loss of control or limit setting on part of others: references to lack of control by others; references to errors or misjudgments by others that might injure the self. (B) Internal obstacles: references to difficulties in setting limits on oneself or problems in disciplining the self; references to errors or misjudgments by self that might harm the self. (C) Interpersonal: arguments or troubles in getting along with others; problems in interpersonal relations, such as inability to make friends.

References to commitments or to a sense of obligation to responsible or constructive social and personal behavior; to obligations to perform well or succeed in a task; to commitment to a task and to carrying it out or completing it (III) *decreased* with grade up to grade 8 ($r = -0.19$, $N = 103$, $p < 0.06$) and then *increased* through grade 12.

*Hope Scale.*[6] References to feelings of optimism about the present or future (H2, + 1) involving others (a) or the self (b) *increased* with age ($r = 0.41$, $N = 103$, $p < 0.001$).

*Human Relations Scale.* Nonevaluative references to any kinds of human relations involving others which specify the person(s) interacted with, but which do not specify the nature of the deeper involvement and which are not classified elsewhere (B2b, + ¼), *increased* with grade ($r = 0.16$, $N = 103$, $p < 0.10$).

Nonevaluative references to any kinds of human relations which are generalized, ambiguous as to person(s) interacted with, and impersonal (B3, −½) *increased* with grade ($r = 0.36$, $N = 103$, $p < 0.001$).

Direct interactions with interviewer (D6b, + ½), not questions, but other direct references such as "you know" or statements addressing interviewer directly by name or as "you" *increased* with grade ($r = 0.40$, $N = 103$, $p < 0.001$).

[6] The hope, human relations, and social alienation–personal disorganization scales are composed of content categories that are weighted positively (+), meaning that these verbal items when they occur indicate some quantity of the psychological state belonging to the scale's name, and content categories that are weighted negatively (−), signifying that these verbal items when they occur subtract some quantity from the psychological state measured by the scale. In addition, some verbal categories are weighted zero (0), indicating that the occurrences of these verbal items do not add to or subtract from the magnitude of psychological dimension being expressed. Whenever content categories from these scales are referred to below, the valence or weight assigned to these categories will be given so that the reader can perceive how these developmental changes might be related to each content analysis scale.

*Social Alienation–Personal Disorganization Scale.* Reference to others unfriendly to self (IB2, + 1/3) *increased* with age ($r = 0.17$, $N = 102$, $p < 0.10$). References to the self helping, being friendly toward others (IC2, – 2) were relatively frequent during kindergarten and first grade and then *decreased* considerably with the second grade and remained relatively unchanged in frequency thereafter ($r = -0.28$, $N = 102$, $p < 0.005$).

References to others helping, being friendly toward self (IC3, – 2) were relatively frequent during grades 1, 2, and 3 and then *decreased* and leveled off in all subsequent grades ($r = -0.28$, $N = 102$, $p < 0.005$).

References to the self being intact, satisfied, healthy, well, with definite positive affect or valence indicated (IIB3a, – 1), *increased* gradually after the third grade ($r = 0.24$, $N = 102$, $p < 0.02$).

References to being intact, satisfied, healthy, well, with flat, factual, or neutral attitudes expressed (IIB3b, – 1), *decreased* with grade ($r = 0.18$, $N = 102$, $p < 0.08$).

Denial of feelings, attitudes, or mental state of the self (IIC, + 3) *increased* with grade ($r = 0.16$, $N = 102$, $p < 0.10$).

Reference to food, good or neutral (IID2, 0), *decreased* with grade ($r = 0.29$, $N = 102$, $p < 0.003$).

References to weather being bad, dangerous, unpleasant, or otherwise negative (not sunny, not clear, uncomfortable, etc.) (IIE1, – 1) *increased* with grade ($r = 0.21$, $N = 102$, $p < 0.03$).

Verbal statements characterized by incomplete sentences, clauses, and phrases and blocking (IIIA2, 0) *decreased* with grade ($r = -0.25$, $N = 102$, $p < 0.01$).

References to obviously erroneous or fallacious remarks or conclusions and illogical or bizarre statements (IIIA3, +2) *decreased* with grade ($r = 0.21$, $N = 102$, $p < 0.03$).

Repetition of ideas in sequence in the form of words separated only by a word (IIIB1, 0) *decreased* with grade ($r = -0.30$, $N = 102$, $p < 0.003$).

Repetition of ideas in sequence in the form of phrases or clauses (separated only by a phrase or clause) (IIIB2, + 1) *decreased* with grade ($r = -0.41$, $N = 102$, $p < 0.001$).

References to the interviewer, other than questions (IVB, + ½), *increased* with grade ($r = 0.37$, $N = 102$, $p < 0.001$).

Religious or biblical references (V, + 1) *increased* with age ($r = 0.21$, $N = 102$, $p < 0.04$).

*Cognitive Impairment Scale.* Cognitive impairment scores *decreased* with grade ($r = -0.22$, $N = 102$, $p < 0.03$).

The cognitive impairment scale contains many, but not all, of the speech categories of the social alienation–personal disorganization scale; those language categories that these two scales have in common have different weights. The two principal categories accounting for the negative correlation of cognitive impair-

ment scores and grade are incomplete sentences, clauses, phrases, blocking (IIIA2, +1) and repetition of phrases and clauses (separated by only a phrase or clause (IIIB2, + 1)).

## DISCUSSION

Piaget (1928, 1947, 1952) systematically studied and traced the development of cognitive and intellectual processes in children, and others have contributed to the understanding of language development in children (Brown and Berko, 1960; Ervin, 1961; Palermo and Jenkins, 1964; Entwisle, 1966; Linneberg, 1966; McNeill, 1966; Ancoshian and Carlson, 1973; Meyer and June, 1973; Costanzo *et al.*, 1973; Miller, 1973; Wiig and Semel, 1974). Relatively little systematic work has been done, however, on the development of the expression of emotions and other psychological states in children as communicated in the semantic or content aspects of speech. The article is an initial report of an investigation aiming to record and analyze the content of speech of children 6-17 with the purpose of describing, in mathematized form, the fears, worries, angers, strivings, and hopes of children as they grow and develop in our society. The intention, here, is to provide a new method of assaying these psychological states in children as they are communicated in the semantics of verbal behavior and to prepare the way to work toward the construct validation of this measurement procedure, much as was done in validating this method of assessing psychological states in adults (Gottschalk and Gleser, 1969).

Children have more than one language "register" (Houston, 1969, 1970): that is, styles of language having in common their appropriateness to a given situation or environment, for example, the language used in school settings and the language used at home or in other settings. Here, the language spoken in response to standardized and ambiguous instructions in a school setting was the language register being studied. In what ways this speech and the language register that children, particularly disadvantaged children, use at home might be similar or different with respect to the content categories examined here would be a worthwhile study.

The present study is only a first step in tracing developmental changes and sexual differences in speech content of children. Single observations of a sample of children stratified at different school grade levels, that is, a cross-sectional sample, do not reflect, with certitude, developmental changes unless the sample is very large. This is a modest-sized sample, not large enough to provide firm answers to the many questions asked of it and the statistical comparisons made. Replications of this study need to be made, not only with children from a similar population, but also with children from other populations. A better research design to map developmental changes of the speech content of children would have been to follow each child and get repeated observations over, at least, a

3-year period. But this was not possible. The longitudinal data available (Loban study) were ideal in some respects in that they followed the same children over a 12-year period, but the pictures used, except one, to evoke speech varied every 2 or 3 years. Different Thematic Apperception Test pictures have been demonstrated to elicit different amounts of anxiety as measured by content analysis (Gottschalk and Gleser, 1969, p. 110) and probably other psychological states as well. So this constitutes a flaw in the Loban data for the purposes of this study. For these reasons, the findings reported here with respect to children's speech are to be regarded as initial approximations.

Subsequent reports will compare the norms and percentiles found in the present study with those found for other samples of children including those of different race, socioeconomic background, and health status. Also, other articles will report construct validation data, using not only psychosocial and behavioral criteria but also biological and medical criteria.

## ACKNOWLEDGMENTS

Daniel E. Bates and Claire A. Cable collected and scored the speech samples, and Herman Birch, Ph.D., provided statistical assistance.

## REFERENCES

Ancoshian, L., and Carlson, J. S. (1973). A study of mental imagery and conversation within the Piagetian framework. *Hum. Develop.* 16: 382-394.

Brown, R., and Berko, J. (1960). Word association and the acquisition of grammar. *Child Develop.* 31: 1-14.

Costanzo, P. R., Coie, J. D., Grument, J. F., and Farnill, D. (1973). A reexamination of the effects of intent and consequences on children's moral judgement. *Child Develop.* 44: 154-161.

Entwisle, D. R. (1966). *Word Associations of Young Children,* Johns Hopkins Press, Baltimore.

Ervin, S. (1961). Changes with age in the verbal determinants of word association. *Am. J. Psychol.* 64: 361-372.

Fuller, G. B. (1969). The Minnesota Percepto-Diagnostic test (revised). *J. Clin. Psychol. Monogr. Suppl.* No. 28. 1-81.

Gleser, G. C., Gottschalk, L. A., and Springer, K. J. (1961). An anxiety scale applicable to verbal samples. *Arch. Gen. Psychiat.* 5: 593-605.

Gleser, G. C., Gottschalk, L. A., Fox, R., and Lippert, W. (1965). Immediate changes in affect with chlordiazepoxide in juvenile delinquent boys. *Arch. Gen. Psychiat.* 13: 291-295.

Gottschalk, L. A. (1971). Some psychoanalytic research into the communication of meaning through language: The quality and magnitude of psychological states. *Brit. J. Med. Psychol.* 44: 131-148.

Gottschalk, L. A. (1972). An objective method of measuring psychological states associated with changes in neural function. *J. Biol. Psychiat.* 4: 33-49.

Gottschalk, L. A. (1974a). A hope scale applicable to verbal samples. *Arch. Gen. Psychiat.* 30: 779-785.

Gottschalk, L. A. (1974b). The application of a method of content analysis to psychotherapy research. *Am. J. Psychother.* 28: 488-499.

Gottschalk, L. A. (1975). Drug effects in the assessment of affective states in man. In Essman, W. B., and Valzelli, L. (eds.), *Current Developments in Psychopharmacology*, Vol. 1, Spectrum Publications, New York.

Gottschalk, L. A., and Frank, E. C. (1967). Estimating the magnitude of anxiety from speech. *Behav. Sci.* 12: 289-295.

Gottschalk, L. A., and Gleser, G. C. (1964). Distinguishing characteristics of the verbal communications of schizophrenic patients. In Association for Research in Nervous and Mental Diseases, *Disorders of Communication*, Vol. 42, Williams and Wilkins, Baltimore, pp. 400-413.

Gottschalk, L. A., and Gleser, G. C. (1969). *The Measurement of Psychological States Through the Content Analysis of Verbal Behavior*, University of California Press, Berkeley.

Gottschalk, L. A., and Hambidge, G. (1955). Verbal behavior analysis: A systematic approach to the problem of quantifying psychologic processes. *J. Project. Techniques* 19: 387-409.

Gottschalk, L. A., and Kaplan, S. M. (1958). A quantitative method of estimating variations in intensity of a psychologic conflict or state. *Arch. Neurol. Psychiat.* 79: 688-696.

Gottschalk, L. A., Gleser, G. C., Daniels, R. S., and Block, S. L. (1958). The speech patterns of schizophrenic patients: A method of assessing relative degree of personal disorganization and social alienation. *J. Nerv. Ment. Dis.* 127: 153-166.

Gottschalk, L. A., Gleser, G. C., Springer, K. J., Kaplan, S. M., Shanon, J., and Ross, W. D. (1960). Effects of perphenazine on verbal behavior patterns. *Arch. Gen. Psychiat.* 2: 632-639.

Gottschalk, L. A., Gleser, G. C., Magliocco, E. B., and D'Zmura, T. L. (1961a). Further studies on the speech pattern of schizophrenic patients: Measuring inter-individual differences in relative degree of personal disorganization and social alienation. *J. Nerv. Ment. Dis.* 132: 101-113.

Gottschalk, L. A., Springer, K. J., and Gleser, G. C. (1961b). Experiments with a method of assessing the variations in intensity of certain psychological states occurring during two psychotherapeutic interviews. In Gottschalk, L. A. (ed.), *Comparative Psycholinguistic Analysis of Two Psychotherapeutic Interviews*, International Universities Press, New York.

Gottschalk, L. A., Gleser, G. C., and Springer, K. J. (1963). Three hostility scales applicable to verbal samples. *Arch. Gen. Psychiat.* 9: 254-279.

Gottschalk, L. A., Gleser, G. C., D'Zmura, T., and Hanenson, I. B. (1964). Some psychophysiological relationships in hypertensive women: The effect of hydrochlorothiazide on the relation of affect to blood pressure. *Psychosom. Med.* 26: 610-617.

Gottschalk, L. A., Cleghorn, J. M., Gleser, G. C., and Iacono, J. M. (1965a). Studies of relationships of emotions to plasma lipids. *Psychosom. Med.* 27: 102-111.

Gottschalk, L. A., Gleser, G. C., Wylie, H. W., and Kaplan, S. M. (1965b). Effects of imipramine on anxiety and hostility levels derived from verbal communications. *Psychopharmacologia* 7: 303-310.

Gottschalk, L. A., Winget, C. N., Gleser, G. C., and Springer, K. J. (1966). The measurement of emotional changes during a psychiatric interview: A working model toward quantifying the psychoanalytic concept of affect. In Gottschalk, L. A., and Auerbach, A. H. (eds.), *Methods of Research in Psychotherapy*, Appleton-Century-Crofts, New York.

Gottschalk, L. A., Stone, W. N., Gleser, G. C., and Iacono, J. M. (1969a). Anxiety and plasma free fatty acids (FFA). *Life Sci.* 8: 61-68.

Gottschalk, L. A., Winget, C. N., and Gleser, G. C. (1969b). Manual of Instructions for Using the Gottschalk-Gleser Content Analysis Scales: Anxiety, Hostility, and Social Alienation–Personal Disorganization, University of California Press, Berkeley.

Gottschalk, L. A., Gleser, G. C., Cleghorn, J. M., Stone, W. N., and Winget, C. N. (1970). Prediction of changes in severity of the schizophrenic syndrome with discontinuation and administration of phenothiazines in chronic schizophrenic patients: Language as a predictor and measure of change in schizophrenia. *Comprehensive Psychiat.* 11: 123-140.

Gottschalk, L. A., Bates, D. E., Waskow, I. E., Katz, M. M., and Olson, J. (1971). Effect of amphetamine or chlorpromazine on achievement strivings scores derived from the content analysis of speech. *Comprehensive Psychiat.* 12: 430-435.

Gottschalk, L. A., Elliott, H. W., Bates, D. E., and Cable, C. G. (1972a). The use of content analysis of short samples of speech for preliminary investigation of psychoactive drugs: Effect of lorazepam on anxiety scores. *Clin. Pharmacol. Ther.* 13: 323-328.

Gottschalk, L. A., Haer, J. L., and Bates, D. E. (1972b). Effect of sensory overload on psychological state. *Arch. Gen. Psychiat.* 27: 451-457.

Gottschalk, L. A., Fox, R. A., and Bates, D. E. (1973). A study of prediction and outcome in a Mental Health Crisis Clinic. *Am. J. Psychiat.* 130: 1107-1111.

Gottschalk, L. A., Stone, W. N., and Gleser, G. C. (1974). Peripheral versus central mechanisms accounting for anti-anxiety effect of propranolol. *Psychosom. Med.* 36: 47-56.

Houston, S. H. (1969). A sociolinguistic consideration of the black English of children in northern Florida. *Language* 45: 599-607.

Houston, S. H. (1970). A reexamination of some assumptions about the language of the disadvantaged child. *Child Develop.* 41: 947-963.

Jacobson, E., Uliana R. L., and Stolzoff, G. (1973). Evaluation and comparison of group therapeutic techniques for inpatient and outpatient for latency age boys. Paper presented at the annual meeting of the Western Psychological Association, Anaheim, Calif.

Linneberg, E. H. (1966). *New Directions in the Study of Language*, M. I. T. Press, Cambridge, Mass.

Loban, W. D. (1963). *The Language of Elementary School Children: A Study of the Use and Control of Language Effectiveness in Communication, and the Relations Among Speaking, Reading, Writing, and Listening*, Research Report No. 1, National Council of Teachers of English, Champaign, Ill.

Loban, W. D. (1966a). *Language Ability, Grades Seven, Eight, and Nine*, OE-30018, Cooperative Research Monograph No. 18, Government Printing Office, Washington, D.C.

Loban, W. D. (1966b). *Problems in Oral English*, Research Report No. 5, National Council of Teachers of English, Champaign, Ill.

Luborsky, L., Docherty, J. P., Todd, T. C., Knapp, P. H., Mirsky, A. F., and Gottschalk, L. A. (1975). A context analysis of psychological states prior to petit mal EEG paroxysms. *J. Nerv. Ment. Dis.* 160: 282-298.

McNeill, D. (1966). *Developmental Psycholinguistics*, Center for Cognitive Studies, Harvard University, Cambridge, Mass. (mimeographed).

Meyer, W. J., and Shane, J. (1973). The form and function of childrens' questions. *J. Genet. Psychol.* 123: 285-296.

Miller, P. H. (1973). Attention to stimulus dimensions in the conservation of liquid quantity. *Child Develop.* 44: 129-136.

Murray, H. A. (1943). *Thematic Apperception Test: Manual*, Harvard University Press, Cambridge, Mass.

Palermo, D. S., and Jenkins, J. J. (1964). *Word Association Norms*, University of Minnesota Press, Minneapolis.

Piaget, J. (1928). *The Child's Conception of the World*, Harcourt Brace, New York.

Piaget, J. (1947). *The Psychology of Intelligence*, Routledge and Kegan Paul, London.

Piaget, J. (1952). *The Child's Conception of Number*, Routledge and Kegan Paul, London.

Wiig, E. H., and Semel, E. M. (1974). Development of comprehension of logicogrammatical sentences by grade school children. *Percept. Motor Skills* 38: 171-176.

# Introduction to Chapter 7

Introductory Comments by L.A. Gottschalk

This study extended the investigation of the content of natural speech of white children to 276 black children and obtained normative measures on four affective states; anxiety, hostility directed outward, hostility directed inward, and ambivalent hostility. It also assessed the effect of an interviewer's race on the speech content of these black children.

Uliana found a significant linear increase in overt hostility outward scores with grade levels ($p < .0001$) and a significant quadratic relationship of covert hostility scores with grade ($p < .002$), where the maximum was between grades five through ten. Total hostility outward scores were found to have both a significant linear ($p < .03$) and quadratic relationship ($p < .006$) with grade level. Furthermore, black male children interviewed by black female interviewers had a significant linear increase with age for overt hostility outward scores ($p < .003$), whereas black female children had a significant linear increase in overt hostility outward scores when interviewed by white female interviewers ($p < .01$).

Male black children had a significant quadratic relationship ($p < .001$)

with grade of their guilt anxiety scores, with a sharp increase in guilt anxiety scores in the seventh and eighth grades. Whereas, females had a barely significant quadratic association ($p < .05$) of their guilt anxiety scores with grade, with the maximum guilt anxiety scores peaking in the fifth and sixth grades.

There was a significant quadratic effect of total anxiety scores and grade obtained by black interviewers ($p < .006$) with the maximum anxiety scores occurring during the ninth and tenth grades. A significant quadratic effect for total anxiety scores and grade was, also, found with white interviewers ($p < .04$), but the peak pattern was difficult to discern.

Significantly higher mean total anxiety scores were obtained with white interviewers than black interviewers ($p < .04$), most of this difference being accounted for by shame anxiety scores.

In contrast to a group of white adults studied by Gottschalk and Gleser,(1969) this group of black children did not have significantly higher shame and separation anxiety scores than males. Nor did male black children have significantly higher mutilation and death anxiety scores than females. There was a tendency, for black male children, to have higher average mutilation anxiety scores (0.63) than female children (0.55) and for black female children to have higher average shame anxiety scores (1.18) than black boys (1.01).

The normative scores for black children on these measures of affect approximated those of white children.

# 7

# Measurement of Black Children's Affective States and the Effect of Interviewer's Race on Affective States as Measured Through Language Behavior

Regina Uliana*

The use of language behavior to study children's emotions has largely been derived from clinical analyses of individual children (Wolman, Lewis, and King, 1972). Wolman (1972) has concluded that of the research into children's language behavior, the major portion has derived from Piaget's theories of cognitive growth, thus leaving experimental research of children's emotions and their various psychological states, as manifested through language, seriously neglected. In the past fifteen years, however, researchers have developed methods used to systematically analyze the semantic contents of speech. These methods have enabled investigators to obtain precise and objective measurements of the kinds and intensities of various psychological states and have added new dimensions to the study of the interrelationship between the verbal behavior and emotions of both adults and children.

Pilot studies of young adults between ages fifteen and seventeen and

*From the Department of Psychiatry and Human Behavior, University of California, Irvine.

boys between ages ten and thirteen, demonstrated that Gottschalk's content analysis method can be applied successfully to young adults and children for purposes of clinical assessment (Gleser et al., 1965; Gottlieb et al., 1967; Jacobson et al., 1973). Most recently this method has been applied to a stratified sample of 110 children selected from a white middle-class area for the purpose of obtaining normative scores (Gottschalk, 1974, 1975, 1976).

However, due to the existence of many diverse subcultures with their respective attitudes, beliefs, and customs, these pilot studies and the sample of white children restrict generalization of the results to but a segment of the children's population. Further sampling and studies of children's language behavior of various subcultures and ethnic groups may help explain the extent to which the normative scores of psychological states derived from the content analysis of their speech can be generalized and would thereby insure that the normative scores are more representative of the total population of children.

When collecting data from different ethnic groups, the effects of a number of factors have been shown to influence the results. One such factor is that of the interviewer's race. Most of the studies studying the racial influence of the interviewer have focused their attention on how much the interviewers affect performance and motivation. For instance, studies investigating the effects of white and black interviewers on black children revealed that an interviewer's race appears to affect performance when black children are performing cognitive tasks as opposed to performing motor skills (Katz et al., 1968; Kennedy and Vega, 1965).

Studies that report the effect of an interviewer's race on the psychological functionings of an interviewee have found that anxiety and hostility scores increased depending upon the interviewer's race and the situational variables (Katz et al., 1964; Baratz, 1967). Katz et al. (1964) found that the influence of the interviewer's race was minimal on black adolescents' hostility scores when they were given "neutral" verbal instructions with neutral instructions meaning that the nature of what was being tested was

not revealed to the subjects. But when using a "non-neutral" set of instructions given by black interviewers, hostility scores decreased with black subjects. Baratz (1967) found that black undergraduates reported more anxiety on Mandler and Sarason's Test Anxiety Questionnaire (1952) when they were tested by white interviewers than when they were tested by black interviewers.

However, Sattler (1970) has suggested that the critical factor seems to be the degree to which the interviewer involves himself in the testing situation. He indicates that standard instructions given to the subject in a school setting tend to minimize the effect of interviewer's race on results. Other investigators have found that the interviewer may be viewed by the subject as part of the teaching staff, thus further minimizing the interviewer's influence (Bryant et al., 1966).

Because of the possible influences of the variable, interviewer's race, the present study was designed with a twofold purpose: 1) to extend the investigation of speech content to black children and thus to obtain normative measures on four types of affective states and 2) to measure the effect of the interviewer's race on the black children's language content. Specifically, this study examined: 1) the affect score of black boys and girls over time for twelve grade levels; 2) the intercorrelations between affect scale scores; and 3) the main effect and interaction effects of the interviewer's race.

Design

The basic paradigm (Table 1) of this intra-black study for examining sex and grade level differences* and for testing interviewer's effects was an hierarchical design group within-treatment analysis of variance (Myers, 1972). By using this procedure, the main effects of grade, sex of subjects and interviewer's race were determinable. Interaction effects of grade and sex of subject, grade and interviewer's race and sex of subject and interviewer's race could also be examined. Further, by determining the main effect of grade

*Grade levels were used in the analyses as a factor rather than age so that the cell sizes would remain uniform.

Table 1

Analysis of Variance: Affective States

| Source | df |
|---|---|
| Between Interviewers | |
| Race | 1 |
| Interviewers/Race | 4 |
| Within Interviewers/Race | |
| Grade* | 5 |
| Race x Grade | 5 |
| Interviewers x Grade/Race | 20 |
| Sex | 1 |
| Race x Sex | 1 |
| Interviewers x Sex/Race | 4 |
| Grade x Sex | 5 |
| Race x Grade x Sex | 5 |
| Interviewers x Grade x Sex/Race | 20 |
| Subject/Interviewer x Grade x Sex/Race | 72 |

*Original twelve grade levels collapsed to 6 levels.

and the interaction effects of grade and sex of subject, and grade and interviewer's race, the necessary data for trend analyses were available.

Subjects

Two hundred and eighty-eight black children, ranging from the first through the twelfth grade and stratified for sex, were selected from a semi-integrated population. A list of schools that had a predominantly black population was provided by the Santa Ana School District, Santa Ana, California. Parent permission letters were distributed to students

in the classrooms. (Although it compromised the generalizability of the sample somewhat by getting the permission of parents,there was no other way to obtain the subjects.) Students who returned their signed letters were then classified according to race, grade, and sex by use of the school directory. An equal number of black female and black male children were randomly selected from this list for each of the twelve grade levels.

Independent Variables

Interviewer's race was the one factor varied in this study. Three white women and three black women selected from a group of college women who responded to an advertisement were used as interviewers. Attempts were made to minimize differences between the interviewers by keeping constant such factors as age, educational level, and general appearance. The six interviewers were either juniors or seniors in college with an average age of twenty-one. A neat and professional appearance was maintained by all interviewers.

Dependent Variables

The Gottschalk and Gleser content analysis system (1969a) was used for analyzing black children's speech content. This approach was selected because of its sophisticated classification system and objectivity. Also, it limited the involvement of the interviewer, reduced rater biases, and used neutral, standard instructions for eliciting speech, thus preventing malingering or falsifying on the part of the subject. In addition, it was easily administered, was designed to tap both conscious and unconscious emotional responses, and was readily scorable (i.e. could be scored by non-professional technicians according to standard procedures). Further, since many young children participated in this study, it was thought best to use this method which, as Bennett (1973) states, obtains the data in a very "natural" way.

Using the Gottschalk and Gleser method (1969a), the dependent variables selected for this study were the four affect scales and their subscales: anxiety total, death anxiety, mutilation anxiety, separation anxiety, guilt anxiety, shame anxiety, and diffuse anxiety; hostility outward total,

hostility outward-overt, and hostility outward-covert; hostility inward, and ambivalent hostility.

The subscale scores in this study were considered both as independent psychological components and as subcomponents of the major scale. Thus, a total of twelve affect variables were analyzed (Gottschalk and Gleser, 1969a). To obtain the final scores for the individual subscales, each score was computed by adding a 0.5 correction factor to the raw score, multiplying by 100, dividing by the number of words spoken and then taking the square root of the corrected score. The total scale scores were computed by the same process, only they contained, as the raw score, the sum of the weighted subscale scores.

Procedures

Interviewers were first trained to give the following instructions while omitting extraneous facial, bodily, and verbal cues that might influence the interviewee:

"My name is____. Please sit here (indicate where subject is supposed to sit.) I have a tape recorder here and here is a microphone. I would like you to speak into this microphone, please.

"This is a study of speaking and conversational habits. Upon a signal from me, I would like you to speak for five minutes about any interesting or dramatic life experience you may have had. Once you have started I will be here listening to you, but I would prefer not to reply to any questions you may feel like asking me until the five minute period is over. Do you have any questions you would like to ask me now before we start? Well, then you may begin."

(If the child is unable to respond, the following instructions are tried):

"I'll tell you what to do; try telling me any stories you like about yourself."

(If the child does not respond after about one minute, the instructions are further modified): "Try telling me any stories about any one you

know (pause) or, try telling me about any television program you have recently seen."

Once trained, each interviewer was randomly assigned two males and two females from each of the twelve grades. They then collected five-minute tape-recorded verbal samples from their assigned subjects. After the speech sample was recorded, each interviewer was instructed to ask the subject not to tell other children what he/she talked about.

Interviews were collected during the morning hours from 8-11. There was no specific grade order in which the children were interviewed, thus eliminating possible order effect.

Typescripts of the verbal samples were independently scored by two technicians for the affect variables. The procedure for scoring is outlined by Gottschalk and Gleser (1969b).

Hypotheses

Although a significant portion of this study was exploratory in nature, it was anticipated that certain results may occur. A list of hypotheses was therefore derived which has been inferred or found from the previous work with adults and white children's speech patterns.

1. Grade Effect. Based on Piaget's (1969) theory of cognitive development, together with Freud's (1933) theory of psychosexual development, it was predicted that there would be an increase of hostility-outward expressions in children's speech content as they approached and reached adolescence.

2. Sex Effect. Based on studies with adults (Gottschalk and Gleser, 1969a) it was expected that females would have significantly higher shame anxiety and separation anxiety scores than males; males would have significantly higher mutilation and death anxiety scores than females and males would have significantly higher hostility-outward scores than females.

3. Sex and Grade Effect. From theories of psychosexual development (Freud, 1933) together with societal sanction of male assertiveness and female non-assertiveness, it was hypothesized that as the children approached

adolescence, there would be a significantly greater increase in male hostility-outward scores than in female hostility-outward scores.

4. Effect of Interviewer's Race. It was hypothesized that with minimal interviewer involvement, the interviewer's race would not have a significant effect on the magnitude of affective states of black children's verbal behavior.

5. Interrelationship between Affect Scores. Based on analysis of adult scores (Gottschalk and Gleser, 1969a) and white children's scores (Gottschalk, 1975, 1976), it was expected that hostility outward scores would correlate positively with ambivalent hostility; shame anxiety would correlate positively with hostility inward scores, and guilt anxiety would correlate positively with hostility-outward scores.

## Results

Only two hundred and seventy-six subjects' verbal scores were used in these final analyses. To compensate for those cells that were empty because of these missing data, the twelve grade levels, representing the factor grade, were collapsed to six levels: grades 1 and 2 = Level 1; grades 3 and 4 = Level 2; grades 5 and 6 = Level 3; grades 7 and 8 = Level 4; grades 9 and 10 = Level 5; grades 11 and 12 = Level 6 (see Table 1).

Main effects. A significant effect of grade was found for total hostility outward scores ($F = 4.01$, df 5/20, $p < .01$) (see Figure 1); for hostility outward subscales overt ($F = 3.98$, df 5/20, $p < .01$) and covert ($F = 4.39$, df 5/20, $p < .01$) (see Figure 2); and for the subscale guilt anxiety ($F = 2.73$, df 5/20, $p < .05$) (see Figure 3). An effect of interviewer's race on total anxiety scores ($F = 9.29$, df 1/4, $p < .04$) was also found to be significant. There were no other significant main effects for grade, sex of subject or interviewer's race.

Interaction effects. An effect was found to be significant for grade by sex of subject on ambivalent hostility scores ($F = 3.32$, df 5/20, $p < .02$) and guilt anxiety scores ($F = 3.05$, df 5/20, $p < .03$). A significant effect of grade by interviewer's race on total anxiety scores was found ($F = 3.05$, df 5/20, $p < .03$). Also, a triple interaction effect of grade by sex of

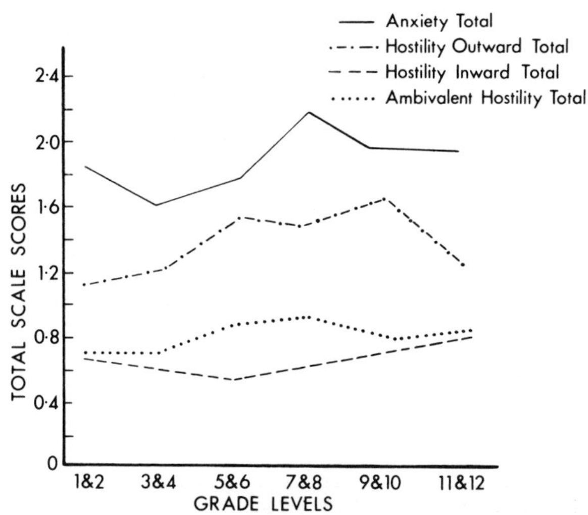


Fig. 1 RELATIONSHIP OF TOTAL SCALE SCORES FOR ANXIETY, HOSTILITY OUTWARD, HOSTILITY INWARD AND AMBIVALENT HOSTILITY TO GRADE LEVEL OF BLACK CHILDREN

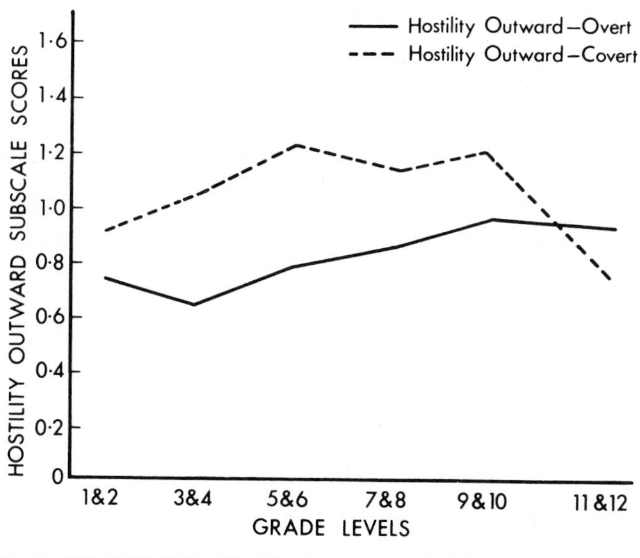


Fig. 2 RELATIONSHIP OF HOSTILITY OUTWARD SUBSCALE SCORES TO GRADE LEVEL OF BLACK CHILDREN

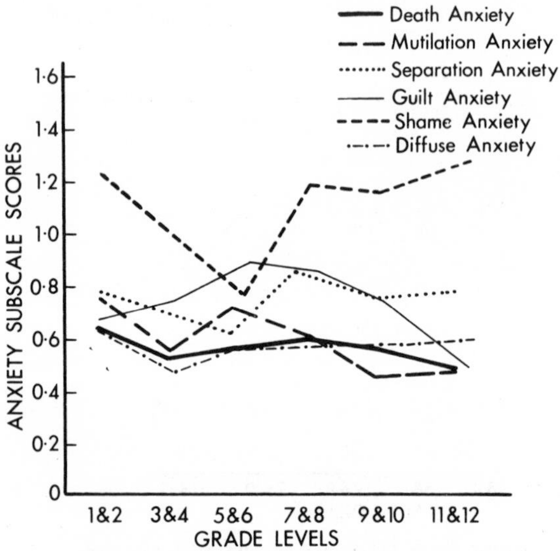


Fig 3 RELATIONSHIP OF ANXIETY SUBSCALE SCORES TO GRADE LEVEL OF BLACK CHILDREN

subject by interviewer's race was found to be significant on the subscale overt hostility outward ($F = 2.74$, df 5/20, $p < .05$).

Trend Analysis. One of the purposes of this study was to examine the children's scores over time. A trend analysis was thus applied for those effects that were found to be significant with respect to the factor grade. It was found that overt hostility outward scores (see Figure 2) had a significant linear increase with age ($F = 15.99$, df 5/270, $p < .0001$), whereas covert hostility outward scores had a significant quadratic effect with grade levels ($F = 10.63$, df 5/270, $p < .002$), where the maximum was between grades five through ten. Total hostility outward scores (see Figure 1) were found to have both a significant linear effect ($F = 4.73$, df 5/270, $p < .03$) and significant quadratic effect ($F = 7.63$, df 5/270, $p < .006$) with the minimum beginning in the first and second grades and rising to a maximum around the ninth and tenth grades.

Since there was also found to be a significant triple interaction

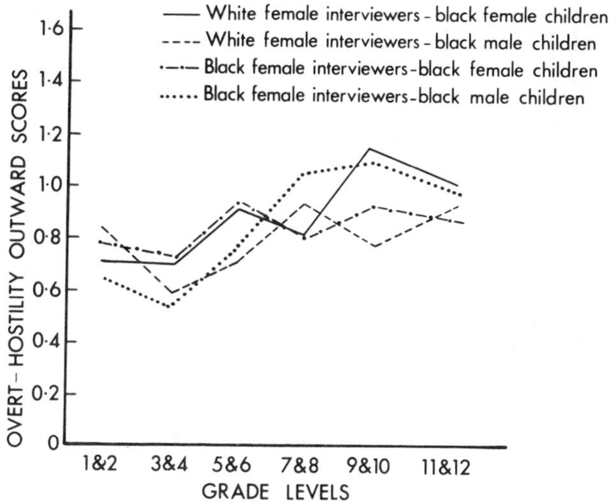


Fig. 4 TRIPLE INTERACTION OF BLACK CHILDREN'S GRADE LEVEL AND SEX BY RACE OF INTERVIEWER ON OVERT-HOSTILITY OUTWARD SCORES

effect with overt hostility outward scores, a trend analysis was made with respect to this interaction. Graphic representations were first made to determine whether comparisons between the sex of the subject for each interviewer's race or between the interviewer's race for each sex of the subject would best show possibilities of interpretation. It was decided, because of a more consistent curve, that looking at trends between interviewer's race for each subject's sex was the more profitable choice (see Figure 4). Results revealed that black male children interviewed by black female interviewers had a significant linear increase with age for overt hostility outward scores ($F = 9.43$, df 5/63, $p < .003$), while black female children had a significant linear increase in overt hostility outward scores when interviewed by white female interviewers ($F = 6.40$, df 5/63, $p < .01$).

The subscale guilt anxiety (see Figure 3) was found to have a significant quadratic effect with grade ($F = 14.34$, df 5/270, $p < .0001$), but since the results also revealed a significant interaction effect of grade

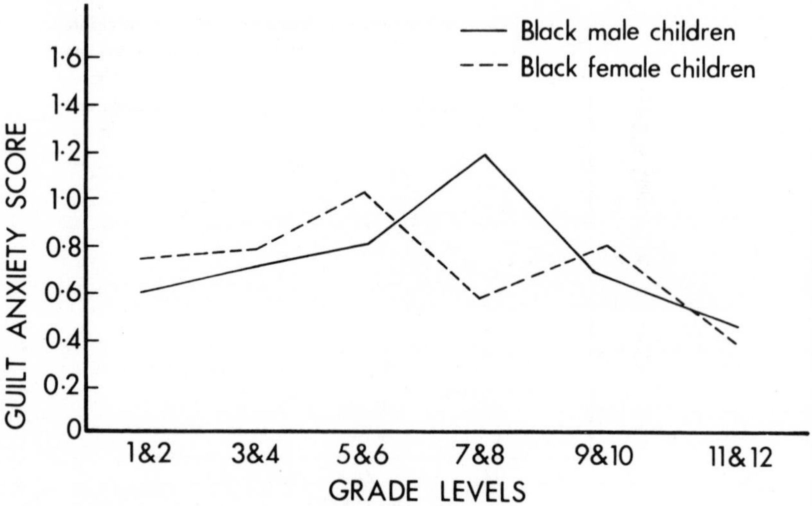


Fig. 5 INTERACTION OF GRADE LEVEL BY SEX OF CHILD ON GUILT ANXIETY SCORES

by sex of subject, trend analysis for males and females was made separately (see Figure 5). Males showed a significant quadratic effect ($F = 11.47$, df 5/131, $p < .001$), with a sharp increase found in the seventh and eight grades. Females had a slightly significant quadratic effect ($F = 3.89$, 5/133, $p < .05$), with the maximum peaking in the fifth and sixth grades and then a less than maximum peak in the ninth and tenth grades.

A trend analysis of the results, showing a significant interaction of grade by sex on ambivalent hostility scores (see Figure 6), revealed that, again, males had a sharp increase in the seventh and eight grades resulting in a significant quadratic effect ($F = 9.81$, df 5/131, $p < .003$). Females, on the other hand, did not appear to have a particular pattern of response.

A trend analysis on the significant interaction of grade and interviewer's race on total anxiety scores (Figure 7) revealed a significant quadratic effect for scores obtained by black interviewers ($F = 7.85$, df 5/133, $p < .006$) with the maximum around the ninth and tenth grades. A

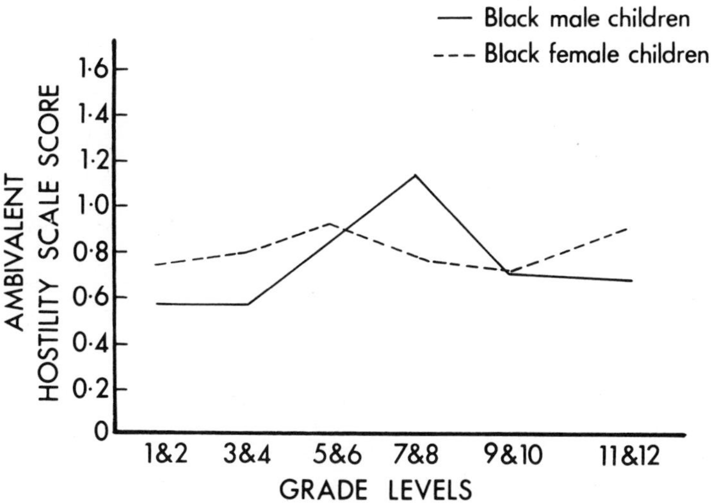


Fig.6 INTERACTION OF GRADE LEVEL BY SEX OF CHILD ON AMBIVALENT HOSTILITY SCALE SCORES

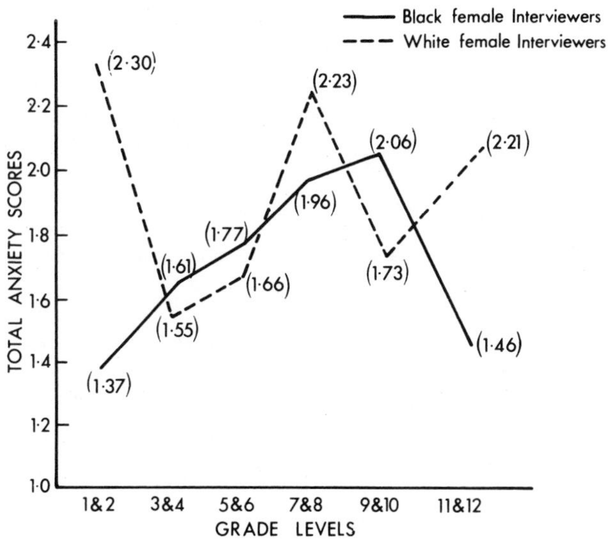


Fig.7 INTERACTION OF BLACK CHILDREN'S GRADE LEVEL BY RACE OF INTERVIEWER ON TOTAL ANXIETY SCORES

significant quadratic effect was also found for scores obtained by white interviewers ($F = 4.23$, df 5/131, $p < .04$). The pattern of this curve fluctuates too much to cite a systematic rise from a minimum to a maximum level.

Intercorrelations of Affect Scale Scores. In addition to the analysis of variance of scores, intercorrelations between affect scores were examined to determine whether or not the results go in the expected direction as was found with adults and white children's scores. Tables 2, 3, 4, and 5 list the intercorrelations and those found to be significant for black and white children, respectively.

Percentiles. Because a portion of this study was to provide normative data, percentiles of the black children's scores are given in the Appendix (see Tables 6-16). Tables 6 and 7 show the percentiles for the total and subscale scores for all 276 black children. Tables 8 and 9 show total and subscale percentile scores for each sex. Table 10 lists the percentile scores for the affect scales according to the race of the interviewer. Tables 11-16 give the distribution of mean anxiety and hostility total and subscale scores divided into four subgroups: for all the black children (N=276); for all the black children according to sex; and for all black children according to the race of the interviewer.

Discussion

The intention of this study was to extend and to provide normative or standardized data for a method of analyzing black children's affective states as they are manifested in their language behavior.

Because this study focused on a particular subculture some potential problematic methodological factors and their possible influence on the normative scores needed to be considered. One factor, that of the interviewer's race, was controlled. Another factor concerned the language behavior of black children. In particular, there has been an on-going controversy centering on whether Black English is another language or simply a dialect of American English. In view of this controversy, it was necessary to consider the possible effects of these language differences on content analysis measures. For instance, any differences between the black and white children's

Table 2

Intercorrelations of the Affect Scores of Black Children (N = 276)

| Affect Measures | Hostility Outward | | | Hostility Inward | Ambivalent Hostility |
|---|---|---|---|---|---|
| | Total | Overt | Covert | | |
| Anxiety Total | 0.40*** | 0.29*** | 0.36*** | 0.45*** | 0.42*** |
| Anxiety Subscales: | | | | | |
| Death | 0.27*** | -0.01 | 0.35*** | 0.16** | 0.11 |
| Mutilation | 0.19*** | 0.10 | 0.20*** | 0.20*** | 0.23*** |
| Separation | 0.20*** | 0.01 | 0.24*** | 0.14** | 0.22*** |
| Guilt | 0.63**** | 0.29*** | 0.65**** | -0.06 | 0.57**** |
| Shame | -0.04 | 0.19*** | -0.12* | 0.55**** | 0.04 |
| Diffuse | 0.02 | 0.13** | -0.01 | 0.08 | 0.11 |
| Hostility Outward Total | | | | 0.02 | 0.31*** |
| Hostility Outward Subscales: | | | | | |
| Overt | | | 0.19** | 0.24*** | 0.31*** |
| Covert | | | | -0.09 | 0.24*** |
| Hostility Inward Total | | | | | 0.15** |
| Ambivalent Hostility Total | | | | | |

* = p<.05
** = p<.01
*** = p<.001
**** = p<.0001

Table 3

Intercorrelations of Anxiety Subscale Scores of Black Children (N = 276)

| Anxiety Subscales | Death | Mutilation | Separation | Guilt | Shame | Diffuse |
|---|---|---|---|---|---|---|
| Death | | 0.19*** | 0.35*** | 0.07 | 0.08 | 0.11 |
| Mutilation | | | 0.23*** | 0.14** | 0.04 | 0.11 |
| Separation | | | | 0.08 | -0.02 | 0.12* |
| Guilt | | | | | -0.05 | -0.04 |
| Shame | | | | | | 0.24*** |
| Diffuse | | | | | | |

* = p<.05
** = p<.01
*** = p<.001

Table 4

Intercorrelations of the Affect Scores of White Children (N = 102)

| Affect Measures | Hostility Outward | | | Hostility Inward | Ambivalent Hostility |
|---|---|---|---|---|---|
| | Total | Overt | Covert | | |
| Anxiety Total | 0.45** | 0.18 | 0.49** | 0.61*** | 0.49** |
| Anxiety Subscales: | | | | | |
| Death | 0.40** | -0.01 | 0.55** | 0.18 | 0.27* |
| Mutilation | 0.24* | 0.00 | 0.35** | 0.52** | 0.29† |
| Separation | 0.29†† | 0.12 | 0.26* | 0.45** | 0.45** |
| Guilt | 0.49** | 0.48** | 0.40** | 0.10 | 0.37** |
| Shame | 0.10 | 0.15 | 0.10 | 0.32** | 0.18 |
| Diffuse | 0.29†† | 0.22† | 0.24* | 0.28†† | 0.24* |
| Hostility Outward Total | | | | 0.05 | 0.32** |
| Hostility Outward Subscales: | | | | | |
| Overt | | | 0.14 | 0.03 | 0.31** |
| Covert | | | | 0.09 | 0.23† |
| Hostility Inward Total | | | | | 0.40** |
| Ambivalent Hostility Total | | | | | |

† = p<.03    * = p<.01
†† = p<.003    ** = p<.001
*** = p<.0001

Table 5

Intercorrelations of Anxiety Subscale Scores of White Children (N = 102)

| Anxiety Subscales | Death | Mutilation | Separation | Guilt | Shame | Diffuse |
|---|---|---|---|---|---|---|
| Death | | 0.27** | 0.24** | 0.16 | 0.06 | 0.20* |
| Mutilation | | | 0.37*** | 0.05 | 0.00 | 0.19* |
| Separation | | | | 0.09 | 0,07 | 0.15 |
| Guilt | | | | | 0.17 | 0.23** |
| Shame | | | | | | 0.25** |
| Diffuse | | | | | | |

* = p<.05
** = p<.01
*** = p<.001

verbal sample scores could be entirely due to peculiarities of idiomatic the or syntactic structures in different cultures. Given the fact that the children being tested were selected from an integrated neighborhood, it was assumed that "strong dialects," as might be found more readily in the South and other areas, would not be predominant, if present at all. In addition, it was thought that grammatical distinctions or differences would not significantly effect results because syntax or grammar does not have, with respect to the measurement method used in this study (Gottschalk and Gleser, 1969a), a direct relationship with the kinds and intensities of the various affective states measured. Grammatical structure functions only to delineate the clauses and phrases which are the scorable units. In short, it is the thematic content, sometimes referred to as the semantic content, that is scored, not the grammatical structure. As an example, a Black English statement may be expressed as, "I be fighting him all the time." In Standard English, the expression may appear as "I am always fighting with him." The item scored is "fighting."

Because it is the thematic content that is scored, difficulties may arise if the meaning of a word is different because of some unusual cultural customs or if the use of slang makes the meaning of what is said ambiguous. If there are cultural differences and these differences are mirrored in language behavior, there is a possibility of misinterpreting words as hostile or anxious when , in fact, the words were not meant to function in such a way.

This idiomatic factor was dealt with in two ways. Gottschalk and Gleser (1969a) have suggested that when there is a question about the affective nature of any word, the scorer may then look at the context in which the word is spoken. If this did not resolve the problem, the use of a Black Glossary (Roberts, 1971) was available. However, problems due to either linguistic structure or use of ambiguous slang did not arise in this study. Because there were no problems with respect to the use of Black English or slang does not mean to say that these children do not speak Black English or use slang. It may be that these black children

speak in Black English but do so more at home or with their peers (Houston, 1969, 1970). They may have restricted themselves to speaking mostly in Standard English because they gave their speech samples in a school setting.

However that may be, in support of the assumption that the Gottschalk content analysis method has potential transcultural use, studies using the method may be found in German (Flegel, 1967; Schöfer, 1974) and Spanish (Delgado, unpublished, 1975). Reports have also shown its usefulness in Australia (Bennett, unpublished doctoral thesis, 1973) and in Canada (Cleghorn et al., 1970).

In a more general light, since validity and reliability studies with the adult population appeared to corroborate the fact that language behavior and intrapsychic states were closely related, it was reasonable to assume, conditionally, that the same relationship held true for the children's population. However, it was understood that there was a need for further validation studies to actually prove such assumptions held true for children*

In the first analysis of the data, which examined grade, sex of subject and effect of interviewer's race, the results confirmed the hypothesis with respect to grade levels that there would be a significant increase in outward hostility scores as children approached and reached adolescence. The hypotheses about sex differences and the interaction effects between grade and sex of the subject, however, were not confirmed. In addition to those hypothesized results, it was found that guilt anxiety, ambivalent hostility, and overt hostility outward scores significantly related either with grade level, with the interaction of grade by sex of subject or with the interaction of grade by sex of subject by interviewer's race.

Trend analysis was applied to the data to determine the changes over time of the significant effects which were found with the factor grade level. Results showed there were several significant quadratic trends. This rise

---

*It is not the purpose of this study to validate these assumptions but rather to obtain normative measures of black children's affective states under the conditions of this study.

in the middle grades which generally represents the ages eleven through fourteen, suggests that there are radical changes in the psychological makeup of these children during these years. Piaget (1969) called this early adolescent stage the "formal operatory level" wherein there appears a "spontaneous development of an experimental spirit." Freud (1933) described early adolescence as the stage wherein the child's fears of castration or rejection are lessened. It may be that the combination of these two processes in the normal child at this age provides him the impetus to express more outward and varied behavior. It appears, at least, in early adolescence of normal black children that affective changes occur about the same time as a certain cognitive state emerges. It also appears that as cognitive growth is measured through language behavior, so, too, can affective changes. It is obvious that further research is necessary before making any definite statements about their relation. But if affective states were found to correlate significantly with stages of cognitive development such findings would provide a fruitful and valuable source for understanding and predicting such things as good or problematic social and psychological adjustment at home and at school, as well as good or poor academic achievement. Such research now seems possible with the use of the content analysis method.

A second analysis showed that controlling for the interviewer's race is necessary when measuring anxiety states, but is not necessary when measuring for hostility states. The mean scores showed that the subscale shame anxiety (i.e. feelings of inadequacy or embarrassment) may have contributed more than other subscales to the increase in total anxiety scores of those children interviewed by white interviewers. It may be that controlling for this subcategory of anxiety alone would lessen the effect of the interviewer's race.

Additional analysis revealed that the intercorrelations of affect scores for these black children were consistent with those found among adults and white children's affect scores. Implications of these findings indicate that interrelationships among the affect scales do not appear to change be-

tween subcultures giving the scales greater transcultural potential.

In general, this study provides additional normative data for the content analysis of children's speech. Combined with the results from the white children's study (Gottschalk, 1975, 1976), it appears that the various psychological states of children can productively be studied through the content analysis of their speech behavior. Further studies will examine groups of children from other subcultures and ethnic groups, including Mexican-American children and emotionally disturbed children from both an inpatient and outpatient psychiatric clinic.

## References

Baratz, S.S. Effects of race of experimenter, instructions, and comparison population upon level of reported anxiety in Negro subjects. J. of Personal. and Soc. Psychol. 7, 194-196 (1967).

Bennett, M.D.J. The emotional response of husbands to suicide attempts by their wives. Unpublished doctoral dissertation, University of Sydney (1973).

Bryant, E.C., Gardner, I., Jr., and Goldman, M. Responses on racial attitudes as affected by interviewers of different ethnic groups. J. of Soc. Psychol. 70, 95-100 (1966).

Cleghorn, J.M., Peterfy, G., Pinter, E.J., and Pattee, C.J. Verbal anxiety and the beta adrenergic receptors: a facilitating mechanism? J. of Nerv. and Ment. Dis. 151, 266-272 (1970).

Delgado, J. Effect of stimulation of cerebral implanted electrodes on the content of human speech. Unpublished manuscript, Madrid (1975).

Dollard, J., and Auld, F., Jr. Scoring Human Motives: A Manual. Yale University Press, New Haven (1959).

Flegel, H. Erassung schizophrener morbiditatsverlaude mit Gottschalks verbaler stichprobe, verglichen mit Wittenborns Rating Scales und der BPRS. Zeitschrift fur Psychotherapie und Medizinische Psychologie 5, 186-194 (1967).

Freud, S. New Introductory Lectures on Psycho-analysis. W.W. Norton and Co., New York (1933).

Freud, S. The Problem of Anxiety. W.W. Norton and Co., New York (1936).

Gleser, G.C., Gottschalk, L.A., Fox, R., and Lippert, W. Immediate changes in affect with chlordiazepoxide in juvenile delinquent boys. Arch. Gen. Psychiat. 13, 291-295 (1965).

Gottlieb, A., Gleser, G.C., and Gottschalk, L.A. Verbal and physiological responses to hypnotic suggestion of attitudes. Psychosom. Med. 24, 172-183 (1967)

Gottschalk, L.A. A hope scale applicable to verbal samples. Arch. Gen. Psychiat. 30, 779-785 (1974).

Gottschalk, L.A. Differences in the content of speech of girls and boys ages six to sixteen, in Mental Health and Children, Vol 3. D.V. Sankar, ed. PJD Publications Ltd, New York (1976).

Gottschalk, L.A. Children's speech as a source of data toward the measurement of psychological states. J. of Youth and Adoles. 5, 11-36 (1976).

Gottschalk, L.A., and Gleser, G.C. The Measurement of Psychological States Through the Content Analysis of Verbal Behavior. University of California Press, Berkeley (1969a).

Gottschalk, L.A., Winget, C.N., and Gleser, G.C. Manual of Instructions for Using the Gottschalk-Gleser Content Analysis Scales: Anxiety, Hostility, and Social Alienation-Personal Disorganization. University of California Press, Berkeley (1969b).

Hafner, A.J., and Kaplan, A.M. Hostility content analysis of the Rorschach and TAT. J. of Proj. Tech. 24, 137-143 (1960).

Houston, S.H. A sociolinguistic consideration of the black English of children in northern Florida. Language, 45, 599-607 (1969).

Houston, S.H. A reexamination of some assumptions about the language of the disadvantaged child. Child Devel. 41, 947-963 (1970).

Jacobson, E., Stolzoff, G.E., and Uliana, R.L. Evaluation and comparison of group therapeutic techniques for inpatient and outpatient for latency

age boys. Paper presented at the meeting of the Western Psychological Association, Anaheim, California (1973).

Katz, I., Robinson, J.M., Epps, E.G., and Waly, P. Effects of race of experimenter and test vs. neutral instructions on the expression of hostility in Negro boys. J. of Soc. Issues, 20, 54-60 (1964).

Mandler, G., and Sarason, S.B. A study of anxiety and learning. J. of Ab. and Soc. Psychol. 47, 166-173 (1952).

Myers, J.L. Fundamentals of Experimental Design, 2nd ed. Allyn and Bacon, Boston (1972).

Piaget, J., and Inhelder, B. The Psychology of the Child. Basic Books, Inc., New York (1969).

Roberts, H.E. The Third Ear: A Black Glossary. The Better Speech Institute of America, Inc., Chicago (1971).

Sattler, J.M. Racial "experimenter effects" in experimentation, testing, interviewing and psychotherapy. Psychol. Bull. 73, 137-160 (1970).

Schöfer, G. Die Gottschalk-Gleser inhaltsanalyse: die messung von aggressivitat und angst in sprachprohen. Auszugweise Ubersetzung aus: 4.u.5., unveroffenthchtes Manuskript, Hamburg (1974).

Wolman, R.N., Lewis, W.C., and King, M. The development of the language of emotions: I. theoretical and methodological introduction. J. of Genet. Psychol. 120, 167-176 (1972).

Table 6

Percentile Scores* for Affect Scales of Black Children (N = 276)

| Percentile | Anxiety Total | Hostility Outward | | | Hostility Inward | Ambivalent Hostility |
|---|---|---|---|---|---|---|
| | | Overt | Covert | Total | | |
| 95........ | 3.32 | 1.69 | 2.54 | 2.72 | 1.34 | 1.62 |
| 90........ | 2.97 | 1.49 | 2.09 | 2.36 | 1.14 | 1.39 |
| 85........ | 2.60 | 1.30 | 1.82 | 2.19 | 0.96 | 1.21 |
| 80........ | 2.47 | 1.18 | 1.57 | 2.01 | 0.83 | 1.08 |
| 75........ | 2.31 | 1.10 | 1.45 | 1.76 | 0.75 | 0.99 |
| 70........ | 2.19 | 0.97 | 1.31 | 1.61 | 0.69 | 0.87 |
| 60........ | 1.99 | 0.84 | 1.08 | 1.42 | 0.58 | 0.72 |
| 50........ | 1.81 | 0.70 | 0.84 | 1.26 | 0.51 | 0.59 |
| 40........ | 1.53 | 0.61 | 0.68 | 1.04 | 0.46 | 0.49 |
| 30........ | 1.28 | 0.52 | 0.56 | 0.81 | 0.40 | 0.43 |
| 25........ | 1.19 | 0.47 | 0.50 | 0.72 | 0.37 | 0.40 |
| 20........ | 1.05 | 0.43 | 0.46 | 0.64 | 0.34 | 0.37 |
| 15........ | 0.86 | 0.41 | 0.43 | 0.58 | 0.31 | 0.35 |
| 10........ | 0.71 | 0.35 | 0.39 | 0.49 | 0.38 | 0.32 |
| 5........ | 0.51 | 0.30 | 0.32 | 0.43 | 0.26 | 0.29 |
| Mean.... | 1.82 | 0.83 | 1.07 | 1.35 | 0.63 | 0.76 |
| s.d..... | 0.89 | 0.44 | 0.69 | 0.74 | 0.37 | 0.52 |

These scores are for Black and White interviewers combined.

Table 7

Percentile Scores for the Anxiety Subscales of Black Children (N = 276)*

| Percentile | Death | Mutilation | Separation | Guilt | Shame | Diffuse |
|---|---|---|---|---|---|---|
| 95..... | 1.28 | 1.52 | 1.52 | 1.88 | 2.63 | 1.10 |
| 90..... | 0.97 | 1.09 | 1.30 | 1.36 | 2.07 | 0.92 |
| 75..... | 0.68 | 0.67 | 0.94 | 0.87 | 1.39 | 0.64 |
| 50..... | 0.43 | 0.45 | 0.65 | 0.58 | 0.84 | 0.46 |
| 25..... | 0.31 | 0 33 | 0.46 | 0.41 | 0.51 | 0.35 |
| 10..... | 0.26 | 0.27 | 0.36 | 0.31 | 0.34 | 0.28 |
| 5..... | 0.25 | 0.25 | 0.31 | 0.27 | 0.29 | 0.27 |
| Mean... | 0.56 | 0.59 | 0.76 | 0.74 | 1.10 | 0.56 |
| s.d.... | 0.35 | 0.40 | 0.40 | 0.51 | 0.83 | 0.31 |

*These scores are for Black and White interviewers combined.

Table 8

Percentile Scores for the Anxiety Scale of Black Children by Race of Interviewer*

| Percentile | Anxiety Total | | Anxiety Subscales | | | | | | | | | | | |
|---|---|---|---|---|---|---|---|---|---|---|---|---|---|---|
| | | | Death | | Mutilation | | Separation | | Guilt | | Shame | | Diffuse | |
| | B | W | B | W | B | W | B | W | B | W | B | W | B | W |
| 95........ | 3.12 | 3.35 | 1.25 | 1.28 | 1.54 | 1.44 | 1.61 | 1.46 | 1.88 | 1.87 | 2.11 | 2.93 | 1.08 | 1.30 |
| 90........ | 2.99 | 2.90 | 0.92 | 1.00 | 1.06 | 1.09 | 1.31 | 1.27 | 1.48 | 1.18 | 1.80 | 2.46 | 0.86 | 0.97 |
| 85........ | 2.56 | 2.59 | 0.82 | 0.87 | 0.82 | 0.83 | 1.11 | 1.10 | 1.25 | 1.04 | 1.54 | 2.02 | 0.77 | 0.87 |
| 80........ | 2.37 | 2.48 | 0.76 | 0.78 | 0.73 | 0.71 | 1.03 | 1.02 | 1.07 | 0.89 | 1.46 | 1.68 | 0.68 | 0.70 |
| 70........ | 2.06 | 2.23 | 0.61 | 0.59 | 0.61 | 0.58 | 0.85 | 0.90 | 0.80 | 0.74 | 1.18 | 1.36 | 0.60 | 0.58 |
| 60........ | 1.85 | 2.08 | 0.49 | 0.48 | 0.51 | 0.50 | 0.75 | 0.76 | 0.67 | 0.62 | 0.97 | 1.14 | 0.52 | 0.50 |
| 50........ | 1.65 | 1.92 | 0.43 | 0.43 | 0.45 | 0.44 | 0.63 | 0.68 | 0.59 | 0.57 | 0.80 | 0.87 | 0.46 | 0.45 |
| 40........ | 1.45 | 1.67 | 0.40 | 0.38 | 0.41 | 0.38 | 0.57 | 0.59 | 0.49 | 0.48 | 0.64 | 0.74 | 0.42 | 0.40 |
| 30........ | 1.16 | 1.45 | 0.34 | 0.32 | 0.36 | 0.34 | 0.50 | 0.48 | 0.45 | 0.42 | 0.55 | 0.58 | 0.38 | 0.36 |
| 20........ | 0.92 | 1.20 | 0.31 | 0.30 | 0.32 | 0.30 | 0.42 | 0.43 | 0.39 | 0.35 | 0.44 | 0.48 | 0.34 | 0.31 |
| 15........ | 0.79 | 0.96 | 0.29 | 0.28 | 0.29 | 0.28 | 0.40 | 0.41 | 0.34 | 0.32 | 0.39 | 0.39 | 0.31 | 0.30 |
| 10........ | 0.63 | 0.73 | 0.27 | 0.26 | 0.28 | 0.26 | 0.36 | 0.36 | 0.32 | 0.30 | 0.35 | 0.34 | 0.29 | 0.27 |
| 5........ | 0.50 | 0.56 | 0.25 | 0.25 | 0.26 | 0.25 | 0.31 | 0.31 | 0.28 | 0.26 | 0.29 | 0.28 | 0.27 | 0.26 |
| Mean.... | 1.72 | 1.93 | 0.56 | 0.56 | 0.59 | 0.59 | 0.76 | 0.76 | 0.78 | 0.70 | 0.99 | 1.20 | 0.55 | 0.56 |
| s.d..... | 0.85 | 0.91 | 0.35 | 0.36 | 0.39 | 0.41 | 0.41 | 0.39 | 0.56 | 0.47 | 0.68 | 0.96 | 0.29 | 0.33 |

*B = Average for Three Black Interviewers (N = 139); W = Average for Three White Interviewers (N = 137).

Table 9

Percentile Scores for the Affect Scales of Black Male (N = 137) and Black Female (N = 139) Children*

| Percentile | Anxiety Total | | Hostility Outward | | | | | | Hostility Inward | | Ambivalent Hostility | |
|---|---|---|---|---|---|---|---|---|---|---|---|---|
| | | | Overt | | Covert | | Total | | | | | |
| | M | F | M | F | M | F | M | F | M | F | M | F |
| 95........ | 3.13 | 3.36 | 1.72 | 1.66 | 2.51 | 2.53 | 2.75 | 2.65 | 1.33 | 1.35 | 1.62 | 1.57 |
| 90........ | 2.70 | 3.06 | 1.48 | 1.50 | 2.16 | 2.08 | 2.38 | 2.36 | 1.14 | 1.13 | 1.42 | 1.26 |
| 85........ | 2.48 | 2.77 | 1.29 | 1.30 | 1.83 | 1.81 | 2.18 | 2.19 | 0.96 | 0.95 | 1.34 | 1.11 |
| 80........ | 2.38 | 2.53 | 1.18 | 1.14 | 1.59 | 1.56 | 1.96 | 2.09 | 0.88 | 0.77 | 1.17 | 1.07 |
| 70........ | 2.18 | 2.20 | 0.96 | 1.00 | 1.25 | 1.32 | 1.59 | 1.60 | 0.72 | 0.67 | 0.81 | 0.90 |
| 60........ | 1.99 | 1.99 | 0.80 | 0.88 | 1.03 | 1.10 | 1.43 | 1.54 | 0.59 | 0.57 | 0.68 | 0.75 |
| 50........ | 1.81 | 1.80 | 0.65 | 0.73 | 0.83 | 0.87 | 1.20 | 1.27 | 0.52 | 0.50 | 0.55 | 0.62 |
| 40........ | 1.56 | 1.53 | 0.56 | 0.66 | 0.61 | 0.72 | 0.96 | 1.09 | 0.47 | 0.46 | 0.47 | 0.54 |
| 30........ | 1.33 | 1.22 | 0.47 | 0.58 | 0.50 | 0.62 | 0.77 | 0.84 | 0.40 | 0.39 | 0.41 | 0.45 |
| 20........ | 1.14 | 0.91 | 0.41 | 0.45 | 0.44 | 0.49 | 0.59 | 0.69 | 0.35 | 0.34 | 0.35 | 0.40 |
| 15........ | 0.93 | 0.82 | 0.38 | 0.43 | 0.42 | 0.46 | 0.53 | 0.63 | 0.31 | 0.31 | 0.33 | 0.36 |
| 10........ | 0.61 | 0.71 | 0.34 | 0.39 | 0.35 | 0.43 | 0.45 | 0.55 | 0.28 | 0.28 | 0.31 | 0.34 |
| 5........ | 0.50 | 0.56 | 0.29 | 0.30 | 0.30 | 0.35 | 0.37 | 0.45 | 0.26 | 0.26 | 0.28 | 0.29 |
| Mean.... | 1.80 | 1.84 | 0.81 | 0.85 | 1.04 | 1.10 | 1.32 | 1.38 | 0.65 | 0.61 | 0.74 | 0.79 |
| s.d. | 0.80 | 0.96 | 0.46 | 0.42 | 0.70 | 0.69 | 0.74 | 0.73 | 0.39 | 0.34 | 0.48 | 0.56 |

*These scores are for the Black and White interviewers combined.

Table 10

Percentile Scores for the Anxiety Subscales of Black Male (N = 137) and Black Female (N = 139) Children*

| Percentile | Death | | Mutilation | | Separation | | Guilt | | Shame | | Diffuse | |
|---|---|---|---|---|---|---|---|---|---|---|---|---|
| | M | F | M | F | M | F | M | F | M | F | M | F |
| 95........ | 1.16 | 1.46 | 1.68 | 1.01 | 1.44 | 1.71 | 1.91 | 1.48 | 2.51 | 2.93 | 1.09 | 1.11 |
| 90........ | 0.92 | 1.00 | 1.29 | 0.80 | 1.24 | 1.37 | 1.52 | 1.27 | 2.07 | 2.07 | 0.88 | 1.00 |
| 75........ | 0.61 | 0.71 | 0.70 | 0.63 | 0.75 | 0.92 | 0.86 | 0.88 | 1.35 | 1.46 | 0.62 | 0.65 |
| 50........ | 0.40 | 0.46 | 0.44 | 0.45 | 0.69 | 0.62 | 0.56 | 0.59 | 0.78 | 0.94 | 0.42 | 0.49 |
| 25........ | 0.31 | 0.32 | 0.32 | 0.33 | 0.47 | 0.45 | 0.39 | 0.43 | 0.47 | 0.58 | 0.32 | 0.38 |
| 10........ | 0.26 | 0.27 | 0.27 | 0.27 | 0.36 | 0.36 | 0.31 | 0.30 | 0.31 | 0.37 | 0.27 | 0.30 |
| 5........ | 0.25 | 0.25 | 0.26 | 0.25 | 0.31 | 0.30 | 0.27 | 0.27 | 0.28 | 0.31 | 0.26 | 0.28 |
| Mean.... | 0.53 | 0.59 | 0.63 | 0.55 | 0.77 | 0.75 | 0.74 | 0.73 | 1.01 | 1.18 | 0.52 | 0.59 |
| s.d..... | 0.34 | 0.36 | 0.45 | 0.35 | 0.38 | 0.42 | 0.55 | 0.48 | 0.76 | 0.90 | 0.27 | 0.34 |

*These scores are for the Black and White interviewers combined.

Table 11

Average Affect Scores from Subgroups of Black Children for Black and White Interviewers Combined

| Subgroups | N | Death | Mutilation | Separation | Guilt | Shame | Diffuse |
|---|---|---|---|---|---|---|---|
| Grades 0-3 | 64 | 1.71 (0.95) | 0.69 (0.34) | 0.95 (0.57) | 1.09 (0.64) | 0.61 (0.38) | 0.68 (0.40) |
| Grades 4-6 | 72 | 1.68 (0.77) | 0.75 (0.44) | 1.19 (0.76) | 1.40 (0.80) | 0.56 (0.29) | 0.76 (0.47) |
| Grades 7-9 | 71 | 2.04 (0.95) | 0.94 (0.51) | 1.16 (0.70) | 1.51 (0.76) | 0.64 (0.37) | 0.86 (0.56) |
| Grades 10-12 | 69 | 1.84 (0.84) | 0.92 (0.40) | 0.96 (0.70) | 1.36 (0.67) | 0.72 (0.43) | 0.74 (0.63) |
| All Grades, 1-12 | 276 | 1.82 (0.89) | 0.83 (0.44) | 1.07 (0.69) | 1.35 (0.74) | 0.63 (0.37) | 0.76 (0.52) |

Note: (    ) = Standard Deviation

Table 12

Average Anxiety Subscales Scores for Subgroups of Black Children for Black and White Interviewers Combined

| Subgroups | N | Death | Mutilation | Separation | Guilt | Shame | Diffuse |
|---|---|---|---|---|---|---|---|
| Grades 0-3 | 64 | 0.56 (0.29) | 0.67 (0.47) | 0.73 (0.38) | 0.68 (0.45) | 1.12 (0.87) | 0.58 (0.34) |
| Grades 4-6 | 72 | 0.57 (0.38) | 0.65 (0.44) | 0.76 (0.37) | 0.85 (0.55) | 0.85 (0.50) | 0.52 (0.30) |
| Grades 7-9 | 71 | 0.57 (0.37) | 0.57 (0.35) | 0.81 (0.46) | 0.84 (0.59) | 1.22 (0.98) | 0.57 (0.30) |
| Grades 10-12 | 69 | 0.52 (0.37) | 0.45 (0.28) | 0.75 (0.40) | 0.57 (0.41) | 1.20 (0.87) | 0.56 (0.30) |
| All Grades, 1-12 | 276 | 0.56 (0.35) | 0.59 (0.40) | 0.76 (0.40) | 0.74 (0.51) | 1.10 (0.83) | 0.56 (0.29) |

Note: (   ) = Standard Deviation

Table 13

Average Anxiety Subscale Scores from Subgroups of Black Children Interviewed by Black Women

| Subgroups | N | Anxiety Total | Anxiety Subscales | | | | |
|---|---|---|---|---|---|---|---|
| | | | Death | Mutilation | Separation | Guilt | Shame | Diffuse |
| Grades 0-3 | 33 | 1.44 (0.85) | 0.59 (0.25) | 0.65 (0.39) | 0.71 (0.37) | 0.71 (0.47) | 0.90 (0.63) | 0.60 (0.37) |
| Grades 4-6 | 36 | 1.73 (0.82) | 0.57 (0.40) | 0.70 (0.51) | 0.77 (0.40) | 0.89 (0.58) | 0.87 (0.52) | 0.50 (0.23) |
| Grades 7-9 | 36 | 2.03 (0.96) | 0.58 (0.38) | 0.55 (0.32) | 0.80 (0.52) | 0.88 (0.66) | 1.20 (0.92) | 0.59 (0.28) |
| Grades 10-12 | 34 | 1.64 (0.64) | 0.49 (0.35) | 0.46 (0.24) | 0.76 (0.32) | 0.63 (0.47) | 1.00 (0.52) | 0.52 (0.25) |
| All Grades, 1-12 | 139 | 1.72 (0.85) | 0.56 (0.35) | 0.59 (0.39) | 0.76 (0.41) | 0.78 (0.56) | 0.99 (0.68) | 0.55 (0.29) |

Note: (    ) = Standard Deviation

Table 14

Average Anxiety Subscale Scores from Subgroups of Black Children Interviewed by White Women

| Subgroups | N | Anxiety Total | Anxiety Subscales | | | | | |
|---|---|---|---|---|---|---|---|---|
| | | | Death | Mutilation | Separation | Guilt | Shame | Diffuse |
| Grades 0-3 | 31 | 1.99<br>(0.97) | 0.56<br>(0.32) | 0.70<br>(0.55) | 0.77<br>(0.39) | 0.65<br>(0.44) | 1.36<br>(1.03) | 0.55<br>(0.32) |
| Grades 4-6 | 36 | 1.64<br>(0.73) | 0.57<br>(0.36) | 0.61<br>(0.36) | 0.74<br>(0.33) | 0.80<br>(0.52) | 0.83<br>(0.50) | 0.54<br>(0.36) |
| Grades 7-9 | 35 | 2.06<br>(0.95) | 0.56<br>(0.37) | 0.59<br>(0.39) | 0.81<br>(0.40) | 0.80<br>(0.51) | 1.23<br>(1.06) | 0.54<br>(0.32) |
| Grades 10-12 | 35 | 2.04<br>(0.96) | 0.55<br>(0.40) | 0.45<br>(0.32) | 0.74<br>(0.46) | 0.52<br>(0.33) | 1.40<br>(1.09) | 0.60<br>(0.33) |
| All Grades, 1-12 | 137 | 1.93<br>(0.91) | 0.56<br>(0.35) | 0.59<br>(0.41) | 0.76<br>(0.39) | 0.70<br>(0.47) | 1.20<br>(0.96) | 0.56<br>(0.33) |

Note: (    ) = Standard Deviation

Table 15

Average Affect Scale Scores from Subgroups of Black Children by Sex of Subject

| Sub-Groups | Anxiety Total | | Hostility Outward | | | | | | Hostility Inward | | Ambivalent Hostility | |
|---|---|---|---|---|---|---|---|---|---|---|---|---|
| | | | Overt | | Covert | | Total | | | | | |
| | M | F | M | F | M | F | M | F | M | F | M | F |
| Grades 0-3 | 1.70<br>(0.95) | 1.71<br>(0.97) | 0.63<br>(0.31) | 0.73<br>(0.37) | 0.89<br>(0.62) | 1.01<br>(0.52) | 1.01<br>(0.67) | 1.17<br>(0.60) | 0.67<br>(0.50) | 0.55<br>(0.22) | 0.59<br>(0.32) | 0.77<br>(0.45) |
| Grades 4-6 | 1.76<br>(0.79) | 1.61<br>(0.76) | 0.67<br>(0.39) | 0.83<br>(0.48) | 1.21<br>(0.76) | 1.17<br>(0.77) | 1.39<br>(0.77) | 1.42<br>(0.85) | 0.58<br>(0.26) | 0.54<br>(0.31) | 0.73<br>(0.39) | 0.79<br>(0.54) |
| Grades 7-9 | 2.06<br>(0.86) | 2.03<br>(1.04) | 0.99<br>(0.55) | 0.90<br>(0.47) | 1.16<br>(0.70) | 1.16<br>(0.71) | 1.55<br>(0.78) | 1.47<br>(0.75) | 0.64<br>(0.38) | 0.64<br>(0.35) | 1.00<br>(0.62) | 0.73<br>(0.46) |
| Grades 10-12 | 1.68<br>(0.57) | 2.01<br>(1.03) | 0.91<br>(0.47) | 0.93<br>(0.33) | 0.87<br>(0.64) | 1.06<br>(0.75) | 1.28<br>(0.66) | 1.44<br>(0.68) | 0.70<br>(0.42) | 0.74<br>(0.43) | 0.64<br>(0.45) | 0.85<br>(0.77) |
| All Grades, 1-12 | 1.80<br>(0.80) | 1.84<br>(0.96) | 0.81<br>(0.46) | 0.85<br>(0.42) | 1.04<br>(0.70) | 1.10<br>(0.69) | 1.32<br>(0.74) | 1.38<br>(0.73) | 0.65<br>(0.39) | 0.61<br>(0.34) | 0.74<br>(0.48) | 0.79<br>(0.56) |

Note: (     ) = Standard Deviation

Table 16

Average Anxiety Subscale Scores from Subgroups of Black Children by Sex of Subject

| Sub-Groups | Death | | Mutilation | | Separation | | Guilt | | Shame | | Diffuse | |
|---|---|---|---|---|---|---|---|---|---|---|---|---|
| | M | F | M | F | M | F | M | F | M | F | M | F |
| Grades 0-3 | 0.55 (0.24) | 0.60 (0.32) | 0.67 (0.54) | 0.67 (0.41) | 0.72 (0.36) | 0.74 (0.40) | 0.62 (0.34) | 0.74 (0.53) | 1.10 (0.95) | 1.15 (0.81) | 0.53 (0.30) | 0.61 (0.38) |
| Grades 4-6 | 0.61 (0.49) | 0.53 (0.22) | 0.74 (0.48) | 0.57 (0.39) | 0.85 (0.40) | 0.66 (0.31) | 0.76 (0.45) | 0.93 (0.63) | 0.83 (0.59) | 0.87 (0.41) | 0.49 (0.24) | 0.56 (0.35) |
| Grades 7-9 | 0.48 (0.23) | 0.66 (0.45) | 0.60 (0.39) | 0.54 (0.31) | 0.77 (0.45) | 0.84 (0.47) | 1.01 (0.74) | 0.68 (0.32) | 1.12 (0.87) | 1.31 (1.08) | 0.51 (0.23) | 0.62 (0.35) |
| Grades 10-12 | 0.48 (0.33) | 0.56 (0.42) | 0.50 (0.35) | 0.41 (0.18) | 0.73 (0.28) | 0.77 (0.49) | 0.57 (0.49) | 0.58 (0.30) | 1.00 (0.57) | 1.42 (1.07) | 0.55 (0.30) | 0.57 (0.29) |
| All Grades, 1-12 | 0.53 (0.34) | 0.59 (0.36) | 0.63 (0.45) | 0.55 (0.35) | 0.77 (0.38) | 0.75 (0.42) | 0.74 (0.55) | 0.73 (0.48) | 1.01 (0.76) | 1.18 (0.90) | 0.52 (0.27) | 0.59 (0.34) |

Note: ( ) = Standard Deviation

# Introduction to Chapter 8

Introductory Comments by Louis A. Gottschalk

Goldine C. Gleser and her coworkers have evaluated psychotherapy with adolescents using the content analysis of verbal samples. Drop outs from psychotherapy (N=44) had significantly higher scores on social alienation-personal disorganization and spoke significantly fewer words than those who started psychotherapy (N=152) (See also Gottschalk, 1974). Also, female drop outs had significantly higher hostility outward scores and lower hostility inward scores than male adolescent drop outs, or those of either sex who remained in psychotherapy.

The affect scores six weeks after the onset of psychotherapy decreased for both a group of adolescents given immediate psychotherapy (N=54) and those who were required to wait for treatment for six weeks (N=66). By twelve weeks, those adolescents who underwent a six week delay in obtaining psychotherapy had higher average scores on axiety, hostility outward, ambivalent hostility, and social alienation-personal disorganization than those adolescents who received psychotherapy for the total twelve weeks. These differences largely disappeared by six months. For those adolescents whose psychothera-

pist obtained psychiatric consultation and supervision early in the psychotherapy, there were significantly lower affect scores six months after the initial assessment on social alienation-personal disorganization as compared to those adolescents whose therapists did not obtain such consultation.

Thus evidence suggests that the psychiatric consultation with the therapist helped the therapist find something about the adolescent to which he could relate positively and this helped the adolescent reach out in a more positive manner to others. This study has not only a valuable contribution to the content analysis of speech with children, but also a solid contribution to psychotherapy research in general.

Reference:

Gottschalk, L.A. The application of a method of content analysis to psychotherapy research. Amer. J. of Psychother. 28, 488-499 (1974).

8

# Evaluation of Psychotherapy with Adolescents using Content Analysis of Verbal Samples

Goldine Gleser, Caroline Winget,
Roslyn Seligman, and Joseph L. Rauh

The content analysis of brief samples of verbal behavior has been used to assess changes in emotional status in a number of studies (Gottschalk and Gleser, 1969), but to our knowledge has not been used previously to evaluate outcome of psychotherapy with adolescents. The present report describes such a study carried out at the Cincinnati Adolescent Clinic.

The Cincinnati Adolescent Clinic began a program of service and research for emotionally and behaviorally disturbed adolescents in 1972. The project had four major objectives:

a. development of a new health care delivery system utilizing non-physician primary care providers;

b. assessment of the effectiveness of the treatment program for adolescent patients;

c. assessment of the effect of a six-week delay in initiating therapy;

d. assessment of the usefulness and effectiveness of consultee-oriented psychiatric consultation for primary care providers.

The first two years of the study comprised a pilot study, enabling us to tighten our design and improve assessment procedures. The resulting research protocol was carefully followed in the subsequent two years (September 1974 to June 1976), using new therapists. It is the data from this latter period that will be presented here.

## Research Design

Three female therapists were employed, representing three disciplines and three levels of professional training: a nurse (B.S.), a social worker (M.S.W.), and a psychologist (Ph.D.). All patients applying to the Clinic with psychological or behavioral problems were assigned randomly within sex and race strata to one of four experimental conditions and to one of the three therapists. The four experimental conditions involved either immediate (conditions I and II) or delayed treatment (conditions III and IV) and either presenting (conditions I and III) or not presenting (conditions II and IV) the patient to a psychiatric consultant in a diagnostic conference. This presentation took place within the first two weeks after therapy was begun, i.e., weeks one or two for those patients treated immediately (condition I) and weeks seven or eight for patients who were delayed (condition III). The consultation was focused on the therapist-patient interaction with the aim of increasing the therapist's interest in and empathy for the patient. In summary, the design required that each of the three therapists treat 14 patients under each of four conditions, yielding 168 patients in all. The 14 patients in each block consisted of four white males, four white females, three black males and three black females.

A total of 260 telephone referrals were obtained to enable us to complete the design. Of these, 43 did not keep their intake appointment, 45 did not actually enter into therapy, and 2 were dropped for administrative reasons. As a part of the intake procedure, each adolescent filled out a self-report checklist of problem statements, the

Adolescent Life Assessment Checklist (ALAC) (Gleser, et al., 1977), and gave a tape recorded five-minute verbal sample. These assessment procedures were repeated at six weeks, 12 weeks, and six months.

Recently, Gottschalk (1975) has reported on the use of the verbal sample technique with children of age 6 to 16. He used instructions appropriate for this age range, but considerably modified from those generally used with adults. Our experience with the pilot sample indicated that little change was needed in the standardized procedure for adolescents in the 11-to-19-year age range. The instructions we used were:

"One of the things we are studying is how people talk and what they talk about. I want you to think for a moment about something in your life, past or present, that is important or interesting to talk about. And then when you are ready, I'll turn on the tape recorder for five minutes. You can ask questions before we turn on the tape recorder, but after you start I'm not supposed to talk until you finish."

In the instructions to the interviewer, it was noted that if the subject wanted further instructions or was very hesitant, the interviewer might suggest that the subject take another minute to think about people and happenings in his life. The interviewer's basic attitude was one of sympathy that the task might seem difficult but assurance that the subject would accomplish it.

The tapes were transcribed and scored by research assistants on the affect scales and on the scale for Social Alienation-Personal Disorganization. Only data for the <u>summary</u> affect scales are reported here; i.e., Anxiety, total Hostility Outward, Hostility Inward, and Ambivalent Hostility. Further description of these scales, together with reliability and validity studies, can be found in Gottschalk and Gleser (1969). Directions for scoring are given in Gottschalk, et al. (1969).

## Results

### Initial Verbal Samples

Initial verbal samples were obtained on 152 of the 168 subjects who started therapy and on 44 of the 45 initial dropouts from therapy. Average scores for these two groups are shown in Table 1. In this table, males and females are reported separately. The main difference between the dropouts and those who started into therapy is that the former group spoke fewer words ($p = .05$) and had higher scores on Social Alienation-Personal Disorganization ($p = .02$) than did those who started therapy. The female dropouts had higher scores on Hostility Outward and lower scores on Hostility Inward than their male counterparts or those of either sex who remained in therapy. Averaged over both groups, females scored significantly higher on Anxiety, Ambivalent Hostility and total words spoken.

Table 2 shows the within-group means, standard deviations and intercorrelations among the five major affect scores and total words. All affect scores are positively intercorrelated and all are nearly independent of the number of words spoken. Anxiety is most highly correlated with all other scores.

## Treatment Outcome

Analysis of the treatment outcome from the viewpoint of the verbal sample evaluation will be presented in two sections. In the first section we will deal with the six and 12-week assessments which were available for 120 individuals who gave verbal samples. An additional 32 subjects completed these assessments but did not give a sufficient verbal sample to be scored. The second section presents the analysis on the 92 patients on whom six-month follow-up verbal samples were obtained.

### Six and 12-Week Assessments

Table 3 shows the initial, six-week and 12-week average verbal

Table 1

Mean Initial Verbal Sample Scores for Dropouts and Those Who Started Therapy

| Dropouts | Females | Males | Total |
|---|---|---|---|
| | N = 24 | N = 20 | N = 44 |
| Anxiety | 2.49 | 1.97 | 2.25 |
| Hostility Outward | 2.11* | 1.44* | 1.80 |
| Hostility Inward | .95 | 1.18 | 1.05 |
| Ambivalent Hostility | 1.78 | 1.26 | 1.54 |
| Social Alienation- | | | |
| Personal Disorganization | 2.57 | 2.50 | 2.54 |
| Total Words | 358 | 354 | 356 |
| **Started Therapy** | **Females** | **Males** | **Total** |
| | N = 79 | N = 73 | N = 152 |
| Anxiety | 2.28 | 2.03 | 2.16 |
| Hostility Outward | 1.72 | 1.67 | 1.70 |
| Hostility Inward | 1.20 | 1.03 | 1.12 |
| Ambivalent Hostility | 1.48 | 1.29 | 1.39 |
| Social Alienation- | | | |
| Personal Disorganization | .50 | .90 | .69 |
| Total Words | 475 | 388 | 433 |

*Significant interaction p < .02.

scores classified by treatment and sex for the 120 adolescents who remained in the project at the time of the 12-week assessment. A multivariate analysis of variance indicated that there were no significant differences at the time of the initial assessment among verbal

Table 2

Means and Average Within-Group* Standard Deviations and Intercorrelations of Initial Verbal Sample Scores

N = 196

| Variable | Means | s.d. | Correlations | | | | | |
|---|---|---|---|---|---|---|---|---|
| | | | Anx. | H.O. | H.I. | A.H. | S.A.-P.D. | T.W. |
| Anxiety | 2.18 | .98 | | .59 | .49 | .70 | .52 | .11 |
| Hostility Outward | 1.72 | .77 | | | .22 | .61 | .40 | .17 |
| Hostility Inward | 1.10 | .64 | | | | .35 | .36 | .08 |
| Ambivalent Hostility | 1.43 | .85 | | | | | .48 | .22 |
| Social Alienation-Personal Disorganization | 1.11 | 4.61 | | | | | | .01 |
| Total Words | 416 | 233 | | | | | | |

*Within race, sex, and dropout-remainder subgroups.

sample score means for treatment condition, therapist, or their interaction. From initial assessment to six weeks, average scores decreased on all scales for both the delay groups (III and IV) and for the immediate treatment groups (I and II). None of the variables differed significantly at six weeks, i.e., there were no important differences in $T_2$ variables controlled for $T_1$ as a function of immediate treatment as opposed to a six-week delay. However, at $T_3$, there was a difference in Ambivalent Hostility ($p = .01$), those treated immediately having the lower score. It might be noted that scores at 12 weeks were also higher for the delay groups than for the two groups treated immediately on Anxiety and Hostility Outward, as well as for Social Alienation-Personal Disorganization, although none of these differences were significant. The delay group had slightly lower average scores on Hostility Inward. At that point, those in the delay groups had had only six weeks of

Table 3

Mean Verbal Affect Scores

Classified by Sex, Treatment Condition and Occasion*#

| | Immediate Present I | | | | | | Immediate Non-Present II | | | | | |
|---|---|---|---|---|---|---|---|---|---|---|---|---|
| | Females (N=16) | | | Males (N=15) | | | Females (N=13) | | | Males (N=10) | | |
| | $T_1$ | $T_2$ | $T_3$ | $T_1$ | $T_2$ | $T_3$ | $T_1$ | $T_2$ | $T_3$ | $T_1$ | $T_2$ | $T_3$ |
| Anxiety | 2.3 | 2.0 | 1.7 | 2.0 | 1.7 | 1.5 | 2.4 | 2.1 | 2.3 | 2.1 | 1.5 | 1.6 |
| Hostility Outward | 1.6 | 1.5 | 1.4 | 1.8 | 1.5 | 1.4 | 1.7 | 1.6 | 1.7 | 1.6 | 1.4 | 1.1 |
| Hostility Inward | 1.3 | 1.2 | 1.1 | 1.0 | 1.0 | 1.0 | 1.1 | 1.4 | 1.2 | 1.0 | .8 | 1.0 |
| Ambivalent Hostility | 1.6 | 1.3 | .8 | 1.1 | 1.3 | 1.2 | 1.5 | 1.2 | 1.2 | 1.3 | .8 | .6 |
| Social Alienation-Personal Disorganization | -.6 | -2.1 | -3.5 | .3 | 2.4 | .7 | 1.5 | -.3 | -.6 | .5 | -1.1 | .8 |
| Total Words | 485 | 424 | 386 | 437 | 434 | 451 | 547 | 499 | 408 | 536 | 409 | 337 |
| | Delay Present III | | | | | | Delay Non-Present IV | | | | | |
| | Females (N=16) | | | Males (N=17) | | | Females (N=18) | | | Males (N=15) | | |
| | $T_1$ | $T_2$ | $T_3$ | $T_1$ | $T_2$ | $T_3$ | $T_1$ | $T_2$ | $T_3$ | $T_1$ | $T_2$ | $T_3$ |
| Anxiety | 2.3 | 2.2 | 2.1 | 2.3 | 1.9 | 1.9 | 2.1 | 1.9 | 1.9 | 1.8 | 1.6 | 2.1 |
| Hostility Outward | 1.6 | 1.7 | 1.8 | 1.7 | 1.3 | 1.2 | 1.8 | 1.4 | 1.6 | 1.6 | 1.4 | 1.6 |
| Hostility Inward | 1.4 | 1.1 | 1.0 | 1.0 | 1.1 | 1.2 | 1.1 | .9 | .9 | 1.1 | .7 | .9 |
| Ambivalent Hostility | 1.4 | 1.5 | 1.8 | 1.4 | 1.1 | 1.2 | 1.6 | 1.2 | 1.0 | 1.3 | 1.1 | 1.1 |
| Social Alienation-Personel Disorganization | 1.2 | -.5 | -.8 | 2.7 | 1.6 | 1.7 | -.3 | -2.6 | -1.7 | -.2 | .4 | .2 |
| Total Words | 466 | 480 | 395 | 386 | 288 | 270 | 511 | 413 | 440 | 363 | 346 | 292 |

*$T_1$ = initial testing; $T_2$ = six weeks; $T_3$ = 12 weeks.

#Means given to only one decimal place for ease in reading.

therapy as compared to the opportunity for 12 weeks of therapy for those who were seen immediately.

Analysis of the data with regard to psychiatric consultation within the immediate and delay conditions revealed some significant effects.

The multivariate F for present versus non-present groups was significant at $p \leq .01$. In the immediate group, Anxiety dropped more by 12 weeks for those who were presented for consultation than for those who were not. No difference was evident at six weeks. On the other hand, Ambivalent Hostility remained higher, on the average, for the presented cases than for those not presented in both the delay and immediate groups. This difference was significant only for the delay group. Total words decreased in all groups, but significantly more by 12 weeks for the immediate-non-present and the delay-present than for other groups.

Further analysis of the data indicated a significant interaction between sex and treatment outcome at 12 weeks ($p = .04$). Male patients obtained lower Anxiety and Hostility Outward scores at 12 weeks with all treatment conditions except delay-non-present (condition IV), whereas females showed comparable decreases only for condition I. Males obtained a significant decrease in Ambivalent Hostility only in condition II, whereas females obtained substantial decreases in conditions I and IV. Social Alienation-Personal Disorganization decreased for females in all conditions but little systematic change was noted for males.

Highly significant differences in corrected affect scores at 12 weeks were attributable to differences among therapists. Table 4 gives verbal score data for the three therapists by immediate versus delay conditions. Changes in verbal affect scores were most marked for Therapist 2 at $T_3$. Although mean Anxiety and Social Alienation-Personal Disorganization scores were markedly higher for this therapist at $T_1$, they decrease at six weeks and again at 12 weeks. At 12 weeks, mean scores for patients assigned to Therapist 2 rank lowest on Anxiety, Hostility Outward, Ambivalent Hostility and Social Alienation-Personal Disorganization. Furthermore, Therapist 2 was unique in achieving a reduction in Ambivalent Hostility in both immediate and delay groups. Therapist 1 patients obtained a more modest decline from $T_1$ to $T_2$ and a

Table 4

Mean Verbal Affect Scores by Therapist,

Immediate vs Delay, and Time of Assessment*

| Therapist 1 | Immediate (N=19) | | | Delay (N=22) | | | Total (N=41) | | |
|---|---|---|---|---|---|---|---|---|---|
| | $T_1$ | $T_2$ | $T_3$ | $T_1$ | $T_2$ | $T_3$ | $T_1$ | $T_2$ | $T_3$ |
| Anxiety | 2.0 | 1.8 | 1.7 | 2.1 | 1.9 | 1.9 | 2.0 | 1.9 | 1.8 |
| Hostility Outward | 1.6 | 1.4 | 1.4 | 1.8 | 1.5 | 1.5 | 1.7 | 1.5 | 1.5 |
| Hostility Inward | 1.0 | 1.1 | 1.1 | 1.3 | 1.0 | 1.2 | 1.1 | 1.0 | 1.1 |
| Ambivalent Hostility | 1.1 | 1.1 | .9 | 1.5 | 1.4 | 1.4 | 1.3 | 1.3 | 1.2 |
| Social Alienation-Personal Disorganization | -.9 | -.1 | -2.2 | 1.4 | .3 | .5 | .3 | .2 | -.7 |
| Total Words | 408 | 365 | 389 | 388 | 378 | 304 | 397 | 372 | 343 |
| Therapist 2 | Immediate (N=18) | | | Delay (N=20) | | | Total (N=38) | | |
| Anxiety | 2.7 | 2.1 | 1.8 | 2.2 | 2.0 | 1.7 | 2.4 | 2.1 | 1.8 |
| Hostility Outward | 1.9 | 1.8 | 1.4 | 1.5 | 1.6 | 1.4 | 1.7 | 1.7 | 1.4 |
| Hostility Inward | 1.1 | 1.1 | 1.3 | 1.0 | .9 | .8 | 1.1 | 1.0 | 1.0 |
| Ambivalent Hostility | 1.7 | 1.3 | 1.1 | 1.3 | 1.2 | .8 | 1.5 | 1.3 | .9 |
| Social Alienation-Personal Disorganization | 2.0 | 1.1 | -.3 | 1.6 | -.6 | -2.3 | 1.7 | .2 | -1.3 |
| Total Words | 538 | 533 | 477 | 471 | 441 | 376 | 503 | 485 | 424 |
| Therapist 3 | Immediate (N=17) | | | Delay (N=24) | | | Total (N=41) | | |
| Anxiety | 2.0 | 1.6 | 1.9 | 2.1 | 1.9 | 2.3 | 2.1 | 1.8 | 2.1 |
| Hostility Outward | 1.5 | 1.4 | 1.5 | 1.7 | 1.2 | 1.7 | 1.6 | 1.3 | 1.6 |
| Hostility Inward | 1.2 | 1.1 | .9 | 1.1 | 1.0 | 1.0 | 1.2 | 1.0 | .9 |
| Ambivalent Hostility | 1.3 | 1.1 | 1.0 | 1.5 | 1.2 | 1.5 | 1.4 | 1.1 | 1.3 |
| Social Alienation-Personal Disorganization | .1 | -1.8 | .1 | -.2 | -.7 | .9 | -.1 | -1.2 | .6 |
| Total Words | 550 | 431 | 331 | 446 | 336 | 375 | 489 | 376 | 357 |

*Means given to only one decimal place for ease in reading.

leveling off for Anxiety, Hostility Outward and Ambivalent Hostility at 12 weeks. Hostility Inward scores for Therapist 1 rose somewhat from $T_2$ to $T_3$, while Social Alienation-Personal Disorganization scores showed a marked drop. On most scales, Therapist 3 showed lowered average scores at $T_2$ and a clear rise to or above mean initial values at 12 weeks. Only on Hostility Inward did scores remain stable at a slight downward slope for Therapist 3, and particularly so with immediate treatment where average scores for the other two therapists rose slightly.

Six-Month Assessment

At six months, 92 of the 120 patients who were providing verbal samples at three months remained in the program. Some of these patients had additional treatment, whereas others simply returned for the six-month assessment. A perusal of initial scores for these 92 (Table 5) and the initial scores for the 120 of Table 3 indicates very similar scores. Thus, it would appear that those dropping out of the project between three months and six months were comparable to those who remained. Affect and Social Alienation-Personal Disorganization scores for groups I and II (immediate treatment) are identical or very slightly higher for those remaining in therapy. The elevation of scores for 48 patients in groups III and IV (delay) was somewhat greater, although still minimal, as compared to the initial scores for 66 patients analyzed from $T_1$ to $T_3$. For all groups, there was some indication that patients who were more verbal remained and those who spoke fewer words dropped out of the assessment procedure. However, this trend was more marked for the delay groups than for the immediate treatment groups.

At six months, as shown in Table 5, the average content scores on verbal behavior for subjects in the four treatment conditions were remarkably similar. Overall, the $T_4$ scores of those in the two delay conditions did not differ from those in the two immediate conditions. However, males had lower scores on Hostility Inward and females had

Table 5

Mean Verbal Affect Scores Initially, at 12 Weeks, and 3 Months, Classified by Treatment Condition*

| Immediate Treatment | Present (N=25) | | | Non-Present (N=19) | | | Total (N=44) | | |
|---|---|---|---|---|---|---|---|---|---|
| | $T_1$ | $T_3$ | $T_4$ | $T_1$ | $T_3$ | $T_4$ | $T_1$ | $T_3$ | $T_4$ |
| Anxiety | 2.1 | 1.6 | 1.7 | 2.4 | 2.1 | 2.1 | 2.2 | 1.8 | 1.9 |
| Hostility Outward | 1.7 | 1.4 | 1.4 | 1.7 | 1.5 | 1.6 | 1.7 | 1.4 | 1.5 |
| Hostility Inward | 1.1 | 1.0 | 1.0 | 1.1 | 1.1 | 1.2 | 1.1 | 1.1 | 1.1 |
| Ambivalent Hostility | 1.3 | 1.1 | 1.1 | 1.4 | .9 | 1.2 | 1.4 | 1.0 | 1.2 |
| Social Alienation-Personal Disorganization | .4 | -1.2 | -.6 | 1.7 | .9 | 1.1 | .9 | -.3 | .1 |
| Total Words | 496 | 446 | 420 | 532 | 373 | 374 | 512 | 414 | 401 |
| Delayed Treatment | Present (N=26) | | | Non-Present (N=22) | | | Total (N=48) | | |
| Anxiety | 2.4 | 2.1 | 1.9 | 2.0 | 1.9 | 1.6 | 2.2 | 2.0 | 1.8 |
| Hostility Outward | 1.8 | 1.6 | 1.7 | 1.7 | 1.6 | 1.5 | 1.8 | 1.6 | 1.6 |
| Hostility Inward | 1.3 | 1.1 | 1.1 | 1.1 | .9 | 1.0 | 1.2 | 1.0 | 1.1 |
| Ambivalent Hostility | 1.4 | 1.5 | 1.4 | 1.5 | 1.0 | 1.3 | 1.5 | 1.3 | 1.3 |
| Social Alienation-Personal Disorganization | 2.6 | 1.2 | -1.0 | 0 | -1.0 | .5 | 1.4 | .2 | -.3 |
| Total Words | 466 | 370 | 390 | 492 | 427 | 361 | 478 | 396 | 377 |
| Total | Present (N=51) | | | Non-Present (N=41) | | | Total (N=92) | | |
| Anxiety | 2.3 | 1.8 | 1.8 | 2.2 | 2.0 | 1.9 | 2.2 | 1.9 | 1.8 |
| Hostility Outward | 1.8 | 1.5 | 1.6 | 1.7 | 1.6 | 1.6 | 1.7 | 1.5 | 1.6 |
| Hostility Inward | 1.2 | 1.0 | 1.0 | 1.1 | 1.0 | 1.1 | 1.2 | 1.0 | 1.1 |
| Ambivalent Hostility | 1.4 | 1.3 | 1.3 | 1.4 | .9 | 1.2 | 1.4 | 1.1 | 1.2 |
| Social Alienation-Personal Disorganization | 1.5 | 0 | -.8 | .7 | -.1 | .8 | 1.2 | 0 | -.1 |
| Total Words | 481 | 407 | 405 | 512 | 401 | 367 | 495 | 404 | 388 |

*Means given to only one decimal place for ease in reading.

lower Ambivalent Hostility scores for immediate as compared to delay treatment (interaction p = .05). There were also no significant differences overall in the average content scores according to whether the group was or was not presented for psychiatric consultation, although those in the non-present condition at six months yielded somewhat higher scores on Social Alienation-Personal Disorganization (+.81 as compared to -.84). This difference is primarily attributable to the females who were significantly lower in Social Alienation-Personal Disorganization when treated in conditions I and III than in II and IV. Also, the females in the non-present condition spoke somewhat fewer words than in the present group, whereas no difference was noted for males.

Two major problems were encountered in analyzing the six-month follow-up data. Both of these problems resulted in a loss of statistical power. First, reduction in sample size resulted in small numbers of cases in some of the cells of our design, making it of questionable value to analyze higher order interactions. Secondly, the correlations between initial verbal samples and six-month scores were very low so that only Ambivalent Hostility scores related significantly to initial scores. Using initial and six-week scores as predictors yielded some increase in predictive power, particularly for Anxiety and Social Alienation-Personal Disorganization scores, but further reduced the degrees of freedom. Thus, while some effects found at 12 weeks continued to hold at follow-up, they were no longer statistically significant.

<u>The Effect of Therapist on Six-Month Average Verbal Sample Scores</u>

Table 6 displays average affect scores by occasion for each of the three therapists. For each of the content variables, the patients assigned to the three therapists yielded highly similar average scores at six months. Average Anxiety scores were reduced as compared to initial scores for all three therapists. Hostility Outward, Ambivalent Hostility and Social Alienation-Personal Disorganization were lowest for those treated by Therapist 1. For Therapist 3, Hostility

Table 6

Mean Affect Scores for Three Therapists

by Time of Assessment*

| | Therapist #1 | | | Therapist #2 | | | Therapist #3 | | |
|---|---|---|---|---|---|---|---|---|---|
| | $T_1$ | $T_3$ | $T_4$ | $T_1$ | $T_3$ | $T_4$ | $T_1$ | $T_3$ | $T_4$ |
| Anxiety | 2.1 | 1.8 | 1.8 | 2.5 | 1.8 | 1.9 | 2.1 | 2.2 | 1.9 |
| Hostility Outward | 1.8 | 1.4 | 1.5 | 1.7 | 1.4 | 1.6 | 1.7 | 1.7 | 1.6 |
| Hostility Inward | 1.2 | 1.1 | 1.1 | 1.1 | 1.0 | 1.0 | 1.2 | 1.0 | 1.2 |
| Ambivalent Hostility | 1.4 | 1.1 | 1.1 | 1.5 | .9 | 1.2 | 1.4 | 1.4 | 1.4 |
| Social Alienation-Personal Disorganization | 1.0 | -.6 | -1.0 | 2.2 | -.3 | 1.0 | .4 | .8 | .6 |
| Total Words | 420 | 371 | 364 | 516 | 438 | 408 | 544 | 404 | 393 |
| N | | 30 | | | 31 | | | 31 | |

*Means given to only one decimal place for ease in reading.

Outward average scores at six months were virtually identical to initial scores, whereas for Therapists 1 and 2, Hostility Outward scores rose slightly from $T_3$ to $T_4$ but remained considerably lower than average initial scores on this variable. On Ambivalent Hostility, and also on Social Alienation-Personal Disorganization, Therapist 3 patients yielded higher scores at $T_4$ than at the time of initial assessment. Scores on Social Alienation-Personal Disorganization for patients assigned to Therapists 1 and 2 were markedly improved at $T_4$ as compared to the average initial scores. For Therapist 3, this improvement occurred only for the groups presented for psychiatric consultation. Significant interactions of therapist with treatment condition occurred for Anxiety and Hostility Inward. This interaction was due to the unusually poor

results shown by Therapist 3 for those of her patients who were treated immediately but not presented for psychiatric consultation.

Six-Month Outcome by Race and Sex of Patient

Table 7 shows the verbal affect scores initially, at 12 weeks, and at six months, by sex and race of patient, averaged over all treatment conditions.

Anxiety: For all groups, Anxiety decreased from $T_1$ to $T_4$. Females, both black and white, started with more Anxiety than their male counterparts and remained more anxious than males at the six-month follow-up. However, six months scores corrected for initial scores did not differ by race or sex.

Hostility Outward: All groups decreased on Hostility Outward except white females whose scores increased from initial to six months. The largest decrease was obtained for black females, followed by white males. Black males, on the average, showed only minimal change in Hostility Outward following therapy. Differences in outcome for race and sex were highly significant, $p < .01$.

Hostility Inward: Black and white females all showed a very modest decrease from initial to six months in average Hostility Inward scores. Black males showed a slight increase on these scales. Differences in outcome were marginally significant ($p = .06$).

Ambivalent Hostility: Ambivalent Hostility scores were higher initially for females compared to males, and for black adolescents compared to white. The post-treatment scores decreased for all except the black males, whose scores increased. The six-month scores were significantly higher for blacks.

Social Alienation-Personal Disorganization: Black males and females had higher Social Alienation-Personal Disorganization scores initially than did the white subgroups. All groups showed a lessening of pathology as measured by this scale, with females showing the greatest improvement.

Table 7

Comparison of Treatment Outcome on Verbal Scores for Groups Categorized by Sex and Ethnic Group

| | Black (N=23) | | | White (N=25) | | | Total | | |
|---|---|---|---|---|---|---|---|---|---|
| Females | $T_1$ | $T_3$ | $T_4$ | $T_1$ | $T_3$ | $T_4$ | $T_1$ | $T_3$ | $T_4$ |
| Anxiety | 2.45 | 1.99 | 1.94 | 2.38 | 2.20 | 2.06 | 2.41 | 2.10 | 2.00 |
| Hostility Outward | 1.91 | 1.87 | 1.34 | 1.60 | 1.62 | 1.86 | 1.75 | 1.74 | 1.61 |
| Hostility Inward | 1.34 | .95 | 1.10 | 1.20 | 1.01 | 1.16 | 1.27 | .98 | 1.13 |
| Ambivalent Hostility | 1.68 | 1.30 | 1.41 | 1.40 | 1.09 | 1.27 | 1.54 | 1.19 | 1.34 |
| Social Alienation-Personal Disorganization | 2.30 | -.23 | -.46 | .09 | -1.94 | -1.24 | 1.15 | -1.12 | -.87 |
| Total Words | 498 | 472 | 389 | 585 | 439 | 423 | 543 | 455 | 406 |
| Males | Black (N=18) | | | White (N=26) | | | Total | | |
| Anxiety | 2.01 | 1.76 | 1.79 | 2.04 | 1.68 | 1.62 | 2.03 | 1.71 | 1.69 |
| Hostility Outward | 1.69 | 1.26 | 1.60 | 1.77 | 1.27 | 1.45 | 1.74 | 1.26 | 1.52 |
| Hostility Inward | 1.10 | 1.22 | 1.16 | 1.00 | .94 | .85 | 1.04 | 1.06 | .98 |
| Ambivalent Hostility | 1.26 | 1.25 | 1.56 | 1.26 | .97 | .87 | 1.26 | 1.08 | 1.15 |
| Social Alienation-Personal Disorganization | 1.33 | 2.71 | 1.58 | 1.12 | .15 | .14 | 1.21 | 1.19 | .73 |
| Total Words | 422 | 329 | 336 | 454 | 365 | 392 | 441 | 350 | 369 |
| Total | | | | | | | | | |
| Anxiety | 2.26 | 1.89 | 1.88 | 2.21 | 1.94 | 1.84 | | | |
| Hostility Outward | 1.81 | 1.60 | 1.46 | 1.69 | 1.44 | 1.65 | | | |
| Hostility Inward | 1.24 | 1.07 | 1.13 | 1.10 | .97 | 1.00 | | | |
| Ambivalent Hostility | 1.50 | 1.28 | 1.48 | 1.33 | 1.03 | 1.07 | | | |
| Social Alienation-Personal Disorganization | 1.88 | 1.06 | .43 | .62 | -.88 | -.54 | | | |
| Total Words | 465 | 409 | 366 | 518 | 401 | 407 | | | |

Total Words: Initially, females were significantly more verbal than males. All groups spoke fewer words, on the average, at the six-month assessment than they did initially, and the difference between the sexes was reduced.

## Discussion

It is evident from the present study that it is possible to use verbal samples with an adolescent population starting as young as 11 years of age with very little, if any, modification of the procedure used with adults. While some young people found this a stressful procedure, only ten per cent of those assessed initially in our study failed to give a scoreable verbal sample. There was a tendency, however, for less verbal adolescents to drop out of our assessment program, resulting in somewhat more missing data than was true for ratings and inventory data. This disadvantage must be weighed against the advantage of obtaining a more subtle evaluation of affect than is usually possible by self-report. We feel that this technique adds a third dimension to the evaluation of psychotherapy, particularly with regard to affects that are seldom reported and often are not fully recognized by the patient.

During the period covered by this study, a stratified normative sample of black and white, male and female adolescents, was assessed, using verbal samples as well as other measures of functioning (Gleser, et al., 1977). The initial average verbal affect scores for the adolescents in the current study were very significantly higher ($p < .001$) than those obtained in this normative sample. The scores for Social Alienation-Personal Disorganization were also higher ($p < .005$). This latter scale has been reported on more fully elsewhere (Winget, et al., 1977). The six-month verbal scores for our patients, while, in general, reduced from their initial values, continued to be somewhat higher than those of their peers who had not been referred for therapy.

A further comparison of initial scores can be made with a sample of 46 incarcerated delinquent male white adolescents, ages 14 to 16 (Gleser, et al., 1965). In the latter study, initial scores were: Anxiety-2.38; Hostility Outward-1.83; Hostility Inward-.81; and Ambivalent Hostility-1.86. The largest difference between these scores and those obtained for our male white sample is for Ambivalent Hostility, which is very significantly higher for the delinquent sample. This score, which is derived from verbal statements regarding destructive, injurious, critical feelings and actions of others toward the self, may be indicative of persons having serious behavior problems rooted in disorders of the self (Kohut, 1971, 1977). While our white male patients evidently had elevated scores on this scale relative to a normative sample, they did not approach the level of the delinquent boys. However, the initial scores of black females and the six-month score for black males approach this level. It appears to us that Ambivalent Hostility may be an important measure by which to gauge one aspect of the stage of narcissistic development in adolescents and young adults.

Turning now to the research design of the therapy per se, it is interesting to note that scores at six weeks decrease for both those given immediate treatment and those who were required to wait for treatment in this interval. A similar result was obtained via self-report and parental report. Evidently, the initial evaluation and expectation of treatment has some positive value in reducing pathology and family conflict in this short period of time. By 12 weeks, some differential effects of the longer treatment period were evident, with those who were delayed yielding higher average scores on Anxiety, Hostility Outward, Ambivalent Hostility and Social Alienation-Personal Disorganization, and lower verbal productiveness than those who received immediate treatment. These small differences largely disappeared by six months for those still giving verbal samples. However, the effect

of delay differed somewhat for females as compared to males. Females decreased in Ambivalent Hostility when treated immediately but showed little or no decrease in this variable when treatment was delayed. Rather, they displayed some reduction in Hostility Inward with delay. Males, on the other hand, decreased but little on Ambivalent Hostility with either treatment regimen but decreased in Hostility Inward with immediate treatment.

The second major question to which our research was addressed was whether consultation by a skilled child psychiatrist would enhance the therapeutic results achieved by our young therapists who had not previously worked with adolescents in the role of primary care providers. As mentioned earlier, this was a single consultation, held shortly after therapy began, and did not involve the consultant meeting with the patient. On the basis of the verbal sample, one major effect was noted. Adolescents who were presented for consultation had lower scores six months after initial assessment on Social Alienation-Personal Disorganization than those who were not presented. The Social Alienation-Personal Disorganization scale was originally devised to discriminate the relative severity of the schizophrenic syndrome and to differentiate schizophrenic from non-schizophrenic individuals. Items are weighted positively as evidence of pathology and negatively as associated with healthy behavior. Items weighted negatively include remarks about self or others well or intact and also remarks about congenial and constructive thoughts, feelings, and actions between individuals. On almost all negatively weighted items the adolescent clinic patients had significantly fewer scoreable remarks than did the normative sample that we tested (Winget, et al., 1977). We believe, therefore, that what the consultation accomplished was to help the therapist find something about the adolescent to which she could relate positively and this, in turn, helped the adolescent reach out in a more positive manner to others. This hypothesis also fits another

finding of our study, namely, that the "presented" group increased more in "tolerance of intimacy" than those not presented.

One puzzling finding in this study was the decrease in total words spoken over the course of therapy and follow-up. On the basis of our pilot study, as well as from the fact that normative subjects spoke more than patients, we would have expected total words to increase over the period of this study. It is possible that the conditions under which the verbal sample was taken produced some negative conditioning. The verbal samples were all obtained by one interviewer who had no contact with the patients except for the purpose of obtaining the assessment data. She purposely maintained a somewhat aloof, objective stance in order not to set up an additional relationship, but this could have been seen as disinterest or disapproval by some of the young people. In the pilot study, verbal samples were obtained by the receptionist who had some contact and conversation with the patients at other times than during assessment. Further work is needed to determine how best to minimize the effect of the interviewer in longitudinal studies.

This report has focused largely on a research project designed to evaluate the effectiveness of delivery of mental health services to adolescents in a special outpatient clinic setting. The research demonstrates the utility of content analysis of brief segments of verbal behavior in assessing psychological states of adolescents in treatment. For many adolescents, such evaluation may yield information on subtle and complex factors in the therapeutic situation.

The lower verbal productivity and higher Social Alienation-Personal Disorganization scores of those who applied for therapy but dropped out after intake has important implications for the delivery of mental health service to adolescents. This pinpointing of poor verbal skills in certain youth suggests the need for greater flexibility in planning treatment modalities for these segments of the adolescent population who have

difficulty relating or communicating to others. Such planning might include greater outreach programming and more emphasis on play therapy, occupational therapy, family therapy, etc., with lowered expectation that "talking" is the important thing.

Summary

The content analysis of verbal behavior obtained under standardized conditions was used to evaluate outcome of therapy with adolescents. One hundred sixty-eight patients were randomly assigned within sex and race strata to one of four experimental conditions and to one of three therapists. The four conditions involved combinations of either immediate or delayed treatment and either presenting or not presenting the patient to a psychiatric consultant. Verbal samples were analyzed for Anxiety, Hostility Outward, Hostility Inward, Ambivalent Hostility, and for Social Alienation-Personal Disorganization.

Dropouts differed from those who started therapy in that the former group spoke significantly fewer words and had significantly higher scores on Social Alienation-Personal Disorganization. There were no significant differences in initial verbal sample scores by condition, nor by therapist assigned, for the 120 adolescents remaining in the project at the time of the 12-week assessment. From initial assessment to six weeks, average scores decreased on all scales for both the delay groups and the immediate treatment groups, and no significant differences in trend were evident. However, at 12 weeks, Ambivalent Hostility was significantly lower in those treated immediately compared to those in the delay condition. Some complex differences were significant for those presented for consultation in contrast to those not presented, and for sex by treatment outcome.

At six months, average content scores on verbal behavior for subjects in the four treatment conditions were remarkably similar. For all conditions, Anxiety decreased from initial assessment to assessment at six months. For Hostility Outward, differences in outcome by race and

sex were highly significant, while for Hostility Inward they were marginally significant. Post-treatment scores on Ambivalent Hostility decreased for all except black males, whose scores increased. All groups showed less pathology at six months than initially as scored by the Social Alienation-Personal Disorganization scale.

It is felt that the content analysis of verbal samples offers an important addition to assessment methods which can be useful in outcome studies with adolescents.

## References

Gleser, G. C., Gottschalk, L. A., Fox, R., and Lippert, W. Immediate changes in affect with chlordiazepoxide. Arch. Gen. Psychiat. 13, 291-295 (1965).

Gleser, G., Seligman, R., Winget, C., and Rauh, J. L. Adolescents view their mental health. J. Youth Adol. 6(3), 249-263, 1977.

Gottschalk, L. A. and Gleser, G. C. The measurement of psychological states through the content analysis of verbal behavior. University of California Press, Berkeley and Los Angeles (1969).

Gottschalk, L. A., Winget, C. N., and Gleser, G. C. A manual for using the Gottschalk-Gleser content analysis scales. University of California Press, Berkeley and Los Angeles (1969).

Kohut, H. The analysis of the self. International Universities Press, New York (1971).

Kohut, H. The restoration of the self. International Universities Press, New York (1977).

Winget, C., Seligman, R., Rauh, J. L., and Gleser, G. C. Social Alienation-Personal Disorganization assessment in disturbed and normal adolescents. (Submitted to Pediatrics.)

# Part II
# Scoring the Content Analysis Scales

Two chapters are included in this section, one (9) entitled "A computerized scoring system for use with content analysis scales" (Gottschalk et al, 1975) and another (10) entitled "Response productivity in verbal content analysis: a critique of Marsden, Kalter, and Ericson" (Gleser and Lubin, 1976). The first chapter in this section indicates that computerization of scoring of these content analysis scales will eventually be quite possible. The second paper discusses the use of percentage scores to control for productivity and verbal content analysis and answers criticisms of Marsden, Kalter, and Ericson (1975) that the Gottschalk-Gleser content analysis scales make erroneous use of percentage scores.

# A Computerized Scoring System for Use with Content Analysis Scales

Louis A. Gottschalk, Catherine Hausmann, and John Seely Brown

COMPUTER ASSISTANCE with the analysis of speech content according to a prearranged system would provide a considerable saving of time, an increase in the uniformity of content analysis, and a more rapid and efficient technique of surveying qualitative and quantitative interrelationships between many different psychological states and biological variables. One of the hurdles to an automated system of speech content analysis has been that a person (instead of a machine) has had to label each word in a speech transcript with the appropriate syntactical tag indicating how the word is used in a sentence. If a computer program were capable of parsing natural language, a vital step forward could be taken in the computer analysis of speech content.

Without the use of an automated parser, several interesting and promising attempts have been made to apply computer techniques to content analysis. Stone[1-3] and others[4] have pioneered a large group of these studies and have developed computer programs capable of classifying content (the General Inquirer System) and of ordering these content categories with one another in interesting ways. Colby[5] has also successfully used a computer to perform content analysis of primitive folk tales from Eskimo, Japanese, and Ixilmaya cultures. In the field of psychiatry and psychology, the attempts to use computer methods to analyze content have been mostly limited to the analysis of various classes of words that manifestly denote certain psychological categories (hostility, love, anxiety, or fear, intellectual processes, and so on).[6]

Most of the automated content analysis projects have been based on single-word or single-phrase tag schemes. The shortcomings of these systems are primarily that they discard too much highly relevant information. For example: (1) They fail to identify who did or felt what about whom. (2) They throw away the meaningful classification of referents such as "it," "that," "which," "those," "these," and so forth, when these are easily comprehended in context by human content-analysis scorers. (3) They ignore the scoring of emotionally charged words that, out of context, cannot be properly classified, such as "get" (in "I'll get you for that"), "dig" (in "I dig you"), or "make" (in "She's on the make").

Our commitment in computer research is to surpass the content analysis of single, isolated words or phrases and to focus on the meaning carried in clauses or sentences and, eventually, in a still broader contextual framework.

---

*From the Communications and Measurement Laboratory, Department of Psychiatry and Human Behavior, College of Medicine, and the Division of Computer Sciences, University of California at Irvine, Irvine, Calif.*

Louis A. Gottschalk, M.D.: *Professor and Chairman, Department of Psychiatry and Human Behavior, College of Medicine;* Catherine Hausmann, B.S.: *Research Associate, Department of Psychiatry and Human Behavior, College of Medicine, and Division of Computer Sciences;* John Seely Brown, Ph.D.: *Assistant Professor, Division of Computer Sciences; University of California at Irvine, Irvine, Calif.*

Our work with computer analysis of the content of speech has progressed slowly over the years 1971 to 1973. In 1971–72 we carried out a pilot study[7] of the feasibility and problems involved in the content analysis of themes contained in interviews, using the hostility outward scale of the Gottschalk-Gleser content analysis method.[8–10] This pilot study made clear some of the difficult problems in an automated approach that sought to identify the subject (agent) and object of an action and the emotional verbs signifying an action or state, the identification of which is clearly prerequisite for applying a content analysis scheme based on the Gottschalk-Gleser hostility scales. This pilot study suggested solutions to some of these problems that formed the basis of our 1972–73 study, the substance of which we are now reporting. We believe that this research demonstrates that the thematic content of natural, spoken language can eventually be computer-analyzed following complex content analysis scales that have proved very useful in research in psychophysiology,[10–12] neuropsychopharmacology,[13–19] psychosomatic medicine,[10,20,21] psychotherapy,[22–25] and general psychiatry.[23,26,27]

## METHODS

Before a computer can successfully mimic the action of a human scorer using the Gottschalk-Gleser content analysis method it must derive a fairly sophisticated representation of the meaning of its input. This is in contradistinction to traditional schemes for computer-driven content analysis, which have found it sufficient to utilize pattern matches against particular words (with and without inflectional endings removed) or against word clusters in order to characterize the essential meaning of its input. In the Gottschalk-Gleser method the presence of a single word or group of words is seldom sufficient for characterizing what score a clause is to receive. Instead, a considerably more detailed analysis of the sentence is mandatory, requiring that the action or theme of the clause along with the actor and recipient of this action be identified. Once these structural elements are isolated, then each can be further analyzed as to the properties it possesses, and then a score for the clause can be determined.

An additional syntactic piece of information that must be gleaned from the structure of a sentence before it can be scored is the existence and scope of a negative. The critical part a negative plays is illustrated by the sentence, "The anteater does not like the red ants." Here the verb "to like," normally a nonhostile, nonscorable verb in the Hostility Directed Outward scale (see Table 1 below), becomes scorable with the addition of the negative "not." A further example is the sentence, "We don't hate bears." This sentence would be scorable without the negative present as self expressing dislike of pets (IB1), but it receives a different content classification with the negative present, namely, denial of dislike, hatred (IIF1).

The scope of the negative becomes important in more complex sentences, such as "He wasn't telling the truth when he said that I like my congressman." If we were looking only at word clusters such as "I like my congressman" we would miss the true intent of the sentence. We must in fact discern the relationships between these clusters; that is, we must find the scope of the negative in the first part of the sentence and discover its effect on the meaning of the second part. In

**Table 1. Hostility Directed Outward Scale: Destructive, Injurious, Critical Thoughts, and Actions Directed to Others**

(I) Hostility Outward—Overt: Thematic Categories

- A3* Self killing, fighting, injuring other individuals or threatening to do so.
- B3 Self robbing or abandoning other individuals, causing suffering or anguish to others, or threatening to do so.
- C3 Self adversely criticizing, depreciating, blaming, expressing anger, dislike of other human beings.
- A2 Self killing, injuring, or destroying domestic animals, pets, or threatening to do so.
- B2 Self abandoning, robbing domestic animals, pets, or threatening to do so
- C2 Self criticizing or depreciating others in a vague or mild manner.
- D2 Self depriving or disappointing other human beings.
- A1 Self killing, injuring, destroying, robbing wildlife, flora, inanimate objects, or threatening to do so.
- B1 Self adversely criticizing, depreciating, blaming, expressing anger or dislike of subhuman, inanimate objects, places, situations.
- C1 Self using hostile words, cursing, mention of anger or rage without referent.

(II) Hostility Outward—Covert: Thematic Categories

- A3* Others (human) killing, fighting, injuring other individuals or threatening to do so.
- B3 Others (human) robbing, abandoning, causing suffering or anguish to other individuals, or threatening to do so.
- C3 Others adversely criticizing, depreciating, blaming, expressing dislike of other human beings.
- A2 Others (human) killing, injuring, or destroying domestic animals, pets, or threatening to do so.
- B2 Others (human) abandoning, robbing domestic animals, pets, or threatening to do so.
- C2 Others (human) criticizing or depreciating other individuals in a vague or mild manner.
- D2 Others (human) depriving or disappointing other human beings.
- E2 Others (human or domestic animals) dying or killed violently in death-dealing situation or threatened with such.
- F2 Bodies (human or domestic animals) mutilated, depreciated, defiled.
- A1 Wildlife, flora, inanimate objects injured, broken, robbed, destroyed, or threatened with such (with or without mention of agent).
- B1 Others (human) adversely criticizing, depreciating, expressing anger or dislike of subhuman, inanimate objects, places, situations.
- C1 Others angry, cursing without reference to cause or direction of anger; also instruments of destruction not used threatening.
- D1 Others (human, domestic animals) injured, robbed, dead, abandoned, threatened with such from any source, including subhuman and inanimate objects, situations (storms, floods, etc.).
- E1 Subhumans killing, fighting, injuring, robbing, destroying each other or threatening to do so.
- F1 Denial of anger, dislike, hatred, cruelty, and intent to harm.

*The number serves to give the weight as well as to identify the category. The letter also helps identify the category.

this example it would allow the sentence to be categorized as self expressing dislike of others (IC3).

In developing a parsimonious theory for how to apply the Gottschalk-Gleser content analysis method the above considerations (plus others) convinced us that we must first derive a description of a clause's syntactic deep structure before attempting to apply our content analysis scheme to it. In so doing we hoped to avoid the fantastic proliferation of special patterns that would otherwise be needed to capture the various syntactic nuances of sentences. What was needed was an efficient parser that contained a sufficiently powerful grammar to characterize the subset of English that is often encountered in psychiatric interviews. The parser chosen for this task was an experimental version of Woods' Augmented Transition Network Parser.[28] This parser was translated into UCI LISP[29] and was slightly modified so as to run on a medium-size PDP-10. Its grammar was enlarged to cover certain linguistic constructions that frequently occurred in our domain of discourse, and a special core resident dictionary (of several hundred entries) was created for the interviews constituting our data base.

Since the Augmented Transition Network Parser has been exceptionally well documented,[28,30] we shall not here provide a detailed description of either how it works[31] or what our version of their basic grammar looks like.[32] We shall instead proceed by example, illustrating the syntactic description produced by the parser and how we make use of this description.

Let us first consider the sentence, "He tore up the calendar page for the new month." It gets parsed as:

```
(SENTENCE DECLARATIVE*
  (NOUN-PHRASE* (PRONOUN He)
    (NUMBER SINGULAR))
  (AUXILIARY* (TENSE PAST))
  (VERB-PHRASE* (VERB tear-up)
    (NOUN-PHRASE (DETERMINER the)
      (ADJECTIVE (NOUN-PHRASE (NOUN calendar)))
      (NOUN page)
      (NUMBER SINGULAR))
      (PREPOSITIONAL-PHRASE (PREPOSITION for)
        (NOUN-PHRASE (DETERMINER the)
        (ADJECTIVE new)
        (NOUN month)
        (NUMBER SINGULAR)))))
```

The syntactic description (or parse) is in the form of a tree with SENTENCE at the top having four branches—DECLARATIVE (the sentence type); NOUN-PHRASE (the subject); AUXILIARY (tense); and VERB-PHRASE (includes the verb, the object, and any verb modifiers). Input sentences in passive voice are transformed into active voice and hence receive the identical structural description the active-voice sentence receives. For example, the following sentences receive the same syntactical description:

"Spinach is not liked by many children."

"Many children do not like spinach."

---

*Abbreviations output by the parser have been expanded for readability.

```
(SENTENCE DECLARATIVE
  NEGATIVE
  (NOUN-PHRASE (ADJECTIVE Many)
               (NOUN child)
               (NUMBER PLURAL))
  (AUXILIARY (TENSE PRESENT))
  (VERB-PHRASE (VERB like)
               (NOUN-PHRASE (NOUN spinach)
                            (NUMBER SINGULAR))))
```

Although the above examples represent only simple sentences (i.e., no embedded sentences, etc.), the parser is capable of handling substantially more complex sentences. However, at present our routines for interpreting (scoring) the output of the parser are restricted to handling nonembedded sentences.

*On Interpreting Syntactic Structures*

In the Gottschalk-Gleser scoring method, the score that a sentence receives depends on the action verb in conjunction with the noun phrases that function as actors and recipients of this action. In addition to isolating these grammatical constituents, we must provide techniques for assigning "meaning" to each of these constituents. Fortunately, a relatively straightforward application of semantic features appears to suffice for this operation. Verbs are assigned features called verb-types ($V_1$–$V_8$), which are listed below:

$V_1$: Causing death or physical injury.
$V_2$: Causing suffering or anguish; robbing; abandoning.
$V_3$: Expressing adverse criticism, anger, blame, dislike, depreciation.
$V_4$: Expressing vague or mild criticism or depreciation.
$V_5$: Depriving; disappointing.
$V_6$: Denial of anger, dislike, hatred, cruelty, or intent to harm.
$V_7$: Cursing.
$V_8$: Dying or killing violently.

These verb-types have been formulated from the Hostility Outward and other Hostility scales (Inward and Ambivalent) of the Gottschalk-Gleser content analysis method. The thematic categories and weights of the Hostility Outward scale are given in Table 1 to help orient the reader.

In order to determine which verb-type a verb is to receive, the infinitive form of the verb is retrieved from the parse and looked up in a feature dictionary. Note that the parser performs the required morphological analysis for stripping the inflectional endings off the verb, yielding its infinitive or root form.

Assigning semantic features to the noun-phrases that function as actors and recipients is slightly more problematic. In the simplest case the noun-phrase receives the semantic features of its head noun (determined by accessing the semantic-feature dictionary with that head noun). If, however, the head noun of a noun-phrase has no "relevant" semantic features but has a modifying prepositional phrase that contains as its head noun a noun that has "relevant" semantic features, then these features are lifted up to function as the semantic markers for the initial noun-phrase. Since this algorithm is completely recursive, it can be repeatedly applied to prepositional phrases that modify previous noun-phrases in

a frantic effort to find some noun in the complex noun-phrase that has usable semantic features. A few samples of this technique will help to illustrate the above discussion.

1. "the little *boy*"

(NOUN-PHRASE (DETERMINER *the*)
  (ADJECTIVE *little*)
  (NOUN *boy*)
  (NUMBER SINGULAR)

Look up "boy" in feature dictionary.
= (+ OTHER + ANIMATE).

2. "the *side* of the *car*"

(NOUN-PHRASE (DETERMINER *the*)
  (NOUN *side*)
  (NUMBER SINGULAR)
  (PREPOSITIONAL-PHRASE (PREPOSITION *of*)
    (NOUN-PHRASE (DETERMINER *the*)
      (NOUN *car*)
      (NUMBER SINGULAR) ) ) )

Look up "side" in feature dictionary. It has no relevant features; so go to prepositional phrase modifying it. Look up the head noun "car" in the feature dictionary.
= (± INANIMATE).

3. "her face"

(POSSESSIVE (NOUN-PHRASE (PRONOUN *she*) ) )
  (NOUN *face*)
  (NUMBER SINGULAR) )

Look up "face" in feature dictionary. It has the special feature (+ PART), which tells the program to look for a preceding possessive, and to look up the head noun of that possessive noun-phrase, "she."
= (+ OTHER + ANIMATE).

### *The Scoring Algorithm*

Our scoring algorithm must decide what the score for the clause (sentence) is to be, after examining the set of features assigned to the above-mentioned noun-phrases and the head verb. In order to piece together this information and to make the correct decision as to what the score for the clause should be, our scorer utilizes an information structure for advice on how to interpret its inputs. This structure is called the scoretree, and it is indexed by the verb-type. For example, the scoretree associated with the verb-type $V_1$ (causing death or

physical injury) is:

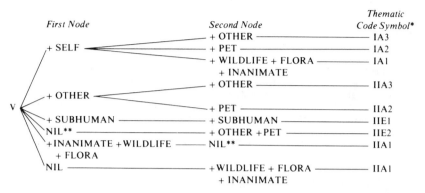

| | *First Node* | *Second Node* | *Thematic Code Symbol** |
|---|---|---|---|
| V | + SELF | + OTHER | IA3 |
| | | + PET | IA2 |
| | | + WILDLIFE + FLORA + INANIMATE | IA1 |
| | + OTHER | + OTHER | IIA3 |
| | | + PET | IIA2 |
| | + SUBHUMAN | + SUBHUMAN | IIE1 |
| | NIL** | + OTHER + PET | IIE2 |
| | +INANIMATE +WILDLIFE + FLORA | NIL** | IIA1 |
| | NIL | +WILDLIFE + FLORA + INANIMATE | IIA1 |

At present each scoretree has only two levels. The first level is made up of tests for the features of the subject of the sentence in question. The second level is composed of tests for the object. The scoring algorithm utilizes the scoretree in the following fashion. First, it determines which scoretree to access by determining the verb-type of the head verb in the clause. It then chooses a first-level node by overlapping the features of the subject (or actor) noun-phrase with the features of successive first-level nodes until some partial match is achieved. It then searches the second-level nodes accessible from the current first-level node overlapping the features of the object (or recipient) noun-phrase with successive nodes until another partial match is achieved. Associated with the second-level node is the score that the total clause is to receive.

In order to unify the various steps that our system goes through in scoring a sentence, we summarize below the results of each step in scoring the sentence, "The garbage man hit my dog with a belt."

The sentence is parsed, yielding the syntactic deep structure:

```
(SENTENCE DECLARATIVE
  (NOUN-PHRASE (DETERMINER the)
    (ADJECTIVE (NOUN-PHRASE (NOUN garbage)))
    (NOUN man)
    (NUMBER SINGULAR)
  (AUXILIARY (TENSE PAST))
  (VERB-PHRASE (VERB hit)
    (NOUN-PHRASE (DETERMINER the)
      (POSSESSIVE (NOUN-PHRASE (PRONOUN I)))
      (NOUN dog)
      (NUMBER SINGULAR)
```

*The number serves to give the weight of this thematic category as well as to identify the category. The letter and Roman numeral also help identify the category. These weights are used to derive the raw and corrected scores in each of the Gottschalk-Gleser psychological scales, the details of which have been described elsewhere.[8]

**Unfeatured subject or object.

(PREPOSITIONAL-PHRASE (PREPOSITION *with*)
(NOUN-PHRASE (DETERMINER *a*)
(NOUN *belt*)
(NUMBER SINGULAR) ) ) )

The head verb, subject (actor), and object (possible recipient) are isolated:

Head verb: *hit*
Subject: (NOUN-PHRASE (DETERMINER *the*) (ADJECTIVE *garbage*) NOUN *man*) )
Object: (NOUN-PHRASE (DETERMINER *the*) (POSSESSIVE (NOUN-PHRASE (PRONOUN *I*) ) ) (NOUN *dog*) (NUMBER SINGULAR) ) (PREPOSITIONAL-PHRASE (PREPOSITION *with*) (NOUN-PHRASE (DETERMINER *a*) (NOUN *belt*) (NUMBER SINGULAR) ) ) )

Each of the above three constituents is assigned a set of semantic features:

Head verb: $V_1$
Subject: (+ OTHER + ANIMATE)
Object: (+ PET + SUBHUMAN + ANIMATE)

The feature of the head verb is used to determine the pertinent scoretree, i.e., $V_1$ (see above for actual scoretree): (1) The first-level node is determined from the features on the subject. (2) The second-level node is determined from the features on the object.

The score associated with the second-level node is output: IIA2. This code symbol (IIA2) gives the weight (2) of this thematic or action category and also serves to identify the category. These weights are used to derive the raw and corrected scores in each of the Gottschalk-Gleser content analysis scales. The details for obtaining final scores on those scales have been described elsewhere.[9,10]

By not integrating the scoretree information directly into the scoring algorithm, we can easily augment and modify this crucial information without having to modify the scoring algorithm. For example, by just changing the scoretree we can use the exact same scoring algorithm for all the different Gottschalk-Gleser scales.

It is difficult to quantify just how well our present computerized scoring method performs. In testing our method out on 100 sentences taken from our manual,[9] we were able to parse and score correctly approximately 60% of them. The sentences below are a representative sample of the kinds of sentences that were handled:

"I sort of upset them with my hours of coming in at nights." (scored ID2—self depriving or disappointing other human beings). For the present we have made the assumption that pronouns like "he," "she," "him," "her," "they," etc., refer to humans. This is a gross assumption and could, in some instances, be erroneous. Note the sentence "The chickens hit their heads." It is not likely that the chickens hit a human head.

"We hit the man on the back of the head with a brick." (scored IIA3—others (human) killing, fighting, injuring other individuals or threatening to do so). Although the complete sentence is parsed, in the present scoring algorithm only the subject, the verb, and the object—in this case, just the first four words—are used to achieve a score.

"The dock has been blown up." (scored IIA1—wildlife, flora, inanimate objects injured, broken, robbed, destroyed, or threatened with such—with or without mention of agent). The parse puts this sentence into active voice, filling in a dummy subject. The scoretree used ($V_1$) has an arc for looking for subjects of this type. The arc looks for a "nil" or unfeatured subject.

"We almost knocked over two gas pumps." (scored IIA1). The verb is parsed as "to knock over." For the present, it is a $V_1$ verb (causing death or physical injury), but if the direct object had been "a bank" it would be a $V_2$ verb (robbing). See the discussion of this problem that follows.

"We picked on my mother a lot." (scored IIC2—others (human) criticizing or depriving other individuals in a vague or mild manner).

"I don't trust him anymore." (scored IC2—self criticizing or depreciating others in a vague or mild manner). The negative "not" makes an unscorable action verb "to trust" into a scorable action.

"I burned a hole in the sofa." (scored IA1—self killing, injuring, destroying, robbing wildlife, flora, inanimate objects or threatening to do so). "Hole" is featureless. The scorer looks to the prepositional phrase modifying it for features.

The Gottschalk-Gleser content analysis method does not claim to score every bit of content relevant to any one psychological state. Rather, it aims to make quantitative differentiations with respect to each psychological state, between verbal samples produced by the same individual on different occasions or between individuals on any occasion. These content analysis scales provide a measure of *relative* magnitude of the emotion or psychological state of people from small samples of their speech. Although at the present stage of development of a computerized scoring method for verbal content about 40% of the content data are lost using an automated method in contrast to a human content analysis technician, perhaps scores from a group of speech samples content-analyzed by a human versus a machine method might intercorrelate highly. As a preliminary test of this question, we selected six 5-min speech samples from the manual[9] and compared the Hostility Directed Outward scores obtained by human content analysis technicians and our computerized scoring system at its present level of development. A Spearman rank difference correlation of 0.80 was obtained between the ranked scores using the two methods. We believe this result, though preliminary, is encouraging and certainly suggests that a fair amount of information can be lost and still not too much disturb the relative ordering of magnitude, by content analysis, of one psychological state.

### *Problems to Be Handled in Future Development of This Computerized System*

It is a property of many verbs that they take on different senses depending on the semantic features of the noun-phrase acting as their direct object. A simple example using the verb "to fire":

1. He fired a gun.
2. He fired a man.
3. He fired a piece of pottery.

In some cases, as with the first two sentences, the change in meaning necessarily dictates a change in the verb's semantic features or verb-type. In

sentence 1 the verb has the verb-type $V_1$ (causing death or physical injury); in sentence 2 it has the verb-type $V_5$ (depriving, disappointing).

Another example of a verb showing this property is "to cut":

He cut her hair.

He cut prices.

He cut a class.

He cut a deck of cards.

He cut the engine.

He cut a song.

It is clear that some way must be found to handle this problem. One way would be to extend the concept of a scoretree by creating a special scoretree for each verb of this type. This would be useful for verbs like "to fire" that have multiple verb-types. The scoretree would allow for disambiguation of the verb's meaning by testing for various kinds of direct objects by looking either for specific words (pottery) or for specific features (+ WEAPON + PROJECTILE).

Another method that would work well with verbs having multiple meanings but only one scorable meaning would require that a list of words or features leading to unscorable senses of the verb be created for each of these problematic verbs. The elements of the list would be checked against the direct object of the sentence in question, and if any of these words or features matched then no scoretree would be accessed and the clause would be scored "nil." Because a special scoretree would not be created with this method, it is a much thriftier approach.

Another problem is that of retrieving recipients that are not direct objects, combined with the problem discussed above. We will illustrate this with the verb "to shoot." Let us look at the sentences:

1. I shot the man.
2. I shot the rifle.
3. I shot at the target.

The first sentence is scored without difficulty. The second sentence is trickier, for it probably does not mean that a hole was put through the rifle. The real recipient of the action is not the direct object, as it is in the first sentence, but some unspecified thing. In the third sentence the object of the prepositional phrase is the recipient. A scoretree for the verb "to shoot" must look for recipients in several places and in a specific order. It must first see whether there is a direct object. If there is one, then it must check to see whether it is a weapon or a projectile from a weapon. If so, or if there is no direct object, then it must look for a prepositional-phrase beginning with "at." The real recipient is probably the noun-phrase within the "at" prepositional-phrase. (Of course, we are always going to come up against such sentences as, "He shot the gun at the park"—an unfortunate ambiguity.) More work must be done on finding ways to characterize the placing of recipients, since their discovery is critical to our scoring scheme.

The third problem, in addition to direct objects changing the meaning of verbs and the unstable placement of recipients in a sentence, is that of single words such as nouns, pronouns, adjectives, etc., implying a scorable action. For example:

"The Sudan raids cause lots of trouble." (IIA3—others killing others or threatening to do so).

"The picture of the killer was in the paper." (IIA3).

"I found a lot of racial prejudice among them." (IIC2—others criticizing others in a vague or mild manner).

"It was just one damned thing after another." (IC1—self cursing).

It is not clear whether there are any systematic and rapid ways of scoring these words. No techniques have been developed yet. A brute-force lookup procedure may be necessary, which is very time-consuming.

Perhaps the most fascinating aspect of this research is the discovery of the amount of inferencing that a human scorer does—something that present-day computers are ill-equipped to handle. One interesting example of this phenomenon is the sentence, "When the lambs are big enough, they end up in the freezer." Using his knowledge of the way the world behaves, the human scorer realizes the implication of lambs ending up in the freezer and scores it IIA2 (others killing pets). Another example: "He knocked over the goldfish bowl." This time the scorer implies a sequence of action not at all explicit in the sentence, which goes something like this: The goldfish bowl is knocked over, dumping both water and fish on the floor; water spreads everywhere (a characteristic of liquids) causing harm to the fish who cannot live without being immersed in it. The scorer codes this clause IIA2 (killing or injuring pets).

A much subtler sentence, requiring knowledge of the views of college students and the significance of troop trains, is, "Some college kids tried to stop a troop train." The scorer scores this one IIC3 (others adversely criticizing, expressing dislike of others). He does not score it this way because of the action alone—trying to stop a train is not equal to expressing dislike of others. Instead he uses his knowledge of the antiwar, antimilitary attitudes of "college kids" and the military aspect of "a troop train" and puts these ideas together into a scenario of political demonstration that one implies as meaning "others adversely criticizing, expressing dislike of others."

Although the present-day field of content analysis is unable to handle these problems requiring the storing of huge amounts of knowledge about the world, we can look to the rising field of artificial intelligence for ideas and possibly future solutions.

## SUMMARY

1. This is a report of the development of a computerized scoring system for use with content analysis scales of speech. The goal has been to surpass the content analysis of single, isolated words in natural language and to focus the analysis on the quality and quantity of meaning carried in clauses or sentences and, eventually, in a broader contextual framework.

2. Using the Gottschalk-Gleser content analysis Hostility scales, the first step taken was the use of an efficient parser that contained a sufficiently powerful grammar to characterize the subset of English that is often encountered in psychiatric interviews. Wood's Augmented Transition Network Parser was modified to run on a PDP-10 computer, and its grammar was enlarged to cover certain linguistic constructions that frequently occur in spoken discourse. In addition, a small dictionary of several hundred entries was created, permitting the maintenance of this dictionary in core.

3. Since the Gottschalk-Gleser content analysis method derives a score on the basis of the action verb in a clause in conjunction with the noun-phrases that function as actors and recipients of this action, a technique was developed for assigning "meaning" to each of these constituents. Accordingly, verbs were assigned semantic features called verb-types based on the thematic categories and weights of the Gottschalk-Gleser Hostility Outward scale.

4. The infinitive form of the verb in each spoken clause was retrieved from the parse and looked up in the semantic-features dictionary. The parser performed the required morphological analysis and stripped the inflectional ending of the verb, yielding its infinitive or root form.

5. The computer next assigned semantic features to the noun-phrases that function as actors and recipients of the action verbs. In the simplest instances, the noun-phrase received the semantic features of its head noun. In more complex instances, for example in prepositional-phrases, noun-phrases were located as semantic markers for the initial noun-phrase.

6. The scoring algorithm for arriving at the score for each clause was obtained after examining the set of semantic features assigned to the above-mentioned noun-phrases and head verb. An information structure (scoretree) was used for advice on how to interpret the combinations of noun-phrases and head verbs, and it was indexed by the verb-type. At present, each scoretree has only two levels; the first level is made up of tests for the features of the subject of the clause in question and the second level is composed of tests for the object. Which scoretree to access is determined by locating the verb-type of the head verb in the clause; the first-level node is obtained by overlapping the features of the subject noun-phrase with the features of successive first-level nodes until some partial match is achieved. The second-level node is located from the first-level node overlapping the features of the object noun-phrase with successive nodes until another partial match is achieved. Associated with the second-level node is the score that the total clause is to receive.

7. In testing this automated method on 100 sentences taken at random from the manual of instructions for using the Gottschalk-Gleser content analysis scales, 60% of them were correctly parsed and scored. As another preliminary test of the information retrieved by this computerized method, six 5-min speech samples were scored by human content analysis technicians, and their scores were compared to the computerized scoring system at its present level of development. A Spearman rank difference correlation of 0.80 was obtained between the ranked scores using the two methods.

8. The shortcomings and further steps to take in the development of this content analysis method are outlined and discussed.

## ACKNOWLEDGMENTS

The technical assistance of Michael Syben, A.B., and Richard R. Burton, A.B., in this study is deeply appreciated.

## REFERENCES

1. Stone PJ, Bales RF, Namewirth JZ, et al: The general inquirer: A computer system for content analysis and retrieval based on the sentence as a unit of information. Behav Sci 7:484 498, 1962

2. Stone PJ, Hunt EB: A computer approach

to content analysis: Studies using the general inquirer system, in Proceedings of the Western Management Science Institute Spring Joint Computer Conference. Reprint #7, Graduate School of Business Administration, University of California, Los Angeles, 1963, pp 241 256

3. Stone PJ, Dunphy DC, Smith MS, et al: The General Inquirer: A Computer Approach to Content Analysis. Cambridge, Mass., M.I.T. Press, 1967

4. Paige JM: Automated content analysis of "Letters from Jenny": A study in individual personality. Department of Social Relations, Harvard University (unpublished paper) 1964

5. Colby BN: A partial grammar of Eskimo folktales. Am Anthropologist 75:645 662, 1973

6. Dahl H: The measurement of meaning in psychoanalysis by computer analysis of verbal contexts. J Am Psychoanal Assoc 22:51 62, 1974

7. Brown JS, Rubinstein R, Vittal J, et al: The feasibility of computer analysis of hostility outward according to the Gottschalk-Gleser content analysis scales. (unpublished paper) 1971

8. Gottschalk LA, Gleser GC, Springer KV: Three hostility scales applicable to verbal samples. Arch Gen Psychiatry 9:254 279, 1963

9. Gottschalk LA, Winget CN, Gleser GC: Manual of Instructions for Using the Gottschalk-Gleser Content Analysis Scales. Los Angeles, Berkeley, University of California Press, 1969

10. Gottschalk LA, Gleser GC: The Measurement of Psychological States from the Content Analysis of Verbal Behavior. Los Angeles, Berkeley, University of California Press, 1969

11. Gottschalk LA, Kaplan SM, Gleser GC, et al: Variations in magnitude of emotion: A method applied to anxiety and hostility during phases of the menstrual cycle. Psychosom Med 24:300 311, 1962

12. Gottschalk LA, Gleser GC, D'Zmura TL, et al: Some psychophysiological relationships in hypertensive women. The effect of hydrochlorothiazide on the relation to affect to blood pressure. Psychosom Med 26:610–617, 1964

13. Gottschalk LA, Gleser GC, Wylie HW, et al: Effects of imipramine on anxiety and hostility levels. Psychopharmacologia 7:303 310, 1965

14. Gleser GC, Gottschalk LA, Fox R, et al: Immediate changes in affect with chlordiazepoxide in juvenile delinquent boys. Arch Gen Psychiatry 13:291 295, 1965

15. Gottschalk LA, Elliott HW, Bates DE, et al: The use of content analysis of short samples of speech for preliminary investigation of psychoactive drugs: Effect of Lorazepam on anxiety scores. Clin Pharmacol Ther 13:323–328, 1972

16. Gottschalk LA, Noble EP, Stolzoff GE, et al: Relationship of chlordiazepoxide blood levels to psychological and biochemical responses, in Garattini S, Mussini E, Randall LO (eds): The Benzodiazepines. New York, Raven Press, 1973, p 257

17. Gottschalk LA, Stone WN, Gleser GC: Peripheral versus central mechanisms accounting for anti-anxiety effect of Propranolol. Psychosom Med 36:47–56, 1974

18. Gottschalk LA, Biener R, Noble EP, et al: Thioridazine plasma levels and clinical response, in Marshall M, Cohn B (eds): Clinical Psychopharmacology, New Research 1974. New York, Jason Aronson, 1974

19. Gottschalk LA: Drug effects in the assessment of affective states in man, in Essman WB, Valzelli L (eds): Current Developments in Psychopharmacology. New York, Spectrum, 1974

20. Gottschalk LA, Cleghorn JM, Gleser GC, et al: Studies of relationships of emotions to plasma lipids. Psychosom Med 27:102–111, 1965

21. Gottschalk LA, Stone WN, Gleser GC, et al: Anxiety levels in dreams: Relation to changes in plasma free fatty acids. Science 153:645–657, 1966

22. Gottschalk LA, Mayerson P, Gottlieb A: The prediction and evaluation of outcome in an emergency brief psychotherapy clinic. J Nerv Ment Dis 144:77–96, 1967

23. Gottschalk LA, Fox RA, Bates DE: Prediction and outcome in a mental health crisis clinic. Am J Psychiatry 130:1107–1111, 1973

24. Gottschalk LA: A hope scale applicable to verbal samples. Arch Gen Psychiatry 30:779–785, 1974

25. Gottschalk LA: The application of a method of content analysis to psychotherapy research. Am J Psychotherapy (in press)

26. Gottschalk LA, Gleser GC: Distinguishing characteristics of the verbal communications of schizophrenic patients, in Disorders of Communication, Assoc Res Nerv Ment Dis (ARNMD) 42:400 413, Baltimore, Williams & Wilkins, 1964

27. Gottschalk LA: An objective method of measuring psychological states associated with changes in neural function. J Biological Psychiatry 4:33 49, 1972

28. Woods WA: Transition network grammar for natural language analysis. Communications of the Association for Computing Machinery 13:10, 1970

29. Bobrow RJ, Burton RR, Lewis D: University of California, Irvine, LISP Manual, University of California at Irvine Technical Report 21, October 1972

30. Woods WA: An experimental parsing system for transition network grammars, in Natural Language Processing. New York, Algorithmics Press, 1973

31. Woods WA, Kaplan RM, Nash-Webber B: The lunar sciences natural language information system: Final report. Bolt Beranek and Newman, Report 2378, June 15, 1972

32. Hausmann CL, Brown JS: Documentation for computerized content analysis system (working paper). 1973

# Response Productivity in Verbal Content Analysis: A Critique of Marsden, Kalter, and Ericson

Goldine C. Gleser
*University of Cincinnati*

Ardie Lubin
*U.S. Naval Health Center, San Diego, California*

**While agreeing with the contention of Marsden, Kalter, and Ericson that use of percentage scores to control for productivity in verbal content analysis can yield erroneous conclusions, exception is taken to their sweeping generalizations in this regard. We particularly refute their inclusion of the Gottschalk-Gleser scales as typical of the unreflecting use of percentage scores. Furthermore, limitations and contradictions are pointed out in the methods they recommend to correct for response productivity.**

In a recent article, Marsden, Kalter, and Ericson (1974) have drawn attention to the important problem of controlling for response productivity in content analysis studies of psychotherapy. They claim that most investigators, who have devised and used verbal content scores, have ignored the problem or have used a method "based on conceptual error, one that does not in fact constitute a control for productivity" (p. 224). The method referred to here is that of expressing the content category frequency (or score, $X$) as a percentage of the total number of units ($T$) coded to all categories.

We share their concern about the erroneous conclusions that can result from the use of a percentage measure where the relation between content score and number of units coded has not been examined. The use of such a ratio implies that the content score for subject $i$ increases linearly as the total number of units increases, in the form

$$X_i = a_i T_i, \quad (1)$$

so that $a_i$ is the characteristic rate at which subject $i$ produces units of the type categorized $X$. This theoretical model can be tested empirically within individuals. Or it can be assumed and the resulting relationship of $T_i$ and $a_i$ can be examined over subjects. In the work of one of us (Gottschalk & Gleser, 1969), the relations between raw scores and number of words were examined extensively in samples from a number of populations before final measures of affects were adopted. In almost every sample, final measures had low, nonsignificant correlations with total words (Gottschalk & Gleser, 1969, p. 18). Judge of our surprise, then, when Marsden et al. (1974) cited the Gottschalk and Gleser measures as typical of the unreflecting erroneous use of percentage scores. Correspondence with Marsden et al. has yielded no change in their position. We think the readers of this journal should have a chance to compare the criticisms of Marsden et al. with the actual methods used by Gottschalk and Gleser so they can make their own judgments of the adequacy with which the problem of verbal fluency is handled. We would also like to comment on some more general issues as well as the dangers of the Marsden et al. solution.

First, let us define the Gottschalk-Gleser measure. It is not a simple percentage of the number of coded units, though the number of words is used as a divisor. The final formula for a verbal affect score is:

$$(f_1w_1 + f_2w_2 + f_3w_3 + \cdots + f_nw_n + .5)^{\frac{1}{2}}/N^{\frac{1}{2}}, \quad (2)$$

where $f_n$ is the frequency of use per observed unit of time for the $n$th type of thematic verbal reference pertinent to the affect being scored, $w_n$ is the weight applied to such thema, and $N$ is the number of words per observed unit of time. It should be noted that the several affect scales do not form a set of mutually exclusive and exhaustive

Requests for reprints should be sent to Goldine C. Gleser, Department of Psychiatry, University of Cincinnati College of Medicine, Cincinnati, Ohio 45267.

categories covering all thema as may be true in some types of content analyses. It is quite possible to find no codable content in a protocol.

Now let us take up the criticisms of Marsden et al.

1. "Percentages are unstable when their denominators are small . . ." (Marsden et al., 1974, p. 225). This exact point was discussed by Gottschalk and Gleser and a solution offered:

"We recommend using only verbal samples of at least 70 or more words because the smaller the number of words in the verbal sample, the less the adequacy or reliability of the sample as a true measure of any psychological variable. A choice of a minimum of 70 words has been arrived at as a rough compromise between reliability of sampling and loss of research data" (Gottschalk & Gleser, p. 67, and see, e.g., pp. 141 and 143).

2. "The score that has presumably been corrected for the effects of productivity ($X/T$) obviously should never be substantially correlated with the measure of productivity ($T$)" (Marsden et al., 1974, p. 225).

Referring to Equation 2, Gottschalk and Gleser (1969) stated that this transformation "with rare exceptions, reduces the correlation between the affect score and number of words essentially to zero" (p. 18).

3. Marsden et al. (1974, p. 226) are concerned that $X/T$ results in a new variable that does not provide direct information about theoretical constructs cast in terms of raw frequencies.

We certainly agree that it is important to devise measures appropriate to the theoretical construct that is being investigated. But we question their assumption that most investigators are interested in the raw frequency of certain words or thema regardless of the quantity of verbal material. Gottschalk and Gleser clearly indicate they are concerned with measures of affect, that they assume these to be measured by the weighted relative frequency of specific thema to verbal references of all kind, and that their final measure should be generalizable over independently obtained verbal samples of variable length. Thus, scores obtained from Equation 2 do represent the theoretical construct in which they are interested. Furthermore, they consider productivity to be an important variable in its own right whose relationship to other variables should be examined in any study using content analysis. (See, e.g., Gottschalk & Gleser, 1969, pp. 156, 208, 283.)

Not only have Marsden et al. seriously misled the readers with regard to the Gottschalk-Gleser scales, but they have provided a very limited and mechanical approach to the problem of controlling verbal content measures for productivity. Let us consider their proposal. Very simply, they suggest that the score $T$-$X$ be used as the measure of response productivity. The partial correlation of each response category with an outside variable $Z$ is then obtained using $T$-$X$ as the variable whose linear effect is removed from $X$ and $Z$. The reason they give for choosing $T$-$X$ to control for productivity is to avoid the "spurious inflation of the correlation" between $X$ and $T$ resulting because $X$ is contained in $T$. Their concern about the part–whole problem seems to stem from a concept of productivity as a secondary or derived variable rather than a basic variable in its own right, independent of the particular content under consideration. That Marsden et al. (1974) see the content score as primary is evident from their statement that "$X$ need not constitute a sizable portion of $T$ to substantially *affect the correlation between* T *and variables with which* X *is correlated*" (p. 226, italics ours). But numerous studies (e.g., Matarazzo, Wiens, & Saslow, 1966) attest to the fact that verbal productivity is an important variable in its own right, usually simpler and more basic than the specific content that is being investigated. If the relation between $X$ and $Z$ can be accounted for by verbal productivity alone, then one does not need an elaborate content analysis to explain the relation. The use of $T$-$X$ as a measure of productivity results in such absurdities as a correlation of $-.26$ and $.21$ with an external variable $Z$ in the same sample, depending on which $X$ is under consideration (see Marsden et al., 1974, Table 2, p. 227). With this changing measure of productivity, how does one interpret the resulting partial correlations? What has been controlled?

Aside from how productivity is measured, the approach of Marsden et al. is misleading in its restrictiveness. They ignore completely the possibility that the pairwise relations between $X$, $T$, and $Z$ may not be linear. Part and partial correlations are based on the assumption of mutually linear relations and have equivocal meaning at best in any other circumstances. Yet nowhere do they suggest examining these relations before deciding on a method of controlling for the effect of productivity. It is interesting, however, that they do recommend an approach suggested by Cronbach (1949). This method takes into account the possibility that relations with $T$ are nonlinear, although Marsden et al. make no mention of this fact. Neither do they mention that Cronbach controls for $T$. Thus, if this method is applied to variables that are linearly related, the result will be the same as that obtained by partialing out $T$, a solution that Marsden et al. had specifically rejected in their 1974 discussion.

We find particularly objectionable the casual treatment given by Marsden et al. (1974) to the development of interpretable measures of a construct. Their only concern is for the specific case in which correlations are obtained with an outside variable. The problem of developing an appropriate measure independent of any specific sample or method of analysis is totally disregarded. Thus, they concluded by taking issue with the use of residual scores, again using Gottschalk and Gleser as their focus of attack. Here they stated without qualification that the practice of using residual scores "incorrectly deals with the part–whole problem and the control of productivity" (p. 228). Their reason for this statement is that "the method neglects to remove from $Z$ its linear effect on $T$ as is properly done by use of the partial correlation coefficient" (p. 228). The important point about a residual score is that it reduces $X$ by that portion of $X$ predictable from $T$ without regard to whether a variable $Z$ has also been observed. Furthermore, if a correlation with an outside variable $Z$ is of interest, whether the linear effect of $T$ should be removed from $Z$ depends on what question is being asked. Correlating the residual score with $Z$ indicates what portion of total variance in $Z$ can be attributed to (or predicted by) $X$ independent of $T$. If one wishes to determine the correlation of $Z$ and $X$ for a fixed value of $T$, then dividing by $(1 - r^2_{ZT})^{\frac{1}{2}}$ yields the partial of which Marsden et al. speak.

In conclusion, we wish to stress that we are not condoning the automatic use of $X/T$ or any other procedure to control for productivity. What we are urging is that measures be developed with appropriate attention to the construct they are intended to operationalize so that research results using such measures can be interpreted meaningfully.

Furthermore, in the analysis of verbal content, controlling for productivity is not enough. What is important is to consider to what extent fluency or productivity accounts for relationships with external variables, regardless of the particular content measures used.

REFERENCES

Cronbach, L. J. Statistical methods applied to Rorschach scores: A review. *Psychological Bulletin*, 1949, *46*, 393–429.

Gottschalk, L. A., & Gleser, G. C. *The measurement of psychological states through the content analysis of verbal behavior.* Berkeley: University of California Press, 1969.

Marsden, G., Kalter, N., & Ericson, W. A. Response productivity: A methodological problem in content analysis studies in psychotherapy. *Journal of Consulting and Clinical Psychology*, 1974, *42*, 224–230.

Matarazzo, R. G., Wiens, A. N., & Saslow, G. Experimentation in the teaching and learning of psychotherapy skills. In L. A. Gottschalk & A. H. Auerbach (Eds.), *Methods of research in psychotherapy.* New York: Appleton-Century-Crofts, 1966.

(Received January 20, 1975)

# Part III
# Neuropsychopharmacological Studies

A survey and appraisal of the application of verbal behavior methods to psychopharmacology has been made by Waskow (1967). In this excellent review, Waskow has described and discussed not only the Gottschalk-Gleser content analysis approach, but that of others.

Neuropsychopharmacological studies have been attractive to Gottschalk and his coworkers because such studies provide an avenue for exploring the relationship in humans of neurochemical correlates to feelings, thoughts, and behavior. The biochemical alterations in the central nervous system induced by psychoactive pharmacological agents, now beginning to be understood, provide an experimental approach to the psychobiochemistry and psychopharmacology of the mind.

Early in the development of his content analysis method, Gottschalk explored the psychological and behavioral changes that were induced by various pharmacological agents. Most of the psychopharmacological studies done by Gottschalk and his colleagues have not had, as an immediate or

urgent goal, the assessment of the effectiveness of a psychopharmacological agent in any specific type of emotional disorder or mental illness, although more recently there have been exceptions to this statement. Rather, the focus has been to determine in what ways the administration of the psychoactive agent has influenced various key psychological states, drives, or psychopathological symptoms, and quite often these psychopharmacological studies have not involved psychiatric patients (for example, Gottschalk et al, 1968). An early application by Gottschalk et al (1956) of content analysis to psychopharmacological studies demonstrated that a dose of 2 to 6 mgs of pipradrol (Meratran - a psychomotor stimulant), as compared to a placebo, significantly increased the number of verbal references to actual or expected accomplishments and strivings for recognition as well as the number of words spoken per three minutes. Ross et al (1963), along a somewhat similar line, asked 80 medical students to write five-minute verbal samples in double-blind, placebo-drug study, in which one third of the students received, by mouth, either a placebo, 10 mgs of dextro-amphetamine, or 65 mgs of amobarbital. A significantly lower mean anxiety score ($p < .05$), using the Gottschalk-Gleser content analysis anxiety scale, was found with amobarbital, as compared with dextroamphetamine or the placebo. Also, more words were written per five minutes, on the average ($p < .10$) by subjects on amphetamine (108) than on the placebo (95) or amobarbital (86). Gottschalk et al (1968) next explored the influence of the subject's mental set or induced attitude on the subject's response to psychoactive medication, using 108 male college students, and having them write ten-minute verbal samples while on either a placebo, secobarbital (90 mg), or racemic amphetamine sulfate (10 mg). The subjects were led to the expectation that they would have one of three possible reactions from the drug they received, including the placebo. Interesting drug and mental set interaction effects were noted.

Gottschalk and his coworkers next carried out several psychopharmacological studies using their content analysis procedure in the assessment of the effects of tranquilizers. In one study (Gleser et al, 1965),

46 juvenile delinquent boys were orally administered 20 mgs of chlordiazepoxide (Librium) in a double-blind, placebo-drug study. Significant decreases were found in anxiety ($p < .01$), ambivalent hostility ($p < .05$), and overt hostility outward scores ($p < .06$) 40 to 120 minutes after ingesting 20 mg of chlordiazepoxide. No psychological changes were found from the content analysis of five-minute verbal samples 24 hours after ingesting 30 mg of chlordiazepoxide. In another study (Gottschalk et al, 1960), 20 dermatologic inpatients (10 men and 10 women, ages range 17 to 79) were given 16 to 24 mg/day of perphenazine (Trilafon) by mouth for one week, alternating with a placebo for one week, using a double-blind, cross-over design. Analysis of the content of five-minute verbal samples obtained from these patients showed, with perphenazine, a reduction of median hostility outward scores in 16 of the 20 patients ($p < .01$) and a significant increase in references to feelings of bodily and emotional well-being ($p < 02$). With perphenazine, there also occurred a decrease in the anxiety scores at the elevated end of the spectrum of anxiety scores derived from speech samples, but this trend did not quite reach a .05 level of confidence. Longitudinal studies of psychopharmacological effects of drugs were next carried out by Gottschalk et al (1968), using the major tranquilizer, thioridazine (Mellaril) and the antidepressant, imipramine (Tofranil) (Gottschalk et al, 1965). Moreover, studies of the content analysis of the speech of individuals administered psychotomimetic drugs (LSD-25, Ditran, Psilocybin) or a placebo showed that people receiving a psychotomimetic drug had significantly higher content analysis scores on the Gottschalk-Gleser congitive and intellectual impairment scale than when they received a placebo (Gottschalk and Gleser, 1969).

References

Gleser, G.C., Gottschalk, L.A., Fox, R., and Lippert, W. Immediate changes in affect with chlordiazepoxide in juvenile delinquent boys. Arch. Gen. Psychiatry 13, 291-295 (1965).

Gottschalk, L.A. and Gleser, G.C. The Measurement of Psychological States

Through the Content Analysis of Verbal Behavior. University of California Press, Berkeley, Los Angeles (1969).

Gottschalk, L.A., Gleser, G.C., Springer, K.J., Kaplan, S.M., Shanon, J., and Ross, W.D. Effects of perphenazine on verbal behavior patterns. Arch. Gen. Psychiatry 2, 632-639 (1960)

Gottschalk, L.A., Gleser, G,C,, and Stone, W.N. Language as a measure of changes in schizophrenia. Effect of a tranquilizer (phenothiazine derivative) on anxiety, hostility, and social alienation-personal disorganization in chronic schizophrenic patients. Presented at Symposium on Language and Thought in Schizophrenia, Newport Beach, California, November (1968).

Gottschalk, L.A., Gleser, G.C., Stone, W.N., and Kunkel, R.L. Studies of psychoactive drug effects on nonpsychiatric patients. Measurement of affective and cognitive changes by content analysis of speech, in Psychopharmacology of Drugs of Abuse, J. Wittenborn, W. Evans, N. Kline, and J. Cole, eds. Charles C. Thomas, Springfield, Illinois (1968)

Gottschalk, L.A., Gleser, G.C., Wylie, H.W., Jr., and Kaplan, S.M. Effects of imipramine on anxiety and hostility levels. Psychopharmacologia 7, 303-310 (1965)

Gottschalk, L.A., Kapp, F.T., Ross, W.D., Kaplan, S.M., Silver, H., MacLeod, J.A., Kahn, J.B., Jr., Van Maanen, E.F., and Acheson, E.H. Explorations in testing drugs affecting physical and mental activity. Studies with a new drug of potential value in psychiatric illness. J.A.M.A. 161, 1054-1058 (1956).

Ross, W.D., Adsett, N., Gleser, G.C., Joyce, C.R.B., Kaplan, S.M., and Tieger, M.E. A trial of psychopharmacologic measurement with projective techniques. J. Proj. Tech. 27, 223-225 (1963)

Waskow, I. The effects of drugs on speech: a review, in Research in Verbal Behavior and Some Neurophysiological Implications. K. Salzinger and S. Salzinger, eds. Academic Press, New York (1967)

The collection of papers in the present volume report studies carried out after the 1969 books published by Gottschalk and his coworkers, and these provide further demonstrations of the range of applications of these content analysis scales.

The papers in this section of neuropsychopharmacology are arranged according to logical groups. The first group of papers explore the effects of certain psychoactive drugs or chemical substances on language content as exemplified in the Gottschalk-Gleser content analysis scales. This section includes a chapter (11) on the "Effects of amphetamine or chlorpromazine on achievement striving scores derived from the content analysis of speech" (Gottschalk et al, 1971), a chapter (12) on "Effects of Diphenylhydantoin on anxiety and hostility in institutionalized prisoners" (Gottschalk et al, 1973), a chapter (13) on "Anxiety and beta adrenergic blockade" which examines the effect of propranolol on anxiety scores (Stone et al, 1973), a chapter (14) exploring the effect of marihuana entitled "Effect of marihuana and placebo marihuana smoking on psychological state and on psychophysiological cardiovascular functioning in anginal patients" (Gottschalk et al, 1977), and a previously unpublished chapter (15) on effects of alcohol on psychological state entitled "A laboratory study of emotional reactions to a stressful film on alcoholic and non-alcoholic subjects" (Parker et al, 1977). Another chapter (16) in this group explores this content analysis method as a means of detecting and establishing the anti-anxiety effect of new drugs, "Content analysis of speech samples to determine effect of Lorazepam on anxiety" (Gottschalk et al, 1972). An original and previously unpublished chapter (17) involves an investigation of the effects of inhalation of 40% nitrous oxide on psychological states as measured by content analysis. It is entitled, "Measurement of subjective effects of nitrous oxide; validation of post-drug questionnaire responses by verbal content analysis of speech samples collected during drug intoxication" (Atkinson).

Another subsection of these neuropsychopharmacological studies

includes chapters which explore, with the Gottschalk-Gleser speech content analysis method, the language characteristics of certain neuropsychiatric syndromes and the extent to which these syndromes are altered by psychoactive drugs. One chapter (18) in this group, "Prediction of changes in severity of the schizophrenic syndrome with discontinuation in administration of phenothiazines in chronic schizophrenic patients: language as a predictor and measure of change in schizophrenia" (Gottschalk et al, 1970) examines carefully the extent to which various verbal categories in the social alienation-personal disorganization scale is influenced by the withdrawal and the administration of phenothiazine derivatives. Two other papers aim to examine subtle speech characteristics of a transient cerebral organic brain syndrome, characterized by temporary impairment of short term memory consolidation, produced by certain benzodiazepine derivatives. These two chapters (19 and 20) are entitled "Effects of triazolam and flurazepam, on emotions and intellectual function" (Gottschalk and Elliott, 1977) and "Effects of certain benzodiazepine derivatives on disorganization of thought as manifested in speech" (Gottschalk, 1977). The last chapter (21) in this subsection involves a study of psychoactive drug, propranolol, to try to explain the mechanism of anxiety-relieving effects of a beta-adrenergic pharmacological agent; this chapter is entitled "Peripheral versus central mechanisms accounting for antianxiety effects of propranolol" (Gottschalk et al, 1974).

A third subsection of this group of neuropsychopharmacological studies involves the investigation of the pharmacokinetics of certain psychoactive drugs and the relationship of individual differences in pharmacokinetics and the clinical response to these specific drugs. These chapters include (22) "Chlordiazepoxide plasma levels and clinical response" (Gottschalk and Kaplan, 1972), a chapter (23) exploring both psychological and biochemical responses to chlordiazepoxide pharmacokinetics entitled "Relationships of chlordiazepoxide blood levels to psychological and biochemical responses" (Gottschalk et al, 1973). Another chapter (24) examines the pharmacokinetics of meperidine (Demerol) and clinical

response "Relationships of plasma meperidine levels to changes in anxiety and hostility" (Elliott et al, 1974). The pharmacokinetics of major tranquilizers and clinical response are explored in a chapter (25) entitled "Thioridazine plasma levels and clinical response" (Gottschalk et al, 1975); another chapter (26) entitled "Plasma levels of mesoridazine and its metabolites and clinical response in acute schizophrenia after a singular intramuscular drug dose" (Gottschalk et al, 1976); and another chapter (27) dealing with pharmacokinetics and clinical response is entitled "Pharmacokinetics of chlordiazepoxide, meperidine, thioridazine, and mesoridazine and relationships with clinical response" (Gottschalk et al, 1975).

A final subsection of these neuropsychopharmacological studies deals with measurement problems involving psychological states and their assessment in this section peculiar to the field of psychopharmacology itself. The one chapter (28) in this section is entitled "Drug effects and the assessment of affective states in man" (Gottschalk, 1975).

# Effect of Amphetamine or Chlorpromazine on Achievement Strivings Scores Derived From Content Analysis of Speech

*By* Louis A. Gottschalk, Daniel E. Bates, Irene E. Waskow, Martin M. Katz, and James Olsson

THIS STUDY IS BASED ON DATA that had been collected in an NIMH research project investigating the psychological states produced by a number of differently acting psychotropic drugs.[14] In this project, small doses of LSD, amphetamine, and chlorpromazine were administered to prisoner subjects, who were tested before and after drug administration on a number of physiological and psychological measures. Results have already been reported on some of the major effects of LSD in this study. The psychological testing included obtaining short samples of the subjects' speech, according to procedures developed by Gottschalk and Gleser.[9] In the present paper, we are reporting on the effects of amphetamine and chlorpromazine on achievement strivings as measured by a content analysis method applied to these speech samples.

The achievement strivings scale used in the present study gained impetus from the work of Friedman and Rosenman,[5,6] who were investigating coronary heart disease in persons who felt driven to achieve under pressure of time. To pursue similar studies, Gottschalk et al.[7] developed a content analysis scale applicable to small samples of speech for measuring achievement strivings and achievement frustration; using this method they compared achievement strivings scores of healthy subjects and medical inpatients with myocardial infarction or coronary insufficiency. They found the group of healthy individuals showed significantly higher scores for total achievement strivings than the scores of three groups of hospitalized patients.[9] They attributed their finds in part to the context in which the individuals spoke. The same achievement strivings scale was later employed to study the effect of a subject's mental set or expectation on the effect of a psychoactive drug, racemic amphetamine, secobarbital, or a placebo.[8] Subjects were randomly assigned to one of nine combinations of these three drugs and three mental sets (amphetamine, secobarbital, and placebo set). Achievement strivings scores were found to be significantly higher with the amphetamine set ("This drug will probably make

*From the Department of Psychiatry and Human Behavior, University of California at Irvine, Irvine, Calif., the Clinical Research Branch, Division of Extramural Research Programs, National Institute of Mental Health, Bethesda, Md., and Friends of Psychiatric Research, Baltimore, Md.*

Louis A. Gottschalk, M.D.: *Chairman, Department of Psychiatry and Human Behavior, University of California, Irvine, Calif.* Daniel E. Bates, B.A.: *Postgraduate Researcher, Department of Psychiatry and Human Behavior, University of California, Irvine, Calif.* Irene E. Waskow, Ph.D.: *Clinical Research Branch, Division of Extramural Research Programs, National Institute of Mental Health, Bethesda, Md.* Martin M. Katz, Ph.D.: *Chief, Clinical Research Branch, Division of Extramural Research Programs, National Institute of Mental Health, Bethesda, Md.* James Olsson, Ph.D.: *Friends of Psychiatric Research, Baltimore, Md.*

you feel more peppy and energetic and cheerful.") and with the amphetamine drug; the drug-set interaction was not significant. Evans and Smith[4] showed that 10 mg of *d*-amphetamine enhanced the need to achieve scores as measured by McClelland's need achievement scale for the Thematic Apperception Test. But in a later paper, Davis, et al.,[1] using 15 mg of *d*-amphetamine, failed to completely duplicate this finding. At one point (55 min postdrug) they found the amphetamine group had *less* achievement imagery than the placebo group.

Since Gottschalk's initial studies, the achievement strivings content analysis scale has undergone minor modification. The present study was performed using the current scale which differs slightly from earlier forms. Therefore, in part, the present study serves as a validation study (Table 1). The standard administration and scoring procedures are discussed in detail elsewhere.[9]

## Materials and Methods

Two studies reported in this research project took place, under the auspices of the NIMH's Psychopharmacology Research Branch, at the Patuxent Institution, a treatment center in Maryland for emotionally disturbed criminal offenders. A total of 80 inmates took part in two studies. In the present paper, data is reported only for the 41 subjects in the amphetamine, chlorpromazine, and placebo groups who produced adequate speech samples in the predrug and at least one postdrug period. There were 30 whites and 11 blacks with a mean age of 26.0 yr and an age range of 21–39. The average education level was 9.7 yr and the average I.Q. was 103.2. All the subjects were given a psychiatric screening to eliminate any possible psychotic or severely disturbed individuals. A more complete description of the subject population, as well as the procedures used in these studies, is presented in Katz et al.[14]

### *Procedure*

After screening, all potential subjects were interviewed, instructed as to the general nature of the research, and given a choice of volunteering or not volunteering for the study. It was explained that the effects of the various drugs would range from mild to moderately strong depending upon the drug and how each person reacted to it. Also, subjects were informed, "Some effects might be pleasant, others might be uncomfortable, and other effects might be quite different than you've had before." An important aspect of the research procedure was the attempt to create—in the instructions given, in the atmosphere of the room, and in the interactions of the staff with the subject—a pleasant, but neutral atmosphere, in which specific expectations on the subject's part would be kept to a minimum.

In the first study, subjects who volunteered were randomly assigned to one of four treatments (11 subjects to each): 50 $\mu$g LSD, 15 mg amphetamine, 50 mg chlorpromazine, and placebo; in the second study, 12 subjects were each randomly assigned to the LSD, amphetamine, and placebo conditions. Results reported in the present paper are based on data for the 18 amphetamine, 8 chlorpromazine, and 15 placebo subjects for whom adequate speech samples were available.

The conditions of the study were double-blind; neither the subjects nor observers knew to which treatment condition a subject was assigned. Each subject was run on a separate day. Before administration of the drug, a psychiatrist and a psychologist administered the base-line physiological and psychological tests. The psychiatrist briefly reiterated the instructions given earlier, and the drugs were then administered orally. An hour later, testing was resumed and was repeated at specified intervals throughout the day. Between testing periods, the research coordinator kept in frequent touch with the subject and tried to maintain a friendly, supportive relationship.

In addition to the speech samples, predrug and postdrug testing was carried out on a

Table 1.—Achievement Strivings Scale

Score all codable clauses. Distinguish between references to the self or others by adding the following notation: (a) self or self and others; (b) others.

I. Vocational, occupational, educational references, including naming and identification.

II. Other constructive activities where emphasis is on work or labor rather than play. Emphasis may be in form of overcoming hardships, obstacles, problems, toward reaching a goal. Exclude all sports and entertainment activities.
   A. Domestic activities: moving; buying or selling major items; decorating, painting, cleaning, cooking, doing chores.
   B. Activities that require some effort or perseverance to carry out or activities done with speed or accuracy, activities involving trying new experiences as in eating new food or traveling to new places (score no more than three in succession of references to traveling to new places). Score references to learning new information or habits, needing to satisfy curiosity, or attempting to unlearn undesirable attitudes or behavior.

III. References to commitment or sense of obligation to responsible or constructive social and personal behavior; to obligation to perform well or succeed in a task; to commitment to a task and to carrying it out or completing it. References to inculcation by others or self of sense of responsibility for one's actions or for welfare of others; responsibility for leadership; evidence of positive superego or ego ideal; evidence of high standards or standards that are hard to live up to (score these even when reference is to fears of not achieving, e.g., "I felt terrible about doing so badly on the test").

IV. Deterrents
   A. External dangers or problems or fear of loss of control or limit setting on part of others. References to lack of control by others; references to errors or misjudgments by others that might injure the self.
   B. Internal obstacles: references to difficulties in setting limits on oneself or problems in disciplining the self; references to errors or misjudgments by self that might harm the self.
   C. Interpersonal: arguments or troubles getting along with others; problems in interpersonal relations, such as inability to make friends.

V. Sports (note that some sports, such as swimming, may be A, B, or C, depending on context).
   A. Spectator.
   B. Team or organized.
   C. Solitary or small group.

VI. Entertainment.
   A. Spectator.
   B. Amateur.
   C. Professional.

number of physiological measures, including blood pressure, body temperature, and pupillary changes; and a number of psychological measures, including the Clyde Mood Scale, Subjective Drug Effects Questionnaire, and Picture Rating Technique.

Speech samples were obtained from both drug and placebo subjects, predrug and postdrug. Subjects were instructed to talk about any interesting or dramatic personal experience and their speech samples were tape-recorded.[9] In the first study subjects were instructed to speak for 5 min, and in the second study, for 3 min. The postdrug speech samples were obtained at approximately 2 hr and 4 hr postdrug. Subsequent scoring of achievement strivings from the verbal samples was performed by content analysis technicians, independ-

Table 2.—Effect of Amphetamine (15 mg), Chlorpromazine (50 mg), or a Placebo on Achievement Strivings Scores

| Treatment | No. | Mean Scores for Achievement Strivings | | |
|---|---|---|---|---|
| | | Verbal Sample 1 | Verbal Sample 2 | Verbal Sample 3 |
| Amphetamine (15 mg) | 16 | 1.33±1.62 | 2.93*±1.94 | 2.13±1.90 |
| Chlorpromazine (50 mg) | 7 | 1.68±1.99 | 0.07±1.71 | 2.00±1.95 |
| Placebo | 14 | 1.39±1.92 | 0.43±1.30 | 1.00±2.50 |

*Significantly greater than the achievement strivings scores from the comparable verbal sample of the placebo group at the 0.01 level when both are adjusted for verbal sample 1.

ent of those who gathered the data at the Patuxent Institution, and blind to the conditions of the study.

Scores on the achievement strivings scale were calculated for each verbal sample and corrected for number of words spoken in the standard manner, i.e., scores were expressed in terms of amount of scoreable thematic items per 100 words.[9] Correcting for number of words in this way, allowed the achievement strivings scores derived from 5-min verbal samples obtained in the first study and the 3-min samples obtained in the second study, to be included together for the statistical analysis (Table 2).

Analysis of covariance with multiple covariates, BMD04V,[3] was used to test for differences between scores for the amphetamine, chlorpromazine, and placebo groups for verbal sample 2 (2 hr postdrug) adjusted for verbal sample 1 (predrug) scores and verbal sample 3 (4 hr postdrug) scores adjusted for verbal sample 1 (predrug) scores. The scores for subjects who did not speak in all three sessions were not included in the statistical analysis. There were two in the amphetamine group, one in the placebo group, and one in the chlorpromazine group who were dropped.

## Results

Covariance analysis revealed that scores for the amphetamine group for verbal sample 2 were significantly higher ($p<0.01$) than comparable scores from the placebo group ($F=19.33$, df=1, 26). But scores for the amphetamine group for verbal sample 3 were not quite significantly higher than the same scores for the placebo group ($F=4.16$, df=1, 26). The covariance analysis indicated that achievement strivings scores derived from verbal sample 2 and verbal sample 3 for the chlorpromazine group were not significantly different than comparable scores from the placebo group ($F=0.46$, df=1, 17 and $F=0.75$, df=1, 17, respectively).

The effect of amphetamine or chlorpromazine on number of words for the first 3 min of all samples was investigated for verbal sample 2 and verbal sample 3, using analysis of covariance (Table 3). Comparing the number of words spoken by the amphetamine group to number of words spoken by the placebo group for verbal samples 2 and 3 adjusted for number of words spoken for verbal sample 1, significantly more words were spoken ($p<0.05$) when subjects were on amphetamine for verbal sample 2 only ($F=6.71$, df=1, 27).

Any possible influence of number of words spoken on achievement strivings scores was examined statistically, and it was found to be negligible. No significant differences were found, also, in number of words spoken in verbal samples

**Table 3.—Effect of Amphetamine (15 mg), Chlorpromazine (50 mg), or a Placebo on Number of Words Occurring in the First 3 Min of Speech Samples**

| Treatment | No. | Mean Number of Words Spoken | | |
|---|---|---|---|---|
| | | Verbal Sample 1 | Verbal Sample 2 | Verbal Sample 3 |
| Amphetamine (15 mg) | 16 | 260.9±124.3 | 315.6*±86.2 | 281.9±126.5 |
| Chlorpromazine (50 mg) | 7 | 311.9±75.1 | 321.7±110.8 | 298.1±95.9 |
| Placebo | 14 | 332.1±108.6 | 287.9±120.3 | 275.3±149.1 |

*Significantly greater than the number of words from comparable verbal sample of the placebo group at the 0.05 level when both are adjusted for verbal sample 1.

2 and 3 from the chlorpromazine group as compared to the equivalent indices from the placebo group.

## Discussion and Conclusion

As previously stated, the present study was designed to ascertain whether amphetamine (15 mg by mouth) could affect achievement strivings scores as measured by the Gottschalk-Gleser Achievement Strivings Scale, a psycholinguistic technique for assessing the relative magnitude of this psychological state. As shown, a relationship was indicated between ingestion of 15 mg of amphetamine and a significant increase in achievement strivings scores 2 hr later. Although there was a similar effect 4 hr later, it was not large enough to be statistically significant. The present study corroborates other studies that single doses of psychomotor stimulants, such as amphetamine, increase the expression of achievement strivings, as assessed by the Gottschalk content analysis procedures[8,10] or the McClelland need achievement scale applied to the Thematic Apperception Test.[1,4] The increased verbal expression of achievement strivings and increased verbal output with amphetamine-like drugs does not necessarily signify, of course, that other achievement behavior will necessarily be concurrently manifested. DiMascio and Buie,[2] after administering 10–15 mg of *d*-amphetamine, found no cognitive or motor improvement. Holliday[12] showed that 10 mg of *d*-amphetamine enhanced performance (in addition and subtraction tasks) of fatigued subjects but failed to demonstrate that 10 mg of *d*-amphetamine facilitated performance over predrug performance. In their earlier mentioned paper, Evans and Smith[4] found amphetamine enhanced performance on two tasks; spatial orientation tests and Guilford's Consequences Test. Yet, Weiss and Laties,[15] based on a comprehensive review of research in the area of athletic events and monitoring tasks up to 1961, contend that amphetamine enhancement of performance is not restricted just to fatigued or bored subjects. Recently Hurst[13] found subjects in self-appraisal tests said that their performance increased somewhat on racemic amphetamine, and increased a great deal on *d*-amphetamine, although neither drug actually affected performances significantly.

The failure to find a significant depressing effect of chlorpromazine as com-

pared to placebo on achievement strivings scores may be due to the small dosage (50 mg) employed in the present study. Davis et al.[1] reported a decrease in achievement strivings scores with 75 mg of oral chlorpromazine as compared to amphetamine. The present study may have had too small a chlorpromazine group (N=7) to allow the drug effect to become apparent or the present study's inability to confirm the findings of Davis et al. may be because our study compared the influence of chlorpromazine to the placebo group instead of the amphetamine group.

In the present study and other similar ones[7,8] the specificity of the effect of amphetamine on spontaneous references to achievement strivings in speech is supported by the fact that anxiety and hostility scores derived by content analysis using the Gottschalk-Gleser method are not increased by amphetamine at these dose levels (10–15 mg orally).

This further psychopharmacological validation of the Gottschalk-Gleser Achievement Strivings Scale justifies further use of this objective content analysis procedure for assessing the magnitude of achievement strivings as a predictor variable or dependent variable in psychiatric and behavioral science research.

## Acknowledgment

Statistical and computing assistance was provided by William H. Fellner, Mathematics Department, University of California, Irvine, and the Health Sciences Computing Facility, UCLA, sponsored by NIH Resources Grant RR-3.

## References

1. Davis, K. E., Evans, W. O., and Gillis, J. S.: The effects of amphetamine and chlorpromazine on cognitive skills and feelings in normal adult males. *In* Evans, W. O., and Kline, N. (Eds.): Psychopharmacology of the Normal Human. Springfield, Ill.: Charles C Thomas, 1968.

2. DiMascio, A., and Buie, D. H.: Psychopharmacology of chlorphentermine and d-amphetamine. Clin. Pharmacol. Ther. 5:174, 1964.

3. Dixon, W. J. (Ed.): Biomedical Computer Programs. Berkley, University of California Press, 1968.

4. Evans, W. O., and Smith, R. P.: Some effects of morphine and amphetamine on intellectual functions and mood. Psychopharmacologia 6:49, 1964.

5. Friedman, M., and Rosenman, R. H.: Association of specific overt behavior patterns with blood cholesterol levels, blood clotting time, incidence of arcus senilis, and coronary artery disease. JAMA 169:1286, 1959.

6. –, and –: Overt behavior patterns in coronary disease: Detection of overt behavior patterns in patients with coronary disease by a new psychophysiologic procedure. JAMA 173:1320, 1960.

7. Gottschalk, L. A., Cleghorn, J. M., and Gleser, G. C.: Studies of inpatients with acute myocardial infarction and coronary insufficiency. Foundations Fund for Research in Psychiatry-Fluid Research Grant. Unpublished Study, 1964. *In* Gottschalk, L. A., and Gleser, G. C. (Eds.): The Measurement of Psychological States Through the Content Analysis of Verbal Behavior. Berkeley, University of California Press, 1969.

8. –, Gleser, G. C., Stone, W. N., and Kunkel, R. L.: Studies of psychoactive drug effects on non-psychiatric patients. Measurement of affective and cognitive changes by content analysis of speech. *In* Evans, W. O., and Kline, N. (Eds.): Psychopharmacology of the Normal Human. Springfield, Ill., Charles C Thomas, 1968.

9. –, –: The Measurement of Psychological States Through the Content Analysis of Verbal Behavior. Berkeley, University of California Press, 1969.

10. –, Kapp, F. T., Ross, W. D., Kaplan, S. M., Silver, H., MacLeod, J. A., Kahn, J. B., Jr., Van Maunen, E. F., Acheson, G. H.:

Explorations in testing drugs affecting physical and mental activity. Studies with a new drug of potential value in psychiatric illness. JAMA 161:1054, 1956.

11. –, Winget, C. N., and Gleser, G. C.: Manual of Instructions for Using the Gottschalk-Gleser Content Analysis Scales: Anxiety, Hostility, and Social Alienation-Personal Disorganization. Berkeley, University of California Press, 1969.

12. Holliday, A. R.: The effects of *d*-amphetamine on errors and correct responses of human beings performing a simple intellectual task. Clin. Pharmacol. Ther. 7:312, 1966.

13. Hurst, P. M.: Dimensions of drug effects upon choice behavior. Psychopharmacol. Bull. 6:32, 1970.

14. Katz, M. M., Waskow, I. E., and Olsson, J.: Characterizing the psychological state produced by LSD. J. Abnorm. Psychol. 73:1, 1968.

15. Weiss, B., and Laties, V.: Enhancement of human performance by caffeine and amphetamines. Pharmacol. Rev. 14:1, 1962.

# Effects of Diphenylhydantoin on Anxiety and Hostility in Institutionalized Prisoners

Louis A. Gottschalk, Lino Covi, Regina Uliana, and Daniel E. Bates

NEARLY THREE DECADES ago a number of reports appeared that diphenylhydantoin was useful in the treatment of behavioral or psychophysiological disorders, characterized by excitement of a nonepileptic nature (Kalinowski and Putnam, 1943; Freyhan, 1945; Kubanek and Rowell, 1946). There were also claims about this time of beneficial effects of diphenylhydantoin with psychopathic behavior (Brill and Walker, 1945) on the grounds that many such patients have abnormal EEGs (Hill and Waterson, 1942). A revival of interest has occurred in diphenylhydantoin as a therapeutic agent in a wide variety of nonepileptic disorders (Turner, 1967; Jonas, 1967), including adult prisoners and juvenile delinquents (Resnick, 1967) and neurotic patients (Haward, 1967).

Klein (1967) observed that diphenylhydantoin's effects were subtle compared to the obvious influences of the phenothiazines and antidepressants and speculated that diphenylhydantoin might function as a "mood stabilizing adjunct." A review of controlled studies over the past few years would seem to support Klein's view that the effects, if any, of diphenylhydantoin on psychiatric manifestations are relatively difficult to detect and may be limited to mood or affect stabilization in selected patients.

Booker et al. (1967) studied three groups of normal college undergraduates (N = 20), divided into three groups receiving either 300 mg of diphenylhydantoin daily for 6 days, placebo for 6 days, or 300 mg of diphenylhydantoin for 6 days followed by 6 days of placebo. No consistent effects attributable to diphenylhydantoin were demonstrated, either on physiological or on psychological tests, including measures of tactile discrimination ability, auditory attention and sustained concentration, motor steadiness, heart rate, vasomotor reactivity, and galvanic skin response.

Case et al. (1969), in a double-blind study on anxious psychiatric outpatients, found no significant drug-placebo differences in effect of diphenylhydantoin (200 mg/day) on anxiety.

Lefkowitz (1969), in a controlled study on 50 institutionalized delinquent

*From the Department of Psychiatry and Human Behavior, College of Medicine, University of California at Irvine, and the Department of Psychiatry and Behavioral Sciences, The Johns Hopkins University School of Medicine, Baltimore, Maryland.*

Louis A. Gottschalk, M.D.: *Professor of Psychiatry, Social Science, and Social Ecology and Chairman of the Department of Psychiatry and Human Behavior, College of Medicine, University of California at Irvine; Director, Psychiatric Residency Training Program and Psychiatric Services, UCI-Orange County Medical Center, Orange, Calif.* Lino Covi: *Assistant Professor of Psychiatry, The Johns Hopkins University School of Medicine, Baltimore, Md.* Regina Uliana, B.A.: *Research Assistant, Communication and Measurement Laboratory, Department of Psychiatry and Human Behavior, University of California at Irvine.* Daniel E. Bates, B.A.: *Postgraduate Researcher, Communication and Measurement Laboratory, Department of Psychiatry and Human Behavior, University of California at Irvine.*

boys, found no greater improvement in disruptive behavior in patients on diphenylhydantoin (200 mg/day) than placebo.

Uhlenhuth et al. (1972) compared the effects of diphenylhydantoin, (300 mg/day) and phenobarbital (90 mg/day) in anxious patients; a slightly more favorable response to phenobarbital, of borderline significance, occurred after 2 weeks and a slightly more favorable response occurred at the end of 10 weeks to diphenylhydantoin.

Boelhouwer et al. (1968), in another double-blind study, investigated the effects of diphenylhydantoin (300 mg/day) and thioridazine (300–600 mg/day), together and separately, on impulsive, antisocial, and aggressive behavior in adolescents and young adults. Patients with a 14 and 6/second positive spiking in the EEG showed a greater response to the combination of drugs than to either drug alone. Patients without positive spiking showed the best response to diphenylhydantoin alone.

Stephens and Shaffer (1970), in a 6-week double-blind cross-over study, with 30 patients carefully selected for high anxiety, irritability, and explosive anger, found that diphenylhydantoin, 300 mg daily, was more effective than diphenylhydantoin, 15 mg daily, used as a placebo, in reducing symptoms of anger, irritability, impatience, and anxiety, as evaluated by self-report and physician ratings.

In contrast to the latter study, Conners et al. (1971) found no significant differences in ratings of the symptoms of young delinquent boys randomly assigned to double-blind treatment with diphenylhydantoin (200 mg/day), methylphenidate (20 mg/day), or placebo for 2 weeks.

The favorable effects of diphenylhydantoin in various psychiatric and behavioral disorders appear to have been observed primarily in uncontrolled clinical studies. Generally, the studies reporting negative results have been better designed and have included a placebo control. The arguments of the proponents of the usefulness of diphenylhydantoin in these psychiatric conditions, in the face of such negative findings, include such points as (1) patients should be selected for various target symptoms, such as high anxiety, explosive temper, and aggressive behavioral outbursts; (2) patients should be administered such medication for many weeks in order to observe good results; and (3) patients with abnormal EEGs may have better results. The skeptics of effectiveness of diphenylhydantoin in these nonepileptic or subictal disorders state that (a) most clinical studies have not ruled out a placebo effect; (b) if there are, indeed, any favorable effects of the kind reported they are weak; and (c) the rating scales and self-report measures used in many of these studies are subject to many errors (e.g., see Wittenborn, 1967, 1972).

## PURPOSE

The purpose of the present study was to explore further the effectiveness of diphenylhydantoin, by a placebo-drug double-blind design, on aggressive and explosive behavior over a 6-month period on inmates of an institution dedicated to the diagnosis and treatment of dangerous and emotionally unstable recidivists. This population had been studied earlier by one of us in a limited pilot trial (Covi and Uhlenhuth, 1969) and in a larger controlled study where an in-

significant trend in favor of diphenylhydantoin controlling overt aggressive behavior was found (Covi and Uhlenhuth, 1968). Some of the same measures used in the pilot and in the larger study were adopted in the present study. In addition, in order to answer the methodological questions always present in a study of sociopathic subjects, an objective content analysis procedure (Gottschalk and Gleser, 1969; Gottschalk, 1972) was adopted that avoids some of the measurement problems occasioned by psychiatric rating scales and self-report measures.

## METHODS

*Subjects.* Forty-two male volunteer inmates in Patuxent Institution, a diagnostic and treatment center of the State of Maryland for emotionally disturbed criminal offenders served as subjects. The subjects were selected by one of us (L.C.) after inspection of their institutional record for the previous 6 months. Only inmates who had reported violations of discipline rules in the previous 6 months were offered the possibility of voluntary participation in the study. At the screening interview the importance of abstaining from all illegally obtained drugs or alcohol was stressed, complete confidentiality for all information given was guaranteed, and a daily payment of 50¢ for each day of participation in the study was offered. The inmates willing to participate then signed a consent form. The subjects average age was 25.36 ± 6.15 and the average educational level was 8.25 ± 1.90.

*Procedure.* Following a double-blind design, 24 of the 44 subjects were randomly assigned to the drug condition and received 300 mg of diphenylhydantoin (DPH) daily by mouth for a 6-month testing period, and the remaining 18 subjects were assigned to the placebo condition for the same period and received approximately 24 mg of DPH daily. A placebo with a few milligrams of DPH was given rather than a simple placebo to avoid informing subjects that a placebo was going to be used and then having to conceal from them whether they received it or not. Medication was administered in a syrup, uniform in taste and appearance for both preparations and packed in individually coded bottles at a hospital pharmacy. The medication was given in a single dose in the morning by a research technician who observed the subject swallow it.

One 5-minute speech sample was obtained from each subject at approximately one month intervals, so that each subject provided a maximum of seven verbal samples from which anxiety and hostility scores were derived. The first verbal sample was obtained predrug, and the day after the obtaining of the predrug verbal sample the medication was started.

The remaining six speech samples were obtained postdrug. In some cases not all subjects gave the required seven verbal samples. 21 subjects were missing at least one of their seven speech samples. 12 subjects were missing as many as four speech samples. Missing samples were the result of refusal of the subject to give a sample, administrative deletion, or problems in staff scheduling.

Speech samples were obtained according to a standard procedure in which subjects were asked to speak for 5 minutes into the microphone of a tape recorder in response to purposely ambiguous instructions to talk about any interesting or dramatic personal life experiences. Typescripts, made from the tape recordings, were scored independently for anxiety, hostility outward, hostility inward, and ambivalent hostility following the Gottschalk-Gleser content analysis method (Gottschalk and Gleser, 1969; Gottschalk, Winget, and Gleser, 1969) by technicians at the University of California, Irvine, who were uninformed about the details and design of the study.

This content analysis method of measuring the magnitude of psychological states is an objective procedure in which the semantic (content) aspect of each grammatical clause is scored according to whether or not it denotes or connotes the theme of a group of weighted content categories that have been empirically found to signify some quanta of a specific psychological dimension, such as, anxiety. The interjudge reliability of scoring such content for any one of about a dozen different psychological scales is repeatedly checked so that the reliability coefficient is 0.85 or above. Extensive construct validation studies have been carried out and previously reported (Gottschalk and Gleser, 1969) establishing the validity of the anxiety, hostility, and other such scales against four types of criterion measures, namely, *psychological* (self-report and clinical rating scales), *biochemical* (plasma free fatty acids, cortisol, insulin, etc.), *physiological* (skin temperature, blood pressure, GSR, etc.), and *pharmacological* (response to

placebo, chlordiazepoxide, lorazepam, perphenazine, thioridazine, imipramine, secobarbital, dextroamphetamine, etc.). Summaries of these reliability and validity studies are available elsewhere (Gottschalk, 1971; Gottschalk, 1972; Gottschalk, 1973). The *anxiety scale* measures conscious and subconscious free anxiety. The *hostility outward scale* measures verbal references to anger directed from the self towards others (*overt hostility outwards*) and from others directed to others (*covert hostility outwards*). The *hostility inwards* scale measures angry and hostile references from the self directed towards the self. The *ambivalent hostility* scale measures verbal references concerning hostile thoughts and actions from others directed to the self.

## RESULTS

As an indicator of change in affect scores over the period of the study, the slope of the scores plotted against the monthly testing intervals was calculated

**Table 1.**

| Affect Scales | Average Slope: Placebo Group | Average Slope: Drug Group | T Value |
|---|---|---|---|
| Anxiety | − 0.045 ± 0.369* | − 0.018 ± 0.345 | 0.24 |
| Hostility outward total | − 0.038 ± 0.162 | 0.093 ± 0.433 | 1.21 |
| Overt hostility outward | − 0.085 ± 0.333 | 0.107 ± 0.399 | 1.65 |
| Covert hostility outward | 0.015 ± 0.090 | 0.023 ± 0.214 | 0.15 |
| Inward hostility | − 0.007 ± 0.124 | − 0.037 ± 0.128 | − 0.76 |
| Ambivalent hostility | 0.060 ± 0.175 | − 0.045 ± 0.203 | − 1.77 |

*Standard deviation.

**Table 2. Anxiety Scores for Subjects Receiving Either Diphenylhydantoin (300 mg/day) or a Placebo (Diphenylhydantoin 24 mg/day)**

| Interval Scores Obtained (In Months)* | Drug (N = 24) X̄ | Drug (N = 24) SD | Placebo (N = 18) X̄ | Placebo (N = 18) SD |
|---|---|---|---|---|
| 1 | 2.01 | 0.84 | 2.11 | 0.87 |
| 2 | 2.28 | 0.84 | 2.19 | 0.80 |
| 3 | 2.23 | 0.91 | 2.45 | 0.90 |
| 4 | 1.97 | 0.76 | 2.12 | 0.54 |
| 5 | 2.13 | 0.69 | 2.43 | 0.78 |
| 6 | 1.66 | 0.55 | 2.11 | 0.79 |
| 7 | 1.70 | 0.87 | 2.29 | 0.75 |

*Scores obtained the first month were predrug and all subsequent scores were postdrug.

**Table 3. Hostility-Out-Total Scores for Subjects Receiving Either Diphenylhydantoin (300 mg/day) or a Placebo (Diphenylhydantoin 24 mg/day)**

| Interval Scores Obtained (In Months)* | Drug (N = 24) X̄ | Drug (N = 24) SD | Placebo (N = 18) X̄ | Placebo (N = 18) SD |
|---|---|---|---|---|
| 1 | 1.42 | 0.61 | 1.73 | 0.77 |
| 2 | 1.68 | 0.70 | 1.97 | 0.87 |
| 3 | 1.29 | 0.64 | 1.53 | 0.74 |
| 4 | 1.36 | 0.53 | 1.40 | 0.56 |
| 5 | 1.82 | 0.87 | 1.69 | 0.85 |
| 6 | 1.22 | 0.73 | 1.56 | 0.79 |
| 7 | 1.41 | 0.84 | 1.58 | 0.63 |

*Scores obtained the first month were predrug and all subsequent scores were postdrug.

for each subject for each of the 6 affect scales (anxiety, hostility outward total, hostility outward overt, hostility outward covert, hostility inward, and ambivalent hostility). A t-test between average slopes for the group of subjects on diphenylhydantoin and for the placebo group was calculated for each affect scale. No significant difference was found between these average slopes for the two groups on any of the 6 affect scales. (See Table 1.)

Tables 2–5 give the average anxiety, total hostility outward, hostility inward, and ambivalent hostility scores per month for both diphenylhydantoin and placebo groups of subjects. These findings are, also, illustrated in Fig. 1. It is clear from the examination of these tables and Fig. 1 that there are no notable differences in these measures during the 6 months of this study.

## DISCUSSION

Our findings that diphenylhydantoin (300 mg/day administered over a 6-month period), as compared to a placebo, does not reduce anxiety and three kinds of hostility in institutionalized, recidivist criminals corroborates the previous findings, using different measures and groups of patients, of the lack of antianxiety and/or antiaggressive effects of diphenylhydantoin (Booker, 1967; Case, 1969; Lefkowitz, 1969; Conners et al., 1971). Moreover, our study indicates these effects do not show up even though the diphenylhydantoin is administered for 6 months.

**Table 4. Hostility In Scores for Subjects Receiving Either Diphenylhydantoin (300 mg/day) or a Placebo (Diphenylhydantoin 24 mg/day)**

| Interval Scores Obtained (In Months)* | Drug (N = 24) | | Placebo (N = 18) | |
|---|---|---|---|---|
| | $\bar{X}$ | SD | $\bar{X}$ | SD |
| 1 | 0.74 | 0.53 | 1.07 | 0.47 |
| 2 | 0.81 | 0.47 | 1.00 | 0.61 |
| 3 | 0.89 | 0.47 | 0.94 | 0.77 |
| 4 | 0.89 | 0.56 | 1.00 | 0.55 |
| 5 | 0.71 | 0.60 | 0.95 | 0.56 |
| 6 | 0.82 | 0.51 | 1.18 | 0.63 |
| 7 | 0.64 | 0.46 | 1.05 | 0.60 |

*Scores obtained the first month were predrug and all subsequent scores were postdrug.

**Table 5. Ambivalent Hostility Scores for Subjects Receiving Either Diphenylhydantoin (300 mg/day) or a Placebo (Diphenylhydantoin 24 mg/day)**

| Interval Scores Obtained (In Months)* | Drug (N = 24) | | Placebo (N = 18) | |
|---|---|---|---|---|
| | $\bar{X}$ | SD | $\bar{X}$ | SD |
| 1 | 1.37 | 0.75 | 1.35 | 0.53 |
| 2 | 1.29 | 0.91 | 1.48 | 0.69 |
| 3 | 0.96 | 0.55 | 1.33 | 0.79 |
| 4 | 1.05 | 0.69 | 1.28 | 0.73 |
| 5 | 1.06 | 0.75 | 1.40 | 0.50 |
| 6 | 1.12 | 0.60 | 1.26 | 0.61 |
| 7 | 1.16 | 0.67 | 1.52 | 0.78 |

*Scores obtained the first month were predrug and all subsequent scores were postdrug.

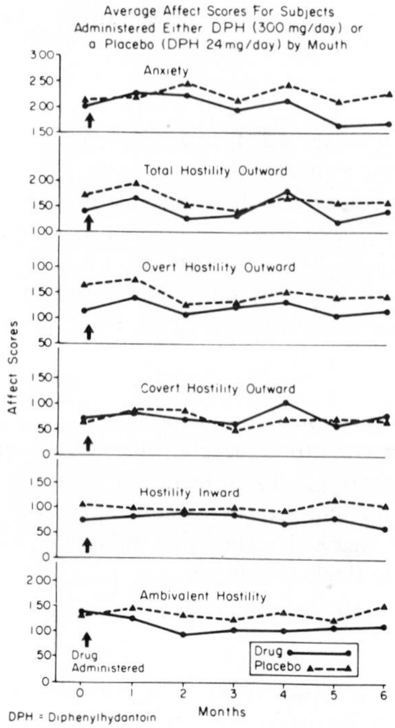


Fig. 1.

Some criticism may be levelled at the significance of our findings on the basis that the psychological measure used, derived as it was from the content analysis of speech, may not relate to overt, destructive, aggressive behavior. Validation studies of these hostility scales (Gottschalk, et al., 1963; Gottschalk et al., 1970), however, have demonstrated significant correlations between hostility scores derived from speech and ratings by independent observers of aggressive behavior (Oken scale, 1960, and the Spitzer et al., Mental Status Schedule, 1967). Also, more recent studies by Freedman et al. (1973) have demonstrated significant correlations between overt hostility outward scores derived by content analysis and hand movements focused towards external objects and, also, covert hostility outward scores and hand movements focused towards the body, especially hand to hand movements; these findings provide evidence that the thoughts we verbalize have some relationship with specific movements we carry out with our body.

A different line of evidence that the content of hostile themes in speech is related to manifestly hostile behavior is the relationship of the magnitude of our hostility scores to the antisocial and aggressive behavior of the groups of péople supplying the speech samples. We have evidence that the hostility scores from antisocial and criminal groups, derived by the content analysis method, are significantly elevated as compared to comparable scores from a normative group of nonpsychiatric subjects (N = 322) composed of employees of Kroger Company (138), medical patients at a Veterans Administration Hospital and

private hospital (76), and college students (108). A group of 16–17-year-old delinquent boys (Gleser et al., 1967) in response to standardized instructions for eliciting the speech samples (i.e., to talk about any interesting or dramatic life experiences) gave speech samples with outward hostility scores averaging 1.82, (which is in the 92nd percentile of a normative group), average ambivalent hostility scores of 1.93, (which is in the 99th percentile of a normative sample), and average hostility inward scores of 0.84 (80th percentile). A group of incarcerated male narcotic addicts at a maximum security institution in Vacaville, California (Elliott et al., 1973) gave speech samples averaging overt outward hostility scores of 1.06 (in the 84th percentile of a normative sample), ambivalent hostility scores of 0.67 (in the 70th percentile), and inward hostility scores of 1.41 (in the 98th percentile). The present group of male criminal subjects from Patuxent had average hostility outward scores of 1.55 (86th percentile), average ambivalent hostility scores of 1.36 (93rd percentile), and average inward hostility scores of 90 (84th percentile of a normative sample). Differences in intelligence or educational level do not account for these findings, for previous studies (Gottschalk and Gleser, 1969, p. 81) have shown there are no relationships between three hostility scales and educational level or intelligence. Hence, these data provide additional evidence, over previous validity studies, that the content-analysis hostility scores bear a quantitative relationship with antisocial, hostile aggressive behavior.

Most of the positive reports about the antihostility and antianxiety effects of diphenylhydantoin have come from uncontrolled studies. The few controlled investigations which offer suggestive evidence of positive effects of diphenylhydantoin (Boelhouwer, 1968; Stephens and Shaffer, 1970; and Uhlenhuth et al., 1972), indicate weak effects. We are inclined to share Klein's view (1967) that diphenylhydantoin effects on the affects, if any, are subtle and difficult to detect. Certainly, other psychoactive drugs have easily detectible effects, in double-blind, placebo-drug studies, when the Gottschalk content analysis method of measuring psychological states is employed: for example, chlordiazepoxide (20 mg orally) significantly lowers anxiety and overt hostility outward scores (Gleser et al., 1965) and chlordiazepoxide (25 mg orally) reduces anxiety scores more when plasma chlordiazepoxide levels in different individuals on such a dosage exceed 0.7 $\mu$g/ml (Gottschalk and Kaplan, 1972); perphenazine significantly lowers hostility outward scores (Gottschalk et al., 1960); hydrochlorothiazide (25–50 mg/day) administered to hypertensive women blocks the positive correlation between hostility outward scores and increases in diastolic blood pressure (Gottschalk et al., 1964); lorazepam (5 mg orally) significantly reduces anxiety scores (Gottschalk et al., 1972); thioridazine (4 mg/kg of body weight orally) significantly reduces social alienation-personal disorganization scores in acute schizophrenics (Gottschalk et al., 1973).

## SUMMARY

(1) In a double-blind, drug-placebo study, a group of 42 emotionally disturbed, male criminals incarcerated at a treatment center with an average age of 25 ± 6 and an average educational level of 8 ± 2, were randomly assigned for a 6-month period to 300 mg of diphenylhydantoin daily by mouth or to a placebo in the form of 24 mg of diphenylhydantoin daily.

(2) Five-minute tape-recorded speech samples, elicited by standardized instructions to "talk about any interesting or dramatic life experiences," were obtained before drug administration and for a 6-month period postdrug. The typescripts of these speech samples were blindly scored, by content analysis technicians unfamiliar with the purpose or nature of this study, for anxiety, total hostility outward, overt hostility outward, covert hostility outward, hostility inward, and ambivalent hostility according to the method of Gottschalk (Gottschalk and Gleser, 1969; Gottschalk et al., 1969).

(3) There were no significant differences between the drug and placebo groups in the magnitude of these anxiety or hostility scores over the 6-month period, as assessed by comparison of the slopes for all the affect scores overtime.

(4) These findings confirm the observations of several other investigators that diphenylhydantoin has a weak effect, if any, as an antianxiety or antihostility agent, even when administered over a 6-month period of time to a group of aggressive, antisocial, criminal offenders.

(5) The relationship and relevance of scores of psychological states derived from the content analysis of speech to manifest behavior is discussed.

## ACKNOWLEDGMENT

We gratefully acknowledge the statistical assistance of Herman Birch, Ph.D., University of California at Irvine, in the evaluation of our data.

## REFERENCES

1. Boelhouwer C, Henry CE, Glueck BC: Positive spiking: a double-blind study on its significance in behavior disorders, both diagnostically and therapeutically. *Am J Psychiatry* 125:473,481, 1968

2. Booker HE, Matthews CG, Slaby A: Effects of diphenylhydantoin on selected physiological and psychological measures in normal adults. Neurology 17:949-951, 1967

3. Brill NQ, Walker EF: Psychopathic behavior with latent epilepsy. J Nerv Ment Dis 101:545-549, 1945

4. Case WG, Rickels K, Brazilian S: Diphenylhydantoin in neurotic anxiety. Am J Psychiatry 126:254-255, 1969

5. Conners CK, Kramer R, Rothschild GH, et al: Treatment of young delinquent boys with diphenylhydantoin sodium and methyl phenidate. Arch Gen Psychiatry 24:156-160, 1971

6. Covi L, Uhlenhuth EH: A controlled study of the effect of diphenylhydantoin (DPH) on dangerous antisocial recidivists. I. Effects on aggressive behavior. Presented at Diphenylhydantoin Conference of the Dreyfus Charita- Foundation, Miami, Florida, 1968.

7. Covi L, Uhlenhuth EH: Methodological problems in the psychopharmacological study of the dangerous antisocial personality, in Garattini S, Sigg EB (eds): Aggressive Behavior. Excerpta Medica Foundation, Amsterdam, 1969, p 326-335

8. Elliott HW, Gottschalk LA, Uliana RL: Relationship of plasma meperidine levels to changes in anxiety and hostility (to be published).

9. Freedman N, Blass T, Rifkin A, et al: Body movements and the verbal encoding of aggressive affect. J Personal Soc Psychol 26: 72-85, 1973.

10. Freyhan FA: Effectiveness of diphenylhydantoin in management of non-epileptic psychomotor excitement-states. AMA Arch Neurol Psychiatry 55:370-374, 1945

11. Gleser GC, Gottschalk LA, Fox R, et al: Immediate changes in affect with chlordiazepoxide in juvenile delinquent boys. Arch Gen Psychiat 13:291-295, 1965

12. Gottschalk LA: (Unpublished data)

13. Gottschalk LA, Biener R, Noble EP: Relationship of thioridazine plasma concentrations, after single oral dose of 4 mg/kg, to clinical response in acute schizophrenic patients: Annual Meeting of American Psychiatric Association, Hawaii, May, 1973

14. Gottschalk LA, Kaplan SA: Chlordiaze-

poxide levels and clinical responses. Comp Psychiatry 13:519–528, 1972

15. Gottschalk LA: An objective method of measuring psychological states associated with changes in neural function. J Biologic Psychiatry 4:33–49, 1972

16. Gottschalk LA, Elliott HW, Bates DE, et al: The use of content analysis of short samples of speech for preliminary investigation of psychoactive drugs: effect of lorazepam on anxiety scores. Clin Pharmacol Therapeut 13: 323–328, 1972

17. Gottschalk LA, Bates DE, Waskow IE, et al: Effect of amphetamine or chlorpromazine on achievement strivings scores derived from content analysis of speech. Compr Psychiatry 12:430–435, 1971

18. Gottschalk LA: Some psychoanalytic research into the communication of meaning through language: the quality and magnitude of psychological states. Br J Med Psychol 44: 131–147, 1971

19. Gottschalk LA, Gleser GO., Cleghorn JM, et al: Prediction of changes in severity of the schizophrenic syndrome with discontinuation and administration of phenothiazines in chronic schizophrenic patients. Compr Psychiatry 11:123–140, 1970

20. Gottschalk LA, Gleser GC: The measurement of psychological states through the content analysis of verbal behavior. Berkeley, Los Angeles, University of California Press, 1969, p. 317.

21. Gottschalk LA, Gleser GC, D'Zmura T, et al: Some psychophysiological relationships in hypertensive women: the effect of hydrochlorothiazide on the relationship of affect to blood pressure. Psychosom Med 26:610–617, 1964

22. Gottschalk LA, Gleser GC, Springer KJ: Three hostility scales applicable to verbal samples. Arch Gen Psychiatry 9:254–279, 1963

23. Gottschalk LA, Gleser GC, Springer KJ: et al: Effects of perphenazine on verbal behavior patterns. Arch Gen Psychiatry 2:632–639, 1960

24. Hill D, Watterson D: Electroencephalographic studies of psychopathic personalities. J Neurol Psychol 5:47, 1942

25. Howard LRC: A study of physiological responses of neurotic patients to diphenylhydantoin. Int J Neuropsychiatry (Suppl) 3: 49–56, 1967

26. Jonas HP: Diagnostic and therapeutic use of diphenylhydantoin in the subictal state and non-epileptic dysphoria. Int J Neuropsychiatry (Suppl) 3:21–29, 1967

27. Klein D: Discussion of psychotropic effect of diphenylhydantoin (DPH). Int J Neuropsychiatry (Suppl) 3:64–66, 1967

28. Kalinowsky L, Putnam TJ: Attempts at treatment of schizophrenia and other non-epileptic psychoses with Dilantin. AMA Arch Neurol Psychiatry 49:414–420, 1943

29. Kubanek JL, Rowell RC: The use of Dilantin in the treatment of psychotic patients unresponsive to other treatment. Dis Nerv Syst 7:1–4, 1946

30. Lefkowitz MM: Effects of diphenylhydantoin in disruptive behavior: Study of male delinquents. Arch Gen Psychiatry 29: 643–651, 1969

31. Oken D: An experimental study of suppressed anger and blood pressure. Arch Gen Psychiatry 2:441–456, 1960

32. Resnick O: The psychoactive properties of diphenylhydantoin; experiences with prisoners and juvenile delinquents. Int Neuropsychiatry (Suppl) 3:30–48, 1967

33. Spitzer RL, Fleiss JL, Burdock EI, et al: The mental status schedule: properties of factor analytically derived scales. Arch Gen Psychiatry 16:479–493, 1967

34. Stephens JH, Shaffer JW: A controlled study of the effects of diphenylhydantoin on anxiety, irritability, and anger in neurotic outpatients. Psychopharmacologia 17:169–181, 1970

35. Turner WJ: The usefulness of diphenylhydantoin in treatment of nonepileptic emotional disorders. Int J Neuropsychiatry (Suppl) 3:8–20, 1967

36. Uhlenhuth EH, Stephens JH, Dim BH, et al: Diphenylhydantoin and phenobarbital in the relief of psychoneurotic symptoms. A controlled comparison. Psychopharmacologia 27: 67–84, 1972

37. Wittenborn JR: Do rating scales objectify clinical impressions? Compr Psychiatry 8:386–392, 1967

38. Wittenborn JR: Reliability, validity, and objectivity of symptom-rating scales. J Nerv Ment Dis 154:79–87, 1972

13

# ANXIETY AND β-ADRENERGIC BLOCKADE

Walter N. Stone, Goldine C. Gleser,
Louis A. Gottschalk

Twenty-four healthy male volunteers were given 60 mg of propranolol hydrochloride (a β-adrenergic blocking agent) or placebo in divided doses given orally during the 12-hours preceding experimental procedures. As a group those subjects receiving propranolol had significantly lower initial anxiety levels measured from speech samples. A stress interview was followed by increases in anxiety scores to comparable levels in both groups.

Plasma free fatty acid (FFA) determinations did not differ significantly for the two groups, either initially or during the experimental period. However, pulse rate at the end of the 55-minute session was significantly lower for subjects on propranolol. The correlation between anxiety scored from the inital speech sample and FFA level was positive and significant for the placebo subjects and negative for the propranolol group. Propranolol administered orally may have value as an antianxiety agent and in addition is seen as providing an avenue for the exploration of psychobiological relationships.

The development of drugs that block autonomic receptors has provided an avenue for the study of the complex interrelationships between autonomic stimulation, affect, and physiological response. In particular, the availability of oral and intravenous forms of a β-adrenergic receptor blocking drug, propranolol hydrochloride, makes possible both laboratory and clinical studies aimed at elucidating the contributions of the autonomic nervous system to the subjective experience of anxiety. In symptomatic patients intravenous injections of propranolol ameliorate feelings of anxiety.[1,2] Similarly, oral administration

This study was supported in part by research funds from the Veterans Administration Hospital, Cincinnati. The drug and matching placebo were supplied by Ayerst Laboratories, New York. Technical assistance was provided by Carolyn Winget and Mary Danzeisen.

of B-blocking drugs to patients is also effective in reducing symptoms of anxiety.[3-7] Autonomically mediated symptoms such as palpitations, sweating, and diarrhea were most noticeably affected in these patients. In contrast to the beneficial effects of β-blockade in patients, Bogdonoff and Estes[8] found that propranolol administered intravenously did not reduce anxiety in volunteers who were anxious to confrontation with a needle. Similiarly, in hypnotized volunteers receiving placebo or propranolol intravenously. Pinter et al[9] and Cleghorn et al[10] did not find differences in anxiety levels measured from verbal samples following stressful or nonstressful suggestions. In these studies with volunteers autonomic blockade was demonstrated by inhibition of lipolysis.

This study was designed to examine the psychobiological effects of a β-adrenergic blocking drug, propranolol, given orally, in volunteer subjects under both nonstress and stress conditions. In previous work from our laboratory, we have demonstrated that anxiety scored from a speech sample correlates positively with base line plasma free fatty acid (FFA) and FFA responsivity to experimental stimuli.[11, 12] Thus, this particular psychobiological relationship was expected to provide a sensitive experimental system in which the effects of β-adrenergic blockade would be carefully monitored. In the present study, we postulated that subjects receiving propranolol would show lower levels of plasma FFA, bradycardia, and decreased initial anxiety, compared to a control group. We also anticipated that the usual correlations between plasma FFA and anxiety would be disrupted. We made no prediction regarding the comparative changes in anxiety or FFA level following stress.

## METHODS

College men ages 21 to 28 were paid volunteers for this double-blind study. They were told that we were studying the effect of a drug which was used in patients with heart disease and might slow their pulse rate. However, our primary interest was in the effect upon their emotions and changes in certain blood chemicals. In connection with this we told the subjects that they would be asked to give two five-minute verbal samples during the morning's study.[13] They were then given an envelope containing either six placebo or six 10 mg propranolol hydrochloride (Inderal) tablets. (In other preliminary studies, we had determined that this dose of propranolol, given orally, significantly reduced resting pulse rates in healthy volunteers, but did not diminish responsivity to the exercise stimulus of the Master's Two-Step test.) The envelopes were coded and randomly assigned to subjects with instructions to take two tablets after dinner, two at bedtime, and two upon arising the morning of the study. Except for the water necessary to swallow the tablets, subjects were instructed not to eat o smoke after the evening meal. Thus, all subjects had fasted 12 to 14 hours at th time speech and blood samples were obtained.

In the morning, preceding the experimental period, the subject rested, sitting quietly for one-half hour. For the remainder of the experimental period, the subject lay on a table with his left arm placed through a screen. He could observe the inital venipuncture but, thereafter, he was screened from seeing further blood samples being taken. Blood samples were obtained through a 19-gauge needle placed in the antecubital vein and secured. A short piece of connecting tubing was attached to a three-way stopcock; one end was available to withdraw blood samples; the other was attached to normal saline, which was slowly infused to prevent clotting in the needle. The initial portion of each sample was discarded to ensure the emptying of the connecting tubing. Blood samples were obtained at the time of venipuncture and at 5, 15, 20, 25, 35, 40, 45, 50, and 55 minutes later. A verbal sample was obtained immediately following the initial blood sample. After collecting the 25-minute blood sample the experimenter moved from behind the screen and interviewed the subject for ten minutes. The focus during the interview was upon life events which upset, worried, or evoked anxiety in the subject. The interviewer was active in searching for these topics but then permitted the subject to speak freely when he seemed to be talking about an area that involved feelings of anxiety. Following the interview, blood was drawn for the 35-minute sample and then the second five-minute sample of speech was obtained. Finally, after the last blood sample was drawn and before removing the indwelling needle, a resting pulse rate was obtained for one minute at the radial artery.

A total of 24 subjects completed the study, 12 in each group. Two technicians independently analyzed the verbal samples for anxiety by the method of Gottschalk and Gleser.[13] The average of the two scores was used in all calculations. The blood samples were analyzed for FFA by the method of Trout et al.[14]

## RESULTS

Average anxiety scores and standard deviations for the propranolol and placebo groups are shown in Table 1. As a group those subjects receiving propranolol had lower anxiety scores on the initial five-minute speech sample than those receiving a placebo ($p < .05$, one-tail Mann-Whitney). Thirty-five minutes later, immediately following the ten-minute interview focused on eliciting anxiety, subjects in both placebo and propranolol groups had increased anxiety scores which no longer differed significantly between the two groups. During the interview, subjects in both groups had considerable scoreable anxiety as indicated in Table 1. It should be noted, however, that these were scores obtained from speech occurring during interactive circumstances, with the interviewer actively pursuing stressful experiences. They are not equivalent to spontaneous speech.

Table 1.—Means and SD of Anxiety Scores From Spontaneous Verbal Samples and Focused Interviews

| | Placebo | | Propranolol | |
|---|---|---|---|---|
| | Mean | SD | Mean | SD |
| Verbal sample, 0-5 min N=12 | 1.32 | .52 | 1.00* | .46 |
| Focused interview, 25-30 min N=10 | 1.79 | .63 | 1.75 | .44 |
| Focused interview, 30-35 min N=10 | 1.99 | .45 | 2.38 | .29 |
| Verbal sample, 35-40 min N=12 | 1.41 | .79 | 1.34 | .43 |

* Significantly different from placebo ($P < .05$) by one-tailed *t*-test.

Data for FFA are presented in the Figure and Table 2. Although the initial levels of FFA appear lower for the drug group, there were no significant differences in either initial or average levels of FFA between subjects receiving propranolol or placebo. Average FFA in the 25-minute period prior to the interview did not differ from the average FFA in the 20 minute period following the interview. In addition, there was no apparent inhibition of FFA mobilization in response to the venipuncture or focused interview in either the drug or placebo group, although those subjects receiving propranolol appear to have a somewhat greater rise in FFA in the first 15 minutes.

A significant, positive correlation ($r = .70$) between FFA averaged over the entire experimental period and anxiety in the initial speech sample was found for subjects receiving placebo, but this correlation was negative ($r = -.55$) and not significant, for those receiving propranolol. The difference in correlation under the two conditions is highly significant ($p < .01$). For both the placebo and drug groups there were no significant correlations between rise in FFA in the 20 minutes following a stimulus (either venipuncture and verbal sample or an interview followed by a verbal sample) and anxiety scored on the verbal sample at the time of the stimulus.

Pulse rates obtained after collection of the blood samples but before removal of the indwelling needle were significantly different ($p < .05$, df 16) for the placebo and drug groups. Those subjects receiving propranolól had an average pulse rate of 52.4/min (SD 5.2); those receiving placeboes had an average rate of 58.5/min (SD 5.6)

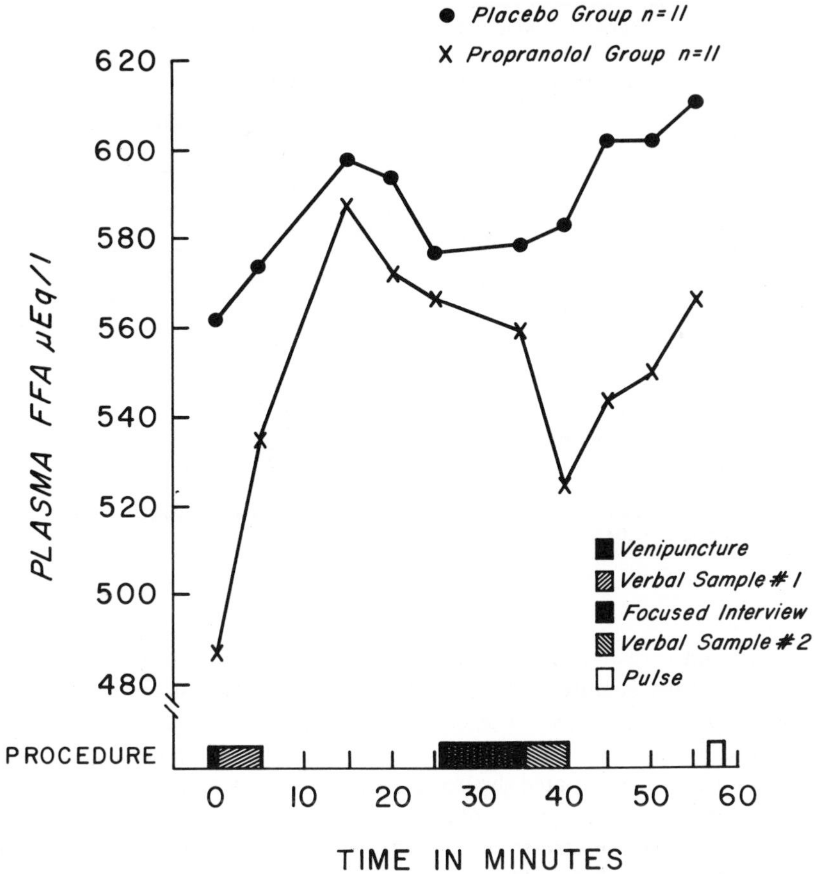


## COMMENT

This report combines into one study two conditions used by other investigators: anxiety and FFA were measured both in a basal state and then following a stress-focused interview. These two conditions roughly correspond to the clinical studies with patients and the laboratory-stress situations with

Table 2.—Means and SD of Averages of FFA Determinations Before and After Focused Interview and Correlations With Anxiety in Verbal Samples

| | | | Correlations With Anxiety Score | |
|---|---|---|---|---|
| | $\bar{X}$ | SD | First 5 min | After Interview |
| | Placebo N = 12 | | | |
| Av FFA μEq/liter, 0-25 min | 600 | 214 | .72* | .09 |
| Av FFA μEq/liter, 35-55 min | 621 | 223 | .69* | .04 |
| | Propranolol N = 12 | | | |
| Av FFA μEq/liter, 0-25 min | 540 | 194 | −.55† | .32 |
| Av FFA μEq/liter, 35-55 min | 538 | 221 | −.56† | .38 |

* Significantly different from zero ($P < .05$).
† Very significantly different from corresponding values in placebo group ($P < .01$).

volunteers. In the resting condition our results are similar to the clinical reports in which anxious symptomatic patients reported decreased anxiety with β-adrenergic blocking drugs. Following the stress-focused interview both the control and drug subjects had greater scoreable anxiety than initially, and the scores no longer differentiated the two-groups, which is similar to the studies on volunteer subjects. Thus, propranolol has antianxiety effects in situations where there is no immediate stress; no antianxiety effects are obtained when the experimental situation includes a stress.

The initial levels of FFA did not differ significantly for the propranolol and placebo groups. Moreover, in both groups FFA increased after the stimuli of a venipuncture and request to talk for five minutes and again after the stress-focused interview and second verbal sample, regardless of whether or not the subject had taken propranolol. Pinter et al[9] found increased adipokinesis following hypnosis and the request to speak for five minutes when propranolol was used, but the rise was smaller than that obtained without the drug. Ripley et al,[15] using propranolol administered intravenously, reported that reliving of past emotional experiences under hypnosis was followed by increases in plasma FFA. Others[8] found no increase in FFA following stress under conditions of β-blockade produced by propranolol received intravenously. Thus, the data indicate that propranolol, at most, only partially inhibits lipolysis following significant stress. One reason for these discrepant results may be the amount of variation in plasma levels of

propranolol. Shand et al[16] found that the plasma levels of propranolol of subjects given uniform intravenous doses of the drug may vary as much as twofold (following oral administration plasma levels may vary sevenfold). On this basis, it would be well to report drug plasma levels in future studies to improve the interpretability of results.

The mechanism by which propranolol reduces anxiety is as yet unclear. Two alternative hypotheses appear possible: (1) propranolol or one of its metabolites may act directly upon the central nervous system (CNS), or (2) propranolol may act by inhibiting sympathetic feedback to the CNS thereby decreasing arousal and/or anxiety.

Animal studies have indicated that propranolol has a direct action upon the CNS. In large doses propranolol has sedative and anticonvulsive action[17×18] and will prolong the hypnotic effect of chloral hydrate.[19] Leonard[20] has demonstrated that propranolol increases glucose uptake and glycogenesis and decreased glycolyses in the mouse brain, an effect not predictable from its peripheral action. Diazepam (valium), a clinically effective antianxiety agent has similar biochemical effects on the CNS.

Despite these provocative findings, as yet there have been no adequate relevant studies on human subjects. A suggestive finding has been reported by Coltart and Shand[21] in an experiment in which exercise-induced tachycardia was inhibited by propranolol. They noted that "the present study has demonstrated a difference between oral and intravenous routes of administration, showing that about three times the plasma levels are required to produce a given effect after intravenous than after oral administration." Most likely a metobolite of propranolol, present in greater amounts after oral administration, is active in producing the $\beta$-adrenergic blockade. Analogously, it is possible that an active metabolite of propranolol, given orally, has a depressant effect upon the CNS which contributes to the antianxiety effect. In this connection, Coltart and Shand,[21] speculating about the clinical response to propranolol in the treatment of angina and hypertension state: "it remains a distinct possibility that a non-specific effect of (oral) propranolol could contribute to its efficacy . . ." and mention the CNS.

The second possibility, that propranolol acts to diminish anxiety through partial blockade of peripheral $\beta$-adrenergic receptors, seems compatible with our findings. This argument posits that afferent stimuli from the peripheral autonomic nervous system act to maintain arousal and/or anxiety of the CNS. Therefore, a decrease in stimuli from the periphery may be associated with a decrease in anxiety. Sufficient $\beta$-adrenergic blockade was attained at the dosage levels used in this study to reduce the pulse rate significantly but not to reduce lipid mobilization. This suggests that different receptor systems have different sensitivities to $\beta$-adrenergic blockade. The decrease in initial anxiety levels and the disruption of the positive correlation between average plasma FFA and

anxiety for the propranolol-treated group supports the idea that these interrelated functions are differentially affected by the β-blockade under resting conditions. With increased external stimuli, this blockade may be overcome, with resultant increase in afferent stimuli to the CNS. Certainly there was increase in plasma FFA following both the stimuli of the venipuncture and request to speak, and the stress-focused interview. A somewhat different interpretation of these findings is presented by Gottschalk et al.[22]

The consistent findings of an antianxiety effect of propranolol in studies utilizing oral dosage suggest that this drug may be a useful psychopharmacological agent. Although the mechanism of action is not entirely clear at this time, there is suggestive evidence that propranolol or one of its metabolites may act either through one or both of the proposed pathways: through β-adrenergic blocking of feedback mechanisms or by direct action on the CNS. Either way, further studies are necessary, with careful monitoring of drug plasma levels, in order to explore effects of varied β-adrenergic drug dosage schedules on a variety of psychobiological systems.

## REFERENCES

1. Turner P, Granville-Grossman KL, Smart JV: Effect of adrenergic receptor blockade on the tachycardia of thyrotoxicosis and anciety state. *Lancet* 2:1316-1318, 1965.

2. Nordenflet O: Orthostatic ECT changes and the adrenergic beta-receptor blocking agent: Propranolol (Inderal). *Acta Med Scand* 178:393-401, 1965.

3. De Risio C, Murmann W: Anxiety and the pulse. *Br Med J* 2-373, 1967.

4. Granville-Grossman KL, Turner P: The effect of propranolol on anxiety. *Lancet* 1:788-790, 1966.

5. Suzman M: An evaluation of the effects of propranolol on the symptoms and electrocardiographic changes in patients with anxiety and hyperventilation syndrome, abstract. *Ann Intern Med* 68:1194, 1968.

6. Wheatley D: Comparative effects of propranolol and chlordiazipoxide in anxiety states. *Br J Psychiatry* 115:1411-1412, 1969.

7. Gallant DM, Swanson WC, Guerrera-Figuero R: A controlled evaluation of propranolol in chronic alcoholic patients presenting the symptomatology of anxiety and tension. *J Clin Pharmacol* 13:41-43, 1973.

8. Bogdonoff MD, Estes EH Jr: Energy dynbamics and acute states of arousal in man. *Psychosom Med* 23:23-32, 1961.

9. Pinter EJ, et al: The influence of emotional stress on fat mobilization. *Am J Med Sci* 254:634-651, 1967.

10. Cieghorn JM, et al: Verbal anxiety and the beta adrenergic receptors. *J Nerv Ment Dis* 151:266-273, 1970.

11. Gottschalk LA, et al: Studies of relationships of emotions to plasma lipids. *Psychosom Med* 27:102-111, 1965.

12. Stone WN, et al: Stimulus, affect, and plasma free fatty acid. *Psychosom Med* 31:331-341, 1969.

13. Gottschalk LA, Gleser GC: *The Measurement of Psychological States Through the Content Analysis of Verbal Behavior*] Berkeley, Calif, University of Calif Press, 1969.

14. Trout DL, Estes EH Jr, Friedberg SJ: Titration of FFA of plasma. *J Lipid Res* 1:199-202, 1960.

15. Ripley HS, Cobb LA, Jones JW: Mobilization of free fatty acids during hypnosis, in *Proceedings of Annual Meeting of the American Psychiatric Association, San Francisco, 1970.* Washington, DC, American Psychiatric Association, 1970.

16. Shand DG, Nuckolls EM, Oates JA: Plasma propranolol levels in adults with observations on four children. *Clin Pharmacol Therap* 11:112-120, 1970.

17. Leszkovsky G, Tardos L: Some effects of propranolol on the central nervous system. *J Pharm Pharmacol* 17:518-519, 1965.

18. Murmann W, Almirante L., Saccani-Guelfi M: Central nervous system effects of four β-adrenergic receptor blocking agents. *J Pharm Pharmacol* 18:317:318, 1966.

19. Laverty R, Taylor KM: Propranolol uptake into the central nervous system and the effect on rat behavior and amine metabolism. *J Pharm Pharmacol* 20:605-609, 1968.

20. Leonard BE: The effect of some β-adrenergic receptor blocking drugs on carbohydrate metabolism in mouse brain. *Neuro-pharmacology* 10:127-144, 1971.

21. Coltart DJ, Shand DG: Plasma propranolol levels in the quantitative assessment of β-adrenergic blockade in man. *Br Med J* 3:731-734, 1970.

22. Gottschalk LA, Stone WN, Gleser GC: Peripheral versus central mechanisms accounting for anti-anxiety effects of propranolol. *Psychosom Med.* 36: 47-56, 1974.

# Effect of Marijuana and Placebo-Marijuana Smoking on Psychological State and on Psychophysiological Cardiovascular Functioning in Anginal Patients

Louis A. Gottschalk,[1,2] Wilbert S. Aronow,[1] and Ravi Prakash[1]

*Received June 28, 1976*

*Ten male anginal patients with angiographically documented coronary artery disease, in a randomized double-blind crossover study, smoked one marijuana cigarette (containing 18 mg of Δ-9-THC) on one morning and one placebo marijuana cigarette (containing 0.05 mg of Δ-9-THC) on a successive morning. Significant increases occurred in average cognitive and intellectual impairment scores, derived from the objective content analysis of 5 min of speech, 30 mins after smoking the marijuana cigarette as compared to the placebo marijuana cigarette, and these scores decreased to near presmoking levels 60 min after smoking. No significant average changes occurred in anxiety or three hostility scale scores following smoking marijuana. Sizable individual differences were noted in the psychological responses to marijuana smoking due, presumably, to personality differences and/or differences in THC pharmacokinetics. Significant psychocardiovascular hemodynamic correlations, as measured by echocardiography, were observed during placebo-marijuana smoking between hostility inward scores and systolic blood pressure and ejection fraction, overt hostility outward scores and diastolic blood pressure, as well as between anxiety scores and stroke volume and left ventricular end-diastolic dimension and left ventricular diastolic volume. These significant psychophysiologic correlations were all eliminated during marijuana smoking. In view of associated findings that marijuana smoking decreased myocardial oxygen delivery, decreased exercise time until the*

[1] Department of Psychiatry and Human Behavior, College of Medicine, University of California at Irvine, Irvine, California, and the Cardiology Section, Medical Service, Long beach Veterans Administration Hospital, Long Beach, California.

[2] Reprint requests should be directed to: Dr. Louis A. Gottschalk, Department of Psychiatry and Human Behavior, College of Medicine, University of California, Irvine, California 92717.

*onset of anginal pain, and increased myocardial oxygen demand in anginal patients, the use of marijuana by such patients is clearly inadvisable.*

## INTRODUCTION

The potential medicinal properties of marijuana and its derivatives, in contrast to its adverse physiological effects, have been a continuing area of scientific inquiry. The present investigation was one of a series of studies exploring the effects of smoking a marijuana cigarette (containing Δ-9-THC) on the cardiovascular and psychological functioning of male anginal patients with documented coronary artery disease. In an earlier study among this series examining the effects of marijuana on cardiovascular hemodynamics, Aronow and Cassidy (1974), in a double-blind study involving patients with angina pectoris due to coronary artery disease, demonstrated that smoking one marijuana cigarette increased the resting heart rate, blood pressure, and venous carboxyhemoglobin level, and decreased the exercise time until the onset of angina pectoris by 48%. Smoking one placebo marijuana cigarette did not significantly change the resting heart rate and blood pressure, but increased the venous carboxyhemoglobin level and decreased the exercise time by 8.6% until angina pectoris. Smoking marijuana significantly decreased the exercise time until angina pectoris more than smoking placebo marijuana ($p < 0.001$). The increase in heart rate and blood pressure which occurred after smoking marijuana increased the myocardial oxygen demand. Also, the increase in carboxyhemoglobin level after smoking marijuana or placebo marijuana decreased the amount of oxygen available to the myocardium.

In another study by this same group of investigators of the effects of smoking marijuana *vs.* placebo marijuana on cardiovascular hemodynamics in anginal patients, Prakash *et al.* (1975) used echocardiography in a double-blind crossover study in ten patients. They found that smoking marijuana increased the heart rate, systolic and diastolic blood pressure, and decreased the end-diastolic volume, stroke index, and ejection fraction, but did not significantly change the end-systolic volume and cardiac index. Whereas, smoking placebo marijuana did not significantly change the heart rate, blood pressure, and end-systolic volume, but decreased the end-diastolic volume and cardiac index as well as decreased (though less than marijuana) the stroke index index and ejection fraction. The cardiovascular hemodynamic changes after smoking placebo marijuana were found to be attributable to carboxyhemoglobin (Aronow *et al.*, 1974). The hemodynamic changes after smoking marijuana, on the other hand, were found to be due to Δ-9-THC (Beaconsfield *et al.*, 1972; Benmouyal *et al.*, 1971; Huy *et al.*, 1972; Johnson and Domino, 1971; Kiplinger and Manno, 1971; Renault *et al.*, 1971; Roth *et al.*, 1973; Tashkin *et al.*, 1973) in addition to carboxyhemoglobin (Aronow *et al.*, 1974).

None of the previous studies of these investigators examined the acute effects of smoking marijuana simultaneously on cognitive and emotional reactions and cardiovascular function. This was the purpose of the present study.

## MATERIALS AND METHODS

Ten men, mean age 48.9 ± 9.1 years (range 38 to 59 years), with classic stable angina pectoris due to angiographically documented coronary artery disease with greater than 75% narrowing of at least one coronary vessel were subjects. Each of the ten patients smoked approximately one pack of cigarettes daily but none was a marijuana smoker.

The subjects were brought to the laboratory and familiarized with the equipment and the procedures before the study was done. Because the determinations of left ventricular dimensions were made intermittently for a period of approximately 135 min, it was of utmost importance that only subjects with distinct and readily obtainable left ventricular dimensions be studied. Therefore, 40 patients were screened in selecting our 10 subjects who had technically satisfactory, easily obtainable echocardiograms.

All subjects were hospitalized on the nights before the two study mornings. The subjects did not smoke for 12 hr prior to the onset of the study each morning or during the study periods except by protocol. The patients were not on any medications except for sublingual nitroglycerin within 2 weeks on this study. The subjects did not receive sublingual nitroglycerin on their study mornings.

On two successive study mornings, at 8:00 AM, with the subject in the fasting state, a control echocardiogram was recorded intermittently for 10 min with an Ekoline-20 ultrasonoscope and a Honeywell strip chart recorder. The subject lay supine in a 15-deg right anterior oblique position throughout the study. The transducer position giving the optimal mitral valve echogram was determined. The transducer was then angled slightly laterally and inferiorly to obtain clear left ventricular septal and posterior wall endocardial echoes. In this position, the mitral echogram was discontinuous and the posterior leaflet was usually better visualized. Using the echoes obtained from the mitral apparatus as landmarks, a reproducible left ventricular dimension could be obtained (Burggraf and Parker, 1974; Feigenbaum *et al.*, 1972; Popp and Harrison, 1970). The left ventricular end-systolic diameter was measured at the point of least separation of the septal and posterior wall endocardial echoes. The left ventricular end-diastolic diameter was measured at the time of the peak of the R wave in the electrocardiogram. Each dimension was averaged for five to ten consecutive cardiac cycles to eliminate respiratory variation.

The left ventricular end-systolic volume (LVESV) and the left ventricular end-diastolic volume (LVEDV) were determined by the cube of their respective diameters multiplied by 1.047 (Burggraf and Parker, 1974; Feigenbaum *et al.*,

1972). Stroke volume (SV), cardiac output (CO), and ejection fraction (EF) were derived as follows:

$$SV = LVEDV - LVESV$$
$$CO = \text{heart rate} \times SV/1000$$
$$EF = SV/LVEDV$$

Blood pressure was recorded by a Roche Arteriosonde 1216 automatic blood pressure monitor. The heart rate was measured from the electrocardiogram recorded simultaneously with the echocardiogram.

Immediately after obtaining these cardiovascular measures and prior to smoking, each subject was asked to talk for 5 min into the microphone of a tape recorder in response to standardized and purposely ambiguous instructions to tell about any interesting or dramatic personal life experiences (Gottschalk and Gleser, 1969; Gottschalk *et al.*, 1969b). The typescripts of these speech samples and of subsequent postsmoking ones obtained were scored blindly by technicians following the objective content-analysis method of Gottschalk and Gleser (1969; Gottschalk *et al.*, 1969b) for anxiety, hostility outward, hostility inward, ambivalent hostility, social alienation-personal disorganization, and cognitive impairment.

After the control measurements were obtained, the subjects smoked in a randomized, double-blind crossover study one marijuana cigarette containing 18 mg of Δ-9-tetrahydrocannabinol (THC) on one morning and one placebo marijuana cigarette containing 0.05 mg of Δ-9-THC on the other morning. The subject inhaled ten puffs of smoke from the marijuana cigarette (approximately ¾ of the cigarette) and ten puffs of smoke from the placebo marijuana cigarette (approximately ¾ of the cigarette). The patient smoked the cigarette at his own pace. The aroma produced by the marijuana and placebo marijuana cigarettes was similar.

Echocardiograms and heart rates were recorded and blood pressure measurements determined immediately after smoking, and 10, 15, 20, 30, 60, 90, and 120 min after smoking marijuana and placebo marijuana. Five-minute speech samples, for the measurement of psychological states through the Gottschalk-Gleser content analysis method, were obtained immediately after smoking and 30, 60, 90, and 120 min later: Fig. 1 summarizes the timing of these procedures.

## RESULTS

### Changes in Average Psychological States Among All Subjects After Smoking Marijuana and Placebo Marijuana

Because two subjects drowsed off occasionally following smoking either marijuana or placebo marijuana, speech samples and, hence, psychological scores were not available for these two subjects at some time periods.

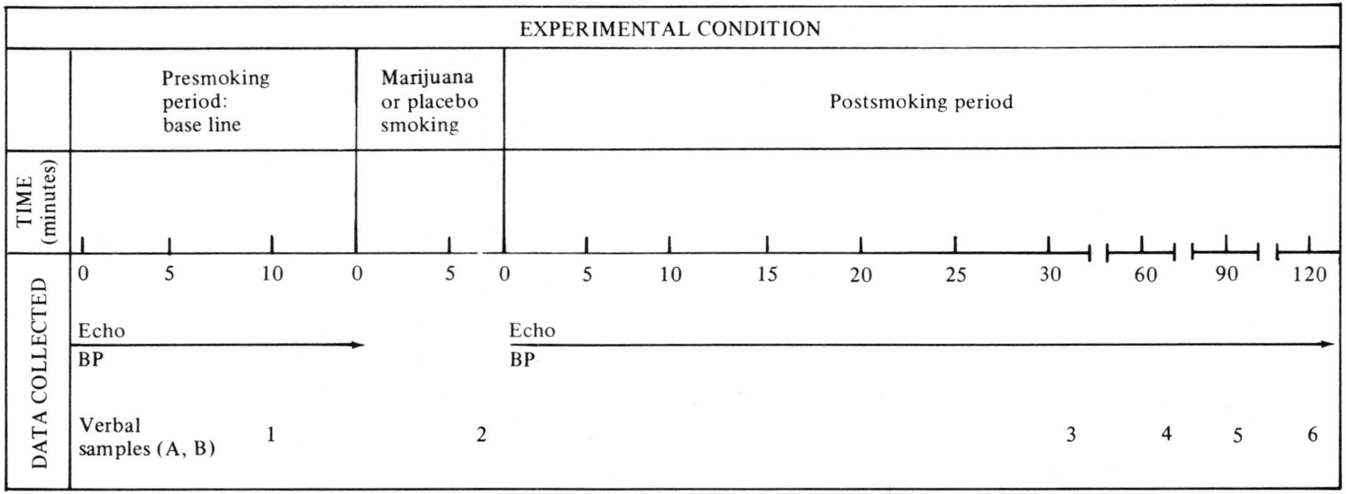


**Fig. 1.** Diagram of procedures: Effect of marijuana and placebo marijuana on cardiovascular and psychological variables. Cardiovascular: Echo: HR, left ventricular end-diastolic volume (EDV); left ventricular end-systolic volume (ESV); EDV-ESV = stroke volume (SV); SV/HR = cardiac output; SV/EDV = ejection fraction; SV/body surface area = stroke index; cardiac output/body surface area = cardiac index. BP: by Roche Arteriosonde 1216 automatic blood pressure monitor. Verbal sample scores: A. Anxiety, hostility outward, hostility inward, ambivalent hostility. B. Social alienation-personal disorganization and cognitive impairment scores.

A significant increase in the average cognitive impairment score (difference = 4.40; N = 8; $p < 0.05$, 2-tail) appeared 30 min after smoking the marijuana cigarette as compared to the placebo marijuana cigarette, and this elevation of average cognitive impairment score decreased to near presmoking levels 60 min after smoking marijuana. A similar increase also occurred in the average social alienation-personal disorganization scores 30 min after smoking the marijuana cigarette, but this increase did not reach a convincing level of statistical significance ($p < 0.10$, 2-tail).

No significant average changes in anxiety and the three hostility scales occurred following marijuana as compared to smoking placebo marijuana.

### Individual Variations in Psychological Responses to Smoking Marijuana

Sizable individual psychological variations were manifested among these subjects. Several subjects (N = 5) had large increases in cognitive impairment scores and social alienation-personal disorganization 30 to 60 min after smoking marijuana; other subjects (N = 4) showed no increases or decreases in these psychological scores. Personality differences and/or differences in THC pharmacokinetics probably account for these marked individual variations, but no corroborative data are available in the present study.

### Intraindividual Correlations Between Psychological and Cardiovascular Variables

Table I summarizes the mean intraindividual correlations between psychological and cardiovascular variables while smoking marijuana in comparison to smoking placebo marijuana. Marijuana smoking canceled the significant psychophysiological correlations occurring during placebo-marijuana smoking between: (i) Hostility inward scores and systolic blood pressure ($r = 0.82, p < 0.001$) and ejection fraction ($r = 0.53, p < 0.05$); (ii) Overt Hostility outward scores and diastolic blood pressure ($r = 0.62$, $p < 0.01$); (iii) Anxiety scores and stroke volume ($r = -0.50, p < 0.05$), left ventricular end diastolic dimension ($r = -0.50, p < 0.05$), and left ventricular diastolic volume ($r = -0.51, p < 0.05$).

## DISCUSSION

### Effects of Marijuana on Psychological Variables

The effects of marijuana smoking on the mean cognitive and intellectual impairment content analysis scores of anginal patients are similar to short-term effects of this substance on mental functioning as noted in other investigations

**Table I.** Mean Intraindividual Correlations Between Psychological and Cardiovascular Variables While Smoking Marihuana (THC) *Versus* Placebo Marijuana

| Psychologic variables | Systolic BP | | Diastolic BP | | Stroke volume | | Left ventricular end diastolic dimension | | Left ventricular end systolic volume | | Left ventricular end diastolic volume | | Ejection fraction | | Stroke index | |
|---|---|---|---|---|---|---|---|---|---|---|---|---|---|---|---|---|
| | THC | Placebo | THC | Placebo | THC | Placebo | THC | Placebo | THC | Placebo | THC | Placebo | THC | Placebo | THC | Placebo |
| Hostility inward | 0.17 | 0.82[d] | 0.08 | 0.43 | | | | | | | | | 0.02 | −0.53[b] | | |
| Overt hostility outward | 0.31 | 0.40 | 0.36 | 0.62[c] | | | | | | | | | | | | |
| Anxiety | | | | | 0.00 | −0.50[b] | 0.08 | −0.50[b] | 0.19 | −0.40 | −0.07 | −0.51[b] | | | 0.00 | −0.48 |

[a] The mean intrasubject correlation coefficient was calculated by first transforming each individual's correlation coefficient into its Fisher's Z equivalent, then finding the mean of those, and finally transforming the mean Z back to a correlation coefficient (Hays, 1963).
[b] $p < 0.05$.
[c] $p < 0.01$.
[d] $p < 0.001$.

(see below). Other agents or conditions which have been noted to increase significantly both cognitive impairment scores and social alienation-personal disorganization scores are other psychotomimetic chemical substances, such as, LSD-25, Ditran, psilocybin (Gottschalk and Gleser, 1969), total or half body irradiation (Gottschalk *et al.*, 1969a), and sensory overload (Gottschalk *et al.*, 1972). Some conditions or agents cause significant increases in only one of these measures; for example, the onset of acute or chronic schizophrenia is specifically associated with large increases in the social alienation-personal disorganization measure, whereas most forms of cerebral organic impairment, whether temporary (e.g., an electroshock treatment) or permanent, produce significant increases in cognitive impairment scores and not social alienation-personal disorganization scores (Gottschalk and Gleser, 1969).

Studies by other investigators using different measures of mental effects have demonstrated that marijuana has varied effects on perception, cognition, and motor function depending on the dose and the type and complexity of the task. Reaction time at low dose is unaffected, but at high dose it is significantly increased (Dornbush *et al.*, 1971); short-term memory, represented by digit span either forward or backward, considered a simple task, is typically unaffected (Waskow *et al.*, 1970); whereas more complex memory tasks are adversely affected, such as the goal-directed serial alternation task (Melges *et al.*, 1970) or tasks in which a delay is interpolated between item presentation and recall (Dornbush *et al.*, 1971; 1972). At low dose levels marijuana subjectively slows the perception of time so that subjects overestimate the passage of time (Clark *et al.*, 1970; Jones and Stone, 1970; Tinklenberg *et al.*, 1972; Weil *et al.*, 1968). Recent data lend support to the idea that memory loss during the intoxicated state and disrupted time-sense may be related (Drew *et al.*, 1972; Miller *et al.*, 1972). Miller (1974) has speculated and offered evidence that the effects of marijuana on cognition are mediated by certain limbic structures, especially the hippocampus, and he has suggested that the biochemical substrate for the effect of marijuana on human subjects is cholinergic.

Although some subjects in the present study had increased anxiety or hostility following marijuana smoking, on the average there were no significant differences in anxiety or hostility scores on comparing the speech samples following marijuana smoking with placebo-marijuana smoking. Significant average increases did occur, however, in the average cognitive impairment scores derived from the speech samples 30 min after smoking marijuana. Not all subjects showed an increase in these scores after smoking marijuana, and this may be due to individual differences in dosage (although each subject smoked identical marijuana cigarettes containing 18 mg of $\Delta$-9-THC) or variations occurring in blood concentrations of the marijuana. Studies of other psychoactive agents (Cash and Quinn, 1970; Usdin, 1970; Gottschalk and Kaplan, 1972; Gottschalk *et al.*, 1972, 1975, 1976; Elliott *et al.*, 1974) have, indeed, indicated that considerable individual variability in psychoactive drug pharmacokinetics follows

similar drug doses and that the clinical response to the drug is related to the drug-blood concentrations of the marijuana. These individual pharmacokinetic variations are the result of different rates of absorption, disposition, metabolism, and pharmacodynamics of Δ-9-THC and its hydroxylated metabolites which are active in varying degrees and collectively account for the observed effects (Domino *et al.*, 1974; Kotin *et al.*, 1973; Mechoulam *et al.*, 1970; Zeidenberg *et al.*, 1973). Δ-9-THC is a good substrate for hepatic microsomal enzymes, so that diseases, drugs, or other conditions which inhibit or activate the liver microsomal enzyme systems may influence the rate of its metabolism (Lemberger, 1973; Low *et al.*, 1973). Perhaps our subjects had different Δ-9-THC pharmacokinetics and those with higher blood levels or half-lives of the pharmacologically active drug had the more marked psychological responses. This possibility must be examined in future studies. Another possibility is that some subjects may be more prone to adverse drug reactions, as Naditch (1974) has demonstrated, for personality or other psychobiological reasons than pharmacokinetic factors. This possibility also merits further investigation.

## Psychophysiological Cardiovascular Correlations

A previous study of the relationship of psychological content analysis scores and cardiovascular variables in 12 hypertensive women patients (Gottschalk *et al.*, 1964) has demonstrated similar psychophysiological cardiovascular relationships to those noted here with anginal male patients, namely, that hostility inward scores correlated significantly with average systolic ($r = 0.47$, $p < 0.05$) and diastolic blood pressure ($r = 0.55$, $p < 0.01$). On the other hand, in the hypertensive women the total hostility outward scores correlated significantly negatively instead of positively (as in the anginal males) with average systolic ($r = -0.50, p < 0.05$) and average diastolic blood pressure ($r = -0.55$, $p < 0.01$). The differences in these psychophysiological correlations may be related to certain characteristics unique to hypertensives in that hypertensives regularly have increases in blood pressure while giving 5-min speech samples; whereas normotensives, such as the anginal patients in this study, regularly have decreases in blood pressure while giving speech samples (Gottschalk *et al.*, 1964; Kaplan *et al.*, 1961). In the study of hypertensive women, as with the anginal males, these correlations disappeared when the hypertensive patients were administered a drug, specifically 25-50 mg/day of hydrochlorothiazide, an antihypertensive diuretic.

Since marijuana has been demonstrated to adversely affect cardiovascular function in anginal patients through decreased myocardial oxygen delivery ard increased myocardial demand (Aronow and Cassidy, 1974; Beaconsfield *et al.*, 1972; Benmouyal *et al.*, 1971; Huy *et al.*, 1972; Johnson and Domino, 1971; Kiplinger and Manno, 1971; Renault *et al.*, 1971; Roth *et al.*, 1973; Tashkin *et al.*, 1973), one might surmise that these effects on cardiovascular

hemodynamics account in large part for the cancellation, during marijuana smoking, of the correlations between affect measures and specific cardiovascular variables. Since marijuana also has acute effects directly on the central nervous system and, hence, on those psychological measures derived from the content analysis of speech, especially the cognitive impairment scale scores, this, too could account for the break-up in the correlations between psychological state and cardiovascular variables during marijuana smoking. Most likely, both central nervous system and peripheral cardiovascular effects of marijuana account for its effects on these psychophysiological correlations.

## SUMMARY AND CONCLUSIONS

Starting as an impartial study seeking some possible therapeutic value from marijuana smoking in the alleviation of anginal pain in patients with coronary artery disease, our series of studies has demonstrated that marijuana-smoking decreased myocardial oxygen delivery and the exercise time until the onset of anginal pain and increased myocardial oxygen demand. In addition, it significantly increased the cognitive impairment of subjects as measured from the content of speech and blocked the usual, nondrug psychocardiovascular correlations. Clearly, for anginal patients marijuana is more a medical hazard than a help.

## ACKNOWLEDGMENT

Michael Isbell, Daniel E. Bates, Claire A. Cable, Wayne Laverty, and Max Warren, provided technical assistance, and Herman Birch gave statistical assistance.

## REFERENCES

Aronow, W. S., and Cassidy, J. (1974). Effect of marihuana and placebo marihuana smoking on angina pectoris. *New Engl. J. Med.* 291: 65.

Aronow, W. S., Cassidy, J., Vangrow, J. S., March, H., Kern, J. C., Goldsmith, J. R., Khemka, M., Pagano, J., and Vawter, M. (1974). Effect of cigarette smoking and breathing carbon monoxide on cardiovascular hemodynamics in anginal patients. *Circulation* 50: 340.

Beaconsfield, P., Ginsburg, J., and Rainsburg, R. (1972). Marihuana smoking: cardiovascular effects in man and possible mechanisms. *New Engl. J. Med.* 287: 209.

Benmouyal, E., Cote, G., and Morin, Y. (1971). A direct action of Δ-9-tetrahydrocannabinol on myocardial contractility. *Clin. Res.* 19: 758 (Abstr.).

Burggraf, G. W., and Parker, J. O. (1974). Left ventricular volume changes after amyl nitrite and nitroglycerine in man as measured by ultrasound. *Circulation* 49: 136.

Cash, W. D., and Quinn, G. P. (1970). Clinical-chemical correlations: an overview. *Psychopharmacol. Bull.* 6: 26.

Clark, L. D., Hughes, R., and Nakashima, E. N. (1970). Behavioral effects of marihuana. Experimental studies. *Arch. Gen. Psychiat.* 23: 193.

Domino, E. F., Rennick, P., and Pearl, J. H. (1974). Dose-effect relations of marijuana smoking on various physiologic parameters in experienced male users — observations on limits of self-titration of smoke. *Clin. Pharmacol. Therap.* 15: 514.

Dornbush, R. L., Fink, M., and Freedman, A. M. (1971). Marihuana, memory, and perception. *Am. J. Psychiat.* 128: 194.

Dornbush, R. L., Clare, G., Zaks, A., Crown, P., Volavka, J., and Fink, M. (1972). 21-day administration of marihuana in male volunteers, in *Current Research in Marihuana,* Lewis, M. F. (ed.), Academic Press, New York, pp. 115-128.

Drew, W. G., Kiplinger, G. F., Miller, L. L., and Marx, M. (1972). Effects of propranolol on marihuana-induced cognitive dysfunctioning. *Clin. Pharmacol. Therap.* 13: 526.

Elliott, H. W., Gottschalk, L. A., and Uliana, R. L. (1974). Relationship of plasma meperidine levels to changes in anxiety and hostility. *Compr. Psychiat.* 15: 57.

Feigenhaum, H., Popp, R. L., Wolfe, S. B., Troy, B. L., Pombo, J. F., Haine, C. L., and Dodge, H. T. (1972). Ultrasound measurements of left ventricle: A correlative study with angiography. *Arch. Internal Med.* 129: 461.

Gottschalk, L. A., and Gleser, G. C. (1969). *The Measurement of Psychological States Through the Content Analysis of Verbal Behavior,* University of California Press, Berkeley.

Gottschalk, L. A., and Kaplan, S. A. (1972). Chlordiazepoxide plasma levels and clinical responses. *Compr. Psychiat.* 13: 519.

Gottschalk, L. A., Gleser, G. C., D'Zmura, T. L., and Hanenson, I. B. (1964). Some psychophysiological relationships in hypertension women. The effect of Hydrochlorothiazide on the relation of affect to blood pressure. *Psychosomat. Med.* 26: 610.

Gottschalk, L. A., Kunkel, R. L., Wohl, T., Saenger, E., and Winget, C. N. (1969a). Total and half body irradiation. Effect on cognitive and emotional processes. *Arch. Gen. Psychiat.* 21: 574.

Gottschalk, L. A., Winget, C. N., and Gleser, G. C. (1969b). *Manual of Instructions for Use of the Gottschalk-Gleser Content Analysis Scales: Anxiety, Hostility, Social Alienation-Personal Disorganization,* University of California Press, Berkeley.

Gottschalk, L. A., Haer, J. L., and Bates, D. E. (1972). Effect of sensory overload on psychological states. *Arch. Gen. Psychiat.* 27: 451.

Gottschalk, L. A., Noble, E. P., Stolzoff, G. E., Bates, D. E., Cable, G. C., Uliana, R. L., Birch, H., and Fleming, E. W. (1973). Relationships of chlordiazepoxide blood levels to psychological and biochemical responses, in *The Benzodiazepenes,* Garattini, S., Mussini, E., and Randall, L. O. (eds.), Raven Press, New York.

Gottschalk, L. A., Biener, R., Noble, E. P., Birch, H., Wilbert, D. E., and Heiser, J. F. (1975). Thioridazine plasma levels and clinical response. *Compr. Psychiat.* 16: 323.

Gottschalk, L. A., Dinovo, E., Biener, R., Birch, H., Syben, M., and Noble, E. P. (1976). Plasma levels of mesoridazine and its metabolites and clinical response in acute schizophrenia after a single intramuscular drug dose, in *Pharmacokinetics, Psychoactive Drug Blood Levels and Clinical Response,* Gottschalk, L. A., and Merlis, S. (eds.), Spectrum Publications, New York.

Hays, W. L. (1963). *Statistics for Psychologists,* Holt, Rinehart and Winston, New York, pp. 530-533.

Huy, N. D., McNicholl, J., and Roy, P. E. (1972). The acute effects of Δ-9-tetrahydrocannabinol (THC) on the left ventricular function of isolated hearts. *Clin. Res.* 20: 910 (Abstr.).

Johnson, S., and Domino, E. F. (1971). Some cardiovascular effects of marihuana smoking in normal volunteers. *Clin. Pharmacol. Therap.* 12: 762.

Jones, R. T., and Stone, G. C. (1970). Psychological studies of marihuana and alcohol in man. *Psychopharmacologia* 18: 108.

Kaplan, S. M., Gottschalk, L. A., Magliocco, D., Rohovit, D., and Ross, W. D. (1961). Hostility in verbal productions and hypnotic dreams of hypertensive patients: Studies of groups and individuals. *Psychosomat. Med.* 23: 311.

Kiplinger, G. F., and Manno, J. E. (1971). Dose-response relationships to cannabis in human subjects. *Pharmacol. Rev.* 23: 339.

Kotin, J., Post, R. M., and Goodwin, F. K. (1973). Delta-9-tetrahydrocannabinol in depressed patients. *Arch. Gen. Psychiat.* 28: 345.

Lemberger, L. (1973). Tetrahydrocannabinol metabolism in man. *Drug Metab. Dispos.* 1: 461.

Low, M. D., Klonoff, H., and Marcus, A. (1973). The neurophysiological basis of the marihuana experience. *Can. Med. Assoc. J.* 108: 157.

Mechoulam, R., Shani, A., Edery, H., and Grunfeld, Y. (1970). Chemical basis for hashish activity. *Science* 169: 611.

Melges, F. T., Tinklenberg, J. R., Hollister, L. E., and Gillespie, H. K. (1970). Marihuana and temporal disintegration. *Science* 168: 1118 (Abst.).

Miller, L. L. (ed.) (1974). *Marihuana Effects on Human Behavior*, Academic Press, New York, pp. 160-188.

Miller, L. L., Drew, W. G., and Kiplinger, G. F. (1972). Effects of marihuana on recall of narrative material and Stroop colour-word performance. *Nature* 237: 172.

Naditch, M. P. (1974). Acute adverse reactions to psychoactive drugs, drug usage, and psychopathology. *J. Abnormal Psychol.* 83: 394.

Popp, R. L., and Harrison, D. C. (1970). Ultrasonic cardiac echography for determining stroke volume and valvular regurgitation. *Circulation* 41: 493.

Prakash, R., Aronow, W. S., Warren, M., Laverty, W., and Gottschalk, L. A. (1975). Effect of marihuana and placebo marihuana smoking on hemodynamics in coronary disease. *Clin. Pharmacol. Therap.* 18: 90.

Renault, P. F., Schuster, C. R., Heinrich, R., and Freeman, D. X. (1971). Marihuana: standardized smoke administration and dose effect curves on heart rate in humans. *Science* 174: 589.

Roth, W. T., Tinklenberg, J. R., Kopell, B. S., and Hollister, L. E. (1973). Continuous electrocardiographic monitoring during marihuana intoxication. *Clin. Pharmacol. Therap.* 14: 533.

Tashkin, D. P., Shapiro, B. J., and Frank, I. M. (1973). Acute pulmonary physiologic effects of smoked marihuana and oral Δ-9-tetrahydrocannabinol in healthy young men. *New Engl. J. Med.* 289: 336.

Tinkleberg, J. R., Kopell, B. S., Melges, F. T., and Hollister, L. E. (1972). Marihuana and alcohol. Time production and memory functions. *Arch. Gen. Psychiat.* 27: 812.

Usdin, E. (1970). Absorption, distribution, and metabolic fate of psychotropic drugs. *Psychopharmacol. Bull.* 6: 4.

Waskow, I. E., Olsson, J. E., Salzman, C., and Katz, M. (1970). Psychological effects of tetrahydrocannabinol. *Arch. Gen. Psychiat.* 22: 97.

Weil, A. T., Zinberg, N. E., and Nelson, J. M. (1968). Clinical and psychological effects of marihuana in man. *Science* 162: 1234.

Zeidenberg, P., Clark, W. C., Jaffe, J., Anderson, S. W., Chin, S., and Malitz, S. (1973). Effect of oral administration of Δ-9-tetrahydrocannabinol on memory, speech, and perception of thermal stimulation results with four normal human volunteer subjects. Preliminary report. *Compr. Psychiat.* 14: 549.

# Introduction to Chapter 15

Introductory Comments by Louis A. Gottschalk

This is one of a number of papers using the Gottschalk-Gleser content analysis scales in the study of the effects of alcohol on affects. It illustrates that the alcoholics studied, in comparison to the nonalcoholics, had significantly higher total anxiety as well as overt hostility outward scores before drinking various doses of alcohol. In response to stressful movies, the alcoholic group had less of a response on scores on affect scores derived from the Mood Adjective Check List (MACL), but there was no significant difference in the affect scores of the two groups after the stress provoked by these films using the Gottschalk-Gleser content analysis measures.

# A Laboratory Study of Emotional Reactions to a Stressful Film in Alcoholic and Non-Alcoholic Subjects

Elizabeth S. Parker, Ronald L. Alkana,

and Ernest P. Noble

From the Department of Psychiatry and Human Behavior, University of California, Irvine.

Supported in part by research grant AA-00252, and Fellowships MH-51714 (to E.S.P.) and AA-00629 (to R.L.A.) from the National Institute on Alcohol Abuse and Alcoholism, ADAMHA. This paper is based on a dissertation submitted (by E.S.P.) in partial fulfillment of the requirements for the Ph.D. degree at the University of California, Irvine.

The authors gratefully acknowledge the help of Dr. Frances Sheridan, and Professor E. Mansell Pattison. We also thank Mr. Robert Gill, Orange County Sheriff's Department, for performing the alcohol readings and Ms. Lauren Babier and Mr. Alan Cochrane who served as research assistants.

---

* Chapter prepared for forthcoming volume, Louis A. Gottschalk (ed.).

Recent years have seen growing concern with understanding the causes of alcoholism. One explanation of alcoholism that has received considerable attention is that alcoholics drink in order to cope with stress (Wexberg, 1951; Ullman, 1952; Higgins, 1953; Lazarus, 1965; Plaut, 1967; Vogel-Sprott, 1972). Stress theories of alcoholism contend that the alcoholic has a low tolerance for frustration (Wexberg, 1951) and poorly developed coping mechanisms (Higgins, 1953; Jellinek, 1960). To alleviate feelings of tension and conflict, the alcoholic learns to use the pharmacological properties of alcohol. Thus drinking is particularly rewarding for the alcoholic who tends to overreact to the stresses and strains of daily life when sober. These rewarding aspects of drinking reinforce it as a behavioral response to stress, thereby setting in motion the cycle of alcohol abuse.

Three conditions implicated in the stress theories of alcoholism form the basis of the present study. They are that:

1. In the sober state, alcoholics will overreact to stressful situations.
2. After drinking alcohol, stress responses will be reduced.
3. Alcohol's stress-reducing effects may be greater for alcoholics than for nonalcoholics.

Unfortunately, in the brief review of studies on stress and alcoholism that follows, inconsistent support for these conditions has been obtained.

Studies comparing sober responses of alcoholics and nonalcoholics to stress have generally yielded conflicting results. Coopersmith (1964) found that alcoholics' autonomic responses to affectively laden words were greater and less discriminating than nonalcoholics, indicating hyperresponsiveness to stress. On the other hand, Rosenberg (1970) reported that alcoholics had less rise in forearm blood flow under stressful task conditions when compared to nonalcoholics, indicating

hyporeactivity to stress. While Chotlos and Goldstein (1967) found that the cardiac responses of alcoholics to emotionally meaningful sounds were more variable than nonalcoholics.

A number of investigators have looked at the effect of alcohol on stress response, although most of these studies have been with nonalcoholic subjects only. Alcohol reduced autonomic responsiveness to loud noise (Carpenter, 1957) and to the frightening experience of a first glider flight (Goddard, 1958). In addition, the inhibitory effect of shock on task performance was reduced by alcohol (Vogel-Sprott, 1967). There is some evidence, however, suggesting that alcohol may enhance responses to stress. Alcohol increased responses to affective stimuli (Coopersmith, 1964) and further impaired task performance under the stressful condition of delayed auditory feedback (Forney and Hughes, 1961).

Systematic research on the effects of alcohol on alcoholic persons is relatively recent. As yet, little is known about the relationship between drinking and the alcoholic's ability to cope with stress. Garfield and McBrearty (1970) examined this question and reported that alcohol decreased alcoholics' reactivity to both stressful and neutral photographs. Unfortunately, the lack of non-alcoholic controls precludes an interpretation about the significance of these findings for alcoholism.

Despite considerable interest in stress and alcoholism, it has not yet been clearly ascertained whether alcoholics are hyper-reactive or hyporeactive to stress, whether alcohol decreases stress responses, or whether alcoholics experience greater stress-reduction after drinking than nonalcoholics. The present study hopes to shed further light on these questions by comparing directly the stress responses of alcoholics and matched nonalcoholic controls under both sober and alcohol conditions. A comparative study was in order as it provided a situation where what was uniquely characteristic of the

alcoholic might be seen in better contrast. A well-developed stress paradigm was selected and stress responses were assessed in a systematic manner.

## METHOD

### Subjects

Twenty-four men, 12 alcoholics and 12 nonalcoholics, participated in this study. Alcoholics were voluntary inpatients at a State Hospital, with a primary diagnosis of "chronic alcoholism" and an average of 8 years of problem drinking. To minimize the effects of withdrawal, only alcoholics who had been without alcohol for at least three weeks were accepted in the study. Nonalcoholics were recruited through advertisements and were paid for their participation.

Alcoholics and nonalcoholics were individually matched for age and education. Their respective mean (± S.D.) ages were 35.6 ± 7.0 years and 36.3 ± 8.8 years and mean (± S.D.) years of school completed were 12.8 (± 2.4) and 13.4 (± 1.4), respectively. Subjects were screened for medical and psychiatric disorders and were not receiving medication during the course of the study. In a pre-experimental interview the procedures of the study were explained to the subjects and written consent was obtained. Drinking history questionnaires were administered to select controls who were moderate drinkers but who did, upon occasion, consume the doses of alcohol being employed. Alcoholics also filled out drinking history questionnaires to measure the extent of their drinking.

### Design and Procedures

Each man participated in a sober (0 ml absolute ethanol per kilogram body weight (ml/kg)), a moderate dose (.67 ml/kg) and a high dose (1.33 ml/kg) session.* Sessions were approximately one week apart

*These doses correspond to 0, 0.55, and 1.1 grams of absolute alcohol per kilogram of body weight (g/kg).

and alcohol conditions were counterbalanced across sessions. Exactly the same protocol was followed in a subject's three sessions. All subjects were tested individually and testing began between 8-9 A.M. after an overnight fast.

Upon arriving at the laboratory, the subject relaxed in his experimental room for a few minutes. He was given his drink which was consumed within 20 minutes in the presence of an experimenter. Mood assessments were taken after the subject finished his drink (Post-Drink Mood) to measure the immediate effect of alcohol on emotions. During the next 50 minutes, the subject performed several cognitive tasks which have been reported elsewhere (Parker et al, 1974). Then mood scores were obtained before and after he watched a stressful film. The experimental protocol is summarized below:

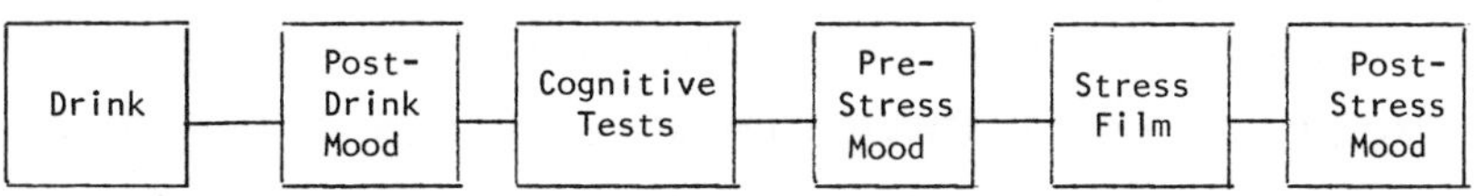


Alcohol was administered in the form of equal volumes of 80 proof whiskey and ice water. The placebo drink in the sober sessions contained colored water in glasses swabbed with whiskey. The high dose of 1.33 ml/kg was sufficient to produce feelings of intoxication in the alcoholics and is comparable to high doses in other studies of nonalcoholics (Ryback et al, 1970; Jones, 1973). Breath samples were taken by means of a breathalyzer before the stress film to estimate blood alcohol concentration (BAC).

The stressor was an industrial accident film which has been used in previous stress research (Lazarus et al, 1965; Nomikos et al, 1968; Koriat et al, 1972). It portrays three mutilating accidents in a woodshop. In the first accident a man lacerates his fingers in a wood planer. Then another worker amputates the tips of his fingers in a saw. In a third accident, a worker is careless with a circular saw, causing a board to be driven through the abdomen of a fellow workman who is shown bleeding in agony. Subjects

viewed the same film in each of their experimental sessions since previous studies have shown that people do not habituate to the woodshop film over three showings (Lazarus, 1968). The advantages of a movie stressor have been well elaborated (Lazarus et al, 1962). It maximizes experimenter control, does not rely on subjects performing a skillful task, and does not employ physical assaults such as shock.

Three times per session mood was measured both by self-reports and content analysis of verbal behavior. Self-reported mood was obtained by the Green-Nowlis Mood Adjective Check List (MACL) (Nowlis, 1965). The MACL is easily administered, sensitive to rapid fluctuations in feelings, sensitive to stressful films, and provides a reliable picture of a broad spectrum of different moods (Nowlis, 1965). A subject checks one of four alternative responses to 33 adjectives according to how he feels at the moment. Each adjective belongs to one of the following 11 functionally independent mood factors: (1) AGGRESSION, (2) ANXIETY, (3) SURGENCY, (4) ELATION, (5) CONCENTRATION, (6) FATIGUE, (7) SOCIAL AFFECTION, (8) SADNESS, (9) SKEPTICISM, (10) EGOTISM and (11) VIGOR. Possible factor scores range from 0 to 9.

The content analysis methods of Gottschalk and coworkers were used as an objective measure of mood (Gottschalk et al, 1969; Gottschalk and Gleser, 1969). These content analysis measures have been used extensively in psychopharmacological research (Gottschalk and Gleser, 1969). Subjects were asked to free associate about their personal life experiences for 5 minutes. Their verbal samples were tape-recorded, transcribed verbatim, and coded by trained technicians on a blind basis according to the Gottschalk-Gleser codes of Anxiety and Hostility-Outward.

## Data Analysis

Affective variables were submitted to analysis of variance using the independent variables of Groups (Alcoholics and Nonalcoholics), Conditions (0, .67 and 1.33 ml ethanol/kg) and, where appropriate, Trials (Pre-Stress and Post-Stress), with Subjects as the random variable

nested within Groups (Kirk, 1968). Post-Drink scores, Pre-Stress versus Post-Stress scores, and Post-Stress minus Pre-Stress scores were analyzed separately. Post-Drink scores describe the immediate effects of alcohol on mood. Comparisons between Pre-Stress and Post-Stress scores reveal the overall effect of the stressor on mood. Difference scores (Post-Stress minus Pre-Stress) were used to simplify the number of independent variables contained in critical interaction terms.

## RESULTS

### Blood Alcohol Concentrations

In the medium dose session, mean (± S.D.) blood alcohol concentrations (BACs) attained by alcoholics and nonalcoholics respectively were .05% (± .01) and .06% (± .01). In the high dose session, BACs for alcoholics and nonalcoholics respectively were .13% (± .02) and .12% (± .01). BACs in the placebo sessions were zero.

### Affective States of Alcoholics and Nonalcoholics

Post-Drink Mood scores indicate that alcoholics displayed greater affective disturbance than the nonalcoholics in all conditions (see Table 1). This is reflected by a significant effect of Groups with no significant Groups X Conditions interaction. Alcoholics had significantly more Anxiety ($p<.01$) and Overt Hostility ($p<.01$) than the nonalcoholics in their verbal samples. They reported significantly more AGGRESSION ($p< .05$), ANXIETY ($p< .01$), and VIGOR ($p< .05$), and less ELATION ($p< .05$) than the nonalcoholics on the MACL.

Both alcoholics and nonalcoholics became more dysphoric when intoxicated. The significant effect of Conditions with no significant Groups X Conditions interaction means that alcohol affected both groups in a similar manner. In the alcohol conditions, verbal samples contained more ANXIETY ($p<.01$). And more AGGRESSION ($p<.05$) and SADNESS ($p<.05$) were reported on the MACL. The significant Groups X Conditions interaction for EGOTISM ($p<.05$) means that this affect

TABLE 1

Post-Drink Mood Scores for the Groups, Alcoholics (A) and Nonalcoholics (NA), in Sober (0 ml/kg), Medium Dose (.67 ml/kg), and High Dose (1.33 ml/kg) Conditions.

| | MEANS | | | | | | ANOVA† | | |
|---|---|---|---|---|---|---|---|---|---|
| | 0 ml/kg | | .67 ml/kg | | 1.33 ml/kg | | Groups | Conditions | Groups X Conditions |
| | A | NA | A | NA | A | NA | df 1,22 | df 2,44 | df 2,44 |
| CONTENT ANALYSIS | | | | | | | | | |
| Anxiety | 2.5 | 1.6 | 2.5 | 1.6 | 3.0 | 2.1 | 21.71** | 10.62** | 0.05 |
| Total Hostility | 1.5 | 1.2 | 1.5 | 1.5 | 1.5 | 1.2 | 2.09 | 0.63 | 0.24 |
| Hostility Overt | 1.2 | 0.8 | 1.3 | 0.8 | 1.3 | 1.1 | 8.83** | 1.38 | 0.55 |
| MACL | | | | | | | | | |
| Aggression | 0.7 | 0.0 | 1.2 | 0.4 | 2.2 | 0.3 | 5.53* | 3.40* | 2.02 |
| Anxiety | 1.1 | 0.3 | 1.6 | 0.3 | 2.3 | 0.2 | 8.57** | 1.01 | 1.71 |
| Surgency | 3.3 | 4.5 | 3.7 | 5.2 | 3.8 | 4.3 | 1.39 | 0.34 | 0.27 |
| Elation | 2.5 | 4.3 | 2.6 | 4.4 | 2.7 | 3.4 | 4.81* | 0.48 | 0.78 |
| Concentration | 5.5 | 6.3 | 5.6 | 6.2 | 5.8 | 5.0 | 0.05 | 0.68 | 1.39 |
| Fatigue | 0.8 | 1.3 | 0.8 | 1.5 | 1.3 | 1.8 | 1.14 | 0.68 | 0.07 |
| Social Affection | 5.8 | 5.5 | 6.3 | 6.8 | 6.3 | 5.9 | 0.00 | 2.43 | 0.56 |
| Sadness | 0.8 | 0.2 | 1.9 | 0.3 | 2.2 | 0.5 | 3.86 | 3.31* | 1.59 |
| Skepticism | 1.6 | 0.9 | 1.8 | 1.3 | 2.6 | 1.3 | 1.09 | 1.54 | 0.66 |
| Egotism | 1.0 | 0.4 | 0.9 | 1.5 | 3.0 | 1.0 | 1.18 | 4.69* | 4.62* |
| Vigor | 6.3 | 3.6 | 5.2 | 3.7 | 5.4 | 3.5 | 4.69* | 0.35 | 0.40 |

† Fs from analysis of variance of Post-Drink Mood Scores

* $p < .05$
** $p < .01$

differentiated the effects of intoxication between alcoholics and nonalcoholics. Nonalcoholics felt more egotistic after the moderate dose than they had in the sober state, while the alcoholics did not become more egotistic until the high dose.

Effect of Stress

Pre-Stress versus Post-Stress comparisons were made across Groups and Conditions to provide a global picture of the effects of the accident film on emotionality (see Table 2). In general, the stressor increased negative affects and decreased positive affects in both groups. After the film there were significant increases in self-reported feelings of AGGRESSION ($p<.05$), ANXIETY ($p<.05$), and SADNESS ($p<.05$), and significant decreases in feelings of SURGENCY ($p<.01$), ELATION ($p<.01$), SOCIAL AFFECTION ($p<.01$), EGOTISM ($p<.01$) and VIGOR ($p<.05$). There was a significant decrease in the verbal sample measure of Anxiety ($p<.05$) after the film.

Differences in Stress Responses Between Alcoholics and Nonalcoholics

Subsequent analysis of the Post-Stress minus Pre-Stress difference scores showed that the stress responses of the alcoholics were considerably less than the nonalcoholics (see Table 3). A significant effect of Groups but no significant Groups X Conditions interaction was found for MACL affects of AGGRESSION ($p<.05$), SADNESS ($p<.05$), SOCIAL AFFECTION ($p<.05$), and EGOTISM ($p<.05$). Thus, after viewing the stress film the alcoholics, as compared to the nonalcoholics, displayed smaller increments in negatively toned feelings (AGGRESSION and SADNESS) as well as smaller decrements in the positively-toned feeling of SOCIAL AFFECTION under both sober and intoxicated conditions.

Effect of Alcohol on Stress Response

The effect of alcohol on stress response was quite different for the alcoholics than for the nonalcoholics. The Groups X Conditions interaction was significant for self-reported feelings of SURGENCY ($p<.05$),

TABLE 2

Pre-Stress and Post-Stress Mood Scores for Groups and Conditions Combined

| | Means | | F† |
|---|---|---|---|
| | Pre-Stress Mood | Post-Stress Mood | df 1,22 |
| CONTENT ANALYSIS | | | |
| Anxiety | 2.4 | 2.3 | 5.24* |
| Total Hostility | 1.4 | 1.5 | 1.32 |
| Hostility Overt | 1.1 | 1.2 | 0.26 |
| MACL | | | |
| Aggression | 0.6 | 1.0 | 6.10* |
| Anxiety | 0.9 | 1.6 | 7.78* |
| Surgency | 3.8 | 2.4 | 28.55** |
| Elation | 3.1 | 1.5 | 38.62** |
| Concentration | 5.6 | 5.8 | 0.60 |
| Fatigue | 1.2 | 1.0 | 0.98 |
| Social Affection | 5.9 | 4.2 | 19.43** |
| Sadness | 1.0 | 1.9 | 6.07* |
| Skepticism | 1.4 | 1.3 | 0.77 |
| Egotism | 1.0 | 0.6 | 8.85** |
| Vigor | 4.5 | 3.9 | 6.57* |

†Fs from comparison of Pre-Stress and Post-Stress Mood Scores from analysis of variance

* $p < .05$
** $p < .01$

ELATION ($p<.01$), and VIGOR ($p<.05$) (see Table 3). Under sober and medium dose conditions the alcoholics were less reactive than the nonalcoholics to the stress. At the high alcohol dose, alcoholics were reacting slightly more than when they were sober, while the non-alcoholics' reactivity diminished.

Relationship Between Self-Reported and Objective Mood Measures

Correlation coefficients were calculated between verbal sample and MACL measures of Anxiety and Hostility for alcoholics and non-alcoholics separately with all Conditions combined (see Table 4). If these two methods were assessing the same underlying affect, then the

TABLE 3

Post-Stress minus Pre-Stress Difference Scores for the Groups, Alcoholics (A) and Nonalcoholics (NA) in Sober (0 ml/kg), Medium Dose (.67 ml/kg) and High Dose (1.33 ml/kg) Conditions.

| | MEANS | | | | | | ANOVA† | | |
|---|---|---|---|---|---|---|---|---|---|
| | 0 ml/kg | | .67 ml/kg | | 1.33 ml/kg | | Groups | Conditions | Groups X Conditions |
| | A | NA | A | NA | A | NA | | | |
| CONTENT ANALYSIS | | | | | | | | | |
| Anxiety | 0.1 | -0.2 | -0.2 | 0.0 | 0.6 | -0.2 | 0.33 | 1.40 | 1.07 |
| Total Hostility | 0.2 | -0.2 | -0.2 | 0.2 | 0.0 | 0.0 | 0.55 | 2.31 | 1.45 |
| Hostility Overt | 0.1 | 0.0 | -0.3 | 0.0 | 0.3 | 0.2 | 0.25 | 2.26 | 0.59 |
| MACL | | | | | | | | | |
| Aggression | -0.1 | 0.4 | 0.3 | 0.9 | -0.3 | 1.1 | 7.00* | 0.64 | 0.70 |
| Anxiety | 0.9 | 1.6 | -0.1 | 1.1 | -0.1 | 1.0 | 3.39 | 2.68 | 0.24 |
| Surgency | -0.8 | -2.3 | -0.2 | -2.9 | -1.3 | -1.1 | 6.08* | 0.36 | 4.81* |
| Elation | -0.6 | -2.3 | -0.8 | -2.6 | -2.4 | -0.9 | 1.71 | 0.13 | 5.57** |
| Concentration | -0.7 | 0.8 | 0.4 | 0.3 | 0.1 | 0.5 | 0.93 | 0.22 | 1.42 |
| Fatigue | -0.1 | -0.8 | -0.5 | -0.1 | -0.2 | 0.2 | 0.00 | 1.00 | 1.96 |
| Social Affection | -0.8 | -2.3 | -1.0 | -3.0 | -0.5 | -2.6 | 5.77* | 0.66 | 0.26 |
| Sadness | 0.4 | 1.7 | 0.4 | 1.5 | -0.4 | 1.9 | 4.37* | 0.15 | 0.76 |
| Skepticism | -0.9 | 0.2 | 0.2 | 0.8 | -0.2 | -0.8 | 1.60 | 3.66* | 2.60 |
| Egotism | -0.1 | 0.0 | -0.8 | 0.1 | -1.3 | -0.2 | 7.63* | 1.34 | 0.86 |
| Vigor | -0.4 | -0.8 | 0.1 | -0.9 | -1.3 | 0.0 | 0.02 | 0.14 | 3.39* |

† Fs from analysis of variance of Post-Stress minus Pre-Stress Difference Scores

* $p < .05$
** $p < .01$

TABLE 4

Correlations (r) between Content Analysis and MACL measures of Anxiety and Hostility for Alcoholics (A) and Nonalcoholics (NA), All Conditions Combined

| | A<br>n = 108 pairs<br>r | NA<br>n = 108 pairs<br>r |
|---|---|---|
| Content Analysis Anxiety and MACL Anxiety | +.28** | -.08 |
| Content Analysis Total Hostility and MACL Aggression | +.15 | +.18 |
| Content Analysis Hostility Overt and MACL Aggression | +.19 | +.06 |

** $p < .01$

larger the correlation coefficient, the more accurate were subjects' self-reports of their internal state. We had thought that the alcoholics might have been less accurate in their self-reports and that the correlations between objective and self-reported measures would be smaller for this group. Only the positive correlation between verbal sample and MACL anxiety scores for the alcoholics was significant ($p<.01$), suggesting that if anything the relationship between objective and self-reported feelings was closer for the alcoholics than the nonalcoholics. It is also possible that the two methods were assessing different emotional components.

## DISCUSSION

The results of this study indicate there are striking differences in the way alcoholics and nonalcoholics cope with stress. Earlier we noted that stress is frequently used as an important variable in explanations of alcoholism despite somewhat inconsistent empirical

support. Whereas stress theories of alcoholism suggest that alcoholics overreact to stress in the sober state, alcoholics in this study displayed hyporesponsiveness to stress. Thus the notion that stress responses of alcoholics and nonalcoholics are different seems to have been supported, however, the nature of this difference was not in the expected direction.

How can we account for the finding that alcoholics, under sober and moderate alcohol conditions, were less responsive to stress than the nonalcoholic subjects? In explaining the hyporeactivity of alcoholics to the stress of task-performance under harassment, Rosenberg (1970) suggested that they may have been deficient in motivation. We doubt that motivational variables can fully account for the responses of the alcoholics in the present study. The alcoholics had volunteered for participation and they appeared interested and concerned with all phases of the experiment. Furthermore, their self-reported levels of CONCENTRATION and FATIGUE were not significantly different from the nonalcoholics.

Perhaps the stress film did upset the alcoholics and they were not reporting their feelings accurately. For example, previous research (Lazarus, 1968) found that personality factors influence the way people report affective responses to stress. Repressive personality types are low reporters but have the same autonomic responses to stress as expressive personalities. If the alcoholics in the present study had repressive personalities, then their inhibited affective reactions on the MACL would reflect a defensive style of reporting. This seems unlikely for two reasons. First, the correlations between self-reported (MACL) and objective (Content Analysis) mood measures were no less for the alcoholics than the nonalcoholics. Had the alcoholics been defensive in their self-reported moods, we would have expected a smaller or negative correlation between these two mood measures for this group of subjects. Second, the alcoholics reported significantly higher levels of affective

disturbance before viewing the stress film which indicates that they were not more inhibited than the nonalcoholics about reporting their feelings.

The alcoholics' hyporesponsiveness to stress may have been a function of their high levels of dysphoria prior to viewing the film. They were significantly more anxious, more hostile, and less elated than the nonalcoholics even before the stress was presented and this type of affective disturbance has been found in other studies of alcoholics (see Barry, 1974). Under sober and moderate alcohol conditions, the alcoholics' emotional distress may have interfered with their ability to perceive, appraise, and/or fully incorporate the stressful nature of the film. This would be analogous to the pattern of highly anxious subjects who fail to respond to experimenter-defined stresses while less anxious subjects are capable of direct and sharp responding (Glickstein et al, 1957). Our clinical observations support this notion. When sober, many alcoholics appear to be so enmeshed in their own personal turmoils that they have difficulty coping directly with new input from their environment. They tend to deny or intellectualize difficult situations and their affective reactions appear blunted.

One of the major paradoxes of alcoholism is that the alcoholic drinks in the face of damaging consequences caused by drinking. There may be a relationship between this paradoxical behavior and the way alcoholics cope with stress. This study found that sober alcoholics displayed inhibited affective responses to stress. Other experimental studies (Vogel-Sprott and Banks, 1965; Weingartner and Faillace, 1971) noted that alcoholics are less able to adjust their performance under punished and presumably stressful conditions than nonalcoholics. In addition, Dudley et al (1974) reported that alcoholics consistently underestimate the significance of changes in their lives. The ability to respond to a stressful situation is an adaptive form of behavior. Upon appraising and reacting to stress, the individual can modify his subsequent behavior to reduce the potential harm he might otherwise

incur. If the alcoholic does not respond to stressful events in his life precipitated by drinking, then the probability that he would make corrective changes is low. This perspective suggests that therapeutic efforts should include an evaluation of how the alcoholic copes with stress when he is sober. If his responses are inappropriate, he might benefit by developing more direct patterns of responding.

One of the most interesting findings from this study involves the effect of high doses of alcohol on stress response. On the basis of stress theories of alcoholism, we expected that alcohol would reduce response patterns with alcoholics experiencing greater stress-mediating effects from alcohol than nonalcoholics. Indeed, nonalcoholics' responses diminished at the high dose in accord with previous studies (Carpenter, 1957; Goddard, 1958). However, the alcoholics, who were hyporesponsive to stress while sober, became more responsive at higher levels of intoxication. In other words, the intoxicated alcoholic began to respond like the sober nonalcoholic, indicating a "normalizing" effect of alcohol on their emotional responses to external stimuli. This enhanced responding may be a rewarding feature of drinking as it would intensify the alcoholics' interaction with his environment.

The very different effect of alcohol on stress responses of alcoholics and nonalcoholics is important in view of the relatively similar effect of alcohol on the baseline affect scores of these two groups. In the absence of stress, alcohol made both alcoholics and nonalcoholics more dysphoric. Thus measurement of general affective state does not yield interesting information about the unique effects of drinking on alcoholics. However, high levels of intoxication result in very different patterns of response for alcoholics indicating that the stress paradigm is helpful in delineating effects of alcohol that are specific to alcoholics. This is, of course, premised on the assumption that a better understanding of why alcoholics drink will be obtained through characterizing responses to drinking that are different from "normal" subjects. Future studies are needed which

study alcoholics' responses to a wider range of stimuli under sober and alcohol conditions. Furthermore, we still need to know how non-hospitalized alcoholics and alcoholics of different types respond under this paradigm.

In conclusion, we would like to present one interpretation that can be drawn from this study. The sober alcoholic exhibits greater emotional disturbance than the nonalcoholic. This enhanced intra-psychic distress may consume the alcoholic's attention and energy and lead him to ignore external stimuli as an adaptive maneuver to prevent his ego from being overwhelmed. The consequence of these internal mechanisms is a blunted reaction to external distress. Alcohol may disengage the alcoholic from his internal distress and change internal adaptive ego perceptions. The intoxicated alcoholic may perceive himself as competent and better able to cope with self and the world. Thus, the sober alcoholic experiences himself as not able to cope with internal stress and must deny external stress, while the intoxicated alcoholic experiences himself as better able to cope with internal stress and can afford the luxury of perceiving external stress.

## SUMMARY

Explanations of alcoholism have suggested that alcoholics may have difficulty dealing with intrapsychic and interpersonal conflicts leading them to use the pharmacological properties of alcohol to alleviate the stresses and strains of daily life. Therefore, the present study systematically examined stress responses in alcoholics and matched nonalcoholic controls under sober and intoxicated conditions. Every subject participated in three experimental sessions and was studied under sober (0 ml ethanol/kg), medium dose (.67 ml/kg) and high dose (1.33 ml/kg) conditions. In each session, affective behavior was assessed by self-reports and content analysis of verbal behavior, before and after subjects viewed a stressful film.

Alcoholics displayed less affective responsiveness to the

experimental stress than nonalcoholics under sober and medium dose conditions. The alcoholics had significantly greater affective disturbance than the nonalcoholics prior to their exposure to stress. Thus it is suggested that alcoholics' blunted reactions to environmental stress may be due to their already high levels of internal disturbance. The contributions of motivational and personality factors in alcoholics' hyporeactivity to stress are discussed. The alcoholics were no less accurate in reporting their affective states than the nonalcoholics. A relationship between inhibited stress responses and maladaptive alcoholic behavior, such as continual drinking in the face of damaging consequences, is suggested.

The high alcohol dose affected stress responses of alcoholics and nonalcoholics in a significantly different manner. At high levels of intoxication, the responses of nonalcoholics diminished, probably reflecting the depressant effects of the drug. However, the reactions of the alcoholics increased indicating a "normalizing" effect of high doses of alcohol on their emotional responses to environmental stimuli. It is suggested that high doses of alcohol may disengage the alcoholic from the internal distresses that inhibited his sober responses to stress. This could be a rewarding aspect of drinking.

## REFERENCES


Barry, H., III. Psychological factors in alcoholism, in The Biology of Alcoholism, Vol.3, Clinical Pathology, B. Kissin and H. Begleiter, eds. Plenum Press, New York (1974).

Carpenter, J. A. Effects of alcohol on skin conductance. Quart. J. Stud. Alcohol 18, 1 (1957).

Chotlos, J. W., and Goldstein, G. Psychophysiological responses to meaningful sounds. J. Nerv. Ment. Dis. 145, 315 (1967).

Coopersmith, S. Adaptive reactions of alcoholics and nonalcoholics.

Quart. J. Stud. Alcohol 25, 262 (1964).

Coopersmith, S. The effects of alcohol on reactions to affective stimuli. Quart. J. Stud. Alcohol 25, 459 (1964).

Dudley, D. L., Roszell, D. K., Mules, J.E. and Hague, W. H. Heroin vs. alcohol addiction: Quantifiable psychosocial similarities and differences. J. Psychosom. Res. 18, 1 (1974).

Forney, R. B., and Hughes, F. W. Delayed auditory feedback and ethanol: Effect on verbal and arithmetical performance. J. Psychol. 52, 185 (1961).

Garfield, Z. H., and McBrearty, J. F. Arousal level and stimulus response in alcoholics after drinking. Quart. J. Stud. Alcohol 31, 832 (1970).

Glickstein, M., Chevalier, J. A., Korchin, S. J., Basowitz, H., Sabshin, M., Hamburg, D. A., and Grinker, R. R. Temporal heart rate patterns in anxious patients. AMA Arch. Neurol. Psychiat. 78, 101 (1957).

Goddard, P. J. Effect of alcohol on excretion of catecholamines in conditions giving rise to anxiety. J. Appl. Physiol. 13, 118 (1958).

Gottschalk, L. A., and Gleser, G. C. The Measurement of Psychological States Through the Content Analysis of Verbal Behavior. University of California Press, Berkeley (1969).

Gottschalk, L. A., Winget, C. N., and Gleser, G. C. Manual of Instructions for Using the Gottschalk-Gleser Content Analysis Scales: Anxiety, Hostility, and Social Alienation-Personal Disorganization. University of California Press, Berkeley (1969).

Higgins, J. W. Psychodynamics in the excessive drinking of alcohol. Arch. Neurol. Psychiat. 69, 713 (1953).

Jellinek, E. M. The Disease Concept of Alcoholism. College and University Press, New Haven (1960).

Jones, B. M. Memory impairment on the ascending and descending limbs of the blood alcohol curve. J. Abnorm. Psych. 82, 24 (1973).

Kirk, R. E. Experimental Design: Procedures for the Behavioral Sciences. Brooks/Cole, Belmont, California (1968).

Koriat, A., Melkman, R., Averill, J. R., and Lazarus, R. S. The self-control of emotional reactions to a stressful film. J. Pers. 40, 601 (1972).

Lazarus, A. A. Toward the understanding and effective treatment of alcoholism. S. African Med. J. 39, 736 (1965).

Lazarus, R. S. Emotions and adaptation: Conceptual and empirical relations, in Nebraska Symposium on Motivation, W. J. Arnold, ed. University of Nebraska Press, Lincoln (1968).

Lazarus, R. S. Opton, E. M., Nomikos, M. S. and Rankin, N. O. The principle of short-circuiting of threat: Further evidence. J. Pers. 33, 622 (1965).

Lazarus, R. S., Spiesman, J. C., Mordkoff, A. M. and Davison, L. A. A laboratory study of psychological stress produced by a motion picture film. Psychol. Monog. 76 (34, Whole No. 553) (1962).

Nomikos, M. S., Opton, E., Averill, J. R. and Lazarus R. Surprise versus suspense in the production of stress reaction. J. Pers. Soc. Psych. 8, 204 (1968).

Nowlis, V. Research with the mood adjective check list, in Affect, Cognition, and Personality, S. S. Tomkins and C. E. Izard, eds. Springer Publ., New York (1965).

Parker, E. S., Alkana, R. L., Birnbaum, I. M., Hartley, J. T. and Noble, E. P. Alcohol and the disruption of cognitive processes. Arch. Gen. Psychiatry 31, 824 (1974).

Plaut, T. F. A., ed. Alcohol Problems, A Report to the Nation by the Cooperative Commission on the Study of Alcoholism. Oxford University Press, New York (1967).

Rosenberg, C. M. Forearm blood flow in response to stress. J. Abnorm. Psychol. 76, 180 (1970).

Ryback, R. S., Weinert, J. and Fozard, J. L. Disruption of short-term

memory in man following consumption of ethanol. Psychonom. Sci. 20, 335 (1970).

Ullman, A. D. The psychological mechanism of alcohol addiction. Quart. J. Stud. Alcohol 13, 602 (1952).

Vogel-Sprott, M. Alcohol effects on human behavior under reward and punishment. Psychopharmacologia 11, 337 (1967).

Vogel-Sprott, M. Alcoholism and learning, in Biology of Alcoholism, Vol. 2, Physiology and Behavior, B. Kissin and H. Begleiter, eds. Plenum Press, New York (1972).

Vogel-Sprott, M.D., and Bank, R.K. The effect of delayed punishment on an immediately rewarded response in alcoholics and nonalcoholics. Behav. Res. Ther. 3, 69 (1965).

Weingartner, H., and Faillace, L.A. Verbal learning in alcoholic patients: Some consequences of positive and negative reinforcement on free-recall learning. J. Nerv. Ment. Dis. 153, 407 (1971).

Wexberg, L.E. Alcoholism as a sickness. Quart. J. Stud. Alcohol 12, 217 (1951).

# Content analysis of speech samples to determine effect of lorazepam on anxiety

*A study is described illustrating the use, in neuropsychopharmacologic studies, of an objective measure of psychological states, such as anxiety, through the content analysis of 5 minute samples of speech. In this report, the psychoactive drug tested was a new benzodiazepine, lorazepam. It was found to exert significant antianxiety effects ($p < 0.05$) as measured by the content analysis method when administered parenterally at a dosage of 5.0 mg. compared to anxiety changes occurring after no drug or 3.0 mg. of lorazepam. Interesting physiological changes in relation to drug dose and anxiety inhibition were followed and are also reported.*

**Louis A. Gottschalk, M.D., Henry W. Elliott, M.D., Ph.D., Daniel E. Bates, B.A., and Claire G. Cable** *Irvine and Vacaville, Calif.*

*The Department of Psychiatry and Human Behavior and the Department of Medical Pharmacology and Therapeutics, College of Medicine, University of California at Irvine, and the Solano Institute for Medical and Psychiatric Research, Vacaville*

This communication illustrates the usefulness of a speech content analysis method for screening psychoactive pharmacologic drugs for antianxiety effects while simultaneously studying their pharmacologic effects on organ systems. Anxiety scores derived from the content analysis of 5 minute speech samples were determined on subjects given either no drug, lorazepam (a new benzodiazepine, 7-chloro-5-[O-chlorophenyl]-1,3 dihydro-3-hydroxy-2H-1,4 benzodiazepine-2-one), in doses of 2.0, 5.0, and 8.0-9.0 mg. intravenously and 3.0, 5.0, and 9.0 mg. intramuscularly, or various doses of pentobarbital or phenobarbital intravenously or intramuscularly. The principal objective of the study was to determine safe sedative and hypnotic doses of lorazepam.

Supported in part by a grant from Wyeth Laboratories, Philadelphia, Pa.

Received for publication June 16, 1971.

Accepted for publication Jan. 7, 1972.

## Materials and methods

***Subjects.*** Thirty-one paid volunteer inmates of the California Medical Facility at Vacaville, who had been medication free for at least 4 weeks, served as subjects. Their average age was 31.4 ± 6.3 years. Groups of 5 subjects each were used. Subjects were not selected because of high anxiety, nor was the study designed

**Table I.** *Mean anxiety scores with standard deviations derived from verbal samples 1, 2, and 3 for all subjects in response to all conditions*

| | *Verbal sample No. 1 (before drug)* | *Verbal sample No. 2 (0.5-2.5 hr. after drug)* | *Verbal sample No. 3 (3.25-7 hr. after drug)* |
|---|---|---|---|
| No drugs (N=6) | 2.05 ± 1.02 | 2.40 ± 0.36 (1.5-2.5 hr.) | 2.10 ± 0.73 (3-6 hr.) |
| Barbiturates (N=4) | 2.85 ± 1.61 | 1.84 ± 1.24 (0.5-1.0 hr.) | 1.90 ± 0.96 (5-6 hr.)* |
| 2.0 mg. Lorazepam, intravenously (N=4) | 2.34 ± 0.65 | 2.25 ± 1.14 (0.5 hr.) | — |
| 3.0 mg. Lorazepam, intramuscularly (N=4) | 1.96 ± 0.43 | 2.31 ± 0.49 (1 hr.) | 1.94 ± 1.08 (6-7 hr.) |
| 5.0 mg. Lorazepam (N=8) | 2.44 ± 0.98 | 1.70 ± 0.79 (1 hr.) | 1.75 ± 0.72 (5-6 hr.) |
| Intramuscular (N=4) | 2.63 ± 1.25 | 1.80 ± 0.67 (1 hr.) | 1.51 ± 0.54 (5-6 hr.) |
| Intravenous (N=4) | 2.25 ± 0.77 | 1.61 ± 0.99 (1 hr.) | 1.99 ± 0.87 (5-6 hr.) |
| 8.0-9.0 mg. Lorazepam (N=5) | 2.66 ± 0.67 | 3.44 ± 2.16 (2.75 and 5.0 hr.)† | 3.05 ± 0.26 (23 hr.) |

Time designations in parentheses are those times after drug at which speech samples were obtained.
*Average anxiety scores for 3 subjects only.
†Average anxiety scores for 2 subjects only.

primarily to evaluate the content analysis method.

***Procedure.*** Four subjects of Group 1 received lorazepam 2 mg. intravenously and one received sodium pentobarbital 100 mg. intravenously. Four of Group 2 received lorazepam 5 mg. intravenously and one received sodium phenobarbital 130 mg. intravenously. Four of Group 3 received lorazepam 5 mg. intramuscularly and one received sodium phenobarbital 260 mg. intramuscularly. Four of Group 4 received lorazepam 3 mg. intramuscularly and one received sodium phenobarbital 120 mg. intramuscularly. The subjects given the barbiturates were chosen at random. All 5 subjects of Group 5 received 8.0 to 9.0 mg. of lorazepam intravenously or intramuscularly. Six prisoners who assisted in the study and therefore were in the same environment but not given any drug served as controls. The nature of the drug and dose was unknown to subjects, to the content analysis technician who scored the verbal samples, and to investigators who performed the physiologic tests.

Speech samples were obtained according to a standard procedure[4, 7] in which subjects were asked to speak for 5 minutes into the microphone of a tape recorder in response to instructions to talk about any interesting or dramatic, personal life experiences. Samples of 80 or more words are reliable, and the typescript of the tape recording can be scored at leisure.* The typescripts of the speech samples were scored for anxiety. In this study, a predrug verbal sample was obtained prior to drug injection, and subsequent verbal samples were obtained at the time specified in Table I.

In the first group, one verbal sample was obtained 0.5 hour before drug administration, but since maximal drug effect did not occur until about one hour

*Directions for scoring samples can be found in the manual by Gottschalk, Winget and Gleser,[7] or samples may be sent for scoring (at cost) to the Communications Research Laboratory, Department of Psychiatry and Human Behavior, University of California, Irvine, College of Medicine, Irvine, Calif. 92664.

after drug administration, the first post-drug verbal samples were taken one hour after drug administration in subsequent studies. With the final group, in which 8.0 to 9.0 mg. of lorazepam was administered, only 2 subjects could provide speech samples on the day of drug administration because of oversedation, but verbal samples were obtained the next morning.

Before drug administration, subjects were observed for alertness, and control values were obtained for standing steadiness, ventilatory response to 5 per cent carbon dioxide, electroencephalograms with the use of needle electrodes, and cardiac output and peripheral resistance by the tilt-table technique. When the drugs were given intravenously, electroencephalogram, electrocardiogram, and electromyogram electrodes were fixed to each subject who was reclining in a semi-Fowler's position, and a drip of 5 per cent dextrose and water was started in a forearm vein. After control electroencephalograms were obtained, the drug was administered intravenously through the tubing, and the electroencephalogram was continuously recorded for 10 minutes. All physiologic tests were repeated approximately one and 5 hours after either intravenous or intramuscular drug administration.

Analysis of covariance, BMD X64, General Linear Hypothesis,[1] was used to test for differences between dose groups for verbal sample No. 2 (0.5 to 2.5 hours after drug) scores adjusted for verbal sample No. 1 (before drug) and for verbal sample No. 3 (3.25 to 7.00 hours after drug) adjusted for verbal sample No. 1.

## Results

***Psychological effects.*** Statistical analysis of changes in anxiety scores before and after 2.0 mg. of lorazepam was omitted because there was no apparent decrease in anxiety. Covariance analysis revealed that anxiety scores for verbal sample No. 2 for the group of subjects receiving 5.0 mg. of lorazepam were significantly lower ($p < 0.05$) than the verbal sample No. 2 anxiety scores from the group of subjects receiving no drug and 3.0 mg. of lorazepam when these scores were adjusted for verbal sample No. 1 (before drug). However, the difference between the same groups was not significant for verbal sample No. 3 adjusted for verbal sample No. 1 ($F = 0.01$, $df = 1, 15$).

Changes in anxiety scores in response to the 8.0 to 9.0 mg. parenteral doses were not analyzed statistically (although the anxiety scores are shown in Table I), because anxiety levels tended to increase rather than decrease (as may occur at the excitement stage of sedation). Also, only 2 subjects were able to speak for verbal sample No. 2 because of drowsiness or sleep, and none was able to do so at the time they were supposed to give verbal sample No. 3. Verbal sample No. 3 was subsequently obtained 23 hours after drug administration.

***Physiologic findings.*** The physiological effects of oral lorazepam in man have been reported in detail elsewhere.[2] It has similar actions parenterally. It is strongly hypnotic, but in hypnotic doses lorazepam produces minimal depression of the respiratory and cardiovascular systems. Even though electroencephalogram pattern changes indicated penetration of the drug into the brain within one minute of intravenous administration (in the form of sleep spindles), subjects noted no immediate effect while maximal effects did not occur until 45 to 60 minutes after injection. Daytime sedation was evident after 2.0 mg. intravenously but more obvious after 3.0 mg. intramuscularly. There was a marked hypnotic effect after 5.0 mg. intravenously and intramuscularly with recovery progressing well 6 hours after drug administration. Doses of 8.0 and 9.0 mg. intramuscularly and intravenously produced Stage I anesthesia for 6 to 8 hours with an obvious "hangover" 22 hours following drug administration, but even with these doses maximal effects did not occur for 45

to 60 minutes, indicating a relatively slow onset of action similar to phenobarbital.

Impairment of performance in the standing steadiness test was related to both duration and magniture of drug action; for example, 3.0 mg. intramuscularly had noticeably more effect than 2.0 mg. intravenously.

Doses of 2.0 and 3.0 mg. of lorazepam did not affect minute volume or response to 5 per cent $CO_2$. However, minute volume was depressed after doses of 5.0 mg. or more, while the response curve to $CO_2$ was shifted to the right, as is characteristic for sedative-hypnotics.

Cardiovascular adaptive mechanisms were not affected by any dose of lorazepam used. Peripheral resistance and cardiac output were not affected in the supine position. Cardiovascular changes following tilt were those expected of normal reflex control of circulation.

### Discussion

The determination of clinical effects of presumptive antianxiety drugs in man has usually involved administration of varying dosages of drugs to sizeable groups of subjects, often by practitioners who are relatively inexperienced in clinical psychopharmacologic research. In addition to difficulties in setting up controlled studies in such early clinical drug evaluations, including placebo-drug comparisons, there are always measurement problems (reliability and validity) involved in assessing changes in the magnitude of anxiety, whether by self-report instruments or behavioral rating scales.

The present report illustrates the usefulness in screening studies of an objective measure of anxiety which does not require a behavioral scientist or psychiatrist in obtaining the raw data for scoring and has the advantage that the subjects do not realize that they are being evaluated for anxiety. In addition, the content analysis technician cannot be influenced by slurred speech or other signs of depression or stimulation, because he works from a typescript. Validation studies of the content analysis measure of anxiety, which establish that it measures conscious and preconscious fear and anxiety, have already been reported in detail.[6]

An example follows of a fragment from a verbal sample which illustrates the Gottschalk-Gleser system of scoring those clauses that have scorable anxiety items, with appropriate symbols designating each category in the anxiety scale (Schedule 1). The diagonal marks indicate grammatical clauses. In Schedule 1, the numbers in parentheses indicate the weights assigned to each scorable content item.

#### Verbal sample coded for anxiety

Total words: 175

Correction Factor $\left(\frac{100}{\text{no. words}}\right)$: 0.5714

Well, let's see. / Traveling nearly 4,000 miles in an airplane for the first time and stopping in various countries provided me with interesting experiences with people. / A somewhat [6a3] frightening experience was / when one of the plane [2c1] engines was found to be defective. / And we learned / just after we were out over the open sea / that it had only been [1a3] corrected temporarily. / Some of [6b3] the passengers were really frightened / but others acted / as if they [6d1] didn't have a worry in the world. / However, these experiences were of necessity brief, and somewhat superficial but quite colorful and enlightening. / I'll have to think of something else now. / A rather interesting experience was / when a group of us used to spar in the gym. / Joe used to get the worst of it. / As a matter of fact, [2b2] whenever he hit someone hard / he [2b2] suffered the most / for he was [2b2] always smashing up his hands. / Another time, we were playing golf with Joe / [3b2] and he fell down / and badly [2b2] skinned up his arms. / We really kidded him about it. /

As can be seen from the scored excerpt of a 5 minute speech sample, the coded notations over clauses scorable for anxiety contain the identification of the type of verbal reference and its weight. The method by which a total score was obtained

**Schedule 1: Anxiety scale***

1. Death anxiety—references to death, dying, threat of death, or anxiety about death experienced by or occurring to:
   a. self (3)
   b. animate others (2)
   c. inanimate objects destroyed (1)
   d. denial of death anxiety (1)
2. Mutilation (castration) anxiety—references to injury, tissue, or physical damage or anxiety about injury or threat of such experienced by or occurring to:
   a. self (3)
   b. animate others (2)
   c. inanimate objects (1)
   d. denial (1)
3. Separation anxiety—references to desertion, abandonment, loneliness, ostracism, loss of support, falling, loss of love or love object, or threat of such experienced by or occurring to:
   a. self (3)
   b. animate others (2)
   c. inanimate objects (1)
   d. denial (1)
4. Guilt anxiety—references to adverse criticism, abuse, condemnation, moral disapproval, guilt, or threat of such experienced by:
   a. self (3)
   b. animate others (2)
   d. denial (1)
5. Shame anxiety—references to ridicule, inadequacy, shame, embarrassment, humiliation, overexposure of deficiencies or private details, or threat of such experienced by:
   a. self (3)
   b. animate others (2)
   d. denial (1)
6. Diffuse or nonspecific anxiety—references by word (see Gottschalk and co-workers,[7] pp. 60-61) or in phrases to anxiety and/or fear without distinguishing type or source of anxiety:
   a. self (3)
   b. animate others (2)
   d. denial (1)

The weights for each subcategory were assigned on the basis of the degree of personal involvement of the speaker and the degree of direct representation of anxiety. These weights are approximations, on an ordinal, rank-order scale; a series of construct validation studies have provided evidence that the weights are justifiable approximations.

*Number in parentheses are the weights.

is shown in Table II. The total raw score for anxiety (or any other affect) is derived by summing the weights of all verbal references made within that category during the verbal sample and then obtaining the sum of scores over all speech categories. This numerical index is adjusted for the varying rates of speech of different people or the same individual on different occasions by adding 0.5 to the raw score and multiplying this sum by 100, divided by the number of words spoken (correction factor). The correction gives an anxiety score per 100 words, avoids the discontinuity occurring whenever no scorable items have occurred in some speech samples, and reduces the correlation between anxiety scores and number of words to zero. A final corrected anxiety score is obtained by the square root of the raw score. This mathematical transformation has been found to reduce skewness in the frequency distribution of anxiety scores and to permit the use of parametric, as well as nonparametric, statistics in the evaluation of data.

**Table II.** *Total scoring of verbal sample coded for anxiety: Correction factor (C.F.) = 0.5714*

| *Subcategory* | *Total weight* | *Raw score* |
|---|---|---|
| Death | 3 | 1.71 |
| 1a3 × 1 | | |
| Mutilation | 9 | 5.14 |
| 2b2 × 4 | | |
| 2c1 × 1 | | |
| Separation | 2 | 1.14 |
| 3b2 × 1 | | |
| Guilt | 0 | — |
| Shame | 0 | — |
| Diffuse | 7 | 4.00 |
| 6a3 × 1 | | |
| 6b3 × 1 | | |
| 6d1 × 1 | | |
| Total | 21 | 11.99 |
| 11.99 + 1/2 C.F. = 12.28 | | |
| Square root = 3.50 | | |

Anxiety scores previously obtained by this method correlate significantly with clinical psychiatric ratings of anxiety, with increase in systolic blood pressure, de-

crease in skin temperature, higher plasma free fatty acid levels in fasting subjects, and greater anxiety scores found in the content of dreams when plasma free fatty acids are elevated.[7] Previous psychopharmacologic studies using this content analysis method have demonstrated that sedative doses of amobarbital (65 mg.) decrease anxiety scores significantly,[8] as do chlordiazepoxide (20 mg.[3] and perphenazine[5] (16 to 24 mg. per day). On the other hand, the antidepressant, imipramine (100 to 300 mg. per day) in nondepressed patients increased anxiety scores.[6]

In the present study we found that lorazepam administered parenterally effectively reduced anxiety at a dosage of 5.0 mg. That this dosage level happens to be noticeably hypnotic and was the lowest dose studied which decreased respiratory stimulant effects of $CO_2$ and minute volume should be further investigated to determine whether there is a functional relationship between the onset of physiologic depression of the respiratory center in response to sedative-hypnotic drugs and effective inhibition of anxiety. It should be noted that barbiturates, which had less apparent sedative effects than 3.0 mg. or more of lorazepam, had some antianxiety effects and that sedative-hypnotics may differ in this regard.

## *References*


1. Dixon, W. J., editor: Biomedical computer programs, Berkeley, 1968, University of California Press.
2. Elliott, H. W., Nomof, N., Navarro, G., Ruelius, H. W., Knowles, J. A., and Comer, W. H.: Central nervous system and cardiovascular effects of lorazepam in man, CLIN. PHARMACOL. THER. **12**:468-481, 1971.
3. Gleser, G. C., Gottschalk, L. A., Fox, R., and Lippert, W.: Immediate changes in affect with chlordiazepoxide in juvenile delinquent boys, Arch. Gen. Psychiatry **13**:291-295, 1965.
4. Gottschalk, L. A., and Gleser, G. C.: The measurement of psychological states through the content analysis of verbal behavior, Berkeley, 1969, University of California Press.
5. Gottschalk, L. A., Gleser, G. C., Springer, K. J., Kaplan, S. M., Shanon, J., and Ross, W. D.: Effects of perphenazine on verbal behavior patterns, Arch. Gen. Psychiatry **2**:632-639, 1960.
6. Gottschalk, L. A., Gleser, G. C., Wylie, H. W., Jr., and Kaplan, S. M.: Effects of imipramine on anxiety and hostility levels, Psychopharmacologia **7**:303-310, 1965.
7. Gottschalk, L. A., Winget, C. M., and Gleser, G. C.: Manual for scoring the Gottschalk-Gleser content analysis scales: Anxiety, hostility, social alienation-personal disorganization, Berkeley, 1969, University of California Press.
8. Ross, W. D., Adsett, N., Gleser, G. C., Joyce, G. R. B., Kaplan, S. M., and Tieger, M. E.: A trial of psychopharmacologic measurement with projective techniques, J. Proj. Tech. **27**: 223-225, 1963.

# Introduction to Chapter 17

Introductory Comments by Louis A. Gottschalk

Atkinson had healthy male volunteers (ages 21 to 30) inhale 40% nitrous oxide for 15 minutes and continue to inhale it for another 5 minutes while giving a speech sample elicited by the standard instructions for the Gottschalk-Gleser method. Following a recovery period of over 20 mintues, a series of self-report measures evaluating the drug experience was administered. Scores derived from the Gottschalk-Gleser scales were correlated with scores on the postdrug self-report scales. There were significant correlations between verbal content scores during intoxication and retrospective self-report scores after intoxication on dimensions of positive affect and negative affect arousal as well as cognitive impairment.

These findings are surprising from two points of view. 1. Psychological state scores derived from the content analysis of speech may not necessarily measure the same psychological dimension assessed by self-report or psychiatric rating scale scores given the same name, e.g., anxiety or hostility, because the states were initially defined differently and/or because different kinds of measurement errors are inherent in self-report and rating

scales (see Chapter 28 ). 2. Drug intoxicated subjects do not always accurately perceive these subjective experiences when sober, especially if there are amnesic effects of the drug. Atkinson's study with nitrous oxide, itself an unusually objective study of the psychological effects of nitrous oxide, demonstrates that, at least with this drug, post-intoxication psychological testing gives a reasonably valid reflection of the subjective experiences of an individual during acute intoxication.

The verbal content scores during acute nitrous oxide intoxication can be used in another way to provide an immediate assessment of the psychological effects of this drug. For example, the verbal content cognitive impairment scores of the subjects during nitrous oxide intoxication were compared to the mean cognitive impairment scores of an adult normative sample of 60 subjects with the following results:

A comparison was made between 60 normative subjects, who gave five minute speech samples following standardized instructions to elicit speech, of the verbal categories of the social alienation-personal disorganization content analysis scale developed by Gottschalk and his coworkers and the average scores on these verbal categories obtained from the five minute speech samples of the 60 subjects who participated in the study of the mental effects occurring with the inhalation of nitrous oxide. Of the 60 subjects in the nitrous oxide study, four subjects were excluded from this comparison because they had less than the 70 word minimum in their speech samples. The subjects under the influence of nitrous oxide showed significantly greater average scores by t-tests*, as compared to the normative subjects, in the following verbal categories indicative of <u>cognitive defect</u>: 1. statements that are inaudible or not understandable (IIIA1, $p < .001$); 2. incomplete

-----------------------------------

*Pooled variance t-tests were used when F-ratios were found to be non-significant. The T-test approximation was used when F-ratios were found to be significant.

p values were from a condensed version of Table 12 of the <u>Biometrika Tables for Statisticians</u> Vol. 1 (ed. 3) edited by E.S. Pearson and H.O. Hartley reproduced in <u>Statistical Methods</u> by G.W. Snedecor and W.G. Cochran, The Iowa State University Press, Ames, Iowa, 1971.

phrases or clauses or blocking (IIIA2, $p < .001$); 3. statements that are illogical or bizarre (IIIA3, $p < .001$); 4. repetition of words separated by no more than a word (IIIB1, $p < .001$); 5. repetition of phrases or clauses separated by no more than a phrase or clause (IIIB2, $p < .005$). Significant differences also occurred in the dimension of social alienation with inhalation of nitrous oxide, namely: 1. significantly fewer statements pertaining to others helping and being friendly towards others (IC1, $p < .001$); 2. significantly fewer statements pertaining to the self helping or being friendly towards others (IC2, $p < .001$); 3. significantly fewer statements pertaining to others helping or being friendly towards the self (IC3, $p < .001$); 4. significantly fewer statements about others being bad, dangerous, ill or malfunctioning (ID1, $p < .05$); 5. significantly fewer statements about others being intact, satisfied, healthy or well (ID2, $p < .001$); 6. significantly fewer statements about the self being intact, satisfied, healthy or well (IIB3a, $p < .001$); 7. significantly more statements about psychological malfunctioning in the self (IIB1b, $p < .01$); 8. significantly more statements about the self malfunctioning due to indeterminate origin (IIB1c, $p < .005$); 9. significantly more statements about not being prepared or able to produce, perform or act (IIB4, $p < .001$); and 10. significantly more statements about the self being controlled or wanting control or asking for control or being obliged or having to do, think or experience something (IIB5, $p < .001$).

These findings indicate that inhalation of nitrous oxide is capable of producing a transient cerebral organic mental disorder that may masquerade as "schizophrenic" in the sense that there are elements of social alienation in the verbal manifestations as well as the congitive defects that typify both acute and chronic organic brain syndromes and schizophrenia.

17

# Measurement of Subjective Effects of Nitrous Oxide: Validation of Post-Drug Questionnaire Responses by Verbal Content Analysis of Speech Samples Collected During Drug Intoxication

Roland M. Atkinson

## INTRODUCTION

How and when to measure subjective effects of consciousness-altering drugs are important experimental design questions, for the nature and validity of subjects' responses may be influenced by the method and timing of inquiries about their drug experience (Barber, 1970; Barr et al., 1972). In this report, I will describe a study of the subjective effects induced by subanesthetic (40%) nitrous oxide ($N_2O$) in 60 healthy young male volunteers. The Gottschalk-Gleser verbal content analytic method (Gottschalk and Gleser, 1969) was applied to five-minute speech samples collected during $N_2O$ intoxication, in an attempt to validate extensive questionnaire data collected after intoxication on dimensions of drug induced emotional responses and cognitive impairment. First I will

---

From the Department of Psychiatry and Human Behavior, College of Medicine, University of California, Irvine. This work was supported by the National Institute on Drug Abuse, grants DA00204 and DA00695. The technical assistance of J. DeWayne Green and Susan J. Hemington, B.A. is gratefully acknowledged. Dr. Atkinson is now Associate Professor of Psychiatry, University of Oregon School of Medicine, and Staff Psychiatrist, Veterans Administration Hospital, Portland, OR 97207.

discuss design considerations, then present and discuss the results of this validation effort.

Questionnaires, adjective checklists and comparable instruments may provide abundant quantifiable data on subjective drug effects, but it is often difficult to choose an optimal time to administer them. Administration during drug intoxication poses several important problems. First, subjects may have difficulty in expressing themselves verbally or in writing, in attending to questions and tasks, and in processing information, for example, interference with short-term memory. Each of these effects has in fact been reported for subanesthetic $N_2O$ (Edwards et al., 1976; Steinberg, 1954; Garfield et al., 1975; Steinberg and Summerfield, 1957; Robson et al., 1960; Parkhouse et al., 1960; Biersner, 1972). A questionnaire introduced during intoxication may also represent a serious intrusion for a subject, who may at this time be especially vulnerable to such phenomena as demand characteristics of the test (Orne, 1962) and evaluation apprehension (Rosenberg, 1969). Both his questionnaire responses and his actual drug experience may thus be altered in a manner difficult or impossible to control. Finally, the time required to complete lengthy questionnaires may exceed the desired duration of drug intoxication. This would have been the case in the present experiment, in which $N_2O$ intoxication was limited to 20 minutes. To avoid these problems, the administration of a questionnaire battery on drug effects was deferred until the intoxication state had ended.

Another set of potentially serious problems is encountered, however, when one elects this common strategy of post-drug assessment. Partial amnesia for the drug experience is a regular consequence of $N_2O$ concentrations above 50% and can occur in some individuals at lower concentrations (Parkhouse et al., 1960). Retrospective distortion by subjects may also occur. Nor are demand characteristics and evaluation apprehension eliminated merely by a change in the timing of tests. Furthermore, even if subjects try to comply with instructions which clearly request them to answer questions based on their best recollection

of the drug experience, their responses in the sober post-drug state may be conditioned at least in part by their sobriety.

For these reasons, it seemed prudent to introduce some measure of drug effects during intoxication, in order to attempt to validate the post-drug data. The Gottschalk-Gleser approach offered several advantages. Collection of a five minute speech sample elicited by the standard instructions represents a brief, unstructured, minimally intrusive intervention during intoxication. The projective form of the method would probably render the data less vulnerable to conscious impression management by subjects than would be the case with questionnaire methods. However, it was anticipated that subjects might encounter psychomotor difficulty in speaking (that is, because of drug induced dysarthria, they might produce unintelligible words) and difficulty attending to the task of speaking (that is, they might fail to speak).

## METHODS

Procedures for the experiment have been described in detail elsewhere (Atkinson et al., 1977a; Atkinson et al., 1977b) and will be presented briefly. The 60 subjects were males, age 21 to 30 years, who responded to ads placed on local college campuses. All were physically and mentally healthy, achieved Shipley-Hartford I.Q. scores $\geq 100$, had not used $N_2O$ non-medically, and had not participated in prior drug or consciousness research. They were each paid $21 for participation in the study. The subjects came individually to the laboratory for a single, 20-minute $N_2O$ inhalation session. Beforehand, they were briefed to refrain from use of psychoactive substances, except caffeine and nicotine, for at least 48 hours prior to the session, and to eat no solid foods after midnight before the session. They were also told in advance that there was a large degree of variation in individual responses to $N_2O$, that we could not predict what their experience would be like, but that, whether pleasant or unpleasant, it would last for only about 20 minutes since major effects

dissipate rapidly when inhalation is terminated. They were also told they could terminate the inhalation session at any point if necessary.

The setting for the session was an attractively decorated, home-like room in a psychophysiology laboratory. The subject sat semi-recumbent in a recliner chair, and was attended by a research assistant who did not interact with him except to give instructions. Nitrous oxide was mixed with oxygen to produce a 40% concentration, by means of a standard, flow-metered anesthesia machine housed in an adjacent instrumentation room. The physician who operated the machine was able to maintain visual and auditory contact with the subject and to monitor respiration. Gas mixtures were pumped through the wall to the subject via a hose-mask system. A non-rebreathing ("one-way") respiratory system was employed. The face mask contained a microphone so that the subject's verbalizations were audible to experimental personnel and could be tape recorded.

After a five-minute practice run on 10% $N_2O$, subjects were instructed to remain quietly introspective during the first 15 minutes of the 40% $N_2O$ inhalation session. Then a five-minute speech sample was collected, elicited by the standard instructions for the Gottschalk-Gleser method. Following this, subjects inhaled pure oxygen for two minutes, before breathing room air again. A 20-minute recovery period followed.

Next a questionnaire battery was administered by another assistant who had not attended the inhalation session. Included were Katz and Waskow's Subjective Drug Effects Questionnaire (SDEQ) (Katz et al., 1968), Pahnke and Richards' Psychedelic Experience Questionnaire (PEQ) (Pahnke, 1963; Pahnke and Richards, 1972), the Multiple Affect Adjective Check List (MAACL) (Zuckerman and Lubin, 1965), and a global rating by subjects of their degree of "high", on a scale from zero to 100, after Jones (1971). For all instruments, subjects were clearly requested to respond according to their best recollection of the drug experience just completed.

Specific Gottschalk-Gleser scales employed were the following: positive affect arousal, two scales: Human Relations and Hope; negative affect arousal, six scales: Total Anxiety, Overt Outward Hostility, Covert Outward Hostility, Total Outward Hostility, Inward Hostility, and Ambivalent Hostility; cognitive impairment, one scale: Cognitive Impairment.

Specific scales from the post-drug questionnaire battery were the following: positive affect arousal, seven scales: SDEQ Total Euhporia, Euphoric Somatic Effects, Euphoric Mood, Euphoric Functioning and Relaxation-and Well-being, PEQ Deeply Felt Positive Mood and global rating of degree of "high"; negative affect arousal, eight scales: SDEQ Total Dysphoria, Dysphoric Somatic Effects, Dysphoric Mood, Dysphoric Functioning and Tension-and-Jitteriness, MAACL Anxiety, Depression and Hostility; cognitive impariment, two scales: SDEQ Improved Cognition and Impaired Cognition.

Scores for Gottschalk-Gleser scales were correlated with scores on post-drug scales, using the Pearson r procedure. It was predicted that Gottschalk-Gleser scale scores for each of the three dimensions, positive affect aroual, negative affect arousal and cognitive impairment, would be correlated with post-drug scale scores on these respective dimensions. For example, it was predicted that scores on the Gottschalk Cognitive Impairment Scale would be directly correlated with scores on the SDEQ Impaired Cognition Scale and inversely correlated with scores on the SDEQ Improved Cognition scale. Pearson r's were thus assessed for significance using a one-tailed method.

## RESULTS

No subject was dropped because of adverse drug effects or procedural problems. As anticipated, dysarthria was common during speech sample collection, so that

most tape recordings contained at least a few unintelligible words. Nevertheless, coherent verbal production was generally quite adequate (mean words per sample =340, s.d. =208). Four subjects were not able to persist in speaking sufficiently to produce a minimum of 75 words required for a meaningful content analysis. Data reported below are based on the responses of the remaining 56 subjects.

Affect Arousal: Correlations between the eight Gottschalk-Gleser affect-related scales and corresponding post-drug affect measures are presented in Tables 1 and 2. Of 120 correlations determined, 96 were in the predicted direction. Of these, 24 achieved statistical significance. Of the 24 correlations in the non-predicted direction, none reached statistical significance. Of the Gottschalk scales, Ambivalent Hostility was most highly correlated with post-drug data: all 15 correlations with post-drug scale scores were in the predicted direction and eight of these achieved statistical significance. Total Outward Hostility and Total Anxiety scores were also correlated significantly with several of the post drug measures. The most notable exception to a general pattern of congruence between affect scores during drug and after drug was the lack of correlation between scores on the Gottschalk Inward Hostility Scale and post drug scores. Ten of the 15 correlations for this scale were in the non-predicted direction, and none of its correlations achieved statistical significance.

Shifting focus to the post-drug scales, one observes that scores on only four of the 15 post-drug affect scales failed to correlate significantly with a single Gottschalk scale. These included one measure of positive affect arousal, the global rating of degree of high, and three measures of negative affect arousal, SDEQ Dysphoric Somatic Effects, SDEQ Tension-and-Jitteriness, and MAACL Hostility.

Cognitive impairment: Scores on the Gottschalk Cognitive Impairment Scale were significantly correlated with two post-drug SDEQ cognition scales in the

TABLE 1

POST-DRUG POSITIVE AFFECT CORRELATES OF GOTTSCHALK AFFECT SCORES (N=56)

| Scales | During-drug (Gottschalk Scales) | | | | | | | |
|---|---|---|---|---|---|---|---|---|
| | Positive | | Negative | | | | | |
| | Human Relations | Hope | Total Anxiety | Outward Hostility Overt | Outward Hostility Covert | Outward Hostility Total | Inward Hostility | Ambivalent Hostility |
| Post-drug | | | | | | | | |
| SDEQ: | | | | | | | | |
| Total euphoria | 0.16 | 0.01 | -0.23* | -0.20 | -0.22* | -0.31* | 0.05 | -0.26* |
| Euphoric-somatic | 0.20 | 0.07 | -0.30* | -0.03 | -0.12 | -0.11 | 0.02 | -0.21 |
| Euphoria-mood | 0.24* | 0.11 | -0.12 | -0.22* | -0.25* | -0.34** | 0.08 | -0.21 |
| Euphoria-functioning | -0.12 | -0.23 | -0.24* | -0.17 | -0.13 | -0.24* | -0.00 | -0.27* |
| Relaxation-well being | 0.11 | 0.03 | -0.08 | -0.18 | -0.21 | -0.31** | 0.12 | -0.24* |
| PEQ: positive mood | 0.26* | 0.10 | -0.18 | -0.25* | -0.21 | -0.35** | 0.11 | -0.13 |
| Degree of "high" | 0.15 | 0.01 | -0.00 | -0.10 | -0.12 | -0.16 | 0.04 | -0.07 |

Pearson r's. All p's one-tailed

* p <.05

** p <.01

TABLE 2

POST-DRUG NEGATIVE AFFECT CORRELATES OF GOTTSCHALK AFFECT SCORES (N=56)

| Scales | During-drug (Gottschalk Scales) | | | | | | | |
|---|---|---|---|---|---|---|---|---|
| | Positive | | Negative | | | | | |
| | Human Relations | Hope | Total Anxiety | Outward Hostility Overt | Outward Hostility Covert | Outward Hostility Total | Inward Hostility | Ambivalent Hostility |
| Post-Drug | | | | | | | | |
| SDEQ: | | | | | | | | |
| Total dysphoria | 0.07 | -0.20 | 0.07 | 0.04 | 0.00 | 0.03 | 0.11 | 0.35** |
| Dysphoria-somatic | 0.01 | -0.19 | -0.07 | 0.01 | -0.16 | -0.08 | 0.03 | 0.22 |
| Dysphoria-mood | 0.00 | -0.21 | 0.01 | 0.02 | 0.04 | 0.03 | 0.05 | 0.35** |
| Dysphoria-functioning | 0.18 | -0.04 | 0.29* | 0.08 | 0.17 | 0.15 | 0.21 | 0.27* |
| Tension-jitteriness | 0.00 | -0.15 | -0.14 | 0.05 | -0.05 | 0.02 | -0.05 | 0.22 |
| MAACL: anxiety | -0.18 | -0.21 | -0.02 | 0.12 | 0.02 | 0.10 | -0.17 | 0.28* |
| Depression | -0.19 | -0.03 | 0.07 | 0.16 | 0.16 | 0.23* | -0.08 | 0.27* |
| Hostility | -0.16 | -0.08 | 0.01 | 0.15 | -0.01 | 0.11 | -0.07 | 0.17 |

Pearson r's. All p's one-tailed

* $p < .05$

** $p < .01$

predicted direction. For the SDEQ Improved Cognition Scale, r=-0.24, while for the SDEQ Impaired Cognition Scale, r=0.25. Both were significant at the .05 level.

## DISCUSSION

Repeated use of the same method over time and use of multiple methods at a given time are both common approaches to assessment of subjective drug effects. The present uncommon design attempts to capitalize on the advantages of two different methods (verbal content analysis vs. questionnaires) applied to the same experience (drug intoxication) at different points in time (during vs. after). Considering the theoretical obstacles to achieving congruence between during-drug Gottschalk scores and post-drug questionnaire scores, that is, the problems related to timing and drug effects surveyed earlier as well as differences in measurement methods, the resulting pattern of small but meaningful correlations is perhaps as surprising as it is face valid.

The verbal sample and questionnaire data tend to offer complementary validation of reportable subjective effects. Most of the significant affect-related correlations (17 of 24) involved post-drug measures of positive affect arousal, rather than negative affect arousal. This may be partially explained by the finding that positive affect arousal was more prominent than negative affect arousal, based on assessment of post-drug data (Atkinson et al., 1977a; Atkinson et al., 1977b). That is, scores ranged further upward on positive affect scales than on negative affect scales. Thus post-drug positive affect scales were probably more sensitive to variation in reportable experience than were the negative affect scales.

With regard to the seven significant correlations between verbal content scale scores and post-drug negative affect scale scores, of interest is the finding that five of these involved the Gottschalk Ambivalent Hostility Scale. Why scores on this scale should be exceptionally well correlated with post-drug

negative affect measures may be understandable as a function of the experimental situation. Subjects were placed in circumstances in which they might well presume that their experience would be affected by an external agency (drug, mask, hose, attendant, overall setting). To the extent that their experience was unpleasant, it is reasonable to expect that the Ambivalent Hostility Scale might be a relatively more sensitive measure for this than other Gottschalk scales, for it is based on verbal content depicting negative personal experiences caused by external agents.

The data support the concept suggested by Pankratz and associates (1972) of general dimensions of positive and negative affect arousal rather than more specific arousal of putative affects implied by the names of the scales used. For example, the Gottschalk Total Anxiety score was not correlated with either the SDEQ Tension-Jitteriness score or the MAACL Anxiety score. However, Total Anxiety scores were significantly correlated with SDEQ Dysphoric Functioning and, negatively as predicted, with several SDEQ euphoria scales. For another example, Gottschalk Total Outward Hostility scores were not significantly correlated with MAACL Hostility scores, but were significantly correlated with MAACL Depression scores and, negatively as predicted, with scores on several post-drug positive affect scales.

Scores on the Gottschalk Inward Hostility scale, based on self-critical and self-destructive verbal content, proved to be uniquely incongruent with post-drug data. This was not a function of low scores, for the mean score on this scale was slightly higher than means for the other hostility scales. The findings suggest that in this sample of young men, self-criticism was independent of drug induced affect arousal.

## CONCLUSIONS

1. The Gottschalk-Gleser verbal content analytic method was applicable to speech samples collected from 56 of 60 subjects intoxicated by 40% $N_2O$.

2. There was a strong, face valid trend of correlation between verbal content scores during intoxication and retrospective questionnaire scores after intoxication, on dimensions of positive affect and negative affect arousal and cognitive impairment.

3. Use of the Gottschalk-Gleser method is recommended in research on subjective effects of drugs employed to produce brief episodes of acute intoxication, to further substantiate findings of post-intoxication testing.

## REFERENCES

Atkinson, R.M., Morozumi, P., Green, J.D., and Kramer, J.C. Nitrous oxide intoxication: subjective effects in healthy young men. Unpublished (1977a).

Atkinson, R.M., Green, J.D., Kramer, J.C., Weijola, M.J., and Chenoweth, D. Prediction of subjective responses to nitrous oxide: role of personality and prior drug use. Unpublished (1977a).

Barber, T.X. LSD, Marihuana, Yoga and Hypnosis. Aldine, Chicago (1970) p. 14.

Barr, H.L., Langs, R.J., Holt, R.R., Goldberger, L., and Klein, G.S. LSD: Personality and Experience. Wiley-Interscience, New York (1972) p. 22.

Biersner, R.J. Selective performance effects of nitrous oxide, Human Factors, 14, 187-194 (1972).

Edwards D., Harris, J.A., and Biersner, R.J. Encoding and decoding of connected discourse during altered states of consicousness. J. Psychol. 92, 97-102 (1976).

Garfield, J.M., Garfield, F.B., and Sampson, J. Effects of nitrous oxide on decision-strategy and sustained attention. Psychopharmacologia. 42, 5-10 (1975).

Gottschalk, L.A. and Gleser, G.C. The Measurement of Psychological States Through the Content Analysis of Verbal Behavior, University of California Press Berkeley (1969).

Jones, R.T. Marihuana-induced "high": influence of expectation, setting and previous drug experience. Pharmacol. Rev. 23, 359-369 (1971).

Katz, M.M., Waskow, I.E., and Olsson J. Characterizing the psychological state produced by LSD. J. Abnorm. Psychol. 73, 1-14 (1968).

Orne, M.T. On the social psychology of the psychological experiment: with particular reference to demand characteristics and their implications. Amer. Psychologist. 17, 776-783 (1962).

Pahnke, W.N. Drugs and Mysticism: an analysis of the relationship between psychedelic drugs and the mystical consciousness. Unpublished doctoral dissertation. Harvard University, Cambridge (1963).

Pahnke, W.M. and Richards, W.A. Psychedelic Experience Questionnaire. Revised, unpublished. Maryland Psychiatric Research Center, Baltimore (1972).

Pankratz, L., Glaudin, V., and Goodmonson, C. Reliability of the Multiple Affect Adjective Check List. J. Personal. Assess. 36, 371-373 (1972).

Parkhouse, J., Henrie, J.R., Duncan, G.M. and Rome, H.P. Nitrous oxide analgesia in relation to mental performance. J. Pharmacol. Exper. Therap. 128, 44-54 (1960).

Robson, J.G., Burns, B.D., and Welt, P.J. The effect of inhaling dilute nitrous oxide upon recent memory and time estimation. Canad. Anaesthetists' Soc. J. 7, 399-410 (1960).

Rosenberg, M.J. The conditions and consequences of evaluation apprehension, in Artifact in Behavioral Research, R. Rosenthal and R.L. Rosnow, eds., Academic Press, New York (1969), pp. 279-349.

Steinberg, H. Selective effects of an anesthetic drug on cognitive behaviour. Quart. J. Exper. Psychol. 6, 170-180 (1954).

Steinberg, H. and Summerfield, A. Influence of a depressant drug on acquisition in rote learning. Quart. J. Exper. Psychol. 9, 138-145 (1957).

Zuckerman, M. and Lubin, B. Manual for the Multiple Affect Adjective Check List. Educational and Industrial Testing Service, San Diego (1965).

# Prediction of Changes in Severity of the Schizophrenic Syndrome with Discontinuation and Administration of Phenothiazines in Chronic Schizophrenic Patients: Language as a Predictor and Measure of Change in Schizophrenia

*By* Louis A. Gottschalk, Goldine C. Gleser, John M. Cleghorn, Walter N. Stone and Carolyn N. Winget

THE PURPOSE OF THIS INVESTIGATION was to explore possible predictors of change in the severity of the schizophrenic syndrome among chronic schizophrenic patients with cessation and administration of phenothiazine chemotherapy. A special feature of this study was the use of five-minute samples of schizophrenic speech to serve as predictor scores and change scores of the schizophrenic symptom complex.[16-18,20,22] An independent set of change scores and predictor scores was provided by the use of the Mental Status Schedule of Spitzer et al.[29-32] and of predictor scores alone by the 16 PF test of Cattell and Eber.[3]

## Materials and Methods

A group of 74 chronic schizophrenic patients, 35 males and 39 females, was selected from the schizophrenic inpatient population at Longview State Hospital in Cincinnati, Ohio, on the following bases: the patients had no complicating medical or neurological illness other than chronic schizophrenia; they were receiving a phenothiazine derivative and no anti-depressant medicament of any kind; they were not mute and were capable of cooperating with the procedures used in the measurements of change. They had the following other characteristics: they had been hospitalized from 6 months to 25 years on the present admission, with a median of 11 years; those hospitalized for the shortest periods had had one to four previous admissions; all patients had been on one of the phenothiazine drugs continually for at least six months (approximately 37% were on trifluoperazine, 19% on fluphenazine, 19% on perphenazine, and the remaining 25% on such drugs as chlorpromazine, thioridazine, or triflupromazine); the patients were all Caucasians and in the age range from 24 to 54, with an average age of 42.9 years.

For the initial assessment of these patients, several procedures were carried out while they were still receiving their phenothiazine medication. Tape-recorded, five-minute verbal samples were obtained from each patient two or three times in the initial week, using the Gottschalk-Gleser method of asking each patient to tell an interesting or dramatic life

---

*Supported in part by Grant T 57-74 from the Foundations Fund for Research in Psychiatry; National Institute of Mental Health Grants MH-08282 and MH-K3-14, 665; and a grant from the Robert Stern Fund.*

Louis A. Gottschalk, M.D.: *Chairman and Professor, Department of Psychiatry and Human Behavior, College of Medicine, University of California at Irvine, Irvine, Calif.* Goldine C. Gleser, Ph.D.: *Professor of Psychology and Director, Psychology Division, Department of Psychiatry, College of Medicine, University of Cincinnati, Cincinnati, Ohio.* John M. Cleghorn, M.D.: *Associate Professor of Psychiatry, Department of Psychiatry, McMaster University Medical School, Hamilton, Ontario, Canada.* Walter N. Stone, M.D.: *Assistant Professor of Psychiatry, Department of Psychiatry, College of Medicine, University of Cincinnati, Cincinnati, Ohio.* Carolyn N. Winget, M.A: *Research Associate, Department of Psychiatry, College of Medicine, University of Cincinnati, Cincinnati, Ohio.*

experience.[15,22]

Each patient was then seen by a psychiatrist or a third-year psychiatric resident who conducted a standardized interview from which he filled out the Mental Status Schedule.[29-32] The 16 PF test, Form A,[3] was administered by a psychologist and research assistant to groups of 6 to 12 patients at any one session. Directions were read aloud and repeated when necessary to make sure that each patient knew what he was to do. Individual attention was given to each person at some point during the time he was answering the test to make sure that he was recording answers correctly and in some cases items were read to him if he was having difficulty reading or understanding the statements. By these means, complete test results were obtained on 35 females and 34 males, or 69 of the 74 patients. The findings from the 16 PF test have been reported elsewhere[11] and will not be presented in detail at this time.

On completion of initial psychological evaluations, all patients had their phenothiazine medication changed, ostensibly, to a new drug, which was actually a placebo of identical appearance to thioridazine. None of the hospital personnel (doctors, nurses, or attendants) was told that a placebo was substituted for the psychoactive drug.

Five-minute speech samples were obtained twice weekly, by the same interviewer whenever possible, from each patient throughout the next eight weeks of the study.

Four weeks after the patients had been taking the placebo, one-half of the group, selected according to Mental Status scores to equate groups, was started on thioridazine in doses comparable to the amount they had been individually receiving in the form of this or any other phenothiazine derivative at the onset of this study (300–1000 mg./day). The other half of the group of patients was continued on the placebo. At this four-week point of the study, all patients were re-evaluated on the Spitzer et al. Mental Status Schedule, and a third evaluation by this measure was done at the end of the eighth week of the study. Different raters were used each time.

Thus, half of the patients were on a placebo for eight weeks and the other half received a placebo for four weeks and then were given the phenothiazine derivative, thioridazine, for four weeks. During the course of this study, if patients became disturbed, they were administered only chloral hydrate (8 cc.) or a placebo by mouth or sodium phenobarbital (0.1 Gm.) intramuscularly. Four patients became difficult to manage during the first four weeks, and had to be dropped from the study.

Typescripts of the five-minute verbal samples were scored independently and blindly by two content analysis technicians for anxiety, hostility outward, hostility inward, ambivalent hostility and social alienation-personal disorganization, following the Gottschalk-Gleser scales. These scales provide an objective procedure for measuring psychological states through the content analysis of small samples of verbal behavior. This method of content analysis, which considers the grammatical clause as the unit of communication of meaning, consists of sets of categories of content, meaning or themes, organized and weighted according to various scaled psychological dimensions. Reliability and validity studies have been reported on scales for measuring, by this method, anxiety,[10,18] three kinds of hostility,[19] social alienation-personal disorganization.[16,17,20,22] and other psychological states.[22]

The Mental Status Schedule, which was completed on each patient during the initial, fourth, and eighth weeks, contains a set of 248 items describing symptoms and behavior to which the psychiatrist responds true or false on the basis of a structured interview with the patient. The authors of this schedule have collected data on over 2000 patients throughout the United States and, at the time of this study, were in the process of determining subscales by means of factor analysis.[29-32] A verimax rotation of the first three principal component factors yielding subscores for neuroticism (feelings and concerns), psychoticism (delusions, hallucinations, grandiosity), and disorientation (confusion, retardation). Forty-two subscales have been derived on more specific and circumscribed symptom clusters.

The 16 PF test claims to measure "functionally unitary and psychologically significant dimensions"[3] as determined by factor analytic and construct validation methods. Standardization tables (1964) provide norms for males in general population based on a substantial number of cases.

All measurements on all patients were computer-analyzed for intercorrelations, means, standard deviations, and other relevant mathematical assessments.

## Results

### *Group Trends in Social Alienation-Personal Disorganization Scores*

Of the 74 patients placed on placebo at the beginning of the study, only four (two males and two females) were discontinued at the end of the first four weeks because of clinical considerations for their well being. These four had required sedatives and had become assaultive or suicidal about the third week on placebo so that it was considered unwise to expose them to the risk of continuing another four weeks on placebo should they happen to be assigned to that group. All four patients decreased steadily in the average number of words they spoke in the five minute sessions, and all but one was mute throughout the third or fourth week. Their scores on the scale for social alienation-personal disorganization increased steadily, with a total average rise of about 10 points in the four weeks. These data, which corroborate the clinical observations, add additional evidence to the validity of the verbal scale for assessing the severity of schizophrenic disorder.

There were a number of occasions for which verbal scores were not available. In some cases data were missing because patients were working or out on pass at the time of some of their scheduled sessions. More often scores were missing because the patient refused to speak or spoke less than the minimum of 45 words needed to obtain a reliable score on the "schizophrenic scale." (At least 70 words are needed to score the affect scales with even a minimum of reliability.) From a previous study validating the verbal measure of social alienation-personal disorganization,[20-22] it was possible to make an estimate of the average score on social alienation-personal disorganization that would be obtained by patients equally disturbed clinically but who spoke little or not at all. On the basis of extrapolations from rating scale scores used as criterion measures against which "schizophrenic" scores from speech samples were compared in this previous study, a score of 8.0 was assigned to verbal samples of up to 45 words and a score of 11.6 to verbal samples in which the subject was completely mute. These estimates helped considerably in obtaining more regular trends. However, six patients spoke so seldom after the first week or two that they were dropped from consideration in analyzing overall longitudinal trends.

The average weekly social alienation-personal disorganization scores of the 64 patients who were followed throughout the study are given in Table 1. Separate averages are provided for those patients who were maintained on placebo throughout the eight weeks and those who received thioridazines the last four weeks. The slopes of the best-fitting linear trend lines for the first and second four-week periods were calculated and the average slopes are indicated in Table 1. These slopes can be interpreted as average weekly rates of change. The average slopes for the first four-week placebo period do not differ significantly between the two groups. The combined average slope of 0.49 for social alienation-personal disorganization scores during the first four weeks is significantly different from a zero slope at the .01 level, indicating an increase in severity of symptomatology during this four-week placebo period.

In the second four-week period for those on placebo, the average scores on the social alienation-personal disorganization scale continued to increase, but

**Table 1.—Average Weekly Social Alienation-Personal Disorganization Scores and Number of Words (per Verbal Sample) from Chronic Schizophrenic Patients**

| Time of Five-Minute Verbal Sample | Group A (Placebo for eight weeks, N = 32) Average Number of Words (per verbal sample) X | s.d. | Group A Average Social Alienation-Personal Disorganization Scores X | s.d. | Group B (Thioridazine last four weeks, N = 32) Average Number of Words (per verbal sample) X | s.d. | Group B Average Social Alienation-Personal Disorganization Scores X | s.d. |
|---|---|---|---|---|---|---|---|---|
| Pre-placebo | 502.0 | 258.7 | 1.9 | 3.5 | 526.0 | 223.6 | 2.0 | 4.0 |
| Week 1 | 407.4 | 247.7 | 1.4 | 4.6 | 438.6 | 221.8 | 2.9 | 4.8 |
| 2 | 411.2 | 258.8 | 2.4 | 5.0 | 429.9 | 243.6 | 2.6 | 5.4 |
| 3 | 416.3 | 282.4 | 2.5 | 4.8 | 392.7 | 189.0 | 4.6 | 7.4 |
| 4 | 410.3 | 282.3 | 3.7 | 5.0 | 364.8 | 238.6 | 3.7 | 7.7 |
| Slope (Wks. 0–4) | −17.6 | 53.0 | 0.48 | 1.10 | −36.6 | 47.3 | 0.50 | 1.41 |
| 5 | 405.5 | 288.5 | 3.6 | 5.7 | 394.3 | 246.5 | 4.3 | 6.1 |
| 6 | 404.0 | 287.2 | 3.4 | 5.6 | 437.8 | 261.2 | 3.5 | 5.8 |
| 7 | 437.8 | 301.0 | 3.7 | 5.6 | 450.9 | 268.1 | 3.2 | 6.6 |
| 8 | 436.4 | 294.0 | 3.9 | 5.6 | 459.6 | 258.5 | 3.6 | 6.1 |
| Slope (Wks. 4–8) | 6.2 | 18.7 | 0.07 | 0.68 | 25.5 | 34.0 | −0.14 | 1.19 |

at a much slower rate. In fact, almost as many of the patients improved as regressed, so that the average slope of .07 was not significant. Clinically there were no further patients who, because of severely disturbed behavior, had to be dropped from the study. The patients who were placed on thioridazine showed some improvement on the average, but again, the average slope of −0.14 was not significantly different from zero. Neither was the difference significant between this average slope and that for patients on placebo. These results are illustrated graphically in Fig. 1.

### *Group Trends in Quantity of Speech*

The number of words spoken each week, on the average, is also given in Table 1 and graphically in Fig. 2. The decrease with placebo during the first four weeks (slope = −27.1 words/week) is very significant ($p < .001$). The difference in slope for the two groups (group A and B) during the placebo period is not significant. In the second four-week period, the patients receiving the active drug (group B) increased their speech at the average rate of 25.5 words per week, a highly significant increase. The placebo group (A) also showed a small rise, but this increase was not significant. The difference in slope for the two treatment groups was highly significant ($t = 2.68$, $p < .01$).

### *Intercorrelations Among Content Analysis Scores of Speech of Chronic Schizophrenics*

Before examining the prediction of individual differences among chronic schizophrenics in response to changes in phenothiazine administration, it is instructive to look briefly at the intercorrelations among various content

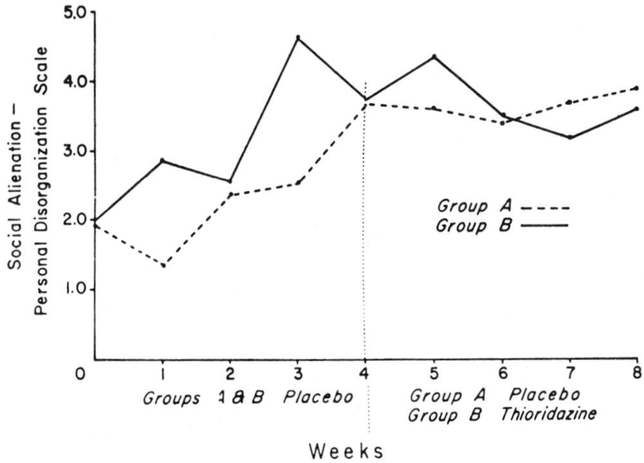


Fig. 1.—Average weekly scores on social alienation-personal disorganization scale for two groups of chronic schizophrenic subjects on two different experimental regimens.

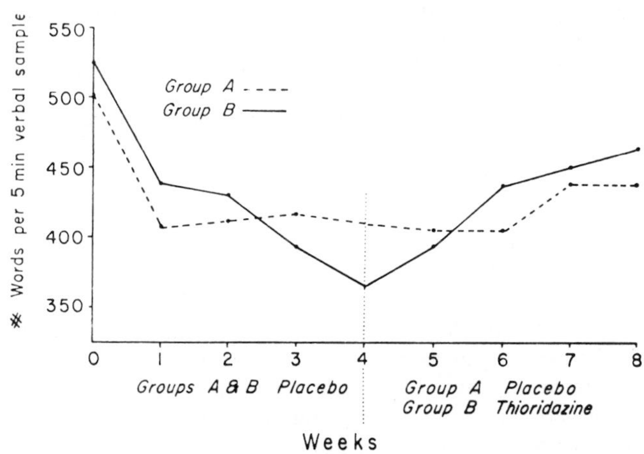


Fig. 2.—Average number of words spoken per verbal sample per week by two groups of chronic schizophrenics.

analysis scores of the speech of these patients obtained in the week prior to the experimental regimen. Table 2 shows the means, standard deviation, and intercorrelations among verbal behavior measures for the 69 chronic schizophrenic patients who were able to cooperate at the beginning of the study. These numbers were obtained by averaging such scores from the two or three verbal samples given by the patient within the week's interval while the patient was on one of the phenothiazine pharmacological agents. Scores for social alienation-personal disorganization correlated significantly ($p < .05$) with ***hostility***

**Table 2.—Intercorrelations Among Verbal Behavior Measures* for Sample of Chronic Schizophrenics (N = 69)**

| Variable | Mean | s.d. | Correlation with variable 2 | 3 | 4 | 5 | 6 | 7 | 8 |
|---|---|---|---|---|---|---|---|---|---|
| 1. Number of Words | 508.8 | 235.2 | −.12 | .15 | .18 | .32 | −.06 | .22 | .01 |
| 2. Anxiety | 1.55 | 0.58 | | .44 | .36 | .51 | .51 | .62 | .35 |
| 3. Overt Hostility Out | 0.72 | 0.34 | | | .23 | .84 | .48 | .69 | .52 |
| 4. Covert Hostility Out | 0.67 | 0.23 | | | | .67 | .10 | .25 | .06 |
| 5. Total Hostility Out | 0.95 | 0.39 | | | | | .37 | .64 | .40 |
| 6. Hostility In | 0.80 | 0.35 | | | | | | .42 | .10 |
| 7. Ambivalent Hostility | 0.80 | 0.42 | | | | | | | .32 |
| 8. Social Alienation-Personal Disorganization | 2.04 | 3.89 | | | | | | | |

* Average of scores on two or three verbal samples taken within interval of one week while patients were on phenothiazine pharmacologic agent.

*outward*, especially *overt hostility outward* (r = .52) (composed of statements of the self being hostile to others) and *ambivalent hostility* (r = .32) (composed of statements of others being hostile to the self) and *anxiety* (r = .35). Covert hostility outward scores (composed of statements of others being hostile to others or hostility inferred from events involving inanimate objects) and *hostility inward* scores (composed of statements about the self being hostile to the self) were not significantly correlated with social alienation-personal disorganization scores. All content analysis scales, except, possibly, total hostility outward, were independent of the number of words spoken.

### *Predictive Aspects of Content Analysis Scores and Changes in Severity of Schizophrenic Syndrome*

Table 3 presents summary data on the principal factor scores (*neuroticism, psychoticism, disorientation*) obtained from the Mental Status Schedule examinations performed initially and after the patients had been on placebo for four weeks. All three factor scores increased significantly after four weeks on placebo relative to the initial values.

Let us examine the correlations between these Mental Status Schedule scores and the verbal behavior measures obtained during the initial week. Here an interesting pattern emerges. The initial scores for social alienation-personal disorganization are not only very significantly correlated ($p < .01$) with *psychoticism* (r = .41) and *disorientation* (r = .43) scores in the initial period, but they are also correlated ($p < .05$) with all three Mental Status factor scales in the follow-up period four weeks later (*psychoticism, r = .52; disorientation, r = .33; neuroticism, r = .29*). Initial overt hostility outward scores (but not covert hostility outwards) obtained while the patients were still on phenothiazine drugs, correlated with and predictive of neurotic (*neuroticism,* r = .34, $p < .01$) and psychotic phenomena (*psychoticism,* r = .31, $p < .05$) as assessed by subscales of the Mental Status Schedule four weeks after discontinuation of phenothiazine drug therapy. Initial hostility inward scores correlated with *neurotic symptoms* (r = .30, $p < .05$) as assessed by the Mental Status Schedule after four weeks off phenothiazine drugs. In contrast to these correlations, initial covert hostility outwards scores, obtained while the

**Table 3.—Correlations Between Verbal Behavior Scores and Mental Status Schedule Factor Scores Obtained from Chronic Schizophrenics (N = 69) Initially While on Phenothiazines and After Four Weeks of Placebo**

| | *Mental Status Schedule Scores* | | | | | |
|---|---|---|---|---|---|---|
| | *Neuroticism* (feelings, concerns) | | *Psychoticism* (delusions, hallucinations) | | *Disorientation* (confusion, retardation) | |
| | $T_1$* | $T_2$* | $T_1$* | $T_2$* | $T_1$* | $T_2$* |
| Mean | 6.4 | 9.6 | 5.6 | 7.3 | 4.1 | 5.7 |
| Standard Deviation | 4.9 | 6.8 | 4.5 | 5.3 | 5.1 | 4.9 |
| Verbal Behavior Scores | | | *Correlations* | | | |
| No. of Words | —.17 | —.03 | —.05 | .17 | —.33 | —.27 |
| Social Alienation-Personal Disorganization | .19 | .29 | .41 | .52 | .43 | .33 |
| Anxiety | .19 | .14 | .17 | .16 | .17 | .14 |
| Overt Hostility Out | .13 | .34 | .22 | .31 | .09 | .00 |
| Covert Hostility Out | —.09 | .02 | —.15 | .06 | —.25 | —.28 |
| Hostility In | .06 | .30 | .03 | .08 | .04 | .09 |
| Ambivalent Hostility | .16 | .20 | .24 | .26 | .03 | —.01 |

* $T_1$ = Initial period while patients were on phenothiazines. $T_2$ = Four weeks after withdrawal of phenothiazine drugs. Italicized correlations are all significant at $p < .05$.

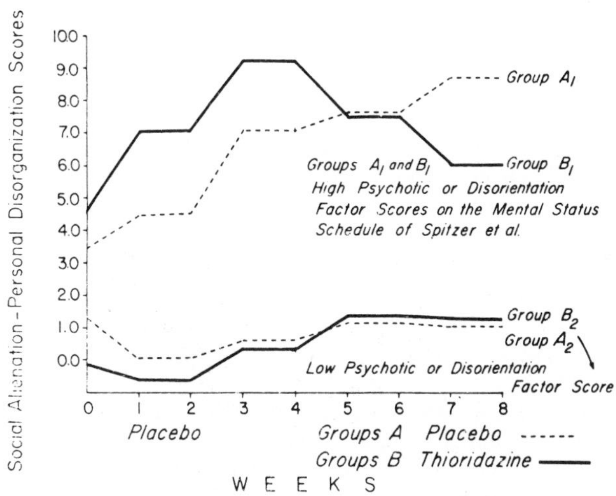


**Fig. 3.**—Social alienation-personal disorganization scores for drug and placebo groups classified on basis of initial mental status factor scores.

chronic schizophrenic patients were still on phenothiazines, correlated *negatively* with the *disorientation* ($r = -.28$, $p < .05$) subscale of the Mental Status Schedule four weeks after drug therapy was terminated.

It is evident that, on the average, patients became increasingly disturbed during the first four weeks that they were on placebo as judged by both the amount and content of their speech samples (Figs. 1 and 2) and from Mental Status Schedule Ratings (Table 3). However, some patients showed almost no deterioration in their behavior, and, if anything, seemed to improve

**Table 4.—Correlations of 16 PF Factors with Initial Scores and Average Rate of Change in Social Alienation-Personal Disorganization**

| 16 PF Scale | Initial Score | Average Rates of Change | | |
|---|---|---|---|---|
| | | First 4 weeks | Last 4 weeks | |
| | (N=69) | (N=69) | placebo (N=30) | drug (N=28) |
| A. Warmth | —.10 | —.20 | —.22 | .00 |
| B. Intelligence | —.25 | —.04 | —.01 | .20 |
| C. Emotional Stability | —.17 | —.21 | .37 | .24 |
| E. Assertiveness | .08 | .04 | —.10 | —.28 |
| F. Enthusiasm | —.16 | —.22 | .04 | —.17 |
| G. Conscientiousness | —.39 | —.17 | .04 | .22 |
| H. Venturesomeness | —.10 | —.10 | .10 | .22 |
| I. Sensitivity | —.10 | .04 | —.07 | .21 |
| L. Distrustfulness | .01 | —.05 | .25 | —.01 |
| M. Autism | .30 | .10 | —.22 | —.01 |
| N. Sophistication | —.30 | —.18 | —.08 | .42 |
| O. Insecurity | .08 | .21 | .08 | —.37 |
| $Q_1$ Free-thinking | —.02 | .15 | —.21 | .25 |
| $Q_2$ Self-sufficiency | .07 | —.10 | .29 | .12 |
| $Q_3$ Self-sentiment | —.32 | —.01 | .06 | .31 |
| $Q_4$ Drive Tension | .11 | .11 | —.32 | —.06 |
| Rate of change first four weeks. | | | —.18 | —.55 |

during the first four weeks on placebo. Even after eight weeks of placebo these patients seemed as well or better off than when they started (Fig. 3).

One of the major interests in this study was trying to find some indicators in the initial data by which one could predict which patients would do well when taken off phenothiazines and which would not. In order to find predictors of response to phenothiazine withdrawal it was necessary to derive some measure to characterize the general trend of scores on the scale of social alienation-personal disorganization for each individual. For this purpose the slopes of the linear trend-line for the first four weeks and for the second four weeks were computed separately for each individual. This method of computing the rate of increase or decrease resulted in a more reliable rate of change measure than would simple difference scores.

Table 4 presents the correlations between the personality factor scores of the 16 PF, and the initial score on social alienation-personal disorganization, and the algebraic slope of the trend-line for social alienation-personal disorganization scores during the first four weeks. For completeness, correlations between 16 PF scores and social alienation-personal disorganization slopes in the last four weeks for patients given placebo and separately for those on thioridazine are also included. (For additional information on 16 PF scores in this study see reference 11.) From the correlations it appears that patients with emotional warmth (A), high emotional stability (C), enthusiasm (F), conscientiousness (G), and shrewdness-sophistication (N), and those who are not particularly insecure (0-) or free thinking (Q-), tend to have the least increment in social alienation-personal disorganization scores over the four weeks after phenothiazine withdrawal. However, none of these zero-order correlations reaches significance at the .05 level. A multiple regression equation was obtained which maximized the multiple correlation using a minimum

Table 5.—Intercorrelations Among Initial Principal Factor and Selected Subscale Scores Derived from Mental Status Schedule and Initial Scores and Average Rate of Change in First Four Weeks for Social Alienation-Personal Disorganization (N = 74)

| | b. | c. | d. | e. | f. | g. | h. | i. | Rate of Change |
|---|---|---|---|---|---|---|---|---|---|
| a. Neuroticism | .39 | .22 | .38 | .02 | .32 | .08 | .16 | .19 | .01 |
| b. Psychoticism | | .12 | .80 | .17 | .07 | .37 | .52 | .41 | .19 |
| c. Disorientation (primary) | | | .04 | .77 | .85 | .22 | .29 | .43 | .31 |
| d. Delusions-Hallucinations | | | | .12 | −.06 | .33 | .34 | .31 | .20 |
| e. Disorientation | | | | | .39 | .17 | .17 | .35 | .30 |
| f. Apathy-Retardation | | | | | | .07 | .20 | .31 | .23 |
| g. Silly Disorganization | | | | | | | .55 | .38 | .31 |
| h. Elated Excitement | | | | | | | | .36 | .18 |
| i. Initial Score Social Alienation-Personal Disorganization | | | | | | | | | .11 |

number of predictors according to the technique suggested by DuBois.[62] Using the six scales, A, C, F, N, O, and $Q_1$ from the 16 PF, a multiple correlation of .389 was obtained. The weights ranged from .08 for insecurity (O) to −.17 for enthusiasm (F). (Note that the predictor scores are such that a high value corresponds to a high rate of increase in social alienation-personal disorganization after phenothiazine withdrawal.)

Intercorrelations among the three principal factor scores and selected factor analytically-derived cluster scores from the Mental Status Schedule, initial scores on social alienation-personal disorganization, and rate of change of these scores over the first four weeks are shown in Table 5. *Disorientation* was the only one of the three principal component Mental Status factors that was significantly correlated with rate of change of social alienation-personal disorganization scores. Among the cluster scores *disorientation*, *apathy-retardation*, and *silly disorganization*, each significantly predicted rate of change scores. The first two of these are highly correlated with the primary disorientation scale, however, and hence are simply giving more specific symptom information

Using the principal factors, a multiple R of .350 was obtained for the weighted sum of *psychoticism* and *disorientation* factor scores. The cluster scores yielded a multiple correlation of .422 for the weighted sum of scores for *disorientation*, *apathy-retardation*, *silly disorganization*, and *delusions-hallucinations*. Thus, the more specific symptom scores appeared to be considerably better predictors than the factor scores. It should be remembered that these scores are probably not as reliable as the more general factor scores and also that there is more opportunity for error to inflate the multiple.

The correlation was obtained between the two sets of predictor scores, i.e., the one from the 16 PF and the one from the Mental Status Schedule symptom clusters, to determine the extent to which they overlapped. The correlation between them was only .33, which, while significant, indicated considerable independence of prediction. The two scores, combined, predicted the average rate of change in social alienation-personal disorganization scores with an R of .497.

Looking again at Table 4, it is evident that individual differences in response to placebo during the second four-week period are not generally predictable from the same set of 16 PF factors as are individual differences in the first four weeks after drug withdrawal. The correlation between rates of change for the two periods is −.18, which is not significantly different from zero. Furthermore, many of the zero-order correlations between the 16 PF scales and rate of change are markedly different for the two periods. For example, the more emotionally stable (C) and self-sufficient ($Q_2$) patient became increasingly socially alienated during the second four weeks, whereas patients who were more free-thinking ($Q_1$) and tense ($Q_4$) in the baseline period showed some improvement.

The correlations between rates of change of social alienation-personal disorganization scores in the first four weeks and those in the last four weeks for subjects on drug was −.55, which is highly significant and indicates that these may be complementary processes. Subjects who showed the greatest increase in social alienation-personal disorganization when they were taken off phenothiazines tended to show the greatest improvement when given an active drug whereas those who did well on placebo tended to lose any gains they had made when they were put back on drugs. This is further borne out by the fact that the linear equation from the combined Mental Status and 16 PF predictors of social alienation-personal disorganization slope for the first period was also correlated −.22 with the slope in the second period for those on thioridazine. (The corresponding correlation for the placebo group is .002).

On examination, the multiple regression equations from the Mental Status Scales, the 16 PF, or the two combined sets of scores appeared to be yielding inflated multiple correlations as the result of the correspondence of a few extreme values. Many intermediate sized changes were being missed and the regression equations did not seem to select those persons who continued to deteriorate with placebo during the second four weeks. Since it was hoped that a simple rule could be found for possible use in decisions to terminate drug therapy, and such a decision does not entail a continuous variable, it was decided to examine the possibility of making the prediction by the use of cut-off scores on the principal Mental Status Schedule factors. By trial and error it was determined that a score of less than seven on both the *psychoticism* and *disorientation* factors selected patients who did not get worse over the eight week period when the drug was withdrawn. On the other hand, a score of seven or greater on either scale indicated a poor prognosis for drug withdrawal. This decision rule actually provided a better separation of patients who did and did not deteriorate with placebo than did the linear regression predictor as measured by a phi coefficient.

Figure 3 shows the scores on the social alienation-personal disorganization scale averaged over successive two-week periods for patients classified according to the multiple cut-off criterion for their assignment to drug or placebo group at the end of the fourth week. Those patients who became mute are not included in these averages. Some interesting features are evident in this figure. The patients who had high *psychoticism* or *disorientation* scores on the initial Mental Status score ($N = 29$) tended to be somewhat more socially

alienated to begin with and remained so throughout the study. This might have been anticipated from the fact that *psychoticism* and *disorientation* scores are positively correlated with scores on social alienation-personal disorganization in the base period.[22] Using a cut-off criterion of 2.0 on the initial social alienation-personal disorganization scores from five-minute verbal samples also divided the chronic schizophrenic patients into those who reacted adversely to discontinuation of phenothiazine medication (scores above 2.0) and those who were relatively unreactive to phenothiazine withdrawal (or administration) during the period of observation.

The average rate of change of scores on the social alienation-personal disorganization scale during the first four weeks was 1.0. Those patients who had low scores on the *psychoticism* and *disorientation* scales of the Mental Status Schedule ($N = 35$) had low average social alienation-personal disorganization scores on their verbal samples, and they continued to have low scores over the entire eight weeks of the study provided they were in the placebo group. If they were put back on drug ($N = 17$) at the end of four weeks, they actually showed a slight (non-significant) increase in social alienation-personal disorganization. Another point of interest is the dip in scores in the first two weeks after drug withdrawal for the low symptom group. This drop has a p value of .10 by a sign test. It will be remembered that over the total duration of this study there was no difference in rate of change scores in the second four-week period for those on drug as compared to placebo. The trend scores in the second period for patients who had scores of seven or higher in *psychoticism* or *disorientation* differ more markedly depending on whether they were given drug or placebo, although the difference still has a probability of approximately .12 of arising by chance.

Since the average number of words spoken in a verbal sample had been noted to decrease when patients were on placebo and increase when they were again given a psychoactive drug, the question arose as to whether individual differences in these trends were also related to the dichotomy of high versus low *psychoticism* and *disorientation* Mental Status Schedule scores. The high symptom group showed an average decrease in the first four weeks of −42.3 words per week, whereas the decrease for the low symptom group was only −15.2 words per week, a difference significant at the .05 level. Those having high scores who were given psychoactive drugs the second four weeks, increased an average of 31.2 words per week as compared to only 0.4 words per week for the placebo group, again a significant difference. For the low symptom groups the corresponding values were 17.5 for those on drug and 11.3 for those on placebo the last four weeks, a non-significant difference.

## Discussion

The intercorrelations among content analysis scores of the speech of schizophrenics indicate that anxiety, overt hostility outward, and ambivalent hostility (but not covert hostility nor hostility inward) are associated with high social alienation-personal disorganization scores. These common variances are not due to occasional scoring of the same content categories in the different scales. Rather, we take those correlations to signify that the sicker schizo-

phrenics are more likely to manifest their disorder in open, destructive aggression, in paranoid ideation, or in higher anxiety. The lack of correlation of social alienation-personal disorganization scores with hostility inward scores indicates that, in our sample of chronic schizophrenics, self-criticism and self-hate, though present, does not contribute to the dimension of severity of the schizophrenic syndrome. Other studies have indicated that our hostility inward scores are associated with various measures of depression.[19] It seems fitting that the social alienation-personal disorganization scale is, hence, not directly concerned with the dimension of hostility inward or, by extension, the dimension of depression. It is of some relevance that hostility inward scores significantly predict (Table 3, $r = .30$) those individuals who will show four weeks later, after withdrawal of phenothiazine drugs, higher scores on the factor of *neuroticism* on the Mental Status Schedule, but these same hostility inward scores will not be predictive of the *psychoticism* or *disorientation* factor scores.

The covert hostility outward scale shows evidence, in this study and with these patients, of being more a measure of relative health than sickness. The covert hostility outward scores (that is, statements of others being hostile to others) do not correlate with scores of social alienation-personal disorganization; rather, the baseline covert hostility outward scores tend to be predictive of those individuals who will not be disoriented later as evaluated on the Mental Status Schedule, four weeks after their tranquilizing pharmacologic agent has been stopped ($r = -.28$, $p < .05$). This finding suggests that the more the schizophrenic patient verbalizes about the hostility among and between others, the more likely is this a sign of relative alertness to external events and, hence, one index of the capacity to test reality. It is noteworthy to consider the ability of the pre-phenothiazine withdrawal scores of social alienation-personal disorganization and overt hostility outward to predict the degree of psychotic exacerbation as assessed by the Mental Status Schedule four weeks after withdrawal of phenothiazine. Elsewhere, with nonpsychotic psychiatric outpatients coming to a brief psychotherapy clinic, Gottschalk et al. observed that high scores on this same "schizophrenic" scale is predictive of those patients who remain the most maladjusted after treatment.[21]

In general, the verbal sample technique for assessing behavior appears to offer a fruitful method for following longitudinal changes in the magnitude of the schizophrenic syndrome and in finding predictors of trend with various types of therapy. The many kinds of problems involved when assessing change in psychiatry and the behavioral sciences have been well documented.[24,34] The use of repeated measures through which one can pass a best-fitting trend line and determine its slope for each subject offers an improved technique for dealing with change, provided the measurement procedure involved is one that can be performed frequently without carry-over effects. Verbal samples are well suited to this requirement.

Considerable evidence that the therapeutic effects of phenothiazines are not maintained following drug withdrawal has been reported in the literature.[1,6] These studies have been reviewed recently by Kamano who points out the need to find an effective method of predicting which patients can tolerate

long periods without drugs and which cannot.[25] The present study is a contribution in this direction. Our findings indicate that, on the average, chronic schizophrenic patients speak progressively fewer words and obtain higher social alienation-personal disorganization scores in the first four weeks after the phenothiazines they are taking are replaced by a placebo. Looking farther, we find that if the psychoactive drug on which the chronic psychotic patient has been maintained has not succeeded in eliminating the more florid schizophrenic symptoms such as delusions and hallucinations or the symptoms of disorientation, apathy, and retardation, then drug treatment should be continued. Chronic patients who are relatively free of such symptoms while on tranquilizing drugs can go at least eight weeks without such medication with no exacerbation of schizophrenic symptoms. They may actually show some symptomatic improvement, possibly because of a decrease of undesirable side-effects. Social alienation-personal disorganization scores over 2 or low covert hostility outward or hostility inward scores on the Gottschalk-Gleser content analysis scales, as well as high *psychoticism* or *disorientation* scores in the Spitzer et al. Mental Status Schedule, are predictive of an adverse response to phenothiazine drug discontinuation.

It is interesting that the number of words spoken in the five-minute interview is also sensitive to pharmacological intervention. A significant difference was found in average rate of change in the number of words spoken for patients on thioridazine as compared to placebo. One reason for the sensitivity of this measure may lie in its objectivity and reliability and in its availability for all subjects. Psychologically, its importance lies in the fact that a low rate of speech is one of the "withdrawal" signs that Goldberg et al. have noted to be among the first symptoms to disappear when patients are treated with phenothiazines.[12] These speech rate symptoms usually improve maximally by the end of five weeks on phenothiazine drugs. We found that at the end of four weeks on thioridazine, speech returned almost to the baseline rate, a finding which is consistent with those of Goldberg and his colleagues. The speech content measure of social alienation-personal disorganization is not only related to evidence (from the Mental Status Schedule) of disorientation and social withdrawal, but also to other schizophrenic symptoms, such as, delusions, hallucinations, belligerence, and memory deficit, all of which Goldberg et al. found continued to abate up to 13 weeks after the start of phenothiazine treatment. In this respect, it is unfortunate that our patients were not followed for a longer period of time.

Several other investigators have looked for predictors of the kinds of reactions that chronic patients may have with the discontinuation of phenothiazine medication. Denber and Bird reported that relapse following withdrawal of chlorpromazine in 1523 patients was related to severity of illness, duration of illness, or length of hospitalization before treatment, but not to duration of hospitalization itself or to clinical diagnosis.[4,5] Others have concluded that there is no relationship between duration of previous chlorpromazine treatment and tendency to regress when chlorpromazine is withdrawn.[14] Freeman and Olson stated that their study of chlorpromazine withdrawal in 96 chronic, hospitalized male psychotics did not provide useful clinical

criteria for identifying those patients who require uninterrupted drug treatment.[9] They mentioned, however, that "sicker patients, particularly those who are confused or show little interest in their environment, tend to be poorer risks for drug discontinuation. . . ." In their study of the withdrawal of perphenazine in 39 male chronic schizophrenics, Whittaker and Hoy reported that it was impossible for them to predict which patients would relapse.[33] Collaborating in a Veterans Administration cooperative study on discontinuing or reducing chemotherapy in chronic schizophrenics, Caffey et al. found no evidence that the probability of relapse was related to diagnosis, length or amount of previous medication, length of hospitalization or age.[2] They also could not substantiate that prestudy psychiatric ratings, using the Inpatient Multidimensional Psychiatric Scale (IMPS)[27] and the Psychotic Reaction Profile (PRP)[26] enabled them to predict which patient would relapse if drugs were discontinued.

We believe that the lack of consistent findings of other investigators, with respect to predictors of which patients will relapse if psychopharmacological agents are discontinued, is due in part to the nature of the change measures previously used and the unreliability involved in deciding when a patient has relapsed. The fact that hospitalized chronic schizophrenics, by definition, are already in a hospital before their phenothiazine medication had been discontinued, makes somewhat indefinite the point at which one decides they have relapsed. In our study of phenothiazine withdrawal, the criteria of change were our objective social alienation-personal disorganization measure and the Mental Status Schedule of Spitzer et al., and the research design did not involve the clinical decision as to whether or not the patient had relapsed.

The present study reemphasizes the difficulty of using chronic schizophrenic patients in large hospitals for the evaluation of new drugs, unless a long washout period from previous drug administration has been allowed. Almost all such patients are on some kind of phenothiazine medication. If they are not, it is very likely they constitute a different population with regard to drug response than those who are continuously maintained on drugs. The latter, again, consists of two types: those who become more floridly psychotic after discontinuing medication and those who remain unchanged or even improve slightly. If such patients were used indiscriminately for new drug studies, experimental results would vary according to the relative proportions of each type of patient in the sample, and the length of time elapsing between medications.

Many further questions are stimulated by the results of this investigation. It would be interesting to know how long the patients characterized as having a good prognosis with drug withdrawal could function reasonably adequately without drugs. Are such patients those who have always functioned marginally with or without drugs or have they had symptoms of disorientation and psychoticism at some prior time which were reduced when a drug was administered, and, most crucially, what accounts for the differential responses of these patients to phenothiazine withdrawal? In this respect, does a difference in metabolic turnover of phenothiazines account for the difference? It may be that the high and low symptom groups are characterized

by differences in the metabolic handling of phenothiazine drugs which would be reflected in differences in the blood levels and/or excretion rates of the phenothiazines. Caffey et al. examined the hypothesis that differential relapse with phenothiazine withdrawal in chronic schizophrenics might be related to some aspects of urine metabolite excretion.[2] Using the Forrest test[8] for urinary metabolite excretion, they could not confirm this hypothesis on their patients. Previously, Forrest and Forrest claimed a correlation of drug excretion rate and relapse pattern could be established in 70 per cent of 20 chronic mental patients in their drug discontinuation.[7] We believe further studies of this relationship are warranted, using other criteria of change of the schizophrenic syndrome, such as our verbal behavior measure.

Another possible explanation of the differential response to phenothiazine withdrawal is that the chronic schizophrenic patients differ with respect to the prior course of the disease process, in their premorbid personality characteristics, and/or in their previous treatment. Aside from the work of Denber and Bird as indicated previously,[4,5] there has been no substantiation of these hypotheses. In this respect, there is some suggestive evidence to support one or more of these explanations from the 16 PF scores, although the differences are not very great.[11] The patients with the more severe symptoms had been hospitalized slightly longer (12.5 versus 9.5 years) but the lengths of stay overlap greatly so that this does not appear to be a crucial factor.

This study raises the possibility that different phenothiazines might be compared fruitfully with respect to the length of time they remain effective after medication is discontinued. While no contrasting effects among phenothiazines were evident for the groups studied here, the number of patients in each group who had been taking any one phenothiazine derivative was rather small. Obviously, further research studies are needed to account for the underlying mechanisms among chronic schizophrenics of the differential response to phenothiazine withdrawal.

## Summary

Seventy-four hospitalized chronic schizophrenic patients, who were able to cooperate with testing and interview procedures, were studied for eight weeks to sequentially evaluate the effect of withdrawal and readministration of phenothiazine medication. The patients, Caucasians of both sexes, in the age range 24–54, had been on some one phenothiazine derivative for at least the previous six months. For the first four weeks all patients were on placebo, while during the next four weeks half were on placebo and half were on thioridazine.

Patients were assessed initially using the standardized Spitzer et al. Mental Status Schedule and the Cattell 16 PF test. In addition, two or three five-minute verbal samples were obtained from each patient in the initial pre-drug withdrawal week to assess the level of social alienation-personal disorganization, hostility, and anxiety by the Gottschalk-Gleser method. Additional verbal samples were obtained twice weekly for the next eight weeks and Mental Status Schedule interviews were obtained at the end of four and eight weeks.

The following results were obtained: (1) Average scores for social aliena-

tion-personal disorganization increased significantly over the first four weeks, indicating increased psychopathology. (2) Those patients who continued on placebo showed little further increase in social alienation-personal disorganization scores in the second four weeks; whereas, those patients who were given thioridazine showed a small, nonsignificant decrease in such scores. (3) The average number of words spoken in a verbal sample decreased significantly for the first four weeks while patients were on placebo. Patients having thioridazine drug the second period showed a significant increase in the number of words spoken. (4) Using multiple correlation techniques with scores obtained during the initial testing period it was possible to predict individual differences in response to phenothiazine withdrawal. A multiple correlation of .39 was obtained using six of the 16 PF factor scales. A multiple correlation of .42 was obtained using four "narrow" factor scales of the Mental Status Schedule. Using both sets of predictors the correlation was .50. (5) Using the general principal factor scores of *psychoticism* and *disorientation* from the Mental Status Schedule, a multiple cut-off criterion of 7 or more in either scale divided the patients into those who gave verbal samples with increasingly high scores in social alienation-personal disorganization when on placebo from those who showed practically no change on this verbal score measure. The same multiple cut-off differentiated those who showed a significant decrease in the number of words spoken in the first period. (6) A cut-off criterion of 2 on the initial social alienation-personal disorganization (content analysis) scores from five minute verbal samples, was also predictive of the chronic schizophrenic patients who were unreactive to phenothiazine drug withdrawal or administration (less than two) and those who reacted with an exacerbation of the schizophrenic syndrome to phenothiazine drug withdrawal or with a decrease in the schizophrenic symptom complex with phenothiazine drug administration (more than two). This cut-off criterion also differentiated those patients who showed a significant decrease in the number of words spoken during the first four week placebo period. (7) The theoretical and practical implications of these findings are discussed.

## ACKNOWLEDGMENTS

We wish to express our appreciation to Dr. John Toppen, Superintendent, for his permission to use the facilities of Longview State Hospital; to the resident psychiatrists and research technicians who assisted in gathering and processing the data; and to the technicians who scored the verbal samples. We thank Drs. Richard Bibb, Mansell Pattison, Eric Hanson, Anthony Gottlieb, Henry Udelmann and Eugene Woods for conducting standardized interviews and afterward filling out the Mental Status Schedule.

## REFERENCES

1. Blackburn, H. L., and Allen, J. L.: Behavioral effects of interrupting and resuming tranquilizing medicine among schizophrenics. J. Nerv. Ment. Dis. 133:303–308, 1961.

2. Caffey, E., Jr., Diamond, L. S., Frank, T. V., Grasberger, J. C., Herman, L., Klett, C. J. and Rothstein, C.: Discontinuation or reduction of chemotherapy in chronic schizophrenics. J. Chron. Dis. 17:347–358, 1964.

3. Cattell, R. B., and Eber, H. W.: Handbook for the Sixteen Personality Factor Questionnaire. Champaign, Ill., Institute for Personality and Ability Testing, 1957 (1964 Supplementation).

4. Denber, H. D. B., and Bird, E. G.: Chlorpromazine in the treatment of mental illness. II. Side effects and relapse rates.

Amer. J. Psychiat. 112:465, 1955.

5. —, and —: Chlorpromazine in the treatment of mental illness. IV. Final results with analysis of data on 1523 patients. Amer. J. Psychiat. 113:972–978, 1957.

6. Diamond, L. S., and Marks, J. B.: Discontinuance of tranquilizers among chronic schizophrenic patients receiving maintenance dosage. J. Nerv. Ment. Dis. 131:247–251, 1960.

6a. Dubois, P. H.: Multivariate Correlation Analysis. New York, Harper, 1957.

7. Forrest, F. M. and Forrest, I. S.: Urine tests for the detection of the newer phenothiazine compounds, drug excretion rates, clinical implications and recent developments in research on phenothiazine drugs. Trans. 4th Veterans Admin. Res. Conf. Chemotherapy in Psychiatry, p. 245, 1960.

8. —, Forrest, I. S., and Mason, A. S.: Review of rapid urine tests for phenothiazine and related drugs. Amer. J. Psychiat. 118: 300–307, 1961.

9. Freeman, L. S., and Alson, E.: Prolonged withdrawal of chlorpromazine in chronic patients. Dis. Nerv. Syst. 23:522–525, 1962.

10. Gleser, G. C., Gottschalk, L. A., and Springer, K. J.: An anxiety measure applicable to verbal samples. Arch. Gen. Psychiat. 5:593–605, 1961.

11. —, and Gottschalk, L. A.: Personality characteristics of chronic schizophrenics in relationship to sex and current functioning. J. Clin. Psychol. 23:349–354, 1967.

12. Goldberg, S. C., Schooler, N. R., and Mattsson, N. B.: Paranoid and withdrawal symptoms in schizophrenia: differential symptom reduction over time. J. Nerv. Ment. Dis. 145:158–162, 1967.

13. —, and Mattsson, N. B.: Schizophrenic subtypes defined by response to drugs and placebo. Dis. Nerv. Syst. 29:153–158, 1968.

14. Good, W. W., Sterling, M., and Holtzman, W. H.: Termination of chlorpromazine with schizophrenic patients. Amer. J. Psychiat. 115:443–448, 1958.

15. Gottschalk, L. A., and Hambidge, G., Jr.: Verbal behavior analysis: a systematic approach to the problem of quantifying psychologic processes. J. Proj. Techn. 19: 387–409, 1955.

16. —, Gleser, G. C., Daniels, R. S., and Block, S.: The speech patterns of schizophrenic patients: a method of assessing relative degree of personal disorganization and social alienation. J. Nerv. Ment. Dis. 127: 153–166, 1958.

17. —, —, Magliocco, B., and D'Zmura, T. L.: Further studies on the speech patterns of schizophrenic patients: Measuring interindividual differences in relative degree of personal disorganization and social alienation. J. Nerv. Ment. Dis. 132:101–113, 1961.

18. —, Springer, K. J., and Gleser, G. C.: Experiments with a method of assessing the variations in intensity of certain psychologic states occurring during two psychotherapeutic interviews. In Gottschalk, L. A., (Ed.). Comparative Psycholinguistic Analysis of Two Psychotherapeutic Interviews. New York, International Universities Press, 1961.

19. —, Gleser, G. C., and Springer, K. J.: Three hostility scales applicable to verbal samples. Arch. Gen. Psychiat. 9:254–279, 1963.

20. —, and Gleser, G. C.: Distinguishing characteristics of the verbal communications of schizophrenic patients. *In:* Disorders of Communication A.R.N.M.D. Vol. 42, pp. 401–413. Baltimore, Williams and Wilkins, 1964.

21. —, Mayerson, P., and Gottlieb, A.: The prediction and evaluation of outcome in an emergency brief psychotherapy clinic. J. Nerv. Ment. Dis. 144:77–96, 1967.

22. —, and Gleser, G. C.: The Measurement of Psychological States Through the Content Analysis of Verbal Behavior. Berkeley, University of California Press, 1969.

23. Green, D. E., Forrest, I. S., Forrest, F. M., and Serra, M. T.: Interpatient variation in chlorpromazine metabolism. Exp. Med. Surg. 23:278–287, 1965.

24. Group for the Advancement of Psychiatry, Committee on Research: Psychiatric Research and the Assessment of Change. Vol. VI, Report No. 63. New York, Group for the Advancement of Psychiatry, pp. 357–478, 1966.

25. Kamano, D. K.: Selective review of effects of discontinuation of drug treatment: Some implications and problems. Psychol. Rep. 19:743–749, 1966.

26. Lorr, M., O'Connor, J. P., and Stafford, J. W.: The psychotic reaction profile. J. Clin. Psychol. 16:241–245, 1960.

27. —, Klett, C. J., McNair, D. M., and Lasky, J. J.: The Manual of the Inpatient

Multidimensional Psychiatric Scale, Palo Alto, Calif., Consulting Psychologists' Press, 1963.

28. Overall, J. E., and Gorham, D. P.: The brief psychiatric rating scale (BPRS). Psychol. Rep. 10:799–812, 1962.

29. Spitzer, R. L., Fleiss, J. L., Burdock, E. I., and Hardesty, A. S.: The mental status schedule; rationale, reliability and validity. Compr. Psychiat. 5:384–395, 1964.

30. —, —, Kernohan, W., Lee, J. D., and Baldwin, I. T.: Mental status schedule. Arch. Gen. Psychiat. 13:448–455, 1965.

31. —: Immediate available record of mental status examination. Arch. Gen. Psychiat. 13:76–78, 1965.

32. —, Fleiss, J,. L., Endicott, J., and Cohen, J.: Mental status schedule: Properties of factor analytically derived scales. Arch. Gen. Psychiat. 16:479–493, 1967.

33. Whittaker, C. B., and Hoy, R. M.: Withdrawal of Perphenazine in chronic schizophrenia. Brit. J. Psychiat. 109:422–427, 1963.

34. Worchel, P., and Byrne, D. (Eds.)): Personality Change. New York, Wiley, 1964.

# Effects of Triazolam and Flurazepam on Emotions and Intellectual Function

Louis A. Gottschalk and Henry W. Elliott

Departments of Psychiatry and Human Behavior, and Medical Pharmacology and Therapeutics, College of Medicine, University of California at Irvine, Irvine, California (92717) and the Solano Institute for Medical and Pharmaceutical Research, Vacaville, California.

ABSTRACT

In a double blind study the psychopharmacological effects on emotions and cognitive functions of single oral doses of the benzodiazepines, triazolam and flurazepam, were observed. As measured by a speech content analysis method 0.25 - 2.0 mg of triazolam significantly decreased total anxiety scores, whereas 30 mg of flurazepam did not. Lower doses of

---

The technical assistance of Daniel Bates, Ph.D. and the statistical assistance of Herman Birch, Ph.D. are hereby acknowledged.

triazolam (0.25 - 0.5 mg) significantly decreased ambivalent hostility scores for at least 240 - 300 minutes postdrug and higher doses (1.0 - 2.0 mg) for at least 60 - 90 minutes. The lower doses also significantly decreased hostility inward scores 60 - 90 minutes postdrug. Flurazepam (30 mg) did not significantly decrease hostility scores. All doses of triazolam and flurazepam used significantly increased social-alienation personality disorganization score scales, this drug effect being limited to the personality disorganization (thought disorder) component of the scale. The effect persisted for flurazepam at 240 - 300 minutes postdrug but was noted only 60 - 90 minutes postdrug for triazolam. The higher doses of triazolam tended to increase cognitive-intellectual impairment scores ($p = 0.08$) but flurazepam and the lower doses of triazolam caused no significant increase in these scores. Of all the psychopharmacologic effects noted, only the anxiety reduction effect of 60 - 90 minutes postdrug was significantly correlated with triazolam dose. Impaired ability to maintain balance correlated with anxiety reduction but not with elevation in social and intellectual impairment scores. This study suggests that the benzodiazepines may transiently impair a certain type of intellectual functioning.

## INTRODUCTION

Preliminary observations by one of us (H.W.E.) during clinical pharmacological trials with triazolam, a new triazolobenzodiazepine, suggested that this psychoactive drug not only is a potent hypnotic agent but may transiently impair memory.

Although there have been previous studies on the effects of drugs as possible enhancers (Evans and Smith, 1964; McGaugh, 1968; Weiss and Laties, 1962) or impairers of memory (Bohdanecky and Jarvik, 1967; Leukel, 1957; Pearlman et al, 1961; Taber and Banuazizi, 1966) or influencers of other aspects of cognitive and intellectual functioning in human or infrahuman subjects, (Latz, 1968; Lehmann and Csank, 1957; Oliverio, 1968) there is a need for more information on these matters. Certain benzodiazepines (e.g., diazepam and lorazepam) have been used with enthusiasm in the practice of medicine for their anterograde amnesic effect by anesthesiologists, obstetricians and dentists. By intravenous administration, and often as the sole preanesthetic medication, diazepam (10-15 mg) can produce anterograde amnesia for at least one-half hour after injection (Clarke et al, 1970; Dundee and Pandit, 1972; Gregg et al, 1974; Wilson and Ellis, 1973). And lorazepam, in intravenous doses of 3 to 5 mg, has been noticed to have even longer amnesic effects (Heisterkamp and Cohen, 1975; Wilson and Ellis, 1973).

Oral doses of flurazepam (15 and 30 mg) and triazolam (0.25 and 0.5 mg) have been noted to impair the performance on various simple cognitive and psychomotor tests 3.5 hours after drug ingestion and 10 hours after the 30 mg dose of flurazepam (Roth et al, 1976).

We are especially interested in both the technical problems in measuring intellectual deficits produced by psychoactive drugs and the possible practical complications and disadvantages of any established transient deficits in mental functioning produced by such drugs, although these amnesic and cognitive effects may be of some therapeutic benefit in certain clinical circumstances. In the present study we focussed, specifically, on the qualitative and quantitative psychological effects of triazolam and flurazepam, as compared to the barbiturate pentobarbital.

Triazolam is a very potent benzodiazepine derivative with a pharmacological profile qualitatively resembling that of diazepam (Elliott et al, 1975). In humans it is shorter acting than diazepam and does not depress the respiratory response to $CO_2$ or affect cardiovascular dynamics in doses 4-8 times the usual hypnotic dose. Single oral doses of 0.25-2.0 mg administered about 9:00 a.m. have dose-related sedative-hypnotic effects ranging from sedation with 0.25 mg to deep sleep lasting about three hours with 2.0 mg. Three of four subjects given 2.0 mg appeared fully recovered at 7 hours, but one subject slept for 6 hours and was severely depressed for 17 hours. Three of four subjects from each group receiving 0.5 mg or more of triazolam failed to remember all or part of the events which occurred during the period of drug action. The relatively short action of therapeutic and even

overdoses of triazolam, together with its minimal effects on respiration and circulation, indicate that it may be superior to hypnotic drugs now available.

## METHODS AND PROCEDURES

Subjects for the present study were healthy incarcerated volunteer adult males with no history of serious chronic disease and no other drug intake for at least 2 weeks prior to trial. State of health was evaluated by history, physical examination, EKG, EEG and laboratory tests (CBC, urinalysis and SMA-12). Informed consent was obtained from all subjects.

All subjects were fasting 10 - 12 hours and were given triazolam (0.25 - 2.0) or flurazepam (30 mg), in capsule form between 9:00 and 11:00 am. The capsule was washed down with a few ounces of water and each subject reclined on his right side for 20 - 30 minutes to facilitate absorption. Six subjects received flurazepam (30 mg), fourteen subjects received triazolam (0.25 - 0.50 mg) and twelve subjects received triazolam (1.0 - 2.0 mg). All trials were double-blind except for the trial of 2.0 mg of triazolam which was single blind.

Following drug administration subjects were observed for drug effects. Five minute speech samples, elicited by the method of Gottschalk (Gottschalk and Gleser, 1969; Gottschalk et al, 1969b) were obtained before drug administration, 60 - 90 minutes, and 240 - 300 minutes following drug administration. One subject who received 2.0 mg of triazolam was too sedated to provide postdrug verbal samples. Typescripts of these tape-recorded speech samples were scored blindly by trained content analysis technicians for anxiety,

hostility outward (overt, covert, and total), social alienation-personal disorganization, and cognitive impairment by the method of Gottschalk and Gleser (1969).

The standing steadiness test, a measure of central nervous system depression as manifested by impairment of balance, (Elliott et al, 1975) was administered predrug and at 30, 60, 120, 180, and 240 minutes post-drug or until return of control values. Scalp EEG's (12 lead), response to $CO_2$, and tilt table test for cardiovascular function were administered between 30 - 120 minutes and 120 - 240 minutes following drug administration and again after 240 minutes if results were still abnormal. Respiratory, cardiovascular, and EEG effects of triazolam have been reported elsewhere (Elliott et al, 1975).

## RESULTS

Table 1 gives average psychological state scores (by content analysis scales) predrug (verbal sample 1), 60 - 90 minutes postdrug (verbal sample 2), and 240 - 300 minutes postdrug (verbal sample 3) for triazolam.

Significant decreases occurred in total anxiety scores with triazolam at both 0.25 - 0.50 mg (N=14; $p < .02$) and 1.00 - 2.00 mg (N=11; $p < .01$) oral doses 60 - 90 minutes postdrug and the anti-anxiety effect persisted 240 - 300 minutes postdrug with the lower dose level ($p < .01$). (See Table 1) The anxiety reduction effect of 30 mg of flurazepam (N=6) was not statistically significant.

Hostility outward scores were not significantly changed at either dose of triazolam. Flurazepam (30 mg) also produced no significant

changes in hostility outward scores.

Hostility inward scores were not significantly changed by flurazepam, but there was a significant decrease ($p < .01$) in hostility inward scores 240 - 300 minutes postdrug after 0.25 - 0.50 mg of triazolam.

There was a significant decrease in ambivalent hostility scores 60 - 90 minutes following the 0.25 - 0.50 mg dose range (N=14. $p < .03$) and 1.00 - 2.00 mg dose range (N=11, $p < .07$) of triazolam, and this decrease persisted 240 - 300 minutes postdrug at the lower dose range ($p < .03$).

Social alienation-personal disorganization scores were significantly increased 60 - 90 minutes following both 0.25 - 0.50 mg (N=14, $p < .02$) and 1.00 - 2.00 mg (N=11, $p < .07$) doses of triazolam as well as 30 mg of flurazepam (N=6, $p < .02$). The significant increase in these scores continued 240 - 300 minutes after the flurazepam ($p < .03$).

Examination of the portion of the social alienation-personal disorganization scale which was adversely influenced by the benzodiazepines, triazolam and flurazepam, indicated that it was the personal disorganization (thought or cognitive disorder) component (Subscale III) that was significantly increased and not the social alienation components (Subscales I and II). This was true 60 - 90 minutes postdrug for both dose ranges (0.25 - 0.50 and 1.00 - 2.00 mg) of triazolam ($p < .001$) and for the lower dose level (0.25 - 0.50 mg) 240 - 300 minutes postdrug ($p < .05$).

Minor non-significant increases did occur 60 - 90 minutes postdrug in cognitive impairment scores after each of the psychoactive drugs administered. However. the only increase in cognitive impairment

TABLE I - Comparison of Average Psychological State (Content Analysis) Scores for Verbal Sample #1 (predrug).

| Psychological State | Triazolam (Dose mg) | N | Verbal Sample (V.S.) #1 |
|---|---|---|---|
| Anxiety | 0.25 - 0.50<br>1.00 - 2.00 | 14<br>11 | 1.99 ± 0.63*<br>1.47 ± 0.78 |
| Hostility Outward Overt | 0.25 - 0.50<br>1.00 - 2.00 | 14<br>11 | 1.10 ± 0.37<br>0.88 ± 0.42 |
| Hostility Outward Covert | 0.25 - 0.50<br>1.00 - 2.00 | 14<br>11 | 0.66 ± 0.27<br>0.84 ± 0.98 |
| Hostility Outward Total | 0.25 - 0.50<br>1.00 - 2.00 | 14<br>11 | 1.28 ± 0.36<br>1.31 ± 0.88 |
| Hostility Inward | 0.25 - 0.50<br>1.00 - 2.00 | 14<br>11 | 0.70 ± 0.41<br>0.50 ± 0.28 |
| Ambivalent Hostility | 0.25 - 0.50<br>1.00 - 2.00 | 14<br>11 | 0.98 ± 0.43<br>0.71 ± 0.54 |
| Social Alienation-Personal Disorganization | 0.25 - 0.50<br>1.00 - 2.00 | 14<br>11 | 0.66 ± 3.21<br>0.57 ± 2.97 |
| Cognitive-Intellectual Impairment | 0.25 - 0.50<br>1.00 - 2.00 | 14<br>11 | 2.43 ± 1.37<br>2.07 ± 0.97 |

*$\overline{X}$ + S.D.
**p = one-tailed test

Table I (continued).. Verbal Sample #2(1 - 1.5 hours postdrug), and Verbal Sample #3 (4 - 5 hours postdrug) at Two Oral Dosage Ranges of Triazolam (0.25 - 0.5 mg and 1.00 - 2.00 mg).

| Verbal Sample (V.S.) #2 | Verbal Sample (V.S.) #3 | V.S.#1 versus V.S.#2 | | V.S. #1 versus V.S. #3 | |
|---|---|---|---|---|---|
| | | t value | p** | t value | p** |
| 1.51 ± 0.65<br>0.82 ± 0.41 | 1.31 ± 0.53<br>1.92 ± 0.79 | 2.44<br>3.10 | .02<br>.01 | 2.52<br>-1.49 | .01<br>.92 |
| 1.08 ± 0.61<br>0.80 ± 0.40 | 0.91 ± 0.56<br>1.01 ± 0.53 | 0.11<br>0.39 | .46<br>.35 | 0.96<br>-1.27 | .18<br>.88 |
| 0.70 ± 0.44<br>0.79 ± 0.47 | 0.77 ± 0.63<br>0.97 ± 1.08 | -0.29<br>0.17 | .62<br>.43 | -0.59<br>-0.50 | .72<br>.69 |
| 1.33 ± 0.57<br>0.99 ± 0.51 | 1.26 ± 0.66<br>1.53 ± 0.96 | -0.27<br>1.20 | .40<br>.13 | 0.09<br>-1.23 | .46<br>.88 |
| 0.47 ± 0.42<br>0.50 ± 0.23 | 0.32 ± 0.15<br>0.54 ± 0.38 | 1.31<br>-0.02 | .11<br>.51 | 3.02<br>-0.29 | .01<br>.61 |
| 0.66 ± 0.34<br>0.50 ± 0.23 | 0.67 ± 0.35<br>0.55 ± 0.33 | 2.18<br>1.63 | .03<br>.07 | 2.18<br>0.92 | .03<br>.19 |
| 3.60 ± 3.29<br>4.39 ± 7.80 | 1.46 ± 2.78<br>1.60 ± 5.99 | -2.35<br>-1.54 | .02<br>.07 | -0.89<br>-0.47 | .20<br>.33 |
| 2.29 ± 2.16<br>4.02 ± 4.34 | 2.23 ± 1.51<br>2.15 ± 1.04 | 0.24<br>-1.46 | .59<br>.08 | 0.54<br>-0.20 | .70<br>.42 |

scores 60 - 90 minutes postdrug approaching significance occurred 60 - 90 minutes following the 1.00 - 2.00 mg dose of triazolam (N=11, $p < .08$).

To determine whether the effect of triazolam on the content analysis scale scores was dose related, multiple regression analyses were performed using the scores for the two postdrug verbal samples as dependent variables. The score for the predrug verbal sample was first entered into the regression equation to control for initial individual variability and then the variable of dose level was entered and tested for significance. Only one content analysis scale score showed a significant result; the anxiety score derived from the first postdrug verbal sample decreased significantly, the higher the triazolam dose (Bates, 1975; Latz, 1968) ($F=4.87$, $p < .05$, one tail).

Standing Steadiness Test. All subjects took the standing steadiness test which consists of counting the number of times per minute that a subject standing on one foot must touch the floor with the elevated foot in order to keep his balance first with eyes open and then with eyes closed (Elliott et al, 1975). Degree of impairment, if any, is scored as: slight = 3-5 touches, moderate = 6-10 touches, marked = 10-30 touches or unable to stand. The findings are summarized as follows:

Flurazepam 30 mg: Of 6 subjects 3 showed no impairment. Two showed slight impairment and 1 moderate impairment with eyes closed. All were normal after 120 minutes.

Triazolam 0.25 mg: Of 4 subjects 2 showed no impairment. One

showed moderate and 1 marked impairment with eyes closed. All were normal after 180 minutes.

Triazolam 0.5 mg: Of 10 subjects 1 showed no impairment. Eight showed slight to marked impairment with eyes open and 9 moderate to marked impairment with eyes closed. One was unable to stand 43 minutes postdrug. All were normal after 210 minutes.

Triazolam 1.0 mg: Of 4 subjects 1 showed moderate impairment with eyes open and 3 were unable to stand for varying periods. All 4 were unable to stand for varying periods with eyes closed. All were normal after 300 mintues.

Triazolam 1.5 mg: Of 4 subjects 1 showed moderate impairment with eyes open and 3 were unable to stand for varying periods. All 4 were unable to stand for varying periods with eyes closed. All were normal after 300 minutes.

Triazolam 2.0 mg: Of 4 subjects all were unable to stand for varying periods with eyes open or closed, one for 17 hours. This subject required 21 hours to recover and was too depressed to provide postdrug verbal samples. The others were normal after 7 hours.

## DISCUSSION

The capacity of the benzodiazepine derivatives to decrease anxiety and hostility levels has been well established (Gleser et al, 1965; Gottschalk et al,1972a) Gottschalk and Kaplan, 1972; Gottschalk et al, 1973; Greenblatt and Shader, 1974). But little attention has been paid to the effects of this class of psychoactive

drugs on cognition and other intellectual processes, except for the previously mentioned amnesic effects, (Clarke et al, 1970; Dundee and Pandit, 1972; Gregg et al, 1974; Heisterkamp and Cohen, 1975; Wilson and Ellis, 1973) effects sought often by obstetricians, anesthesiologists, and dentists. The present study clearly indicates that triazolam, a new benzodiazepine derivative, is like other benzodiazepines we have studied; (Gleser et al, 1965; Gottschalk et al, 1973) it is an effective anti-anxiety agent as well as an inhibitor of certain kinds of hostility, namely, hostility directed inward and ambivalent hostility scores (the latter based on statements made by the speaker connoting hostile activities from external sources directed towards the self.) The anti-anxiety effect of triazolam, at the oral dose level of 0.25 to 0.50 mg or 1.00 to 2.00 mg, was not significantly different by co-variance analysis than the anti-anxiety and anti-hositlity effects of 30 mg of flurazepam orally. Why the larger dose of triazolam (1.00 - 2.00 mg) did not have as prolonged an anti-anxiety effect as the smaller dose (0.25 - 0.50 mg) is not clear to us, at this time; plasma concentration studies of triazolam exploring the pharmacokinetics and clinical response of this drug may provide an answer to this question.

What invites more scrutiny here is the finding that social alienation-personal disorgnization (content analysis) scores were significantly elevated 60 - 300 minutes after ingestion of triazolam and flurazepam. The social alienation-personal disorganization scale measures a psychological dimension which at one extreme (high scores) distinctly typifies the major features of the schizophrenic syndrome,

shades into syndromes psychiatrically labelled "borderline states" (Middle range scores), and includes the variability of transient social withdrawal or the verbal inarticulateness which typifies the verbal communications of normal, everyday life (low scores). At the 75th percentile, a sample of 113 known chronic schizophrenic patients had an average social alienation-personal disorganization scale score of 7.9; a sample of 29 acute schizophrenic patients had an average social alienation-personal disorganization score of 3.6; and a sample of 60 "normal" employed individuals had an average social alienation-personal disorganization score of -1.2 (Gottschalk, 1976; Gottschalk and Gleser, 1969). It is of interest that our subjects in the present psychopharmacological study had average predrug social alienation-personal disorganization scores of 0.62, which is in the 29th percentile of the above described sample of chronic schizophrenic patients and in the 90th percentile of normative subjects. Postdrug (60 - 90 minutes) following oral triazolam, the social alienation-personal disorganization scores of our subjects were elevated to an average of 3.95, which was in the 52nd percentile of our reference chronic schizophrenic patients and above the 95th percentile of normative adult subjects. Postdrug (240 - 300 minutes) following triazolam the social alienation-personal disorganization scores remained elevated to an average of 1.52, which was in the 35th percentile of our reference chronic schizophrenic and above the 95th percentile of normative adult subjects. Besides the schizophrenic syndrome, other conditions are known to change

significantly the total social alienation-personal disorganization scale scores. The administration and withdrawal of phenothiazines in schizophrenic patients can, respectively, significantly decrease and increase these scores (Gottschalk et al, 1975; Gottschalk et al, 1970). Psychotomimetic drugs (Ditran, Psilocybin, and LSD) may increase these scores (Gottschalk and Gleser, 1969). So may cerebral organic brain syndromes, but these conditions can be usually differentiated to a large extent by the cognitive and intellectual impairment (content analysis) scale of Gottschalk (Gottschalk and Gleser, 1969). To complicate the measurement issue, two studies (Bates, 1975; Gottschalk et al, 1972b) have demonstrated that sensory overload in the form of 45 minutes of exposure to chaotic visual and auditory stimuli can also significantly increase social alienation-personal disorganization scores in normal subjects, and that the greater the field dependence of these subjects, as measured by the method of Witkin et al (1962), the greater the increase in these scores with exposure to sensory overload.

The capacity of triazolam to elevate significantly scores of social alienation-personal disorganization was shared by another benzodiazepine derivative, flurazepam (30 mg) in the present study. In fact, significant elevations of social alienation-personal disorganization scores occurred not only 60 - 90 minutes following oral ingestion of flurazepam, but also 240 - 300 minutes later. As previously indicated, it is the personal disorganization (thought disorder) component of this measure which is adversely affected by triazolam and flurazepam rather than the social alienation component.

So this psychoactive drug effect is dissimilar from the total verbal behavior typifying the schizophrenic syndrome, but rather it falls within the cognitive-intellectual component of psychological dysfunction. Presumably, the language disturbance we have noted is an accompaniment of the amnesic effects which have been noted with the benzodiazepines, including triazolam.

Clearly, further examination of the effects of other benzodiazepine derivatives on social alienation-personal disorganization scores and on other measures of social and cognitive impairment is required to determine whether these effects occur in response to other benzodiazepine derivatives. We have enough data here to indicate that certain benzodiazepines are capable, after a single dose, of significantly disrupting certain kinds of cognitive and/or intellectual processes. Furthermore, this phenomenon, outlasts the anti-anxiety effects of these drugs. Hence, presumably the neurobiochemical events underlying these phenomena, that is, anti-anxiety and increase of personal disorganization scores are not identical, though in some way possibly interrelated.

The lack of uniform or pronounced increases in the scores of the cognitive and intellectual impairment scale, a speech content analysis measure designed specifically to detect and quantitate certain kinds of general cerebral organic impairment, (Gottschalk and Gleser, 1969) suggests that the cognitive, and intellectual changes observed with triazolam and flurazepam are of a type that need better definition. The cognitive and intellectual impairment scale was not designed to

directly measure recent memory defects or interferences in memory consolidation or recall. Its validation was based on scores obtained with patients having recently received electroshock treatment or diagnosed as suffering from various kinds of acute or chronic cerebral organic syndromes (e.g., chronic brain syndrome due to alcoholism, senile psychosis, brain tumor, cerebral arteriosclerosis, etc.). This measure registers transient or permanent impairment of brain functioning of some kinds, (Gottschalk and Gleser, 1969; Gottschalk and Kunkel, 1966; Gottschalk et al,1969a), but like many other measures of intellectual malfunction it cannot directly differentiate attentional factors or interference in perceptual registration from irreversible brain damage, all of which can influence the evaluation of memory. A broader battery of tests of memory and other cognitive functions should be used in future research in this area.

Our findings with the standing steadiness test are of interest from several points of view. The fact that only 3 out of the 6 subjects on flurazepam showed no impairment on the standing steadiness test suggests that the increase of social alienation-personal disorganization scores is probably not a result of the same neurobiological mechanism responsible for the maintenance of balance. There does appear, however, to be some relationship between psychopharmacological anti-anxiety or anti-hostility effects and the impairment of the ability to balance oneself on one foot. Such colloquial and metaphorical language expressions as "he is not a well-balanced person" were obviously not based on neuropsychopharmacological observations that the greater the impairment of balance induced by a psychoactive pharmacological agent the more likely there would be an associated decrease in irrational anxiety.

REFERENCES

1. Bates, D.E.: The effect of sensory overload on behavioral and biochemical measures, Unpublished Doctoral Dissertation, University of California at Irvine, 1975.
2. Bohdanecky, Z., and Jarvik, M.E.: Impairment of one trial passive avoidance learning in mice by scopolamine, scopolamine methylbromide, and physostigmine, Int. J. Neuropharmacology 6:217-222, 1967.
3. Clarke, P.R.F., Eccersley, P.S., Frisley, J.P., and Thorton, J.A.: The amnesic effect of diazepam (Valium), Br. J. Anaesth. 42:690-697, 1970.
4. Dundee, J.W., and Pandit, S.K.: Anterograde amnesic effects of pethidine, hyoscine and diazepam in adults, Br. J. Pharmacol. 44: 140-144, 1972.
5. Elliott, H.W. Navarro, G., Kokka, N., and Nomof, N.: Early phase I evaluation of sedatives, hypnotics as minor tranquilizers, in Kagan, F., Harwood, T., Rickels, K., Rudzik, A.D., and Sorer, H., editors: Hypnotics - methods of development and evaluation, New York, 1975, Spectrum Publications, Inc., pp. 87-104.
6. Evans, W.O., and Smith, R.P.: Some effects of morphine and amphetamine on intellectual functions and mood, Psychopharmacologia 6:49-56, 1964.
7. Gleser, G.C., Gottschalk, L.A., Fox, R., and Lippert, W.: Immediate changes in affect with chlordiazepoxide in juvenile delinquent boys, Arch. Gen. Psychiatry 13:291-295, 1965.

8. Gottschalk, L.A.: Children's speech as a source of data toward the measurement of psychological states, J. of Youth & Adolescence 5:11-36, 1976.

9. Gottschalk, L.A., Biener, R., Noble, E.P., Birch, H., Wilbert, D., and Heiser, J.F.: Thioridazine plasma levels and clinical response, Compr. Psychiatry 16:323-337, 1975.

10. Gottschalk, L.A., Elliott, H.W., Bates, D.E., and Cable, C.G.: The use of content analysis of short samples of speech for preliminary investigation of psychoactive drugs: effect of Lorazepam on anxiety scores, Clin. Pharmacol. Ther. 13:323-328, 1972a.

11. Gottschalk, L.A., and Gleser, G.C.: The measurement of psychological states through the content analysis of verbal behavior, Berkeley, Los Angeles, 1969, University of California Press.

12. Gottschalk, L.A., Gleser, G.C., Cleghorn, J.M., Stone, W.N., and Winget, C.N.: Prediction of changes in severity of the schizophrenic syndrome with discontinuation and administration of phenothiazines in chronic schizophrenic patients: language as a predictor and measure of change in schizophrenia, Comp. Psychiat. 11:123-140, 1970.

13. Gottschalk, L.A., Haer, J.L., and Bates, D.E.: Effect of sensory overload on psychological state, Arch. Gen. Psychiatry 27:451-457, 1972b.

14. Gottschalk, L.A., and Kaplan, S.A.: Chlordiazepoxide plasma levels and clinical responses, Compr. Psychiatry 13:519-527, 1972.

15. Gottschalk, L.A., and Kunkel, R.L.: Changes in emotional and intellectual functioning after total body radiation, in Saenger, E.L., Friedman, B.J., Keriakes, J.G., and Perry, H., editors: Metabolic changes in humans following total body radiation, Washington, D.C., 1966. Report period February 1960 through April 1966, Research Grant DA-49-146-XZ315 to Univ. of Cincinnati, College of Medicine, Cincinnati, Ohio, from the Defense Atomic Support Agency.

16. Gottschalk, L.A., Kunkel, R.L., Wohl, T.H., Saenger, E.L., and Winget, C.N.: Total and half body irradiation: effect on cognitive and emotional processes, Arch. Gen Psychiatry 21:574-580, 1969a.

17. Gottschalk, L.A., Noble, E.P., Stolzoff, G.E., Bates, D.E., Cable, C.G., Uliana, R.L., Birch, H., and Fleming, E.W.: Relationships of chlordiazepoxide blood levels to psychological and biochemical responses, in Garattini, S., Mussini, E., and Randall, L.O., editors: Benzodiazepenes, New York, 1973, Raven Press, pp. 257-283.

18. Gottschalk, L.A., Winget, C.N., and Gleser, G.C.: Manual of instructions for use of the Gottschalk-Gleser content analysis scales, Berkeley, Los Angeles, 1969b,University of California Press.

19. Greenblatt, D.J., and Shader, R.I.: Benzodiazepenes in clinical practice, New York, 1974, Raven Press.

20. Gregg, J.M., Ryan, D.E., and Levin, K.H.: The amnesic actions of diazepam, J. Oral Surg. 32:651-664, 1974.

21. Heisterkamp, D.V., and Cohen, P.J.: The effect of intravenous premedication with lorazepam, (Ativan), pentobarbitone or diazepam on recall, Br. J. Anaesth. 47:79-81, 1975.

22. Latz, A.: Cognitive test performance of normal human adults under the influence of psychopharmacological agents: a brief review, in Efron, D.F., Cole, J.O., Levine, J., and Wittenborn, J.R., editors: Psychopharmacology: a review of progress 1957-1967, Washington, D.C., 1968, U.S. Government Printing Office, Public Health Service Publication No. 1836, pp. 83-90.

23. Lehmann, H.E., and Csank, J.: Differential screening of phrenotropic agents in man, J. of Clin. and Experimental Psychopath. and Q. Rev. of Psychiatry and Neurology 18:222-235, 1957.

24. Leukel, F.P.: The effect of ECS and pentothal anesthesia on maze learning and retention, J. Comp. Physiol. Psychol. 50:300-306, 1957.

25. McGaugh, J.L.: Drug facilitation of memory and learning, in Efron, D.H., Cole, J.O., Levine, J., and Wittenborn, J.R., editors: Psychopharmacology, a review of progress 1957-1967, Washington, D.C., 1968, U.S. Government Printing Office, Public Health Service Publication No. 1836.

26. Oliverio, A.: Neurohumoral systems and learning, in Efron, D.H., Cole, J.O., Levine, J., and Wittenborn, J.R., editors: Psychopharmacology, a review of progress 1957-1967, Washington, D.C., 1968, U.S. Government Printing Office, Public Health Service Publication No. 1836, pp 867-878.

27. Pearlman, C.A., Sharpless, S.K., and Jarvik, M.E.: Retrograde amnesia produced by anesthetic and convulsant agents, J. Comp. Physical. Psychol. 54:109-112, 1961.

28. Roth, T., Kramer, M., and Lutz, T.: The effects of hypnotics on sleep, performance, and subjective state, unpublished manuscript, 1976.

29. Taber, R.I., and Banuazizi, A.: $CO_2$-induced retrograde amnesia in a one-trial learning situation, Psychopharmacologia 9:382-391, 1966.

30. Weiss, B., and Laties, V.G.: Enhancement of human performance by caffeine and the amphetamines, Pharmacol. Rev. 14:1-36, 1962.

31. Wilson, J., and Ellis, F.R.: Oral premedication with lorazepam (Ativan): a comparison with heptabarbitone (Medomin) and diazepam (Valium), Br. J. Anaesth. 45:738-744, 1973.

32. Witkin, H.A., Faterson, H.F., Goodenough, D.R., and Karp, S.A.: Psychological differentiation, New York, 1962, John Wiley and Sons.

# EFFECTS OF CERTAIN BENZODIAZEPINE DERIVATIVES ON DISORGANIZATION OF THOUGHT AS MANIFESTED IN SPEECH

LOUIS A. GOTTSCHALK, M.D.

*From the Department of Psychiatry and Human Behavior, College of Medicine, University of California, Irvine, California 92717*

ABSTRACT

**1. Typescripts of tape-recorded five-minute speech samples were obtained before and 30 to 300 minutes after the administration of single doses of chlordiazepoxide (25 mg. orally), lorazepam (3 and 5 mg. intramuscularly; and 2 and 5 mg. intravenously), triazolam (0.25-2.0 mg. orally), and flurazepam (30 mg. orally) and 4 weeks after chronic daily doses of diazepam (15 mg. orally/day) and lorazepam (3 mg. orally/day).**

**2. The typescripts were scored blindly for form and content changes in cognitive-intellectual function. All of the benzodiazepine derivatives, under all conditions and doses, were associated with adverse cognitive effects, the most consistent being significant increases in: (a) words or remarks that were not understandable or were inaudible, and (b) blocking or incomplete sentences, clauses or phrases.**

**3. In the study of the effect of a single oral dose of chlordiazepoxide (25 mg.) on cognitive function in 18 chronically anxious patients, more significant increases in the verbal signs of cognitive dysfunction occurred in the 11 patients whose peak chlordiazepoxide blood levels were 0.70 ug./ml. or above.**

**4. The implications are discussed of these temporary adverse cognitive effects accompanying the usual therapeutic mild tranquilizing effects of these drugs.**

## INTRODUCTION

In a recent report Gottschalk and Elliott[1] observed that single oral doses of the benzodiazepine derivatives, triazolam (0.25-2.0 mg.) and flurazepam (30 mg.), significantly elevated signs of disorganization and repetition of ideas occurring in five-minute speech samples 60 to 90 minutes after drug administration. These speech changes are concomitants of other evidence of impairment of intellectual function that has been noted with such pharmacological agents. That is, various benzodiazepine derivatives have been used in the practice of medicine for their anterograde amnesic effect by anesthesiologists, obstetricians, and dentists. For instance, by

The technical assistance of Regina L. Uliana, Ph.D., Julie Hoigaard, B.A., and Michael Syben, B.A. and the statistical assistance of Herman Birch, Ph.D. are hereby acknowledged with appreciation.

intravenous administration, and often as the sole preanesthetic surgical medication, diazepam (5 to 15 mg.) can produce anterograde amnesia in 50 to 90 percent of adults, the peak effect occurring in 2 to 3 minutes and the effect lasting 20 to 30 minutes.[2-5] And lorazepam, in intravenous doses of 3 to 5 mg., has been observed to have even longer amnesic effects.[4,6] Oral doses of flurazepam (15 and 30 mg.) and triazolam (0.25 and 0.5 mg.) have been noted to impair the performance of various simple cognitive and psychomotor tests 210 minutes after ingestion of both drugs and 600 minutes after the 30 mg. dose of flurazepam.[7] Since the speech changes indicative of intellectual dysfunction that Gottschalk and Elliott[1] observed with triazolam and flurazepam are likely to be superficial manifestations of more complex transient cerebral dysfunction, such as, anterograde amnesia, it was considered appropriate to determine whether such speech changes occur with other benzodiazepine derivatives and to learn more specifically what these changes are.

## METHODS AND PROCEDURES

The five-minute speech samples and related data for the present study were obtained from previous studies involving the benzodiazepines in which the effect of these pharmacological agents was examined on anxiety and hostility as derived from the content analysis of speech samples.[8,9,10,11]

Speech samples were content-analyzed by technicians, unfamiliar with the purpose of this study, for social alienation-personal disorganization scale and cognitive-intellectual impairment scale scores, according to the method of Gottschalk and Gleser[12] (See Schedule I and II in Appendix). The social alienation-personal disorganization scale is a validated measure derived from the objective content analysis of short speech samples. It measures the magnitude of withdrawal from and dislike of social relations as well as the degree of cognitive-intellectual impairment or thought disorder. It can be divided into three major subscales: I. Interpersonal references; II. Intrapersonal references; and III. Disorganization and repetition.[12-17] The cognitive-intellectual impairment scale was developed from verbal content categories used in the social alienation-personal disorganization scale but reweighted so as to differentiate the speech of individuals with certain types of cerebral organic impairment, whether transient or permanent, such as, organic brain syndrome due to chronic alcoholism, arteriosclerosis, senile psychosis, postelectroshock treatment, from the thinking disorder associated with schizophrenia.[12,15]

For the purposes of the present study, verbal categories from the social alienation-personal disorganization scale (which includes all the verbal categories from the cognitive impairment scale) were scored from the available five minute speech samples. "Original" weights (Reference 12, pages 42-44) were used in comparing scores derived from speech samples obtained before and after drug administration, for these weights are common to both the thought disorder portion of the social alienation-personal disorganization scale and the cognitive impairment scale.

I. *Chlordiazepoxide* (25 mg. orally in a single dose)

A previously reported study[8,10] demonstrated that out of 18 subjects those subjects with higher blood levels of chlordiazepoxide following ingestion of a standard dose of

25 mg. of chlordiazepoxide were more likely to have a greater decrease in anxiety scores as measured through the content analysis of speech. These data were re-examined and further analyzed to determine the effect of chlordiazepoxide on social alienation-personal disorganization and cognitive impairment scores. In this study, 18 anxious subjects (14 males and 4 females), who had not taken any drugs of any kind for at least 4 weeks, participated in double-blind, drug-placebo, cross-over study, balanced for order, in which nine of the subjects first took a placebo capsule and the other nine first took 25 mg. of chlordiazepoxide in capsule form at 8:00 a.m. after 12 hours of fasting. Each subject, at least one week later, took the capsule, containing either a placebo or chlordiazepoxide, that had not been ingested on the previous occasion. On the average, 90 minutes postdrug and, again, 140 minutes postdrug, each subject gave a five-minute tape-recorded speech sample in response to standardized instructions.[13] Blood was drawn at these times for plasma chlordiazepoxide assays, which were performed by the method of Schwartz and Postma.[18]

II. A. *Lorazepam* (3.0 and 5.0 mg. intramuscularly in a single dose)

II. B. *Lorazepam* (2.0 and 5.0 mg. intravenously in a single dose)

*Methods and Procedures:* This was a study demonstrating the anti-anxiety effects of lorazepam as measured by the method of the content analysis of speech.[9] Twenty-six paid volunteer inmates of the California Medical Facility at Vacaville, who had been medication free for at least 4 weeks, served as subjects. Their average age was 31.4 ±6.3 years. Groups of 5 subjects each were used. Subjects were not selected because of high anxiety levels.

Four subjects of Group 1 received lorazepam 2 mg. intravenously and one received sodium pentobarbital 100 mg. intravenously. Four of Group 2 received lorazepam 5 mg. intravenously and one received sodium phenobarbital 130 mg. intravenously. Four of Group 3 received lorazepam 5 mg. intramuscularly and one received sodium phenobarbital 260 mg. intramuscularly. Four of Group 4 received lorazepam 3 mg. intramuscularly and one received sodium phenobarbital 120 mg. intramuscularly. The subjects given the barbiturates were chosen at random. Six prisoners, who assisted in the study and therefore were in the same environment but not given any drug, served as controls. The nature of the drug and dose was unknown to subjects, to the content analysis technician who scored the verbal samples, and to investigators who performed various psychologic tests.

Speech samples were obtained according to standardized instructions[12,15] in which subjects were asked to speak for 5 minutes into the microphone of a tape recorder in response to instructions to talk about any interesting or dramatic, personal life experiences. The typescripts of the speech samples were scored for anxiety. In this study, a predrug verbal sample was obtained prior to drug injection, a second verbal sample was obtained 30 to 150 minutes after drug injection, and the third verbal sample was obtained 195 to 420 minutes after drug injection.

In the first group, only one verbal sample was obtained 30 minutes after drug administration, but since maximal drug effect did not occur until about 60 minutes after drug administration, the first postdrug verbal samples were taken 60 minutes after drug administration in subsequent studies.

II. C. *Lorazepam* (3.0 mg./day orally for 4 weeks)

*Methods and Procedures:* This was a study aiming to compare different methods (self-report scales, rating scales, and content analysis scales) of assessing the magnitude in psychological states.[11] It involved a double-blind, placebo-drug investigation

examining the differences in psychological effects resulting from the oral administration of lorazepam (3 mg./day), diazepam (15 mg./day) or a placebo to a randomly selected group of 35 outpatients over a 4 week period.

The sample of psychiatric outpatients was obtained from the Symptomatic Volunteer Clinic at Philadelphia General Hospital. These outpatients were suffering from neurotic anxiety and tension of at least moderate degree, with or without somatization and depression.

The measures used to assess psychological dimensions before and during drug treatment were: (1) the Gottschalk-Gleser Content Analysis Scales;[12] (2) the Hopkins Symptom Checklist (HSCL), a 52-item self-report measure originally developed by Parloff, Kelman and Frank;[19] (3) the Hamilton Anxiety Scale, a 13-item rating scale which has been cluster-analyzed into an emotional and somatic cluster,[20] (4) the Physician Questionnaire, 1 16-item rating scale consisting of an emotional and somatic cluster.[21]

For the present portion of this study, we shall concern ourselves only with the content analysis scales which were scored blindly for social alienation-personal disorganization scores by content analysis technicians in the Communications and Measurement Laboratory, University of California at Irvine, from 5-minute speech samples obtained by two research assistants, following standardized procedures of eliciting speech[12] from the psychiatric outpatients in Philadelphia.

III. *Diazepam* (15 mg./day for 4 weeks)

*Methods and Procedures:* The five minute speech samples used for this study with diazepam (15 mg.) given daily for 4 weeks were obtained in the investigation[11] described above for lorazepam (3 mg./day for 4 weeks).

IV. *Flurazepam* (30 mg. orally in a single dose)

*Methods and Procedures:* Subjects for this study[1] were healthy incarcerated volunteer adult males with no history of serious chronic disease and no other drug intake for at least 2 weeks prior to trial. State of health was evaluated by history, physical examination, EKG, EEG and laboratory tests (CBC, urinalysis and SMA-12). Informed consent was obtained from all subjects.

All subjects were fasting 10 to 12 hours and were given triazolam (0.25-2.0) or flurazepam (30 mg.) in capsule form between 9:00 and 11:00 a.m. The capsule was washed down with a few ounces of water and each subject reclined on his right side for 20 to 30 minutes to facilitate absorption. Six subjects received flurazepam (30 mg.), fourteen subjects received triazolam (0.25-0.50 mg.), and twelve subjects received triazolam (1.0-2.0 mg.). All trials were double-blind except for the trial of 2.0 mg. of triazolam which was single blind.

Following drug administration subjects were observed for drug effects. Five minute speech samples, elicited by the Gottschalk-Gleser method[12,15] were obtained before drug administration, 60 to 90 minutes, and 240 to 300 minutes following drug administration. One subject who received 2.0 mg. of triazolam was too sedated to provide postdrug verbal samples. Typescripts of these tape-recorded speech samples were scored blindly by trained content analysis technicians for anxiety, hostility outward (overt, covert, and total), social alienation-personal disorganization, and cognitive impairment by the method of Gottschalk and Gleser.[15]

V. *Triazolam* (0.25-2.00 mg. orally in a single dose)

*Methods and Procedures:* The five-minute speech samples analyzed to observe the

effect of triazolam 0.25-2.0 mg. orally in a single dose were obtained in the same study summarized above[1] under flurazepam (30 mg.).

## RESULTS

I. *Chlordiazepoxide* (25 mg. orally in a single dose)

There were no significant differences between total social alienation-personal disorganization scores obtained 90 minutes and 140 minutes after oral chlordiazepoxide. However, the *disorganization and repetition subscale* scores showed a significant increase over this 50 minute period (N=18; 2.65 ± 0.91 → 3.25 ± 1.17, t=2.13, $p < .025$, one tail) in all 18 subjects, in whom the chlordiazepoxide peak plasma levels ranged from 0.26 to 1.63 ug./ml. An even greater increase ($p < .01$) in disorganization and repetition subscale scores occurred in those 11 subjects whose chlordiazepoxide peak plasma concentrations were 0.70 ug./ml. or higher. (See Table I)

The increase in the *disorganization and repetition subscale* scores* may be accounted for by an increase in the categories: *blocking or incomplete sentences, clauses, or phrases* (IIIA2) and *repetition of ideas in sequence — phrases or clauses (separated only by a phrase or a clause)* (IIIB2). The increase in scores for *repetition of ideas in sequence — phrases or clauses* reached statistical significance ($p < .025$) in the 11 subjects whose chlordiazepoxide peak plasma concentrations were 0.70 ug./ml. or higher, whereas the increase in scores for *blocking or incomplete sentences, clauses, or phrases* was significant for all 18 subjects. (See Table II)

II. A. *Lorazepam* (3.0 and 5.0 mg. intramuscularly in a single dose)

The total social alienation-personal disorganization scores* of 4 subjects one hundred and twenty minutes after receiving 3.0 and 4 subjects receiving 5.0 mg. of lorazepam intramuscularly increased significantly (N=8; 4.76 ± 1.57 → 6.71 ± 2.74, t=-2.35, $p < .03$, one tailed). It was the *disorganization and repetition subscale* which accounted primarily for this increase (N=8; 2.58 ± 0.77 → 4.11 ± 1.16, t=-5.41, $p < .001$), one tailed). From this subscale, references to *remarks or words that are not understandable or inaudible* (IIIA1) significantly increased (N=8; 0.31 ± 0.29 → 0.83 ± 0.62, t=-1.89, $p < .05$), *blocking or incomplete sentences, clauses, phrases* (IIIA2) significantly increased (N=8; 0.29 ± 0.17 → 0.73 ± 0.60, t=-1.89, $p < .05$), and also *repetition of words in sequence* significantly increased (N=8; 0.88 ± 0.69 → 1.29 ± 0.76, t=-1.91, $p < .05$).

---

* Original weights (Reference 12, pages 42-44)

Table I — *Mean differences between social alienation-personal disorganization (SA-PD) Scores* obtained about 90 minutes and 140 minutes after oral chlordiazepoxide (25 mg.).*

| Groups | Time (min.) | | Total Scores | I. Interpersonal References | II. Intrapersonal References | III. Disorganization and Repetition References |
|---|---|---|---|---|---|---|
| | | | Social Alienation-Personal Disorganization Scales | | | |
| 18 | 90 | mean | 4.56 | 0.71 | 1.10 | 2.65 |
| | | s.d. | 1.99 | 1.17 | 1.10 | 0.91 |
| | 140 | mean | 4.39 | 0.27 | 0.90 | 3.25 |
| | | s.d. | 2.37 | 0.93 | 1.12 | 1.17 |
| | T-Test | | 0.28 | 1.17 | 0.76 | 2.13† |
| 11 | 90 | mean | 4.56 | 0.99 | 1.16 | 2.39 |
| | | s.d. | 2.31 | 1.29 | 1.09 | 0.94 |
| | 140 | mean | 4.41 | 0.24 | 0.86 | 3.38 |
| | | s.d. | 2.42 | 0.86 | 0.98 | 1.16 |
| | T-Test | | 0.16 | 1.46 | 1.21 | 2.75†† |

* Scores determined from original weights
** $p < .05$ (one-tail)
† $p < .025$ (one-tail)
†† $p < .01$ (one-tail)

Table II — *Mean differences between social alienation-personal disorganization Items of subscale III (using original weights) obtained about 90 minutes and 140 minutes after oral chlordiazepoxide (25 mg.).*

| Group | Time (min.) | | IIIA1 | IIIA2 | IIIA3 | IIIB1 | IIIB2 |
|---|---|---|---|---|---|---|---|
| | | | Subscale III: Disorganization and Repetition References | | | | |
| | | | Signs of Disorganization | | | Repetition of Ideas in Sequence | |
| 18 | 90 | mean | 0.34 | 0.62 | 0.04 | 0.67 | 0.99 |
| | | s.d. | 0.31 | 0.39 | 0.07 | 0.52 | 0.53 |
| | 140 | mean | 0.42 | 0.86 | 0.11 | 0.62 | 1.25 |
| | | s.d. | 0.37 | 0.44 | 0.24 | 0.57 | 0.51 |
| | T-Test | | 1.03 | 2.07* | 1.14 | 0.42 | 1.72† |
| 11 | 90 | mean | 0.33 | 0.53 | 0.05 | 0.61 | 0.88 |
| | | s.d. | 0.24 | 0.35 | 0.08 | 0.56 | 0.49 |
| | 140 | mean | 0.38 | 0.82 | 0.15 | 0.69 | 1.34 |
| | | s.d. | 0.34 | 0.32 | 0.30 | 0.64 | 0.40 |
| | T-Test | | 0.39 | 2.02* | 1.02 | 0.42 | 2.27** |

† $p < .10$ (one-tail)
* $p < .05$ (one-tail)
** $p < .025$ (one-tail)

II. B. *Lorazepam* (2.0 and 5.0 mg. intravenously in a single dose)

One hundred and twenty minutes after intravenous administration of 2.0 and 5.0 mg. lorazepam there was an increase in total social alienation-peraonal disorganization scores (N=8; 1.63 ± 2.26 → 3.41 ± 2.19, t=-1.58, $p < .09$, one tailed). Again, it was the *disorganization and repetition subscale* which accounted for this increase (N=8; 1.34 ± 1.01 → 2.64 ± 1.07, t=-2.49, $p < .025$, one tailed). From this subscale, references to *remarks or words that are not understandable or inaudible* (IIIA1) increased significantly (N=8; 0.11 ± 0.10 → 1.09 ± 0.66, t=-4.22, $p < .004$, one tailed) and references to *blocking or incomplete sentences, clauses, or phrases* (IIIA2) also increased significantly (N=8; 0.06 ± 0.09 → 0.31 ± 0.23, t=-3.38, $p < .005$, one tailed).

II. C. *Lorazepam* (3.0 mg. orally per day for 4 weeks)

Two weeks after daily oral administration of lorazepam (3.0 mg.), total social alienation-personal disorganization scale scores increased in seven subjects (2.31 ± 2.53 → 5.44 ± 2.47, t=-2.47, $p < .025$, one tailed). It was not only *disorganization and repetition subscale* (III) scores which accounted for this increase (N=7; 1.72 ± 0.39 → 2.45 ± 1.19, t=-1.49, $p < 0.09$), but also the content category *interpersonal references* (I) (-0.08 ± 1.28 → 1.50 ± 1.34, t=-1.94, $p < .05$). References *to self helping, being friendly towards others* (IC2) significantly decreased (N=7; 0.38 ± 0.48 → 0.23 ± 0.41, t=-2.58, $p < .04$), whereas references to *blocking or incomplete sentences, phrases, or clauses* IIIA2) increased but not significantly (N=7; 0.43 ± 0.47 → 0.65 ± 0.36, t=-1.26, $p < .15$).

III. *Diazepam* (15 mg. orally per day for 4 weeks)

Two weeks after daily oral administration of diazepam (15 mg.), total social alienation-personal disorganization scale scores of 8 subjects did not increase but decreased, though not significantly (N=8; 4.45 ± 2.61 → 3.51 ± 3.34, t=1.27, $p < 0.14$). However, there was a significant increase after 2 weeks of daily drug ingestion in *disorganization and repetition subscale* (III) scores (N=8; 2.07 ± 1.14 → 3.00 ± 1.41, t=-3.21, $p < .01$).

References to *remarks or words that are not understandable or inaudible* (IIIA1) increased but not significantly (N=8; 0.59 ± 0.67 → 0.82 ± 0.98, t=-1.38, $p < .12$) and so did references to *blocking or incomplete sentences, clauses, or phrases* (IIIA2) (N=8; 0.47 ± 0.39 → 0.73 ± 0.43, t=-1.69, $p < .08$).

IV. *Flurazepam* (30 mg. orally in a single dose)

One hundred twenty minutes after ingestion of 30 mg. of flurazepam

there was a significant increase in total social alienation-personal disorganization scores (N=6; 2.83 ± 1.58 → 5.71 ± 2.18, t=-1.99, $p < .05$). This increase can be accounted for by increases in subscale content category *intrapersonal references* (II) (N=6; -0.47 ± 1.23 → 1.44 ± 1.09, t=-2.64, $p < .025$) and subscale content category *disorganization and repetition* (III) (N=6; 2.86 ± 1.01 → 3.64 ± 1.95, t=-1.50, $p < .09$).

This dose of flurazepam significantly decreased references to *self unfriendly to others* (IB1) (N=6; 0.19 ± 0.22 → 0.00, t=2.20, $p < .05$) and references to *others unfriendly to self* (IB2) (N=6; 0.16 ± 0.18 → 0.00, t=2.20, $p < .05$). This dose of flurazepam also significantly increased references to *remarks or words that are not understandable or inaudible* (IIIA1) (N=6; 0.35 ± 0.18 → 1.09 ± 0.91, t=-2.20, $p < .05$).

V. *Triazolam* (0.25-2.00 mg. orally in a single dose)

One hundred twenty minutes after oral administration of 0.25-0.50 mg. of triazolam, total social alienation-personal disorganization scores significantly increased (N=14; 3.17 ± 3.07 → 6.13 ± 3.22, t=-2.12, $p < .025$). A significant increase in these scores also occurred 120 minutes after ingestion of 1.00-2.00 mg. of triazolam (N=11; 3.88 ± 3.30 → 7.49 ± 6.07, t=-1.97, $p < .04$). This increase was primarily due to a significant increase in *disorganization and repetition subscale scores* (III) with the 0.25-0.50 mg. doses (N=14; 2.40 ± 1.31 → 3.81 ± 1.91, t=-3.57, $p < .002$) and the 1.00-2.00 mg. doses (N=11; 2.51 ± 1.85 → 6.95 ± 5.10, t=-3.33, $p < .004$) of triazolam. These combined doses of triazolam (0.25-2.00 mg.) significantly decreased references to *others unfriendly to the self* (IB2) (N=25; 0.30 ± 0.35 → 0.12 ± 0.25, t=2.36, $p < .03$), references to *feeling intact, satisfied, healthy, or well* (IIB3b) (N=25; 0.99 ± 0.82 → 0.42 ± 0.51, t=3.26, $p < .003$), references to *being controlled, feeling controlled, wanting control or being obliged to do, think, or experience something* (IIB5) (N=25; 0.64 ± 0.63 → 0.29 ± 0.48, t=2.66, $p < .01$). These same dosage ranges significantly increased references to *remarks or words that are not understandable or inaudible* (IIIAI) (N=25; 0.48 ± 0.75 → 2.07 ± 2.73, t=-3.15, $p < .005$) and references to *blocking or incomplete sentences, clauses, or phrases,* (IIIA2) (N=25; 0.52 ± 0.61 → 1.38 ± 1.68, t=2.75, $p < .01$).

## DISCUSSION

All of the benzodiazepine derivatives investigated here (lorazepam, diazepam, chlordiazepoxide, triazolam, and flurazepam) had temporary adverse effects on cognitive function as measured from the objective content analysis of five-minute speech samples obtained 30 to 300 minutes after taking single doses of these drugs, either orally, intramuscularly or

intravenously. Similar adverse effects were observed 4 weeks after chronic daily oral doses of diazepam and lorazepam, but these effects did not quite reach statistical significance, possibly because chronic daily dosage with the benzodiazepines induces increased metabolism of these drugs and lower blood levels[22] as well as increased tolerance to the pharmacological effects.[23] The most consistent major adverse and significant effects detected were increases in: (1) Words or remarks that were not understandable or inaudible. (2) Blocking or incomplete sentences, clauses, and phrases. To what extent these changes in the form and/or content of speech reflect more profound deficiencies in cognitive or intellectual function should be explored further. Also, whether similar effects occur with other sedative-hypnotic drugs needs clarification. Our limited data indicates that one hundred twenty minutes after four subjects received either 100 mg. i.v., 120 mg. i.m., 130 mg. i.v., or 260 mg. i.m. of phenobarbital, there was no change in *disorganization and repetition subscale* scores. As noted in the introduction to this report, anterograde amnesic effects have been previously reported in response to various benzodiazepines (lorazepam, diazepam, flurazepam, and triazolam), and the speech defects observed here are consistent with such transient memory impairment.

The benzodiazepines studied here and at the doses employed have been demonstrated elsewhere[8,9,10,11,24] to be capable of producing significant decreases in anxiety and/or hostility outward scores in the content of speech. Whether these anti-anxiety or anti-hostility effects are a result of the cognitive disturbances produced by the benzodiazepines or a concomitant with no causal relationship cannot be ascertained from the data thus far available. The implications of the present findings, however, in combination with the previous findings of anterograde amnesic effects with these benzodiazepines should not be taken lightly or ignored, for at the present time the medical and legal profession do not regard the taking of a single daily therapeutic dose or multiple such doses of these drugs as interferring with the mental competence or responsibility or an individual. This idea should be questioned and examined further.

Certainly, the alleviation of human distress by these medicaments has long been well established. Some, hopefully transient, cognitive and intellectual deficiencies and side effects may be of minor importance in comparison to the beneficial effects of these tranquilizing sedative-hypnotics. Nevertheless, both physician and patient should be alerted to such potential cognitive-intellectual side effects.

*References:*

1. Gottschalk, L.A., and Elliott, H.W.: Effects of triazolam and flurazepam on emotions and intellectual function. *Research Comm. in Psychology, Psychiatry, and Behavior.* 1:575-595, 1977.

2. Clarke, P.R.F., Eccersley, J.P., Frisby, J.P., and Thornton, J.A.: The amnesic effect of diazepam (Valium). *Brit. J. Anaesth. 42:*690-697, 1970.

3. Dundee, J.W., and Pandit, S.K.: Anterograde amnesic effects of pethidine, hyoscine, and diazepam in adults. *Br. J. Pharmac. 40:*140-144, 1972.

4. Wilson, J., and Ellis, F.R.: Oral premedication with lorazepam (Ativan): a comparison with heptabarbitone (Medomin) and diazepam (Valium). *Brit. J. Anaesth. 45:*738-744, 1973.

5. Gregg, J.M., Ryan, D.E., and Levin, K.H.: The amnesic actions of diazepam. *J. Oral Surgery 32:*651-664, 1974.

6. Heisterkamp, D.V., and Cohen, P.J.: The effect of intravenous premedication with lorazepam (Ativan), pentobarbitone or diazepam on recall. *Br. J. Anaesth. 47:*79-81, 1975.

7. Roth, T., Kramer, M., and Lutz, T.: The effects of hypnotics on sleep, performance, and subjective state. Evaluations of New Drugs and Clinical Psychopharmacology. International Symposium, Tirrenia, Italy, Sept., 1975.

8. Gottschalk, L.A., and Kaplan, S.A.: Chlordiazepoxide plasma levels and clinical response. *Compr. Psychaitry 13:*519-527, 1972.

9. Gottschalk, L.A., Elliott, H.W., Bates, D.E., and Cable, C.G.: Content analysis of speech samples to determine effect of Lorazepam on anxiety. *Clin. Pharma. & Therap. 13:*323-328, 1972.

10. Gottschalk, L.A., Noble, E.P., Stolzoff, G.E., Bates, D.E., Cable, C.G., Uliana, R.L., Birch, H., and Fleming, E.W.: Relationship of chlordiazepoxide blood levels to psychological and biochemical responses, in *Benzodiazepines.* S. Garattini, E. Mussini, and L.O. Randall (eds). New York, Raven Press, 1973. pp. 257-283.

11. Gottschalk, L.A., Hoigaard, J., Birch, H., and Rickels, K.: The measurement of psychological states: relationship between Gottschalk-Gleser content analysis scores, and Hamilton Anxiety Rating scale scores, Physician Questionnaire Rating scale scores and Hopkins Symptom Checklist scores. Ch 6 in, *Pharmacokinetics, Psychoactive Drug Blood Levels and Clinical Response.* L.A. Gottschalk and S. Merlis (eds). New York, Spectrum Pub., 1976.

12. Gottschalk, L.A., and Gleser, G.C.: *The Measurement of Psychological States Through the Content Analysis of Verbal Behavior.* Los Angeles, Berkeley, Univ. of California Press, 1969.

13. Gottschalk, L.A., Gleser, G.C., Daniels, R.S., and Block, S.L.: The speech pattern of schizophrenic patients: a method of assessing relative degree of personal disorganization and social alienation.' *J. Nerv. Ment. Dis. 127:*153-166, 1958.

14. Gottschalk, L.A., Gleser, G.C., Magliocco, E.B., and D'Zmura, T.L.: Further studies on the speech patterns of schizophrenic patients. Measuring inter-individual differences in relative degree of personal disorganization and social alienation. *J. Nerv. Ment. Dis. 132:*101-113, 1961.

15. Gottschalk, L.A., Winget, C.N., and Gleser, G.C.: *Manual of Instructions for Using the Gottschalk-Gleser Content Analysis Scales — Anxiety, Hostility, Social Alienation-Personal Disorganization.* Los Angeles, Berkeley, Univ. of California Press, 1969.

16. Gottschalk, L.A., Gleser, G.C., Cleghorn, J.M., Stone, W.N., and Winget, C.N.: Prediction of changes in severity of the schizophrenic syndrome with discontinuation and administration of phenothiazines in chronic schizophrenic patients: language as a predictor and measure of change in schizophrenia. *Compr. Psychiatry 11:*123-140, 1970.

17. Gottschalk, L.A., and Gleser, G.C.: Distinguishing characteristics of the verbal communication of schizophrenic patients, in *Disorders of Communication.* Association for Research in Nervous and Mental Diseases 42:400-413. Baltimore, William and Wilkins, 1964.

18. Schwartz, M.A., and Postma, E.: Metabolic N-demethylation of chlordiazepoxide. *J. Pharmacol. Sci. 55:*1358, 1966.

19. Parloff, M.B., Kelman, H.C., and Frank, J.D.: Comfort, effectiveness, and self-awareness as criteria of improvement in psychotherapy. *Amer. J. Psychiatry 3:*343-351, 1954.

20. Hamilton, M.: The assessment of anxiety states by rating. *Br. J. Med. Psychol. 32:*50-55, 1950.

21. Rickels, K., and Howard, K.: The Physician Questionnaire: a useful tool in psychiatric drug research. *Psychopharmacologia 17:*338-344, 1970.

22. Kanto, J., Iisalo, E., Lehtinen, V., and Salminen, J.: The concentration of diazepam and its major metabolites in the plasma after an acute and chronic administration. *Psychopharmacologia 36:*123-131, 1974.

23. Hillestad, L., Hansen, T., Melson, H., and Drivenes, A.: Diazepam metabolism in normal man. I. Serum concentration and clinical effects after intravenous, intramuscular, and oral administration. *Clin. Pharmacol. Ther. 16:*479-484, 1974.

24. Gleser, G.C., Gottschalk, L.A., Fox, R., and Lippert, W.: Immediate changes in affect with chlordiazepoxide in juvenile delinquent boys. *Arch. Gen. Psychiatry 13:*291-295, 1965.

## APPENDIX

SCHEDULE I

*Content Analysis Scale of (Schizophrenic) Social Alienation and Personal Disorganization*

| Scores (Weights) | | |
|---|---|---|
| Modified* | Original† | Categories and Scoring Symbols‡ |
| | | I. Interpersonal references (including fauna and flora). |
| | | A. To thoughts, feelings or reported actions of avoidance, leaving, deserting, spurning, not understanding of others. |
| 0 | +1 | 1. Self avoiding others. |
| +1 | +1 | 2. Others avoiding self. |
| | | B. To unfriendly, hostile, destructive thoughts, feelings, of actions. |
| +1 | +1 | 1. Self unfriendly to others. |
| +1/3 | +1 | 2. Others unfriendly to self. |

SCHEDULE I — *Continued*

| Scores (Weights) | | |
| --- | --- | --- |
| Modified* | Original† | Categories and Scoring Symbols‡ |
| | | C. To congenial and constructive thoughts, feelings, or actions. |
| -2 | -1 | 1. Others helping, being friendly towards others. |
| -2 | -1 | 2. Self helping, being friendly towards others |
| -2 | -1 | 3. Others helping, being friendly towards self. |
| | | D. To others (including fauna, flora, things and places). |
| 0 | +1 | 1. Bad, dangerous, low value or worth, strange, ill, malfunctioning. |
| -1 | -½ | 2. Intact, satisfied, healthy, well. |
| | | II. Intrapersonal references. |
| | | A. To disorientation-orientation, past, present, or future. (Do not include all references to time, place, or person, but only those in which it is reasonably clear the subject is trying to orient himself or is expressing disorientation with respect to these. Also, do not score more than one item per clause under this category.) |
| +2 | +1 | 1. Indicating disorientation for time, place, or person or other distortion of reality. |
| 0 | -½ | 2. Indicating orientation in time, place, person. |
| 0 | +½ | 3. Indicating attempts to identify time, place, or person without clearly revealing orientation or distorientation. |
| | | B. To self. |
| 0 | +1 | 1a. Physical illness, malfunctioning (references to illness or symptoms due primarily to cellular or tissue damage). |
| +1 | +1 | 1b. Psychological malfunctioning (references to illness or symptoms due primarily to emotions or psychological reactions *not secondary* to cellular or tissue damage). |
| 0 | +1 | 1c. Malfunctioning of indeterminate origin (references to illness or symptoms not definitely attributable either to emotions or cellular damage). |
| -2 | -½ | 2. Getting better. |
| -1 | -1 | 3a. Intact, satisfied, healthy, well; definite positive affect or valence indicated. |
| -1 | -1 | 3b. Intact, satisfied, healthy, well; flat, factual, or neutral attitudes expressed. |
| +½ | +½ | 4. Not being prepared or able to produce, perform, act, not knowing, not sure. |
| +½ | +1 | 5. To being controlled, feeling controlled, wanting control, asking for control or permission, being obliged or having to do, think, or experience something. |
| | | C. Denial of feelings, attitudes, or mental state of the self. |
| | | D. To food. |
| 0 | +1 | 1. Bad, dangerous, unpleasant or otherwise negative; interferences or delays in eating; too much and wish to have less; too little and wish to have more. |
| 0 | -½ | 2. Good or neutral. |
| | | E. To weather. |
| -1 | -½§ | 1. Bad, dangerous, unpleasant or otherwise nega- |

SCHEDULE I — *Continued*

| Scores (Weights) Modified* | Original† | Categories and Scoring Symbols‡ |
|---|---|---|
| | | tive (not sunny, not clear, uncomfortable, etc.) |
| -1 | -1 | 2. Good, pleasanr or neutral. |
| | | F. To sleep. |
| 0 | +1 | 1. Bad, dangerous, unpleasant or otherwise negative; too much, too little. |
| 0 | -½ | 2. Good, pleasant or neutral. |
| | | III. Miscellaneous. |
| | | A. Signs of disorganization. |
| +1 | +1 | 1. Remarks or words that are not understandable or inaudible. |
| 0 | +1 | 2. Incomplete sentences, clauses, phrases; blocking. |
| +2 | +1 | 3. Obviously erroneous or fallacious remarks or conclusions; illogical or bizarre statements. |
| | | B. Repetition of ideas in sequence. |
| 0 | †½ | 1. Words separated only by a word (excluding instances due to grammatical and syntactical convention, where words are repeated, e.g., "as far as," "by and by," and so forth. Also, excluding instances where such words as "I" and "the" are separated by a word). |
| +1 | +1 | 2. Phrases, clauses (separated only by a phrase or clause). |
| | | New Items |
| +1 | 0 | IV. A. Questions directed to the interviewer. |
| +½ | 0 | B. Other references to the interviewer. |
| +1 | 0 | V. Religious and biblical references. |

* These weights are a revision of the weights described in our 1961 publication so as to indicate the findings obtained in the study herein reported. These weights are more sensitive and discriminatory in cross-sectional studies and studies involving the task of differentiating schizophrenics from nonschizophrenics. They can be used satisfactorily in longitudinal investigations. Note that categories signifying evidence of the schizophrenic syndrome are given positive weights and vice versa.

† Described in our 1958 publication. These weights may be more sensitive in longitudinal studies. Note that the direction of scoring is reversed as compared to the weights given in our 1958 publication to conform with the modified weights.

‡ For the rules for scoring the categories, see our manual (Gottschalk *et al.*, 1969).

§ Scored +½ for the first two in a verbal sample and thereafter this item is scored -1.

SCHEDULE II

*Cognitive and Intellectual Impairment Scale*

| Weights | Content Categories and Scoring Symbols |
|---|---|
| | I. Interpersonal References (including fauna and flora). |
| | B. To unfriendly, hostile, destructive thoughts, feelings, or actions. |
| -½ | 1. Self unfriendly to others. |

SCHEDULE II — *Continued*

| Weights | Content Categories and Scoring Symbols |
|---|---|
| | C. To congenial and constructive thoughts, feelings, or actions. |
| -½ | 1. Others helping, being friendly toward others. |
| -½ | 2. Self helping, being friendly toward others. |
| -½ | 3. Others helping, being friendly toward self. |
| | II. Intrapersonal References. |
| +3 | A. To disorientation-orientation, past, present or future (do not include all references to time, place, or person, but only those in which it is reasonably clear the subject is trying to orient himself or is expressing disorientation with respect to these; also, do not score more than one item per clause under this category). |
| | B. To self. |
| -½ | 1. Injured, ailing, deprived, malfunctioning, getting worse, bad, dangerous, low value or worth, strange. |
| +¼ | 3. Intact, satisfied, healthy, well. |
| +1 | 5. To being controlled, feeling controlled, wanting control, asking for control or permission, being obliged or having to do, think or experience something. |
| +1 | C. Denial of feelings, attitudes, or mental state of the self. |
| | D. To food. |
| -1 | 2. Good or neutral. |
| | III. Miscellaneous. |
| | A. Signs of disorganization. |
| +1 | 2. Incomplete sentences, clauses, phrases; blocking. |
| | B. Repetition of ideas in sequence. |
| +1 | 2. Phrases, clauses (separated only by a phrase or clause). |
| +½ | IV. A. Questions Directed to the Interviewer. |

# Peripheral Versus Central Mechanisms Accounting for Antianxiety Effects of Propranolol

LOUIS A. GOTTSCHALK, MD, WALTER N. STONE, MD, AND GOLDINE C. GLESER, PHD

A β-adrenergic blocking agent, propranolol (60 mg orally in three divided doses over a 12-hr period), significantly reduced basal anxiety scores in 12 healthy, nonanxious subjects as compared to a placebo in another 12 similar subjects. In response to a 10-min stress interview, anxiety scores increased to equal levels, whether subjects were on propranolol or a placebo. On placebo, anxiety scores correlated positively (+0.70) with average plasma FFA. On propranolol, anxiety scores correlated negatively (−0.55) with plasma FFA and the average pulse rate was significantly lowered. The experimental findings suggest that basal or resting anxiety may be maintained by peripheral afferent autonomic biofeedback, and the latter can be reduced by β-adrenergic blocking agents; whereas, the magnitude of acutely aroused anxiety is mediated more through the central nervous system.

The development of drugs that block autonomic receptors has provided one avenue for the study of the complex interrelationships between affects, autonomic stimulation, and physiological response. The availability of oral and intravenous forms of a beta adrenergic receptor blocking drug (beta blocking), propranolol, makes possible both laboratory and clinical studies aimed at elucidating the role of the autonomic nervous system in the experience of anxiety. Antianxiety effects of beta adrenergic receptor blockade have been demonstrated in anxious psychiatric patients after single or multiple intravenous injections of propranolol (1,2). Similarly, continued oral administration of beta blocking drugs to patients has been reported to be effective in reducing symptoms of anxiety (3,4,5,6). Autonomically mediated symptoms such as palpitations, sweating, and diarrhea have been most noticeably affected in these patients. A second approach to studying beta adrenergic blockade has involved the study of its effects on experimental stress and anxiety. In contrast to the beneficial effects of beta adrenergic blockade with anxious symptomatic patients, Bogdonoff and Estes (7) found that intravenous propranolol did not reduce anxiety in volunteers who were anxious to confrontation with a hypodermic needle. Similarly, in hypnotized volunteers receiving placebo or intravenous propranolol, Pinter et al. (8) and Cleghorn et al. (9) did not find differences in anxiety levels, derived from the content analysis of verbal samples, following stressful or nonstressful suggestions. In these studies, utilizing volunteers, autonomic blockade was demonstrated by a lowering of plasma FFA.

From the University of California, Irvine, California, and the University of Cincinnati, Cincinnati, Ohio.

Address reprint requests to: L.A. Gottschalk, M.D., Dept. of Psychiatry and Human Behavior, College of Medicine, University of California, Irvine, California 92664.

Received for publication February 20, 1973; revision received May 29, 1973.

## PURPOSES

The present study was designed to examine the psychobiological effects of

oral doses of a beta adrenergic blocking drug, propranolol, in volunteer subjects, under both nonstressful and stressful conditions. We aimed to determine whether reducing the autonomic correlates of anxiety, through such pharmacologic means, reduced the basal (resting) anxiety level, but did not necessarily reduce the subject's capacity to respond with increased anxiety to stressful stimuli. The decreased afferent biofeedback from the cardiovascular system and other adrenergic pathways when the subjects were on propranolol, we reasoned, would proportionately reduce the subject's feelings of anxiety—as adjudged from decreased visceral and somatic reactions —in the resting state, but he might still be aroused to higher anxiety levels through interpersonal interactions contrived to evoke anxiety.

In previous work, we demonstrated that anxiety scores, derived from a speech sample by an objective content analysis method (10) correlated positively with the level of average plasma Free Fatty Acids (FFA) and the increase in FFA to experimental stimuli (11,12). Furthermore, the rise in FFA during a 15 min interval after the onset of REM sleep correlated with anxiety scores derived from the content analysis of dreams reported after being awakened from this REM sleep (13). The work of other investigators (14,15,16) indicates that an increase of plasma FFA in fasting human subjects is a sensitive indicator of the secretion of primary and secondary catecholamines which are hydroxylated on the beta carbon of the side chain. From this we concluded that our previous studies (11,12,13) demonstrate that the Gottschalk-Gleser anxiety score covaries with the secretion of certain catecholamines in the bloodstream and that plasma FFA (in fasting subjects) can be used as an indirect, sensitive measure of adrenergic secretion.

In the present study, we postulated that subjects receiving propranolol orally would show decreased anxiety, bradycardia, and lower levels of plasma FFA compared to the placebo group. We selected an oral dose of propranolol (60 mg over a 12 hr period) that we had found, from a previous, unpublished pilot study, would significantly lower resting heart rate in medically healthy males: we thought that this same dose level would be likely to lower fasting and resting plasma FFA.

## METHODS

Nonanxious college men, aged 21–28, served as paid volunteers for this double-blind, placebo-propranolol study. Subjects were told that we were studying the effect of a drug that might change their heart rate, but we were primarily interested in the effect upon their emotions and changes in certain biochemicals in their blood. Subjects were told that they would be asked to give two five-min speech samples (10) during a one-hr morning experimental period. They were then given an envelope containing either six placebo or six 10-mg propranolol tablets. The envelopes were coded and randomly assigned to subje ts with instructions to take two tablets after dinner, two at bedtime, and two upon arising the morning of the experimental procedure. Except for the water necessary to swallow the tablets, subjects were instructed not to eat or smoke after the evening meal. Thus, all subjects had fasted 12–14 hours by the

time speech and blood samples were obtained.

In the morning, just preceding the experimental period, the subject rested sitting quietly for one-half hr. For the remainder of the experimental period, the subject lay on a table and his left arm was placed through a screen. He could observe the initial venipuncture, but thereafter he was screened from seeing further blood samples being taken so that the sight of his own blood might not evoke anxiety and any associated biochemical reactions.

Blood samples were obtained through a 19-gauge needle placed in the antecubital vein and secured. A short piece of connecting tubing was attached to a three-way stopcock; one end was available to withdraw blood samples; the other was attached to normal saline, which was slowly infused to prevent clotting in the needle. The initial portion of each sample was discarded to ensure the emptying of the connecting tubing. Blood samples were obtained at the time of venipuncture and at 5, 15, 20, 25, 35, 40, 45, 50, and 55 min later.

A five-min verbal sample was obtained immediately following the initial blood sample in response to standardized and purposely ambiguous instructions to speak into the microphone of a tape recorder about any interesting or dramatic personal life experiences. After collecting the 25-min blood sample, the experimenter moved from behind the screen and interviewed the subject for 10 min. The focus during this interview was upon life events which upset, worried, or evoked anxiety in the subject. The interviewer actively searched for these topics but permitted the subject to speak freely when he seemed to be talking about an area that involved feelings of anxiety. Following this "stress" interview, blood was drawn for the 35-min, FFA sample, and then a second five-min sample of speech was obtained. After the final blood sample was obtained and before removing the indwelling needle, resting pulse rate was obtained for one min at the radial artery.

A total of 24 subjects completed the study, 12 in each group. Two content analysis technicians independently analyzed the two five-min speech verbal samples and two five-min segments of the verbalizations of each subject during the stress interview for anxiety by the method of Gottschalk and Gleser (10). The average of the two scores was used in all calculations. The blood samples were analyzed for FFA by the method of Dole (14) as modified by Trout et al. (17).

## RESULTS

Average anxiety scores and standard deviations for the propranolol and placebo groups are shown in Table 1. As a group, those subjects who received propranolol had significantly lower anxiety scores on the first five-min speech sample than those receiving a placebo ($p < 0.05$, one-tail Mann-Whitney). Thirty-five min later, immediately following the 10 min interview focused on eliciting anxiety, subjects in both placebo and propranolol groups had increased anxiety scores, and there was no longer a significant difference in anxiety scores between the two groups. During the stress interview, subjects in both groups had higher scoreable anxiety, as indicated in Table 1.

Data for plasma FFA are presented in Table 2. Although the average values of FFA were lower for the propranolol groups than for the placebo group at each

**TABLE 1. Means and Standard Deviations of Anxiety Scores from Spontaneous Verbal Samples and Focused Interviews**

| | Placebo Mean | s.d. | Propranolol Mean | s.d. |
|---|---|---|---|---|
| Verbal Sample (0–5 min) ($N$ = 12) | 1.32 | 0.52 | 1.00[a] | 0.46 |
| Focused Interview (25–30 min) ($N$ = 10) | 1.79 | 0.63 | 1.75 | 0.44 |
| Focused Interview (30–35 min) ($N$ = 10) | 1.99 | 0.45 | 2.38 | 0.29 |
| Verbal Sample (35–40 min) ($N$ = 12) | 1.41 | 0.79 | 1.34 | 0.43 |

[a]Significantly different from control ($p < 0.05$) by one-tailed t-test.

**TABLE 2. Means and Standard Deviations of Averages of FFA Determinations Before and After Focused Interview and Correlations with Anxiety in Verbal Samples**

| | Plasma FFA Levels (μEq/L) | | Correlations with Anxiety Score | |
|---|---|---|---|---|
| | Mean | s.d. | First 5 min | After Interview |
| | | Placebo ($N$ = 12) | | |
| Ave. FFA (0–25 min) | 600 | 214 | 0.72[a] | 0.09 |
| Ave. FFA (35–55 min) | 621 | 223 | 0.69[a] | 0.04 |
| | | Propranolol ($N$=12) | | |
| Ave. FFA (0–25 min) | 540 | 194 | −0.55[b] | 0.32 |
| Ave. FFA (35–55 min) | 538 | 221 | −0.56[b] | 0.38 |

[a]Significantly different from zero ($p < 0.05$).
[b]Very significantly different from corresponding values in placebo group ($p < 0.01$).

determination, there were no significant differences between the groups at any of the time periods or between levels of FFA averaged over time periods. Both groups showed the typical rise in FFA levels following a venipuncture and the request to speak for five min that we have reported in previous studies (11,12). A similar rise in FFA levels followed the stress interview and second verbal sample. Average plasma FFA in the 25-min period prior to the "stress" interview did not differ from the average FFA in the 20-min period following the interview for either placebo or propranolol group.

A significant, positive correlation ($r$ = 0.70) between anxiety scores (from the first speech sample) and plasma FFA levels averaged over the entire experimental period was found for subjects receiving placebo. But this correlation was negative ($r = -0.55$) and not significant, for those receiving propranolol. The difference in correlation under the two conditions was highly significant ($p \angle$ 0.01) Pulse rates for the placebo and drug groups at the end of the 55-min session were significantly different ($p \angle$ 0.05, d.f. 16). Those subjects receiving propranolol had average pulse rate of 52.4/min.

(s.d.=5.2); those receiving placebo had an average rate of 58.5/min. (s.d.=5.6).

## DISCUSSION

Our results with nonanxious subjects are similar to the clinical reports in which symptomatically anxious patients reported decreased anxiety with beta adrenergic blocking drugs. Our subjects, receiving 60 mg of propranolol orally in three divided oral doses over a 12–14 hr period, had significantly lower anxiety scores than the placebo group. This anxiety-decreasing effect of propranolol was rather remarkable because our subjects were not selected on the basis of their being anxious; the average anxiety score of the placebo group at the beginning to the experimental period (1.32) was, as a matter of fact, only at the 42nd percentile, for a group of normative subjects ($N$=282) and at the 25th percentile for a group of psychiatric outpatients ($N$=107) using our anxiety scale (10, p. 70).

Following the stress-focussed interview, both the control and drug subjects had greater scoreable anxiety than initially, and the scores no longer differentiated the two groups. In this respect our results are similar to those obtained by Pinter et al. (8) and Cleghorn et al. (9) who reported no differences in anxiety levels following stressful and nonstressful suggestions in hypnotized subjects receiving intravenous propranolol.

Levels of plasma FFA did not differ for the propranolol and placebo groups, although they were consistently lower in all subjects on propranolol. In both groups, plasma FFA increased after the stimuli of a venipuncture and request to talk for five min and again after the stress-focussed interview, regardless of whether or not the subject had taken propranolol. These findings are also consistent with those reported by Pinter et al. (8), who found increased plasma FFA following hypnosis and five min of free speech in both propranolol and placebo subjects although the FFA rise was smaller in the placebo group. Ripley et al. (18) also reported plasma FFA increases following hypnosis in spite of beta adrenergic blockade.

The propranolol group had a significantly lower resting pulse than the placebo group at the end of the experiment, indicating some adrenergic blocking effect of propranolol.

What is the mechanism by which propranolol reduces anxiety? We propose two alternative or interlocking hypotheses:

(1) *The beta adrenergic blocking agent reduces peripheral beta adrenergic neural transmission and, hence, the afferent feedback from the peripheral nervous system to the central nervous system. The consequent reduction of these adrenergic visceral and somatic autonomic correlates of anxiety reduces the anxiety-reinforcing aspect of afferent biofeedback to the central nervous system.*

If this hypothesis explains the mechanism of anxiety reduction by propranolol, basal anxiety levels should be reduced, compared to anxiety levels with placebo, but the arousability of anxiety levels through the central nervous system should be unchanged. This is, indeed, what we found in our study. Resting or basal anxiety levels were reduced in the propranolol group, compared to the placebo group, but the capacity of the subjects to respond with increased anxie-

ty to a stressful interview was as marked in the propranolol as in the placebo group. To us, this strongly suggests that the reduction of peripheral afferent messages to the central nervous system, from deactivated beta adrenergic innervations, decreased this mechanism of maintenance of anxiety levels.

Along this line of reasoning, the James-Lange theory (19) defined emotion as the perception of bodily changes, namely, that the arousal and maintenance of fear was initiated peripheral to the central nervous system; "I fear because I run," rather than "I run because I fear," was the paradigm by which the James-Lange theory of emotions signified that afferent feedback from excited visceral and somatic innervations resulted in the subjective experience of fear or anxiety. Cannon's (20) objections to the James-Lange theory of emotions suggested that bodily changes have little importance as determinants of emotional experience and that emotions could be experienced without the occurrence of bodily changes.

Different aspects of anxiety may involve different mechanisms, namely, the *maintenance of anxiety* (through afferent biofeedback—consistent with the James-Lange theory—or other neurochemical mechanisms) and the *arousal of anxiety* (through direct nervous system stimulation—consistent with the Cannon theory). Some experimental support for the importance of afferent autonomic biofeedback in the maintenance of fear responses has been provided by Wynne and Solomon (21) who demonstrated that dogs with bilateral sympathectomies had reduced resistance to the extinction of conditioned aversion responses. These same conditioned aversion reactions were resistant to extinction without surgical and/or pharmacological blocking of autonomic innervation.

Valins (22), in an excellent critical review of the literature, has presented evidence from human studies that peripheral bodily changes can function as determinants as well as correlates of emotions. Bodily changes initiate cognitive processes that influence subjective and behavioral reactions to emotional stimuli. Manipulating the perception of bodily changes—pharmacologically, naturally, or by deception—permits the arousal or inhibition of emotional behavior and the prediction of individual differences in such behavior. However, bodily changes alone have little effect on emotions if an individual does not attribute these changes to emotional stimuli.

In further substantiation of the capacity of peripheral bodily changes to influence the magnitude of emotions, the bradycardia serves as a marker of some beta adrenergic blocking effect. Also, the reversal of the significant positive correlation (+0.70) between anxiety scores and the average plasma FFA levels when our subjects were on placebo by the administration of the beta adrenergic blocker (−0.50) supports the idea that, ordinarily, anxiety levels and peripheral adrenergic activity (as observed indirectly through following plasma FFA levels in fasting subjects) are functionally interrelated and the greater the anxiety level the more adrenergic secretion. The break-up of this functional interrelationship between anxiety and adrenergic activity by a beta adrenergic blocking agent may be achieved through reducing the biofeedback mechanism, although admittedly some other effect on the intervening variables in the chain of events (for example, a decrease in functional brain

catecholamine or brain glucose—see below) may also account for the break-up of this positive correlation

(2) *The beta adrenergic blocking agents have a direct effect on the central nervous system, as well as the peripheral nervous system, and this central effect primarily accounts for the decrease in the basal anxiety level.*

Cannon's theory of emotions (19) held that the affect of fear or anxiety originates in the central nervous system and the visceral and somatic concomitants of anxiety are secondary to the arousal of this affect. In support of this hypothesis is the observation that some individuals can evoke mental images of anxious situations and bring on signs of peripheral autonomic activation, such as, tachycardia, decreased blood flow in the fingers, lowering of skin temperature, and so forth. The report of Gottschalk et al. (13) of a significant correlation between increased plasma FFA the greater the anxiety scores from the content of 15 min of REM dreaming supports this view indirectly, for increasing plasma FFA (e.g. by eating food) does not in itself increase anxiety but increasing the anxiety level does increase plasma FFA. And the parenteral injection of adrenalin or noradrenalin does not necessarily evoke the subjective reaction of anxiety (23, 24). Nisbett and Schacter (24) have demonstrated that the recognition by an individual that an emotional stimulus has caused one's body to react can result in a reevaluation of the emotional stimulus and a more intensely perceived stimulus can heighten the subject's emotional reaction.

The facts are not yet all in with respect to the neurochemical mediation of anxiety in the central nervous system. A traditional viewpoint is that adrenalin, noradrenalin, or other catecholamines, acting as neurotransmitters across synapses in the brain, are involved as chemical mediators in the fear response and that various pharmacological "antianxiety" agents (tranquilizers and sedative-hypnotics) in various ways reduce the functional and available catecholamines at the synaptic level. Presumably, beta adrenergic blocking agents, which can and do pass through the blood-brain barrier, could be capable of reducing the level of certain catecholamines in specialized adrenergic pathways of the brain so that anxiety levels would be decreased. In this connection Bonn et al. (25), in a double-blind sequential trial, found a significant antianxiety effect with anxious patients using a beta adrenergic blocking agent (practolol, 400 mg per day) that does not readily enter the brain; these findings support the hypothesis that peripheral rather than central beta receptor blockade accounts for antianxiety effects of beta adrenergic blockers. But such findings do not rule out central actions of propranolol, a drug which does enter the brain. A different neurochemical mechanism that could explain the effect of propranolol on anxiety is the finding by Leonard (26) that propranolol increases glucose uptake and glycogenesis and decreases glycolysis in the mouse brain, an effect not predictable from its peripheral action. These findings with propranolol parallel those reported by Gey (27) with two clinical antianxiety agents (chlordiazepoxide and diazepam) that also reduce glycolysis in rat brain, apparently at the phase of glucose phosphorylation. Gey suggests that these benzodiazepenes may achieve their antianxiety effects by reducing the rate of glycolysis in the

brain, which is very sensitive to changes in glucose metabolism. It is, hence, quite conceivable that propranolol may directly lower anxiety levels via this specific neurochemical route. In support of a direct sedative effect of propranolol on the brain is the finding that in large doses propranolol has sedative and anticonvulsive properties (28, 29) and will prolong the hypnotic effect of chloral hydrate.

If this second hypothesis accounting for the antianxiety effect of propranolol were to prevail, we would not expect to find that anxiety in our propranolol group would be aroused to similar levels as in our placebo group under the circumstances of a stressful interview. We are inclined, hence to favor our first hypothesis as primarily accounting for the antianxiety effect of propranolol.

It may well be, however that both antianxiety mechanisms of action that we have postulated are involved, both the reduction of peripheral afferent feedback and the direct central effect. What is missing in resolving these issues is to what extent do the benzodiazepenes, barbiturates and other sedative-hypnotic drugs reduce the arousability of anxiety with stressful stimuli? There is evidence that rats (30) pretreated with oxazepam and humans (31) pretreated with chlordiazepoxide do show decreased plasma FFA responses to stressful stimuli, which suggests that propranolol's antianxiety effect is achieved through a different neurochemical mechanism than with the benzodiazepines. We have considered other viewpoints concerning the implications of our findings elsewhere (32).

The dosage of propranolol used in the present study was not high enough to inhibit lipolysis substantially in all subjects. A higher dose over a longer time period might eventuate in primarily a direct central effect. Additional studies, using larger doses of propranolol, including subjects with higher anxiety levels, would be useful in further exploring this matter.

In the meantime, we suggest that the idea of reducing the basal anxiety level of individuals by reducing afferent biofeedback from the peripheral nervous system is an approach to the management of anxiety that also merits further exploration.

The old controversy involving the James-Lange and Cannon theories regarding the origin and maintenance of emotions, and whether or not the sensation of emotions originates in the peripheral nervous system or central nervous system may seem out-dated in terms of our advances in the neuropsychopharmacology and neurophysiology. But these old theories point up two polarized viewpoints on the psychophysiology of emotions that separately contain valid descriptions concerning the arousal and maintenance of emotions; both theories, we think, are true rather than one or the other. Keeping these two possibilities in mind can sharpen the directions of our psychosomatic and somatopsychic research and the conclusions we draw from our experimental findings.

## SUMMARY

Twenty-four healthy volunteers were given 60 mg of propranolol (a β-adrenergic blocking agent) or placebo divided into three equal oral doses during the twelve hr preceding a 55-min experimental procedure. After 12 hr on propranolol, subjects receiving propranolol had sig-

nificantly lower average anxiety scores, as measured by the content analysis of speech, than subjects on placebo. The correlation between these anxiety scores and the average of five plasma free fatty acid determinations, obtained every 5–10 min over a 25-min interval, was positive and significant for the 12 subjects on placebo ($r$=0.70) and negative for the 12 propranolol subjects ($r$=–0.55); the difference between these correlations was highly significant ($p < 0.01$). A 10-min stress interview beginning 25 min after the start of the experimental procedure was followed by an increase in the average anxiety scores to similar levels in both propranolol and placebo groups. Pulse rate at the end of the 55-min session was significantly lower ($p < 0.05$) for subjects on propranolol. Plasma FFA determinations, though lower with propranolol, did not differ significantly for the two groups.

The significance of these findings in terms of the James-Lange and Cannon theories of emotion is examined. Our experimental results suggest that the antianxiety effects of propranolol are achieved, at least in part, by reducing the afferent autonomic biofeedback to the central nervous system, a process which ordinarily helps maintain the level of anxiety-fear, but which does not necessarily inhibit the capacity of the organism to respond with anxiety-fear to stressful stimuli perceived through auditory and visual pathways.

*This study was supported in part by research funds from the Veterans Administration Hospital, Cincinnati, Ohio. The drug and matching placebo were supplied by Ayerst Laboratories, New York. Technical assistance was provided by Carolyn Winget and Mary Danzeisen.*

## References


1. Turner P, Granville-Grossman KL, Smart JV: Effect of adrenergic receptor blockade on the tachycardia of thyrotoxicosis and anxiety state. Lancet 2:1316–1318, 1965
2. Nordenfelt O: Orthostatic ECG changes and the adrenergic beta-receptor blocking agent: propranolol (Inderal). Acta Med Scand 178:393–401, 1965
3. De Risio C, Murmann W: Anxiety and the pulse. Brit Med J 2:373, 1967
4. Granville-Grossman KL, Turner P: The effect of propranolol on anxiety. Lancet 1:788–790, 1966
5. Suzman M: An evaluation of the effects of propranolol on the symptoms and electrocardiographic changes in patients with anxiety and hyperventilation syndrome. (Abstr) Ann Int Med 68:1194, 1968
6. Wheatley D: Comparative effects of propranolol and chlordiazepoxide in anxiety states. Brit J Psychiat 115:1411–1412, 1969
7. Bogdonoff MD, Estes EH Jr: Energy dynamics and acute states of arousal in man. Psychosom Med 23:23–32, 1961
8. Pinter EJ, Peterfy G, Cleghorn JM, Pattee CJ: The influence of emotional stress on fat mobilization: The role of endogenous catecholamines and the -adrenergic receptors. Amer J Med Sci 254:634–651, 1967
9. Cleghorn JM, Peterfy G, Pinter EJ, Pattee CJ: Verbal anxiety and the beta adrenergic receptors: A facilitating mechanism? J Nerv Ment Dis 151:266–273, 1970
10. Gottschalk LA, Gleser GC: The Measurement of Psychological States Through the Content Analysis of Verbal Behavior. Berkeley, Univ Calif Press, 1969
11. Gottschalk LA, Cleghorn JM, Gleser GC, Iacono JM: Studies of relationships of emotions to plasma lipids. Psychosom Med 27:102–111, 1965

12. Stone WN, Gleser GC, Gottschalk LA, Iacono JM: Stimulus, affect, and plasma fatty acid. Psychosom Med 31:331–341, 1969
13. Gottschalk LA, Stone WN, Gleser GC, Iacono JM: Anxiety levels in dreams: Relation to changes in plasma free fatty acids. Science 153:654–657, 1966
14. Dole VP: Relation between non-esterified fatty acids in plasma and metabolism of glucose. J Clin Invest 35:150–154, 1956
15. Gordon RS Jr, Cherkes A: Unesterified fatty acid in human blood plasma. J Clin Invest 35:206, 1956
16. Mueller PS, Horowitz D: Plasma free fatty acid and blood glucose responses to analogues of norephinephrine in man. J Lipid Res 3:251, 1962
17. Trout DL, Estes EH Jr, Friedberg SJ: Titration of FFA of plasma: A study of current methods and a new modification. J Lipid Res 1:199–202, 1960
18. Ripley HS, Cobb LA, Jones JW: Mobilization of free fatty acids during hypnosis, in Proceedings of Annual Meeting of the American Psychiatric Association, San Francisco, 1970
19. James W: The Principles of Psychology. New York, Holt, 1890
20. Cannon WB: Bodily Changes in Pain, Hunger, Fear and Rage. New York, Appleton, 1915
21. Wynne LC, Solomon RL: Traumatic avoidance learning: acquisition and extinction in dogs deprived of normal peripheral autonomic function. Genet Psychol Monogr 52:241–284, 1955
22. Valins S: The perception and labeling of bodily changes, in Physiological Correlations of Emotion. Edited by P Black, New York, Academic, 1970
23. Schachter S, Singer JE: Cognitive, social, and physiological determinants of emotional state. Psychol Rev 69:379–399, 1962
24. Nisbett RE, Schachter S: Cognitive manipulation of pain. J Exp. Soc Psychol 2:227–236, 1966
25. Bonn JA, Turner P, Hicks DC: Beta-adrenergic-receptor blockade with practolol in treatment of anxiety. Lancet 1:814–815, 1972
26. Leonard BE: The effect of some β-adrenergic receptor blocking drugs on carbohydrate metabolism in mouse brain. Neuropharmacol 10:127–144, 1971.
27. Gey KF: Effect of benzodiazepines on carbohydrate metabolism in rat brain, In The Benzodiazepines, Edited by Garattini S, Mussini E, Randall, LO, New York, Raven Press, 1973
28. Leszkovsky G, Tardos L: Some effects of propranolol on the central nervous system. J Pharm Pharmac 17:518–519, 1965
29. Murmann W, Almirante L, Saccani-Guelfi M: Central nervous system effects of four β-adrenergic receptor blocking agents. J Pharm Pharmac 18:317–318, 1966
30. Khan, AV, Forney RB, Hughes FW: Plasma free fatty acids in rats after shock modified by centrally active drugs. Arch Intern Pharmacodyn, 151:466, 1964
31. Brown ML, Sletten IW, Kleinman KM, Karol B: Effect of oxazepam on physiological responses to stress in normal subjects. Curr Ther Res 10:543, 1968
32. Stone, WN, Gleser, GC, Gottschalk, LA: Anxiety and adrenergic blockade, Arch Gen Psychiat. (in press), 1973.

# Chlordiazepoxide Plasma Levels and Clinical Responses

By Louis A. Gottschalk and Stanley A. Kaplan

THIS IS A REPORT of one aspect of a research program involving the exploration of psychoactive drug plasma levels and the associated clinical responses. The special focus of the study being reported is the relationship of chlordiazepoxide blood levels (92 ± 20 minutes after the ingestion of 25 mg of chlordiazepoxide in 18 anxious individuals who fasted ten to 12 hours) to changes in anxiety, hostility, and other psychological levels.

No one has reported finding any definite relationship between chlordiazepoxide drug levels and the degree of emotional response. Very recent studies on the blood levels and half-life of chlordiazepoxide and its metabolites have not dealt with clinical responses.[31]

Many studies have been carried out examining the effect of the oral administration of chlordiazepoxide on anxiety or hostility. In general, there is substantial evidence that chlordiazepoxide in single or repeated doses can reduce anxiety/fear. Depending on the research design and measurement instruments some investigators report a decrease in hostility or aggression with chlordiazepoxide,[12,27,35] whereas others report increases in certain kinds of hostility.[10,28,34]

A previous study using an objective method of measuring anxiety and three kinds of hostility (hostility outward, hostility inward, and ambivalent hostility through the content analysis of speech has demonstrated that chlordiazepoxide (20 mg) by mouth, compared to a placebo, significantly decreased anxiety, overt hostility outward, and ambivalent hostility in 16-17-year-old juvenile delinquent boys.[12]

The present study aimed not only to replicate findings from this earlier investigation, but also to extend the study to explore the influence of blood levels of this psychoactive pharmacological agent on the clinical response.

## PROCEDURE

### *Subjects*

Subjects participating were paid volunteers who were in good physical health and free of any disabling medical disorders. There were selected, in all, 18 anxious subjects (14 males and 4 females) psychiatrically screened by a preliminary interview so that they all had anxiety levels equal to or greater than 4 on the anxiety rating scale of the Overall-Gorham Brief Psychiatric Rating Scale.[26] In addition, they were carefully interviewed to be certain that they were not currently taking drugs of any kind and had not done so for at least four weeks, and they were told not to drink alcohol, coffee, or to smoke tobacco for 24 hours before each testing period. Subjects who were using any hormonal medication, such as birth control pills and so forth, were, of course, rejected from participation in this study.

---

*From the Department of Psychiatry and Human Behavior, University of California at Irvine, Irvine, Calif. and the Orange County Medical Center, Orange, Calif.*

*Supported in part from Grant MH-20174 from the National Institute of Mental Health; and also from a Grant-in-Aid from Hoffmann-LaRoche, Inc.*

## METHOD

Subjects were told simply that this was a study of the relationship of emotions, especially anxiety, to body chemistry and the effect of a small dose by mouth of a mild tranquilizer or a placebo on these emotions. Furthermore, they were advised they would have to come to the Mental Health Outpatient Clinic, Orange County Medical Center, twice in the morning for about one and one-half hours on each occasion, at least one week apart, after eating a supper the previous night between 6:00 and 8:00 p.m. and fasting thereafter until the experimental session began.

The research utilized a double-blind, cross-over design balanced for order, nine of the subjects taking a placebo capsule first and the other nine first taking 25 mg of chlordiazepoxide in capsule form. Since all subjects were anxious, paid volunteers and not registered inpatients or outpatients at the Medical Center, they were given two identical capsules (one containing a placebo and the other chlordiazepoxide) after being accepted for the study and fully instructed which capsule to take before their first and second visits to the Clinic. Instructions were so designed that ingestion of the capsules took place about one and one-fourth hours before collection of psychological and biochemical data was carried out. On checking the actual time of ingestion of each subject's capsules, the average time between ingestion and the start of data collection was 92 minutes, the standard deviation was ± 20, and the range was from 60 to 145 minutes. Actual measurement of chlordiazepoxide blood levels, reassuringly, revealed that subjects did take their placebo and chlordiazepoxide capsules at designated times so that the cross-over design was perfectly balanced.

On arrival for the experimental procedure the subjects were first quizzed briefly about when they had had supper the previous evening, what time they had taken their capsule, and whether or not they had taken any other drugs of any kind. If they had taken any other drugs than those specified, or the fasting since the preceding night's supper had been violated, the experimental procedure was not carried any further. Such subjects were either dropped from the study and replaced by another individual or if it was possible to arrange without compromising the research design, the subject was asked to return on another occasion.

Subjects were then asked to lie down on a bed, they were permitted to relax and get comfortable for about 15 minutes, one of the subject's arms was put through a cloth screen so that the subject could not see the next procedure although he was told what was going on, and then an indwelling intravenous catheter was inserted in an antecubital vein and normal saline solution was allowed to infuse slowly into the vein to prevent clotting of blood. The system was so arranged that blood could be withdrawn from the subject without the subject knowing when it was being withdrawn. Immediately after insertion of the intravenous catheter (time zero), 20-25 cc. of blood was withdrawn and put into a heparinized tube. At ten minute intervals thereafter, for a total of 50 minutes, similar amounts of blood were withdrawn for biochemical determinations. At time zero minutes and at 50 minutes, the subject was asked to give a five-minute speech sample into the microphone of a tape recorder in response to standardized instructions to talk for five minutes about any interesting or dramatic personal life experiences; this is the data collection procedure for the objective measurement of psychological states according to the procedure of Gottschalk and Gleser.[13,16]

The heparinized blood samples were immediately, as drawn, stored in chipped ice until the experiment was over; then, after spinning down, the supernatant plasma was pipetted off and rapidly frozen. Biochemical determinations were subsequently carried out on the 18 subjects. Plasma-free fatty acids were determined by the method of Antonis,[1] triglycerides by the method of Kessler and Lederer,[21] glucose by the method of Frings, Ratcliff, and Dunn,[9] cortisol by the method of Butte and Noble (1969),[4] cholesterol by the method of Huang, Chen, Wefler, and Raftery,[20] uric acid by the method of Musser and Ortegoza,[25] insulin by the method of Hales and Randle,[18,19] calcium by the method of Gitelman,[11] chlordiazepoxide and metabolites by the method of Schwartz and Postma,[30] creatinine by the Technicon method,[33] glutamic oxalacetic transaminase (SGOT) and lactic dehydrogenase (LDH) according to Kessler et al.,[22] and alkaline phosphatase following the method of Morgenstern et al.[23]

Typescripts of the five-minute speech samples were scored blindly for the magnitude of various psychological states according to the Gottschalk-Gleser method[13] by content analysis technicians who were unfamiliar with the purpose of the research. Scores were obtained from all speech samples on anxiety, hostility outward (total, overt, and covert), hostility inward, ambivalent hostility (based on self-references to others making hostile remarks about the speaker), human relations, and achievement strivings.[13]

All these data were punched on IBM cards and various statistical analyses were carried out, using a 360 and an 1130 IBM computer. Dixon computer[18] programs or other statistical analyses were used as indicated.

## RESULTS

### *Chlordiazepoxide Plasma Levels*

Chlordiazepoxide plasma levels resulting from the ingestion of 25 mg of chlordiazepoxide were obtained at zero and 50 minute points of the experimental sessions. These plasma levels ranged from 0.26 to 1.63 μg/ml. (see Table 1). Levels of metabolites of chlordiazepoxide were absent or negligible in the plasma samples examined.

Table 1 shows that if the chlordiazepoxide plasma level at the beginning (time zero) of the experimental period was low, it was likely to be low also 50 minutes later; when initial plasma levels were high, the subsequent plasma levels were also high. This point is emphasized in the high correlation ($r = 0.81$) between first and second chlordiazepoxide plasma levels. The chlordiazepoxide plasma levels were not correlated with the time interval between ingestion of the drug and the time of drawing the blood sample for chlordiazepoxide determination ($r = 0.05$ at zero minutes and $r = -0.12$ at 50 minutes). Also, body weight of the subject or sex did not appear to have an appreciable influence on the drug blood level.

**Table 1. Chlordiazepoxide Plasma Levels at Beginning of Experimental Period (time zero) and at Termination (time 50 minutes)***

| Subjects | Sex | Weight (lb) | Chlordiazepoxide Plasma Level at time zero (μg/ml) | Time After Ingestion of Drug (min) | Chlordiazepoxide Plasma Level at Time 50 min (μg/ml) | Time After Ingestion of Drug (min) |
|---|---|---|---|---|---|---|
| 1 | F | 107 | 1.46 | 105 | 1.63 | 155 |
| 2 | F | 130 | 1.43 | 90 | 1.09 | 140 |
| 3 | M | 135 | 1.29 | 59 | 1.16 | 109 |
| 4 | M | 180 | 1.29 | 70 | 1.06 | 120 |
| 5 | F | 120 | 1.22 | 105 | 0.88 | 155 |
| 6 | M | 175 | 1.15 | 105 | 0.87 | 155 |
| 7 | M | 157 | 1.00 | 75 | 1.02 | 125 |
| 8 | M | 180 | 0.98 | 90 | 0.77 | 140 |
| 9 | M | 165 | 0.88 | 100 | 1.07 | 150 |
| 10 | M | 185 | 0.80 | 105 | 0.80 | 155 |
| 11 | F | 135 | 0.77 | 145 | 0.76 | 195 |
| Mean | | | 1.12 | 95.36 | 1.01 | 145.36 |
| S.D. | | | 0.24 | 23.01 | 0.25 | 23.01 |
| 12 | M | 160 | 0.79 | 90 | 0.67 | 140 |
| 13 | M | 172 | 0.68 | 78 | 0.80 | 128 |
| 14 | M | 198 | 0.62 | 90 | 0.80 | 140 |
| 15 | M | 170 | 0.42 | 90 | 0.36 | 140 |
| 16 | M | 208 | 0.40 | 80 | 0.34 | 130 |
| 17 | M | 140 | 0.34 | 70 | 0.89 | 120 |
| 18 | M | 165 | 0.26 | 110 | 0.32 | 160 |
| Mean | | | 0.50 | 86.86 | 0.59 | 136.86 |
| S.D. | | | 0.20 | 12.75 | 0.25 | 12.75 |
| Mean Total | | | 0.88 | 92.05 | 0.85 | 142.05 |
| S.D. | | | 0.38 | 19.67 | 0.31 | 19.67 |

*Two sets of means are given to distinguish those subjects whose chlordiazepoxide plasma levels exceeded or were less than 0.70 μg/ml.

*Chlordiazepoxide Plasma Levels and Anxiety Scores*

Taking all 18 subjects and comparing anxiety scores when the subjects were on placebo as compared to when they were on chlordiazepoxide, at the beginning of the experiment (time zero), there was essentially no difference between the anxiety scores on these two occasions (anxiety score 2.49 with placebo versus anxiety score 2.47 with chlordiazepoxide).

Again, taking all 18 subjects and comparing their anxiety scores when they were on placebo as compared to when they were on chlordiazepoxide, at a time 50 minutes after the beginning of the experiment, there was a trend for anxiety scores to be less (see Table 2) when the subjects were on chlordiazepoxide, but this trend was not statistically significant ($t = 1.56$, $p < 0.10$). Also, there was a trend, nonsignificant but yet of interest, for higher chlordiazepoxide plasma levels at time zero to be associated with greater decreases in anxiety from zero to 50 minutes ($r = 0.26$).

It is reasonable to assume that there would be no noticeable effect on anxiety scores if the plasma levels of chlordiazepoxide of our subjects did not reach levels which were effective pharmacologically during the experimental period. Accordingly, if one eliminates from consideration all subjects who had chlordiazepoxide plasma levels, either at the beginning of the experiment (time zero) or at the end of the experiment (time 50 minutes) that were less than 0.70 μg somewhat different results were obtained than if all 18 subjects were included. (A chlordiazepoxide plasma level of 0.70 μg/ml. was chosen as a rough cut-off level because of findings by Schwartz, Postma, and Gaut[31] that peak plasma levels ranged from 0.78 to 1.24 μg/ml. over a period from two to four hours after the ingestion of 20 mg of chlordiazepoxide in six normal, nonanxious subjects.) Taking the 11 subjects whose plasma levels of chlordiazepoxide were consistently above 0.70 μg/ml. during the experimental period and comparing the anxiety scores at 50 minutes after the beginning of the experiment when the subjects were on placebo as compared to being on chlordiazepoxide, there was a significant decrease in the anxiety score when the subjects were on chlordiazepoxide ($t = 2.52$, $p < 0.025$). Also, there was significantly greater decrease in anxiety scores from the beginning of the experimental (time zero) to 50 minutes later when the subjects were on chlordiazepoxide ($t = 2.05$, $p < 0.05$) (see Table 2).

On the 11 subjects whose chlordiazepoxide blood levels were 0 70 μg/ml. or above during the experimental period there was a slight, nonsignificant trend ($r = 0.16$) for higher chlordiazepoxide plasma levels at time zero to be correlated with greater decreases in anxiety scores from the beginning of the experiment to 50 minutes later.

**Table 2. Average Anxiety Scores With Anxious Subjects on either Chlordiazepoxide (25 mg) or Placebo. (Group 18 Constitutes the Total Group, Whereas Group 11 Includes Only Those Eleven Subjects Whose Chlordiazepoxide Plasma Levels Were > 0.70 μg/ml)**

| Group | Time (min) | Anxiety Scores: Placebo | Anxiety Scores: Chlordiazepoxide | Mean Diffs | Significance |
|---|---|---|---|---|---|
| 18 | 0 | 2.49 | 2.47 | −0.02 | $t = -0.07$, $p = NS$ |
| | 50 | 2.62 | 2.24 | −0.38 | $t = -1.56$, $p < 0.10$ |
| Mean diffs | | +0.13 | −0.23 | −0.36 | $t = -1.61$, $p < 0.10$ |
| 11 | 0 | 2.48 | 2.47 | −0.01 | $t = 0.03$, $p = NS$ |
| | 50 | 2.59 | 2.07 | −0.52 | $t = -2.25$, $p < 0.025$ |
| Mean diffs | | +0.11 | −0.40 | −0.51 | $t = -2.05$, $p < 0.05$ |

*Chlordiazepoxide Plasma Levels and Hostility Scores*

There was a trend for hostility scores to decrease more with chlordiazepoxide as compared to a placebo, especially total hostility outward ($t = -1.37$, $p < 0.10$, $N = 18$; $t = 1.69$, $p < 0.10$, $N = 11$) and ambivalent hostility ($t = -1.27$, $p < 0.15$, $N = 11$), but these decreases did not reach a convincing level of significance (see Tables 3-5).

With all 18 subjects, the greater the chlordiazepoxide level at time zero the greater the decrease in ambivalent hostility scores ($r = 0.42$, $p < 0.05$, one-tail test).

No other correlations of interest approaching significance were found with other hostility scores using all 18 subjects. When only the 11 subjects, both of whose

**Table 3. Average Hostility Outward Scores With Subjects on either 25 mg Chlordiazepoxide (Chl) or a Placebo (Pl). (For Explanation of Group 18 and Group 11 See Table 1)**

| | | Hostility Outward Scores | | | | | | | |
|---|---|---|---|---|---|---|---|---|---|
| | Time | Overt | | Covert | | Total | | Mean | |
| Group | (min) | Pl | Chl | Pl | Chl | Pl | Chl | Diffs | Significance |
| 18 | 0 | 1.13 | 1.33 | 1.02 | 0.99 | 1.60 | 1.69 | +0.09 | t = 0.45, p = NS |
| | 50 | 1.23 | 1.15 | 1.04 | 0.81 | 1.72 | 1.45 | −0.27 | t = −1.28, p < 0.15 |
| Mean diffs | | +0.10 | −0.18 | +0.02 | −0.18 | +0.12 | −0.24 | −0.36 | t = −1.37, p < 0.10 |
| | 0 | 1.04 | 1.40 | 1.06 | 1.05 | 1.60 | 1.77 | +0.17 | t = 0.56, p = NS |
| | 50 | 1.17 | 1.08 | 1.04 | 0.75 | 1.69 | 1.36 | −0.33 | t = −1.32, p < 0.15 |
| Mean diffs | | +0.13 | −0.32 | 0.02 | −0.30 | +0.09 | −0.41 | −0.50 | t = −1.69, p < 0.10 |

**Table 4. Average Hostility Inward Scores with Subjects on either Chlordiazepoxide (25 mg) or a Placebo. (For Explanation of Group 18 and Group 11 See Table 1)**

| | | Hostility Scores | | | |
|---|---|---|---|---|---|
| | Time | | Chlordiaze- | Mean | |
| Group | (min) | Placebo | poxide | Diffs | Significance |
| 18 | 0 | 1.16 | 1.05 | −0.11 | t = −0.54, p = NS |
| | 50 | 1.02 | 1.17 | +0.15 | t = 0.61, p = NS |
| Mean diffs | | −0.14 | +0.12 | +0.26 | t = 0.97, p = NS |
| 11 | 0 | 1.05 | 1.03 | −0.02 | t = −0.05, p = NS |
| | 50 | 0.90 | 1.12 | 0.22 | t = 0.85, p = NS |
| Mean diffs | | −0.15 | +0.09 | +0.24 | t = 0.70, p = NS |

**Table 5. Average Ambivalent Hostility Scores with Subjects on either Chlordiazepoxide (25 mg.) or a Placebo. (For Explanation of Group 18 and Group 11 See Table 1).**

| | | Ambivalent Hostility Scores | | | |
|---|---|---|---|---|---|
| | Time | | Chlordiaze- | Mean | |
| Group | (min) | Placebo | poxide | Diffs | Significance |
| 18 | 0 | 1.34 | 1.36 | +0.02 | t = 0.08, p = NS |
| | 50 | 1.33 | 1.27 | −0.05 | t = −0.25, p = NS |
| Mean diffs | | −0.01 | −0.09 | −0.08 | t = −0.35, p = NS |
| 11 | 0 | 1.38 | 1.38 | 0 | t = 0.02, p = NS |
| | 50 | 1.42 | 1.08 | −0.34 | t = −1.33, p < 0.15 |
| Mean diffs | | +0.04 | −0.30 | 0.34 | t = −1.27, p < 0.15 |

Table 6. Correlations Between Chlordiazepoxide Plasma Levels (at Time Zero) and Changes in Hostility Scores

| Blood level | Changes in Hostility Scores From Zero to 50 Minutes | | | | |
|---|---|---|---|---|---|
| | Total Hostility Out, 50–0 | Overt Hostility Out, 50–0 | Covert Hostility Out, 50–0 | Hostility In, 50–0 | Ambivalent Hostility 50–0 |
| $Chlordiazepoxide_0$ (N = 11) | 0.82 | 0.80 | 0.37 | −0.47 | −0.15 |
| $Chlordiazepoxide_0$ (N = 18) | 0.07 | 0.02 | 0.02 | −0.25 | −0.42 |

chlordiazepoxide levels were above 0.70 μg/ml. were used, however, significant correlations occurred between chlordiazepoxide plasma levels (at time zero) and total hostility outward (r = 0.82) due principally to the correlation with overt hostility outward (r = 0.80). The correlation between chlordiazepoxide plasma levels and ambivalent hostility scores fell to - 0.15 when only those subjects (N = 11) were considered. (see Table 6).

*Chlordiazepoxide Plasma Levels and Other Psychological States*

There was a trend for chlordiazepoxide plasma levels, using all 18 subjects, to correlate negatively (- 0.31) with achievement strivings scores derived from the five minute speech samples and obtained at time zero and positively (0.28) with difference scores from time zero to time 50. Correlations between chlordiazepoxide plasma levels and human relations scores were essentially zero.

Chlordiazepoxide plasma levels and their relationship to various biochemical variables and psychobiochemical correlates have been reported in detail elsewhere.[15]

## DISCUSSION

There have been very few studies examining human individual differences in drug blood levels of new psychoactive drugs after ingestion of a standardized oral dose. More scarce have been examinations of the relationships between drug blood levels and clinical response in human subjects.

The present study illustrates that a wide range of differences in chlordiazepoxide plasma levels is obtained in 18 anxious individuals receiving identical dosages (25 mg) of this pharmacological agent by mouth. The differences in plasma level cannot be attributed, in our study, to differences in elapsed time between ingestion of the drug and drawing the blood sample for chlordiazepoxide determination, nor to body weight, nor to sex. Differences in drug absorption time might account for these widely ranging chlordiazepoxide plasma levels; more likely, we believe, are individual differences in drug metabolism.

Animal studies have revealed marked differences among different genetic strains of animal species in drug blood levels achieved with standardized dosages. Also, in human subjects given similar parenteral dosages of psychoactive drugs, marked differences in blood levels have been found using imipramine, chlorpromazine, thioridazine, and meperidine.[5,8,17,36] Moreover, the presence in the body of other psychoactive agents, e.g., sedatives, hypnotics, or tranquilizers, have been found to influence the metabolism and turn-over rate of certain psychoactive drugs.

The findings reported here illustrate the importance of individual differences in drug metabolism and the bearing such differences can have on drug efficacy. This study

suggests exploring how to detect and influence psychoactive drug metabolism to maximize desired pharmacological effects.

A previous study using the same content analysis method of deriving anxiety and hostility scores[12] also showed a significant reduction in anxiety, overt hostility outward, and ambivalent hostility after 20 mg of chlordiazepoxide in 16–17-year-old delinquent boys. The present study strongly suggests that the plasma level of an antianxiety agent, such as chlordiazepoxide, must be sufficient or exceed a certain level before an antianxiety effect is achieved by most individuals.

This study contributes some information on the issue as to whether or not chlordiazepoxide is capable of increasing hostility levels in anxious subjects. Apparently, a single oral dose of 25 mg of chlordiazepoxide does not raise hostility levels while it lowers anxiety scores in anxious subjects. In fact, the higher the plasma level of chlordiazepoxide the greater the decrease in ambivalent hostility scores. Curiously, however, when one uses for such a calculation the 11 subjects whose chlordiazepoxide levels were 0.70 μg/ml or above, a correlation of 0.82 is obtained between the chlordiazepoxide plasma level at the beginning of the experimental period (time zero) and the increase in hostility outward scores from zero to 50 minutes during the experimental session. Most of this correlation is accounted for by the overt hostility outward component ($r = 0.80$) of the hostility outward rather than the covert hostility outward component ($r = 0.37$). These findings occur in the face of a mild but not quite significant decrease in hostility outward scores and ambivalent hostility when subjects are on chlordiazepoxide as compared to when they are on a placebo. Our findings contrast and supplement those of DiMascio and his co-workers.[2,7,10,28] In these studies subjects received mild tranquilizers (chlordiazepoxide or oxazepam or a placebo for one week) in contrast to a single dose, as in the study being reported. In the most recent report by this group,[10] chlor 'iazepoxide (10 mg tid) for one week reduced anxiety (as measured by the Scheier and Cattell self-report test[29]) in high and medium anxious subjects (as assessed by the Taylor Manifest Anxiety scale). Chlordiazepoxide was found to increase significantly ambivalent hostility scores in high anxious subjects while oxazepam increased hostility inward scores[28] using the Gottschalk Content Analysis Hostility Scale.[14] Hostility scores from the Buss-Durkee Hostility Inventory[3] also apparently increased with chlordiazepoxide. Our study cannot disprove that perhaps with more prolonged administration of minor tranquilizers an increase in some kind of hostility may occur in some individuals.

Besides the fact that there may well be different effects on psychological states of single dose and multiple doses of psychoactive pharmacological agents, there are also differences in results that may be obtained depending on the psychological measuring technique used. For instance, the Buss-Durkee, the Scheier and Cattell, and Taylor Manifest Anxiety scales are all self-report procedures for assessing psychological states, and as such these measurement procedures are subject to the effects of suggestion or covering up. Individuals reporting about themselves using these methods are aware what is being measured and may expose only what they want to about themselves instead of how they really feel. The Gottschalk-Gleser content analysis method, on the other hand, does not reveal to the subject what psychological dimensions are really being measured, and this method is designed to give an assessment of a psychological state more than a psychological trait. Hence, the latter procedure may not necessarily give identical results to the former measurement methods.

## SUMMARY

(1) This was a double-blind, drug-placebo, cross-over study examining the effects on several psychological states of a single oral dose of chlordiazepoxide (25 mg) on 18 chronically anxious subjects.

(2) Plasma levels of chlordiazepoxide ranged from 0.26 to 1.63 μg/ml. These plasma levels were not correlated with the time interval between ingestion of the drug and time of drawing the blood sample for chlordiazepoxide determination (average time interval 92 minutes, range 60 to 145 minutes), nor with body weight or sex.

(3) Anxiety, hostility outward, and ambivalent hostility scores tended to decrease ($p < 0.10$) over the 50-minute observation period of this study when subjects were on chlordiazepoxide as compared to a placebo. But a statistically significant decrease in anxiety scores ($p < 0.025$) during this time period occurred only in those 11 subjects whose chlordiazepoxide plasma levels exceeded 0.70 μg/ml. The decrease in hostility outward, hostility inward, and ambivalent hostility scores, when these subjects were on chlordiazepoxide, did not reach a convincing level of significance.

(4) Chlordiazepoxide plasma levels of all 18 subjects correlated with scores on anxiety (- 0.26), ambivalent hostility (- 0.42) and achievement strivings (- 0.31). Chlordiazepoxide blood levels of the 11 subjects whose levels exceeded 0.70 μg/ml also correlated with hostility outward scores (0.82) and hostility inward scores (- 0.47).

(5) Implications of these findings are discussed as well as directions for future research.

## ACKNOWLEDGMENT

We acknowledge gratefully the professional advice of Ernest P. Noble, the statistical assistance of Herman Birch, and the technical assistance of Daniel E. Bates and Claire A. Cable.

## REFERENCES

1. Antonis, A.: Semiautomated method for the colorimetric determination of plasma free fatty acids. J. Lipid Res. 6:307, 1965.

2. Barrett, J. E., and DiMascio, A.: Comparative effects on anxiety of the "minor tranquilizers" in "high" and "low" anxious student volunteers. Dis. Nerv. Syst. 27:483, 1966.

3. Buss, A. H., and Durkee, A.: An inventory for assessing different kinds of hostility. J. Consult. Psychol. 21:343, 1957.

4. Butte, J. C., and Noble, E. P.: Simultaneous determination of plasma or whole blood cortisol and corticosterone. Acta Endocrinol. 61:678, 1969.

5. Cash, W. D., and Quinn, G. P.: Clinical-chemical correlations: an overview. Psychopharmacol. Bull. 6:26, 1970.

6. Cohen, I. M., and Harris, T. H.: Effects of chlordiazepoxide in psychiatric disorders. Southern Med. J. 54:1271, 1969.

7. DiMascio, A., and Barrett, J. E.: Comparative effects of oxazepam in "high" and "low" anxious student volunteers. Psychosomatics 6:298, 1965.

8. Elliott, H., Gottshalk, L., and Uliana, R.: Meperidine blood levels and clinical response. Unpublished data.

9. Frings, S. F., Ratcliff, C. R., and Dunn, R. T.: Automated determination of glucose in serum or plasma by a direct 0-toluidine procedure. Clin. Chem. 16:282, 1970.

10. Gardos, G., DiMascio, A., Salzman, C., and Shader, R. I.: Differential actions of chlordiazepoxide and oxazepam on hostility. Arch. Gen. Psychiat. (Chicago) 18:757, 1968.

11. Gitelman, H. J.: An improved automated procedure for the determination of calcium in biological specimens. Anal. Biochem. 18:521, 1967.

12. Gleser, G. C., Gottschalk, L. A., Fox, R., and Lippert, W.: Immediate changes in affect with chlordiazepoxide in juvenile delinquent boys. Arch. Gen. Psychiat. (Chicago) 13:291, 1965.

13. Gottschalk, L. A., and Gleser, G. C.: The Measurement of Psychological States Through the Content Analysis of Verbal Behavior. Berkeley, University of California Press, 1969.

14. —, —, and Springer, K. J.: Three hostility scales applicable to verbal samples. Arch. Gen. Psychiat. (Chicago) 9:254, 1963.

15. —, Noble, E. P., Stolzoff, G. L., Bates, D. E., Cable, C. G., Uliana, R. L., Birch, H., Fleming, J.: Relationship of chlordiazepoxide blood levels to psychological and biochemical responses. *In* Garattini, S., and Leonardi, A., (Eds.): Proceedings of International Symposium on Benzodiazepenes. New York, Raven Press, 1972.

16. —, Winget, C. N., and Gleser, G. C.: Manual of Instructions for Using the Gottschalk-Gleser Content Analysis Scales: Anxiety, Hostility, Social Alienation-Personal Disorganization. Berkeley, University of California Press, 1969.

17. Green, D. E., Forrest, I. S., Forrest, F. M., and Serra, M. T.: Interpatient variation in chlorpromazine metabolism. Exp. Med. Surg. 23:278, 1965.

18. Dixon, W. J. (Ed.): Biomedical Computer Programs. Berkeley, University of California Press, 1968, p. 1.

19. Hales, C. N., and Randle, P. J.: Immunoassay of insulin with insulin antibody precipitate. Biochem. J. 88:137, 1963.

20. Huang, T. C., Chen, C. P., Wefler, V., and Raftery, A.: A stable reagent for the Liebermann–Burchard reaction. Anal. Chem. 33:1405, 1961.

21. Kessler, G., and Lederer, H.: Fluorometric Measurement of Triglycerides. *In* Skeggs, L. T., Jr., (Ed.): Automation in Analytical Chemistry. New York, Mediad, 1966, p. 341.

22. —, Rush, R. L., Leon, L., Delea, A., and Cupiola, R.: Automated 340 nm measurement of SGOT, SGPT, and LDH. Clin. Chem. 16:530, 1970.

23. Morgenstern, S., Kessler, G., Auerbach, J., Flor, R. V., and Klein, B.: Automated p-nitrophenylphosphate serum alkaline phosphatase procedure for the auto analyzer. Clin. Chem. 11:876, 1965.

24. Murray, N.: Covert effect of chlordiazepoxide therapy. J. Neuropsychiat. 3:168, 1962.

25. Musser, A. W., and Ortigoza, C.: Automated determination of uric acid by the hydroxylamine method. Tech. Bull. Registry of Med. Technol. 36:21, 1966.

26. Overall, J. E., and Gorham, D. R.: The brief psychiatric rating scale. Psychol. Rep. 10:799, 1962.

27. Randall, L. A., and Schallek, W.: Pharmacological activity of certain benzodiazepenes. *In* Efron, D. H. et al. (Eds.): Psychopharmacology: A Review of Progress, 1957–1967, Washington, D. C., Public Health Service Publication No. 1836, U. S. Government Printing Office, 1968, p. 153.

28. Salzman, C., DiMascio, A., Shader, R. I., Harmatz, J. S.: Chlordiazepoxide, expectation, and hostility. Psychopharmacol. 14:38, 1969.

29. Scheier, I. H., and Cattell, R. B.: Handbook and Test Kit for the IPAT 8-Parallel form anxiety battery. Champaign, Ill. Institute for Personality and Ability Testing, 1960.

30. Schwartz, M. A., and Postma, E.: Metabolic N-demethylation of chlordiazepoxide. J. Pharmacol. Sci. 55:1358, 1966.

31. —, —, and Gaut, Z.: Biological half-life in chlordiazepoxide and its metabolite, demoxepam, in man. J. Pharmaceut. Sci. 60:1500, 1971.

32. Sternbach, L. H., Randall, L. O., and Gustafson, S. R.: 1, 4-Benzodiazepenes (chlordiazepoxide and related compounds). *In* Psychopharmacological Agents, Gordon, M. (Ed.), Vol. 1, p. 199. Academic Press, New York.

33. Technicon Methodology N-14b.: Technicon Instrument Corporation, Tarrytown, N. Y., 1965.

34. Tobin, J. M., Bird, I. F., and Boyle, D. E.: Preliminary evaluation of Librium (R0-0690) in the treatment of anxiety reactions. Dis. Nerv. Syst. 21:11, 1960.

35. —, and Lewis, N. D. C.: New psychotherapeutic agent, chlordiazepoxide. Use in treatment of anxiety states and related symptoms. JAMA 174:1242, 1960.

36. Usdin, E.: Absorption, distribution, and metabolic fate of psychotropic drugs. Psychopharmacol. Bull. 6:4, 1970.

# RELATIONSHIPS OF CHLORDIAZEPOXIDE BLOOD LEVELS TO PSYCHOLOGICAL AND BIOCHEMICAL RESPONSES

**Louis A. Gottschalk, Ernest P. Noble, Gordon E. Stolzoff, Daniel E. Bates, Claire G. Cable, Regina L. Uliana, Herman Birch, and Eugene W. Fleming**

*Department of Psychiatry and Human Behavior, University of California at Irvine, and the Orange County Medical Center, Irvine, California*

## I. INTRODUCTION

This is a report on one aspect of a research program involving the exploration of psychoactive drug blood levels and the associated clinical and biochemical responses. The special focus of this study is placed on the relationship of chlordiazepoxide blood levels (after the ingestion of 25 mg of chlordiazepoxide in 18 chronically anxious, fasting subjects) to changes in anxiety, hostility, and other psychological levels, as well as to certain biochemical substances considered responsive to alterations in the magnitude of emotions.

Very few studies are available on the relationship of chlordiazepoxide blood levels and clinical response in humans. No one has reported finding any definite relationship between the blood level of this drug and the degree of emotional response. Recent studies of chlordiazepoxide blood levels and half-life (Schwartz, Postma, and Gaut, 1971) have not examined the relationship of these to clinical response.

On the other hand, many studies have been carried out examining the effect of the oral administration of chlordiazepoxide on anxiety or hostility. In general, there is substantial evidence that chlordiazepoxide in single or repeated doses can reduce anxiety and fear. Depending on the research design and measuring instruments, some investigators report a decrease in hostility or aggression with chlordiazepoxide (Tobin and Lewis, 1960; Gleser, Gottschalk, Fox, and Lippert, 1965; Randall and Schallek, 1968), whereas others report increases in certain kinds of hostility (Tobin, Bird, and

Boyle, 1960; Gardos, DiMascio, Salzman, and Shader, 1968; Salzman, DiMascio, Shader, and Harmatz, 1969).

Previous studies, using the same objective content-analysis method of measuring anxiety and three kinds of hostility (outward, inward, and ambivalent) as in the present investigation, have demonstrated that chlordiazepoxide (20 mg orally) significantly decreased anxiety, overt hostility outward, and ambivalent hostility in 16- to 17-year-old juvenile delinquent boys (Gleser et al., 1965) when compared to a placebo. Also, in studies using the same content-analysis procedure for measuring psychological states, anxiety scores in individuals fasting 10 to 12 hr have been found to be significantly correlated with average free fatty acid levels over a 50-min period as well as with the increase in free fatty acid levels from 0 to 20 min after a venipuncture with an intravenous indwelling catheter (Gottschalk, Cleghorn, Gleser, and Iacono, 1965; Gottschalk, Stone, Gleser, and Iacono, 1969*a*; Stone, Gleser, Gottschalk, and Iacono, 1969). In these studies, positive correlations were also found between hostility scores, especially inward and ambivalent hostility, and plasma triglycerides, cholesterol, and corticosteroid levels, but not with free fatty acid levels.

The aim of the present study was not only to replicate findings from these earlier investigations, but also to extend them to explore other psychobiochemical relations and to investigate the influence of blood levels of psychoactive pharmacological agents on these psychobiochemical relationships.

## II. PROCEDURE

*Subjects*: The participating subjects were paid volunteers, in good physical health. Eighteen anxious subjects (14 male and 4 female) were selected; they were psychiatrically screened by a preliminary interview so that they all had anxiety levels equal to or greater than 4 on the anxiety rating scale of the Overall-Gorham Brief Psychiatric Rating Scale (Overall and Gorham, 1962). In addition, they were carefully interviewed to ascertain that they were not currently taking drugs of any kind and had not done so for at least 4 weeks; they were told not to drink alcohol or coffee or to smoke tobacco for 24 hr before each testing period. Subjects who were using any hormonal medication, such as birth control pills, were rejected from participation in this study.

## III. METHODS

Subjects were told, in simple terms, that the purpose of this study was to

explore the relationship of various emotions, especially anxiety, to body chemistry, as well as the effect of a small oral dose of a mild tranquilizer or placebo on these psychochemical associations. Furthermore, they were advised that they would have to come to the Mental Health Outpatient Clinic, Orange County Medical Center on two mornings, at least one week apart, for about 90 min on each occasion, after eating supper the previous night between 6:00 and 8:00 p.m. and fasting thereafter until the experimental session began.

The research utilized a double-blind, crossover design, balanced for order. Nine of the subjects took a placebo capsule first and the other nine first took 25 mg of chlordiazepoxide in capsule form. Since all subjects were chronically anxious, paid volunteers, they were given two identical capsules (one containing a placebo and the other chlordiazepoxide) after being accepted for the study, and fully instructed which capsule to take before their first and second visits to the Clinic. Instructions were so designed that ingestion of the capsules took place about 75 min before the collection of psychological and biochemical data. The actual average time between ingestion and the start of data collection was 92.05 min, the standard deviation was $\pm$ 19.67, and the range was from 60 to 145 min. Actual measurement of chlordiazepoxide blood levels reassuringly revealed that subjects did take their placebo and chlordiazepoxide capsules at designated times so that the crossover design was balanced.

On arrival for the experimental procedure, the subjects were first questioned briefly about when they had had supper the previous evening, what time they had taken their capsule, and whether or not they had used other drugs of any kind. If they had taken any other drugs than those specified or if the fasting since the preceding night's supper had been violated, the experimental procedure was terminated. Such subjects were either dropped from the study and replaced by another individual or, if it could be arranged without compromising the research design, the subject was asked to return on another occasion.

Subjects were then asked to lie down on a bed, and they were permitted to relax and get comfortable for about 15 min. One arm was put through a cloth screen so that the subject could not see the next procedure although he was told what was going on. An indwelling intravenous catheter was then inserted in an antecubital vein, and normal saline solution was allowed to infuse slowly into the vein to prevent clotting of blood. The system was so arranged that blood could be withdrawn from the subject without his knowledge. Immediately after insertion of the intravenous catheter (time zero), 20 to 25 cc of blood was withdrawn and put into a

heparinized tube. At 10-min intervals thereafter, for a total of 50 min, similar amounts of blood were withdrawn for biochemical determinations. At time zero and at 50 min, the subject was asked to give a 5-min sample speech into the microphone of a tape recorder in response to standardized instructions to talk about any interesting or dramatic personal life experiences. This is the data collection procedure for the objective measurement of psychological states according to the method of Gottschalk and Gleser (1969).

The heparinized blood samples were immediately placed in ice. They were then subjected to centrifugation in the cold, and plasma was separated and stored frozen for subsequent biochemical determinations. Plasma free fatty acids were determined by the method of Antonis (1965), triglycerides by the method of Kessler and Lederer (1966), glucose by the method of Frings, Ratcliff, and Dunn (1970), cortisol by the method of Butte and Noble (1969), cholesterol by the method of Huang, Chen, Wefler, and Raftery (1961), uric acid by the method of Musser and Ortigoza (1966), insulin by the method of Hales and Randle (1963), calcium by the method of Gitelman (1967), chlordiazepoxide by the method of Schwartz and Postma (1966), creatinine by the Technicon method (1965), glutamic oxalacetic transaminase (SGOT) and lactic dehydrogenase (LDH) according to Kessler, Rush, Leon, Delea, and Cupiola (1970), and alkaline phosphatase following the method of Morgenstern, Kessler, Auerbach, Flor, and Klein (1965).

Typescripts of the 5-min speech samples were scored blindly for the magnitude of various psychological states according to the Gottschalk-Gleser method (1969) by content-analysis technicians who were unfamiliar with the purpose of the research. Scores were obtained from all speech samples on anxiety, hostility outward (total, overt, and covert), hostility inward, ambivalent hostility (based on self-references to others making hostile remarks about the speaker), human relations, and achievement strivings (Gottschalk and Gleser, 1969).

All these data were punched on IBM cards, and various statistical analyses were carried out using a 360 IBM computer and an 1130 IBM computer. Dixon (1969) computer programs or other statistical analyses were used as indicated.

## IV. RESULTS

### A. Chlordiazepoxide blood levels

Chlordiazepoxide blood levels resulting from the ingestion of 25 mg of

TABLE I. *Chlordiazepoxide blood levels at beginning of experimental period (time zero) and at termination (time 50 min)*

| Subjects | Sex | Weights (lb) | Chlordiazepoxide blood level at time zero (μg/ml) | Time after ingestion of drug (min) | Chlordiazepoxide blood level at time 50 min (μg/ml) | Time after ingestion of drug (min) |
|---|---|---|---|---|---|---|
| 1 | F | 107 | 1.46 | 105 | 1.63 | 155 |
| 2 | F | 130 | 1.43 | 90 | 1.09 | 140 |
| 3 | M | 135 | 1.29 | 59 | 1.16 | 109 |
| 4 | M | 180 | 1.29 | 70 | 1.06 | 120 |
| 5 | F | 120 | 1.22 | 105 | 0.88 | 155 |
| 6 | M | 175 | 1.15 | 105 | 0.87 | 155 |
| 7 | M | 157 | 1.00 | 75 | 1.02 | 125 |
| 8 | M | 180 | 0.98 | 90 | 0.77 | 140 |
| 9 | M | 165 | 0.88 | 100 | 1.07 | 150 |
| 10 | M | 185 | 0.80 | 105 | 0.80 | 155 |
| 11 | F | 135 | 0.77 | 145 | 0.76 | 195 |
| Mean* | | | 1.12 | 95.36 | 1.01 | 145.36 |
| s.d. | | | 0.24 | 23.01 | 0.25 | 23.01 |
| 12 | M | 160 | 0.79 | 90 | 0.67 | 140 |
| 13 | M | 172 | 0.68 | 78 | 0.80 | 128 |
| 14 | M | 198 | 0.62 | 90 | 0.80 | 140 |
| 15 | M | 170 | 0.42 | 90 | 0.36 | 140 |
| 16 | M | 208 | 0.40 | 80 | 0.34 | 130 |
| 17 | M | 140 | 0.34 | 70 | 0.89 | 120 |
| 18 | M | 165 | 0.26 | 110 | 0.32 | 160 |
| Mean* | | | 0.50 | 86.86 | 0.59 | 136.86 |
| s.d. | | | 0.20 | 12.75 | 0.25 | 12.75 |
| Mean total | | | 0.88 | 92.05 | 0.85 | 142.05 |
| s.d. | | | 0.38 | 19.67 | 0.31 | 19.67 |

* Two sets of means are given to distinguish those subjects whose chlordiazepoxide blood levels exceeded or were less than 0.70 μg/ml.

chlordiazepoxide were obtained at 0- and 50-min points of the experimental sessions. These blood levels ranged from 0.26 to 1.63 $\mu$g/ml. Blood levels of metabolites of chlordiazepoxide were absent to negligible.

Table I shows that if the chlordiazepoxide blood level at the beginning (time zero) of the experimental period was low, it was likely to be low also 50 min later. When initial blood levels were high, the subsequent blood levels were also high. This point is emphasized in the high correlation ($r = 0.81$) between the first and second chlordiazepoxide blood levels. The chlordiazepoxide blood levels were not correlated with the time interval between ingestion of the drug and the time of drawing the blood sample for chlordiazepoxide determination ($r = 0.05$ at 0 min and $-0.12$ at 50 min). Also, the body weight or sex of the subject did not appear to have an appreciable influence on the drug blood level.

### B. Chlordiazepoxide blood levels and anxiety scores

Taking all 18 subjects at zero time and comparing anxiety scores between when the subjects were on placebo and when they were on chlordiazepoxide, essentially no difference between the anxiety scores on these two occasions was obtained (anxiety score was 2.49 with placebo versus 2.47 with chlordiazepoxide).

Again, comparing the anxiety of all 18 patients when they were on placebo or on chlordiazepoxide, at 50 min after the beginning of the experiment, there was a trend for anxiety scores to be lower (see Table II) when the subjects were on chlordiazepoxide, but this trend was not statistically significant ($t = -1.56$, $p < 0.10$). Also, there was a trend, nonsignificant but still of interest, for higher chlordiazepoxide blood levels at time zero to be associated with greater decreases in anxiety from 0 to 50 min ($r = 0.26$).

It is reasonable to assume that there would be no noticeable effect on anxiety scores if the blood levels of chlordiazepoxide of our subjects did not reach levels which were effective pharmacologically during the experimental period. Accordingly, if we eliminated from consideration all subjects who had chlordiazepoxide blood levels at either the beginning (time zero) or the end of the experiment (time 50 min) that were less than 0.70 $\mu$g/ml, we obtained somewhat different results than if we included all 18 subjects. (A chlordiazepoxide blood level of 0.70 $\mu$g/ml was chosen as a rough cutoff level because of findings by Schwartz, Postma, and Gaut (1971) that peak blood levels ranged from 0.78 to 1.24 $\mu$g/ml over a period of 2 to 4 hr after the ingestion of 20 mg of chlordiazepoxide in six normal subjects.) Comparing the anxiety scores of the 11 subjects whose blood levels of

chlordiazepoxide were consistently above 0.70 μg/ml when they were on placebo and on chlordiazepoxide 50 min after the beginning of the experiment, chlordiazepoxide resulted in a significant decrease in the anxiety scores ($t = -2.52$, $p < 0.025$). Also, there was a significantly greater decrease in anxiety scores between the beginning of the experiment and 50 min later in the chlordiazepoxide-treated subjects ($t = -2.05$, $p < 0.05$) (Table II).

TABLE II. *Average anxiety scores with anxious subjects on either chlordiazepoxide (25 mg) or placebo*

| Group | Time (min) | Anxiety scores: Placebo | Anxiety scores: Chlordiazepoxide | Mean difference | Significance |
|---|---|---|---|---|---|
| 18 | 0 | 2.49 | 2.47 | −0.02 | $t = -0.07$, $p =$ n.s. |
| | 50 | 2.62 | 2.24 | −0.38 | $t = -1.56$, $p < 0.10$ |
| Mean difference | | +0.13 | −0.23 | −0.36 | $t = -1.61$, $p < 0.10$ |
| 11 | 0 | 2.48 | 2.47 | −0.01 | $t = 0.03$, $p =$ n.s. |
| | 50 | 2.59 | 2.07 | −0.52 | $t = -2.25$, $p < 0.025$ |
| Mean difference | | +0.11 | −0.40 | −0.51 | $t = -2.05$, $p < 0.05$ |

Group 18 constitutes the total group, whereas Group 11 includes only those 11 subjects whose chlordiazepoxide blood levels were > 0.70 μg/ml.

Of the 11 subjects whose chlordiazepoxide blood levels were 0.70 μg/ml or above during the experimental period, there was a slight, nonsignificant trend ($r = 0.16$) for higher chlordiazepoxide blood levels at time zero to be correlated with greater decreases in anxiety scores from the beginning of the experiment to 50 min later.

### C. Chlordiazepoxide blood levels and hostility scores

There was a trend for hostility scores to decrease more with chlordiazepoxide than with placebo, especially total hostility outward ($t = -1.37$, $p < 0.10$, N = 18; $t = -1.69$, $p < 0.10$, N = 11) and ambivalent hostility ($t = -1.27$, $p < 0.15$, N = 11). However, these decreases did not reach a statistically convincing level of significance (Tables III-V).

With all 18 subjects, the greater the chlordiazepoxide level at time zero, the greater the decrease in ambivalent hostility scores ($r = -0.42$, $p < 0.05$, one-tail test) (Table VI).

No other correlations of interest approaching significance were found with other hostility scores using all 18 subjects. When only the 11 subjects

TABLE III. *Average hostility outward scores with subjects on either 25 mg chlordiazepoxide (Chl) or a placebo (Pl)*

| | | Hostility outward scores | | | | | | | |
|---|---|---|---|---|---|---|---|---|---|
| | | Overt | | Covert | | Total | | | |
| Group | Time (min) | Pl | Chl | Pl | Chl | Pl | Chl | Mean difference | Significance |
| 18 | 0 | 1.13 | 1.33 | 1.02 | 0.99 | 1.60 | 1.69 | +0.09 | $t = 0.45$, $p =$ n.s. |
| | 50 | 1.23 | 1.15 | 1.04 | 0.81 | 1.72 | 1.45 | −0.27 | $t = -1.28$, $p < 0.15$ |
| Mean difference | | +0.10 | −0.18 | +0.02 | −0.18 | +0.12 | −0.24 | −0.36 | $t = -1.37$, $p < 0.10$ |
| 11 | 0 | 1.04 | 1.40 | 1.06 | 1.05 | 1.60 | 1.77 | +0.17 | $t = 0.56$, $p =$ n.s. |
| | 50 | 1.17 | 1.08 | 1.04 | 0.75 | 1.69 | 1.36 | −0.33 | $t = -1.32$, $p < 0.15$ |
| Mean difference | | +0.13 | −0.32 | −0.02 | −0.30 | +0.09 | −0.41 | −0.50 | $t = -1.69$, $p < 0.10$ |

For explanation of groups, see Table II.

TABLE IV. *Average hostility inward scores with subjects on either chlordiazepoxide (25 mg) or a placebo*

| | | Hostility scores | | | |
|---|---|---|---|---|---|
| Group | Time (min) | Placebo | Chlordiazepoxide | Mean difference | Significance |
| 18 | 0 | 1.16 | 1.05 | −0.11 | $t = -0.54$, $p =$ n.s. |
| | 50 | 1.02 | 1.17 | +0.15 | $t = 0.61$, $p =$ n.s. |
| Mean difference | | −0.14 | +0.12 | +0.26 | $t = 0.97$, $p =$ n.s. |
| 11 | 0 | 1.05 | 1.03 | −0.02 | $t = -0.05$, $p =$ n.s. |
| | 50 | 0.90 | 1.12 | 0.22 | $t = 0.85$, $p =$ n.s. |
| Mean difference | | −0.15 | +0.09 | +0.24 | $t = 0.70$, $p =$ n.s. |

For explanation of groups, see Table II.

TABLE V. *Average ambivalent hostility scores with subjects on either chlordiazepoxide (25 mg) or a placebo*

| | | Ambivalent hostility scores | | | |
|---|---|---|---|---|---|
| Group | Time (min) | Placebo | Chlordiazepoxide | Mean difference | Significance |
| 18 | 0 | 1.34 | 1.36 | +0.02 | $t = 0.08$, $p =$ n.s. |
| | 50 | 1.33 | 1.27 | −0.05 | $t = -0.25$, $p =$ n.s. |
| Mean difference | | −0.01 | −0.09 | −0.08 | $t = -0.35$, $p =$ n.s. |
| 11 | 0 | 1.38 | 1.38 | 0 | $t = 0.02$, $p =$ n.s. |
| | 50 | 1.42 | 1.08 | −0.34 | $t = -1.33$, $p < 0.15$ |
| Mean difference | | +0.04 | −0.30 | −0.34 | $t = -1.27$, $p < 0.15$ |

For explanation of groups, see Table II.

TABLE VI. *Correlations between chlordiazepoxide blood levels (at time zero) and changes in hostility scores*

| | Changes in hostility scores from zero to 50 min | | | | |
|---|---|---|---|---|---|
| Blood level | Total hostility out $_{50-0}$ | Overt hostility out $_{50-0}$ | Covert hostility out $_{50-0}$ | Hostility in $_{50-0}$ | Ambivalent hostility $_{50-0}$ |
| Chlordiazepoxide$_0$ (N = 11) | 0.82 | 0.80 | 0.37 | −0.47 | −0.15 |
| Chlordiazepoxide$_0$ (N = 18) | 0.07 | 0.02 | 0.02 | −0.25 | −0.42 |

whose 0- and 50-min chlordiazepoxide levels were above 0.70 μg/ml were used, however, significant correlations occurred between chlordiazepoxide

blood levels (at time zero) and total hostility outward ($r$ = 0.82), due principally to the correlation with *overt* hostility outward ($r$ = 0.80). The correlation between chlordiazepoxide blood levels at time zero and ambivalent hostility scores fell to —0.15 when only those subjects (N = 11) were considered (Table VI).

### D. Chlordiazepoxide blood levels and other psychological states

There was a trend for chlordiazepoxide blood levels, using all 18 subjects, to correlate negatively (—0.31) with achievement strivings scores derived from the 5-min speech samples and obtained at time zero and positively (0.28) with difference scores from time 0 to time 50. Correlations between chlordiazepoxide blood levels and human relations scores were essentially zero.

### E. Chlordiazepoxide blood levels and biochemical correlates

The biochemical correlates of chlordiazepoxide blood levels are given in Table VII. Those of possible interest are boldface. It should be noted that chlordiazepoxide blood levels among the total group (N = 18) and the group of 11 whose blood levels exceeded 0.70 $\mu$g/ml are included in these calculations as well as the chlordiazepoxide level at zero ($\text{chlordiazepoxide}_0$) and 50 min ($\text{chlordiazepoxide}_{50}$). There tended to be a negative correlation between chlordiazepoxide blood levels and the average plasma free fatty acids ($r$ = —0.26, —0.15, —0.32, —0.19), average triglycerides ($r$ = —0.43, 0.01, —0.39, —0.33), average glucose (r = —0.73, —0.50, —0.80, —0.71), and average insulin ($r$ = —0.11, —0.55, —0.17, —0.52). The correlations between initial chlordiazepoxide blood levels (time zero) and average cortisol levels tended to be positive ($r$= 0.21, 0.26), but between chlordiazepoxide levels at 50 min and average cortisol, these correlations tended to be negative ($r$ = —0.30). The correlations between chlordiazepoxide levels and SGOT ($r$ = —0.44, —0.34, —0.28, —0.16), and creatinine ($r$ = —0.37, —0.25, —0.20, —0.25) also tended to be negative. The correlations between chlordiazepoxide blood levels and $\text{triglycerides}_{10\text{-}20}$ tended to be positive ($r$ = 0.38, 0.11, 0.48, 0.42).

One must exercise caution in drawing final conclusions about the significance of any of the correlations in Table VII without further replication, especially because of the large number run and the probability that 5 out of 100 correlations could be expected to be significant by chance alone. Nevertheless, many of these correlations provide research leads and hypotheses

TABLE VII. *Correlations between chlordiazepoxide blood levels and biochemical variables*

| Blood levels | Chlordiazepoxide$_0$ (N=18) | Chlordiazepoxide$_0$ (N=11) | Chlordiazepoxide$_{50}$ (N=18) | Chlordiazepoxide$_{50}$ (N=11) |
|---|---|---|---|---|
| FFA av. | −0.26 | −0.15 | −0.32 | −0.19 |
| Triglyceride av. | **−0.43** | 0.01 | −0.39 | −0.33 |
| Trig$_{20-0}$ | −0.36 | **−0.46** | −0.38 | −0.23 |
| Trig$_{40-20}$ | 0.38 | 0.11 | **0.48** | **0.42** |
| Glucose av. | **−0.73** | **−0.50** | **−0.80** | **−0.71** |
| Cortisol av. | 0.21 | 0.26 | −0.05 | −0.30 |
| Insulin | −0.11 | **−0.55** | −0.17 | **−0.52** |
| SGOT | **−0.44** | −0.34 | −0.28 | −0.16 |
| Creatinine | −0.37 | −0.25 | −0.20 | −0.25 |
| LDH | 0.17 | 0.44 | 0.12 | **0.53** |

(N=18) = All 18 subjects

(N = 11) = The 11 subjects whose blood levels of chlordiazepoxide exceeded 70 μg/ml.

FFA, free fatty acid; Trig$_{20-0}$, difference between Trig at 20 and 0 min; LDR, lactic dehydrogenase; SGOT, glutamic oxalacetic transaminase.

that may serve as guidelines for further studies. Let us point out some of the possible guideposts.

Any set of correlations (e.g., along the rows in Table VII) that is uniform and at least moderately negative or positive may describe a linear relationship between two variables (e.g., chlordiazepoxide and average blood glucose). Any set of correlations that uniformly changes sign when chlordiazepoxide levels at zero are compared with levels at 50 min may indicate that chlordiazepoxide has a biphasic relationship with the dependent variable (e.g., chlordiazepoxide may initially stimulate and later depress average cortisol secretion). Any set of correlations that changes sign when one biochemical variable is compared over time in its relationship with chlordiazepoxide (e.g., triglycerides$_{20-0}$ and triglycerides$_{40-20}$) may indicate a curvilinear (biphasic) association with chlordiazepoxide. Any set of correlations that changes consistently in magnitude with the blood concentration of chlordiazepoxide being considered (e.g., chlordiazepoxide and insulin) may indicate a curvilinear association (e.g., with blood insulin).

Comparing average plasma free fatty acid and triglyceride levels every 10 min when the subjects were on chlordiazepoxide or placebo (see Figs. 1 and 2 and Table VIII), there was a significant elevation, as statistically assessed by analysis of variance, of both of these lipids when the subjects were on chlordiazepoxide (free fatty acids, $F = 9.166$, $p < 0.01$; triglycerides, $F = 11.496$, $p < 0.001$ two-tailed test). Also, creatinine blood levels

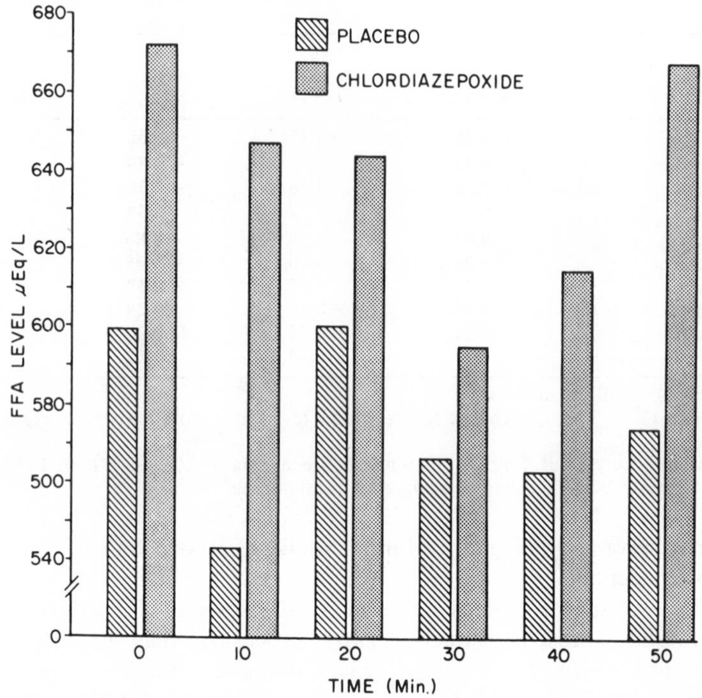


FIG. 1. Comparison of average free fatty acid levels under chlordiazepoxide and placebo conditions (N = 18).

were significantly lower under drug as compared to placebo conditions ($t = 7.22$; $p < 0.001$).

No significant differences were found, however, in blood glucose levels under the drug as compared to the placebo conditions.

In Table IX we have given the correlations between blood insulin and glucose, under chlordiazepoxide and placebo conditions for the 18 subjects. The expected negative correlations between insulin levels and glucose are revealed under placebo conditions, but with chlordiazepoxide this hypoglycemic effect of insulin no longer prevails.

### F. Psychological states and biochemical correlates

Correlations between anxiety, hostility, other psychological states, and various biochemical substances in plasma, during the placebo and drug conditions, are presented in Table X.

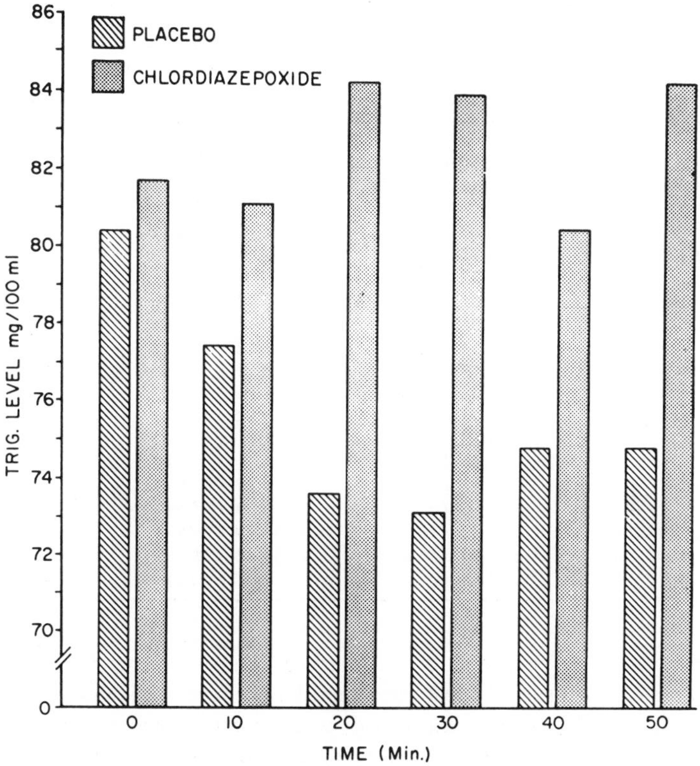


FIG. 2. Comparison of average triglyceride levels under chlordiazepoxide and placebo conditions (N = 18).

Except for correlations that have been observed in previous studies, the correlations listed in Table X should be interpreted with caution. (See also above comments regarding Table VII.) The boldface numbers do, however, suggest hypotheses that are useful for heuristic purposes and merit further exploration.

The positive correlation ($r = 0.35$), during placebo conditions, between anxiety scores and average plasma free fatty acids, although not quite significant (one-tailed test), was typically significant in our previous studies (Gottschalk et al. 1965, 1969*a*). Also, the positive correlation of hostility outward scores with cortisol level ($r = 0.42$) corresponded with previous findings (Gottschalk et al., 1969*a*), but the negative correlation of hostility outward scores with cholesterol level during the placebo condition ($r = -0.35$) was counter to a usually positive correlation in earlier studies.

TABLE VIII. *Means and standard deviations of biochemical variables under chlordiazepoxide and placebo conditions*

| Biochemical variable | Conditions: Drug | Conditions: Placebo | Significance |
|---|---|---|---|
| FFA av. | 640.02 (196.02) | 574.19 (223.75) | $p < 0.01$ |
| $FFA_{20-0}$ | −27.61 (176.25) | 1.11 (194.50) | — |
| $FFA_{40-20}$ | −29.44 (135.72) | −37.78 (113.71) | — |
| Triglyceride av. | 82.66 (32.74) | 75.71 (25.68) | $p < 0.001$ |
| $Trig_{20-0}$ | 2.67 (20.50) | −6.67 (20.40) | — |
| $Trig_{40-20}$ | −3.78 (13.14) | 1.17 (15.90) | — |
| Glucose av. | 85.30 (8.87) | 85.34 (8.78) | — |
| $Gluc_{20-0}$ | 0.61 (6.16) | 1.72 (17.14) | — |
| $Gluc_{40-20}$ | −2.01 (7.50) | −3.11 (8.92) | — |
| Cortisol av. | 11.69 (5.86) | 11.62 (6.08) | — |
| $Cortisol_0$ | 11.84 (6.55) | 12.79 (7.41) | — |
| $Cortisol_{50}$ | 11.52 (7.45) | 9.76 (5.33) | — |
| Cholesterol | 176.11 (83.09) | 179.94 (26.96) | — |
| Uric acid | 5.48 (0.83) | 5.71 (1.04) | — |
| Calcium | 8.49 (0.71) | 8.11 (1.31) | — |
| Insulin | 16.56 (5.68) | 18.17 (8.79) | — |
| SGOT | 9.16 (4.25) | 6.29 (3.01) | $p < 0.10$ |
| Alkaline phosphatase | 30.22 (10.34) | 32.00 (9.36) | — |
| LDH | 114.44 (36.47) | 119.22 (28.88) | — |
| Creatinine | 0.88 (0.12) | 1.04 (0.12) | $p < 0.001$ |

Especially to be noted is the marked change in correlation between certain scores for psychological states and biochemical variables under chlordiazepoxide conditions as compared to placebo conditions. These signify, we believe, psychoactive drug effects influencing either one or both factors in the correlate. We can be more certain of this likelihood in the case of previously observed correlations done under no-drug conditions (e.g., anxiety scores with average blood free fatty acids, or hostility outward scores with blood cortisol). With correlations that have never been previously looked at, when a reversal of sign occurs in a fairly high correlation coefficient, under drug conditions as compared to placebo conditions, the possibility is similarly increased that this change reflects a psychoactive drug effect, acting either on the central nervous system or peripherally or both.

TABLE IX. *Correlations of blood insulin and glucose* ($N = 18$)

| Condition | $Gluc_0$ | $Gluc_{10}$ | $Gluc_{20}$ | $Gluc_{30}$ | $Gluc_{40}$ | $Gluc_{50}$ |
|---|---|---|---|---|---|---|
| Chlordiazepoxide | 0.08 | 0.03 | 0.08 | 0.12 | 0.21 | 0.14 |
| Placebo | −0.69 | −0.19 | −0.25 | −0.19 | −0.59 | −0.13 |

$Gluc_0$ = blood glucose at zero min; $Gluc_{50}$ = blood glucose at 50 min.

TABLE X. *Correlations of psychological state scores with biochemical variables under chlordiazepoxide and placebo conditions (N = 18)*

| Biochemical variables | Anxiety | | Hostility out $total_o$ | | Hostility $in_o$ | | Hostility $ambivalent_o$ | | Achievement $strivings_o$ | | Human $relations_o$ | |
|---|---|---|---|---|---|---|---|---|---|---|---|---|
| | Drug | Placebo | Drug | Placebo | Drug | Placebo | Drug | Placebo | Drug | Placebo | Drug | Placebo |
| FFA av. | —0.18 | **0.35** | —0.15 | **0.48**** | | | **—0.35** | —0.11 | —0.29 | **—0.55**** | 0.24 | —0.43* |
| $FFA_{20-0}$ | | | | | | | | | | | | |
| $FFA_{40-20}$ | | | 0.11 | **—0.56**** | **—0.43*** | 0.05 | | | **0.42*** | —0.32 | 0.16 | **0.47**** |
| Triglyceride av. | | | | | | | | | | | | |
| $Trig_{20-0}$ | —0.22 | **0.41*** | | | —0.32 | 0.22 | 0.07 | **0.45*** | —0.12 | **0.41*** | | |
| $Trig_{40-20}$ | 0.24 | **—0.46**** | 0.14 | **—0.39** | | | | | | | | |
| Glucose av. | | | | | | | —0.32 | —0.14 | | | **—0.40*** | —0.21 |
| $Glucose_{20-0}$ | | | **0.48**** | 0.14 | | | | | | | 0.16 | **—0.36** |
| $Glucose_{40-20}$ | | | | | | | | | | | —0.36 | 0.27 |
| Cortisol av. | | | **—0.41*** | 0.29 | | | —0.19 | **—0.46**** | | | 0.36 | **—0.43*** |
| $Cortisol_0$ | | | —0.29 | **0.42*** | | | —0.27 | **—0.48**** | | | **0.58**** | **—0.43*** |
| $Cortisol_{50}$ | | | **—0.39** | 0.17 | | | —0.05 | **—0.52**** | | | 0.05 | —0.32 |
| $Cortisol_{50-0}$ | | | —0.13 | **—0.47**** | | | | | | | **—0.45*** | 0.21 |
| Cholesterol | | | 0.11 | —0.35 | **0.40*** | 0.10 | **0.33** | —0.24 | | | **—0.35** | —0.33 |
| Uric acid | | | | | | | —0.12 | —0.34 | | | 0.17 | **—0.51**** |
| Calcium | | | | | | | **—0.38** | —0.25 | | | **0.35** | **—0.59**** |
| Insulin | | | | | | | 0.29 | **0.53**** | 0.38 | **—0.44**** | **—0.47**** | —0.01 |

Boldface correlations are of possible interest.
* $p < 0.10$ (two-tailed test).
** $p < 0.05$ (two-tailed test).
Trig = Triglycerides.

## V. DISCUSSION

There have been very few studies examining human individual differences in drug blood levels of new psychoactive drugs after ingestion of a standardized oral dose. Even more scarce are examinations of the relationships between drug blood levels and clinical response in human subjects.

The present study illustrates that a wide range of differences in chlordiazepoxide blood levels is obtained in 18 anxious individuals receiving identical dosages (25 mg) of this pharmacological agent by mouth. The differences in blood levels cannot be attributed, in our study, to differences in time elapsed between ingestion of the drug and drawing the blood sample for chlordiazepoxide determination, nor to body weight, nor to sex. Differences in drug absorption time might account for these widely ranging chlordiazepoxide blood levels; more likely, we believe, are individual differences in drug metabolism.

Animal studies have revealed that genetic factors can account for the marked differences in drug blood levels achieved with standardized dosages. Also, in human subjects given similar parenteral doses of psychoactive drugs, marked differences in blood levels have been found using imipramine, chlorpromazine, thioridazine, and meperidine (Green, Forrest, Forrest, and Serra, 1965; Usdin, 1970; Cash and Quinn, 1970; Elliott, 1971). Moreover, the presence in the body of other psychoactive agents (e.g., sedatives, hypnotics, or tranquilizers) has been found to influence the metabolism and the half-life of certain psychoactive drugs.

The findings of the present study suggest the importance of individual differences in drug metabolism and the bearing such differences can have on drug efficacy. Our study points the way toward the importance of further investigations of the type reported here, and invites the eventual exploration of how to detect and influence psychoactive drug metabolism to maximize desired pharmacological effects.

The present investigation reveals a low correlation ($r = -0.26$) between chlordiazepoxide blood levels in 18 anxious subjects and a decrease in anxiety scores, over a 50-min observation period, and a significant correlation ($r = -0.42$, $p < 0.05$, one-tailed test) between drug blood levels and a decrease in ambivalent hostility scores. Correlations between drug blood levels and psychological reactions of 11 of the subjects whose drug blood levels exceeded 0.70 $\mu$g/ml revealed an interesting positive correlation ($r = 0.82$) between hostility outward scores and drug blood levels.

Examination of the decreases in anxiety and hostility scores over the 50-min observation period with all 18 subjects taking chlordiazepoxide (25

mg), compared to changes in these scores with a placebo, showed not quite significant ($p < 0.10$) decreases in anxiety, hostility outward, and ambivalent hostility scores. However, when changes in psychological studies were examined in those 11 anxious subjects whose chlordiazepoxide blood levels were 0.70 mg/ml or above, a significant decrease occurred in anxiety scores ($p < 0.025$) when subjects were on chlordiazepoxide rather than placebo. Comparative decreases in hostility scores ($N = 11$) with chlordiazepoxide still did not reach a convincing level of significance.

Previous studies using the same content-analysis method of deriving anxiety and hostility scores (Gleser et al., 1965) also showed a significant reduction in anxiety, overt hostility outward, and ambivalent hostility after 20 mg of chlordiazepoxide in 16- to 17-year-old delinquent boys. The present study strongly suggests that the blood level of an antianxiety agent such as chlordiazepoxide must be sufficient or exceed a certain level before an antianxiety effect is achieved by most individuals.

Our findings that chlordiazepoxide blood levels in 18 subjects (Table VII) tend to be negatively correlated with average blood free fatty acids ($r = -0.26$), triglycerides ($r = -0.43$), glucose ($r = -0.73$), creatinine ($r = -0.37$), and, in the 11 subjects having higher chlordiazepoxide levels, with insulin ($r = -0.55$), point to rather varied metabolic and neurogenic effects that cannot be easily understood by one explanatory mechanism.

This study contributes some information regarding the ability of chlordiazepoxide to increase hostility levels in anxious subjects. Apparently, a single oral dose of 25 mg of chlordiazepoxide does not raise hostility levels while it lowers anxiety scores in anxious subjects. In fact, the higher the blood level of chlordiazepoxide, the greater the decrease in ambivalent hostility scores. Curiously enough, however, when one uses for such a calculation the 11 subjects whose chlordiazepoxide levels were 0.70 $\mu$g/ml or above, a correlation of 0.82 is obtained between the chlordiazepoxide blood level at the beginning of the experimental period (time zero) and the increase in hostility outward scores from 0 to 50 min during the experimental session. Most of this correlation is accounted for by the overt hostility outward component ($r = 0.80$) rather than the covert hostility outward component ($r = 0.37$). These findings occur in the face of a slight but not quite significant decrease in hostility outward scores and ambivalent hostility when subjects are on chlordiazepoxide as compared to placebo. Whereas our findings on hostility are in contrast to those of DiMascio and his coworkers, our results on anxiety supplement them. In their studies (DiMascio and Barrett, 1965; Barrett and DiMascio, 1966; Gardos et al., 1968; Salzman et al., 1969), subjects received mild tranquilizers for 1 week

(chlordiazepoxide or oxazepam or a placebo) in contrast to a single dose in the present study. In the most recent report by this group (Gardos et al., 1968), chlordiazepoxide (10 mg t.i.d.) for 1 week reduced anxiety (as measured by the Scheier and Cattell, 1960, self-report test) in high and medium anxious subjects (as assessed by the Taylor Manifest Anxiety Scale). Chlordiazepoxide was found to increase significantly ambivalent hostility scores in highly anxious subjects, whereas oxazepam increased hostility inward scores (Salzman et al., 1969), using the Gottschalk content-analysis hostility scale (1963). Hostility scores from the Buss-Durkee Hostility Inventory (1957) also, apparently, increased with chlordiazepoxide. Our study cannot disprove that, perhaps with more prolonged administration of minor tranquilizers, an increase in some kind of hostility may occur in some individuals.

Besides the fact that there may well be different effects on psychological states of single and multiple doses of psychoactive pharmacological agents, there are also differences in results that may be obtained depending on the psychological measuring technique used. For instance, the Buss-Durkee, the Scheier and Cattell, and Taylor Manifest Anxiety Scales are all self-report procedures for assessing psychological states, and, as such, these measurement procedures are subject to the effects of suggestion or covering up. Individuals reporting about themselves, using these methods, are aware of what is being measured and may expose only that which they want to reveal instead of how they actually feel. The Gottschalk-Gleser Content-Analysis Method (1969), on the other hand, does not reveal to the subject what psychological dimensions are really being measured, and this method is designed to give an assessment of a psychological trait. Hence, the latter procedure may not necessarily give identical results to the former measurement methods.

The elevation of plasma free fatty acid levels (and triglycerides) with a single dose of chlordiazepoxide, as compared to a placebo, in a relatively nonstressful experiment is of interest. Other investigators (Martelli and Corsico, 1969) have noted that chlordiazepoxide (40 mg/kg, i.p.) elevates plasma free fatty acids in female albino rats. There is evidence (Martelli and Corsico, 1969) that this lipomobilizing effect of chlordiazepoxide may occur through the mechanism of blocking the enzyme phospodiesterase which, in turn, like theophylline, prevents the inactivation of cyclic 3′, 5′-AMP and, hence, of adipose tissue lipase (Hynie, Krishna, and Brodie, 1966; Butcher and Baird, 1969). Oxazepam (30 mg in a single dose) has been demonstrated to keep plasma free fatty acid levels lower than a placebo (Brown, Sletten, Kleinman, and Korol, 1968) during a planned stress-

ful experiment in which human subjects received mild electroshocks or the threat of such. Similarly, Khan, Forney, and Hughes (1964) have demonstrated that chlordiazepoxide (20 mg/kg) administered to rats will block the rise in free fatty acids more effectively than pentobarbital (5 mg/kg), or ethanol (0.55 g/kg), or after repeated electroshocks (2 sec every min for 90 min). Our study is a natural-history, relatively nonstressful study; under these circumstances, chlordiazepoxide, in a single dose, elevates blood free fatty acids and triglycerides rather than having a notable effect on blocking the elevation of these lipids through stress-induced adrenergic mechanisms. In our study, at the same time, anxiety scores were significantly reduced when chlordiazepoxide blood levels exceeded 0.70 $\mu$g/ml. In the study of Brown et al. (1968), when a stressful electroshock stimulus was applied to human subjects, oxazepam blocked free fatty acid elevation as compared to a placebo. The free fatty acid level with placebo in the Brown et al. study reached 670 $\mu$equiv/liter with electroshock, whereas in our study average free fatty acids ranged from 540 to 600 $\mu$equiv/liter when the subjects were on placebo and from 595 to 670 on chlordiazepoxide. Apparently, a single dose of chlordiazepoxide, possibly in contrast to oxazepam, may mobilize lipids as much as a stress stimulus. We propose that the lipomobilizing effect of a single dose of chlordiazepoxide involves metabolic mechanisms peripheral to the central nervous system, possibly through blocking the influence of phosphodiesterase, which permits cyclase to activate cyclic AMP, which in turn activates adipose tissue lipase. At the same time, the lowering of anxiety scores in our study demonstrates the simultaneous neurochemical inhibition of adrenergic activation through the central nervous system. Since our subjects were not purposely stressed, the capacity of chlordiazepoxide to block the lipomobilizing effect of stress was not elicited; rather, the peripheral metabolic effect of chlordiazepoxide appeared to predominate.

In contrast to other investigators (Rutishauser, 1963; Sternbach, Randall, and Gustafson, 1964; Satoh and Iwamoto, 1966) who observed that chlordiazepoxide produced short-lasting increases in blood glucose in fasted rats, we found no significant differences in blood glucose levels with chlordiazepoxide or a placebo. This hyperglycemic effect of chlordiazepoxide is believed to be an indirect action, due in part to activation of adrenergic mechanisms. In female rats, such a hyperglycemic effect does not occur when the dose level is less than 30 mg/kg, i.p., and it lasts for at least 4 hr when the dosage reaches 60 mg/kg, i.p. (Arrigoni-Martelli and Toth, 1969). The absence of such a hyperglycemic effect in our subjects, who received only 25 mg per mouth, is most likely the result of a relatively low dosage.

Our findings suggest that chlordiazepoxide (25 mg) may have a mild initial stimulating influence on cortisol blood levels and a suppressing effect on insulin secretion. More definitely, it blocks the hypoglycemic effect of insulin (Table IX). These and other biochemical effects of 25 mg of chlordiazepoxide seem to be considerable, although not heretofore noted. We have no evidence that these biochemical effects are advantageous or disadvantageous for human beings, any more than suppressing anxiety or other psychological states may or may not be deleterious. We believe strongly that these effects of this benzodiazepine should be investigated further to improve our understanding of mechanism of action and side effects.

The capacity of a small oral dose of chlordiazepoxide to change radically the typical psychobiochemical correlations of anxiety with blood free fatty acids, and hostility with blood cortisol levels, should be of interest. Our demonstration that other less well-substantiated correlations between psychological states and biochemical variables are also markedly influenced tends to corroborate the likelihood that small doses of psychoactive drugs such as chlordiazepoxide may have widespread peripheral and central nervous system effects as well as a variety of metabolic effects. Such findings underline how careful an investigator should be about attributing psychoactive drug effects to only one biological mechanism or pathway and, particularly, to the one on which he has focused attention. Biological pathways other than the intended ones may be influential in leading to the observed effects.

The apparent biochemical correlates of various psychological states that we have demonstrated here and the modification of these correlations with a psychoactive drug suggests a possible research avenue involving the detection and estimation of the magnitude of various psychological states through biochemical measures.

## VI. SUMMARY

(1) We performed a double-blind, drug-placebo, crossover study examining the effects on several psychological states and on a variety of biochemical substances in the blood, including chlordiazepoxide blood levels, of a single oral dose of chlordiazepoxide (25 mg) on 18 anxious subjects.

(2) Blood levels of chlordiazepoxide ranged from 0.26 to 1.63 $\mu$g/ml. These blood levels were not correlated with the time interval between ingestion of the drug and time of drawing the blood sample for chlordiazepoxide determination (average time interval 92 min, range 60 to 145

min), nor with body weight or sex.

(3) Anxiety, hostility outward, and ambivalent hostility scores tended to decrease ($p < 0.10$) over the 50-min observation period of this study when subjects were on chlordiazepoxide, as compared to a placebo. However, a statistically significant decrease in anxiety scores ($p < 0.025$) during this time period occurred only in those 11 subjects whose chlordiazepoxide blood levels exceeded 0.70 μg/ml. In these subjects, the decrease in hostility outward and ambivalent hostility scores, when the subjects were on chlordiazepoxide, did not reach a convincing level of significance.

(4) Chlordiazepoxide blood levels of all 18 subjects correlated with scores on anxiety (—0.26), ambivalent hostility (—0.42), achievement strivings (—0.31), average blood free fatty acids (—0.26), average triglycerides (—0.43), glucose (—0.73), and creatinine (—0.37). Chlordiazepoxide blood levels of the 11 subjects whose levels exceeded 0.70 μg/ml also correlated with hostility outward scores (0.82), hostility inward scores (—0.47), and with blood insulin (—0.55).

(5) Chlordiazepoxide, at this single oral dosage (25 mg), in comparison to a placebo, significantly elevated plasma free fatty acids ($p < 0.01$) and triglycerides ($p < 0.001$) but had no effect on glucose. This lipomobilizing effect is thought to be due to blocking of the enzyme phosphodiesterase, allowing cyclase to activate cyclic AMP and, hence, adipose tissue lipase.

(6) The significant negative correlations of blood insulin levels with blood glucose, when the same subjects were on placebo, were blocked when the subjects were administered the chlordiazepoxide. There was some slight evidence that chlordiazepoxide might stimulate cortisol secretion initially and suppress it 50 min later.

(7) A series of correlations between various psychological states and biochemical variables in the blood under placebo conditions were reversed when the subjects were on chlordiazepoxide: e.g., anxiety correlated with average free fatty acids (placebo 0.35, chlordiazepoxide —0.18); hostility outward with cortisol (placebo 0.42, chlordiazepoxide —0.29); achievement strivings with average triglyceride (placebo —0.32, chlordiazepoxide 0.42); achievement strivings with insulin (placebo —0.44, chlordiazepoxide 0.38); and human relations with cortisol (placebo —0.43, chlordiazepoxide 0.58). These changes in psychobiochemical relationships, associated with ingestion of 25 mg of chlordiazepoxide, suggest the influence of a variety of intervening variables, including metabolic and neurochemical influences on the peripheral and central nervous system.

(8) Implications of these findings are discussed as well as directions for future research.

## ACKNOWLEDGMENTS

This study has been supported in part by U.S. Public Health Service research grant MH-20174 from the National Institute of Mental Health, and by a grant-in-aid from Hoffmann-La Roche Inc.

## REFERENCES

Antonis, A. (1965): Semiautomated method for the colorimetric determination of plasma free fatty acids. *Journal of Lipid Research,* 6:307

Arrigoni-Martelli, E., and Toth, E. (1969): Effect of chlordiazepoxide on glucose metabolism in rats. In: *European Society for the Study of Drug Toxicity. Toxicity and Side-Effects of Psychotropic Drugs; Proceedings of the Meeting Held in Paris,* Series No. 145, p. 73. Excerpta Medica Foundation, Amsterdam.

Barrett, J. E., and DiMascio, A. (1966): Comparative effects on anxiety of the "minor tranquilizers" in "high" and "low" anxious student volunteers. *Diseases of the Nervous System,* 27:483.

Brown, M. L., Sletten, I. W., Kleinman, K. M,. and Korol, B. (1968): Effect of oxazepam on physiological responses to stress in normal subjects. *Current Therapeutic Research,* 10:543.

Buss, A. H., and Durkee, A. (1957): An inventory for assessing different kinds of hostility. *Journal of Consulting Psychology,* 21:343.

Butcher, R. W., and Baird, C. E. (1969): The regulation of cyclic AMP and lipolysis in adipose tissue by hormones and other agents. In: *Drugs Affecting Lipid Metabolism,* edited by W. L. Holmes, L. A. Carlson, and R. Paoletti. Plenum Press, New York, p. 5.

Butte, J. C., and Noble, E. P. (1969): Simultaneous determination of plasma or whole blood cortisol and corticosterone. *Acta Endocrinologica,* 61:678.

Cash, W. D., and Quinn, G. P. (1970): Clinical-chemical correlations: An overview. *Psychopharmacology Bulletin,* 6:26.

Cohen, I. M., and Harris, T. H. (1969): Effects of chlordiazepoxide in psychiatric disorders. *Southern Medical Journal,* 54:1271.

Cuparencu, B., Ticsa, I., Safta, L., Rosenberg, A., Mocan, R., and Brief, G. A. (1969): Influence of some psychotropic drugs on the development of experimental atherosclerosis. *Cor et Vasa, International Journal of Cardiology,* 11:112.

DiMascio, A., and Barrett, J. E. (1965): Comparative effects of oxazepam in "high" and "low" anxious student volunteers. *Psychosomatics,* 6:298.

Elliott, H. W., Gottschalk, L. A., and Uliana, R. L. (1973): Relationship of plasma meperidine levels to changes in anxiety and hostility. *Psychopharmacologia,* (*in press*).

Frings, S. F., Ratcliff, C. R., and Dunn, R. T. (1970): Automated determination of glucose in serum or plasma by a direct O-toluidine procedure. *Clinical Chemistry,* 16:282.

Gardos, G., DiMascio, A., Salzman, C., and Shader, R. I. (1968): Differential actions of chlordiazepoxide and oxazepam on hostility. *Archives of General Psychiatry,* 18: 757.

Gitelman, H. J. (1967): An improved automated procedure for the determination of calcium in biological specimens. *Analytical Biochemistry,* 18:521.

Gleser, G. C., Gottschalk, L. A., Fox, R., and Lippert, W. (1965): Immediate changes in affect with chlordiazepoxide in juvenile delinquent boys. *Archives of General Psychiatry,* 13:291.

Gottschalk, L. A., Cleghorn, J. M., Gleser, G. C., and Iacono, J. M. (1965): Studies of relationships of emotions to plasma lipids. *Psychosomatic Medicine,* 27:102.
Gottschalk, L. A., and Gleser, G. C. (1969): *The Measurement of Psychological States Through the Content Analysis of Verbal Behavior.* University of California Press, Berkeley.
Gottschalk, L. A., Gleser, G. C., and Springer, K. J. (1963): Three hostility scales applicable to verbal samples. *Archives of General Psychiatry,* 9:254.
Gottschalk, L. A., Stone, W. N., Gleser, G. C., and Iacono, J. M. (1969*a*): Anxiety and plasma free fatty acids (FFA). *Life Sciences,* 8:61.
Gottschalk, L. A., Winget, C. N., and Gleser, G. C. (1969*b*): *Manual of Instructions for Using the Gottschalk-Gleser Content Analysis Scales: Anxiety, Hostility, Social Alienation-Personal Disorganization.* University of California Press, Berkeley.
Green, D. E., Forrest, I. S., Forrest, F. M., and Serra, M. T. (1965): Interpatient variation in chlorpromazine metabolism. *Experimental Medicine and Surgery,* 23:278.
Hales, C. N., and Randle, P. J. (1963): Immunoassay of insulin with insulin antibody precipitate. *Lancet,* 1:200.
Hales, C. N., and Randle, P. J. (1963): Immunoassay of insulin with insulin antibody precipitate. *Biochemical Journal,* 88:137.
Huang, T. C., Chen, C. P., Wefler, V., and Raftery, A. (1961): A stable reagent for the Liebermann-Burchard reaction. *Analytical Chemistry,* 33:1405.
Hynie, S., Krishna, G., and Brodie, B. B. (1966): Theophylline as a tool in studies of the role of cyclic adenosine 3′,5′-monophosphate in hormone-induced lipolysis. *Journal of Pharmacology and Experimental Therapeutics,* 153:90.
Kessler, G., and Lederer, H. (1966): Fluorometric Measurement of Triglycerides. In: *Automation in Analytical Chemistry,* edited by L. T. Skeggs, Jr., Mediad, Inc., New York, p. 341.
Kessler, G., Rush, R. L., Leon, L., Delea, A., and Cupiola, R. (1970): Automated 340-nm measurement of SGOT, SGPT, and LDH. *Clinical Chemistry,* 16:530.
Khan, A. U., Forney, R. B., and Hughes, F. W. (1964): Plasma free fatty acids in rats after shock as modified by centrally active drugs. *Archives of International Pharmacodynamics,* 151:466.
Martelli, E. A., and Corsico, N. (1969): On the mechanism of lipomobilizing effect of chlordiazepoxide. *Journal of Pharmacy and Pharmacology,* 21:59.
Morgenstern, S., Kessler, G., Auerbach, J., Flor, R. V., and Klein, B. (1965): Automated p-nitrophenylphosphate serum alkaline phosphatase procedure for the auto analyzer. *Clinical Chemistry,* 11:876.
Murray, N. (1962): Covert effect of chlordiazepoxide therapy. *Journal of Neuropsychiatry,* 3:168.
Musser, A. W., and Ortigoza, C. (1966): Automated determination of uric acid by the hydroxylamine method. *Technical Bulletin of Registry of Medical Technologists,* 36:21.
Opitz, K. (1965): Einfluss von Psychopharmaka auf die nichtveresterten Fettsaüren im Blutsplasma. *Experientia,* 21:462.
Overall, J. E., and Gorham, D. R. (1962): The brief psychiatric rating scale. *Psychological Reports,* 10:799.
Randall, L. O., and Schallek, W. (1968): Pharmacological activity of certain benzodiazepines. In: *Psychopharmacology: A Review of Progress, 1957-1967,* edited by D. H. Efron, *et al.,* p. 153. Public Health Service Publication No. 1836, U.S. Government Printing Office, Washington, D.C.
Rutishauser, M. (1963): Beeinflussung des Kohlenhydralstoffwechsels des Rattenhirns durch Psychopharmaka mit sedativer Wirkung. *Naunyn-Schmiedebergs Archiv für Pharmakologie und Experimentelle Pathologie,* 245:396.
Salzman, C., DiMascio, A., Shader, R. I., and Harmatz, J. S. (1969): Chlordiazepoxide, expectation, and hostility. *Psychopharmacologia,* 14:38.

Satoh, T., and Iwamoto, T. (1966): Neurotropic drugs, electroshock, and carbohydrate metabolism in the rat. *Biochemical Pharmacology,* 15:323.

Scheier, I. H., and Cattell, R. B. (1960): *Handbook and Test Kit for the IPAT 8-Parallel Form Anxiety Battery.* Institute for Personality and Ability Testing, Champaign, Illinois.

Schwartz, M. A., and Postma, E. (1966): Metabolic N-demethylation of chlordiazepoxide. *Journal of Pharmacological Sciences,* 55:1358.

Schwartz, M. A., Postma, E., and Gaut, Z. (1971): Biological half-life in chlordiazepoxide and its metabolite, demoxepam, in man. *Journal of Pharmaceutical Sciences,* 60:1500.

Sternbach, L. H., Randall, L. O., and Gustafson, S. R. (1964): 1,4-Benzodiazepines (chlordiazepoxide and related compounds). In: *Psychopharmacological Agents,* edited by M. Gordon., Vol. 1. Academic Press, New York, p. 199.

Stone, W. N., Gleser, G. C., Gottschalk, L. A., and Iacono, J. M. (1969): Stimulus, affect and plasma free fatty acids. *Psychosomatic Medicine,* 31:331.

Technicon Methodology N-14b. (1965): Technicon Instrument Corporation, Tarrytown, New York.

Tobin, J. M., Bird, I. F., and Boyle, D. E. (1960): Preliminary evaluation of LIBRIUM (RO-0690) in the treatment of anxiety reactions. *Diseases of the Nervous System.* 21:11.

Tobin, J. M., and Lewis, N. D. C. (1960): New psychotherapeutic agent, chlordiazepoxide. Use in treatment of anxiety states and related symptoms. *Journal of the American Medical Association,* 174:1242.

Usdin, E. (1970): Absorption, distribution, and metabolic fate of psychotropic drugs. *Psychopharmacology Bulletin,* 6:4.

# Relationship of Plasma Meperidine Levels to Changes in Anxiety and Hostility

Henry W. Elliott, Louis A. Gottschalk, and Regina L. Uliana

*Six adult male former drug users were given single 100-mg doses of meperidine by the intramuscular route and an additional six were administered 100-mg doses by the oral route in a single-blind situation. Anxiety and hostility were measured by speech-content analysis before and after drug administration and correlated with plasma concentrations of meperidine. Significant decreases in anxiety and outward overt hostility scores occurred 1 to 1.5 hr postdrug when plasma meperidine concentrations were high, with return of these affect scores toward predrug values at 6 hr when plasma concentrations of meperidine were falling. Meperidine was found to resemble sedative-hypnotics in its effects on anxiety and hostility. Significant correlations were noted between plasma meperidine concentration and decrease in anxiety and hostility inward scores. The findings are consistent with the hypothesis that narcotic abuse is enhanced through the psychological effects of these drugs. Key words: meperidine, anxiety, hostility, drug abuse.*

THE narcotic analgesics have multiple actions on the central nervous system, including the production of euphoria, tranquility, and somnolence, which may be responsible in large part for their abuse potential.[1] It is possible that changes in anxiety and hostility may accompany or play a role in these effects, and quantitation of such changes would be useful in interpreting the actions of narcotic analgesics in both therapeutic and abuse situations. Moreover, the correlations of changes in anxiety and hostility with blood meperidine concentrations would also be of interest. This report describes the effects of single 100-mg doses of meperidine HCl, intramuscularly and orally, on anxiety and hostility levels and on plasma concentrations of meperidine base in adult male former narcotic users. Anxiety and hostility were measured by a speech-content-analysis method.

## MATERIALS AND METHODS

### *Subjects*

Twelve paid volunteer male inmates, average age 37.2 years, range 27–46 years, of the California Medical Facility at Vacaville, with a history of street narcotic use, but who were medication-free for at least 4 weeks, served as subjects. Subjects were not selected because of high anxiety or hostility levels; informed consent was obtained from all participants prior to initiating the study.

### *Procedure*

Two single-blind experiments were performed, one for parenteral and one for oral formulations of meperidine. The identity of the drug and dose were unknown to the subjects and to the content-analysis technician who scored the verbal samples.

---

*From the Department of Medical Pharmacology and Therapeutics and the Department of Psychiatry and Human Behavior, College of Medicine, University of California, Irvine, and the Solano Institute for Medical and Psychiatric Research, Vacaville, Calif.*

Henry W. Elliott, M.D., Ph.D.: *Professor and Chairman, Department of Medical Pharmacology and Therapeutics, College of Medicine, University of California, Irvine.* Louis A. Gottschalk, M.D.: *Professor and Chairman, Department of Psychiatry and Human Behavior, College of Medicine, University of California, Irvine; Director of Psychiatric Service, Orange County Medical Center.* Regina L. Uliana, A.B.: *Research Assistant, Department of Psychiatry and Human Behavior, College of Medicine, University of California, Irvine.*

*Supported in part by a research project grant from the National Institute of Mental Health, Bethesda, Md. (MH-20174-02) and by a grant from Wyeth Laboratories, Philadelphia, Pa.*

Plasma concentrations of meperidine base were determined using gas-liquid chromatography by the method of Knowles, White, and Ruelius.[2]

Anxiety and hostility levels were determined by the speech-content-analysis method of Gottschalk and Gleser.[3] Five-minute verbal samples were obtained pre-drug ($VS_1$), 63–104 min post-drug ($VS_2$), and 360–397 min post-drug ($VS_3$) from six randomly chosen subjects given 100 mg meperidine intramuscularly, and on another day, from the remaining six subjects given meperidine 100 mg orally.

The speech samples were obtained according to a standard procedure[3,4] in which the subjects spoke for 5 min into the microphone of a tape recorder in response to instructions to talk about any interesting or dramatic personal life experiences. The typescripts of the tape recordings were scored for relevant thematic or semantic variables by a content-analysis technician, unfamiliar with the purpose or design of this study, following validated scales of a variety of psychological dimensions, specifically, anxiety and hostility outward (overt and covert), hostility inward, and ambivalent hostility. Pre-drug and post-drug values were compared and correlated with plasma concentrations of meperidine base at the approximate time of obtaining the speech samples.

A brief description of the content-analysis scales and some examples of their previous applications may be in order. All the affect scores are derived from the frequency of occurrence of certain specified themes per grammatical clause of a typescript of the verbal behavior. Not merely "manifest" anxiety, such as "I was afraid," but also "latent" anxiety (or hostility) is scored, such as, "others are afraid" or "I lost my balance" or "I am to blame" or "the car was completely wrecked." The validity of these scales has been checked against four types of criterion measures: psychological (self-reports and rating scales), physiological (especially, autonomic measures), biochemical, and pharmacological.[3] Anxiety scores previously obtained by this content-analysis method correlate significantly with clinical psychiatric ratings of anxiety, with increase in systolic blood pressure, decrease in skin temperature, and higher plasma free fatty-acids levels in fasting subjects (a sensitive, indirect measure of adrenergic activation). Previous psychopharmacologic studies have demonstrated that sedative doses of amobarbital (65 mg) decrease anxiety scores significantly,[5] as do chlordiazepoxide, 20 mg[6] and 25 mg;[7] perphenazine, 16–24 mg/day;[8] and lorazepam, 5 mg.[9] On the other hand, the antidepressant imipramine (100–300 mg/day) in nondepressed patients increases anxiety scores.[10] Hostility outward (total) scores are made up of two subscale scores, *overt hostility outward,* which is derived from verbal statements directly indicative of the speaker's hostility to external objects, and *covert hostility outward,* which is derived from utterances by the speaker denoting hostile thoughts or actions to others. *Hostility inward* scores are derived from angry and hostile assertions made by the self (the speaker) about the self. *Ambivalent hostility* scores are derived from thematic contents that denote hostile or destructive thoughts or activities originating from external objects (people, things, or events) and directed toward the self (that is, the speaker).[11] Previous psychopharmacologic studies have demonstrated that these hostility outward scores are increased by repeated doses of imipramine (100–300 mg/day) in nondepressed subjects,[10] and decreased by a single dose of chlordiazepoxide[6,9] or repeated doses of perphenazine (16–25 mg/day)[8] or thioridazine.[12]

## RESULTS

In the intramuscular study, mean plasma concentrations of meperidine, in nanograms per milliliter, were 249.9 at 60 min, 257.6 at 90 min, and 142.4 at 360 min, and there was a wide range of plasma concentrations across the six subjects for comparable post-drug time intervals (see Table 1).

In the oral study, corresponding mean plasma meperidine concentrations were, in nanograms per milliliter, 97.9 at 60 min, 114.7 at 90 min, and 51.7 at 360 min. The peak concentrations were approximately half those attained after intramuscular administration, and the biological half-life was approximately 6–7 hr, slightly longer than the 5–6 hr half-life after intramuscular administration. The range of meperidine plasma concentrations also varied widely over the six subjects who took the drug orally (see Table2).

The effects of meperidine 100 mg intramuscularly or orally or both on anxiety and hostility by the method of content analysis of verbal samples are presented in

**Table 1. Meperidine Blood Levels of Six Subjects (in Nanograms of Meperidine Base/Milliliter of Plasma) Receiving 100 mg of Meperidine Intramuscularly**

| Time After IM Injection of 100 mg Meperidine | Subjects | | | | | | |
|---|---|---|---|---|---|---|---|
| | A | C | H | O | M | P | Mean |
| 1 hr | 170.5 | 167.4 | 185.6 | 335.5 | 319.9 | 320.3 | 249.9 |
| 1.5 hr | 192.2 | 170.4 | 200.7 | 344.3 | 340.7 | 299.6 | 257.6 |
| 6 hr | 122.7 | 121.5 | 105.8 | 203.0 | 159.3 | 142.0 | 142.4 |

**Table 2. Meperidine Blood Levels of Six Subjects (in Nanograms of Meperidine Base/Milliliter of Plasma) Receiving 100 mg of Meperidine by Mouth**

| Time After Oral Ingestion of 100 mg Meperidine | Subjects | | | | | | |
|---|---|---|---|---|---|---|---|
| | G | B | H | A | J | T | Mean |
| 1 hr | 238.8 | 0 | 127.3 | 89.7 | 101.2 | 30.2 | 97.9 |
| 1.5 hr | 185.0 | 56.4 | 131.4 | 78.2 | 152.1 | 85.1 | 114.7 |
| 6 hr | 50.0 | 88.8 | 31.3 | 37.6 | 72.5 | 30.2 | 51.7 |

Table 3. Fortunately all subjects had relatively high pre-drug anxiety scores (about the 90th percentile for a normative sample) and hostility scores (about the 70th percentile). Statistical analysis (by a two-tailed t test) indicated significant decreases in average anxiety and outward hositility scores 1–1.5 hr post-drug, with return toward pre-drug values 6 hr post-drug. The most significant differences ($p<0.01$) were noted when both groups of six subjects were combined, but data suggestive of decreased anxiety and hostility scores with 100 mg of meperidine were obtained from each separate group of six subjects, whether the route of drug administration was oral or intramuscular.

Table 4 presents the Pearson product moment correlations of meperidine plasma concentrations with the affect scores of the second verbal sample and with the difference scores of verbal sample two minus verbal sample one. The estimated plasma concentration at the time of verbal sample two was used and was calculated by interpolation between the values at 1 hr and 1½ hr.* In addition, before combining the oral and intramuscular groups to find an overall correlation, the values of the meperidine concentration were standardized for each group.

Significant ($p<0.05$) to near significant correlations between meperidine plasma concentrations and *decreases* in anxiety and hostility inward scores were observed. Also, the greater the plasma meperidine concentration the less the decrease in

*Interpolations were made using the following formula:

$$C_{VS} = \frac{T_{VS} - 60'}{30'} (C_{90} - C_{60}) + C_{60}$$

where $C_{VS}$ = concentration at time of verbal sample; $T_{VS}$ = time verbal sample taken; $C_{90}$ = concentration at 90 min; $C_{60}$ = concentration at 60 min.

**Table 3. Average Affect Scores, Separate and Combined, for Subjects Receiving Meperidine by the IM (I) and Oral (O) Routes**

| Time | Anxiety | | | Outward Hostility (Overt) | | | Outward Hostility (Covert) | | | Outward Hostility (Total) | | | Ambivalent Hostility | | | Hostility Inward | | |
|---|---|---|---|---|---|---|---|---|---|---|---|---|---|---|---|---|---|---|
| | O+I | O | I | O+I | O | I | O+I | O | I | O+I | O | I | O+I | O | I | O+I | O | I |
| Pre-drug (av) | 2.57 | 2.74 | 2.41 | 1.06 | 1.06 | 1.07 | 0.63 | 0.49 | 0.78 | 1.21 | 1.18 | 1.25 | 0.67 | 0.76 | 0.58 | 1.41 | 1.73 | 1.09 |
| (SD) | ±0.97 | ±1.33 | 0.50 | ±0.54 | ±0.76 | ±0.27 | ±0.37 | ±0.33 | ±0.38 | ±0.56 | ±0.70 | ±0.46 | ±0.28 | ±0.30 | ±0.25 | ±0.73 | ±0.85 | ±0.44 |
| 1–1.5 hr | 1.85† | 1.82† | 1.88* | 0.77‡ | 0.87* | 0.68† | 0.73 | 0.43 | 1.01 | 1.02 | 0.87* | 1.16 | 0.60 | 0.48* | 0.72* | 1.09* | 1.11* | 1.07 |
| post-drug | ±0.79 | ±1.08 | 0.46 | ±0.45 | ±0.62 | ±0.19 | ±0.60 | ±0.18 | ±0.75 | ±0.68 | ±0.66 | ±0.74 | ±0.35 | ±0.18 | ±0.46 | ±0.67 | ±0.82 | ±0.56 |
| 6–6.5 hr | 2.28 | 1.97 | 2.59 | 0.89 | 0.62 | 1.12 | 0.60 | 0.42 | 0.79 | 0.99 | 0.66 | 1.31 | 0.58 | 0.60 | 0.55 | 1.27 | 1.19 | 1.36 |
| post-drug | ±1.02 | ±1.20 | 0.77 | ±0.43 | ±0.37 | ±0.33 | ±0.31 | ±0.16 | ±0.32 | ±0.50 | ±0.40 | ±0.36 | ±0.35 | ±0.45 | ±0.25 | ±0.63 | ±0.79 | ±0.48 |

*Significantly lower than the pre-drug score at $p < 0.10$, two-tail test.
† Significantly lower than the pre-drug score at $p < 0.05$, two-tail test.
‡ Significantly lower than the pre-drug score at $p < 0.01$, two-tail test.

**Table 4. Correlations of Meperidine Plasma Concentrations (Standard Scores) With Affect Scores for Subjects Receiving Meperidine by the Oral (O) and IM (I) Routes, Separate and Combined**

| Affect Scores | Anxiety | | | Hostility Out (Overt) | | | Hostility Out (Covert) | | | Hostility Out Total | | | Ambivalent Hostility | | | Hostility In | | |
|---|---|---|---|---|---|---|---|---|---|---|---|---|---|---|---|---|---|---|
| | O+I $N=12$ | O $N=6$ | I $N=6$ | O+I $N=12$ | O $N=6$ | I $N=6$ | O+I $N=12$ | O $N=6$ | I $N=6$ | O+I $N=12$ | O $N=6$ | I $N=6$ | O+I $N=12$ | O $N=6$ | I $N=6$ | O+I $N=12$ | O $N=6$ | I $N=6$ |
| $VS_{2-1}$ | −0.39 | −0.72* | −0.11 | −0.37 | −0.42 | −0.39 | 0.46 | 0.84† | 0.27 | 0.12 | 0.54 | −0.04 | −0.24 | −0.54 | −0.16 | −0.57* | −0.66 | −0.61 |
| $VS_2$ | −0.37 | −0.41 | −0.35 | −0.36 | −0.73* | −0.55 | 0.03 | 0.64 | 0.10 | 0.25 | 0.73* | −0.18 | −0.26 | −0.16 | −0.36 | −0.64† | −0.65 | −0.67* |

$VS_{2-1}$ = difference between affect scores derived from verbal sample two minus verbal sample one
$VS_2$ = affect scores derived from second verbal sample (obtained 63–82 min after administration of drug).
*Significant at $p < 0.05$, one-tailed test.
† Significant at $p < 0.01$, one-tailed test.

covert hostility outward scores, and, on the average, *covert* hostility outward scores were least affected post-drug of any of the hostility scores.

## DISCUSSION

The wide variations in meperidine plasma concentrations at similar time intervals post-drug and occurring with the same doses (100 mg) of meperidine, administered either orally or parenterally, should be of considerable interest to both clinicians and basic scientists. While wide interindividual variations in drug metabolism have been reported with other psychoactive drugs,[7,13–15] including major and minor tranquilizers and antidepressants, this range of variation occurring with a synthetic narcotic analgesic has not been previously emphasized. From the basic science point of view, such interindividual variations should stimulate investigation of the enzymatic differences, genetic and acquired, between people responsible for such variations in the rate of breakdown of such psychoactive drugs. Also these findings should alert clinical investigators exploring the mechanisms of action and usefulness of narcotic antagonists that interindividual variations may be quite broad.

The capacity of meperidine for significant anti-anxiety effect and reduction of overt hostility outward (using an objective content-analysis measure of these psychological states) indicates that, by these behavioral criteria, meperidine has psychopharmacological actions similar to sedative–hypnotic agents and minor tranquilizers.[3,7–9] The attractiveness of narcotic drugs for individuals occasionally or chronically using them is consistent with these psychological effects.

That the plasma concentration of meperidine tends to be correlated with the amount of reduction of anxiety and hostility inward may provide a clue as to which individuals are likely to become habituated to the use of such drugs: namely, those individuals whose plasma concentrations of narcotics, after receiving a standard dose, reach higher levels and in whom the relative half-life of the drug is longer. Such a speculation, of course, needs to be investigated further.

A significant *decrease* in hostility outward scores with a single dose of psychoactive drug but a simultaneous *correlation* of higher hostility outward scores with higher plasma concentrations of the drug has been noted with chlordiazepoxide.[7] Other investigators[16,17] have reported increases in hostility outward scores with decreases in anxiety scores, using these content–analysis scales, in some patients receiving continuous oral doses of certain benzodiazepene derivatives, and these investigators have suggested the explanation of a release or disinhibition effect of these drugs on the central nervous system. But the work of these investigators should not be confused with our data, which are based on single-dose instead of continuous-dose studies and which include relating the plasma concentration of the psychoactive drug to decreases or increases of anxiety and different kinds of hostility. We do not know exactly why an anti-anxiety and anti-hostility agent, such as meperidine appears to be when given in a single dose, is associated with *increases* instead of decreases in covert hostility outward scores, the greater the plasma concentration of the drug. Such findings are useful and have heuristic value in broadening our perspectives with regard to the types of hostility (and anxiety) that may be differentially affected by psychoactive drugs and the

more subtle interactions of pharmacological agents on the psychobiological processes in man.

Obviously our sample of subjects in this study is small, and our findings at this preliminary stage can only point the direction for further investigation.

## REFERENCES


1. Martin WR: Desirable effects of narcotics—euphoria, tranquility, and somnolence, in: DiPalma JR (ed): Drill's Pharmacology in Medicine (ed 4). New York, McGraw-Hill, 1971, p 370
2. Knowles JA, White GR, Ruelius HW: Determination of meperidine in human plasma and urine by gas-liquid chromatography. Analytical Letters 6:281, 1973.
3. Gottschalk LA, Gleser GC: The Measurement of Psychological States Through the Content Analysis of Verbal Behavior. Berkeley, University of California Press, 1969
4. Gottschalk LA, Winget CM, Gleser GC: Manual of Instructions for Using the Gottschalk-Gleser Content Analysis Scales: Anxiety, Hostility, Social Alienation-personal Disorganization. Berkeley, University of California Press, 1969
5. Ross WD, Adsett N, Gleser GC, et al: A trial of psychopharmacologic measurement with projective techniques. J Proj Tech Pers Ass 27:223, 1963
6. Gleser GC, Gottschalk LA, Fox R, Lippert W: Immediate changes in affect with chlordiazepoxide in juvenile delinquent boys. Arch Gen Psychiatry 13:291, 1965
7. Gottschalk LA, Kaplan SA: Chlordiazepoxide blood levels and clinical response. Compr Psychiatry 13:519, 1972
8. Gottschalk LA, Gleser GC, Springer KJ, et al: Effects of perphenazine on verbal behavior patterns. Arch Gen Psychiatry 2:632, 1960
9. Gottschalk LA, Elliott HW, Bates DE, Cable CG: Content analysis of speech samples to determine effect of lorazepam on anxiety. Clin Pharmacol Ther 13:323, 1972
10. Gottschalk LA, Gleser GC, Wylie HW Jr, Kaplan SA: Effects of imipramine on anxiety and hostility levels. Psychopharmacologia 7:303, 1965
11. Gottschalk LA, Gleser GC, Springer KJ: Three hostility scales applicable to verbal samples. Arch Gen Psychiatry 9:254, 1963
12. Gottschalk LA, Gleser GC, Cleghorn JM, et al: Prediction of changes in severity of the schizophrenic syndrome with discontinuation and administration of phenothiazines in chronic schizophrenic patients. Compr Psychiatry 11:123, 1970
13. Green DE, Forrest IS, Forrest FM, Serra MT: Interpatient variation with chlorpromazine metabolism. Exp Med Surg 23:278, 1965
14. Cash WD, Quinn GD: Clinical-chemical correlations: An overview. Psychopharmacol Bull 6:26, 1970
15. Usdin E: Absorption, distribution, and metabolic fate of psychotropic drugs. Psychopharmacol Bull 6:4, 1970
16. Gardos G, Di Mascio A, Salzman C, Shader RI: Differential actions of chlordiazepoxide and oxazepam on hostility. Arch Gen Psychiatry 18:757, 1968
17. Salzman C, Di Mascio A, Shader RI, Harmatz JS: Chlordiazepoxide, expectation, and hostility. Psychopharmacologia 14:38, 1969

# Thioridazine Plasma Levels and Clinical Response

Louis A. Gottschalk, Robert Biener, Ernest P. Noble, Herman Birch, Donald E. Wilbert, and Jon F. Heiser

THERE IS SOME EVIDENCE that standardized oral doses of psychoactive pharmacologic agents do not necessarily result in similar blood levels or clinical responses to these drugs, presumably because of different rates of absorption or elimination, rate of metabolic breakdown, other biologic factors affecting pharmacokinetics, or differing etiologies of the psychopathologic processes.[1–8]

The main purpose of this research project was to examine the relationship of a single, standardized oral dose of a phenothiazine derivative, thioridazine, to the resulting drug blood levels and clinical responses in acute schizophrenic patients. It was hypothesized that there would be individual differences in pharmacokinetics and the associated clinical responses. Another purpose was to search for predictors of favorable responses to a single drug dose. It was intended that the findings and hypotheses derived from the present and similar single-dose studies would be applied to continuous-dose thioridazine therapeutic studies of schizophrenia.

## METHODS

### *Subjects*

A total of 25 acute schizophrenic patients was selected from the Psychiatric Service, Orange County Medical Center, whose ages ranged from 21 to 55, without significant history of hepatic or cardiorenal disease or chronic alcoholism or other drug abuse. All subjects were drug-free for at least 4 weeks or longer prior to participation in this investigation. No other medications of any kind except thioridazine were given to the subjects during this experimental period. In addition to the selection of these patients being based on the independent diagnosis and consensus of schizophrenia by three psychiatrists, high scores on the major features of schizophrenia from three psychiatric rating scales and an objective speech-content analysis measure served as corroborative evidence of the diagnosis of severe acute schizophrenia.

### *Experimental Design*

The design involved a placebo-drug, single-oral-dose, non-crossover study, double-blind in the assessment of all measures, except for the scoring of three of the behavioral rating scales by a psychiatrist (R.B.). The study extended over a period of 10 days. The thioridazine (4 mg/kg) and inactive placebo were administered orally in an identical liquid vehicle. Diversified measures of psychiatric change were used—psychiatric rating scales based on ratings by a psychiatrist and scales based on

---

*From the Department of Psychiatry and Human Behavior, University of California at Irvine, Irvine, Calif., and the Psychiatric Service, Orange County Medical Center, Orange, Calif.*

Louis A. Gottschalk, M.D.: *Professor and Chairman;* Robert Biener, M.D.: *Assistant Research Psychiatrist;* Ernest P. Noble, Ph.D., M.D.: *Professor;* Herman Birch, Ph.D.: *Assistant Research Psychologist;* Donald E. Wilbert, M.D.: *Assistant Clinical Professor;* Jon F. Heiser, M.D.: *Adjunct Assistant Professor; Department of Psychiatry and Human Behavior, College of Medicine, University of California at Irvine.*

*Supported in part by NIMH Research Project Grant MH-20174 from the Psychopharmacology Branch, Bethesda, Md., and by a research grant from Sandoz, East Hanover, N.J.*

technician-trained content analysis of speech—because of the possibility that some measures of clinical change might respond more sensitively than others to blood drug levels. The following baseline measures were obtained before the administration of any medication:

1. A battery of three behavioral rating scales: namely, the Overall-Gorham Brief Psychiatric Rating Scale BPRS,[9] the Hamilton Depression Rating Scale,[10] and the Wittenborn Rating Scale.[10] Preliminary to data collection using these rating scales, videotapes of the responses of acute schizophrenic patients in seven evaluative interviews by one psychiatrist (R.B.) were viewed and rated by two other psychiatrists (D.W. and J.H.) to check the interrater reliability of scoring these behavioral rating scales.

2. A daily 5-min tape-recorded speech sample from the patient for the objective measurement of the severity of the schizophrenic syndrome (social alienation–personal disorganization scale) by means of the content analysis method of Gottschalk and Gleser.[11,12]

3. Fasting plasma biochemical levels (including the SMA-12* and plasma phenothiazine content) as well as clinical laboratory hematologic data (complete blood count and other blood indices).

4. Complete urinalysis (including a screening test for sedative-hypnotics and phenothiazines).

After obtaining these baseline measures, at 8:00 A.M. on day 1, each patient received an oral dose of the liquid placebo.

For the total 10 days of observation in the hospital, 5-min speech samples were obtained each morning at 8:00 A.M. On days 3, 6, and 8 of observation, following the tape recording of the speech sample, ratings were again made on the three behavioral rating scales.

On day 6 before breakfast and following the morning evaluative interview for rating the patient's behavior, blood was again drawn for the SMA-12 determination and plasma thioridazine concentration. Then, while the patient was still fasting (12–14 hr), a single dose (4 mg/kg) of oral liquid thioridazine concentrate was given. Blood was drawn for plasma thioridazine determinations 1, 4, and 8 hr, and 1, 2, 3, and 4 days postdrug.

The 5-min speech samples were scored by content-analysis technicians, unfamiliar with the nature of this study, for social alienation–personal disorganization, hostility, anxiety, and hope scores by the method of Gottschalk and Gleser.[11,12] Behavioral Rating Scale items and factors were scored and factor analyzed with the assistance of the Early Clinical Drug Evaluation Unit (E.C.D.E.U.) of the Psychopharmacology Branch, National Institute of Mental Health. Plasma thioridazine levels were measured by the fluorometric method of Pacha.[13] Since this method is not thought to be specific for thioridazine, but also measures metabolites, thioridazine and its metabolites were checked by a modification[14,15] of the gas-chromatographic procedure of Curry and Mould.[16] Blood chemistry (SMA-12) was autoanalyzed in the Clinical Laboratory of the Orange County Medical Center. Statistical assessment of all data, including determination of plasma thioridazine half-life and area under the curve, were carried out by use of the Dixon Biomedical Computer Programs[17] and the Statistical Package for Social Sciences.[18]

## RESULTS

### *Reliability of Scoring the Psychiatric Rating Scales (Overall-Gorham Brief Psychiatric Rating Scale, Hamilton Depression Scale, Wittenborn Rating Scale)*

Preliminary to final data collection, three psychiatrists (R.B., D.W., and J.H.) rated the relative magnitude of the behavioral and psychologic dimensions by viewing seven videotaped interviews. A measure of agreement, A, was calculated[19] between these ratings which is sensitive not only to the correlations among the ratings, but also to differences between mean ratings and between variability of ratings. The means of the A statistic for the three scales were: Overall-Gorham BPRS, 0.82; Hamilton, 0.80; and Wittenborn, 0.76. The indices of interrater reliability of scoring these three rating scales are in a satisfactory

*SMA 12: total protein, albumin, calcium, phosphorus, cholesterol, uric acid, creatinine, total bilirubin, alkaline phosphatase, CPK, LDH, transaminase SGOT.

range for psychiatric measurements, although the reliability index for the Wittenborn Scale is at the margin of acceptability. All the psychiatric ratings used in the data analyses of this study were done by only one (R.B.) of the three psychiatrists.

The interscorer reliability of the technicians scoring the social alienation–personal disorganization scale exceeded 0.85.

*Thioridazine Plasma Concentrations following Ingestion of 4 mg/kg*

Thioridazine plasma concentrations determined by the fluorometric method were compared to the results obtained on the same frozen plasma samples 6–12 months later, using the gas-chromatographic method. The intercorrelation of the plasma concentrations 4 hr postdrug determined by the two analytical methods was highly significant ($r = 0.61$, $N = 25$, $p < 0.001$).

The concentrations of plasma thioridazine obtained using the original gas-chromatographic procedure of Curry and Mould[16] were, as expected, lower than those obtained by the fluorometric method.[13] This can be explained by the expected greater specificity of the gas chromatographic method. No metabolites were detected within 30 min from the 3% OV-17 gas chromatograph column, using the Curry and Mould method. The modification[14] of the Curry and Mould method gave results for thioridazine plasma concentration which were also lower than the fluorometric results; but this modified method revealed the presence of mesoridazine and another metabolite.[14,15] Following the pharmacokinetics of the single oral dose of thioridazine with the modified gas-chromatographic method, it was noted that the plasma thioridazine concentration reached a maximum from 1 to 4 hr and then decreased, whereas the mesoridazine level reached its maximum between 4 to 8 hr, and the metabolite, identified as sulforidazine (thioridazine-S-sulfone), about 8 hr postdrug. Twenty-four and forty-eight hours after drug administration, thioridazine and the two metabolites noted above were still measurable in the blood plasma.

All of the other pharmacologic findings and their relationships with clinical findings given in this report were obtained by the fluorometric method. The average half-life for all patients was $24.0 \pm 8.0$ hr; for the male patients it was $22.8 \pm 5.2$ hr, and for female patients it was $25.5 \pm 10.6$ hr. Although there was no significant difference between the mean half-lives of male and female patients, females were significantly more variable than males in their thioridazine half-lives ($F = 4.15$; $p < 0.05$, two-tailed test).

Peak blood levels were obtained in the period of 0.5–8.0 hr. Average peak value for males was 6.0 μg/ml (range 3.5–8.2 μg/ml) and for females, 6.0 μg/ml (range, 2.5–13.2 μg/ml).

The individual range of variations of the plasma concentrations of thioridazine after the standard oral dose of 4 mg/kg was quite marked and can be seen from the curves in Fig. 1. Significant intercorrelations occurred between such pharmacokinetic variables[17] as total area (area under the time curve) and half-life ($r = 0.65$, $p < 0.001$), peak level and total area ($r = 0.75$, $p < 0.001$), half-life and elimination rate ($r = -0.74$, $p < 0.001$), and peak hour with total area ($r = 0.40$, $p < 0.05$).

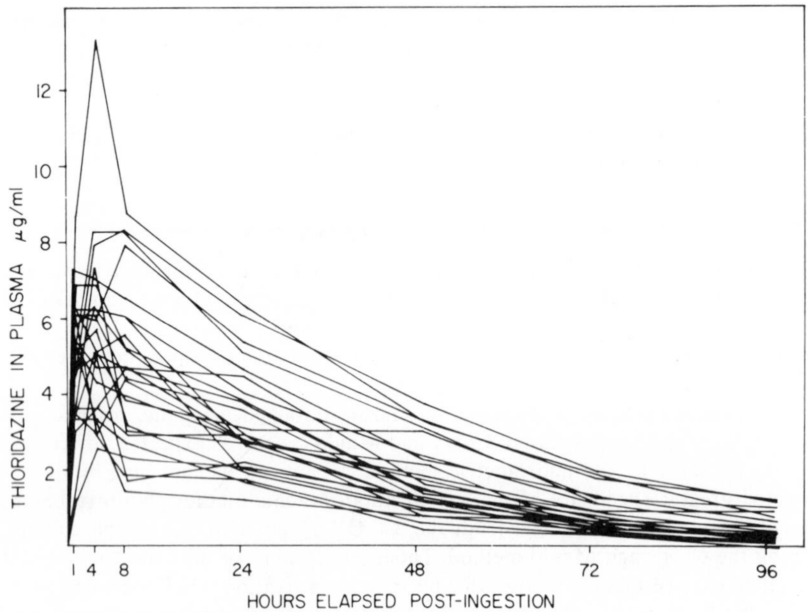


**Fig. 1.** **Changes in thioridazine plasma concentrations following ingestion of 4 mg/kg in 25 schizophrenic patients.**

*Pretreatment and Posttreatment Scores of Various Behavioral and Psychologic Measures*

For each of the 18 items of the Overall-Gorham BPRS and for each of the major factors of the BPRS, Hamilton Depression, and Wittenborn Rating Scales, an overall analysis of variance was first performed. This was followed by statistical tests for the comparison between the immediately predrug score (day 6) and the average of the scores prior to that and also by tests for the comparison between the postdrug score (day 8) and the average of the scores prior to that.[20] If the first comparison did not show a significant decrease in morbidity, whereas the second did, then it would be reasonable to conclude that the thioridazine, and not merely the passage of time in the hospital decreased the psychiatric morbidity scores (Table 1).

*Rating scale scores.* Overall-Gorham Brief Psychiatric Rating Scale Pretreatment (day 1) and posttreatment (BPRS) scores (day 8) for all separate 18 dimensions of the BPRS are given in detail in Table 1. Nine BPRS scores showed significant decreases postdrug (day 8) as compared to the scores over all predrug days (days 1, 3, and 6): (1) Conceptual Disorganization ($p < 0.001$), (2) Guilt Feelings ($p < 0.01$), (3) Mannerisms and Posturing ($p < 0.01$), (4) Grandiosity ($p < 0.05$), (5) Depressive Mood ($p < 0.05$), (6) Hostility ($p < 0.05$), (7) Hallucinatory Behavior ($p < 0.001$), (8) Unusual Thought Content ($p < 0.001$), and (9) Blunted Affect ($p < 0.01$). Anxiety and Suspiciousness both showed a nonsignificant decreasing trend ($p < 0.10$) postdrug. No significant increases in any of the other BPRS categories occurred following drug administration.

When behavioral changes over the 6-day predrug period were examined, two BPRS items showed a significant fall on day 6 as compared to day 1: Guilt Feelings ($p < 0.05$) and Grandiosity ($p < 0.05$). We may assume that nondrug treatment factors (milieu and psychotherapy) or the course of the schizophrenic syndrome itself accounted for these improvements.

The 18 items of the BPRS have been factor-analyzed into four factors.[10] Although our patients showed apparent decreases after drug administration in all four of these factors, significant average decreases occurred in two factors only, Depression ($p < 0.01$) and Thinking Disorder ($p < 0.001$). Anergia showed an average decrease at the 0.10 level of significance.

The Hamilton Depression Scale has been divided into four factors. Three of these factors showed significant average decreases after drug administration (day 8) compared to the average of predrug days 1, 3, and 6: Sleep Disturbance ($p < 0.01$), Anxiety/Depression ($p < 0.05$), and Apathy ($p < 0.01$) (see Table 1).

Of the six factors from the Wittenborn Rating Scale, one showed a significant average decrease after drug administration (day 8) as compared to predrug days 1, 3 and 6: Depression-Retardation ($p < 0.05$). The Paranoia and the Excitement factors showed an average decrease at the 0.10 level of significance (see Table 1).

*Social alienation–personal disorganization content analysis scores.* Scores on the social alienation–personal disorganization scale, derived by content analysis of the 5-min speech samples, were compared for the predrug (days 1–6) and postdrug periods. Because speech samples were not obtained on some days for a few subjects, the analysis of the social alienation–personal disorganization scores had to be done in a manner different from that of the rating scales. To determine whether there was any predrug trend, lines of best fit were first found for each patient's predrug scores plotted against days; the mean of the slopes of these lines was tested to see if it differed from zero. The mean slope was 0.18, which did not differ significantly from zero ($t = 0.55$).

Subsequently, each set of postdrug speech samples was tested against the mean of all the predrug speech samples using the t test for matched data. Where a patient was missing a postdrug speech sample, his predrug scores did not enter the analysis. The average total social alienation–personal disorganization scores decreased significantly 24 hr (day 7; $t = -2.41$, $p < 0.05$) and 48 hr (day 8; $t = -2.09$, $p < 0.05$) following drug administration (see Table 2). A brief nonsignificant worsening of the average social alienation–personal disorganization scores occurred 1 hr after thioridazine ingestion, but within 4 hr after ingestion this effect had disappeared.

Since 5-min speech samples were obtained daily over the 10-day period of observation of this study, scores derived by content analysis of these verbalizations afforded an opportunity to follow daily changes in schizophrenic functioning, in response to hospitalization and placebo ingestion (day 1) and active drug ingestion (day 6). Figure 2 diagrams these day-to-day changes in average total social alienation–personal disorganization scores.

The social alienation–personal disorganization scale has five subcategory scale scores: (1) Interpersonal References (social alienation), (2) Intrapersonal References, (3) Disorganization and Repetitive Thinking, (4) Questions directed to the interviewer, and (5) Religious References. The beneficial effect of a single dose of thioridazine ingestion appeared to be most marked 24 hr postdrug on the

**Table 1. Means of Behavioral Rating Scores Before (Day 0, Day 3, Day 6) and After (Day 8) Oral Dose of Thioridazine (4 mg/kg)**

| | | | | | Overall F | | Day 8 Versus Previous Days | | Day 6 Versus Previous Days | |
|---|---|---|---|---|---|---|---|---|---|---|
| Behavioral Rating Scores | Day 0 | Day 3 | Day 6 | Day 8 | *F* | *P** | *F* | *P** | *F* | *P*† |
| BPRS items | | | | | | | | | | |
| 1 Somatic Concern | 3.24 | 3.32 | 3.12 | 3.00 | 0.48 | NS | | | | |
| 2 Anxiety | 4.32 | 4.28 | 4.20 | 3.92 | 1.22 | NS | 3.38 | 0.10 | 0.25 | NS |
| 3 Emotional Withdrawal | 2.96 | 3.64 | 3.44 | 3.32 | 2.06 | NS | | | | |
| 4 Conceptual Disorganization | 5.08 | 4.80 | 4.76 | 3.84 | 8.28 | 0.001 | 23.10 | 0.001 | 0.61 | NS |
| 5 Guilt Feelings | 4.64 | 4.96 | 4.40 | 4.16 | 4.31 | 0.01 | 7.11 | 0.01 | 3.94 | 0.05 |
| 6 Tension | 4.08 | 3.72 | 3.88 | 3.64 | 1.19 | NS | | | | |
| 7 Mannerisms and Posturing | 4.12 | 3.88 | 4.08 | 3.36 | 3.02 | 0.05 | 8.24 | 0.01 | 0.11 | NS |
| 8 Grandiosity | 3.52 | 3.12 | 2.88 | 2.68 | 4.27 | 0.01 | 5.98 | 0.05 | 4.23 | 0.05 |
| 9 Depressive Mood | 4.08 | 4.04 | 3.92 | 3.52 | 2.09 | NS | 5.83 | 0.05 | 0.42 | NS |
| 10 Hostility | 4.08 | 3.80 | 4.40 | 3.60 | 2.68 | 0.10 | 4.05 | 0.05 | 3.13 | NS |
| 11 Suspiciousness | 4.84 | 4.60 | 4.84 | 4.28 | 1.52 | NS | 3.74 | 0.10 | 0.21 | NS |
| 12 Hallucinatory Behavior | 4.16 | 4.00 | 4.00 | 2.72 | 6.91 | 0.001 | 20.47 | 0.001 | 0.07 | NS |
| 13 Motor Retardation | 2.20 | 2.88 | 2.52 | 2.76 | 2.41 | 0.10 | 1.03 | NS | 0.01 | NS |
| 14 Uncooperativeness | 2.52 | 3.48 | 3.36 | 3.20 | 2.83 | 0.05 | 0.07 | NS | 1.33 | NS |
| 15 Unusual Thought Content | 5.96 | 6.12 | 6.04 | 4.88 | 10.36 | 0.001 | 30.69 | 0.001 | 0.00 | NS |
| 16 Blunted Affect | 4.64 | 4.76 | 4.75 | 4.12 | 3.30 | 0.05 | 9.57 | 0.01 | 0.09 | NS |
| 17 Excitement | 3.24 | 3.16 | 3.40 | 2.80 | 0.91 | NS | | | | |
| 18 Disorientation | 2.20 | 1.68 | 1.60 | 1.52 | 2.80 | 0.05 | 2.09 | NS | 2.29 | NS |

| | | | | | | | | | | |
|---|---|---|---|---|---|---|---|---|---|---|
| BPRS factors | | | | | | | | | | |
| Depression (1,2,5,9) | 4.07 | 4.15 | 3.91 | 3.65 | 3.33 | 0.05 | 7.93 | 0.01 | 1.82 | NS |
| Thinking Disorder (4,8,11,12,15) | 4.71 | 4.53 | 4.50 | 3.68 | 10.95 | 0.001 | 31.50 | 0.001 | 0.46 | NS |
| Anergia (3,7,13,16) | 3.48 | 3.79 | 3.70 | 3.39 | 2.23 | 0.10 | 3.42 | 0.10 | 0.18 | NS |
| Excitement-Disorientation (17,18) | 2.72 | 2.42 | 2.50 | 2.16 | 1.79 | NS | | | | |
| Hamilton depression factors | | | | | | | | | | |
| Sleep Disturbance (4,5,6) ‡ | 2.22 | 2.25 | 2.13 | 1.71 | 3.61 | 0.05 | 9.57 | 0.01 | 0.01 | NS |
| Somatization (11,12,13,14,15) | 2.06 | 2.05 | 1.99 | 1.83 | 1.02 | NS | | | | |
| Anxiety/Depression (1,2,3,9,10) | 2.95 | 3.02 | 2.89 | 2.68 | 2.50 | 0.10 | 6.58 | 0.05 | 0.70 | NS |
| Apathy (7,8,17) | 3.20 | 3.50 | 3.51 | 3.03 | 4.28 | 0.01 | 9.17 | 0.01 | 1.28 | NS |
| Wittenborn factors | | | | | | | | | | |
| Anxiety (1,2,3,4) ‡ | 2.52 | 2.66 | 2.61 | 2.47 | 1.25 | NS | 2.04 | | 0.05 | |
| Somatic-Hysterical (5,6,7) | 1.76 | 1.88 | 1.83 | 1.81 | 0.28 | NS | 0.02 | | 0.01 | |
| Obsessive-Compulsive-Phobic (8,9,10) | 1.85 | 1.88 | 1.91 | 1.84 | 0.18 | NS | 0.25 | | 0.28 | |
| Depressive Retardation (11,12,13) | 2.61 | 2.71 | 2.53 | 2.40 | 3.24 | 0.05 | 6.74 | 0.05 | 2.16 | NS |
| Excitement (14,15) | 2.16 | 2.28 | 2.22 | 2.00 | 1.52 | NS | 3.79 | 0.10 | 0.00 | NS |
| Paranoia (16,17) | 3.34 | 3.50 | 3.33 | 3.14 | 1.65 | NS | 3.57 | 0.10 | 0.41 | NS |

*Two-tailed test.

†One-tailed test.

‡The items for these factors were obtained from the Hamilton depression and Wittenborn rating scales.[10]

**Table 2. Mean Changes in Social Alienation-personal Disorganization Scores Before and After Administration of a Single Dose of Oral Thioridazine (4mg/kg) (Mean ± SD)**

| Social Alienation-Personal Disorganization Scores | Predrug | Postdrug | | | | | Difference Scores Predrug to 24 hr Later* | *p* (two-tailed) |
|---|---|---|---|---|---|---|---|---|
| | 0 hr | 1 hr | 4 hr | 8 hr | 24 hr | 48 hr | | |
| Total | 13.08 ± 8.15 | 14.84 ± 6.23 | 12.52 ± 6.61 | 10.70 ± 7.1 | 8.51 ± 8.70 | 9.78 ± 7.17 | −4.56 ± 10.84 | 0.025 |
| Subscale 1, Interpersonal references | −0.59 ± 2.31 | −0.88 ± 2.25 | −0.66 ± 1.02 | −1.08 ± 2.19 | −1.81 ± 2.16 | −1.04 ± 1.36 | −1.31 ± 2.99 | 0.025 |
| Subscale 2, Intrapersonal references | 4.33 ± 2.99 | 5.07 ± 1.93 | 4.04 ± 2.15 | 3.80 ± 3.86 | 3.14 ± 3.52 | 3.17 ± 2.64 | −1.11 ± 5.02 | NS |
| Subscale 3, Disorganization and repetition | 8.17 ± 5.09 | 8.54 ± 5.62 | 7.68 ± 4.29 | 6.72 ± 3.42 | 6.22 ± 5.18 | 6.93 ± 4.45 | −1.93 ± 5.26 | 0.05 |
| Subscale 4, Questions directed to interviewer | 0.87 ± 0.97 | 1.49 ± 1.28 | 1.13 ± 0.91 | 0.81 ± 0.77 | 0.66 ± 0.64 | 0.61 ± 0.57 | −0.24 ± 1.08 | NS |
| Subscale 5, Religious references | 0.30 ± 0.78 | 0.62 ± 1.44 | 0.32 ± 1.04 | 0.45 ± 0.84 | 0.32 ± 0.85 | 0.10 ± 0.18 | 0.05 ± 0.96 | NS |

*Two patients who did not produce a scorable response on one of the two occasions are eliminated from the analysis.

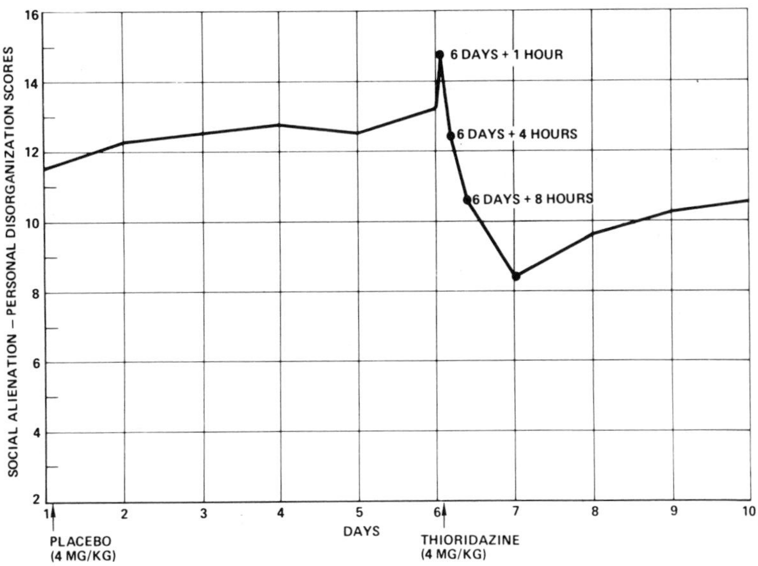


**Fig. 2. Changes in average total social alienation-personal disorganization scores pre- and post-drug.**

following subcategory scales: Interpersonal References ($p < 0.025$) and Disorganization and Repetitive Thinking ($p < 0.05$).

*Correlations of Indices of Plasma Thioridazine Concentration With Measures of Clinical Response*

*Behavorial rating scales.* A large number of ratings of psychiatric change decreased significantly in relationship to indices of plasma thioridazine concentration, specifically, plasma level (on day 8), half-life, and area under curve (up to day 8 or through day 10). Table 3 gives correlations of thioridazine plasma concentrations with behavioral changes 2 days after ingestion of thioridazine (4 mg/kg). Among the Brief Psychiatric Rating Scale factors, several of the indices of plasma thioridazine concentration correlated significantly with decreases in either the Depression, Thinking Disorder, or Excitement-Disorientation factors. Among the Hamilton Depression Scale factors, several indices of plasma thioridazine concentration correlated significantly with decreases in either the Sleep Disturbance or Anxiety/Depression factors. Among the Wittenborn factors, one plasma thioridazine concentration index correlated significantly with a decrease in the Excitement and Paranoia factors.

*Content analysis scales.* When the social alienation–personal disorganization scale scores were followed as a measure of clinical change, clinical improvement 24 hr as well as 48 hr after drug ingestion was examined because these measures were available 24 hr postdrug (whereas the behavioral rating scale scores were not) and because maximal and significant improvement in the social alienation–personal disorganization scores appeared 24 hr postdrug. However, 24 hr after

Table 3. Correlations of Thioridazine Plasma Concentrations With Behavioral Changes Two Days After Thioridazine (4 mg/Kg) by Mouth

| Behavioral Measures (days 8 minus 6) | Plasma Concentration (day 8) | Area (Area under curve up to day 8) | Half-life | Area Under Entire Curve |
|---|---|---|---|---|
| Brief Psychiatric Rating Scale factors | | | | |
| 1. Depression | −0.42* | −0.42* | −0.41* | −0.46* |
| 2. Thinking Disorder | −0.41* | −0.26 | −0.26 | −0.28 |
| 3. Anergia | −0.19 | −0.03 | 0.05 | 0.00 |
| 4. Excitement-Disorientation | −0.42* | −0.30 | −0.39† | −0.36† |
| Hamilton Depression Scale factors | | | | |
| 1. Sleep Disturbances | −0.14 | −0.46* | −0.27 | −0.50‡ |
| 2. Somatization | −0.39† | −0.15 | 0.06 | −0.08 |
| 3. Anxiety/Depression | −0.29 | −0.44* | −0.25 | −0.45* |
| 4. Apathy | −0.36† | −0.25 | −0.05 | −0.24 |
| Wittenborn factors | | | | |
| 1. Anxiety | −0.39† | −0.30 | −0.21 | −0.36† |
| 2. Somatic-Hysterical | −0.38† | −0.04 | 0.06 | 0.01 |
| 3. Obsessive-Compulsive-Phobic | −0.34† | +0.21 | 0.03 | +0.21 |
| 4. Depressive-Retardation | −0.29† | −0.34† | −0.11 | −0.28 |
| 5. Excitement | −0.41* | −0.19 | −0.35† | −0.24 |
| 6. Paranoia | −0.47* | −0.33 | −0.06 | −0.26 |

†$p < 0.10$.
*$p < 0.05$.
‡$p < 0.01$.
$p$ values obtained using two-tailed test.

thioridazine ingestion, no significant cross correlations were found between the various indices of drug plasma concentration and scores of social alienation–personal disorganization. At 48 hr postdrug, there were also no significant correlations between drug plasma levels and social alienation–personal disorganization scores.

Because there was so much interindividual variation in the social alienation–personal disorganization measures, especially during the first 24 hr postdrug, intraindividual correlations between social alienation–personal disorganization scores and plasma levels of thioridazine were examined. There was no evidence that, for most of the patients, the higher the drug plasma concentration the less the social alienation–personal disorganization scores when these variables were examined concomitantly at time 0 (just before drug administration) and at 1, 4, 8, and 24 hr postdrug. However, the higher the predrug social alienation–personal disorganization scores, the more likely there were negative intraindividual correlations between the thioridazine plasma levels and social alienation–personal disorganization scores during the first 24 hr postdrug (i.e., the higher the thioridazine plasma levels the lower the social alienation–personal disorganization scores). Specifically, of the 19 calculable correlations for which data were available, there was no overlap between the intraindividual correlations (predominantly negative) of the 10 patients whose predrug social alienation–personal disorganization scores were in the upper half and the intraindividual correlations (predominantly positive) of the 9 patients whose predrug scores were in the lower half (a Mann-Whitney U Test = 0, $p < 0.001$). This finding suggests strongly

that, in using thioridazine with acute schizophrenic patients, the sicker patients are more likely to show a significant relationship between drug blood levels and clinical improvement.

In addition, it is reasonable to believe that decreases in the magnitude of various dimensions of the schizophrenic syndrome tend to follow, rather than occur concomitantly with, changes in drug plasma concentration. This appears to be the case, for when these variables are examined in such a way that social alienation–personal disorganization scores for all patients, regardless of the severity of their predrug clinical status, are correlated with thioridazine plasma levels one time point earlier than the social alienation–personal disorganization scores,* there are found 16 negative intraindividual correlations (the higher the drug plasma levels the lower the social alienation–personal disorganization scores) and five positive correlations. A sign test indicates this difference in negative and positive correlations is significant ($p < 0.03$). When the correlations using longer lag periods, that is, longer time intervals between the psychoactive drug plasma level and the subsequent clinical response, are studied, no significant trends appear. Ideally, of course, it would be preferable if plasma levels and social alienation–personal disorganization scores were examined at equal intervals postdrug for the purposes of this kind of statistical evaluation, but such data were not available in the present study.

### *Predictors of Favorable Response to a Single Dose of Thioridazine (4 mg/kg) by Mouth*

*Thioridazine plasma concentrations as predictors of clinical response.* As Table 3 indicates, various indices of thioridazine plasma concentration can be regarded as predictors of favorable clinical responses in a number of factors from the rating scales (Depression, Thinking Disorder, and Excitement-Disorientation factors from the BPRS; Sleep Disturbance and Anxiety/Depression from the Hamilton Depression Scale; and Excitement and Paranoia factors from the Wittenborn Scale).

*Behavioral and psychologic indices as predictors of plasma thioridazine concentration.* Social alienation–personal disorganization scores predrug (on day 1) correlated 0.44 ($p < 0.03$) with postdrug thioridazine half-life and 0.43 ($p < 0.03$) with area under curve. Looking at the subscales, significant correlations with blood level indices occurred only with subscale 1 scores (Interpersonal references) on day 1 which correlated 0.39 ($p < 0.05$) with thioridazine half-life and subscale 3 scores (Disorganization and Repetition) which correlated 0.51 ($p < 0.01$) with thioridazine half-life and 0.43 ($p < 0.05$) with area under curve.

None of the predrug behavioral rating scale scores appeared to predict indices of thioridazine plasma concentration to a significant extent except the BPRS Excitement-Disorientation factor predrug (day 3), which correlated 0.46 ($p < 0.02$)

---

*A lag period of social alienation–personal disorganization (SA–PD) scores one time point after the drug plasma level such that drug plasma level at time 0 was matched with SA-PD score at 1 hr postdrug, drug plasma level at 1 hr postdrug was matched with the SA-PD score 4 hr postdrug, drug plasma level at 4 hr postdrug was matched with SA-PD score 8 hr postdrug, and so forth through 24 hr postdrug.

with peak plasma thioridazine concentration, and the Hamilton Depression Scale Sleep Disturbance factor predrug (on day 3), which correlated 0.38 ($p < 0.06$) with peak plasma thioridazine concentration.

*Predrug clinical laboratory data as predictors.* Intercorrelations of predrug clinical laboratory data and indices of plasma thioridazine concentration were examined. Of the various significant or borderline significant correlations, the negative correlations of predrug RBC, basophiles, monocytes, urine albumin, cholesterol with half-life, area under curve, or peak level look interesting. Also, similar correlations that are positive are of interest. These include predrug hemoglobin, mean corpuscular hemoglobin concentration (MCHC), alkaline phosphatase, CPK, and polymorphonuclear leukocytes. Certainly, any such predictive correlations, if they hold up with further studies, will be of considerable interest from a basic and clinical science point of view. For all the correlations run, there are not many significant ones, and the validity of any one of these should be held in doubt until replication data are available. We see these correlations, as we see all of our predictor data at this time, as leads (hypotheses) to be tested in future investigations.

## DISCUSSION

### *Thioridazine Plasma Concentrations*

The variability of plasma thioridazine half-life, over all 25 patients, as indicated by the standard deviation (± 8.0 hr) and Fig. 1, is considerable. Presumably, these differences are due to genetic or other biologic differences.[1,5,22] The significantly greater variability noted in female patients, if it holds up with future studies, may be due to the influence of the menstrual cycle, and hence female sex hormones, on drug metabolism. As previously noted, patient-to-patient variability of this proportion has been reported with other psychoactive parmacologic agents.

These observed individual differences in the pharmacokinetics of a drug are thought to be related to differences in absorption, distribution, elimination and the activity of hepatic enzymes which metabolize these drugs. These drug-metabolizing enzymes are not the usual enzymes of intermediary metabolism, but are believed to have been developed in evolution to permit the organism to dispose of liposoluble substances—hydrocarbons, alkaloids, terpenes, and sterols—ingested in food, which would accumulate to very high levels if they were not converted to excretable derivatives.[28]

Kinetically, the plasma level may not be a good index of the amount of drug attached to receptor sites, especially if these sites are located in the central nervous system. However, if the psychoactive drug passes freely through the blood-brain barrier, as the phenothiazines do, plasma concentrations of the drug may be proportional to the amount of drug reaching receptor sites and hence may be related to clinical effect. That possibility, indeed, was one of the major working hypotheses of this present investigation. Another hypothesis was that, although it is probable that most of the thioridazine may become bound to protein in the plasma, and there are individual differences in the amount of drug so bound, the amount of free drug is in continual equilibrium with that bound to protein. Hence

it may not be necessary at this time to determine the proportion of drug free and bound to protein to establish meaningful relationships between pharmacokinetics and clinical response.

The significant correlations across patients between decreased factor scores from the psychiatric rating scales with indices of plasma thioridazine concentration 48 hr after ingestion of 4 mg/kg of thioridazine and the intraindividual correlations between improvement in social alienation–personal disorganization (content analysis) scores and plasma drug concentration within 24 hr demonstrate that plasma concentration of this drug does, indeed, relate to degree of clinical improvement, at least for a single drug dose, Further studies of continuous drug doses with schizophrenic patients will be necessary to determine to what extent our findings generalize to the usual clinical psychopharmacologic practices in the treatment of schizophrenia.

Positive correlations between plasma drug level and clinical improvement have also been reported with other psychoactive drugs, for example, chlordiazepoxide,[7,21] meperidine,[8] imipramine,[25] amitriptyline,[26] and nortryptyline,[27] especially with drug responders. Our findings support the growing view that clinical response in psychopharmacology should be monitored more by plasma concentration than by dose.

We are in the process of replicating these findings in further ongoing single-dose studies using intramuscular mesoridazine (2 mg/kg) and multiple-dose studies lasting up to 8 weeks using oral thioridazine. In these new studies, we are following the plasma concentrations of thioridazine and its metabolites using both fluorometric and gas chromotographic analytical methods.

## SUMMARY

1. The relationship between indices of plasma thioridazine concentration (half-life, area under curve, peak level) and clinical response was examined over a 10-day period in 25 patients with severe to moderately severe acute schizophrenia following a single oral dose (on day one) of a placebo and of thioridazine, 4 mg/kg (on day 6). This was a preliminary study, and the findings obtained here are being tested in continuous dose studies of schizophrenic patients.

2. Significant improvement in only 2 of 18 Overall-Gorham BPRS items occurred predrug (days 1–6), namely, in Guilt ($p < 0.05$) and Grandiosity ($p < 0.05$). No predrug improvement was observed in the other BPRS items, Hamilton Depression Scale Ratings, Wittenborn Scale Ratings, or Gottschalk-Gleser social alienation–personal disorganization scores derived by content analysis from 5-min speech samples.

3. Following the single dose of thioridazine, a significant average decrease was noted within 24 hr in the social alienation–personal disorganization scores, and within 48 hr in nine subscales of the BPRS, two of four factor scores of the BPRS, three of four Hamilton Depression Rating Scale factors, and one of six Wittenborn Rating Scale factors. The manifestations of the schizophrenic syndrome showing such significant improvement included Thought Disorder, Conceptual Disorganization, Apathy, Anxiety, and Depression.

4. Significant correlations were found between indices of plasma thioridazine

levels and favorable clinical responses on certain behavioral and psychologic features of the schizophrenic syndrome.

5. Suggestive evidence was obstained which points to some predrug behavioral and clinical laboratory data that may serve as predictors of thioridazine pharmacokinetics.

## ACKNOWLEDGMENT

The technical assistance or advice of Eugene Dinovo, Ph.D., Ardie Lubin, Ph.D., Michael Soyben, Daniel Bates, Regina Uliana, Julia Hoigaard, and the Early Clinical Drug Evaluation Unit, Psychopharmacology Branch, NIMH, Biometrics Division, George Washington University, Washington, D.C. are hereby acknowledged.

## REFERENCES

1. Green DE, Forrest IS, Forrest FM, et al: Interpatient variation chlorpromazine metabolism. Exp Med Surg 23:278-287, 1965

2. Hammer W, Idesträm CH, Sjöqvist F: Chemical control of antidepressant drug therapy in Proceedings of the First International Symposium on Antipressiant Drugs. Amsterdam, Excerpta Medica, 1966, pp 301-310

3. Hammer W, Sjoqvist F: Plasma level of monomethyl tricyclic antidepressants during treatment with imipramine-like compounds. Life Sci 6:1895-1903, 1967

4. Hollister LE, Curry SH, Derr JE, et al: Studies of delayed action medication. Clin Pharmacol Ther 11:49-59, 1970

5. Usdin E: Absorption, distribution, and metabolic fate of psychotropic drugs. Psychopharmacol Bull 6:4-25, 1970

6. Cash WD, Quinn GP: Clinical-chemical correlations: an overview. Psychopharmacol Bull 6:26-33, 1970

7. Gottschalk LA, Kaplan SA: Chlordiazepoxide plasma levels and clinical responses. Compr Psychiatry 13:519-528, 1972

8. Elliott HW, Gottschalk LA, Uliana RL: Relationship of plasma meperidine levels to changes in anxiety and hostility. Compr Psychiatry 15:57-61, 1974

9. Overall JE, Gorham DP: The brief psychiatric rating scale (BPRS). Psychol Rep 10:799-812, 1962

10. Guy W, Bonato RR: Manual for the ECDEU Assessment Battery, Second Revision. Chevy Chase, Maryland, National Institute of Mental Health, U.S. Dept. of Health, Education, and Welfare, 1970

11. Gottschalk LA, Gleser GC: The Measurement of Psychological States Through the Content Analysis of Verbal Behavior. Los Angeles, University of California Press, 1969

12. Gottschalk LA, Winget CN, Gleser GC: Manual of Instructions for Using the Gottschalk-Gleser Content Analysis Scales. Los Angeles, University of California Press, 1969

13. Pacha WL: A method for the fluorometric determination of thioridazine or mesoridazine in plasma. Experientia 25:103-104, 1969

14. Dinovo EC, Gottschalk LA, Nandi BR, et al: A method for measuring thioridazine, mesoridazine, metabolites and other phenothiazines in plasma. J Pharmaceut Sci (in press)

15. Gruenke L, Craig J, Dinovo E, et al: Identification of a metabolite of thioridazine and mesoridazine from human plasma. Res Commun Chem Pathol Pharmacol 10:221-225, 1975

16. Curry SH, Mould GD: Gas chromatographic identification of thioridazine in plasma and method for routine assay of the drug. J Pharm Pharmacol 21:674-677, 1969

17. Dixon WJ (ed): Biomedical Computer Programs. Berkeley, University of California Press, 1972

18. Nie NH, Bent DH, Hull CH: Statistical Package for the Social Sciences. New York, McGraw-Hill, 1970

19. Robinson WS: The statistical measurement of agreement. Am Sociol Rev 22:17, 1957

20. Myers JL: Fundamentals of Experimental Design. Boston, Allyn and Bacon, 1966, ch 13

21. Gottschalk LA, Noble EP, Stolzoff GE, et al: Relationships of chlordiazepoxide blood levels to psychological and biochemical responses, in Garattini S, Mussini E, Randall LO (eds): The Benzodiazepines. New York, Raven, 1973

22. Brodie BB, Reid WD: The value of determining the plasma concentration of drugs in animal and man, in La Du, Markel, Way (eds): Fundamentals of Drug Metabolism and Drug Disposition. Baltimore, Williams & Wilkins, 1971

23. Curry SH: Determination of nanogram quantities of chlorpromazine and some of its me-

tabolites in plasma using gas-liquid chromatography with an electron-capture detector. Anal Chem 40:1251–1255, 1968

24. Curry SH, Marshall JHL: Plasma levels of chlorpromazine and some of its relatively nonpolar metabolites in psychiatric patients. Life Sci 7:9–17, 1968

25. Glassman AH, Perel JM: Plasma levels of imipramine and clinical outcome, in Gottschalk LA, Merlis S (eds): Pharmacokinetics, Psychoactive Drug Blood Levels, and Clinical Response. New York, Spectrum, 1975

26. Braithwaite RA, Goulding R, Theano G, et al: Plasma concentration of amitriptyline and clinical response. Lancet 1:1297–1300, 1972

27. Burrows G, Scoggins BA, Turecek LR, et al: Plasma nortriptyline and clinical response. Clin Pharmacol Ther 16:639–644, 1974

28. Brodie BB, Maickel RP: Comparative biochemistry of drug metabolism, in Brodie BB, Erdos EG (eds): Proceedings of the First International Pharmacological Meeting, vol 6. Oxford, Pergamon, 1961, pp 299–324.

# *Plasma Levels of Mesoridazine and its Metabolites and Clinical Response in Acute Schizophrenia After a Single Intramuscular Drug Dose*

L.A. GOTTSCHALK
E. DINOVO
R. BIENER
H. BIRCH
M. SYBEN
E.P. NOBLE

Previous studies of the pharmacokinetics of single, standardized, oral doses of chlordiazepoxide (25 mg),[1,2] meperidine (100 mg)[3] and thioridazine (4 mg/kg)[4] have been carried out by our research group. These have revealed quite marked individual differences in blood plasma concentrations or other pharmacokinetic indices of these psychoactive drugs and have shown, furthermore, that the clinical responses to these drugs are related in magnitude to these pharmacological variables. Standardized intramuscular doses of meperidine (100 mg)[3] and chlordiazepoxide (20 mg)[5] have also indicated wide individual variations in the resulting plasma concentrations, with higher average plasma concentration after meperidine occurring intramuscularly rather than orally; whereas chlordiazepoxide intramuscularly has been found to result in significantly lower plasma levels of chlordiazepoxide 1 and 2 hours after administration than after a similar oral dose.

As part of this continuing research program, the aim of the present study was to examine the pharmacokinetics and clinical response after

intramuscular administration of a single dose of mesoridazine (2 mg/kg) in acute schizophrenic patients and to compare the pharmacokinetics of a single intramuscular dose of mesoridazine in acute schizophrenic patients with that in normal subjects.

## METHODS AND PROCEDURES

### Subjects

The subjects for this study were 10 acute schizophrenic patients who had no evidence of medical disease by history and physical examination, had no history of alcoholism or drug abuse, and had not been receiving any psychoactive drugs for at least 4 weeks. These characteristics were checked by an SMA-12,* an SMA-6,** and a urine drug screen. These patients presented themselves at the Psychiatry Service, Orange County Medical Center, and the diagnosis of acute schizophrenia was made by an admitting psychiatrist and confirmed by another staff psychiatrist. The diagnosis of severely ill, floridly symptomatic schizophrenia was confirmed through comparison of a profile analysis of the patients' Brief Psychiatric Rating Scale scores[6,7] to a group of psychiatrists' diagnostic stereotype profiles for a variety of schizophrenic and other functional psychotic categories. Also, the patients' average pre-drug social alienation/personal disorganization speech content analysis score was $9.99 \pm 5.10$, the mean of which is in the 85th percentile of such scores for a group of 113 known chronic schizophrenic patients and in the 100th percentile of a group of 29 known acute schizophrenic patients.[8]

Other subjects for this study included 6 normal (nonschizophrenic) subjects who were college students participating in this investigation as paid volunteers.

### Method

The experimental design involved a placebo-drug, single intramuscular dose, non-crossover study, double-blind in the assessment of all measures except the scoring of the three behavioral rating scales by a psychiatrist (R.B.). The study extended over a period of 10 days. The mesoridazine (2 mg/kg) and inactive placebo (sterile normal saline) were administered intramuscularly. Diversified measures of psychiatric change were used, including psychiatric rating scales based on ratings by a psychiatrist and

*SMA-12: total protein, albumin, calcium, phosphorus, cholesterol, uric acid, creatinine, total bilirubin, alk. phosphates, CPK, LDH, transaminase SGOT.

**SMA-6: chlorides, bicarbonate, potassium, sodium, BUN, glucose.

scales based on technician-trained content analysis of speech, because of the possibility that some measures of change might respond more sensitively than others to blood drug levels. The following baseline measures were obtained before the administration of any medication:

(1) *A battery of 3 behavioral rating scales, recommended as measurement tools by the Early Clinical Drug Evaluation Unit (ECDEU) of the Psychopharmacology Branch of the National Institute of Mental Health,*[9] *namely, (a) the Overall-Gorham Brief Psychiatric Rating Scale (BPRS),*[10] *(b) the Hamilton Depression Rating Scale, and (c) the Wittenborn Rating Scale.* In a previous study,[4] we determined that the interrater reliability on these scales of the rating psychiatrist (R.B.) with two other psychiatrists was satisfactory.

(2) *A daily 5-minute tape-recorded speech sample from the patient for the objective measurement of the severity of the schizophrenic syndrome (social alienation/personal disorganization scale) and other psychological states by means of the content analysis method of Gottschalk and Gleser.*[8,11]

(3) *Fasting plasma biochemical levels (including the SMA-12, SMA-6 and plasma phenothiazine content) as well as clinical laboratory hematological data (complete blood count, hematocrit, and other blood indices).*

(4) *Complete urinalysis (including a screening test for sedative-hypnotics and phenothiazines).*

After obtaining these baseline measures, at 8 A.M. on day 1, each patient received an intramuscular injection of the placebo (normal saline).

On the 6th day, before breakfast and following the morning evaluative interview for rating the patient's behavior, blood was again drawn for the SMA-12 and SMA-6 determinations and plasma mesoridazine concentration. Then, while the patient was still fasting (12–14 hours) a single dose (2 mg/kg) of intramuscular mesoridazine was given.

After this single dose of mesoridazine, 5-minute speech samples and blood for plasma mesoridazine determinations were obtained 1, 4 and 8 hours later, and 1, 2, 3 and 4 days later before breakfast.Behavioral ratings on the three scales were obtained before breakfast 1 and 2 days post-drug.

For the total 10 days of observation in the hospital, 5-minute speech samples were also obtained each morning at 8 A.M. On the 1st, 6th, 7th, and 8th days of observation, following the tape recording of the 5-minute speech samples, ratings were made on the three behavioral rating scales.

The 5-minute speech samples were coded by content analysis technicians, unfamiliar with the nature of this study, for social alienation/personal disorganization scores by the method of Gottschalk and Gleser.[8,11] Behavioral Rating Scale items and factors were scored with the assistance of the Early Clinical Drug Evaluation Unit (ECDEU) of the Psychopharmacology Branch, National Institute of Mental Health. Plasma mesoridazine levels were measured by the fluorometric method of Pacha,[12]

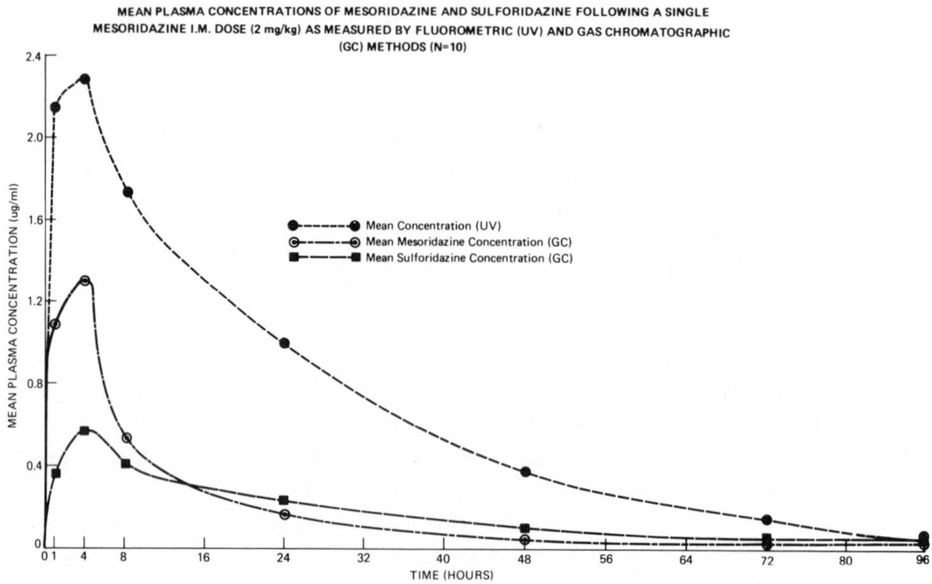


Figure 1

and since this method is not thought to be specific for mesoridazine but also measures metabolites, mesoridazine and its metabolites were checked by a modification[13] of the gas chromatographic procedure of Curry and Mould.[14] Blood chemistry (SMA-12 and SMA-6) was performed in the Clinical Laboratory of the Orange County Medical Center. Statistical assessment of all data, including determination of plasma mesoridazine half-life, area under the curve, and peak level were carried out by use of Biomedical Computer Programs[15] and the Statistical Package for Social Sciences.[16]

## RESULTS

### Mesoridazine Plasma Levels by Fluorometry (UV) and Gas Chromatography (GC) in Acute Schizophrenics and Normal Subjects

Table I gives plasma mesoridazine concentrations at 1, 4, 8, 24, 48, 72, and 96 hours post-drug for the 10 schizophrenic patients, and Table II gives plasma mesoridazine concentration at 1, 4, 8 and 24 hours post-drug for the 6 normal subjects using both fluorometric and gas chromatographic analytical methods. Missing data from the normal subjects, due to an insufficient quantity of blood or to a dropping out of one subject from further participa-

**Table I.** Mesoridazine Pharmacokinetics, Schizophrenic Patients (N = 10), with Single Dose (2 mg/kg, i.m.)

| Patient | Method | | Mesoridazine Blood Concentrations in μg/ml | | | | | | | | | | |
|---|---|---|---|---|---|---|---|---|---|---|---|---|---|
| | | | Time in Hours Post-Drug | | | | | | | Area Under Curve | Half-Life | Peak | Time of Peak |
| | | | 1 | 4 | 8 | 24 | 48 | 72 | 96 | | | | |
| BM | (Spectrophotofluorometer) | | 3.76 | 3.76 | 2.58 | 1.53 | 0.32 | 0.18 | 0.02 | 86.85 | 14.61 | 3.85 | 1.45 |
| GS | (Spectrophotofluorometer) | | 0.99 | 0.87 | 0.47 | 0.18 | 0.00 | 0.00 | 0.00 | 11.35 | 6.50 | 1.03 | 1.49 |
| YP | (Spectrophotofluorometer) | | 1.40 | 1.37 | 1.06 | 0.48 | 0.09 | 0.07 | 0.02 | 30.16 | 12.75 | 1.49 | 1.74 |
| LF | (Spectrophotofluorometer) | | 0.72 | 0.84 | 0.87 | 1.17 | 1.28 | 0.82 | 0.48 | 290.68 | 190.38 | 1.04 | 5.41 |
| DB | (Spectrophotofluorometer) | | 2.04 | 1.73 | 1.25 | 0.30 | 0.07 | 0.01 | 0.00 | 27.77 | 8.17 | 1.40 | 2.09 |
| DC | (Spectrophotofluorometer) | | 2.15 | 2.20 | 1.39 | 0.25 | 0.73 | 0.03 | 0.02 | 44.03 | 12.22 | 2.27 | 1.68 |
| VB | (Spectrophotofluorometer) | | 1.79 | 2.90 | 2.13 | 0.87 | 0.14 | 0.03 | 0.00 | 53.59 | 10.56 | 2.80 | 3.48 |
| JP | (Spectrophotofluorometer) | | 2.47 | 2.35 | 2.57 | 1.70 | 0.21 | — | 0.00 | 88.45 | 20.53 | 2.77 | 2.20 |
| AV | (Spectrophotofluorometer) | | 2.02 | 2.09 | 1.97 | 1.69 | 0.90 | 0.26 | 0.12 | 105.44 | 30.65 | 2.26 | 2.30 |
| LB | (Spectrophotofluorometer) | | 4.16 | 5.00 | 2.92 | 1.45 | 0.39 | 0.05 | 0.04 | 84.48 | 10.13 | 4.95 | 2.26 |
| | | Means | 2.15 | 2.29 | 1.72 | 1.01 | 0.37 | 0.16 | 0.09 | | | | |
| BM | (Gas Chromatograph) | | 1.52 | 1.21 | 0.53 | 0.00 | 0.00 | 0.00 | 0.00 | 11.29 | 3.27 | 1.67 | 1.69 |
| GS | (Gas Chromatograph) | | 0.60 | 0.20 | 0.00 | 0.00 | 0.00 | 0.00 | 0.00 | 0.19 | 2.85 | 0.60 | 1.00 |
| YP | (Gas Chromatograph) | | 0.44 | 0.57 | 0.32 | 0.06 | 0.02 | 0.00 | 0.00 | 6.29 | 5.05 | 0.62 | 2.37 |
| LF | (Gas Chromatograph) | | 0.32 | 0.28 | 0.27 | 0.27 | 0.21 | 0.16 | 0.07 | 29.28 | 64.71 | 0.31 | 0.17 |
| DB | (Gas Chromatograph) | | 0.25 | 0.43 | 0.51 | 0.00 | 0.00 | 0.00 | 0.00 | 6.96 | 3.59 | 0.49 | 5.18 |
| DC | (Gas Chromatograph) | | 0.82 | 0.93 | 0.50 | 0.15 | 0.00 | 0.00 | 0.00 | 10.70 | 5.54 | 1.01 | 2.25 |
| VB | (Gas Chromatograph) | | 0.64 | 2.54 | 1.16 | 0.00 | 0.00 | 0.00 | 0.00 | 19.83 | 2.63 | 1.93 | 3.79 |
| JP | (Gas Chromatograph) | | 1.40 | 1.19 | 0.58 | 0.38 | 0.00 | — | 0.00 | 18.30 | 8.45 | 1.46 | 0.35 |
| AV | (Gas Chromatograph) | | 1.70 | 1.37 | 0.92 | 0.36 | 0.10 | 0.00 | 0.00 | 24.38 | 9.38 | 1.75 | 0.36 |
| LB | (Gas Chromatograph) | | 3.06 | 4.70 | 0.89 | 0.31 | 0.00 | 0.00 | 0.00 | 26.75 | 1.70 | 4.02 | 2.45 |
| | | Means | 1.10 | 1.30 | 0.53 | 0.17 | 0.05 | 0.03 | 0.01 | | | | |

Table II. Mesoridazine Pharmacokinetics, Normal Subjects (N = 6), with Single Dose (2 mg/kg, i.m.)

| Subject | | | Mesoridazine Blood Concentrations in $\mu g/ml$: Time in Hours Post-Drug 1 | 4 | 8 | 24 | Area Under Curve | Half-Life | Peak | Time of Peak |
|---|---|---|---|---|---|---|---|---|---|---|
| TW | (Spectrophoto-fluorometer) | | 0.65 | 0.65 | 0.52 | 0.23 | 14.87 | 13.27 | 0.70 | 1.86 |
| BC | | | 2.10 | 1.92 | 1.32 | 0.47 | 32.82 | 9.29 | 2.18 | 1.53 |
| WS | | | 1.28 | 1.14 | 0.58 | 0.26 | 14.62 | 6.46 | 1.34 | 1.50 |
| TO | | | 1.43 | 2.51 | 1.80 | 1.12 | 64.73 | 16.64 | 2.30 | 3.77 |
| BK | | | 0.50 | 1.10 | 0.63 | — | | | | |
| MO | | | 1.64 | 1.97 | 2.10 | — | | | | |
| | | Means | 1.27 | 1.55 | 1.16 | 0.52 | | | | |
| TW | (Gas Chromatograph) | | 0.31 | — | — | 0.05 | | | | |
| BC | | | 0.78 | 1.05 | 0.52 | 0.00 | 8.88 | 2.59 | 1.13 | 2.77 |
| WS | | | 0.34 | 0.66 | 0.27 | 0.17 | 7.06 | 5.90 | 0.57 | 3.12 |
| TO | | | 0.94 | 0.53 | — | 0.35 | | | | |
| BK | | | 0.09 | 0.10 | — | — | | | | |
| MO | | | 0.26 | 0.22 | 0.19 | — | | | | |
| | | Means | 0.45 | 0.51 | 0.33 | 0.14 | | | | |

tion in this study by the 24th hour post-drug, accounts for incomplete data in Table II.

For both the schizophrenic patients and normal subjects there was a wide range of blood concentrations at comparable time periods post-drug. The plasma concentrations of mesoridazine were considerably less as determined by gas chromatographic (GC) analysis than by fluorometric (UV) analysis, which verifies the lack of specificity for the fluorometric method of analysis. (see Fig. 1).

One subject, LF, showed an extremely long half-life, as determined by both analytic methods (see footnote a, Table III). The half-life of mesoridazine by the GC method, excepting patient LF, ranged from 1.70–9.38 hours (N = 9) with a median of 5.05. For normals, the half-life ranged from 2.59–5.90 hours (N = 2) by GC. Median plasma concentration 1 hour post-drug by GC was 0.73 ug/ml (N = 10) for the schizophrenic patients and 0.33 ug/ml (N = 6) for the normals. Intercorrelations between various mesoridazine pharmacokinetic variables, as assayed by both the UV and GC analytic methods, are given in Table III.

Most of the observed difference between the plasma concentrations for mesoridazine, as determined by the fluorometric and gas chromatographic methods, can be explained by the presence of one or more metabolites of mesoridazine that are co-measured with mesoridazine in the fluorometric assay but not in the gas chromatographic assay. One of these

**Table III.** Intercorrelations of Mesoridazine Pharmacokinetic Variables (N = 9)[a]

| Pharmacokinetic Variables | Peak Level | | Peak Hour | | Half-life | | Total Area[b] | |
|---|---|---|---|---|---|---|---|---|
| | GC | UV | GC | UV | GC | UV | GC | UV |
| Peak level | | | | | | | | |
| GC | | .88** | .31 | | −.28 | | .84** | |
| UV | | | | .27 | | .03 | | .67* |
| Peak hour | | | | | | | | |
| GC | | | | .55 | −.64 | | .15 | |
| UV | | | | | | .20 | | .34 |
| Half-life | | | | | | | | |
| GC | | | | | | .82* | .21 | |
| UV | | | | | | | | .75* |
| Total area | | | | | | | | |
| GC | | | | | | | | .84** |
| UV | | | | | | | | |

*$p < .05$
**$p < .005$

[a] Patient L.F.s pharmacokinetic variables were omitted from this table because she was found to have an elevated LDH (330; normal range, 90–200) and CPK (204; normal range, 25–145), though a SGOT within normal limits, and an extremely long GC mesoridazine half-life (64.71) and GC sulforidazine half-life (180.0), indicative of probable acute hepatic dysfunction because of heavy, brief drinking of alcohol just prior to hospital admission.

[b] **Total area** – The area (in ug/ml by hours) under the curve that was fitted to the points representing plasma mesoridazine concentration against time separately for each patient and after drug administration. The curve was fitted using a nonlinear least squares computer program.[15]

metabolites was observed within 1 hour after drug administration and reached its maximum plasma concentration about 4 hours post-drug. This major metabolite of mesoridazine was positively identified as sulforidazine (thioridazine-S-sulfone) by means of gas chromatography/mass spectrometry and comparative TLC and GC of known standard and subjects' plasma extracts.[17,18] Table IV gives sulforidazine plasma concentrations 1, 4, 8, 24, 48, 72 and 96 hours post-drug in our 10 acute schizophrenic patients, and 1, 4, 8 and 24 hours post-drug in a few normal subjects.

## Changes in Clinical Response after a Single Dose of Mesoridazine

Table V summarizes changes in the manifestations, as adjudged by the behavioral rating scales, of acute schizophrenia after the single intramuscular dose of mesoridazine (2 mg/kg). Significant decreases in the behavioral rating scale scores 24–48 hours post-drug are evident in the BPRS factor scores of Depression ($p < .01$), Thinking Disorder ($p < .001$),

**Table IV.** Mesoridazine Metabolite (Sulforidazine) Blood Concentrations*

| Subjects | | | Time in Hours Post-Drug | | | | | | | Area Under Curve | Half-Life | Peak | Time of Peak |
|---|---|---|---|---|---|---|---|---|---|---|---|---|---|
| | | | 1 | 4 | 8 | 24 | 48 | 72 | 96 | | | | |
| BM | Schizophrenics | | .58 | .80 | .58 | .18 | 0 | 0 | 0 | 12.78 | 8.57 | .81 | 2.96 |
| GS | | | .18 | .13 | .13 | 0 | 0 | 0 | 0 | 2.24 | 7.63 | .18 | 1.24 |
| YP | | | .16 | .19 | .15 | .09 | .01 | .02 | 0 | 4.95 | 15.84 | .19 | 2.52 |
| LF | | | .25 | .34 | .22 | .30 | .32 | .29 | .14 | 81.14 | 180.00 | .31 | 3.71 |
| DB | | | .05 | .05 | .05 | 0 | 0 | 0 | 0 | .81 | 7.29 | .06 | 2.42 |
| DC | | | .34 | .46 | .34 | .20 | .05 | 0 | 0 | 11.04 | 14.82 | .45 | 2.91 |
| VB | | | .10 | .62 | .45 | .14 | 0 | 0 | 0 | 9.16 | 6.12 | .54 | 5.74 |
| JP | | | .49 | .69 | .49 | .35 | 0 | 0 | 0 | 16.19 | 14.49 | .67 | 3.04 |
| AV | | | .29 | .49 | .52 | .47 | .23 | .02 | 0 | 25.07 | 25.40 | .57 | 6.85 |
| LB | | | 1.11 | 1.74 | .83 | .71 | .25 | 0 | 0 | 36.36 | 14.86 | 1.48 | 2.85 |
| | | Means | 0.36 | 0.55 | 0.38 | 0.24 | 0.09 | 0.03 | 0.01 | | | | |
| TW | Normals | | .09 | — | — | .03 | | | | | | | |
| BC | | | .42 | .59 | .40 | — | | | | | | | |
| WS | | | .12 | .20 | .12 | .08 | | | | | | | |
| TO | | | .28 | .44 | .28 | .24 | | | | | | | |
| BK | | | .04 | .10 | — | .07 | | | | | | | |
| MO | | | .12 | .23 | .20 | — | | | | | | | |
| | | Means | .18 | .31 | .25 | .15 | | | | | | | |

*The standards for sulforidazine were derived by taking the ratio we have found between the peak height of mesoridazine and the peak height of sulforidazine for the same concentration.

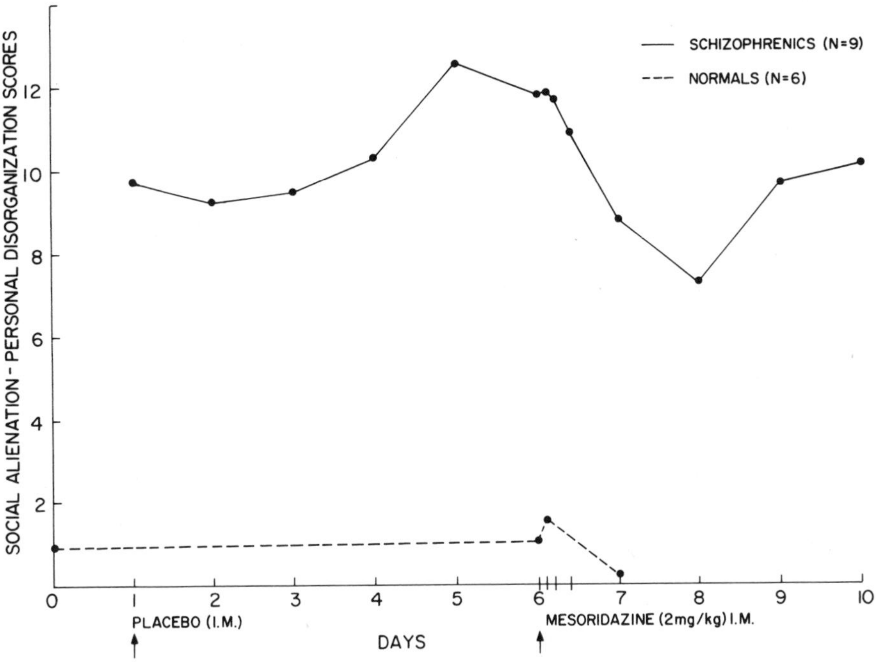


FIG. 2. Average Social Alienation-Personal Disorganization Scores After A Single Placebo 8 Mesoridazine (2 mg/kg) I.M. Injection.

Anergia ($p < .001$), Excitement-Disorientation ($p < .01$); the Hamilton Depression Rating Scale factor scores of Sleep Disturbance ($p < .001$), Anxiety-Depression ($p < .001$), Apathy ($p < .001$); and the Wittenborn Rating Scale factor scores of Anxiety ($p < .01$), Depressive Retardation ($p < .01$), Excitement ($p < .01$) and Paranoia ($p < .001$). No significant changes occurred in these behavioral rating scores during the first 6 days pre-drug even after a placebo intramuscular injection on day 1, except for a decrease in the Anergia factor scores ($p < .05$) of the BPRS; a larger decrease in the Anergia factor scores ($p < .001$) followed the injection of mesoridazine on day 6.

The changes in the social alienation/personal disorganization scale scores before and after the injection of mesoridazine (2 mg/kg) are illustrated in Fig. 2. A significant *decrease* in the social alienation/personal disorganization scale scores ($-3.17 \pm 3.86$; $t = 2.59$; $p < .01$) occurred 24 hours post-drug in 9 of the 10 acute schizophrenic patients; since one of the 10 patients was mute before drug administration, this patient's scores were omitted in these calculations. There was essentially no change in the average social alienation/personal disorganization scale scores 24 hours post-drug in the normal subjects. The average pre-drug social alienation/personal disorganization scale score of the acute schizophrenic

**Table V.** Improvement in Behavioral Ratings (Brief Psychiatric Rating Scale, Hamilton Depression Scale, and Wittenborn Scale) with Single Dose of Mesoridazine (2 mg/kg, i.m.)

| | Mesoridazine Study No. 1 | | | | | | | | |
|---|---|---|---|---|---|---|---|---|---|
| | Day 1 | Day 6 | Day 7 | Day 8 | Overall F | F 7 vs. 6 & 1 | F° 6 vs. 1 | F 8 vs. 7 | F 8 & 7 vs. 6 & 1 |
| BPRS Items | | | | | | | | | |
| 1. Somatic concern | 2.30 | 2.50 | 1.90 | 2.20 | 1.03 | 2.74 | 0.33 | 0.74 | 2.02 |
| 2. Anxiety | 3.80 | 4.00 | 2.70 | 3.00 | 6.15** | 15.18*** | 0.32 | 0.71 | 17.43*** |
| 3. Emotional withdrawal | 3.80 | 3.00 | 2.50 | 2.00 | 11.30*** | 10.36** | 6.14** | 2.40 | 25.37*** |
| 4. Conceptual disorganization | 5.60 | 5.00 | 3.40 | 3.80 | 17.18*** | 39.38*** | 2.95* | 1.31 | 47.29*** |
| 5. Guilt | 3.80 | 3.90 | 3.90 | 3.30 | 1.10 | 0.02 | 0.07 | 2.40 | 0.83 |
| 6. Tension | 4.00 | 4.40 | 3.20 | 3.40 | 6.35** | 13.96*** | 1.67 | 0.42 | 16.95*** |
| 7. Mannerism and posturing | 5.00 | 4.70 | 3.10 | 3.30 | 20.27*** | 44.56*** | 0.98 | 0.44 | 59.40*** |
| 8. Grandiosity | 3.60 | 3.50 | 2.70 | 3.10 | 3.11* | 8.86** | 0.09 | 1.47 | 7.77** |
| 9. Depressive mood | 3.40 | 3.50 | 3.00 | 3.20 | 0.75 | 2.05 | 0.08 | 0.30 | 1.86 |
| 10. Hostility | 4.20 | 4.30 | 3.50 | 3.40 | 5.85** | 10.13** | 0.13 | 0.13 | 17.28*** |
| 11. Suspiciousness | 4.70 | 4.50 | 3.30 | 3.40 | 17.06** | 36.33*** | 0.64 | 0.16 | 50.37*** |
| 12. Hallucinatory behavior | 3.80 | 3.80 | 1.60 | 1.50 | 16.89** | 27.17*** | 0.00 | 0.04 | 42.61*** |
| 13. Motor retardation | 2.30 | 2.10 | 2.40 | 1.80 | 1.23 | 0.47 | 0.35 | 3.16 | 0.18 |
| 14. Uncooperativeness | 3.90 | 3.50 | 2.60 | 2.30 | 12.27*** | 17.60*** | 1.75 | 0.98 | 34.09*** |
| 15. Unusual thought content | 5.30 | 5.20 | 3.70 | 3.80 | 12.09*** | 25.59*** | 0.08 | 0.08 | 35.95*** |
| 16. Blunted affect | 4.60 | 4.00 | 3.30 | 3.50 | 5.08** | 10.06** | 2.71 | 0.30 | 12.22** |
| 17. Excitement | 4.00 | 3.90 | 2.70 | 3.20 | 4.91** | 13.59** | 0.07 | 1.63 | 13.04** |
| 18. Disorientation | 1.60 | 1.30 | 1.10 | 1.00 | 2.12 | 2.48 | 1.37 | 0.15 | 4.85* |

| | | | | | | | | | |
|---|---|---|---|---|---|---|---|---|---|
| **BPRS Factors** | | | | | | | | | |
| Depression 1,2,5,9 | 3.32 | 3.48 | 2.88 | 2.92 | 3.98* | 8.36** | 0.51 | 0.06 | 11.37** |
| Thinking disorder 4,8,11,12,15 | 4.60 | 4.40 | 2.94 | 3.12 | 7.32*** | 87.67*** | 1.08 | 0.88 | 116.74** |
| Anergia 3,7,13,16 | 3.92 | 3.45 | 2.82 | 2.65 | 13.60*** | 19.64*** | 4.47* | 0.61 | 35.73*** |
| Excite.-disorient. 17,18 | 2.80 | 2.60 | 1.90 | 2.10 | 4.62** | 11.16** | 0.52 | 0.52 | 12.81** |
| **Hamilton Factors** | | | | | | | | | |
| Sleep disturbance 4,5,6 | 2.42 | 2.19 | 1.27 | 1.50 | 5.67** | 13.54** | 0.51 | 0.51 | 15.99*** |
| Somatization 11,12,13,14,15 | 1.52 | 1.69 | 1.52 | 1.49 | 0.44 | 0.24 | 0.77 | 0.03 | 0.52 |
| Anxiety-depression 1,2,3,9,10 | 3.17 | 2.92 | 2.21 | 2.33 | 6.23** | 13.61** | 0.90 | 0.21 | 17.57*** |
| Apathy 7,8,17 | 3.89 | 3.62 | 2.87 | 2.71 | 11.14*** | 17.96*** | 1.19 | 0.41 | 31.84*** |
| **Wittenborn Factors** | | | | | | | | | |
| Anxiety 1,2,3,4 | 2.48 | 2.48 | 2.08 | 2.00 | 4.89** | 8.06** | 0.00 | 0.21 | 14.46** |
| Somatic-hysterical | 1.33 | 1.63 | 1.37 | 1.56 | 1.06 | 0.45 | 2.21 | 0.96 | 0.01 |
| Obsessive compulsive phobic 8,9,10 | 1.57 | 1.60 | 1.53 | 1.57 | 0.05 | 0.11 | 0.04 | 0.04 | 0.08 |
| Depressive retardation 11,12,13 | 2.43 | 2.33 | 2.13 | 1.93 | 6.50** | 5.49 | 0.67 | 2.65 | 16.16** |
| Excitement 14,15 | 2.45 | 2.50 | 1.80 | 2.00 | 3.28* | 8.48* | 0.03 | 0.56 | 9.23** |
| Paranoia 16,17 | 3.40 | 3.30 | 2.50 | 2.80 | 7.51*** | 20.09*** | 0.21 | 1.88 | 20.43** |

°One-tailed tests
*p < .05
**p < .01
***p < .001

**Table VI.** Significant or Consistent Correlations Between Various Indices of Drug Plasma Concentration After Single I.M. Dose of Mesoridazine (2 mg/kg) and Changes in Behavioral Ratings (N = 9)

| | | | | | | Indices of Drug Pharmacokinetics | | | | | | | | | |
|---|---|---|---|---|---|---|---|---|---|---|---|---|---|---|---|
| | | | | | | GC conc | | GC area | | GC half-life | | GC peak | | GC peak hour | |
| **Changes in Behavioral Ratings** | UV conc | UV area | UV half-life | UV peak | UV peak hr | mesoridazine | sulforidazine | mesoridazine | sulforidazine | mesoridazine | sulforidazine | mesoridazine | sulforidazine | mesoridazine | sulforidazine |
| Brief Psychiatric Rating Scale Factors | | | | | | | | | | | | | | | |
| Anergia | | | | | | | | | | | | | | | |
| 24 hrs post-drug | .07 | .00 | –.47 | .45 | .23 | .00 | .12 | .11 | .11 | –.41 | –.54 | .31 | .39 | .28 | –.24 |
| 48 hrs post-drug | –.68** | –.57* | –.56 | –.29 | –.57* | –.67** | –.76** | –.75** | –.68** | –.27 | –.57* | –.56 | –.42 | .09 | –.68** |
| Wittenborn Scale Factors | | | | | | | | | | | | | | | |
| Somatic-hysterical | | | | | | | | | | | | | | | |
| 24 hrs post-drug | –.53 | –.43 | –.13 | –.47 | –.52 | –.60* | –.59* | –.61* | –.55 | –.01 | –.16 | –.57 | –.63* | –.34 | –.10 |
| 48 hrs post-drug | –.38 | –.66** | –.47 | –.42 | –.62* | –.19 | –.40 | –.76** | –.68** | –.13 | –.38 | –.64* | –.65* | –.21 | –.38 |

Two-tail tests

*p $<$ .10 UV = spectrophotofluorometer

**p $<$ .05 GC = gas chromatograph

patients (9.99± 5.10) was significantly greater ($t = 3.90$; $p < .005$), as would be expected, than the comparable average pre-drug score (0.98± 2.87) of the normal subjects.

### Correlations between Indices of Drug Plasma Concentration after a Single I.M. Dose of Mesoridazine and Changes in Behavioral Ratings

There were only a few correlations which suggested a relationship between some drug concentration measures and clinical improvement. When patient L.F. was eliminated, the remaining 9 patients showed an association between higher mesoridazine and sulforidazine concentrations in the blood at 48 hours and improvement on the BPRS Anergia scale at 48 hours. A similar relationship with Anergia was seen with area-under-the-curve for mesoridazine and sulforidazine. (See Table VI, where negative correlations indicate association of drug concentration measures with a *decrease* in psychiatric morbidity scores.) Another clinical measure that evinced some relationship between improvement and blood concentration measures was the Somatic-Hysterical Factor of the Wittenborn Rating Scale. The various correlations may again be seen in Table VI.

These correlations of drug level with clinical improvement appeared with the nonspecific fluorometric (UV) method as well as with the more specific gas chromatographic (GC) analytical method. Other than with these two clinical measures, no significant correlations between pharmacokinetic variables and behavioral rating scale scores occurred with a single I.M. injection of mesoridazine.

### Social Alienation/Personal Disorganization Scores and Indices of Mesoridazine Plasma Concentrations

Pre-drug social alienation/personal disorganization scores ($N = 9$) had low positive correlations with post-drug fluorometric mesoridazine peak levels ($r = .35$) and area-under-curve ($r = .36$). Although these correlations did not reach a convincing level of significance, they are mentioned because a previous study[4] examining social alienation/personal disorganization scores ($N = 25$) as predictors of thioridazine concentration, using the Pacha fluorometric assay method[12] after a single oral dose of thioridazine (4 mg/kg), revealed a significant positive correlation between the average pre-drug social alienation/personal disorganization scores in 25 patients with thioridazine half-life (0.44, $p < .03$) and area-under-curve (0.43, $p < .03$).

No significant correlations were found between indices of mesoridazine plasma concentration and changes in social alienation/personal disorganization scores 24 and 48 hours post-drug.

Looking at individual correlations between drug plasma concentrations and social alienation/personal disorganization scores revealed that 4 of the 10 patients showed lower social alienation/personal disorganization scores the higher were their plasma mesoridazine levels over 24 and 48 hours post-drug. These 4 patients were the most clear-cut favorable responders to the single mesoridazine injection as adjudged from changes in post-drug social alienation/personal disorganization scores. Another 3 patients were slight favorable responders and 3 were non-responders to the mesoridazine. Apparently, whether or not a patient responds favorably to a given dose of a psychoactive drug constitutes another factor as to the nature of correlations between drug plasma levels and clinical responses. The response of the schizophrenic syndrome to a single dose of a phenothiazine may not have much relationship to the response of this syndrome to continuous doses. Hence, before making more of these preliminary findings than warranted, more pertinent data need to be collected.

## DISCUSSION

As in our previous findings with a single oral dose of thioridazine (4 mg/kg), the administration of mesoridazine (2 mg/kg) intramuscularly was associated with a wide variation in plasma concentrations, peak drug blood level, peak drug level hour, half-life and area-under-the-curve as well as significant decreases within 24 to 48 hours of various measures of the schizophrenic syndrome. These measures include social alienation/personal disorganization scores of the Gottschalk-Gleser Content Analysis Scale, the factors of Thinking Disorder, Excitement-Disorientation and Depression of the Overall-Gorham Brief Psychiatric Rating Scale, the factors of Sleep Disturbance and Apathy of the Hamilton Depression Scale, and the factors of Anxiety-Excitement and Paranoia of the Wittenborn Scale. These findings with single doses of phenothiazine are unexpected in that these crucial characteristics of the schizophrenic syndrome have usually been considered to require a much longer time than 1 or 2 days to begin to respond favorably to psychoactive drug medication. Certainly our patients were still quite schizophrenic 48 hours after receiving the single dose of these phenothiazines, but significant average improvement had appeared in comparison to their pre-drug mental status. Usually psychoactive drug treatment of acute schizophrenia has been considered to require weeks to begin to make its effect manifest on the schizophrenic syndrome. While such rapid initial effects of the phenothiazines on the schizophrenic syndrome do not shed any penetrating light on the etiological theories of schizophrenia, that is, the genetic,

biochemical or psychosocial ones, these empirical findings must be compatible with these theories for the latter to maintain their explanatory value if not their actual validity.

Both our thioridazine and mesoridazine single-dose studies do reveal that there are frequent significant correlations between the indices of psychoactive drug blood levels and the nature and degree of the clinical therapeutic response. Although our present study using mesoridazine involves only 10 acute schizophrenic patients, suggestive evidence has been presented to show that mesoridazine effects somewhat different behavioral-psychological changes as compared to thioridazine, if not in the degrees and dimensions of improvement (Table V), at least on the basis of comparing the quite different correlates of thioridazine plasma indices and their associated clinical responses (Table VI). The correlations reported in our previous thioridazine study[4] were based on drug plasma concentrations measured by the nonspecific fluorometric method of Pacha,[12] whereas in the present mesoridazine study these correlations were based on both the fluorometric and gas chromatographic assays. Comparing the correlations in the two studies using the fluorometric procedure indicates that a single oral dose (4 mg/kg) of thioridazine, while not having any more marked beneficial effect on the schizophrenic syndrome than a single intramuscular dose of mesoridazine (2 mg/kg), was associated with a different pattern of improvement among the behavioral ratings 48 hours post-drug. The thioridazine plasma indices correlated with improvement in the Depression, Thinking Disorder and Excitement-Disorientation factors of the BPRS, with the Sleep Disturbance and Anxiety/Depression factors of the Hamilton Depression Scale and with the Excitement and Disorientation factors of the Wittenborn Scale; whereas the single-dose behavioral beneficial effect of an intramuscular injection of mesoridazine (2 mg/kg) was associated with significant correlations of the drug level indices only with improvement in Anergia factor scores of the BPRS and the Somatic-Hysterical factor scores of the Wittenborn Scale. These correlational differences strongly suggest that the parent drug thioridazine has pharmacological effects, either quantitatively or qualitatively, somewhat different from those of its metabolites, mesoridazine and sulforidazine.

With only single doses of mesoridazine, we find the parent drug is rapidly broken down to sulforidazine. On the average, more sulforidazine than mesoridazine was circulating in the blood plasma 24 hours after intramuscular injection of mesoridazine (Fig. 1). The differential clinical effects of sulforidazine could not be precisely separated from the effects of mesoridazine in the present study, even though the correlates of drug and metabolite plasma concentration and clinical response could be separately determined and examined.

Comparing the pharmacokinetics of a single dose of mesoridazine in

acute schizophenics and normals did not reveal any marked differences. With respect to clinical response, of course, the normal subjects have no schizophrenic target symptoms and, hence, are not affected clinically similarly to the schizophrenic patients. The normal subjects were, however, obviously very heavily sedated by the mesoridazine and hypotensive reactions were prominent.

A major issue in single-dose psychoactive drug studies of pharmacokinetics is whether such research gives information on what the pharmacokinetics is likely to be during continuous and multiple-dose drug administration. We have entertained the hypothesis that single-dose drug administration would provide useful data to predict reasonably well what the average drug plasma concentration would be during continuous and multiple-drug dose. We have also speculated that those patients who improved the most with a single-drug dose would be likely to show most rapid improvement with continuous drug treatment. Recently Davis et al.[19] have offered some data, using butaperazine as the psychoactive agent, that supports the former hypothesis. We have been obtaining single-dose data with mesoridazine (2 mg/kg) or thioridazine (4 mg/kg) followed 4 days after the administration of the single dose with continuous daily dose administration of thioridazine for 3–6 weeks. Preliminary examination of the relationship of single-dose pharmacokinetics to multiple-dose pharmacokinetics with 6 patients, using the fluorometric analytical method, gives corroborative evidence ($r = .91$, $p < .02$) that peak plasma level following single-dose treatment predicts average drug plasma concentration with continuous daily drug treatment. If these preliminary findings receive further corroboration, and if a relationship is found between chronic plasma levels and clinical response, such relationships between single-dose and multiple, continuous dose pharmacokinetics/clinical response will be useful in monitoring patient treatment with psychoactive drugs.

## SUMMARY

(1) This study investigated the relationship of the pharmacokinetics of mesoridazine to its clinical response. Ten acute schizophrenic patients, without the history of any complicating medical disorder or chronic alcoholism or previous psychoactive drug administration for at least 4 weeks preceding hospital admission, were administered a single placebo intramuscular injection of normal saline on the 1st day of the study, and 6 days later were administered a single dose of mesoridazine (2 mg/kg) intramuscularly. A group of 6 normal volunteers were also administered a placebo intramuscular injection of normal saline, and 6 days later were administered a single intramuscular dose of mesoridazine (2 mg/kg) in the same mental hospital setting.

(2) On the 1st and 6th days pre-drug and the 7th and 8th days post-drug, all patients were assessed on three behavioral rating scales: the Overall-Gorham Brief Psychiatric Rating Scale, the Hamilton Depression Rating Scale and the Wittenborn Rating Scale. Also, all patients gave 5-minute speech samples in response to standardized instructions on the 6-pre-drug days and for 4 days post-drug for the measurement of Social Alienation/Personal Disorganization according to the content analysis method of Gottschalk and Gleser. The 6 normal subjects were assessed for clinical response pre-drug and post-drug by the same measurement procedures on a somewhat modified schedule.

(3) Pharmacokinetic analyses, including plasma concentration, peak level, half-life, area-under-time-concentration-curve and peak hour were determined by the spectrophotofluorometric method of Pacha and a modification (Dinovo et al.[17]) of the gas chromatographic method of Curry and Mould.[14]

(4) Pharmacokinetic indices showed wide individual variation among patients and normals, and while normal subjects tended to have lower indices, these differences were not statistically significant. Significant decreases in all clinical measures of the schizophrenic syndrome occurred within 24 hours post-drug among the schizophrenic patients but, as expected, not among the normal subjects. No significant pre-drug decreases in the clinical measures following placebo administration were observed, except for the average BPRS Anergia factor score, which decreased significantly following the injection of mesoridazine.

(5) The Anergia factor scores of the BPRS and the Somatic-Hysterical factor scores of the Wittenborn Scale showed significant improvement related to drug plasma peak level, area-under-curve, or half-life, using both UV and GC analytic methods; not only mesoridazine, but its major metabolite following a single-drug dose, sulforidazine, showed the above pharmacokinetic/clinical response correlations, suggesting that this metabolite is pharmacologically active. These correlations were different from those found in a previous study examining the relationship between thioridazine pharmacokinetic variables after a single oral dose (4 mg/kg) and the same clinical responses measures, though overall improvement of the schizophrenic syndrome occurring with mesoridazine (2 mg/kg) or thioridazine (4 mg/kg) was similar.

(6) The relevance of such single-dose studies to continuous-dose studies was demonstrated by a preliminary investigation with 6 schizophrenic patients showing that single-dose peak drug levels are significantly positively correlated with continuous-dose average drug plasma level.

## ACKNOWLEDGMENTS

This study was supported in part by a research grant (MH 20174-02) from the Psychopharmacology Branch, NIMH, and a research grant-in-aid from Sandoz Co. R. Bina, M.A. Nandi and D.E. Bates lent technical assistance and J. Overall, Ph.D., provided consultation on assessment of BPRS scale scores.

## REFERENCES

1. Gottschalk, L.A., Kaplan, S.A.: Chlordiazepoxide plasma levels and clinical responses. *Compr. Psychiatry* 13:519–28, 1972.
2. Gottschalk, L.A., Noble, E.P., Stolzoff, G.E., Bates, D.E., Cable, C.G., Uliana, R.L., Birch, H., Fleming, E.W.: Relationships of chlordiazepoxide blood level to psychological and biochemical responses. In *The Benzodiazepines,* edited by S. Garattini, E. Mussini, L. Randall. New York, Raven Press, 1973.
3. Elliott, H., Gottschalk, L.A., Uliana, R.L.: Relationships of plasma meperidine levels to changes in anxiety and hostility. *Compr. Psychiatry* 15:57–61, 1974.
4. Gottschalk, L.A., Biener, R., Noble, E.P., Birch, H., Wilbert, D.E., Heiser, J.F.: Thioridazine plasma levels and clinical response. *Compr. Psychiatry* 16:323-337, 1975.
5. Gottschalk, L.A., Dinovo, E.C., Biener, R.: Effect of oral and intramuscular routes of administration on serum chlordiazepoxide levels and the prediction of these levels from pre-drug fasting serum glucose concentrations. *Res. Comm. Chem. Path. Pharm.* 8:697–702, 1974.
6. Overall, J.E., Gorham, D.P.: A pattern probability model for the classification of psychiatric patients. *Behav. Sci.* 8:108–16, 1963.
7. Overall, J.E.: A configural analysis of psychiatric diagnostic stereotypes. *Behav. Sci.* 8:211–19, 1963.
8. Gottschalk, L.A., Gleser, G.C.: *The Measurement of Psychological States Through the Content Analysis of Verbal Behavior.* Berkeley, Los Angeles, University of California Press, 1969.
9. Guy, W., Bonato, R.R.: *Manual for the ECDEU Assessment Battery,* 2nd rev. Chevy Chase, Maryland, National Institute of Mental Health, U.S. Dept. of Health, Education and Welfare, 1970.
10. Overall, J.E., Gorham, D.P.: The brief psychiatric rating scale (BPRS). *Psychol. Rep.* 10:799–812, 1962.
11. Gottschalk, L.A., Winget, C.N., Gleser, G.C.: *Manual of Instructions for Use of the Gottschalk-Gleser Content Analysis Scales: Anxiety, Hostility, and Social Alienation-Personal Disorganization.* Berkeley, Los Angeles, University of California Press, 1969.
12. Pacha, W.L.: A method for the fluorometric determination of thioridazine or mesoridazine in plasma. *Experientia* 25:103–04, 1969.
13. Dinovo, E.C., Gottschalk, L.A., Nandi, B.R., Geddes, P.G.: A method for measuring thioridazine, mesoridazine, metabolites and other phenothiazines in plasma. *J. Pharm. Sci.* (in press).
14. Curry, S.H., Mould, G.D.: Gas chromatographic identification of thioridazine in plasma and method for routine assay of the drug. *J. Pharm. Pharmacol.* 21:674–77, 1969.
15. Dixon, W.J. (ed.): *BMD: Biomedical Computer Programs X-Series Supplement.* Berkeley, Los Angeles, University of California Press, 1972.
16. Nie, N.H., Bent, D.H., Hull, C.H.: *Statistical Package for the Social Sciences.* New York, McGraw-Hill, 1970.

17. Dinovo, E.C., Gottschalk, L.A., Noble, E.P., Biener, R.: Isolation of a possible new metabolite of thioridazine and mesoridazine from human plasma. *Res. Comm. Chem. Path. Pharm.* 7:489–96, 1974.
18. Gruenke, L.D., Craig, J.C., Dinovo, E.C., Gottschalk, L.A., Noble, E.P., Biener, R.: Identification of a metabolite of thioridazine and mesoridazine from human plasma. *Res. Comm. Chem. Path. Pharm.* 10:221–25, 1975.
19. Davis, J.M., Janowsky, D.S., Sekerke, I., Manier, H., El-Yousef, M.K.: The pharmacokinetics of Butaperazine in plasma. In *The Phenothiazines and Structurally Related Drugs,* edited by I. Forrest, C. Carr, E. Usden. New York, Raven Press, 1974.

# PHARMACOKINETICS OF CHLORDIAZEPOXIDE, MEPERIDINE, THIORIDAZINE, AND MESORIDAZINE AND RELATIONSHIPS WITH CLINICAL RESPONSE

Louis A. Gottschalk, Eugene C. Dinovo, Robert S. Biener, Herman Birch

Pharmacokinetic studies of single, standardized, oral or intra-muscular doses of chlordiazepoxide (25mg) (Gottschalk, et al, 1972, 1973, 1974), meperidine (100mg) (Elliott et al 1974), oral thioridazine (4 mg/kg) (Gottschalk et al, 1975a), and intramuscular mesoridazine (2 mg/kg) (Gottschalk et al, 1975b) have revealed quite marked individual differences in blood plasma concentrations, peak plasma levels, half-lives, and area-under-the-curve plotting blood concentration against time. Furthermore, these studies have indicated that the clinical responses to these drugs are significantly related to the magnitude of some of these various pharmacokinetic indices. For example, in our chlordiazepoxide studies, anxiety, hostility outward, and ambivalent hostility scores, as measured by the method of content analysis of verbal samples, tended to decrease ($p < .10$) over a fifty minute observation period when subjects were on chlordiazepoxide compared to a placebo. However, a statistically significant decrease in anxiety scores ($p < .025$) during this time period occurred only in those 11 subjects whose chlordiazepoxide blood levels exceeded .70 mcg/ml; no significant decreases occurred in anxiety scores of the subjects whose blood chlordizaepoxide blood levels were less than .70 mcg/ml. In the meperidine study, there was a significant correlation between meperidine plasma levels, after either oral or intramuscular administration, and decrease in anxiety scores. In the single dose oral thioridazine study, involving the administration of this major tranquilizer to 25 acute schizophrenic patients, significant decreases occurred in measures of the schizophrenic syndrome 24-48 hours postdrug among the schizophrenic patients, as measured by the following: Overall-Gorham Brief Psychiatric Rating Scale, (Overall and Gorham, 1962); Hamilton Depression Rating Scale, and Wittenborn Rating Scale (Guy and Bonato, 1970) and in Gottschalk-Gleser (1969) content analysis scale scores measuring the severity of the schizophrenic syndrome in terms of social alienation-personal disorganization. Also, thioridazine plasma pharmacokinetic indices correlated with improvement in the Depression. Thinking, Disorder, and Excitement-Disorientation factors of the BPRS; with Sleep Disturbance and Anxiety/Depression factors of the Hamilton Depression scale;

and with the Excitement and Paranoia factors of the Wittenborn scale. In the mesoridazine study, in which the drug was administered intramuscularly to ten acute schizophrenic patients, again there was a significant improvement in the rating scale and content analysis scale indices of the schizophrenic syndrome, but here significant correlations of drug concentration indices were with improvement in Anergia factor scores of the BPRS and the Somatic-Hysterical factor scores of the Wittenborn scale. These differences in correlations between the two studies, strongly suggested that the parent drug, thioridazine, had somewhat different pharmacological effects, either quantitatively or qualitatively, than its metabolite, mesoridazine and sulforidazine (the latter being another metabolite of thioridazine and mesoridazine detectable after a single dose of these drugs — Dinovo et al, 1974; Gruenke et al, 1975).

## RESEARCH AIMS

Although these single dose psychoactive drug studies have been very useful, in that they have demonstrated conclusively the wide individual variations in the pharmacokinetics of psychoactive drugs as well as the relationships of various pharmacokinetic indices to anti-anxiety and anti-schizophrenic manifestations, there are certain important questions they have not answered. They have not provided information on what the drug concentrations in the blood are likely to be during continuous dose drug administration and they have not been able to tell us to what extent a favorable reponse to a single dose of a phenothiazine is predictive of the kind and degree of clinical response with continuous drug dosage. With respect to the latter issue, psychoactive drug treatment of acute schizophrenia has usually been considered to require weeks to begin to make its effect manifest in the schizophrenic syndrome. Many of our acute schizophrenic patients in the single dose thioridazine and mesoridazine studies have had, however, marked beneficial responses to a single dose of these phenothiazines, although some patients have had little or no favorable clinical response. Combining single dose and multiple dose phenothiazine studies in the same schizophrenic patients would let us pursue the leads obtained in our single dose studies and permit us to determine whether examining the single dose pharmacokinetics and clinical response in each patient might be of practical significance in terms of optimal drug dose and probable clinical response in long term pharmacotherapy of the schizophrenic syndrome.

## METHOD

In the present report, we will relate findings with 10 acute schizophrenic patients who initially received a single dose of intramuscular mesoridazine (2 mg/kg), followed four days after this single dose of mesoridazine with daily dose treatment, over a three to eight week period, of oral thioridazine (4 mg/kg).

(There is *no* generally accepted definition of a formal thought disorder. Therefore, a consistent set of criteria were used for the selection of our research patients, diagnosed as having an "acute schizophrenic episode.")

Our previous studies with single dose oral thioridazine (Gottschalk et al, 1975) and intra-muscular mesoridazine (Gottschalk 1975) have demonstrated that thioridazine is first metabolized to the pharmacologically active mesoridazine (thioridazine-S-sulfoxide) which is in turn metabolized to the pharmacologically active sulforidazine (thioridazine-S-sulfone) (Dinovo et al, 1974, 1975; Gruenke et al, 1975). No other metabolites have been positively identified after a single dose by gas chromatography. After continuous daily dosage with thioridazine (4 mg/kg), however another metabolite has been detected and we have identified it as thioridazine-R-sulfoxide. We wondered whether these very similar phenothiazines, thioridazine and mesoridazine or their metabolites, might have some similarities after a single dose in certain aspects of their pharmacokinetics (peak concentration, peak hours, half-life, area-under-the-time-concentration-curve, absorption constant, elimination constant) within each individual so that one or more of these indices might serve as a predictor of the steady state drug concentration with daily continuous dose treatment with thioridazine.

Our aims in this combined single dose followed by continuous dose drug study, hence, were as follows:

1. To determine whether those who responded to a single dose of mesoridazine were more likely to respond more favorably during continuous dosage with thioridazine.

2. To determine whether any pharmacokinetic indices during the single dose study were predictors of the average blood levels during continuing daily doses of thioridazine.

3. To look for any relationship between the plasma level of the parent drug or its metabolities and the development of any adverse side-effects associated with administration of thioridazine.

4. To examine the equilibrium established between blood and spinal fluid concentration of thioridazine and its metabolities in patients receiving continuous daily administration of this drug.

## RESULTS

Our study is incomplete, for data from additional patients need to be obtained and data already collected need yet to be analyzed. We can report here, however, some preliminary findings, which may or may not hold up with more data.

1. *Do acute schizophrenic patients who respond favorably to a single dose of intramuscular mesoridazine respond more favorably to continous oral thioridazine?*

In our group of 10 acute schizophrenic patients, we noted 3 who were

non-responders to both mesoridazine and thioridazine. Two of these patients improved considerably during the first six predrug days of the study, after receiving on the first day a placebo injection of mesoridazine, and these two patients had minimal improvement or got worse in the various behavioral measures of the schizophrenic syndrome after administration of the phenothiazines. The other non-responder showed minimal improvement or aggravation of the schizophrenic syndrome at the standardized dosage level used. There were no discernible pretreatment characteristics among these three schizophrenic patients that could provide us clues that these patients would either respond spontaneously and without drug therapy with considerable improvement to hospitalization or would be unresponsive to the dose of thioridazine used. All three patients had marked disturbances in thought disorder, apathy or anergia, hallucinatory or delusional manifestations typical of acute schizophrenia. Though they appear, at this point, to be indistinguishable from the patients who were more responsive to phenothiazine therapy, we intend to analyze pertinent data further to determine whether they can be discriminated. We have collected a group of another 10 acute schizophrenic patients from among 35 other schizophrenic patients in our two previous studies, that were relatively unresponsive to a single dose treatment of thioridazine or mesoridazine, and we will reexamine the characteristics of this combined pool of patients.

Preliminary analysis of our data with all 10 patients in the present study suggests that the kind and degree of the psychological response to a single dose of intramuscular mesoridazine may predict the likelihood of a favorable psychological response with continuous daily treatment with oral thioridazine.

When the improvement in a rating scale score (as measured by the difference between the score 24 hours postdrug and the immediately predrug score) was correlated with the average on that rating scale of the first three weeks of the continuous drug dose phase of the study, the correlations were generally negative, and sometimes significantly so. At first glance this would imply that the more a patient improved in the single dose phase of the study the worse he was during the continuous dose phase. However, we think another explanation is more reasonable. The patients who were worse initially had more room to improve with the acute dose and showed larger change scores, although after the change they still may have been worse than the patients who were less sick initially. If the initially sicker patients remained sicker during the continuous dose phase and the healthier remained healthier, the negative correlations would be explained.

Therefore we looked at the results in a different manner. We attempted to determine how well a patient's clinical status 24 hours after a single drug dose predicted his clinical status during the continuous dose phase over and above what his predrug clinical status would predict. To this end we calculated partial correlations, correlating patients' 24 hour postdrug single dose clinical rating scale scores with continuous dose phase scores while partialling out or eliminating the effect of inital clinical status as measured just before the

administration of the single dose of mesoridazine. The results of this statistical evaluation were as follows:

1. The BPRS Thinking Disorder Factor score 24 hours after the single drug dose correlated 0.66 ($N = 8$, $p < .05$) with the average BPRS Thinking Disorder Factor score after the multiple drug dose.

2. The Wittenborn Somatic-Hysterical Factor score 24 hours after the single drug dose correlated 0.80 ($N = 8$, $p < .009$) with the average Wittenborn Somatic-Hysterical Factor score after the multiple drug dose.

3. The Wittenborn Obsessive Compulsive Phobic Factor score 24 hours after the single drug dose correlated 0.92 ($N = 8$, $p < .001$) with the Wittenborn Factor score after the multiple drug dose.

Multiple regression predictor equations can be written for these relationships, for example, for the relationship between the short term and long term drug effect on thought disorder: BPRSLF2 - 0.18 + 0.35 BPRS6F2 + 0.44 BPRS7F2 ($p < .01$) where BPRSLF2 is the average BPRS factor score for thought disorder during long term drug administration, BPRS6F2 is the BPRS factor score for thought disorder predrug and on day 6 of the study, and BPRS7F2 is the thought disorder factor score 24 hours after the single drug dose.

II. *Were there any pharmacokinetic indices during the single intramus[ cular dose study which might predict average blood levels during continuous daily doses of thioridazine? The answer seems to be "probably*]"

It is to be noted, here, that the fluorometric method (Pacha, 1969) is a non-specific assay that measures thioridazine, mesoridazine, and metabolites without distinguishing between them; whereas, the gas chromatographic method is capable of specifically assaying and distinguishing thioridazine and its various metabolites (Curry and Mould, 1969; Dinovo et al, 1975).

Following a single dose of intramuscular mesoridazine, mesoridazine half-life (by GC) correlated .86, ($N = 5$, $p < .07$) and mesoridazine area-under-the-curve correlated .86 ($p < .07$) with the average mesoridazine blood concentration over the first three weeks of daily oral thioridazine.

Following a single dose of intramuscular mesoridazine, sulforidazine area-under-the-curve (by GC) correlated significantly positively ($r = 0.88$, $N = 6$, $p < .02$) with the average sulforidazine blood concentration over the first three weeks of daily oral thioridazine.

III. *Were there any pharmacokinetic indices demonstrated with the single dose of mesoridazine that predicted the behavioral response after continuous daily doses of thioridazine? Yes*]

The mesoridazine area-under-the-curve (for the first 24 hours postdrug measured by the fluorometric method) correlated significantly ($N = 10$) with improvement in many different average rating scale scores (over 3 weeks) following chronic administration of oral thioridazine:

BPRS Depression Factor score ($r = 67$, $p < .04$)

BPRS Thinking Disorder Factor score ($r = .78$, $p < .007$)

BPRS Anxiety-Depression Factor score ($r = .94$, $p < .001$)
Hamilton Anxiety-Depression score ($r = .60$, $p < .06$)
Hamilton Apathy Factor score ($r = .84$, $p < .003$)
Wittenborn Anxiety Factor score ($r = .61$, $p < .06$)
Wittenborn Depression-Retardation Factor score ($r = .61$, $p < .06$)

Sulforidazine half-life (by GC) following a single dose of intramuscular mesoridazine, correlated negatively significantly ($r = 0.65$, $N = 10$, $p < .04$) with the average BPRS Excitement-Disorientation Factor score during the first three weeks after daily continuous oral thioridazine. The longer the sulforidazine half-life after a single dose of mesoridazine, the lower the BPRS Excitement-Disorientation Factor score with daily continuous oral thioridazine.

Sulforidazine half-life, after a single dose of intramuscular mesoridazine, did not correlate significantly negatively with the average BPRS Thought Disorder Factor score ($r = 0.52$, $N = 10$, $p < .20$) during daily continuous oral thioridazine treatment.

Mesoridazine peak (by GC), following the single intramuscular dose of mesoridazine, correlated negatively with the average BPRS Thought Disorder Factor score ($r = 0.58$, $N = 9$, $p < .10$) during daily continuous oral thioridazine.

The mesoridazine peak hour (by the fluorometric method), following the single intramuscular dose of mesoridazine correlated positively with the average Hamilton Somatization Factor score ($r = 0.59$, $N = 10$, $p < .09$), the average Hamilton Apathy Factor score ($r = 0.67$, $N = 9$, $p < .05$), and the average Wittenborn Somatic-Hysterical Factor score ($r = 0.89$, $N = 9$, $p < .001$), the average Wittenborn Depression-Retardation Factor score ($r = 0.64$, $N = 9$, $p < 10$), and the average Wittenborn Paranoia Factor score ($r = 0.59$, $N = 9$, $p < .09$) during daily continuous oral thioridazine. Sulforidazine peak hour (by GC) after a single dose of intramuscular mesoridazine, correlated positively with average BPRS Anergia Factor score ($r = 0.72$, $N = 10$, $p < .02$), average Hamilton Somatization Factor Score ($r = 0.63$, $N = 10$, $p < .05$), average Hamilton Anxiety-Depression Factor score ($r = 0.73$, $N = 10$, $p < .02$), average Hamilton Apathy Factor score ($r = o.68$, $N = 10$, $p < .03$), Wittenborn Anxiety Factor score ($r = .83$, $N = 10$, $p < .003$), average Wittenborn Obsessive-Compulsive Factor score ($r = 0.64$, $N = 10$, $p < .05$), average Wittenborn Depression-Retardation Factor score ($r = 0.91$, $N = 10$, $p < .001$), average Wittenborn Excitement Factor score ($r = 0.62$, $N = 10$, $p < .05$), average Wittenborn Paranoia Factor score ($r = 0.56$, $N = 10$, $p < .09$).

IV. *Were any adverse side effects observed and were these noted to be associated with any pharmacodynamic variables?*

One patient developed abnormal EKG changes and this patient had unusually high sulforidazine plasma levels about two weeks before these EKG changes appeared, but the sulforidazine plasma levels, as well as the plasma levels of mesoridazine and thioridazine, fell abruptly about one week before the abnormal EKG changes appeared. Whether the change, that is, decrease, in

phenothiazine blood concentration or the preceding high levels of a metabolite, such as, sulforidazine, accounted for the EKG abnormalities, that persisted for 3 weeks after their onset, we do not know at this time. Obviously, more data needs to be obtained.

V. *What are the relationships between blood and spinal fluid concentra[ tions of thioridazine and its metabolites?*

On one of our acute schizophrenic patients, we did lumbar punctures to obtain cerebrospinal fluid samples for assay of the concentration of thioridazine and its metabolites three and five weeks after daily administration of oral thioridazine (4 mg/kg). We did so in order to determine whether there are fixed individual or group ratios between plasma concentrations of these pharmacological substances. To our surprise no traces of these chemical substances could be detected in the spinal fluid. Thioridazine or mesoridazine could be detected and approximately 95% recovered after adding these substances to clean samples of human cerebrospinal fluid. Also, these drugs and their metabolites could be detected and recovered in the brain tissue of mice after intraperitoneal injection by our research team.

We must, tentatively, conclude that, though thioridazine and its metabolites pass through the blood-brain barrier and readily become attached to receptor sites and brain tissues, these pharmacological agents do not diffuse into the lumbar spinal fluid, even after 3 or more weeks of continuous daily dosage with this drug or are so rapidly removed by the binding sites of the brain that none can be detected at the level of sensitivity of our assay method (.05 ug/mi).

## DISCUSSION

On the basis of our preliminary studies, there appear to be some predictive relationships between the pharmacokinetic and clinical responses among schizophrenic patients to a single dose of a phenothiazine and the average drug blood concentration and clinical response during continuous daily pharmacotherapy of schizophrenia. Davis et al (1974) have reported that peak blood levels of butaperazine, after a single drug dose, are highly correlated with the average blood concentration after continuous drug dose. Pharmacokinetic formula for predicting effective drug concentration have been provided by Goldstein et al (1974), but how well these apply to the phenothiazines and other psychoactive drugs needs confirmation. Other research reporting the relationship of clinical response to a single drug dose and the clinical response after multiple drug dose is rare in psychopharmacology. It is likely in the future, as our technology improves, monitoring of blood concentration and other pharmacokinetic indices of psychoactive medication will become routine. But there are depressed patients and schizophrenic patients who are non-responders to psychoactive drugs, regardless of the blood levels obtained. We need to be

able to ascertain, without prolonged clinical trial-and-errors and as soon as possible with the advent of a treatment program, which psychiatric patients are favorable responders to the appropriate pharmacological agents when blood levels are adequate and which patients are non-responders and, hence, require a different treatment regimen. We intend to pursue these research goals as well as others in the area of pharmacokinetics and clinical response.

## BIBLIOGRAPHY

1. Curry SH and Mould GD: Gas chromatographic identification of thioridazine in plasma and method for routine assay of the drug. *J Pharm Pharmac* 21:674-677, 1969.

2. Davis JM, Janowsky DS, Sekerke I, Manier H and El Yousef MK: The Pharmacokinetics of Butaperazine in Plasma in Forrest IS, Carr CJ, and Usden E (eds): *The Phenothiazines and Structurally Related Drugs*. New, Raven Press, 1974.

3. Dinovo EC, Gottschalk LA, Nandi BR, and Geddes DG: A method for measuring thioridazine, mesoridazine, metabolites, and other phenothiazines in plasma. *J Pharmac Sci* 65:667-669, 1976.

4. Dinovo EC, Gottschalk LA, Noble EP, and Biener R: Isolation of a possible new metabolite of thioridazine and mesoridazine from human plasma. *Res Comm Chem Path Pharm* 7:489-496, 1974.

5. Elliott H., Gottschalk LA, Uliana RL: Relationships of plasma meperidine levels to changes in anxiety and hostility. *Compr Psychiatry* 15:57-61, 1974.

6. Goldstein A, Aronow L and Kalman SM: *Principles of Drug Action: The Basis of Pharmacology*. 2nd edition. New York, John Wiley, 1974.

7. Gottschalk LA, Biener R, Noble EP, Birch H, Wilbert DE, Heiser JF: Thioridazine plasma levels and clinical response. *Compr Psychiatry* 16:323-337, 1975a.

8. Gottschalk LA, Dinovo E, Biener R: Effect of oral and intramuscular routes of administration on serum chlordiazepoxide levels and the prediction of these levels from predrug fasting serum glucose concentrations. *Res Comm Chem Path Pharm* 8:697-702, 1974.

9. Gottschalk LA, Dinovo E, Biener R, Birch H, Syben M, Noble EP: Plasma levels of mesoridazine and its metabolites and clinical response in acute schizophrenia after a single intramuscular dose. In Gottschalk LA and Merlis S (eds): *Pharmacokinetics, Psychoactive Drug Levels, and Clinical Response*. New York, Spectrum Publications, 1975b.

10. Gottschalk LA and Gleser GC: *The Measurement of Psychological States Through the Content of Verbal Behavior*. Berkeley, Los Angeles, University of California Press, 1969.

11. Gottschalk LA, Kaplan SA: Chlordiazepoxide plasma levels and clinical responses. *Compr Psychiatry* 13:519-528, 1972.

12. Gottschalk LA, Noble EP, Stolzoff GE, Bates DE, Cable CG, Uliana RL, Birch H, and Fleming EW: Relationships of chlordiazepoxide blood level to psychological and biochemical responses. In Garattini S, Mussini E, Randall L (eds): *The Benzodiazepines*. New York, Raven Press, 1973.

13. Gruenke LD, Craig JC, Dinovo EC, Gottschalk LA, Noble EP, and Biener R: Identification of a metabolite of thioridazine and mesoridazine from human plasma. *Res Comm Chem Path Pharm* 10:221-225, 1975.

14. Guy W, Bonato RR: *Manual for the ECDEU Assessment Battery*. 2nd revision, Chevy Chase, Maryland, National Institute of Mental Health, U.S. Dept. of Health, Education and Welfare, 1970.

15. Overall JE, Gorham DP: The brief psychiatric rating scale (BPRS). *Psychol Rep* 10:799-812, 1962.

16. Pacha WL: A method for the fluorometric determination of thioridazine or mesoridazine in plasma. *Experientia* 25:103-104, 1969.

# DRUG EFFECTS IN THE ASSESSMENT OF AFFECTIVE STATES IN MAN

By LOUIS A. GOTTSCHALK

## INTRODUCTION

In the study of drug effects in man, we are hindered by incomplete knowledge ragarding the neurophysiology, neurochemistry, and neuropharmacology of human behavior and subjective experience. We know that the site and mechanism of action of pharmacological agents involves neurons, their synapses, and the facilitation or inhibition of neural transmission across these synapses. We have a number of interesting hypotheses (Cooper *et al.*, 1970; Himwich, 1970; Weil-Malherbe and Szara, 1971; Barchas and Usdin, 1973; Snyder *et al.*, 1974; Davis and Janowsky, 1974; Janowsky *et al.*, 1974; Schildkraut, 1974) that attempt to explain the pathogenesis of mental disorders and the mechanism of action of psychoactive drugs which involve pharmacological actions of biochemical neurotransmittors substances, such as the biogenic amines; for example, norepinephrine, dopamine, serotonin and tryptamine. But we cannot very easily study these internal processes directly in man; instead, we have to extrapolate what information is available mostly from studies with animals. Our studies of such drug effects with human beings require us to administer a drug to a person and, without knowing exactly where or how it works, to observe the behaviors and subjective experiences that are evoked by the drug. This is the limited kind of understanding we have of the psychological effects and mechanism of action of most of the psychoactive drugs, an understanding that can be empirically based but which does not provide a precise and detailed level of understanding of neuropsychopharmacological processes. It leaves room for much error, makes us guess what the major intervening variables are, forces us to specify carefully the personality dimensions we are trying to influence by the drug, and obliges us to measure those personality dimensions which might be undergoing adverse changes as well as the dimensions which are changing in a favorable direction.

Moreover, no tenable theoretical basis for the pharmacotherapy of personality disorders has been proposed that can be neatly integrated with extant theories of the pathogenesis of neurosis or behavior disorders. In this sense, there is no justification for referring to any class of psychoactive drugs as "antineurotic," for there is no evidence that any psychoactive drugs influence "neurosis" or character disorders per se, though these drugs appear to influence some concomitants of these psychiatric disorders, such as anxiety, hostility, depression, the schizophrenic syndrome, memory processes, or cognitive and intellectual processes. There is better rationale, at this time, in limiting pharmacological terminology to describing a drug action and referring to psychoactive drugs as "hypnotics," "sedatives," "minor" and "major tranquilizers," "energizers," "psychotomimetics" than to imply by using

psychiatric terminology ("antineurotic" or "antipsychotic" drugs) that these drugs influence the cause or causes of mild or severe personality syndromes.

An important step in accurately assessing the effects of pharmacological agents on personality and behavior is to distinguish the effects of non-drug factors from drug effects on these psychological variables. These non-drug factors include the effect of the personality and attitudes of the individual administering the drug (Rickels, 1963; Uhlenhuth *et al.*, 1966; Gottschalk, 1968b), the context or milieu in which the drug is given (Sabshin and Ramot, 1956), demographic and personality characteristics of the patient (Rickels, 1963, 1968), the physiological state of the patient, the route of drug administration, and so forth. Proper controls and research design, including placebo-drug and double-blind procedures, are necessary to determine the causal role of pharmacological agents on personality changes. Rather than assessing haphazard or nonspecified manifestations of personality changes occurring with pharmacotherapy, the expected changes need to be specified so that other investigators can replicate the reported findings if necessary. Instead of changes being reported vaguely as "improved" or "unimproved" in order to be able to ascribe personality changes to drug effects, it is important to describe changes occurring with drug administration in terms of qualitative and quantitative changes. Furthermore, when some form of psychotherapy or other therapy is also included in the total therapeutic program, the investigator should specify the areas and dimensions of personality change which he plans or hopes these other change agents will influence and to differentiate these, if possible, from the personality changes which he hopes that the psychoactive drugs will affect. Failure to be specific on these crucial issues leads to the perpetuation of conflicting findings in psychopharmacological research, a lack of verification with respect to the actual pharmacological effect of the drug, and an inability to differentiate between psychoactive drug effects and possible effects of the interaction of drug effects with other factors which are capable of influencing psychological dimensions.

Another important step in studying drug effects is to select appropriate, reliable and valid measures of personality change. The measures of personality change should be related, if possible, to the investigator's theory of personality structure and organization. For example, an investigator following a behavioral theory of personality might not rely on verbal reports of the magnitude of an individual subjective state of anxiety, but rather rely more on observable behavioral signs of tension. Whereas a psychodynamically oriented investigator might be more likely to select a self-report measure of change or some other measure from which the quality and quantity of the patient's subjective experience can be evaluated.

Because so many factors other than psychoactive drugs are capable of influencing the personality variables being measured in psychopharmacological studies, including the passage of time and the natural history of the personality disorder, the use of adequate controls is imperative. Subtle aspects of the doctor–patient relationship (Rickels *et al.*, 1966, 1968; Sapolsky, 1965; Gottschalk and Gleser, 1969), the context in which treatment is given or the treatment setting itself (Sabshin and Ramot, 1956; Rashkis and Smarr, 1957; Sabshin and Eisen, 1957; Rickels *et al.*, 1965; Uhlenhuth *et al.*, 1966), the patient's mental set toward the drug, induced consciously or unconsciously by the pharmacotherapist (Sabshin and Ramot, 1956; Fisher *et al.*, 1964; Uhlenhuth and Park, 1964; Uhlenhuth *et al.*, 1966; Gottschalk *et al.*, 1968), the patient's personality (Gottschalk *et al.*, 1956; Rickels *et al.*, 1964; McLaughlin *et al.*, 1965; Rickels and Downing, 1966), the pharmacotherapist's attitudes (Rickels, 1968; Gottschalk, 1968b), the effect of other treatment programs occurring in conjunction with the drug therapy (Rashkis and Smarr, 1957; Chassan and Bellak, 1966), all of these influences, and many more (Rickels, 1968) confound the issue as to which agent, if any, is primarily responsible for the personality changes that are observed. An investigator preparing to embark on a psychopharmacological study for the first time is advised to read the GAP Report, entitled "Some Observations on Controls in Psychiatric Research" (1959), "Psychiatric Research and the Assessment of Change" (1966), and "Pharmacotherapy and Psychotherapy: Paradoxes, Problems, and Progress" (1974), as well as other chapters in this volume in order to get some background on the research issues and methods involved in the field of neuropsychopharmacology.

## THE SCOPE AND VARIETY OF PSYCHOACTIVE DRUG EFFECTS

### Qualitative and Quantitative Effects

Psychoactive drugs have been designed by their manufacturers and used by clinicians to effect a variety of qualitative and quantitative psychological changes. These include: (1) reduction of anxiety or fear, (2) reduction of anger and hostility to others, (3) reduction of anger and hostility toward the self, (4) reduction of depression, (5) reduction of the severity of the schizophrenic syndrome, (6) increase in achievement strivings and other aspects of constructive performance, (7) increase in feelings of well-being, pleasure, euphoria, (8) increase in the psychedelic state, (9) production of amnesia, (10) improvement in learning speed or memory consolidation, (11) improvement in social adjustment and interpersonal relations. The qualitative variety of these psychological events ranges from affects (fear, hostility, depression, joy) to cognitive and

intellectual processes, motivational processes (achievement strivings), psychiatric syndromes (schizophrenia, mania, depression), and memory processes (amnesia, memory enhancement). In this chapter there will be a primary focus on drug effects on affecting states.

### Time or Duration Effects

Psychoactive drugs may be administered for short-term effects or long-term effects. That is, these drugs may be given to influence *psychological states* which are transient and short-lived subjective experiences or to influence *psychological traits* which are long-lasting experiences. For example, they may quiet immediate anxiety or chronic anxiety. In the former instance, only one or two doses of an antianxiety agent may be prescribed, and in the latter instance repeated doses of a drug may be required. Or the affective response that needs change may not be steadily excessive affect, but very labile affect, that is affect that is too easily and rapidly aroused at relatively slight provocation. The different time characteristics of the psychological states that are to be modified by drugs may require different kinds of drugs to achieve the desired effect or the same drugs at different doses, using the same or different routes of administration. Also, different measurement methods and tools may be necessary to determine whether these goals are actually accomplished.

### Direct or Indirect Effects

Since we are not certain how most psychoactive drugs achieve their pharmacological effects, alhtough some progress has been made in explaining the action of some drugs in terms of their effects on neurotransmitter substances and their influence on impulse transmission at neural synapses, we cannot be sure whether the clinical effects noted with drugs are direct or indirect. For example, propranolol, a beta-adrenergic blocking agent, has definite antianxiety effects (Stone *et al.*, 1973). There is some evidence that though this drug may accomplish its antianxiety effect to some extent through central nervous system pharmacological action, there is also evidence that by its action on the peripheral nervous system through its beta-adrenergic blocking effect on autonomic nervous system synapses, it blocks the anxiety-reinforcing afferent biofeedback of the autonomic correlates of anxiety (Gottschalk *et al.*, 1974c) and, if so, the latter mechanism of action could be regarded as an indirect effect. Likewise, the effectiveness of the phenothiazenes on the dimension of thought disorder in schizophrenia may not be due to any specific action on this psychological dimension, say, but the direct effect of reducing the amount of a postulated psychotomimetic catecholamine metabolite (Weil-Malherbe and Szara, 1971; Mandell *et al.*, 1971) but it may simply exercise a sedative-

hypnotic action, reducing the hallucinatory or other perceptual distortions of the schizophrenic patient and, hence, indirectly permitting the patient's thinking processes to become more coherent and logical and less fragmented (Gottschalk *et al.*, 1974b). Moreover, meperidene, which is an excellent analgesic (direct effect?), is also a good anxiety-reducing (indirect effect?) drug (Elliott *et al.*, 1974). These issues remain debatable, for we do not have all the empirical evidence we need to decide them. These matters need continued searching inquiry and, whenever possible, clarification so that we can advance the science of neuropsychopharmacology.

## BIOLOGICAL FACTORS INFLUENCING DRUG EFFECTS

Besides the specific type of pharmacological agent in terms of the classification of sedative-hypnotics, mild tranquillizers, major tranquilizers, psychomotor stimulants, and anti-depressants, other factors influence drug effects. These include drug blood concentration, pharmacokinetics, route of administration, drug interactions, and so forth.

### Drug Blood Concentration

There is increasing evidence that similar doses of psychoactive agents, whether administered orally or parenterally, eventuate in a wide range of drug blood concentrations (Green *et al.*, 1965; Hammer and Sjoqvist, 1966; Usdin, 1970; Gottschalk *et al.*, 1972, 1973b, 1974b; Elliott *et al.*, 1974).

There is also evidence that with single drug doses, the drug plasma level is correlated with the clinical response (Cash and Quinn, 1970; Gottschalk *et al.*, 1972, 1973b, 1974b; Elliott *et al.*, 1974). There is less evidence in continuous drug dose studies that drug plasma levels are associated with different degrees of clinical responses, for research of this kind is just getting underway. But some studies of this sort have indicated drug plasma levels influence the magnitude of clinical response (Cash and Quinn, 1970; Braithwaite *et al.*, 1972; Burrows *et al.*, 1972; Serrano *et al.*, 1973).

The fact that with standardized doses of drugs these wide ranges of drug plasma levels do occur and that the drug plasma level is related to the clinical response clearly indicates that differences in drug plasma concentration may account for variations in clinical response.

### Route of Drug Administration

Usually parenteral administration of drugs produces more rapid and higher drug peaks and a shorter half-life than oral administration under fasting condi-

tions. Hence, clinical responses are likely to be variously associated with the route of administration.

There are exceptions to the above, and with certain drugs, e.g., chlordiazepoxide (Gottschalk *et al.*, 1974a), oral administration of the drug at the same dose level as intramuscular administration is associated with a higher drug plasma concentration. See also diphenylhydantoin (Serrano *et al.*, 1973; Wilensky and Lawden, 1973). So, these facts need to be recognized when comparing drug effects under different routes of drug administration.

### Drug Interaction

Drug interaction is the modification of an effect of one drug by the presence of another, whether by direct or indirect means. Such interactions may affect absorption, distribution, receptor action, metabolism, or excretion. Drug interactions may be beneficial or harmful, and they may vary from one individual to another or across species and they may or may nto be of clinical significance (Goldstein *et al.*, 1974, pp. 819-827).

So the administration of more than one psychoactive drug simultaneously can influence drug effect. Moreover, various foodstuffs, insecticides, tobacco, and coffee can influence the activation or inhibition of hepatic microsomal enzymes (Conney and Burns, 1971) which metabolize psychoactive drugs. Besides human genetic differences, the immediately previous history of drug use and exposure to various food and nonfood chemical substances alter the availability of these hepatic enzymes which break down the organic molecules of drugs. These factors account, in part, for the wide interindividual variation in pharmacokinetics and drug plasma concentrations, which in turn are capable of influencing drug effects.

## MEASUREMENT TOOLS AND PROCEDURES ASSESSING AFFECTIVE STATES IN MAN

In this section the measurement tools and procedures available for assessing affective states are examined. But first, some definitions are in order with respect to affective states.

### Affective States

Affects are usually considered to be distinct from emotions, "affects" referring to the subjective and psychological states that can motivate behavior. "Emotions" are usually defined as including the physiological concomitants of these psychological states. On the other hand, many authors make no precise distinction between affects and emotions, and there will be no distinction made between these two terms here.

Affects are usually short-lived lasting from minutes to hours, sometimes a few days. With certain psychoactive disorders, such as psychoneuroses, psychoses, or organic cerebral disorders, e.g. delirium, affects may become long-lasting.

### Psychological States versus Traits

The distinction between short-term affects and longer term affects are often classified as *psychological states,* which are brief transient reactions, and *psychological traits,* which are the typical, habitual characteristics of an individual.

### Mood

Mood refers to affective characteristics which are relatively longer lasting (days to weeks or months) than affects. The term in psychiatry has primarily been used with respect to the dimension of depression on the one extreme and mania on the other. Manic-depressive reactions or mania or depression separately are referred to as affective disorders. In this chapter, affective states are used in a wider sense than in this more narrow denotation.

### Anxiety versus Fear

Anxiety psychodynamically refers to irrational apprehension; whereas, fear refers to apprehension concerning a real, external danger or threat. Similar distinctions could be made about all affects or moods, that is, are they irrational responses, responses to perceptual or cognitive distortions or the confusion of past memories and events with the present or are the affects experienced tied to reality for time, place, and person? Here, no such distinction will be made between anxiety and fear or between other irrational and rational affects, not because this distinction should never be made, but because most of the objective measuring instruments used to assess these affects cannot make these distinctions (except for careful and persisting and inquiry through the clinical interview) and, also, because psychoactive drugs appear to modify affective states, at least for brief intervals, whether or not they rest on rational bases.

## MEASUREMENT TOOLS AND PROCEDURES IN ASSESSING PSYCHOACTIVE DRUG EFFECTS

There are three major objective methods of measuring drug effects: self-report scales, behavioral rating scales, and the objective content analysis of speech or handwriting.

## Self-Report Scales

Self-report scales are designed to give the patient an opportunity to describe his subjective distress, and since it is the patient's subjective distress that ordinarily accounts for seeking treatment, such self-report scales would appear to be a plausible criterion of drug effects. Affective states may be assessed in terms of an individual's self-report directly about *affects* or in terms of associated *somatic dysfunctions, cognitive and intellectual dysfunctions*, or actual overall *performance dysfunctions*. Unfortunately, the subject may respond to self-report measures in terms of his traits as much as in terms of his state. Or it may be that the patient's self-descriptions are more in terms of the kind of person that the patient believes himself to be rather than descriptions of the subjective state in which he currently finds himself. Self-report inventories of somatic discomfort, although useful, are not sufficient as measures of affects because many patients who have significant subjective affects do not suffer appreciable somatic distress. And there are patients of hypochondriacal or hysterical disposition who tend to exaggerate or perhaps use real or imagined somatic distress without experiencing appreciable affects. Similarly, impaired performance is not found in some affectively disturbed patients who, with great psychic discomfort, mobilize their energy and continue to perform well. The possibility that self-report inventories designed to assess transient affective states will be confounded with characterological traits is commonly recognized and should be a concern for all clinical investigators.

Two of the most generally used self-report inventories in psychopharmacological research are the Psychiatric Outpatient Mood Scales (POMS) and the Symptom Check List (SCL). Review of four different studies using the POMS (McNair *et al.*, 1964, 1965, 1970; Pillard and Fisher, 1967) indicates that the POMS is capable of assessing situational anxiety, but not necessarily the same anxiety which is reduced by antianxiety medication. Also, had not a distinction been made between high acquiescent and low acquiescent patients, the POMS would not have shown an anxiety-reducing effect for chlordiazepoxide in the 1970 study (McNair *et al.*, 1970). In four studies using the Symptom Check List (Lipman *et al.*, 1968; Lipman *et al.*, 1969; Uhlenhuth *et al.*, 1968; Rickels *et al.*, 1971), the use of the SCL was accompanied by inconsistencies and failures which were as notable as the successes. Apparently this self-report inventory has not as yet advanced to the status of a primary criterion that can be depended on to show drug effects.

These various reports based on the POMS and SCL provide evidence that chemcial compounds which are in common use and known to be effective as antianxiety or antidepressant agents may or may not be distinguished from a pharmacologically inert placebo on the basis of scores based on the outpatient

use of self-report inventories. Specifically, the discrimination of a psychoactive drug, based on these self-report measures, was found to be a function of the severity of the illness or of the attitudes of the physician or of the personality of the patient or of the nature of the clinic. Wittenborn states (Wittenbron, 1974, p. 11) that "limited and inconsistent findings in these various reports may be an indication of the limitations in the adequacies of these self-report inventories as criteria. Since dependable validity has not been established for these inventories, the results may be a better guide to the appropriate conditions for using the inventory than to the appropriate conditions for using the drug."

Self-report measures are useful, but they should not be regarded as sufficient criteria for drug effects. Self-report inventories however are not necessarily a less desirable alternative to rating scales. Rating scales do not distinguish between patients in the same way as self-report inventories and in spite of their fallibility, self-report inventories offer an approach to the assessment of subjective manifestations which may not be correctly perceived and reported by raters. Disadvantages present in self-report measures may be summarized as follows. Since the patient is describing his own behavior, characteristic psychological defense mechanisms may obscure an accurate evaluation of his subjective state, and actual psychopathological processes may color or distort his perspective. Also, as Downing *et al.* (1971) have indicated, the patients self-assessments may be influenced by a number of other biases, such as a desire to please the physician, and to a lesser degree by such factors as "social desirability" (Edwards, 1959). Finally, it may be difficult for the patient to precisely evaluate the severity of his condition, for he may not have the professional experience of a clinician in making these judgments (Prusoff *et al.*, 1972).

### Psychiatric Rating Scales

With psychiatric rating scales, assessments are made by a trained observer, usually a psychiatrist or clinical psychologist. Hence, the rater customarily has had some experience in measuring psychopathological phenomena and usually he has had some experience and practice in administering these rating scales. The clinician is free to assess the status of the patient from a range of behavioral and affective cues, verbal and nonverbal. His judgments are likely to be less constricted by the distortions inherent in this self-report approach, and he is capable of accurately establishing the pattern as well as the level of severity of the patient's symptom profile (Derogatis *et al.*, 1972).

The ratings of clinicians are not necessarily better or more valid than the self-reports of patients. The clinical interviewer gains objectivity and detachment, but he sacrifices familiarity with the patient; his sphere of reference is

limited to the immediate interview situation. Also clinicians are not free from systematic distortions. Definite biases or "orientations" regarding clinical interpretation may be introduced in the formal training and cultural background of the clinician (Cooper *et al.*, 1969; Gurland *et al.*, 1969, 1970; Fisher *et al.*, 1971). Also, subtle personality characteristics, usually long preceding the professional training of the rater and labeled countertransference by some clinicians (Orr, 1960), may distort the perceptions and emotional reactions of the rater vis-a-vis the patient. Also, other studies indicate (Gottschalk, 1971) that different interviewers may evoke varying emotional responses from the same patients. Finally, agreement between independent clinical observers is often only moderate.

A number of studies (Park *et al.*, 1965; Paykel *et al.*, 1970; Prusoff *et al.*, 1972) have shown that agreements between clinical observations and patient's self-reports vary widely. Derogatis *et al.* (1971) found great similarities in the assessment of symptom dimensions between psychiatrist and outpatients, but also noticed distinctions between the two, particularly in lower class patients. Technically trained clinicians are, for the most part, more discriminating than patients. The consensus seems to be that these two forms of assessment each contribute unique information to the overall clinical evaluation of patients as well as providing a certain amount of common data concerning the patient's clinical status. Provided that a consistent and compatible set of scales can be made available, the ideal method would be to employ both of these different kinds of scales on different occasions and under certain conditions. One or the other technique will be subject to distortion, but rarely will both be equally vulnerable to the same sources of error. Since accurate identification of the basis in nature of disagreement between self-report and clinical boservation has not progressed very far at the present time, the optimal strategy would seem to involve using both methods to maximize the validity of clinical appraisals or, even better, to include the use of a third method of measuring psychological states, namely, the systematic content analysis of language behavior (Gottschalk, 1974c,d).

## Content Analysis Scales

In psychopharmacological studies, besides self-report measures and rating scales, there is yet another method of measuring changes in psychological states that may be influenced by psychoactive pharmacological agents and this is the method of content analysis of verbal behavior. As previously indicated, self-report procedures have certain shortcomings, including providing the possibility of malingering or faking and the opportunity for various responses sets such as social desirability, acquiescence, and deviance (Anastasi, 1968:

Wittenborn, 1974). Rating scales also pose measurement problems involving reliability, halo effects (such as the tendency of raters to be unduly influenced by a single favorable or unfavorable trait), error of central tendency (that is, the tnedency to rate persons in the middle of a scale and to avoid extreme positions), and leniency error (the reluctance of many raters to assign unfavorable ratings) (Anastasi, 1968; Wittenborn, 1967, 1972). The content analysis of an individual's speech or handwritten communications offers a third alternative approach to the evaluation of psychoactive drug effects that, under proper circumstances, can avoid some of the measurement problems of self-report and rating scales.

Waskow (1967) has thoroughly reviewed the literature on the effects of drugs on content of speech, and she has described a variety of approaches. Marsden (1965) has reviewed content analysis has elaborated on the application of content analysis to psychotherapy research (Gottschalk, 1974d) and to the measurement of emotions (Gottschalk, 1974c).

There is one content analysis procedure which has been widely applied to research problems in psychophysiology, psychotherapy, and neuropsychopharmacology, the method of Gottschalk (Gottschalk and Hambidge, 1955; Gottschalk *et al.*, 1956; Gottschalk and Gleser, 1969; Gottschalk *et al.*, 1969c; Gottschalk, 1971, 1972, 1974a,b,c,d). The specific focus here will be on the Gottschalk content analysis procedure as it applies to neuropsychopharmacological research.

## THE CONTENT-ANALYSIS METHOD OF GOTTSCHALK AND CO-WORKERS

### Summary Description of the Procedure, Reliability, and Construct-Validation Studies

This measurement method utilizes a function that is uniquely human, namely, speech and its content or semantic aspects. The development of this method has involved a long series of steps. It has required that the psychological dimensions to be measured (for example, anxiety, hostility outward, hostility inward, cognitive or intellectual impairment, achievement strivings, social alienation-personal disorganization be carefully defined; that the content, the lexical cues, be spelled out from which a receiver of any verbal message infers the occurrence of the psychological states; that the linguistic, principally syntactical, cues conveying intensity be specified; that differential weights be assigned for semantic and linguistic cues whenever appropriate; and that a systematic means be arrived at of correcting for the number of words spoken per unit time so that one individual can be compared to others or to himself on

different occasions with respect to the magnitude of a particular psychological state. The method also requires that a formal scale of weighted content categories be specified for each psychological dimension to be measured; that research technicians be trained to score these typescripts of human speech (much as biochemical technicians are trained to run various chemical determinations by following prescribed procedures); and that the interscorer reliability of two trained content technicians using the same scale by 0.85 or above (a modest but respectable level of consensus in the behavioral sciences for these kinds of measurements). Moreover, a set of construct-validation studies have had to be carried out to ascertain exactly what this content analysis procedure was measuring, and these validation studies have included the use of four kinds of criterion measures: psychological (self-report and behavioral rating scales), physiological, pharmacological, and biochemical. On the basis of these construct-validation studies, changes have been made in the content categories and the associated weights of each specific scale in the direction of maximizing the correlations between the content analysis scores with these various criterion measures.

Construct validation of any behavioral or psychological test instrument requires repeated reexamination and retesting, in new situations, of the variables being evaluated. After initial validation studies were completed for verbal behavior measures of such psychological states as anxiety, hostility outward and hostility inward, social alienation-personal disorganization (an objective dimension constituting the main features of schizophrenia), cognitive and intellectual impairment, achievement strivings, a large variety of additional investigations was carried out using these verbal behavior measures. These further investigations have provided considerable data on the ways in which such verbal behavior scores relate to other relevant measurable phenomena. These data have afforded solid evidence as to how the psychological states measured by this verbal behavior measure "fit" with other empirical data.

The details of the reliability and validity studies and the specific investigations pinning down each point have been published over the past 20 years. They have recently been collected in two books, and these describe many newer unpublished investigations on the subjects (Gottschalk and Gleser, 1969; Gottschalk *et al.*, 1969c).

## Summary of Theoretical Framework and Scoring Procedures

A brief comment on the theoretical framework from which this measurement approach has developed: The theoretical approach has been truly eclectic and includes behavioral and conditioning theory, psychoanalytic clinical hypotheses, and linguistic theory.

The formulation of these psychological states has been deeply influenced by the position that they all have biological roots. Both the definition of each separate psychological state and the selection of the specific verbal content items used as cues for inferring each state were influenced by the decision that whatever psychological state was measured by this content analysis approach should, whenever possible, be associated with some biological characteristic of the individual in addition to some psychological aspect or some social situation.

The scoring or content-analysis technician applying this procedure to typescripts of tape-recorded speech need not worry, however, about approaching the work of content analysis with one theoretical orientation or another; rather, he carefully follows a strictly empirical approach, scoring the occurrence of any content or themes in each grammatical clause of the speech according to a "cookbook," namely, various well-delineated language categories constituting each of our verbal behavior scales. A manual (Gottschalk *et al.*, 1969c) is available which indicates what verbal categories should be looked for, and how much the occurrence of each one is to be weighted. The technician, then, follows prescribed mathematical calculations leading up to a final score for the magnitude of any one psychological state or another.

## Standard Instructions for Eliciting Verbal Behavior

The instructions to elicit speech from a research subject have been purposely relatively ambiguous and nonstructured, except that a report of personal or dramatic life experiences has been requested. Such instructions have been used because of an initial aim to probe the immediate emotional reactions of patients or subjects instead of the typical or habitual ones and to minimize reactions of guarding or covering up. Standardized instructions were used, also, in order to compare individuals in a standard context so that demographic and personality variables could be explored and investigated, while holding relatively constant the influence of such variables as the instructions for eliciting the speech, the interviewer, the context, and the situation. The effects of varying these noninterviewee variables have subsequently been investigated, one by one, after reliable and valid content analysis scales were developed.

The principal standard instructions used in the Gottschalk content analysis procedure to elicit 5-minute verbal samples are as follows: "This is a study of speaking and conversation habits. Upon a signal from me I would like you to speak for five minutes about any interesting or dramatic personal life experiences you have had. Once you have started I will be here listening to you, but I would prefer not to reply to any questions you would feel like asking me until the five minute period is over. Do you have any questions you would like to ask me now before we start? Well, then you may begin."

These instructions are designed to simulate roughly a projective test situation. The lack of verbal responsiveness of the examiner during the period the subject is speaking, plus a conscious attempt on the part of the examiner to keep at a minimum any nonverbal cues that might indicate his reactions to the subject, tend to give the interviewer the quality of "blank screen" on which the subject projects some part of the gamut of his reactions to any vaguely similar life situation within his past experience. What the subject talks about during any one verbal sample depends in large part on what psychological conflicts or states are being experienced at the time and what orienting and appraising states or conflicts are most highly aroused by the stimulus-situation eliciting the speech. These psychological states determine how the subject perceives the experimental situation and what events are retrieved from his remote or recent memory storage system. The standardized nature of the situation in which the verbal samples are elicited minimizes the interviewer as a variable influencing the interviewee's psychological state and leaves the interviewee's reactions (appropriate and inapporpriate) as a predominant variable in the interpersonal interaction, very similar to the projective test situation.

## Other Types of Language Behavior to Which This Content Analysis Procedure May Be Applied

The content analysis procedures can be and have been applied to interview material, psychotherapeutic, diagnostic, or otherwise. These content analysis scales can be applied to different kinds of language material obtained in a variety of situations and in both spoken and written form. The typed data can be broken down into equal temporal units (for example, 2- or 5-minute segments). Or the units can be based on the number of words spoken by one or both participants (or more if they are present); for example, consecutive 500-word sequences of the speaker's can be coded for content. Depending on the purpose and research design of the study period, these content analysis scales have also been applied to dreams, projective test data (specifically, tape-recordings of Thematic Apperception Test responses), to written verbal samples, and even to literature, letters, public speeches, and any other type of language material.

Actually, most of the reliability and validity studies on this method have been done on small samples of speech, 2 to 5 minutes in duration, obtained in response to the standard instructions given above. For this reason, normative, percentile, and other scores of affects and psychological states derived by this content analysis method cannot be uncritically generalized to verbal behavior obtained by other means than by the standardized procedure.

## Example of One Content Analysis Scale and Its Application

An example of the simplest Gottschalk content analysis scale, the Anxiety Scale, is shown below, followed by an example of a coded and scored speech sample. Six subtypes of anxiety are included in the total anxiety score: death anxiety, mutilation anxiety, separation anxiety, guilt anxiety, shame anxiety, and diffuse anxiety.

### SCHEDULE I
### Anxiety Scale

1. Death anxiety—references to death, dying, threat of death, or anxiety about death experienced by or occurring to:
   a. self (3)
   b. animate others (2)
   c. inanimate objects (1)
   d. denial of death anxiety (1)
2. Mutilation (castration) anxiety—references to injury, tissue or physical damage, or anxiety about injury or threat of such experienced by or occurring to:
   a. self (3)
   b. animate others (2)
   c. inanimate objects destroyed (1)
   d. denial (1)
3. Separation anxiety—references to desertion, abandonment, ostracism, loss of support, falling, loss of love or love object, or threat of such experienced by or occurring to:
   a. self (3)
   b. animate others (2)
   c. inanimate objects (1)
   d. denial (1)
4. Guilt anxiety—references to adverse criticism, abuse, condemnation, moral disapproval, guilt, or threat of such experienced by:
   a. self (3)
   b. animate others (2)
   d. denial (1)
5. Shame anxiety—references to ridicule, inadequacy, shame, embarrassment, humiliation, over-exposure of deficiencies or private details, or threat of such experienced by:
   a. self (3)
   b. animate others (2)
   d. denial (1)
6. Diffuse or nonspecific anxiety—references by work of phrase to anxiety and/or fear without distinguishing type or source of anxiety.
   a. self (3)
   b. animate others (2)
   d. denial (1)

The verbal sample illustrates the system of scoring those clauses which have scorable anxiety items, with appropriate symbols designating each category in the anxiety scale. The numbers in parentheses in the verbal sample indicate the weights assigned to each scorable content item. The diagonal marks indicate grammatical clauses. A detailed description and discussion of scoring procedures, with many examples, is provided in "A Manual for Using the Gottschalk-Gleser Content Analysis Scales" (Gottschalk *et al.*, 1969c).

**EXAMPLE I**
**Verbal Sample No. 1 Coded for Anxiety**

| | |
|---|---|
| **Name of Subject:** | |
| **(Male psychiatric inpatient)** | **Interviewer:** |
| **Date:** | **Total Words: 187** |
| **Name of Study:** | **Correction Factor: 0.5348** |

5a3
What do you want me to say? / I don't know what to talk about. / Well
5a3
let's see . . . / I don't know what to talk about, Doc. / Uh I've been
here for about four months / and uh had a pretty rough time of it. /
And and uh my wife, she wants me to stay here / as long as I can. /
6a3
I I told her / I would. / Our babies, they get on my nerves, my little
babies. / Sometimes I don't get no sleep. / (pause) Got a little
2b2 2b2
cat at home. / It got hurt, / it got a broken leg / and I had to get
1b2
that fixed. / (Pause) I had a pretty rough time of it. / My dad, I lost
3a3
my dad in '51, / now only got two brothers living. / And they never
3a3 4a3
come to see me. / I guess / it's pretty much my fault. / And uh my
wife she she changes her mind all the time. / I think / she's kind
6b2 4b2
of nervous too. / She thinks / she hears people saying bad things
6a4
about her. / I get sort of frightened and scared about it all. / I
don't know / what else I can tell you. / That's all / I can think of. /

## Illustrations of Applications of the Gottschalk Content Analysis Scale of Verbal Behavior

To understand and appreciate the applicability of any measurement procedure in assessing psychoactive drug effects, it is helpful to be familiar with the ways in which demographic factors, diseases, physiological, biochemical, and other variables are related to the psychological dimensions measured by the method. Some demographic, psychophysiological, and psychobiochemical relationships will first be summarized followed by a review of some neuropsychopharmacological findings relevant to the assessment of affective states.

### Some Deographic Factors Influencing Emotions (Gottschalk and Gleser, 1969)

#### Anxiety and Intelligence

An analysis of variance of the verbal anxiety scores for 90 individuals employed at the same company (Kroger) reveals a significant negative trend in anxiety with IQ level ($p<0.05$), the lowest IQ group having the highest anxiety scores ($r$ = 0.28). Since the task involves extemporaneous speaking into a microphone, an activity for which individuals with the lower IQ sometimes feel inadequate, higher shame anxiety is elicited with the lower IQ, and it is this anxiety subscale that accounts for the negative correlation with IQ (see Fig. 1).

#### Anxiety and Sex Differences

No sex differences have been found in large samples of individuals for total anxiety scores, but in six separate subscale scores for anxiety, we have found in normative samples (173 males and 109 females), higher scores for females on separation and shame anxiety as compared to males; males have significantly higher scores on death and mutilation anxiety (see Fig. 2).

#### Anxiety and Age

The relationship between age and anxiety has been examined in several samples of adults and no evidence of a linear relationship has been found. One subscale of anxiety, however, evidently increases consistently with age. In three separate samples of people correlations of 0.25, 0.24, and 0.28 were found between age and death anxiety. Such a relationship makes sense, since death appears increasingly important and threatening as one grows older.

#### Hostility Scores and Race

In several series of studies, lower hostility outward scores were found in Negroes as compared to Caucasians. The difference between the hostility outward scores in black as compared to white people is more marked among

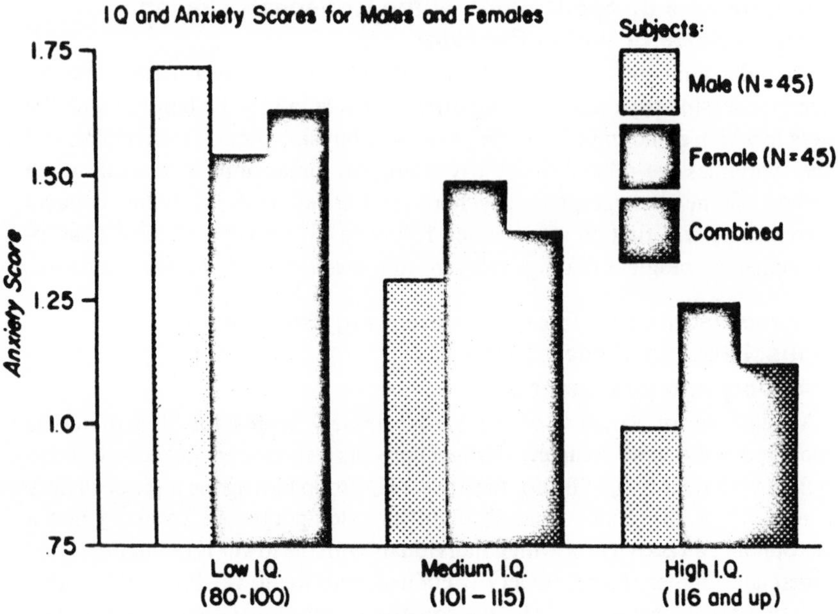


Fig. 1

females. This finding has been thought to be due either to the suppression of hostility in Negroes, or to the fact that most of these verbal samples were collected by white interviewers.

### Hostility Outward Scores and Sex

There has been found a significant trend for higher hostility outward scores to be present in the 5-minute verbal samples of males as compared to females. This sex difference is probably related to endocrine differences, higher hostility outward probably being secondary to male sex hormones (Gottschalk, 1968c).

### Some Psychophysiological Relationships

### Anxiety and Skin Temperature

The higher the anxiety scores derived from our content analysis method, the greater the fall in skin temperature during the giving of the speech sample. The evidence follows.

A group of 12 high school boys 16–17 years of age gave three 5-minute verbal samples on each of two separate occasions while continuous measurements of skin temperature were being taken and the boys were in a hypnotic

state (Gottlieb *et al.*, 1967). The anxiety scores from the six verbal samples obtained under hypnosis were negatively correlated with the change in skin temperature occurring during the giving of the 5-minute verbal sample for each student separately, using a rank-order correlation. Ten of the 12 correlations were negative ($p<0.04$), yielding an averaging intrasubject correlation of −0.31.

A corroborative study, examining the correlations between five sequences of two 50-minute psychotherapeutic interviews and continuous measures of skin temperature (Gottschalk *et al.*, 1961), revealed a significant negative correlation between the anxiety scored in each5-minute interval and the change in skin temperature from the beginning to the end of each 5-minute interval (Gottschalk and Gleser, 1969).

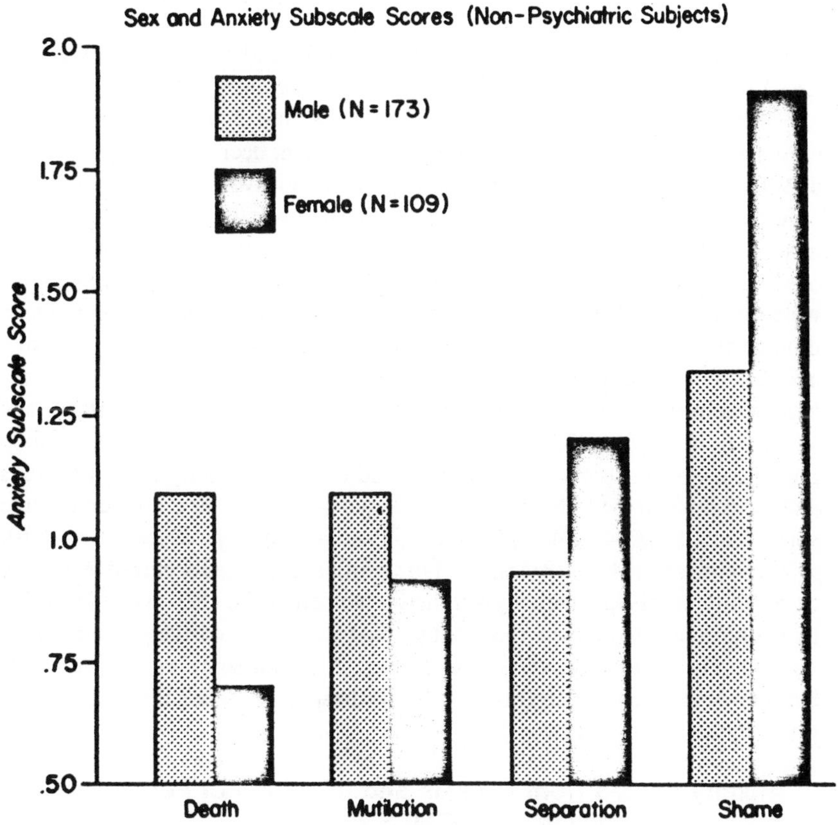


Fig. 2

### Coronary Artery Disease and Anxiety and Hostility Scores

Miller (1965), using hostility content analysis scales, studied 34 patients with the diagnosis of myocardial infarction and a control group of 34 medical patients free of coronary artery disease. The patients were matched for race, sex, education, and intelligence. The patients with coronary artery disease were found to score higher on measures of hostility inward ($p<0.01$) and ambivalent hostility ($p<0.06$) than the noncoronary medical patients, but not on either overt or covert hostility outward. The coronary group also scored higher on anxiety ($p<0.01$) than the noncoronary group of medical patients.

### Essential Hypertension and Anxiety and Hostility Scores

A small group of hypertensive patients obtained significantly higher hostility outward scores ($p<0.05$) as compared to the hostility outward scores from normotensive patients (Kaplan *et al.*, 1961).

Two psychophysiological studies (Kaplan *et al.*, 1961; Gottschalk *et al.*, 1964) have shown that blood pressure tends to increase significantly among hypertensives following talking for 5 minutes into a tape-recorder in the presence of another person in contrast to significant decreases of systolic and diastolic blood pressure occurring among nonmotensives after such an event.

In another study (Gottschalk *et al.*, 1964), levels of verbal anxiety and hostility, blood pressure, and pulse rate of 12 hypertensive women were observed over two different 3-week periods. During these periods, the patients were receiving 25–50 mg per day of hydrochlorothiazide (an antihypertensive diuretic with no known psychoactive action on the central nervous system) or a placebo. While the women were taking the placebo, significant positive correlations were obtained between their hostility inward scores and their average systolic ($r = 0.47, p<0.05$) and average diastolic ($r = 0.55, p<0.01$) blood pressures. Positive correlations were found between hostility outward scores and the change in their blood pressure taken before and after giving a 5-minute verbal sample ($r = 0.46$, $p<0.05$—systolic blood pressure; $r = 0.50$, $p<0.05$—diastolic blood pressure). No significant changes occurred in anxiety or hostility levels of these hypertensive women while they were receiving hydrochlorothiazide, even though the blood pressure of these women fell significantly while they were on this drug. Also, all significant correlations between blood pressure and hostility levels disappeared when the women were given hydrochlorothiazide.

### Anxiety Scores from Dreams and Inhibition of Penile Erection with Rapid Eye Movement (REM) Sleep

Karacan *et al.* (1966) studied the relationships of penile erections during episodes of rapid eye movement (REM) sleep and the anxiety scores derived

from the tape-recorded dreams reported upon awakening from such periods of sleep. A statistically significant association was found between anxiety scores from such dreams and the lack of penile erections.

Bell, Stroebel, and Prior (1971) have further demonstrated that anxiety scores derived from dream content analysis correlate with scrotal muscle reflexes during the dream.

### The Relationship of the Magnitude of Emotions, as Determined from Content Analysis of a Tape-Recorded Interview, and Paroxysmal Electroencephalographic Activity

A 20-year-old single white male, Army private, an inpatient at Walter Reed Army Hospital in Washington, D.C., for the study of the etiology of grand mal seizures he developed during military duty in the absence of a history of head injury, was found to have frequent high amplitude bursts of slow wave paroxysmal activity on his electroencephalogram (Gottschalk, 1955). Several hourly sessions of EEG recordings were carried out while he was interviewed. The tape-recordings of the interviews were synchronized with his EEG recordings so that the content of what he was saying could be related to the paroxysmal EEG activity. Sixteen 30-word segments of his speech occurring just before a paroxysmal EEG event were selected from these interviews as well as sixteen 30-word segments which were not immediately followed by abnormal EEG activity. Content-analysis technicians were asked to score these 30-word segments for total negative affects, including negative as well as positive emotions (scores derived from the Human Relations Scales, a measure of the capacity for congenial human relationships) (Gottschalk, 1968a).

Paroxysmal EEG activity was found to be preceded significantly more often by a higher total affect score ($p<0.05$) than normal EEG activity (see Fig. 3). Total anxiety ($p<0.05$) and hostility inward ($p<0.05$) scores were found to account principally for this finding; whereas hostility outward, ambivalent hostility, and positive affect scores were not significantly related to the abnormal paroxysmal EEG activity (Gottschalk *et al.*, 1972).

### Some Psychobiochemical Relationships

### Studies of Relationships of Emotions to Plasma Lipids

A natural history study (Gottschalk, 1968c; Gottschalk *et al.*, 1965a) disclosed different relationships between several types of emotions and blood lipids in a group of 24 men who had fasted 10 to 12 hours. Findings were cross-validated in a study of a second group of 20 men. Anxiety scores have a significant positive correlation with plasma free fatty acids (FFA) in both groups—a sign of catecholamine (adrenergic) secretion. Three types of hostility scores, however, had an essentially zero correlation with plasma free fatty

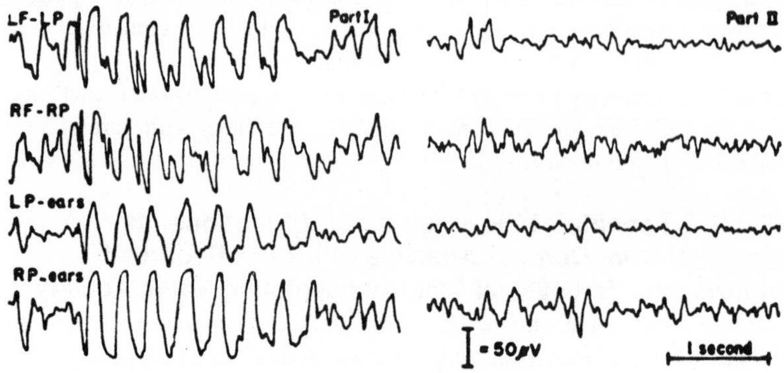


FIGURE 3
EEG: PAROXYSMAL BRAIN WAVE ACTIVITY
PART I: PT. RESTING WITH EYES CLOSED.
PART II: EYES CLOSED: PT. COUNTING SILENTLY.

acids. More anxious men tended to have higher free fatty acid levels and sharper rises in FFA than nonanxious men in a reaction to a venipuncture and free associating for 5 minutes. There was evidence for positive correlations between plasma triglyceride levels and both anxiety and hostility inward scores as well as for total hostility outward scores and levels of blood cholesterol. Stone *et al.* (1969) found that nonathlete, college students tended, as a group, to have higher plasma free fatty acid responses to the same anxiety levels than college students who were athletes (either on the football or swimming teams) (see Fig. 4 and Table I).

## Anxiety Levels and Dreams: Relation to Changes in Plasma Free Fatty Acids

Blood samples for determination of plasma free fatty acids were obtained throughout the night by means of an indwelling venous catheter. The first blood sample was drawn at the onset of rapid eye movements (REM) and the second after 15 minutes of these eye movements. Subjects were then awakened and asked to relate their dreams; a third sample was drawn 15 to 25 minutes later. Anxiety scores derived from 20 dreams of nine subjects had significant positive correlations with increases in free fatty acids occurring during REM sleep. There were no consistently positive correlations with hostility scores derived from the same dreams. These findings indicate that anxiety aroused in dreams triggers the release of catecholamines into the circulation and these catecholamines mobilzie proportional amounts of plasma free fatty acid from body fat (Gottschalk *et al.*, 1966).

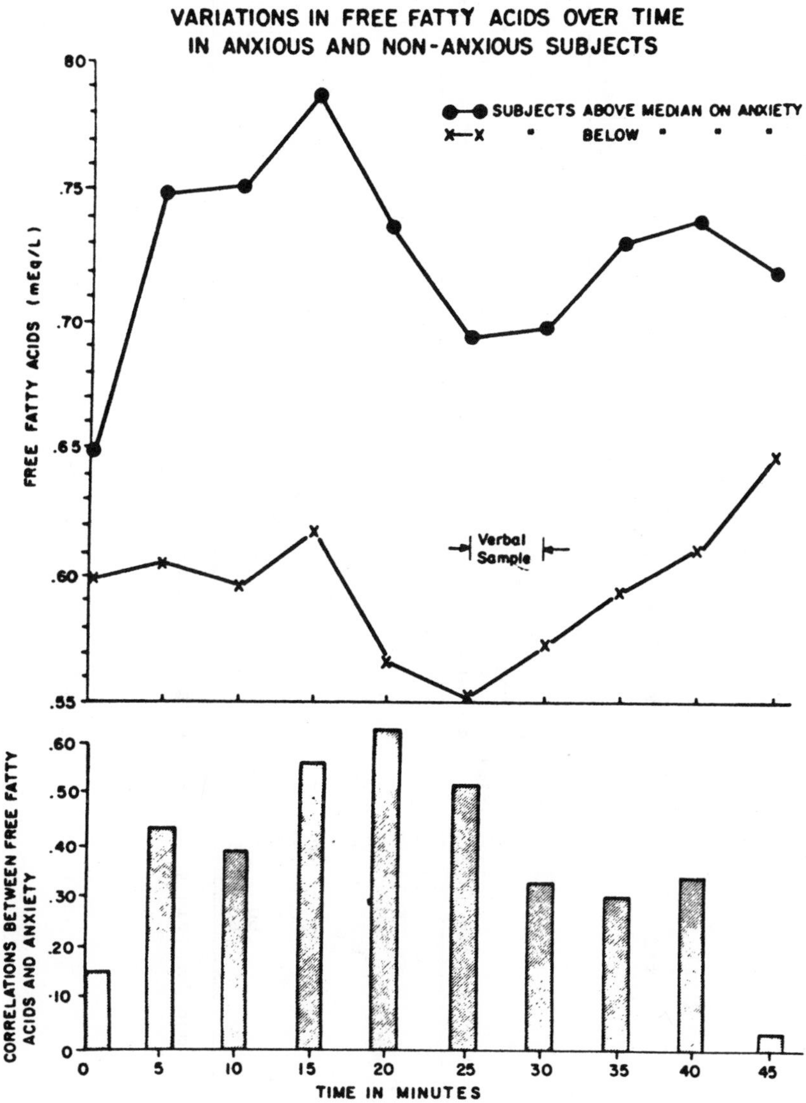

VARIATIONS IN FREE FATTY ACIDS OVER TIME
IN ANXIOUS AND NON-ANXIOUS SUBJECTS
SUBJECTS ABOVE MEDIAN ON ANXIETY
" BELOW " " "
Verbal Sample
FREE FATTY ACIDS (mEq/L)
80
.75
.70
.65
.60
.55
CORRELATIONS BETWEEN FREE FATTY ACIDS AND ANXIETY
.60
.50
.40
.30
.20
·10
0
0
5
10
15
20
25
30
35
40
45
TIME IN MINUTES


Fig. 4

Table I

Correlations among Lipids and Verbal Affect Measures

| Measure | Mean | s.d. | Serum lipids | | Immediate affect scores | | | | | |
|---|---|---|---|---|---|---|---|---|---|---|
| | | | | | | Hostility | | | | |
| | | | | | | Outward | | | | |
| | | | Triglycerides | Av. free fatty acids | Anxiety | Overt | Covert | Total | Inward | Ambivalent |
| Cholesterol, mg. %* | 185.10 | 29.36 | .30 | -.13 | -.24 | .51 | .08 | .37 | -.28 | -.03 |
| Triglycerides, mg. % | 59.35 | 35.64 | --- | .17 | .26 | -.03 | -.11 | -.18 | .47 | .07 |
| Av. free fatty acids, mEq/L | .66 | .13 | --- | --- | .44 | -.08 | -.07 | .00 | .36 | .04 |
| Anxiety | 1.29 | .53 | --- | --- | --- | .14 | .00 | .08 | .52 | .42 |
| Hostility outward | | | | | | | | | | |
| Overt | .64 | .28 | --- | --- | --- | --- | .32 | .87 | -.03 | .47 |
| Covert | .56 | .26 | --- | --- | --- | --- | --- | .72 | .02 | .02 |
| Total | .81 | .35 | --- | --- | --- | --- | --- | --- | -.08 | .33 |
| Hostility inward | .60 | .22 | --- | --- | --- | --- | --- | --- | --- | .04 |
| Ambivalent hostility | .66 | .33 | --- | --- | --- | --- | --- | --- | --- | --- |

*Age was not partialed out for this group, since the age range was extremely limited.

### Corticosteroid Levels and Hostility and Anxiety

Five-minute verbal samples, elicited by the standardized method, were analyzed for hostility and anxiety scores and correlated with corticosteroid levels of 28 nonpsychotic male medical patients (Gottschalk, 1968c; Gottschalk and Gleser, 1969). A correlation of +0.40 was obtained between hostility outward levels and the average plasma 17-hydroxycorticosteroid levels; the correlation was higher with the corticosteroid level obtained 1 hour after the 5-minute sample was obtained (+0.47) than that obtained 1 hour before this time (+0.31). No correlation was found between plasma 17-hydroxycorticosteroids and anxiety and hostility inward scores. In these studies, the psychochemical relationships have been observed at relatively low levels of arousal for these emotions, that is, in situations where there was no contrived stress and in which the data was collected in a natural history setting. Such facts may account for why anxiety did not arouse corticosteroid secretion in these studies.

### Anxiety and Hostility Levels and Phases of the Menstrual Cycle

Five-minute verbal samples given daily by small numbers of women for periods up to 3 months have indicated that different women have different cycles of anxiety and hostility, depending on their own personal reactions to the changing hormonal levels of their cycles. Across individuals, however, women as a group show a transient decrease of anxiety and hostility at the time of ovulation, presumably related to the secretion of luteinizing hormone. Also, they show an increase in anxiety premenstrually using our content analysis method (Gottschalk *et al.*, 1962; Ivey and Bardwick, 1968). Recent studies (Silbergeld *et al.*, 1971) have shown that the birth control pill, Enovid, smoothes out and blocks the significant fluctuations in anxiety and hostility previously observed during the menstrual cycle by this content analysis method.

### Some Neuropsychopharmacological Relationships

### Anxiety and Hostility in Response to Psychoactive Drugs

Many studies have been carried out using this content analysis procedure in neuropsychopharmacological investigations. In almost all of these studies the double-blind, cross-over design has been used. These studies have been of considerable interest because they afford a means of influencing the neurochemical environment of the brain and of observing the behavioral and psychological effect as measured through speech.

The minor tranquilizer, chlordiazepoxide, in 46 juvenile delinquent boys

administered 20 mg of the drug, as compared to a placebo, produced significant decreases in anxiety, ambivalent hostility, and overt hostility outward 40 to 120 minutes after ingesting the chlordiazepoxide (Gleser *et al.*, 1965).

In another study (Gottschalk *et al.*, 1960) 20 dermatological inpatients (10 men and 10 women) were given perphenazine, 16 to 24 mg a day by mouth for 1 week alternating with a placebo for 1 week, using a double-blind, cross-over design. Analysis of the content of 5-minute verbal samples obtained from these patients showed a reduction of hostility outward scores with perphenazine (16–24 mg/day) in 16 of the 20 patients ($p<0.01$) and a decrease in anxiety scores at the elevated end of the spectrum of the anxiety scores.

Another study showed an increase in anxiety and overt hostility out scores derived from verbal samples in patients receiving the antidepressant drug, imipramine (100–300 mg/day), as compared to a placebo (Gottschalk *et al.*, 1865b).

Gottschalk and his co-workers (Gottschalk and Kaplan, 1972; Gottschalk *et al.*, 1973b), in a double-blind, placebo-drug, cross-over study with 18 anxious subjects demonstrated that chlordiazepoxide (20 mg by mouth) significantly reduced anxiety scores, as assessed by 5-minute speech samples, only in those subjects whose chlordiazepoxide plasma concentrations exceeded 0.70 $\mu$g/ml. Hostility scores, though decreased when subjects were on chlordiazepoxide, were not significantly lowered. Interesting relationships between chlordiazepoxide plasma levels, biochemical changes, and changes in psychological state scores were also revealed by this study.

Gottschalk *et al.* (1972) demonstrated that lorazepam parenterally (4–5 mg), as compared to a placebo, could significantly lower anxiety scores derived from the speech of a small sample ($N = 8$) of incarcerated prisoners, and a paradigm of this type was suggested as a method of screening antianxiety, antidepressant, and other new psychoactive drugs.

Elliott *et al.* (1974), using the Gottschalk content analysis procedure, demonstrated that the amount of reduction of anxiety and hostility scores of male prisoners was highly correlated with meperidine plasma levels whether administered (100 mg) by mouth or intramuscularly; in this study meperidine at this dose significantly reduced anxiety and certain hostility levels as compared to a placebo.

Gottschalk *et al.* (1974c) gave propranolol (40 mg by mouth), a beta-adrenergic blocking agent, or a placebo to 20 nonanxious college students in a cross-over design. Resting anxiety scores, derived from the content analysis of speech samples, were significantly lowered when the subjects were on propranolol, but their capacity to respond with increased anxiety under the circums-

tances of a stress interview was not influenced by propranolol. The reduction of resting anxiety scores by propranolol was thought to be a consequence of a decrease in the afferent biofeedback to the central nervous system of autonomic physiological correlates of anxiety which are capable of sustaining anxiety levels; this mechanism did not prevent direct arousal of anxiety through the stress interview process.

Gottschalk *et al.* (1973a) found that diphenylhydantoin (400 mg/day by mouth), as compared to a placebo, administered over a period of 6 months to 43 imprisoned recidivist offenders, produced no changes in average anxiety or hostility scores as measured from weekly 5-minute speech samples over the 6-month period.

Currently, Rickels and Gottschalk (1974) are studying the effects of lorazepam on anxiety and depression in psychiatric outpatients and are measuring the changes in psychiatric symptoms with self-report, rating, and the Gottschalk content analysis scales. Although many self-report and rating scales have already been used in the construct-validation studies for the Gottschalk content analysis scales, it is anticipated that this study will provide further data useful in the comparison of these different measurement approaches in psychoactive drug studies.

In a longitudinal study of 74 hospitalized chronic schizophrenic patients (Gottschalk *et al.*, 1970), content analysis scores and Mental Status Schedule Scale scores (Spitzer *et al.*, 1964, 1965, 1967) were obtained before and after withdrawal of maintenance doses of phenothiazine medication by a substitution of a placebo. Overt hostility outward content analysis scores from 5-minute speech samples before phenothiazine drug withdrawal were predictive of neurotic ($r = 0.34$) and psychotic ($r = 0.31$) phenomena, as adjudged from the Mental Status Schedule, appearing 4 weeks after discontinuation of phenothiazine drug therapy. Also, covert hsotility outward scores correlated negatively with Mental Status Schedule disorientation scores ($r = 0.28$) 4 weeks after stopping phenothiazine drug therapy.

## Social Alienation-Personal Disorganization Scores (A Measure of the Severity of the Schizophrenic Syndrome) from Content Analysis of Speech

In the above described study of 74 chronic schizophrenic patients (Gottschalk *et al.*, 1970), schizophrenic patients with social alienation-personal disorganization scores greater than 2.0 before phenothiazine drug withdrawal were very sensitive to discontinuation and readministration of phenothiazine, that is, got rapidly worse with drug withdrawal and better with

readministration of drug. Whereas, patients with social alienation-personal disorganization scores of less than 2.0 (while on phenothiazine) were relatively clinically unreactive to drug withdrawal or administration.

Preliminary studies (Gottschalk *et al.*, 1974b) of the relationship of single dose thioridazine (after 4 mg/kg by mouth to 25 patients) and/or mesoridazine plasma concentrations (after 2 mg/kg intramuscularly to 10 patients) in acute schizophrenic patients indicated that social alienation-personal disorganization scores derived from speech samples were significantly decreased by this major tranquilizer within 24 hours and the decreases in these scores were correlated with higher plasma concentrations of this piperidine phenothiazine, whether the drug was given orally or intramuscularly. (See also Gottschalk *et al.*, 1973c.) All these patients were acute, medically healthy schizophrenic patients, who had not received any other psychoactive drug for at least 4 weeks prior to participation in these studies.

Other findings of interest in this research were as follows. Predrug social alienation-personal disorganization scores, derived from 5-minute speech samples, were significantly correlated with post drug thioridazine half-life ($r = 0.44$, $p<0.03$) (Gottschalk *et al.*, 1974b). Also, social alienation-personal disorganization scores in this study correlated significantly predrug ($r = -0.46$, $p<0.01$) and postdrug ($r = -0.53$, $p<0.01$) with the Social Assets Scale of Luborsky *et al.* (1973), indicating that the fewer the social assets score, based on a 5-minute self-administered questionnaire on one's past personal and family history, the greater the social alienation-personal disorganization content analysis scores.

## Achievement Striving Scores, Derived from the Content Analysis of 5-Minute Verbal Samples, as They Relate to Induced Mental Set or Psychomotor Stimulants

One study (Gottschalk *et al.*, 1968) with college students has shown that telling these students that a pill would make them "more peppy and energetic" (whether the pill was a placebo, 90 mg of secobarbital, or 10 mg of dextroamphetamine) significantly increased the achievement striving scores of these students, as derived from 5-minute speech samples, regardless of the medication they were administered. On the other hand, dextroamphetamine (10 mg) by mouth also significantly increased achievement striving scores, regardless of the set induced. This study demonstrated that induced mental set and drug effect can be additive.

In another study (Gottschalk *et al.*, 1971a) similar achievement striving scores were found to be significantly higher ($p<0.01$) in the 5-minute speech samples of a large group of male prisoners ($N = 33$) at the Patuxent, Maryland,

penitentiary when they had ingested *d*-amphetamine (15 mg) than when they had taken a placebo capsule.

## Cognitive and Intellectual Impairment Measured from 5-Minute Samples of Speech

Preliminary development has been carried out on a content analysis scale derivable from 5-minute samples of speech, which measures the magnitude of cognitive and intellectual impairment. The purpose of this scale is to assess the magnitude of transient and reversible changes in general cognitive and intellectual function as well as irreversible changes, all due principally to brain dysfunction and minimally to transient and emotional changes in the individual (Gottschalk and Gleser, 1969). At its present state of development, this content-analysis scale of cognitive and intellectual impairment is capable of differentiating patients with organic brain syndromes from nonbrain damage patients and individuals. Correlational studies with two measures of irreversible brain damage, the Halstead Battery (1947) and the Trail Making Test (Reitan, 1958) on a group of 20 subjects, male and female, ranging in age from 40 to 84 showed satisfactory correlations with both of these measures (Halstead Battery, $r = 0.55$, and Trail Making Test, $r = 0.48$).

Gottschalk and Gleser (1969) used these verbal content analysis scores to investigate the effects of LSD-25 and a placebo on the social alienation-personal disorganization scores of a group of college student volunteers. They showed that LSD-25 and a placebo on the social alienation-personal disorganization scores of a group of college student volunteers. The showed that LSD-25 did not influence scores on the social alienation-personal disorganization scale anymore than did a placebo. But LSD-25 did sginificantly increase scores on th cognitive impairment scale. In another study, the same investigators examined the effects of LSD-25, Ditran (JB329), and Psilocybin on behavior. In this study the effect of these psychotomimetic drugs on the dimension of cognitive-intellectual impairment was to produce more signs of cognitive impairment in the speech of normals than occurs without drugs in the speech of schizophrenics. Most recently, Waskow *et al.* (unpublished) found, using institutionalized prisoners as subjects, that LSD (50$\mu$g) as compared to a placebo did significantly increase scores on both the social alienation-personal disorganization and the cognitive-intellectual impairment content-analysis scales. These data suggest that, at least in some kinds of subjects, psychotomimetic drugs are more likely to induce a transient organic brain syndrome than a functional mental disorder.

Another study (Gottschalk *et al.*, 1969a), using the cognitive-intellectual impairment scale, explored the effect of total and half-body irradiation on

intellectual functioning. This study provided suggestive evidence of temporary impairment of such functioning immediately after exposure to such radiation.

A recent study with a potent new benzodiazepine, triazolam (Elliott and Gottschalk, 1974), indicated that a single oral dose (0.25–2.0 mg) of this drug in 20 subjects reduced anxiety (content analysis) scores and subjects were amnesic that they had taken the drug, which was reflected in significantly increased social alienation-personal disorganization and cognitive-intellectual impairment scores 2 hours but not 6 hours after drug ingestion. Whereas, pentobarbital (100 mg) by mouth, in an additional 10 subjects in the same study, reduced anxiety (content analysis) scores without influencing immediate memory consolidation in the form of elevating either cognitive-intellectual impairment or social alienation-personal disorganization scores over the same time period.

The cognitive-intellectual impairment scale, at its present stage of development, measures general intellectual functioning rather than the functioning of any specific part of the brain.

## SUMMARY

This is a review of the methodological approaches involved in the measurement of affects and their changes in neuropsychopharmacology. Definitions are given of psychological states, traits, moods, affects, emotions, affective disorders, and related subjects. Because many events and factors other than the use of psychoactive drugs can influence affects and similar psychological states of interest, these are not only enumerated, but also the necessity of taking them into consideration in fashioning one's research design in studying such drugs is emphasized.

The major objective methods of measuring affects in psychopharmacology are by means of self-report scales, behavioral rating scales by independent observers, and content analysis scales of verbal behavior. Self-report scales and rating scales are attractive in that they are not difficult to use, but they have various shortcomings with respect to validity. Specifically, self-report scales provide the possibility of malingering or faking and the opportunity for various response sets, such as, social desirability, acquiescence, and deviance. And behavioral rating scales introduce measurement problems involving reliability, halo effects, errors of central tendency, and leniency errors.

Verbal behavior is easy to elicit by standardized methods for content analysis, but the objective scoring of content according to well-validated content analysis scales requires trained content analysis technicians. A review is provided of the theoretical bases and various applications of the content analysis scales of Gottscalk and his co-workers in the measurement of affects

because this method is newer and less well known than the self-report and behavioral rating scale approaches and because the sensitivity, specificity, and versatility of this method can thereby be better appreciated. Psychopharmacological studies using these content analysis measures are reviewed in detail.

In psychopharmacological research, it is considered at this time, wise to employ all three of these types of measures of affects in order to get observational data from three points of view and to compensate for the possible error variance of any one method.

## REFERENCES


Anastasi, A. (1968): *Psychological Testing*. Third Edition. The Macmillan Company, New York.

Barchas, J., and Usdin, E. (1973): (Eds.) *Serotonin and Behavior*. Academic Press, New York.

Bell, A.I., Stroebel, C.F., and Prior, D.D. (1971): Interdisciplinary study of the scrotal sac and testes correlating psychophysiological and psychological observations. *Psychoanal. Quart.* *40*:415-434.

Braithwaite, R.A., Gouldine, R., Theano, G., Bailey, J., and Coppen, A. (1972): Plasma concentration of amitriptylene and clinical response. *Lancet* *1*:1297-1300.

Burrows, G.D., Davies, B., and Scoggins, B.A. (1972): Plasma concentration of nortriptylene and clinical response in depressive illness. *Lancet* *2*:619-623.

Cash, W.D., and Quinn, G.P. (1970): Clinical-chemical correlations: An overview. *Psychopharmacol. Bull.* *6*:26-33.

Chassan, J.B., and Bellak, L. (1966): An introduction to intensive design in the evaluation of drug efficacy. In: *Methods of Research in Psychotherapy*, edited by L.A. Gottschalk and A.H. Auerbach, pp. 478-499, Appleton-Century-Crofts, New York.

Cooper, J.E., Kendell, R.E., Gurland, B.J., Sartoris, N., and Farkas, T. (1969): Cross-national study of diagnosis of the mental disorders: Some results from the first comparative investigation. *Amer. J. Psychiat.* *125*:21-29 (Supplementary).

Cooper, J.R.,Bloom, F.E., and Roth, R.H. (1970): *The Biochemical Basis of Neuropharmacology*, Oxford University, New York.

Committee on Research. Group for the Advancement of Psychiatry. (1959): *Some observations on controls in psychiatric research*, Group for Advancement of Psychiatry, Report No. 42, New York.

Committee on Research. Group for the Advancement of Psychiatry. (1966): *Psychiatric research and the assessment of change*, Group for Advancement of Psychiatry, Report No. 68, New York.

Committee on Research. Group for Advancement of Psychiatry. (1974): *Pharmacotherapy and psychotherapy: Paradoxes, problems, and progress*, Group for the Advancement of Psychiatry, Report No. 93, New York.

Davis, J.M., and Janowsky, D. (1973): Amphetamine and methylphenidate psychosis. In: *Frontiers in Catecholamine Research*, edited by E. Usdin and S.H. Snyder, pp. 977-982, Pergamon Press, New York, New York.

Derogatis, L.R., Klerman, G.L., and Lipman, R.S. (1972): Anxiety states and depressive neuroses: Issues in nosological discrimination. *J. Nerv. Ment. Dis.* *155*:392-403.

Derogatis, L.R., Lipman, R.S., Covi, L., and Rickels, K. (1971): Neurotic symptom dimen-

sions: As perceived by psychiatrists and patients of various social classes. *Arch. Gen. Psychiat.* *24*:454-464.

Downing, R., Rickels, K., Wittenborn, J.R., and Mattsson, N.B. (1971): Interpretation of data from investigations assessing the effectiveness of psychotropic agents. In: *Principles and Problems in Establishing the Efficacy of Psychotropic Agents*, edited by J. Levine, B. Schiele, and L. Bouthilet, US Public Health Service, Chevy Chase, Maryland.

Edwards, A.L. (1959): Social desirability and personality test construction. In: *Objective Approaches to Personality Assessment*, edited by B.M. Bass and I.A. Berg, pp. 100-118, Van Nostrand, New York.

Elliott, H.W., and Gottschalk, L.A. (1974): Effect of a new benzodiazepine, triazolam, on anxiety, hostility, social alienation-personal disorganization, and cognitive-intellectual impairment. (In preparation.)

Elliott, H.W., Gottschalk, L.A., and Uliana, R.L. (1974): Relationship of plasma meperidine levels to changes in anxiety and hostility. *Comprehen. Psychiat.* *15*:57-61.

Fisher, S., Cole, J.O., Rickels, K., and Uhlenhuth, E.N. (1964): Drug-set interaction: The effect of expectations on drug response in outpatients. *Neuropsychopharmacology* *3*:149-156.

Gleser, G.C., Gottschalk, L.A., Fox, R., and Lippert, W. (1965): Immediate changes in affect with chlordiazepoxide. *Arch. Gen. Psychiat.* *13*:291-295.

Goldstein, A., Aronow, L., and Kalman, S.M. (1974): *Principles of Drug Action: The Basis of Pharmacology*, second edition, John Wiley and Sons, Inc., New York.

Gottlieb, A.A., Gleser, G.C., and Gottschalk, L.A. (1967): Verbal and physiological responses to hypnotic suggestion of attitudes. *Psychosom. Med.* *29*:172-183.

Gottschalk, L.A. (1974a): A hope scale applicable to verbal samples. *Arch. Gen. Psychiat.* *30*:779-785.

Gottschalk, L.A. (1972): An objective method of measuring psychological states associated with changes in neural function. *J. Biol. Psychiat.* *4*:33-49.

Gottschalk, L.A. (1974d): The application of a method of content analysis ot psychotherapy research. *Amer. J. Psychother.*, in press.

Gottschalk, L.A. (1974b): Differences in the content of speech of girls and boys ages six to sixteen. In: *Studies on Childhood Psychiatric and Psychological Problem*, edited by D.V. Sankar, PJD Publications, Ltd., Westbury, New York, in press.

Gottschalk, L.A. (1968c): The measurement of hostile aggression through the content analysis of speech: some biological and interpersonal aspects. In: *Biology of Aggressive Behavior*, edited by S. Garattini and E.B. Sigg, pp. 299-316, Excerpta Medical Foundation, Amsterdam, The Netherlands.

Gottschalk, L.A. (1955): Psychologic conflict and electroencephalographic patterns. Some notes on the problem of correlating changes in paroxysmal electroencephalographic patterns with psychologic conflicts. *Arch. Neurol. Psychiat.* *73*:656-662.

Gottschalk, L.A. (1974c): Quantification and psychological indicators of emotions: The content analysis of speech and other objective measures of psychological states. In: *Psychiatry in Medicine, Psychosomatic Medicine*, edited by Z.J. Lipowski, in press.

Gottschalk, L.A. (1968a): Some applications of the psychoanalytic concept of object relatedness: preliminary studies of a human relations scale applicable to verbal samples. *Comprehen. Psychiat.* *9*:608-620.

Gottschalk, L.A. (1968b): Some problems in the evaluation of the use of psychoactive drugs, with or without psychotherapy, in the treatment of non-psychotic personality disorders. In:

*Psychopharmacology: A Review of Progress, 1957-1967*, edited by D.H. Efron, pp. 255-269, PHS Publication No. 1836, Washington, D.C., U.S. Government Printing Office.

Gottschalk, L.A. (1971): Some psychoanalytic research into the communication of meaning: The quality and magnitude of psychological states. *Brit. J. Med. Psychol. 44*:131-147.

Gottschalk, L.A., Bates, D.E., Waskow, I.E., Katz, M.M., and Olsson, J. (1971a): Effect of amphetamine or chlorpromazine on achievement striving scores derived from content analysis of speech. *Comprehen. Psychiat. 12*:430-436.

Gottschalk, L.A., Biener, R., and Dinovo, E. (1974a): Effect of oral and intramuscular routes of administration on serum chlordiazepoxide levels and the prediction of these levels from predrug serum glucose concentrations. *Res. Commun. Chem. Pathol. Pharmacol.*, in press.

Gottschalk, L.A., Biener, R., Noble, E.P., Birch, H., Wilbert, D., and Heiser, J. (1974b): Thioridazine plasma levels and clinical response. In: *Psychopharmacology and Social Science*, edited by M. Marshall and B. Cohn, Jason Aronson, Inc., New York, in press.

Gottschalk, L.A., Cleghorn, J.M., Gleser, G.C., and Iacono, J.M. (1965a): Studies of relationships of emotions to plasma lipids. *Psychosom. Med. 27*:102-111.

Gottschalk, L.A., Covi, L., Uliana, R., and Bates, D.E. (1973a): Effect of diphenylhydantoin on anxiety and hostility in institutionalized prisoners. *Comprehen. Psychiat. 14*:503-511.

Gottschalk, L.A., Elliott, H.W., Bates, D.E. and Cable, C.G. (1971b): Content analysis of speech samples to determine effect of lorazepam on anxiety. *Clin. Pharmacol. Therapeut. 13*:323-328.

Gottschalk, L.A., and Gleser, G.C. (1969): *Measurement of Psychological States Through the Content Analysis of Verbal Behavior*. University of California Press, Berkeley, California.

Gottschalk, L.A., Gleser, G.C., Cleghorn, J.M., Stone, W.N., and Winget, C.N. (1970): Prediction of changes in severity of the schizophrenic syndrome with discontinuation and administration of phenothiazines in chronic schizophrenic patients: Language as a predictor and measure of change in schizophrenia. *Comprehen. Psychiat. 11*:123-140.

Gottschalk, L.A., Gleser, G.C., D'Zmura, T.L., and Hanenson, I.B. (1964): Some psychophysiological relationships in hypertensive women. The effect of hydrochlorothiazide on the relationship of affect to blood pressure. *Psychosomatic Med. 26*:610-617.

Gottschalk, L.A., Gleser, G.C., Springer, K.J., Kaplan, S.M., Shanon, J., and Ross, W.D. (1960): Effects of perphenazine on verbal behavior patterns. *Arch. Gen. Psychiat. 2*:632-639.

Gottschalk, L.A., Gleser, G.C., Stone, W.N., and Kunkel, R.L. (1968): Studies of psychoactive drug effects on nonpsychiatric patients. In: *Psychopharmacology of the Normal Human*, edited by W. Evans and N. Kline, pp. 162-188, Charles C. Thomas, Springfield, Illinois.

Gottschalk, L.A., Gleser, G.C., Wylie, H.W., and Kaplan, S.M. (1965b): Effects of imipramine on anxiety and hostility levels. *Psychopharmacologia 7*:303-310.

Gottschalk, L.A., Haer, J.L., and Bates, D.E. (1972a): Effect of sensory overload on psychological state. *Arch. Gen. Psychiat. 27*:451-457.

Gottschalk, L.A., and Hambidge, G. (1955): Verbal behavior analysis: A systematic approach to the problem of quantifying psychological processes. *J. Proj. Tech. 19*:387-409.

Gottschalk, L.A., and Kaplan, S.A. (1972b): Chlordiazepoxide levels and clinical response. *Comprehen. Psychiat. 13*:519-528.

Gottschalk, L.A., Kaplan, S.M., Gleser, G.C., and Winget, C.N. (1962): Variations in magnitudes of emotions: A method applied to anxiety and hostility during phases of the menstrual cycle. *Psychosom. Med. 24*:300-311.

Gottschalk, L.A., Kapp, F.T., Ross, W.D., Kaplan, S.M., Silver, H., MacLeod, J.A., Kahn,

J.B., Jr., Van Maanen, E.F., and Acheson, G.H. (1956): Explorations in testing drugs affecting physical and mental activity. *J. Amer. Med. Ass. 161*:1054-1058.

Gottschalk, L.A., Kunkel, R.L., Wohl, T. Saenger, E., and Winget, C.N. (1969a): Total and half body irradiation. Effect on cognitive and emotional processes. *Arch. Gen. Psychiat. 21*:574-580.

Gottschalk, L.A., Noble, E., and Elliot, H. (1973c): Preliminary studies of relationships between psychoactive drug blood levels and clinical responses: Chlordiazepoxide, meperidine and thioridazine. *Psychopharmacol. Bull. 9*:40-43.

Gottschalk, L.A., Noble, E.P., Stolzoff, G.E., Cable, C.G., Uliana, R.L., Birch, H., and Fleming, E.W. (1973b): Relationships of chlordiazepoxide blood levels to psychological and biochemical responses. In: *Benzodiazepines*, edited by S. Garattini, E. Mussini and L.O. Randall, pp. 257-283, Raven Press, New York.

Gottschalk, L.A., Springer, K.J., and Gleser, G.C. (1961): Experiments with a method of assessing the variations in intensity of certain psychological states occurring during two psychotherapeutic interviews. In: *Comparative Psycholinguistic Analysis of Two Psychotherapeutic Interviews*, edited by L.A. Gottschalk, Ch. 7, International Universities Press, New York.

Gottschalk, L.A., Stone, W.N., and Gleser, G.C. (1974c): Peripheral versus central mechanisms accounting for anti-anxiety effect of propanolol. *Psychosom. Med. 36*:47-56.

Gottschalk, L.A., Stone, W.N., Gleser, G.C., and Iacono, J.M. (1969b): Anxiety and plasma free fatty acid (FFA) levels. *Life Sci. 8*:61-68.

Gottschalk, L.A., Stone, W.N., Gleser, G.C., and Iacono, J.M. (1966): Anxiety levels in dreams: Relation to changes in plasma free fatty acids. *Science 153*:654-657.

Gottschalk, L.A., Winget, C.N., and Gleser, G.C. (1969c): *Manual of Instructions for Using the Gottschalk-Gleser Content Analysis Scales: Anxiety Hostility, and Social Alienation-Personal Disorganization.* University of California Press, Berkeley, California.

Green, D.E., Forrest, I.S., Forrest, F.M., and Serra, M.T. (1965): Interpatient variation in chlorpromazine metabolism. *Exp. Med. Surg. 23*:278-287.

Gurland, G., Fleiss, J.L., Cooper, J.E., Kendell, R.E., and Simon, R. (1969): Cross-national study of diagnosis of the mental disorders: Some comparisons of diagnostic criteria from the first investigation. *Amer. J. Psychiat. 125*:30-38, (Suppl.).

Gurland, B., Fleiss, J.L., Cooper, J.E., Sharpe, L., Kendell, R.E., and Roberts, P. (1970): Cross-national study of diagnosis of mental disorders: Hospital diagnoses and hospital patients in New York and London. *Comprehen. Psychiat. 11*:18-25.

Halstead, W.D. (1947): *Brain and Intelligence*. University of Chicago Press, Chicago, Illinois.

Hammer, W., and Sjoqvist, F. (1967): Plasma level of monomethyl tricyclic antidepressants during treatment with imipramine-like compounds. *Life Sci. 6*:1895-1903.

Himwich, H.E. (1970): Indoleamines and the depressions: In: *Biochemistry, Schizophrenias, and* Affective Illnesses, edited by H.E. Himwich, pp. 230-282, Williams and Wilkins, New York.

Janowsky, D.S., El-Yousef, M.K., and Davis, J.M. (1974): Acetylcholine and depression. *Psychosom. Med. 36*:248-257.

Kaplan, S.M., Gottschalk, L.A., Magliocco, E.B., Rohovit, D.D., and Ross, W.D. (1961): Hostility in verbal productions and hypnotic dreams of hypertensive patients: Studies of groups and individuals. *Psychosom. Med. 23*:311-322.

Karacan, I., Goodenough, D.R., Shapiro, A., and Starker, S. (1966): Erection cycle during sleep in relation to dream anxiety. *Arch. Gen. Psychiat. 15*:183-189.

Lipman, R.S., Covi, L., Rickels, K., Uhlenhuth, E.H., and Lazar, R. (1968): Selected measures of change in outpatient drug evaluation. In: *Psychopharmacology: A Review of Progress,*

edited by D.H. Efron, J.O. Cole, J. Levine, and J.R. Wittenborn, U.S. Government Printing Office, Washington, D.C.

Lipman, R.S., Rickels, K., Covi, L., Derogatis, L.R., and Uhlenhuth, E.H. (1969): Factors of symptom distress. *Arch. Gen. Psychiat. 21*:328-338.

Luborsky, L., Docherty, J.P., Knapp, P., and Gottschalk, L.A. (1974): A context analysis of psychological states prior to petit-mal seizures. *J. Nerv. Ment. Dis.* In press.

Luborsky, L., Todd, T.C., and Katcher, A.N. (1973): A self-administered social assets scale for predicting physical and psychological illness and health. *J. Psychosom. Res. 17*:109-120.

McLaughlin, B.E., Chassan, J.B., and Ryan, F. (1965): Three single-case studies comparing diazepam and meprobamate: An application of intensive design. *Comprehen. Psychiat. 6*:128-136.

McNair, D.M., Fisher, S., Kahn, R.J., and Dropplemen, L.F. (1970): Drug-personality interaction in intensive outpatient treatment. *Arch. Gen. Psychiat. 22*:128-135.

McNair, D.M., Goldstein, A.P., Lorr, M., Cibelli, L.A., and Roth, I. (1965): Some effects of chlordiazepoxide and meprobamate with psychiatric outpatients. *Psychopharmacologia 7*:256-265.

McNair, D.M., and Lorr, M. (1964): An analysis of mood in neurotics. *J. Abnorm. Soc. Psychol. 69*:620-627.

Mandell, A.J., Buckingham, B., and Segal, D. (1971): Behavioral, metabolic, and enzymatic *N*-methylating system. In: *Brain Chemistry and Mental Disease*, edited by B.T. Ho and W.M. McIsaac, pp. 37-60, Plenum Press, New York.

Marsden, G. (1965): Content-analysis studies of therapeutic interviews: 1954-1964. *Psychol. Bull. 68*:298-321.

Miller, C.K. (1965): Psychological correlates of coronary artery disease. *Psychosom. Med. 27*:257-265.

Orr, D. (1954): Transference and countertransference: A historical survey. *J. Amer. Psychoanal. Ass. 2*:621-670.

Park, L.C., Uhlenhuth, E.H., Lipman, R.S., Rickels, K., and Fisher, S. (1965): A comparison of doctor and patient improvement ratings in a drug (meprobamate) trial. *Brit. J. Psychiat. 111*:535-540.

Paykel, E.S., Prusoff, B.A., Kleman, G.L., and Dimascio, A. (1970): Self report and clinical interview ratings in depression. Paper presented at the Ninth Annual Meeting of the ACNP, San Juan, Puerto Rico, Dec. 9-11.

Pillard, R.C., and Fisher, S. (1967): Effects of chlordiazepoxide and secobarbital on film-induced anxiety. *Psychopharmacologia 12*:18-23.

Prusoff, B.A., Klerman, G.L. and Paykel, E.S. (1972): Concordance between clinical assessments and patient's self-report in depression. *Arch. Gen. Psychiat. 26*:546-552.

Rashkis, H.A., and Smarr, E.R. (1957): Drug and milieu effect with chronic schizophrenia. *Arch. Neurol. Psychiat. 78*:89-96.

Reitan, R.M. (1958): Validity of the Trail-Making Test as an indicator of organic brain damage. *Percept. Motor Skills 8*:271-276.

Rickels, K. (1968): (Ed.) *Non-specific Factors in Drug Therapy*, Charles C. Thomas, Springfield, Illinois.

Rickels, K. (1963): Psychopharmacologic agents: A clinical psychiatrist's individualistic point of view. Patient and doctor variables. *J. Nerv. Ment. Dis. 138*:540-549.

Rickels, K., Cattell, R., MacAfee, A., and Hesbacker, P. (1965): Drug response and important external events in the patient's life. *Dis. Nerv. Sys. 26*:782-786.

Rickels, K., and Downing, R. (1966): Compliance and improvement in drug-treated and placebo-treated neurotic outpatients. *Arch. Gen. Psychiat. 14*:631-633.

Rickels, K., and Gottschalk, L.A. (1974): Collaborative studies of effects of lorazepam on anxiety and depression in psychiatric outpatients. Comparison of content analysis, self-report, and rating scale scores, in preparation.

Rickels, K., Lipman, R.S., Park, L.C., Covi, L., Uhlenhuth, E.H., and Mock, J.E. (1971): Drug, doctor warmth, and clinic setting in the symptomatic response to minor tranquilizers. *Psychopharmacologia 20*:128-152.

Rickels, K., Ward, C.H., and Schut, L. (1964): Different populations, different drug responses, comparative study of two antidepressants, each used in two different patient groups. *Amer. J. Med. Sci 247*:328-335.

Sabshin, M.D., and Eisen, S.B. (1957): The effects of word tension on the quality and quantity of tranquilizer utilization. *Ann. N.Y. Acad. Sci. 67*:746-757.

Sabshin, M., and Ramot, J. (1956): Pharmacotherapeutic evaluation and the psychiatric setting. *Arch. Neurol. Psychiat. 75*:362-370.

Sapolsky, A. (1965): Relationship between patient-doctor compatibility, mutual perception, and outcome of treatment. *J. Abnormal Psychol. 70*:70-76.

Schildkraut, J.J. (1974): The current status of biological criteria for classifying the depressive disorders and predicting responses to treatment. *Psychopharmacol. Bull. 10*:5-25.

Serrano, E.E., Raye, D.B., Hammer, R.H., and Wilder, B.V. (1973): Plasma diphenyhydantoin values after oral and intramuscular administration of diphenyhydantoin. *Neurology 23*:311-317.

Silbergeld, S., Brast, N., and Noble, E.P. (1971): The menstrual cycle: A double-blind study of mood, behavior, and biochemical variables with Enovid and a placebo. *Psychosomatic Med. 33*:411-428.

Simon, R.S., Fisher, B., Fleiss, J.L., Gurland, B.J., and Sharp, L. (1971): Relationship between psychopathology and British- or American-oriented diagnosis. *J. Abnormal Psychol. 78*:26-29.

Snyder, S.H., Banerjee, S.P., Yamamura, H.I., and Greenberg, D. (1974): Drugs, neurotransmitters, and schizophrenia. *Science 184*:1243-1253.

Spitzer, R.L., Fliess, J.L., Burdock, E.O., and Hardesty, A.S. (1964): The mental status schedule: rationale, reliability, and validity. *Comprehensive Psychiat. 5*:384-395.

Spitzer, R.L., Fliess, J.L., Endicott, J., and Cohen, J. (1967): Mental status schedule: properties of factor analytically derived scales. *Arch. Gen. Psychiat. 16*:479-493.

Spitzer, R.L., Fliess, J.L., Kernohan, W., Lee, J.C., and Baldwin, I.T. (1965): Mental status schedule. *Arch. Gen. Psychiat. 13*:448-455.

Stone, W.N., Gleser, G.C., and Gottschalk, L.A. (1973): Anxiety and beta adrenergic blockade. *Arch. Gen. Psychiat. 29*:620-622.

Stone, W.N., Gleser, G.C., Gottschalk, L.A., and Iacono, J.M. (1969): Stimulus, affect and plasma free fatty acids. *Psychosomatic Med. 31*:331-341.

Uhlenhuth, E.H., Lipman, R.S., Rickels, K., Fisher, S., Covi, L., and Park, L.C. (1968): Predicting the relief of anxiety with meprobamate. *Arch. Gen. Psychiat. 19*:610-630.

Uhlenhuth, E.H., and Park, L.C. (1964): The influence of medication (imipramine) and doctor in relieving depressed psychoneurotic outpatients. *J. Psychiat. Res. 2*:101-122.

Uhlenhuth, E.H., Rickels, K., Fisher, S, Park, L.C., Lipman, R.S., and Mock, J. (1966): Drug, doctor's verbal attitude, and clinic setting in the symptomatic response to pharmacotherapy. *Psychopharmacologia (Berlin) 9*:392-418.

Usdin, E. (1970): Absorption, distribution, and metabolic fate of psychotropic drugs. *Psychopharmacol. Bull. 6*:4-25.

Waskow, I. (1967): The effects of drugs on speech: A review. In: *Research in Verbal Behavior and Some Neurophysiological Implications*, edited by K. Salzinger and S. Salzinger, pp. 355-382, Academic Press, New York.

Weil-Malherbe, H., and Szara, S.I. (1971): *The Biochemistry of Fucntional and Experimental Psychoses*. Charles C. Thomas, Springfield, Illinois.

Wilensky, A.J., and Lawden, V.A. (1973): Inadequate serum levels after intramuscular administration of diphenylhydantoin. *Neurology 23*:318-324.

Wittenborn, J.R. (1967): Do rating scales objectify clinical impression? *Comprehensive Psychiat. 8*:386-392.

Wittenborn, J.R. (1972): Reliability, validity, and objectivity of symptom-rating scales. *J. Nerv. Ment. Dis. 154*:79-87.

Wittenborn, J.R. (1974): Self-report inventories as criteria for anxiety-allaying medications. Unpublished manuscript.

Zeidenberg, P., Perel, J.M., Kanzler, M., Wharton, R.N., and Malitz, S. (1971): Clinical and metabolic studies with imipramine in man. *Amer. J. Psychiat. 127*:57-62.

# Part IV

# Psychophysiological and Psychosomatic Studies

In this section, there has been included a series of papers involving psychophysiological, psychobiochemical, and psychosomatic studies. The first chapter (Chapter 29) is a review paper and is entitled "Quantification and psychological indicators of emotion: the content analysis of speech and other objective measures of psychological states" (Gottschalk, 1974). The other chapters include two chapters on the relationship of psychologic states to plasma free fatty acids (a good indirect indicator of the arousal of plasma adrenergic secretions in human subjects), and these are Chapter 30, "Anxiety and plasma free fatty acids (FFA)" (Gottschalk et al, 1969) and Chapter 31, "Stimulus affect and plasma free fatty acids" (Stone et al, 1969). Another chapter, Chapter 32, involves an investigation of emotional states as trigger mechanisms in epileptic manifestations and is entitled "A content analysis of psychological states prior to petit mal EEG paroxysms" (Luborsky et al, 1975). Another chapter, Chapter 33, is a psychochemical study that demonstrates that one of the biochemical indicators of the arousal of adrenergic substances in the blood stream is highly correlated with anxiety scores as measured by the Gottschalk-Gleser content analysis

scores; this chapter is entitled "Changes in serum dopamine-beta-hydroxylase activity during group therapy" (Silbergeld et al, 1975). Other chapters include a paper, Chapter 34, entitled "The relationship of the manifest content of dreams to duration of childbirth in primiparae" (Winget and Kapp, 1972), and Chapter 35 entitled "Male anxiety during sleep" (Bell, 1975). An original and previously unpublished chapter (36) using the Gottschalk-Gleser content analysis scales applied to German subjects is entitled "Alexithymia: a comparative study of verbal behavior in psychosomatic and psychoneurotic patients" (von Rad et al).

# QUANTIFICATION AND PSYCHOLOGICAL INDICATORS OF EMOTIONS: THE CONTENT ANALYSIS OF SPEECH AND OTHER OBJECTIVE MEASURES OF PSYCHOLOGICAL STATES

Louis A. Gottschalk, M.D.[1]

*University of California College of Medicine*
*Irvine, California*

ABSTRACT–1. Reliable and valid measurement of affects, emotions, and moods has posed a problem for psychiatric and psychophysiological research as the demand has grown for more sensitive, precise, and objective assessment methods than the method of clinical impressionistic evaluation. There are three major methods in current use for assessing these psychological variables: self-report scales, behavioral rating scales, and the content analysis of verbal behavior.

2. Self-report inventories give an individual an opportunity to describe his subjective state, and their major advantage is that what the person is actually experiencing may not be correctly perceived by external observers. Disadvantages of the self-report method include the possibility that the subject may malinger or fake or may not be in good communication with his own feelings so that he gives a distorted report about them.

3. Psychiatric rating scales have the advantage of putting a trained observer to the task of assessment, and the clinician rater has the option of using a broad range of behavioral and affective cues, verbal and nonverbal, in following this method. But since such raters are not free from systematic distortion and thorough familiarity with the subject of observation is infrequent, all relevant information to make a valid assessment is often not available. Moreover, different interviewers may evoke varying emotional responses from the same person.

4. Objective content analysis of verbal behavior can avoid most of the shortcomings of the self-report and observer rating methods, so long as reasonably standardized procedures are used for eliciting verbal behavior and other key features of scientific methodology are followed. A disadvantage of the content analysis method is that it is time-consuming and requires training and quality checks to carry out accurate content analysis coding. On the other hand, reliable and valid measurement procedures in all fields of research take time and care.

5. A brief review is provided of the variety of findings and applications of the content analyses method of measuring feeling states, and these applications include the research areas of psychotherapy, psychophysiology, and neuropsychopharmacology.

There are relatively few objective measures of immediate, labile emotional states, such as anxiety or hostility. Most psychological tests have been designed to measure general traits or typical behavior and thus are fairly insensitive to

[1] Professor and Chairman, Department of Psychiatry and Human Behavior, College of Medicine, University of California, Irvine, California (92664).

small changes in labile emotional response. Moreover, such tests can seldom be used in longitudinal studies because of a tendency for the responses evoked in the testing situation to become learned or stereotyped.

The fact that there is a paucity of objective indices of immediate psychological states makes difficult the development of a valid method of measuring such variables, since no direct criteria are available. Thus, it is necessary to proceed by slow and tedious steps, using various indirect methods of assessing validity.

Before reviewing the measurement tools and procedures in use and available for assessing emotional states, some definitions will be provided of what will be considered, here, as falling under the broad classification of "emotions."

## DEFINITIONS

### *Affects and Emotions*

Affects are sometimes considered to be distinct from emotions—"affects" referring to the feeling states that can be the result of or can motivate behavior, and "emotions" referring to these affects but in addition including the physiological concomitants of these psychological states. Many authors make no precise distinction between affects and emotions. Here, there will be no differentiation made between affects, emotions, and other feeling states.

Affects are usually short-lived, lasting from minutes to hours, sometimes a few days. With certain personality disorders, such as psychoneuroses, psychoses, or organic cerebral disorders, e.g., delirium, affects may become much more long-lasting, possibly weeks or months.

### *Psychological States Versus Traits*

Psychological states are usually relatively transient subjective reactions; psychological traits are, typically, habitual feeling states characteristic of an individual. Both psychological states and traits are usually accompanied by specific behavior patterns.

### *Mood*

Mood refers to affective characteristics which are relatively longer lasting (days to weeks or months) than affects. In psychiatry the term has primarily been used in reference to the dimension of depression on the one extreme and mania on the other—that is, manic-depressive reactions or mania or depression are referred to as affective disorders. In this paper, the term affective states will be used more widely than this narrow connotation of affective disorder. The use of the term "mood" here will thus refer to affects or emotions of sustained duration, usually short of the duration of traits.

*Anxiety Versus Fear*

Anxiety psychodynamically refers to irrational apprehension, whereas fear refers to apprehension concerning a real, external danger or threat. Similar distinctions could be made about all affects or emotions; that is, are the emotions irrational responses, i.e., responses to perceptual or cognitive distortions or to the confusion of past memories and events with the present or the future, or are they experienced reality-bound for time, place, and person? Here, no such distinction will be made between anxiety and fear or other affects, not because this distinction should never be made, but because most objective measuring instruments used to assess these affects do not or cannot make these distinctions and also because psychophysiological reactions appear to be produced by affective states, at least for brief intervals, whether or not they rest on rational bases.

## MEASUREMENT TOOLS AND PROCEDURES USED IN ASSESSING PSYCHOLOGICAL VARIABLES

There are three major methods of measuring psychological variables: self-report scales, behavioral rating scales, and the objective content analysis of verbal behavior.

*Self-Report Measures*

Self-report measures of emotions, for example, of hostility-aggression, have been constructed with items derived from the MMPI [1-5] and from independent sources [5-8]. Most of these measures consist of items chosen on the basis of face validity [1, 4, 9], and others have been selected by virtue of their empirical relationship to clinical ratings of aggressiveness [2, 3]. The self-report inventories have been compared with projective techniques, learning tasks, and clinical and other self-ratings, with varying degrees of success [7, 10-12]. In general, it has been found that the more similar the criterion measure is to a self-report procedure, the better is the correlation between the criterion measure and self-report inventory. Factor analysis of some of the hostility inventories [6, 8] has indicated two subclasses of items, labeled "aggression" and "hostility," but the distinction in items usually has not been maintained in the final scores derived from these inventories. In the most recent and most carefully worked out of the MMPI derived hostility inventories, that of Buss [12], these subclasses have been considered meaningfully distinct and thus have been maintained in the final score.

All self-report inventories, including the various adjective checklists [13-15] commonly used to assess affect level or prevailing mood, primarily tap conscious attitudes acceptable enough to the subject to be acknowledged. They would seem to be of limited usefulness, therefore, in studying relationships in which suppressed or repressed affects or emotions may play a major part.

Projective tests such as the Rorschach and TAT have traditionally provided evaluations of deeper, more enduring personality traits, but in this role the tests have been somewhat unwieldy to manipulate and difficult to quantify. Thus, in the last decade or so quite a bit of effort has been directed toward developing content scales of the responses from these projective tests to overcome these difficulties [16-24]. In the assessment of hostility, for example, some of the scales are divided into an overt and a covert hostility portion and include weights reflecting the intensity of the hostility expressed. Hafner and Kaplan [25] found a differing relationship between the overt and covert portions of their hostility scales, depending on whether applied to the Rorschach or the TAT. The overt and covert portions showed a high positive correlation on the Rorschach but a significant negative one on the TAT. Further, there was no correlation between the hostility scores on the Rorschach and TAT.

A difference in the meaning of hostility scores on the Rorschach and TAT was also noted by Buss [12] when comparing his hostility self-report inventory with the two projectives. His inventory scores correlated with a modified, multiple-choice form of the TAT [26] but not with Rorschach scores. Out of the vast array of conflicting results, obtained from studies relating hostility scales derived from projective tests to overt behavioral aggression, Buss found certain general trends appearing. He noted that a) hostile content scales yield a direct relationship to overt behavior; b) gross weights are as successful as more highly differentiated weights in this regard; and c) correlations are higher when less ambiguous stimuli are used and when subjects are more aware of their hostile feelings. These findings have led Buss to suggest that self-report inventories provide as good a measure of aggressive behavior as projective tests.

Self-report scales are designed to give an individual the opportunity to describe his subjective state, and since it is subjective distress that ordinarily accounts for a patient seeking treatment, such self-report scales would appear to be a plausible criterion of emotional or affective disturbances. Affective states may be assessed in terms of an individual's self-report directly about *affects* or in terms of associated *somatic dysfunction, cognitive and intellectual dysfunction*, or actual overall *performance dysfunction*. Unfortunately, the individual may respond to self-report measures in terms of his traits as much as in terms of his state. Or it may be that the subject's self-description is more in terms of the kind of person that he believes himself to be rather than a description of the subjective state in which he currently finds himself. Self-report inventories of somatic discomfort, although useful, are not sufficient as direct measures of affects because many people who have significant subjective affects do not suffer appreciable somatic distress. And there are individuals of hypochondriacal or hysterical disposition who tend to exaggerate or perhaps use real or imagined somatic distress without experiencing appreciable affect. Similarly, performance is impaired in some affectively disturbed patients who, with great psychic

discomfort, mobilize their energy and continue to perform well. The possibility that self-report inventories designed to assess transient affective states will be confounded with characterological traits is commonly recognized and should be a concern for all clinical investigators.

Two of the most generally used self-report inventories in psychopharmacologic research are the Psychiatric Outpatient Mood Scales (POMS) [27-29] and the Symptom Check List (SCL) [30, 31], both of which have been used extensively in psychopharmacological research. Review of four different studies using the POMS [27-29, 32] indicates that the POMS is capable of assessing situational anxiety but not necessarily the same kind of anxiety which is reduced by antianxiety medication. Also, had a distinction not been made between high acquiescent and had low acquiescent patients not been available, the POMS would not have shown an anxiety-reducing effect for chlordiazepoxide in the study. In four studies using the SCL [30, 31, 33, 34] the use of the SCL was accompanied by inconsistencies and failures which were as notable as the successes. It would appear that this self-report inventory has not as yet advanced to the status of a primary criterion that can be depended upon to show psychoactive drug effects, but this does not necessarily mean it is not a useful and valid measure of psychological reactions associated with other events.

These various reports based on the POMS and SCL provide evidence that pharmacological agents which are in common use and known to be effective may or may not be distinguished from placebo on the basis of scores based on the use of self-report inventories. Specifically, the discrimination of a psychoactive drug, using these self-report measures, was found to be a function of the severity of the illness, the attitudes of the physician, the personality of the patient, or the nature of the clinic. Self-report measures are, thus, useful but should not be regarded as sufficient criteria for detecting psychoactive drug effects. Self-report inventories, however, are not necessarily a less desirable alternative to rating scales. Rating scales do not distinguish between subjects in the same way as self-report inventories and in spite of their fallibility, self-report inventories offer an approach to the assessment of subjective manifestations which may not be correctly perceived and reported by raters.

Disadvantages present in self-report measures may be summarized as follows. Since the subject is describing his own behavior, characteristic psychological defense mechanisms may obscure an accurate evaluation of his subjective state and actual psychopathologic processes may color or distort his perspective; for instance, the subject may malinger or fake. Also, as Downing et al [35] have indicated, the patient's self-assessments may be influenced by a number of other biases such as a desire to please the physician, and to a lesser degree by such factors as "social desirability" [36]. Finally, it may be difficult for the patient to evaluate precisely the severity of his condition, for he does not have the professional experience of a clinician in making his judgments [37].

### *Psychiatric Rating Scales*

With psychiatric rating scales, assessments are made by a trained observer—a psychiatrist, clinical psychologist, psychiatric social worker, and so forth. Hence, the rater customarily has had some experience in measuring psychopathologic phenomena and administering these rating scales. The clinician is free to assess the status of the patient from a range of behavioral and affective cues, verbal and nonverbal. His judgments are likely to be less constricted by the distortions inherent in this self-report approach, and he is capable of accurately establishing the pattern as well as the level of severity of the patient's symptom profile [38].

But the ratings of clinicians are not necessarily better or more valid than the self-reports of patients. While the clinical interviewer gains objectivity and detachment, he sacrifices familiarity with the patient; his sphere of reference is limited to the immediate interview situation. Nor are clinicians free from systematic distortions: definite biases or "orientations" regarding clinical interpretation may be introduced in the formal training and cultural background of the clinician [39-42]. Likewise, subtle personality characteristics, usually long preceding the professional training of the rater and labelled countertransference by some clinicians [43], may distort the perceptions and emotional reactions of the rater vis-a-vis the patient. Studies by Gottschalk et al. [44, 45] indicate that different interviewers may evoke varying emotional responses from the same patients. Finally, agreement between independent clinical observers is often only moderate.

A number of studies [37, 46, 47] have shown that agreements between clinical observations and patient's self-reports vary widely. Derogatis et al. [48] found great similarities in the assessment of symptom dimensions between psychiatrist and outpatients but also noticed distinctions between the two, particularly in lower class patients. Technically trained clinicians are, for the most part, more discriminating than patients. The consensus seems to be that these two forms of assessment each contribute unique information to the overall clinical evaluation of patients as well as providing a certain amount of common data concerning the patient's clinical status. Provided that a consistent and compatible set of scales could be made available, the ideal method of measuring psychological states might be to employ both kinds of scales on different occasions and under certain conditions. One or the other technique would be subject to distortion, but rarely would both be equally vulnerable to the same sources of error. Since accurate identification of the basis of disagreement between self-report and clinical observation has not progressed very far at the present time, the optimal strategy would seem to involve using both of these methods to maximize the validity of clinical appraisals or, even better, to include the use of a third method of measuring psychological states, namely, the content analysis of verbal behavior.

### *Content Analysis Procedures*

Besides self-report measures and rating scales, content analysis of verbal behavior is yet another method of measuring changes in psychological states. Self-report procedures have certain shortcomings [49], the least of which is providing the possibility of malingering or faking. Rating scales also pose measurement problems [50] involving reliability, halo effects (such as the tendency of raters to be unduly influenced by a single favorable or unfavorable trait), error of central tendency (the tendency to rate persons in the middle of a scale and to avoid extreme positions), and leniency error (the reluctance of many raters to assign unfavorable ratings). The content analysis of an individual's speech or handwritten communications offers a third alternative approach to the evaluation of psychoactive drug effects that, under proper circumstances, can bypass some of these measurement problems.

Waskow [51] has thoroughly reviewed the literature on the effects of psychoactive drugs on content of speech and has described a variety of approaches. Marsden [52] has reviewed content analysis studies of therapeutic interviews and Gottschalk [53] has elaborated more recently on the application of content analysis to psychotherapy research.

The Gottschalk method of content analysis procedure [54-56] is one content analysis method that has been applied extensively to research problems in psychophysiology, psychotherapy, and neuropsychopharmacology; the specific focus here will be on the Gottschalk content analysis procedure as it applies to psychophysiological research.

### *Summary Description of the Procedure, Reliability, and Construct Validation Studies*

The measurement method that has been developed by Gottschalk and his co-workers utilizes a function that is uniquely human, namely, language and its content or semantic aspects. The development of this method has involved a long series of steps. It has required that the psychological dimensions to be measured (for example, anxiety, hostility outward, hostility inward, hope, cognitive-intellectual impairment, achievement strivings, social alienation-personal disorganization, and so forth) be carefully defined; that the content, the lexical cues, be spelled out from which a receiver of any verbal message infers the occurrence of the psychological states; that the linguistic, principally syntactical, cues conveying intensity be specified; that differential weights be assigned for semantic and linguistic cues whenever appropriate; and that a systematic means be arrived at to correct for the number of words spoken per unit time so that one individual can be compared to others or to himself on different occasions with respect to the magnitude of a particular psychological

state. The method requires, also, that a formal scale of weighted content categories be specified for each psychological dimension to be measured; that research technicians be trained to score these typescripts of human speech (much as biochemical technicians are trained to run various chemical determinations by following prescribed procedures); and that the interscorer reliability of two trained content technicians using the same scale be 0.85 or above (a modest but respectable level of consensus in the behavioral sciences for these kinds of measurements). Moreover, a set of construct-validation studies have had to be carried out to ascertain exactly what this content analysis procedure was measuring, and these validation studies have included the use of four kinds of criterion measures: psychological (self-report and behavioral rating scales), physiological, pharmacological, and biochemical. On the basis of these construct-validation studies, changes have been made in the content categories and the associated weights of each specific scale in the direction of maximizing the correlations between the content analysis scores with these various criterion measures.

Construct-validation of any behavioral or psychological test instrument requires repeated reexamination and retesting, in new situations, of the variables being evaluated. After initial validation studies were completed for verbal behavior measures of such psychological states as anxiety, hostility outward and hostility inward, social alienation-personal disorganization (an objective dimension constituting the main features of schizophrenia), cognitive and intellectual impairment, and achievement strivings, a large variety of additional investigations have been carried out using these verbal behavior measures. These further investigations have provided considerable data on the ways in which such verbal behavior scores relate to other relevant measurable phenomena.

### *Summary of Theoretical Framework and Scoring Procedures*

A brief comment on the theoretical framework from which this measurement approach has developed: The theoretical approach has been eclectic and includes behavioral and conditioning theory, psychoanalytic clinical hypotheses, and linguistic theory.

The formulation of these psychological states has been influenced by the position that they all have biological roots. Both the definition of each separate psychological state and the selection of the specific verbal content items used as cues for inferring each state were influenced by the decision that whatever psychological state was measured by this content analysis approach should—whenever possible—be associated with some biological characteristic of the individual in addition to some psychological aspect or some social situation.

The scoring or content-analysis technician applying this procedure to typescripts of tape-recorded speech need not worry, however, about approaching the work of content analysis with one theoretical orientation or another; rather,

he carefully follows a strictly empirical approach, scoring the occurrence of any content or themes in each grammatical clause of the speech according to a "cookbook," namely, various well-delineated language categories constituting each of our verbal behavior scales. A manual [56] is available which indicates what verbal categories should be looked for, and how much the occurrence of each one is to be weighted. The technician, then, follows prescribed mathematical calculations leading up to a final score for the magnitude of any one psychological state or another.

### *Standard Instructions for Eliciting Verbal Behavior*

The instructions to elicit speech from a research subject have been purposely relatively ambiguous and nonstructured, except that a report of personal or dramatic life experiences has been requested. Such instructions have been used because of an initial aim to probe the immediate emotional reactions of patients or subjects, instead of the typical or habitual ones, and to minimize reactions of guarding or covering up. Standardized instructions are used, also, in order to compare individuals in a standard context so that demographic and personality variables can be explored and investigated, while holding relatively constant the influence of such variables as the instructions for eliciting the speech, the interviewer, the context, and the situation. The effects of varying these noninterviewee variables have subsequently been investigated, one by one, after reliable and valid content analysis scales were developed.

The standard instructions used in the Gottschalk content analysis procedure to elicit five minute verbal samples are: "This is a study of speaking and conversation habits. Upon a signal from me I would like you to speak for five minutes about any interesting or dramatic personal life experiences you have had. Once you have started I will be here listening to you, but I would prefer not to reply to any questions you might feel like asking me until the five minute period is over. Do you have any questions you would like to ask me now before we start? Well, then you may begin."

These instructions are designed to simulate roughly a projective test situation. The lack of verbal responsiveness of the examiner during the period when the subject is speaking, plus a conscious attempt on the part of the examiner to keep at a minimum any nonverbal cues that might indicate his reactions to the subject, tend to give the examiner in the total situation the quality of "blank screen" on which the subject projects some part of the gamut of his reactions to any vaguely similar life situation within his past experience. What the subject talks about during any one verbal sample depends in large part on what psychological conflicts or states most probably are being experienced at the time and what states or conflicts are most highly mobilized by the stimulus eliciting speech. These psychological states determine how the subject perceives the experimental situation and what events are retrieved from his remote or recent

memory storage system. The standardized nature of the situation in which the verbal samples are elicited minimizes the interviewer as a variable influencing the interviewee's psychological state and leaves the interviewee's reactions (appropriate and inappropriate) as a predominant variable in the interpersonal interaction.

*Other Types of Language Behavior to Which This Content Analysis Procedure May Be Applied*

The content analysis procedures can be, and have been applied to interview material—psychotherapeutic, diagnostic or otherwise. These content analysis scales can be applied to different kinds of language material obtained in a variety of situations and in both spoken and written form. Most of the reliability and validity studies have been done on small samples of speech, three to five minutes in duration, obtained in a response to standard instructions. The typed data can be broken down into equal temporal units (for example, two of five minute segments). Or the units can be based on the number of words spoken by one or both participants (or more if they are present); for example, consecutive 500 word sequences of the speaker's can be coded for content. Depending on the purpose and research design of the study period, these content analysis scales have also been applied to interviews, dreams, projective test data (specifically, tape-recordings of Thematic Apperception Test responses), written verbal samples, and even literature, letters, public speeches, and any other type of language material.

*Example of the Hostility Content Analysis Scale and its Application*

Three of the Gottschalk content analysis scales, the Hostility Scales, are shown here (see Schedules 1, 2 and 3), followed by an example of two coded and scored speech samples.

The following example illustrates the system of scoring on the three hostility scales. These fragments of two five-minute verbal samples have been broken down into their component grammatical clauses (complete or elliptical), and those clauses which are scorable on one or more scales are marked with the appropriate symbols. The first symbol, a Roman numeral, indicates the type of hostility; the second symbol, a single small letter, indicates a subcategory of verbal items; the third symbol identifies the weight assigned to the thematic category scored. In the following examples, hostility inward scoring is designated with a I, ambivalent hostility is designated with a II, and all scoring on the hostility directed outward scale is enclosed in parentheses, the (I) denoting overt hostility outward and the (II) denoting the covert portion of the scale.

## SCHEDULE 1

### Hostility Directed Outward Scale: Destructive, Injurious, Critical Thoughts and Actions Directed to Others

| (I) Hostility Outward–Overt | | (II) Hostility Outward–Covert | |
|---|---|---|---|
| | *Thematic Categories* | | *Thematic Categories* |
| a 3* | Self killing, fighting, injuring other individuals or threatening to do so. | a 3* | Others (human) killing, fighting, injuring other individuals or threatening to do so. |
| b 3 | Self robbing or abandoning other individuals, causing suffering or anguish to others, or threatening to do so. | b 3 | Others (human) robbing, abandoning, causing suffering or anguish to other individuals, or threatening to do so. |
| c 3 | Self adversely criticizing, depreciating, blaming, expressing anger, dislike of other human beings. | c 3 | Others adversely criticizing, depreciating, blaming, expressing anger, dislike of other human beings. |
| a 2 | Self killing, injuring or destroying domestic animals, pets, or threatening to do so. | a 2 | Others (human) killing, injuring, or destroying domestic animals, pets, or threatening to do so. |
| b 2 | Self abandoning, robbing, domestic animals, pets, or threatening to do so. | b 2 | Others (human) abandoning, robbing, domestic animals, pets, or threatening to do so. |
| c 2 | Self criticizing or depreciating others in a vague or mild manner. | c 2 | Others (human) criticizing or depreciating other individuals in a vague or mild manner. |
| d 2 | Self depriving or disappointing other human beings. | d 2 | Others (human) depriving or disappointing other human beings. |
| | | e 2 | Others (human or domestic animals) dying or killed violently in death-dealing situation or threatened with such. |
| | | f 2 | Bodies (human or domestic animals) mutilated, depreciated, defiled. |
| a 1 | Self killing, injuring, destroying, robbing wildlife, flora, inanimate objects or threatening to do so. | a 1 | Wildlife, flora, inanimate objects, injured, broken, robbed, destroyed or threatened with such (with or without mention of agent). |
| b 1 | Self adversely criticizing, depreciating, blaming, expressing anger or dislike of subhuman, inanimate objects, places, situations. | b 1 | Others (human) adversely criticizing, depreciating, expressing anger or dislike of subhuman, inanimate objects, places, situations. |

* The number serves to give the weight as well as to identify the category. The letter also helps identify the category.

**SCHEDULE 1 cont.**

(I) Hostility Outward–Overt cont.

c 1 Self using hostile words, cursing, mention of anger or rage without referent.

(II) Hostility Outward–Covert cont.

c 1 Others angry, cursing without reference to cause or direction of anger; also instruments of destruction not used threateningly.

d 1 Others (human, domestic animals) injured, robbed, dead, abandoned or threatened with such from any source including subhuman and inanimate objects, situations (storms, floods, etc.).

e 1 Subhumans killing, fighting, injuring, robbing, destroying each other or threatening to do so.

f 1 Denial of anger, dislike, hatred, cruelty, and intent to harm.

**SCHEDULE 2**

**Hostility Directed Inward Scale: Self-Destructive, Self-Critical Thoughts and Actions**

I. Hostility Inward

*Thematic Categories*

a 4* References to self (speaker) attempting or threatening to kill self, with or without conscious intent.

b 4 References to self wanting to die, needing or deserving to die.

a 3 References to self injuring, mutilating, disfiguring self or threats to do so, with or without conscious intent.

b 3 Self blaming, expressing anger or hatred to self, considering self worthless or of no value, causing oneself grief or trouble, or threatening to do so.

c 3 References to feelings of discouragement, giving up hope, despairing, feeling grieved or depressed, having no purpose in life.

a 2 References to self needing or deserving punishment, paying for one's sins, needing to atone or do penance.

b 2 Self adversely criticizing, depreciating self; references to regretting, being sorry or ashamed for what one says or does; references to self mistaken or in error.

c 2 References to feelings of deprivation, disappointment, lonesomeness.

a 1 References to feeling disappointed in self; unable to meet expectations of self or others.

b 1 Denial of anger, dislike, hatred, blame, destructive impulses from self to self.

c 1 References to feeling painfully driven or obliged to meet one's own expectations and standards.

* The number serves to give the weight as well as to identify the category. The letter also helps identify the category.

## SCHEDULE 3

### Ambivalent Hostility Scale: Destructive, Injurious Critical Thoughts and Actions of Others to Self

II. Ambivalent Hostility

*Thematic Categories*

a 3* Others (human) killing or threatening to kill self.

b 3 Others (human) physically injuring, mutilating, disfiguring self or threatening to do so.

c 3 Others (human) adversely criticizing, blaming, expressing anger or dislike toward self or threatening to do so.

d 3 Others (human) abandoning, robbing self, causing suffering, anguish, or threatening to do so.

a 2 Others (human) depriving, disappointing, misunderstanding self or threatening to do so.

b 2 Self threatened with death from subhuman or inanimate object, or death-dealing situation.

a 1 Others (subhuman, inanimate, or situation), injuring, abandoning, robbing self, causing suffering, anguish.

b 1 Denial of blame.

A detailed description of the scoring procedures for these three hostility scales, with many examples, is provided in a *Manual* [56].

*Example 1.* Male high school student: Note especially hostility out.

(Ib1)<br>
"This pledging period you go through/is kind of stupid./ Take for instance last<br>
IIb3 (IIa3) (Ic2)<br>
Sunday/when they beat us up. / I can't see/what they accomplish/when they take<br>
(IIa3) (Ib1)<br>
someone/ and give him five or ten swats./ And some of the stupid things they make<br>
you do/like running around a car/when you're at a red light/is very dangerous./<br>
(IIe2)<br>
Somebody can get killed/when they pull some of these stunts off./ So I didn't feel in<br>
(Ib1)<br>
too pleasant a mood/when I answered that questionnaire;/ and I put down every way<br>
(Ib1) (Ib1)<br>
/ I felt sore/ that I could./ That's the way / I felt. / And coming down here to take<br>
this test is an example./ I wanted to come./ But before I came in this room / the guys<br>
(IIa3) IIb3 (IIf1) (Ib1)<br>
take us / and we get punched again and all./ I didn't mind / but what the heck's the<br>
(Ic3) (IIa3) IIb3<br>
sense of it./ It's not their right / to kick you through the floor, every time they feel<br>
Ib1 (Ic3)<br>
like it. / Because you have as much right on this earth / as they do."/

*Example 2.* Woman psychiatric inpatient: Note especially hostility inward.

(IId3)
"The most interesting part of my life is / why my sister and them want to put me
(IId3)
away / and why they want to take my kids away from me./ It all started back / when
(IId1) (Ib1)
my mother died / and it's getting worser and worser./ When I want to start drinking /
(Id2) (IIf1)
I don't pay the kids any attention./ I don't leave them alone in the house or nothing./
IIc3 IIc3
My sisters and them, they just say / I'm crazy / and make fun of me./ And they don't
IId3
want me around them. / I want them to let my life alone / and let me be happy / and
IId3 Ib2
don't make me miserable / I want to get all this drinking and stuff out of me./ They
IId3 (Ic2) Ib2
keep bothering me./ I got away from them once / and stopped drinking / and I was
Ib2
doing real good/ and then I started drinking again / and that just kept getting worser./
Ic3 Ia4
And sometimes I get to the place/I just don't care./ Sometimes it seems/like I want to
Ia4 Ib1
take my life / and I done tried that three times / and I don't want that to happen
Ic3
anymore / because I got my kids to raise up./ And I'm just in misery / and there's
IIa1
something / that I just want to get away from all the time."/

## NEUROSCIENCE APPLICATIONS OF THE GOTTSCHALK SCALES

### *Some Demographic Factors Influencing Emotions [55]*

*Anxiety and Intelligence.* An analysis of variance of the verbal anxiety scores for ninety individuals employed at the same company (Kroger) reveals a significant negative trend in anxiety with IQ level ($p < 0.05$), the lowest IQ group having the highest anxiety scores ($r = -0.28$). Since the task involves extemporaneous speaking into a microphone, an activity for which individuals with the lower IQ sometimes feel inadequate, higher shame anxiety is elicited with the lower IQ, and it is this anxiety subscale that accounts for the negative correlation with IQ.

*Anxiety and Sex Differences.* No sex differences have been found in large samples of individuals for total anxiety scores, but in six separate subscale scores for anxiety, in normative samples (173 males and 109 females), higher scores for females have been found on separation and shame anxiety as compared to males. Males have significantly higher scores than females on death and mutilation anxiety. Recently, Gottschalk [57] has reported some similarities and differences in the content of speech of boys and girls ages six to sixteen (N = 109).

*Anxiety and Age.* The relationship between age and anxiety has been examined in several samples of adults and no evidence of a linear relationship has

been found. One subscale of anxiety, however, evidently increases consistently with age. In three separate samples of people correlations of 0.25, 0.24, and 0.28 were found between age and death anxiety. Such a relationship seems to make sense, since death appears increasingly important and threatening as one grows older.

*Hostility Scores and Race.* In several series of studies, lower hostility-out scores were found in Negroes as compared to Caucasians. The difference between the hostility outward scores in black as compared to white people is more marked among females. This finding has been thought to be due either to the suppression of hostility in Negroes or to the fact that most of these verbal samples were collected by white interviewers. Studies are currently being carried out to test these hypotheses.

*Hostility Outward Scores and Sex.* There has been found a significant trend for higher hostility outward scores to be present in the five minute verbal samples of males as compared to females. This sex difference is probably related to endocrine differences, higher hostility outward probably being secondary to male sex hormones [58].

### *Psychophysiological Findings*

*Anxiety and Skin Temperature.* The higher the anxiety scores derived from our content analysis method, the greater the fall in skin temperature during the giving of the speech sample. The evidence follows.

A group of twelve high school boys sixteen to seventeen years of age gave three five minute verbal samples on each of two separate occasions while continuous measurements of skin temperature were being taken and the boys were in a hypnotic state [59]. The anxiety scores from the six verbal samples obtained under hypnosis were negatively correlated with the change in skin temperature occurring during the giving of the five minute verbal sample for each student separately, using a rank-order correlation. Ten of the twelve correlations were negative ($p < 0.04$), yielding an averaging intrasubject correlation of $-0.31$.

A corroborative study, examining the correlations between five minute sequences of two fifty minute psychotherapeutic interviews and continuous measures of skin temperature [60], revealed a significant negative correlation between the anxiety scored in each five minute interval and the change in skin temperature from the beginning to the end of each five minute interval [55].

*Studies of Relationships of Emotions to Plasma Lipids.* A natural history study [61, 62] disclosed different relationships between several types of emotions and blood lipids in a group of twenty-four men who had fasted ten to twelve hours. Findings were cross-validated in a study of a second group of twenty men. Anxiety scores had a significant positive correlation with plasma

free fatty acids (FFA) in both groups; elevated plasma free fatty acids in fasting subjects are a sign of catecholamine (adrenergic) secretion. Three types of hostility scores, however, had an essentially zero correlation with free fatty acids. More anxious men tended to have higher free fatty acid levels and sharper rises in FFA than nonanxious men in a reaction to a venipuncture and free-associating for five minutes. There was evidence for positive correlations between plasma triglyceride levels and both anxiety and hostility inward scores as well as for total hostility outward scores and levels of blood cholesterol. Stone et al. [63] found that nonathlete college students tended as a group to have higher plasma free fatty acid responses to the same anxiety levels than college students who are athletes (either on the football or swimming teams).

*Anxiety Levels and Dreams: Relation to Changes in Plasma Free Fatty Acids.* Blood samples for determination of plasma free fatty acids were obtained throughout the night by means of an indwelling venous catheter. The first blood sample was drawn at the onset of rapid eye movements (REM) and the second after fifteen minutes of these eye movements. Subjects were then awakened and asked to relate their dreams; a third sample was drawn fifteen to twenty-five minutes later. Anxiety scores derived from twenty dreams of nine subjects had significant positive correlations with changes in free fatty acids occurring during REM sleep. There were no consistently positive correlations with hostility scores derived from the same dreams. These findings indicate that anxiety aroused in dreams triggers the release of catecholamines into the circulation and these catecholamines mobilize proportional amounts of plasma free fatty acid from body fat [64].

*Anxiety Scores from Dreams and Inhibition of Penile Erection with Rapid Eye Movement (REM) Sleep.* Karacan et al. [65] studied the relationships of penile erections during episodes of rapid eye movement (REM) sleep and the anxiety scores derived from the tape-recorded dreams reported upon awakening from such periods of sleep. A statistically significant association was found between anxiety scores from such dreams and the lack of penile erections. Bell, Stroebel and Prior [66] have further demonstrated that anxiety scores derived from dream content analysis correlate with scrotal reflexes during the dream.

*Corticosteroid Levels and Hostility and Anxiety.* Five minute verbal samples, elicited by a standardized method, were analyzed for hostility and anxiety scores and correlated with corticosteroid levels of twenty-eight nonpsychotic male medical patients [55]. A correlation of +0.40 was obtained between hostility outward levels and the average plasma 17-hydroxycorticosteroid levels; the correlation was higher with the corticosteroid level obtained one hour after the five minute sample was obtained (+0.47) than that obtained one hour before this

time (+0.31). No correlation was found between plasma 17-hydroxycorticosteroids and anxiety and hostility inward scores. In Gottschalk's studies, the psychochemical relationships have been observed at relatively low levels of arousal for anxiety and other emotions, that is, in situations where there was no contrived stress and in which the data were collected in a natural history setting. These facts may account for why anxiety was not highly correlated with corticosteroid secretion.

### *Neuropsychopharmacological Studies*

*Anxiety and Hostility Levels and Phases of the Menstrual Cycle.* Five-minute verbal samples given daily by small numbers of women for periods up to three months have indicated that different women have different cycles for anxiety and hostility, depending upon their own personal reactions to the changing hormonal levels of their menstrual cycles. Across individuals, however, women as a group show a transient decrease of anxiety and hostility at the time of ovulation, possibly related to the secretion of luteinizing hormone. Also, they show an increase in anxiety premenstrually using content analysis scores [67, 68]. Recent studies [69] have shown that the birth control pill, Enovid (norethynodrel with mestranol), smoothes out and blocks the significant fluctuations in anxiety and hostility previously observed during the menstrual cycle by this content analysis method.

*Anxiety and Hostility in Response to Psychoactive Drugs.* Many studies have been carried out using this content analysis procedure in neuropsychopharmacological investigations. In almost all of these studies the double-blind, cross-over design has been used. These studies have been of considerable interest because they afford a means of influencing the neurochemical environment of the brain, and observing the behavioral and psychological effect as measured through speech.

The minor tranquilizer, chlordiazepoxide, in forty-six juvenile delinquent boys administered 20 mg of the drug, as compared to a placebo, produced significant decreases in anxiety, ambivalent hostility, and overt hostility outward forty to one hundred and twenty minutes after ingesting the chlordiazepoxide [70].

In another study [71] twenty dermatologic inpatients (ten men and ten women) were given perphenazine, 16 to 24 mg a day by mouth for one week alternating with a placebo for one week, using a double-blind, cross-over design. Analysis of the content of five minute verbal samples obtained from these patients showed a reduction of hostility outward scores with perphenazine (16-24 mg/day) in sixteen of the twenty patients ($p < 0.01$) and a decrease in anxiety scores at the elevated end of the spectrum of the anxiety scores.

Another study showed an increase in anxiety and overt hostility-out scores derived from verbal samples in patients receiving the antidepressant drug, imipramine (100-300 mg/day) as compared to a placebo [72].

Gottschalk and his co-workers [73, 74], in a double-blind, placebo-drug, cross-over study with eighteen anxious subjects demonstrated that chlordiazepoxide (20 mg by mouth) significantly reduced anxiety scores, as assessed by five-minute speech samples, only in those subjects whose chlordiazepoxide plasma concentrations exceeded 0.70 μg/ml. Hostility scores, though decreased when subjects were on chlordiazepoxide, were not significantly lowered. Interesting relationships between chlordiazepoxide plasma levels, biochemical changes, and changes in psychological state scores were, also, revealed by this study.

Gottschalk et al. [75] demonstrated that lorazepam parenterally (4-5 mg), as compared to a placebo, could significantly lower anxiety scores derived from the speech of a small sample (N = 8) of incarcerated prisoners, and a paradigm of this type was suggested as a method of screening anti-anxiety, anti-depressant, and other new psychoactive drugs.

Elliott et al. [76], using the Gottschalk content analysis procedure, demonstrated that the amount of reduction of anxiety and hostility scores of male prisoners was highly correlated with meperidine plasma levels whether administered (100 mg) by mouth or intramuscularly; in this study meperidine at this dose significantly reduced anxiety and certain hostility levels as compared to a placebo.

Propranolol (40 mg by mouth), a beta adrenergic blocking agent, or a placebo, was administered to twenty non-anxious college students in a cross-over design [77, 78]. Resting anxiety scores, derived from the content analysis of speech samples, were significantly lowered when the subjects were on propranolol, but the subjects' capacity to respond with increased anxiety under the circumstances of a stress interview was not influenced by propranolol.

Preliminary studies [79] of the relationship of thioridazine (after 4 mg/Kg by mouth to twenty-five patients) and/or mesoridazine plasma concentrations (after 2 mg/Kg intramuscularly to ten patients) in acute schizophrenic patients indicate that social alienation-personal disorganization scores (a measure of the severity of the schizophrenic syndrome) derived from speech samples are significantly decreased by this major tranquilizer within twenty-four hours and the decreases in these scores are correlated with higher plasma concentrations of this piperidine phenothiazine.

Currently, Gottschalk and Rickels [80] are studying the effects of lorazepam on anxiety and depression in psychiatric outpatients and are measuring the changes in psychiatric symptoms with self-report, rating, and the Gottschalk content analysis scales. Although many self-report and rating scales have already been used in the construct-validation studies for the Gottschalk content analysis scales, it is anticipated that this study will provide further data useful in the

comparison of these different measurement approaches in psychoactive drug studies.

Gottschalk et al. [81] have found that diphenylydantoin (400 mg/day by mouth), as compared to a placebo administered over a period of six months to forty-three imprisoned recidivist offenders produced no changes in average anxiety or hostility scores as measured from weekly five-minute speech samples.

*Achievement Striving Scores, Derived from the Content Analysis of Five-Minute Verbal Samples, as They Relate to Induced Mental Set or Psychomotor Stimulants.* One study [82] with college students has shown that telling these students that a pill would make them "more peppy and energetic" (whether the pill was a placebo, 90 mg of secobarbital, or 10 mg of dextroamphetamine) significantly increased the achievement striving scores of these students, as derived from five-minute speech samples, regardless of the medication they were administered. On the other hand, dextroamphetamine (10 mg) by mouth also significantly increased achievement striving scores, regardless of the set induced. This study demonstrated that induced mental set and drug effect can be additive.

In another study [83] similar achievement striving scores were found to be significantly higher ($p < 0.01$) in the five-minute speech samples of a large group of male prisoners ($N = 33$) at the Patuxent, Maryland, penitentiary when they had ingested dextroamphetamine (15 mg) than when they had taken a placebo capsule.

*Cognitive and Intellectual Impairment Measured from Five-Minute Samples of Speech.* Preliminary development has been carried out on a content analysis scale derivable from five-minute samples of speech, which measures the magnitude of cognitive and intellectual impairment. The purpose of this scale is to assess the magnitude of transient and reversible changes in general cognitive and intellectual function as well as irreversible changes, all due principally to brain dysfunction and minimally to transient and emotional changes in the individual [55]. At its present state of development, this content-analysis scale of cognitive and intellectual impairment is capable of differentiating patients with organic brain syndromes from nonbrain-damaged patients and individuals. Correlational studies with two measures of irreversible brain damage, the Halstead Battery [84] and the Trail Making Test [85] on a group of twenty subjects, male and female, ranging in age from forty to eighty-four showed satisfactory correlations with both of these measures (Halstead Battery, $r = 0.55$, and Trail Making Test, $r = 0.48$).

Gottschalk and Gleser [55] used these verbal content analysis scores to investigate the effects of LSD-25 and a placebo on the social alienation-personal disorganization scores of a group of college student volunteers. They showed that LSD-25 did not influence scores on the social alienation-personal

disorganization scale any more than did a placebo. But LSD-25 did significantly increase scores on the cognitive impairment scale. In another study, the same investigators examined the effects of LSD-25, Ditran (JB329), and psilocybin on behavior. In this study the effect of these psychotomimetic drugs on the dimension of cognitive-intellectual impairment was to produce more signs of cognitive impairment in the speech of normals than occurs without drugs in the speech of schizophrenics. Most recently, it has been found, using institutionalized prisoners as subjects, that LSD (50 mg) as compared to a placebo, did significantly increase scores on both the social alienation-personal disorganization and the cognitive-intellectual impairment content-analysis scales. These data suggest that, at least in some kinds of subjects, psychotomimetic drugs are more likely to induce a transient organic brain syndrome than a functional mental disorder.

Another study [86], using the cognitive-intellectual impairment scale, explored the effect of total and half body irradiation on intellectual functioning. This study provided suggestive evidence of temporary impairment of such functioning immediately after exposure to such radiation.

This particular scale, at its present stage of development, measures general intellectual functioning rather than the functioning of any specific part of the brain.

*Social Alienation-Personal Disorganization and Hope Scores Derived from Content Analysis of Speech, as Measures of Pharmacokinetic and Clinical Effects of a Single Oral Dose (4 mg/Kg) of Thioridazine to 25 Acute Schizophrenic Patients.* Twenty-five acute, medically healthy schizophrenic patients, who had not received any other psychoactive drug for at least four weeks prior to participation in this study, were given one oral dose of thioridazine (4 mg/Kg). Pre-drug social alienation-personal disorganization scores, derived from five-minute speech samples, were significantly correlated with post-drug thioridazine half-life ($r = 0.44$, $p < .03$) and area-under-curve ($0.43$, $p < .03$). Also, during the first twenty-four hours post-drug, the higher the plasma thioridazine levels the lower the social alienation-personal disorganization scores [57].

In this same study, predrug Hope scores correlated significantly with the amount of improvement in the Depression factor scores of the Overall Gorham Brief Psychiatric Rating Scales [87].

### *The Relationship of the Magnitude of Emotions and Paroxysmal Electroencephalographic Activity*

A 20-year-old single white male, Army private, an inpatient at Walter Reed Hospital in Washington, D.C. for the study of the etiology of grand mal seizures he developed during military duty in the absence of a history of head injury, was found to have frequent high amplitude bursts of slow wave paroxysmal activity

on his electroencephalogram [88]. Several hourly sessions of EEG recordings were carried out while he was interviewed. The tape-recordings of the interviews were synchronized with his EEG recordings so that the content of what he was saying could be related to the paroxysmal EEG activity. Sixteen thirty-word segments of his speech occurring just before a paroxysmal EEG event were selected from these interviews as well as sixteen thirty-word segments which were not immediately followed by abnormal EEG activity. Content-analysis technicians were asked to score these thirty-word segments for total negative affects, including negative as well as positive emotions (scores derived from the Human Relations Scales, a measure of the capacity for congenial human relationships) [89].

Paroxysmal EEG activity was found to be preceded significantly more often by a higher total affect score ($p < 0.05$) than normal EEG activity. Total anxiety ($p < 0.05$) and hostility inward ($p < 0.05$) scores were found to account principally for this finding; whereas hostility outward, ambivalent hostility, and positive affect scores were not significantly related to the abnormal paroxysmal EEG activity [90].

## REFERENCES


1. Cook WW, Medley DM: Proposed hostility and pharisaic-virtue scales for the MMPI. J Appl Psychol 38:414-18, 1954
2. Schultz SD: A differentiation of several forms of hostility by scales empirically constructed from significant items on the Minnesota Multiphasic Personality Inventory. Unpublished doctor's dissertation. Pennsylvania State College, 1954
3. Fischer MG: The prediction of assaultiveness in hospitalized mental patients. Unpublished doctor's dissertation. Pennsylvania State University, 1956
4. Siegel SM: The relationship of hostility to authoritarianism. J Abnorm Soc Psychol 52:368-73, 1956
5. Lorr M, McNair DM, Michaux WW, Raskin A: Frequency of treatment and change in psychotherapy. J Abnorm Soc Psychol 64:281-92, 1961
6. Bass BM: Development of a structured disguised personality inventory. J Appl Psychol 40:393-97, 1956
7. Buss AH, Durkee A, Baer M: The measurement of hostility in clinical situations. J Abnorm Soc Psychol 52:84-86, 1956
8. Guilford NP: Personality. New York, McGraw-Hill, 1959
9. Moldawski P: A study of personality variables in patients with skin disorders. Unpublished doctor's dissertation. Iowa State University, 1953
10. Dinwiddie TW: An application of the principle of response generalization to the prediction of aggressive responses. Unpublished doctor's dissertation. Catholic University of America, 1954
11. Smith JG: Influence of failure, expressed hostility, and stimulus characteristics on verbal learning and recognition. J Pers 22:475-93, 1954
12. Buss AH: The Psychology of Aggression. New York, John Wiley, 1961
13. Nowlis V, Nowlis HH: The description and analysis of mood. Ann NY Acad Sci 65:345-55, 1956
14. Zuckerman M: The development of an affect adjective check list for the measurement of anxiety. J Consult Psychol 24:457-62, 1960
15. Clyde DV: Clyde Mood Scale. Washington, D.C., George Washington University, 1961
16. Elizur A: Content analysis of the Rorschach with regard to anxiety and hostility. J Proj Techn 13:247-84, 1949

17. Walker RG: A comparison of clinical manifestations of hostility with Rorschach and MAPS test performance. J Proj Techn 15:444-60, 1951
18. DeVos AH: A quantitative approach to affective symbolism in Rorschach responses. J Proj Techn 16:133-50, 1952
19. Finney BC: Rorschach test correlates of assaultive behavior. J Proj Techn 19:6-17, 1955
20. Gluck MR: The relationship between hostility in the TAT and behavioral hostility. J Proj Techn 19:21-26, 1955
21. Gluck MR: Rorschach content and hostile behavior. J Consult Psychol 19:475-79, 1955
22. Murstein BI: The projection of hostility on the Rorschach and as a result of ego-threat. J Proj Techn 20:418-28, 1956
23. Stone H: The TAT aggressive content scale. J Proj Techn 20:445-52, 1956
24. Wirt RD: Ideational expression of hostile impulses. J Consult Psychol 20:185-89, 1956
25. Hafner AJ, Kaplan AM: Hostility content analysis of the Rorschach and TAT. J Proj Techn 24:137-43, 1960
26. Hurley JR: The Iowa picture interpretation test: a multiple choice version of the TAT. J Consult Psychol 19:372-76, 1955
27. McNair DM, Lorr M: An analysis of mood in neurotics. J Abnorm Soc Psychol 69:620-27, 1964
28. McNair DM, Goldstein AP, Lorr M, Cibelli LA, Roth I: Some effects of chlordiazepoxide and meprobamate with psychiatric outpatients. Psychopharmacologia 7:256-65, 1965
29. McNair DM, Fisher S, Kahn RJ, Dropplemen LF: Drug-personality interaction in intensive outpatient treatment. Arch Gen Psychiat 22:128-35, 1970
30. Lipman RS, Covi L, Rickels K, et al: Selected measures of change in outpatient drug evaluation, in Psychopharmacology: A Review of Progress, 1957-1967. Edited by Efron DH, Cole JO, Levine J, Wittenborn JR. Washington, D.C., U.S. Government Printing Office, 1968
31. Lipman RS, Rickels K, Covi L, et al: Factors of symptom distress. Arch Gen Psychiat 21:328-38, 1969
32. Pillard RC, Fisher S: Effects of chlordiazepoxide and secobarbital on film-induced anxiety. Psychopharmacologia 12:18-23, 1967
33. Uhlenhuth EH, Lipman RS, Rickels K, et al: Predicting the relief of anxiety with meprobamate. Arch Gen Psychiat 19:619-30, 1968
34. Rickels K, Lipman RS, Park LC, et al: Drug, doctor warmth, and clinic setting in the symptomatic response to minor tranquilizers. Psychopharmacologia 20:128-52, 1971
35. Downing R, Rickels K, Wittenborn JR, Mattsson NB: Interpretation of data from investigations assessing the effectiveness of psychotropic agents, in Principles and Problems in Establishing the Efficacy of Psychotropic Agents. Edited by Levine J, Schiele B, Bouthilet L. Chevy Chase, Maryland, US Public Health Service, 1971
36. Edwards AL: Social desirability and personality test construction, in Objective Approaches to Personality Assessment. Edited by Boss BM, Berg IA. New York, Van Nostrand, 1959
37. Prusoff BA, Klerman GL, Paykel ES: Concordance between clinical assessments and patients' self-report in depression. Arch Gen Psychiat 26:546-52, 1972
38. Derogatis LR, Klerman GL, Lipman RS: Anxiety states and depressive neuroses: issues in nosological discrimination. J Nerv Ment Dis 155:392-403, 1972
39. Cooper JE, Kendell RE, Gurland BJ, et al: Cross-national study of diagnosis of the mental disorders: some results from the first comparative investigation. Amer J Psychiat 125:21-29 (Suppl), 1969
40. Gurland B, Fleiss JL, Cooper JE, et al: Cross-national study of diagnosis of the mental disorders: some comparisons of diagnostic criteria from the first investigation. Amer J Psychiat 125:30-38 (Suppl), 1969
41. Gurland B, Fleiss JL, Cooper JE, et al: Cross-national study of diagnosis of mental disorders: hospital diagnoses and hospital patients in New York and London. Comprehens Psychiat 11:18-25, 1970
42. Simon RS, Fisher B, Fleiss JL, et al: Relationship between psychopathology and British–or American–oriented diagnosis. J Abnorm Psychol 78:26-29, 1971

43. Orr D: Transference and countertransference: a historical survey. J Amer Psychoanal Assoc 2:621-70, 1954
44. Gottschalk LA, Kapp FT, Ross WD, et al: Explorations in testing drugs affecting physical and mental activity. JAMA 161:1054-58, 1956
45. Gottschalk LA: Some psychoanalytic research into the communication of meaning: the quality and magnitude of psychological states. Brit J Med Psychol 44:131-47, 1971
46. Park LC, Uhlenhuth EH, Lipman RS, et al: A comparison of doctor and patient improvement ratings in a drug (meprobamate) trial. Brit J Psychiat 111:535-40, 1965
47. Paykel ES, Prusoff BA, Klerman GL, DiMascio A: Self report and clinical interview ratings in depression. Paper presented at the Ninth Annual Meeting of the ACNP, San Juan, Puerto Rico, Dec. 9-11, 1970
48. Derogatis LR, Lipman RS, Covi L, Rickels K: Neurotic symptom dimensions: as perceived by psychiatrists and patients of various social classes. Arch Gen Psychiat 24:454-64, 1971
49. Wittenborn JR: Do rating scales objectify clinical impressions? Comprehens Psychiat 8:386-92, 1967
50. Wittenborn JR: Reliability, validity, and objectivity of symptom-rating scales. J Nerv Ment Dis 154:79-87, 1972
51. Waskow I: The effects of drugs on speech: a review, in Research in Verbal Behavior and Some Neurophysiological Implications. Edited by Salzinger K, Salzinger S. New York, Academic Press, 1967
52. Marsden G: Content-analysis studies of therapeutic interviews: 1954-1964. Psychol Bull 68:298-321, 1965
53. Gottschalk LA: The application of a method of content analysis to psychotherapy research. Amer J Psychother 28:488-99, 1974
54. Gottschalk LA, Hambidge G: Verbal behavior analysis: a systematic approach to the problem of quantifying psychologic processes. J Proj Techn 19:387-409, 1955
55. Gottschalk LA, Gleser GC: The Measurement of Psychological States Through the Content Analysis of Verbal Behavior. Berkeley, University of California Press, 1969
56. Gottschalk LA, Winget CN, Gleser GC: Manual of Instructions for Using the Gottschalk-Gleser Content Analysis Scales: Anxiety, Hostility, and Social Alienation-Personal Disorganization. Berkeley, University of California Press, 1969
57. Gottschalk LA: Differences in the content of speech of girls and boys ages six to sixteen, in Studies on Childhood Psychiatric and Psychological Problems. Edited by Sankar DV. Westbury, New York, PJD Publications, 1975
58. Gottschalk LA: The measurement of hostile aggression through the content analysis of speech: some biological and interpersonal aspects, in Biology of Aggressive Behavior. Edited by Garattini S, Sigg EB. Amsterdam, Excerpta Medica Foundation, 1968
59. Gottlieb AA, Gleser GC, Gottschalk LA: Verbal and physiological responses to hypnotic suggestion of attitudes. Psychosom Med 29:172-83, 1967
60. Gottschalk LA, Springer KJ, Gleser GC: Experiments with a method of assessing the variations in intensity of certain psychological states occurring during two psychotherapeutic interviews, in Comparative Psycholinguistic Analysis of Two Psychotherapeutic Interviews. Edited by Gottschalk LA. New York, International Universities Press, 1961
61. Gottschalk LA, Cleghorn JM, Gleser GC, Iacono JM: Studies of relationships of emotions to plasma lipids. Psychosom Med 27:102-11, 1965
62. Gottschalk LA, Stone WN, Gleser GC, Iacono JM: Anxiety and plasma free fatty acid (FFA) levels. Life Sci 8:61-68, 1969
63. Stone WN, Gleser GC, Gottschalk LA, Iacono JM: Stimulus, affect and plasma free fatty acids. Psychosom Med 31:331-41, 1969
64. Gottschalk LA, Stone WN, Gleser GC, Iacono JM: Anxiety levels in dreams: relation to changes in plasma free fatty acids. Science 153:654-57, 1966
65. Karacan I, Goodenough DR, Shapiro A, Starker S: Erection cycle during sleep in relation to dream anxiety. Arch Gen Psychiat 15:183-89, 1966
66. Bell AI, Stroebel CF, Prior DD: Interdisciplinary study of the scrotal sac and testes correlating psychophysiological and psychological observations. Psychoanal Quarter 40:415-34, 1971

67. Gottschalk LA, Kaplan SM, (Cleser GC, Winget CN:) Variations in magnitudes of emotions: a method applied to anxiety and hostility during phases of the menstrual cycle. Psychosom Med 24:300-11, 1962
68. Ivey ME, Bardwick JM: Patterns of affective fluctuation in the menstrual cycle. Psychosom Med 30:336-48, 1968
69. Silbergeld S, Brast N, Noble EP: The menstrual cycle: a double-blind study of mood, behavior, and biochemical variables with Enovid and a placebo. Psychosom Med 33:411-28, 1971
70. Gleser GC, Gottschalk LA, Fox R, Lippert W: Immediate changes in affect with chlordiazepoxide. Arch Gen Psychiat 13:291-95, 1965
71. Gottschalk LA, Gleser GC, Springer KJ, et al: Effects of perphenazine on verbal behavior patterns. Arch Gen Psychiat 2:632-39, 1960
72. Gottschalk LA, Gleser GC, Wylie HW, Kaplan SM: Effects of imipramine on anxiety and hostility levels. Psychopharmacologia 7:303-10, 1965
73. Gottschalk LA, Kaplan SA: Chlordiazepoxide levels and clinical response. Comprehens Psychiat 13:519-28, 1972
74. Gottschalk LA, Noble EP, Stolzoff GE, et al: Relationships of chlordiazepoxide blood levels to psychological and biochemical responses, in Benzodiazepines. Edited by Garattini S, Mussini E, Randall LO. New York, Raven Press, 1973
75. Gottschalk LA, Elliott HW, Bates DE, Cable CG: Content analysis of speech samples to determine effect of lorazepam on anxiety. Clin Pharmacoi Ther 13:323-28, 1971
76. Elliott HW, Gottschalk LA, Uliana RL: Relationship of plasma meperidine levels to determine effect of lorazepam on anxiety. Clin Pharmacol Ther 13:323-28, 1971
77. Stone WN, Gleser GC, Gottschalk LA: Anxiety and beta adrenergic blockade. Arch Gen Psychiat 29:620-22, 1973
78. Gottschalk LA, Stone WN, Gleser GC: Peripheral versus central mechanisms accounting for anti-anxiety effect of propanolol. Psychosom Med 36:47-56, 1974
79. Gottschalk LA, Biener R, Noble EP, et al: Thioridazine plasma levels and clinical response. Comprehens Psychiat 1975 (in press)
80. Gottschalk LA, Rickels K: Collaborative studies of effects of lorazepam on anxiety and depression in psychiatric outpatients: comparison of content analysis, self-report, and rating scale scores. 1975 (in preparation)
81. Gottschalk LA, Covi L, Uliana R, Bates DE. Effect of diphenylhydantoin on anxiety and hostility in institutionalized prisoners. Comprehens Psychiat 14:503-11, 1973
82. Gottschalk LA, Gleser GC, Stone WN: Studies of psychoactive drug effects on non-psychiatric patients: measurement of affective and cognitive changes by content analysis of speech, in Psychopharmacology of the Normal Human. Edited by Evans W, Kline N. Springfield, Illinois, Charles C Thomas, 1968
83. Gottschalk LA, Bates DE, Waskow IE, et al: Effect of amphetamine or chlorpromazine on achievement striving scores derived from content analysis of speech. Comprehens Psychiat 12:430-36, 1971
84. Halstead WD: Brain and Intelligence. Chicago, University of Chicago Press, 1947
85. Reitan RM: Validity of the Trail-Making Test as an indicator of organic brain damage. Percept Mot Skills 8:271-76, 1958
86. Gottschalk LA, Kunkel RL, Wohl T, et al: Total and half body irradiation: effect on cognitive and emotional processes. Arch Gen Psychiat 21:574-80, 1969
87. Gottschalk LA: A hope scale applicable to verbal samples. Arch Gen Psychiat 30:779-85, 1974
88. Gottschalk LA: Psychologic conflict and electroencephalographic patterns: some notes on the problem of correlating changes in paroxysmal electroencephalographic patterns with psychologic conflicts. Arch Neurol Psychiat 73:656-62, 1955
89. Gottschalk LA: Some applications of the psychoanalytic concept of object relatedness: preliminary studies of a human relations scale applicable to verbal samples. Comprehens Psychiat 9:608-20, 1968
90. Gottschalk LA: An objective method of measuring psychological states associated with changes in neural function. J Biol Psychiat 4:33-49, 1972

# 30

# Anxiety and Plasma Free Fatty Acids (FFA)

L.A. Gottschalk[1], W.M. Stone[2], G.C. Gleser[3], and J.M. Iacono[4]

Department of Psychiatry and Human Behavior, College of Medicine, University of California Irvine, Irvine, California, 92664[1]; College of Medicine, University of Cincinnati and the Veterans Administration Hospital, Cincinnati, Ohio 45229[2,3] Department of Medicine and Nutrition Laboratory, College of Medicine, University of Cincinnati, Cincinnati, Ohio 45229[4].

(Received 23 September 1968; in final form 4 November 1968)

Abstract

Anxiety-fear and not hostility, as measured by an objective method using the content analysis of five-minutes of speech, can mobilize plasma free fatty acids (FFA) from fat stores in fasting subjects. The average rise in plasma FFA 20 minutes after beginning to speak is significantly correlated (positively) with the average anxiety scores derived from these speech samples. On three different days this psychochemical correlation is absent when examined a second time within 25 minutes after a previous assessment of anxiety from a speech sample.

The relationship between the arousal of emotions and changes in plasma FFA levels has been explored by a number of investigators. It has been demonstrated that FFA levels increase in response to external stress, e.g., before examinations or surgery[1]; in response to hypnotic suggestion[2]; in reaction to the pain of a venipuncture or the request to speak extemporaneously for five minutes[3,4]

Gottschalk et al.[4] have noted a peak increase in FFA values occurring 15-20 minutes after speaking extemporaneously five minutes and also a maximal correlation between FFA and anxiety-fear occurring about 20 minutes after such verbal behavior. Moreover, a significant correlation has been reported[5] between anxiety assessed by content analysis of dream reports and the amount of change occurring in plasma FFA during the first 15 minutes of dreaming, dream-time being ascertained by the rapid eye movement (REM) method[6,7]. We report here a further investigation of the temporal relationship between anxiety and plasma FFA under conditions of minimal stress involving only the experimental subjects' experiencing a venipuncture and talking extemporaneously for five minutes at two specified times during each experimental session.

## Procedure

Twelve college men, ages 18-23, were paid volunteers for this study. The students were told that the purpose of this study was to explore relationships between emotional states and changes in certain chemicals in the blood stream. They were instructed not to eat after the evening meal and were asked to report to the research laboratory at 7:15 a.m. the following morning. Each of the subjects was thus in a 12-14 hour state of fasting during a total of three morning periods of observation, usually spaced at weekly intervals.

The subject was told that at two different periods during each of the three mornings of observation, he would be asked to give a five-minute tape-recorded talk about any personal experiences of his choice. The typescripts of these tape-recorded five-minute speech samples, analyzed by a method of content analysis,[8,9,10,11] were used for the determination of emotional state. Each morning in the laboratory preceding the experimental period, the subject rested quietly for one-half hour. For the remainder of the experimental period, the sub-

ject lay supine, and his left arm was placed through a small opening in a screen. He could observe an initial venipuncture, but, thereafter he was screened from seeing further blood samples being taken. A 19-gauge needle was inserted into the antecubital vein and secured. A short piece of connecting tubing was attached to a three-way stop-cock; one end was available to withdraw blood samples without carrying out further venipunctures. The other was attached to a bottle of normal saline which was slowly infused to prevent clotting in the indwelling needle. The initial portion of each sample was discarded to assure emptying the residual saline from the connecting tubing. Blood samples were obtained at the time of venipuncture and 5, 15, 20, 25, 35, and 45 minutes later.

At each experimental session, verbal samples were obtained according to one of three schedules: A. 25 minutes after obtaining the first blood sample and 45 minutes thereafter; B. immediately after obtaining the first blood sample and 45 minutes thereafter; C. immediately after obtaining the first blood sample and 25 minutes thereafter.

The order in which the subjects followed these schedules was balanced according to a Latin Square design. Blood samples were taken before the subject gave a verbal sample, and the venipuncture needle was not withdrawn until after completion of the verbal sample at the 45-minute timing.

The verbal samples were analyzed independently for anxiety and hostility by two content-analysis technicians, who were unacquainted with the design of this research, using the method of Gottschalk and Gleser[8,9,10,11]. The blood samples were analyzed for plasma free fatty acids by the method of Dole[12] as modified by Trout _et al_.[13].

## Results

1. As in earlier studies (Gottschalk _et al_, 1965) substantial positive

correlations (r = .39, .49, .49, $p < .05$) were obtained over subjects in each of the three experimental sessions between anxiety scores derived from the first verbal sample (of the two verbal samples produced in each session) and average FFA levels throughout the 45-minute time interval, whether the first verbal sample was obtained at 0 or at 25 minutes after the venipuncture. In these instances, as well as in our previous studies, the maximal correlations between the anxiety scores obtained from any of these (first) verbal samples and plasma FFA levels occurred 15 to 25 minutes after the venipuncture, with only one exception.

Hostility scores, as in our preceding work[4,5] were not consistently correlated in the same direction with average plasma FFA levels (hostility out, r = .26, -.42, .42; hostility in, r = -.04, .26, .03).

2. Anxiety scores derived from a second verbal sample obtained during any one of the three experimental sessions did not correlate with the average FFA levels (r = .16, .08. .00) obtained during that experimental session, even though the overall average anxiety derived from second verbal samples produced during an experimental session was not appreciably different in magnitude from the average anxiety calculated from first verbal samples. For example, when a second verbal sample was obtained 25 minutes after a venipuncture (the first verbal sample having been obtained immediately following the venipuncture), the correlation between average FFA and anxiety scores decreased to .16 (using Schedule C). When the second verbal sample was obtained 45 minutes after the venipuncture, average plasma FFA and anxiety scores correlated .08 (using Schedule A) and .00 (using Schedule B).

3. The beginning of a verbal sample was followed by a rise in plasma FFA in the succeeding 20 minutes. For this group of subjects, the rise in plasma

FFA following a verbal sample was greater, on the average, than the rise of FFA following a venipuncture alone. A venipuncture alone was followed in the succeeding 20 minutes by an average increase in FFA of only 14$\mu$ Eq/L. When the verbal sample was requested immediately after the venipuncture, the corresponding increase in FFA in 20 minutes was 57$\mu$ Eq/L. A verbal sample produced 25 minutes after the venipuncture was followed by an average plasma FFA increase of 48$\mu$ Eq/L in the succeeding 20 minutes, a change which was significantly different ($p < .05$) from the average decrease of 30$\mu$ Eq/L obtained in the subsequent 20 minutes when no verbal sample was elicited 25 minutes after the venipuncture.

4. The subject's average rise in plasma FFA 20 minutes after starting to give a verbal sample (either at 0' or 25' after the venipuncture) correlated positively with his average level of anxiety assessed from these verbal samples across the entire group of subjects ($r = +.65$, $p < .05$ by analysis of covariance, between subjects). However, for any one individual, on the average, the correlation between his anxiety scores and the subsequent rise in his FFA was only +.15 (by analysis of covariance within subjects). The correlation over all subjects and experimental conditions was $r = .31$.

5. When anxiety scores derived from a verbal sample were correlated with the change in FFA in the preceding 20 minutes, rather than the subsequent 20 minutes, the correlations over subjects and over the three experimental trials were both less than .10. That is to say under the conditions of the present study, no relationship existed between anxiety scores derived from verbal samples and the changes in FFA over the preceding 20 minutes.

## Discussion

This study corroborates the findings in our previous studies [4,5] indi-

cating that anxiety, but not hostility, is correlated with plasma FFA levels in the fasting individual. In the present study we have shown, in addition, that anxiety at low levels of arousal, is significantly associated with a transient increase (up to about 20 minutes after beginning to speak) in circulating plasma FFA. Our previous findings indicate that even while asleep and before recounting a dream, the more anxiety in the dream content the higher the associated rise in plasma FFA[5]. The present study indicates that the more anxiety in five minutes of telling stories about one's life to an investigator-interviewer, the greater the increase in FFA levels.

Of additional interest in the present study is the finding that this psychochemical linkage has a relative refractory period when this specific psychochemical correlation is examined, on three different experimental days, within 25 minutes after a previous similar assessment of the anxiety level by means of a method[8,9,10,11] requiring the subject to talk for five minutes about any interesting or dramatic life experiences. The relative refractoriness of this psychochemical linkage to the average FFA level is no longer present when using the anxiety score derived from a first verbal sample obtained during an experimental session one or two weeks later. What accounts for this temporary weakening of this psychosomatic relationship within a twenty-five or forty-five minute time period is a matter of speculation. Unfortunately, our research design does not enable us to determine what the correlation would be between plasma FFA and anxiety scores from second verbal samples obtained more than one hour after an initial verbal sample.

One possible explanation for our finding is that, immediately after the system has been once activated, the humoral substances and associated neurogenic pathways that mediate between these psychologic and biochemical

variables are temporarily in a relative refractory state, and a period of recovery is necessary for this psychosomatic pathway to operate at a maximal correlation. It is known that certain circulating catecholamines are capable of mobilizing plasma free fatty acids[14,15,16] through the activation of a lipase which catalyzes the production of plasma free fatty acids from the body's fat deposits. This lipase may still be catalyzing the production of free fatty acids from body fat for some considerable time after its activation without any quantitative relationship to the circulating catecholamines or the initial releasing stimulus for these chemical substances, namely, the magnitude of anxiety.

Other investigators[17,18,19] have noted a "first-time" effect in psychoendocrine relationships due to the stress resulting from the novelty of an experimental situation. Our finding differs from the so-called "first-time" effects reported thus far in that our psychophysiological data indicate a recovery of plasma FFA responsivity to the mild variations in magnitude of anxiety generated by our subjects giving a verbal sample a week or two later in the same experimental situation.

It is clear that the interesting psychochemical relationships we have observed point to a need for further research in this area.

## References


1. M.D. BOGDONOFF and E.H. ESTES, JR. Psychosom. Med. 23,23 (1961)

2. J.R. FISHMAN, P.S. MUELLER, and V. STOEFFLER. Psychosom Med. 24,522 (1962)

3. A.J. COPPEN and A.G. HEZEY. J. Psychosom. Res. 5,56 (1960)

4. L.A. GOTTSCHALK, J.M. CLEGHORN, G.C. GLESER, and J.M. IACONO. Psychosom. Med. 27, 102 (1965)

5. L.A. GOTTSCHALK, W.N. STONE, G.C. GLESER, and J.M. IACONO Science, 153, 645-657 (1966)

6. E. ASERINSKY and N. KLEITMAN. Science, 118, 273 (1953)

7. E. ASERINSKY and N. KLEITMAN. J. Appl. Physiol. 8, 1 (1955)

8. L.A. GOTTSCHALK, K.J. SPRINGER, and G.C. GLESER, in Comparative Psycholinguistic Analysis of Two Psychotherapeutic Interviews (edit. by Gottschalk, L.A.), 115 (International Univ. Press, New York, 1961).

9. L.A. GOTTSCHALK, G.C. GLESER, AND K. J. SPRINGER, Arch. Gen. Psychiat., 9, 254 (1963)

10. G.C. GLESER, L.A. GOTTSCHALK, and K.J. SPRINGER. Arch. Gen. Psychiat., 5, 593 (1961)

11. L.A. GOTTSCHALK and G.C. GLESER , (Univ. of Calif. Press, Berkeley, Los Angeles, New York, 1969).

12. V.P. DOLE., J. Clin. Invest., 35, 150 (1956)

13. D.L. TROUT, E.H. ESTES, JR. and S.J. FRIEDBERG., J. Lipid Res., 1, 119 (1960)

14. R.S. GORDON, JR. and A. CHERKES., J. Clin. Invest. 35, 206 (1956)

15. R.J. HAVEL and A. GOLDFIEN., J. Lipid Res., 1, 102 (1960)

16. P.S. MUELLER and D. HORWITZ., J. Lipid Res. 3, 251 (1962)

17. A. HAMBURG., in Ultrastructure and Metabolism of the Nervous System, (edit. by S. Corey), (Williams and Wilkins, Baltimore, 1966).

18. J.W. MASON, J.V. BRADY and W.T. TOLSON, in Endocrine and the Central Nervous System XLVII 227 A.R.N.M.D., (Williams and Wilkins, Baltimore, 1966)

19. G. C. CURTIS, M. L. FOGEL, D. McEVOY, and C. ZARATE., Psychosom. Med., 28, 766 (1966)

This study was supported in part by PHS Grant K3-MH-14, 665 and by research funds from the V.A. Hospital, Cincinnati, Ohio.

# Stimulus, Affect, and Plasma Free Fatty Acid

WALTER N. STONE, MD, GOLDINE C. GLESER, PhD, LOUIS A. GOTTSCHALK, MD,* and JAMES M. IACONO, PhD

In healthy young men average levels of plasma free fatty acid (FFA) correlated with anxiety, which had been measured by content analysis of speech samples in an initial sample, but not with that measured in a second sample obtained during a 45-min experimental period. The correlation was significant whether the first verbal sample was obtained immediately or 25 min after the beginning of the experimental period. A second verbal sample obtained at the 25- or 45-min point in the session did not correlate with the average FFA per experimental session. Fasting FFA levels were lower in well-conditioned athletes as contrasted to nonathletes, and after 9 hr, as opposed to 14 hr, fasting. The request for and production of a verbal sample acted as a stimulus effecting a rise in FFA. This rise correlated significantly with anxiety scores derived from the verbal samples. Typically anxious subjects showed the greatest FFA responsivity. The present group of college athletes had a minimal average FFA rise following venipuncture. They also showed decreased variability in FFA with repeated experimental exposure. These findings support the hypothesis that adaptation can occur.

WHILE FREE FATTY ACIDS (FFA) are mobilized as an immediate source of energy for muscular activity,[1] they have also been shown to be related to emotional arousal accompanying certain noxious procedures not requiring muscular activity.

A number of different researchers utilizing various stimuli have shown an increase in plasma FFA with emotional arousal. In these studies, the nature of the affect was determined from the experimental procedure, the subject's reported response, or the observations of a member of the research team. Correlations of amount of emotional arousal with rise in FFA level were attempted in several instances. Cardon and Gordon[2] stressed a group of subjects with a sham traumatic biopsy procedure, and found a rise in FFA level following the stress. They suggested that fear was the dominant affect. Bogdonoff *et al*[3] described a marked rise in FFA level during a stress interview in which "all subjects became more or less heatedly involved in conversation." Bogdonoff *et al*[4] also demonstrated a rise in FFA level associated

---

From the Department of Psychiatry, University of Cincinnati College of Medicine, and the Veterans Administration Hospital, Cincinnati, Ohio.

Presented at the Annual Meeting, American Psychosomatic Society, Boston, March 31, 1968.

Received for publication April 22, 1968; final revision received April 14, 1969.

*Present address: Department of Psychiatry and Human Behavior, University of California, California College of Medicine, Irvine, Calif.

with fear of a venipuncture. A similar response occurred during an important 15-min oral examination.[5] Havel and Goldfien[6] demonstrated an increase in FFA level during an experimental procedure which they described as evoking "anxiety of discomfort." Carlson *et al*,[7] using a stress situation involving the sorting of steel balls with minimal variation in size under the pressure of time and distracting noises and lights, obtained increases in levels of FFA and an increase in urinary catecholamine excretion. Fishman *et al*[8] found variations in plasma FFA with induced hypnotic suggestion. These studies demonstrate that there is an increase in plasma FFA level with a variety of stressful situations and accompanying affect arousal.

We have been interested in differentiating the specific affects of emotional arousal associated with mobilization of FFA at low levels of stress. Utilizing a 5-min sample of free associative speech in which the affects of anxiety-fear and hostility-anger were separately quantifiable, we[9] found that the rise in FFA level following a venipuncture was correlated with anxiety in a verbal sample spoken 25 min after the venipuncture. In addition, the average levels of FFA during the experimental period were significantly correlated with anxiety scores in the verbal sample. There were no significant correlations between FFA levels or changes and hostility scores. Further corroboration of the association between rise in FFA level and arousal of anxiety, rather than hostility, was obtained by a study of plasma FFA changes during dreaming. There was a positive correlation between increase in FFA during the first 15 min of a REM cycle and anxiety scored from a dream report given immediately upon awakening after the 15-min REM period.[10]

The present studies were undertaken to explore further some of the questions raised by these findings. We wished to replicate the finding that anxiety was related to average level and rise of FFA following a venipuncture, and to determine whether a change in the time of obtaining a verbal sample would alter this relationship. We had suggested that our measure of anxiety 25 min following a venipuncture was a reflection of anxiety at the time of venipuncture. However, this was an assumption that needed further verification by obtaining verbal samples at the time of the venipuncture. In addition, we noted that in some groups there was a rise in FFA following the verbal sample and wondered if the production of the verbal sample itself acted as a stimulus for mobilizing anxiety and its biochemical correlates.

## Methods

Two experimental groups of college men, ages 18–23, were paid volunteers for these studies. They were told that the purpose of the study was to explore relationships between emotional states and changes in certain chemicals in the blood. The main group of 12 students, all members of college athletic teams, were instructed not to eat after the evening meal and were asked to report to the laboratory at 7:15 AM the following morning. Thus, all of the subjects were in a 12- to 14-hr state of fasting during three morning periods of observation.

The subject was told that on each of the three mornings he would be studied he would be asked to give a "5-min verbal sample" at two periods during the morning's trial. Preceding the experimental period, the subject rested, sitting quietly for ½ hr. For the remainder of the experimental period, the subject lay on a table and his left arm was placed through a screen. He could observe the initial venipuncture, but, thereafter, he was screened from seeing further blood samples being taken. A 19-gauge needle was placed in the antecubital vein and secured. A short piece of connecting tubing was attached to a three-way stopcock; one end was available to withdraw blood samples; the other was attached to normal saline, which was slowly infused to prevent clotting in the needle. The initial

portion of each sample was discarded to ensure the emptying of the connecting tubing. Blood samples were obtained at the time of venipuncture and at 5, 15, 20, 25, 35, and 45 min later.

At each experimental session verbal samples were obtained according to one of three schedules: Schedule A, 25 and 45 min after obtaining the first blood sample; Schedule B, immediately and 45 min after obtaining the first blood sample; Schedule C, immediately and 25 min after obtaining the first blood sample.

The order in which the subjects followed these schedules was balanced according to a Latin-square design. The blood samples were taken before the subject related each verbal sample, and the needle was not withdrawn until completion of the verbal sample at the 45-min timing.

Another group of 26 subjects—16 athletes and 10 nonathletes—followed the same experimental procedure. They were instructed to give verbal samples immediately following the venipuncture and 45 min later (Schedule B). Twelve of these subjects repeated the procedure on two occasions—once having fasted from dinner about 6:00 PM the preceding evening (a fast of 14 hr), and once having dinner and then a sandwich and milk "snack" at 11:00 PM (a fast of 9 hr). The other 14 subjects were studied on only one occasion after fasting 14 hr.

Two technicians independently analyzed the verbal samples for anxiety and hostility by the method of Gottschalk and Gleser.[11,12] The blood samples were analyzed for FFAs by the method of Dole[13] as modified by Trout *et al.*[14]

## Results

### *Average FFA and Relationship to Anxiety*

Table 1 shows the anxiety scores determined from the verbal samples and the average FFA during the 45-min period of study for the 12 subjects on each of the three experimental mornings. Anxiety scores in the first verbal sample, whether obtained at 0 or 25 min after the venipuncture, correlated positively with the *average* FFA for that experimental period. There was no difference in these correlations if the verbal sample was obtained at either of the two time periods (0 or 25 min), provided this was the initial sample of speech. Anxiety scores in the second verbal sample correlated poorly with the average level

TABLE 1. ANXIETY SCORES AND AVERAGE FFA* DETERMINATIONS FOR EACH SUBJECT ON THREE SCHEDULES

| | | *Schedule A* | | | *Schedule B* | | | *Schedule C* | | | | | |
|---|---|---|---|---|---|---|---|---|---|---|---|---|---|
| | | *Anxiety* | | | *Anxiety* | | | *Anxiety* | | | *Anxiety (av)* | | |
| *Subject No.* | *Schedule order* | *25 min* | *45 min* | *FFA* (av)* | *0 min* | *45 min* | *FFA (av)* | *0 min* | *25 min* | *FFA (av)* | *1st VS* | *2nd VS* | *FFA (av 3 sessions)* |
| 1 | BCA | 0.30 | 0.60 | 403 | 1.30 | 0.64 | 700 | 0.84 | 1.42 | 356 | 0.81 | 0.89 | 486 |
| 2 | CAB | 1.36 | 2.06 | 603 | 1.00 | 2.42 | 460 | 2.86 | 1.16 | 610 | 1.74 | 1.88 | 558 |
| 3 | CBA | 1.64 | 2.32 | 614 | 2.43 | 2.38 | 771 | 1.80 | 2.40 | 850 | 1.96 | 2.37 | 745 |
| 4 | ACB | 1.12 | 0.80 | 621 | 1.10 | 0.88 | 556 | 1.30 | 2.76 | 587 | 1.17 | 1.48 | 588 |
| 5 | BAC | 0.97 | 2.14 | 357 | 2.37 | 2.52 | 601 | 1.71 | 0.28 | 700 | 1.69 | 1.65 | 553 |
| 6 | ABC | 1.68 | 1.08 | 489 | 1.62 | 2.55 | 386 | 1.53 | 0.78 | 730 | 1.61 | 1.47 | 568 |
| 7 | ACB | 0.30 | 0.88 | 417 | 0.56 | 0.74 | 390 | 0.32 | 0.80 | 354 | 0.39 | 0.82 | 387 |
| 8 | CBA | 1.59 | 0.70 | 597 | 1.29 | 0.95 | 341 | 1.20 | 0.68 | 471 | 1.36 | 0.78 | 470 |
| 9 | BAC | 1.42 | 1.14 | 687 | 1.88 | 2.72 | 437 | 1.33 | 1.32 | 613 | 1.54 | 1.73 | 579 |
| 10 | ABC | 1.22 | 2.66 | 619 | 2.40 | 0.97 | 566 | 2.27 | 1.63 | 534 | 1.96 | 1.75 | 573 |
| 11 | BCA | 2.10 | 1.75 | 531 | 1.90 | 1.46 | 1021 | 2.20 | 1.70 | 509 | 2.07 | 1.64 | 687 |
| 12 | CAB | 1.20 | 1.76 | 334 | 1.09 | 1.21 | 341 | 2.10 | 1.60 | 429 | 1.46 | 1.52 | 368 |
| AVERAGE | | 1.24 | 1.49 | 523. | 1.58 | 1.62 | 548 | 1.62 | 1.38 | 562 | 1.48 | 1.50 | 547 |

* FFA is measured in microequivalents per liter.

TABLE 2. Product-Moment Correlations of Average FFA with Affect Scores on Verbal Samples Obtained at Different Times During Experimental Procedure

| | *Schedule A* | *Schedule B* | *Schedule C* | *Combined* |
|---|---|---|---|---|
| Anxiety | | | | |
| 0 min | — | 0.49 | 0.39 | 0.44 |
| 25 min | 0.49 | — | 0.16 | 0.29 |
| 45 min | 0.08 | 0.00 | — | −0.03 |
| Hostility out | | | | |
| 0 min | — | −0.42 | 0.26 | −0.14 |
| 25 min | 0.42 | — | 0.02 | 0.17 |
| 45 min | −0.13 | −0.19 | — | −0.16 |
| Hostility in | | | | |
| 0 min | — | 0.26 | −0.04 | 0.14 |
| 25 min | 0.03 | — | 0.07 | 0.10 |
| 45 min | 0.35 | 0.29 | — | 0.32 |
| Ambivalent hostility | | | | |
| 0 min | — | 0.20 | 0.18 | 0.18 |
| 25 min | 0.37 | — | −0.36 | −0.05 |
| 45 min | 0.07 | 0.64 | — | 0.37 |

of FFA. The correlation of anxiety with average FFA was higher when the second verbal sample was obtained 25 min rather than 45 min after the venipuncture (Table 2). Hostility scores from either the first or second verbal sample did not correlate in a consistent fashion with the average FFA.

Subjects who were more anxious at the time of their first verbal sample of a session had higher levels of FFA than those who were less anxious. Table 3 shows that for all subjects and sessions the correlation of anxiety in the initial verbal sample with average FFA was +0.52 ($p < 0.01$, one tail). Anxiety for an individual, averaged for the three experimental mornings, correlated +0.69 with average FFA ($p < 0.01$, one tail).

TABLE 3. Correlations of Average FFA with Anxiety in the Initial Verbal Sample

| *Anxiety* | *r* | *p* |
|---|---|---|
| All subjects and sessions | 0.52 | 0.01 |
| Across individuals averaged over three sessions | 0.69 | 0.01 |
| Sessions within the individual | 0.37 | 0.05 |

The correlation within the individual between levels of anxiety and FFA from one session to another was +0.37 ($p < 0.05$, one tail). The extent to which anxiety and FFA *levels* for a given individual covaried from session to session did not differ significantly from the extent to which they covaried from individual to individual.

### *Response of FFA To Stimuli of Venipuncture or Speaking and Relationship To Anxiety*

Figure 1 illustrates the variation in plasma FFA over time for the three schedules. Correlations between anxiety scores in the verbal samples and FFA at each sampling point are shown in Fig. 2. With regard to anxiety determined from the first verbal sample, it may be noted that when the venipuncture and verbal sample occurred together at Time 0′ (Schedules B and C), the maximal correlation between FFA and anxiety occurred 20–25 min later. In contrast, there was a slight decrease in the correlation between FFA and anxiety during the first 20- to 25-min period when the verbal sample was obtained 25 min after

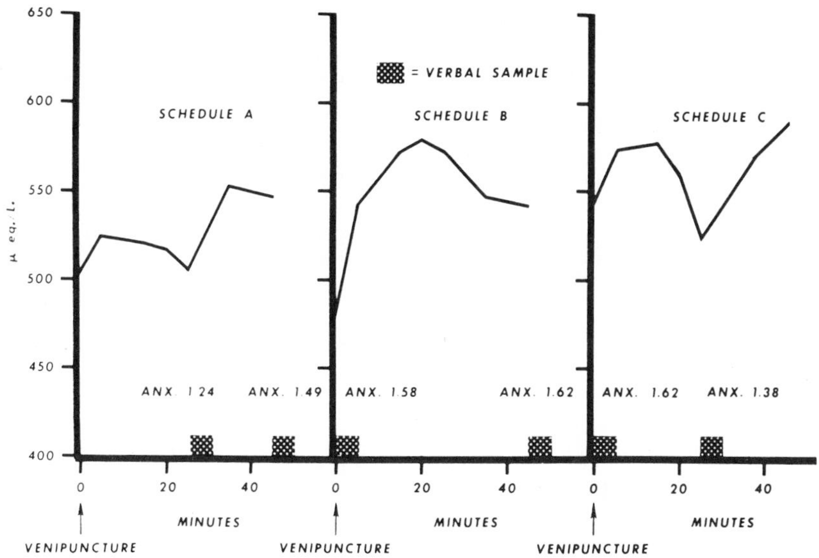


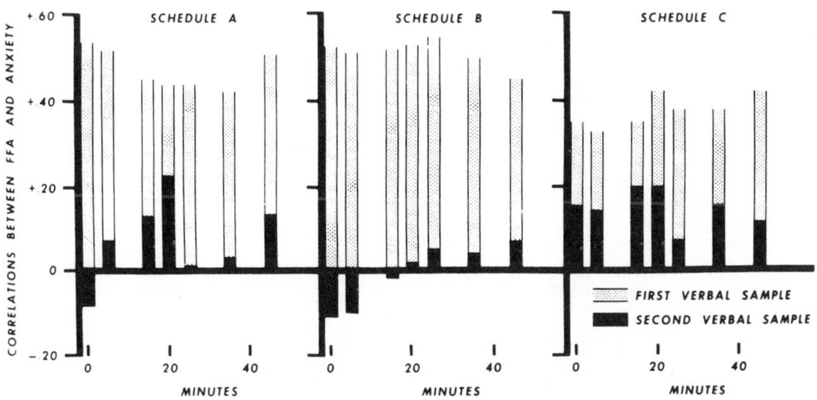


FIG 1 *(top)*. Changes in plasma free fatty acids after venipuncture and verbal sample. N = 12 for each schedule. FIG 2 *(bottom)*. Correlations between anxiety scores and free fatty acids at each sampling point for the three schedules.

the venipuncture (Schedule A). Moreover, following the verbal sample at 25 min in Schedule A, the correlations again increased to a maximum at 45 min. The correlations between FFA and anxiety in the second verbal samples did not follow a consistent pattern, and were generally below $r = +0.20$.

Three different conditions provided data with regard to changes in FFA following a stimulus: (1) venipuncture alone (one trial per subject—Schedule

TABLE 4. FFA* Determinations by Subject at Selected Times Under Each Verbal Sampling Schedule

| Subject No. | FFA: Schedule A | | | | FFA: Schedule B | | | | FFA: Schedule C | | | |
|---|---|---|---|---|---|---|---|---|---|---|---|---|
| | *0 min* | *20 min* | *25 min* | *45 min* | *0 min* | *20 min* | *25 min* | *45 min* | *0 min* | *20 min* | *25 min* | *45 min* |
| 1 | 440 | 380 | 440 | 380 | 590 | 690 | 680 | 730 | 380 | 330 | 280 | 420 |
| 2 | 560 | 620 | 620 | 620 | 430 | 460 | 450 | 490 | 650 | 560 | 550 | 690 |
| 3 | 490 | 610 | 590 | 730 | 590 | 790 | 850 | 790 | 840 | 870 | 780 | 850 |
| 4 | 570 | 570 | 540 | 670 | 470 | 560 | 580 | 600 | 530 | 570 | 510 | 630 |
| 5 | 360 | 380 | 330 | 330 | 490 | 670 | 630 | 610 | 590 | 690 | 680 | 790 |
| 6 | 470 | 490 | 510 | 510 | 380 | 410 | 430 | 370 | 670 | 750 | 690 | 670 |
| 7 | 400 | 430 | 410 | 430 | 380 | 380 | 390 | 390 | 330 | 350 | 380 | 370 |
| 8 | 590 | 570 | 560 | 610 | 360 | 370 | 370 | 290 | 530 | 430 | 420 | 500 |
| 9 | 650 | 680 | 690 | 670 | 350 | 450 | 470 | 500 | 680 | 570 | 570 | 620 |
| 10 | 570 | 670 | 550 | 630 | 500 | 620 | 590 | 530 | 520 | 550 | 510 | 540 |
| 11 | 610 | 500 | 490 | 530 | 850 | 1170 | 1070 | 910 | 470 | 530 | 490 | 550 |
| 12 | 330 | 310 | 330 | 350 | 360 | 370 | 370 | 290 | 350 | 490 | 430 | 420 |
| Average | 503.3 | 517.5 | 505.0 | 538.3 | 479.2 | 578.3 | 573.3 | 541.7 | 545.0 | 557.5 | 524.2 | 587.5 |

* Measured in microequivalents per liter.

A); (2) venipuncture and verbal sample at 0 min (two trials per subject–Schedules B and C); (3) verbal sample at 25 min (two trials per subject–Schedules A and C). One other condition served as a partial control, ie, no venipuncture or verbal sample at 25 min (one trial per subject–Schedule B). Table 4 shows the levels of FFA at 0, 20, 25, and 45 min for each subject. The changes in FFA during the two 20-min time periods (0–20 min and 25–45 min) indicate the response to the differing kinds and amount of stimulation–ie, venipuncture, venipuncture and verbal sample together, and verbal sample alone.

As shown in Table 5, on the average, the venipuncture alone did not evoke a notable change in FFA (14 μEq/liter) for the 12 subjects. However, subjects responded to the stimulus of producing a verbal sample with a definite rise in FFA. This effect can be seen when the venipuncture and verbal sample occurred at the same time or following the production of a verbal sample 25 min after the venipuncture. Under these two conditions, the rise in FFA in the succeeding 20 min was 56 and 48 μEq/liter, respectively.

For all subjects and experimental conditions that included a verbal sample followed by at least 20 min of observation (four trials for each of the 12 subjects), there was a positive correlation between the anxiety in the verbal sample and the rise in FFA in the succeeding 20 min ($r = +0.31$, $p < 0.05$; Table 6). The subjects who had higher average anxiety scores for the four trials had larger average increases in FFA ($r = +0.65$, $p < 0.01$). When individual trials for a subject were considered, the correlation between anxiety levels and increase in FFA for each of the 12 individuals across his own four experimental trials averaged only $r = +0.15$. Stated another way, over a series of four trials the more anxious the individual, the greater his average rise in FFA. However, we cannot state with any confidence, for a specific individual and trial, that because he is more anxious than usual he will have a greater increase in FFA.

TABLE 5. Average Change in FFA During the 20-Min Interval Following Either Venipuncture or Verbal Sample

| *Experiment* | *Tests (No.)* | *FFA (av change in μEq/Liter)* |
|---|---|---|
| Venipuncture (Schedule A) | 12 | +14 |
| Venipuncture + V.S. (T: 0 min Schedule B and C) | 24 | +56 |
| V.S. (T: 25 min Schedule A and C) | 24 | +48 |
| No venipuncture or V.S. (T: 25 min Schedule B) | 12 | −32 |

### *Factors Altering Relationships Between FFA and Stimuli*

Prior life experiences of the subject can affect his FFA level and response to experimental conditions.

Previous experience with the experimental procedure diminished the variability of the FFA determinations during a subsequent trial. The variability was greatest during the first trial. The correlation between variability in plasma FFA and the order of the trial was $r = -0.30$ ($p = 0.07$) for 36 trials on 12

BLE 6. Correlations of Anxiety and Change in FFA During the 20-Min Interval Following a Verbal Sample

| *Anxiety* | *r* | *p* |
|---|---|---|
| All subjects and experimental trials | 0.31 | 0.05 |
| Across individual averaged over four trials | 0.65 | 0.01 |
| Trials within the invididual | 0.15 | NS |

subjects. FFA and anxiety levels also diminished, but these trends did not approach significance.

Physical conditioning of experimental subjects significantly altered levels of FFA (Fig. 3). Of the 26 college students mentioned above, 16 were members of university football or swimming teams. The other 10 subjects were nonathletes. The athletes had significantly lower average FFA levels than did the nonathletes ($p < 0.01$) and also showed less response to a venipuncture.

The length of fasting time prior to the study affected the level and responsivity of FFA. The average level of FFA was higher ($p = 0.07$) for the trial following the 14-hr fast as compared to that following the 9-hr fast. The rise in FFA in the first 20 min after venipuncture was also greater ($p < 0.05$) for the longer fast (Fig 4).

## Discussion

Anxiety scores from the verbal sample obtained immediately following the venipuncture in the studies reported above both substantiate and extend our earlier work indicating a relationship between anxiety and FFA levels. We found a significant positive correlation between average FFA and anxiety in

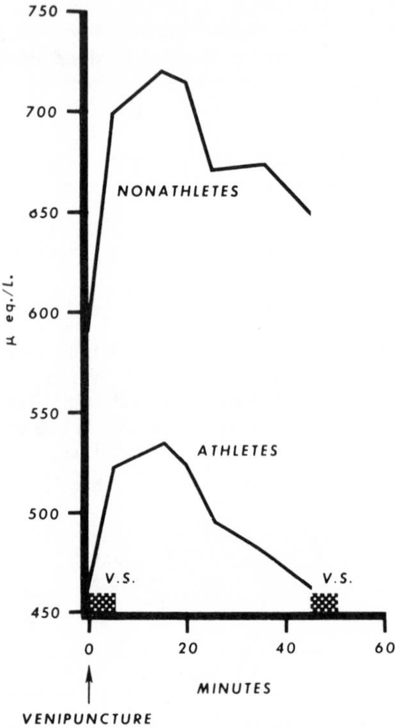


FIG 3. Comparison of free fatty acid levels and response of college athletes and nonathletes to venipuncture and verbal sample (V.S.).

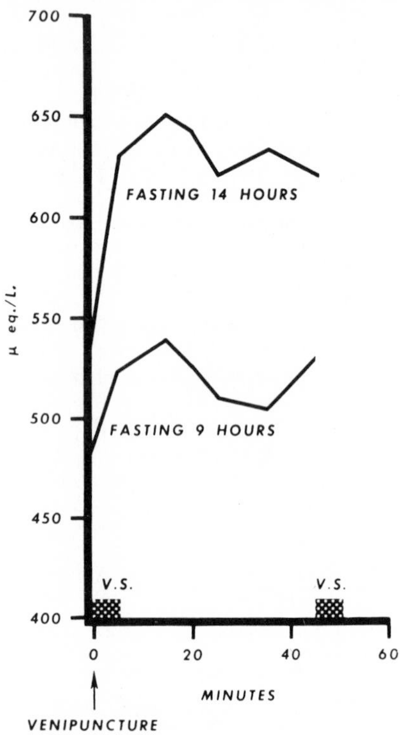


FIG 4. Free fatty acid change following venipuncture and verbal sample (*V.S.*) after 9 and 14 hr fasting.

the first verbal sample of each experimental session whether obtained at 0 or 25 min. Thus the timing of the *first* verbal sample is not critical to the relationship.

Once a verbal sample had been produced, some alteration apparently occurred in the relationship between anxiety and plasma FFA levels within a session, as indicated by the nonsignificant correlation between anxiety scores in a second verbal sample and average FFA within the 45-min study period. We did not find that anxiety scores were necessarily less the second time a subject gave a verbal sample during any one experimental session. In fact, the average anxiety in the first and second verbal samples of a session was essentially equal for the group as a whole, although the scores for any particular subject may have differed substantially. There was only a low positive correlation between successive anxiety scores within an experimental session, but the two scores were not completely unrelated.

These findings do not specify the mechanism by which anxiety in the initial verbal sample relates to average FFA, but may serve as additional indirect support for the hypothesis that our measure of anxiety is directly related with the amount to which certain catecholamines are secreted into the circulation and serve to mobilize FFA from body fat depots. For the present, we assume, until more concrete evidence can be obtained, that the change in anxiety that takes place in the 25 min. between first and second verbal samples during an experimental session, coupled with an ongoing chain of biochemical events set in motion by anxiety measured in the first verbal sample, accounts for the lack of correlation between anxiety scores derived from *second* verbal samples and the average plasma FFA per session. Anxiety scores derived from first verbal samples of these same subjects on subsequent experimental days *did* correlate significantly with the average plasma FFA obtained on those specific days. Thus, the reduction in correlation is transient.

Levels of plasma FFA were influenced by factors other than anxiety. The selection of homogeneous populations subjected to identical pre-experimental conditions was crucial when the effects of the experimental procedures were being studied. Two groups of subjects who seemed similar except for physical conditioning through rigorous athletic participation were shown to have significantly different levels of FFA (Fig 3). Similarly, variation of the prestudy fasting period in the 9- to 14-hr range affected the levels of FFA (Fig 4). Gordon and Cherkes[15] and Albrink and Neuwirth[16] also have reported gradual increases in FFA levels with lengthening periods of fasting. Failure to control carefully for dietary factors and physical conditioning may obscure subtle relationships between emotions and plasma FFA.

The present study extended and refined some of our previous findings. First, our impression that the act of talking—ie, producing a verbal sample itself—acts as an arousal process or stimulus activating a rise in plasma FFA level in most subjects, was verified. Secondly, we found that there are some types of subjects who do not show a FFA response to a venipuncture: For the subjects in the present study there was only a small rise in FFA values on the average in the 20-min period following venipuncture alone (Schedule A), despite the fact that the anxiety scores obtained from verbal samples 25 min after the venipuncture were about equivalent to those obtained by subjects in our previously published studies. Furthermore, using this schedule (A), the individual changes in plasma FFA in the 20 min following the venipuncture were uncorrelated with anxiety scores obtained from the first verbal sample at

25 min. These findings taken together imply an extremely limited differential FFA response to venipuncture. Evidently the subjects, all of whom were well-conditioned varsity athletes, had had many experiences with physical contact and pain and hence were possibly adapted to a minor pain stimulus such as the venipuncture encountered in this experimental situation. On the other hand, the lower levels of FFA responsivity of our athletic subjects could be less a matter of adaptive learning and more a matter of differential rates of lipid metabolism, as compared to nonathletes, on the basis of their muscle mass and their state of physical conditioning.

According to the work of Sapira and Shapiro,[17] who measured cardiovascular reactivity, changes in plasma FFA and catecholamine excretion in response to stressful stimuli of a cold pressor test and ischemic pain tend to support the adaptation theory. They found that adrenergic responses, as measured by plasma FFA and catecholamine excretion, decreased with repetition of the same stimulus, while cardiovascular responses remained constant. Although these authors had no direct measure of affect arousal they suggested that repetition of the same stimulus might evoke reduced emotional response which would be reflected in the decrease in catecholamine excretion and lesser rise in FFA. For the most part, their hypothesis was not supported by our data, since neither the anxiety nor FFA levels of our subjects decreased significantly over the three experimental trials. On the other hand, the variability of plasma FFA determinations per session decreased with repeated experimental exposure.

## Summary

In healthy young men, average levels of plasma FFA correlated with anxiety measured by content analysis of speech samples in an initial sample, but not with that measured in a second sample obtained during a 45-min experimental period. The correlation was significant whether the first verbal sample was obtained immediately or 25 min after the beginning of the experimental period. A second verbal sample obtained at the 25- or 45-min point in the session did not correlate with the average FFA per experimental session.

Fasting FFA levels were lower in well-conditioned athletes as contrasted to nonathletes; 9 as opposed to 14 hrs fasting was associated with a lower average plasma FFA level.

The request for and production of a speech sample was followed by a rise in the FFA level in the succeeding 20 min for most of these subjects. The subject's average FFA level increase correlated significantly with the average of his anxiety scores derived from verbal samples produced immediately prior to the rise. Thus, the more typically anxious subjects tended to show the most FFA responsivity.

The present group of college varsity athletes, on the average, did not show a FFA rise following the venipuncture as had our subjects in previously published studies. Also there was a significant decrease in the variability of plasma FFA over the three experimental sessions in which each subject participated. These findings support the hypothesis suggested by Sapira and Shapiro of an adaptive mechanism that decreases the responsivity of plasma FFA with repetition of the same stimulus.

*Veterans Administration Hospital*
*3200 Vine St*
*Cincinnati, Ohio 45220*

## References

1. Steinberg, D. Dynamics of FFA mobilization and utilization. *Prog Biochem Pharmacol 3:*139, 1967.

# A CONTEXT ANALYSIS OF PSYCHOLOGICAL STATES PRIOR TO PETIT MAL EEG PAROXYSMS

LESTER LUBORSKY, PH.D.,[1] JOHN P. DOCHERTY, M.D.,[2] THOMAS C. TODD, PH.D.,[3] PETER H. KNAPP, M.D.,[4] ALLAN F. MIRSKY, PH.D.,[4] AND LOUIS A. GOTTSCHALK, M.D.[5]

This is the first report in the literature of an application of the rigorous symptom-context method for determining the nature of the psychological antecedents of petit mal EEG paroxysmal activity. The activity is defined by the presence of a 3 cycle/second spike and wave on the EEG which is recorded concurrently while the patient is speaking his thoughts freely during interviews. The content of the patient's speech before each petit mal episode is compared with the content of speech during non-paroxysmal periods. Three petit mal patients were examined in this way for four sessions each. (Total petit mal EEG paroxysms for patient no. 1 were 19, patient no. 2 were 25, and patient no. 3 were 55.) For the first patient, strong psychological antecedents were found before petit mal EEG paroxysms as compared with comparison periods from the same patient. These consisted of such usual negative affects as feeling depressed and blocked. For the two other patients, only a few psychological antecedents discriminated significantly and these were not of the same type across the three patients. We conclude that the patients differ in amount and type of psychological antecedents. The differences may be attributed to differences in the type of petit mal and/or differences in the psychological component to the petit mal. The differences among the patients are probably not related to the average length of the paroxysms since we have shown that the relationships with the duration were generally insignificant. The paroxysms occurred more often during the patient's silence than during the patient's speech (for two of the three patients)—talking probably requires more focused attention than silence; more focused attention or activity tends to reduce these episodes.

The "broad context" in which symptoms emerge has been the focus of much psychosomatic research. Such research tends to be retrospective, to consider symptoms with gradual or undefined point of onset, and to deal with stable personality or social variables. A good example is the relating of general level of "life stress" to the amount of respiratory illness (9). In contrast, "immediate context" studies, such as

[1] Professor of Psychology in Psychiatry, University of Pennsylvania School of Medicine, 207 Piersol Building, Philadelphia, Pennsylvania 19104.

This report is an expansion of one presented at the annual meeting of the American Psychosomatic Society in Washington, D.C., March 20–22, 1970. Support in part was provided by United States Public Health Service Research Grant MH-15442, Research Scientist Award MH-40710 to Dr. Luborsky, Research Scientist Award MH-14915 to Dr. Mirsky, and Postdoctoral Research Fellowship Award MH-37854 to Dr. Todd.

We are grateful for the suggestions and help of Drs. John Paul Brady, Reuben Kron, Aaron Katcher, Stuart Rosenthal, Jim Mintz, Henry Bachrach, and Roberta B. Harvey, Marilyn Johnson, Freda M. Greene, and Marjorie Cohen.

[2] Department of Psychiatry, Yale University School of Medicine, New Haven, Connecticut.

[3] Philadelphia Child Guidance Clinic, Philadelphia, Pennsylvania.

[4] Department of Psychiatry, Boston University School of Medicine, Boston, Massachusetts.

[5] Department of Psychiatry and Human Behavior, University of California College of Medicine, Irvine, California.

those on momentary forgetting (11), include symptoms having a well defined point of onset, and the variables investigated are those which may fluctuate from moment to moment. An extensive review of the psychosomatic literature revealed only 23 of such studies (13).

The best controlled of the immediate context studies employ the "symptom-context method" (11, 12) consisting of recordings of a patient's behavior just before, during, and just after a symptom's appearance. These "symptom" data are then compared with those of matched comparison periods in which the symptom did not occur—in this way we can estimate the unique characteristics of the context immediately surrounding the symptom.

So far, only three recurrent symptoms have been studied by the symptom-context method: momentary forgetting, stomach pain, and migraine headache. For all three it could be argued that a bias was introduced by dependence upon the patient's report for learning of the occurrence of the symptom—a patient at times *has* the option of not reporting the symptom, or reporting it after a delay. Also, because such symptoms are known to the observer only when reported, some of the uniformities discovered might reflect the beginnings of the intention to report, not something more integral to the symptom. There may also be a lag in reporting, so that a context could reflect the *effects* of a symptom, rather than its antecedents. Ideally then, for the application of this method: a) the symptom should be independently observable; b) its duration should be clearly demarcated; and c) its frequency of occurrence should be sufficient to allow for statistical treatment of the data.

The study of seizure disorder meets these methodological requirements. The attacks have a clear onset and can be monitored physiologically. The EEG may be used to register the symptom reliably so that we are not dependent upon the patient's report. In fact, the attack often occurs without the awareness of either the patient or the observer.

Applying the symptom-context method to petit mal epilepsy is especially necessary, in view of the opposing opinions about the presence of psychological antecedents in episodes of petit mal. Many of the clinical neurologists and some psychophysiologists (15, 21, 22) tend to conclude that psychological antecedents are not present or not important with petit mal.

On the contrary, much psychosomatic research maintains that seizure disorders of many kinds are psychosomatic entities (1, 2, 7, 20). Also, the fact that experimentally induced seizures have been shown to be amenable to classical conditioning suggests that seizures might be precipitated by psychological variables (10, 17, 18). In fact, investigators of petit mal epilepsy in the last 20 years have tried to capture these prior psychological states—with some clinical success, but without adequate controls. Seven studies deal with the immediate onset conditions of petit mal (or similar) episodes (2-6, 23, 24). They report prior affects such as rage, depression, blocking of emotion, unfocused attention, frustration, passivity, lack of control, anxiety, and helplessness. Inspection of this list suggests that two types of psychological states may be crucial: a) an increase in some form of negative affect; and b) an increase of unfocused attention of the form that may exist during reverie. Unfortunately, in every study only one judge—a therapist or a researcher—was responsible for deciding which affect was present, and there was no control by comparison with nonsymptom occasions.

Neither opinion, either for or against the presence of significant psychological antecedents of petit mal, has a proper evidential basis. Because of the rigor of the symptom-context method, our results should have special power for deciding whether some, all, or no patients have such psychological antecedents before petit mal.

Our study consists primarily of an examination of the psychological antecedents of three patients' petit mal EEG paroxysms followed by a brief discussion of two additional factors which might influence the psychological antecedents: the appearance of the EEG epileptic activity during speech *vs.* during silence, and the length of the episode.

## *Procedures*

This study is based on the interview protocols of three patients with recurrent EEG paroxysms clearly marked in their actual positions in the interview. The criterion for a petit mal EEG paroxysm was the presence on the EEG of a period of 3 cycle/second spike and wave activity. To be precise, our focus of study is on the correlates of *preparoxysmal EEG activity.* The three patients are Mr. ES from Dr. Louis Gottschalk, and Miss NC and Mr. ST from Dr. Peter Knapp.

For each patient the EEG paroxysmal contexts in four sessions were analyzed. Segments of the patient's words before EEG paroxysms ("symptom" segments) were selected. For purposes of comparison, segments of the patient's words which were not near paroxysmal activity ("comparison" segments) were randomly selected. Three methods of evaluating the segments were applied for each patient: a) free or intuitive judgments; b) clinical ratings of variables; c) objective scoring of variables. These methods will be described in the course of presenting the first patient, Mr. ES. Our aims in using a variety of methods were: a) to try to assess the essential ingredients of the psychological antecedents of petit mal; and b) to learn more about what each method can contribute to this kind of research on symptom formation. We were especially interested in the judge's ability to distinguish between symptom and comparison segments when he was free to generate his own hypotheses in comparison with his performance when he was given a specific quality to judge.

### MR. ES

Mr. ES had been intensively studied 19 years ago; the description of the patient is taken mainly from that study[6] (6).

"The patient was a 24-year-old Army private of Polish-Catholic origin . . . his first seizure occurred at the age of 23, when he was returning to his military post after a 3-day leave. It was exceedingly important to him never to make a mistake, break rules, or provoke displeasure in persons of authority. In the service of such strong deference and obedience to authority, he anxiously hurried back to his post and checked in several seconds before the 'deadline.' Fifteen minutes later he had his first epileptic seizure, a grand mal spell. He had another seizure 2 days later, and on the next day still another one. . . . On admission to the hospital he was agitated, very tense, and depressed. He had somatic symptoms involving every body system. Among other things he complained of hypersalivation, of hearing difficulty, of disturbances of the sense of taste and smell. He said that he had episodes during which he felt 'pins and needles' from the neck down, and during which he felt that he could not move his hands, wherever he put them—on his lap, on his chest, or so on. He had a persistent feeling he was doomed to die suddenly . . ." (p. 656).

Neurological and medical studies, including blood counts, urinalyses, cerebrospinal fluid studies, a glucose tolerance test, skull X-rays, and pneumoencephalogram, were all within normal limits. Repeated electroencephalographic studies revealed bursts of symmetrical and synchronous 3 cycle/second spike and wave activity. In addition, there was clear evidence of theta activity in the background, predominantly on the right side, with some indication of a right temporal focus of abnormality (Figure 1).

"His seizures occurred three to four times per week during the first 2 months of hospitalization, although he was given diphenylhydantoin sodium and phenobarbitol. Seizures were most frequently nocturnal and began to occur three to six times in rapid succession. Then they gradually decreased in frequency over the next

[6] Reprinted by permission from the A.M.A. Arch. Neurol. Psychiatry, *73:* 656–662, 1955, and the author.

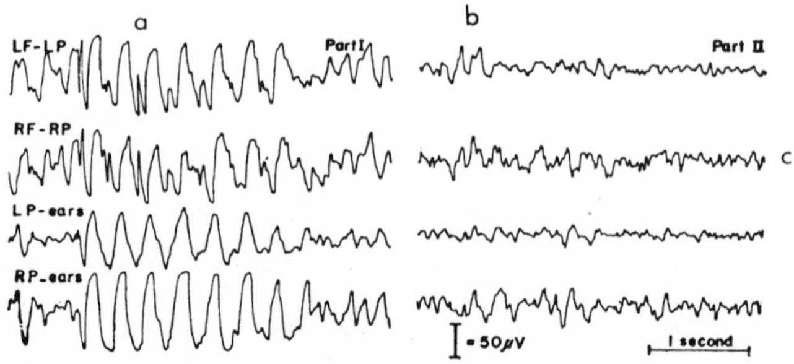


FIG. 1. EEG paroxysmal brain wave activity (Mr. ES). *Part I.* Pt. resting with eyes closed. *Part II.* Eyes closed. Pt. counting silently. *a.* This is indubitably 3/second spike and wave activity. *b.* This is theta activity (about 5 cps). *c.* This is, in general, compatible with a right-sided slow wave predominance but from this sample one could not argue that there was a right *temporal* predominance.

month, and none occurred during the last two months of observation" (p. 657).

Because this patient's "seizures," except for his grand mal attacks, were manifest only on the EEG but not clinically, they will be referred to more precisely as "EEG paroxysmal" states, or "paroxysms."

"Personality studies revealed he was a perfectionist, scrupulous, very religious young man. He was exceedingly dependent on his parents, obsessively preoccupied with the fear he might disappoint or hurt his mother. He emphasized that his mother taught him the 'difference between right and wrong,' and he said that he became anxious when he did not live up to the standards she inculcated in him. He was boastful of what he considered his exemplary behavior—absolutely no smoking, no drinking, no sex—and he was scornful of soldiers more self-indulgent in these respects. His precollege occupational interests had been in becoming either a mortician or a clergyman. He was operating a successful mortuary business before being drafted into military service.

During his hospitalization, lasting 5 months, studies were made of psychological factors associated with the occurrence of paroxysmal electroencephalographic patterns. He was interviewed during six electroencephalographic recordings, the interviews occurring in the middle period of each 45 to 60 minutes of recording, while he was resting supine with eyes closed.

The activity of talking with someone in itself was found to significantly reduce the frequency of paroxysms (greater than a duration of 1 second) of high voltage slow activity in this patient. The effect of other types of external and internal stimuli on the frequency of paroxysmal electroencephalographic activity was observed. Repeated external auditory stimuli—loud and startling sounds, noises, or music—had no effect whatsoever on the frequency of paroxysms . . . Having the subject count silently by 3's eliminated the paroxysms completely for a period of 10 minutes.

Since, for this subject, talking with his physician and doing on request silent simple arithmetic significantly 'suppressed' the frequency of his slow wave paroxysms, it was a problem to determine whether or not any specific emotional conflicts might either suppress or provoke abnormal cerebral electrical discharges. At no time did talking or silent counting increase the frequency of paroxysms beyond the rate they occurred when he was awake but silent. In order to determine the relationship of psychologic conflicts and the rate of electroencephalographic paroxysms in this patient, it was necessary to find out whether a transient release from the usual suppressor effect of verbal communication occurred at any specific times during the interviews. That is, were there to be found any common themes, conflicts, or situations, expressed in the patient's verbalizations or in the interactions of the patient and the interviewer, preceding the occurrence of a slow wave burst in his electroencephalogram?" (p. 657).

Further clues about the onset conditions were suggested by the patient's description of a severe "spell": "Recently I bit my tongue something terrible. When I wake up from a spell I have a headache and my arms hurt. Most of the spells occur when I'm asleep. It seems that if I get excited or worked up, 1 or 2 days later I get a spell. I notice I'm very irritable lately. I make scenes of little things. I catch myself doing this and I wonder why. I get sorry for hollering at people." One hypothesis, then, was that when the patient gets "excited" or angry at others as well as at himself, he may be more prone to the attacks.

"Study of electronic tape-recorded interviews with this patient, synchronized with the electroencephalographic record, indicated that *slow wave paroxysms* occurred roughly *within 30 seconds* after he expressed a fear of being criticized adversely or repudiated or after he criticized and repudiated himself. The thought of repudiation of himself by his mother and father, God, the Army, doctors, nurses, or the investigator appeared to be just as commonly followed by a slow wave paroxysm. The effect of this psychologic state (presumably severe separation anxiety) appeared to eliminate transiently the suppressing effect of verbal communication on his abnormal electroencephalographic slow wave bursts. Furthermore, actual adverse criticism of the patient by the investigator or another person was found to be followed by the slow paroxysmal cerebral electrical activity during certain recording sessions; no such paroxysmal activity occurred for 20 minutes of blander interviewing before and after such criticism.

Without any changes in anticonvulsant medication, the total frequency of this patient's paroxysms of cerebral dysrhythmia decreased over a period of 2 months, when the investigator attempted to help him feel acceptable and likeable. And when the patient's self-criticism was not allayed, but abetted, the paroxysmal rate tended to increase. Concomitantly, with a decrease in the brief seizure patterns observed in the electroencephalograms, the patient's clinical status improved. No changes in seizure frequency were observed after he was taken off of anticonvulsant medication during the third month of hospitalization" (p. 658).

The present reanalysis of data was based upon verbatim transcripts of four interviews with concurrent recording of the EEG from which 19 symptom segments and 19 comparison segments were extracted. Most symptom segments contain about 30 patient-words preceding EEG paroxysmal activity; each comparison segment contains 30 words preceding a randomly selected control point when no such activity was present. The following is a sample of the first four symptom segments containing a sufficient number of patient-words for the analyses.

NO. 1 (NO. 13)

Mr. ES: I cried and cried and cried. In fact, I cried most of the time. Some nurses are so irritable, they make everybody want to hate them.

NO. 2 (NO. 14)

T: You get so mad at people, you could almost kill them.

Mr. ES: I guess I don't appreciate life; I guess I just want it to be a basket of roses.

NO. 3 (NO. 16)

Mr. ES: Mother is looking forward to my getting well. I do, but it hurts to read the letters of my mother and my sister. It's hard to read sister's letters.

NO. 4 (NO. 17)

Mr. ES: She was sick before I came home.

T: How do you feel about sister?

Mr. ES: Sister and I were always close. I know she is *always* sincere in what she says.

*Free or intuitive judgments.* The set of 38 segments was first given to each of five independent judges with a "free" instruction: "The patient whose interview is included in these segments was subject to short EEG paroxysmal episodes lasting from 1 second to a few seconds. His interview was conducted while EEG leads were attached, so that the EEG paroxysmal ac-

tivity could be recorded. Decide for each segment whether it is one that came before a symptom (symptom segment) or before a comparison point when no such activity was present on the EEG (comparison segment). Half of these 38 segments are symptom segments and half are comparison segments. Please proceed by first dividing the 38 into 19 symptom and 19 comparison segments, and then rank all 38, with the top one the most certain to have come before a symptom, and the 38th the most certain to be a comparison segment."

Since presence of affect is the most common hypothesis in the literature and commonly reported by judges, and by Gottschalk (6), the judge was then given the same set of segments with the "affect-clue" instruction: "Please do the same ranking, but this time rank it in terms of the following clue—*the presence of high negative affect, especially involving anger or criticism to others or self.*"

Finally, the judge was given the complete transcripts of the four interviews with a small blank at the end of each of the 38 points. The instructions were the same as the "affect" instructions.

These procedural variations were aimed at learning the factors governing the judgment process. We could compare: a) the basic global free instruction; b) the "affect-clue" instruction; c) the same "affect" instruction applied after the judge read the entire session (to learn whether knowing the entire session offers any advantage over knowing only the segment); d) the above three variations, but using only the judges' two-category judgments of symptom *vs.* comparison (to check our assumption that ranking all segments would be better than a two-category judgment).

Accuracy of judgments (*i.e.*, in discriminating symptom from nonsymptom comparison segments) for all three combined conditions was significant at the .01 level.[7] The "affect instruction" and "affect instruction with entire sessions" were each significant at the .01 level, but the "free instruction" ratings by themselves were not significant.[8] There was no significant difference among conditions. When questioned after the free instruction ranking, most judges seemed to have relied on the amount of negative affect in making their ratings. It is of special interest that knowing the whole session did not significantly improve their judgments. Finally, the two-category judgments involve some loss of information (a finding which has been reported in other research).[9]

*Clinical ratings on 18 variables.* Three bases were important in the selection: a) some were precursors of the three symptoms studied so far by the symptom-context method; b) others were from a review of studies of the immediate antecedents of a variety of symptoms; c) several were from a review of studies of the patient's state immediately before petit mal attacks.

Each of the 38 segments was rated on the 18 variables by two judges independently (HB and MJ) on a 5-point scale from 1 (little) to 5 (much).

A high percentage of these variables differentiated symptom from comparison segments at the 5 per cent level or better (Table 1) despite difficulties of rating such short segments and despite the consequently low reliabilities on some variables (for example, separation anxiety, feeling blocked by therapist, lack of control, new attitude, tiredness, attention difficulty). These vari-

[7] Results for five judges were analyzed, using a repeated measurements analysis of variance design comparing differences among conditions to the judges × conditions interaction. (This error term has 8 *df.*)

[8] It may be objected that the increase in score (nonsignificant) from the free instruction task to the affect instruction task merely represents a practice effect. Anticipating this problem, we had two judges repeat the free instruction task before proceeding to the affect task, and they showed no change in score. In addition, the scores on the third task, the in-context rating, showed no improvement over the second task with the affect instruction.

[9] *E.g.*, Lincoln, Kristina. An intercorrelational study of some factors relating to therapeutic sensitivity. Dissertation, Grad. School of Arts and Sciences, Dept. of Psychology, New York University, June, 1971. The ranking judgments for affect instructions using entire sessions were significantly better than the two-category judgments for the same condition.

TABLE 1

*Summary of Differentiating Variables between Symptom Segments vs. Comparison Segments*

| More Before EEG-Paroxysmal Activity | | More Before EEG-Nonparoxysmal Activity | |
|---|---|---|---|
| Mr. ES | p-value | Miss NC | p-value |
| Blocked | .002 | Hostility | .05 |
| Depression | .002 | Hostility-out (G-G) | (.10) |
| Involvement with T | .002 | Speech disturbance (Mahl) | .05 |
| Hostility | .01 | | |
| Reference to T | .01 | Mr. ST | |
| Anxiety | .05 | | |
| Helplessness | .05 | Ambivalent hostility (G-G) | .025 |
| Hopelessness | .05 | | |
| Blocked by T | .05 | | |
| Lack of control | .05 | | |
| Guilt | .05 | | |
| Hostility to T | .05 | | |
| Anxiety (Gottschalk-Gleser) | .05 | | |
| Hostility-in (G-G) | .01 | | |
| Schizophenic (G-G) | .05 | | |
| Mr. ST | | | |
| Cognitive disturbance (LL) | .01 | | |

ables with low reliability were mainly ones where both raters saw little evidence of the variable. The three most differentiating variables (.002 level) were: feeling blocked, depression, and involvement with therapist. Variables which differentiated at the .01 level were: hostility to therapist, and at any explicit reference to the therapist. At the .05 level were: anxiety, helplessness, hopelessness, feeling blocked by the therapist, lack of control, guilt, hostility to therapist. (The depressive and hostile content is obvious on inspection of the four examples provided above.)

*Objective scoring on seven variables.* A precise scoring of the affect preceding petit mal EEG paroxysms is offered by Gottschalk and Gleser's (8) measures of negative affect—anxiety, hostility-out, hostility-in, and ambivalent hostility. These measures are based upon independent judges' objective scoring of the patient's words alone. Table 1 includes results of a comparison of 16 preparoxysmal and 16 nonpreparoxysmal verbal samples. Cognitive disturbance (Luborsky, in preparation) and speech disturbance (14) were also tried. (Three of the 19 samples had to be dropped because of the insufficient number of words.) We learned from these analyses that total negative affect, anxiety, and hostility-in were significant at the .05 level. Hostility-out and ambivalent hostility did not reach significant levels. Discrimination between preparoxysmal verbal samples was improved by including positive affects (Gottschalk Human Relations Scale) along with negative affect ($p < .01$). Positive affect by itself showed a slight trend ($p < .10$). This supports the hypothesis that high affect, positive or negative, tends to be associated with EEG paroxysmal activity. In conclusion, the Gottschalk measures provide a more precise statement than we had—a confirmation that high negative affect was indeed distinguishing, but specifically it was anxiety and hostility-in that were most relevant.[10]

[10] Because so many significant findings emerged for Mr. ES, it is reasonable to ask to what extent these results represent some common cluster of variables. A cluster analysis was performed on the correlations among the 24 rated variables and the average ratings from the three conditions of instruction. Two strong and distinct clusters emerged. One "negative affect" cluster (median

*Conclusions about Mr. ES.*

1. By rating and objective scoring methods, the differentiation is large, mainly on the types of negative affect variables preceding a variety of psychosomatic symptoms (13). It is informative to compare our findings with those from the clinical analysis. Gottschalk (6, p. 658) had concluded that "slow wave paroxysms occurred within 30 seconds after he expressed a fear of being criticized adversely or repudiated, or after he criticized and repudiated himself." Furthermore, Gottschalk (6, p. 658) noted that "adverse criticism of the patient by the investigator or another person was found to be followed by paroxysmal cerebral electrical activity. . . ." Our independent symptom-context analyses confirm that increased expression of affect precedes the paroxysmal EEG activity. *Negative affect,* generally especially anger or criticism to others or the self, is significantly associated with EEG paroxysms. Specifically in terms of the Gottschalk-Gleser measures, *high negative affect is relevant, but especially high anxiety and hostility-in.* High positive affect also tends to be associated with onset of EEG paroxysms. In sum, Gottschalk's (6) clinical impression, based on paying attention to the content of patients' verbalizations immediately before the abnormal EEG activity, was corroborated and precisely specified in kind and amount, but also expanded by virtue of the present method.

2. Judgments made from the contents of the entire interviews are not significantly better than those made from the segments alone *on these variables.*[11] This is a finding of interest in terms of the amount of information helpful in making clinical judgments of interview data.

3. A methodological finding of interest is that ranking according to degree of certainty yielded somewhat greater differentiation than simple, dichotomous judgment of the segments, but only when the judge had ample information upon which to base his judgment (as provided by the total session context).

4. Judges can quickly and easily evaluate the context preceding the onset of an attack with highly significant differentiation of these contexts from control (comparison) contexts. This differentiation can be achieved by providing the judges with the affect-clue instruction, but cannot when they are using free or intuitive judgment.

### MISS NC

Both Miss NC and Mr. ST were studied at Boston University Medical Center. The interviews were scheduled for the same time of day, each day. The patients made no changes in their medical routines and appeared to follow instructions about not eating breakfast. During the interviews they were recumbent or semirecumbent, with the interviewer seated at about a 45-degree angle to the left and front. Patients could move their extremities, provided no contact was made with the EEG electrodes. After a preliminary period in their first interview, they were instructed to close their eyes in order to decrease the amount of artifact in the EEG record.

One channel of a 4-channel Harvard Instrument Company write-out recorded the EEG, using amplifiers from the Lexington Instrument Company. A pair of

intercorrelation, .47) consisted of 13 variables: concern about supplies, anxiety, helplessness, hopelessness, blocked, lack of control, guilt, depression, anxiety (Gottschalk-Gleser), hostility-in (G-G), total affect (G-G), average rating with affect instructions, and average rating with affect instructions in context of entire session. The second cluster (median intercorrelation, .59) might be labeled "interaction with therapist" (blocked by T, hostility to T, reference to T, involvement with T, and "schizophrenic thought scale" (G-G). The two clusters are relatively independent (median intercorrelation, .12). Both clusters are highly related to differentiation between symptom and control segments. Twelve of the 13 variables in the negative affect cluster differentiate between symptom and control (mean $t$-value = 2.71, $p < .01$). All five variables in the interaction with therapist cluster yield significant differentiation between symptom and control segments (mean $t$-value = 2.95, $p < .01$). Hostility was the only variable which produced significant differentiation, which was not included in either of the two clusters.

[11] In another study (16) we have shown again that this conclusion is warranted, except for one class of variables involving judgments of empathy.

electrodes on the opposite side served as a back-up channel, which could be switched on in the event of failure of the primary pair. Placements were fronto-central. The patients' previous participation in petit mal studies using multichannel recordings provided extensive EEG data with which to compare our own records. Two investigators each read the EEG independently, and subsequently went over the records together, identifying as definite paroxysmal activity those EEG bursts to which both had given a high confidence rating (almost all were .5 second or longer). In most of the "experimental" sessions only the single channel was used. The single channel recording was rarely ambiguous in identifying such activity, and review of the multichannel recordings usually resolved such ambiguities.

To establish the correspondence of EEG and the voice record, a time marker delivered auditory signals into the tape recorder and visual signals into the polygraph at 1-minute intervals. One investigator synchronized the record of attacks from the EEG tracing with the typescript, using a stopwatch to pinpoint the exact words being uttered by the patient as the petit mal burst occurred. (The matching accuracy was approximately ±2 seconds from the initiation of the petit mal burst.)

The diagnostic evaluation of Miss NC clearly indicated petit mal activity (as illustrated in Figure 2). Before going further into our data analyses procedures, a brief introduction to Miss NC is presented.[12]

Miss NC is a 16-year-old girl who has had petit mal epilepsy since the age of 10. This was first noticed by a teacher at school when she had a spell subsequent to being asked to climb a ladder. She has had only one single grand mal which occurred in school 4 years earlier. She is under fair drug control; bursts are noted by her mother in the early morning. These spells are characterized by brief periods of staring; no automatism or myoclonic components have appeared. She is presently under the care of a neurologist, receiving Zarontin and Valium three times a day. The patient tends to forget her midday dosage. Her parents feel that her condition is aggravated "if something important is coming up," and also, they feel, just before her menses, when they describe her as "moody."

There is no history of difficulty at birth. The patient was a full term baby and had no birth or neonatal complications, walked at 11 months, and talked at about the same time. No recent serious illness was reported. She is described as being the brightest of the three children, having maintained an 88 average up until the 8th grade of parochial school. Her marks deteriorated after she was transferred, for financial reasons, to a public school.

The patient is the oldest of three children. The others are healthy. Her parents are 39 years of age. At one time the father was treated for peptic ulcer. A maternal aunt suffered from grand mal seizures subsequent to a head injury during pregnancy. She gradually deteriorated to the point where commitment to a hospital was necessary. The patient's mother fears a similar outcome for her. There is no history of any other seizure disorder in the family. The parents are described as happily married. Mr. C was unemployed or a while and Mrs. C supported the family as a stitcher in a clothing factory. The family is a closely knit one, and both parents are cooperative in any venture which might possibly help their daughter. They encourage her to participate in activities with her peers, and take pride in her social success.

*Procedure for evaluating the interview samples.* The first four sessions of Dr. Peter Knapp's interviews with Miss NC were selected for study. Within these, 75 segments (each on a separate page) of 50 words each were selected for rating by judges. One third of these were segments which came before 3 cycle/second paroxysmal EEG activity (symptom segments). The remaining two thirds were segments chosen by an arbitrary randomization procedure from the remaining parts of the interview where no such paroxysmal activity was present (comparison segments). These comparison segments were selected so that they were at least 200 words away from the point of paroxysmal activity. A sample of two symp-

[12] From the original evaluation in Knapp, P., and Rosenthal, S., 1968. Unpublished paper.

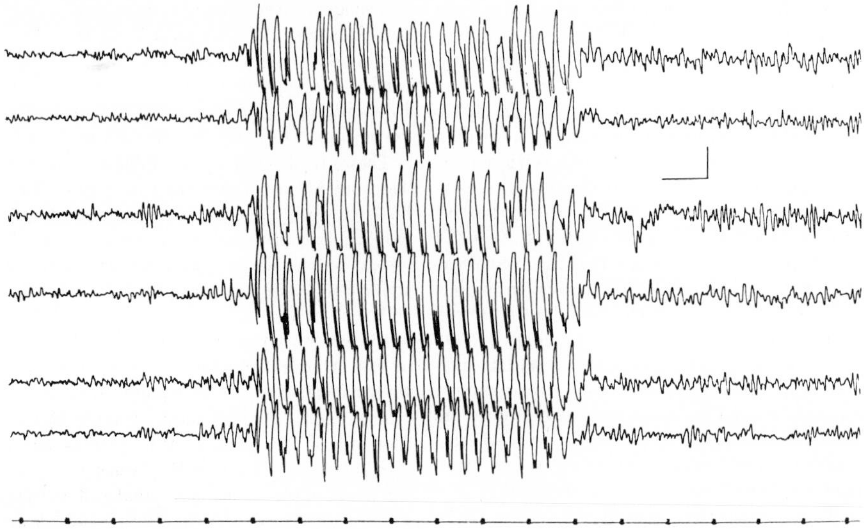

FIG. 2. Example of spike-wave burst recorded from patient Miss NC. The calibration signal is 1 second and 50 $\mu$V. The identity of the six recording channels (starting at the top) is as follows: $F_3$–$C_3$, $C_3$–$P_3$, $P_3$–$O_1$, $F_4$–$C_4$, $C_4$–$P_4$, $P_4$–$O_2$. These abbreviations are in accordance with the "10-20" systems as described by Penfield and Jasper (19).

tom segments is presented below to facilitate understanding of the results.

NO. 1

Miss NC: Um, we used to go walking a lot down to Lincoln Park of y-know, places of amusement, on to the beach.

T: Uh-huh. And what else?

Miss NC: Those are the main places we used to go. Or else we used to go fishing or bicycle riding. There weren't too many dances in the summertime 'cause it was so warm. We jus' go ridin' around.

NO. 2

Miss NC: . . . all the subjects that you have to take. And you take business, commercial college course, general, agriculture. There was this man that came to school one day after English class; this girl came and got me, and his name is Mr. Russo—he wanted to talk to me about—um.

*Free or intuitive judgments.* We began with judges' sortings of 75 50-word segments—25 preparoxysmal segments and 50 comparison segments. (Because we had so much more data for Miss NC, we doubled the number of comparison segments.) Also, because there were now 75 segments, they were judged using a sort with 11 piles (instead of rankings). The sortings were done three times, just as before, according to free instruction, affect instruction, and affect instruction in the context of the entire interview session.

Although the mean ratings are close to the chance expectation of 5.00 [13] (the free instruction mean is 5.22, affect instruction 5.40, and in-context instruction 5.36), the results are consistently in the opposite direction of that which was predicted. If "high affect" instructions were associated with seizures, the means should be lower

[13] The statistical method was an analysis of variance design similar to that described for Mr. ES, but based on four judges. None of the *F*-ratios reached the .10 level of significance.

than 5.00. For 10 of the 11 judgments for the three combined conditions, discrimination is in the "wrong" direction. When the data are scored on a dichotomous basis, there is the same tendency for results to be in the opposite direction, although this tendency is less marked.

*Clinical ratings of 18 variables.* We proceeded to the second type of analysis—ratings by two independent judges (RH and TT) of all 75 segments. The variables and the method were the same as for Mr. ES. The two judges highly agreed in their ratings, except for "separation anxiety," "emergence of new attitudes," and "tired"—there were almost no occurrences to be scored for those. Several other variables also had moderately low rates of occurrence. Table 1 shows the results using the pooled ratings of the two judges. "Hostility" is the only one of the 18 variables which is significant at the .05 level, but in the wrong direction—the comparison segments have more hostility than the symptom segments.

*Objective scoring of seven variables.* We went on with content analyses of 51 200-word segments—19 symptom segments and 42 comparison( control) segments. Six of the 25 symptom and eight of the 50 comparison segments were not included because they would have overlapped with other segments.) Only one judge made these scorings, but reliability of these scoring systems is reported to be high (8). The scales were Gottschalk and Gleser's hostility-out, hostility-in, ambivalent hostility, anxiety, schizophrenic, Mahl's speech disturbance index (14) and Luborsky's cognitive disturbance index (in preparation). One of these, speech disturbance, gave significant differentiation at the $p < .05$ level, and another, hostility-out, at the $p < .10$ level, but both of these are again in the wrong direction (Table 1). Furthermore, the 200-word segments were divided into first and second 100-word units to see whether, when the words were closer to the symptom, there would be a trend toward increase in the variables, as we had found in all other similar analyses of symptom onset (12), but no such trend occurred.

*Conclusions about Miss NC.* For this patient, the three clinical judgments conditions were not significant and both the clinical ratings and objective scores yielded little, *i.e.,* only two significant differentiations at the 5 per cent level (out of 25 variables)—the preparoxysmal segments had *less* rated hostility and speech disturbance. These two are not atypical in direction for this patient—all those which approached significance were consistent with these. The direction of the differences is opposite from those for the previous patient, Mr. ES.

MR. ST

The procedures were the same as for Miss NC and analyses were essentially those applied to the other two patients. A sample of the EEG evaluation clearly is consistent with the diagnosis of petit mal (Figure 3). Dr. Stuart Rosenthal conducted the free-association interviews. The following history is from the original evaluation.

Mr. ST is a 25-year-old man who has had petit mal epilepsy since 10 years of age. His aunt noticed his frequent "stares" at this time and brought them to his parents' attention. A year following that, the patient had his first grand mal attack. These invariably followed a bout of near continuous petit mal attacks, and occurred approximately three times a month until his sophomore year of high school when medication decreased their frequency to once every 3 to 6 months. His last grand mal attack was 5 years ago. At the time of study, he was having one to three "absences" on a "good" day, going from one every 2 days to dozens daily. Much of this variability was dependent upon his financial ability to adhere to his medical regimen, although this regimen was only partially effective.[14] Mr. ST was supposed to take half a tablet of Mysoline three times a day and two capsules of Dilantin twice daily. An earlier experience with barbiturates revealed that they made him lethargic. This patient's seizures are characterized by several seconds of staring, accompanied by myoclonic movements of the left lower lip and the fingers of the left upper

[14] Mr. ST's medication was changed after the period of study resulting in somewhat better control of his seizures.

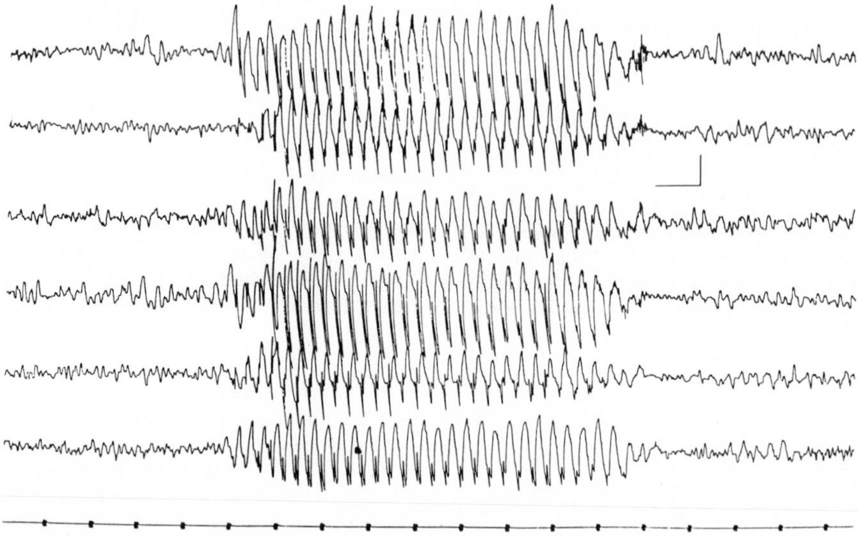

FIG. 3. Example of spike-wave burst recorded from patient Mr. ST. The calibration signal is 1 second and 50 $\mu$V. The identity of the six recording channels (starting at the top) is as follows: $F_3$–$C_3$, $C_3$–$P_3$, $P_3$–$O_1$, $F_4$–$C_4$, $C_4$–$P_4$, $P_4$–$O_2$. These abbreviations are in accordance with the "10-20" system as described by Penfield and Jasper (19).

extremity. There is an associated amnesia for immediately preceding events. Automatisms are not present. He believes that anxiety and lack of sleep predispose him to more bursts. Although there is no aura, Mr. ST states he can predict a "bad" day by vague tenseness and "not feeling like myself." On the other hand, he believes that seizures are infrequent when he is mentally and physically active, and that seizure duration is inversely related to frequency. He attempted to abort earlier grand mal attacks by counting and claims success for this maneuver.

There is no history of prenatal, neonatal, or developmental abnormalities for this patient other than epilepsy. He is the second oldest of five children. His siblings are in good health, and there is no history of epilepsy in the family. The father is a manufacturer—successful, affable, and in good health. The mother, who is sensitive, warm, and active, is employed and abhors the role of housewife. The parents are happily married, financially comfortable, and religious, but tolerate the patient's more "liberal" behavior. The patient moved to Massachusetts from another eastern state in his early adolescence and came under the care of a "specialist." He later attended a small college for three semesters, where he majored in art, but found the milieu stultifying and transferred to a school in Boston on the advice of his instructor. His progress there has been considerable; he won an art scholarship for study abroad. He intends to use this after a year. After some hesitation because of religious differences, he married and has two small children, both healthy.

The first four preparoxysmal segments are presented to help the reader understand this patient's manner of expressing himself.

NO. 21

Mr. ST: . . . anyway this was a bone of contention between us as far as getting married and everything and this postponed the whole business and we just kind of—you know—put it out of our minds—you know—thinking—you know

—not even thinking—you know just going on—you know. . .

NO. 27

Mr. ST: . . . the marriage—you know—you know—they should really be notified about the marriage—you know—about being married. As a matter of fact, I had sent M.—(wife) back to—y-y-you still want me y- are you still interested in all this business? Um—okay—so anyway, as a matter of fact. . . .

NO. 20

Mr. ST: . . . way, whose name is C. ——, but everyone calls her Peach.

T: Is she?

Mr. ST: Is she a peach? Yes, she is. Uh, and she—uh—ma—sh—cousin and I were very good friends. We were the same age and apparently she just noticed it one day when I was coming home from sch—when I was home.

NO. 101

Mr. ST: . . . though they didn't have the money—they would have—they just didn't know any better, and the doctor felt that he could handle it himself, until it got to the point where—uh—I don't know—they sent me to (hospital) and—you know—gave me the—you know—diagnostic thing. . .

*Free or intuitive judgments.* Five clinical judges were asked to attempt to discriminate between the 55 symptom segments and the 55 comparison segments.[15] As with Miss NC, 11 scale points were used, but the Q-sort procedure was abandoned as being unnecessarily cumbersome. The mean rating for symptom segments was 6.06, compared to 6.26 for the comparison segments. This difference was in the expected direction for four of the five judges; however, this difference was far from statistically significant.

*Clinical rating of 18 variables.* The same 18 variables were judged (by RH and MJ) on the 110 segments. None of these variables showed significant differences, or even trends, at the .10 level.

*Objective scoring of seven variables.* Among these, two were significant discriminators—Gottschalk and Gleser's ambivalent hostility was *lower* (.025) before paroxysmal activity and cognitive disturbance was ***higher*** (.01) before paroxysmal activity (Table 1).

*Conclusions about Mr. ST.* The results appeared to be more similar to those for Miss NC than to those for Mr. ES. (It is of interest that the EEG characteristics are also more similar to Miss NC than to Mr. ES.) In contrast to Mr. ES, only a few variables reached significant levels of discrimination. Ambivalent hostility was *less* prominent before paroxysmal activity. Increase in cognitive disturbance before paroxysmal activity was most discriminating for Mr. ST—the reader can easily see these in the examples; *e.g.*, there is a build-up of many vague circumlocutions such as "you know," and "I don't know."

### *Appearance of EEG Paroxysms during Speech vs. during Silence*

At least two investigators have shown that petit mal are more likely to occur in silence than during speaking (6, 24). In both studies the finding was based on comparison of EEG paroxysmal activity frequency during a half-hour or longer period of silence with that during a comparable period of an interview. Our own analysis is the first which inspects the location of EEG paroxysmal activity within an interview—specifically comparing frequency of EEG paroxysmal activity during the patient's speech, the therapist's speech, the silence after the patient's speech, and the silence after the therapist's speech. The attack frequency in Table 2 can be compared with the actual amount of speech *vs.* silence in each of the four interviews. Two of the three patients show deviation from the ex-

[15] The two conditions employing the "affect clue" were not used for Mr. ST because at this point in the research we felt that more precise information of this kind was provided by the rated variables.

TABLE 2

*Frequency of EEG Paroxysmal Activity in Relation to Patient and Therapist Speech vs. Silence (in Comparison with Actual Time Spent in Speech vs. Silence in the Four Interviews)*

| | | P Speech | T Speech | Silence | |
|---|---|---|---|---|---|
| | | | | After P speech | After T speech |
| Mr. ES | EEG paroxysms | .44 | .00 | .56 | .00 |
| | Time spent in speech | .67 | .05 | .22 | .05 |
| Miss NC | EEG paroxysms | .17 | .17 | .52 | .13 |
| | Time spent in speech | .40 | .17 | .31 | .11 |
| Mr. ST | EEG paroxysms | .93 | .02 | .03 | .02 |
| | Time spent in speech | .94 | .03 | .02 | .01 |

pected proportions. Both Mr. ES and Miss NC show *more* than the expected proportion of episodes in the silence after the patient's speech (as compared with the actual proportion of the interview containing silence after the patient's speech).[16] Similarly, both show fewer episodes during the patient's speech than would be expected on the basis of proportion of interview time devoted to the patient's speech. For Mr. ST there was essentially no deviation from the expected proportions.

In sum, two of the three patients show more petit mal EEG activity when they cease talking than when they are talking—a finding consistent with that reported by other investigators using a slightly different method. The effect seems to be a function of focused *vs.* unfocused attention, as Gottschalk showed by presenting a variety of tasks to Mr. ES. Gottschalk found that counting by 3's was even more potent than speaking in reducing episodes; in fact, it abolished them. Talking usually entails greater focusing of attention than silence does. Gottschalk therefore has suggested that EEG paroxysms which appear *during a patient's talking* should have stronger psychological antecedents than those which appear during silence. We had sufficient data to test this possibility only for Mr. ES. There was no tendency for psychological antecedents to be greater for episodes which occurred while Mr. ES was talking.

[16] For Mr. ES, $\chi^2 = 17.2$, $df = 2$, $p < .01$. For Miss NC, $\chi^2 = 6.0$, $df = 2$, $p < .05$. For Mr. ST, $\chi^2 = .10$, $df = 1$, N.S.

### *Duration of EEG Paroxysms and Psychological Antecedents to Them*

If psychological factors are involved in the precipitation of EEG paroxysms, it seems a reasonable expectation that there would be more of them before longer ones. No prior research has been reported on this, although some other investigators must have considered the importance of the factor since they dropped episodes of 1 second or less [e.g., Gottschalk (6), and Zegans (24)].

Dropping attacks which were less than 1 second in duration had virtually no effect on the results for Miss NC or Mr. ST. Data on duration of attacks were not available for a sufficient number of Mr. ES's episodes to justify this type of analysis.

For Miss NC, however, there were available data on the duration of 18 of the 25 episodes. For these 18, correlation of length of the episodes with the 18 clinical variables was generally *positive* and higher than similar correlations with symptom *vs.* comparison segments. No clear tendency was shown by the seven objectively scored variables. *Hopelessness* was the only variable reaching statistical significance for this small sample ($r = .57$, $p < .05$;) *i.e.*, the longer the episode, the more hopelessness.

To examine this issue for Mr. ST, the duration of the paroxysmal activity for each of the 55 symptom segments was correlated with the 25 variables previously used. Where two episodes occurred in close proximity (three instances), an average duration was used. No significant relationships

were obtained. The two largest correlations were hostility-out ($r = .25$) and hopelessness ($r = .22$). (Neither of these variables had shown any discrimination between symptom and comparison segments. Their correlations with symptom *vs.* comparison segments scored 1 and 0, were .02 and −.03, respectively.) Neither cognitive disturbance nor ambivalent hostility showed significant correlations with duration of episode. Cognitive disturbance was in the same direction ($r = .14$); ambivalent hostility was not rated as occurring in any of the symptom segments.

In conclusion, therefore, correlations of the contents before an EEG paroxysm with its *duration* did not usually reveal substantial relationships, although more of a relationship for Miss NC than for Mr. ST.

### *Discussion and Conclusions*

1. Our purpose was to report the first application of the symptom-context method to evaluating the psychological antecedents in three petit mal patients. The significant antecedents of 3 cycle/second spike and wave activity for all three patients are summarized in Table 1. If one's expectations were that all such patients should be like Mr. ES, then our results represent a failure of replication; if, however, one's expectations had been that patients differ in amount and type of psychological antecedents, then our results are a confirmation. For Mr. ES, strong psychological antecedents were found. These consisted of the types of negative affects frequently reported before many psychosomatic symptoms; *e.g.*, feeling depressed, blocked, hostile (13). For Miss NC and Mr. ST there were a few significant differences but these were difficult to interpret.[17] Our findings of marked individual differences in psychological antecedents for the three patients, because of the method by which they were established, have a unique place in the literature on antecedents of petit mal epilepsy.[18]

2. *Across* all three patients there are no clearly consistent psychological antecedents. The nearest possibility of a consistent antecedent is some form of hostility, but

[17] However, for Miss NC (and to a lesser extent Mr. ST) the direction of the correlations suggests that the patient was *less* affectively aroused in the preparoxysmal periods. This direction appears to be similar to findings on a girl with petit mal (24).

It is of interest that a prior method using whole sessions [12] also turned up similar small but *significant* findings on these two patients. The first approach in the first four sessions (with Miss NC) was to attempt "blind" prediction, picking "stress points" where they predicted that seizure activity would occur. This proved too difficult a task, but led to hypotheses about the stresses that *post hoc* seemed associated with seizure activity. Applying these to the next four sessions, one judge tried with some success to separate ("blind") preseizure contexts from randomly selected nonseizure contexts. The distribution of "hits" in 42 textual interruptions in interviews 5 to 8 had an insignificant $\chi^2 = 3.43$, $p < .10$, $p > .05$. The investigators used a similar approach on material from Mr. ST. Here a judge *ranked* segments ("blind") according to predicted likelihood that petit mal would be present. In two of four interviews, results were significant (using the Mann Whitney $U$-test) at $p < .05$. The judges felt that detailed study might yield progressively more refined hypotheses, particularly when the approach is supplemented by quantitative linguistic indices, and when the record contains audiovisual material leading up to the exact seconds before seizure onset.

[18] Further studies are planned in order to identify which patients have strong psychological antecedents (like Mr. ES) and which have weak ones (like Miss NC and Mr. ST). We have begun to obtain videotape recordings for each patient so that the data for learning the antecedents would not be limited to the lexical analyses. Additional information will be provided by measures of respiration and nonparoxysmal EEG to provide an estimate of the baseline EEG patterns which precede the seizure activity. Then, rather than rely only on single predictors, multiple regression analyses will determine the best combination of the antecedent psychological and physiological variables for predicting the seizures of each patient. We have also begun to extend the scoring on one patient (Mr. ST) for cognitive disturbance and speech disturbance throughout entire sessions. The results suggest that there is the onset of a build-up on these two variables about 300 words before the seizure; the seizure occurs about 100 words past the peak on these variables (from work in progress by Luborsky, L., and Wagner, A.). Finally it will be important to learn whether petit mal patients with different types of antecedents are differentially susceptible to psychological (and other) treatment procedures which aim at reducing or abolishing the seizures, such as counting by 3's or feedback training.

the particular hostility variable differs for each patient *and* both for Miss NC and Mr. ST the relationship is inverse—hostility is *greatest* before EEG *non*paroxysmal periods.

3. The difference in magnitude of the findings for Mr. ES *vs.* for Miss NC and Mr. ST is impressive—can we understand the difference? In view of the limitations of our study to only three patients, the answers must be speculative.

a. The psychological differences in the patients may reflect physiological differences in the nature of their convulsive disorder. For both Miss NC and Mr. ST, the onset of disorder was in childhood and was characterized by typical "absence" spells, *i.e.*, clinically manifest episodes. These indicators, as well as the EEG pattern, would characterize these patients as having "classical" or "typical" petit mal. For Mr. ES, however, the disorder apparently began in adulthood, which would make it statistically a relatively rare type of petit mal. The petit mal EEG paroxysmal activity was not associated with clinically manifest episodes. The EEG was also suggestive of a right temporal lobe focus, which is compatible, perhaps, with a diagnosis of secondary bilateral synchrony subsequent to a cortical focus of abnormality. Inspection of the tracings suggests abnormally slow background activity in Mr. ES's record, which may also be compatible with the diagnosis of cortical damage or dysfunction. The data are insufficient to establish that the behavioral differences between Mr. ES and the other two patients are a function of these clinical-diagnostic differences; however, the presence of temporal lobe abnormality in Mr. ES may provide some clue which bears watching in future studies of such patients. Of particular interest might be those patients with the mixed diagnosis of generalized epilepsy (petit mal) in the presence of localizing or focal features.

b. Miss NC and Mr. ST may be more inhibited than Mr. ES about putting their feelings into words. This could make a lot of difference since the patient's words determine the ratings and scores on the personality variables. However, this point is more speculative than the preceding one because we have no estimate of the amount of experienced freedom to express feelings. It is true, nevertheless, that Mr. ES was in a form of combined psychotherapy and petit mal exploration while Miss NC and Mr. ST were primarily in a petit mal exploration.

c. The differences are probably not related to the average length of the episodes of petit mal EEG paroxysms since we have shown that the relationships with duration were slight and uneven—insignificant for Mr. ST and only slightly related for Miss NC.

4. One suggestive finding emerged about the operation of the various types of evaluations of the onset conditions for symptoms: the free or intuitive judgments by themselves did not reach significance levels for any of the patients, not even for Mr. ES who had such large differences by the rating and scoring methods. Apparently symptom *vs.* nonsymptom distinctions are difficult for a judge to make, unless he is judging a specific variable (as has also been shown (12) for similarly analyzed data before patients' reports of stomach pain).

5. The petit mal EEG paroxysms occurred more often during the patient's silence than during the patient's speech (for two of the three patients). Talking probably reflects more focused attention than silence; more focused attention or activity tends to reduce the frequency of attacks.

REFERENCES

1. Allen, I. M. The emotional factor and the epileptic attack. New Zealand Med. J., *55:* 297–308, 1956.
2. Barker, W. The petit mal attack as a response within the CNS to distress organism environment situations. Psychosom. Med., *10:* 73–94, 1948.
3. Freedman, D. A., and Adatto, C. P. On the precipitation of seizures in an adolescent boy. Psychomsom. Med., *30:* 437–447, 1968.
4. Goldie, L., and Green, J. A. study of the psychological factors in a case of sensory reflex epilepsy. Brain, *82:* 505–524, 1959.
5. Gottschalk, L. A. Effects of intensive psychotherapy on epileptic children. Arch. Neurol. Psychiatry, *70:* 361–384, 1953.

6. Gottschalk, L. A. Psychologic conflict and electro-encephalographic patterns. Arch. Neurol. Psychiatry, *73:* 656–662, 1955.
7. Gottschalk, L. A. The relationship of psychologic state and epileptic activity: Psychoanalytic observations on an epileptic child. In *Psychoanalytic Study of the Child, Vol. XI,* pp. 352–380. International Universities Press, New York, 1956.
8. Gottschalk, L., and Gleser, G. *The Measurement of Psychological States Through the Content Analysis of Verbal Behavior.* University of California Press, Berkeley, 1969.
9. Holmes, T. H., and Rahe, R. H. The Social Readjustment Rating Scale. J. Psychosom. Res., *11:* 213–218, 1967.
10. Kreindler, A. *Experimental Epilepsy.* Elsevier Publ. Co., New York, 1965.
11. Luborsky, L. New directions in research on neurotic and psychosomatic symptoms. Am. Sci., *58:* 661–668, 1970.
12. Luborsky, L., and Auerbach, A. H. The symptom-context method: Quantitative studies of symptom formation in psychotherapy. J. Am. Psychoanal. Assoc., *17:* 68–99, 1969.
13. Luborsky, L., Docherty, J. P., and Penick, S. The onset conditions for psychosomatic symptoms: A review of quantitative studies. Psychosom. Med., *35:* 187–204, 1973.
14. Mahl, G. Disturbances and silences in the patient's speech in psychotherapy. J. Abnorm. Soc. Psychol., *53:* 1–15, 1956.
15. Merritt, H. *Neurology.* Lea and Febiger, Philadelphia, 1963.
16. Mintz, J., and Luborsky, L. Segments versus whole sessions: Which is the better unit for psychotherapy process research. J. Abnorm. Psychol., *78:* 180–191, 1971.
17. Morrell, F., and Naquet, R. Conditioning of generalized hypersynchronous discharge in cats with epileptogenic lesions. Electroencephalogr. Clin. Neurophysiol., *8:* 728, 1956.
18. Naquet, R., and Morrell, F. Conditioning of hypersynchronous discharges of the myoclonic type induced by Cardiazol injection into the cat. Electroencephalogr. Clin. Neurophysiol., *8:* 728, 1956.
19. Penfield, W., and Jasper, H. *Epilepsy and the Functional Autonomy of the Human Brain.* Little, Brown, Boston, 1954.
20. Rahrer, J., Ganis, F. M., and Shaffer, J. W. Intercorrelations between affect, urinary 17-hydroxycorticosteroid levels and epileptic convulsions. Psychosom. Med., *29:* 144–150, 1967.
21. Small, J. D., Stevens, J. R., and Milstein, V. Electroclinical correlates of emotional activation of the EEG. J. Nerv. Ment. Dis., *138:* 146–155, 1964.
22. Stevens, J. R. Emotional activation of the EEG in patients with convulsive disorders. J. Nerv. Ment. Dis., *128:* 339–351, 1959.
23. Yeager, L. L., and Gianoscol, A. J. Psychological stress and petit-mal variant, a telemeter study. Case Rep., Am. J. Psychiatry, *119:* 996–997, 1963.
24. Zegans, L., Kooi, K., Waggoner, R., and Kemph, J. Effects of psychiatric interview upon paroxysmal cerebral activity and autonomic measures in a disturbed child with petit mal epilepsy. Psychosom. Med., *26:* 151–161, 1964.

# Changes in Serum Dopamine-β-Hydroxylase Activity during Group Psychotherapy

SAM SILBERGELD, PHD, MD, RONALD W. MANDERSCHEID, MA, PATRICIA H. O'NEILL, MSN, FRIEDHELM LAMPRECHT, MD, AND LORENZ K. Y. NG, MD

This psychobiological study investigates married-couple group psychotherapy from pre- and postsession serum dopamine-β-hydroxylase (DBH) determinations, the Free Association Test (FAT), and a Postsession Questionnaire (PSQ). Experimental manipulations permit controls for the assessment of DBH variations. Group, gender, and individual linear regression analyses are interpreted by a stressor-destressor typology. DBH levels significantly increase during psychotherapy. Increments are comparable with those from physical work. Most variability in DBH is predicted from a small set of psychological variables. Psychological stressors and destressors show psychobiochemical individuality. Implications of psychological stressors for psychosomatic vulnerability are discussed.

## INTRODUCTION

This pilot study is the first to consider a catecholamine-synthesizing enzyme as an index for classifying affect and behavior during married-couple group psychotherapy. Although numerous operational indicators of emotional arousal exist (1), the measurement of dopamine-β-hydroxylase (DBH) activity may differentiate psychological variables on the basis of sympathetic nervous system activity. Such differentiation can be relevant for prediction and understanding of psychological stressors and their relationship to psychosomatic vulnerability.

DBH catalyzes the hydroxylation of dopamine to norepinephrine (2). This enzyme localizes in the noradrenergic vesicle of sympathetic nerves (3) and in the chromaffin granules of the adrenal medulla (4). DBH has a much longer circulating half-life than catecholamines (5). In the rat, partial chemical sympathectomy diminishes (6) and immobilization stress increases serum DBH activity (7). In man, rapid increases in plasma DBH during stresses associated with increased sympathetic nerve activity (cold pressor test and exercise) are similar in magnitude and time course to the elevations of serum DBH activity in rats subjected to immobilization stress (8). In both man and the rat, DBH activity occurs in sera and apparently not in the formed elements of the blood (6). Serum DBH activity is much greater in humans than in other species studied. Physiological data suggest that DBH is discharged into the circulation *in vivo* during periods of catecholamine release by either sympathetic nerves or the adrenal medulla (6). The correlation found between plasma norepinephrine and DBH

From the Mental Health Study Center, NIMH, Adelphi, Maryland 20783, and the Division of Clinical and Behavioral Research, NIMH, Bethesda, Maryland 20014.

Tables showing by-session analyses for the Postsession Questionnaire and the Free Association Test, as well as for the regression analyses by group and by gender, are available from the senior author.

Address reprint requests to: Sam Silbergeld, PhD, MD, Mental Health Study Center, 2340 University Boulevard East, Adelphi, Maryland 20783.

Received for publication September 3, 1974; revision received January 20, 1975.

activity in patients with essential hypertension supports other evidence that DBH is a potentially useful index of sympathetic function (9–11). However, cautions are to be noted (12–15). Adrenal DBH has been suggested as an approach to assessment of premortem stress (16). The current state of knowledge encourages small-scale, longitudinal, clinical investigation of DBH as an indicator of affect and behavior.

Multiple approaches are needed for experimental evaluation of mood and behavior (17). In the present study, a Postsession Questionnaire (PSQ) measures self (S), peer (P), and therapist (T) ratings on a series of affect parameters for each group member at every session. Pre- and postsession Free Association Tests (FAT) (18,19) permit the content analysis of verbal behavior for specific types of anxiety and hostility. The FAT can reflect preconscious and /or unconscious thought content, while the PSQ permits measurement of conscious affect.

The following specific questions and expectancies have oriented the analyses reported in this paper. Does group psychotherapy influence serum DBH activity? Psychotherapy is both a threat- and a stress-inducing experience (20) that may be detectable through an appropriate biochemical indicator of sympathetic nervous system arousal. Which measured affects and behaviors relate to changes in serum DBH activity during group psychotherapy? Threatening and stressful ones are expected to do so. If serum DBH discriminates among affects and behaviors, how responsive is it to intensity changes within these? Since DBH varies directly with the degree of physical exertion, one expects similar variation with psychological exertion, especially threat or stress.

## METHOD

### Therapy Group

Five married couples participated in 15 sessions of brief group psychotherapy. Two years later, the same 10 individuals completed an additional 15 sessions. The data reported here derive from the latter experience. Mean age is 37 and mean length of marriage 14 years. Education averages six years beyond high school. All husbands are ministers. Two wives are employed outside the home, one as a minister and the other as a nurse. All couples have two or more children.

### Affect Data

Prior to and following each therapy session, a 5 min FAT (18,19) was completed by each member. The FAT recordings were scored by verbal content analysis for anxiety and hostility dimensions. These 13 FAT variables are delineated in Table 1. At the end of each session, group members also rated themselves and other members on 16 affect and behavior parameters by means of the PSQ. The two cotherapists, a psychiatrist and a psychiatric nurse, rated each member in the same manner. Thus, each PSQ variable yields three ratings for each member at every session: self-evaluation (S), mean peer evaluation (P), and mean therapist evaluation (T). These 16 PSQ variables are shown in Table 1.

### DBH Assay

Blood samples were obtained by venipuncture from each group member prior to and following sessions 1, 3, 5, 6, 10, 11, and 15.[1] These blood samples were immediately placed on ice and centrifuged

---

[1]These seven sessions were selected for serum DBH determinations in order to evaluate the first and last session of each phase of the group therapy model. One middle session was included in order to assess the impact of a long session. For analytic and research purposes, the 15 therapy sessions are structurally characterized as triphasic: (1) control, (2) innovation, and (3) effect. Each of these consecutive phases consists of five successive sessions. The middle session of each phase is approximately 8 hr, instead of the customary 2 hr, in duration. Sessions 1 and 2 are designed to have minimal therapeutic and therapist activity.

**TABLE 1. Affect and Behavior Variables from Postsession Questionnaire (PSQ) and Free Association Test (FAT)**

| PSQ[a] | FAT[b] |
|---|---|
| Comfort | Death Anxiety |
| Effectiveness | Mutilation Anxiety |
| Insight | Separation Anxiety |
| Communication | Guilt Anxiety |
| Anxiety | Shame Anxiety |
| Hostility | Diffuse Anxiety |
| Discouragement | Total Anxiety |
| Self-Centeredness | Hostility Outward, Overt |
| Controlling | Hostility Outward, Covert |
| Involvement | Total Hostility Outward |
| Helpfulness | Hostility Inward |
| Group Influence | Ambivalent Hostility |
| Popularity | Total Inward and Ambivalent Hostility |
| Self-Confidence | |
| Avoidance of Emotion by Intellectualization | |
| Overall Behavioral Change Since First Group Session | |

[a] In order to evaluate each group member except the therapists, three ratings were obtained for all PSQ variables at the end of each session: Self (S), Peer (P), and Therapist (T). Scores for PSQ variables range from 0 through 10. 0 = lowest; 1–2 = very low; 3–4 = low; 5 = average; 6–7 = high; 8–9 = very high; 10 = highest.

[b] An FAT was completed by each group member before (pre) and after (post) all sessions. For discussion of the scoring method, see Gottschalk and Gleser (19). A derived measure, delta FAT, equals the difference between post- and presession scores.

10,000 × G for 10 min at 40°C. The sera were removed, and aliquots were frozen and stored for later DBH analyses. Serum DBH activity was assayed essentially by the method of Weinshilboum and Axelrod (6), with a modified pH of 5.5. Results from the 131 analyzed samples (excludes venipuncture failures and breakage of tubes) are expressed as nmoles of $\beta$-phenylethanolamine/ml/hr (Table 1 and Fig. 1).

Acquisition of blood samples is often associated with anxiety, hostility, and unpleasantness (21). In order to minimize such effects, the same physical milieu and the same technician were used throughout all pre- and postsession blood withdrawals.

## Data Analysis

Several statistical techniques are employed. The t-test for independent samples is used to assess gender differences in the affect and DBH variables.[2] Stepwise linear regression[3] measures the strength and direction of covariation between the psychological variables and changes in DBH activity levels. These analyses are done for the entire group, for each gender separately, and for each individual.[4] The Biomedical Computer Program BMD02R (24) is used for the regression analyses.[5]

[2]In rejecting the null hypothesis in statistical tests, a result will be considered a trend or suggestive difference if $P < 0.10$, significant if $P < 0.05$, and very significant if $P < 0.01$.

[3]Several statistical issues (22) surround stepwise regression. These focus upon the probabilistic interpretations associated with partial F. For present purposes, no probabilistic statements have been made or used. A 3% increment to the explained variance defines the "cutoff point," rather than the probabilities associated with the partial F. This procedure is designed to mitigate the problem of interpretation.

[4]By-person stepwise regressions represent a relatively novel application of correlational techniques advocated by Lykken (23). Recurrent observations on the same individual constitute the sample, and variables are the units of analysis. Since the present data

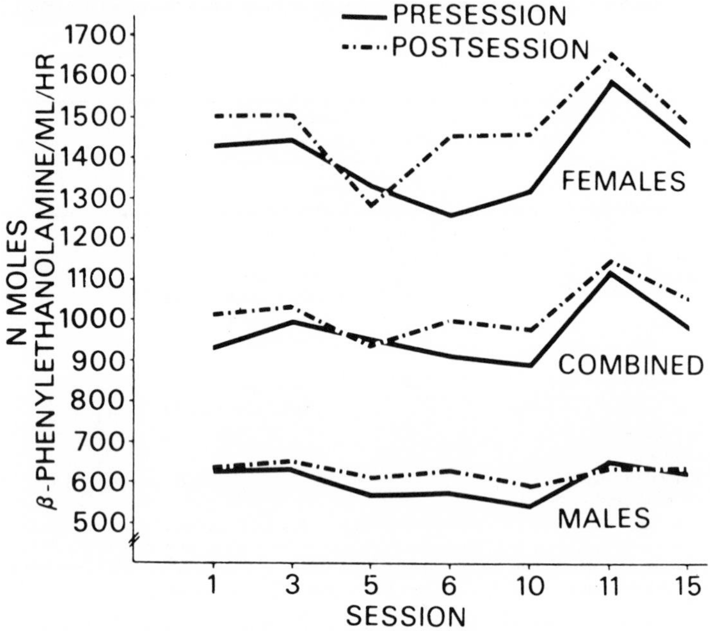


Fig. 1. Mean presession and postsession serum DBH activity levels by session for combined and separate genders. Continuous lines specify presession means; interrupted lines, postsession.

In order to evaluate changes in DBH activity, two measures are constructed: (a) delta DBH = postsession minus presession DBH activity; and (b) kappa DBH = postsession minus mean for all presession DBH activity scores. Delta DBH does not take into consideration fluctuations in presession activity due to idiosyncratic experiences apart from the therapy group. Kappa DBH corrects for such variation at the individual level. Consequently, kappa is expected to be more sensitive to changes in DBH activity during the sessions.

## Summary of Variables

To summarize, data were obtained for the following 93 variables: 48 Postsession Questionnaire (PSQ) variables derived from 16 self (S), 16 peer (P), and 16 therapist (T) ratings; 39 Free Association Test (FAT)

consist of multiple observations for each variable across time, scores are statistically dependent. However, the same degree of dependency exists throughout the data. Thus, the by-person equations are comparable. Since the major focus is on individual differences rather than generalizability of equational structure, the technical problems associated with this application are less acute. Because of statistical dependency, patterns of relationships among variables will be reinforced, thus overestimating percentage of explained variance. Actual percentages range between those observed for the by-gender regressions and those for the by-person regressions.

[5]This program computes a sequence of multiple linear regression equations in a stepwise manner. One independent variable is added at each step. The criterion for selection is the magnitude of the partial correlation with the dependent variable controlling for other independent variables already in the equation. Variables are added until a prespecified condition is met, e.g., increment to percent variance explained falls below a declared level.

variables from 13 presession, 13 postsession, and 13 change measures (delta FAT = postsession minus presession FAT score); four dopamine-β-hydroxylase (DBH) variables, i.e., presession DBH activity, postsession DBH activity, delta DBH, and kappa DBH; gender; and session number.

## RESULTS

Table 2 specifies pre- and postsession DBH activity levels for each of the 10 group members. By session, females in this study exhibit significantly higher DBH activity levels than males ($P < 0.05$) with the exception of the first presession ($P < 0.10$).[6] Similarly, when DBH activity levels are averaged for all sessions, females show significantly higher levels than males for pre- and postsession determinations ($P < 0.001$). However, delta DBH indicates only one significant ($P < 0.05$) gender difference. Males show larger changes during session 5. Similarly, kappa DBH exhibits gender variations for only two sessions. Males are significantly higher ($P < 0.05$) during session 5 and females during session 15. Averaged for all sessions, delta and kappa DBH do not show gender differences. These results imply that in this sample, pre- and postsession activity levels are gender-linked even though the measures of change, delta and kappa DBH, apparently are not.

Analyses of Table 2 data (*t*-test for dependent samples) have been performed for

[6] In a private communication, Lamprecht and Kopin report mean basal DBH activity levels for 46 females ($\bar{X}$ = 464.8; SEM = 7.7) and 75 males ($\bar{X}$ = 526.7; SEM = 7.0). Others (15) do not indicate gender differences in activity levels. These findings suggest that the females in the present study may have usually high basal DBH activity levels.

**TABLE 2. Serum Activity Levels of Dopamine-β-Hydroxylase (DBH) for Females and Males by Session**[a]

| Subject[b] | | Session 1 | 3 | 5 | 6 | 10 | 11 | 15 | Mean ± SEM[c] |
|---|---|---|---|---|---|---|---|---|---|
| 1F | Pre | 2205 | 1837 | 1930 | 1429 | 1711 | 1911 | 1906 | 1847 ± 89 |
| | Post | 1970 | 1917 | 1837 | 1792 | 1892 | 1931 | 1935 | 1896 ± 23 |
| 2F | Pre | — | — | 928 | 1041 | — | 1476 | 1110 | 1139 ± 119 |
| | Post | — | — | 964 | — | — | 1292 | 1227 | 1161 ± 100 |
| 3F | Pre | 1282 | 999 | 1062 | 1016 | 996 | 1155 | — | 1085 ± 46 |
| | Post | 1324 | 992 | 984 | 1169 | 1270 | 1357 | 1176 | 1182 ± 56 |
| 4F | Pre | 797 | 1120 | 999 | 1046 | 905 | 871 | 1042 | 969 ± 43 |
| | Post | 919 | 1112 | 902 | 1047 | 865 | 1045 | 1093 | 998 ± 38 |
| 5F | Pre | — | 1836 | 1745 | 1798 | 1692 | 2572 | 1693 | 1889 ± 139 |
| | Post | 1783 | 2002 | 1718 | 1830 | 1831 | 2701 | 1980 | 1978 ± 127 |
| 1M | Pre | 974 | 997 | 854 | 917 | 821 | 1103 | 1035 | 957 ± 38 |
| | Post | 955 | 1013 | 954 | 1011 | 983 | 983 | 1004 | 986 ± 9 |
| 2M | Pre | 476 | 482 | 396 | 399 | 348 | 446 | 276 | 403 ± 28 |
| | Post | 453 | 502 | 406 | 438 | 487 | 473 | 493 | 465 ± 13 |
| 3M | Pre | 350 | 341 | 256 | 248 | 255 | 261 | 346 | 294 ± 18 |
| | Post | 344 | 343 | 262 | 285 | 320 | 271 | 326 | 307 ± 13 |
| 4M | Pre | 1031 | 1075 | 1032 | 1036 | 1020 | 1164 | 1121 | 1068 ± 21 |
| | Post | 1088 | 1098 | 1162 | 1175 | 918 | 1167 | 1034 | 1092 ± 35 |
| 5M | Pre | 331 | 281 | 321 | 273 | 293 | 299 | 371 | 310 ± 13 |
| | Post | 342 | 297 | 278 | 246 | 266 | 299 | 324 | 293 ± 13 |

[a] Serum activity is expressed as nmoles β-phenylethanolamine/ml/hr for before (pre) and after (post) the indicated sessions.

[b] F = female, M = male. Corresponding numbers represent spouses.

[c] Results are expressed as mean ± standard error of the mean.

pre- to postsession changes in DBH activity by and across sessions for females, males, and combined genders. By session, females show increases ($P < 0.10$) for sessions 6, 10, and 15, and males do so for session 6. Males increase significantly ($P < 0.05$) during session 3, and females decrease ($P < 0.10$) during session 5. The combined genders show significant increases for sessions 6 and 10, and a trend increase for session 3. Across-session analyses suggest an upward change for females, and significant increments for males ($P < 0.05$) and combined genders ($P < 0.001$). Figure 1 illustrates these variations in DBH activity levels. Postsession activity tends to be higher than presession activity levels for both genders. These results suggest that the therapy session is accompanied by an increment in DBH activity level.[7]

Two experimental manipulations serve as controls for the assessment of variations in serum DBH activity (see footnote 1). In comparison to all others, sessions 1 and 2 of the group therapy are designed to minimize therapeutic and therapist activity. Significant changes in DBH activity levels are not observed during session 1. This contrasts with the other six sessions for which enzyme determinations are made. The second manipulation occurs during phase 2 only. As homework assignments, each group member scores FAT transcripts previously made by themselves and unidentified others. This innovation, the subject of a future publication, is designed to catalyze the therapeutic process by increasing awareness of self and peer FAT anxiety. It is expected to generate higher levels of psychological threat and stress during the phase 2 sessions. Consequently, increments in DBH activity levels should be larger for these sessions. Table 2 and Fig. 1 confirm this.

Table 3 compares female and male S, P, and T evaluations from the 16 PSQ parameters. For these analyses, data are averaged for all sessions. The self-evaluations show that for 9 of 16 parameters, males rate themselves notably higher than females, viz., Comfort, Insight, Hostility, Discouragement, Self-Centeredness, Controlling, Popularity, Self-Confidence, and Avoidance of Emotion by Intellectualization. Females do not score themselves significantly higher in a single instance. When evaluated by peers, females are notably higher for Effectiveness, Insight, and Overall Behavioral Change. Males are rated higher by peers for Self-Centeredness, Controlling, Self-Confidence, and Avoidance of Emotion by Intellectualization. Therapists evaluate females higher for Effectiveness, Insight, Popularity, and Overall Behavioral Change. Therapists rate males higher for Self-Centeredness, Controlling, and Avoidance of Emotion by Intellectualization. Similar results are observed when the data are examined for each session.

In general, males tend to evaluate themselves higher for both desirable, e.g., Insight, and what might be considered male stereotypic characteristics, e.g., Controlling and Avoidance of Emotion by Intellectualization. A different pattern is observed for the P evaluations in that females are rated higher for several desirable characteristics. Males are scored higher for parameters commensurate with a dominant male role. T ratings are more congruent

---

[7]In terms of percent, pre- to postsession DBH activity changes range from 0% to 79%. Changes > 10% are not likely to represent assay error (15). Calculations show that for 19 of 64 (30%) instances, the levels increased > 10%. For 6 of 64 (9%), the levels decreased > 10%. Overall, in 45 of 64 (70%) instances, activity levels increased to some extent during the session ($P < 0.01$ by z-test for difference of proportions). These results imply that DBH activity is likely to increase during the therapy session.

**TABLE 3. Mean ± SEM Postsession Questionnaire (PSQ) Scores from Self (S), Peer (P), and Therapist (T) Ratings for Females (F) and Males (M)[a–f]**

| | PSQ-S | | | PSQ-P | | | PSQ-T | | |
|---|---|---|---|---|---|---|---|---|---|
| Variables | F Mean ± SEM | M Mean ± SEM | Sig.[a–e] | F Mean ± SEM | M Mean ± SEM | Sig.[a–e] | F Mean ± SEM | M Mean ± SEM | Sig.[a–e] |
| Comfort | 4.60±0.14 | 5.59±0.14 | e | 4.76±0.10 | 4.71±0.09 | a | 5.39±0.18 | 5.41±0.18 | a |
| Effectiveness | 5.12±0.17 | 5.31±0.16 | a | 5.37±0.09 | 5.10±0.08 | c | 5.87±0.12 | 5.49±0.12 | c |
| Insight | 5.33±0.18 | 5.77±0.20 | b | 5.50±0.10 | 5.22±0.09 | c | 5.95±0.11 | 5.40±0.13 | d |
| Communication | 5.76±0.20 | 5.63±0.17 | a | 5.62±0.12 | 5.57±0.11 | a | 6.26±0.10 | 6.18±0.09 | a |
| Anxiety | 5.41±0.21 | 5.27±0.23 | a | 5.41±0.14 | 5.34±0.13 | a | 5.19±0.17 | 4.90±0.16 | a |
| Hostility | 4.04±0.25 | 4.85±0.21 | c | 4.68±0.15 | 4.39±0.13 | a | 3.97±0.13 | 4.11±0.12 | a |
| Discouragement | 3.91±0.25 | 4.88±0.21 | d | 4.63±0.14 | 4.39±0.12 | a | 3.69±0.12 | 3.57±0.09 | a |
| Self-Centeredness | 3.51±0.23 | 5.08±0.20 | e | 3.92±0.08 | 4.31±0.13 | c | 3.83±0.15 | 5.09±0.16 | e |
| Controlling | 3.44±0.22 | 4.81±0.20 | e | 3.97±0.10 | 4.29±0.13 | b | 3.68±0.12 | 4.67±0.14 | e |
| Involvement | 6.35±0.22 | 6.44±0.20 | a | 6.20±0.18 | 5.99±0.13 | a | 6.89±0.11 | 6.79±0.11 | a |
| Helpfulness | 5.25±0.16 | 5.32±0.18 | a | 5.41±0.11 | 5.23±0.09 | a | 6.09±0.09 | 5.93±0.10 | a |
| Group Influence | 5.23±0.17 | 6.21±0.61 | a | 5.58±0.10 | 5.46±0.12 | a | 6.31±0.11 | 6.27±0.13 | a |
| Popularity | 5.39±0.14 | 5.73±0.14 | b | 5.87±0.11 | 5.85±0.15 | a | 6.16±0.10 | 5.73±0.11 | d |
| Self-Confidence | 5.13±0.13 | 5.62±0.13 | d | 5.25±0.08 | 5.42±0.06 | b | 5.57±0.11 | 5.59±0.11 | a |
| Avoidance of Emotion | 2.99±0.18 | 5.00±0.21 | e | 3.75±0.06 | 4.36±0.14 | e | 3.57±0.11 | 4.57±0.14 | e |
| Overall Behavioral Change | 5.19±0.15 | 5.30±0.23 | a | 5.27±0.09 | 5.06±0.08 | b | 5.89±0.12 | 5.48±0.11 | c |

[a]Not significant.
[b]$P < 0.10$.
[c]$P < 0.05$.
[d]$P < 0.01$.
[e]$P < 0.001$.
[f]Means are calculated from scores for all sessions. Results derive from *t*-test for independent samples.

with P than with S. Self-Centeredness, Controlling, and Avoidance of Emotion by Intellectualization are consistently rated higher for males across the three modes of evaluation. Effectiveness, Insight, and Overall Behavioral Change are scored notably higher for females by P and T assessment.

Table 4 presents presession, postsession, and delta FAT (postsession minus presession FAT) scores for females and males, averaged for all sessions. Pre and *post scores* refer to actual magnitudes and should be distinguished from delta, a measure of change. For presession FAT scores, significant differences are not detected between genders. However, for postsession scores, females average significantly higher ($P < 0.05$) on Death and Separation Anxiety, and all Hostility Outward categories. Males are higher on Hostility Inward and Total Inward and Ambivalent Hostility. By delta FAT, females show significantly larger increases for all of the Hostility Outward categories. Males show significantly larger increases for Hostility Inward.

By stepwise regression analysis, delta and kappa DBH have been predicted from 48 PSQ (S, P, and T), 10 delta FAT, gender, session number, and presession DBH activity variables. These analyses are based on data from the 10 group members. The criterion for inclusion of an independent variable is a 3% or greater increment to explained variance. For delta DBH, 16 variables explain approximately 65% of the variance. This analysis substantiates the previously described *t*-tests. Since gender does not enter the equation, sex differences in delta DBH do not seem likely even when other significant predictors are controlled. The session variable does enter the equation; with other predictors controlled, delta DBH increases more during later sessions. For kappa DBH, 11 variables explain about 65% of the variance. The session and gender variables are among these predictors. Each explains about 5% of the variance. The impact of session order is similar for delta and kappa DBH. For the gender variable, the partial regression coefficient suggests males may have positive and females negative kappa DBH values.[8] As expected, fluctuations in presession DBH activity levels have only slight impact ($b = 0.02$) on kappa. Generally, delta FAT Hostility varies inversely while delta FAT Anxiety varies directly with delta and kappa DBH. PSQ-S Anxiety varies directly with kappa.

The same series of independent variables is employed in stepwise regressions performed for females and males separately. The total percentage of explained variance has been incremented substantially above that observed in the analyses performed on the entire sample. For delta DBH, these percentages are 77% for females (11 variables) and 87% for males (7 variables). The corresponding figures for kappa DBH are 86% (7 variables) and 86% (9 variables), respectively.

The two regressions for females indicate that several of the delta FAT Anxiety categories are strong positive predictors of increase in delta and kappa DBH. For example, a single unit increase in delta FAT Separation Anxiety results in a 285 unit increase in kappa DBH. This variable alone explains about 37% of the variance in kappa DBH. Delta FAT Hostility Outward, Overt, is a strong inverse predictor of kappa DBH for females. PSQ-P Hostility follows the same pattern with respect to

[8]This finding varies from the original *t*-test results. The gender difference only emerges after 9 predictor variables have entered the regression equation. Consequently, the relationship would not be detected in a simple *t*-test analysis.

**TABLE 4. Mean ± SEM Free Association Test (FAT) Scores for Females (F) and Males (M)[a–f]**

| Variables | Pre | | | Post | | | Delta | | |
|---|---|---|---|---|---|---|---|---|---|
| | F Mean ± SEM | M Mean ± SEM | Sig.[a–e] | F Mean ± SEM | M Mean ± SEM | Sig.[a–e] | F Mean ± SEM | M Mean ± SEM | Sig.[a–e] |
| A. Anxiety: | | | | | | | | | |
| Death | 0.44±0.04 | 0.48±0.04 | *a* | 0.38±0.02 | 0.34±0.01 | *b* | −0.05±0.04 | −0.15±0.05 | *a* |
| Mutilation | 0.49±0.05 | 0.51±0.04 | *a* | 0.36±0.02 | 0.36±0.02 | *a* | −0.14±0.05 | −0.16±0.05 | *a* |
| Separation | 0.77±0.07 | 0.65±0.06 | *a* | 0.62±0.06 | 0.44±0.03 | *d* | −0.17±0.09 | −0.17±0.06 | *a* |
| Guilt | 1.15±0.08 | 1.12±0.08 | *a* | 1.21±0.08 | 1.39±0.09 | *a* | 0.14±0.10 | 0.25±0.11 | *a* |
| Shame | 0.85±0.08 | 0.91±0.08 | *a* | 1.24±0.10 | 1.24±0.09 | *a* | 0.41±0.12 | 0.33±0.12 | *a* |
| Diffuse | 1.19±0.07 | 1.21±0.08 | *a* | 0.99±0.06 | 0.89±0.06 | *a* | −0.22±0.10 | −0.32±0.09 | *a* |
| Total | 2.28±0.09 | 2.27±0.07 | *a* | 2.29±0.09 | 2.25±0.08 | *a* | 0.03±0.11 | 0.00±0.10 | *a* |
| B. Hostility: | | | | | | | | | |
| Outward, Overt | 1.07±0.07 | 1.12±0.10 | *a* | 1.36±0.09 | 1.14±0.08 | *b* | 0.29±0.10 | −0.02±0.12 | *c* |
| Outward, Covert | 0.59±0.04 | 0.57±0.06 | *a* | 0.84±0.06 | 0.61±0.06 | *d* | 0.24±0.08 | 0.04±0.08 | *b* |
| Outward, Total | 1.22±0.07 | 1.25±0.11 | *a* | 1.62±0.09 | 1.31±0.09 | *c* | 0.40±0.10 | 0.03±0.14 | *c* |
| Inward | 0.94±0.06 | 0.90±0.06 | *a* | 0.91±0.06 | 1.10±0.07 | *c* | −0.03±0.07 | 0.20±0.10 | *b* |
| Ambivalent | 0.59±0.05 | 0.62±0.06 | *a* | 0.66±0.06 | 0.74±0.07 | *a* | 0.08±0.07 | 0.07±0.10 | *a* |
| Inward and Ambivalent | 1.12±0.07 | 1.10±0.07 | *a* | 1.12±0.07 | 1.36±0.08 | *c* | 0.00±0.08 | 0.21±0.10 | *a* |

[a–e]See Table 3.

[f]Means for pre- (before session), post- (after session), and delta (post minus pre) FAT scores are displayed. These means are calculated from scores for all sessions. Results derive from *t*-test for independent samples.

delta DBH. Generally, PSQ-S variables emerge early in the regressions, but appear after the most predictive delta FAT variables.

The delta FAT Anxiety variables are important predictors of change in DBH activity for females, but not for males. However, delta FAT Hostility variables are strong inverse predictors of delta DBH for males. For example, a single unit increase in delta FAT Ambivalent Hostility is accompanied by a 48 unit decrease in delta DBH. This variable alone explains 18% of the variance. PSQ-T Hostility functions in a similar manner within the kappa DBH equation. For females and males, PSQ-S variables are important predictors of delta DBH. For males, P and T ratings are apparently the best predictors of kappa DBH.

Tables 5 and 6 display by-person regressions for females and males, respectively. As compared with preceding analyses, a substantial increase has been achieved in percentage of variance explained. Not more than four variables are required to explain practically all variance in delta and kappa DBH for any individual. In general, partial regression coefficients are larger for females than males. Other results (t-test) imply that females and males do not differ significantly in delta or kappa DBH. Thus, this difference in magnitude of b suggests a greater physiological sensitivity to change in affect and behavior for these females.

One may note the diversity of affect and behavior variables predictive of change in DBH for any single individual. Physiological stressors are defined by positive regression coefficients; destressors, by negative coefficients. For example, kappa DBH activity for female 1F indicates that perceived Self-Confidence serves as a destressor, while perceived Effectiveness is a stressor. Tables 5 and 6 also illustrate the contrast in plus and minus signs for the same psychological variable among different individuals, i.e., affects and behaviors predictive of DBH are idiosyncratic. In other words, the same affect or behavior may be physiologically stressing for one person and destressing for another. For example, delta DBH increases with Total Inward and Ambivalent Hostility for female 1F. On the other hand, the same affect varies inversely with delta DBH for female 3F. These relationships outline a DBH indicator system. Results in Tables 5 and 6 support the conclusion that DBH can serve as a psychobiochemical indicator in psychotherapy.

## DISCUSSION

The present study is the first to show that serum DBH activity is significantly increased during group psychotherapy. Increased levels of this enzyme have been reported under conditions of acute physical (8,25) and cardiac (9–11) stress. Inhibitors of DBH have shown effectiveness against human hypertension (26). By contrast, DBH apparently decreases for a number of conditions involving hypofunction of the sympathetic nervous system, e.g., Parkinson's disease (27), Down's syndrome (28), and familial dysautonomia (29). A number of factors determine normal DBH blood values. Differences in basal DBH may be due to different rates of enzyme removal from the circulation, quantity of releasable DBH, rate of release, access of DBH to the circulation (30), genetic (11,31,32) and familial factors (31), and mode of assay (9). Wetterberg et al. (11) find little variability in human DBH activity as a function of time. Diurnal as well as monthly variations are slight. In a recent review, Geffen (15) notes

**TABLE 5. Partial Regression Coefficient (*b*) and Percent Explained Variance (% $s^2$) for Postsession Questionnaire (PSQ) and Free Association Test (FAT) Variables Predictive of Delta and Kappa Changes in Dopamine-β-Hydroxylase (DBH) Activity for Each Female Separately**[a,b]

| Subject | Delta DBH Variable | *b* | % $s^2$ | Kappa DBH Variable | *b* | % $s^2$ |
|---|---|---|---|---|---|---|
| 1F | Hostility, Inward and Ambivalent, FAT-*A* | 324 | 65.7 | Anxiety, PSQ-T | − 83 | 71.5 |
| | | | | Self-Confidence, PSQ-S | − 40 | 8.9 |
| | | | | Effectiveness, PSQ-S | 31 | 11.5 |
| | | | | Helpfulness, PSQ-T | − 34 | 5.4 |
| | Total (1 variable) | | 65.7 | Total (4 variables) | | 97.3 |
| 2F | Overall Behavioral Change, PSQ-P | 247 | 100.0 | Insight, PSQ-P | −331 | 99.9 |
| | Total (1 variable) | | 100.0 | Total (1 variable) | | 99.9 |
| 3F | Hostility, Inward and Ambivalent, FAT-*A* | −131 | 99.1 | Hostility, Inward and Ambivalent, FAT-*A* | −116 | 99.0 |
| | Total (1 variable) | | 99.1 | Total (1 variable) | | 99.0 |
| 4F | Popularity, PSQ-T | 3 | 64.8 | Self-Centeredness, PSQ-P | −119 | 66.6 |
| | Controlling, PSQ-T | −100 | 19.5 | Diffuse Anxiety, FAT-*A* | 104 | 13.3 |
| | Group Influence, PSQ-P | − 74 | 5.6 | Effectiveness, PSQ-S | 40 | 13.7 |
| | Total Anxiety, FAT-*A* | 54 | 9.1 | Shame Anxiety, FAT-*A* | 58 | 4.2 |
| | Total (4 variables) | | 99.0 | Total (4 variables) | | 97.8 |
| 5F | Avoidance of Emotion, PSQ-P | 351 | 85.4 | Separation Anxiety, FAT-*A* | 346 | 92.5 |
| | Session Number | 11 | 5.4 | Hostility, Inward and Ambivalent, FAT-*A* | 251 | 3.3 |
| | Overall Behavioral Change, PSQ-T | −101 | 8.8 | | | |
| | Total (3 variables) | | 99.6 | Total (2 variables) | | 95.8 |

[a] PSQ ratings derive from self (S), peer (P), and therapist (T) evaluations for each group member. Delta FAT (FAT-*A*) measures changes from presession to postsession, i.e., FAT-*A* = postsession minus presession FAT scores. Changes in DBH activity are defined as follows: delta DBH = postsession minus presession DBH activity; kappa DBH = postsession minus mean of all presession DBH activity levels.

[b] Results derive from stepwise linear regression. Session number and presession DBH activity are included among the initial variables.

**TABLE 6. Partial Regression Coefficient (*b*) and Percent Explained Variance (%$s^2$) for Postsession Questionnaire (PSQ) and Free Association Test (FAT) Variables Predictive of Delta and Kappa Changes in Dopamine-β-Hydroxylase (DBH) Activity for Each Male Separately[a]**

| Subject | Delta DBH | | | Kappa DBH | | |
|---|---|---|---|---|---|---|
| | Variable | *b* | %$s^2$ | Variable | *b* | %$s^2$ |
| 1M | Ambivalent Hostility, FAT-*A* | −109 | 73.3 | Diffuse Anxiety, FAT-*A* | −32 | 81.7 |
| | Self-Centeredness, PSQ-P | 163 | 14.3 | Group Influence, PSQ-S | −1 | 9.6 |
| | Communication, PSQ-S | 41 | 10.9 | Group Influence, PSQ-T | −15 | 7.6 |
| | Total (3 variables) | | 98.5 | Total (3 variables) | | 98.9 |
| 2M | Overall Behavioral Change, PSQ-P | 89 | 78.2 | Separation Anxiety, FAT-*A* | −27 | 94.9 |
| | Session Number | 8 | 20.7 | Comfort, PSQ-P | 6 | 3.3 |
| | Total (2 variables) | | 98.9 | Total (2 variables) | | 98.2 |
| 3M | Hostility, Inward and Ambivalent, FAT-*A* | −23 | 84.8 | Popularity, PSQ-T | 72 | 67.2 |
| | Insight, PSQ-T | 16 | 5.9 | Hostility Outward, Covert, FAT-*A* | −62 | 22.2 |
| | Comfort, PSQ-S | −13 | 3.1 | Communication, PSQ-T | −32 | 4.8 |
| | | | | Separation Anxiety, FAT-*A* | 33 | 4.0 |
| | Total (3 variables) | | 93.8 | Total (4 variables) | | 98.2 |
| 4M | Involvement, PSQ-T | −45 | 75.9 | Involvement, PSQ-T | −81 | 63.1 |
| | Helpfulness, PSQ-S | 28 | 8.9 | Discouragement, PSQ-P | 97 | 9.7 |
| | Avoidance of Emotion, PSQ-S | −17 | 9.4 | Insight, PSQ-P | −342 | 20.1 |
| | Session Number | −6 | 4.1 | Self-Confidence, PSQ-P | 265 | 7.1 |
| | Total (4 variables) | | 98.3 | Total (4 variables) | | 100.0 |
| 5M | Helpfulness, PSQ-T | 6 | 68.9 | Popularity, PSQ-T | 32 | 39.9 |
| | Controlling, PSQ-P | 18 | 8.1 | Overall Behavioral Change, PSQ-T | 27 | 56.3 |
| | Self-Confidence, PSQ-T | 24 | 16.4 | | | |
| | Total (3 variables) | | 93.4 | Total (2 variables) | | 96.2 |

[a]See Table 5, footnotes *a* and *b*.

Kagan's typology and stepwise regression yields results that illustrate psychobiochemical individuality, i.e., interpersonal differences are shown in response to identical stimuli (37). For example, among married couples, the same affect can be a stressor for one spouse and a destressor for the other.

This initial report would like to direct attention to the need for psychobiochemical methods and techniques: (1) to serve as ancillary tools for clinical assessment of affect and behavior; (2) to permit evaluation of the effectiveness of different therapy models; and (3) to help specify the psychological correlates of vulnerability to psychosomatic illness. The present pilot study develops one paradigm for approaching these broad problems. Preliminary efforts are underway to ascertain the validity of the DBH indicator system. Though encouraging, such work will require replication by others.

## SUMMARY

This pilot study investigates dopamine-$\beta$-hydroxylase (DBH) as an indicator of psychological affect and behavior. Postsession Questionnaire (PSQ), Free Association Test (FAT), and serum DBH data derive from 10 individuals in 15-session, married-couple group psychotherapy. Two experimental manipulations serve as controls for the assessment of variations in DBH activity.

Analyses of DBH show that psychological threat and stress engendered in psychotherapy are accompanied by increases in DBH activity levels. These findings contrast with those observed during the control session in which therapeutic and therapist activity was minimized. Even though higher levels of DBH activity occur in the females examined, two measures of change in DBH, delta and kappa, show no gender variations.

Among the psychological variables, men rate themselves higher on desirable and male stereotypic descriptors. Peers and therapists agree not only in rating females higher on desirable characteristics, but also in rating males higher on descriptors apparently congruent with a dominant male role. FAT anxiety and hostility dimensions show that gender differences emerge during group psychotherapy. Females exhibit larger increases for all of the Hostility Outward categories; males do so for Hostility Inward. These FAT results concur with the clinical importance of hostility expression for this group of ministers and wives.

A stressor-destressor typology and stepwise linear regression show that serum DBH activity can serve as an index for psychological affect and behavior. Specific psychological variables correlate with increases or decreases in serum DBH activity. Delta and kappa DBH are increasingly more predictable from affect and behavior variables by group, gender, and individual regression analyses. Examination of the by-person regression results suggests that psychological stressors and destressors are idiosyncratic to specific individuals. These findings support the conclusion that DBH can serve as a psychobiochemical indicator in psychotherapy.

*The authors are grateful to Dorothy P. Simmons for assistance in data analysis and editing, Terri D. Harris for technical assistance, and Charles P. Pautler and Donald S. Rae, Division of Computer Systems, for computer programming. Comments by Drs. J. Axelrod, F. Holloway, I. Kopin, E. Noble, and two anonymous editors have been most helpful.*

fluctuations over a 24-hr cycle and increasing activity during youth. The magnitude of changes in serum DBH activity with threat or stress is not as great as the range of normal values in a control population (7,8,31). Present results confirm this for both delta and kappa DBH.

Planz and Palm (25)[9] report a range of plasma DBH activity greater than 80-fold (4 to 340 units) for 34 resting volunteers, with a mean ± SEM increase of 25 ±3% after maximum workload. In the present study,[9] the individual basal levels vary about 11-fold (248 to 2572 units). For each individual, the sessions showing maximal percent increase in delta and kappa DBH have been selected. These percent changes derived from delta and kappa have been averaged for the 10 individuals. For delta, the resultant mean ± SEM = 24 ±6%; for kappa, 16 ±3%. The average maximal stress load recorded immediately after brief, married-couple group psychotherapy and physical work seem comparable.

Weinshilboum et al. (31)[9] measure serum DBH activity in 227 normal adults who range in age from 19 to 64 years. Among these adult subjects, DBH activity does not change with age, and gender differences are not observed. The range varies from less than 50 to 2200 units. Unlike the other two studies, current results suggest gender variations in DBH activity levels for the present sample. However, delta and kappa DBH are not gender-linked.

Gender differences in the conscious psychological affects appear to depend on mode of evaluation, i.e., S, P, or T. By PSQ-S, males rate themselves higher than females. Fewer gender variations are noted for PSQ-P and PSQ-T. However, when differences are detected, peer and therapist evaluations generally agree. Preconscious and unconscious FAT data show no gender differences in average presession scores. Postsession FAT scores indicate females are higher on all Hostility Outward dimensions and males are higher on Inward and Total Inward and Ambivalent Hostility. Delta FAT differences tend to correspond with these findings. In a group of ministers and wives, the hostility variables might be expected to play a key role in the therapeutic process since management of hostility constitutes a central clinical problem.

In his discussion of the current state of biochemical studies relevant to human feelings, Mandell (33) predicts future development of physiochemical gauges for estimating stress tolerance, consistency of performance, and proneness to psychosomatic disease. As measures of psychological stress, biochemical reactions may provide precise pancultural standards whose variations are minor compared to other response modes (34) In general, present results support the potential usefulness of instruments such as the FAT and PSQ for measuring psychological variables correlated with changes in neural functions. These results also extend psychobiochemical studies relating FAT parameters to plasma hydrocorticosteroid levels, lipids, and catecholamines (17–19). The present study fulfills criteria expressed by Luborsky, Docherty, and Penick (35) for psychophysiological indicators needed to explain stress responses.

Kagan (36) presents a typology of stress analogous to alertness or calm by discriminating stressor and destressor emotions. In the present study, the use of

[9]DBH substrate conditions and units vary among the three studies discussed; nmoles octopamine/ml plasma/20 min for Planz and Palm, nmoles β-phenylethanolamine/ml sera/hr for Weinshilboum et al. and for the present study. For comparative purposes, one needs to note these variations in units.

## REFERENCES

1. Bridges PK: Recent physiological studies of stress and anxiety in man. Biol Psychiatry 8:95–112, 1974
2. Kaufman, S, Friedman S: Dopamine-β-hydroxylase. Pharmacol Rev 17:71–100, 1965
3. Potter L, Axelrod J: Properties of norepinephrine storage particles of the rat heart. J Pharmacol Exp Ther 142:299–305, 1963
4. Kirshner N: Pathway of noradrenaline formation from dopa. J Biol Chem 226:821–825, 1957
5. Rush RA, Geffen LB: Radioimmunoassay and clearance of circulating dopamine-β-hydroxylase. Circ Res 31:444–452, 1972
6. Weinshilboum R, Axelrod J: Serum dopamine-beta-hydroxylase activity. Circ Res 28:307–315, 1971
7. Weinshilboum RM, Kvetnansky R, Axelrod J, Kopin IJ: Elevation of serum dopamine-β-hydroxylase activity with forced immobilization. Nature New Biol 230:287–288, 1971
8. Wooten GF, Cardon PV: Plasma dopamine-β-hydroxylase activity. Arch Neurol 28:103–106, 1973
9. Geffen LB, Rush RA, Louis WJ, Doyle AE: Plasma dopamine-β-hydroxylase and noradrenaline amounts in essential hypertension. Clin Sci 44:617–620, 1973
10. Schanberg SM, Stone RA, Kirshner N, et al.: Plasma dopamine-β-hydroxylase: a possible aid in the study and evaluation of hypertension. Science 183:523–525, 1974
11. Wetterberg L, Aberg H, Ross SB, Froden O: Plasma dopamine-β-hydroxylase activity in hypertension and various neuropsychiatric disorders. Scand J Clin Lab Invest 30:283–289, 1972
12. DeChamplain J: Report on the discussion of the fourth session. Pharmacol Rev 24:427–430, 1972
13. Horwitz D, Alexander RW, Lovenberg W, Keiser HR: Human serum dopamine-β-hydroxylase: relationship to hypertension and sympathetic activity. Circ Res 32:594–599, 1973
14. Reid JL, Kopin IJ: Significance of plasma DBH activity as an index of sympathetic neuronal function (to be published)
15. Geffen L: Serum dopamine-β-hydroxylase as an index of sympathetic function. Life Sci 14:1593–1604, 1974
16. Silbergeld S, Kvetnansky R, Sigalos GL, et al.: Levels of adrenal catecholamine-synthesizing enzymes after postmortem treatment in rats and after necropsy in human beings. J Lab Clin Med 77:290–297, 1971
17. Silbergeld S, Brast N, Noble EP: The menstrual cycle: a double-blind study of symptoms, mood and behavior, and biochemical variables using Envoid and placebo. Psychosom Med 33:411–428, 1971
18. Gottschalk LA: An objective method of measuring psychological states associated with changes in neural function: content analysis of verbal behavior. Biol Psychiatry 4:33–49, 1972
19. Gottschalk LA, Gleser GC: The measurement of psychological states through the content analysis of verbal behavior. Los Angeles, California, University of California Press, 1969
20. Spielberger CD: Conceptual and methodological issues in anxiety research, in Anxiety: Current Trends in Theory and Research, Vol. II (edited by CD Spielberger). New York, Academic Press, 1972, pp. 481–493
21. Frankenhaeuser M: Experimental approaches to the study of human behavior as related to neuroendocrine functions, in Society, Stress and Disease, Vol. I, Psychosocial Environment and Psychosomatic Diseases (edited by L Levi). London, Oxford University Press, 1971, pp. 22–35
22. Pope PT, Webster JT: The use of an F-statistic in stepwise regression procedures. Technometrics 14:327–340, 1972
23. Lykken DT: Multiple factor analysis and personality research. J Exp Res Pers 5:161–170, 1971
24. Dixon WJ (editor): BMD Biomedical Computer Programs. Los Angeles, California, University of California Press, 1973
25. Planz G, Palm D: Acute enhancement of dopamine-β-hydroxylase activity in human plasma after maximum workload. Eur J Clin Pharmacol 5:255–258, 1973
26. Hidaka H, Asano T, Takemoto N: Analogues of fusaric (5-butylpicolinic) acid as potent inhibitors of dopamine-β-hydroxylase. Molec Pharmacol 9:172–177, 1973
27. Freedman LS, Roffman M, Goldstein M: Changes in human serum dopamine-β-hydroxylase activity in various physiological and pathological states, in Frontiers in Catecholamine Research (edited by E Usdin, SH Snyder). New York, Pergamon Press, 1973, pp. 1109–1114
28. Wetterberg L, Gustavson KH, Backstrom M, et al.: Low dopamine-β-hydroxylase activity in Down's syndrome. Clin Genet 3:152–153, 1972

29. Weinshilboum RM, Axelrod J: Reduced plasma dopamine-β-hydroxylase activity in familial dysautonomia. N Engl J Med 285:938–942, 1971
30. Freedman LS, Ebstein RP, Park DH, et al.: The effect of cold pressor test in man on serum immunoreactive dopamine-β-hydroxylase and on dopamine-β-hydroxylase activity. Res Commun Chem Pathol Pharmacol 6:873–878, 1973
31. Weinshilboum RM, Raymond FA, Elveback LR, Weidman WH: Serum dopamine-β-hydroxylase activity: sibling-sibling correlation. Science 181:943–945, 1973
32. Wooten GF, Eldridge R, Axelrod J, Stern RS: Elevated plasma dopamine-β-hydroxylase activity in autosomal dominant torsion dystonia. N Engl J Med 288:284–287, 1973
33. Mandell AJ: The status of research in biochemical psychiatry. Biol Psychiatry 7:153–159, 1973
34. Averill JR, Opton EM jun, Lazarus RS: Cross-cultural studies of psychophysiological responses during stress and emotion, in Society, Stress and Disease, Vol. I, Psychosocial Environment and Psychosomatic Diseases (edited by L Levi). London, Oxford University Press, 1971, pp. 110–124
35. Luborsky L, Docherty JP, Penick S: Onset conditions for psychosomatic symptoms: a comparative review of immediate observation with retrospective research. Psychosom Med 35:187–204, 1973
36. Kagan A: Epidemiology and society, stress and disease, in Society, Stress and Disease, Vol. I, Psychosocial Environment and Psychosomatic Diseases (edited by L Levi). London, Oxford University Press, 1971, pp. 36–48
37. Hamburg D, in: Synopsis of the general discussion, intervening variables determining the interindividual variation in psychological and physiological response, the biochemical individuality, in Society, Stress and Disease, Vol. I, Psychosocial Environment and Psychosomatic Diseases (edited by L Levi). London, Oxford University Press, 1971, p. 459

# THE RELATIONSHIP OF THE MANIFEST CONTENT OF DREAMS TO DURATION OF CHILDBIRTH IN PRIMIPARAE

Carolyn Winget, MA and Frederic T.Kapp, MD

This report compares manifest dream content during pregnancy with subsequent duration of childbirth in primiparae. One hundred pregnant women were screened in a prenatal clinic to rule out potential complications of labor due to mechanical causes or disease processes. Recent dreams obtained from 70 of these women were scored for anxiety, threat, hostility, motility and themes of pregnancy. The scoring of the manifest dream content was compared with the duration of subsequent childbirth as assessed by Friedman's criteria. Both anxiety and threat were significantly most frequent in the dreams of the short labor group (under 10 hours) and least frequent in the dreams of the prolonged labor group (over 20 hours). The implications of these findings are discussed in terms of the function of dreaming as an adaptive mechanism for coping with an impending normal life crisis.

From the University of Cincinnati, College of Medicine, Department of Psychiatry.
Address for reprint requests: Carolyn Winget, Department of Psychiatry, Cincinnati General Hospital, Cincinnati, Ohio 45229.
Received for publication September 13, 1971

The influence of psychologic factors on labor, and especially on the duration of childbirth in women having their first babies, has been investigated by obstetricians, psychologists and psychiatrists for many years (1-6). Fears and anxieties about the inevitable delivery and the new role of motherhood have been considered important contributing causes in prolonged labor in which mechanical or medical reasons are absent. The demonstration that the epinephrine blood level rises with fear and anxiety (7, 8) and that such increases interfere with uterine contractions (9) offers a possible mechanism to explain how such psychologic factors interact with and influence uterine physiology during labor.

The assessment of the role of psychic conflict in childbirth is complicated because denial and repression are defense mechanisms used frequently by pregnant women to avoid facing their fears and anxieties. Cramond (10) described suppression and repression as typical characteristics of the "dysfunction temperament" in women with uterine dysfunction during labor. Kennedy (11) pointed out difficulties in eliciting and measuring anxiety, fear and tension in pregnant women which he hypothesized caused or contributed to the syndrome of inefficient uterine action during labor.

In this study, we have used the dreams of pregnant women in an attempt to circumvent their defenses to obtain data on underlying fears and anxieties.

Childbirth, with its ubiquitous concerns, provides a fertile soil for the action of psychogenic influences. The expectant mother's attitude toward her coming infant, her readiness for motherhood, her changing self-image and her whole life situation contribute to the psychic influences on her delivery. Expectations and fears of childbirth are intensified with the beginning of labor, and previously existing psychic conflicts are often reactivated.

One might think that the process of birth unfolds in accordance with specific, inherent, biologically determined mechanisms and that it is insulated against external and internal psychologic influences. If delivery were a purely physiologic process, it would be subject to far fewer individual variations than it is, but an event involving greatly heightened inner tension and a tremendous physical upheaval must produce important psychic concomitants. Complications of childbirth, such as prolonged labor due to inefficient uterine action, supply us with clues regarding the role of psychic factors in its course.

Why does the pregnant uterus, after remaining for months subject only to minor and occasional contractions, suddenly go into powerful and efficient action which within a few hours rids the uterus of the contents which it has borne for such a long time? We still do not have a clear answer to this question. However, a significant role in the onset of labor is undoubtedly played by the maturing physiology of the fetus as well as that mother. We know that the uterine musculature is sensitive to the intricate balance between the hormones of the fetus and those of the mother. The series of events that culminates in labor

involves, and may be triggered by the maturation of the fetal endocrine system, particularly the pituitary and adrenal glands. The various secretions of these glands affect the physiology of the mother via the placenta. A feedback mechanism probably initiates labor by affecting the hormonal production of the placenta as well as the maternal endocrine glands which in turn affect the uterus directly. In other words, the initiation of labor is an exceedingly complex affair mediated by intricate and interlocking hormonal controls (12).

Nor do the complexities end here. Obstetricians, as well as those in the behavioral sciences, have been interested in separating out and learning more about the relationships of psychic influences on uterine functioning. Bickers (13) reported hyperactivity of the nonpregnant uterus in patients subjected to fearful stimuli. Kelly (14) reported a similarity of uterine stimulatory responses to hypnotically recalled fear and that produced by intravenous catecholamines.

Epinephrine in low dosage inhibits spontaneous as well as oxytocin-induced human uterine contractions. Norepinephrine, on the other hand, promotes an increase of uterine motility (15). It is also established that catecholamine levels tend to be elevated during stressful situations (7). Garcia and Garcia (9) have presented evidence of higher plasma levels of catecholamines in women undergoing abnormal labor than in their "normal" counterparts. Thus there is reasonable evidence to support the hypothesis that psychic stress influences uterine motility via shifts in endogenous catecholamine levels.

As part of an ongoing study of variables influencing uterine action during labor, a research team at the University of Cincinnati Medical Center has been attempting to validate the usefulness of a structured interview based on 10 predictive variables isolated in a previous postpartum study by one of us (5). Included in the interview is a request that the pregnant woman tell the interviewer her most recent dream.

In an early psychoanalytically oriented study, Helena Deutsch (16) described some typical themes and their representations and meanings in dreams during pregnancy. Babies are often the subject of such dreams. Sometimes the child of the dream is advanced in development as evidenced by walking or talking. In these dreams, according to Deutsch, the expectant mother fulfills, in fantasy, her wishes to bear the child and mother it, wishes that she has gnawing doubts about her ability to fulfill. Other pregnant women express the negative side of their ambivalence to childbirth and motherhood by dreaming of giving birth to infants who are deformed or dead.

In studying the manifest content of 100 dreams of 14 pregnant women, Van de Castle (17) noted that during the last trimester approximately 35% of their dreams contained references to a baby or child. In contrast, reference to a baby or child occurred in only about 5% of the dreams of nonpregnant women included in his and Calvin Hall's normative sample of college women (18).

Gillman (19) reported on dreams during first pregnancy in his investiga-

tion of the relation of the psychologic stress of pregnancy to subsequent maternal adaptation. He concluded that the dreams of pregnant women are useful in delineating how individuals come to grips with their new role. Coleman (20) found the dreams of his pregnant subjects useful in the exploration of their psychologic state during first pregnancy. Cheek (21) discussed the significance and usefulness of dreams in predicting which pregnant women would be "poor-risk" obstetric patients and would, therefore, need special attention in coping with childbirth. Epstein (22), in a study of pregnant women, explored the relation between waking levels of expressed concern over the stress of childbirth and the manifest portrayal of pregnancy themes in the content of recalled dreams.

The purpose of this paper is to report further on some of the dimensions of the manifest dream content in pregnant women, as well as to describe some interesting relationships which have emerged between types of dream content and subsequent duration of labor in primiparae.

## MATERIALS AND METHODS

### *Subjects*

One hundred successive, presumably healthy, primigravidae were selected for study. Women with potential dystocia due to mechanical difficulties such as borderline or abnormally small pelvic capacity were ruled out as were those with diabetes, hypertension or other illnesses which sometimes affect delivery. Each subject was studied in a prenatal clinic during the third trimester of her first pregnancy. In general, the subjects were from the lower or lower-middle classes, with a mean age of 18 (range: 15 to 26 years). Most of the subjects, 75%, were black, and 67% were unmarried.

### *Data Collection*

The records of the local Maternal and Infant Care Agency were screened each week to secure the names of all primigravidae requesting care at two prenatal clinics. Each subject was then given a semi-structured interview attempting to discover her attitudes toward variables thought to be central to adaptation to pregnancy and motherhood. A request for the most recent dream was made within the context of sleep difficulties. In addition, each subject filled out a Defense Mechanisms Inventory (23). A report of these aspects of our study will be made later.*

*The authors wish to express their appreciation for the participation in data collection to Mrs. Fanny Nicholes and Mrs. Rita Seifert, Research Assistants in the Department of Psychiatry, and Dr. Donald E. Wilbert, Senior Resident in Psychiatry.

*Assessment of Length of Childbirth*

Contrary to our initial expectation that length of labor would provide the "hard" data of this study, we found that much effort was required to approach a valid and reliable assessment of this variable. Ultimately, as outlined by Friedman (24), it was found most useful to take into account the sum of three separate phases of the childbirth process:[+]

1. *The Latent Phase of Stage One of Labor*. This is defined as beginning with the onset of regular uterine contractions, as perceived by the subject, and extending to that point in time when cervical dilatation suddenly accelerates. A member of the research group conducted postpartum interviews in an effort to improve the reliability of the subjective judgments regarding the time of the onset of labor.

2. *The Active Phase of Stage One of Labor*. This phase extends from the time of acceleration to full dilatation of the cervix—ie, approximately from 3 to 10 cm.

3. *The Second Stage of Labor*. This is defined as the period from the end of the active phase (cervix fully dilated) to the delivery of the infant.

Overall, we found a modest but significant correlation between the summed duration of the latent and active phases of stage one and the duration of the second stage, indicating that these measures were not independent of one another. On the basis of these data, therefore, we chose to use the sum of all three measurements as our estimate of the duration of childbirth.

Of the original 100 subjects selected for potentially normal delivery, 30 were subsequently excluded. Eighteen did not report dreams and four could recall only a childhood dream. Other subjects dropped included: 2 in which the weight of the babies were under 2500 g; 1 instance of overt prenatal emotional problems; 2 subjects whose labor data were of questionable reliability; and 1 subject who was 14 years of age. Also excluded were 2 women who underwent cesarean sections due to a previously undetected pelvic disproportion.

*Content Analysis of Dreams*

Dreams were abstracted from the interview records and coding was carried out blindly. The Threat Scale of Framo *et al* (25) and three affect scales of Gottschalk and Gleser (26, 27) were used to test the hypothesis that psychic stress affects uterine action in childbirth. We also coded for motility (28) because of the possibility that the amount of movement in fantasy life may be related to the

---

[+]The authors wish to thank Dr. Tom P. Barden and Mrs. Kay Bornemann, Research Assistant, both of the Department of Obstetrics and Gynecology, for the painstaking work which was required for these measurements.

duration of labor. Finally, we coded for the frequency of overt themes of childbirth and babies because previous studies (17, 19, 20) had reported the centrality of these themes in the dreams of pregnant women.

## RESULTS

The 70 women in this study were divided into three categories on the basis of total childbirth time as contained in the obstetric record. Group I were the 31 women who delivered in less than 10 hours. Group II was an intermediate group of 31 women whose childbirth time ranged from over 10 to 20 hours. Group III, the Prolonged Labor Group, consisted of 8 women whose childbirth time was over 20 hours. Most obstetricians consider 20 hours as the cutting point for defining abnormal length of labor (29). Race, marital status and age were not significant factors in the distribution of the subjects among the three groups. Nor did whether or not a subject told a dream during the interview relate to subsequent length of labor.

Table 1 summarizes the results of the analysis of the manifest dream content for our three groups of primiparae categorized as to duration of childbirth. The results indicate:

1. There was a significant relationship ($P < .01$) between frequency of dreams with anxiety in the manifest content and duration of childbirth. Anxiety as measured by the Gottschalk-Gleser scale was present in over 80% of the dream reports of those who subsequently delivered in less than 10 hours but was scoreable in only 25% of the dreams of the Prolonged Labor Group. The women who were intermediate in frequency of anxiety themes were also intermediate in length and labor.

2. Scoring for themes of threat revealed similar but slightly attentuated significant differences ($P < .05$).* This is to be expected in view of the conceptual similarity of the Threat Scale and the scale for measuring Anxiety. The vector of the threat—ie, whether it was directed toward the self or toward another object, did not differentiate the dreams of the three groups.

3. Hostility, both that directed outward and to the self, showed trends toward being highest in those women with the shortest labor time as compared with the intermediate and prolonged labor groups.

4. Average motility scores suggested that the higher the movement scores in dreams, the shorter the labor time, although this finding was also not statistically significant.

5. Overt themes of babies, labor and delivery room were present in about

*If the 4 women omitted because their reported dreams were recalled from childhood rather than from their period of pregnancy are included, the statistical significance of anxiety increases to ($P < .001$) and that for threat to ($P < .01$).

**Table 1. Dream Content and Duration of Childbirth**

| Dream Variable Present | Total Duration of Childbirth in 70 Cases: Less than 10 hr (N=31) N | % | Over 10 but less than 20 hr (N=31) N | % | More than 20 hr (N=8) N | % | |
|---|---|---|---|---|---|---|---|
| Anxiety | 25 | 81 | 14 | 45 | 2 | 25 | $\chi^2=12.21$ $P<.01$ |
| Threat | 24 | 77 | 15 | 48 | 3 | 37 | $\chi^2=7.10$ $P<.05$ |
| Hostility–outward | 16 | 52 | 11 | 36 | 2 | 25 | ns |
| Hostility–inward | 14 | 45 | 6 | 19 | 2 | 25 | ns |
| Average motility score | 14 | | 12 | | 10 | | ns |
| Baby–labor–delivery theme | 11 | 36 | 11 | 36 | 4 | 50 | ns |

one-third of the dreams of all the subjects but did not differentiate the short, intermediate and long labor groups.

## DISCUSSION

The physiology of the pregnant woman is designed to nuture the growing fetus and is tuned to a serene, contented waiting. Even women who are ususally tense and liable to anxiety are often surprised by their calmness during pregnancy. They do not have the same emotional responses which they would have otherwise to environmental stresses. To this physiologically determined self-satisfied state is added the indulgence of the culture which allows and encourages the self-centered attitude of the pregnant woman.

A woman's emotional state during pregnancy is determined by her physiologic status as well as her personality structure and only secondarily is it influenced by personal attitudes toward external factors such as the legitimacy of her pregnancy. We found no difference in duration of childbirth by marital status. This agrees with the findings of Steward and Bernard (30) and of Eysenck (31) who found that emotional problems presumed to be associated with illegitimacy did not lead to difficult labor.*

*Some of our interview data leads us to the conclusion that the current social scene with its sharply changing concepts of sex and marriage make it even less likely today to find marital status influencing duration of labor.

An important psychic task of the pregnant woman is to differentiate the growing child within from herself so that when delivery occurs she will accept the newborn infant as a separate individual. To the extent that this differentiation is not worked through, the delivery will be experienced as a painful separation, as though a part of the body were being lost. In other words, an important task of the pregnant woman is to prepare to deliver the child from herself both physically and psychologically.

Most women, pregnant for the first time, anticipate the coming childbirth as a major crisis. Yet, in spite of this anticipation, concern about childbirth remains in the background during the contented, hormonally well-balanced pregnancy of those women who have a normal desire for motherhood. Toward the end of pregnancy, however, the contented mood is often dimmed by tense expectations, by fear of pain, by fear of being damaged or of dying and concern for the well-being of the unborn child. Many women, even the well adjusted, become dubious of the outcome of their pregnancy when the time of delivery nears. They question their courage to bear the pain and their capacity and willingness to assume the responsibilities of being a mother.

We found that pregnant women in whom anxiety and threat themes are missing from their dreams are more likely to undergo prolonged labor due to inefficient uterine action than their counterparts whose dreams contain anxiety and threat. This supports the hypothesis that the function of the dream is an attempt to master, in fantasy, an anticipated stress in waking life. It is consistent with Maeder's (32) idea that dreams contain attempts at solving conflicts by providing practice in the dream for subsequent waking actions. Modern students of the dream—eg, Erikson (33), French and Fromm (34) and Bonime (35) have emphasized that dream work is dominated by the need to find a solution for current pressing conflicts. Investigators such as Jones (36), Witkin and Lewis (37), and Cartwright (38) have demonstrated problem-solving behavior during dreaming.

We think that the attempt to solve an intense ongoing conflict in the dream utilizes technics successful in dealing with previously stressful situations. Dreams characteristically contain elements representing current or anticipated problems as well as representations of earlier conflicts with which the individual had wrestled. This intermingling of the current problem which the dreamer is attempting to solve with those conflicts successfully coped with in the past is used by the dreamer as a kind of template to work out a solution. The blending of past and present in the attempted solution, often represented in the dream by metaphor or by analogy, frequently gives the dream its seemingly meaningless or bizarre manifest content.

Our study suggests that pregnant women who dream during the last trimester of stressful themes or feelings of anxiety and other negative affects are attempting to cope with the anticipated crisis of the delivery. Those women who

do not face the coming stressful situation by attempting to deal with it in their dreams are more likely to resort to mechanisms of denial and repression of the anticipated threat. It is interesting to note that there was a marked tendency for those who subsequently underwent prolonged childbirth to report briefer dreams than their counterparts in both the short and intermediate duration groups. We hypothesize that for some women the anticipated trauma of childbirth is too great to be allowed even symbolic or displaced expression in dreams. When labor is initiated, their lack of psychologic preparation, as evidenced by the absence of anxiety and threat in their dreams before labor ensues, may lead to increased anxiety with its concomitant abnormalities in catecholamine blood levels. Such women are tenser both psychologically and physiologically than the women who have used dreaming as a psychologic immunization to prepare themselves for the approaching confinement.

Dream reports during pregnancy provide a useful clinical and research tool for circumventing the defenses of denial and repression and can lead to a better understanding of the underlying dynamics of how a woman copes with the crisis of childbirth. For some women, even though there is little conscious awareness of the nature of the imminent stress of childbirth, dreaming can function to mobilize and integrate adaptive mechanisms and thus perform a major function in coping with one of the important stresses in a woman's life.

## SUMMARY

As part of an investigation of prolonged labor in primigravidae, recent dreams were secured from women during the last trimester of their pregnancy. We used these dreams to tap anxiety and fear which were difficult to assess by ordinary interview technics because of their repression or denial. When delivery data were available, cases of disproportion, breech birth or unreliable labor data were dropped from the study and the remaining women were assigned to one of three labor groups: a) total labor of less than 10 hours (N = 31); b) 10 to less than 20 hours (N = 31); c) 20 hours or over (N = 8). All women had previously been screened for mechanical problems and diseases that may affect duration of childbirth. There were no significant demographic differences in the composition of these three groups. Overall the mean age was 18; almost 80% of the women were Negro, and about 65% were single.

Dreams were abstracted from interview records and scored blindly for anxiety, threat, hostility, motility and themes of babies, pregnancy and delivery. Both anxiety (Gottschalk-Gleser scale) and threat (Framo et al scale) were significantly most frequent in the dreams of the short labor group (under 10 hours) and least frequent in the dreams of the prolonged labor group (over 20 hours). In addition, a comparison of the three groups showed a trend in the short

labor group toward greater hostility and more motility in dream content. The implications of these findings are discussed in terms of the function of dreaming as an adaptive mechanism for coping with an impending normal life crisis.

## REFERENCES


1. Jeffcoate TNA, Baker K, Martin RH: Inefficient uterine action. *Surg Gynecol Obstet* 95:257, 1952.
2. Castallo MA, Wainer AS: Prolonged labor. *M Clin N Am* 39:1801, 1955.
3. Hetzel BS, Bruer B, Poidevin LOS: A survey of the relation between certain common antenatal complicatons in primiparas and stressful life situations during pregnancy. *J Psychosom Res* 5:175, 1961.
4. Rosengren WR: Some social psychologic aspects of delivery room difficulties. *J Nerv Ment Dis* 132:515, 1961.
5. Kapp FT, Hornstein S, Graham VT: Some psychologic factors in prolonged labor due to inefficient uterine action. *Comp Psychiat* 4:9-18, 1963.
6. Chertok L: *Motherhood and personality, Psychosomatic Aspects of Childbirth*] London, Tavistock, 1969.
7. Elmadjiian, F, Hope JM, Lamson ET: Excretion of epinephrine and norepinephrine under stress. *J Clin Endocrinol* 17:608, 1957.
8. Euler US, Lundberg U: Effect of flying on the epinephrine excretion in Air Force personnel. *J Appl Phys* 6:551, 1953.
9. Garcia CR, Garcia ES: Epinephrine-like substances in the blood and their relation to uterine inertia. *Am J Obstet Gynecol* 69:812, 1955.
10. Cramond WA: Psychological aspects of uterine dysfunction. *Lancet* 2:1241, 1954.
11. Kennedy C: Incoordinate uterine action. *Edinburgh Med J* 56:445, 1949.
12. Quilligan EJ: The initiation of labor. *Hosp Prac* 44-49, 1968.
13. Bickers W: Uterine contraction patterns: effects of psychic stimuli on the myometrium. *Fertil Steril* 7:268, 1956.
14. Kelly JV: Effect of fear upon uterine motility. *Am J Obstet Gynecol* 83:576, 1962.
15. Barden TP, Stander RW: Effects of adrenergic blocking agents and catecholamines in human pregnancy. *Am J Obstet Gynecol* 102:226-235, 1968.
16. Deutsch H: *The Psychology of Women.* Vol 2, New York, Grune and Stratton, 1945, p 126-201; 202-258.
17. Van de Castle RL, Kinder P: Dream content during pregnancy. *Psychophys* 4:373, 1968.
18. Hall CS, Van de Castle RL: *The Content Analysis of Dreams*. New York, Appleton-Century-Crofts, 1966.
19. Gillman RD: The dreams of pregnant women and maternal adaptation. *Am J Orthopsychiat* 38:668-692, 1968.
20. Coleman AD: Psychological state during first pregnancy. *Am J Orthopsychiat* 39:788-797, 1969.
21. Cheek DB: Some newer understandings of dreams in relation to threatened abortion and premature labor. *Pacif Med Surg* 73:379-384, 1965.
22. Epstein LRS: Dreams of pregnant women. PhD dissertation, University of Kansas, 1969.
23. Gleser GC, Ihilevich D: An objective instrument for measuring defense mechanisms. *J Consult Clin Psych* 33:51-60, 1969.

24. Friedman EA: *Labor: Clinical Evaluation and Management.* New York, Appleton-Century-Crofts, 1967.

25. Framo JL, Osterweil J, Boszormenyi-Nagy I: A relationship between threat in the manifest content of dreams and active-passive behavior in psychotics. *J Abnorm Soc Psychol* 65:41-47, 1962.

26. Gottschalk LA, Gleser GC: The measurement of psychological states through the content analysis of verbal behavior. Berkeley and Los Angeles: University of California Press, 1969.

27. Gottschalk LA, Winget CN, Gleser GC: A manual for using the Gottschalk-Gleser content analysis scales. Berkeley and Los Angeles: University of California Press, 1969.

28. Whitman RM, Pierce C, Maas J, Baldridge B: Drugs and dreams. *II: Imipramine and prochlorperazine. Comp Psychiat* 2:219-226, 1961.

29. Friedman EA: An objective method of evaluating labor. *Hosp Prac* July:82-87, 1970.

30. Stewart DB, Bernard RM: A clinical classification of difficult labor and some examples of its use. *J Obstet Gynecol Br Emp* 61:318, 1954.

31. Eysenck SBG: Personality and pain assessment in childbirth of married and unmarried mothers. *J Ment Sc* 107:417, 1961.

32. Maeder A: The dream problem. *Nerv Ment Dis Monog Series,* 22, 1916.

33. Erikson EA: The dream specimen of psychoanalysis. *J Am Psychoanal Assoc* 2:5-56, 1954.

34. French TM, Fromm E: *Dream Interpretation: A New Approach.* New York, Basic Books, 1964.

35. Bonime W: *The Clinical Use of Dreams.* New York, Basic Books, 1962.

36. Jones RM: *The New Psychology of Dreaming.* New York, Grune and Stratton, 1970.

37. Witkin HA, Lewis HB: The relation of experimentally induced presleep experiences to dreams. *J Am Psychoanal Assoc* 13:819-849, 1965.

38. Cartwright RD: The effect of dream opportunity on daytime problem resolution: A preliminary report of a pilot study. Presented at APSS, Santa Fe, New Mexico, 1970.

# MALE ANXIETY DURING SLEEP

ANITA I. BELL, New York

This report is a step in a chain of events which started in 1957 with the observation that the scrotal sac and testes had virtually been ignored in Freud's writings and in the Grinstein Index. Child and adolescent analysis and that of adults as well revealed material which indicated that the scrotal sac and testes played a significant role in male anxiety, separate and apart from the erotic role of the penis.

One way screen observations of cases in supervision as well as more intensive supervision immediately after each therapy hour seemed to further confirm the importance of such material.

This observation was followed by an interdisciplinary study in which young college students were given a structured psychiatric interview while being monitored for psychophysiological responses (Bell *et al.*, 1971). Subjects were wired to a polygraph to obtain readings on GSR, SPR, EKG, EEG and respiration. In addition to a penile strain gauge, a scrotal strain gauge was used to measure testicular retractions. In addition, Ag-AgCl Beckman electrodes measured the activity of the dartos and cremaster muscles. This study (Bell *et al.*, 1971) confirmed the clinical hypothesis that sac and testes respond physiologically to anxiety-provoking experiences.

Up to the present, studies involving the male genital during sleep have concerned themselves only with penile activity during REM and NREM. Fisher (1966), who introduced the psychoanalytic meanings of dreams as related to the penile cycle of tumescence and detumescence during sleep, did not use scrotal instrumentation, nor did he consider the psychoanalytic implications of the scrotum and testes.

In a pilot sleep study (Bell, 1972) the same instrumentation and technique as described in the interdisciplinary psychophysiological study was used with the addition of the standard equipment for sleep studies according to Rechtschaffen & Kales (1968) including EEG and EOG monitoring. Each subject was interviewed by the author who is an experienced child, adolescent and adult analyst. A complete developmental history was elicited, psychological and medical, as well as present day difficulties, if any. Three subjects were studied for three baseline nights and four to eight nights with content awakenings. The subjects were told that we were studying the male genital during sleep.

These subjects were awakened whenever a scrotal complex response (SCR) appeared on the polygraph, regardless of sleep stage. There were 80 SCR awakenings, 35 during REM, 45 in NREM, and of the dartos, 9 occurred in REM and 58 in NREM. Content reports associated with an SCR were rated for anxiety in manifest content according to the Gottschalk–Gleser scale (Gottschalk *et al.*, 1969) by a blind rater and by a psychiatrist. In this paper only dreams rated as showing high anxiety are included.

Among the recurring motifs in these dreams are: (1) *anxiety over the scrotal instrumentation:* which included a strain gauge and electrodes; (2) *symbolic references to scrotal sac and testes:* which included the number *two,* bicycle wheels, cars as total genital or other mechanical devices, also ticks or bugs, jewels, fuses and light bulbs as scrotal symbols. (Many will object to our evaluation of symbolic content. But the kind of content which appears when only the penile gauge is applied versus that with scrotal instrumentation is food for thought.) (3) repeated instances of *fear of bodily injury* and, finally, (4) subjects' *fear of homosexual attack* by the male technician.

Subjects' dreams will be reported first and rated according to manifest content. These will then be compared with one of Freud's own dreams and his discussion of it, and dream material reported by Fisher in his sleep research.

*Dream 1.* a.m. report, night 1, non-awakening.

A 21-year-old subject, who did not seem anxious and was very cooperative, during his first non-awakening night reported dreaming of cleaning his windows, ticks crawling all over his body—he saw them in the crotch and on the arms; they were dark ticks, two at the base of the shaft of his penis. He picked off one on the right arm. On polygraph, the cremaster tracing went flat. The experimenter noted a question: 'Did he pick an electrode off? He did.' This dream was rated high anxiety by Gottschalk–Gleser scale.

*Dream 2.* a.m. report, non-awakening, marked dartos, SCR. penile blip, sustained testicular retraction;
recall 3 anxiety 3

I was dreaming that *there was a car of mine that was in an accident and the left and the right side door was pushed in.* We took the door off, put it in the garage or apart. And I remember going to Mary's place for another car, to find another door to fit the car... My father had a car. My car had been hit on one side. The door was hit in. We took the smashed door off. We kept all three cars together in a lot right *outside the house*... I remember incidents... of like trying to get the door, and I can remember once we went to look for doors at this place, I guess nearby, and this guy right in back of me, tailgating, trying to cut me off. *When the guy was tailgating, I can remember being mad at him, like, ' What's this guy doing? He's crazy. He's really driving like a maniac.'* There was an intersection coming up and he was going to go left there, and he was coming up, trying to pass me on the left, one of those things. Another part, too, we went to our house, we just got there and there was this *big radio set* or something and as we tuned it in... I was changing stations and a *fuse blew.* That's when I woke up now.

Another subject seemed very much at ease on the nights when the chief investigator had been in the lab and assisted with electrodes as the occasion required. This particular night he was told that the author would leave and that the male technician would be there alone. He had seemingly accepted this and showed no noticeable anxiety, yet woven into his dream we see considerable fear of the male technician as life-threatening and the wish that the author would stay. From his comments, he considered her a good mother figure. The degree of anxiety about the male technician and scrotal instrumentation is illustrated by his dream, reported on the morning of his third non-awakening night:

*Dream 3.* a.m. report, night 3, dartos, SCR active all stages;
recall 3 anxiety 3

I was living in a house with someone who is my uncle or some guy I just trusted, and he had me hooked up to electrodes except we slept in boxes, very much like *coffins.* And I slept there. I guess I set up a regular pattern because I seemed to have accepted it in the dream. One night, my cousin's car—she's about 18 now—her car broke down, near the place, or somehow she was stranded near there and it was at the house. I fell for her, but she told me that I was *sleeping in a coffin, giving my life to this guy*, but I didn't believe it because he was a nice guy, but I walked around, so I walked around when *she was there with all the electrodes on.* I figured I'd plug them back in or something, and I don't know the sequence but I found out that he was a *vampire* and he was stealing my life [laugh] *he was stealing my life with the electrodes*, and *she couldn't leave* because her car was still broken and *I wanted her to stay anyway*, but she didn't and went to another house. *And I visited her at the house and it blew some of the experiment 'cause I took all the electrodes with me.* There was more people at her house and *they questioned me about the electrodes*, and I guess that's all, you know I'm having the experiment...

I can remember kissing my cousin, except there is *something about her face*, I can't place yet, but it was distorted. Well, it became mechanical or non-aligned. She looked like my cousin, but when I got close it wasn't but I still wanted to kiss the person, whoever it was, maybe the face would be off, the mouth would be over by the ear or there was something wrong, but I kissed her anyway. I think I went back and found out that *he was exposed as taking my life*, so I don't know what happened. I don't know how the dream finishes up. I know that he was exposed. I guess that *everything was left hanging*. Nothing got solved.

This subject became increasingly anxious as the nights went on. In fact, by the eighth night he was annoyed and said so. He dreamed it, too: he dreamed that he was ' getting paid to answer silly questions '. He had had surgery as a child—one kidney had been removed—and the whole idea of a hospital was frightening to him. Yet he wanted to work in a hospital. His wish to work in a hospital seems to have been an attempt to master the overwhelming castration threat caused by the surgery and loss of the kidney. (We have reported a child therapy case in which kidney and testicles were equated, Bell, 1968.)

Symbolically, his anxiety content expressed

itself in testicular terms, i.e. ticks, cars, machines, mechanical devices. He dreamed the following on an awakening night:

*Dream 4.* Stage 2.

I was trying to figure why I should wake up from sewing. When you told me to wake up, I was sewing. There was a genital *machine* and it was all set to go, so I was going to sit down and see what went. It was something new to do. I never sewed before . . . The *showcase was robbed in the store;* there was *no jewels* or nothing in it. The sewing machine was on top of the counter.

Previously we found this subject dreaming about running around with the wires, then coming back and plugging them in. This dream seemed to be an attempt to further master his anxiety. He dreamed he was sewing—probably what had been cut by the surgeons. The next statement tells us that the showcase was robbed, the *jewels were gone*. The castration had already taken place. One kidney had been removed. Testes are commonly referred to as jewels; when paratroopers are putting on their gear, they are cautioned to beware of ' the family jewels ', i.e. don't damage your testicles. These associations constitute castration fears in terms of kidney, sac and testes. No phallic symbols appear.

Both these subjects dreamed about accidents or damage to their cars. Two doors, one on each side, were mentioned. The electrodes, one on each side of the scrotal sac, would provide the external stimulus.

A third subject brought out the same idea. He was slightly older than the other two, and married. He seemed relaxed, but during his sleep he made movements which seemed to be warding off being hit by someone. Having observed these repetitive movements the author asked the subject if he had been hit as a child. He replied that his father had a bad temper and used to hit him around the head.

The content that follows was in response to an awakening with SCR and a rating of high anxiety on the Gottschalk–Gleser scale.

*Dream 5.* Stage: awake.

I was thinking about an event that happened to me, oh, years ago. It was something that actually happened. It was just a weird thing. My father hit this guy with a car and it was just a weird thing. But I was thinking about it in reference to the police in the town where my parents live . . . My father hit this kid on a bicycle, and he was really freaked out about it. He was like in shock. I was just sort of re-picturing that. No one actually saw the accident except for himself, and I was picturing it to myself as I guess I imagine it would have looked.

From the manifest content, this dream also indicates a danger to the body. I have often come across riding on a bicycle as a masturbatory symbol. Symbolically, the body as phallus (the usual analytic interpretation) has the *added factor* of two *round wheels*, which could be representative of two testes. This is from the viewpoint of a child analyst who depends on drawings rather than verbalizations for material.

In this dream there is the possible element that the father with the big car castrates the boy for masturbating. Again the castration refers to both the sac and both testes (two wheels) and the penis.

All subjects dreamed of cars in connexion with bodily danger. This leads to the conjecture that for today's male in our culture, the car with its complicated motor may be used to symbolize the entire genital, i.e. penis, sac and testes.

Mentation which was elicited when SCRs appeared involved danger to the body and symbolically the testes were involved. All of these dreams were rated as involving high anxiety. The fact that subjects wore instrumentation on *both the penis and the scrotum* (plus the fact that the actual dream content indicated *symbolically* the presence of scrotal testicular elements) made it easier to *concretely* ascertain that what the psychoanalyst considers anxiety referable only to the penis is *in actuality referable to the scrotum.* Thus it is possible that castration anxiety includes fears of loss of the testes as well as the penis. If we had followed Freud's idea that dreams are the royal road to the unconscious and symbolism is the lock that opens the door, psychoanalysis would not be ' falling from its pinnacle ' today and psychiatry would not be tagging along.

It might be argued that evaluation of the dream material derives only from the manifest dream content. Subjects of the experiment were not in therapy. However, this gives us a basis of comparison with Fisher's work and with some of the dreams by Freud and others.

*Dream* 1 shows ticks as electrodes, but possibly testicular symbols as well, with ticks at the

base of the shaft, where in fact electrodes had been placed.

*Dream* 2, when evaluated from the perspective of dream symbolism, is indicative of genital anxiety. From clinical study we know that in the mind of the male, young or old, his car represents his power, i.e. his genital. Freudian analysts have always considered it a phallic symbol. However, the elements of *two sides* (the 'two doors were pushed in') would also be scrotal, i.e. two testicles in a sac. The electrodes were on either side of the scrotum. The thrust of the motor in front could be considered phallic, and the danger to the rear (tailgating) would involve the anal threat and also the threat of the technician, who was positioned behind. Also, the subject perceived the electrodes placed on either side of the scrotum with a current running through them as dangerous.

## Discussion

There are many questions that merit attention here. Why are males reluctant to touch or look too closely at the scrotal part of another male? (Clinically and in paediatrics we have found this to be so.) Is this too closely linked with homosexuality? Is it the taboo against dirt and sex? Is it the fear of destruction by another male? Or is it a warding off of unconscious desires to be touched or stroked by another male, in this case the male technician?

The anxiety of both the male technician when an electrode got loose or had to be checked and the anxiety of the male subject were enormous. One subject sweated so much that the thermostat had to be turned down and the electrodes fell off due to moisture. The technician also sweated and showed considerable anxiety. In addition the technician, who was an intuitive and sensitive young man with superior intelligence, had an incredible block about the anatomy and physiology of the scrotum. Even though a member of the urology staff explained the anatomy, he was unable to comprehend the placement of the equipment. This was all the more remarkable because he had been a subject at other laboratories and had no difficulty in placing the electrodes on himself. Only after the author, a much older female M.D., repeatedly explained and assisted in a very casual manner was he able to place the equipment on the subjects properly. As we talked over what had happened, he realized his block and its basis. In sharp contrast, the female technician had no such difficulty, nor did the subjects react with anxiety to her or to the chief investigator.

During the previously reported study of psychiatric interviews in the waking state (Bell *et al.*, 1971), the male psychophysiologist was unable to put the electrodes on the subjects himself or even be present while they were being applied. He gave the subjects a drawing of the area and detailed instructions so that they could do it themselves; then he went out of the room. He was most uncomfortable about the experiment. If any difficulties with the electrodes occurred, he checked the polygraph and then instructed the subjects verbally about how to rectify the problem. Just the idea of seeing, to say nothing of touching the scrotum of another male, was upsetting.

Freud considered dreams as 'the royal road to the unconscious' and described symbol as follows:

> Symbolism is perhaps the most remarkable chapter of the theory of dreams. In the first place, since symbols are *stable translations*, they realize to some extent the ideal of the ancient as well as of the popular interpretation of dreams, from which, with our technique, we had departed widely. They allow us in certain circumstances to *interpret a dream without questioning the dreamer, who indeed would in any case have nothing to tell us about the symbol* (Freud, 1916, p. 151, my italics).

Freud has reported a number of dreams which show very clearly symbolic reference to the sac and testes (Freud, 1900, pp. 360, 366, 388) but for the most part he did not interpret them, nor do his followers. Perhaps an answer may be found in one of Freud's own dreams, reported in 1900, when he was 44 years of age. (Within a year or two he had a Steinach operation.) It is a most impressive example of an anxiety dream directly connected with a painful scrotal stimulus. It rates high anxiety according to the Gottschalk–Gleser scale. The defences used are denial and displacement. As he himself says,

> In fact, I have only noted a single dream in which an objective and painful source of stimulus is recognizable; and it will be most instructive to examine the effect which the external stimulus produced in this particular dream.
> *I was riding on a grey horse, timidly and awkwardly to*

*begin with, as though I were only reclining on it. I met one of my colleagues, P., who was sitting high on a horse, dressed in a tweed suit, and who drew my attention to something (probably to my bad seat). I now began to find myself sitting more and more firmly and comfortably on my highly intelligent horse, and noticed that I was feeling quite at home up there. My saddle was a kind of bolster, which completely filled the space between its neck and crupper. In this way I rode straight* IN BETWEEN TWO VANS. *After riding some distance up the street, I turned round and tried to dismount, first in front of a small open chapel that stood in the street frontage. Then I actually did dismount in front of another chapel that stood near it. My hotel was in the same street; I might have let the horse go to it on its own, but I preferred to lead it there. It was as though I should have felt ashamed to arrive at it on horseback. A hotel ' boots ' was standing in front of the hotel; he showed me a note of mine that had been found, and laughed at me over it. In the note was written, doubly underlined: ' No food ' and then another remark (indistinct) such as ' No work ', together with a vague idea that I was in a strange town in which I was doing* NO WORK [italics original, emphases mine].

It would not be supposed at first sight that this dream originated under the influence, or rather under the compulsion, of a painful stimulus. But for some days before I had been suffering from boils which made every movement a torture; and finally a boil the size of an apple had risen at the base of my scrotum, which caused me the most unbearable pain with every step I took. Feverish lassitude, loss of appetite and the hard work with which I nevertheless carried on—all these had combined with the pain to depress me. I was not properly capable of discharging my medical duties. There was, however, one activity for which, in view of the nature and situation of my complaint, I should certainly have been less fitted than for any other, and that was—riding. And this was precisely the activity in which the dream landed me: it was *the most energetic denial of my illness that could possibly be imagined* [my italics]. I cannot in fact ride, nor have I, apart from this, had dreams of riding. I have only sat on a horse once in my life and that was without a saddle, and I did enjoy it. But in this dream I was riding as though I had no boil on my perineum—or rather *because I wanted not to have one*. My saddle, to judge from its description, was the poultice which had made it possible for me to fall asleep. Under its assuaging influence, I had probably been unaware of my pain during the first hours of sleep. The painful feelings had then announced themselves and sought to wake me; whereupon the dream came and said soothingly: ' No! Go on sleeping! There's no need to wake up. You haven't got a boil; for you're riding on a horse, and it's quite certain that you couldn't ride if you had a boil in that particular place.' And the dream was successful. The pain was silenced, and I went on sleeping (Freud, 1900, pp. 229–230).

It is striking that Freud calls this the most important form of denial and yet in all subsequent discussions about castration he focuses almost entirely on the penis. There is also the wish for sexual activity, the two chapels one with the open door, and the reference to the note, the laughter and the indistinct remark ' such as " no work " '.

It is quite possible that Freud would have wanted to repress, deny and displace to the penis any memories of so painful an experience to his most vulnerable and ' dirty ' area. From previous studies (Bell, 1956, 1964, 1965, 1968) it has been noted that although not consciously perceived by the adult male, a long since forgotten taboo about cleanliness during the bowel training days is stirred up along with the prohibitions about touching the ' dirty ' scrotal area. Thus he associates sex with dirt. These unsettling associations connected with the scrotal area constitute one of the big stumbling blocks to the acceptance of the scrotal area as having significance. In fact, it seems to be one of the biggest obstacles towards a more thorough understanding of male castration anxiety, male chauvinism, male homosexuality and bisexuality. Thus it is understandable that Freud overlooked the scrotal symbols (cf. Bell, 1961) in his subsequent work (e.g. in his 1909–1911 additions to the ' Interpretation of Dreams ', Freud, 1900, pp. 360–362, 366, 388, see further below).

To illustrate: familiar to those using Freudian concepts is the case of the Rat Man (Freud, 1909*b*) in which a fascinating account of his ideas about his testicles are revealed in two dreams (Bell, 1961). The Rat Man had one undescended testicle. There are particular dreams and associations which indicate that he was quite often preoccupied with his undescended testicle. When trying to describe a wartime torture he became sufficiently anxious to have to leave the couch and walk about the room. This torture consisted of a pot being turned upside down on the buttocks of a prisoner into which some rats had been put. Freud points out that the Rat Man had unconsciously wished just such a punishment on his father. The steps may be found in detail in the text. As we shall soon see, this may have been because he considered his father responsible for his undescended testicle. Two dreams in the text seem to reveal these

ideas. During the hour in question, Freud stated: ' Quite unsuspectingly he told me that one of his testicles was undescended, but his potency was very good.' (Example of displacement and denial.) ' In a dream he had met a captain *who only had his badge of rank on the right side and one of the three stars was hanging down* ' (1909*b*, p. 295, my italics). (Whether this refers to the one testicle that hangs down, or whether it means his penis, is open to question. However, the shape of a star has a greater similarity to the testicle than to the penis.) ' He pointed out the analogy to his cousin's operation.' Inasmuch as his cousin's operation had involved the removal of both ovaries and the dream content reveals a one-sided badge of rank where two should have been, we have the right to suspect that he associates his own missing testicle with his cousin's missing ovaries.

In the text he has a further fantasy. If a rat bites, it will be put to death by man. He had been severely beaten by his father for biting. To use Freud's own words, ' he could truly be said to find a living likeness of himself in the rat. According to his earliest and most momentous experiences, rats were children.'

The second dream seems to indicate that the Rat Man tried to tell how he lost one testicle, and at the hands of a man. He dreamed

> that he went to the dentist to have a bad tooth pulled out. He pulled one out but it was not the right one, but *the one next to it*, which only had something slightly wrong with it. When it had come out, he was astonished at its size (1909*b*, p. 315, my italics).

Freud had dealt with the tooth as a penis symbol which led to associations about masturbation. An addendum to the dream on the following day (p. 317), however, indicated that the tooth really did not look like a tooth but like a tulip bulb to which he gave the association of slices of onions. ' He did not accept the further association of " orchids " to his cryptorchidism,' says Freud. Yet Freud stated it was an operation for pulling out his tail. So, too, with the other obvious fact that the very large tooth could only be his father's. He finally admitted this as being a *tu quoque* and a revenge against his father.

Although this dream even today would be interpreted as the tooth being the equivalent of the penis, if we consider the phrase, ' He pulled one out, but it was not the right one, but the one next to it, which only had something slightly wrong with it ', I think that by virtue of the side-by-side quality of these two teeth and the bulbous form, they could represent the testicles, one of which indeed had something wrong with it—it was not there. In fact, Freud himself gives a clue when he remarks on the difficulty the patient had to see the interpretation in terms of the penis. It seems to me that in this dream the Rat Man indicates that it is a male figure, this time a dentist, who is doing the castrating and, as is to be expected, the testicle is involved. If we look at the torture administered by the cruel captain and consider the possibility that the circumstances of such a torture could involve devouring the testicles, the parallel becomes clearer:

> It is my father who is responsible for my missing testicle because of the cruel punishment he administered to me. I wish the same punishment on him.

*This underlines the danger of beating little boys on the back-side or in general. Such beatings cause testicular retractions and frequently libidinize this area.* It is quite possible that the Rat Man was concerned about his testicles and may have lumped penis and testicles together. In fact, he used to bend over and examine his genitals from behind as well as in front, a common activity among males—but never talked about.

It is of interest that the following examples given in ' The Interpretation of Dreams ' (1900) show how Freud overlooked the testicular significance of teeth. There are many other examples which have not been included in this paper.

Dream:

> *He was being treated by two university professors of his acquaintance instead of by me. One of them was doing something to his penis. He was afraid of an operation. The other was pushing against his mouth with an iron rod, so that he lost* ONE OR TWO *of his teeth. He was tied up with* FOUR *silk cloths* (p. 386, italics original, emphases mine).

The symbolism of *two* links testicles with teeth in this dream but is overlooked. Freud states:

But I may draw attention to another parallel to be found in linguistic usage. In our part of the world the act of masturbation is vulgarly described as '*sich einen ausreissen*' or '*sich einen herunterreisen*' (literally, 'pulling one out' or 'pulling one down'). I know nothing of the source of this terminology or of the imagery on which it is based; but 'a tooth' would fit very well into the first of the two phrases (p. 388).

So would testicles. *Again Freud omits an activity that many, many boys indulge in after defecation and after masturbation.* While sitting on the toilet seat after defecating they feel a retraction and in response to this feeling they try to pull down the testicles or reassure themselves that they are down. This is particularly true of the early teenager who is preoccupied with this area (Bell, 1965). After masturbating they frequently look in the mirror as the Rat Man did, and then worry that they have injured themselves when they discover that the left testicle hangs lower—a normal occurrence, but most often repressed. One young man, aged 21, after reading this remarked, 'You mean I've been worrying about that all these years for nothing!'

Freud's contributions to this theme are even more enlightening in other writings. He it was, in fact, who pointed out the importance of particular details in analysing dreams. In the *Interpretation of Dreams* (1900, pp. 360–362) he presented a dream in which a hat symbolized the male genital. This hat was of a peculiar shape: '*Its middle piece was bent upward and its side pieces hung down in such a way that one side was lower than the other.*' It was on the detail of the two side pieces hanging down unevenly that Freud pointed out the importance of 'details of this kind that point the way in determining an interpretation'. Yet he did not pursue the full significance of these details as related to the sac and testes.

An excellent description of the male genital in symbolic terms was listed by Freud in the same work:

... *Then someone broke into the house and she was frightened and called out for a policeman. But he had quietly gone into a church, to which a number of steps led up, accompanied* BY TWO TRAMPS. *Behind the church there was a hill and above it a* THICK WOOD. *The policeman was dressed in a helmet, brass collar and cloak. He had a brown beard. The* TWO TRAMPS, WHO WENT ALONG PEACEABLY *with the policeman,* HAD SACK-LIKE APRONS TIED ROUND THEIR MIDDLES. *In front of the church a path led up to the hill; on both sides of it there grew grass and brushwood, which became thicker and thicker, and at the top of the hill, turned into regular wood* (p. 366, italics original, emphases mine).

This dream describes the male organ as frightening, including the scrotal components in the form of '*two* tramps' who went with the policeman as less frightening. Again we find *two* included as symbolic of sac and testes. In a dream reported to the author by a female patient there were two red roses side by side. Her associations led to her memory of seeing a male baby's genitals when she was ten years old.

Another dream reported by Freud shows the symbol of *two* related to teeth and flying, which could well have had to do with retractions of the testes.

*He was attending a performance of* '*Fidelio*' *and was sitting in the stalls at the Opera beside L., a man who was congenial to him and with whom he would have liked to make friends.* SUDDENLY *he flew through the air right across the stalls, put his hand to his mouth and pulled out* TWO *of his teeth* (pp. 385–6, italics original, emphases mine).

It reminds me of the comment of a four-year-old regarding the movement of his testes: 'They'll jump out of my mouth!' or of the Mexican saying, 'I got so scared, my testicles jumped up to my throat.' The quality of movement and the use of *two* should by now be obvious.

Although Freud *describes* the symbolic aspects of the sac and testes, their significance is never developed by him. In 1909 Freud made his famous remark (1909*a*) in his paper on a phobic five-year-old boy, 'Little Hans': 'It is remarkable what a small degree of interest the little sac with its contents arouses in the child.' What made him change his mind? Did the scrotal abscess dream he reported in 1900 intensify his defences of denial, repression and displacement to the penis?

Fisher (1966) in his study of 'Dreaming and Sexuality' states:

The observations I have presented demonstrate something that has not heretofore been known—that dreaming in the male is accompanied, on a physiological level, by massive sustained *genital* excitation.

Actually he was referring only to the penis. He, like Freud, ignored the scrotal sac and testes, as did other sleep researchers, Dement, Aserinsky, Kleitman and others. Fisher's prediction of anxiety in terms of rapid detumescence dovetails with what we found by measuring SCR, but he discussed only REM mentation and REM is associated with penile tumescence only. It does not give us complete information about the total genital. If we awakened for SCRs consistently, we found NREM anxiety mentation with *no* associated changes in the penile range. Also, the mental content indicated symbolic references to the sac and testes. In this instance our findings did not agree with Fisher, but supplement his findings.

Fisher states about male subjects, ' Males showed a great deal of castration anxiety and fears of homosexual assault aroused by the passive position assumed in sleep.' However, he does not include the testicular retractions, neither in his thinking nor in his instrumentation.

Since Fisher evaluates his material psychoanalytically, there are parallels which can be drawn between the present work and Freud's and Fisher's. In such studies the symbolic factors can play a considerable role.

Fisher (1966) makes the following observations:

> The initial marked tumescence may begin some minutes before the onset of the REMP or as late as 18 minutes after it. In the latter instance, we obtain a prolonged flat record indicating inhibition of erection . . . We were particularly interested in dream content associated with flat portions of the records . . . compared with the content from awakenings after a considerable degree of erection had been attained.

The information that we have recorded in our recent study (Bell, 1971) shows that these flat penile portions associated with inhibitions of erection are also associated with anxiety which are marked by an SCR.

Further, Fisher evaluates the dream of a subject as follows:

> The third episode lasted, according to the subject, a matter of minutes. His brother returned to the car and the subject looked at the lake and saw some really strange fish in the water. They were red and had spines and looked like sharks. They came right on the land to get him and he was *forced to climb a tree*. He was scared that they would bite him, that they would come out of the water, that they would rub against him with their sharp scales and do him in. He was hitting at them with a branch when he was awakened by the buzzer. It was *clearly this part of the dream that was associated with the rapid detumescence.*

Such findings are open to ambiguous interpretations unless a more complete gathering of the data is possible, which becomes possible only if both penis and scrotum are taken into account. For example, when the subject was in danger he was ' forced to climb a tree '. It is possible that he had a scrotal testicular retraction and contraction. If Fisher had measured the scrotum at that moment, he might have found an SCR.

Fisher continues:

> It was evident from the subject's association that he suffers from severe anxieties about sexual relations with women and that he unconsciously thinks of the female genital as a dangerous, biting organ.

I would ask at this point, dangerous to what? Penis—or sac and testes? Subjects in the present study who wore monitoring equipment for both *never pulled off the penile gauge but many times the scrotal instrumentation was pulled off.* For the male, *any threat of injury carries with it fear of injury to the scrotum,* which from prepuberty on is enormously sensitive. Consequently, it is unwise to overlook this area when talking of injury to the male genital.

Philip Roth (1967) eloquently illustrates the importance of the testicle in his book *Portnoy's Complaint.* The following quote expresses this well:

> Sometimes during my ninth year one of my testicles apparently decided it had had enough of life down in the scrotum and began to make its way north. At the beginning I could feel it bobbing uncertainly just at the rim of my pelvis—and then, as though its moment of indecision had passed, entering the cavity of my body, like a survivor being dragged up out of the sea over the hull of a lifeboat . . .
>
> And there it nestled, secure at last behind the fortress of my bones, leaving its foolhardy mate to chance it alone in that boy's world of football cleats and picket fences, sticks and stones and pocket-knives, all those dangers that drove my mother nearly mad with worry, and about which I was warned and warned and warned. And warned again. And again. And again. So my left testicle took up residence in the vicinity of the inguinal canal. By pressing a

finger in the crease between my groin and my thigh, I could still, in the early weeks of the disappearance, feel the curve of its jellied roundness; but then came nights of terror when I searched my guts in vain, searching all the way up to my rib cage —alas, the voyager had struck off for regions uncharted and unknown. Where was it gone to! How high and how far before the journey would come to an end! Would I one day open my mouth to speak in class, only to discover my left nut out on the end of my tongue?

Compare this with verbalizations of four-year-old boys (Bell, 1968) who concretely express the idea that their testes would jump all the way up and 'jump out of my mouth'. I have frequently seen residuals in the form of stammering both in adults and children when this topic came up for discussion.

In school we chanted, along with our teacher, *I am the Captain of my fate, I am the Master of my soul* and meanwhile, within my own body, an anarchic insurrection had been launched by one of my privates—which I was utterly helpless to put down?

For some six months, until its absence was observed by the family doctor during my annual physical examination, I pondered my mystery, more than once wondering—for there was no possibility that did not enter my head, *none*—if the testicle could have taken a dive backwards towards the bowel and there begun to convert itself into just such an egg as I had observed my mother yank in a moist yellow cluster from the dark interior of a chicken whose guts she was emptying into the garbage. What if breasts began to grow on me, too? What if my penis went dry and brittle, and one day, while I was urinating, snapped off in my hand? Was I being transformed into a girl? Or worse, into a boy such as I understood (from the playground grapevine) that Robert Ripley of *Believe It Or Not* would pay ' a reward ' of a hundred thousand dollars for? Believe it or not, there is a nine-year-old boy in New Jersey who is a boy in every way, *except he can have babies.*

Who gets the reward? Me, or the person who turns me in? How accurately does he express the age-old wish of the male child—to have babies, and to grow breasts!

## Summary

These sleep studies, although preliminary, bear out earlier clinical observations:

1. Anxiety is directly connected with scrotal instrumentation.
2. The castration fear in the male is primarily vested in any injury or threat to the scrotal area.
3. Symbolic representation of scrotal sac and testes is observed in dream material.
4. There were elements of fear of homosexual desires. Whether they are particular unto these males merits further study of more cases.

In view of the aforementioned findings, it would be important to take anxiety measurements from (1) penis only; (2) scrotum (sac and testes) only; (3) total genital: each with male technician and a female technician on the same subject in counterbalanced order.

At the present state of our knowledge, no studies on sleep stages which include the scrotum as well as the penis have been reported. This deprives us of any basis of comparison. It also raises a question. Should previous research which measured only penile changes be re-evaluated because of the possibility of experimenter bias?

Freud, Fisher—to say nothing of all the literature in psychoanalytic reports, including even the responses to Rorschach stimuli which show testicular symbols but are never interpreted as such—furnish an overwhelming number of examples of scrotal material that has been overlooked. Psychoanalytic interpretations are subjective, hence open to question. There are now specific polygraph indications of scrotal anxiety which can be correlated with the dream content of an awakening. Further research is indicated to explore this area. Previous research, influenced by classical Freudian thinking, has tended to fit all findings into a rigid format which omits the scrotum.

It is indeed worthy of study to discover why the average ' experienced ' psychoanalyst and therapist is so emotionally upset by this area and why even the old guard analyst needs to completely ignore it.

This paper is dedicated to the memory of the late Arthur Shapiro, M.D.

Dr Bell is Clinical Professor of Psychiatry, Georgetown University Medical School, Washington D.C. and Temporary Attending Psychiatrist, Montefiore Hospital.

## Acknowledgements

The author is indebted to Drs Herbert Weiner and Howard Roffwarg for use of the Sleep Laboratory, Montefiore Hospital, Bronx, New York. She wishes to acknowledge the assistance of Barry Schwartz, M.D., Urologist and Dr Rosalind Cartwright, Frances Gwozdz, the late Dr Arthur Shapiro, and Harvey Cohen for valuable suggestions; Dr J. Arlow for suggestions on organization; and Arthur Firl and Julia Baker, technicians.

The first part of this paper was presented as abstract and published as a short communication at the First European Congress on Sleep Research, Basel, 1972; the second part was presented as abstract, by title only, APSS meeting, Jackson Hole, Wyoming, 1973.

## References


BELL, A. I. (1961). Some observations on the role of the scrotal sac and testicles. *J. Am. psychoanal. Ass.* **9,** 261–286.

BELL, A. I. (1964). Bowel training difficulties in boys: prephallic and phallic considerations. *Am. J. Child Psychiat.* **3,** 577–590.

BELL, A. I. (1965). The significance of scrotal sac and testicles for the prepuberty male. *Psychoanal. Q.* **34,** 182–206.

BELL, A. I. (1968). Additional aspects of passivity and feminine identification in the male. *Int. J. Psycho-Anal.* **49,** 640–647.

BELL, A. I. (1972). The scrotal sac and testes during sleep: psychological correlates and mental content. (Presented to the First European Congress of Sleep Research, Basel, Switzerland; unpublished.)

BELL, A. I., STROEBEL, G. F. & PRIOR, D. D. (1971). Interdisciplinary study of the scrotal sac and testes correlating psycho-physiological and psychological observations. *Psychoanal. Q.* **40,** 415–434.

FISHER, C. (1966). Dreaming and sexuality. In R. M. Loewenstein *et al.* (eds.), *Psychoanalysis—A General Psychology. Essays in Honor of Heinz Hartmann.* New York: Int. Univ. Press.

FREUD, S. (1900). The interpretation of dreams. *S.E.* **4–5.**

FREUD, S. (1909*a*). Analysis of a phobia of a five-year-old boy. *S.E.* **10.**

FREUD, S. (1909*b*). Notes upon a case of obsessional neurosis. *S.E.* **10.**

FREUD, S. (1916). Introductory lectures on psychoanalysis. X. Symbolism in dreams. *S.E.* **15.**

GOTTSCHALK, L. A., WINGATE, C. N. & GLESER, G. C. (1969). *Manual of Instructions for Using the Gottschalk–Gleser Content Analysis Scales: Anxiety, Hostility, and Social Alienation-Personal Disorganization.* Berkeley: Univ. of Calif. Press.

RECHTSCHAFFEN, A. & KALES, A. (1968). *A Manual of Standardized Terminology, Techniques and Scoring System for Sleep Stages of Human Subjects.* Washington D.C.: U.S. Publ. Health Serv. Publication.

ROTH, P. (1967). *Portnoy's Complaint.* New York: Random House.

# Introduction to Chapter 36

Introductory Comments by Louis A. Gottschalk

This contribution by von Rad and his associates is a contribution in both psychosomatic and psychotherapeutic research. The authors seek to determine, through objective analysis of the language patterns in the diagnostic clinical interviews of a group of 40 psychosomatic and 40 psychoneurotic patients, whether there is, indeed, a relative deficiency in the emotional expression of psychosomatic patients. Using a resourceful and imaginative research design, these investigators test a hypothesis, encapsulated in the terms "alexithymia" or "pensée opératoire," which states that psychosomatic patients are blocked from using language which expresses emotions and avoid thoughts or feelings which reveal affects. They demonstrate that psychosomatic patients, in the first thousand words of the diagnostic clinical interview, have significantly lower anxiety and hostility scores on the Gottschalk-Gleser content analysis scales, and they make significantly more use of denials of affect as compared to psychoneurotic patients. They also demonstrate that certain stories told by these patients, as well as the speech of these patients in the diagnostic interviews, contain fewer emotionally-laden words among the psychosomatic patients and that more interventions are required by the interviewer with psychosomatic patients than psychoneurotic patients.

Dr. von Rad and his coworkers also explore the relationship of certain kinds of hostility and associated anxious affects among these two groups of patients, much as has been done by Witkin et al (1968) and Gottschalk and Gleser (1969) as well as by Lewis, and Schöfer et al in separate chapters (Chapter 47 and

Chapter 5 ) in this book. Their finding of a comparatively high correlation between hostility inward and shame anxiety scores in the psychosomatic patients in contrast to relatively high hostility outward and guilt anxiety scores in the psychoneurotic patients is a differentiation worth exploring further.

Among this research group's contributions to psychotherapy research is the demonstration that excerpts of clinical interviews can be used fruitfully to answer psychodynamically-oriented questions.

# Alexithymia: a Comparative Study of Verbal Behavior in Psychosomatic and Psychoneurotic Patients

M. von Rad, M. Drücke, W. Knauss, and F. Lolas

This investigation was prompted by the observation - which up to now has only been explained in a clinical casuistic way and has been the subject of many theories - of a certain pattern of symptoms, which can be seen as a typical, but not obligatory characteristic of psychosomatic patients and which has been given varying titles: 'infantile personality' (Ruesch, 1948), 'pensée opératoire' (Marty et al, 1963), alexithymia (Sifneos, 1973), psychosomatic phenomenon (Stephanos, 1973). These designations, reflecting different accentuations, apply to a phenomenon which, in short, attempts to describe the following observations and hypotheses: in contrast to neurotic patients, psychosomatic patients show 1. a conspicuous lack of fantasy, 2. a typical 'concretistic' technical manner of thinking, 3. a pronounced incapability to express feelings or even to experience them, 4. a certain type of object relationships ('projective reduplication') and 5. a large degree of social conformity.

-------------------------

*From the Psychosomatic Clinic of the University of Heidelberg, Director: Professor Dr. W. Brautigam

These observations are at present in part hotly discussed and the reason for this lies, in our opinion, in often premature attempts to account for the phenomenon aetiologically - as to whether it is genetically determined (Heiberg, 1977), localisable in tne brain (MacLean, 1949; Nemiah, 1973; Hoppe, 1975), related to social status (Cremerius, 1977), explicable psychodynamically (Marty et al, 1963; Stephanos, 1973), or whether it is, in fact, only a product of the examination situation, of the doctor-patient relationship (Wolff, 1977). What is lacking initially are empirical investigations which provide data on the phenomenon by means of a controlled comparison.

When planning the total investigation, of which only some of the results of the verbal analysis will be presented here, we started from the premise that it would be desirable to examine fantasy and the capacity for emotional expression with objectifiable parameters at different levels using different stimuli with the same patient group. The method of examining such variables, in particular the content analysis of psychotherapeutic interviews can itself be set at different levels and this had led to a number of different approaches (Holsti, 1968; Marsden, 1971). We selected two different approaches which in some ways are almost diametrically opposed. We examined psychoneurotic and psychosomatic patients on the one hand (Part I) at the classical content analytical 'atmostic' level of the frequency distribution of the more formal lexical constituents of speech samples and, on the other hand, (Part II) at the level of a more content-oriented 'pragmatic' procedure (Marsden, 1971), taking in the context and the communication aspect of verbal expressions.

For the latter approach the content analysis procedure developed by Gottschalk and Gleser seemed to us to be especially suitable for four reasons: 1. it was developed with extensive regard to basic psychoanalytic premises and thus it belongs in the same frame of reference as that from which the clinical hypotheses being investigated here have arisen. 2. It has been validated, tested, and extended under the most varying conditions

for more than twenty years - this is particularly true of the anxiety and hostility scales - and has, inter alia, also been applied to psychotherapeutic interviews (Gottschalk and Kaplan, 1958; Gottschalk et al, 1961, 1963, 1966; Gottschalk, 1969). 3. The interpretative possibilities for coding are limited, as the interpretative elements are integrated into the scales themselves and do not have to be provided first by the - psychologically trained - coder. 4. This is one of the decisive reasons why the procedure is also transferrable to the German language, as a study of 200 'normal persons' (Schöfer, 1977) has shown. Thus using the Gottschalk-Gleser procedure, the nature and extent of actual affects which are relatively close to consciousness can be measured in the way in which they are expressed verbally, in the interview situation for example, e.g. in an overt, covert or denied form.

## Methods

Using the five basic characteristics associated with alexithymia, we set up a series of special hypotheses regarding the verbal behavior of psychosomatic patients which are specified with the reporting of our results.

We set up two comparative groups (in the sequence of their arrival in our outpatient department) each with 40 patients, with (a) wholely dominant psychic complaints ('neurotics') and (b) somatic complaints with an organ-destructive process ('psychosomatics') who were matched for (1) intelligence, (measured by the Raven test), (2) age, (3) sex and (4) approximately, social status.

## Patients

Group I, neurotics, contained only classical neuroses without any important physical complaints. Group II, psychosomatic patients, included patients with peptic ulcer, ulcerative colitis, neurodermatitis, bronchial asthma, essential hypertension, psoriasis, and others. A condition here was that the organ-destructive psychosomatic symptom had to have been manifest within the last two years. All the patients came to our outpatient department, i.e. they were not bed-ridden. (For detailed infor-

Table 1

Comparison of Social Status of the Psychoneurotic and Psychosomatic Groups

| | I Psychoneurotic Group | II Psychosomatic Group |
|---|---|---|
| | Parents | |
| Unskilled | 4 | 8 |
| Independent | 13 | 10 |
| Employed staff | 19 | 16 |
| Professional people | 3 | 4 |
| "Social climber" | 9 | 4 |
| | Patients | |
| Unskilled | 1 | 5 |
| Independent | 6 | - |
| Employed staff | 16 | 23 |
| Students | 9 | 5 |
| Professional people | 2 | 2 |
| "Social climber" | 15 | 8 |
| Secondary school | 9 | 19 |
| "0"-Level | 9 | 8 |
| "A"-Level | 15 | 6 |
| Mode of Referral: | | |
| Spontaneous | 20 | 8 |
| Physician/other persons | 20 | 32 |

Table 2

Survey of the Matched Samples

| | I Psychoneurotic Group N=40 | II Psychosomatic Group N=40 |
|---|---|---|
| Diagnostic categories | narcissistic..............6 | peptic ulcer...........14 |
| | depressive ...............7 | unceritive colitis.....11 |
| | depressive-narcissistic...5 | neurodermitis...........5 |
| | obsessional...............4 | asthma..................3 |
| | obsessional-depressive....2 | psoriasis...............2 |
| | hysterical................3 | others..................5 |
| | hysterical-depressive....11 | |
| | hysterical-obsessive......2 | |
| Age (Average) | ........................28,1 | ......................28,9 |
| Sex | | |
| Male | ........................14 | ......................16 |
| Female | ........................26 | ......................24 |
| Intelligence (Average - Raven Test) | | |
| Within normal range | ........................29 | ......................29 |
| Above normal range | ........................11 | ......................11 |
| Socioeconomic class (without house-wifes N=11) | | |
| Lower class | ........................4 | ......................8 |
| Middle class | ........................30 | ......................27 |
| Mode of referral | | |
| Spontaneous | ........................20 | ......................8 |
| Physician/Other persons | ........................20 | ......................32 |

mation on the patient sample, in particular with regard to social variables, see B. Viertmann, 1976).

Procedures

We carried out the investigation at various levels: 1. by tests, (Rorschach, Giessen and the card 3 BM of the TAT); 2. by an unfinished ('open-ended') story and 3. by a first psychoanalytical interview. In making this choice of the instruments of investigation we were led by the following considerations: we wished to investigate at various levels (test alone, test in twos, doctor-patient dyad) and to investigate off-shoots of 'fantasy' or 'feelings' under different contexts (optical, acoustic, bipersonal) and more or less 'abstract' conditions or stimulants (more abstract story, concrete picture), in so far as they are reproduced in speech. The TAT, story, and first interview were tape-recorded, transcribed, and evaluated.

The sequence of investigations was always as follows. After the first short contact in the outpatient department, the patient was asked to come in for the first test (Giessen test: self and ideal image). Then

---

*The story we made up for the purpose of the investigation was read to the patient slowly by the tester twice and in such a way that the sex of the main character in the story agreed with that of the patient. It was stated that it was important for the story to have an end. It ran as follows:

'The long walk had made him/her very tired; the rucksack weighed down on his back and his footsteps were heavy. In the morning, when they started out on their family excursion, the sun had been shining and they had all been in good spirits.

Now it was late. A dark cloud came up over the horizon and he noticed that he found it a bit sinister. Looking at the cloud mother said: "How quickly it gets dark here in the mountains - we musn't loose any time." Only a short time later it was completely dark; a cold whistling wind blew thick fragments of mist across the path. Suddenly he was startled to find that he was alone. Before him there was a

the interview there was an average of 36.6 adjectives from Group I patients as compared to 29.5 ($p < 0.01$) for Group II patients, in the TAT 6.7 as compared to 5.4 (not significant) and in the 'story' 7.8 as compared to 5.0 ($p < 0.05$).

4. Frequency of grammatically incomplete sentences

Prompted by Bernstein's investigations on the 'restricted code' (Bernstein, 1972), which some authors relate to the verbal behavior of psychosomatic patients (Bräutigam, 1974), we assumed that psychosomatic patients would use incomplete and grammatically incorrect sentences considerably more frequently than neurotic patients. We defined incomplete and incorrect sentences by 1. lack of a subject, verb or important part of the sentence, 2. incorrect constructions of a grammatic or formal nature.

This assumption was confirmed. Group I patients used on the average 36, and Group II patients on the average used 45 incomplete sentences. The difference is highly significant ($p < 0.01$). Of course, agreement in a single, merely formal parameter is far from being proof of the assumption that psychosomatic patients use a restricted code as suggested by Bernstein (1972), an assumption which appears problematical at all events. (The findings are compiled in Table 3)

5. Frequency of speech sequences of over 70 words in the interview

Prompted by investigations by Overbeck (1974, 1975), who succeeded in determining some typical differences in the verbal behavior of neurotic and psychosomatic patients in the course of four psychotherapy treatments, we set up the hypothesis that psychosomatic patients, with their pronounced dependence on concrete orientation and on help from the therapist, would have more difficulty in producing long word-sequences by themselves without interruption. As a unit of measure, we chose continuous speech sequences by the patient of more than 70 words, in which the interviewer did not intervene and in which there were no long pauses. This magnitude, which was taken at random, corresponds to a rather long unit of speech, of the kind which is liable to occur in a psychoanalytic interview. It is also

Table 3.

Psychoneurotic and Psychosomatic Patients: Quantitative Differences in Verbal Samples

A. Structural Aspects

| Patients' Speech-Sample (absolute numbers) | | | I. Psychoneurotic Group | | | II Psychosomatic Group | | | | |
|---|---|---|---|---|---|---|---|---|---|---|
| | | | n | mean | SD | n | mean | SD | t | P |
| Quantity | Words (TAT) | | 39 | 165.97 | 109.76 | 35 | 132.35 | 117.68 | 1.27 | |
| | Words (story) | | 38 | 211.73 | 144.99 | 33 | 134.14 | 99.85 | 2.62 | <0.05 |
| Frequency | I | * | 39 | 67.17 | 12.86 | 40 | 60.84 | 13.83 | 2.09 | <0.05 |
| | One (Man) | * | 39 | 3.46 | 4.54 | 40 | 5.05 | 4.71 | 1.52 | |
| | Auxiliary Verbs | * | 39 | 61.58 | 16.72 | 40 | 76.05 | 13.11 | 4.25 | <0.01 |
| | Adjectives/Adverbs | * | 39 | 36.56 | 13.13 | 40 | 29.51 | 8.47 | 2.82 | <0.01 |
| | Adjectives/Adverbs (TAT) | | 39 | 6.28 | 5.23 | 35 | 5.53 | 3.89 | 1.05 | |
| | Adjectives/Adverbs (story) | | 38 | 7.76 | 7.30 | 33 | 4.96 | 3.81 | 1.93 | <0.05 |
| | Incomplete sentences | * | 39 | 36.23 | 12.75 | 40 | 44.97 | 14.09 | 2.87 | <0.01 |

*Patients' first 1000 words during the interview.

psychosomatic patients. The restriction of the transcribed text for scoring of thematic content to the verbal behavior of the patient is permissible inasmuch as Gottschalk and his coworkers (Gottschalk and Frank, 1967; Gottschalk and Gleser, 1969) have demonstrated that para-language variables are essentially redundant and serve to clarify the verbally expressed affective content rather than to communicate new affective content.

## Hypotheses and Results

### I. The Frequency of Different Parameters in TAT, Story, and Interview

#### 1. Word quantity in TAT and 'story'

We assumed that the TAT and the 'story' present different stimuli for the patient's fantasy, which would be reflected in the word quantity produced. In accordance with the initial hypotheses, it was to be expected that psychosomatic patients would use fewer words than neurotics as a consequence of their limited access to their fantasy life. In the TAT, patients from group I (neurotics) produced on the average 165 words as compared to 132 words in group II (psychosomatic patients). This shows a clear trend, but is not significant. In the 'story', group I patients produced on the average of 211 words, and group II patients spoke 134 words, which is a significant difference ($p < 0.05$).

We interpret this difference between the responses of the two groups of patients to the TAT and 'story' as follows: the optical stimulus of the TAT picture is more concrete, more graphic, constantly present and can always be referred to, and in this way it responds better to the concretistic thought of psychosomatic patients. In comparison, continuing a story makes higher demands on abstraction capabilities, on the capacity to free oneself from an object and abandon oneself to fantasy. It can also be assumed that, in terms of development, sight, being a modality which is closer to touch, develops earlier and requires less 'psychic structure' than hearing.

2. Frequency of the words 'I' and 'one' in the interview

As early as 1958, Shands demonstrated the deficiencies in the emotional expression of psychosomatic patients in a detailed and differentiated manner with verbatim records. They were rediscovered later by the French school under the designation 'pensée opératoire' (Marty and De M'Uzan, 1963) and by the Boston group as 'alexithymia' (Sifneos, 1973). Shands gives a point which we have followed up on a purely formal plane here, namely, that psychosomatic patients do not use the word 'I' in an emotionally meaningful context. In contrast, different authors (Mitscherlich, 1967; Brede, 1972; Overbeck, 1975) have pointed out, time and again, that the psychosomatic patient is over-adapted and makes an effort to attain outer inconspicuousness. We have assumed that both hypotheses would be reflected in a complementary way at the word level: that psychosomatic patients would use the word 'I' less and the word 'one' more than neurotic patients.

This was confirmed: group I patients used the word 'I' significantly more frequently ($p < 0.05$) than patients in group II (mean value 67 as compared to 60 times). On the other hand, group I patients used 'one' more rarely than group II patients (on average 3.4 as compared to 5 times); this is a trend in the direction expected, but is not significant.

3. Frequency of auxiliary verbs, verbs and adjectives

We assumed that the closer affinity to conrete things and to action would also be reflected in a less differentiated and simpler word usage among psychosomatic patients. We, therefore, presumed that psychosomatic patients would use more ('simple') auxiliary verbs than neurotic patients.

This was confirmed. Group I patients used an average of 61 auxiliary verbs. Group II patients used an average of 76. This difference is highly significant ($p < 0.01$). On the other hand, there is no significant difference in the use of main verbs (87 as compared to 83). This was to be expected. Also, our assumption that the number of adjectives and adverbs, which tend to make out the colour of the language, would differ to the disfavor of the psychosomatic patients was also confirmed. In

the patient was given an appointment for another test period, in which first of all the Rorschach, then the TAT, and finally the 'story'* was recorded. Then, at his third appointment, the patient came to a first psychoanalytic interview, the first half hour of which was also taped. The interviews were carried out in such a way that each of the six interviewers met almost exactly the same number of patients from each group. It was agreed in a preliminary discussion that the interviewer should run the conversation in his own style but should pay attention to two points: 1. he should conduct the interview concentrating on complaints, i.e. he should get as exact a picture of the complaints as possible and 2. he should ask about the patient's inner experience as the occasion arose (e.g., "How do you feel when you are 'depressive'?" What was it like when...?" "What went on inside you when...?").

All the interviewers were psychoanalysts. As a members of a clinic and participants in a regular outpatient conference, it can, perhaps, be assumed that they have a certain basic conformity in their manner of conducting a first interview, apart from the concentration on complaints

---

fork in the path, around him only the dark night and the howling of the wind.'

We based the draft of the story on the following considerations: 1. It should describe a concrete incident in such a way as to offer an incentive for affective participation by way of identification with the main character, while not leaving the sphere of concrete tangibility. 2. Although the setting is one of realistic action, the background of the story was purposefully left vague and undefined so that it could serve as a screen for projection. 3. The story was intended to indicate a family situation in which, however, only the mother-child relationship is explicit. The patient is thus free to continue the story using two or more persons. 4. The dramatic climax of the story is the loss of an object - in view of the fact that such loss experiences are very frequently described by many authors with regard to the precipitation of the psychosomatic process.

as mentioned above. However, the question of the comparability of the interview situation with all 80 patients, i.e. of the variability of the interaction effect between interviewer and patient naturally arises. This was not examined for itself, but on the basis of the comparable clinical and theoretical training of the interviewers and the instruction to pay particular attention to the complaints of the patients, a situational comparability can be taken to exist.

Data Analysis

The evaluations of Part I were done by an assistant who was not familiar with the hypotheses; the only exception was that the determination of the 'affect-laden' words was done by two of the authors independently and in duplicate. As a unit for investigation, we took the first 1000 words of the patient in the interview in order to have the same unit for all of them. (This corresponds roughly to 10 minutes of an interview).

In Part II of the examination, 2 members of our team coded the first 1000 words of the patient, transcribed from the first interview, the anxiety and hostility scales of Gottschalk and Gleser, (1969). Careful training was given and the interrater reliability when using the method - a detailed description of which (Gottschalk and Gleser, 1969; Gottschalk, 1971) can be omitted here - reached the standard of more than .85 required by Gottschalk and his coworkers. The speech sample was thus not obtained using the 'standard instruction' often given, in which an individual is asked to talk for five minutes about an interesting event, but the speech sample was taken from a natural clinical situation. The interviewer's expressions were not taken into account, for in this investigation we were less interested in the interaction between patient and interviewer and more in the speech content expressed by the patient. The speech sample was taken from the first psychoanalytic diagnostic interview because we believed that a clinical interview situation which is as natural as possible, was the best source of information to compare with the clinical situation in which the initial observations were made noting differences in emotional expression between psychoneurotic and

the lowest limit of a word sample to which the Gottschalk-Gleser method for the quantitative registration of certain affects can be reliably applied.

In the interview, Group I patients used such speech sequences of over 70 **words** an average of 4.4 times; Group II patients, 3.5 times. This difference is significant ($p < 0.05$).

6. Frequency of interviewer intervention in the interview

On the basis of the same assumption (see 5.), we expected that the therapist would intervene more frequently in interviews with psychosomatic patients. We defined as an intervention an expression by the therapist which contained at least one word (or more), but not semi-verbal utterances, such as, 'hm'.

Interviewers did intervene an average of 18.7 times with Group I patients and 25.1 times with Group II patients in our two patient samples. This difference is significant ($p < 0.05$) and agrees with the results of Overbeck (1975). A variance analysis of the six individual interviewers relating to the frequency of the intervention showed that there was no difference between them with respect to interventions. (Each interviewer met about the same number of patients from Groups I and II). There was, however, a significant difference regarding the amount of words they used. It is perhaps an inadmissible interpretation, and it is certainly an open question, as to whether one can relate the conformity in the intervention frequency more to the patient samples and the difference in word count more to the individual style of the interviewer.

7. Frequency of 'affect-laden' words in the interview, the TAT, and the 'story'

One of the basic premises given above states that psychosomatic patients have, in contrast to neurotic patients, difficulties in expressing their feelings. The investigation of such a complex phenomenon gives rise to many methodological problems, beginning with the choice of the parameter which should be used to investigate it. We started from the hypothesis that the difficulties which psychosomatic patients

have in expressing their feelings must be reflected in some way in their use of words. So we limited ourselves to the verbal level and conjectured that psychosomatic patients would use less 'affect-laden' words than neurotic patients. We defined as 'affect-laden' only those nouns, adjectives or verbs in which an unambiguous manifest tone of feeling was evident. What was decisive was that the tone of feeling explicit in the word was comprehensible without long interpretations being used; it had to be direct and colloquial and have an expression of affect, of whatever kind, as a primary denotation. In accordance with the differentiation made by Sifneos (1973), these would be words which express feelings (e.g. fear, insecurity, hoping, suffering, sinister, happy, etc.). In a few cases of doubt, we kept to the meaning given in the Wehrle-Eggers dictionary (1968) in which emotional terms are set down lexically.

It was clear to us that this in no way gives a quantifying expression of the 'total affective content' of the speech samples. Nor can it be taken as an indication of it, as affect can be expressed in many ways without using any affective words in the above sense. The hypothesis was merely that when the psychosomatic patients showed this kind of difficulty in expressing affects, one would expect to find it reflected at the simple word level as well.

Group I patients used 18.6, and Group II patients 12.9 'affect-laden' words in the interview. The difference is highly significant ($p < 0.01$). In the TAT, Group I patients had 4.8 and Group II patients 3.2 affect-laden words on average; this difference is not significant. In contrast to this in the 'story', Group I patients had an average of 2.7 as compared to Group II patients with 1.2; this difference is significant ($p < 0.05$). If, in addition, one compares the variability of the affect-laden words used, i.e. the number of different affect-laden words in the interview, patients from Group I had an average of 10.9 words, and Group II patients an average of 7.9 words. This difference too is highly significant ($p < 0.01$). In contrast, no difference could be found in the interviewers;

on average they used 3.2 affect-laden words with Group I patients and 3.3 affect-laden words with Group II patients.

Here again it is interesting to note that it is only in the TAT that the differences are not significant, although they follow the tendency expected. This could be attributed to the greater concreteness and actual presence of the stimulus, as discussed above.

The differences between the groups of patients with respect to the average use of words in the interview as well as the relatively limited variability of affect-laden words of the psychosomatic patients, tends to support the concept of alexithymia as a characteristic of psychosomatic patients. The finding that the interviewers did not use more affect-laden words with psychosomatic patients, although they intervened significantly more often because of the emotional constriction of these patients, helps substantiate the idea that the findings are not an outcome of interviewer behavior.

II. Measurement of Anxiety and Hostility in the Interview Using the Gottschalk-Gleser method

Here again the initial hypothesis was that it would be possible to differentiate between psychoneurotic and psychosomatic patients. We supposed that, in accordance with the hypothesis of their limited capability for affective communication, psychosomatic patients would, in general, express quantitatively less anxiety and hostility in a psychoanalytic interview, and that it would be possible to differentiate them sufficiently reliably from the psychoneurotic group on this basis alone. Furthermore, we expected typical correlations between the anxiety and hostility sub-scales; especially, in the psychosomatic patients, a high correlation between the shame anxiety and the hostility directed inwards was expected. Observations of other patient groups in the psychiatric interview and using the standard instructions to elicit speech suggest such hypotheses (Witkin et al, 1968; Gottschalk and Gleser, 1969; Gottschalk, 1971).

Table 4.

Psychoneurotic and Psychosomatic Patients: Quantitative Differences in Verbal Samples

B. Dyadic Aspects

| Patients speech samples (absolute numbers) | | I. Psychoneurotic Group | | | II Psychosomatic Group | | | | |
|---|---|---|---|---|---|---|---|---|---|
| | | n | mean | SD | n | mean | SD | t | P |
| Word sequence (more than 70) | * | 39 | 4.44 | 1.96 | 40 | 3.51 | 1.97 | 2.12 | < 0.05 |
| Affect-laden words | * | 39 | 18.67 | 10.29 | 40 | 12.94 | 7.13 | 2.89 | < 0.01 |
| Affect-laden words (TAT) | | 39 | 4.87 | 4.15 | 35 | 3.28 | 4.35 | 1.62 | |
| Affect-laden words (story) | | 38 | 2.79 | 3.55 | 33 | 1.25 | 1.90 | 2.39 | < 0.05 |
| Affect-laden words (variability) | * | 39 | 10.90 | 4.92 | 40 | 7.92 | 3.94 | 2.96 | < 0.01 |
| Interviewers speech sample (absolute numbers) | | | | | | | | | |
| Interventions | * | 39 | 18.70 | 10.90 | 40 | 25.10 | 15.50 | 2.09 | < 0.05 |
| Affect-laden words | * | 39 | 3.20 | 3.55 | 40 | 3.30 | 3.78 | 0.13 | |

* Patients' first 1000 words during the interview

If one regards the values derived from the interview as a whole, one important finding can be seen at first glance: in general psychosomatic patients exhibit lower values than the psychoneurotic patients in all the anxiety and hostility scales (with only one exception). Differences of particular significance are found in the total anxiety and its sub-scales guilt anxiety** and shame anxiety**, in the hostility directed inwards and in the total hostility directed inwards ($p < 0.001$).* Lower values for the psychosomatic patients, which are significant, are found too in the separation anxiety** ($p < 0.01$) and in the ambivalent hostility ($p < 0.05$), while in the total hostility directed outwards the boundary of significance is just missed. The only exception is the sub-scale mutilation anxiety**, in which psychosomatic patients show slightly (non-significantly) higher values, which can no doubt be explained by the actually higher physical threat to this group of patients.

We also wished to know whether the total scores, i.e., the three individual values of the total hostility directed outwards, the total hostility directed inwards and the total anxiety, taken together, made

---

*For the use of the category 'total hostility directed inwards' (a compilation in the scale of the hostility directed inwards and the ambivalent hostility) which Gottschalk himself did not allow for, we are indebted to G. Schöfer who has recently demonstrated the usefulness and justification of this category (Schöfer, 1977b).

** Anxiety subscale scores were calculated by adding 0.5 to the total weighted anxiety subscale score, multiplying by one hundred, dividing by the number of words in the speech sample, and taking the square root of the result. Namely, the corrected anxiety subscale score = $\sqrt{\frac{100\ (\Sigma fxwx + 0.5)}{\text{Number of words}}}$,

where $\Sigma fxwx$ represents the sum of all weighted scores on the anxiety subscale in the speech sample. This method of arriving at the corrected anxiety subscale scores has been recommended and used by Gottschalk recently (1976), thought it is not the same as the procedure used earlier by Gottschalk and Gleser (1969, pp 74-78).

Table 5

Differences Between Psychoneurotic and Psychosomatic Patients. Gottschalk-Gleser Anxiety subscales and Hostility Scales Derived from Verbal Samples

A. Psychoanalytic Interview (Patients first 1000 words)

| Scales | Psychoneurotic Group | | | Psychosomatic Group | | | | |
|---|---|---|---|---|---|---|---|---|
| Anxiety Subscales | n | mean | SD | n | mean | SD | t | p |
| Death | 39 | .39 | .28 | 40 | .35 | .26 | .71 | |
| Mutilation | 39 | .33 | .19 | 40 | .35 | .31 | -.35 | |
| Separation | 39 | .83 | .50 | 40 | .57 | .34 | 2.69 | <0.01 |
| Guilt | 39 | .82 | .57 | 40 | .44 | .32 | 3.72 | <0.001 |
| Shame | 39 | 1.28 | .54 | 40 | .73 | .49 | 4.72 | <0.001 |
| Diffuse | 39 | 1.03 | .54 | 40 | .73 | .49 | 2.52 | <0.05 |
| Total anxiety | 39 | 2.23 | .54 | 40 | 1.63 | .50 | 5.17 | <0.001 |
| Hostility scales | | | | | | | | |
| Hostility out overt | 39 | .84 | .58 | 40 | .64 | .39 | 1.79 | |
| Hostility out covert | 39 | .41 | .29 | 40 | .33 | .24 | 1.40 | |
| Total hostility out | 39 | .93 | .62 | 40 | .69 | .45 | 1.92 | |
| Hostility inwards | 39 | 1.49 | .49 | 40 | .99 | .41 | 4.88 | <0.001 |
| Ambivalent hostility | 39 | .90 | .51 | 40 | .71 | .26 | 2.06 | <0.05 |
| Total hostility in | 39 | 1.78 | .54 | 40 | 1.23 | .40 | 5.13 | <0.001 |

a sufficiently distinct differentiation of the two groups possible. In accordance with the $T^2$ test procedure of Hotelling, there are at three degrees of freedom f = 12.3 (df 3/75: $p<0.001$). This means that the psychosomatic patients in our patient collective can be differentiated from the psychoneurotic patients high significantly solely on the basis of the total values of the Gottschalk-Gleser anxiety and hostility scales.

A survey of the various intercorrelations between the individual anxiety and hostility scales (separate) for the group of psychosomatic and the group of psychoneurotic patients is given in Tables 6 and 7. Altogether our hypotheses are confirmed here too: with the neurotic patients there are high correlations between guilt anxiety and hostility (both directed outwards and ambivalent) in particular, but also between total anxiety and total hostility directed inwards. In contrast the psychosomatic patient shows a typical pattern of high correlation between shame anxiety and hostility directed inwards as well as between separation anxiety and ambivalent hostility. We shall return to these points later.

Finally, we were interested in the category of negation and denial, for according to the theory of many psychoanalysts it is denial which plays a decisive role as a defense mechanism in the development and persistence of psychosomatic symptoms (Nemiah, 1973). Following a suggestion from Gottschalk (1976), we first of all determined the raw denial values alone of each scale and then compared them between the two groups of patients - separately from the other categories of the scales. In contrast to the findings for the affect scales given above, the result was pronounced and almost reversed: the group of psychosomatic patients had considerably higher raw denial values than the group of psychoneurotic patients in all the anxiety and hostility scales, with only one exception. Only with the hostility directed outward scores do we find a considerably higher value for the psychoneurotics. If the significance of this difference is assessed according to the number of patients who expressed denials for a certain scale, i.e., not according to the total value of the denials, a chi square value of 4.1 or 5.4 respectively is found for the hostility directed inwards and the diffuse anxiety scales (after Yates correction); both are significant (df 1: $p < 0.05$). With the hostility directed outwards there was only a clear trend to the favor of the neurotic group, but this difference was not significant. Thus these findings demonstrate that the psychosomatic

Table 6

Correlations Between Gottschalk-Gleser Anxiety Subscales and Hostility Scales Derived from Verbal Samples of Psychoneurotic Patients (Group I)

A. Psychoanalytic Interview (Patients first 1000 words)

| Scale | Death | Mutilation | Separation | Guilt | Shame | Diffuse | Total Anxiety |
|---|---|---|---|---|---|---|---|
| Overt hostility out | -.00 | .13 | -.03 | .40* | -.15 | -.09 | .04 |
| Covert hostility out | .42** | .18 | .01 | .09 | -.17 | -.07 | -.03 |
| Total hostility out | .10 | .18 | -.00 | .35* | -.16 | -.05 | .02 |
| Hostility in | -.08 | -.19 | .15 | .29 | .21 | -.12 | .24 |
| Ambivalent hostility | -.09 | -.23 | .04 | .61** | .20 | -.05 | .19 |
| Total hostility in | -.09 | -.28 | -.30 | .56*** | .27 | -.17 | .37* |

* = $p < 0.05$

** = $p < 0.01$

*** = $p < 0.0001$

Table 7.

Correlations between Gottschalk-Gleser Anxiety Subscales and Hostility Scales Dervied from Verbal Samples of Psychosomatic Patients (Group II)

A. Psychoanalytic Interview (Patients first 1000 words)

| Scale | Death | Mutilation | Separation | Guilt | Shame | Diffuse | Total Anxiety |
|---|---|---|---|---|---|---|---|
| Overt hostility out | -.16 | -.29 | .20 | .04 | .18 | -.20 | -.06 |
| Covert hostility out | .10 | -.09 | .13 | .05 | .22 | -.02 | .11 |
| Total hostility out | -.11 | -.27 | .21 | .05 | .21 | -.18 | -.04 |
| Hostility in | -.06 | -.04 | .04 | .22 | .52** | .18 | .43** |
| Ambivalent hostility | .03 | .04 | .38* | .28 | .42** | -.16 | .32** |
| Total hostility in | -.05 | -.03 | .25 | .28 | .53*** | .10 | .50** |

* = $p < 0.05$
** = $p < 0.01$
*** = $p < 0.001$

hostility directed inwards and the diffuse anxiety scales.

## Discussion

We are of the opinion that the results which we are presenting here are of too general and nonspecific to establish an etiological basis for alexithymia. Nevertheless, it should be kept in mind that all our findings do not contradict the concept of the French school (to which this investigation is indebted for its hypotheses) and, in particular, do not contradict the observations of J. McDougall (1974). However, our findings do not enable us to determine whether the psychosomatic phenomenon should be looked on as an inherent or acquired deficiency, whether massive global defence mechanisms (denial) play a decisive role, or whether the psychosomatic symptom should be seen rather as an adaptive measure produced by the ego. Certainly very many different, and, in individual cases, varying conditions must take place - perhaps a narcissistic deficit based on the failure of the early mother-child dyad, perhaps a specific psychodynamic conflict, but unspecific stresses as well or a vulnerability in certain areas of personality ('psychosomatic sector') may be responsible, possibly as a result of a partially unsuccessful desomatisation, and finally, no doubt, also a proneness which is present at birth (somatic predisposition) which serves as a substrate to give the factors mentioned above their pathogenicity. The effect of social variables, such as, those of social status, with their socially specific interaction patterns, have not yet even been alluded to.

We should like first to discuss a methodological problem which is inherent in this work, namely, the choice of verbal behavior as the object of the investigation, as it is, clearly, highly dependent on education and social status. Our patient samples were, indeed, matched exactly with regard to intelligence, but with regard to professions there were slight differences and with regard to schooling a number of differences to the disfavor of the psychosomatic group. This difference, which viewed

in the overall context is only slight, may have some minimal influence on verbal behavior, despite the matched intelligence. We believe, however, that this factor alone cannot explain the differences in the findings, which are very distinctive.

As far as the results of the classical content-analytical tests in Part I are concerned, one finding seems to us to be of particular significance in the light of the surprisingly distinct differences between the two groups of patients. This is the absence throughout of significant results with the TAT card 3 BM. Naturally, we must ask in how far this relatively monotonous card with the 'depressive' sunken figure allows relatively less play for the creative fantasy, merely in view of its outer monotony. Here, however, a more convincing explanation seems to us be that it is rather the concrete tangible presence and availability of the optical stimulus which allows the psychosomatic patient to express himself purely quantitively in the same way as neurotic patients (rather as if he were describing a picture). This explanation, if it is correct, would not only agree with the hypotheses concerning concretistic thought among psychosomatic patients, but it would also indirectly explain the differences which arise more clearly from the story, where these conditions of concrete availability do not exist to that degree. Without a doubt, the interpersonal communications in the initial psychoanalytic interview is the situation in which the requirement is emphasized to express feelings and describe individual problems in a lively and imaginative way. It is here that the uncertainty of being able to meet the doctor's expectations, the attempt to hold fast to what one 'does', and the 'emptiness of the relationship' (Marty et al, 1963) of the psychosomatic patient is most distinct. The latter is reflected indirectly in the significantly increased intervention frequency of the interviewer, a finding which agrees with Overbeck's (1974, 1975) results, and supports De M'Uzan's contention that the analyst should make an 'energetic contribution' in conversation with the psychosomatic patient.

Indications of an affective 'emptiness of the relationship' and to

'pseudonormality' among psychosomatic patients are also found in the content analytic study of anxiety and hostility using the Gottschalk-Gleser scales. Particularly with total anxiety scores and with guilt, shame, and separation anxiety scores, and with hostility directed inwards scores, psychosomatic patients exhibit significantly lower values than psychoneurotic patients. In our conviction this is related to the interpersonal interview situation in which the most personal difficulties and problems are involved and can become conscious with the result that a particular sensitivity towards one's own weakness and insecurity may arise. However, it appears that psychosomatic patients handle this situation differently from psychoneurotics: 1. they express far fewer feelings, purely quantitatively. Whether they simply do not have the feelings to that extent in the interview situation or whether they do not let them become conscious or are unable to express them on the basis of certain defense mechanisms (denial) must remain an open question. 2. Apart from this purely quantitative aspect, we can observe a different pattern of dealing with affect by the two Groups in the interview situation on the basis of intercorrelations of various affect scores. With the psychoneurotic patients, a significant correlation between guilt anxiety and hostility directed outwards as well as ambivalent hostility was found, a finding which Gottschalk also observed with outpatient psychiatric patients, of whom one may assume that many were neurotic (Gottschalk, 1971). On the other hand, with psychosomatic patients an unambiguous correlation between guilt anxiety and hostility directed inwards as well as ambivalent hostility is found, also a correlation which has been repeatedly observed with various patient groups and with normal persons (Witkin et al, 1966, 1968; Gottschalk and Gleser, 1969; Gottschalk, 1971). It is in these correlations that our two patient groups differ.

The different sources and psychological meaning of shame and guilt has been examined repeatedly and carefully during the past few years (Witkin et al, 1966; Piers and Singer, 1953, Lewis, 1971; Stierlin, 1974). Shame anxiety is related to important other people, before whose judgement one

would like to 'sink into the ground' and under whose disapproving gaze one is painfully aware of one's own weakness. Thus, in terms of psychological development, it is a very early feeling which belongs more to the pre-Oedipal stage. Guilt on the other hand refers to a more mature psychic structure, which has created its own inner standards by which it measures itself. Thus guilt is a later emotion which belongs more to the Oedipal stage, which relates not to another person but to oneself. With all possible caution, one can perhaps say that the significant correlation between shame and hostility directed inwards scores does, at least, not contradict the theory that psychosomatic disease is a very early disturbance and confirms the picture of the psychosomatic patient as a particularly object-dependent person who is symbiotically dependent on a partner. (On the other hand the high correlation between guilt and hostility directed outwards, which we do not find with our psychosomatic patients, is not surprising with neuroses as they are more Oedipal disturbances.)

A very significant element here - although its real weight is hard to define - is the fact that our results are based alone on the first 1000 words of the patient in a psychoanalytic interview. (The Gottschalk-Gleser findings from the TAT card and the 'story' cannot be considered here.) Most of Gottschalk's and Schöfer's findings were gained using the standard instructions for eliciting speech (Schöfer, 1976, 1977; Gottschalk, 1977). This is a method by which the interviewer asks the interviewee to talk about any interesting or dramatic life experiences and is then silent. This procedure represents a bipersonal interaction situation far less than a psychoanalytic interview. As a result, all the comparisons mentioned with other results can only be interpreted with great caution. This is especially true of the attempt at quantitative comparisons with a normal population (Gottschalk and Gleser, 1969; Schöfer, 1976) in which our neurotic patients lie clearly above the norm particularly in total anxiety, hostility directed inwards and in guilt and shame anxiety. On the other hand, the values for our psychosomatic patients (perhaps with the exception of the increased

hostility directed inwards scores) are astonishingly close to the normal values reported by Schöfer and Gottschalk. If one attempts such a methodologically problematic comparison at all, this seems - taken at face value - to suggest the super- or pseudo-normality of psychosomatic patients. We should, however, like to risk the viewpoint that a patient who is reporting to his therapist his complaints and his needs would see himself under more compulsion to give expression to his feelings and sufferings than in response to the more anonymous and impersonal standard instructions. This would mean that the affect scores derived from the clinical interviews of our psychosomatic patients were lower than what one would expect them to be. This certainly will be rewarding to check it out in later studies.

Finally, another basic problem should be mentioned, which is of special interest for our considerations. By the express determination of the authors, the Gottschalk-Gleser method measures mainly actual, possibly quickly changing, conscious or relatively conscious affects and only to a lesser extent preconscious or 'bound' affects. Thus our results only permit conclusions about the actual condition of the psychosomatic and psychoneurotic patients during the interview and should not be interpreted in the sense of stable traits of personality. The authors point out also, however, that bound affects are also recorded by their affect scales at "the level of the relevant autonomic arousal," and here in particular by psychological mechanisms of displacement and denial of the verbal items concerned (Gottschalk and Gleser, 1969). The same is presumably true for high intercorrelations which can reflect typical psychological conflict patterns.

In this light our results in the sub-category 'denial' take on a special accent, for they prompt the question as to whether psychosomatic patients do not keep up their apparent normality, among other things, by a high degree of denial. This applies particularly to hostility directed inwards and diffuse anxiety, in which they differ significantly from neurotic patients. In other words, it is just that affect which

has reached a high correlation in the evaluation of the scales as a typical conflict-resolving pattern that is strongly denied. With the psychosomatic patient, it is particularly the shame anxiety and the diffuse anxiety which is aggressively resolved inwards. With the psychoneurotic, rather the hostility directed outwards which is guiltily experienced. We think that it is just these findings which support the hypotheses stated at the beginning and perhaps demonstrate a certain contradiction to Nemiah's supposition that denial does not play a decisive role with psychosomatic patients (Nemiah, 1973, 1975).

In conclusion, it can be said that in the investigation of speech samples of psychosomatic and psychoneurotic patients, using both classical content analytical methods of frequency counts and with the 'pragmatic' method of Gottschalk and Gleser, certain typical behavior patterns of psychosomatic patients become clear in the examination situation whose psychodynamic interpretation agrees well with the hypotheses stated initially on "alexithymia" and the "pensée opératoire." In our opinion, the findings confirm, at various levels, the existence of this so-called 'psychosomatic phenomenon', but do not at present permit any empirically substantiated statements about its etiology.

## SUMMARY

Verbal samples obtained from 40 psychoneurotic and 40 psychosomatic patients, matched with respect to age, sex, intelligence and some social indicators were examined using different methods of content analysis. It was postulated that the restricted fantasy life and difficulty in expressing feelings attributed to psychosomatic patients would be reflected at speech level (TAT verbal responses, completion of an open-ended story, psychoanalytic interviews).

I.

In a sample consisting of the first 1000 words of the patient during the interview, psychosomatic patients were found to use the personal pronoun 'I' less frequently and to use fewer affect-laden words, but to

exhibit higher scores for auxiliary verbs and incomplete sentences than psychoneurotics. With psychosomatic patients interviewer intervention was more frequent. This difference cannot be traced back to interviewer variables and interviewing style (variance analysis).

II.

The measurement of anxiety and hostility using the Gottschalk-Gleser scales gave the following results: with total anxiety in particular, and its sub-units guilt, shame, separation and diffuse anxiety, and with hostility directed inwards and with ambivalent hostility, the psychosomatic patients showed lower values than the neurotic patients did, which were in part highly significant. Typical correlations of the individual affect scales, which differentiated between the two groups, were also found, as was a distinct distribution of the denial values, which were seen to be in part significanlty increased for psychosomatic patients.

Both at a purely verbal level and with the Gottschalk-Gleser method the results confirm the existence of the 'psychosomatic phenomenon' ('alexithymia' - 'pensee operatoire'), in our opinion, but they do not up to now permit any empirically substantiated statements concerning its aetiology.

References

Bernstein, B. Sozialization und Sprachverhalten. Pädagogischer Verlag Schwann, Düsseldorf (1972).

Bräutigam, W. Pathogenetische Theorien und Wege der Behandlung in der Psychosomatik. Nervenarzt 45, 354-363 (1974).

Brede, K. Sozioanalyse psychosomatischer Störungen. Athenäum Verlag, Frankfurt (1972).

Cremerius, J. Psychosomatic disorders: Class specific and/or structur-specific neuroses? Psychother. Psychosom. (in print).

Gleser, G.C., and Lubin, A. Response productivity in verbal content

analysis: a critique of Marsden, Kalter, and Ericson. J. of Consulting and Clinical Psychology 44, 508-510 (1976).

Gottschalk, L.A. Childrens speech as a source of data toward the measurement of psychological states. J. of Youth and Adolescence 5, 11-36 (1976)

Gottschalk, L.A. Some psychoanalytic research into the communication of meaning through language: the quality and magnitude of psychological states. Br. J. Med. Psychol. 44, 131-147 (1971).

Gottschalk, L.A. and Frank, E.C. Estimating the magnitude of anxiety from speech. Behav. Sci. 12, 289-295, 1967.

Gottschalk, L.A. and Gleser, G.C. The Measurement of Psychological States Through the Content Analysis of Verbal Behavior. Univ. of California Press, Los Angeles, Berkeley (1969).

Gottschalk, L.A., Gleser, G.C., and Springer, K.J. Three hostility scales applicable to verbal samples. Arch. Gen. Psychiatry 9, 254-279 (1963).

Gottschalk, L.A. and Kaplan, S.M. A quantitative method of estimating variations in intensity of a psychologic conflict or state. Arch. Neurol. Psychiatry 79, 688-696 (1958).

Gottschalk, L.A., Springer, K.J., and Gleser, G.C. Experiments with a method of assessing the variations in intensity of certain psychological states occurring during two psychotherapeutic interviews, Ch. 7, in Comparative Psycholinguistic Analysis of Two Psychotherapeutic Interviews. L.A. Gottschalk, ed. International Universities Press, New York (1961).

Gottschalk, L.A., Winget, C.N., and Gleser. G.C. Manual of Instructions for Using the Gottschalk-Gleser Content Analysis Scales. University of California Press, Los Angeles, Berkeley (1969).

Gottschalk, L.A., Winget, C.N., Gleser, G.C., and Springer, K.J. The measurement of emotional changes during a psychiatric interview: a working model toward quantifying the psychoanalytic concept of affect, in Methods of Research in Psychotherapy. L.A. Gottschalk

and A.H. Auerbach, eds. Appleton-Century-Crofts, New York (1966).

Heiberg, A. Alexithymia - an inherited trait? Psychother. Psychosom. (in print).

Hoppe, H. Die Trennung der Gehirnhälften. Psyche 29, 919-940 (1975).

Holsti, O.R. Content analysis, in The Handbook of Social Psychology, Vol. II. G. Lindzey and E. Aronson, eds. 596-692 (1968).

Lewis, H.B. Shame and Guilt in Neurosis. International Universities Press, New York (1971).

MacLean, P.D. Psychosomatic disease and the "Visceral Brain." Psychosom. Med. 11, 338-353 (1949).

Marsden, G. Content-analysis studies of psychotherapy: 1954 through 1968, in Handbook of Psychotherapy and Behavior Change. A.E. Bergin and S.L. Garfield, eds. 345-407 (1971).

Marsden, G., Kalter, N., and Ericson, W.A. Response productivity: a methodological problem in content analysis studies in psychotherapy. J. of Consulting and Clinicical Psychology 42, 224-230 (1974).

Marty, P., De M'Uzan, M. La "pensée opératoire." Rev. Franc. Psychoanal. 27, suppl., 1345-1356 (1963).

Marty, P., De M'Uzan, M., u. David Ch. L'investigation psychosomatique. Press Univ. France, Paris (1963).

McDougall, J. The psychosoma and the psychoanalytic process. Int. Rev. Psycho-Anal. 1, 437-459 (1974).

Mitscherlich, A. Krankeit als Konflikt II, ed. Suhrkamp, Frankfurt (1967).

Nemiah, J.C. Psychology and psychosomatic illness: reflections on theory and research methodology. Psychother. Psychosom. 22, 106-111 (1973).

Nemiah, J.C. Denial revisited: reflections on psychosomatic theory. Psychother. Psychosom. 26, 140-147 (1975).

Nemiah, J.C. and Sifneos, P. Affect and fantasy in patients with psychosomatic disorders, in Modern Trends in Psychosomatic Medicine. O.W. Hill, ed. Butterworths, London (1970).

Nemiah, J.C. and Sifneos, P. Psychosomatic illness: a problem in communication. Recent research in psychosomatics. Psychother. Psychosom. 18, 154-160 (1970).

Overbeck, G. Objecktivierende und relativierende Beiträge zur Pensée opératoire der französischen Psychosomatik. Habilitationsschrift. GieBen (1975).

Overbeck, G. u Brahler, E. Eine Beobachtung zum sprechverhalten von patienten mit psychosomatischen Störungen. Vorläufiger Bericht. Dynamische Psychiatrie 7, 100-108 (1974).

Piers, G. and Singer, M.D. Shame and Guilt. Charles C. Thomas, Springfield, Illinois (1953).

v. Rad, M., u. Vierthmann, B. Psychosomatische und psychoneuroticsche Patienten im Vergleich. III Selbst- und Idealbild im GeiBen-Test. Vortragsmanuskript.

Ruesch, J. The infantile personality. Psychosom. Med. 10, 134-144 (1948).

Schöfer, G. Erfassung affektiver Veränderungen durch Sprachinhalts-analyse im Psychotherapieverlauf. Bibliotheca Psychiatrica, Nr. 154, 55-61 (1976).

Schöfer, G. Das Gottschalk-Gleser-Verfahren: Eine Sprachinhalts-analyse zur Erfassung und Quantifizierung von aggressiven und ängstlichen Affekten. Zt. Psychosom. Med. und Psychoanalyse 23, 86-102 (1977a).

Schöfer, G. The Gottschalk-Gleser Analysis of Speech: A Normative Study. (Dependencies of hostile and anxious affects from sex, sex of the interviewer, socioeconomic class and age). (1977b).

Shands, H. An approach to the measurement of suitability for psycho-therapy. Psychiatric Quarterly 32, 501-522 (1958).

Sifneos, P. The prevalence of "alexithymic" characteristics in psychosomatic patients. Psychother. Psychosom. 22, 255-262 (1973).

Sifneos, P. Problems of psychotherapy of patients with alexithymic

characteristics and physical disease. Psychother. Psychosom. 26, 65-70 (1975).

Stephanos, S. Analytisch-psychosomatische Therapie. Jb. Psychoanal. suppl. 1 (1973).

Stierlin, H. Shame and Guilt in Family Relations. Reprinted the Archives of General Psychiatry 30 (1974).

Viertmann, B. Eine empirische Untersuchung zum "psychosomatischen Phänomen" mit Hilfe des GieBen-Tests. Dissertation, Heidelberg (1976).

Vogt, R., Bürckstümmer, G., Ernst, L., Meyer, K. u. v. Rad, M. Differences of fantasy life in psychosomatic and psychoneurotic patients. Psychother. Psychosom.(In press).

Wehrle, H. und Eggers, H. Deutscher Wortschatz 1 und 2. Fischer Verlag, Frankfurt (1968).

Witkin, H.A., Lewis, H.B., and Weil, E. Shame and guilt reactions of more differentiated and less differentiated patients early in therapy. Presented at the Annual Meeting of the American Psychological Association. New York (1966).

Witkin, H.A., Lewis, H.B., and Weil, E. Affective Reactions and patient-therapist interactions among more differentiated and less differentiated patients early in therapy. J. Nerv. Ment. Dis. 146, 193-208 (1968).

Wolff, H.H. The contribution of the interview situation to the apparent restriction of fantasy life and emotional experience in psychosomatic patients. Psychother. Psychosom. (In press).

Zepf, S. Die Sozialisation des psychosomatischen Kranken. Campus, Frankfurt (1976).

# Part V

# Somatic Studies and Studies of Environmental Effects on Psychological Processes

Three papers comprise this section, and they concern effects of external or environmental effects of psychological reactions. Chapter 37 is entitled "Total and half body irradiation: effect on cognitive and emotional processes" (Gottschalk et al, 1969). Another chapter, (38) originally presented at an annual meeting of the American Neurosurgical Society (1970), is entitled "An objective method of measuring psychological states associated with changes in neural function: content analysis of verbal behavior" (Gottschalk, 1972). A third paper, Chapter 39, in this series deals with the effects of excessive visual and auditory stimuli on psychological states, and it is entitled "Effect of sensory overload on psychological state" (Gottschalk et al, 1972).

37

# Total and Half Body Irradiation

## Effect on Cognitive and Emotional Processes

*Louis A. Gottschalk, MD, Irvine, Calif; Robert Kunkel, MD; Theodore H. Wohl, PhD; Eugene L. Saenger, MD; and Carolyn N. Winget, MA, Cincinnati*

THE effects on mental processes of the exposure of the human central nervous system to irradiation has not been investigated extensively because of the potentially hazardous and irreversible results on living human tissue. The available information on this subject has had to be extrapolated from experimental laboratory studies on infrahuman animals or gleaned from the accidental exposure of man or from the analysis of the symptoms of the survivors irradiated at Nagasaki and Hiroshima.

More recently it has also been possible to obtain some information on this subject from the performance of patients with advanced neoplastic disease who have been treated with whole body radiation. The latter source of data is the only planned type of investigation of radiation effect on human beings that is feasible at present and, hence, any information available by this means cannot fail to add to our inadequate knowledge on this subject. This paper is a report of a study of the acute mental reactions of patients with metastatic neoplasms exposed to total or partial body radiation.

Submitted for publication April 30, 1969.

From the departments of psychiatry (Dr. Kunkel, and Carolyn Winget), radiology (Dr. Saenger), and psychology (Dr. Wohl), University of Cincinnati, College of Medicine, Cincinnati General Hospital, and Cincinnati Veterans Administration Hospital, Cincinnati, and the Department of Psychiatry and Human Behavior (Dr. Gottschalk), College of Medicine, University of California Irvine, Irvine, Calif.

Reprint requests to Department of Psychiatry and Human Behavior, College of Medicine, University of California Irvine, Irvine, Calif 92664 (Dr. Gottschalk).

### Procedure

Sixteen patients at the Cincinnati General Hospital or the Cincinnati Veterans Administration Hospital with advanced neoplastic disease were selected for partial or total body irradiation. Selection of patients was carried out by radiotherapists of the Department of Radiology, University of Cincinnati, College of Medicine based on their clinical judgment as to which patients would be likely to benefit most from the treatment.[1] Selection of patients was based on the following criteria: (1) The patients had "solid" tumors. Patients with lymphoma were excluded. (2) Relatively good nutritional status with ability to maintain weight. (3) Normal renal function. (4) Stable hemogram in the control period. In these studies each patient served as his own control, so that postradiation changes were then compared to preexposure observations. The pretreatment control period was of one to three weeks in duration.

In each case the patient was advised that the therapy might be beneficial to him but that it was experimental in nature. Informed consent was obtained in all cases. No other methods of palliative treatment for neoplastic disease were administered to these patients over the duration of this study.

Soon after being selected for radiation therapy, the patients were asked to speak for five minutes into the microphone of a tape recorder in response to standardized instructions given by one of us (R.K.) to

talk about any interesting or dramatic life experiences. Two research technicians blindly and independently scored each clause of these speech samples according to categories of meaning or content in specific scales developed by Gottschalk and Gleser,[2] and by using an empirically derived formula, objective base-line scores were obtained for several complex psychological variables, such as cognitive and intellectual impairment, anxiety, hostility, and hope. The reliability and validity of these so-called content analysis measures have been reported elsewhere.[3,4]

Then the patients were tested by a psychologist using the Halstead Battery[5] (a series of tests of intellectual function requiring the use of a range of simple to highly complex sensorimotor abilities) and the Wechsler-Bellevue Adult Intelligence Scale (an intelligence test). Furthermore, a brief battery of tests of intellectual impairment was administered largely derived from Reitan.[6-8] The latter psychological measures included a screening test for aphasia, the digit span, digit symbol, and similarities tests (derived from the Wechsler-Bellevue Scale—tasks for conceptualization, association, and memory), finger tapping tests (simple tests of sensorimotor coordination under the pressure of time), and the Trail Making Test[8] (another measure of organic cerebral function).

After psychological testing the patients were brought to the cobalt 60 teletherapy unit for treatment. During the preexposure period, several sham irradiations were given to permit accurate dosimetry and obtain cooperation of the patient. The sham radiation was also instituted as a control to provide some base line from which to compare actual effects of radiation on cognitive and emotional processes. All sham radiation preceded actual radiation sessions. There was no discussion with the patient of possible subjective reactions resulting from the treatment. Other physicians, nurses, technicians, and ward personnel were instructed not to discuss postirradiation symptoms or reactions with the patient. This precaution was carefully followed so as to standardize and minimize "iatrogenic" factors in influencing whatever subjective reactions the patients might have to the radiation.

With all patients, the actual radiation was given in a single exposure of one half to one hour duration rather than in fractionated exposures. Exposure rates were 3 to 6 roentgens (R)/min. The exposure intensity ranged from 50 to 300 R. Half the radiation dose was given laterally. The patient was then rotated and the remaining half of the dose was given through the opposite lateral portal. Further details of dosimetry are available elsewhere.[1]

Before and after sham radiation, a tape-recorded five-minute verbal sample was obtained from each patient by asking the patient to talk about any interesting or dramatic life experiences. Immediately after each verbal sample was obtained, the short battery of tests of cognitive function derived from Reitan was administered. The same measures were obtained, in the same sequence and by the same investigators, before and after actual radiation, one day postradiation, three days postradiation, and one, two, four, and six weeks postradiation.

The five minute verbal samples were analyzed for content independently by two research technicians using the Gottschalk-Gleser method.[2-4] Successive average scores over each time period for each patient were obtained for cognitive and intellectual impairment, anxiety, hostility, and hope. The results of the Halstead Battery, the Wechsler-Bellevue Adult Intelligence Scale, and the short battery of modified Halstead-Reitan tests were processed and evaluated by two psychologists.

## Results

Due mostly to their physical illness, it was not possible for all of the patients to complete every battery of tests, especially after the initial testing. Relevant intellectual characteristics of the patient sample were as follows: a low-educational level (ranging from 0 to eight years of education with a mean of 4.2 years), a low-functioning intelligence quotient (ranging from 63 to 112 on the full-scale of the Wechsler-Bellevue with a mean of 84.5), and a strong evidence of cerebral organic deficit in the baseline (preradiation) measure of most of the patients. The latter evidence was a Halstead Impairment Index ranging from 0.50 to 1.00 with a mean of 0.77 and a Trail Making

**Table 1.—*Relevant Characteristics of Patients Receiving Total or Half Body Radiation***

| PT No. | Sex | Race | Age (yr) | Educational Level (yr) | Wechsler-Bellevue Verbal IQ | Wechsler-Bellevue Perform IQ | Wechsler-Bellevue Full-Scale IQ | Halstead Impairment Index | Trail Making Test A | Trail Making Test B | Trail Making Test A & B |
|---|---|---|---|---|---|---|---|---|---|---|---|
| 050 | M | W | 80 | 5 | 107 | 117 | 112 | 0.88 | 7 | 2 | 9 |
| 051 | M | W | 66 | 7 | 101 | 96 | 99 | 0.88 | 8 | 3 | 11 |
| 055 | F | N | 56 | 2 | 70 | 79 | 72 | 0.88 | — | — | — |
| 056 | M | N | 53 | 0 | 79 | 80 | 89 | 0.50 | 7 | 1 | 8 |
| 057 | F | N | 57 | 7 | 85 | 72 | 79 | 0.70 | — | — | — |
| 058 | F | N | 48 | 8 | 86 | 84 | 84 | 0.63 | 5 | 2 | 7 |
| 059 | M | W | 42 | 8 | 105 | 82 | 99 | 0.63 | 4 | 2 | 6 |
| 060 | F | N | 49 | 3 | 92 | 82 | 87 | 0.75 | 5 | 0 | 5 |
| 061 | F | N | 64 | 0 | 61 | 71 | 63 | 0.67 | — | — | — |
| 062 | M | N | 60 | 5 | 86 | 82 | 83 | 0.75 | 1 | 1 | 2 |
| 064 | F | N | 55 | 8 | 70 | 66 | 67 | 0.70 | 4 | 1 | 5 |
| 065 | F | N | 84 | 6 | 115 | 100 | 109 | 0.50 | 7 | 1 | 8 |
| 066 | M | N | 63 | 1 | 71 | 58 | 63 | 1.00 | 1 | 0 | 1 |
| 067 | F | N | 52 | 8 | 81 | 69 | 74 | 1.00 | 4 | 0 | 4 |
| 068 | F | N | 73 | 0 | 88 | 100 | 89 | 1.00 | 1 | 0 | 1 |
| 070 | M | N | 62 | 0 | 80 | 89 | 83 | 0.88 | 1 | 1 | 2 |
| 9 Female, 13 Negro<br>7 Male, 3 White | | | | | | | | | | | |
| Mean | | | 60.2 | 4.2 | 86.0 | 82.9 | 84.5 | 0.77 | 3.4 | 0.8 | 4.3 |
| Range | | | 42-84 | 0-8 | 61-115 | 58-117 | 63-112 | .50-1.00 | 1-8 | 0-3 | 1-11 |

**Table 2.—*Cognitive and Intellectual Impairment Scores Before and After Sham and Actual Radiation****

| Lower only | Initial | Pre-sham | Post-sham | Pre-rad | Post-rad | 1 day | 3 day | 1 wk | 2 wk | 4 wk | 6 wk |
|---|---|---|---|---|---|---|---|---|---|---|---|
| 065 | −0.31 | 1.03 | 1.07 | −0.30 | 0.44 | 0 | −0.14 | 1.36 | 2.42 | 0.17 | 0.69 |
| 064 | 1.76 | 2.07 | 2.89 | 1.60 | 3.53 | 2.23 | 1.64 | 2.48 | 2.70 | 3.80 | 2.36 |
| 066 | 2.86 | 2.13 | 1.31 | 3.19 | 2.42 | 1.48 | 3.97 | 2.33 | 2.77 | 2.41 | 3.37 |
| 067 | 4.22 | 1.33 | 4.18 | 1.27 | 2.76 | 3.57 | 1.15 | 4.08 | 1.89 | 2.78 | 0.08 |
| Upper only | | | | | | | | | | | |
| 056 | 1.64 | 1.45 | −2.66 | — | 0.80 | — | — | — | −0.10 | — | — |
| 050 | 1.22 | — | — | 0.77 | 1.13 | 1.62 | −0.40 | — | — | — | — |
| 055 | 4.72 | 2.94 | 3.22 | 0.68 | 1.13 | 0.84 | 1.08 | 1.90 | 0.80 | 0.57 | 2.29 |
| Total body radiation | | | | | | | | | | | |
| 060 | 5.21 | −0.21 | 1.28 | −2.47 | 2.92 | −0.74 | −0.59 | −2.65 | −0.47 | −1.03 | — |
| 062 | 2.44 | 0.95 | 2.75 | 0.74 | 3.35 | 4.05 | −0.99 | 2.26 | 1.28 | 0.87 | — |
| 058 | −0.27 | −1.07 | — | −1.47 | 0.44 | — | −0.31 | 0.80 | 0.04 | — | — |
| 057 | — | 0.36 | 0.36 | 2.28 | 3.40 | 3.28 | 0.75 | 0.57 | 5.07 | 2.59 | 0.94 |
| 051 | 1.25 | −1.82 | 1.16 | 0.73 | 0.20 | −0.23 | −0.91 | 0.90 | — | — | — |
| 061 | 0 | 0 | — | 1.11 | — | 1.56 | −0.25 | 3.54 | — | — | 1.52 |
| 059 | 1.27 | 1.36 | — | −0.35 | — | 2.33 | 0.39 | 1.06 | 0.38 | 1.33 | — |
| 070 | 2.49 | 3.93 | 2.56 | 0.80 | — | 1.79 | 1.55 | −0.23 | 3.05 | 1.79 | 2.37 |
| Mean | 1.92 | 1.08 | 1.65 | 0.61 | 1.88 | 1.68 | 0.50 | 1.42 | 1.65 | 1.53 | 1.70 |

* Missing data on some patients—because of the fluctuating severity of their illness—accounts for our not giving complete data on all patients. One patient was dropped from the initial 16 in the tabulation of intellectual impairment scores because of the large amount of missing data.

**Table 3.—*Cognitive and Intellectual Impairment Scores Ranked Within Nine Patients***

| Patient No. | Pre-sham | Post-sham | Pre-rad | Post-rad | 1 day | 3 day | 1 wk |
|---|---|---|---|---|---|---|---|
| 065 | 5 | 6 | 1 | 4 | 3 | 2 | 7 |
| 064 | 3 | 6 | 1 | 7 | 4 | 2 | 5 |
| 066 | 3 | 1 | 6 | 5 | 2 | 7 | 4 |
| 067 | 3 | 7 | 2 | 4 | 5 | 1 | 6 |
| 055 | 6 | 7 | 1 | 4 | 2 | 3 | 5 |
| 060 | 5 | 6 | 2 | 7 | 3 | 4 | 1 |
| 062 | 3 | 5 | 2 | 6 | 7 | 1 | 4 |
| 057 | 1 | 2 | 5 | 7 | 6 | 4 | 3 |
| 051 | 1 | 7 | 5 | 4 | 3 | 2 | 6 |
| Sum | 30 | 47 | 25 | 48 | 35 | 26 | 41 |

$\chi^2 = 13.047$ for 6 df.
$P \leq 0.05$.

Index (A+B) ranging from 1 to 11 with a mean of 4.3. (Scores on the Halstead Impairment Index of greater than 0.30 are considered indicative of cerebral organic deficit, and scores less than 13 on the Trail Making Test suggestive of the same.) Other characteristics of this sample of patients—sex, age, and race—are given in Table 1.

At the dosage levels of radiation to which these patients were exposed, evidence of a worsening of cognitive functioning after actual radiation appeared to depend on the specific measure of transient intellectual impairment used as a criterion. The brief battery of tests derived from Reitan, administered before and after sham and actual total body radiation, showed no directional trends. Whereas, the cognitive and intellectual impairment scores derived from the Gottschalk-Gleser content analysis scales gave some evidence of reversible organic cerebral impairment occurring after body irradiation (see Table 2).

These data were analyzed by the Friedman nonparametric test for matched groups. Complete data over the seven occasions from presham to first week postradiation were available for only nine patients; the ranks over rows for the scores of each of these nine patients are shown in Table 3. The column sums of ranks show a significant difference ($\chi^2 = 13.05$, $P \leqslant 0.05$). The lowest column sums are associated with presham, preradiation, and three-day postradiation, while the highest column sums come from postsham and postradiation. In further multiple comparisons by the Wilcoxon matched-pairs test (one-tailed) the only significant differences obtained in verbal behavior scores of intellectual impairment were between pre- and postradiation ($P \leqslant 0.025$) and postradiation and three days after radiation ($P \leqslant 0.01$). Because of the small number of cases available for these statistical evaluations, it was not considered appropriate to break down the group further to determine whether area of body irradiation influenced the effect of radiation on intellectual functioning. Although we have indicated the area of irradiation in our patients in Table 2, we feel there is at this point insufficient information available to warrant analyzing this dimension further.

To determine whether the obtained difference between sham and real radiation effects was significant, a method of difference scores was used, subtracting presham from postsham and preradiation from postradiation scores and comparing these differences by the Wilcoxon test. This difference was not significant.

Even though the difference between presham and postsham radiation was not statis-

**Table 4.—*Means and SD for Four Affect Scales Before and After Irradiation Treatment***

| Affects | | Initial | Pre-sham | Post-sham | Pre-actual Treatment | Post-actual Treatment | 1 day | 3 day | 1 wk | 2 wk | 4 wk | 6 wk |
|---|---|---|---|---|---|---|---|---|---|---|---|---|
| Anxiety | (N) | 15 | 14 | 12 | 15 | 14 | 13 | 14 | 12 | 12 | 9 | 7 |
| | Mean | 1.54 | 1.72* | 1.05* | 1.69* | 1.33* | 1.03 | 1.43 | 1.17 | 1.38 | 1.18 | 1.12 |
| | SD | 0.60 | 0.93 | 0.46 | 0.86 | 0.69 | 0.56 | 0.74 | 0.56 | 0.56 | 0.71 | 0.55 |
| Hostility out | Mean | 0.75 | 0.70 | 1.22 | 1.06 | 0.91 | 0.99 | 0.84 | 0.82 | 0.72 | 0.59 | 0.92 |
| | SD | 0.38 | 0.47 | 0.90 | 0.77 | 0.72 | 0.64 | 0.53 | 0.50 | 0.34 | 0.18 | 0.83 |
| Ambivalent hostility | Mean | 0.59 | 0.75 | 0.75 | 0.86 | 0.52 | 0.69 | 0.67 | 0.56 | 0.62 | 0.48 | 0.83 |
| | SD | 0.34 | 0.52 | 0.86 | 0.59 | 0.37 | 0.65 | 0.51 | 0.55 | 0.80 | 0.20 | 0.74 |
| Hostility in | Mean | 0.77 | 0.96 | 0.92 | 0.92 | 0.98 | 0.87 | 0.76 | 0.69 | 0.77 | 0.92 | 0.91 |
| | SD | 0.41 | 0.62 | 0.69 | 0.47 | 0.65 | 0.69 | 0.39 | 0.30 | 0.51 | 0.46 | 0.40 |

* Presham plus preactual treatment scores > postsham plus postactual treatment scores ($P < 0.02$).

tically significant (ranked scores of 30 and 47 respectively) and the difference between preactual and postactual radiation was significant (ranked scores of 25 and 48 respectively), the lack of statistical significance between sham and actual radiation effects casts a little doubt on whether actual radiation verbal symbolic effects are, indeed, more pronounced than sham radiation effects.

The evidence of worsening of intellectual functioning obtained from verbal samples may be due to some undetermined factors in the treatment situation rather than a radiation effect. But in view of the detrimental consequences that could occur, as a result of human error, if irradiation at the dosage level we have used could impair cognitive or verbal symbolic processes, we prefer to play safe and accept the probability that radiation of such a magnitude can interfere, at least temporarily in some individuals, with these intellectual processes.

The changes noted in cognitive and intellectual scores from verbal samples were not likely due to anxiety or hostility. In Table 4 are some of the objective content analysis scores of emotional reactions to the radiation. Since these affect scores are relatively normal in distribution[2-4] the means were compared by the correlated *t*-test. The number of subjects in a given comparison was the number for whom scores were available over all conditions. The mean anxiety scores obtained prior to sham and actual radiation were significantly higher ($P \leqslant 0.02$) than the anxiety scores immediately following sham and actual radiation, using the Gottschalk-Gleser Anxiety Scale. No significant pretreatment and posttreatment differences were found in three types of hostility scores (out, in, and ambivalent) derived from the verbal samples.

In 16 of these patients, a correlation of +0.38 ($P \leqslant 0.08$) was obtained between hope scores obtained from the first five-minute verbal sample given by these patients and the duration of survival (in days) of these patients after receiving actual body radiation. Moreover, the third day postradiation, the average hope scores from five-minute verbal samples of ten cancer patients who returned home that day (+5.42) were compared (by a Mann Whitney U-Test) to the comparable hope scores of six patients obliged by their illness to remain in the hospital (+1.9). The average hope scores of the group of patients returning home was significantly higher ($P \leqslant 0.01$) than the average hope scores of the patients having to remain in the hospital.

## Comment

Information is limited about the effects of ionizing radiation on man's intellectual and emotional performance. Zellmer[9] reviewed data compiled by the Atomic Bomb Casualty Commission[10,11] describing the clinical signs and symptoms of five groups of accidental human exposures[12] and a report[13] of the performance of patients with advanced neoplastic disease treated with total-body radiation. Zellmer concluded that a medically healthy population of military personnel might be considered 100% effective for performing all tasks for the first hour following acute total-body exposure of 600 rad or less, occasional vomiting being the only untoward reaction limiting performance for some individuals. (A *rad* is a unit of measurement of the *absorbed* dose of ionizing radiation. A *roentgen* is a measure of radiation exposure. A *rad* varies with the type of tissue irradiated and is not always equivalent to a *roentgen*.) During the first day Zellmer conjectured that only those receiving the 500 to 600 rad exposure should have any weakness, and their efficiency should not be impaired more than 20%. By the second day, almost all persons in the 500 to 600 rad groups, about 50% of those in the 400 rad group, and 25% of those in the 300 rad group would require hospitalization, and their efficiency would be impaired proportionately. After the third day, the need for hospitalization would decline rapidly and would not have to be considered for the remaining personnel until two to three weeks after radiation.

Laboratory studies of rats exposed to total-body irradiation have shown no change in learning or retention of learned tasks[14-16] receiving from 100 to 1,000 R. A decrease in activity of rats immediately following exposure to 100 to 1,000 R of whole body X-irradiation was reported by Jones et al[17] and Fields.[16] Also, Kimeldorf et al[18] demonstrat-

ed that rats exposed to 500 R showed a significant decrease, as compared to a control group, in the time they could swim before exhaustion overtook them, and this finding was corroborated by Furchtgott.[19] Thus, in the rat, where the LD 50/30 is 600 to 700 R, the first demonstrable loss in cognitive function was after exposure to about 500 R total-body irradiation. But this loss was not evident in the learning or retention of learned tasks or in the performance of tasks which did not require sustained muscular effort.

With the rhesus monkey, in a controlled study, Riopelle[20] found no difference in delayed responses in monkeys irradiated with 400 R. But a decrease in activity—scratching and grooming—was noted in rhesus monkeys after 400 R by Leary and Ruch[21] and by McDowell and Brown.[22] In summary, sublethal doses of total-body radiation up to the LD 50/30 dose (about 500 R in the rhesus monkey) may have an immediate, mild weakening effect manifested by a decrease in undirected activity. However, in these animals, where motivation was high, there was no decrease in performance of highly complicated or discriminative tasks, according to Kaplan and Gentry,[23] Kaplan et al,[24] and Melching and Kaplan.[25]

Our own studies with human subjects also indicate a fair resistance to emotional and cognitive dysfunction with total or half-body irradiation given as palliative treatment to debilitated patients of low-educational level with metastatic carcinoma. At dosages ranging from 50 to 300 R our patients with preradiation signs of cerebral organic impairment, showed no evidence of a worsening of mentation using a brief (Halstead-Reitan) battery selected to detect potentially reversible changes in intellectual function. However, the suggestive transient impairment of cognitive and intellectual Impairment Scale applied to the content of five-minute samples of speech, raises the question whether certain types of mental functioning may be interfered with by irradiation from the cobalt 60 teletherapy unit. This finding would be more convincing if the difference between sham and actual radiation effects had also been statistically significant. The fact that our sample of patients before radiation therapy already had signs of functional cerebral organic intellectual impairment might make them more susceptible to worsening of their cognitive functioning with nonspecific stress. The study of a more normal intellectual group of subjects would be a valuable comparison if such a sample were available for such investigations. In any event, further studies using these measures need to be done, to replicate the observed findings and to determine how dose and exposed body area influence these signs of mental malfunction.

The increase in transient anxiety before sham and actual radiation as compared to the anxiety levels immediately after sham or actual radiation indicates that irradiation itself certainly does not increase an individual's anxiety level, but the apprehension about any unknown treatment is an emotional stress that can arouse anticipatory anxiety or fear. Whether elevated pretreatment anxiety can accentuate signs of post-treatment organic cerebral impairment (ie, within a time period of one hour) should be explored. There is evidence, for example, that transient anxiety, as measured by the Gottschalk-Gleser content analysis method can elevate plasma-free fatty acids in the 15 to 20 minute period following speaking for five minutes.[26,27] The fact that no directional trend was observed in three kinds of hostility before and after radiation indicates that changes in these emotions did not account for the changes seen in the intellectual impairment scores.

The suggestive evidence of a relationship of survival time to an objective (content analysis) psychological measure of hopefulness is in line with the clinical observation (Goldfarb et al[28]) that a sick or dying patient's emotional attitude about life and the value of human relationships can, to some extent, influence life expectancy.

**Summary**

A group of 16 patients with metastatic carcinoma was given total or half body irradiation as palliative treatment at dosages ranging from 50 to 300 R by means of a cobalt 60 teletherapy unit.

On nine patients for whom data were complete, evidence of transient impairment of intellectual function ($P \leqslant 0.02$) appeared

immediately after actual irradiation and persisted one day later, using the criterion of an intellectual impairment scale applied to the content of short samples of speech. A lack of statistical significance between sham and actual radiation effects raised a question whether actual radiation verbal symbolic effects were, indeed, more pronounced than sham radiation effects. No evidence of a worsening of mentation was obtained with sham or actual radiation using different criteria of impaired intellectual function (derived from Reitan).

A significant increase in pretreatment anxiety (but not in hostility) was found in the patients ($P \leqslant 0.02$). Also, in 16 patients higher initial hope scores were associated with a shorter period of hospitalization ($P \leqslant 0.01$) and a longer survival time ($P \leqslant 0.08$).

This work has been supported by the Defense Atomic Support Agency, DOD under contract DA-49-146-XZ-315, and by a US Public Health Service Research Career Award (MK-K3-14, 665) to Dr. Gottschalk.

Harold Perry, MD, and Harry Horowitz, MD, of the Radioisotope Division, Radiology Department, University of Cincinnati, College of Medicine, selected patients for radiological therapy. Phyllis H. Moenster, MA (of the Neuropsychology Laboratory, Cincinnati Veterans Administration Hospital) administered the Halstead Battery and Modified Halstead-Reitan Battery neuropsychological tests of mental impairment and Arnold Binder, PhD, University of California, Irvine, provided statistical consultation.

## References

1. Saenger, E.L., et al: Metabolic Changes in Humans Following Total Body Irradiation, *DASA 1844 Progress Report in Research Project DA-49-146-XZ-315 (Defense Atomic Support Agency, Washington, DC)*, (Feb) 1960-(April) 1966.

2. Gottschalk, L.A., and Gleser, G.C.: *The Measurement of Psychological States Through the Content Analysis of Verbal Behavior*, Berkeley, Calif: University of California Press, 1969.

3. Gleser, G.C.; Gottschalk, L.A.; and Springer, K.J.: An Anxiety Scale Applicable to Verbal Samples, *Arch Gen Psychiat* **5**:593-605 (Dec) 1961.

4. Gottschalk, L.A.; Gleser, G.C.; and Springer, K.J.: Three Hostility Scales Applicable to Verbal Samples, *Arch Gen Psychiat* **9**:254-279 (Sept) 1963.

5. Halstead, W.D.: *Brain and Intelligence*, Chicago: University of Chicago Press, 1947.

6. Reitan, R.M.: Investigation of the Validity of Halstead's Measures of Biological Intelligence, *Arch Neurol Psychiat* **73**:28-35 (Jan) 1955.

7. Reitan, R.M.: Qualitative Versus Quantitative Mental Change Following Brain Damage, *J Psychol* **46**:339-346 (Oct) 1958.

8. Reitan, R.M.: Validity of the Trail Making Test as an Indicator of Organic Brain Damage, *Percept Motor Skills* **8**:271-276 (Aug) 1958.

9. Zellmer, R.W.: Human Ability to Perform After Acute Sublethal Radiation, *Military Med* **126**:681-687 (Sept) 1961.

10. Oughterson, A.W., et al: *Statistical Analysis of the Medical Effects of the Atomic Bomb*, Oak Ridge, Tenn: US Atomic Energy Commission, Technical Information Service (p 1-288) (Feb) 1955.

11. Oughterson, A.W., and Warren, S.: "Medical Effects of the Atomic Bomb in Japan," in *National Nuclear Energy Series, VIII*, New York: McGraw-Hill Book Company, Inc., 1956.

12. Thoma, G.E., and Wald, N.: The Diagnosis and Management of Accidental Radiation Injury, *J Occup Med* **1**:421-447 (Aug) 1959.

13. Payne, R.B.: Effects of Ionizing Radiation on Human Psychomotor Skills, *US Armed Forces Med J* **10**:1009-1021 (Sept) 1959.

14. Furchtgott, E.: Effects of Total Body X-Irradiation on Learning: An Exploratory Study, *J Comp Physio Psychol* **44**:197-203 (Feb) 1951.

15. Arnold, W.J.: Maze Learning and Retention after X-Irradiation of the Head, *J Comp Physio Psychol* **45**:358-361 (Aug) 1952.

16. Fields, P.E.: The Effects of Whole Body X-Radiation Upon the Psychological Abilities of White Rats, *Amer Psychologist* **10**:415-416 (Aug) 1955.

17. Jones, D.C., et al: Effect of X-Irradiation on Performance of Volitional Activity by the Adult Male Rat, *Amer J Physiol* **177**:243-250 (May) 1954.

18. Kimeldorf, D.J., et al: Effect of X-Irradiation Upon the Performance of Daily Exhaustive Exercise by the Rat, *Amer J Physiol* **174**:331-335 (Sept) 1953.

19. Furchtgott, E.: Behavioral Effects of Ionizing Radiations, *Psychol Bull* **53**:321-334 (July) 1956.

20. Riopelle, R.J.: Spatial Delayed Response With Monkeys, *J Comp Physio Psychol* **52**:746-753 (Dec) 1959.

21. Leary, R.W., and Ruch, T.C.: Activity, Manipulation, Drive, and Strength in Monkeys Subjected to Low-Level Irradiation, *J Comp Physio Psychol* **48**:336-342 (Aug) 1955.

22. McDowell, A.A., and Brown, W.L.: Some Effects of Nuclear Radiation Exposure on the Behavior of the Rhesus Monkey, *USAF School of Aviation Medicine Report No. 58-58*, 1958.

23. Kaplan, S.J., and Gentry, G.: Some Effects of a Lethal Dose of X-Radiation Upon Memory: A Case History Study, *USAF School of Aviation Medicine Project No. 21-3501-0003, Report No. 2*, (May) 1954.

24. Kaplan, S.J., et al: Some Effects of a Lethal Dose of X-Radiation Upon Retention in Monkeys, *USAF School of Aviation Medicine Project No. 21-3501-0003, Report No. 8*, (p 1-10) (Aug) 1954.

25. Melching, W.H., and Kaplan, S.J.: Some Effects of a Lethal Dose of X-Radiation Upon Retention: Studies of Shock Avoidance Motivation, *USAF School of Aviation Medicine Project No. 21-3501-0003, Report No. 9*, (p 1-8) (Aug) 1954.

26. Gottschalk, L.A., et al: Studies of Relationships of Emotions to Plasma Lipids, *Psychosom Med* **27**:102-111 (March-April) 1965.

27. Gottschalk, L.A., et al: Anxiety Levels in Dreams: Relation to Changes in Plasma Free Fatty Acids, *Science* **153**:654-657 (Aug 5) 1966.

28. Goldfarb, C.; Driesen, J.; and Cole, D.: Psychophysiologic Aspects of Malignancy, *J Psychiat* **123**:1545-1552 (June 12) 1967.

# An Objective Method of Measuring Psychological States Associated with Changes in Neural Function: Content Analysis of Verbal Behavior[1]

Louis A. Gottschalk[2]

*Received March 11, 1971*

*A new method is described for objectively recording and measuring emotional and cognitive changes in human subjects in whom natural or experimental variations in neural status have occurred. The method involves the content analysis of tape-recorded and transcribed speech, by technicians trained to follow validated scales of a variety of psychological dimensions. Well-tested scales are available for measuring the magnitude of anxiety, hostility outward, hostility inward, social alienation-personal disorganization (schizophrenic syndrome), cognitive and intellectual impairment, capacity for congenial human relations, achievement strivings, health-sickness, dependency, and so forth. A review of numerous psychophysiological, psychobiochemical, and psychopharmacological studies is provided to illustrate the possible usefulness of this procedure in various kinds of research in the neurosciences.*

## INTRODUCTION

A not infrequent problem encountered by neural scientists is the objective recording and measurement of changes in emotional and cognitive function of human subjects in whom natural or experimental changes in neural status have

[1] Presented, in modified form, at the Annual Meeting of the American Neurosurgical Society, Ojai, California, March 26, 1970.

[2] Department of Psychiatry and Human Behavior, College of Medicine, University of California at Irvine, Irvine, California.

occurred. An objective method has been developed—involving the content analysis of verbal behavior—which is especially applicable to this problem. The method allows collection of the raw data, namely, tape-recorded speech, by the neural scientist, himself, or by a research technician, if preferable.

## THE CONTENT ANALYSIS METHOD OF MEASURING PSYCHOLOGICAL STATES

The measurement method that I have developed with my associates utilizes a function that is uniquely human, namely, speech and its content or semantic aspects. The development of this method has involved a long series of steps. It has required that the psychological dimensions to be measured (for example, anxiety, hostility outward, hostility inward, cognitive or intellectual impairment, achievement strivings, social alienation-personal disorganization, and so forth) be carefully defined; that the content, the lexical cues, be spelled out from which a receiver of any verbal message infers the occurrence of the psychological states, that the linguistic, principally syntactical, cues conveying intensity be specified, that differential weights be assigned for semantic and linguistic cues whenever appropriate; and that a systematic means be arrived at of correcting for the number of words spoken per unit time so that one individual can be compared to others or to himself on different occasions with respect to the magnitude of a particular psychological state. The method requires, also, that a formal scale of weighted content categories be specified for each psychological dimension to be measured; that research technicians be trained to score these typescripts of human speech (much as biochemical technicians are trained to run various chemical determinations by following prescribed procedures); that the inter-scorer reliability of two trained content technicians using the same scale be 0.85 or above (a modest but respectable level of consensus in the behavioral sciences for these kinds of measurements). Moreover, a set of construct-validation studies have had to be carried out to ascertain exactly what this content analysis procedure was measuring, and these validation studies have included the use of four kinds of criterion measures: psychological, physiological, pharmacological, and biochemical. On the basis of these construct-validation studies, changes have been made in the content categories and the associated weights of each specific scale in the direction of maximizing the correlations between the content analysis scores with these various criterion measures.

Construct-validation of any behavioral or psychological test instrument requires repeated reexamination and retesting, in new situations, of the variables being evaluated. After initial validation studies were completed for verbal behavior measures of such psychological states as anxiety, hostility outward and hostility inward, social alienation-personal disorganization (an objective dimension constituting the main features of schizophrenia), cognitive and intellectual

impairment, achievement strivings, a large variety of additional investigations have been carried out using these verbal behavior measures. These further investigations have provided considerable data on the ways in which such verbal behavior scores relate to other relevant measurable phenomena. These data have afforded solid evidence as to how the psychological states measured by our verbal behavior measures "fit" with other empirical data (Gleser *et al.*, 1961; Gottschalk *et al.*, 1958; 1960; 1961*a, b*; 1963; 1964).

A brief comment on the theoretical framework from which our measurement approach has developed: our theoretical approach has been truly eclectic in that we have borrowed heavily from behavioral and conditioning theory, psychoanalytic clinical hypotheses, and linguistic theory. The scoring or content-analysis technician applying our procedure to typescripts of tape-recorded speech need not worry, however, about approaching the work of content analysis with one theoretical orientation or another; rather, he carefully follows a strictly empirical approach, scoring the occurrence of any content or themes in each grammatical clause of the speech according to a "cookbook," namely, various well delineated language categories constituting each of our verbal behavior scales. A manual (Gottschalk *et al.*, 1969*b*) is available which indicates what verbal categories should be looked for, and how much the occurrence of each one is to be weighted. The technician, then, follows prescribed mathematical calculations leading up to a final score for the magnitude of any one psychological state or another.

The formulation of these psychological states has been deeply influenced by the position that they all have biological roots. Both the definition of each separate psychological state and the selection of the specific verbal content items used as cues for inferring each state were influenced by the decision that whatever psychological state was measured by this content analysis approach should—whenever possible—be associated with some biological characteristic of the individual in addition to some psychological aspect or some social situation.

The details of the reliability and validity studies and the specific investigations pinning down each point have been published over the past 13 years. They have recently been collected in two books, and these books describe many newer unpublished investigations on the subject (Gottschalk and Gleser, 1969; Gottschalk *et al.*, 1969*b*).

These content analysis scales can be applied to different kinds of language material obtained in a variety of situations and in both spoken and written form. Most of our reliability and validity studies have been done on small samples of speech, 3 to 5 min in duration, obtained in a response to standard instructions. The instructions to elicit speech from a research subject have been purposely relatively ambiguous and nonstructured, except that a report of personal or dramatic life experiences has been requested. We were led to use such instructions because of our initial aim to probe the immediate emotional

reactions of our interviewees, instead of the typical or habitual ones, and to minimize reactions of guarding or covering up. We settled on using standardized instructions, also, in order to compare individuals in a standard context so that demographic and personality variables could be explored and investigated, while holding relatively constant the influence of such variables as the instructions for eliciting the speech, the interviewer, the context, and the situation. The effects of varying these noninterviewee variables have subsequently been investigated, one by one, after reliable and valid content analysis scales were developed.

The standard instructions we have used to elicit many 5 min verbal samples are typically typed on a three-by-five card and are read aloud to the subject prior to turning on the tape-recorder. They read: "This is a study of speaking and conversation habits. Upon a signal from me I would like you to speak for 5 min about any interesting or dramatic personal life experiences you have had. Once you have started I will be here listening to you, but I would prefer not to reply to any questions you would feel like asking me until the 5 min period is over. Do you have any questions you would like to ask me now before we start? Well, then you may begin."

These instructions are designed to simulate roughly a projective test situation. The lack of verbal responsiveness of the examiner during the period the subject is speaking, plus a conscious attempt on the part of the examiner to keep at a minimum any nonverbal cues that might indicate his reactions to the subject, tend to give the examiner in the total situation the quality of "blank screen" on which the subject projects some part of the gamut of his reactions to any vaguely similar life situation within his past experience. We find that what the subject talks about during any one verbal sample depends in large part on what psychological conflicts or states are being most probably experienced at the time and what states or conflicts are most highly mobilized by the stimulus eliciting speech. These psychological states determine how the subject perceives the experimental situation and what events are retrieved from his remote or recent memory storage system. The standardized nature of the situation in which the verbal samples are elicited minimizes the interviewer as a variable influencing the interviewee's psychological state and leaves the interviewee's reactions (appropriate and inappropriate) as a predominant variable in the interpersonal interaction.

These content analysis procedures can be, and have been applied to interview material, psychotherapeutic, diagnostic or otherwise. The typed data can be broken down into equal temporal units (for example, 2 of 5 min segments). Or the units can be based on the number of words spoken by one or both participants (or more if they are present); for example, consecutive 500 word sequences of the speaker's can be coded for content. Depending on the purpose and research design of the study period, these content analysis scales have also been applied to dreams, projective test data (specifically, tape-

recordings of Thematic Apperception Test responses), to written verbal samples, and even to literature, letters, public speeches, and any other type of language material.

An example of the simplest content analysis scale we have developed, the Anxiety Scale, is shown below, followed by an example of a coded and scored speech sample. Six subtypes of anxiety are included in the total anxiety score: death anxiety, mutilation anxiety, separation anxiety, guilt anxiety, shame anxiety, and diffuse anxiety.

## SCHEDULE 1

### Anxiety Scale

1. Death anxiety–references to death, dying, threat of death, or anxiety about death experienced by or occurring to:
   a. self (3)
   b. animate others (2)
   c. inanimate objects (1)
   d. denial of death anxiety (1)
2. Mutilation (castration) anxiety–references to injury, tissue or physical damage, or anxiety about injury or threat of such experienced by or occurring to:
   a. self (3)
   b. animate others (2)
   c. inanimate objects destroyed (1)
   d. denial (1)
3. Separation anxiety–references to desertion, abandonment, ostracism, loss of support, falling, loss of love or love object, or threat of such experienced by or occurring to:
   a. self (3)
   b. animate others (2)
   c. inanimate objects (1)
   d. denial (1)
4. Guilt anxiety-references to adverse criticism, abuse, condemnation, moral disapproval, guilt, or threat of such experienced by:
   a. self (3)
   b. animate others (2)
   d. denial (1)
5. Shame anxiety–references to ridicule, inadequacy, shame, embarrassment, humiliation, overexposure of deficiencies or private details, or threat of such experienced by:
   a. self (3)
   b. animate others (2)
   d. denial (1)
6. Diffuse or nonspecific anxiety–references by work of phrase to anxiety and/or fear without distinguishing type or source of anxiety.
   a. self (3)
   b. animate others (2)
   d. denial (1)

The verbal sample illustrates the system of scoring those clauses which have scorable anxiety items, with appropriate symbols designating each category in

the anxiety scale. The numbers in parentheses in the verbal sample indicate the weights assigned to each scorable content item. The diagonal marks indicate grammatical clauses. A detailed description and discussion of scoring procedures, with many examples, is provided in *A Manual for Using the Gottschalk-Gleser Content Analysis Scales* (Gottschalk *et al.*, 1969*b*).

## EXAMPLE 1

### Verbal Sample #1 Coded for Anxiety

Name of Subject:<br>
(Male psychiatric inpatient) Interviewer:<br>
Date: Total Words: 187<br>
Name of Study: Correction Factor: 0.5348

5a3<br>
What do you want me to say? / I don't know what to talk about. / Well, let's<br>
5a3<br>
see . . . / I don't know what to talk about, Doc. / Uh I've been here for about<br>
four months / and uh had a pretty rough time of it. / And and uh my wife, she<br>
6a3<br>
wants me to stay here / as long as I can. / I I told her / I would. / Our babies,<br>
they get on my nerves, my little babies. / Sometimes I don't get no sleep. /<br>
2b2 2b2<br>
(Pause) Got a little cat at home. / It got hurt, / it got a broken leg / and I had<br>
1b2<br>
to get that fixed. / (Pause) I had a pretty rough time of it. / My dad, I lost my<br>
3a3 3a3<br>
dad in '51, / now only got two brothers living. / And they never come to see<br>
4a3<br>
me. / I guess / it's pretty much my fault. / And uh my wife she she changes her<br>
6b2<br>
mind all the time. / I think / she's kind of nervous too. / She thinks / she hears<br>
4b2 6a4<br>
people saying bad things about her. / I get sort of frightened and scared about<br>
it all. / I don't know / what else I can tell you. / That's all / I can think of. /

## ILLUSTRATIONS OF NEUROSCIENCE APPLICATIONS OF THE GOTTSCHALK CONTENT ANALYSIS SCALE OF VERBAL BEHAVIOR

### Some Demographic Factors Influencing Emotions (Gottschalk and Gleser, 1969)

#### *Anxiety and Intelligence*

An analysis of variance of the verbal anxiety scores for 90 individuals employed at the same company (Kroger) reveals a significant negative trend in

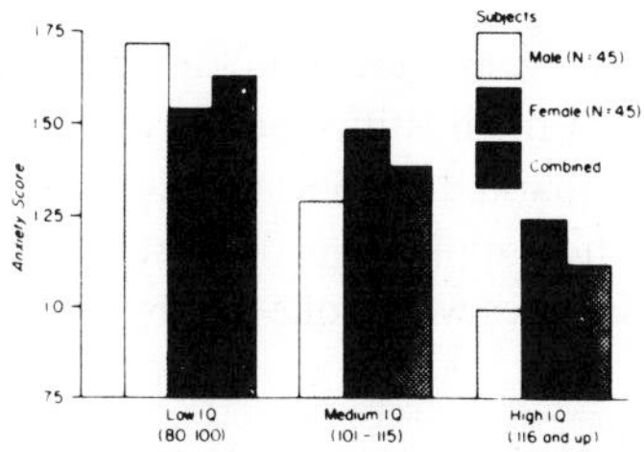


**Fig. 1.** IQ and anxiety scores for males and females.

anxiety with IQ level ($p < 0.05$), the lowest IQ group having the highest anxiety scores ($r = -0.28$). Since the task involves extemporaneous speaking into a microphone, an activity for which individuals with the lower IQ sometimes feel inadequate, higher shame anxiety is elicited with the lower IQ, and it is this anxiety subscale that accounts for the negative correlation with IQ (*see* Fig. 1).

## *Anxiety and Sex Differences*

No sex differences have been found in large samples of individuals for total anxiety scores, but in six separate subscale scores for anxiety, we have found in normative samples (173 males and 109 females), higher scores for females on separation and shame anxiety as compared to males; males have significantly higher scores on death and mutilation anxiety (*see* Fig. 2).

## *Anxiety and Age*

The relationship between age and anxiety has been examined in several samples of adults and no evidence of a linear relationship has been found. One subscale of anxiety, however, evidently increases consistently with age. In three separate samples of people we have found correlations of 0.25, 0.24, and 0.28 between age and death anxiety. Such a relationship makes sense, since death appears increasingly important and threatening as one grows older.

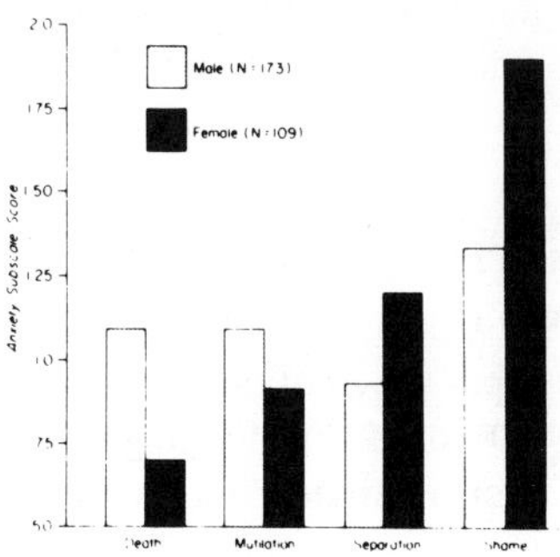


**Fig. 2.** Sex and anxiety sub-scale scores (non-psychiatric subjects).

### *Hostility Scores and Race*

In several series of studies, lower hostility-out scores were found in Negroes as compared to Caucasians. The difference between the hostility outward scores in black as compared to white people is more marked among females. This finding has been thought to be due either to the suppression of hostility in Negroes, or to the fact that most of these verbal samples were collected by white interviewers.

### *Hostility Outward Scores and Sex*

There has been found a significant trend for higher hostility outward scores to be present in the 5 min verbal samples of males as compared to females. This sex difference is probably related to endocrine differences, higher hostility outward probably being secondary to male sex hormones (Gottschalk, 1968*a*).

## Psychophysiological Findings

### *Anxiety and Skin Temperature*

The higher the anxiety scores derived from our content analysis method, the greater the fall in skin temperature during the giving of the speech sample. The evidence follows.

A group of twelve high school boys 16-17 years of age gave three 5 min verbal samples on each of two separate occasions while continuous measurements of skin temperature were being taken and the boys were in a hypnotic state (Gottlieb *et al.*, 1967). The anxiety scores from the six verbal samples obtained under hypnosis were negatively correlated with the change in skin temperature occurring during the giving of the 5-min verbal sample for each student separately, using a rank-order correlation. Ten of the twelve correlations were negative ($p < 0.04$), yielding an averaging intrasubject correlation of −0.31.

A corroborative study, examining the correlations between 5-min sequences of two 50-min psychotherapeutic interviews and continuous measures of skin temperature (Gottschalk *et al.*, 1961*b*), revealed a significant negative correlation between the anxiety scored in each 5-min interval and the change in skin temperature from the beginning to the end of each 5-min interval (Gottschalk and Gleser, 1969).

### *Studies of Relationships of Emotions to Plasma Lipids*

A natural history study (Gottschalk, 1968*a*; Gottschalk *et al.*, 1965*a*) disclosed different relationships between several types of emotions and blood lipids in a group of 24 men who had fasted 10 to 12 hr. Findings were cross-validated in a study of a second group of 20 men. Anxiety scores have a

significant positive correlation with plasma free fatty acids (FFA) in both groups—a sign of catecholamine (adrenergic) secretion. Three types of hostility scores, however, had an essentially zero correlation with free fatty acids. More anxious men tended to have higher free fatty acid levels and sharper rises in FFA than nonanxious men in a reaction to a venipuncture and free associating for 5 min. There was evidence for positive correlations between plasma triglyceride levels and both anxiety and hostility inward scores as well as for total hostility outward scores and levels of blood cholesterol. We have found (Stone *et al.*, 1969) that nonathlete, college students tend, as a group, to have higher plasma free fatty acid responses to the same anxiety levels than college students who are athletes (either on the football or swimming teams) (*see* Fig. 3 and Table I).

*Anxiety Levels and Dreams: Relation to Changes in Plasma Free Fatty Acids*

Blood samples for determination of plasma free fatty acids were obtained throughout the night by means of an indwelling venous catheter. The first blood

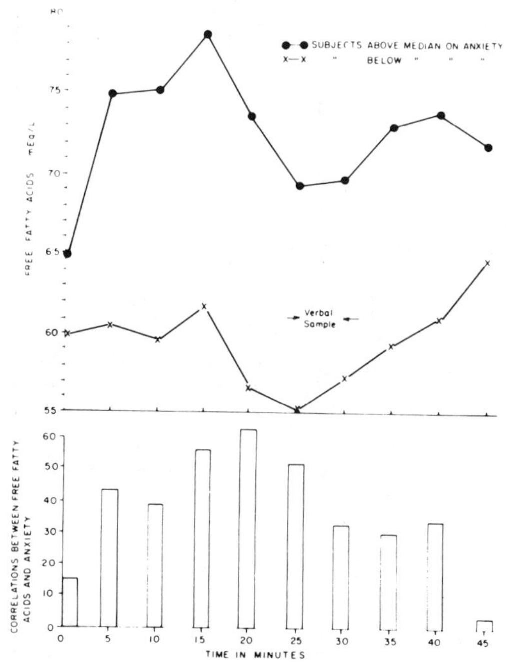


**Fig. 3.** Variations in free fatty acids over time in anxious and nonanxious patients (Group II).

**Table I.** Correlations Among Lipids and Verbal Affect Measures

| Measure | Mean | SD | Serum lipids | | Immediate affect scores | | | | | | |
|---|---|---|---|---|---|---|---|---|---|---|---|
| | | | | | | Hostility | | | | | |
| | | | | | | Outward | | | | | |
| | | | Triglycerides | Av. free fatty acids | Anxiety | Overt | Convert | Total | Inward | Ambivalent |
| Cholestérol, mg %[a] | 185.10 | 29.36 | 0.30 | −0.13 | −0.24 | 0.51 | 0.08 | 0.37 | −0.28 | −0.03 |
| Triglycerides, mg % | 59.35 | 35.64 | – | 0.17 | 0.26 | −0.03 | −0.11 | −0.18 | 0.47 | 0.07 |
| Av. free fatty acids, mEq/L | 0.66 | 0.13 | – | – | 0.44 | −0.08 | −0.07 | −0.00 | 0.36 | 0.04 |
| Anxiety | 1.29 | 0.53 | – | – | – | 0.14 | 0.00 | −0.08 | 0.52 | 0.42 |
| Hostility outward | | | | | | | | | | |
| Overt | 0.64 | 0.28 | – | – | – | – | 0.32 | 0.87 | −0.03 | 0.47 |
| Covert | 0.56 | 0.26 | – | – | – | – | – | 0.72 | 0.02 | 0.02 |
| Total | 0.81 | 0.35 | – | – | – | – | – | – | −0.08 | 0.33 |
| Hostility inward | 0.60 | 0.22 | – | – | – | – | – | – | – | 0.04 |
| Ambivalent hostility | 0.66 | 0.33 | – | – | – | – | – | – | – | – |

[a] Age was not partialed out for this group, since the age range was extremely limited.

sample was drawn at the onset of rapid eye movements (REM) and the second after 15 min of these eye movements. Subjects were then awakened and asked to relate their dreams; a third sample was drawn 15 to 25 min later. Anxiety scores derived from 20 dreams of nine subjects have significant positive correlations with changes in free fatty acids occurring during REM sleep. There were no consistently positive correlations with hostility scores derived from the same dreams. These findings indicate that anxiety aroused in dreams triggers the release of catecholamines into the circulation and these catecholamines mobilize proportional amounts of plasma free fatty acid from body fat (Gottschalk *et al.*, 1966).

### *Anxiety Scores from Dream and Inhibition of Penile Erection with Rapid Eye Movement (REM) Sleep*

Karacan *et al.* (1966) studied the relationships of penile erections during episodes of rapid eye movement (REM) sleep and the anxiety scores derived from the tape-recorded dreams reported upon awakening from such periods of sleep. A statistically significant association was found between anxiety scores from such dreams and the lack of penile erections.

### *Corticosteroid Levels and Hostility and Anxiety*

Five-minute verbal samples, elicited by our standardized method, were analyzed for hostility and anxiety scores and correlated with corticosteroid levels of 28 nonpsychotic male medical patients (Gottschalk *et al.*, 1969*a, b*). A correlation of +0.40 was obtained between hostility outward levels and the average plasma 17-hydroxycorticosteroid levels; the correlation was higher with the corticosteroid level obtained 1 hr after the 5-min sample was obtained (+0.47) than that obtained 1 hr before this time (+0.31). No correlation was found between plasma 17-hydroxycorticosteroids and anxiety and hostility inward scores. In our own studies, the psychochemical relationships have been observed at relatively low levels of arousal for these emotions, that is, in situations where there was no contrived stress and in which the data was collected in a natural history setting. These facts may account for why both anxiety and hostility did not arouse corticosteroid secretion in our studies.

### *Anxiety and Hostility Levels and Phases of the Menstrual Cycle*

Five-minute verbal samples given daily by small numbers of women for periods up to three-months have indicated that different women have different cycles of anxiety and hostility, depending upon their own personal reactions to the changing hormonal levels of their cycles. Across individuals, however, women as a group show a transient decrease of anxiety and hostility at the time of ovulation, presumably related to the secretion of luteinizing hormone. Also, they show an increase in anxiety premenstrually using our content analysis

method (Gottschalk *et al.*, 1962; Ivey and Bardwick, 1968). Recent studies (Silbergeld *et al.*, 1971) have shown that the birth control pill, Enovid, smoothes out and blocks the significant fluctuations in anxiety and hostility previously observed during the menstrual cycle by our method.

## Anxiety and Hostility in Response to Psychoactive Drugs

We have done many studies using our content analysis procedure in neuropsychopharmacological investigations. In almost all of our studies we have used the double-blind, cross-over design. These studies have been of considerable interest to us because they afford a means of influencing the neurochemical environment of the brain, and observing the behavioral and psychological effect as measured through speech. The minor tranquilizer, chlordiazepoxide, in 46 juvenile delinquent boys administered 20 mg of the drug, produced significant decreases in anxiety, ambivalent hostility, and overt hostility outward 40 to 120 min after ingesting the chlordiazepoxide (Gleser *et al.*, 1965). In another study (Gottschalk *et al.*, 1960) 20 dermatologic inpatients (10 men and 10 women) were given perphenazine, 16 to 24 mg a day by mouth for one week alternating with a placebo for one week, using a double-blind, cross-over design. Analysis of the content of 5-min verbal samples obtained from these patients showed a reduction of hostility outward scores with perphenazine in 16 of the 20 patients ($p < 0.01$) and a decrease in anxiety scores at the elevated end of the spectrum of the anxiety scores. Another study showed an increase in anxiety and overt hostility-out scores derived from verbal samples in patients receiving the antidepressant drug, imipramine, as compared to a placebo (Gottschalk *et al.*, 1965*b*).

The implications of these findings is that the neurochemical changes produced by these pharmacological agents are a functional decrease in utilizable catecholamines in the brain with tranquilizers, such as chlordiazepoxide and perphenazine, and an increase in such catecholamines with the administration of the antidepressant psychoactive drugs such as imipramine (Schildkraut *et al.*, 1968).

## Achievement Striving Scores, Derived from the Content Analysis of Five-Minute Verbal Samples, as they Relate to Induced Mental Set of Psychomotor Stimulants

One study (Gottschalk *et al.*, 1968) on college students has shown that telling these students that a pill would make them "more peppy and energetic" (whether the pill was a placebo, 90 mg of secobarbital, or 10 mg of dextroamphetamine) significantly increased the achievement striving scores of these students, as derived from 5-min speech samples, regardless of the

medication they were administered. On the other hand, dextroamphetamine (10 mg) by mouth also significantly increased achievement-striving scores, regardless of the set induced. This study demonstrated that induced mental set and drug effect can be additive.

In another study (Gottschalk *et al.*, 1971) similar achievement-striving scores were found to be significantly higher ($p < 0.01$) in the 5-min samples of a large group of male prisoners ($N = 33$) at the Patuxent, Maryland, penitentiary when they had ingested dextroamphetamine (15 mg) than when they had taken a placebo capsule.

### The Relationship of the Magnitude of Emotions, as Determined from Content-Analysis of a Tape-Recorded Interview, and Paroxysmal Electroencephalographic Activity

A 20-year-old single white male, Army private, an inpatient at Walter Reed Army Hospital in Washington, D.C., for the study of the etiology of grand mal seizures he developed during military duty in the absence of a history of head injury, was found to have frequent high amplitude bursts of slow wave paroxysmal activity on his electroencephalogram (Gottschalk, 1955). Several hourly sessions of EEG recordings were carried out while he was interviewed. The tape-recordings of the interviews were synchronized with his EEG recordings so that the content of what he was saying could be related to the paroxysmal EEG activity. Sixteen 30-word segments of his speech occurring just before a paroxysmal EEG event were selected from these interviews as well as sixteen 30-word segments which were not immediately followed by abnormal EEG activity. Content-analysis technicians were asked to score these 30-word segments for total negative affects (anxiety and hostility scores combined) and for total effects, including negative as well as positive emotions (scores derived from our Human Relations Scales, a measure of the capacity for congenial human relationships) (Gottschalk, 1968*b*).

Paroxysmal EEG activity was found to be preceded significantly more often by a higher total effect score ($p < 0.05$) than normal EEG activity (*see* Fig. 4). Total anxiety ($p < 0.05$) and hostility inward ($p < 0.05$) scores were found to account principally for this finding; whereas hostility outward, ambivalent hostility, and positive affect scores were not significantly related to the abnormal paroxysmal EEG activity.

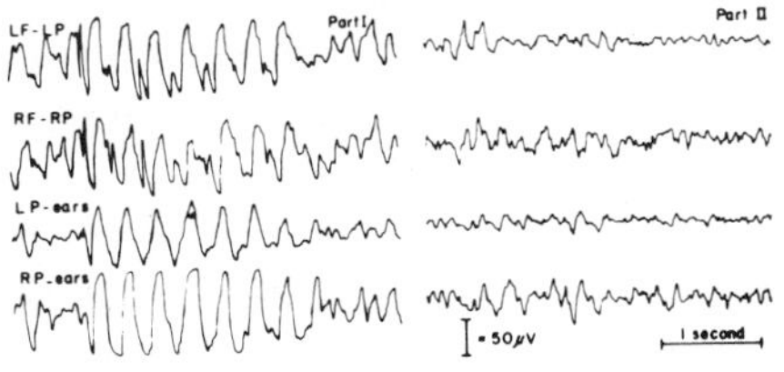

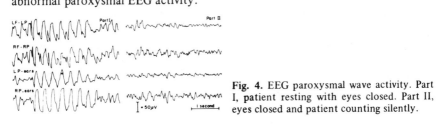

**Fig. 4.** EEG paroxysmal wave activity. Part I, patient resting with eyes closed. Part II, eyes closed and patient counting silently.

## Cognitive and Intellectual Impairment Measured from Five-Minute Samples of Speech

Preliminary development has been carried out on a content analysis scale derivable from 5-min samples of speech, which measures the magnitude of cognitive and intellectual impairment. The purpose of this scale is to assess the magnitude of transient and reversible changes in general cognitive and intellectual function as well as irreversible changes, all due principally to brain dysfunction and minimally to transient and emotional changes in the individual (Gottschalk and Gleser, 1969). At its present state of development, this content-analysis scale of cognitive and intellectual impairment is capable of differentiating patients with organic brain syndromes from nonbrain damage patients and individuals. Correlational studies with two measures of irreversible brain damage, the Halstead Battery (1947) and the Trail Making Test (Reitan, 1958) on a group of twenty subjects, male and female, ranging in age from 40 to 84 showed satisfactory correlations with both of these measures (Halstead Battery, $r = 0.55$, and Trail Making Test, $r = 0.48$).

Gottschalk and Gleser (1969) used these verbal content analysis scores to investigate the effects of LSD-25 and a placebo on the social alienation-personal disorganization scores of a group of college student volunteers. They showed that LSD-25 did not influence scores on the social alienation-personal disorganization scale anymore than did a placebo. But LSD-25 did significantly increase scores on the cognitive impairment scale. In another study, the same investigators examined the effects of LSD-25, Ditran (JB329), and Psilocybin on behavior. In this study the effect of these psychotomimetic drugs on the dimension of cognitive-intellectual impairment was to produce more signs of cognitive impairment in the speech of normals than occurs without drugs in the speech of schizophrenics. Most recently, Waskow *et al.* (*unpublished*) found, using institutionalized prisoners as subjects, that LSD (50 μg) as compared to a placebo, did significantly increase scores on both the social alienation-personal disorganization and the cognitive-intellectual impairment content-analysis scales. These data suggest that, at least in some kinds of subjects, psychotomimetic drugs are more likely to induce a transient organic brain syndrome than a functional mental disorder.

Another study, recently published (Gottschalk *et al.*, 1969*c*) using the cognitive-intellectual impairment scale explored the effect of total and half body irradiation on intellectual functioning. This study provided suggestive evidence of temporary impairment of such functioning immediately after exposure to such radiation.

We believe that this scale, at its present stage of development, measures general intellectual functioning rather than the functioning of any specific part

of the brain. The possible usefulness of this scale, as well as some of our other scales, during stimulation or functional impairment of various parts of the human brain is obvious.

## DISCUSSION

This review of previous studies using this objective method of assessing the magnitude of various psychological states provides an idea of its potential usefulness in many kinds of research in the neural sciences. In our own research, we have been eager to collaborate with neuroscientists who might be involved in stimulating or interfering with the function of various parts of the central nervous system. Many of the complex psychological and behavioral reactions to stimulation of electrodes implanted in the central nervous system in humans could most likely be measured by this content analysis procedure.

New neuropsychopharmacological studies using this content analysis method are revealing that the intravenous administration of barbiturates, benzodiazepine derivatives (e.g., chlordiazepoxide or diazepam), or placebo indicate that this procedure is a very sensitive and accurate method of detecting potentially new anti-anxiety pharmacological agents. Moreover, new neurochemical studies are in process to explore relationships with some of the psychological variables objectively measurable by this approach and endocrines such as testosterone, estrogens, insulin, growth hormone, corticosteroids, ACTH, and so forth.

The biggest step we are seeking is the development of a computer program for the content analysis of speech from our scales directly from a typescript. This time-saving breakthrough will probably take about a decade. When such computerization can be accomplished many exciting psychological correlates of brain function in the neural sciences will be possible.

## REFERENCES

Gleser, G. C., Gottschalk, L. A., and Springer, K. J. (1961). An anxiety scale applicable to verbal samples. *Arch. Gen Psychiat.* **5**: 593.

Gleser, G. C., Gottschalk, L. A., Fox, R., and Lippert, W. (1965). Immediate changes in affect with chlordiazepoxide in juvenile delinquent boys. *Arch. Gen. Psychiat.* **13**: 291.

Gottlieb, A., Gleser, G. C., and Gottschalk, L. A. (1967). Veral and psychological responses to hypnotic suggestion of attitudes. *Psychosomat. Med.* **29**: 172.

Gottschalk, L. A. (1955). Psychologic conflict and electroencephalographic patterns. Some notes on the problem of correlating changes in paroxysmal electroencephalographic patterns with psychologic conflicts. *Arch. Neurol. Psychiat.* **73**: 656.

Gottschalk, L. A. (1968*a*). The measurement of hostile aggression through the content analysis of speech: Some biological and interpersonal aspects, in *Biology of Aggressive Behavior*, Garattini, S. and Sigg, E. B. (eds.), Excerpta Medica Foundation, Amsterdam, the Netherlands.

Gottschalk, L. A. (1968*b*). Some applications of the psychoanalytic concept of object relatedness: Preliminary studies on a human relations scale applicable to verbal samples. *Comprehensive Psychiat.* **9**: 608.

Gottschalk, L. A., and Gleser, G. C. (1969). *The Measurement of Psychological States Through the Content Analysis of Verbal Behavior*, University of California Press, Berkeley and Los Angeles.

Gottschalk, L. A., Gleser, G. C., Daniels, R. S., and Block, S. L. (1958). The speech patterns of schizophrenic patients: A method of assessing relative degree of personal disorganization and social alienation. *J. Nervous Mental Disease* **127**: 153.

Gottschalk, L. A., Gleser, G. C., Springer, K. J., Kaplan, S. M., Shanon, J., and Ross, W. D. (1960). Effects of perphenazine on verbal behavior patterns. *Arch. Gen. Psychiat.* **2**: 632.

Gottschalk, L. A., Gleser, G. C., Magliocco, E. B., and D'Zmura, T. L. (1961*a*). Further studies on speech patterns of schizophrenic patients. Measuring inter-individual differences in relative degree of personal disorganization and social alienation. *J. Nervous Mental Disease* **132**: 101.

Gottschalk, L. A., Springer, K. J., and Gleser, G. C. (1961*b*). Experiments with a method of assessing the variations in intensity of certain psychological states occurring during two psychotherapeutic interviews, in *Comparative Psycholinguistic Analysis of Two Psychotherapeutic Interviews*, Gottschalk, L. A. (ed.), International Universities Press, New York.

Gottschalk, L. A., Kaplan, S. M., Gleser, G. C., and Winget, C. N. (1962). Variations in magnitude of emotion: A method applied to anxiety and hostility during phases of the menstrual cycle. *Psychosomat. Med.* **24**: 300.

Gottschalk, L. A., Gleser, G. C., and Springer, K. J. (1963). Three hostility scales applicable to verbal samples. *Arch. Gen. Psychiat.* **9**: 254.

Gottschalk, L. A., Gleser, G. C., D'Zmura, T., and Hanenson, I. B. (1964). Some psychophysiological relationships in hypertensive women. The effect of hydrochlorothiazine on the relation of affect to blood pressure. *Psychosomat. Med.* **26**: 610.

Gottschalk, L. A., Cleghorn, J. M., Gleser, G. C. and Iacono, J. M. (1965*a*). Studies of relationships of emotions to plasma lipids. *Psychosomat. Med.* **27**: 102.

Gottschalk, L. A., Gleser, G. C., Wylie, H. W., and Kaplan, S. M. (1965*b*). Effects of imipramine on anxiety and hostility levels derived from verbal communications. *Psychopharmacologia* **7**: 303.

Gottschalk, L. A., Stone, W. N., Gleser, G. C., and Iacono, J. M. (1966). Anxiety levels in dreams: relation to changes in plasma free fatty acids. *Science* **153**: 654.

Gottschalk, L. A., Gleser, G. C., and Stone, W. N. (1968). Studies of psychoactive drugs effects on non-psychiatric patients. Measurement of affective and cognitive changes by content analysis of speech, in *Psychopharmacology of the Normal Human*, Evans, W., and Kline, N. (eds.), Charles C. Thomas, Springfield, Ill.

Gottschalk, L. A., Stone, W. N., Gleser, G. C., and Iacono, J. M. (1969*a*). Anxiety and plasma free fatty acid (FFA) levels. *Life Sci.* **8**: 61.

Gottschalk, L. A., Winget, C. N., and Gleser, G. C. (1969*b*). *Manual of Instructions for Using the Gottschalk-Gleser Content Analysis Scales: Anxiety, Hostility, and Social Alienation-Personal Disorganization*, University of California Press, Berkeley, Los Angeles.

Gottschalk, L. A., Kunkel, R. L., Wohl, T., Saenger, E., and Winget, C. N. (1969*c*). Total and half body irradiation. Effect on cognitive and emotional processes. *Arch. Gen. Psychiat.* **21**: 574.

Gottschalk, L. A., Bates, D. E., Waskow, I. E., Katz, M. M., and Olsson, J. (1971). Effect of amphetamine or chlorpromazine on achievement strivings scores derived from content analysis of speech. *Comprehensive Psychiat.* **12**: 430.

Halstead, W. D. (1947). *Brain and Intelligence*, University of Chicago Press, Chicago.

Ivey, M. E., and Bardwick, J. M. (1968). Patterns of affective fluctuation in the menstrual cycle. *Psychosomat. Med.* **30:** 336.

Karacan, I., Goodenough, D. R., Shapiro, A., and Starker, S. (1966). Erection cycle during sleep in relation to dream anxiety. *Arch. Gen Psychiat.* **15:** 183.

Reitan, R. M. (1958). Validity of the Trail Making Test as an indicator of organic brain damage. *Percept. Motor Skills* **8:** 271.

Schildkraut, J. J., David, J. M., and Klerman, G. L. (1968). Biochemistry of depressions, in *Psychopharmacology: A Review of Progress, 1957-1967*, U.S. Government Printing Office, Public Health Service Publication No. 1836, Washington, D.C. pp. 625-648.

Silbergeld, S., Brast, N. and Noble, E. P. (1971). The menstrual cycle: a double-blind study of mood, behavior, and biochemical variables with Enovid and a placebo. *Psychosomat. Med.* **33:** 411.

Stone, W. N., Gleser, G. C., Gottschalk, L. A. and Iacono, J. M. (1969). Stimulus, affect, and plasma free fatty acids. *Psychosomat. Med.* **31:** 331.

# Effect of Sensory Overload on Psychological State

## Changes in Social Alienation-Personal Disorganization and Cognitive-Intellectual Impairment

Louis A. Gottschalk, MD; John L. Haer, PhD; and Daniel E. Bates, BA, Irvine, Calif

**Ten male and ten female subjects were shown a 43-minute, high-intensity sound color movie contrived to evoke a psychedelic experience. Five-minute tape-recorded speech samples and Rod and Frame tests were obtained from each subject before and immediately after exposure to the sound movie.**

**Content analysis scores of the speech samples showed a significant increase in social alienation-personal disorganization scores ($P < .025$, one-tailed test) and cognitive-intellectual impairment scores ($P < .005$, one-tailed test) after exposure to the sensory overload experience. The degree of field dependence, derived from the Rod and Frame test, significantly predicted which subjects would have the largest increases in cognitive-intellectual impairment scores ($r = .48$, $P < .025$, one-tailed test).**

The aim of this study was to determine whether any temporary pathological psychological states might be produced by excessive auditory and visual stimulation. The criteria for assessing such psychological changes were changes in the content of speech measured by the Gottschalk-Gleser social alienation-personal disorganization scale and the cognitive-intellectual impairment scale. The relevance of techniques for producing states of sensory deprivation has been reviewed elsewhere.[1-4] In this report we are designating the procedure in which a subject receives excessive atypical sensory stimulation as "sensory overload." No major work has been undertaken in which deviant psychological states have been brought on by having subjects inundated with excessive sensory stimulation.

Drug-induced altered states of consciousness have been investigated using the same psycholinguistic scales employed in this study. Gottschalk and Gleser[5] used these verbal content analysis scales to investigate the effects of lysergic acid diethylamide (LSD-25) and a placebo on the social alienation-personal disorganization and cognitive-intellectual impairment scores of a group of college student volunteers. They showed that LSD-25 did not produce manifestations of schizophrenia (increase in social alienation-personal disorganization scores) anymore than did a placebo. But LSD-25 did promote cognitive impairment and, in this sense, did induce a toxic mental disorder rather than a functional one. In another study, the same investigators examined the effects of LSD-25, piperidyl benzilate (Ditran) and psilocybin on verbal behavior. In this exploratory study the effect of these psychotomimetic drugs was to produce more signs of cognitive impairment in the speech of normals than occurs without drugs in the speech of schizophrenics. Most recently, however, Waskow et al (unpublished data) found, using institutionalized prisoners as subjects, that LSD (50μg) as compared to a placebo, did significantly increase scores on both the social alienation-personal disorganization and the cognitive and intellectual impairment Gottschalk-Gleser scales.

Accepted for publication Nov 2, 1971.

From the Communications and Measurements Laboratory, Department of Psychiatry and Human Behavior, College of Medicine, University of California, Irvine, Calif.

Reprint requests to the Department of Psychiatry and Human Behavior, Orange County Medical Center, 101 S Manchester Ave, Orange, Calif 92668 (Dr. Gottschalk).

### Method

**Subjects.**—Ten male and ten female Caucasians voluntarily served as subjects. (Mean age, 27.6 years; mean educational level, 15 years.) Seven subjects were students, three were artists, and the remainder were employed in semiprofessional or skilled occupations. Although two of the 20 subjects were undergoing psychotherapy, neither exhibited serious evidence of psychiatric impairment. All of the subjects had heard of the project through informal sources. Hence, all exhibited curiosity about an experience "involving light and sound."

**Apparatus.**—The Sensory Overload Apparatus was constructed in the shape of a geodesic dome upon the inside of which a visual presentation, a movie, was projected. The dome was 6 feet high and 11 feet in diameter. The interior walls and dome were painted white and the floor upon which the subject reclined was carpeted. Access to the interior of the dome was via a small door which, from a view on the inside, blended with the walls.

A standard visual presentation was accomplished by projecting a 16-mm film through an 8-inch lens located in the center of the floor of the interior dome space. Since the movie projector was located under the floor of the interior dome space, subjects were usually not aware of the technique of presentation. The image that the lens projected matched the circular interior dome space sufficiently so that a relatively clear image was projected over about two thirds of the ceiling and walls. The subjects experienced being surrounded by a total environment of color and sound.

The 16-mm film was in color and lasted 43 minutes. The film was made with the intention of simulating visual and auditory aspects of a quasihallucinatory experience. Twelve minutes of the film consisted of changing abstract images. Three 30-second segments projected a diffuse red light, and the remainder of the film was composed of sequences relating to a variety of themes: birth, death, violence, eroticism, views of outer space, nature, surgical procedures, and so forth. The themes selected were assumed to tap conscious and unconscious levels of significance for all subjects. The short segments were spliced together randomly or were shown in split second shots, so that the "flow" of the film defied customary expectations. Most subjects did not think of themselves as "merely watching a movie"; rather they felt caught up in an engrossing experience that was intense, colorful, and replete with arousing images and sequences nonlogically linked.

A tape recorder was used to supply the standard auditory presentation through inconspicuous speakers in the dome space wall. The intensity of sound was judged extremely loud but bearable. Sounds were taken from recordings of sound effects and electronic music. These unusual sounds were juxtaposed in a manner so that sometimes the music complemented the visual presentation and sometimes was antagonistic to it. All subjects reported that the sound seemed to converge on them from all directions.

**Procedures.**–The subjects were individually interviewed and tested before and after exposure to the overload. Prior to the experimental procedures, personal background data were obtained, including motives for participating in the experiment. Then, subjects were given the Rod and Frame test,[6] a test of space perception (lining up rods in a rectangular box), and a test of ability to estimate the passage of time. A five-minute electronic tape-recorded verbal sample was next obtained from the subjects by asking each one to speak about any interesting or dramatic personal life-experiences. The specific instructions given to subjects and the standardized procedures for scoring the speech samples are discussed elsewhere.[7] Finally, subjects filled out the Multiple Affective Adjective Checklist, a device which provides measures of anxiety, depression, and hostility.[8]

Subjects were then placed in the Sensory Overload Apparatus for about 45 minutes. They were requested to lie on their backs under the dome and were assured that the experimenter would remain in the room outside. No additional instructions were given. Subjects who asked questions about the experiment were told that they would be given information afterward. After the 45 minutes they were taken to an adjoining room and asked to give another five-minute verbal sample. Then they filled out the Multiple Affective Adjective Checklist and were again given the Rod and Frame, space perception, and time-estimation tests. After the testing was concluded, subjects were asked to enlarge on portions of their verbal reports of their experiences.

Typescripts of the five-minute speech samples were scored blindly for social alienation-personal disorganization and cognitive and intellectual impairment (Tables 1 and 2) by content analysis technicians uninformed as to the details of this study.

The social alienation-personal disorganization content analysis scale, also called the "schizophrenic scale," has been validated against a number of criterion measures: (1) A set of three psychiatric rating scales covering the dimensions of "intrapsychic phenomena," "behavioral patterns," "personal habit patterns," both cross-sectionally (152 schizophrenic patients for one occasion) and longitudinally (18 schizophrenic patients for up to six months).[5,9-11] (2) The Mental Status Schedule of Spitzer et al.[5,12-15] (3) Portions of the Cattell 16PF[5,16,17] pertaining to schizophrenia. Other construct validation studies have pursued: (1) The extent to which the verbal items in the scale discriminate schizophrenic speech (acute and chronic) as compared to the speech of randomly selected psychiatric outpatients, general medical patients, and a large nonmedical normative sample of subjects[11] and (2) the degree to which this scale predicts and follows changes in the relative severity of the schizophrenic syndrome with administration and withdrawal of a major tranquilizer, thioridazine, in 69 chronic schizophrenic patients.[15] These studies indicate that the social alienation-personal disorganization scale measures a psychological dimension at one extreme congruent with the schizophrenic syndrome and at the nonpsychotic end of this continuum delineates various degrees of withdrawal and alienation from human relations or lapses in logical coherent thinking processes that might be labeled "schizoid" trends. Social alienation-personal disorganization scores obtained from pretreatment five-minute speech samples of patients coming to a Mental Health Crisis Clinic have been found to be predictive of an unfavorable post-treatment outcome probably because the scores reflect schizoid tendencies in these patients.[18] Scores from five-minute samples of

Table 1.—Social Alienation and Personal Disorganization (Schizophrenic) Scale

| Weights | Content Categories and Scoring Symbols |
|---|---|
| | **I. Interpersonal references (including fauna and flora).** |
| | A. To thoughts, feelings, or reported actions of avoiding, leaving, deserting, spurning, not understanding of others. |
| 0 | 1. Self avoiding others. |
| +1 | 2. Others avoiding self. |
| | B. To unfriendly, hostile, destructive thoughts, feelings, or actions. |
| +1 | 1. Self unfriendly to others. |
| +1/3 | 2. Others unfriendly to self. |
| | C. To congenial and constructive thoughts, feelings, or actions. |
| −2 | 1. Others helping, being friendly toward others. |
| −2 | 2. Self helping, being friendly toward others. |
| −2 | 3. Others helping, being friendly toward self. |
| | D. To others. |
| 0 | 1. Being bad, dangerous, strange, ill, malfunctioning, having low value or worth. |
| −1 | 2. Being intact, satisfied, healthy, well. |
| | **II. Intrapersonal references.** |
| +2 | A. To disorientation—references indicating disorientation for time, place, person, or other distortion of reality—past, present, or future (do not score more than one item per clause under this category). |
| | B. To self. |
| 0 | 1a. Physical illness, malfunctioning (references to illness or symptoms due primarily to cellular or tissue damage). |
| +1 | 1b. Psychological malfunctioning (references to illness or symptoms due primarily to emotions or psychological reactions not secondary to cellular or tissue damage). |
| 0 | 1c. Malfunctioning of indeterminate origin (references to illness or symptoms not definitely attributable either to emotions or cellular damage). |
| −2 | 2. Getting better. |
| −1 | 3a. Intact, satisfied, healthy, well: definite positive affect or valence indicated. |
| −1 | 3b. Intact, satisfied, healthy, well; flat, factual or neutral attitudes expressed. |
| +½ | 4. Not being prepared or able to produce, perform, act, not knowing, not sure. |
| +½ | 5. To being controlled, feeling controlled, wanting control, asking for control or permission, being obliged or having to do, think, or experience something. |
| +3 | C. Denial of feelings, attitudes, or mental state of the self. |
| | D. To food. |
| 0 | 1. Bad, dangerous, unpleasant, or otherwise negative; interferences or delays in eating; too much and wish to have less; too little and wish to have more. |
| 0 | 2. Good or neutral |
| | E. To weather. |
| −1 | 1. Bad, dangerous, unpleasant, or otherwise negative (not sunny, not clear, uncomfortable, etc.). |
| −1 | 2. Good, pleasant, or neutral. |
| | F. To sleep. |
| 0 | 1. Bad, dangerous, unpleasant, or otherwise negative, too much, too little. |
| 0 | 2. Good, pleasant, or neutral. |
| | **III. Disorganization and repetition.** |
| | A. Signs of disorganization. |
| +1 | 1. Remarks or words that are not understandable or audible. |
| 0 | 2. Incomplete sentences, clauses, phrases; blocking. |

Table 1.—Social Alienation and Personal Disorganization (Schizophrenic) Scale (Continued)

| Weights | Content Categories and Scoring Symbols |
|---|---|
| +2 | 3. Obviously erroneous or fallacious remarks or conclusions; illogical or bizarre statements. |
| | B. Repetition of ideas in sequence. |
| 0 | 1. Words separated only by a word (excluding instances due to grammatical and syntactical convention, where words are repeated, eg, "as far as," "by and by," and so forth; also excluding instances where such words as "I" and "the" are separated by a word). |
| +1 | 2. Phrases or clauses (separated only by a phrase or a clause). |
| | **IV. References to the interviewer.** |
| +1 | A. Questions directed to the interviewer. |
| +½ | B. Other references to the interviewer. |
| +1 | **V. Religious and biblical references.** |

Table 2.—Cognitive and Intellectual Impairment Scale

| Weights | Content Categories and Scoring Symbols |
|---|---|
| | **I. Interpersonal references (including fauna and flora).** |
| | B. To unfriendly, hostile, destructive thoughts, feelings, or actions. |
| −½ | 1. Self unfriendly to others. |
| | C. To congenial and constructive thoughts, feelings, or actions. |
| −½ | 1. Others helping, being friendly toward others. |
| −½ | 2. Self helping, being friendly toward others. |
| −½ | 3. Others helping, being friendly toward self. |
| | **II. Intrapersonal references.** |
| +3 | A. To disorientation-orientation, past, present, or future (do not include all references to time, place, or person, but only those in which it is reasonably clear the subject is trying to orient himself or is expressing disorientation with respect to these; also do not score more than one item per clause under this category). |
| | B. To self. |
| −½ | 1. Injured, ailing, deprived, malfunctioning, getting worse, bad, dangerous, low value or worth, strange. |
| +¼ | 3. Intact, satisfied, healthy, well. |
| +1 | 5. To being controlled, feeling controlled, wanting control, asking for control or permission, being obliged or having to do, think or experience something. |
| +1 | C. Denial of feelings, attitudes, or mental state of the self. |
| | D. To food. |
| −1 | 2. Good or neutral. |
| | **III. Miscellaneous.** |
| | A. Signs of disorganization. |
| +1 | 2. Incomplete sentences, clauses, phrases; blocking. |
| | B. Repetition of ideas in sequence. |
| +1 | 2. Phrases, clauses (separated only by a phrase or clause). |
| +1 | **IV. A. Questions directed to the interviewer.** |

speech are more indicative of a state than a trait, but the average of scores from repeated measures over time provides an index closer to a trait measure.

The cognitive-intellectual impairment scale was derived originally from the social alienation-personal disorganization (schizophrenic) scale after it was noted that scores from a brain-function impaired sample of patients showed a distribution that was similar to scores from a sample of acute and chronic schizophrenics.[11] Speech content and form items that distinguished the speech of people with a transient or irreversible brain dysfunction from schizophrenic speech were selected from the social alienation-personal disorganization scale and assigned new weights to maximize this distinction.[19] Further refinement of these weights was achieved using the Halstead Battery[20] and the Trail-Making test[21] as criterion measures to discriminate more precisely signs in speech of organic brain dysfunction. Further modifications in weights assigned to these speech items were made after observing changes in cognitive-intellectual impairment scores in patients with acute brain syndromes that were reversible, eg, before, during, after the electroshock therapy.[5] This scale measures a state of generalized brain-function impairment, largely a different function of cognition and mentation than the disorganization of thinking which may occur in the schizophrenic syndrome. It has, however, proved sensitive in detecting significant temporary worsening in the intellectual functioning of patients receiving partial or total body-irradiation.[22] And in studies previously referred to in this report, LSD-25, piperidyl benzilate, or psilocybin have been found more consistently and significantly to increase scores on the cognitive-intellectual impairment scale than on the social alienation-personal disorganization scale.

## Results

Comparison of the mean of social alienation-personal disorganization scores at preexposure (1.99 ± 3.16) and for postexposure (3.96 ± 2.94) in the Sensory Overload Apparatus showed there was a significant difference ($t = 2.101$, $P < .025$) using a one-tailed test. Comparison of the mean of cognitive and intellectual impairment scores for preexposure (2.23 ± 1.41) to the mean score at postexposure (3.85 ± 1.89) also showed there was a significant change ($t = 3.401$, $P < .005$) using a one-tailed test (Table 3).

The correlation of preexposure field dependence-independence scores and change scores for social alienation-personal disorganization was +0.36, and the correlation of field dependence-independence scores with cognitive-intellectual impairment change scores was $r = +0.48$ ($P < .025$, one-tailed test) (Table 4). The relationships between subjects' Rod and Frame test scores and their social alienation-personal disorganization scores, preexposure and postexposure, were $r = -0.33$ and $r = +0.26$, respectively. There was no relationship ($r = +0.08$) between the ranking of subjects on social alienation-personal disorganization scores before and after the sensory overload experience. Also, there was no significant correlation ($r = +0.24$) between subjects' ranking on preexposure cogni-

Table 3.—Content Analysis Scale Score Derived From Five-Minute Speech Samples Taken Before and After Exposure to a Sensory Overload Experience

| Scales | Mean Preexposure Scores | Mean Postexposure Scores | t | P-Value (One-Tailed) |
|---|---|---|---|---|
| Social alienation-personal disorganization | 1.99 ± 3.16 | 3.96 ± 2.94 | 2.101 | .025 |
| Cognitive-intellectual impairment | 2.23 ± 1.41 | 3.85 ± 1.89 | 3.401 | .005 |

Table 4.—Intercorrelation of Scores*

| | Social Alienation-Personal Disorganization Scores | Cognitive-Intellectual Impairment Scores |
|---|---|---|
| | **Preexposure Scores** | |
| Field dependence-independence scores (preexposure) | −.33 | −.36 |
| | **Postexposure Scores** | |
| | +.14 | +.26 |
| | **Changes Scores** | |
| | +.36 | +.48 ($P < .025$, one-tailed) |

* Intercorrelations of social alienation-personal disorganization scores and cognitive-intellectual impairment scores (derived from content analysis of five-minute speech samples taken before and after exposure to a sensory overload experience) with preexposure field dependence-independence scores (Rod and Frame test).

Table 5.—Changes in Content Analysis Subcategory Scores of Social Alienation: Personal Disorganization Scores Before and After Sensory Overload Exposure

| Sub-category Item | Weights* | No. Subjects Using Category, %† Pre-exposure | Post-exposure | Total Weighted Scores Pre-exposure | Post-exposure | Mean Scores Including SD‡ Preexposure | Postexposure | t= | P<§ |
|---|---|---|---|---|---|---|---|---|---|
| IA1 | 0 | ... | ... | ... | ... | ... | ... | ... | ... |
| A2 | +1 | 26(05) | 11(02) | 1.49 | 0.45 | 0.30 ± 0.17 | 0.23 ± 0.04 | 07 | .15 |
| IB1 | +1 | 42(08) | 42(08) | 3.75 | 3.65 | 0.47 ± 0.36 | 0.46 ± 0.39 | 33 | .33 |
| B2 | +⅓ | 32(06) | 21(04) | ±1.90 | 0.65 | 0.27 ± 0.47 | 0.22 ± 0.16 | 15 | .21 |
| IC1 | −2 | 32(06) | 11(02) | −4.92 | −0.74 | −0.82 ± 0.50 | −0.37 ± 0.15 | 01 | .025 |
| C2 | −2 | 84(16) | 53(10) | −25.18 | −19.14 | −1.57 ± 1.32 | −1.91 ± 2.57 | 65 | NS |
| C3 | −2 | 53(10) | 0( 0) | −10.44 | 0.00 | −1.05 ± 1.07 | 0.00 ± 0.00 | 0 | .005 |
| ID1 | 0 | ... | ... | ... | ... | ... | ... | ... | ... |
| D2 | −1 | 53(10) | 53(10) | −8.55 | −5.45 | −0.86 ± 0.67 | −0.55 ± 0.46 | 41 | .25 |
| IIA | +2 | 21(04) | 53(10) | 3.55 | 8.35 | 0.89 ± 1.23 | 0.84 ± 0.45 | 22 | .05 |
| IIB1a | 0 | ... | ... | ... | ... | ... | ... | ... | ... |
| 1b | +1 | 63(12) | 16(03) | 7.26 | 1.63 | 0.61 ± 0.37 | 0.54 ± 0.26 | 11 | .01 |
| 1c | 0 | ... | ... | ... | ... | ... | ... | ... | ... |
| IIB2 | −2 | 05(01) | 0( 0) | −0.52 | 0.00 | −0.52 ± 0.00 | 0.00 ± 0.00 | ... | NS |
| B3a | −1 | 63(12) | 47(09) | −6.35 | −8.07 | −0.53 ± 0.36 | −0.90 ± 0.57 | 42 | .25 |
| B3b | −1 | 74(14) | 63(12) | −10.87 | −9.47 | −0.78 ± 0.48 | −0.79 ± 0.93 | 40 | NS |
| B4 | +½ | 79(15) | 42(08) | 3.54 | 2.30 | 0.24 ± 0.15 | 0.29 ± 0.31 | 40 | NS |
| B5 | +½ | 53(10) | 47(09) | 2.53 | 2.81 | 0.53 ± 0.19 | 0.31 ± 0.21 | 67 | NS |
| IIC | +3 | 58(11) | 58(11) | 18.17 | 18.83 | 1.65 ± 1.26 | 1.72 ± 0.97 | 56 | .42 |
| IID1 | 0 | ... | ... | ... | ... | ... | ... | ... | ... |
| D2 | 0 | ... | ... | ... | ... | ... | ... | ... | ... |
| IIE1 | −1 | 11(02) | 0( 0) | −1.09 | 0.00 | −0.54 ± 0.55 | 0.00 ± 0.00 | ... | NS |
| E2 | −1 | 0( 0) | 0( 0) | 0.00 | 0.00 | 0.00 ± 0.00 | 0.00 ± 0.00 | ... | NS |
| IIF1 | 0 | ... | ... | ... | ... | ... | ... | ... | ... |
| IIF2 | 0 | ... | ... | ... | ... | ... | ... | ... | ... |
| IIIA1 | +1 | 89(17) | 100(19) | 25.62 | 37.00 | 1.51 ± 1.03 | 1.95 ± 1.31 | 39 | NS |
| A2 | 0 | ... | ... | ... | ... | ... | ... | ... | ... |
| A3 | +2 | 26(05) | 26(05) | 2.39 | 7.84 | 0.60 ± 0.15 | 1.31 ± 1.06 | 16 | NS |
| IIIB1 | 0 | ... | ... | ... | ... | ... | ... | ... | ... |
| B2 | +1 | 100(19) | 94(18) | 23.14 | 25.17 | 1.22 ± 0.78 | 1.40 ± 1.11 | 92 | NS |
| IVA | +1 | 47(09) | 26(05) | 2.20 | 1.38 | 0.24 ± 0.18 | 0.28 ± 0.20 | 27 | .06 |
| IVB | +½ | 89(17) | 84(16) | 18.66 | 7.58 | 0.48 ± 0.43 | 0.45 ± 0.37 | 61 | NS |
| V | +1 | 21(04) | 05(01) | 1.40 | 0.48 | 0.34 ± 0.30 | 0.48 ± 0.00 | ... | NS |

* Positive weights indicate increased alienation or disorganization.
† Numbers in parentheses indicate actual number of subjects.
‡ Means represent scores only for those responding to that subcategory.
§ Test of significance using Wilcoxon Matched-Pairs Signed-Ranks test.

tive and intellectual impairment scores and their postexposure ranking.

A detailed examination was carried out of the changes in content categories occurring in the five-minute speech samples in response to the sensory overload experience. The Wilcoxon Matched-Pairs Signed-Ranks test was used to compare the magnitude of these changes in preexposure and postexposure scores for each subject and within each category. The major changes accounting for increased scores in the dimension of social alienation-personal disorganization were found to be in the following subcategories: (1) fewer references to others being

Table 6.—Changes in Content Analysis Subcategory Scores of Cognitive-Intellectual Impairment Scores Before and After Sensory Overload Exposure

| Subcategory Item | Weights* | No. Subjects Using Category, %† | | Total Weight Scores | | Mean Scores Including SD‡ | | | |
|---|---|---|---|---|---|---|---|---|---|
| | | Preexposure | Postexposure | Preexposure | Postexposure | Preexposure | Postexposure | t= | P<§ |
| IA1 | 0 | ... | ... | ... | ... | ... | ... | ... | ... |
| A2 | 0 | ... | ... | ... | ... | ... | ... | ... | ... |
| IB1 | −½ | 42(08) | 42(08) | −1.88 | −1.82 | −0.23 ± 0.18 | −0.23 ± 0.20 | 33 | .33 |
| B2 | 0 | ... | ... | ... | ... | ... | ... | ... | ... |
| IC1 | −½ | 32(06) | 11(02) | −1.23 | −0.19 | −0.20 ± 0.12 | −0.09 ± 0.07 | 01 | .025 |
| C2 | −½ | 84(16) | 53(10) | −6.29 | −4.78 | −0.39 ± 0.33 | −0.48 ± 0.64 | 65 | ... |
| C3 | −½ | 53(10) | 0 | −2.61 | ... | −0.26 ± 0.27 | 0.00 ± 0.00 | 0 | .005 |
| ID1 | 0 | ... | ... | ... | ... | ... | ... | ... | ... |
| D2 | 0 | ... | ... | ... | ... | ... | ... | ... | ... |
| IIA | +3 | 21(04) | 53(10) | 5.33 | 12.51 | 1.33 ± 1.02 | 1.25 ± 0.67 | 22 | .05 |
| IIB1a | −½ | 32(06) | 16(03) | −2.14 | −0.91 | −0.36 ± 0.45 | −0.30 ± 0.19 | 16 | .40 |
| 1b | −½ | 63(12) | 16(03) | −3.65 | −0.81 | −0.30 ± 0.18 | −0.27 ± 0.13 | 11 | .01 |
| 1c | −½ | 32(06) | 47(09) | −0.80 | −2.66 | −0.13 ± 0.06 | −0.30 ± 0.24 | 20 | .13 |
| B2 | 0 | ... | ... | ... | ... | ... | ... | ... | ... |
| B3a | +¼ | 63(12) | 47(09) | 1.59 | 2.02 | 0.13 ± 0.09 | 0.22 ± 0.14 | 42 | .25 |
| B3b | +¼ | 74(14) | 63(12) | 2.72 | 2.37 | 0.19 ± 0.12 | 0.20 ± 0.23 | 40 | NS |
| B4 | 0 | ... | ... | ... | ... | ... | ... | ... | ... |
| B5 | +1 | 53(10) | 47(09) | 5.05 | 5.61 | 0.50 ± 0.38 | 0.62 ± 0.43 | 67 | NS |
| IIC | +1 | 58(11) | 58(11) | 6.06 | 6.24 | 0.55 ± 0.42 | 0.57 ± 0.30 | 56 | .42 |
| IID1 | 0 | ... | ... | ... | ... | ... | ... | ... | ... |
| D2 | −1 | 0 | 05(01) | −0.20 | 0.00 | 0.00 ± 0.00 | −0.20 ± 0.00 | 0 | NS |
| IIE1 | 0 | ... | ... | ... | ... | ... | ... | ... | ... |
| IIE2 | 0 | ... | ... | ... | ... | ... | ... | ... | ... |
| IIF1 | 0 | ... | ... | ... | ... | ... | ... | ... | ... |
| F2 | 0 | ... | ... | ... | ... | ... | ... | ... | ... |
| IIIA1 | 0 | ... | ... | ... | ... | ... | ... | ... | ... |
| A2 | +1 | 79(15) | 100(19) | 15.92 | 29.29 | 1.06 ± 0.69 | 1.54 ± 0.75 | 23 | .005 |
| A3 | 0 | ... | ... | ... | ... | ... | ... | ... | ... |
| IIIB1 | 0 | ... | ... | ... | ... | ... | ... | ... | ... |
| B2 | +1 | 100(19) | 95(18) | 23.14 | 25.17 | 1.22 ± 0.78 | 1.40 ± 1.11 | 92 | NS |
| IVA | +½ | 47(09) | 26(05) | 0.96 | 0.63 | 0.12 ± 0.09 | 0.14 ± 0.10 | 27 | .06 |
| IVB | 0 | ... | ... | ... | ... | ... | ... | ... | ... |
| V | 0 | ... | ... | ... | ... | ... | ... | ... | ... |

* Positive weights indicate increased impairment.
† Numbers in parentheses indicate actual number of subjects.
‡ Means represent scores only for those responding to that subcategory.
§ Test of significance using Wilcoxon Matched-Pairs Signed-Ranks test.

friendly toward the self (verbal category notation IC3, $P < .005$); (2) fewer references to others being friendly towards others (IC1, $P < .025$); (3) more references to disorientation (IIA, $P < .05$); (4) more references to others avoiding the self (IA2, $P < .15$). References to psychological malfunctioning (IIB1b, $P < .01$) and questions directed to the interviewer (IVA, $P < .06$), which one might expect would occur more prominently after sensory exposure, actually occurred less frequently, but with more magnitude in the instance of subcategory IVA (Table 5).

The major changes accounting for increased scores in the dimension of cognitive-intellectual impairment were shown to be in the following categories: (1) More incomplete sentences, clauses, phrases; blocking (IIIA2, $P < .005$); (2) fewer references to others being friendly toward self (IC3, $P < .005$); (3) fewer references to others being friendly towards others (IC1, $P < .025$); (4) fewer references to psychological malfunctioning (IIB1b, $P < .01$); (5) more references to disorientation (IIA, $P < .05$). References to malfunctioning of indeterminate origin (IIB1c), usually a verbal category not suggestive of cognitive-intellectual impairment, actually tended to occur somewhat more prominently after sensory exposure ($P < .13$). Also, subcategory IVA, slightly indicative of cognitive impairment, again occurred less frequently but with greater magnitude after sensory overload ($P < .06$) (Table 6).

The results appear to show that several content categories (IC1, IC3, IIA) of the dimensions of social alienation-personal disorganization and cognitive-impairment undergo modifications in the same directions in reaction to the sensory overload experience. On the other hand, in response to the overload stimulation, more references to others avoiding the self (IA2) help produce increased scores in the social alienation-personal disorganization scale, whereas, more incomplete sentences, etc (IIIA2) and fewer references to psychological malfunctioning (IIB1b) contribute to greater scores in the cognitive-intellectual impairment scale.

The data and results derived from other measures obtained in this study have been reported elsewhere.[23,24]

### Comment

The results indicate that experience in the Sensory Overload Apparatus produces a measurable increase in the subjects' social alienation-personal disorganization scores (a measure congruent with the relative severity of the schizophrenia) and cognitive-intellectual impairment scores (brain function disorder).[5] Those who had higher social alienation-personal disorganization scores before being exposed to the excessive sensory stimulation were not necessarily those most affected by the experience. Likewise, the brain-function impairment change over subjects was not predictably related to preexposure scores, though there was a trend, which did not quite reach a statistically convincing level of significance, for subjects with higher cognitive-intellectual impairment scores before exposure to have higher postexposure scores ($r = +.24$).

High Rod and Frame test scores indicate high field dependence, as contrasted to field independence,[6] ie, perceptual and cognitive function influenced by contextual field. It is plausible that a chaotically organized, intense, visual and auditory sensory overload will be likely to impair significantly the cognitive function of field-dependent individuals to a greater extent than field-independent subjects, and this is, indeed, what we have found.

The detailed examination of the specific changes in speech categories of the two psychological dimensions in reaction to the sensory experience is interesting, but it raises as many questions as it answers. It would appear that we have obtained evidence that both impairment of brain function and sociopsychological function are induced by sensory overload. Our criteria, however, of these functions contain some common denominators which, though weighted differently in order to detect these presumably different mental conditions, show changes in similar directions. We must argue, at this time, however, that if there is any fault in our measurements, it is not in the discriminatory capacity of our measurement tools (ie, the two content analysis scales), but in the complexity of nature which permits sociopsychological dysfunction to be associated with disturbances of brain function and vice versa. We continue to be concerned, however, with maximizing the specificity of the two content analysis measures used in this study, and the data obtained here will be considered in making possible future changes in the weights assigned to content categories.

Various authors[25-28] have elucidated extraneous variables which influence and bias the results obtained in sensory deprivation studies. The variables most emphasized are: (1) the subjects' preexperimental expectation; (2) the subjects' individual motivation either in accordance with or against the expectations; and (3) problems in using free or quasifree methods of eliciting data from the subjects. The content analysis method we have used here, which gives no indication of what psychological dimensions are being scored, copes in part with the effect of suggestion or expectation in influencing our results.

On inquiry, a surprisingly high number of our subjects (12 out of 20) had had prior experience with LSD or mescaline. This fact leads us to wonder whether our group of subjects might have been especially prone to seek or have psychedelic experiences. Subjects, however, with no prior drug experience reported significantly more subjective alterations of consciousness (not including scores of social alienation-personal disorganization and cognitive-intellectual impairment) than individuals who had taken such drugs.[21]

We have no idea of the psychophysiological mechanism accounting for the capacity of our subjects to have such schizophrenic-like or organic brain-function-like disturbances in response to the type of sensory overload stimuli to which we exposed them. Obviously, to answer such questions further studies need to be carried out with a variety of other subjects and with a control exposure in the Sensory Overload Apparatus without stimulation by the color sound movie.

### References


1. Ziskind E: A second look at sensory deprivation. *J Nerv Ment Dis* 138:223-232, 1964.
2. Ziskind E, Augsburg T: Hallucinations in sensory deprivation. *Dis Nerv Syst* 28:721-726, 1967.
3. Brawley P, Pos R: The informational underload (sensory deprivation) model in contemporary psychiatry. *Canad Psychiat Assoc J* 12:105-124, 1967.
4. Pos R, Rzadki EJ, McElroy JF, et al: Research into the informational underload (sensory deprivation) hypothesis of mental illness: Preliminary report. *Canad Psychiat Assoc J* 12:135-145, 1967.
5. Gottschalk LA, Gleser GC: *The Measurement of Psychological States Through the Content Analysis of Verbal Behavior.* Berkeley, University of California Press, 1969.
6. Witkin HA, Kyk RB, Paterson HF, et al: *Psychological Differentiation.* New York, John Wiley & Sons Inc, 1962.
7. Gottschalk LA, Winget CN, Gleser GC: *Manual of Instructions for Using the Gottschalk-Gleser Content Analysis Scales.* Berkeley, University of California Press, 1969.
8. Zuckerman M, Lubin B: *Manual for the Multiple Affect Adjective Check List.* San Diego, Calif, Education and Industrial Testing Service, 1965.
9. Gottschalk LA, Gleser GC, Daniels RS, et al: The speech patterns of schizophrenic patients: A method of assessing relative degree of personal disorganization and social alienation. *J Nerv Ment Dis* 127:153-166, 1958.
10. Gottschalk LA, Gleser GC, Magliocco EB, et al: Further studies on the speech patterns of schizophrenia patients: Measuring interindividual differences in relative degree of personal disorganization and social alienation. *J Nerv Ment Dis* 132:101-113, 1961.
11. Gottschalk LA, Gleser GC: Distinguishing characteristics of the verbal communications of schizophrenic patients, in Rioch D, Weinstein E (eds): *Disorders of Communication.* Baltimore, William & Wilkins Co, 1964, vol 42, pp 400-413.
12. Spitzer RL, Fleiss JL, Burdock EI, et al: The mental status schedule: Rationale, reliability, and validity. *Compr Psychiat* 5:384-395, 1964.
13. Spitzer RL, Fleiss JL, Kernohan W, et al: Mental status schedule. *Arch Gen Psychiat* 13:448-455, 1965.
14. Spitzer RL, Fleiss JL, Endicott J, et al: Mental status schedule: Properties of factor analytically derived scales. *Arch Gen Psychiat* 16:479-493, 1967.
15. Gottschalk LA, Gleser GC, Cleghorn JM, et al: Prediction of changes in severity of the schizophrenic syndrome with discontinuation and administration of phenothiazines in chronic schizophrenic patients: Language as a predictor and measure of change in schizophrenia. *Compr Psychiat* 11:123-140, 1970.
16. Cattell RB, Eber HW: *Handbook for the 16 Personality Factor Questionnaire.* Champaign, Ill, Institute for Personality and Ability Testing, 1957 (1964 supplementation).
17. Gleser GC, Gottschalk LA, Stone WN, et al: Changes in the severity of social alienation-personal disorganization in chronic schizophrenic patients: Psychometric and psychopharmacologic factors, in Sankar DVS (ed): *Schizophrenia: Current Concepts in Research.* New York, P.J.D. Publications Ltd., 1969, pp 51-69.
18. Gottschalk LA, Mayerson P, Gottlieb A: The prediction and

evaluation of outcome in an emergency brief psychotherapy clinic. *J Nerv Ment Dis* 144:77-96, 1967.

19. Gottschalk LA, Kunkel RL: Changes in emotional and intellectual functioning after total body radiation, in Saenger EL, et al (eds): *Metabolic Changes in Humans Following Total Body Radiation.* Report Period February 1960 through April 1966 to Defense Atomic Support Agency, Washington, DC, Research grant DA-49-146-XZ-315.

20. Halstead WD: *Brain and Intelligence.* Chicago, University of Chicago Press, 1947.

21. Reitan RM: Validity of the trail-making test as an indicator of organic brain damage. *Percept Motor Skills* 8:271-276, 1958.

22. Gottschalk LA, Kunkel RL, Wohl TH, et al: Total and half-body irradiation: Effect on cognitive and emotional processes. *Arch Gen Psychiat* 21:574-580, 1969.

23. Haer JL: Alteration in consciousness induced by sensory overload. *J Stud Consciousness* 3:161-169, 1970.

24. Haer JL: Field dependency in relation to altered states of consciousness. *J Percept Motor Skills* 33:192-194, 1971.

25. Jackson CW, Pollard JC: Some nondeprivation variables which influence the "effects" of experimental sensory deprivation. *J Abnorm Psychol* 7:383-388, 1966.

26. Kandel EJ, Myers TI, Murphy DB: Influence of prior verbalizations and instructions on visual sensations reported under conditions of reduced sensory input, abstract. *Amer Psychologist* 13:334, 1958.

27. Orne MT, Scheib LE: The contribution of nondeprivation factors in the production of sensory deprivation effects: The psychology of the "panic button." *J Abnorm Soc Psychol* 68:3-12, 1964.

28. Reed GF: Preparatory set as a factor in the production of sensory deprivation phenomena. *Proc Royal Soc Med* 55:1010-1014, 1962.

# Part VI

# Psychokinesic Studies

These chapters involve examinations of the association of psychologic states to various non-verbal neuromuscular activities. One chapter, Chapter 40, is entitled, "A study of the representation of anxiety in chronic schizophrenia"(Steingart et al, 1977). Another, Chapter 41, is entitled "Body movements in the verbal encoding of aggressive affect" (Freedman et al, 1973). Another chapter, Chapter 42, is entitled "The psychoanalytic study of hand-mouth approximations" (Gottschalk, 1974). A chapter follows (43) entitled "A study of the relationship of nonverbal to verbal behavior: effect of lip caressing on hope and oral references as expressed in the content of speech" (Gottschalk and Uliana, 1976). A final chapter (44) is entitled "Further studies on the relationship of nonverbal to verbal behavior: effect of lip caressing on shame, hostility, and other variables as expressed in the content of speech" (Gottschalk and Uliana, 1977).

40

# A STUDY OF THE REPRESENTATON OF ANXIETY IN CHRONIC SCHIZOPHRENIA

Irving Steingart, Stanley Grand, Reuben Margolis, Norbert Freedman, and Charles Buchwald

This research is a part of a series of inter-related studies conducted with both normal subjects and clinical populations which utilize certain kinetic and linguistic aspects of communication behavior as indices for the status of thought organization. The present study examines the dialogue communication behavior of a group of chronic, male schizophrenics, and demonstrates a relation between these same indices of communication behavior and types of anxiety expression.

## INTRODUCTION

The present paper is part of an ongoing research program which utilizes attributes of hand movement and attributes of language construction which occur in spontaneous language performance as indices of the organization of communication behavior. Communicative behavior is *both* sign behavior and the basis for other sorts of inference making. The researcher must make a choice as to what use such data are put. Recently, Winer, Devoe, and Geller (1972) stressed this important distinction with respect to hand movements. Hand movements, then may be interpreted as either coded meanings or hand movements may be understood simply as attributes which tell us something about the properties of an individual's behavior during communication. The same distinction applies to the analysis of language behavior. Conventional categories of content analysis emphasize sign properties while more formal

attributes of language construction can be used as a basis for inference about organizational properties of an individual's behavior.

Certain categorizations of language behavior, together with certain classifications of hand movement behavior which accompany spontaneous speech, constitute for us important indices of cognitive organization during an act of communication. We gave evidence which links such language construction and hand movement behavior to clinical remission as well as paranoid and depressive psychopathology (Steingart & Freedman, 1972; Steingart & Freedman, in press) adaptation among clinically normal but blind subjects (Blass, Freedman, & Steingart, 1974), and discrimination between field independent (F-I) and field dependent (F-D) cognitive style among normal subjects in a situation of monologue communication (Freedman, O'Hanlon, Oltman, & Witkin, 1972; Steingart, Freedman, Grand, and Buchwald (1975). However, with respect to this sighted normal population, we also found that in a dialogue communication situation no differences in language behavior were present between field-independent and field-dependent subjects. We thus came to consider that dialogue communication has intrinsic supportive effects that can obscure important individual differences among sighted, normal subjects. We thus came to consider that dialogue communication has intrinsic supportive effects that can obscure important individual differences among sighted, normal subjects. We thus elected to study dialogue communication behavior with a group of subjects whose psychopathology is associated with more vulnerable communication behavior, a group of chronic schizophrenics, and obtained further evidence about the relevance of our hand movement and language measures for the assessment of cognitive organization during an act of communication (Grand, Steingart, Freedman, & Buchwald, 1975). Thus, we are led to expect that, if we can identify these differences in the organization of communication behavior, such differences should also relate to differences in developmental levels and functions served by anxiety expression in a group of chronic schizophrenics. When we speak about differences in "developmental levels" of anxiety expression we refer to expected changes in the *content* of anxiety experience co-ordinated with stages of personality development (Erikson, 1963). Anxiety experience also is expected to change in *function* with personality development. What at first is a disorganized and disorganizing traumatic anxiety experience is expected to change into a *signal* like function which alerts the organism to anticipate a possible danger, and thus enhances the possibility of effective response (Freud, 1926; Leeper, 1948).

Pavey (1968), in a recent review of relevant literature about language behavior, laments the neglect of any effort to apply more contemporary formulations about language behavior to research in schizophrenia. Indeed, in a still more recent review of the psycholinguistic literature, Fillenbaum (1971) cites no research which attempts to apply these more recent formulations about

language performance and competence to schizophrenic pathology. One, still more recent, exception to his barren state of affairs is the important work conducted by Lindenfeld (1972; 1973; in press). Lindenfeld's work suggests that, in general, there appears to be an inverse relation between degree of syntactic complexity (such as would be inferred from a Chomskyan model of grammar) and the amounts of body movement during spontaneous speech, and that this kind of relation between body movement and syntax occurs with both normal and various types of psychopathological populations. But Lindenfeld's approach does not utilize certain of our classifications of *body touching* hand movements which we consider to have important implications for the organization of communication behavior, and thus, we expect, will show congruence with language performance complexity.

Further, we utilize classifications of language behavior which involve language function together with syntactic complexity. First, we dichotomize speech according to how sentence elaboration primarily is achieved. Sentences can become elaborated by grammatical coordination devices, or certain kinds of apositive formations, which have been established by developmental research to be relatively immature types of acquisition of grammatical skill (Hunt, 1970). Such sentence elaboration —which we term narrative language—is (roughly) inferred in a generative-transformation model of grammar to reflect the operation of "conjoining" transformational activities (Lyons, 1968).

All remaining sentence elaborations we term complex language. These sentences appear in spontaneous, surface structure speech as full or abridged kinds of complex sentences. They represent, developmentally, the acquisition of more mature sorts of grammatical skills (Hunt, 1970), and are (roughly) inferred to reflect the operations of various kinds of "embedding" transformations (Lyons, 1968). We then make a second, further distinction within Complex language. Complex Portrayal contrasted to complex conditional language construction pivots about different *functional* uses to which an individual puts his grammatical, embedding skills for the structuring of experience. This orientation toward language behavior derives from Piaget's seminal work about the development of intelligence (Piaget,1923).

## METHOD

### *Patient Selection and Clinical Interview*

Sixteen male, chronic schizophrenic patients comprised the subjects for this study. An audio-video tape was made of a clinical interview which was conducted with each of these 16 patients. The interview was an open-ended, unstructured exploration into the patient's current activities, social relation-

ships, and feeling states. A 10-minute segment, beginning five minutes after the start of the interview, was the basis for the data for our study. All patients had been receiving some form of phenothiazine medication and were placed on placebo one week prior to the present study. At the time of the study, the still possible presence of phenothiazine was checked by an evaluation of extrapyramidal symptoms, and none was found. According to the Hollingshead index (Hollingshead & Redlich, 1958), there were no significant differences among our patients for level of education, job status, etc. Further details about patient selection and other procedures for data collection can be found elsewhere (Grand, Freedman, & Steingart, 1973).

*Assessment of the Organization of Communication Behavior*

Our present methods of analyzing kinetic and linguistic behavior form video-recorded interviews have been reported in detail elsewhere (Freedman, Blass, Rifkin, & Quitkin, 1973; Steingart & Freedman, 1972). Here we shall simply outline our approach. Briefly, the analysis of hand movement behavior has focused on movements of the hands which accompany speech. All hand movements are classified in terms of two broad domains of acitivity: a class of object-focused movements, and a class of body-focused movements. Object-focused movements are communicative acts closely linked to the rhythm and content of speech, and may qualify, punctuate, illustrate, or depict some verbalized or partially unverbalized aspect of thought. The chief characteristic of body-focused movements is that the hands are involved in some stimulation of the body or its adornments. Thus, by definition, body-focused activity bears no manifest relation to the rhythm or content of speech, and, with one exception, is continuous in nature.

Three levels of object-focused activity have been delineated: *Speech primacy* movements which are qualifying and punctuating motions, subordinate to the rhythm of speech and lacking representational quality; *Representational* movements which are a supplement to the verbal utterance and in which some referent, an object, an idea, or feeling state, is given physical and visible representation; *Nonrepresentational* movements consisting of groping, pointing, or depicting gestures where the primary mode of expression is in the motor realm, relatively autonomous from the verbal flow. These categories of movement suggest a progression in the level of integration of speech and movement behavior from subordination, to supplementation, to substitution of movement for the flow of speech. Two judge percentage agreement for the identification of an object-focused movement act is 86%, and category assignment agreement as to type of object-focused act is 70% (Freedman, 1972). Three levels of body-focused activity have been delineated which are distinguishable in terms of the relative degree of organization of the movements

themselves: *Descrete body touching* consists of brief and instrumental acts of body stimulation or the touching of a body adornment such as a tie. *Continuous body touching* consists of continuous stimulation by the hand as agent of some body part other than the hands, or a body adornment; *Continuous finger-to-hand activity* consists of repetitive and unpatterned continuous stimulation of the fingers and / or hands. These categories suggest a progression from relatively circumscribed and integrated movements to relatively diffuse and unpatterned movements. These levels of object- and body-focused activity form the empirical basis for observing the integration of kinetic activity during discourse.

Our approach to language behavior follows form both naturalistic observations of the development of children's language (Piaget, 1923), as well as controlled studies of the development of syntactic maturity (Hunt, 1970), which suggest that language shows an increasingly complex function which enables an individual to move from simple description of essentially unintegrated events, to complex patterned relationships among experiences, to that kind of structuralization of reality established by a conditional (contingency) framework. Briefly, three categories of grammatically coherent surface sentence structures are identified.

*Simple narrative language* behavior consists of surface, simple sentence structures, i.e. simple independent clauses which are not even coordinated to other simple sentences, and so not contain adjectival, adverbial, or propositional modifying material about time or quantity. The overwhelming predominance of such surface simple sentences are of the simple, active declarative form, and represent grammatically the simples level of grammatical skill such as would be inferred from the point of view of a Chomskyan model of grammar (Lyons, 1968). *Complex Portrayal language* consists of surface, complex sentence structures which enable an articulation of some *patterned* interrelation among experiences, through various sorts of grammatical embedding devices (Lyons, 1968), but still only descriptive. *Conditional language* behavior also includes surface, complex sentence structures but now embedding devices bring about the articulation of a *causal, deductive,* or *purposive matrix (i.e.*), a conditional or contingency framework), which is *applied* to immediate experience by the selection of particular subordinate conjections, etc. There is another kind of Conditional language behavior which involves a contiguous placement of two sentences (any combination of simple and complex). The syntax of the second sentence can establish a conditional framework by the introductory use of some kind of causal or illative (inference making) coordinating conjunction, or the introductory deployment of a demonstrative adjective, etc.[1]

The deployment of each type of language behavior is calculated in terms of the percentage clause output relative to the total number of clauses produced which make up grammatically coherent sentences. Any possible effects of skewness are corrected by an arc sine transformation. Two judge reliability, for

both sentence identification and for coding of sentence type, has been established to be better than 90% (Steingart & Freedman, 1972)

*Assessment of Anxiety Expression*

The verbal responses of the subjects were transcribed, sent to Gottschalk's laboratory, and scored for the presence of different types of anxiety using Gottschalk's Content Analysis Scales (Gleser, Gottschalk, & Springer, 1961). The presence of anxiety in this study is evaluated by means of five scales and the following are examples actually gathered from our subjects: *Separation Anxiety*, e.g., " . . . he threw me out of the house . . ."; *Guilt Anxiety*, e.g., ". . . maybe it was my fault that he died." *Shame Anxiety*, e.g., " . . . but I can't . . . I don't tell this to anyone." *Diffuse Anxiety*, "I was really scared." *Mutilation Anxiety*, " . . . cause I only see on one eye."[2]

A weighted scoring procedure is used allowing for the measurement of intensity of each of these anxiety expressions. For instance, another example of diffuse anxiety which would be considered as less intense because the anxiety is attributed to another, would be" . . . she had a nervous breakdown." Another instance of guilt anxiety which would be considered less intense, because of the use of denial, would be:" . . . but I'm not guilty about anything."

The subject's verbal output is unitized into grammatical clause units, and each unit is scored for the presence of one or more of the anxiety categories. Affect scores are expressed as rates per 100 words and are corrected for skewness by means of a square root transformation. Gleser and Gottschalk (1961) report a two judge product-moment for total anxiety scores of .86 and a mean rank-order correlation for the five categories used here of .80.

## RESULTS

Our data analysis proceeds in three steps. First, we examine the intercorrelations we obtained between the two sets of communication measures which we studied—hand movements and language behavior. Next, we use such intercorrelations as basis to rank order our subjects in terms of the organization of their communication behavior. Finally, we look for connections between type of anxiety expression and organization of communication behavior among our subjects.

The intercorrelations among our hand movement and language behavior measures are depicted in Table 1.

It should be noted that the significant intercorrelations we obtained establish a congruent pattern with respect to the organization of communication behavior. Simple narrative language utilizes, relatively, the simplest sorts of language behavior possible for grammatically coherent speech. It is this kind of

TABLE 1

INTERCORRELATIONS AMONG THE ORGANIZATION OF HAND MOVEMENT AND LANGUAGE BEHAVIOR MEASURES

| | Hand movement, object focused | | | Hand movement, body focused | | |
|---|---|---|---|---|---|---|
| Language behavior | Speech primacy | Representational | Non-representational | Finger-to-hand | Continuous body touching | Discrete body touching |
| Fragmented | −.01 | −.05 | .20 | .43 | −.10 | −.10 |
| Simple narrative | −.11 | −.40 | .10 | .56* | −.36 | −.76** |
| Complex portrayal | .43 | .43 | .12 | .00 | −.15 | .00 |
| Total conditional | −.20 | .13 | −.03 | −.57* | .60* | .61* |

* $p < .05$, two-tailed.
** $p < .01$, two-tailed.

language behavior which is significantly and positively correlated with a kind of body touching which morphologically is completely unpatterned. Finger-to-hand activity involves no functional assignment whatsoever between one part of the body (the hand) acting as agent upon some other part of the body (or its adornment). Simple narative language is significantly and negatively correlated with discrete body touching. This latter kind of hand movement is a type of body touching which not only is patterned (hand as agent acting upon some body part, or its adornment, as object) but also appears as an instrumental act such as relieving an itch, adjusting a tie, etc. Conditional language utilizes not only more complex grammatical skills for sentence embeddings but also employs such skills for the purpose of structuring some type of contingency framework for experience. It is this kind of language behavior which is significantly and negatively correlated with finger-to-hand activity, while it is significantly and positively correlated with both continuous and discrete body touching.

Next, we identified the eight subjects with the highest sum ranks on these five, significantly intercorrelated hand movement and language construction measures, and the remaining eight subjects with the lowest sum ranks. These two groups are called, respectively, our high versus low organization-of-communication behavior groups.[3] These two groups of subjects are then contrasted in terms of their anxiety expression scores. It will be recalled that our hypotheses are directional. We expect our high level of oganization-of-communication behaviour group to possess greater amounts of developmentally more advanced kinds of anxiety content and function in contrast to our low group. Rather than compare the high and low groups on each of the Gottschalk anxiety scales, we factor analyzed the anxiety scores.[4] *We expected the factoring to yield separate content and function factors. Comparison of the high and low groups on such*

TABLE 2

FACTOR LOADINGS OF GOTTSCHALK (1961) ANXIETY SCALES AND MEAN FACTOR SCORES BETWEEN HIGH- AND LOW-ORGANIZATION-OF-COMMUNICATION BEHAVIOR GROUPS

| Anxiety scale | Loading | High *M* | High *SD* | Low *M* | Low *SD* | *t* |
|---|---|---|---|---|---|---|
| Factor 1 | | .16 | .90 | −.16 | .67 | .80, *ns* |
| Shame | .70 | | | | | |
| Mutilation | .66 | | | | | |
| Diffuse | .30 | | | | | |
| Guilt | .21 | | | | | |
| Separation | −.13 | | | | | |
| Factor 2 | | .31 | .82 | −.31 | .48 | 1.84* |
| Diffuse | −.62 | | | | | |
| Guilt | .59 | | | | | |
| Shame | .14 | | | | | |
| Separation | .02 | | | | | |
| Mutilation | .00 | | | | | |

* $p < .05$, one-tailed.

*factors would avoid the problem of multiple t* tests on the same population using the Gottschalk anxiety scales and allow us to test directional hypotheses. A principle components factor analysis was performed with squared multiple correlations in the diagonal in order to focus on common variance. A varimax rotation of the two factors with more than two per cent trace yielded the factors shown in Table 2.

Factor 2 appears to be the hypothesized function factor, having high positive loading of guilt anxiety and a high negative loading of diffuse anxiety. Factor 1 doesn't quite fulfill our expectations of a content factor: mutilation and shame load in the same positive direction but separation only has a very low, albeit expected, negative loading. In fact, separation may be a very small (1.8% trace) third factor. A comparison of factor scores, between our high versus low organization-of-communication behavior groups, only is significant for the anxiety function factor (Factor 2 ).

## DISCUSSION

Our data do indicate that differences in how cognitive organization is revealed by communicative behavior—even differences among a group of marginally adjusted, chronic, male schizophrenics who are not exactly notable

for their cognitive skills (Silverman, 1964)—are linked to certain important differences in anxiety expression. Parenthetically, all of our chronic, male schizophrenics are characterized as extemely field dependent (Engelhardt, Freedman, & Margoles, 1957-1967) so that such a measure of cognitive style would not have discriminated differences either in the communication behavior or affect expression of our subjects.

It is only the incidence of what is termed in the Gottschalk scales diffuse (nonsignal) anxiety, and guilt anxiety, which appears to be connected to the communication behavior of our subjects. The incidence of separation anxiety versus mutilization anxiety and shame anxiety in our subjects, a distinction which is at least justified on clinical, developmental grounds (Erikson, 1963), shows no such connection with the organization of our subjects' communication behavior.

Why do we obtain differences in anxiety expression between diffuse (non-signal) anxiety and guilt anxiety, and not in anxiety expressions of separation, mutilation, and shame? We would like to offer an explanation—admittedly ad hoc which relates what we believe we are tapping with our measures to our particular research population. If we take into account the results of our factor analysis of the Gottschalk scales, we can consider that diffuse and guilt anxiety reflect extremes of a functional dimension of anxiety experience for our subjects irrespective of any particular anxiety content. We can interpret Factor 2 as an anxiety function factor and describe it in information processing terms. Diffuse anxiety is nonsignal anxiety. It defines the lowest level of information processing of an anxiety experience which is traumatic in information processing of terms in that all that is represented is the anxiety experience itself, with no cognition as to what the anxiety is about or where it is. Guilt anxiety can be taken to reflect a final, critical advance in the signal function of anxiety. Now danger has become internalized in a manner that makes it *relatively autonomous* from situational determinants. Inasmuch as the source of anxiety is now firmly represented as something which exists within the individual, and thus anxiety experience now will be determined by the individual's behavior, a much more effective control over anxiety experience is made possible compared to either diffuse trauma or anxiety generated by some situational circumstance. The significance of such an interiorization of anxiety experience—i.e., the acquisition of guilt anxiety—for personality organization was emphasized by Freud (1926) and continues to be emphasized in the clinical literature in terms of the maintenance of self-esteem (Kohut, 1971).

We have stressed throughout that we consider our language behavior and hand movement measures to reflect the status of cognitive organization in communication behavior. As such, it may be considered that our communication measures would possess, for any individual, a closer connection to anxiety function (Factor 2) than anxiety content. Expressions of shame and mutilation

obviously involve anxiety content about self-representation (Factor 1). We expected that anxiety content about such narcissistic injury would be related (through a high, negative loading) to separation anxiety about loss of love from a significant other, but at least for our subjects this did not occur. If we interpret our research measures in this way, together with how we have defined different sorts of information processing for anxiety experience in response to our factor analysis, it is perhaps to be expected that an extreme, marginally adjusted group of subjects will only show extreme differences in the function (information processing) of anxiety experience with no difference in any kind of anxiety content.[5] This kind of reasoning leaves the door open for any future research which might demonstrate further differentiations in the information processing communication behavior, with neurotic and clinically normal subjects who can be presumed to possess more complex personality organizations compared to our subjects.[6]

Finally, we should like to turn our attention to a possible implication of our research for theories of emotion, which exhibit the widest possible diversity. Some theorists maintain that to consider that a phenomenon of emotion itself exists is illusionary, and that the construct ought to be redefined simply as a (high) point on a sleep-tension dimension (Lindsley, 1951) or some continuum of activation (Woodsworth & Schlossberg, 1954). Other theories essentially pivot about whether emotions should be considered to exist as separate entities which independently enter into the organism's ceaseless information processing (Izard, 1971; Tomkins & McCarter, 1964) versus theorists who formulate emotions as some part of the information processing activity itself (Leeper, 1948).

The data and implication of this study, as well as our other research with these language behavior and hand movement measures, is that they do signify important differences in the status of information processing (cognitive organization) during communication behavior. It might prove possible in future research to utilize our hand movement and language behavior measures as independent variables, and then devise experimental manipulations for some hypothesized effect upon the information processing of emotional experience. If such an experimental manipulation can be devised, then the resultant data might contribute to this important question about the nature of the relationship between emotions and cognition.

## FOOTNOTES

This research was supported in part by Grants MH—14383, MH-1983, and MH-5090 awarded by the National Institute of Mental Health, United States Public Health Service. Requests for reprints should be sent to Irving

Steingart, Department of Psychiatry, Downstate Medical Center, Box 88, 450 Clarkson Avenue, Brooklyn, New York 11203.

1. Contiguous instances of conditional language account for less than 3% of our entire language sample, and; if we were to omit this type of conditional language behavior, our results would remain the same.

2. A sixth type of anxiety— death anxiety—has not been utilized for this study inasmuch as the developmental significance of this anxiety is not readily apparent from manifest content.

3. A further examination of the Hollingshead index (Hollingshead & Redlich, 1958) findings for these subjects revealed no significant differences between our high and low groups.

The basis for these ratings was as follows: The higher the percentage of narrative behavior the lower the rank; the higher the percentage of conditional behavior the higher the rank; the higher the time spent in continuous finger-to-hand movement the lower the rank; the higher the time spent in continuous body touching the higher the rank; the higher the time spent in discrete body touching the higher the rank.

Other analyses of this data make it clear that the *joined* consideration of these five hand movement and language behavior measures provides information about anxiety expression which is not reflected in the individual correlations between these same five measures and our subjects' anxiety scores. None of these five selected hand movement and language behavior measures is significantly correlated with total word output. Also, it may be claimed that there is some intrinsic relation between guilt expression and language construction such that guilt anxiety requires a conditional form. Gottschalk (Gleser & Gottschalk, 1961) gives the following examples of guilt anxiety: "I felt terrible about the lies;" "His family thought I was unfit;" "I had guilty feelings about having relations with a married man." These three examples of guilt anxiety would, respectively, be coded as instances of simple narrative, complex portrayal, and complex conditional language behavior.

4. No such factor analytic examination of these scales exists according to our examination of the literature and personal correspondence with Prof. Gottschalk.

5. This includes another comparison conducted between our high versus low group for separation anxiety.

6. We have comparative data (Steingart, Freedman, et al., 1975) which indicates that normals produce about three times as much of the kind of (conditional) language behavior associated with guilt interiorization in *half* of the dialogue time used by our chronic schizophrenics. However, uncontrolled variables of age, sex, education, etc., enter into this comparison.

## REFERENCES


Blass, T., Freeman, N., & Steingart, I. Body movement and verbal encoding in the congenitally blind. *Perceptual and Motor Skills,* 1974, 39, 279-293.

Engelhardt, D. (Principal investigator), Freedman, N., & Margolis, R. (Co-principal investigator). A study of ataractics in schizophrenic outpatients. U.S.P.H.S. Grant no. 01983, 1957-1967.

Erikson, E.H. *Childhood and society* (2nd ed.). New York: Norton, 1963.

Fillenbaum, S. Psycholinguistics. *Annual Review of Psychology,* 1971, 22, 251-308.

Freedman, N. The analysis of movement behavior during the clinical interview. In A. Siegman & B. Pope (Eds.), *Dyadic communications in interviews.* New York: Pergamon Press, 1972.

Freedman, N., O'Hanlon, J., Oltman, P., & Witkin, H.A. The imprint of psychological differentiation on kinetic behavior in varying communicative contexts. *Journal of Abnormal Psychology,* 1972, *79,* 239-258.

Freedman, N., Blass, T., Rifkin, A., & Quitkin, F. Body movements and the verbal encoding of aggressive affect. *Journal of Personality and Social Psychology,* 1973, 26, 72-85.

Freud, S. (1926). Inhibitions, symptoms, and anxiety. (J. Strachey, ed. and trans.). London: Hogarth Press, 1961.

Gleser, G., Gottschalk, L.A., & Springer, R. J. An anxiety scale applicable to verbal samples. *Archives of General Psychiatry,* 1961, *5,* 593-604.

Gottschalk, L., Winget, C., & Gleser, C. *Manual of instructions for using the Gottschalk-Gleser Content Analysis Scales: Anxiety, hostility, social alienation-personal disorganization.* Berkeley: University of California Press, 1969.

Grand, S., Freedman, N., & Steingart, I. A study of the representation of objects in schizophrenia. *Journal of the American psychoanalytic Association,* 1973, *21* 399-434.

Hunt, K.W. Syntactic maturity in school children and adults. Monographs of the Society for Research in Child Development, 1970, *35,* (1,Serial No.134).

Izard, C.E. *The face of emotion.* New York: Appleton-Century Crofts, 1971, 468-480.

Kohut, H. The analysis of the self. A systematic approach to the psychoanalytic treatment of narcissistic personality disorders. *The monograph Series of the Psychoanalytic Study of the Child,* 1971 (No. 4).

Leeper, R.W. A motivational theory of emotion to replace "emotion as disorganized response." *Psychological Review,* 1948, *55,* 5-21.

Lindenfeld, J. In search of psychological factors of linguistic variation. *Semiotica,* 1972,*5*: 350-361.

Lindenfeld, J. Affective states and the syntactic structure of speech. *Semiotica,* 1973, *8*: 368-375.

Lindenfeld, J. Syntactic structure and kinesic phenomena in communicative events. *Semiotica,* 1974, 12, 61-73.

Lindsley, D.M. Emotion. In S.S. Stevens (Ed.), *Handbook of experimental psychology.* New York: John Wiley, 1951.

Lyons, S. *Introduction to theoretical linguistics.* London: Cambridge University Press, 1968.

Pavey, D. Verbal behavior in schizophrenia: A review of recent studies. *Psychological Bulletin,* 1968, 70, 164-178.

Piaget, J. *The language and thought of the child.* (1923). (M. Labain, trans) New York: Meridian Books, 1955.

Silverman, J. The problem of attention in research and theory in schizophrenia. *Psychological Review,* 1964, 71, 352-379.

Steingart, I., & Freedman, N. A language construction approach for the examination of self-object representaton in varying clinical states. R.R. Holt and E. Peterfreund, Vol I, 1972, 132-178.

Steingart, I & Freedman, N. The organization of body-focused kinetic behavior and language construction in schizophrenic and depressed states. Donald D. P. Spense (ed.) *Psychoanalysis and Contemporary Science,* (Ed.) Donald P., Spence, Vol. IV, New York: Macmillan Co., 1975.

Steingart, I., Freedman, N., Grand, S., & Buchwald, C. Personality organization and language behavior: The imprint of psychological differentiation on language behavior in varying communication conditions. *Journal ofPsycholinguistic Research,* 1975, *4,* 241-255.

Tomkins, S.S. & McCarter, R. What and where are th primary affects? Some evidence for a theory. *Perceptual and Motor Skills,* 1964, 18, 119-158.

Weiner, M., Devoe, S., & Geller, J. Nonverbal behavior and nonverbal communication. *Psychological Review,* 1972, 185-214.

Woodworth, R.S. & Schlossberg, H.S. *Experimental Psychology.* New York; Holt, Rinehart & Winston, 1954.

Steingart, I., & Freedman, N. A language construction approach for the examination of self/object representation in varying clinical states. [illegible]

Steingart, I., & Freedman, N. The organization of body-focused kinesic behavior and language construction in [illegible] states. In D. P. Spence (Ed.), [illegible] (Vol. 4). New York: [illegible]

Steingart, I., Freedman, N., Grand, S., & Buchwald, C. Personality organization and language behavior: The imprint of psychological differentiation on language behavior in varying communication conditions. Journal of Psycholinguistic Research, 1975, 4, 241-255.

Tomkins, S. S., & McCarter, R. What and where are the primary affects? Some evidence for a theory. Perceptual and Motor Skills, 1964, 18, 119-158.

Wiener, M., Devoe, S., [illegible] Nonverbal behavior and nonverbal communication. Psychological Review, 1972, 79, [illegible]

Woodworth, R. S., & Schlosberg, H. Experimental psychology. New York: Holt, Rinehart & Winston, 1954.

# BODY MOVEMENTS AND THE VERBAL ENCODING OF AGRESSIVE AFFECT[1]

NORBERT FREEDMAN,[2] THOMAS BLASS,[3] ARTHUR RIFKIN, and FREDERIC QUITKIN

The relationship between kinetic behavior, defined by a scoring system of object- and body-focused hand movements, and direction of verbal aggression was examined. Motor behavior and concomitant verbal samples were scored from videotaped interview segments of 24 college students. Intercorrelational analysis revealed that object-focused movements were related to overt hostility ($r = .49$) and that this relationship varied with subcategories of such movements: for speech primacy, $r = .49$; for representational, $r = .36$; and for nonrepresentational motor primacy movements, $r = .09$. Body-focused movements were related to covert hostility ($r = .53$) and specifically to hand-to-hand motions ($r = .52$). Analysis of peak-trough periods within interviews revealed significant covariations between movements and forms of hostility. Qualitative clause-by-clause analysis elucidated the nature of the movement-hostility contiguity. Results were interpreted in terms of the differential role of object-and-body-focused movements in the encoding of affect.

Herman Melville, in his morality novel of Billy Budd, has fashioned a hero whose tragic flaw was his dearth of words and violence of action. In a climactic episode of the story, Billy, confronted by both captain and tormenter, seething with unverbalized rage, cannot utter a sound; yet with one stroke of his hand, fells his adversary. As he faced his accuser, Billy

found himself in a convulsed tongue-tie, straining forward in an agony of ineffectual eagerness to obey the injunction to speak . . . and then, in the next instant, quick as a flame from a discharged cannon at night, his right arm shot out and Claggart dropped to the deck [p. 62].

Only rarely do the motions of the body have such dramatic consequences and only rarely are they so disconnected from any verbal utterance. Most body movements during discourse, as we hope to show, are intimately interwoven with the spoken word, and when they are, they may ease the inclusion of the hostile thought into the verbal flow—and perhaps prevent the violence of a Billy Budd.

Movements of the body, of hands, head, or legs, that emerge in the course of a communicative situation are data that have been of central interest to the clinical researcher. The brunt of this interest stems from the assumption that kinetic behavior constitutes a language of interpersonal relations. Such behavior has been regarded as communication that in analogic form defines the implicit relationship of two participants in a given social context (Watzlawick, Beavin, & Jackson, 1967). However, body movements in interviews are linked not only to social context but also to speech and, hence, are a reflection of more central representational functions; they are the body's participation in the symbolizing process. Another source of interest in the study of body movements, then, derives from the view that kinetic behavior points not only to social transactions, but to the transformation of thought into words. Dittmann and Llewellyn (1969), for example, have linked the occurrence of body movements to the phonemic rhythm of speech and have suggested their role in syntactic planning. Mahl (1968) has described anticipatory body movements in which motor behavior anticipates the unverbalized. In our research, we proceed from the assumption that the organization of body movements varies in its relationship to the verbal utterances and that such variation may be an objective indicator of the ease of transforming thoughts into words—of the relative difficulty in verbal encoding. When movements are phased in with rhythm and content of speech, they may serve to facilitate verbal encoding; yet, when there is a lack of congruence, they may actually interfere with the process of verbal representation.

A coding system that defines units of motor expression having different relationships to speech has been developed from videotape recorded interviews (Freedman, 1971; Freedman & Hoffman, 1967). Central to this method of analysis is the distinction between a class of object-focused and a class of body-focused hand movements. Object-focused movements are discrete acts, generally pointing away from the body, and are closely phased in with rhythm and content of speech: They may punctuate, qualify, illustrate, or concretize what is being said. In contrast, in body-focused activity, we can observe not only self-

ministration but a form of movement activity which is continuous in nature and apparently split off from speech. In our work, we have elaborated various subcategories of object and body-focused movements, and these categories further delineate the functional difference between units of motor expression. Thus, within object-focused movements, there are speech-primacy gestures—the movements that punctuate and qualify what is said but do not represent the content of thought itself. Within body-focused movements, there are hand-to-hand motions, a continuous rubbing and stroking of the hands onto each other repetitively without any effort to depict what is being said. Here, then, are different forms of kinetic expression describing different levels of integration of motor-speech linkage and pointing, presumably, to varying difficulties in encoding and representing.

In ongoing and completed studies, we have been able to link object- and body-focused movements to independent measures of linguistic and cognitive functioning. The occurrence of object-focused movements was found to be embedded in syntactically more complex language structure, whereas the appearance of body-focused movements, specifically hand-to-hand motions, seem to occur with less complex language structure and with a verbal product that is punctuated by silences. The prevalence of these classes of hand movements could also be associated with relatively stable indicators of cognitive style: Body-focused, specifically hand-to-hand motions were more frequent among cognitively less differentiated (field dependent) individuals whereas a trend suggesting a relative saliency of speech-primacy, object-focused gestures was noted among more differentiated (field independent) individuals (Freedman, O'Hanlon, Oltman, & Witkin, 1972). These observations indicate that movements during an interview, defined in terms of speech-relatedness, may point to a relative difficulty in articulating and encoding experiences and, moreover, that such motor behavior may be a visible indicator of a higher or lower level of psychological differentiation.

In the present study, we shall extend our observatons of object- and body-focused movements. We shall shift from observations concerning the encoding of relatively formal thought to the encoding of meaningful chunks of affective experiences, specifically aggression. The motor system has a particular relevance to the expression of aggressive promptings. Darwin (1929) has held that motor behavior has a survival function and becomes enlisted as a vehicle in the event of attack. Freud (1925) viewed the motor channel as a major pathway in the expression of aggression, and he described clinical phenomena such as resistiveness and negation which revealed themselves motorically. Such thoughts would suggest that motor manifestations in interviews may constitute derivatives of aggressive drive. However, in attempting to link speech-related movements to the expression of aggression, we are not concerned with the presence of aggressive affect per se. Indeed, feelings of rage and anger may be most conspicuously displayed by other forms of nonverbal expression, such as

the expression of the face (Ekman, Sorenson, & Friesen, 1969). Rather, kinetic manifestations linked to speech are more likely to be indicative of an ability to encode the hostile promptings into the verbal content. In this study, then, we wish to link the prevalence of speech-related movements with forms of articulated aggression.

Speech-related movements are visible indicators of psychological structure on the kinetic level; the articulation of aggression may be an indicator of psychological structure in the verbal level. In studying the possible link between speech-related movements and forms of articulated aggression, it is important to distinguish between overt and direct aggression and covert and denied forms of aggression. When the aggressive intent, vis-a-vis the object, is incorporated into the self (e.g., "I hate him"), we are likely to observe a more differentiated psychological structure. Several empirical studies have demonstrated a relationship between overt verbal aggression and psychological differentiation (Silverman, 1966; Witkin, Lewis, & Weil, 1968). There is, however, a more intrinsic rationale for an expected association between the overt expression of hostile feelings during an interview and more differentiated kinetic organization. Differentiation refers to the articulation of functional boundaries in various channels of expression. Thus, in the verbal representation of overt aggression, there are clear boundaries between the self and the object of hostility. In linguistic terms, the self is in the subject position and the hated object in the predicate position. On the kinetic level, when motor acts are linked to the rhythmic quality of speech, the speaker established boundaries and coherent chunks of thought out of the continuous flow of the verbal utterance. He may do so, of course, not only with the motions of his hands but also with motions of his head or legs. Conversely, when the representation of aggressive feelings in verbal content is indirect, when the source of attack is not clearly perceived, there are no clear boundaries between self and nonself. In turn, in the kinetic behavior, motor expression tends to transcend the boundaries of rhythmic chunks and is continuous in nature.

We are now in a position to spell out the objective of the study in operational terms. It is expected that individuals characterized by a high level of object-focused, and specifically speech-primacy, movements will reveal a high level of overt hostility in the verbal content of the interview; conversely, individuals with a prevalence of body-focused, and specifically hand-to-hand, activity are expected to reveal their feelings in verbal forms which avoid overt expression of hostility. The empirical examination of these hypotheses is made possible by the method of content analysis developed by Gottschalk, Winget, and Gleser (1969). The system provides for the scoring of hostility and other forms of affect. Hostility is analyzed in terms of overtness of verbal aggression resulting in the following four scoring categories: overt, covert, ambivalent hositility, and hostility in. It thus becomes possible to obtain a quantitive index

of different modes of aggression from verbal data which are temporally contiguous to the appearance of the movement behavior; the former derived from the audio track, the latter from the video track of the recorded interview.

The expected link between indexes of psychological structure observed on the kinetic level with forms of articulation of hostility is not limited to variations among individuals. We are interested in the study of psychological structure not only as an aspect of individual style but as a reflection of the variations in structure in different states. One of the heuristic advantages in defining the structure from interview data both in kinetic terms and in terms of the verbal articulation is that we may be able to observe the ebb and flow of psychological organization as it occurs in different states. Such fluctuations can then be traced in different phases of treatment or in the course of a single interview following different forms of intervention. It is a further objective of this study to trace the covariation of structure on the kinetic and affective level as it occurs in the course of a single interchange.

## METHOD

The method involves the independent evaluation of concomitantly obtained samples of kinetic and verbal behavor derived from a structured interview situation. The data are part of a larger study on the relationship between body movements in interviews and cognitive style. For a detailed presentation of the procedure for this study, see Freedman et al. (1972).

The subjects were 24 female college students, predominantly of Jewish descent and native Americans: 12 had previously been identified as field dependent and 12 as field independent. Each subject was asked to participate in an experiment on "speech patterns." The subjects were interviewed by a research psychiatrist who assumed a warm and receptive role and spent about 20 minutes establishing rapport and discussing relatively neutral issues pertaining to the subject's social and college activities. After this warm-up period, the interviewer introduced a 5-minute "association task" in which he asked the subject, using instructions modified from Gottschalk et al. (1969), to talk about "something personally meaningful and significant" without interruption. The speech and kinetic behavior data derived from this association task formed the basis of this study.

As part of the larger study, there were various sources of data that were not included in this report. The subjects were also exposed to a second interviewer who behaved in a cold and detached manner. For 16 subjects, this cold condition preceded the warm encounter, and for 8 subjects, the cold followed the warm condition. There are several reasons for excluding the data from the cold interview condition from the present report. Not only is the warm condition a more neutral one for the study of movement-affect relationships but

the cold condition also tended to suppress object-focused movements and thus was not suitable for the correlational analysis with affect expression. We shall, however, evaluate the impact of a preceding cold encounter on the relationship between movement and aggression in the subsequent warm encounter. Also the role of cognitive style (field dependence) was not examined since the primary goal of this article was the exploration of the movement-affect relationship.

Videotaped interviews were scored for the occurrence of different types of object- and body-focused movements, and transcripts from audio tapes were scored for the expression of aggression.

*Assessment of Kinetic Behavior*

As previously stated, all hand movements are identified as either object or body focused. Each of these major divisions of movement activity is further analyzed in terms of various subcategories.

*Analysis of object*—focused movements. Object-focused movements, by definition, are those hand movements that are intimately linked to the rhythmic and/or content aspects of speech. The movements have a characteristic directionality in that they tend to occur at distance from the body surface and usually do not involve body touching. The attribute of speech relatedness allows for a further definition of the nature of this movement-speech linkage ranging from instances where movements appear subordinate to the verbal statement to instances where movements appear to be the primary carrier of the message. It is possible to make a functional distinction of object-focused movements on the basis of their tendency to organize, supplement, or substitute for the verbal statement. These functions may be operationally defined by three object-focused movements: speech primacy, representational motor primacy, and nonrepresentational motor primacy.

The defining characteristic of the class of speech-primacy movements is their subservience to the spoken word. These hand movements closely parallel the formal and rhythmic properties of speech. One kind of speech-primacy movement is the punctuating movement. In this movement, the hand traverses a path that is essentially straight and devoid of any molding qualities, and the movements in beatlike fashion emphasize what is being said. Another kind of speech-primacy movement is that which we have labeled the minor qualifier. This category includes repetitive gestures that appear to qualify what is being said but that contain no representational or content properties. Descriptively, these movements tend to be small, involving often simply a turning of the wrists. They are well delineated, but not staccatolike movements.

Motor-primacy movements may also be closely phased in with the rhythmic properties of speech. Yet, their defining characteristic is that the expression of some content message has been relegated to the motor realm.

Some partially articulated image, feeling state, or thought is externalized by the movement of the hands. The judgment of relative motor primacy is always made by reference to the spoken word. We have distinguished various kinds of motor-primacy movements. The two major subdivisions are representational and nonrepresentational motor-primacy movements.

In the case of representatonal motor-primacy movements, an image having clearly definable space and time referents, a feeling state, or an abstract idea is given motor expression. Representational movements are frequently literal outlines of a picture image, sometimes a condensation of it, and vary in the goodness of fit between what is described and what is depicted by gesture. In these representational acts, gestures provide considerably more information than is carried by speech alone, and in this sense, are regarded as a kind of motor-primacy activity.

Nonrepresentational motor-primacy movements lack a verbally described referent and thus appear to have a substitutive function, vis-a vis the verbal message. Two instances of nonrepresentational gestures are pointing and speech failure. In the case of pointing, gestures are not used to represent but to point at a person or thing in the immediate environment (the room) or outside (the building across the street). Speech failures are either groping movements in which the individual struggles with word finding or incongruities between word and gesture.

While all object-focused movements bear a relation to speech, the identification of the foregoing three categories reflect important differences in the function of the movement vis-a-vis what is being uttered. Indeed, the three categories of speech primacy, representational motor primacy, and nonrepresentational motor-primacy appear to describe ordinal steps ranging not only from speech to motor primacy but perhaps also from greater to lesser integration of kinetic behavior with the verbal flow.

*Analysis of body*—focused movements. The defining characteristic of body-focused movements is that the hands are involved in some form of stimulation of the body or its adornments. By definition, body-focused activity bears no manifest relationship to rhythm or content of speech and, with one exception, is continuous in nature. Body-focused movements are further analyzed in terms of their organization.

Three categories of body-focused activity are distinguished: continuous hand-to-hand movements, continuous body touching, and discrete body touching.

*Continuous hand-to-hand movements.* These movements involve the continuous stimulation of the hands or fingers by each other, one on the other or one on itself. Descriptively, the quality of hand-to-hand movements is repetitive and stereotyped, involving rubbing or stroking of fingers; these motions often give the appearance of fidgetiness. In contrast to body touching, what is absent

in these motions is the functional division by which one hand acts as agent upon the body surface.

*Continuous body touching*. These are continuous and repetitive motions that entail the touching of some specific body part or its adornment by the hand. The important conceptual distinction in continuous body touching is that a particular locus of the body, lips, neck, arms, legs, is selected for soothing or stroking. In body touching, there appears to be the functional division in which the hand acts as agent upon the body as object. To the extent that body touching involves a "thing" object, such as manipulation of pen, ring, or necklace, we appear to be dealing with a more symbolic form of self-stimulation in which the focus is displaced from the body surface onto another object. Previously (Freedman, 1971), we had distinguished between direct (involving skin surface stimulation) and indirect body touching (involving touching of clothing and accessories). These movements, however, were found to be functionally equivalent and thus are grouped into a single category.

As noted, the majority of body-focused movements appear as continuous activity. Hence, the two categories of body-focused activities are expressed in time scores. As the best overall index, we are computing a total continuous body-focused movement score consisting of the two constituents.

*Discrete body touching*. While the majority of body-focused movements are continuous in nature, there are body-focused movements that are discrete and noncontinuous, for example, pulling a skirt, touching the eye, or stroking the chin. These movements tend to be brief, lasting 3 seconds or less, and tend to have a terminal structure (relieving an itch, adjusting a garment). Discrete body touching similar to continuous body touching in that a specific body area is selected for self-stimulation. However, the movements are more circumscribed both by their time-limited nature and their terminal structure.

*Scores used in the analysis of the data*. Object-focused movements, in view of their assumed relation to speech,are computed in terms of rates that take into account the subject's total word output. An object-focused movement rate is defined by the formula frequency object-focused movement X 100/total words. Such rates are determined separately for total object-focused movements and its three subcategories. Total continuous body-focused movements, as well as continuous hand-to-hand and body touching are expressed in time scores and refer to number of seconds spent in a particular type of activity per 5-minute period. For discrete body touching, movements are counted as single acts, and incidence of such acts is determined for the 5-minute sample.

Reliability of scores between two observers as well as test-retest evaluations have been reported elsewhere (Freedman et al., 1972).

### *Assessment of Hostility from Verbal Content*

The verbal responses of the subjects were transcribed and scored for the presence of different types of hostility expression using Gottschalk's content

analysis scales (Gottschalk et al., 1969). This content-analytic method is a technique for determining the presence of different kinds of affect in a verbal sample.

The presence of hostility is evaluated by means of four scales tapping the following types of hostility: overt hostility out—statements scored under this category are those that refer to aggressive or hostile feelings as having emanated from the speaker (e.g., "I felt an aversion to him from the very first"); covert hostility out—statements scored under this category are those in which aggression or hostility is attributed to others as either active agents of aggression or passive recipients of aggression or in which there is a denial of hostile feelings (e.g., "The police handcuffed her boyfriend before carrying him into emergency"); hostility in—these are statements dealing with thoughts, actions, and feelings that are self-critical, self-destructive, or self-punishing (e.g., "I cut both my wrists two years ago"); ambivalent hostility—verbal statements scored in this scale are all themes about destructive, injurious, critical thoughts and actions of others toward the self (e.g., "None of her family liked my drinking").

A weighted scoring procedure is used, allowing for measurement of intensity of affect. The subject's verbal output is unitized into grammatical clause units, and each unit is scored for the presence of one or more of the affect categories. Affect scores are expressed as rates per 100 words and are corrected for skewness by means of a square root transformation. (For further details of the scoring procedure, see Gottschalk et al., 1969).

## RESULTS

In determining the association between speech-related movements and articulation of aggression, three phases in the analysis of the data can be delineated: (*a*) the covariation of kinetic behavior scores with hostility scores among individuals (correlational analysis), (*b*) the covariation of kinetic behavior and hostility scores within interviews, and (*c*) a qualitative examination concerning the nature of the aggression-movement relationship.

### *Covariations of Kinetic Behavior with Hostility Scores among Individuals*

Based on the sample of 24 subjects, correlations between object-focused movements and hostility scores are presented in Table 1, and correlations between body-focused movements and hostility scores are shown in Table 2. It had been expected that object-focused movements would be associated with the overt expression of aggression, and body-focused movements with a tendency to express nonovert forms of aggression—covert hostility, hostility in, or ambivalent hostility. In considering the obtained relationships for total object-focused movements (Table 1), it can be noted that subjects high in this type of activity did, as expected, express their aggression overtly ($r = 48$, $p < .01$). In further considering the obtained findings for total continuous body-focused movements

TABLE 1
CORRELATIONS BETWEEN CATEGORIES OF OBJECT-FOCUSED ACTIVITY AND CATEGORIES OF VERBAL HOSTILITY

| Class of object-focused movement | Categories of verbal hostility | | | |
|---|---|---|---|---|
| | Overt | Covert | Hostility in | Ambivalent |
| Total object focused | .48** | −.35* | .11 | .38* |
| Speech primacy | .49** | −.35* | .14 | .29 |
| Motor primacy | .45* | −.16 | −.03 | .39* |
| Representational | .36* | −.37* | .05 | .27 |
| Nonrepresentational | .09 | −.07 | −.05 | .41* |

*Note.* $N = 24$.
* $p < .05$.
** $p < .01$.

(Table 2), it was noted that subjects high in such self-manipulatory activity did not express aggression overtly (there were no significant correlations), yet they did express hostility (see Table 1 and Table 2) covertly ($r = .53$, $p < .01$). While these findings would seem to confirm the hypothesis, a somewhat different picture emerges when the subcategories of both object- and body-focused movements are examined.

The correlations involving the subcategories of object-focused movements shown in Table 1 suggest ordinal steps in the association between movement behavior and expression of hostility. The strongest link was observed between speech-primacy object-focused movements and overt hostility ($r = .49$, $p < .01$); next there was a significant correlation between representational motor-primacy gestures ($r = .36$, $p < .05$); and, finally, when nonrepresentational motor-primacy gestures (pointing or groping movements) were considered, there was no longer any significant correlation with overt hotility scores. Indeed, this last class of object-focused movement is positively linked to ambivalent hostility ($r = .41$, $p < .05$), a correlation that accounts for the apparently contradictory association between total object-focused movements and ambivalent hotility. There were also sets of negative correlations consistent with the above trends: Namely, individuals high in total object-focused, speech-primacy, or representational gestures are *not* likely to reveal covert hostility ($r = -.35, -.35$, and $-37$, respectively, all $ps < .05$). Clearly, then, not all object-focused movements are linked to the encoding of hostile affect. Yet, specifically, those object focused gestures that organize what is said appear to be part of a communicative context in which aggressive feelings can be verbalized more readily.

A similar qualification to the overall findings(see Table 3) can be noted when various aspects of body-focused activity are considered. Whereas we had

TABLE 2

CORRELATIONS BETWEEN CATEGORIES OF BODY-FOCUSED ACTIVITY AND CATEGORIES OF VERBAL HOSTILITY

| Class of body-focused movement | Categories of verbal hostility | | | |
|---|---|---|---|---|
| | Overt | Covert | Hostility in | Ambivalent |
| Total continuous body-focused | −.10 | .53* | −.03 | −.26 |
| Continuous hand to hand | .01 | .52* | .01 | .02 |
| Continuous body touching | −.20 | .04 | −.04 | −.22 |
| Discrete body touching | .02 | −.17 | −.20 | −.04 |

*Note.* $N = 24$.
* $p < .01$.

TABLE 3

SUMMARY OF ANALYSIS OF VARIANCE OF OVERT HOSTILITY AS A FUNCTION OF SPEECH-PRIMACY MOVEMENTS AND PREINTERVIEW STRESS

| Source | *df* | *MS* | *F* |
|---|---|---|---|
| Speech primacy (A) | 1 | .13 | 6.50* |
| Interview condition (B) (stress versus no stress) | 1 | .02 | 1.00 |
| A × B | 1 | 0 | 0 |
| Error | 20 | .02 | |

* $p < 025$.

observed earlier that total body-focused movements are significantly associated with covert hotility, this finding can be accounted for exclusively by one subcategory—hand-to-hand movements. Subjects high in hand-to-hand activity were likely to express their anger covertly ($r = .52$, $p < .01$). Neither continuous nor discrete body touching was linked to any form of verbal aggression. It must be added that the correlation between hand-to-hand movements and covert hostility may be somewhat of an overestimate since hand-to-hand movement scores revealed a very skewed distribution: 10 of the 24 subjects had extremely high scores. (A pointbiserial correlation dichotomizing hand-to-hand movements into high and low scores was .49, $p < .01$). It is, thus, not body-focused activity per se but only the more repetitive and inarticulate quality of self-ministration that forms part of a communicative context in which the direct expression of aggressive affect is difficult to attain.

The question was raised whether the foregoing associations between motor behavior and affect expression may have been prompted by factors in the communicative setting. It will be recalled that certain subjects were exposed to a cold and rejecting listener prior to the interview segment under scrutiny. Did such an antecedent experience stir aggressive affect and thus evoke redundant responses on both the motor and verbal level? Or, does the motor-affect linkage hold even when such preinterview stress is absent? We checked this issue by evaluating subjects with and without preinterview stress. The two kinetic variables yielding the highest correlation with hostility scores, namely, speech-primacy and hand-to-hand movements, were so studied.

In Table 3, we present a summary of the analysis of variance of overt hostility scores for subjects high and low in speech-primacy movements, with and without preinterview stress. There was a significant speech-primacy movement effect ($F = 6.50$, $p < .025$) but no significant interview condition or interaction effects. A corresponding analysis of variance was carried out for covert hostility scores among subjects high and low in hand-to-hand motions and differing in preinterview stress. The results of this analysis, summarized in Table 4, revealed again that there was a significant kinetic behavior effect ($F = 6.12$, $p < .025$) yet no significant interview condition or interaction effects. It may then be concluded that an individual's propensity to use speech-primacy gestures as part of the communicative repertoire is likely to be linked to the emergence of overt hostility. Conversely, the propensity to use hand-to-hand motions is linked to the expression of covert hostility. Furthermore, such relationships can be obtained regardless of antecedent stress experiences. This conclusion does not negate the possibility that the nature of the communicative task, the request to associate and to talk about something significant and personally relevant for 5 minutes, may itself have been an important factor in prompting hostile affect.

*Covariation of Kinetic Behavior and Hostility Scores within Interviews*

The correlations between kinetic behavior and hostility scores presented thus far do not (see Table 4) demonstrate convincingly any intrinsic connnection between movement and affect. Indeed, it is possible for individuals high in speech-primacy or hand-to-hand motions to differ on attributes other than movement behavior, attributes that may account for differences in the verbal expression of aggression.[4] It was felt that even stronger evidence could be provided if the co-occurrence of kinetic behavior and hostility could be demonstrated temporally within the same individual. To what extent does the expression of hostility occur during periods of peak movement activity or to what extent does it occur during trough periods? An answer to these questions requires the concomitant tracing of the saliency of movement scores and affect

TABLE 4

SUMMARY OF ANALYSIS OF VARIANCE OF COVERT HOSTILITY AS A FUNCTION OF HAND TO HAND MOVEMENTS AND PREINTERVIEW STRESS

| Source | *df* | *MS* | *F* |
|---|---|---|---|
| Hand to hand (A) | 1 | .49 | 6.12* |
| Interview condition (B) (stress versus no stress) | 1 | .22 | 2.75 |
| A × B | 1 | .02 | .25 |
| Error | 20 | .08 | |

* $p < .025$.

scores over the course of the 5-minute interview span. Such an analysis is made possible by the fáct that both movement and hostility scores occur in bursts and are thus amenable to the analysis of peaks and troughs.

Toward this end, subjects high in speech-primacy and hand-to-hand movements were selected to trace the occurrence of overt and covert hostility, respectively. Six subjects with high-speech-primacy-movement scores and adequate prevalence of overt hostility scores were chosen for this analysis. Only three subjects with high-hand-to-hand-movement scores could be selected. There were several subjects who had continuous hand-to-hand motions throughout the 5-minute association task without let up, and for these, an analysis of peak and trough periods was not possible. The 5-minute interview sample was divided into twenty 15-second segments. Using the 15-second segment as the basic unit, a frequency distribution of speech-primacy-movement scores per unit was obtained for each subject. A median split was then employed dichotomizing the distribution for each subject and defining any given segment as representing either a peak or trough of movement activity. Finally, using the verbal transcript, the number of hositility clauses occurring during peak and trough units was determined. Weighted mean hostility scores per segment (using Gottschalk's scoring criteria) could then be computed. These segment scores

[4] Indeed, there was considerable overlap between the subject's speech-primacy movement score and her level of sychological differentiation as measured by tests of field dependence: 8 of the 10 "high" hand-to-hand movement subjects were identified as field dependent. An individual's propensity to reveal speech-primacy movements may point to her cognitive style and, more generally, to a communicative style. In view of the small number of deviant cases in the present sample, we are not in a position to evaluate the possible interaction between movement score and cognitive style on the articulation of aggression.

TABLE 5

MEAN WEIGHTED OVERT HOSTILITY SCORES FOR PEAK AND TROUGH SPEECH-PRIMACY PERIODS

| Subject number | Peak speech-primacy period | Trough speech-primacy period |
|---|---|---|
| 1 | .90 | .27 |
| 2 | .91 | .33 |
| 3 | .75 | .88 |
| 4 | .90 | .44 |
| 5 | .66 | .38 |
| 6 | .58 | .37 |
| *M* | .78 | .44 $t = 2.92$* |

* $p < .025$, one-tailed; $df = 5$.

could then be used to arrive at a mean segment score for each individual's peak and trough period.

The mean overt hostility scores for each of the six high-speech-primacy subjects during peak and trough periods are listed in Table 5. It can be noted that overt hostility scores were higher for five of the six subjects during peak periods than during trough periods. For all six subjects combined, the mean for peak periods was .78, for trough periods, .44 ($t = 2.92$, $p < .025$, one-tailed). Similar peak and trough examination of covert hostility scores for the three subjects high in hand-to-hand movements is presented in Table 6. In spite of the small number of cases, (see Table 6) observations were consistent with expectations. All three subjects revealed higher covert hostility scores during peak than during trough periods. For the three subjects combined, during peak hand-to-hand movement periods, the mean was 2.40; during trough periods, / 3.25, it was 1.36 ($t =$, $p < .05$, one-tailed test).

## *Qualitative Examination of the Movement Affect Relationship*

There appears to be convincing evidence that speech-primacy gestures are part of a context in which overtly hostile thoughts are readily encoded and that hand-to-hand motions are part of a context in which covertly hostile thoughts predominate. Yet, common sense observations tell us that such movements are part and parcel of everyday usage and occur in speech not even remotely touching upon aggressive themes. Moreover, aggression, as we have just seen in the peak-trough analysis, may occur without punctuating or qualifying gestures in evidence. How can we explicate the role of motor activity in the verbal encoding of aggressive thought?

TABLE 6

MEAN WEIGHTED COVERT HOSTILITY SCORES FOR PEAK AND TROUGH HAND-TO-HAND PERIODS

| Subject number | Peak hand-to-hand period | Trough hand-to-hand period |
|---|---|---|
| 1 | 1.80 | .50 |
| 2 | 2.40 | 2.00 |
| 3 | 3.00 | 1.60 |
| *M* | 2.40 | 1.36 $t = 3.25$* |

* $p < .05$, one-tailed; $df = 2$.

Our line of explication entails the localization of speech-primacy movements in clauses adjacent to the hostile utterances. We thus scrutinize the field surrounding the clause, ascertaining whether a movement precedes, coincides with, or follows the aggressive theme. (Such an analysis, of course, could not be carried out for hand-to-hand movements inasmuch as these represent time scores and the pinpointing of movement and clauses is not possible.)

From such observations, no quantitative statement can be made concerning movement locus in relation to the hostility-carrying clause. Movements were observed antecedent to, concomitant with, or subsequent to the clause. However, a surprising qualitative finding emerged: namely, that in many instances when the expression of aggressive themes was direct, unequivocal, and blatant, speech-primacy movements, particularly minor qualifiers, dropped out. Such a dropout of gestures during clauses occurred in two patterns: those in which gestures preceded and those in which they followed hostility-carrying clauses.

An example of the first situation, that is, of an instance in which the movement precedes the affect discharge phrase, can be noted in the following sequence of three overt hostility clauses taken from Subject R. The subject was talking about her experiences in sensitivity training:

/I didn't think [minor qualifier] I'd like it/
/because [minor qualifier] I never believed in it/
/I thought it was phony/

Note how a gradual build-up to the third and most intensely hostile clause occurs

with no visible hand movements coninciding with that clause. It is as if the speech-primacy movement paved the way, enabling the subject to express her feelings ("It was phony."). When she verbalizes these feelings, the movement drops out.

An example of the second type of movement-hostility,contiguity, that is, of speech-primacy movements following an unequivocal expression of hostility, is provided by a subject talking about a member of her group:

/I personally don't care for him/
/because he's nasty to everybody/
/and I don't think that's the way [minor qualifier]
to get [minor qualifier] people to like you/

Here, the first clause ("I personally don't care for him"), showing a clearly hostile feeling, is unaccompanied by gesture. The movement occurs later in what seems to be an attempt to soften the harshness of the initially hostile statement.

These observations, although informal, point up the fact that while movement and hostility themes are correlated, they are not redundant sources of information. Rather, gestures appear to be instrumental in paving the way for the encoding of the hostile promptings. Kinetic expressions may then help the person to build up to a pitch so that the stirred affect can be articulated, *or* the movement may be employed to mollify and soften the impact of hostile strivings if these are felt to be too intense.

In summary, object- and body-focused hand movements during an association task were linked to forms of verbal aggression among individuals,within individuals between segments of interviews, and possibly also between clauses. Specifically:

1. Individuals high in object-focused movements revealed more overt hostility in their verbal associations than did those low in object-focused movements: Individuals high in body-focused activity expressed more covert hostility than subjects who were low in body-focused activity.

2. There were significant variations in the link of overt and covert hostility scores within the different subcategories of object- and body-focused movements. (*a*) Within object-focused movements, overt hostility was linked most strongly to speech-primacy movements, less to representational motor-primacy, and not at all to nonrepresentatonal movements. This last variable was correlated with ambivalent hostility. (*b*) Within body-focused movements, hand-to-hand movements were significantly associated with covert hostility, but continuous and discrete body touching was not.

3. The associations between speech-primacy movements and overt hostility as well as hand-to-hand motions and covert hostility was further tested by a peak-trough analysis within interviews. During peak speech-primacy segments, there was more overt hostility than during trough segments and during peak hand-to-hand activity, there was more covert hostility than during trough segments.

4. In an attempt to explicate the movement-hostility relationship, we attempted to locate speech-primacy gestures in clauses preceding, coinciding with, and following aggressive themes. During intense verbal expression of hostility, gestures often dropped out. Movements either preceded (paved the way for) or followed (mollified) the hostile thought.

## DISCUSSION

In this article, we have been concerned with the contribution of body movements to the verbal encoding of aggressive stirrings. We have presented data that link different forms of speech-related movements to the encoding of meaningful chunks of affective, specifically hostile, thoughts.[5] Yet, there was nothing in the data that would indicate that hand movements constitute direct expressions of aggressive feelings; rather, it would seem more appropriate to assert that these movements are indicative of a visible kinetic-linguistic organization in the communicative flow which defines the relative difficulty in verbalization, that is, whether certain kinds of transformations may or may not take place.[6] Moreover, we suspect that the occurrence of object- and body-focused movements point up the communicative conditions conducive to what in psychoanalytic theory has been termed the neutralization of drive; that through the study of body motions in interviews, we may identify the presence of those psychological structures that may facilitate symbolization rather than discharge or action.

If, indeed, the motions, wiggles, and fidgets that invariably accompany ordinary speech define ongoing psychologic structure and the ability to verbalize, then a series of further questions may be posed, stimulated by the data of the present study: (*a*) What is the specific form of kinetic-linguistic organization that is part of verbalization or verbalization failure?[7] (*b*) What is the role of motility per se in the verbalization of aggressive bursts? (*c*) Finally, what is the role of aggressive drive in mediating the possiblity for verbalization?

### *Kinetic Structure Associated with Verbalization and Verbalization Failure*

We have proceeded from the assumption that movements during speech constitute the body's paritcipation in the symbolizing process—the process of

establishing representations (Werner & Kaplan, 1967). Movements, from this vantage point, are not only symbols or signals, but depending on their form or organization, are part processes which, in varying ways, contribute to the overall effort of articulating experiences. The kinetic behavior system during monologue or dialogue is not necessarily a language system as has been suggested by Birdwhistell (1970). Dittmann (in press), in a recent critique of Birdwhistell's work, has argued congently that not all movements are identifiable as discrete and categorical units and that they lack super and subordinate structure, two criteria that linguists have proposed as being requisite for a communication system to be considered a language. Kinetic behavior during interviews also is qualitatively distinct from the kind of gestural expression observed in the interactions between infants and mothers, a signalling system almost exclusively devoid of verbal form. Considered as a part process, the more the motions of the body dovetail with the verbal flow, the more likely are we to observe a structure in which verbalization is facilitated; yet, when movements are split off or are dissociated, verbalization is likely to be interfered with. These considerations have guided the development of our scoring system. We have operationally defined movements not in terms of content, that is, what they signify, but in terms of formal categories, asking of each gesture whether it appears to have an organizing or representational function, or whether it seems to constitute essentially nonrepresentational discharge action.

Our original expectation had been that object-focused movements, phased in with rhythm and speech content, would be linked with verbalization of overt aggression while body-focused movements, continuous and unrelated to speech, would be linked to a difficulty in expressing aggression overtly. In a broad and statistical sense, this proved to be so. Yet,it also proved to be an oversimplification. The expectation was challanged by the range of correlations within object- and body-focused movements. On the basis of data from this and earlier studies, it seems mandatory that we distinguish independent lines of structuralization with both object- and body-focused movements.

Within the broad class of object-focused activity, structuralization is defined by the relationship of the movement to the spoken word. Do the movements appear to have an organizing, supplementing or substitutive role? We have seen that as observations shift from speech-primacy gestures, the verbalization of overt hostility becomes more difficult. The facts, then, accord well with the expectations; as movements are phased in with speech, verbalization of aggression becomes more overt; as movements become nonrepresentational and dischargelike in character, the aggressive intent cannot be expressed directly. Although much work is yet to be done in specifying scoring criteria, it seems that a dimension of structuring within object-focused movements emerges.

Within the category of body-focused activity, which by definition is not

related to speech, structuralization can be defined by the morphology of the movements themselves, and empirical observations corroborate the assumptions of different levels of organization within this domain of kinetic behavior. Hand-to-hand motions have been considered the most diffuse form of body-focused activity. Previously (Freedman et al., 1972), this class of behavior was linked to a lower level of psychological differentiation (field dependence). Now we find it to be correlated with covert hostility. The question may be raised why hand-to-hand motions did not also correlate with hostility in. Hostility in is also an indicator of the difficulty in encoding overtly hostile thoughts and has been empirically linked to limited differentiation (Witkin, Lewis, & Weil, 1968). The difference seems to lie in the conditions of observation and subject population. In the Witkin et al. (1968) study, observations were based on patients in psychotherapy and in such a setting of self-revelation, hostility in is a likely response. In the present study, normal volunteer subjects were asked to "associate" in front of a relative stranger, a situation that may be expected to more readily stir up hostile affect. Indeed, the mean hostility in scores were lower than the mean overt hostility scores.

Body touching during speech, in contrast to hand-to-hand motions, is a representational gesture in which the individual selects a body part out of the available context and seems to articulate and depict some body experience. When such nonverbal representation takes place, there appears to be no interference with verbal encoding. Neither continuous nor discrete body touching revealed correlations with any hostility variables. Futher, there is preliminary clinical evidence that hand-to-hand motions and body touching also have their distinct linguistic correlates. Thus, in observations of schizophrenic patients who revealed pervasive hand-to-hand activity also had more fragmented syntax in their language. Depressed patients who revealed a predominance of continuous body touching showed more complex syntax in their speech.[8] There is, then, a rational and empirical basis to distinguish greater or lesser articulation within body-focused as well as object-focused activity.[9]

*Role of Motility in Verbalization and Verbalization Failure*

In the peak-trough analysis as well as in the qualitative analysis of the data, we have used the classes of speech primacy and hand-to-hand motions as criterion units that signify higher and lower structures in the communicative flow. We have done so partly on empirical grounds in that they yielded the highest correlation with aggression scores, but we have done so also on rational grounds in that they constitute extremes of organization within object- and body-focused movements, respectively. These two categories of kinetic activity are undoubtedly part of an orchestrated cluster of events. Such different levels of organization can probably be observed in various vehicles of expression, be they

postural, vocal, or syntactic. Yet, the questions may be asked: What is the role of motility, itself, that makes structure and verbalization possible? Are the movements simply a signpost of the kind of organization in which articulation of aggression can occur? Or, do the movements, when they emerge in rhythmic chunks, have a primary organizing function?

Mahl (1970) has argued that movements are not only expressive, but that they have attributes that may prime, anticipate, and pave the way toward articulation. The present study was primarily correlational in nature and there was no hard evidence to support such a priming function of motility. Yet, the peak-trough analysis has revealed that there exists an envelope of kinetic behavior surrounding a particular "hostility" phrase. Thus, with speech-primacy movements, a single phrase may be surrounded by a long string of qualifying or punctuating gestures that have little to do with hostile thought; or as we have seen in the qualitative analysis of the data, a gesture may pave the way for a direct expression of hostility. The envelope surrounding covertly hostile expressions is equally striking. Three or four covertly aggressive clauses are surrounded by a continuous string of hand motions, or perhaps more properly termed a grid, which prevents the expression of overt hostility. These observations of an envelope of kinetic activity surrounding aggressive themes suggest that our categories of gestural behavior are not necessarily expressive of affect but constitute activities preparing for and anticipating the as yet unverbalized. Or, they may indicate the kinetic mobilization for the repression or suppression of what must remain silent.

There are anecdotal clinical observations that argue that the organization of movements themselves set up different states of attention. Ferenczi, in a series of charming vignettes, has delineated how restrictive motions may conserve the clarity of thought (like the chunking of speech-primacy movements) (1926b), and in another essay entitled "Embarrassed Hands" (1926a), he presents an outline of the psychological states created by movements that are much akin to our hand-to-hand category: the splitting of attention, the loss of the automotism of gestures which is required for the effective communication of thought, and the loss or threatened loss of the intentionality to convey a central thought to a listener. Speech-primacy and hand-to-hand movements may indeed be indicative of quite different states of consciousness occurring in the course of an interchange.

*Role of the Aggressive Drive*

It is evident from what has been presented that the kinetic-linguistic organization defined by the categories of object- and body-focused movements may govern the verbalization of a range of affective experiences not limited to aggression. That different forms of aggression were specifically linked to motor

behavior in this study may be attributed to the nature of the experimental situation: the demand to talk and to associate in front of a stranger, a doctor, a psychiatrist. Rather interestingly, the subjects revealed little annoyance with their interviewer directly, hostility appearing by indirection in the content of the stories told.

To be sure, the intensity of aggression provoked in the situation of this study was mild, yet it was strong enough to be linked to body movements which point to the different ways in which the hostile promptings may be processed. The very mildness of the stress (a far cry from stress-induction experiments) make the present observations relevant to a range of clinical phenomena. Thus, the data have suggested that in a simple talking task, through observation of visible behavior, we may gain clues concerning the processing of aggression in those clinical conditions and in those phases of treatment where neutralization of aggression is an issue. It may well be that the rhythmic participation of body movements in articulated thought constitutes an operational definition of neutralized drive.

When the aggressive drive becomes very intense, the kinetic behavior system (movements of hands, feet or head) is probably no longer relevant. Even in the qualitative analysis of the data, we noted that at moments of more intense rage, hand movements dropped out. With intense rage, man is likely to be immobilized,and the most frightening person is not one who gesticulates profusely but one who is immobile. There is empirical evidence that in such instances of intense unverbalized rage, other nonverbal channels become enlisted. The presentation of an intensely sadistic motion picture has been shown to activate the muscles of the face (P. Ekman, personal communication, (1971) and the excessive sensitivity to intrusions on their personal space has been found to be a characteristic of individuals with histories of violent behavior (Kinzel, 1970). How to neutralize the unverbalized or unverbalizable rage of a Billy Budd is not yet within our ken.

## REFERENCES


Balkanyi, C. On Verbalization. *International Journal of Psychoanalysis*, 1964, 46, 64-74.

Birdwhistell, R. *Kinesics and context*. Philadelphia: University of Pennsylvania Press, 1970.

Darwin, C. *The expression of emotions in man and animals*. New York: Appleton, 1929.

Dittmann,m A. Review of R. Birdwhistell, *Kinesics and context*. *Psychiatry*, in press.

Dittmann, A., & Llewellyn, L. Body movement and speech rhythm in social conversation. *Journal of Personality and Social Psychology*, 1969, 11, 98-106.

Efron, D. *Gestures and environment*. New York: King's Crown, 1941.

Ekman, P., Sorenson, E., & Friesen, W. Pan-cultural elements in facial displays of emotion. *Science* , 1969, 164, 86-88.

Ferenczi, S. Embarrassed hands (1914). In, *Further contributions to the technique and theory of psychoanalysis*. London: Hogarth Press, 1926. (a)

Ferenczi, S. Thinking of muscle innervation (1919). In, *Further contributions to the technique and theory of psychoanalysis*. London: Hogarth Press, 1926. (b)

Freedman, N. The analysis of movement behavior during the clinical interview. In A. Siegman & B. Pope (Eds.), *Studies in dyadic communication*.New York: Pergamon Press, 1971.

Freedman, N., O'Hanlon, J., Oltman, P., & Witkin, H.A. The imprint of psychological differentiation on kinetic behavior in varying communicative contexts. *Journal of Abnormal Psychology*, 1972, 79, 239-258.

Freedman, N., & Hoffman, S.P. Kinetic behavior in altered clinical states: An approach to the objective analysis of motor behavior during clinical interviews. *Perceptual and Motor Skills*, 1967, 24, 525-539.

Freud, S. *Negation*. Vol. 19. London: Hogarth Press, 1925.

Gottschalk, L., Winget, C., & Gleser, C. *Manual of instructions for using the Gottschalk-Gleser Content Analysis Scales: Anxiety, hostility, social alienation-personal disorganization* .Berkeley: University of California Press, 1969.

Hoffman, S.P. *An empirical study of representational hand movements*. (Doctoral dissertation, New York University) Ann Arbor, Mich.: University Microfilms, 1968, No. 69-7960.

Jackson, J.H. *Selected writings of John Hughlings Jackson*. Vol. 2, London: Staples, 1968.

Kinzel, A. Body-buffer zone in violent prisoners. *American Journal of Psychiatry*, 1970, 127, 59-64.

Mahl, G.F. Gestures and body movements in interviews. In J. Shlien (Ed.), *Research in psychotherapy*. Vol. 3, Washington, D.C.: American Psychological Association, 1968.

Mahl, G.G. *Expressive behvior during the analytic process*. Unpublished manuscript, Yale University, 1970.

Melville, H. *Billy Budd*. New York: Washington Square, 1963.

Rosenfeld, H. Instrumental affiliative functions of facial and gestural expressions. *Journal of Personality and Social Psychology*, 1966, 4, 65-72.

Silverman, L.H. A technique for the study of psychodynamic relationships: The effects of subliminally presented aggressive stimuli in the production of pathological thinking in a schizophrenic population. *Journal of Consulting Psychology*, 1966, 30, 103-111.

Watzlawick, P., Beavin, J., & Jackson, D. *Pragmatics of human communications*. New York: Norton, 1967.

Werner, H., & Kaplan, B. *Symbol formation*. New York: Wiley, 1967.

Witkin, H.A., Lewis, H.B., Weil, E. Affective reactions and patient-therapist interactions among more differentiated and less differentiated patients early in therapy. *Journal of Nervous and Mental Disease*, 1968, 146, 193-208.

42

# THE PSYCHOANALYTIC STUDY OF HAND-MOUTH APPROXIMATIONS

LOUIS A. GOTTSCHALK, M.D.

THE OPPORTUNITY TO STUDY the relationship between the content of free association and a repeated physical gesture was provided by the psychoanalysis of a 40-year-old married psychologist. During his treatment this patient not infrequently moved one hand from alongside his body toward his mouth and then fingered his lips, oral cavity, nose, or cheek, or rubbed his closed eyes with his fingers or fist. It was decided to investigate the relationship of the content of his free associations and these various hand-face approximations.

The content of verbal material during psychoanalysis and its correlation with various behaviors or manifestations of the involuntary nervous system have long been of interest to analysts. Ferenczi (1912) wrote of the relationship of associative content to a variety of transient symptoms during the psychoanalytic session. I have reported psychoanalytic observations on the recurring epileptic manifestations of an eight-year-old boy (Gottschalk, 1956) and on the psychophysiological relationship between the content of free associations and paroxysmal electroencephalographic activity in a 24-year-old soldier subject to grand mal seizures (Gottschalk, 1955), and my findings have been reconfirmed by a more rigorous analysis of the data (Luborsky et al., 1970, 1974). Luborsky (1964, 1967, 1970) has examined the content of speech accompanying symptomatic behavior in psychoanalytic and psychotherapeutic interviews and compared it with the speech of control interviews. His formalizing of the use of control sessions in such studies constituted a methodological advance in that patients could be used as their own controls in assessing the frequency of occurrence of par-

ticular behavioral events. Luborsky and Auerbach (1969) have reminded us that this kind of psychoanalytic research, which they refer to as the "symptom-context method," can yield unique data about the interrelationship between the content of associations and various symptoms (such as the report that one has forgotten what one was about to say) and relating the forgetting to the immediately preceding and following stream of associative content. In these kinds of correlations lie the evidence and cues from which psychoanalysts, functioning not only as clinicians but as scientists, prove that certain psychological events are to varying degrees outside the level of one's awareness, yet influence behavior or physiological processes.

More specifically related to the subject of this paper is Rangell's (1954) study of the psychology of poise in relation to its perioral origins and the relation of adult behavior to fetal behavior with respect to this character trait. Adatto (1957) reported on the analysis of an adult patient's pouting, a facial expression with oral origins later used by the patient to express displeasure at the mother's feeding a younger sibling. More recently Adatto (1970) has reported on "snout-hand behavior" in an adult male analysand whose snout-hand activity represented, among other things, "a residual infantile wish in the transference being acted out in a masturbatory equivalent of face rubbing" (p. 826).

## Brief Résumé of the Patient's Analysis

Before he began his analysis, the patient, a psychologist, was an unusually mature, perceptive man, with a long-standing penchant for self-reflection and introspection. Some combination of these traits—and probably others that cannot be specified—made it possible for him to start his analysis and get well involved in it with a minimum of defensiveness and intellectualization. This is not to say that he presented himself as the acme of "normality" and "mental health." Rather, he could at the onset detail systematically and lucidly his lifetime traumas and experiences and his ensuing neurotic struggles and real achievements. He was able to delineate those genetic and psychodynamic factors that he understood and those areas of comprehension which eluded him and apparently left him with recurring symptoms. These symptoms included:

occasional doubts about his real abilities; disturbing feelings that his wife—an attractive woman—did not sufficiently match his ideal of feminine beauty (the important missing characteristic being fuller breasts); occasional impotence (in the form of loss of erection during intercourse or retarded ejaculation); and chronic, nonallergic rhinitis.

During his treatment, B. made excellent progress in the analysis and resynthesis of himself. This was evidenced by dynamic and structural changes as well as by definite symptomatic changes. His chronic rhinitis became practically nonexistent. His episodes of sexual impotence stopped. His self-concept of possibly being inadequate or damaged (depicted, for example, in dreams by having a false tooth or being minus a jawbone) disappeared. B.'s mind was a busy and inquiring one, yet critical and skeptical about easy or hastily arrived-at formulations.

The earlier portions of his analysis were characterized by a mother transference. His mother died of an infection when he was five months old. His rearing was taken over by a paternal aunt, but he later spent much time with another aunt and his paternal grandmother, all three women having the role of mother surrogate for him. His father, an architect, was so grief-stricken at the death of B.'s mother that he played a relatively minor role in B.'s rearing for several years.

The manifest theme of his first dream in analysis was of his sucking on the breasts of a young woman and finding the milk sweet. The second dream dealt with a frightening erotic attraction to three women, his three mother surrogates. It is likely that the focus of the analysis on early mother-child relationships was enhanced by B.'s wife becoming pregnant with the couple's second child about three months before his analysis started; she gave birth to a baby girl six months after the beginning of his analysis.

Frustration of oral-passive urges in the analytic situation led him to reflect that though he lost his mother while he was still nursing at the breast, he was overindulged by his substitute "three mothers," certainly till the age of four. At the age of four he developed a strange malady—obviously a conversion reaction—consisting of his being unable to walk. After ailing for several weeks he was tricked into a recovery, by being tempted to go after a gift, a fuzzy toy animal. Analysis revealed that this episode of "paralysis" was triggered

by the marriage and first pregnancy of one of his aunts, his principal mother surrogate at that time, and his anxiety at losing his place in her affections. Anal smearing fantasies and impulses toward the analyst and key parental figures appeared, which were superseded and defended against by reaction formations and a preoccupation with cleanliness and orderliness. These anal reactions were re-enactments of the aggressive reactions he had to early childhood frustrations of dependency. The reaction formations to the hostile aspect of these anal urges were presumably quick to develop because of the threat of further withdrawal of love and support.

At this point he disclosed that prepubertally he had had an eating problem characterized by his subsisting primarily on milk and candy. With adolescence this eating pattern gave way to a more balanced menu, and with this change in diet there arose a reaction formation against passive dependence: he all but made a fetish of independence, self-reliance, and autonomy. Whereas at an earlier age he fantasied a reunion with his deceased mother in a far-off place or that his mother was nearby, always watching over him, he renounced or forgot about these solaces. In adolescence, he renounced his adherence to and faith in religion. In analysis, being able to trace the vicissitudes of his oral needs and frustrations, he could realize the defensive and self-defeating nature of his excessive striving for independence and repudiation and intolerance of his legitimate and appropriate need for support and love.

When this kind of material came into focus in the transference, he initially expressed inappropriate resentment and bitterness toward the analyst, and when the defensive nature of this resentment was pointed out—that it was a cover-up for his affection—he burst into tears of relief and insight.

In his teens he overidealized the girls he dated, and avoided having sexual relationships with them, for he saw them as madonnas. He feared open aggression toward men, and such aggression was inhibited early. The suppression of aggression toward older men was instilled by a grandfather who was quite firm though friendly, and by the threat of blackmail by an older boy and his younger brother after the patient, as a boy, had threatened and then struck the younger boy with a knife. The guilt-ridden repressed urges to get rid of interferences with his sources of supplies of love and support emerged at this time, and these destructive impulses were

traced through a variety of relationships, from his favorite aunt's first child to his own son and, later, his daughter. Fear of his own aggression was increased by separation anxiety and fear of retaliation for his hostile aggression.

During the later portion of his analysis, the transference manifested itself mostly as a father-uncle transference, characterized by phallic competitive urges, a feeling of inferiority, fear of retaliation, and thoughts of renouncing ambitious striving intermingled with new zest and self-confidence.

The termination of his analysis was associated with a continuing sense of self-assurance and equanimity. He now had a capacity to love his wife more intimately withcut the preoccupation that her breasts were too small. His nonallergic vasomotor rhinitis—previously unresponsive to a variety of medical treatments—was cured and, finally, he was more assertive and creative in his professional work.

To help give the flavor of the patient's analysis, I shall present some of his first and last dreams in the analysis.

Session 3

*Dream:* "I had a dream about a girl with well-developed breasts, 17 or 18 years of age. I remember kissing on her breasts. They had a sweetish taste."

*Associations:* "Mother died at 20 years of age when I was five months old. I was weaned off breast to bottle at this time. Dream seems like a wish to recapture my mother. I have reaction formation to this—to be self-sufficient and not obligated to people."

Session 4

*Dream:* "The scene was like a circus. You'd go on a ride between sheets, like canvas. You'd take off your coat first and go on the dock between two sheets. After that you'd go in the basement to a restaurant. Some of my friends were with me. One said, I'm too old for this. The dream was somewhat scary."

*Associations:* "Wish to return to the womb via labia. My associations to the man who said, 'I'm too old for this,' leads to two thoughts: (1) I'm too old to get into psychoanalysis and (2) I'm too old to regress to the oral pleasures of the womb."

Session 12

*Dream:* "I was in the market place. There were vendors. There were two apples, I stole. I threw the apples somewhere with the idea I'd pick them up later. Then I picked up another apple and I believe I paid for it. I bit into the apple and it had a double layer—reddish outside layer and different color on inside."

*Associations:* "Double-layered apple is like a fetus in a mother. Also like an embryo. The scene of dream is like place where I lived when mother died and where I was then raised. I don't know what dream means. There were other parts to dream: dark corridors and dimly lit rooms."

(Analyst: "Why did you steal two apples?")

"I don't know. They were big apples. I rolled them into place between buildings. I took them in quick succession. I don't know why two? Mother and child. Two people."

(Analyst: "How about two breasts?")

"That could be. They weren't red but were yellowish. Can I get this only by stealing, by tricks or deception? It opens up a lot of ideas. I have vague thought that after my mother died, my father didn't care much about me, didn't want to see me. Maybe he was depressed. Maybe father blamed me or I blamed father for mother's death."

Session 14

*Dream:* "I was buying pencils at a store. People pushed ahead of me at a cash register and got there first. I went to somebody complaining that some people pushed me out of line. This man I spoke to said I should speak up. I went back to the counter and I had an old pencil and I got back in line, but I never did get the three new pencils I wanted."

*Associations:* "I associate man I spoke to with my father. He told me to get back there and speak up. The person behind the counter, behind the cash register, was a male but I'm not sure. Pencils are phallic. I envied phalluses of other kids. Person behind the cash register was maybe you or an older woman psychologist I know. I used to wrestle with a female—a maid—who had large breasts when I was about seven or eight. She was well built. Had large breasts. I'd attack her from ambush and she'd giggle.

"I get the thought of urinating in females—especially a prostitute or my wife or your wife—as a punishment for their behavior. Also this is an infantile theory of impregnation. This is a wish to impregnate one. Three pencils—why three? Penis and two testicles. My wife is pregnant, is due in about six months. I don't have any question that this is my baby."

(Analyst: "Pencils are like phalluses. Are you interested in writing?")

"I am interested in writing. Have written many diaries and poetry. A big ambition to write but I have felt I didn't have enough talent. I have strongest admiration for writers. I have hoped that psychoanalysis would help liberate certain energies there that are bound. After last hour had a burst of energy—as if inhibitions fell off. This gave me an inkling what I might achieve in psychoanalysis."

Session 15

*Dream:* "I had a dream about what would happen if I didn't get a medal from you for something."

*Associations:* "I expect something from this analysis. Since I'm not getting it I'll not do things for you. Fantasy of sucking a penis. Semen is like milk. Fantasy of putting you in a pit with a lot of other people and many people spitting on you. Memory of having six or eight teeth removed by a rough dentist. I had low level of anesthesia. My aunt B. was along. They were milk teeth. I didn't want to say that. Dream could be related to my rage and wanting to bite off the breast."

Session 586

"Feelings of shame and disgust at my crying at the idea of separation and object loss."

Analyst interprets patient's harsh self-criticism of his sadness and urge to cry and suggests his paternal grandfather made him feel crying was "sissified."

Session 587

Analyst turns down radio in waiting room outside of office when patient complains of loudness of woman singer on radio.

SESSION 588

*Dream:* "A young woman came to visit me. She was pretty. Looked familiar. The house was like a mansion. I asked my aunt or cousin to have her wait and went to shave or dress. I was older than she and thought she was maybe too young for me. I think she was interested in me because I was a psychologist. I was divorced. I hoped she might be interested in me and something might come of our meeting."

*Dream:* "A woman older than I—I was an adolescent in this dream—was going to swim around the bay. She went under—submerged and disappeared. The water within a nearby enclosure was calm, and outside of it, it was wild and churning.

"The woman didn't come up and I got concerned and tried to see her down in the water. I could see many sea animals and coral, but I couldn't see her.

"I went to a doctor's room for help, and he was sleeping. I wanted to wake him up to tell him about the woman, but I didn't dare awaken him. Suddenly, he woke up spontaneously and looked at me, and he became my grandfather—my mother's father and not the other grandfather I talk about.

"He told me to get a coat and a rope. He said I needed a coat because it was cold outside. But it wasn't that cold outside when the woman had dived into the water. The rope was to throw a line to the woman to rescue her. Then, my son John woke me up."

*Associations:* "The first dream represents a wish to find a youthful reincarnation of my mother. The second dream is a wish to have you, my psychoanalyst, or my maternal grandfather, rescue my mother and bring her back from the dead. I feel now some impatience and disappointment with you."

## Procedure

The patient was seen for 612 analytic sessions over a period of almost four years. During one phase of his analysis, beginning in the second year and lasting six months, verbatim notes were kept of his associations as well as notations about the placement and movement of his hands and fingers. On many random occasions the patient's analytic sessions were tape-recorded, and the tapes were transcribed and then erased. The analyst's notations of the patient's hand movements were then edited into the verbatim transcripts.

About six years after the termination of the patient's analysis these progress notes were systematically studied in an investigation of the temporal relationship between hand-mouth activity and the content of associations.

### Method I

The data obtained in the psychoanalytic situation were analyzed in several different ways. In Method I, the analyst reviewed handwritten notes or verbatim transcripts (including hand-movement observations) and impressionistically summarized the content and flow of free associations. Needless to say, the summaries indicate the nature of the patient's transference to the analyst at the time.

To illustrate this procedure, I shall present a random selection of summaries of the hand movements and free associations produced by this patient during a segment of the middle phase of his analysis. A clear-cut relationship between perioral hand movements and nonsexual and sexual child-mother associations is never quite established by this procedure, for child-mother associations occurred when the patient's hands were at his sides and away from the face or "snout" area. Nevertheless, an elusive patterning of associational content and hand location does become apparent, which defies simple formulation and easy consensus among different psychiatrists examining these chronological sequences. My own attempt to synthesize these hand-movement-verbal-content relationships follows the summaries.

Other psychodynamic relationships and psychokinesic formulations are possible, and I invite the generation of alternative hypotheses. In my opinion, the psychoanalytic situation is a good source of clinical hypotheses. The empirical verification of these hypotheses is often difficult and time-consuming, and may involve statistical evaluation of the data. I will describe such an assessment procedure after reviewing the results of Method I.

## Summary of patterns of content of patient's free associations and hand movements

### Sample 1 (12/21/64)

*Fingering lips and nose while reporting dreams.*
Very active involvement with people in dream.
Flirtation with a woman.

Meeting with woman in a hotel for a year.
Other "flirtatious" episodes.
Becoming very interested in a woman.

SAMPLE 2 (12/22/64)

*Hands at sides during telling of a dream.*
Relationship with dead body of a woman in dream.
Feelings of guilt over relations with dead woman—the interest in the breasts.
"Love and mother are two words I have not used."
*Beginning to finger lips and chin.*
Thoughts of dead husband of woman.
Feeling depressed.
Reminded of dictator whose body was blown up by a woman terrorist.
Feelings of shame; became half woman himself to cope with loss of mother (in early childhood).

SAMPLE 3 (12/23/64)

*Hands at sides.*
Nonsexual relationship of self with a man.
Relationship of another man with a *thin* girl.
Therapeutic relationship with a little boy.

SAMPLE 4 (12/30/64)

*Holding and fingering chin and not lips.*
*Dream 1*
Intercourse with a woman.
*Dream 2*
At a restaurant with grandmother.
Father tells about his sex life with women.

SAMPLE 5 (1/15/65)

*Fingers alternately on chin and over lips.*
Both hand locations associated with involvement with people but when hands on lips there are more references to megalomania and to women.

SAMPLE 6 (1/6/65)

*Hands at sides.*

Rebellious. Not much to say. Angry at a teacher.

*Fingers around mouth and rubbing lips.*

Shortly preceded by memories of getting enema from grandmother.

Experiencing gastrointestinal disturbance; recalling cramps and diarrhea he recently had.

*Fingers in mouth and rubbing nose and left eye.*

Had cramps deep in abdomen last Sunday.

Recall of explosive diarrhea.

Diarrhea followed mother-in-law's leaving after visit to his home.

Dream about wife.

*Fingers resting steadily on lips.*

Wife's cooking.

Mother-in-law wants his children to have better religious education.

His not saying prayers before mealtime.

*Fingers away from mouth but on face.*

Shortly preceded by his referring to guilt at not saying prayers before meals.

Ambivalence toward mother-in-law.

Repudiation of mother-in-law.

*Fingering lips briefly.*

Mother-in-law returns to stay with him after auto accident.

Mother-in-law—irritated by her.

Mother-in-law—thinks of him as a stranger.

Irritated at mother-in-law because she licks her fingers after she eats a tart.

Mother-in-law licks knife and he does not.

He used to lick fingers but was taught this was bad manners.

*Taking fingers away from mouth and face.*

Immediately preceded by psychoanalyst pointing out, for the first time, that the expression of his oral tensions and urges is curbed by his shame, but that he is not against touching his fingers to his lips during psychoanalytic sessions.

Talks about putting his fingers in his mouth.

Mother-in-law putting her fingers in mouth too stimulating to him.

Slobbers on his cigarettes.

Bites pipe stems.

Mother-in-law irritating because she indulges self too much.

His mouth area "is most invested."

Sample 7 (1/13/65)

*Hand on cheek.*

Immediately preceded by reporting headache yesterday in reaction to frustrated dependence.

Eyes hurt with headache.

Shame at revealing himself a "crybaby."

Wish for analyst to have eye pain rather than self.

Tendency to cover up his feelings.

*Tongue around lips, hands away from face.*

Immediately preceded by report he recalled crying when young female cousin died.

Grandmother comforted him after a boy hit him on head and cheek.

*Hands move away from face and then return to cheek.*

Trying to control feelings.

Stoicism.

*Fingers briefly rub nose and lips.*

Immediately preceded by statement "one thing I couldn't prevent was blushing." "I wanted a stoical facade."

*Fingering in mouth and between teeth.*

People seeing the little boy in him and this makes him feel ashamed.

Fear of depending on others.

Trying to cover up urge to cry over feeling like an orphan.

Sample 8 (1/26/65)

*Hands near but not on lips.*

Rage and murderous urges.

Frustrated in sex and dependence.

Castration anxiety.

*Hands on mouth or lips.*

Sex with women.
Difficulty performing sex adequately.

## Summary of the above and other psychokinetic sequences observed in patient B

1. The analysand touches a part of his anatomy related to a psychological or biological function he is experiencing and describing.

2. The relationship of the hand activity and position to the content of thought may be very concrete or highly symbolic.

3. The predominance of one type of thought content and hand activity at one area of the body can be influenced and changed with psychoanalytic intervention; likewise, the relationship may remain fairly stable in patterning without specific analytic intervention (i.e., interpretive comments or calling patient's attention to specific hand movements and thought contents).

4. Immediately before, during, or after hand movements near or at his mouth, the patient's thoughts concern a longing for the breast or for the whole body, or to be part of a woman, in a sexual or nonsexual context. These associations tend to be affectionate or positive rather than negative.

5. Hand movements away from the mouth area or static hand positions away from this area (e.g., hands at sides) are more often associated with the expression of negative affects toward people.

6. More specifically, touching the lips and mouth is often related to talking about women and intimacy and gastrointestinal function. The latter more often occurs when a finger is inserted into the mouth.

7. Touching the eyelids is often related to talking about seeing or understanding.

8. Touching the abdomen is associated with the expression of thoughts about the vagina and sexual intercourse.

9. Touching the nose is associated with sexual interest in forbidden women or discussing diarrhea following his mother-in-law's leaving his home.

### Method II

Transcripts of 14 psychoanalytic sessions, tape-recorded over a one-year period, were divided into the smallest possible communi-

cation units (grammatical clauses). (Notations of hand movements were not included in the typescripts.) Two content-analysis technicians independently scored each clause, according to an object-relations scale (see Schedule 1), for references to females (F), males (M), sexually unspecified humans (O), and inanimate objects (I), and for valence: positive (+), neutral (=), and negative feelings (—,h) toward any objects. Differences in classification by the two technicians were subsequently resolved by review and consensus. Each clause was then scored for the accompanying hand position: hand touching mouth or lips (I), hands on face but not touching lips (II), and hands away from face (III). Eight hundred and thirty-six statements were scored along the three dimensions: object relations, valence, and hand position during utterance.

### SCHEDULE 1
### OBJECT-RELATIONS SCALE

O: other(s), sex unspecified, in unspecified or neutral relationship(s)
O+: other(s), sex unspecified, in pleasant, gratifying, affectionate relationship(s)
O—: other(s), sex unspecified, in unpleasant, ungratifying, frustrating relationship(s)
Oh: other(s), sex unspecified, in hateful relationship(s)
S: self, in unspecified or neutral relationship(s)
S+: self, in pleasant, gratifying, affectionate relationship(s)
S—: self, in unpleasant, ungratifying, frustrating relationship(s)
Sh: self, in hateful relationship(s)
F: female(s), in unspecified or neutral relationship(s)
F+: female(s), in pleasant, gratifying, affectionate relationship(s)
F—: female(s), in unpleasant, ungratifying, frustrating relationship(s)
Fh: female(s), in hateful relationship(s)
M: male(s), in unspecified or neutral relationship(s)
M+: male(s), in pleasant, gratifying, affectionate relationship(s)
M—: male(s), in unpleasant, ungratifying, frustrating relationship(s)
Mh: male(s), in hateful relationship(s)
I: inanimate object(s), in unspecified or neutral relationship(s)

I+: inanimate object(s), in pleasant, gratifying, affectionate relationship(s)
I—: inanimate object(s), in unpleasant, ungratifying, frustrating relationship(s)
Ih: inanimate object(s), in hateful relationship(s)
A: animate (subhuman) object(s), in unspecified or neutral relationship(s)
A+: animate (subhuman) object(s), in pleasant, gratifying, affectionate relationship(s)
A—: animate (subhuman) object(s), in unpleasant, ungratifying, frustrating relationship(s)
Ah: animate (subhuman) object(s), in hateful relationship(s)

RULES FOR OBJECT-RELATIONS SCALE

1. Score as many object-relations events as occur, according to the above categories, per grammatical clause.
2. Whenever combinations of the above object-relations content categories occur, score these as combinations by connecting different object-relations notations with a plus sign. For example, female, self, interacting with others pleasantly = $F_+ + S_+ + O_+$; or male, self, liking female, but disliking inanimate object = $M_+ + S_+ + F_+ \quad I_-$.

There was no reason to expect the statements to be equally distributed among the categories within any dimension and, in fact, they were not. In the object-relations classification, 53% of the statements were about males, 20% were about females, 16% were about humans of unspecified sex, and 11% were about inanimate objects. This finding, by the way, is consistent with those of an earlier study (Gottschalk and Gleser, 1969, pp. 262f.) that indicated that in general males make many more verbal references to males (excluding all self-references) and females make many more references to females. In the valence classification, 49% of the statements were neutral, 35% were negative, and 16% were positive. In the hand-position classification, 49% of the statements were made during position II, 34% during position I, and 17% during position III.

More important than the question of how the statements are distributed among the dimensions is the question of interaction

between one dimension and another. For example, does the proportion of statements referring to different objects vary from one hand position to another? Does the proportion of statements of different valence vary with hand position? Figure 1 presents the findings relevant to these questions: The proportion of female responses decreases as one goes from hand position I to hand position II, and hand position III is accompanied by fewer positive and more neutral responses than are hand positions II and I.

There is a significant relationship, in this patient, between the position of the hand and the kind of object he is likely to mention ($\chi^2 = 15.28$, $df = 6$, $p < .02$). The proportion of female references made during hand position I is significantly greater than the proportion made during positions II and III ($\chi^2 = 8.95$, $df = 1$, $p < .01$) (Castellan, 1965). The number of female references made

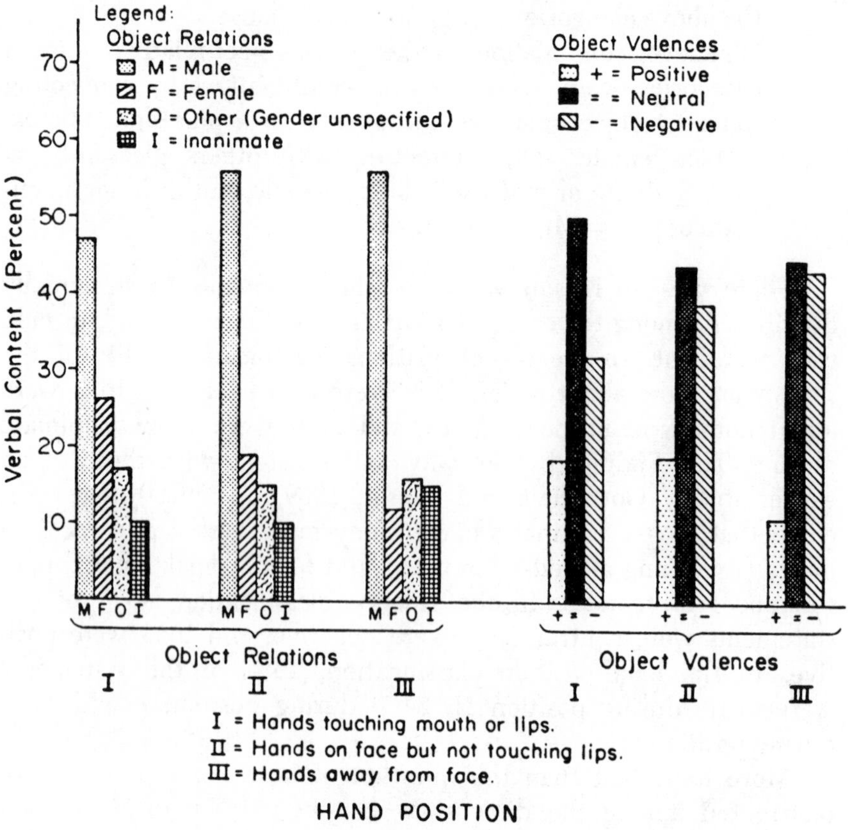


FIGURE 1

during hand position II is larger than the number made during hand position III ($\chi^2$ of 2.67, $df = 1$), but the difference is not quite significant ($p < .10$).

A similar statistical analysis on the relationship between hand position and valence revealed a significant association ($\chi^2 = 9.84$, $df = 4$, $p < .05$). The ratio of neutral statements to positive statements during hand position III is 5.19, whereas the comparable ratio during hand positions I and II combined is 2.82, a statistically significant difference ($\chi^2 = 4.58$, $df = 1$, $p < .05$).

Another way to look at the data is to determine whether there is a consistent tendency over the 14 sessions for a particular object reference or valence to be associated with a particular hand position. Unfortunately not all hand positions occurred in every session; so sessions that lacked a particular hand position could not be included in some analyses, thus weakening the statistical evaluation. Nevertheless some trends were noted. In nine out of 11 sessions the proportion of negative statements was higher during hand position II than during hand position I (sign test, $p < .01$). In eight out of eight sessions the proportion of negative statements was higher during hand position III than during hand position I ($p < .01$). In seven out of eight sessions the proportion of female references was higher during hand position I than during hand position III ($p < .05$). In ten out of 11 sessions the proportion of references to females or positive references to all objects was higher during hand position I than during hand position II ($p < .01$). In six out of eight sessions the proportion of such references was higher during hand position I than during hand position III ($p < .05$).

Another finding, not related to hand position, is of an interaction between object references and valence ($\chi^2 = 42.60$, $df = 6$, $p = .001$): female references were more likely to be positive than were nonfemale references ($\chi^2 = 24.71$, $df = 1$, $p < .001$), and male references were more likely to be positive than inanimate or other sex-unspecified references ($\chi^2 = 5.81$, $df = 1$, $p < .02$).

## Discussion

One of the first analysts to write about psychoanalysis and body movements was Deutsch (1952), who coined the term "analytic posturology" to encompass the psychoanalytic study of posture

and gesture. He found in patients' gestures and postures evidence for underlying drives and defenses, such as conflicts between masculine and feminine tendencies; for example, flexion of the hand meant the assumption of a passive feminine position. Deutsch (1959) found meaning in each individual gesture and to a large extent perceived a one-to-one relationship between the gesture and the underlying drive. He (1966, pp. 167–168) gave three basic principles to serve as guidelines for understanding of body movements: (1) Unconscious emotional needs which cannot be discharged verbally lead to mobility and postural behavior. (2) The nature of certain postural activities is revealed when they occur in association with specific verbalized mental contents, especially repetitive patterns of simultaneous body and thought expressions. (3) Knowledge of the patient's personality helps clarify the meaning of his gestures. A patient's motor patterns may change as he alternately identifies with and rejects various incorporated objects. Needles (1959) noted the occurrence of gesticulation in the psychoanalytic situation, and emphasized its regressive aspects. Scheflen (1964, 1966) spent many years as a student of "kinesics" under Birdwhistell (1952, 1960, 1970). By filming parts of psychotherapeutic and psychoanalytic treatments and carefully examining the content of speech and body movements, Scheflen has given us probably the most comprehensive understanding, from a psychoanalyst's point of view, of the relationship between these different channels of communication. One of his major findings is that, contrary to Deutsch's view, the meaning of body movements depends not necessarily on contiguity with any *specific* verbalized mental contents, but on the social and personal context in which they occur and certainly on what has preceded their appearance. Scheflen (1966) held that only rarely is the meaning of a single gesture clear and then only in the simplest instances. Instead, he noted complex patterns of communication in which the body language was only one detail; to be understood it must be considered in its complicated interaction with the patient's verbal behavior. Haggard and Isaacs (1966) filmed micromomentary facial movements during psychotherapeutic sessions, movements hardly discernible to the naked eye, and were able to relate 25% of them to what the patient was saying. Though the latter kind of observation is of no immediately obvious use to the clinician, it does add to the

body of evidence that even the most minute body movements signify and possibly substitute for the semantic and vocal modalities of communication. Gottschalk and Frank (1967) reported strong evidence of the redundancy of the semantic and vocal (paralanguage) channels of communication and, by extension, the motor channels. They emphasized the survival value to our distant ancestors, running away from predators, of sending messages of danger to others, simultaneously, through all avenues of communication: by content, vocally (tone of voice and cadence), and motorically (by posture and gesture). We, the distant inheritors of the capacity to survive, must have inherited the tendency to issue the same message in every way possible.

The opportunity to make very refined observations provided by the psychoanalytic situation enables the scientist to see that body motion can influence thought content and vice versa, and one modality of communication may, at times, substitute for another.

The second procedure described here, exploring the relationship of hand movements to the content of free associations, is not by any means considered to be an exhaustive analysis of these relationships, but rather as a fruitful approach to testing the hypotheses generated by the first method described, which is a clinical impressionistic one. It is clear that the clinical impressionistic approach is a rich source of hypotheses for understanding the connections between psychodynamics and motor activity. The more objective and rigorous methods involved in the second procedure have demonstrated precisely the bases for our clinical impressions. In this man, thoughts of women, or of gratifying relationships with any objects regardless of gender, are more often associated with hand placement on or near his mouth than with hand placement away from his face. Verbalizations of neutral or negative feelings toward objects occur less often when his hand is touching his lips than when it is not. In most instances these findings reach a convincing level of statistical significance, raising our clinical impressionistic observations (or hypotheses) to the level of facts.

The microanalysis of these relationships between hand movements and verbal content has many implications, both for developmental theory and for clinical psychoanalysis. The importance for psychoanalytic technique not only of observing body movements but also of inquiring about them at appropriate times, becomes

obvious. Since the gender of the objects discussed and the valence of the speaker toward all objects are clearly associated with where this patient puts his hands while he free associates, there may well be significant associations between mental content and body movements in other patients too. An analyst could be badly misled in his interpretation of such a patient's underlying psychodynamics, and certainly in comprehending the nature of the transference, if he did not have the additional data of how this patient's hand movements relate to his associations. The analyst would do well to observe the analysand's motor activities for some time to determine whether he can detect what content has been added to or subtracted from the patient's verbal associations with recurring similar motor activity. If the analyst believes he discerns a patterned relationship, he might do well to keep his hypothesis to himself and test whether the analysand has any awareness of such a relationship. To embark here on an essay on psychoanalytic technique with respect to the timing and nature of interventions by the analyst concerning verbal and nonverbal communications is, however, not my purpose. The main points to be emphasized here are that a patient's "free associations" are not "free" and are not entirely revealed by his speech. Others, including Freud (1913, 1914, 1917), have also pointed out how unfree "free associations" are. Wilhelm Reich's (1949) pioneer observations about character armoring and body activity as a façade for deeper covert motivations and conflicts are reconfirmed by this case study.

Developmentally, I believe that this study illustrates how the steps toward autonomy and self-sufficiency are aided by body activity. The patient's touching his oral area with his fingers evokes memories and associations of a supportive type, of females and of good objects, affects, and ideation. It is not sufficient to dismiss these as autoerotic or masturbatory equivalents and thus to imply that they are pathological remnants or signs of an unresolved narcissism or mother fixation. Fleeting, nonfeeding hand-mouth or hand-face movements typify every living human being, regardless of how well subliminated are his drives. An appropriate and valuable ego function is provided by this analysand's sampling his environment with the positive perspectives (references to females or positive references to all objects) evoked when his hand is in the oral area and the negative perspectives aroused when his hands are

at his side. Somewhere between these perspectives—influenced by the ideation and affects evoked from his own memory bank—lies a true appraisal of external reality. This two-way frame of reference permits more accurate plotting of the position of external stimuli indicated by all incoming messages in all sensory modalities. When he learns that an external object will not respond in terms of his needs, he can temporarily evoke the kinds of memories and thoughts of objects that give hope and pleasure, though transient (by touching his lips), which in turn keep him searching for satisfaction in spite of temporary adversity and frustration.

No doubt obesity and alcoholism are unrelenting attempts to evoke a childhood, mother-child paradise, through self-mastery and autonomy. But in these conditions the remedy—that is, the transient sense of equanimity afforded by oral stimulation—has become an end in itself, to the destruction of the balanced function of the rest of the organism.

Rangell (1954) has emphasized the importance of stimulation—by food, alcohol, smoking, self-initiated perioral muscle tightening, and so forth—of the snout area in the maintenance of poise, an attitudinal posture which lends the person a semblance of equanimity or an actual sense of inner satisfaction. The present report, especially of the psychodynamic aspects of hand movements toward the perioral area or elsewhere, provides more information about kinesic activities which enhance poise. The analysis of this patient brings out the adaptive function of hand-mouth actions, illustrating how they lay a groundwork for the maintenance of self-sufficiency and autonomy. The potency of oral stimulation in enhancing the ego's integrative capacity to deal with the frustrations of everyday life is demonstrated.

One may well raise the question whether touching the hand to the mouth evokes memories of oral satisfactions and the like or, conversely, whether thoughts and feelings of an oral kind elicit movement of the hand to the mouth: That is, what is cause and what is effect? A statistical evaluation from a natural-history study of the type reported here cannot convincingly answer this question. An experimental study in progress, however, provides some data which bear on this question: 20 subjects were asked to free-associate for two separate five-minute periods while they rubbed their lips with their fingers, and for two separate five-minute periods while

they kept their hands away from their faces. This study clearly reveals that in some persons lip touching definitely influences the content of thought, as reflected in speech, in the direction of evoking memories related to oral functions, whereas in other persons mental contents defending against oral preoccupations predominate (Gottschalk and Uliana, 1974).

That psychokinesic relationships differ from person to person should not be surprising; similar findings have been reported by investigators of psychosomatic correlations (Engel, Reichsman, and Anderson, 1971; Luborsky et al., 1970, 1974), who found that well-verified psychological and somatic correlates observed within one person do not necessarily occur within others.

## References


Adatto, C. P. (1957), On Pouting. *J. Amer. Psychoanal. Assn.*, 5:245–249.

——— (1970), Snout-Hand Behavior in an Adult Patient. *J. Amer. Psychoanal. Assn.*, 18:823–830.

Birdwhistell, R. L. (1952), *Introduction to Kinesics*. Louisville, Kentucky: University of Louisville Press.

——— (1960), Kinesics and Communication. In: *Explorations in Communication*, ed. E. Carpenter & M. McLuhan. Boston: Beacon Press.

——— (1970), *Kinesics and Context*. Philadelphia: University of Pennsylvania Press.

Castellan, M. J., Jr. (1965), On the Partitioning of Contingency Tables. *Psychol. Bull.*, 64:330–338.

Deutsch, F. (1952), Analytic Posturology. *Psychoanal. Quart.*, 21:196–214.

——— (1959), On the Formation of the Conversion Symptom. In: *On the Mysterious Leap from the Mind to the Body*, ed. F. Deutsch. New York: International Universities Press, pp. 59–72.

——— (1966), Some Principles of Correlating Verbal and Non-verbal Communication. In: *Methods of Research in Psychotherapy*, ed. L. A. Gottschalk & A. H. Auerbach. New York: Appleton-Century-Crofts, pp. 166–184.

Engel, G., Reichsman, F., & Anderson, D. (1971), Behavior and Gastric Secretion: III. Cognitive Development and Gastric Secretion in Children with Gastric Fistula. (Abstr.) *Psychosom. Med.*, 33:472.

Ferenczi, S. (1912), On Transitory Symptom-Constructions during the Analysis. In: *Sex in Psychoanalysis*. New York: Brunner, 1950, pp. 193–212.

Freud, S. (1913), On Beginning the Treatment (Further Recommendations on the Technique of Psycho-Analysis I). *Standard Edition*, 12:123–144. London: Hogarth Press, 1958.

——— (1914), Remembering, Repeating and Working Through (Further Recommendations on the Technique of Psycho-Analysis II). *Standard Edition*, 12:147–156. London: Hogarth Press, 1958.

——— (1917), Introductory Lectures on Psycho-Analysis, Part III. Lecture XIX: Resistance and Repression. *Standard Edition*, 16:286–302. London: Hogarth Press, 1963.

Gottschalk, L. A. (1955), Psychologic Conflict and Electroencephalographic Patterns. Some Notes on the Problem of Correlating Changes in Paroxysmal Electroencephalographic Patterns with Psychologic Conflicts. *A.M.A. Arch. Neurol. Psychiat.*, 73:656–662.

——— (1956), The Relationship of Psychologic State and Epileptic Activity. Psychoanalytic Observations on an Epileptic Child. *The Psychoanalytic Study of the Child*, 11:352–380. New York: International Universities Press.

——— & Frank, E. C. (1967), Estimating the Magnitude of Anxiety from Speech. *Behav. Sci.*, 12:289–295.

——— & Gleser, G. C. (1969), *The Measurement of Psychological States through the Content Analysis of Verbal Behavior.* Berkeley, Cal.: University of California Press.

——— & Uliana, R. (1974), An Experimental Study of Influence of Hand-Mouth Stimulation on Content of Free Association. Unpublished manuscript.

Haggard, E. A., & Isaacs, K. S. (1966), Micromomentary Facial Expressions as Indicators of Ego Mechanisms in Psychotherapy. In: *Methods of Research in Psychotherapy*, ed. L. A. Gottschalk & A. H. Auerbach. New York: Appleton-Century-Crofts, pp. 154–165.

Luborsky, L. (1964), A Psychoanalytic Research on Momentary Forgetting during Free-Association. *Bull. Philadelphia Assn. Psychoanal.*, 14:119–137.

——— (1967), Momentary Forgetting during Psychotherapy and Psychoanalysis: A Theory and Research Method. In: Motives and Thought: Psychoanalytic Essays in Honor of David Rapaport, ed. R. R. Holt. *Psychol. Issues*, Monogr. 18/19: 175–217. New York: International Universities Press.

——— (1970), New Directions in Research on Neurotic and Psychosomatic Symptoms. *Amer. Sci.*, 58:661–668.

——— & Auerbach, A. H. (1969), The Symptom-Context Method. Quantitative Studies of Symptom Formation in Psychotherapy. *J. Amer. Psychoanal. Assn.*, 17:68–99.

——— Docherty, J. P., Knapp, P., & Gottschalk, L. (1970), The Symptom-Context Method of Measuring the Psychological State prior to Petit-Mal Seizures. (Abstr.) *Psychosom. Med.*, 32:557.

——— ——— Todd, T. C., Knapp, P., Mirsky, A., & Gottschalk, L. A. (1974), A Content Analysis of Psychological States prior to Petit-Mal Seizures. *J. Nerv. Ment. Dis.*, in press.

Needles, W. (1959), Gesticulation and Speech. *Internat. J. Psycho-Anal.*, 40:291–294.

Rangell, L. (1954), The Psychology of Poise. *Internat. J. Psycho-Anal.*, 35:313–332.

Reich, W. (1949), *Character Analysis*, 3rd ed. New York: Orgone Institute Press.

Scheflen, A. E. (1964), The Significance of Posture in Communication Systems. *Psychiatry*, 27:316–331.

——— (1966), Natural History Method in Psychotherapy: Communicational Research. In: *Methods of Research in Psychotherapy*, ed. L. A. Gottschalk & A. H. Auerbach. New York: Appleton-Century-Crofts, pp. 263–289.

# A Study of the Relationship of Nonverbal to Verbal Behavior: Effect of Lip Caressing on Hope and Oral References as Expressed in the Content of Speech

Louis A. Gottschalk and Regina L. Uliana

THIS STUDY was an outgrowth of a previous psychoanalytic investigation in which the content of speech was observed when an analysand periodically fingered his mouth or nose during psychoanalytic therapy. In this earlier study, the analysand was noted to speak significantly more frequently of women and to attach positive valences towards all objects when he was touching his oronasal area as compared to when his hands were at his side.[1] In this natural history study, where the hand–mouth activity appeared spontaneously during the psychoanalytic process involving one patient and clearly served a self-supporting function leading to a temporary feeling of independence and security for the analysand, there was no information enabling one to generalize how commonly hand–mouth activity of this sort evoked such specific speech content in others. Also, except for the inferences one might make on the basis of temporal relationships, it could not be determined whether the hand–mouth contact evoked certain memories and thoughts and, hence, such speech content, or whether this speech content and its associated mental content caused the hand–mouth activity.

An experimental study with a group of individuals, in which the hand–mouth activity would be systematically alternated with a hand position away from the face, was seen as one means of pursuing the question of cause-and-effect relationships, and specifically of charting the ways in which such kinesic activity was capable of influencing verbal content. On a broader basis, such a study was seen as a possible method of contributing to our understanding of the interplay of early life experiences and object relations on mental content, as well as enlarging our understanding of the effect of hand–mouth activities on memory retrieval and on the processing of new mental content as expressed and objectified in the verbalization of hope and optimism.

---

*From the Department of Psychiatry and Human Behavior, College of Medicine, University of California at Irvine, Irvine, Calif.*

Louis A. Gottschalk, M.D.: *Professor of Psychiatry, Social Science, and Social Ecology and Chairman of the Department of Psychiatry and Human Behavior, College of Medicine, University of California at Irvine, Irvine, Calif., and Director, Psychiatric Residency Training Program and Psychiatric Services, UCI-Orange County Medical Center, Orange, Calif.;* Regina Uliana, B.A.: *Research Assistant, Communication and Measurement Laboratory, Department of Psychiatry and Human Behavior, University of California at Irvine, Irvine, Calif.*

*Presented at the meeting of the Maurice Levine Society, Department of Psychiatry, College of Medicine, University of Cincinnati, October 12, 1974.*

*Reprint requests should be addressed to Dr. Louis A. Gottschalk, Department of Psychiatry and Human Behavior, College of Medicine, University of California at Irvine, Irvine, Calif. 92664.*

## MATERIALS AND METHODS

### *Subjects*

Twenty college students, 10 males and 10 females, with a mean age of 21.45 yr, were paid volunteers for this study. Only those subjects who reported, during an initial interview, that they were in good general health and that they had not taken any drugs (i.e., depressants or psychoactive drugs) during the preceding month, were allowed to participate in the study. Further, only those women who were not on birth control pills were offered the possibility of participating in the study.

### *Procedure*

Each subject gave four 5-min speech samples in the presence of one of the authors; each 5-min period was accompanied by either hand-position A (hands at one's side) or hand-position B (one hand caressing one's lips), balanced for both men and women in either the sequence ABBA or BAAB to control for possible order effects. The speech was elicited by asking each subject to talk for 5 min about any interesting or dramatic life experiences following standardized instructions used previously in many investigations of content analysis of speech.[2,3] Speech samples were tape-recorded in full view of the subjects, and these tapes were later transcribed.

After giving the four 5-min speech samples, each subject completed the following measures.

(1) Each participant completed the Luborsky et al. Social Assets Scale,[4] which is a self-report procedure constructed of 33 weighted items relating to an individual's psychosocial background, including details of parent–child relations, parent loss, sibship, educational level, and so forth (see Schedule 1). The composite score from this measure is called a "social assets" scale score, and this measure has been found valuable in predicting improvement from brief psychiatric hospitalization and

**Table 1. Correlations of Social Assets Scale Scores (Luborsky) and Various Behavioral and Psychological Measures Before (days 1, 3, and 6) and After (day 8) Thioridazine (4 mg/kg) by Mouth in Acute Schizophrenic Patients. (*N* = 25)**

| Behavioral or Psychological Measure | Social Assets Scale (Luborsky) | | | |
|---|---|---|---|---|
| | Day 1 | Day 3 | Day 6 | Day 8 |
| BPRS | | | | |
| 1. Depression | | | | −0.45§ |
| 2. Thinking Disorder | | | | |
| 3. Anergia | −0.54‡ | −0.64* | −0.59† | −0.37 |
| 4. Excitement-disorientation | | | | −0.56† |
| Hamilton Depression Scale | | | | |
| 1. Sleep disturbance | | | | |
| 2. Somatization | −0.37 | −0.47§ | −0.31 | −0.44§ |
| 3. Anxiety depression | | | | |
| 4. Apathy | −0.28 | −0.37 | −0.45§ | −0.23 |
| Wittenborn Scale | | | | |
| 1. Anxiety | | | | |
| 2. Somatic-hysterical | −0.36 | −0.36 | −0.16 | −0.42§ |
| 3. Obsessive-compulsive-phobic | | | | −0.37 |
| 4. Depression retardation | −0.40§ | −0.33 | −0.37 | −0.45§ |
| 5. Excitement | | | | −0.45§ |
| 6. Paranoia | | | | |
| Social Alienation-Personal Disorganization Scale | | | −0,46§ | −.53‡ |

*$p < .001$.
†$p < .005$.
‡$p < .01$.
§$p < .05$.

**Table 2. Average Number of Words Spoken During Five Minutes For Each Condition: Hands at Side (A) and Hand Lightly Rubbing Lips (B)**

| Hand Position | |
|---|---|
| A | B |
| 467.5 | 422.5 |
| 682.5 | 668.5 |
| 594.5 | 417.5 |
| 817.5 | 809.5 |
| 896 | 736 |
| 1066.5 | 1088 |
| 769.5 | 808.5 |
| 911 | 829 |
| 894 | 867 |
| 857 | 824 |
| 558 | 493 |
| 441.5 | 356 |
| 618.5 | 616.5 |
| 587 | 712.5 |
| 762 | 684 |
| 619 | 638.5 |
| 792 | 731.5 |
| 869 | 946 |
| 1114.5 | 1049 |
| 437.5 | 370.5 |
| Means = 737.75 | 703.40 |
| SD = 195.97 | 212.42 |

T-test for total number of words spoken between condition (A) hands at side and condition (B) hand rubbing lips ($t = 2.14$; $N = 20$; $p < .05$; two-tail).

the frequency and severity of episodes of certain specific illnesses (herpes simplex, arthritis).[4] This social assets scale score, in 25 acute schizophrenic patients, was significantly negatively correlated ($r = -0.46$, $p < .01$) pretreatment with social-alienation personal-disorganization content analysis scores (a measure of the relative severity of the schizophrenic syndrome derived from the content analysis of speech[3] with the Anergia Factor ($r = -0.59$, $p < .005$) of the Overall–Gorham Brief Psychiatric Rating Scale,[5] and with the Apathy Factor ($r = -0.46$, $p < .05$) of the Hamilton Depression Scale,[6] as well as with various other measures from these patients 2 days post-treatment and after a single oral dose of thioridazine (4 mg/kg)[7,8] (see Table 1).

(2) Subjects completed a questionnaire designed by the authors, composed of 21 questions about various aspects of the subjects' history of oral activities (see Schedule 2).

The typescripts of the speech samples were then content-analyzed (without the content-analysis technician knowing the hand position with which the speech sample was associated) for the dependent variables of this study: (1) Hope scale scores,[3,9] which are derived from a verbal content analysis scale composed of seven content categories (four weighted positively and three weighted negatively) counted for their frequency of occurrence within each grammatical clause of 3–5 min of verbal communication. This scale was devised to measure the intensity of the optimism that a favorable outcome is likely to occur, not only in one's personal earthly activities, but also in cosmic phenomena and even in spiritual or imaginary events. The total hope scale score is arrived at by summating the weights of all relevant hope content categories used per speech sample and expressing this raw score in terms of a corrected score per 100 words spoken, so that these scores can be compared within an individual over different occasions and between individuals, regardless of the total number of words spoken during the 5 min of speech (see Schedule 3). (2) Object Relations Scale,[1] which classifies each reference to "objects" for references to females, males, sexually unspecified humans, inanimate objects, and for the expression of positive and negative feelings toward any object (Schedule 4). (3) Oral references occurring in the speech samples (see Schedule 5).

## RESULTS

### *Effect of Hand Position on Number of Words per Five-Minute Speech Sample*

On the average, the subjects spoke significantly fewer words during the 5-min period when they caressed their lips than when they kept their hands at their sides ($t = 2.14, p < .05$) (see Table 2).

### *Effect of Hand Position on Hope Scale Scores*

Total hope scale scores were not significantly different when the subjects were touching their lips as compared to when they had their hands at their sides. However, considering separately the seven content categories of the hope scale, there were more verbal references during lip caressing ($t = -1.84, N = 20, p < .08$, two-tail test) to the frequency of use per 100 words of the content category of "*not* being or *not* wanting to be or *not* seeking to be the recipient of good fortune, good luck, or God's favor or blessing" (hope scale content category H5, see Table 3 and Schedule 3).

When the group of subjects with social assets scale scores in the highest 33% was compared with the group having social assets scale scores in the lowest 33%, it was discovered that significantly higher hope scores were produced by the groups of subjects having higher social assets scores for both hand-positions A ($t = 2.62, p < .05, N = 12$) and B ($t = 2.70, p < .025, N = 12$). Also, the group of subjects with the lower social assets scores tended to have greater increases in hope scores (B-A) while touching their lips ($t = 1.84, N = 12, p < .05$, one-tail) than the group with the higher social assets scores (see Table 4). Likewise, as Table 5 indicates, the subjects who had the greater increases in total hope scores during hand–mouth approximation, as compared to when their hands were at their sides (B-A), tended to be those who had the lower social assets scores ($t = -2.21, N = 12, p < .05$, one-tail). These findings were in line with prior hypotheses.

Correlations between hope scores and social assets scale scores were 0.42 during hand position A, 0.29 during hand position B, and −0.31 for B-A. There were no significant correlations between total hope scale scores and total oral references under either or both experimental hand conditions.

**Table 3. Average Hope Content Category (Subscale) Scores For Both Conditions, Hands At Side (A) and Hand Lightly Rubbing Lips (B), for 20 Subjects**

| Hand Position | | Hope Content Category Scores H1 | H2 | H3 | H4 | H5 | H6 | H7 |
|---|---|---|---|---|---|---|---|---|
| A | Mean | 0.77 | 0.67 | 0.09 | 0.09 | 0.08 | 0.62 | 0.36 |
| | SD | 0.55 | 0.53 | 0.19 | 0.12 | 0.09 | 0.50 | 0.28 |
| B | Mean | 0.87 | 0.65 | 0.10 | 0.06 | 0.17 | 0.50 | 0.40 |
| | SD | 0.49 | 0.38 | 0.16 | 0.08 | 0.21 | 0.43 | 0.40 |
| | T-test and *p* Value | −0.84 | 0.14 | −0.47 | 1.70 | −1.84* | 1.10 | −0.38 |

$N = 20$.
*$p < .08$ (two-tail).

**Table 4. Relationship of Mean Hope Scale Scores for Each Hand Position (Hands at Side–A and Hand Lightly Rubbing Lips–B) with Ranked Social Assets Scale Scores**

| Subject's Sex | Ranked Social Assets Scale Scores | Hand Position | | |
|---|---|---|---|---|
| | | A | B | B–A |
| M | 8.50 | 0.27 | 0.27 | 0.00 |
| F | 6.00 | −0.92 | 0.52 | 1.44 |
| M | 4.50 | 1.51 | 1.74 | 0.23 |
| F | 3.50 | 1.31 | 0.86 | −0.45 |
| F | 3.50 | 4.01 | 1.85 | −2.16 |
| F | 3.50 | 3.24 | 1.30 | −1.94 |
| F | 3.00 | 1.18 | −0.08 | −1.26 |
| M | 2.50 | 0.84 | −1.46 | −2.30 |
| M | 2.50 | 0.00 | 0.03 | 0.03 |
| M | 1.50 | 1.51 | 1.18 | −0.33 |
| F | 1.00 | 1.63 | 1.86 | 0.23 |
| M | 0.00 | −0.88 | 0.70 | 1.58 |
| M | −0.50 | −0.23 | 0.49 | 0.72 |
| F | −1.00 | 1.64 | 1.51 | −0.13 |
| M | −1.50 | 0.78 | 1.34 | 0.56 |
| F | −1.50 | −2.23 | 0.23 | 2.46 |
| M | −2.50 | −0.56 | −0.05 | 0.51 |
| M | −2.75 | −0.22 | −0.23 | −0.01 |
| F | −5.00 | −1.40 | −0.57 | 0.83 |
| F | −7.00 | −0.43 | −0.31 | 0.12 |
| Means | 0.91 | 0.55 | 0.56 | 0.01 |
| SD | 3.75 | 1.52 | 0.90 | 1.22 |

Difference between means of hope scale scores derived from speech samples elicited from subjects with highest $\frac{1}{3}$ and lowest $\frac{1}{3}$ social assets scale scores during hand-position A ($t = 2.62$; $N = 12$; $p < .05$; two-tail).

Difference between means of hope scale scores derived from speech samples elicited from subjects with highest $\frac{1}{3}$ and lowest $\frac{1}{3}$ social assets scale scores during hand-position B ($t = 2.70$; $N = 12$; $p < .025$; two-tail).

Difference between means of hope scale change scores (B–A) associated with highest $\frac{1}{3}$ and lowest $\frac{1}{3}$ social assets scale scores ($t = 1.84$; $N = 12$; $p < .05$; one-tail).

### *Effect of Hand Position on Intercorrelations Between Hope Scale Scores with Affect Scores and Object Relations Scores*

The intercorrelations were examined between hope scale scores, and anxiety scale, hostility outward scale, and object relations scale scores derived from speech samples given during the two hand positions. When the hands were by the subjects' sides (position A), the affect scores were significantly negatively correlated with hope scores. Specifically, hope scores correlated negatively with total anxiety scores ($r = -0.64$, $p < .002$), and most of this correlation could be accounted for by the correlation of hope scores with guilt anxiety ($r = -0.67$, $p < .001$) and diffuse anxiety ($r = -0.62$, $p < .003$). Hope scores correlated significantly negatively with total hostility outward scores ($r = -0.55$, $p < .01$) and most of this association could be accounted for by the negative correlation of hope scores with overt hostility outward scores ($r = -0.51$, $p < .02$). Such negative correlations between hope scores and affects have been previously

Table 5. Relationship of Ranked Hope Scale Difference Scores (B–A) Associated With Social Assets Scale Scores

| Subject's Sex | Ranked B–A's | Social Assets Scale Scores |
|---|---|---|
| F | 2.46 | −1.50 |
| M | 1.58 | 0.00 |
| F | 1.44 | 6.00 |
| F | 0.83 | −5.00 |
| M | 0.72 | −0.50 |
| M | 0.56 | −1.50 |
| M | 0.51 | −2.50 |
| F | 0.23 | 1.00 |
| M | 0.23 | 4.50 |
| F | 0.12 | −7.00 |
| M | 0.03 | 2.50 |
| M | 0.00 | 8.50 |
| M | −0.01 | −2.75 |
| F | −0.13 | −1.00 |
| M | −0.33 | 1.50 |
| F | −0.45 | 3.50 |
| F | −1.26 | 3.00 |
| F | −1.94 | 3.50 |
| F | −2.16 | 3.50 |
| M | −2.30 | 2.50 |
| Mean | 0.01 | 0.91 |
| SD | 1.22 | 3.75 |

Difference between means of social assets scale scores associated with highest $\frac{1}{3}$ and lowest $\frac{1}{3}$ hope scale difference scores (B–A) during hand-position B and A ($t = -2.21$; $N = 12$; $p < .05$; one-tail).

demonstrated with other groups of subjects,[9] including children ages 6–16 (hope × anxiety scores, $r = -0.46$, $N = 109$, $p < .001$; hope × hostility outward scores, $r = -0.45$, $N = 109$, $p < .001$) and adults (hope × anxiety scores, $r = -0.19$, $N = 91$, $p =$ NS; hope × hostility outward scores, $r = -0.26$, $N = 91$, $p < .05$). As might be expected, the hope scores produced under the conditions of the subjects' hands being at their sides correlated significantly positively ($r = 0.86$, $p < .001$) with the positive valence side of the object relations scale scores.

However, these significant correlations of hope scores with total anxiety, guilt anxiety, diffuse anxiety, hostility outward, and object relations scores all disappeared, that is, became *not* significant, when the subjects caressed their lips with a finger (hand-position B) while they gave speech samples.

### *Effect of Hand Position on Intercorrelations Between Object Relations Scale Scores and Affect Scores*

Object relations scores correlated significantly negatively with total anxiety scores ($r = -0.51$, $p < .02$) and hostility outward scores ($r = -0.48$, $p < .03$) from speech samples produced when the subjects held their hands at their side (hand-position A). When these same subjects were touching their lips (hand-position B), content analysis scores derived from speech samples given under this condition showed no correlation between object relations and total anxiety scores

and a significant negative correlation ($r = -0.52$, $p < .02$) between object relations and hostility outward scores.

*Effect of Hand Position on Object Relations Scale Scores*

Four of the subjects consistently (during both occasions) expressed more positive feelings associated with objects while lip stroking, and four other subjects consistently voiced more negative feelings, that is, lower object relations scores, while lip stroking. Three out of these four subjects with increased object relations scores during hand-position B also had more references to women during hand-position B than during hand-position A. These three subjects, one male and two females, had similar quantitative changes in their references to objects while lip stroking, as did the psychoanalytic patient studied by Gottschalk.[1] Three (all males) of the four subjects who had decreased object relations scores during lip stroking had fewer references to women during this hand position (B). No consistent intraindividual correlations occurred between hope scale scores and object relations scale scores; among the eight subjects noted above, four of these intercorrelations were positive and four were negative.

These findings indicate that the associations of more verbal references to women and/or the expression of more positive or fewer negative feelings to all objects when one's finger is stroking the lips are not unique to the psychoanalytic patient studied by Gottschalk and alluded to in the beginning of this paper.[1] But the present study also clearly demonstrates that hand–mouth activity may be consistently associated with fewer verbal references of these kinds of even with no consistent pattern of verbal behavior of these specific kinds.

Certainly, the present study, on the basis of its experimental design, indicates that the nature and location of hand activity can influence the expression of different speech contents in different individuals. So, the doubt we were left in with the Gottschalk psychoanalytic and natural history study[1] as to the cause-and-effect relationship of hand–mouth activity to specific speech and mental contents has been resolved by means of the present experimental study. We have demonstrated that certain specific hand–mouth activities can, indeed, evoke certain speech contents. Our present study, however, does not disprove that certain mental or speech contents may stimulate hand–mouth activity.

## RELATIONSHIP OF RESPONSES ON ORAL HISTORY QUESTIONNAIRE AND HOPE SCALE SCORES*

Some of the responses on the oral history questionnaire were found to be related to increases in hope scale scores under the conditions of the two hand posi-

*To determine possible relationships between hope scale scores and the kinds of answers on the oral history questionnaire, subjects' mean B-A scores were determined for each answer to each question.

T-tests were then determined between the mean B-A scores for each possible comparison. Those comparisons that had an answer with two or fewer responses were omitted.

To insure that the probability of obtaining a false positive result was not greater than .05 for any one question, the Scheffe technique[10] was used. There were no significant comparisons using the Scheffe technique. However, those comparisons that had significant t-tests are suggestive of areas where future research may be fruitful.

A word of caution: the Scheffe technique was used with answers for any one question and does not take into account the total number of questions on the questionnaire. When this study is replicated, we intend to examine those questions that showed interesting t-test scores in the present study.

Table 6. Mean Male and Female Content Category (Subscale) Scores for Condition A (Hands at Side)

| Sex N = 20 | | Hope Content Category Scores | | | | | | |
|---|---|---|---|---|---|---|---|---|
| | | H1 | H2 | H3 | H4 | H5 | H6 | H7 |
| Male | Mean | 0.50 | 0.48 | 0.05 | 0.06 | 0.07 | 0.46 | 0.26 |
| | SD | 0.29 | 0.40 | 0.08 | 0.08 | 0.10 | 0.27 | 0.22 |
| Female | Mean | 1.03 | 0.85 | 0.13 | 0.12 | 0.08 | 0.79 | 0.46 |
| | SD | 0.63 | 0.59 | 0.25 | 0.15 | 0.08 | 0.62 | 0.32 |
| | T-test and *p* Value | −2.42* | −1.64 | −0.97 | −1.13 | −0.25 | −1.54 | −1.63 |

$^*p < .05$ (two-tail).

Mean Male and Female Content Category (Subscale) Scores for Condition B (Hand Lightly Rubbing Lips)

| Sex N = 20 | | Hope Content Category Scores | | | | | | |
|---|---|---|---|---|---|---|---|---|
| | | H1 | H2 | H3 | H4 | H5 | H6 | H7 |
| Male | Mean | 0.77 | 0.60 | 0.09 | 0.05 | 0.22 | 0.49 | 0.39 |
| | SD | 0.32 | 0.39 | 0.12 | 0.06 | 0.24 | 0.50 | 0.38 |
| Female | Mean | 0.97 | 0.70 | 0.12 | 0.06 | 0.12 | 0.50 | 0.40 |
| | SD | 0.61 | 0.37 | 0.20 | 0.10 | 0.18 | 0.38 | 0.43 |
| | T-test and *p* Value | −0.92 | −0.59 | −0.41 | −0.28 | 1.05 | −0.05 | −0.06 |

tions. Because one might expect, by chance, that at least one of the 21 questions could show significant differences, these findings should be interpreted very cautiously and must be replicated.

*Question 1.* Subjects who said they were breast-fed in infancy had significantly greater increases (B-A) in hope scores when their hand was lightly rubbing their lips ($t = 2.27$, $N = 13$, $p < .05$, two-tail).

*Question 6.* Subjects who said they did not chew their fingernails had significantly higher increases in hope scale scores than subjects who reported chewing their fingernails a little ($t = -2.31$, $N = 13$, $p < .05$, two-tail).

*Question 12.* Subjects who reported *rarely getting cold or canker sores* in or around the mouth had greater increases in hope scores with hand–mouth touching (B-A) than those who said they got cold sores *once in a while* ($t = -2.17$, $N = 19$, $p < .05$, two-tail).

*Question 18.* Subjects who reported drinking *several times a week* had higher hope score increases with hand-position B than those who said they drank *only several times a month* ($t = 1.52$, $N = 7$, $p < .10$, one-tail).

### *Male and Female Differences*

No total hope-scale-score sexual differences occurred in this study with either hand position. Women made significantly more references than men ($t = -2.42$, $N = 20$, $p < .05$, two-tail) to the self or others getting or receiving help, advice, support, sustenance, confidence, esteem (hope scale content category H1) when their hands were at their sides (see Table 6). Otherwise, no significant sexual

differences in hope subscale content categories occurred with either of the two hand positions.

However, males had more references than females to food while they were lightly rubbing their lips than when their hands were at their sides ($t = -2.40$, $N = 20$, $p < .05$, two-tail). Females had significantly more references than males to food when their hands were at their sides ($t = 2.26$, $N = 20$, $p < .05$, two-tail).

There were significantly more oral anatomical references by both sexes during hand–mouth approximation than with hands at sides ($t = -2.20$, $N = 20$, $p < .05$, two-tail).

## DISCUSSION

### *Methodology*

The study of nonverbal behavior and the examination of what it communicates or what verbal behavior it substitutes for or any other ramifications of nonverbal behavior has been a shared research enterprise of dancers, choreographers, actors, linguists, anthropologists, behavioral scientists, mental health professionals, and many others. The methodological approaches to the study of kinesics, that is, nonverbal behavior, by the different disciplines vary quite widely, and when the disciplines are committed to the stringent use of the scientific method, those workers persevering with such constraints almost invariably choose the natural science method over the experimental method. An elegant example of the natural science approach applied to studies of kinesics, as these relate to paralanguage and semantic channels of communications, is the work of Scheflen.[11] The work of Norbert Freedman and his co-workers[12,13] also deserves recognition as sophisticated natural science research in this area. Experimental studies, involving manipulation of independent variables, such as total body, face, or extremity movements, while dependent variables, such as speech content, other behavioral or physiological variables, are observed, have been avoided, possibly because such studies may be considered by the naturalists as "artificial" (which natural scientists would generally say about any experimental studies involving behavior) or because the methodological and theoretical problems using the experimental method seem too formidable to researchers interested in nonverbal behavior.

In any event, the present work is somewhat of a novelty. Depending upon the reader's disciplinary and scientific persuasion, the results may seem disappointing and limited to some and exciting and of heuristic value to others.

Psychiatric and psychoanalytic research within the treatment situation has been more noted for its hypothesis-generating results than its well-validated hypothesis-testing achievements. The inclination of the scientist-therapist who works in both the fields of psychotherapy and behavioral science has been to generate hypotheses from the psychotherapeutic situation and to test these hypotheses carefully and experimentally outside of the treatment situation, in other settings than those in which the original empirical data was observed. The present study is an example of this latter kind of research. How complex the relationships of mental and speech content with past history and with changes in hand position are, however, well-illustrated in the present study. Clinicians and behavioral scientists should take note of the capacity of lip stroking to break up

significant intercorrelations between hope, object relations, anxiety, and hostility outward scores prevailing with hand positions alongside the body. Certainly, the findings we are reporting here strongly support the clinical viewpoint that kinesic activity cannot be ignored in following and assessing psychodynamic and psychoeconomic changes during the psychotherapeutic interview.

*Other Possible Analyzable Speech-Content*

Hope scale, object relations scale, anxiety, and hostility outward speech content, as well as oral and nasal references were examined as dependent variables in the present study. Many, many other speech-content variables might have been analyzed and will be analyzed in the future. It is probably safe to assume that such hand–mouth activities as described herein influence other mental content and, hence, speech content, than that described here. We were interested in the specific dependent variables studied here because we were curious about and interested in determining the extent to which a specific type of nonverbal activity can influence object references and the valence of feelings expressed towards these objects, attitudes of hope, optimism, and references to oral activities or anatomical parts. We also wanted to learn more about the effect of an individual's past history, particularly with respect to past nurturance and oral stimulation and habits, on the dependent variables studied. Our findings in the present paper do, indeed, indicate that there are specific influences on the form and content of speech resulting from hand–mouth touching, and it is likely that there are many more influences on verbal behavior content and form which we have not yet explored.

*The Importance of an Individual's Past History on Current Content of Speech*

Summarizing our findings with respect to the influence of a person's past history on current speech content and the susceptibility of a person's expression of specific changes in speech content in response to specific kinds of nonverbal behavior, our study suggests fascinating relationships between past experience and present behavioral manifestations. When subjects fingered their lips, there was more likely to be an increase in hope scores if: (1) the subjects had lower social assets scale scores, (2) they had been breast fed, (3) they did not chew their fingernails, (4) they rarely got cold or canker sores around the mouth, and (5) they drank alcohol several times a week instead of several times a month. These findings suggest that college students with lower social assets (made up of the ingredients of the Luborsky Social Assets Scale), with minimal psychological or biological deterrents to pleasurable oral stimulation, expressed more hope when they publicly caressed their lips than individuals who do not have these traits or experiences. In all individuals, lip caressing evoked more verbal references to not wanting to be the recipient of good fortune, luck, or God's blessing or favor, and stimulated more oral-anatomical references and, by males, more references to food. It is, frankly, difficult to locate a single hypothesis explaining these findings, and it is likely that there is none. It is unnecessarily speculative to try to pin down explanations for these relationships, for we really do not have enough details about each individual subject's life history. We do intend to examine whether there are any specific patterns of associated responses to specific items from the

social assets scale, such as early parent loss, parental chronic illness, parental rejection, and so forth, which account primarily for the observed relationships between social asset scale scores and the kinds of responses subjects had to lip touching.

Freedman et al.[12,14] distinguished between object-focused and body-focused movements of the hands; object-focused hand movements are movements or gestures which involve or point to objects external to the speaker and are associated with increased Gottschalk–Gleser overt hostility outward speech-content analysis scores; whereas, body-focused hand movements do not tend to be temporally related to specific verbalizations, but they are associated with increased covert hostility outward speech-content analysis scores. The hand–mouth hand movements studied here would fall into the classification of body-focused hand movements described in the study by Freedman and his co-workers. We have not yet examined whether, in the experimental situation we have studied, there is relatively increased covert hostility outward during hand–mouth movements. Since Freedman's group was studying individuals in a natural history situation, findings in an experimental situation such as ours may be dissimilar from his.

Does hand–lips touching enhance an individual's sense of security, feeling of optimism, and hope? Or does such activity in experimental situations mobilize super-ego and ego-ideal constraints and inhibitions against openly and publicly indulging in oral pleasures and, hence, evoke decreased hope scores, at least in one hope subscale, namely, in the form of increased expressions of not wanting to be favored, blessed, or rewarded? The latter seems to be a possibility, as adjudged from our findings, but the more our subjects had a history of some psychosocial deprivation, the more likely any sense of shame or embarrassment attendant to hand–lip activities seemed to be overcome, perhaps by lingering unfulfilled needs. In further examination of our data, we will explore whether or not shame anxiety or other anxiety-content analysis scores are influenced by the hand–mouth activity.

In closing, we say that our intent is to do further studies of this sort, and with more data, we feel sure we can obtain more specific conclusions.

## ACKNOWLEDGMENT

The authors wish to thank Herman Birch, Ph.D., who provided statistical consultation and Julia Hoigaard, A.B., who provided technical assistance.

## REFERENCES

1. Gottschalk LA: The psychoanalytic study of hand-mouth approximations, in Goldberger L (ed): Psychoanalysis and Contemporary Science, vol 3. New York, International Universities Press, 1974

2. Gottschalk LA, Hambidge G Jr: Verbal behavior analysis: A systematic approach to the problem of quantifying psychological processes. J Proj Tech 19:387–409, 1955

3. Gottschalk LA, Gleser GC: The Measurement of Psychological States Through the Content Analysis of Verbal Behavior. Berkeley, University of California Press, 1969

4. Luborsky L, Todd TC, Katcher AN: A self-administered social assets scale for predicting physical and psychological illness and health. J Psychosom Res 17:109–120, 1973

5. Overall JE, Gorham DP: The brief psychiatric rating scale (BPRS). Psychol Rep 10:799–812, 1962

6. Guy W, Bonato RR: Manual for the ECDEU Assessment Battery, (sec rev). Chevy Chase, Md., NIMH, USDHEW, 1970

7. Gottschalk, LA, Biener R, Bates D, et al: Depression, hope, and social assets. 1974 (unpublished study)

8. Gottschalk LA, Biener R, Noble EP, et al: Thioridazine plasma levels and clinical response. Compr Psychiatry 16:323-337, 1975

9. Gottschalk LA: A hope scale applicable to verbal samples. Arch Gen Psychiatry 30:779-785, 1974

10. Myers JL: Fundamentals of Experimental Design (ed 1). Boston, Allyn and Bacon, 1966

11. Scheflen A: Natural history method in psychotherapy: Communicational research, in Gottschalk LA, Auerbach AH (eds): Methods of Research in Psychotherapy. New York, Appleton-Century-Crofts, 1966

12. Freedman N, O'Hanlon J, Oltman P, et al: The imprint of psychological differentiation on kinetic behavior in varying communicative contexts. J Abnorm Psychol 79:239-258, 1972

13. Grand S, Freedman N, Steingart I: A study of the representation of objects in schizophrenia. J Am Psychoanal Assoc 21:399-434, 1973

14. Freedman N, Blass T, Rifkin A, et al: Body movements and the verbal encoding of aggressive affect. J Pers Soc Psychol 23:72-85, 1973

# APPENDIX

## SCHEDULE 1
## SOCIAL ASSETS SCALE*
## SCORING WEIGHTS FOR SOCIAL INFORMATION FORM

*Occupation*

2.0 professional—executive
1.0 proprietor—small business
0.5 white-collar worker
0.5 student
0.0 blue-collar (skilled worker)
0.0 retired
0.0 housewife
−1.0 unskilled laborer
−2.0 unemployed

Husband's or wife's occupation scored same as above.

Father's and mother's occupation scored same as above (previously scored father's occupation for subjects under 21 and omitted mother's occupation).

*Sex (included in revised scale, but not scored)*

0.0 male
0.0 female

*Race*

0.0 white
−1.5 black
−1.0 Oriental
−1.0 American Indian
−1.0 other

*Religious preference (included in revised scale, but not scored)*

0.0 Protestant
0.0 Catholic
−1.0 Jewish
−0.5 Other
0.0 None

*Present marital status*

| student | | nonstudent |
|---|---|---|
| 0.0 | married, never divorced, separated, or widowed | 1.0 |
| −1.0 | married, previous divorce, separation, or death of spouse | 0.0 |
| −1.0 | divorced, separated, or widowed | −1.0 |
| 0.0 | never married | −1.0 |

*Home*

1.0 living with spouse and children
0.5 living with spouse, no children
−0.5 living with children or family (no husband or wife)
0.0 living alone
0.0 living with each other

*From Luborsky et al, 1973.

*Education*

| | | | |
|---|---|---|---|
| 2.0 | graduate degree | −1.0 | some high school |
| 1.5 | some graduate school | −1.5 | finished grade school |
| 1.0 | college graduate | −2.5 | some grade school |
| 0.5 | some college | −3.0 | no grade school |
| 0.0 | high school graduate | | |

(Father's and mother's education scored same as above. Added to revised scale.)

*School record*

| | | | |
|---|---|---|---|
| 1.5 | excellent | −1.0 | barely passed |
| 1.0 | good | −2.0 | frequent failure |
| 0.0 | fair | | |

*Times moved within the last year*

| | | | |
|---|---|---|---|
| 0.0 | have not moved | −2.0 | 5 times |
| 0.0 | 1 time | −2.0 | 6 times |
| −0.5 | 2 times | −2.5 | 7 times |
| −1.5 | 3 times | −2.5 | 8 times |
| −2.0 | 4 times | −2.5 | 9 times or more |

*Birthplace (dropped from revised scale)*

0.0 U.S.A. −1.0 Foreign

Father's birthplace scored same as birthplace (dropped from revised scale).
Mother's birthplace scored same as birthplace (dropped from revised scale).

| Mother | | Father |
|---|---|---|
| 0.0 | living | 0.0 |
| 0.0 | died when I was over 20-yr-old | 0.0 |
| −1.0 | died when I was 16–20-yr-old | −1.0 |
| −1.5 | died when I was 10–15-yr-old | −1.0 |
| −2.0 | died when I was 6–9-yr-old | −2.0 |
| −2.5 | died before I was 6-yr-old | −2.9 |

*Parents' marital status*

| | |
|---|---|
| 0.5 | yes } my parents are living together (do not score "no" if one of the following items is scored). |
| −1.0 | no } |
| −0.5 | my parents were separated when I was over 20-yr-old |
| −1.0 | my parents were separated when I was 16–20-yr-old |
| −1.0 | my parents were separated when I was 10–15-yr-old |
| −2.0 | my parents were separated when I was 6–9-yr-old |
| −2.0 | my parents were separated before I was 6-yr-old |

*Health in early childhood*

1.0 good 0.0 fair −2.0 poor

*When you were growing up, did your parents have trouble finding money for necessities?*

−2.0 often −1.0 sometimes 0.0 rarely

*When you were growing up, did your mother have to work outside of the home to earn money?*

−1.0 yes 0.0 no

*Did your father or mother ever have the following illnesses?*

−1.0 for each illness circled; 0.0 for those not circled.

arthritis, asthma, bladder trouble, colitis, diabetes, hay fever, heart condition, high blood pressure, neuralgia or sciatica, nervous breakdown, epilepsy, stomach trouble, skin condition.

*When you were growing up, were either of your parents in poor health?*

| | | | |
|---|---|---|---|
| −2.0 | all of the time | 0.0 | rarely |
| −1.0 | frequently | 0.5 | never |

*When you were growing up, did your parents quarrel?*

| | | | |
|---|---|---|---|
| −2.0 | all of the time | 0.0 | rarely |
| −1.0 | frequently | 0.0 | never |

*Thinking back to the time when you were growing up, did you ever feel that*

- −1.0 father spends too little time with me
- −1.0 mother wants to run her children's lives
- −1.0 mother does not understand me
- 1.0 my parents are always proud of their children

*Job history (on revised scale, students fill out on basis of father's employment; married women on basis of husband's employment)*

| Students male | Students female | | Nonstudents male | Nonstudents female |
|---|---|---|---|---|
| 1.0 | 1.0 | I was employed continuously at the same position for the last 2 yr | 1.0 | 1.0 |
| 1.0 | 1.0 | I was employed continuously during the past 2 yr, but my place of employment changed | 1.0 | 1.0 |
| 0.0 | 0.0 | I was out of work sometimes for the past 2 yr. | −1.0 | 0.0 |
| 0.0 | 0.0 | I was unemployed in the past 2 yr. | −2.0 | 0.0 |

*I was born in*

- 0.0 a big city
- 0.0 a small city (like Camden or Wilmington).
- 0.0 a small town
- −1.0 a farm or rural area

*Church attendance (dropped from revised scale)*

- 0.5 I attend church regularly and am active in church work.
- 0.5 I attend church regularly but am inactive in church work.
- 0.0 I attend church sometimes.
- 0.0 I never attend church.

*Social group membership (dropped from revised scale)*

- 1.0 I am active in one or more social groups
- 0.0 I am not very active
- −0.5 I belong to no social groups

*Friends*

- 0.5 I have many close friends
- 0.5 I have some close friends
- 0.5 I have only a few close friends
- −2.0 I have no friends

*Number of children (count total number)*

| Student | | Nonstudent |
|---|---|---|
| 0.0 | None | −1.0 |
| 0.0 | 1 | 0.5 |
| −0.5 | 2–3 | 0.0 |
| −1.5 | 4–5 | 0.0 |
| −3.0 | 5 or more | −1.5 |

*Home ownership (on revised form, students fill out on basis of family of origin)*

- 1.0 I own my own home
- 0.0 I rent my home

*Automobile (on revised form, students fill out on basis of family of origin)*

- 0.0 there is an automobile available for family use
- −1.0 there is no automobile available

*Television (on revised form, students fill out on basis of family of origin)*

- 0.0 we have a television at home
- −1.0 we have no television at home

*Physical condition*

- 1.5 my physical health is usually very good
- 1.0 my physical health is usually good
- 0.0 I am occasionally ill
- −1.0 I am frequently ill
- −2.0 I am chronically ill

*Cigarette smoking*

- 0.0 I do not smoke
- −0.5 I smoke 5–10 cigarettes per day

−0.5 I smoke 11–20 cigarettes per day
−2.0 I smoke 1 pack a day
−2.0 I smoke 20–30 cigarettes per day
−2.5 I smoked 2 packs or more in the past 2 days

*Were you disabled by illness or accident?*
0.0 for periods of less than 1 wk
−0.5 for periods of less than 1 mo
−1.5 for as long as 6 wk
−2.5 continuously

*If unmarried, are you:*
1.0 engaged
1.0 going steady
0.5 dating several (men, women) frequently
−1.0 dating several (men, women) infrequently
−1.5 no dating

*Interests including work (added to revised scale)*
2.0 I have several major interests which are consistently absorbing and extremely gratifying.
1.0 I have a number of interests which are usually interesting and enjoyable.
0.0 I have one major interest which is usually absorbing and satisfying.
0.0 I have a number of interests which occupy me from time to time, with a good deal of shifting from one area to another.
−1.0 I find it difficult to maintain an interest in anything for an extended period of time.

## SCHEDULE 2
## QUESTIONNAIRE REGARDING ORAL HISTORY

NAME ________________ DATE ________________

1. Do you know whether you were bottle or breast fed as an infant?
   A. ________ Breast
   B. ________ Bottle
   C. ________ Both breast and bottle
   D. ________ Don't know
2. How long were you on the breast and/or bottle?
   ________ 0–3 mo
   ________ 4–8 mo
   ________ 9–12 mo
   ________ 13–18 mo
   ________ 19–23 mo
   ________ 24 or more
3. Have you had any dental or gum problems?
   ________ When?
   ________ What kind? (Please mention specifically)
4. Have you had any oral injuries, blemishes, diseases, or oral surgery? ________ Yes ________ No
   ________ When?
   ________ What kind?
5. When you're nervous do you tend to eat?
   ________ More?
   ________ Less?
   ________ Eating habits do not change
6. Did you ever chew your finger nails? ________ Yes ________ No
   ________ Often
   ________ Little
   ________ Not at all

7. Do you still bite your nails? _______ Yes _______ No
   _______ Often
   _______ Little
   _______ Not at all
8. Do you chew pencils or toothpicks?
   _______ Often
   _______ Little
   _______ Not at all
9. Do you have difficulty talking freely with (please circle)
   Friends, Parents, Students, Teachers, Employers, Intimates?
10. Did you ever stutter or stammer? _______ Yes _______ No
   If so, was it
   _______ Mild
   _______ Moderate
   _______ Severe
11. Do you like tart foods as much as sweet flavored ones?
   _______ Yes
   _______ No
12. Do you get a lot of cold sores or canker sores in or around the mouth?
   _______ Rarely
   _______ Once in a while
   _______ Often
13. Do you smoke cigarettes, cigars, or a pipe? (circle which one)
   _______ Yes
   _______ No
14. If you do smoke, how often?
   _______ Daily
   _______ Weekly
   _______ Monthly
   _______ Not at all
15. Do you chew tobacco? _______ Yes _______ No
   _______ Often
   _______ Little
   _______ Not at all
16. Do you smoke marijuana? _______ Yes _______ No
17. How often have you used marijuana in the past 12 mo?
   _______ Not at all
   _______ Daily
   _______ Several times a wk
   _______ Several times a mo
   _______ About once a mo
   _______ Less than once a mo
18. How often have you used alcohol in the past 12 mo?
   _______ Not at all
   _______ Daily
   _______ Several times a wk
   _______ Several times a mo
   _______ Once a mo
   _______ Less than once a mo
19. Do you usually drink
   _______ Wine
   _______ Beer
   _______ Whiskey
   _______ Gin
   _______ Other

20. On the average, how many drinks do you have when you drink?
 ________ One
 ________ Two
 ________ Three
 ________ Four
 ________ More than four
21. When you're nervous, do you tend to smoke
 ________ More
 ________ Less
 ________ Not at all
22. Do you have any other oral habits, problems, difficulties, or taboos that have not been mentioned so far? ________ Yes ________ No
 Please specify ______________________________________________

## SCHEDULE 3
## HOPE SCALE

| Weights | | Content Categories and Coding Symbols |
|---|---|---|
| +1 | H1 | References to self or others getting or receiving help, advice, support, sustenance, confidence, esteem (A) from others (B) from self. |
| +1 | H2 | Reference to feelings of optimism about the past, present, or future, (A) others (B) self. |
| +1 | H3 | References to being or wanting to be or seeking to be the recipient of good fortune, good luck, God's favor or blessing, (A) others (B) self. |
| +1 | H4 | References to any kinds of hopes that lead to a constructive outcome, to survival, to longevity, to smooth-going interpersonal relationships. (This category can be scored only if the word "hope" or "wish" or a close synonym is used.) |
| −1 | H5 | References to not being or not wanting to be or not seeking to be the recipient of good fortune, good luck, God's favor or blessing. |
| −1 | H6 | References to self or others not getting or receiving help, advice, support, sustenance, confidence, esteem, (A) from others (B) from self. |
| −1 | H7 | References to feelings of hopelessness, losing hope, despair, lack of confidence, lack of ambition, lack of interest, feelings of pessimism, discouragement, (A) others (B) self. |

## SCHEDULE 4
## OBJECT-RELATIONS SCALE

| | |
|---|---|
| O | Other(s), sex unspecified, in unspecified or neutral relationship(s) |
| O+ | Other(s), sex unspecified, in pleasant, gratifying, affectionate relationship(s) |
| O− | Other(s), sex unspecified, in unpleasant, ungratifying, frustrating relationship(s) |
| Oh | Other(s), sex unspecified, in hateful relationship(s) |
| S | Self, in unspecified or neutral relationship(s) |
| S+ | Self, in pleasant, gratifying, affectionate relationship(s) |
| S− | Self, in unpleasant, ungratifying, frustrating relationship(s) |
| Sh | Self, in hateful relationship(s) |
| F | Female(s), in unspecified or neutral relationship(s) |
| F+ | Female(s), in pleasant, gratifying, affectionate relationship(s) |
| F− | Female(s), in unpleasant, ungratifying, frustrating relationship(s) |
| Fh | Female(s), in hateful relationship(s) |

| | |
|---|---|
| M | Male(s), in unspecified or neutral relationship(s) |
| M+ | Male(s), in pleasant, gratifying, affectionate relationship(s) |
| M− | Male(s), in unpleasant, ungratifying, frustrating relationship(s) |
| Mh | Male(s), in hateful relationship(s) |
| I | Inanimate object(s), in unspecified or neutral relationship(s) |
| I+ | Inanimate object(s), in pleasant, gratifying, affectionate relationship(s) |
| I− | Inanimate object(s), in unpleasant, ungratifying, frustrating relationship(s) |
| Ih | Inanimate object(s), in hateful relationship(s) |
| A | Animate (subhuman) object(s), in unspecified or neutral relationship(s) |
| A+ | Animate (subhuman) object(s), in pleasant, gratifying, affectionate relationship(s) |
| A− | Animate (subhuman) object(s), in unpleasant, ungratifying, frustrating relationship(s) |
| Ah | Animate (subhuman) object(s), in hateful relationship(s) |

### *Rules for Object-Relations Scale*

(1) Score as many object–relations events as occur, according to the above categories, per grammatical clause.

(2) Whenever combinations of the above object–relations content categories occur, score these as combinations by connecting different object–relations notations with a plus sign. For example, female, self, interacting with others pleasantly = $F_+ + S_+ + O_+$; or male, self, liking female, but disliking inanimate object = $M_+ + S_+ + F_+ I_-$.

## SCHEDULE 5
## CLASSIFICATION OF ORONASAL FUNCTIONS AND ACTIVITIES

A. Oral functions and activities
B. Oral anatomical references
C. Nonfood objects or substances placed on lips or in mouth
D. Food references and references to other substances ingested
E. Speech references
F. Oral diseases
G. Words referring to taste, appetite, smells, hunger, thirst
H. Nasal functions and activities
I. Nasal anatomical references

# Part VII

# Papers on Psychotherapy

The first chapter (45) of this series is a review of some possible applications of content analysis to research in psychotherapy, and it is entitled "The application of a method of content analysis to psychotherapy research" (Gottschalk, 1974). Another paper on psychotherapy research by Gottschalk et al (1973), Chapter 46, is entitled "A study of prediction and outcome in a Mental Health Crisis Clinic." Then a series of papers by other authors follow. These include a chapter (47) entitled "Using content analysis to explore shame, guilt, and neurosis" (Lewis, 1977), which is previously unpublished and for which a separate commentary has been prepared. Another original and previously unpublished paper on psychotherapy research (Chapter 48) is entitled "Possible applications of the Gottschalk-Gleser content analysis of speech in psychotherapy research" (Schöfer et al, 1977); this paper is one of three papers in this volume by a group of German investigators from the University of Hamburg, and it is introduced by a separate commentary. A final paper in this section deals more with the application of content analysis to the teaching of psychotherapy than psychotherapy research. As Chapter 49, it is entitled "The teaching of psychotherapy by use of brief typescripts" (Kepecs, 1977).

# FURTHER STUDIES ON THE RELATIONSHIP OF NON-VERBAL TO VERBAL BEHAVIOR: EFFECT OF LIP CARESSING ON SHAME, HOSTILITY, AND OTHER VARIABLES AS EXPRESSED IN THE CONTENT OF SPEECH

Louis A. Gottschalk and Regina L. Uliana*

## INTRODUCTION

This study grew out of a psychoanalytic therapeutic investigation in which a patient's speech was recorded before and after he periodically touched different parts of his body. Two types of observations were made during this psychoanalysis on these psychokinetic sequences; (1) impressionistic evaluations of the relationships between hand movements and the content of free-associations, and (2) independent and objective scoring of the content of speech and its statistical relationship to hand movements and placements. These two types of assessment of the data of observation gave results which supplemented one another, the former method allowing more broad generalizations but less certainty and the latter method enabling more specific evaluations and greater potential for statistical assessment of probabilities.

Some of the main observations noted by the impressionistic method were as follows.

1. If the analysand moved his hands, he generally touched a part of his anatomy related to a psychological or biological function he was experiencing or describing. The relationship of the hand activity and position to the content of his speech could be very concrete or symbolic.

---

[1]From the Department of Psychiatry and Human Behavior, College of Medicine, University of California at Irvine, California 92717. Herman Birch, Ph.D., provided statistical consultation.

2. Hand movements around his mouth or lips tended to be associated with talking about women, a longing for the breast or for the whole body or to be part of a woman, in a sexual or nonsexual context. These associations tended to be affectionate or positive rather than negative.

3. Touching his eyelids was often related to talking about seeing or understanding.

4. Touching his abdomen was often associated with thoughts about the vagina and sexual intercourse.

5. Touching his nose was associated with sexual interest in forbidden women, diarrhea, or disliked women.

6. These psychokinetic relationships remained fairly stable and unchanging without specific analytic intervention. They could be altered, however, by interpretive comments or, sometimes, by simply calling the patient's attention to specific hand movements and thought contents.

The more objective method of content analysis provided statistically significant evidence that the analysand spoke more frequently of women and expressed positive feelings toward all objects (animate and inanimate) when he was touching his oronasal areas as compared to when his hands were at his side (Gottschalk, 1974).

In this natural history study, where the hand-mouth activity appeared spontaneously during the psychoanalytic situation and where the hand movements around the oronasal area served a soothing function leading to a temporary feeling of security and the capacity to feel separate and autonomous from the analyst, there was of course no information enabling one to generalize how commonly such hand-mouth activity might evoke such specific speech content in others. Also, except for the inferences one might make on the basis of temporal relationships, it could not be determined whether the hand-mouth contact did, indeed, evoke certain memories and thoughts and, hence, such speech content or whether this directly observable and recordable speech content and its underlying unrecordable associated mental content caused the hand-mouth activity.

One approach to exploring the cause and effect aspects of such kinesic-semantic relationships was considered to be an experimental study with a group of individuals, in which the hand-mouth activity would be systematically alternated with a hand position away from the face. On a broader basis, such an experimental method, in contrast to the natural history method, was seen as a means of exploring the ways in which such kinesic activity would affect speech content and of contributing to our understanding of the interplay of early life experiences and object relations on mental content.

## METHODS AND PROCEDURES

*Subjects.* Twenty college students, 10 males and 10 females, with a mean age of 21.45 were paid volunteers for this study. Only those subjects who

reported, during an initial interview, that they were in good general health and that they had not taken any drugs, for example, depressants or psychoactive drugs, during the preceeding month were allowed to participate in the study. Furthermore, because the use of birth control pills has been demonstrated to influence speech content (Silbergeld et al, 1971), although the phases of the menstrual cycle can also do so (Gottschalk et al, 1962, Ivey and Bardwick, 1968), only women who were not taking such hormones were offered the possibility of participating in the study.

*Procedure.* Each subject gave 4 five-minute speech samples, in the presence of one of the authors (RU). Each five-minute period of speech was accompanied by either hand-position A (hands at one's side) or hand-position B (one hand caressing one's lips), balanced for both men and women in wither the sequence ABBA or BAAB to control for possible order effects. The speech was elicited by asking each subject to talk for 5 minutes about any interesting or dramatic life experiences following standardized instructions used previously in many investigations of content analysis of speech (Gottschalk and Hambidge, 1955; Gottschalk and Gleser, 1969). Speech samples were tape-recorded in full view of the subjects, and these tapes were later transcribed.

After giving the 4 five-minute speech samples, each subject completed the following measures:

1. The Luborsky et al (1973) Social Assets Scale, which is a self-report procedure constructed of 33 weighted items relating to an individual's pscycho-social background, including details of parent-child relations, parent loss, sibship, educational level and so forth (See Schedule 1). The composite score from this measure is called a "social assets" scale score, and this measure has been found valuable in predicting improvement from brief psychiatric hospitalization and the frequency of episodes and severity of certain specific illnesses (herpes simplex, arthritis). This social assets scale score, in 25 acute schizophrenic patients, was significantly negatively correlated ($r = -0.46, p < .01$) before treatment with a major tranquilizer with social alienation-personal disorganization content analysis scores (a measure of the relative severity of the schizophreic syndrome derived from the content analysis of speech, (Gottschalk and Gleser, 1969), with the Anergia Factor ($r = -0.59$, $p < .005$) of the Overall Gorham Brief Psychiatric Rating Scale (1962), and the Apathy Factor ($r = -0.46, p < .05$) of the Hamilton Depression Scale (Guy and Bonato, 1970). The predrug social assets scores were also significantly correlated with various other measures from these patients 2 days after a single oral dose of thioridazine (4 mg/kg) (Gottschalk et al, 1974, 1975). (See Table 1)

2. A questionnaire designed by the authors, composed of 22 questions about various aspects of the subjects' history of oral activities (see schedule 2).

The typescripts of the speech samples were then content analyzed, without the content analysis technician knowing the hand position with which the speech sample was associated, for the dependent variables of this study:

a. Hope scale scores (Gottschalk and Gleser, 1969; Gottschalk, 1974),

Table 1

Correlations of Social Assets Scale Scores (Luborsky) and Various Behavioral and Psychological Measures Before (days 1, 3, and 6) and After (day 8) Thioridazine (4mg/kg) by Mouth in Acute Schizophrenic Patients (N = 25)

| Behavioral or Psychological Measure | Social Assets Scale (Luborsky) | | | |
|---|---|---|---|---|
| BPRS | Day 1 | Day 3 | Day 6 | Day 8 |
| 1. Depression | | | | -0.45* |
| 2. Thinking Disorder | | | | |
| 3. Anergia | -0.54** | -0.64**** | -0.59*** | -0.37 |
| 4. Excitement-Disorientation | | | | -.56*** |
| Hamilton Depression Scale | | | | |
| 1. Sleep Disturbance | | | | |
| 2. Somatization | -0.37 | -0.47* | -0.31 | -0.44* |
| 3. Anxiety Depression | | | | |
| 4. Apathy | -0.28 | -0.37 | -0.45* | -0.23 |
| Wittenborn Scale | | | | |
| 1. Anxiety | | | | |
| 2. Somatic-Hysterical | -0.36 | -0.36 | -0.16 | -0.42* |
| 3. Compulsive-Phobic | | | | -0.37 |
| 4. Retardation | -0.40* | -0.33 | -0.37 | -0.45* |
| 5. Excitement | | | | -0.45* |
| 6. Paranoia | | | | |
| Social Alienation-Personal Disorganization Scale | | | -0.46* | -.53** |

*p .05
**p .01
***p .005
****p .001

which are derived from a verbal content analysis scale composed of 7 content categories (4 weighted positively and 3 weighted negatively) counted for their frequency of occurrence within each grammatical clause of verbal communication. This scale was devised to measure the intensity of the optimism that a favorable outcome is likely to occur, not only in one's personal earthly activities, but also in cosmic phenomena and even in spiritual or imaginary events. The total hope scale score is arrived at by summating the weights of all relevant hope content categories used per speech sample and expressing this raw score in terms of a corrected score per 100 words spoken, so that these scores can be compared within an individual over different occasions and between individuals, regardless of the total number of words spoken during the five minutes of speech (See Schedule 3 for the Hope Scale).

b. Hostility scale scores (Gottschalk et al, 1963; Gottschalk and Gleser, 1969). (See Schedule 4). These are validated content analysis scales covering three types of conscious and preconscious hostility: hostility outward, overt and covert; hostility inward, and ambivalent hostility.

c. Anxiety scale scores (Gottschalk et al, 1961; Gleser et al, 1961; Gottschalk and Gleser, 1969). (See Schedule 5). These are validated content analysis scales covering conscious and preconscious total anxiety with six anxiety subscales: death anxiety, mutilation anxiety, separation anxiety, guilt anxiety, shame anxiety, and diffuse anxiety.

d. Object Relations Scale (Gottschalk, 1974), which classifies each reference to "objects" for references to females, males, sexually unspecified humans, inanimate objects, and for the expression of positive and negative feelings toward any object (Schedule 6).

e. Oral references occurring in the speech samples (See Schedule 7 for the classification of Oral References).

In a previous report (Gottschalk and Uliana, 1976), we described and discussed our initial findings in this psychokinesic study, and we will summarize them here.

1. Subjects, on the average, spoke significantly fewer words ($t = 2.14$, $p < .05$) during the five minute period when they caressed their lips than when they kept their hands at their sides.

2. There were more verbal references per 100 words during lip caressing ($t = -1.84$, $N = 20$, $p < .08$, two-tail test) to *not* being or *not* wanting to be or *not* seeking to be the recipient of good fortune, good luck, or God's favor or blessing (Hope scale content category No. 5).

3. In line with a prestudy hypothesis, the group of subjects with lower social assets scale scores (lower 1/3) tended to have greater increases in hope scores (B-A) while touching their lips ($t = -1.84$, $N = 12$, $p < .05$, one-tail) than the group with the higher (higher 1/3) social assets scale scores. Likewise, the subjects who had the greater increases in total hope scores during hand-mouth

approximation, as compared to when their hands were at their sides, tended to be those subjects who had the lower social assets scale scores ($t = -2.21$, $N - 12$, $p <$ .05, one tail).

4. When the subjects had their hands at their sides (position A), significant negative correlations of their hope scale scores occurred with total anxiety ($r = -0.64$, $p < .002$),guilt anxiety ($r = =0.67+$ $p < .001$)+ diffuse anxiety ($r = -0.62$, $p <$ .003), total hostility outward ($r = -0.55$, $p < .01$), and overt hostility outward scores ($r = -0.51$, $p < .02$). Significant positive correlations occurred between their hope scale scores and object relations scores ($r = -0.86$, $p < .001$) while their hands were at their sides. When these subjects changed their hand position and caressed their lips with a finger (position B), all these significant correlations disappeared, that is , became non-significant, except for the negative correlation between hope and overt hostility outward ($r = -0.45$, $p < .05$).

5. When the subjects held their hands at their sides (position A), their object relations scale scores correlated significantly negatively with total anxiety scores ($r = -0.51$, $p < .02$) and guilt anxiety scores ($r = -0.51$, $p < .02$). When these same subjects fingered their lips (position B), no correlations occurred between object relation and total anxiety scores ($r = -0.06$) or guilt anxiety scores ($r = 0.06$).

6. Four of the subjects consistently made a preponderance of references to objects of all kinds (animate and inanimate) associated with positive affects while fingering their lips ($0.91 \pm 0.33$), and four other subjects consistently voiced more negative feelings ($0.37 \pm 0.18$; $t = 5.14$, $p < .02$) associated with verbal references to objects while lip stroking. Three out of four subjects with increased object relations scores during lip stroking (hand position B) also had more references to women during hand position B than during hand position A. These three subjects, one male and two females, had similar quantitative changes in their references to objects while lip stroking as did the psychoanalytic patient studied by Gottschalk (1974). Three (all males) of the four subjects who had decreased object relations score during lip stroking had fewer references to women during this hand position (B).

7. *Male-female differences.* Women made significantly more verbal references than men ($t = -2.42$, $N = 20$, $p < .05$, two-tail)to the self or others getting or receiving help, advice, support, sustenance, confidence, esteem (Hope Scale content category H-1) when their hands were at their sides. Males had more references to food than females while they were lightly rubbing their lips ($t = -2.40$, $N = 20$, $p < .05$, two-tale). Females had significantly more references than males to food when their hands were at their sides ($t = 2{,}26$, $N = 20$, $p < .05$). Finally, there were significantly more oral anatomical references by both sexes during hand-mouth approximation than with hands at sides ($t = -2.20$, $N = 20$, $p <$ .05, two-tail).

8. There was more likely to be an increase in hope scale scores when subject fingered their lips if:

a. the subjects had lower Social Assets scale scores;
b. they had been breast fed;
c. they did not chew their fingernails;
d. they rarely got cold or canker sores around the mouth.

*Additional Results*. Further analysis of data obtained in our study of 20 subjects, 10 males and 10 females, has revealed the following additional, heretofore unpublished, findings.

## RELATIONSHIP BETWEEN HOSTILITY OUTWARD SCORES AND HAND ACTIVITY

Freedman et al (1972, 1973), doing natural and non-experimental studies, noted that hand movements involving the body (body-focused hand movements) were associated with increased covert hostility outward content analysis scores and, moreover, that hand movements involving objects external to the speaker (object-focused hand movements) were associated with increased overt hostility outward scores derived from their speech. These findings prompted our examining whether in an experimental situation there was an increase in covert hostility outward scores in the speech of our subjects while they caressed their lips as compared to when they positioned their hands at their sides.

There were no significant differences between average overt hostility outward or covert hostility outward scores and hand activity when the subjects' hands were at sides or fingering their lips.

## SHAME AND GUILT ANXIETY (SUPER EGO OR EGO IDEAL CONSTRAINTS) AND LIP FINGERING

The previous natural history study of Gottschalk with a psychoanalytic patient (1974) and the experimental study with 20 subjects in which hand movements were alternated systematically as part of a research design (Gottschalk and Uliana, 1976) indicated that in some individuals caressing one's own lips enhanced an individual's sense of security and evoked positive feelings, possibly by mobilizing pleasant memories of supportive, nurturing women. But some individuals in the experimental study, judging from the content of their speech, apparently were reminded of unpleasant feelings and tended to have fewer thoughts of women when fingering their lips. In these and other subjects

Table 2

Effect of Hand Position and Sex on Shame Anxiety Scores

| Hand Position | Males (N=10) | Females (N=10) |
|---|---|---|
| A | 0.65 ±0.33 | 0.79 0.41 |
| B | 0.85 ±0.39 | 0.70 ±0.30 |

who were not soothed and supported by lip fingering did such activity in an experimental situation arouse super-ego and ego-ideal constraints and inhibitions against openly and publicly indulging in oral pleasures? Some support for this conclusion seems to be available in the finding of an average increase in the number of references in the speech of the 20 subjects, when fingering their lips, to not wanting to be favored, blessed, or rewarded (Hope Scale category item H-5, 0.08 ± .09 with hand position A versus 0.17 ± 0.2 category with hand position B: $p < .08$, two-tail). Accordingly, several analyses were carried out examining various relationships occurring between shame and guilt anxiety and lip fingering.

There was a non-significant interaction effect between sex and hand position ($p < .10$ by analysis of variance) such that lip fingering was associated with an increase in shame anxiety scores in males as predicted ($t = -1.59$, $N = 10$, $p < .10$) and with a decrease in shame anxiety scores in females (See Table 2).

Average shame anxiety scores of both sexes showed a significant difference under the two hand positions, namely, hands at sides (0.72 ± 0.37) and at lips (0.77 ±0.35). The same is true of average guilt anxiety scores under the two hand conditions.

An attempt was made to test the psychodynamic hypothesis that the subjects who had the most amount of increased hopefulness during lip fingering were individuals who had higher amounts of guilt or shame. The 20 subjects were divided into a subgroup of 6 subjects whose hope scores increased the least during lip fingering, as compared to when they had their hands at their side, and

a subgroup of six subjects whose hpoe scores increased the least during lip fingering. Neither guilt anxiety scores nor shame anxiety scores showed any significant differences in these two subgroups.

The six subjects with the highest average shame and guilt anxiety scores and the six subjects with the lowest average shame and guilt anxiety scores derived from speech samples given during lip fingering (hand condition B) were identified. The six subjects with the highest shame anxiety scores showed an average increase in negative valences associated with references to objects during lip fingering as compared to the position when hands were at the sides (B-A = -0.50, ± 0.48). Whereas,.the six subjects with the lowest shame anxiety scores showed, on the average, a decrease in negative valences associated with references to objects with lip fingering B-A = 0.38 ±0.73). The difference in these mean change scores for negative valences associated with object references was statistically significant ($t = 2.47$; $p < .05$, two-tail). (See Table 3). No significant differences in change scores occurred in other components of the Object Relations scale scores (positive valences and references to males or females) or Hope scale scores in these high and low shame and guilt anxiety groups of subjects.

## EVIDENCES OF SEXUAL DIFFERENCES IN THE PSYCHODYNAMIC EFFECTS OF LIP FINGERING

Previous data analysis revealed that lip fingering eliminated significant negative correlations between various affect scores (anxiety and hostility) and hope scale and positive object relations scores. We wondered whether these intercorrelations as well as the dynamic effect of lip fingering were uniform across the sexes. Hence, possible sexual differences in these intercorrelations were analyzed with the following results.

Males, while they had their hands at their sides, had significant positive correlations between separation anxiety scores and verbal references to inanimate objects with neutral valence ($r = 0.69, p < .03$), to all inanimate objects ($r = 0.69$, $p < .03$), and to total negative valences but no significant correlations occurred between any components of the Object Relations scale and guilt or shame anxiety scores. Whereas, when fingering their lips males lost all significant correlations between separation anxiety and any kinds of verbal references to inanimate objects or negative valences. But they developed significant negative correlations between guilt anxiety scores and references to males with positive valence ($r = -0.69, p < .03$), references to females with neutral valence ($r = -0.67$, $p < .03$), to females with all valences ($r = -0.66, p < .041$), and references to inanimate objects with negative valence ($r = 0.69$, $p < .03$). No correlations occurred between shame anxiety scores and object relations.

Table 3

Differences of Responses in Speech Content to Lip Fingering in High and Low Shame Anxiety Subjects

| Subject # | Shame Anxiety Scores | Changes (B-A) in Negative Valences (Feelings) Associated with Object References During Lip Fingering (B) as Compared to Hands at Side (A) |
|---|---|---|
| 11 | 1.49 | -0.31 |
| 12 | 1.30 | -0.58 |
| 4 | 1.25 | 0.16 |
| 3 | 0.99 | -0.99 |
| 5 | 0.99 | -0.18 |
| 1 | 0.98 | -1.09 |
| 13 | 0.51 | -0.36 |
| 14 | 0.49 | 1.67 |
| 10 | 0.45 | 0.10 |
| 18 | 0.38 | 0.17 |
| 17 | 0.27 | 0.75 |
| 19 | 0.22 | -0.04 |

Females, while holding their hands at their sides, had a significant negative correlation between separation anxiety scores and references to males with positive valence ($r = -0.63, p < .05$); and a significant negative correlation between guilt anxiety scores and references to others with neutral valence (regardless of gender) ($r = -0.64, p < .05$); a significant positive correlation between guilt anxiety scores and references to other females with negative feelings ($r = 0.95, p < .001$), and a significant positive correlation between shame anxiety scores and references to females with negative feelings ($r = -0.95, p < .001$). Whereas, while fingering their lips, females had significant positive correlations between separation anxiety scores and references to inanimate objects with negative feelings ($r = 0.68, p < .03$);and between guilt anxiety scores and references to positive feelings toward males ($r = 0.70, p < .03$). No significant correlations occurred among the women while fingering their lips, between

shame anxiety scores and any components of the object relations scale content categories.

Significant correlations of males and females taken separately between hostility scores and all components of the object relations scale content categories, during the two different hand positions, showed numerous changes, including reversals. They will not be detailed here.

There were no significant effects produced among either males or females on the magnitude of positive affects or valences by lip fingering as compared to the hands-at-side position.

## DISCUSSION

Our studies indicate that there are individual differences with respect to the effects of hand-mouth activity on speech content and, by extension, mental events, including perceptions and the evocation of memories. Though lip fingering significantly reduced the average rate of speech of 20 subjects, five subjects spoke an increased number of words over a five-minute period. Though lip fingering evoked evidence of positive, optimistic, pleasurable feelings in a few people, other individuals had negative and unpleasant feelings during such motor activity. Some individuals were induced to speak more hopefully during lip caressing; whereas, others were not so affected

What are the reasons for these individual differences and for the capacity of some of us to be soothed and comforted by our touching a part of our facial anatomy and others to be unaffected or, even, to have negative responses?

Developmental psychology, learning theory, and clinical psychoanalytic theory would, in general, be in agreement that a person's childhood experience and later past history could likely account for these differences. There is supportive evidence from our studies that past experience can account, in part, for the variety of responses to hand-mouth movements.

Individuals with a past history of relative childhood psychosocial deprivation (lower social assets Scale scores), including, less satisfactory parenting, limited education, and so forth, were among the group of subjects having significantly greater increases in hope scores during lip fingering than subjects with higher social assets scores. Likewise, subjects who had been breast fed and who did not have the history of chewing their fingernails were more likely than others to have an increase in hope scores when fingering their lips.

There is always a possiblility of constitutional or genetic factors playing a part in the kind of response of an individual to lip fingering or any other kinetic activity. Our studies in this area were not well designed to examine such a possibility. A few leads can be derived from our findings that may be pertinent.

Subjects who rarely got cold or canker sores around the mouth were more likely to have an increase in hope scale scores when fingering their lips.

Since cold or canker sores are a result of a localized infection with the herpes simplex virus, such a finding would seem to point to the involvement of a genetic factor. However, this virus is ubiquitous and it typically finds a nidus for localized infection with localized trauma. The common cold, dental work, lip biting, pipe smoking, and so forth can trigger the onset of cold or canker sores around the mouth. While it is understandable why someone with cold sores around the mouth may not enjoy or be soothed with lip rubbing, it is not so clear why such a person would be predisposed not to enjoy lip rubbing when no oral cold sores are present. Also, if lip sucking, biting, or chewing—which behavior can itself lead to oral cold sores—were genetically determined (which is highly questionable), then perhaps we would have some evidence.

Male-female differences in response to lip fingering could be seen as evidence of a biological factor accounting for varying responses to lip caressing. We found that males had significantly ($p < .05$) more references to food than females when lip fingering. Also, males tended to have more shame anxiety than females ($p < .10$) when fingering their lips. And females gave significantly more verbal references to getting or receiving help, advice, support, or esteem than males when their hands were at their sides, and away from their lips. But many aspects of sexual role are learned in our society (Money, 1955; Stoller, 1968) and sex differences in behavioral responses cannot be automatically attributed to hereditary factors and/or hormonal differences.

Response differences, to kinesic activity, such as lip fingering, could result not only from unmet dependency needs in childhood, but also from adult inculcations and warnings that certain kinds of hand-body activity are taboo. We are much more familiar in the clinical literature with case histories of the sexual inhibitions and associated neuroses resulting presumably from parental disapproval of hand-genital stimulation. Lip and nose fingering and finger sucking are often subjected to parental ridicule and scolding. We could not establish, however, that average shame or guilt anxiety scores were significantly different in our subjects under the different hand conditions. But we did note that significant negative correlations between hope and object relations scores with anxiety and hostility scores derived from content analysis of speech when hands were at one's side tended to disappear completely with lip fingering. This suggests that our research design, permitting and requiring public lip fingering as it did, may have provided a partial sanction to dissociate old taboos and, hence, shame or guilt, from feelings of hopefulness and optimism.

Studies of psychokinesics should distinguish between natural-science and experimental observations. Most research workers in the area of kinesics, that is, non-verbal behvior, choose the natural science method over the experimental method. Examples of the natural science method, stemming from a psychoanalytic orientation, are the studies of Deutsch (1966) and Scheflen (1966). Deutsch has been credited with catalyzing the awakening interest in body

communication. He found in the patient's gestures and postures evidence for underlying drives and defenses. To a large extent, he perceived a one-to-one relationship between a gesture and underlying drive and/or defense. The evidence for Deutsch's system for interpreting kinesics consisted of its plausibility, internal coherence, and consistency with some aspects of psychoanalytic theory. For Scheflen, however, matters were more complicated. He held that only rarely was the meaning of a single gesture clear and then only in the simplest instances, as in pointing out directions to a location. Scheflen noted complex patterns of communication in which the body language was one element and to be understood it must be considered in its complicated interaction with the patient's verbal behavior. Deutsch believed that non-verbal behavior frequently took the place of verbal behavior or customarily did so, for example, in expressing unconscious, unverbalized drives or defenses. How one might objectively validate that a gesture or posture represented a deeply unconscious mental event was never elaborated, except on the basis of plausibility and internal consistency. Scheflen was more likely to study a piece of non-verbal behavior and fit it into a larger pattern of commmunication extending over as long as 15 minutes. Hence, he was more likely to see the non-verbal behavior as mirroring, emphasizing, or otherwise modulating the semantic or paralanguage facets of the communication process.

The work of Norbert Freedman and his co-workers (1972; Grand et al, 1973) continues the line of inquiry of Deutsch and Scheflen as sophisticated natural science research in psychokinesis. The investigation of these workers adds scientific rigor and the application of the mathematical assessment of data of observation to the intuition and breadth of these earlier workers. The present conference on "Communication Structures and Psychic Structures" organized by Norbert Freedman is a culmination of the stimulation and contributions of this group to the field (Freedman and Grand, 1977).

While the natural science approach to this field of inquiry has predominated, the experimental approach has been used occasionally. Experimental studies, involving manipulation of independent variables, such as, total body, face, or extremity movements, while dependent variables, such as, speech content or other behavioral or physiological variables are recorded, have been avoided. This avoidance has been based on the notion that the experimental method would be "artificial" and because the methodological and theoretical problems using the experimental method are difficult and challenging.

The use of the experimental method in the present report to supplement and pursue unanswerable questions arising from a natural science study, specifically, a therapeutic psychoanalysis, is one way in which the two methodological approaches may fruitfully interdigitate to add scientific information in the area of psychokinesis. In so doing, we must remind ourselves that one method is not a simple substitute for the other. The findings that prevail

under the conditions of a natural science approach may not obtain under the conditions of the experimental method and vice versa.

What advice or guidelines can basic research of the kind here in psychokinetics offer the practicing psychotherapist? The surest advice is, I am afraid is almost banal: do not ignore but carefully watch what your patient is doing with his gestures, postures, and other body movements while talking. When the question arises what do the body movements mean, we do not seem to have come much beyond the level of understanding of Deutsch and Scheflen. Some specific movements do, as Deutsch suggested, tend to signify specific things. On the other hand, as Scheflen insisted, the message of any specific body movement may change in varying communication contexts and settings. Body movements may influence the psychodynamic interrelationships between speech content in such a way that the intercorrelations between the magnitude of certain affects and other psychological states may be enhanced or diminished among a group of subjects. There is no simple formula that has been discovered for discerning the precise effects of such kinesic-psychological activities within one individual. Knowing what these interrelationships are for one individual will not necessarily help predict what they will be within another individual. The main solution to this problem is to *keep an eye on your patient* and try to learn his formula. Remember that a significant correlation between some aspects of his verbal associations and body position can disappear when he moves, for example, his fingers to his lips. In this connection, other studies examining various psychosomatic relationships have revealed that a drug (hydrochlorothiazide) can eliminate the significant correlation between hostility outward (content analysis ) scores and blood pressure (Gottschalk et al, 1964) and that marihuana smoking can cancel the usually significant relationship between certain affect (content analysis) scores and various hemodynamic variables (Gottschalk et al, 1977). That a non-drug event, lip fingering, can also terminate usually significant psychodynamic correlations in the speech of subjects, indicates the potency of some body movements.

## REFERENCES

1. Deutsch, F. Some principles of correlating verbal and non-verbal communication. In *Methods of Research in Psychotherapy*. L.A. Gottschalk and A.H. Auerbach (Eds) New York: Appleton-Century-Crofts, 1966, pp. 166-184.

2. Gleser, G.C., Gottschalk, L.A., and Springer, K.J. An anxiety scale applicable to verbal samples. *Arch. Gen. Psychiatry* 5: 593-605, 1961.

3. Freedman, N. and Grand, S., (Eds) *Communicative Structures and Psychic Structures* New York: Plenum Press, 1977.

4. Gottschalk, L.A. A hope scale applicable to verbal samples. *Arch. Gen. Psychiatry* 30: 779-785, 1974.

5. Gottschalk, L.A. The psychoanalytic study of hand-mouth approximations. In *Psycho[ analysis and Contemporary Science*. L. Goldberger and V.H. Rosen (Eds) Vol. 3 New York: International Universities Press, Inc., 1974.

6. Gottschalk, L.A., Aronow, W.S., and Prakash, R. Effect of marihuana and placebo-marihuana smoking on psychological state and on psychophysiological cardiovascular functioning in anginal patients. *Bio Psychiatry* 12: 255-266, 1977.

7. Gottschalk, L.A., Biener, R., Bates, D., and Syben, M. Depression, hope, and social assets. Unpublished study, 1974.

8. Gottschalk, L.A., Bierner, R., Noble E.,P., Birch, H., Wilbert, D.E., and Heiser, J.F. Thioridazine plasma levels and clinical response. *Compr. Psychiatry* 16: 323-337, 1975.

9. Gottschalk, L.A. and Gleser, G.C. *The Measurement of Psychological States Through the Content Analysis of Verbal Behavior*. Berkeley: University of California Press, 1969.

10. Gottschalk, L.A., Gleser, G.C., D'Zmura, T., and Hanenson, I.B. Some psychophysiological relationships in hypertensive women. The effect of hydrochlorothiazide on the relation of affect to blood pressure. *Psychosom. Med.* 26: 610-617, 1964.

11. Gottschalk, L.A., Gleser, G.C., and Springer, K.J. Three hostility scales applicable to verbal samples. *Arch. Gen. Psychiatry* 9: 254-279, 1963.

12. Gottschalk L.A. and Hambidge, G. Jr. Verbal behavior analysis: A systematic approach to the problem of quantifying. *J. Proj. Tech.* 19: 387-409, 1955.

13. Gottschalk, L.A., Kaplan, S.M., Gleser, G.C., and Winget, C.N. Variations in magnitude of emotion: A method applied to anxiety and hostility during phases of the menstrual cycle. *Psychosom. Med.* 24: 300-311, 1962.

14. Gottschalk, L.A., Springer, K.J. and Gleser, G.C. Experiments with a method of assessing the variations in intensity of certain psychological states occurring during two psychotherapeutic interviews. Ch. 7 in *Comparative Psycholinguistic Analysis of Two Psychotherapeutic Interviews*. L.A. Gottschalk (Ed) New York: International Universities Press, 1961.

15. Ivey, M. and Bardwick, J.M. Patterns of affective fluctuation in the menstrual cycle. *Psychosom. Med.* 30: 336-348, 1968.

16. Money, J., Hampson, J.G., and Hampson, J.L. Hermaphroditism: Recommendation concerning assignment of sex, change of sex, and psychological mangagement. *Bull, Johns Hopkins Hospital* 97: 284-300, 1955.

17. Silbergeld, S., Brast, N., and Noble, E.P. The menstrual cycle: A double-blind study of mood, behavior, and biochemical variables with Enovid and a placebo. *Psychosom. Med.* 33: 411-428, 1971.

18. Stoller, R.J. Sex and Gender: *The Development of Masculinity and Feminity*. New York: Science House, 1968.

Schedule 1

Questionnaire Regarding Oral History

NAME____________________ DATE____________________

1. Do you know whether you were bottle or breast fed as an infant?
   A. ________Breast
   B. ________Bottle
   C. ________Both breast and bottle
   D. ________Don't know

2. How long were you on the breast and/or bottle?
   ________ 0- 3 months
   ________ 4- 8 months
   ________ 9-12 months
   ________13-18 months
   ________19-23 months
   ________24 or more

3. Have you had any dental or gum problems?
   ______When? ______What kind? (Please mention specifically)

4. Have you had any oral injuries, blemishes, diseases, or oral surgery?
   ____Yes ____No ________When? ________What kind?

5. When you're nervous do you tend to eat?
   ____More? ____Less? ____Eating habits do not change

6. Did you ever chew your finger nails? ____Yes ____No
   ________Often ________Little ________Not at all

7. Do you still bite your nails? ____Yes ____No
   ________Often ________Little ________Not at all

8. Do you chew pencils or toothpicks?
   ________Often ________Little ________Not at all

9. Do you have difficulty talking freely with (Please circle)
   Friends, Parents, Students, Teachers, Employers, Intimates?

10. Did you ever stutter or stammer? ____Yes ____No
    If so, was it ____Mild ____Moderate ____Severe

11. Do you like tart foods as much as sweet flavored ones?
    ______Yes ______No

12. Do you get a lot of cold sores or canker sores in or around the mouth?
__________Rarely __________Once in a while __________Often

13. Do you smoke cigarettes, cigars, or a pipe? (Circle which one)
__________Yes __________No

14. If you do smoke, how often?
________Daily ________Weekly ________Monthly ______Not at all

15. Do you chew tobacco? __________Yes __________No
__________Often __________Little __________Not at all

16. Do you smoke marijuana? __________Yes __________No

17. How often have you used marijuana in the past 12 months?
____________Not at all
____________Daily
____________Several times a week
____________Several times a month
____________About once a month
____________Less than once a month

18. How often have you used alcohol in the past 12 months?
____________Not at all
____________Daily
____________Several times a week
____________Several times a month
____________Once a month
____________Less than once a month

19. Do you usually drink?
_____Wine _____Beer _____Whiskey _____Gin _____Other

20. On the average, how many drinks do you have when you drink?
_____One _____Two _____Three _____Four _____More than four

21. When you're nervous do you tend to smoke?
________More ________Less ________Not at all

22. Do you have any other oral habits, problems, difficulties, or taboos that have not been mentioned so far? ___Yes ___No
Please specify________________________________________

# The Application of a Method of Content Analysis to Psychotherapy Research*

LOUIS A. GOTTSCHALK, M.D.† | *Irvine, Calif.*

*A content analysis method applicable to speech and its thematic aspects is described from the point of view of its eclectic theoretical basis and the operational steps whereby the magnitude of psychologic states can be derived from verbal behavior. Through the application of this procedure, though global interrelationships of relevant variables in the process of psychotherapy may be lost, precise measurement of specific psychologic states can be obtained.*

## *A Content Analysis Method for Measuring Psychologic States*

A content analysis method of measuring psychologic states has been developed that analyzes communication data which are uniquely human, namely, speech and its content or semantic aspects (1). The initial goal in the development of this method was to probe the immediate emotional reactions of subjects or patients, instead of the typical or habitual ones (traits), and to minimize reactions of guarding or covering up. Hence, the instructions to elicit speech from research subjects were purposely relatively ambiguous and nonstructured; customarily, speakers were asked to tell about personal or dramatic life experiences or simply to free-associate. In many early studies, standardized instructions were used, also, in order to compare individuals in a standard context so that demographic and personality variables could be explored and investigated, while holding relatively constant the influence of such variables as the instructions for eliciting speech, the nature and personality of the interviewer, the context, and the situation. The effects of varying these noninterviewee variables were subsequently investigated, one by one, after reliable and valid content analysis scales were developed.

The development of this measurement method has involved a long series of steps. It has required that the psychologic dimensions to be measured (for example, anxiety, hostility outward, hostility inward, cognitive and intellectual impairment, achievement strivings, social alienation-personal disorganization, hope, human relations, dependency, health-sickness, and so

* Presented at the annual Meeting of the Society for Psychotherapy Research, Philadelphia, Pa., June 15, 1973.

† Professor and Chairman, Department of Psychiatry and Human Behavior, College of Medicine, University of California at Irvine, Irvine, Calif. 92664.

forth) be precisely defined, that the lexical cues be carefully pinpointed by which a receiver of any verbal messages infers the occurrence of any of these psychologic states, and that the linguistic, principally syntactic, cues conveying intensity (for example, the word "very" in the proper context) be specified. Next, differential weights were assigned to these semantic and linguistic cues conveying magnitude of a subjective experience whenever appropriate. Next, a systematic means was arrived at of correcting for the number of words spoken per unit time so that one individual could be compared to himself on different occasions or to others with respect to the magnitude of any particular psychologic state.

This content analysis method requires, also, that a formal scale of weighted content categories be specified for every psychologic dimension to be measured and that research technicians be trained to score these typescripts of human speech according to any one scale at an interscorer reliability of 0.85 or above. Moreover, a set of construct-validation studies had to be carried out to recheck exactly what each content analysis scale measured, and these validation studies have included the use of four kinds of criterion measures: psychologic, physiologic, pharmacologic, and biochemical. On the basis of these construct-validation studies, changes have been made in the content categories and their assigned weights of each specific scale, in the direction of maximizing the correlations between the content analysis scores with these various independent criterion measures.

The theoretical framework from which this measurement approach has developed has been an eclectic one and includes behavioral and conditioning theory, psychoanalytic clinical theory, and linguistic theory. In addition, the formulation of these psychologic states has been deeply influenced by the position that they all have biologic roots. Both the definition of each separate psychologic state and the selection of the specific verbal content items used as cues for inferring each state have been influenced by the decision that whatever psychologic state was measured by this content analysis approach should—whenever possible—be associated with some biologic characteristic of the individual in addition to some psychologic aspect or some social situation.

The content analysis technician applying this procedure to typescripts of tape-recorded speech has not had to worry about approaching the work of content analysis following one theoretical orientation or another. Rather, the technician follows a strictly empirical approach, scoring the occurrence of any content or themes in each grammatical clause of speech according to a "cookbook," namely, sets of various, well-delineated language categories making up each of the separate verbal behavior scales. A *Manual* (2) is available which indicates what verbal categories should be looked for and how much the occurrence of each one is to be weighted. Following initial

coding of content in this way, the technician, then, follows prescribed mathematical calculations leading up to a final score for the magnitude of any one psychologic state or another.

This content analysis procedure can be and has been applied to interview material—psychotherapeutic, diagnostic, or otherwise. The content analysis scales can be applied to different kinds of language materials obtained in a variety of situations in both spoken and written form. Most of the reliability and validity studies have been done on small samples of speech, three to five minutes in duration, obtained in response to standard instructions. The typed data can be broken down into equal temporal units (for example two to five minute segments). Or the units can be based on the number of words spoken by one or both participants (or more if they are present); for example, consecutive 500-word sequences of the speakers can be coded for content. Depending on the purpose or research design of the study, these content analysis scales have also been applied to dreams, projective test data (specifically, tape recordings of Thematic Apperception Test responses) to written verbal samples, and even to literature, letters, public speeches, and any other type of language material.

### *"Tooling Up" this Content Analysis Method for Psychotherapy Research*

One of the shortcomings of any content analysis procedure is that it discards valuable data, data which might be of considerable usefulness to the usual psychotherapist in his global approach to his psychotherapeutic roles. A content analysis method could never supplant, in my opinion, the broad perspectives of a psychotherapist nor the psychotherapist's ability to synthesize many different points of view in listening to and reacting to a community of forces. The value in psychotherapy research of a content analysis method lies more in its capacity to give objective assessments about the magnitude of specific psychologic states. As such, high level measurement precision is reached while global interrelationships may be lost. Such precise and accurate assessments of specific psychologic dimensions may have considerable usefulness, for example, in the prediction of treatment outcome.

### *Prediction of Treatment Outcome*

These content analysis scales have been used with encouraging success in a wide variety of studies on prediction of therapeutic outcome.

1. In a Brief Psychotherapy Clinic at the Cincinnati General Hospital, five-minute speech samples were obtained from 22 clinic patients before assignment for psychotherapy. A tape-recorded standardized interview was used to rate psychiatric change (the Psychiatric Morbidity Scale), in terms of functional adaption, along four dimensions: psychologic, interpersonal, vocational, and somatic (3). Pretreatment Human Relations scores derived

from spoken verbal samples correlated with post-treatment Psychiatric Morbidity Scale scores ($r = -.66$, $N = 22$, $p < .01$). Also, pretreatment social alienation-personal disorganization scores correlated with post-treatment Psychiatric Morbidity Scale scores 7 to 10 weeks later ($r = .39$, $N = 22$, $p < .05$). In other words, pretreatment social alienation-personal disorganization scores predicted unfavorable therapeutic outcome and pretreatment human relations scores predicted favorable outcome in this study.

2. A similar investigation of outcome in a Crisis Intervention Clinic at the Orange County Medical Center in Orange, California indicated that pretreatment Human Relations scores correlated negatively ($r = -.26$, $p < .05$, $N = 35$) with post-treatment Psychiatric Morbidity Scores obtained 7 to 10 weeks later. Pretreatment Hope scores correlated significantly ($p < .05$) with greater change (improvement) in social alienation-personal disorganization scores only for those patients in the Actual Treatment Group and these same Hope scores correlated significantly ($p < .01$) with decreased change in Human Relations scores only for those patients in the Actual Wait Group. Several studies have indicated a high negative intercorrelation ($r = -.37$, $N = 22$, $r = -.58$, $N = 109$, $p < .001$) between social alienation-personal disorganization scores and human relations scores (1). Human Relations scores and Hope scores as might be expected, are highly positively correlated (4), for example, in an adult group of 54, $r = .68$, ($p < .005$) and in a group of 109 school children, $r = .51$ ($p < .001$).

In the Orange County Medical Center study, a randomly selected Waiting List group were asked to wait six weeks for treatment instead of receiving it immediately; with these patients, Human Relations scores and Hope scores correlated poorly with post-treatment Psychiatric Morbidity Scale scores ($r = -.18$ and $r = .17$ respectively), that is, nonsignificantly with the treatment outcome measure as compared to those patients treated immediately (5).

3. Social alienation-personal disorganization scores were predictors of a favorable response to a major tranquilizer (thioridazine) among 75 chronic schizophrenic patients at Longview State Hospital, Cincinnati, Ohio. Patients with pretreatment social alienation-personal disorganization scores greater than 2.0 were highly responsive to the administration or withdrawal of this phenothiazine derivative, and patients with pretreatment scores less than 2.0 were essentially unresponsive to administration or withdrawal of this tranquilizer (6).

4. A very recent study of the relationship of psychoactive drug blood levels to clinical response has revealed that when a single standard oral dose of thioridazine (4 mg/kg) was administered to 25 patients with acute schizophrenia at the Orange County Medical Center, predrug social alienation-personal disorganization scores were predictive of postdrug indices of plasma thioridazine concentration, such as the thioridazine half-life ($r = .44$, $p <$

.03) and area-under-the-curve of decreasing drug levels with time ($r = .43$, $p < .03$). Moreover, the degree of improvement among these schizophrenic patients over the first 48 hours postdrug, in terms of factor scores from the Overall-Gorham Brief Psychiatric Rating Scale, the Hamilton Depression Rating Scale, and the Wittenborn Rating Scale, was highly correlated positively with these indices of plasma thioridazine concentration (7).

5. Pretreatment Human Relations scores ($r = .40$, $p < .05$) and Hope scores ($r = .38$, $p < .05$) were predictive of survival time of patients ($N = 16$) with metastatic cancer receiving partial or total body irradiation from radioactive cobalt (8). Further studies with 20 or more such cancer patients replicated the positive correlational trends observed in the initial study (4).

6. Hope scores were derived from five-minute speech samples obtained from psychiatric patients coming to the emergency room of a general hospital in Pittsburgh, Pennsylvania. These scores significantly predicted those patients who would seriously follow up with treatment recommendations (9).

7. Anxiety scores were derived from reports of dreams given by women in the third trimester of pregnancy attending an Outpatient Ob-Gyn Clinic at the Cincinnati General Hospital. The absence of anxiety in these dreams was highly predictive of women who would undergo prolonged labor during childbirth (10). From these early studies, one can see that various psychologic dimensions, derived from the content analysis of language behavior, are predictive of a number of biologic as well as psychosocial, processes.

It is my intention, using a fuller range of my content analysis scales, to explore the predictive value of combinations of these content analysis scores for more complex outcomes. For example, what children or adults are likely to evidence continuing sociopathic or criminal behavior? Which individuals are most readily analyzable, if analyzability can be described in objective and operational terms?

### *Use of These Content Analysis Scales in Psychosomatic or Psychophysiologic Research*

Research in psychotherapy, for some investigators, leads to studies involving scrutiny of psychosomatic or psychophysiologic relationships. There is a growing body of evidence that these content analysis scales not only measure psychologic constructs that are associated with observable changes in the voluntary and involuntary nervous system, but that these content analysis scales are qualitatively and quantitatively sensitive to many pertinent parameters.

1. During two psychotherapeutic interviews, recorded under the direction of Albert Scheflen, M.D. in Philadelphia a number of years ago, the patient's skin temperature was continually recorded along with the patient-therapist

interchanges. Every five-minute segment of the patient's verbal interactions was scored for anxiety, by a content analysis technician using the anxiety scale, and the change in skin temperature before and after each five-minute segment was noted. A significant correlation ($p < .02$) was found between the anxiety score from each five-minute speech interval and the decrease in skin temperature (11).

2. The decrease of skin temperature of adolescent boys (ages sixteen to seventeen) while giving a speech sample, was found to be significantly correlated ($p < .04$) with the anxiety score derived from five-minute speech samples (12).

3. Hostility outward scores, derived from brief speech samples, correlated significantly ($r = .50$; $p < .05$) with increases in diastolic blood pressure in women with essential hypertension; also, inward hostility scores correlated with average diastolic blood pressures ($r = .55$, $p < .01$) (13).

4. From simultaneously tape-recorded interviews and electroencephalograms of a twenty-year-old male patient, high amplitude bursts of paroxysmal electroencephalographic activity were found to be preceded by higher anxiety ($p < .05$) and hostility inward ($p < .05$) scores dreived by content analysis from 30-word segments of speech occurring just before a paroxysmal EEG burst than from similar 30-word speech samples not followed by such abnormal electroencephalographic activity (14).

5. The anxiety scores from the dreams of one group of men were found to be significantly correlated with an increase of plasma free fatty acids ($r = .62$; $p < .01$), which is a sensitive indicator of the immediate secretion of adrenergic substances (15). The dream anxiety scores from another group of men were significantly correlated with a decrease in penile tumescence (16).

6. This content analysis method was employed to explore further and to verify independently relationships clinically noted between various psychodynamic conflicts and coping mechanisms revealed during the psychoanalysis of a patient who occasionally during an analytic session touched or rubbed his lips, mouth, or nose (17). Detailed notes were made of the free associations before and after such hand-mouth movements and on many occasions these sequences were tape-recorded. The clinical psychoanalytic formulation of these hand-mouth approximations was that they provided a source of comfort and feelings of security and bolstered the patient's ability to function independently and autonomously at times when he experienced a sense of distance or lack of support outside of or within the transference relationship to the analyst. A content analysis technician, unfamiliar with the nature of this investigation, blindly scored the typescripts of these tape-recordings, some taken when the patient's hands were at his side and some when one hand was fingering his oral or nasal area, on a simple object relations content analysis

scale in which male, female, and inanimate references were counted and on another scale indicating whether positive, negative, or neutral valences were attached to these object references. Significantly more female and/or positive references were found to be uttered by the patient whenever such hand-mouth approximations occurred. Evidence of the evocation of such verbal contents from the memory bank of the patient, by his voluntary hand-mouth contacts, corroborated the clinical psychoanalytic impression of a security and autonomy-supporting facet to the patient's hand mouth activities.

7. Freedman *et al.* (18) have explored the relationship of hostility scores, derived from speech samples by this content analysis method, to movements of the hands. Motor behavior and concomitant verbal samples were scored from videotaped interview segments of 24 college students. Intercorrelational analysis revealed that external object-focused movements were related to overt hostility outward ($r = .49$). Body-focused movements were related to covert hostility ($r = .53$) and specifically to hand-to-hand motions ($r = .53$). Analysis of peak trough periods within interviews revealed significant covariations between movements and forms of hostility. Qualitative clause-by-clause analysis elucidated the nature of the movement-hostility contiguity. Results of this study were interpreted in terms of the differential role of the external object and body-focused movements in the encoding of affect.

*Psychopharmacologic Studies Employing Content Analysis*

In our drug society, a serious investigator in psychotherapy research, whether doing outcome or process research, cannot ignore the fact that about 65 per cent of patients, whether they come to a Mental Health Outpatient Clinic or a General Medical Clinic are taking some kind of psychoactive drug, either by prescription or via the sharing of drugs from relatives or friends or from an over-the-counter source (19). This percentage does not include such psychoactive agents as alcohol, coffee, and tobacco. Controlled studies, using this content analysis method with a sizable number of commonly used psychoactive drugs, have demonstrated that these medicaments significantly alter an individual's psychologic state. As such, the open or covert use of such psychoactive drugs may confound the researcher of psychotherapy who may be involved in noting and measuring changes in the same psychologic continua that are influenced by pharmacologic agents. I believe it is, hence, quite relevant to give examples of the many content analysis studies I and my co-workers have done which indicate these psychopharmacologic influences.

1. Twenty dermatologic inpatients (10 men and 10 women) were given 16 to 24 mg a day of perphenazine by mouth for one week alternating with a placebo for one week, using a double-blind, crossover design (20). Analysis of the content of five-minute speech samples obtained from these patients

showed a reduction of hostility outward scores with perphenazine in 16 of the 20 patients ($p < .01$) and a decrease in anxiety scores among those patients who had elevated predrug anxiety scores.

2. Forty-six juvenile delinquent, sixteen to seventeen-year-old boys were administered 20 mg of chlordiazepoxide or a placebo. Using the content analysis of five-minute verbal samples, significant decreases were found in anxiety, ambivalent hostility, and overt hostility outward 40 to 120 minutes after ingesting the chlordiazepoxide (21).

3. A significant increase occurred in anxiety and overt hostility outward scores, derived from verbal samples in nondepressed outpatients receiving the antidepressant drug, imipramine, as compared to a placebo (22).

4. An oral dose of 15 mg of dextroamphetamine, as compared to a placebo or 25 mg of chlorpromazine, in a group of 33 incarcerated criminals at Patuxent Institution, Baltimore, significantly increased achievement strivings scores derived from five-minute speech samples (23).

5. Content analysis of speech of individuals administered psychotomimetic drugs (LSD-25, Ditran, or psilocybin) or a placebo showed that people receiving psychotomimetic drugs do not have higher average anxiety or hostility scores, but do have significantly higher content analysis scores on a Cognitive and Intellectual Impairment Scale than when they receive a placebo (1).

6. The relationship of plasma drug level and clinical response was studied in a double-blind, drug-placebo, crossover study, in which the antianxiety effects of a single oral dose of chlordiazepoxide (25 mg) on 18 chronically anxious paid volunteers were observed. Though the subjects had the same oral drug dose, their plasma levels of chlordiazepoxide ranged from 0.26 to 1.63 $\mu$g/ml; and only those 11 subjects whose plasma chlordiazepoxide levels exceeded 0.70 $\mu$g/ml had a statistically significant decrease in anxiety scores, as measured from five-minute speech samples (24).

7. Six ex-street addicts, incarcerated in Vacaville Institution, California were administered 100 mg of meperidine (Demerol) by mouth and another six received the same dose intramuscularly. Significant decreases occurred, one hour postdrug, in both groups of subjects in anxiety and hostility scores, as derived from verbal samples (25). A significant correlation occurred between plasma meperidine concentrations and decrease in anxiety scores.

8. A group of 12 male college students gave five-minute speech samples, after 12 to 14 hours of fasting, following ingestion of either a placebo or propranolol (40 mg), the latter being a beta adrenergic blocking agent. Resting anxiety scores were significantly lower ($p < .05$) when the subjects were on propranolol, but there was no difference, under the drug or placebo condition, in the magnitude of anxiety aroused in reaction to a stress interview. These findings plus heart rate and plasma free fatty acid reduction

in response to propranolol in this specific study suggest that propranolol reduces anxiety primarily by reducing the afferent feedback to the central nervous system of autonomic nervous system correlates of anxiety (26).

*Shame and Guilt as it Influences Psychotherapy*

Helen B. Lewis (27) has written extensively about how guilt-ridden, as compared to shame-ridden individuals, are psychodynamically organized, especially with respect to their aggression and hostility. To independently verify her clinical differentiations of guilt and shame, as well as the relationship of these affects to various kinds of hostile affects, she sent segments of the typescripts of tape-recorded psychotherapeutic interviews for independent and blind scoring of anxiety and hostility by content analysis. Content analysis, according to the scales, showed that guilt anxiety scores correlated significantly and positively with hostility outward scores in the same speech samples and shame anxiety scores correlated significantly and positively with hostility inward scores (see also 1, p. 114 ff.) Of further interest, in these elaborate psychotherapy studies, is the finding that patients with high guilt anxiety content analysis scores tend to be perceptually and cognitively organized in the direction of field independence, as assessed by the Rod-and-Frame Test (28) and that patients who have shame anxiety content analysis scores are field dependent. These affective perceptual-cognitive orientations definitely influence the course of psychotherapy and the nature of the psychotherapeutic interventions necessary to effect therapeutic change.

*Content Analysis in the Measurement of Change with Covert Behavior Conditioning*

A group of 20 paid volunteer college students gave one five-minute speech sample a week for three weeks in response to instructions to talk about any interesting or dramatic personal life experiences. Although the person who elicited these speech samples deadpanned and spoke no words while the subject gave his speech sample, with half the subjects the interviewer covertly nodded his head in assent and with the other half he wagged his head negatively whenever the subject used the words "I" or "we." When the trends for the second half of each verbal sample were analyzed, it was found that there was a significant differential trend ($p < .025$). The group receiving negative reinforcement had a very significant decreasing trend in self-references; whereas the positively reinforced group made about the same number of self-references in all three session (1, p. 237 ff).

*Computer Programming of Content Analysis*

One of the problems in a content analysis system of the kind described here is the training time required to obtain high reliability of coding content

according to any one scale and the other is the time required to score accurately typescripts of interviews. Different content analysis scales require different amounts of time to score—which includes coding content, tallying scores, calculating raw and corrected scores. The total time range for these operations is from 10 to 60 minutes per five-minute speech sample per scale.

In collaboration with John S. Brown, Ph.D. and Cathy Hausman, B.S., Computer Sciences Division, University of California at Irvine and with the technical assistance of Michael Syben from my laboratory, some definite progress has been made toward developing a completely automated system for analyzing the content of natural language according to our hostility outward scale (29). A parsing program was first developed, adapted in part from the LSP program (Lunar System, NASA). This computer program is capable of parsing natural language in a highly accurate fashion, far beyond the precision currently necessary for the level of detail and comprehension of the computerized content analysis procedure we have developed at this moment. In our present computer system, the denotation of hostility outward is assessed only from verbs. The specification of the agent that initiates or carries out the hostility and the object on whom the hostile action is focused requires our specifying the subject of the verb (a noun, pronoun, or phrase) and the direct or indirect object, and these operations are also carried out by our computer program. Admittedly, considerable meaning is lost by ignoring hostile content conveyed in adverbs, adjectives, or certain types of noun or pronoun referents. But the computer program has proved capable of correctly scoring 70 out of a series of 100 clauses scorable for hostility outward and taken from the *Manual* for scoring these hostility scales (2). Also, a nonparametric correlation of 0.91 was obtained between hostility outward scores derived from six five-minute speech samples (totaling around 3,000 words) scored by hand (that is, by trained content analysis technicians) compared to scores obtained from our computer program. We are encouraged by these breakthroughs, and we plan to continue the development of a sophisticated computer program for the content analysis of these content analysis scales.

## SUMMARY

1. This is a review of the possible applications of the content analysis method of Gottschalk and his co-workers in outcome and process research in psychotherapy. A description of this method of measuring psychologic states is provided, including the eclectic theoretical framework from which this measurement approach has been developed, some operational details on how scores are derived from this content analysis procedure, and the reliability and construct validation criteria and studies which have been carried out on these scales.

2. It is emphasized that the application of content analysis to psychotherapy is primarily in its capacity to give objective assessments of the magnitude of specific psychologic states.

3. Brief reviews are supplied of research using this content analysis instrument in the prediction of outcome, in psychosomatic or psychophysiologic research involving psychotherapy, and in psychopharmacologic studies which have relevance to psychotherapy research.

## REFERENCES


1. Gottschalk, L. A. and Gleser, G. C. *The Measurement of Psychological States Through the Content Analysis of Verbal Behavior.* University of California Press, Berkeley, 1969.
2. Gottschalk, L. A., Winget, C. N., and Gleser, G. C. *Manual of Instructions for Using the Gottschalk-Gleser Content Analysis Scales: Anxiety, Hostility, and Social Alienation-Personal Disorganization.* University of California Press, Berkeley, 1969.
3. Gottschalk, L. A., Mayerson, P. and Gottlieb, A. The Prediction and Evaluation of Outcome in an Emergency Brief Psychotherapy Clinic. *J. Nerv. Ment. Dis.*, 144:77, 1967.
4. Gottschalk, L. A. A Hope Scale Applicable to Verbal Samples. *Arch. Gen. Psychiat.*, 30:779, 1974.
5. Gottschalk, L. A., Fox, R. A., and Bates, D. E. A Study of Prediction of Outcome in a Mental Health Crisis Clinic. *Am. J. Psychiat.*, 130:101, 1973.
6. Gottschalk, L. A., Gleser, G. C., Cleghorn, J. C., Stone, W. N., and Winget, C. N. Prediction of Changes in Severity of the Schizophrenic Syndrome with Discontinuation and Administration of Phenothiazines in Chronic Schizophrenic Patients: Language as a Predictor and Measure of Change in Schizophrenia. *Compr. Psychiat.*, 11:123, 1970.
7. Gottschalk, L. A., Biener, R. A., Noble, E. P., Birch, H., Wilbert, D. E., and Heiser, J. F. Thioridazine Plasma Levels and Clinical Response. In *Psychopharmacology and Social Science,* Marshall, M. and Cohn, B., Eds. J. Aronson, New York, 1974.
8. Gottschalk, L. A., Kunkel, R. L., Wohl, T., Saenger, E., and Winget, C. N. Total and Half Body Irradiation. Effect on Cognitive and Emotional Processes. *Arch. Gen. Psychiat.*, 21:574, 1969.
9. Perley, J., Winget, C. N., and Placci, C. Hope and Discomfort as Factors Influencing Treatment Continuance. *Compr. Psychiat.*, 12:557, 1971.
10. Winget, C. N. and Kapp, C. N. The Relationship of the Manifest Content of Dreams to Duration of Childbirth in Primiparae. *Psychosom. Med.*, 34:313, 1972.
11. Gottschalk, L. A., Springer, K. J. and Gleser, G. C. Experiments with a Method of Assessing the Variations in Intensity of Certain Psychological States Occurring during two Psychotherapeutic Interviews. In *Comparative Psycholinguistic Analysis of Two Psychotherapeutic Interviews,* Gottschalk, L. A., Ed. International Universities Press, New York, 1961.
12. Gottlieb, A., Gleser, G. C., Gottschalk, L. A. Verbal and Physiological Responses to Hypnotic Suggestion of Attitudes. *Psychosom. Med.*, 24:172, 1967.
13. Gottschalk, L. A., Gleser, G. C., D'Zmura, T., and Hanenson, I. B. Some Psychophysiological Relationships in Hypertensive Women. The Effect of Hy-

drochlorothiazide on the Relation of Affect to Blood Pressure. *Psychosom. Med.,* 26:610, 1964.
14. Gottschalk, L. A. An Objective Method of Measuring Psychological States Associated with Changes in Neural Function. *J. Biol. Psychiat.,* 4:33, 1972.
15. Gottschalk, L. A., Stone, W. N., Gleser, G. C., and Iacono, J. M. Anxiety Levels in Dreams: Relation to Changes in Plasma Free Fatty Acids. *Science,* 153: 654, 1966.
16. Karacan, I., Goodenough, D. R., Shapiro, A., and Starker, S. Erection Cycle during Sleep in Relation to Dream Anxiety. *Arch. Gen. Psychiat.,* 15:183, 1966.
17. Gottschalk, L. A. A Psychoanalytic Study of Hand-Mouth Approximation. In *Psychoanalysis and Contemporary Science.* International Universities Press, New York, 1974.
18. Freedman, N., Blass, T., Rifkin, A., and Quitkin, F. (1972). Body Movements and the Verbal Encoding of Aggressive Affect. *J. Personality Soc. Psychol.,* 26:72, 1973.
19. Gottschalk, L. A., Bates, D. E., Fox, R. A., and James, J. M. Patterns of Psychoactive Drug Use Found in Samples from a Mental Health Clinic and a General Medical Clinic. *Arch. Gen. Psychiat.,* 25:395, 1971.
20. Gottschalk, L. A., Gleser, G. C., Springer, K. J., Kaplan, S. M., Shanon, J., and Ross, W. D. Effects of Perphenazine on Verbal Behavior Patterns. *Arch. Gen. Psychiat.,* 2:632, 1960.
21. Gleser, G. C., Gottschalk, L. A., Fox, R., and Lippert, W. Immediate Changes in Affect with Chlordiazepoxide in Juvenile Delinquent Boys. *Arch. Gen. Psychiat.,* 13:291, 1965.
22. Gottschalk, L. A., Gleser, G. C., Wylie, H. W., and Kaplan, S. D. Effects of Imipramine on Anxiety and Hostility Levels Derived from Verbal Communications. *Psychopharmacologia,* 7:303, 1965.
23. Gottschalk, L. A., Bates, D. E., Waskow, I. E., Katz, M. M. and Olsson, J. Effect of Amphetamine or Chlorpromazine on Achievement Strivings Scores Derived from Content Analysis of Speech. *Compr. Psychiat.,* 12:420, 1971.
24. Gottschalk, L. A., Noble, E. P., Stolzoff, G. E., Bates, D. E., Cable, C. G., Uliana, R. L., Birch, H., and Fleming, E. W. Relationships of Chlordiazepoxide Blood Levels to Psychological and Biochemical Responses. In *Benzodiazepines,* Garattini, S., Mussini, R., and Randall, L. O. Eds., Raven Press, New York, 1973.
25. Elliott, H. W., Gottschalk, L. A., Uliana, R. L. (1973). Relationship of Plasma Meperidine Levels to Changes in Anxiety and Hostility. *Compr. Psychiat.,* 15:57, 1974.
26. Gottschalk, L. A., Stone, W. N., and Gleser, G. C. Peripheral versus Central Mechanisms Accounting for Anti-Anxiety Effects of Propranolol. *Psychosom. Med.,* 36:47, 1974.
27. Lewis, H. B. *Shame and Guilt in Neurosis.* International Universities Press, New York, 1971.
28. Witkin, H. A. Perception of Body Position and of the Visual Field. *Psychol. Monogr.,* 63:1, 1949.
29. Gottschalk, L. A., Hausman, C., and Brown, J. S. A Computerized Scoring System for Use with Content Analysis Scales. *Compr. Psychiat.,* (in press) 1974.

# A Study of Prediction and Outcome in a Mental Health Crisis Clinic

BY LOUIS A. GOTTSCHALK, M.D., RUTH A. FOX, M.D., AND DANIEL E. BATES

*Sixty-eight patients who came voluntarily to a crisis intervention clinic were randomly assigned to one of two groups. Those in the first group received immediate intervention therapy while those in the second were put on a waiting list. By the end of six weeks (and after minor changes in the makeup of the groups were taken into account) there was no significant difference in the psychiatric morbidity scores of the two groups; both had improved. The authors used a variety of pretreatment and posttreatment measures and found that the best predictor of a patient's condition at the end of six weeks was his pretreatment psychiatric morbidity score. The authors conclude that individuals vary in both their reactions to life crises and their therapeutic needs and that the central issue may not be the recovery itself, but the difficulty and pain with which it is achieved.*

WE UNDERTOOK THIS STUDY of patients who seek treatment at a mental health crisis clinic for several reasons: 1) to determine whether patients who receive brief crisis-oriented psychotherapy, with or without concomitant psychoactive drug therapy, show greater improvement in functioning than patients who are kept on a waiting list without immediate treatment; 2) to identify pretreatment variables that might serve as predictors of which patients will profit most from clinic treatment; and 3) to attempt to replicate the findings of a similar research study that had been undertaken previously in Cincinnati, Ohio (1).

## METHOD

The subjects were patients who came voluntarily to the Mental Health Crisis Intervention Clinic, Orange County Medical Center, because of some life situation or emotional experience with which they had serious difficulty in coping.

To minimize observer bias, all patients were screened, evaluated on pretreatment, and posttreatment variables were evaluated by a member of the research team rather than by the treatment team. The following measures were used:

*Content analysis scores derived from five-minute speech samples.* At the beginning of a tape-recorded interview, the patients were asked to talk for five minutes about any interesting or dramatic life experiences they had ever had. From the typescripts of these speech samples, various psychological scores (Social Alienation-Personal Disorganization, Human Relations, Hope) were obtained by means of the Gottschalk-Gleser content analysis method, a measurement procedure for which satisfactory reliability and validity have been established (2). The Social Alienation-Personal Disorganization Scale is especially designed to distinguish schizoid trends and the schizophrenic syndrome, but it also functions effectively as a discriminator of general psychiatric morbidity (2). The Human Relations Scale measures the patient's current and typical desire for gratifying, supportive, and constructive human relationships (3). The Hope Scale measures the degree of optimism, sense of purpose in existence, and the positive outlook expressed by the subject (4). All five-minute speech samples were scored independently by content analysis technicians who had been trained to code speech according to the Gottschalk-Gleser method with high reliability and who were completely blind to the identity of the patients and the purpose of the study.

*Psychiatric Morbidity Scale (PMS).* A standardized psychiatric interview was tape-recorded. The interview was designed to elicit the current psychiatric symptoms and to establish the degree to which these psychiatric problems had disturbed the patient's typical functioning level. The patients were asked to talk about the problems that led to their coming to the clinic. They were specifically asked about current psychological symptoms, such as anxieties, depression, and fears; current behavioral signs, such as excessive drinking, not fulfilling family responsibilities, or crying; current interpersonal problems, such as withdrawal from or expression of anger toward people; and current somatic symptoms, such as cardiac palpitation, insomnia, or weakness. On the basis of a patient's responses, a psychiatric morbidity score was obtained by a method that has been described and tested elsewhere (1).

Approximately six weeks after the initial interview, we obtained another five-minute speech sample and a follow-up tape-recorded, standardized interview that were identical in format to the initial measures. The same interviewer took both sets of measures. The format of the interview and the PMS have been published recently in slightly modified form (5).

The authors are with the Department of Psychiatry and Human Behavior, College of Medicine, University of California at Irvine, Irvine, Calif. 92664, where Dr. Gottschalk is Professor and Chairman, Dr. Fox is Clinical Instructor, and Mr. Bates is Research Associate. Dr. Gottschalk is also Director, Psychiatric Services, Orange County Medical Center, Orange, Calif.

The authors wish to thank Gunnar Mazaroups, M.D., for his technical assistance and Herman Birch, Ph.D., for his statistical assistance.

The initial scoring of the interviews was done by the research interviewer. They were then rescored by a research associate who listened to the recordings but had no information on whether the patient had received immediate crisis intervention psychotherapy or had been asked to wait. The interrater reliability on the PMS for 92 interviews was 0.73 ($p<.001$), a level that indicates there was no observer bias. This high level of reliability and lack of observer bias indicates that this study approximated a single-blind design.

*Ego strength and weakness scores.* Paper and pencil tests and questionnaires were also administered to the patients when they came to the clinic. These included the Jacobs Ego Strength and Ego Weakness Scales (6), Barron Ego Strength Scale (7), and the Anant Belongingness Scale (8).

*Embedded Figures Test scores.* The relatively small number of patients who could cooperate were administered the Embedded Figures Test (9), a measure of field dependence-independence.

A patient who impressed the research interviewer as probably requiring immediate psychiatric hospitalization or as having serious medical problems was not accepted for this study. Only about eight percent of all patients coming to the crisis clinic fell into this category. The remaining patients were randomly assigned to either a therapy group (Assigned Treatment Group) or to a waiting-list group (Assigned Wait Group). Patients in the Assigned Wait Group were told that there were no immediate opportunities for them to receive psychiatric assistance, but that their names would be placed on a waiting list, which meant they would have to wait about six weeks to begin their treatment. Those who were in the Assigned Treatment Group received brief crisis psychotherapy within one hour of the initial evaluation and subsequently received from one to six treatment sessions from a psychiatrist, clinical psychologist, psychiatric social worker, or mental health associate. At the discretion of the psychiatrist who was consulted on the treatment plans for all patients, psychoactive medication was also prescribed for some patients. The crisis psychotherapy that was given to the patients was patterned after the crisis intervention treatment described by others (10 12).

## RESULTS

On careful inquiry at the time of the follow-up interviews, we learned that a sizable number of patients initially assigned to the treatment group or to the waiting group (put on a waiting list) switched groups, that is, some of those who were in the treatment group did not appear for treatment and some of those who were in the waiting group obtained treatment elsewhere. The occurrence of these shifts from group to group and the number of dropouts (patients who failed to reappear at the clinic and could not be contacted in spite of strenuous efforts to do so) were recorded. The changes in the initial random assignments of the patients to a treatment or waiting list group are illustrated in figure 1.

FIGURE 1
*Changes in Initial Assignments of Patients*

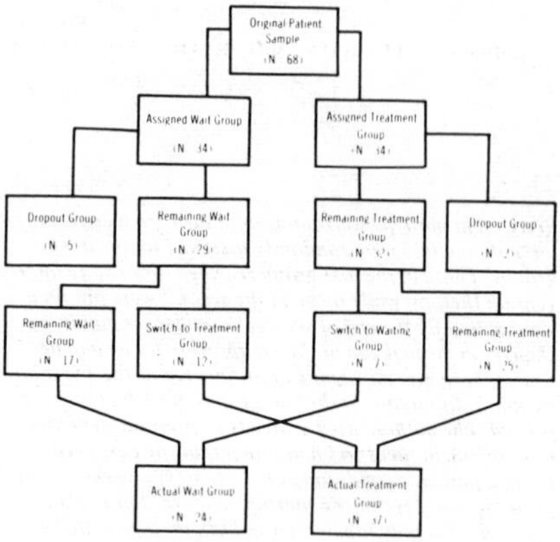


### *Demographic Data*

The average age of the entire sample of 68 patients was 32.01 years (standard deviation [S.D.] = 10.07); the average educational level was 11.54 grades (S.D. = 2.31). Eleven of the 68 patients were Mexican-Americans and the remainder were Caucasians. In the Hollingshead-Redlich two-factor classification system, none of the patients was in class I, three were in class II, 14 were in class III, 24 in IV, 16 in V, and 11 were not classified.

The Cincinnati sample (1) had a social class distribution that was very similar to that of our southern California sample, but the racial composition was different. Thirty-eight percent of the patients in the Cincinnati sample were black, while 16 percent of our California sample were Mexican-Americans.

### *Pretreatment Measures*

After eliminating the dropouts, the Assigned Treatment Group and Assigned Wait Group were compared on the pretreatment measures using Student's t test. The differences in these scores were not significant.

All patients had been asked in the interview about their use of psychoactive drugs. After eliminating the dropouts, we compared the pretreatment scores of patients who had taken psychoactive drugs before treatment with those of patients who had not. The average Barron Ego Strength Scale scores were significantly lower ($t = 2.16$, $p<.05$) for those who had been using psychoactive medications before treatment (16.90) than for those who had not (19.43). PMS scores and Embedded Figures scores tended to be higher and Hope scores to be lower for the patients who had been using psychoactive medications, but these differences were not significant.

*Posttreatment Scores*

The 37 patients in the Actual Treatment Group had an average of 2.7 treatment sessions (S.D. = 1.6), which ranged in duration from 20 to 50 minutes. We cannot assume that there is an absolute uniformity in the treatment over successive sessions because we are dealing with different therapists with varying skills spending varying periods of time with different patients. The Actual Treatment Group patients, however, definitely received more "treatment" than the patients in the Actual Wait Group, who received only the tape-recorded interviews.

An analysis of covariance[1] was performed on the posttreatment PMS scores, which were individually adjusted with reference to the pretreatment levels. Using a $2 \times 2 \times 2 \times 2$ factorial design, the patients were categorized by their actual conditions of treatment (Actual Treatment Group versus Actual Wait Group and psychoactive medication during treatment period versus no psychoactive medication during treatment period), by the experimental conditions they were assigned to (Assigned Treatment Group versus Assigned Wait Group), and by pretreatment drug use (users versus nonusers). We hoped that these last two categorizations would allow us to isolate subpopulations of the total experimental group and perhaps control for the self-selection into treatment conditions by the patients who switched groups. However, no significant differences or interactions were found.

A similar analysis of covariance was performed in which posttreatment Social Alienation-Personal Disorganization Scales were individually adjusted with reference to pretreatment levels. No significant differences or interactions were found.

*Prediction of Outcome*

On the basis of the correlations among various measures, a prediction equation for posttreatment Psychiatric Morbidity Scale scores ($PMS_2$) was obtained. The predictive pretreatment measures were the PMS scores ($PMS_1$), Social Alienation-Personal Disorganization Scale scores ($SAPD_1$), and Human Relations Scale scores ($HRS_1$). For the Actual Treatment Group (N = 33),[2] a multiple correlation of +0.62 was obtained; the prediction equation was $Z(PMS_2) = 0.506\ Z(PMS_1)\quad 0.237\ Z(HRS_1)\quad 0.007\ Z(SAPD_1)$. For the Actual Wait Group (N = 22), R = +0.57 and the prediction equation was $Z(PMS_2) = 0.408\ Z(PMS_1) + 0.049\ Z(HRS_1) + 0.340\ Z(SAPD_1)$.

These were the same variables that were found to have predictive value in an earlier and somewhat similar study conducted in Cincinnati (1). In that study too, the major predictive variable, the one that accounted for most of the multiple correlation, was the pretreatment Psychiatric Morbidity Scale ($PMS_1$). This meant that the more disturbed the patient was initially, the less favorable his outcome was six weeks or more later. The greater his initial interest in and motivation for satisfying human relationships ($HRS_1$) and the less his Social Alienation and Personal Disorganization ($SAPD_1$), the better the outcome six weeks later. (In the present study, however, these last two predictors were weaker than in the Cincinnati study.) In the Cincinnati study, the multiple correlation was +0.54 and the prediction equation was $Z(PMS_2) = 0.380\ Z(PMS_1)\quad 0.580\ Z(HRS_1)\quad 0.164\ Z(SAPD_1)$.

Simple inspection of the beta weights will show that there were some differences in the prediction formulas for the Actual Treatment and Actual Wait Groups that suggest that certain people are more likely to improve with crisis treatment than without it, although the average amount of improvement in the two groups showed no difference.

TABLE 1

*Partial Correlations of Pretreatment Measures with Posttreatment Psychiatric Morbidity Scores ($PMS_2$)*

| | Posttreatment Morbidity Scores ($PMS_2$) | | | |
|---|---|---|---|---|
| | Actual Treatment Group | | Actual Wait Group | |
| Pretreatment Scores | Correlation | N | Correlation | N |
| Social Alienation-Personal Disorganization | +0.16 | 35 | +0.32 | 23 |
| Human Relations | 0.26 | 35 | 0.18 | 22 |
| Hope | 0.03 | 35 | +0.17 | 23 |
| Jacobs Ego Strength | 0.10 | 32 | 0.27 | 23 |
| Jacobs Ego Weakness | +0.06 | 32 | 0.08 | 23 |
| Barron Ego Strength | +0.11 | 33 | +0.02 | 24 |
| $PMS_1$ | +0.58 | 37 | +0.46 | 24 |
| Embedded Figures Test | +0.53 | 17 | +0.18 | 17 |

*Intercorrelations*

Table 1 gives the partial correlations between the posttreatment PMS scores and eight pretreatment measures. The $PMS_2$ scores are corrected for correlation with the $PMS_1$ scores. The correlations for the Actual Treatment Group and Actual Wait Group tended to be in a similar range on all measures except the Embedded Figures Test ($EFT_1$). Table 1 shows that pretreatment Hope scores correlated significantly ($p < .05$) with greater change (improvement) in the Social Alienation-Personal Disorganization scores only for those patients in the Actual Treatment Group, and these same Hope scores correlated significantly ($p < .01$) with less change in Human Relations scores only for those patients in the Actual Wait Group. Also, the Embedded Figures Test scores correlated significantly ($p < .05$) with increases in Human Relations scores for the Actual Wait Group ($r = +.62$) but not for the Actual Treatment Group ($r = \ .14$) among those patients for whom we were able to obtain Embedded Figures Test scores (table 2).

These findings again suggest that certain types of people may be more inclined to improve when receiving

[1] The analysis followed the general linear hypothesis model, using the BMDS64 program of Dixon (13) specifically.

[2] The multiple R could only be calculated for patients without missing scores.

TABLE 2
*Correlations Between Pretreatment Scores and Difference Scores (Measures of Improvement)*

| Correlations* | Actual Treatment Group | | | Actual Wait Group | | |
|---|---|---|---|---|---|---|
| | Correlation | N | Significance | Correlation | N | Significance |
| $EFT_1$ and $(HRS_2-HRS_1)$ | 0.14 | 16 | n.s. | +0.62 | 15 | $p<.05$ |
| Barron Ego Strength$_1$ and $(PMS_2-PMS_1)$ | +0.37 | 33 | n.s. | +0.24 | 23 | n.s. |
| Jacobs Ego Weakness$_1$ and $(PMS_2-PMS_1)$ | 0.28 | 32 | n.s. | 0.13 | 22 | n.s. |
| Hope$_1$ and $(SAPD_2-SAPD_1)$ | +0.42 | 34 | $p<.05$ | +0.31 | 23 | n.s. |
| $PMS_1$ and $(PMS_2-PMS_1)$ | 0.65 | 37 | $p<.01$ | 0.55 | 23 | $p<.01$ |
| Hope$_1$ and $(HRS_2-HRS_1)$ | 0.33 | 33 | n.s. | 0.66 | 22 | $p<.01$ |

*Abbreviations: EFT = Embedded Figures Test; HRS = Human Relations Scale; PMS = Psychiatric Morbidity Scale; SAPD = Social Alienation-Personal Disorganization Scale.

brief contact crisis treatment, while others, who are obliged to wait four to six weeks for such treatment, undergo some improvement with only the prospect of receiving treatment in the near future. On the other hand, in both groups, the sicker patients are likely ($p<.01$) to have less improvement, as indicated by the significant negative correlations ($r=-.65$ and $r=-.55$) between the pretreatment PMS scores ($PMS_1$) and the change occurring in such scores ($PMS_2-PMS_1$). These observed differences in the presumptive predictors of outcome in the Actual Treatment and Actual Wait Groups should, of course, be replicated in further studies.

## DISCUSSION

Other investigators comparing treatment outcome in a treatment group versus a waiting list group have not mentioned switches of patients from one assigned group to another. The switches of patients from one of our originally randomly assigned groups to another makes us wonder whether our experience is unique or whether other investigators have simply failed to note and document such occurrences. This phenomenon, we suspect, is commonplace and poses an obstacle to securing randomly selected groups, a procedure that is necessary for making meaningful statistical comparisons between groups.

After seven patients dropped out, our remaining Assigned Wait Group patients manifested somewhat more psychiatric disability than our Assigned Treatment Group. Then, after some patients switched from one group to another, the Actual Treatment Group patients now had more dysfunction than the Actual Wait Group. This change appears to result from the high psychiatric morbidity of patients who switched from the Assigned Wait Group to the Actual Treatment Group.

### *Use of Pretreatment Psychoactive Medication*

The fact that the crisis center patients who took psychoactive medication before treatment initially had significantly lower Barron Ego Strength scores and a stronger tendency to have higher PMS scores than other patients emphasizes that the use of pharmacologic agents, in itself, designates a subgroup of patients who are generally more incapacitated than other patients. That most of the patients taking psychoactive drugs did not receive these drugs by prescription from a physician but from "over-the-counter" sources or from relatives or friends suggests that this relative incapacity is not physician-induced. We cannot be certain whether lower ego strength or higher psychiatric morbidity is brought on by or precedes the use of psychoactive drugs, but we are inclined to believe that it precedes drug use.

We have found that patients who receive an average of 2.7 treatment sessions of 20 to 50 minutes each are improved, but no more improved at the end of six weeks than those who are still waiting for therapy. There are a number of possible explanations for these findings; we suspect that choosing among these alternatives will be influenced by whether one believes in the value of crisis intervention treatment. The alternatives include:

1. If a diagnostic and evaluative interview by a researcher who does not assume the role of a therapist is as effective as specific crisis intervention therapy carried out by a therapist, then it is the nonspecific aspects of the human relationship with a professional in the clinic that accounts for the improvement in the crisis patient's functioning six weeks after coming to the clinic. This conclusion would be a blow to those mental health professionals who assert that training in crisis intervention psychotherapy requires the inculcation of goals, techniques, and attitudes in the therapist. We find the hypothesis that crisis intervention therapy has specific, as well as nonspecific, features attractive, but more evidence is needed to support this view.

2. Crisis intervention may have been available in some form from friends and relatives outside the crisis clinic for the patients who were in the Actual Wait Group. This would account for the considerable improvement of these patients in six weeks.

3. Most patients suffering from life crises recover spontaneously within six weeks regardless of the kind of care they receive (10, 14). Klerman and Cole (15) also as-

serted that 50 to 60 percent of patients with acute depression and acute anxiety reactions recover within two to six weeks without receiving psychoactive drugs or any other form of treatment.

4. The analysis of covariance design, which adjusts for differences in initial (pretreatment) scores, may be statistically elegant but pragmatically inadequate; this procedure may not take into account important initial differences in the relative values of the pretreatment measures for our two groups.

5. The comparative amount of functional improvement in two groups of patients, each receiving different treatment programs, may not be the relevant issue; the central issue may be how much discomfort and suffering these patients had to undergo in the process of recovering from their crises. This issue was not addressed in this study.

Our study, at first glance, suggests the radical view that, with the exception of patients needing hospitalization, crisis intervention clinic patients may not need to be seen for specific crisis treatment since a diagnostic interview that is not focused on therapy may be of equal avail. We think that to hold such a view firmly is premature, but that our study has heuristic value in this connection. More credible is the notion that "naturally" recuperative tendencies help people over life crises in a six-week period. Whether recovery is more comfortable and easier with crisis intervention is a different issue and may indeed be the essential difference in the experience of treated and waiting-list patients. We know, for instance, that minor surgery can be equally successful with or without anesthesia and that the healing rate of an infection is not appreciably influenced by an analgesic. But the suffering and pain experienced by patients in these situations is considerably reduced by an anesthetic or analgesic. Hence, this facet of treatment and outcome needs to be examined in evaluating the effectiveness of crisis intervention treatment as well as the comparative degree of functional improvement of the patient six weeks after coming to a crisis clinic.

Usually, crisis intervention aims at improving the coping mechanisms of patients so that they become more resilient in the face of later, similar life crises. Here again, our study did not examine this facet of outcome. We know of no controlled studies that have sought to demonstrate decisively that this important goal of crisis therapy has ever been attained; but we believe, on the basis of impressionistic longitudinal clinical observations, that experienced psychotherapists are capable of achieving such goals.

*Prediction of Outcome*

The prediction formulas for a favorable outcome for our two groups are similar to the prediction formula obtained in the earlier study with patients of approximately similar socioeconomic background in Cincinnati (1). The differences that exist between the two prediction formulas may be attributable to ethnic-racial differences in the two samples. Small differences in the beta weights of the prediction formula for our Actual Treatment and Actual Wait Groups and the correlation of the Embedded Figures scores with the outcome measures suggest that the people who improve with brief crisis therapy in our crisis center may be different from those who improve while waiting six weeks for such therapy (tables 1 and 2). If so, other investigators (16 18) who claim that there is very little functional difference between treated and waiting patients at the time of follow-up may be missing the differences in the types of people involved. It would appear that some patients have the capacity to respond favorably only with human interactions while others respond to stress with great resilience and respond very little, or even negatively, to specific human therapeutic intervention.

REFERENCES

1. Gottschalk LA, Mayerson P, Gottlieb A: Prediction and evaluation of outcome in an emergency brief psychotherapy clinic. J Nerv Ment Dis 144:77 96, 1967
2. Gottschalk LA, Gleser GC: The Measurement of Psychological States Through the Content Analysis of Verbal Behavior. Los Angeles, University of California Press, 1969
3. Gottschalk LA: Some applications of the psychoanalytic concept of object relatedness: preliminary studies on a human relations scale applicable to verbal samples. Compr Psychiatry 9:608 620, 1968
4. Gottschalk LA: A hope scale applicable to speech samples. Arch Gen Psychiatry (in press)
5. Gottschalk LA, Brown SB, Bruney EH, et al: An evaluation of a parents' group in a child-centered clinic. Psychiatry 36:157 171, 1973
6. Jacobs MA, Pugatch D, Spilken A: Ego strength and ego weakness. J Nerv Ment Dis 147:297 307, 1968
7. Barron F: An ego strength scale which predicts response to psychotherapy. J Consult Psychol 17:327 333, 1953
8. Anant SS: Belongingness, anxiety, and self-sufficiency. Psychol Rep 20:1137 1138, 1967
9. Witkin HA, Dyk RB, Faterson HF, et al: Psychological Differentiation. New York, John Wiley & Sons, 1962
10. Caplan G: Principles of Preventive Psychiatry. New York, Basic Books, 1964
11. Bellak L, Leonard S: Emergency Psychotherapy and Brief Psychotherapy. New York, Grune & Stratton, 1965
12. Bergin AE, Garfield SL (eds): Handbook of Psychotherapy and Behavior Change: An Empirical Analysis. New York, John Wiley & Sons, 1971
13. Dixon WJ: BMD Biomedical Computer Programs: X-Series Supplement. Los Angeles, University of California Press, 1969
14. Gottschalk LA: Some problems in the evaluation of the use of psychoactive drugs, with or without psychotherapy, in Psychopharmacology: A Review of Progress, Public Health Service Publication 1836. Edited by Efron DE, Cole JO, Levine J, et al. Washington, DC, US Government Printing Office, 1968, pp 255 269
15. Klerman GL, Cole JO: Clinical pharmacology of imipramine and related antidepressant compounds. Pharmacol Rev 17:101 141, 1965
16. Barron F, Leary TF: Changes in psychoneurotic patients with and without psychotherapy. J Consult Psychol 19:239 245, 1955
17. Goldstein AP: Patients' expectancies and nonspecific therapy as a basis for (un)spontaneous remission. J Clin Psychol 16:399 403, 1960
18. Endicott NA, Endicott J: "Improvement" in untreated psychiatric patients. Arch Gen Psychiatry 9:575 585, 1963

# Introduction to Chapter 47

Introductory Comments by Louis A. Gottschalk

Lewis illustrates how she has used the Gottschalk-Gleser method of analyzing content to examine the role of shame and guilt in neurosis and to explore sex differences in superego style. Lewis became interested in the phenomenology of shame and guilt via three avenues: the failure of psychoanalytic therapy for some patients, her research in field-dependence and field-indepedence, and the observation that there is an affinity between shame, depression, and hysteria and guilt, paranoia, and obsessive-compulsive neurosis. Obviously, thoroughly conversant with the pertinent psychoanalytic literature on the subject, Lewis reviews current superego theory and then skillfully demonstrates with clinical data that when shame cannot be discharged symptoms of depression/hysteria appear and when guilt cannot be discharged symptoms of paranoia/obsession occur. This chapter is, in its own right, a sensitive and perceptive contribution to the psychoanalytic therapy of the archaic conscience and it offers valuable insights and suggestions for the psychodynamically oriented psychotherapist. The Gottschalk-Gleser content analysis method takes its proper place as a tool, a procedure, that could be useful in pursuing the stimulating hypotheses Lewis proposes.

# Using Content Analysis to Explore Shame and Guilt in Neurosis

Helen Block Lewis

"...if we could monitor a stream of consciousness, we would get a jumble that would have to be washed out through a sieve..."

Leon Edel *The Modern Psychological Novel*

It was William James (1890) who invented the metaphor, "stream of consciousness," to describe our inner experience, which both "welcomes and rejects...all the while it thinks" (p.284). Almost simultaneously, Freud was suggesting (Breuer and Freud, 1893) that unresolved conflict governs the rejecting and welcoming design of the "sieve." Using the dream as a model, Freud (1900) introduced us to a microscopic analysis of the way unresolved conflict creates primary-process transformation of consciousness which can become symptoms.

Freud's microscopic analysis of the content of consciousness was, of necessity, geared to the exposition of particular dreams and symptom-formations. Its use in symstematic research required the development of reliable measuring instruments which, while adequately reflecting Freud's theory of the workings

of unresolved conflict in consciousness, could take quantifiable readings of the affects of the stream. Gottschalk and Glesser's method of analyzing verbal content for implied affects is among the most useful of such instruments, as this volume attests. In this chapter, I shall describe the way it has been of use in my studies of the role of shame and guilt in neurosis (Lewis, 1971), and of sex differences in superego style (Lewis, 1976). I shall also suggest some hypotheses which the Gottschalk-Gleser method may help us to pursue.

A connection between neurotic symptom formation and an "archaic" superego was first hypothesized by Freud (1923) in The Ego and the Id. This formulation was basic to Freud's 1924 notion of "moral masochism." It led to the work of Reik (1941), Bibring (1953), Menaker (1953) and Berliner (1958), among others, in elucidating the way in which symptoms form under the press of "archaic guilt" toward significant introjects. In this formulation, guilt was the generic term for shame as well. Although superego functioning was implicated in neurosis, the phenomenology of guilt and shame remained a relatively neglected area of psychoanalytic observation and there was a special neglect of shame. Some notable exceptions were the works of Piers and Singer (1953) and Erikson (1956). But it was a sociologist, Helen Lynd (1958) who pioneered in psychoanalytic work by devoting a whole book to shame and its relation to identity development.

My own focus on the phenomenology of superego states of shame and guilt grew out of three main sources. The first was an effort to understand the reasons for failures of psychoanalytic work with my own patients and those of other analysts. These were patients who returned for treatment after an apparently successful analysis with a superego even more critical and cruel than it had been before analysis began. Their vocabulary of self-blame had been increased by psychoanalytic terms. That the self of these patients had assumed the burden of unanalyzed transference hostility seemed evident. My attention was drawn, in particular, to unanalyzed shame in the transference as a source of the patients' increased vulnerability to a renewal of symptoms.

Another influence propelling me into the microanalysis of shame and guilt has been my work on field dependence (Witkin, Lewis, Hertzman, Machover,

Meissner and Wagner, 1954). Since 1954, there has been mounting evidence that cognitive style and forms of pathology are related to each other (Witkin, Dyk, Faterson, Goodenough and Karp, 1962, Witkin, 1965). In earlier clinical accounts of psychoanalytic work with neurotic patients (Lewis, 1958; 1959), I used field dependence as a "tracer element" for following characteristic behavior and transference phenomena during treatment. In particular, the patients' perceptual style focused attention on the manner and extent of individuation of the self from significant "others." A field-dependent patient was described as readily merging herself with the surround. She was self-effacing; when she was self-conscious, it was in an awkward and shy way. A field-independent patient, also a woman, was described as having an organized self which took the initiative in vigilantly defending her place in the field. Differences between field-dependent and field-independent patients were also traced in the organization of the self in dreams.

Making a link between these characteristics of the self and characteristic functioning of the superego was one step in a line of reasoning which supposed that the superego functioned differently in field-dependent and field independent patients. A field-dependent mode of superego functioning would be shame; while a field-independent mode would be guilt. Both modes could be associated with an equally severe or malfunctioning superego. In an experimental study, these hypotheses were put to test and confirmed (Witkin, Lewis and Weil, 1968). Our study made excellent use of the Gottschalk-Gleser method and is reported elsewhere in this volume.

A third source of my continuing interest in the phenomenology of shame and guilt was an early observation that each superego mode leads to its own path or symptom formation. Specifically, there is an affinity between shame and depression and between shame and the hysterias. The hypothesis that guilt is a major component of obsessional and paranoid states has been available to us since Freud's (1909) unravelling of the Rat-Man's symptoms. The well-established fact that women are more prone to depression and hysteria parallels both the sex differences in field dependence, and a sex difference in proneness to shame. It also makes intuitive sense of our finding that

field-dependent patients were more shame-prone than guilt-prone (Witkin, et al, 1968).

The transcripts of the psychotherapy sessions collected in the course of our study of field-dependent and field-independent patients contained many examples of sequences from undischarged shame and guilt into different paths of symptom formation. It is particularly in this area that systematic studies of sequences from shame and guilt into symptom formation might make use of the Gottschalk-Gleser method.

In the course of my work on the phenomenology of shame and guilt, I found it necessary to make a number of emendations in the construct of the superego. I shall briefly review some of the trouble-spots I found in psychoanalytic theory of the superego.

Because psychoanalytic theory was late in developing the conceptual distinction between the self and the ego, shame has been regarded as a lower-order or more primitive kind of state than guilt. This is an error which results from the fact that the source of shame has usually a more "external" locus than the source of guilt. Localization of the source of an experience or originating "out there" does not mean that the experience itself is not an internalized one. Although the stimulus to shame often appears to arise from someone or some circumstance outside the self, shame is a state of the ego which would not be possible if internalized judges (the superego) were not also devaluing the self.

A second difficulty in the superego construct arises from the fact that Freud described its evolution in terms of a male model: the superego arises out of the internalized castration threat. Freud had, of course, distinguished a second route of identification leading to superego formation: anaclitic identifications. These were thought to precede the defensive identifications formed under the castration threat. Anaclitic identifications also involve threat - but of a complicated punishment known as "loss-of-love;" this loss of parental love becomes loss of "self-love" via loss of esteem in their eyes, i.e., shame. Both males and females develop anaclitic identifications out of which shame arises. And anaclitic identifications or "loving"

identifications, as they are sometimes called, continue to develop throughout the individual's childhood. But because anaclitic identifications begin early in relation to mother, and because males must renounce some of their feminine identifications (while females need not), the shame which arises out of anaclitic identifications, or "loss-of-love," was automatically assigned by androcentric thinking to an inferior place in a hierarchy of controls. Shame is still conceptualized in modern writings as a "flooding of the ego with unneutralized exhibitionism" (Kohut, 1971, p. 181), instead of as a complicated superego state in which the self images itself vicariously in the eyes of the "other."

Anaclitic and defensive identifications are by no means mutually exclusive and they are often difficult to distinguish from one another. Although castration anxiety operates as a threat of personal harm, its potency also derives from the fact that the threatening parent is beloved. Identifications set in motion by the fear of the parents may initiate and be superseded by identifications based upon admiration or love of them. This is, in fact, one of the ways in which masochistic persons remain unaware of the extent to which they fear and exaggerate their own moral failures. By assuming that the castration threat and the threat of "loss-of-love" are equally advanced developmentally, it is possible to conceptualize shame and guilt as phenomenologically different modes of the superego.

A third problem in superego theory lies in the formulations we make about the nature of human nature. I have recently come to speculate that the superego is not only a set of drive controls, but a way of maintaining affectional bonds with significant, internalized "others." The self accepts guilt or shame (or both) rather than lose its loving attachment to its introjects. Shame and guilt are uniquely human states which arise out of the fact that human beings are cultural animals. I have recently argued (Lewis, in press) that the cultural nature of humanity makes it reasonable to postulate an innate human affectionateness--an "affectional system," as the Harlows (1965) call it. This biologically given affectional system forms the context within which the culture's moral precepts are absorbed by an

individual. This view of human nature is different from the individualistic and mechanistic formulations which characterize Freud's metapsychology, in contrast to his clinical writings (Bowlby, 1969). Emphasizing the affectional base for superego states brings with it a re-casting of shame and guilt as intrinsically social responses. Shame and guilt are internalized controls not only for the sake of the individual's survival, but for the survival of his or her profoundest attachments. It is this characteristic which makes it possible for some people to sacrifice their lives in acts of principled heroism or martyrdom, rather than betray their superegos.

In a case of "watching" in a child patient (Lewis, 1963) I suggested that shame functions particularly as a protection against the loss of self-boundaries which is implicit in absorbed sexual fantasy, i.e., in states of longing for attachment experience. Shame functions as a sharp, in fact, painful reminder that fantasy experience of the "other" is vicarious. Shame brings into focal awareness both the self and the "other," with the imagery that the other rejects the self. It thus helps to maintain the sense of separate identity, by making the self the focus of experience. This notion about the function of shame is similar to Lynd's (1958) description of how shame can spur the sense of identity. It also parallels Erikson's (1956) observation that shame is the opposite of autonomy, but with the emendation that it is the opposite of the autonomy of the self rather than of the ego. This formulation, while recognizing the apparent "narcissism" in shame, regards it as a phenomenon in which the self is experienced "at the quick," at the same moment that it is maintaining an affectional tie.

I turn now to some examples of the phenomenology of shame and guilt, and to sequences in which the two superego states lead to different paths of symptom formation. My underlying premise is that symptom formation occurs when both shame and guilt cannot be discharged. The state which is to the forefront of the person's experience is one determinant of whether symptoms of depression/hysteria or obsession/paranoia will appear. I shall suggest

at many points how the Gottschalk-Gleser method has been used to check some hypotheses and how it may be used to check others.

There are intrinsic characteristics of the too superego states which impede their discharge. Difficulties in coping with and discharging shame and guilt may be grouped under three main headings: DIFFICULTIES IN

RECOGNIZING ONE'S PSYCHOLOGICAL STATE:

Shame and guilt are often fused and therefore confused.

This is a result of their common origin as modes of repairing lost affectional bonds. The clearest example of their fusion occurs when both states are evoked by a moral transgression. The two states then tend to fuse under the heading of guilt. (The dictionary confirms this observation by terming shame an acute or "emotional" sense of guilt (Lewis, 1971)). But shame of oneself is likely to be operating underneath guilt for transgression.

The self-reproaches that are likely to be formed as guilty ideation develops might run as follows: how could I have done that; what injurious thing to have done; how I hurt so-and-so; what a moral lapse that act was; what will become of that or of him now that I have neglected to do it, or injured him. How should I be punished or make amends. Mea culpa! Simultaneously, ashamed ideation says: how could I have done that; what an idiot I am--how humiliating; what a fool, what an uncontrolled person--how mortifying, how unlike so-and so, who does not do such things; how awful and worthless I am. Shame! Since, in this kind of instance, the ideation of being ashamed of oneself is the same as that of guilty self-reproach, the shame component, although an acute affect, is buried in the guilty ideation. A current of aggression, however, has been activated against the whole self, in both one's own and "other's" eyes. This current of shame can keep both guilty ideation and shame affect active even after appropriate amends have been made.

The stimulus to shame is two-fold: moral and "nonmoral" shame.

Shame may be evoked in connection with guilt, as an acute form of it, or it may be evoked by competitive defeat, sexual rebuff, social snub, invasion of personal privacy or being ridiculed. Ausubel (1955) has drawn attention to the two-fold stimulus evoking shame, distinguishing between moral and "nonmoral" shame. When nonmoral shame is evoked, it readily connects with moral shame. For example, under the press of shame for competitive defeat or sexual rebuff, one can begin an immediate search for moral lapses or transgressions which make sense of the injury one has suffered. Conversely, as we have seen, in the preceding example, moral shame is difficult to distinguish from guilty ideation. Shame thus has a potential for a wide range of associative connections between transgressions and failures of the self and for "stimulus generalizations" such that shame for defeat or snub evokes guilt for transgression. Shame and guilt states are thus easily confused with one another by the experiencing person, although an observer may have a clearer view of the affects.

One question which arose in our therapy study (Witkin, et al, 1968) was whether there would be such great overlap between shame and guilt that the two states would not be distinguishable in our transcripts. This turned out not to be the case: in only a small minority (16.1%) of the "spurts" of shame and guilt did we find them in the same 500 word unit. It thus appears that the person experiencing shame and guilt is likely to confuse them. But a microscopic analysis of verbal content shows them appearing at different moments.

Another very useful purpose to which the Gottschalk-Gleser method may be put is the monitoring of the ebb and flow of patients' shame and guilt reactions during therapeutic sessions. One unexpected finding of our therapy study (Witkin et al, 1968) was that field-dependent patients showed an increase in total guilt anxiety in their second psychotherapy session as compared to their first. It is possible to speculate that this increase in guilt may have been the result of (unconscious) hostility evoked against the therapist in connection with acute but unidentified

shame. For example, one (field-dependent) patient, a man, put it this way:

P:... ... I'll tell you something. The last two times I been depressed when I left here. Not that - when I was talking I wasn't depressed. It's after I leave. That bothers me.

T: Have you wondered about that?

P: Yes.

T: What thoughts do you have?

P: I .. I made a joke of it to my sister, That's all. But uh.. (inaud) laugh out of it. I said, I don't know what's the matter this this guy, he's so nosy. (laugh)

T: Do you think that's the aspect of the situation that makes you depressed?

P: I don't know.

T: Well, I know you don't know, but I wondered if that's what you feel.

P: I feel like an idiot sometimes. When I think what I told you...m - m (pause). But it has some bearing I suppose. (Italics mine)

"I feel like an idiot sometimes when I think what I told you" is an excellent phenomenological description of shameful imagery of himself vis-a-vis the therapist. In the next communication he also describes the accompanying burst of hostility - entirely self-directed - which accompanies feeling like an idiot. He starts thinking, he says, "What the hell am I telling him now." But the patient's hostility is throttled by his own awareness that it is "unwarranted," in other words, by the patient's own sense of justice or guilt. The outcome is a "joke" in which he ridicules himself (and the therapist) for being nosy. What the patient experiences consciously is being depressed after he leaves session. This seems a clear example of the affinity between undischarged shame feeling and depressed mood.

Another patient, a (field dependent) woman says the following in retrospect about her first session:

P: (slight laugh) Last time, uh, when I first came in, I was uhm and I started talking to you, I was upset, but I didn't know about what. And

uhm, I sort of felt I was on the verge of tears, but I didn't know why, therefore, I really didn't mention it because I felt ridiculous. There was no reason.

The patient clearly is aware that she felt ridiculous (ashamed) because she was on the verge of tears. But she also is trying to say that something about talking to the therapist evoked a threat of tears. This unknown threat might well be the feeling of humiliation which is evoked by being a patient, in this instance, a female patient in treatment with a male therapist.

This excerpt also illustrates the affinity between shame and diffuse anxiety. Since the target of hostility in shame is the self, and the self is not an easily specifiable object, shame is experienced as tension or diffuse anxiety (or being on the verge of tears) but not knowing about what. In our study (Witkin et al, 1968), we predicted and confirmed a connection between field dependence and diffuse anxiety. The connection between shame and diffuse anxiety also needs to be pursued systematically. The question could be pursued using the Gottschalk method and an independent measure either of shame state or of diffuse anxiety.

A wide variety of painful superego states exist, in which shame merged with guilt in varying degrees.

Feeling ridiculous, embarrassment, chagrin, mortification, humiliation and dishonor are all variants of shame states, each with its own admixture of guilt and hostility. Embarassment or chagrin, evoked without too much underlying guilt can yield to good-humored laughter. When one has trouble righting oneself after feeling ridiculous or embarrassed, there is usually underlying guilt. Dishonor is the most serious shame state, since it carried the clear implication of personal guilt signifying both a serious crime and a personal failure. In any case, recognizing one's own psychic state usually required the help of a sympathetic observer who has done some introspection of his or her own states. The Gottschalk-Gleser method has a clear potential of use in dissecting complicated superego states,

if only because it can detect the simultaneous operation of anxiety and hostility in neighboring clauses of speech.

DIFFICULTIES IN THE FUNCTIONING OF THE SELF IN SHAME AND GUILT. SHAME IS ABOUT THE SELF (GUILT IS ABOUT THINGS DONE OR UNDONE).

Shame is about the self; it is thus an apparently "narcissistic" reaction, evoked by a lapse from the ego-ideal. An ego-ideal is difficult to spell out rationally; shame thus can be a subjective, "irrational" reaction. Adults regard shame as an "irrational" reaction which is more appropriate to childhood, especially if it occurs outside the context of moral transgression.

In shame, there is what Laing (1960) calls an implosion of the self. The body gestures and attitudes include head bowed, eyes closed, body curved in on itself, making the person as small as possible. At the same time that it seeks to disappear, the self may be dealing with an excess of autonomic stimulation, blushing, or sweating or diffuse rage, experienced as a "flood" of sensations. Shame is thus regarded by adults as a primitive reaction, in which body functions have gone out of control. It is regarded as an irrational reaction for this reason also.

Except for ideation which is often identical with that of guilt, shame is a relatively wordless state. The experience of shame often occurs in the form of imagery, of looking or being looked at. Shame may also be played out in imagery of an internal colloquy, in which the whole self is condemned by the "other." There is, however, a relatively limited vocabulary of scorn. The wordlessness of shame, its imagery of looking, together with the concreteness of autonomic activity make shame a primitive, "irrational" reaction, to which there is difficulty applying a rational solution. One is often ashamed of being or having been ashamed. Shame thus compounds itself out of an intrinsic difficulty in finding a "rational" place for it in the adult's psychic life.

So, for example, the same field dependent patient who was on the verge of tears and ashamed of herself because it was so ridiculous puts her dilemma this way: (The patient had entered treatment because she has a facial tic or "twitches.")

P: (laugh). I think I'd be interested in -well, I - think if I could get rid of the twitches, I'd get rid of the feelings that go with it, you know. But uh I guess if I had these things and I didn't care whether I had them or not, I guess it wouldn't matter either. I don't know (slight laugh). But I don't see how I couldn't care ... you know?

The patient is clearly aware that if she didn't care about having tics, i.e., if she were not ashamed of them,she would be better off. But she doesn't see how she could manage not to be ashamed of them. Rationally, she is quite aware of the fact that she really need not be ashamed of them but also aware that her feelings are not so easily persuaded. The patient is thus expressing a frequent dilemma in shame reactions: they occur in spite of one's better judgment, and compound themselves by making us ashamed that we are ashamed.

Perhaps because it feels like so primitive and "irrational" a state, shame is connected to a specific defense of hiding or running away. It is a state in which the mechanism of denial seems particularly to occur. Denial makes shame difficult for the person experiencing it to identify even though there is a strong affective reaction. The person often does not know what has hit him or her. (See above, p. for the patients' not knowing what they are upset about.)

The same patient who felt like an idiot when he thought of what he told his therapist illustrates the wordlessness of a shame reaction in an excerpt from the transcript which comes shortly before the patient has his burst of ridicule at himself and at his "nosy" therapist. Patient and therapist are talking about the patient's difficulties in school and the patient has begun to remark about the therapist's personal characteristics in what is clearly (to an observer) some state of envy. The patient is describing that his own school work is so difficult because one is competing against

"brilliant people." There is a very long pause.

T: What were you thinking?

P: Mm - , nothing.. that I can remember anyway.

T: Tm?

P: Nothing that I can remember. If I was thinking.

T: You looked sort of depressed. Is that the way you were feeling?

P: I was.. I have been depressed for quite a while. I don't know what I .. (hm?) I don't know what I think when I (inaud) like that. Sometime I just stare at something. (p) Wake up eventually. I don't know what the heck happens in between. (Long pause.)

Another kind of defense against shame appears to operate before any affective state is evoked. This defense, which is best described as "by-passing" shame feeling, does not obliterate the recognition of shame events, but appears to prevent the development of shame feeling. This by-passing of shame is accomplished by a "distancing" maneuver. The self views itself from the standpoint of the "other," but without much affect. The person wonders what he would think of himself if he were in the position of the "other." The content of the ideation in question concerns shame events, but without shame affect. Shame affect is by-passed and replaced by watching the self from a variety of viewpoints, including that of the "other." The following excerpt from the transcript of a (field-independent) male patient is shortly going to talk about masturbation illustrates the phenomenon of by-passing shame. The excerpt begins after a long pause.

T: What are you thinking?

P: I don't know. I have this feeling that there's something (mm,mm) I felt myself almost wince a second ago, and I was trying to think of what it is that I'm, you know. I was also thinking of what I would do if I were the therapist ... and I had a patient facing me (mm) and uh just what significance I would give to each of his movements and the like. This is something that uh I didn't think about to my knowledge for some time - this is what would I do if I were the other (inaudible).

The patient has clearly shifted the position of the self into the posi-

tion of the observer in an effort to ward off shame feeling. The primary process nature of his ideation is subtly expressed in his wondering what significance the observer would give to each of his "movements." Our knowledge that the patient is caught in a state of shame about masturbation makes his use of the term "movements" interpretable as a "concrete" (primary-process)outcome of the conflict in which he is caught. The shift in position of the self into the position of the observer who observes the self also illustrates the "doubleness" of shame experience and its affinity for the development of "scenes in an internal theater" (Breuer and Freud, 1893) in which the self and the other play out their roles.

Guilt, in contrast, is about things--acts or failures to act, or thoughts, for which one bears responsibility. It is often difficult, however, to assess the degree of one's responsibility or to assess the extent of injury which one has committed. It is also difficult to assess what reparation or amends one owes to balance the scales of justice. It is difficult, further, to assess the extent of punishment which one ought to bear in retribution for one's guilty conduct. An "objective" assessment of the extent of responsibility and of punishment seems to exist and require adherence. Heider (1958) has investigated the phenomenology of guilt and punishment. He describes punishment (p. 27) as "P harming O because O harmed or acted against the objective order as P understands it."

When guilt is evoked, it can merge into a "problem" in the rational assignment of motivation, responsibility and consequences. As the guilty person becomes involved in these problems, it can happen that guilty affect subsides, while ideation about the events continues. Guilt thus has an affinity for "isolation of affect," leaving a residuum of "insoluble dilemma" or worry thoughts, but without the person being necessarily aware that he or she is in a state of guilt.

The objective character of guilt and the affinity between it and rational assignment of responsibility can result in the person's becoming very busy in making amends for his guilt or in an insoluble dilemma of thought about his guilt. The self is active in this pursuit. It is intact and self-

propelled, in contrast to the self's divided functioning in shame.

Here, for example, is the transcript of the opening of the first therapy session of a (field-independent) woman patient. It illustrates the "thing" quality of guilt. The bothersome thing is that the patient cannot now decide "whose fault it is" that she does not have an orgasm during intercourse.

P: I don't know where to begin, uh, even when I had gone to Dr. --- a lot of things were really bothering me. Now I dont' feel so turbulent. I just think that whatever was bothering me then is still bothering me really. At the time I went to him it was a problem of sexual adjustment with my husband. I was married in June and it's no problem but, it doesn't bother me as much. I think it's taken a different form. I, I used to really resent him very much and I didn't like love-making and I still don't, but I don't think it's my fault so much any more. The thing that made me, I don't think I was frigid, uhm, I said "maybe it was me" and now I think maybe it's not. Maybe it's both of us. And maybe it's him just as much and maybe it's not all me."

This excerpt illustrates also, the relative lack of affect - the isolation of affect - which occurs in connection with an insoluble dilemma of "is it my fault or his fault?" Since the "problem" is apparently an objective one and involving the just apportionment of blame, acute affect which catches the self "at the quick" is absent in this guilty train of thought. As the patient puts it, she is not so "turbulent" now, although she is aware that at times she can be. The unconscious gratification of being in morally elevated state also sometimes keep the state of guilt active beyond the time of expiation. "He who despises himself," wrote Nietzsche (1937), "thereby esteems himself as the despiser ... When we train our conscience, it kisses as it bites." The self, then, may be caught in its own unconscious pride in being guilty, thus prolonging guilt rather than discharging it.

Here is a sequence in which a (field-independent) male patient, (the patient who wondered what he would think of himself if he were therapist) opens the same session by telling of his "good feeling" in obeying his conscience. Very shortly afterward, he is in an inexorable state of guilt

for defying his conscience. The concrete "problem" or guilty act is not getting out of bed when he should.

P: I won a small-sized battle yesterday ... I did as much work as I could and I went right and took the exam and mm and uh felt very good about it... Funny, today I was here at about 2:30 just to make sure I wouldn't be late, and I was fairly anxious to get here today."

Although the patient was not directly saying so, he was so proud of his obeying his own conscience that he wanted to share with the therapist his good feeling over winning the "small-sized battle." The patient's use of the term "funny" (which would rate a shame anxiety score) represents his own registration of ("childish") pride in his (and the therapist's) achievement.

But on the morning of this session, the patient who had awakened early enough to go job-hunting, got out of bed and then said to himself: "What the hell ... and then I got right back in bed and couldn't sleep but I refused to get out of bed again." In the wake of this transgression the patient begins a characteristic tirade of guilty ideation not only about staying in bed, but about widely generalized faults:

P: And uh I think I've grown accustomed to this life of uh, getting up when I please, not working, having no responsibility other than school and perhaps the feeling of responsibility toward home, but I keep destroying all chances of getting a job."

The flow of his guilt cannot be stopped by the therapist's intervention:

T: Mm, there must be a reason.

P: Yeah, no doubt. Uh, I don't know, it - I was thinking it's possible that I don't want additional responsibility - you know that, with having a job, but somehow that just seems like rationalization to me.

When one is in a state of guilt, benign explanations of the reasons for one's conduct seem like rationalizations!

DIFFICULTIES IN DISCHARGING HOSTILITY IN SHAME AND GUILT

SHAME-RAGE, WHICH ORIGINATES ABOUT THE SELF IS DISCHARGED BACK DOWN UPON THE SELF.

Whether it is evoked in the context of moral transgression or outside it, shame involves a failure by comparison with an internalized ego-ideal. There is thus, an implied framework of negative comparison with others. In the painful experience of being unable to live up to the standards of an admired "imago," attention is often focused on the "other," admired figure. Fascination with the "other" and sensitivity to the "other's" treatment of the self can ease the acute feeling of shame, while at the same time it renders the self still more vulnerable to shame. Shame is close to the feeling of awe. It is the feeling state to which one is more susceptible when one has fallen in love. The "other" is a prominent and powerful force in the experience of shame.

In shame, hostility against the self is experienced in the passive mode. The self feels not "in control" but overwhelmed and paralyzed by the hostility directed against it. One could "crawl through a hole," or "sink through the floor" or "die" with shame. The self feels small, helpless and childish. When, for example, there is unrequited love, the self feels crushed by the rejection. So long as shame is experienced, it is the "other" who is experienced as the source of hostility. Retaliatory hostility against the rejecting other is almost simultaneously evoked. But it is humiliated fury, or shame-rage, which is not considered "justified." The self is still in part experienced as the object of the "other's " scorn. Hostility against the "other" is trapped in this directional bind. To be furious and enraged with someone because one is unloved by him renders one easily and simultaneously guilty for being furious. Evoked hostility is readily redirected back against the vulnerable self.

For shame to occur there must be an emotional relationship between the

person and the "other" such that the person cares what the other thinks or feels about the self. In this affective tie the self does not feel autonomous or independent, but dependent and vulnerable to rejection. Shame is a vicarious experience of the significant other's scorn. A "righting" tendency often evoked by shame is the "turning of the tables." Evoked hostility presses toward triumph over or humiliation of the "other," i.e. to the vicarious experience of the other's shame. But the "other" is simultaneously beloved or admired, that guilt is evoked for aggressive wishes. Or the image of "other" may be devalued; but in this case one has lost an admired or beloved object. Shame-based rage is readily turned back against the self, both because the self is in a passive position vis-a-vis the "other" and because the self values the "other."

A prediction which results from this phenomenological analysis is that there should be a particularly strong association between shame and self-directed hostility. This prediction was confirmed in our therapy study (Witkin, et al, 1968), and in a subsequent study by Safer (1975).

The position of the self as the initiator of guilt, and the determiner or judge of extent of responsibility puts the self "in charge" of the hostility directed against the self. It also puts the self in charge of the distribution of hostility, as well as the assessment of the happenings in the field. This active role of the self in guilt opens the possibility that hostility may be directed not only against the self, but against the "other" and other forces in the field, thus creating an affinity between guilt and projection of hostility.

The prediction resulting from this phenomenological analysis is that there should be a tendency for guilt to be accompanied by hostility directed out as well as hostility directed against the self. Our therapy study (Witkin et al, 1968) showed a clear association between guilt and hostility going in both directions, in contrast to the close association between shame and self-directed hostility.

A particularly instructive example of a sequence from shame into guilt and thence into paranoid ideation comes from the transcript of a field-

independent male patient whose therapist had been interpreting (with some derision) the grandiosity of the patient's ego-ideal. It is easy for an observer to be amused by another person's ego-ideal and also easy to evoke shame in the person whose ego-ideal is under inspection especially since it is difficult to spell out a rationale for one's own strivings.

The patient had entered treatment for chest pains which had no organic base. He connected his symptoms to an "ego-ideal or something that I'm setting up." The patient had a characteristic way of describing his chest pains; he kept saying that he "receives" the pain. The patient had been arguing with the therapist that his ambitions were necessary and inevitable in his life circumstances. In the midst of their dispute about the wisdom of amibition, the therapist called the patient's attention to his peculiar mode of speech about the pains. The patient laughed (most likely with embarrassment, although he did not say so) and several times assured the therapist that he, the patient, knew no one was giving him his pains. At the end of this hour, the patient was suddenly moved to ask the therapist about the microphone in the room. This in spite of the fact that the microphone had been discussed at the opening session of the therapy and this was now the third session.

The patient opened his next hour by telling the therapist the following: P: I was sort of curious last week about that microphone. It developed, on questioning, that the patient had had a fantasy which he himself labeled as "weird," "illogical" and "improbable," to the effect that the therapist had sent a copy of the transcript of the therapy session to the school where the patient studies. His exact words are important because they pick up the theme of sending and "receiving" which had been a particular focus of the patient's embarrassment and had evoked the patient's need to reassure the therapist that he, the patient, was not crazy, since he knew he was not "receiving" chest pains from anyone. Here is the text of the primary process transformation which has the patient in "weird" fantasy of the therapist's betrayal made necessary out of "duty."

P: Well, yeah, I just thought that maybe you were drawing severe

conclusions and that someone should know about it at school. And some administrative officer should know about me ... mm And I was just wondering, 'cause no one's ever known that I sort of ... ah ... had funny ideas or what (laugh) (inaudible). Just a normal human being ... and now .. the picture's changed. I just thought that maybe uh I just thought that maybe you were sending them out of duty or something...some way (laugh) (inaudible) some way 'cause what's gonna happen if he does do it though.

The patient's shame and anger had been evoked by the therapist's interpretation, but it is hostility which has no "rationale" since the therapist is benign. The patient is in a state of guilt vis-a-vis the therapist for the patient's own shame-rage. The outcome is a paranoid fantasy which is very compelling, in spite of the patient's better judgment. And the content of the fantasy concretizes "receiving" and "sending" information about the severe conclusions which the therapist must be drawing about the patient's peculiarities, and which the therapist is compelled to make known on pain of the therapist's being in a state of guilt toward the authorities who should be notified. In this fantasy, both patient and therapist are an insoluble dilemma of guilt.

As I have shown in Shame and Guilt in Neurosis (Lewis, 1971) re-analysis of Freud's cases from the point of view of undischarged shame and guilt clearly supports the connection between shame and depression/hysteria and between guilt and obsessional neurosis. For example, the small fragment of practically verbatim account of conversation with Lucy R. about being in love with her employer reads as follows: (Breuer and Freud, 1893, p. 117).

"Were you ashamed of loving a man?" Freud asked. "no" came the answer from Lucy. "I'm not unreasonably prudish. We are not responsible for our feelings." But, she went on, "it was so distressing to me because he is my employer and I am in service and live in his house. I don't feel the same complete independence toward him that I could toward anyone else. I am a poor girl and he is a rich man. People would laugh at me if they had any idea of it." Lucy says that she is not ashamed and not guilty - as indeed in reason she need not be. She characteristically denies shame as we all

automatically do. But she goes on to recite in detail the state of shame which result from an equality of status. The Gottschalk-Gleser scoring of Lucy's description of her feelings would rate shame scores, especially the last sentence.

Dora, similarly, was in a state which Freud (1905) described as "mortification" at her father's betrayal of her. But neither Freud nor Dora had room in their cognitive systems for the humiliated fury which accompanies mortification at personal betrayal. Both agreed that her rage was "exaggerated" since neither her father nor Herr K. "had made a formal agreement in which she was the object of barter" (Freud, 1905, p.34). In this system, which Dora and Freud shared, the shame of personal betrayal is by implication, not in the same status as guilt for breaking a contract. And indeed, shame is "subjective," i.e., only about the self, whereas guilt is "objective," i.e., about events or things in the world.

In the case of the Rat-Man, Freud (1909, p.159) tells us that the patient spontaneously began his free associations at his first session by speaking about "a friend of whom the patient had an extraordinarily high opinion. The patient used to go to his friend when he was tormented by some criminal impulse and ask him whether he despised him as a criminal. His friend used to give him moral support by assuring him that he (the patient) was a man of irreproachable conduct and had probably been in the habit from his (the friend's) youth onward of taking a dark view of his own life."

The Rat-Man's obsessions were about terrible events for which he, the patient, would be responsible (guilty) and they developed out of the patient's chronic sense of guilt. I have been able to show that each obsessional outbreak was actually stirred by some by-passed shame in the patient's experience. (Lewis, 1971).

A complicated interaction clearly exists, in which sex, cognitive style and superego mode all influence primary process symptom formation. Using the Gottschalk-Gleser method of microscopic analysis of the stream of consciousness has made it possible to unravel some of the complicated interplay of forces governing the formation of psychopathology.

## References


Ausubel, D. Relationships between Shame and Guilt in the Socializing Process. Psychological Review, 62,378-390 (1955).

Berliner, B. The Role of Object - relations in moral masochism. Psychoanalytic Quarterly, 27,38-56 (1958).

Bibring, E. The Mechanism of Depression in Affective Disorders. P. Greenacre, ed. International Universities Press, New York (1953).

Bowlby, J. Attachment and Loss, Vol. I, Basic Books, New York (1969).

Breuer, J. and Freud, S.Studies on Hysteria, Standard Edition, Vol. 2, (1893-1895).

Erikson, E. Identity and the Life Cycle. J. Amer. Psychoana. Assoc. 4,56-121 (1956).

Freud, S. The Ego and the Id. Standard Edition, Vol. 19, (1923).

Freud, S. The Interpretation of Dreams. Standard Edition, Vol. 4-5, (1900-1901).

Freud, S. The Economic Problem of Masochism. Standard Edition, Vol. 19, (1924).

Freud, S. Fragments of an Analysis of a Case of Hysteria. Standard Edition, Vol. 5, (1905).

Freud, S. Notes upon a Case of Obsessional Neurosis. Standard Edition, Vol. 10, (1909).

Gottschalk, L.A. and Gleser, G.C. The Measurement of Psychological States Through the Content Analysis of Verbal Behavior. University of California Press, Los Angeles (1969).

Harlow, H., and Harlow N. The Affectional Systems in Behavior of Non Human Primates. A.M. Schrier, H. Harlow, and F. Stollnitz, eds. Vol. 2, Academic Press, New York (1965).

Heider, F. The Psychology of Interpersonal Relations. John Wiley and Sons, New York (1958).

James, W. Principles of Psychology. Vol. I, Henry Holt and Co., New York (1890).

Kohut, H. The Analysis of the Self. International Universities Press, New York (1971).

Laing, R. The Divided Self. Quadrangle Books, Chicago (1960).

Lewis, H. Over-differentiation and Under-individuation of the Self. Psychoanalysis and the Psychoanalytic Review, 45,21-35 (1958).

Lewis, H. Organization of the Self as reflected in Manifest dreams. Psychoanalytic Review. 46,21-35 (1959).

Lynd, H. On Shame and the Search for Identity. Harcourt, Brace, New York (1958).

Lewis, H. A case of watching as a defense against an oral incorporation fantasy. Psychoanalytic Review, 50,68-80 (1963).

Lewis, H.B. Shame and Guilt in Neurosis. International Universities Press, New York (1971).

Lewis, H.B. Psychic War in Men and Women. New York University Press, New York (1976).

Menaker, E. Masochism: A defense reaction of the ego. Psychoanalytic Quarterly, 22,205-220 (1953).

Nietzsche, F. The Philosophy of Nietzsche. Modern Library Edition, New York (1937).

Piers, G. and Singer, M. Shame and Guilt, Clarks C. Thomas, Springfield, Ill. (1953).

Reik, T. Masochism in Modern Man. Grove Press, New York (1941).

Safer, J. Unpublished dissertation. The New School for Social Research Graduate Faculty (1975).

Witkin, H., Lewis,H., Hertzman, M., Madiofer, K., Weissner, P., and Wagner, S. Personality Through Perception. Harper and Bro., New York (1954).

Witkin, H., Dyk, R., Faterson, H., Goodenough, D., and Karp, S. Psychological Differentiation, John Wiley and Sons, New York (1962).

Witkin, H., Lewis, H., and Weil, E. Affective reactions and patient-therapist interaction among more differentiated and less differentiated patients early in therapy. J. Nerv. Ment. Dis. 146,193-208 (1968).

# Introduction to Chapter 48

Introductory Comments by Louis A. Gottschalk

In this chapter, the research team of Schofer and his coworkers make some innovative and original contributions to the application of the Gottschalk-Gleser content analysis scales to psychotherapy research. They focus, initially, on the units of verbal communication to be analyzed from tape-recorded transcriptions of psychotherapy, and they suggest three kinds of units which lend themselves best towards approaching a variety of research problems in psychotherapy; (1) the single clause or simple sentence; (2) separate patient statements, demarcated from beginning to end, by therapists' statements; and (3) individual psychotherapeutic sessions. As with all the other chapters in this book, this chapter has to be read thoroughly to be appreciated for its meaty quality and its creative introduction of rigorous scientific methodological approaches and measurement techniques to the study of psychodynamically-oriented psychotherapy.

Among the highlights of this chapter, there should be included the discovery of sequential patterns of the expression of one type of affect

during a therapeutic session along a curve showing a progressive decrease of the magnitude, over time, of this specific affect and a corresponding increase, followed by a diminishment of other associated affects. Schofer and his coworkers appear to have demonstrated such recurring patterns with mathematical certainty. If these findings can be replicated, the suscepti-bility to therapeutic interventions of these patterns of the ebb-and-flow of these associated emotions will be of great interest. Another highlight of this chapter is the exploration of what portions of the psychothera-peutic hour are likely to represent the affective arousals occurring during the whole psychotherapeutic hour. Research data is presented which strongly suggests that the affect scores from the first patient's state-ment (790 words), the longest single statement of the patient (uninter-rupted and continuous monologue), and the last statement correlate highly with the affect scores derived from the total psychotherapeutic hours. Whereas, the first speech sample and the single longest statement of the patient provide scores which correlate significantly with hostility directed inward scores, ambivalent hostility scores, and anxiety scores derived from content analysis of the total psychotherapeutic session. These findings supply valuable information towards simplifying and condensing the time-consuming task of microanalytic analysis of a long series of psychotherapeutic sessions.

# Possible Applications of the Gottschalk-Gleser Content Analysis of Speech in Psychotherapy Research*

Gert Schöfer, Friedrich Balck, Uwe Koch**

One of the main reasons which led to the development of the Gottschalk-Gleser content analysis of speech was that Louis A. Gottschalk, in the early nineteen fifties, was looking for psychological instruments with which he could measure immediate and changing affects of patients in interview or psychotherapy situations. The existing psychological instruments (self report, description by others, and projective tests) did not meet these requirements: 1. they intended to measure permanent traits; 2. with the exception of projective instruments, they generally could not measure unconscious aspects; and 3. their application within an interview or therapeutic situation would immediately change the situation or could not be applied. Not much has changed in regard to these three points, apart from the development of rating and content analytic instruments, whose use during

---

*Granted by the German Research Society, Sonderforschungsbereich 115 - Projekt C4

** Department of Psychosomatic Medicine (Chairman Prof.Dr.Dr.A.-E. Meyer) II. Med., University of Hamburg, GFR

the last 20 years has spread considerably. Both types of instruments can be applied to already gathered materials without creating a test situation. The fact that it is applicable to natural text material is, also, one of the great advantages of the Gottschalk-Gleser method.

For several understandable reasons the development of this instrument took the course of creating a standardized situation with standard instructions for eliciting speech and the instrument has been mainly used under these circumstances. The use of the instrument in research on psychotherapy is, therefore, at the present time still at an early state of development. Since one abstains from using the standard instructions for eliciting speech in psychotherapy, one must newly define the summarizing unit*, which so far as a rule has been a five-minute speech sample, in order to analyze material from psychotherapeutic sessions. Even though there is an attempt by Gottschalk (1966) to split interview material into five-minute units, such a division of interviews is a merely physical approach and does not, as a rule, go along with natural speech units, which arise in the process of an interview. Defining units on the basis of their number of words, e.g., 500 words, as well as using time units (2 to 5 minutes) would neglect the natural structure of an interview. Aspects which belong together could be torn

---

*Gottschalk and Gleser are using three classification of units in their instruments:

1. Coding unit: The single grammatical clause to which a coding can be attributed.
2. Summarizing unit: A text for which a score can be calculated. It can be defined by time (5 minutes), number of words, or topic (for instance dream report) etc.
3. Contextual unit: The necessarily wider context which must be taken into consideration in some cases to score the single clause, if the clause cannot be coded by its content alone.

Beside these three units, we see a further one, we want to call it "Thematic unit." This means, that in a broader text you often find parts with more and parts with less codings, and often the single parts are related with different themes. So we suggest, that a specific affect or affect pattern may be connected with a specific theme. The existence of this unit should be examined in the future more precisely.

apart artificially or separate phenomena could artificially be combined. In a therapeutic session, we see three natural units as being possible:

1. the single clause (or sentence, consisting of a subject and predicate);
2. the individual statement of the patient or the therapist, which means that one verbal unit of a partner is framed by two statements of the other partner;
3. the total therapy session

The <u>single clause (or sentence)</u> is the smallest natural unit and is the unit of coding at the same time. This way a sequence of codings can be studied. Working with units of codification creates new problems though:

a) As a rule, not every sentence contains a measurable affect. Rather, to the contrary, only relatively few sentences have an affective content. Therefore, one finds a sequence of sentences without codings into which a few sentences with codings of affects are interspersed.

b) If one does not want to neglect sentences without a coding of affects, one would have to introduce a new category, namely "no codings," which would dominate in comparison to the other codings.

c) The "sentence unit" is smaller than the postulated "thematic unit." It also would not take into consideration several assumptions about the mode of usage of affects in speech. For instance, it is possible to express an affect with a certain intensity in a single sentence directly ("I hate him" = high amount of affect) and in the two following sentences one might not find any coding. Another possibility would be to express the same intensity of affect in three sentences in a very indirect way or through denial (low amount of affect). In a larger unit this difference cancels out, since in that case one multiplies frequency and weight.

These single "sentence units" have their advantage, too: it is possible to observe how directly or indirectly affects will be expressed, and these units could make it possible to get an insight into how individual patients deal with affects.

The <u>single statement</u> of a partner in a dialogue seems to us the most

natural unit. This is based on the assumption that the partner of a conversation stops speaking when he has expressed a certain content or if the other partner starts speaking in case he wants to comment on one of the previously expressed contents. This unit may come closer to the concept of "thematic unit" and describes the natural dialogue most adequately. But the delineation of these units does create problems: besides expressing a certain content in a dialogue, many short statements may be made which cannot be scored in a content analytic way, for instance, introjections, agreements, questions, etc. (e.g. "yes", "hm", "who?", etc.). In addition, there is a problem, which has been mentioned by Gottschalk and Gleser, that speech samples below a certain number of words ($< 70$ words) cannot be scored reliably.

To use the whole therapy session as a unit would not be detailed enough for many research questions, since one receives hardly any information about the processes of changing affects within the hour. For other questions, however, for instance the measurement of changes of affect of the patient over several therapeutic sessions, this unit is very practicable and no technical difficulties arise as would in using smaller units.

Gottschalk et al (1966) analyzed a one-hour interview by dividing the interview into five-minute sections. By calculating affective scores for the patient, for the interviewer, and for both together ("dyadic score") this summarizing unit (time intervals) could show a process within the interview, since the scores in the five-minute units varied. Using sentence units, Kepecs (see Chapter 49) attempted to find in interview sections, processes and dependencies of affects on other variables. Von Rad (see Chapter 36) analyzed interviews of psychosomatic patients and of psychoneurotic patients in taking the first thousand words of a patient from the interviews and scoring in a traditional manner.

## Results

Our team has done studies in all three levels of units mentioned above. We want to show, with an example of each, the possible avenues

of research in the field of psychotherapy suggested by our studies.

1. Sentence unit

From a 19-hour psychotherapy, all patient statements were grouped according to which specific hostile affect they started with. We found 242 such statements. The breakdown and the mean frequencies of the individual codings are shown in Table 1.

Then the sequence of affect codings for single sentences within such a patient statement were looked at, while sentences without coding were neglected. Taking a group, in which all initial codings were identical, and calculating the frequencies of the affect codings at specific locations in the sequence, relatively typical sequences were found (See illustration 1a and 1b). This is demonstrated for Hostility Directed Outward overt (HDOo) and Hostility Directed Inward (HDI).

The illustration shows on the horizontal line the location in the sequence within the patient's statement. On the vertical line is found the frequencies of different codings in percent. Illustration 1a shows the sequences of the group, in which the initial coding is hostility directed outward, overt (HDOo). Obviously the frequency of the HDOo-coding at the first location is 100%, and the frequency of the others, 0%.

At the second location, the frequency of HDOo-codings is still 50%, and the frequency of the others between 10% and 20%. From the second to the sixth location in the sequence, the frequency of HDOo-codings decreases around 10%. Frequencies of the other codings increase slightly. One can clearly see that the first coding in the sequence is so dominant that in the following locations this HDOo-coding always remains the most frequent one. A comparison with the sequences starting with a hostility directed inward (HDI)coding, shows a similar result (See illustration 1b). Here also, with the exception of the fourth session, the coding at the beginning remains the most frequent one. Yet in contrast to the HDO-group, there is a further coding, ambivalent hostility (AH) which grows more important in the course of the sequence.

Table 1.

Frequency of the sequences of the single groups and mean frequencies of the codings per sequence

| | HDOo Group | HDOc Group | HDI Group | AH Group | total |
|---|---|---|---|---|---|
| Number of Sequences | 95 | 33 | 67 | 47 | 242 |
| Mean of Frequency per Sequence | 6.91 | 7.18 | 6.07 | 6.4 | 6.61 |

For both groups it can be clearly seen, though, that the initial coding is dominant. We have tested this result with the Chi-square test and have shown that the frequencies of the specific codings differ highly significantly.

This part of our study shows that an analysis using sentence units makes it possible to analyze structures of hostile affects in psychotherapy. The question arises, if the described behavior is typical for this specific patient or if it can be found also with other individuals. In order to answer these questions, we have analyzed speech samples of 200 subjects in the same manner and have found very similar results. They suggest the conclusion that probably there is a lawful sequence of affect codings. Furthermore, we found that not only the first coding influences the following, but that there is an inner law of codification, meaning that an affect, which arises, generates to a certain extent other specific affects (Balck, 1977).

2. Statement unit

The same 19-hour therapy was also analyzed in regard to the question, whether affective changes could be observed on the level of statements (Schöfer, 1976a). Each therapy session was divided up into speech samples by scoring all patient statements (in between two statements by the

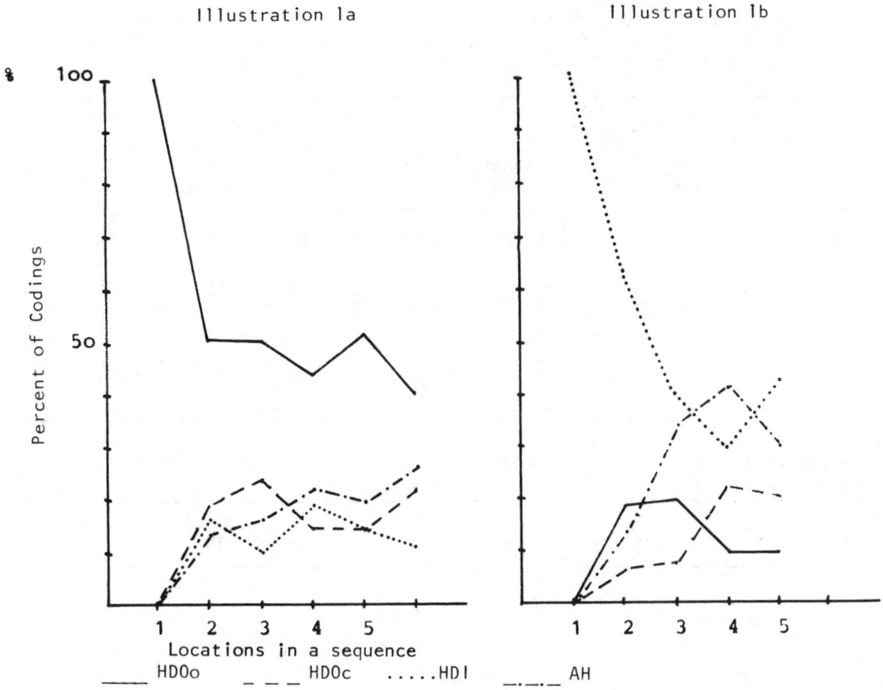


Illustration l: Changes of frequencies in percent of codings in a sequence. The initial coding remains dominant; in addition, frequencies of the other codings (1. ... = locations in the sequence)

Illustration la: (HDOo-group) First coding in the sequence = HDOo

Illustration lb: (HDI-group) First coding in the sequence = HDI

therapist), which contained at least 90 words. The raw scores were transformed with the formula:

$$\sqrt{\frac{100 \times (\text{raw score} + 0.5)}{\text{Number of words}}}$$

Results of the eleventh therapy session are demonstrated in Illustration 2 as an example. Each point on the specific curve of affect shows the affect score of the associated patient statement. One can find states of affect, which remain prominent over several patient statements (e.g.

Table 2: Frequencies of the individual codings at individual locations in the sequence (2. ... 5. ...) for the HDOo- and for the HDI-group. In the lowest line: Chi-square-scores with significancy.

| | 2. | | 3. | | 4. | | 5. | |
|---|---|---|---|---|---|---|---|---|
| | HDOo Group | HDI Group | HDOo Group | HDI Group | HDO Group | HDI Group | HDO Group | HDI Group |
| HDOo | 48 | 12 | 40 | 11 | 30 | 4 | 29 | 3 |
| HDOv | 18 | 4 | 19 | 4 | 10 | 9 | 8 | 6 |
| HDI | 16 | 42 | 8 | 22 | 13 | 12 | 8 | 13 |
| AH | 13 | 9 | 13 | 19 | 15 | 17 | 11 | 9 |
| Total Number of Codings | 95 | 67 | 80 | 56 | 68 | 42 | 56 | 31 |
| $Chi^2$ | 36.21*** | | 29.91*** | | 12.38** | | 14.22** | |

** .01 df = 3

*** .001

hostility directed outward overt (HDOo) is high between the 9th and the 16th statement, hostility directed inward (HDI) being low at the same time). One can observe several such complexes of affects in an hour, which go along with or without simultaneous changes of other affects. In Illustration 2, with each type of hostility the type of anxiety correlating with it is marked as a broken line. One finds trends for the specific affects, which, expressed as statistical correlations, are partly independent, partly dependent.

One can conclude, therefore, that by using patient statement units affective changes and correlations in a therapeutic session can be demonstrated.

3. Hour unit

Taking the total number of words of the patient in a therapeutic session and calculating the affect coding on that basis, one arrives at

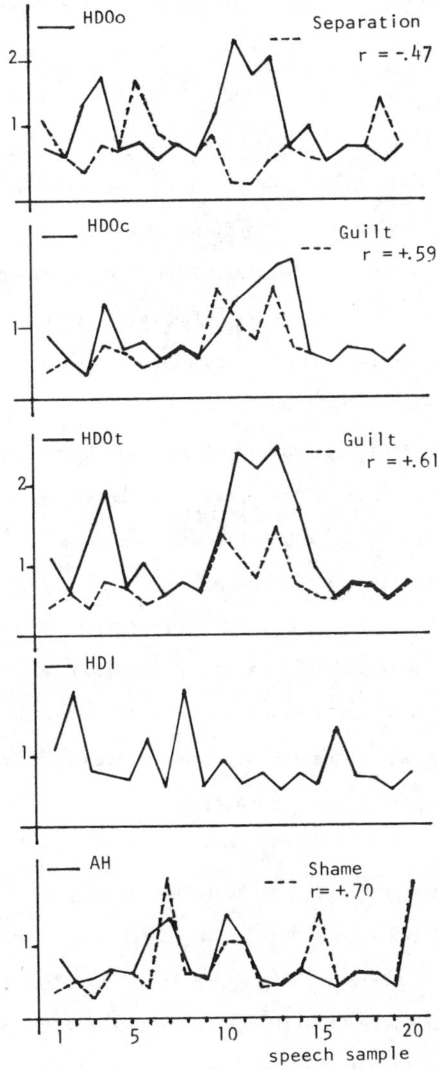


Illustration 2: Processes of the individual modes of hostility (———) with the correlating anxieties (-----) in a therapeutic session. The correlation coefficients are found in the illustration.

a score of a session for each specific affect. This can also be done for the therapist and, furthermore, a "dyadic score" as described by Gottschalk et al (1966) can be calculated, which we have so far not done.

In one study (Schöfer, 1976 b) we got a session score by combining all patient statements having more than 90 words of the 19-hour therapy (by using 17 transcribed hours). Sessions 2 and 5 could not be transcribed because of technical deficiencies. The total number of words of the patient was not considered, but the deviation of the scores is rather small. Illustration 3 shows the trends of the individual affects over the 19 hours. All affects in the course of the therapy have a tendency to decrease which can be shown by the negative correlation with the sequence of hours. To point out a special phenomenon, we have combined all affects into a "total affect." Here two hours, namely the 9th and the 14th, are prominent, because of their high scores of affect. (The phenomenon can also be observed by looking at individual affects.) Looking at the protocols of the therapy and into the retrospectives of the therapy sessions given by the therapist after each hour, one can observe two outstanding features in connection with both increases of affects:

1. In both therapy sessions, the patient relapsed into her symptom, (strong itching of the skin).
2. After both hours the therapist expressed his skepticism in regard to a successful outcome of the therapy. In each of the following sessions this skepticism turned into optimism going along with a strong decrease in affectivity of the patient as Illustration 3 demonstrates.

This shows that analyzing a therapy in "hour units" can be a possibile approach towards describing a therapeutical process and towards identifying outstanding hours, which then can be more thoroughly studied. Since the scoring of total hours and of long therapies is a very taxing endeavour, we have tried to give an answer to the question,

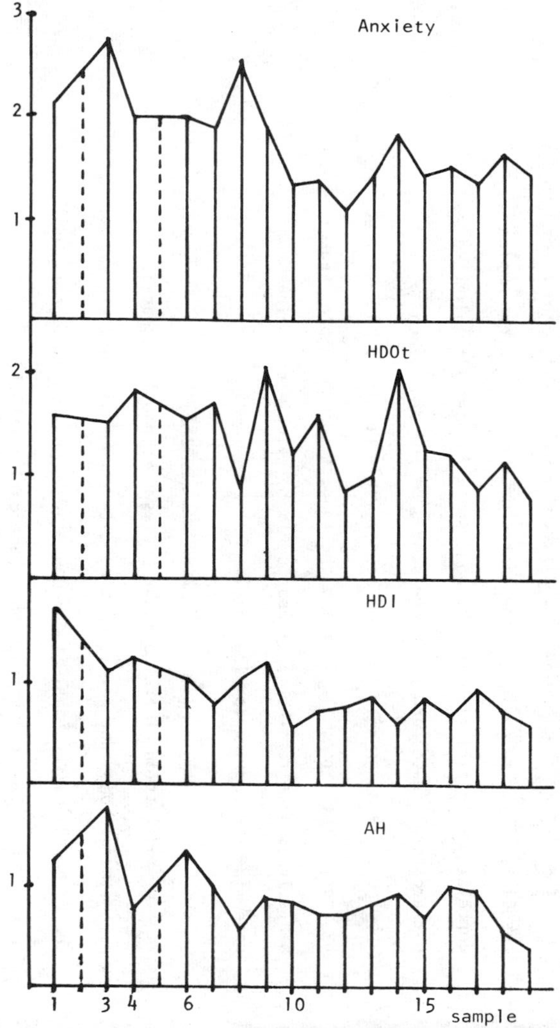

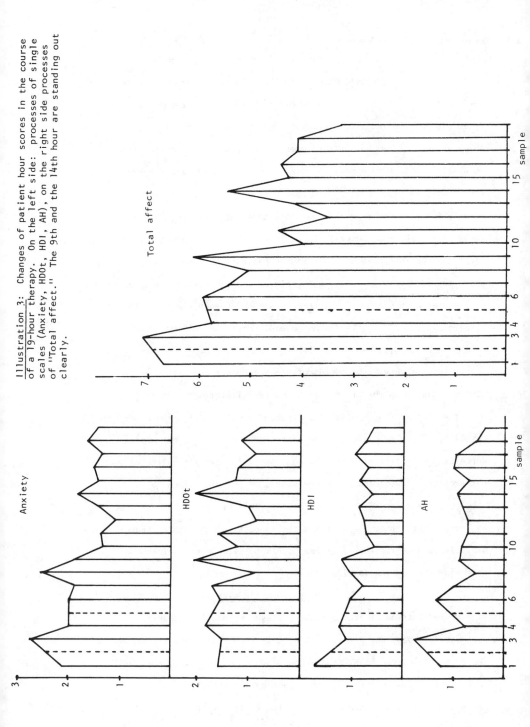

Illustration 3: Changes of patient hour scores in the course of a 19-hour therapy. On the left side: processes of single scales (Anxiety, HDOt, HDI, AH), on the right side processes of "Total affect." The 9th and the 14th hour are standing out clearly.

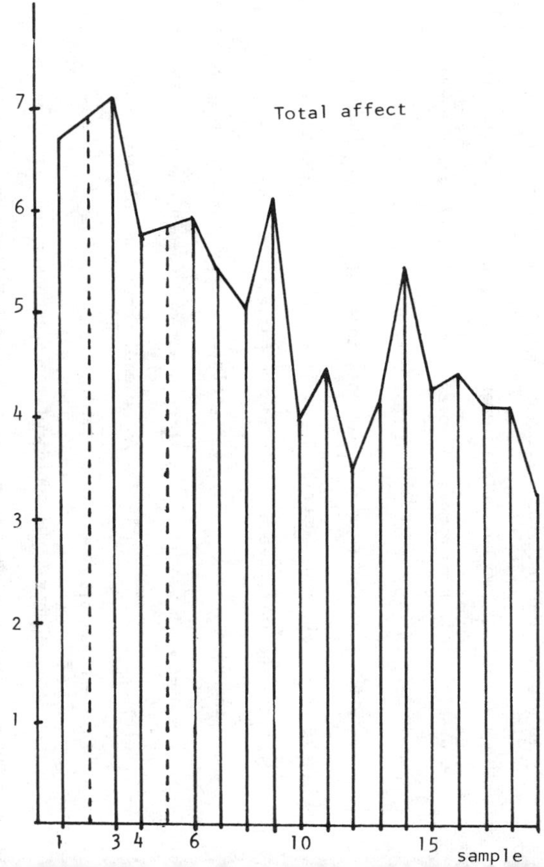

whether one can find sections of a psychotherapeutic session representative of the total hour score, in order to reduce the amount of coding. By looking at the individual session, we had noticed that frequently there are one or two patient statements, which differ from the others because of their high number of words. Out of the 17 scored therapy hours, we found 10, in which one speech sample contained more than 500 words. Our idea was that this patient statement would be important (central for the whole hour). In addition to this, we assumed that the first and the last speech sample of the patient would be important ones, too. In order to test this, we correlated (part-whole correlation) the hour scores with scores of the three described speech samples. The results are shown in Table 3. As an additional control, we considered a 4th speech sample, namely the 7th patient statement.

As Table 3 shows, the scores of the speech samples with more than 500 words and also the first speech samples significanlty correlated with the hour scores in hostility directed inward (HDI), ambivalent hostility (AH), and anxiety. The scores of the last speech samples correlated significantly with the hour score in hostility directed outward total (HDOt) and HDI. The scores of the 7th speech sample show no correlation with the hour score. This result would mean that by scoring the first, the last and the longest speech samples representative scores for the total hour could be calculated, which would economize the scoring considerably.

## Summary and Discussion

The application of the Gottschalk-Gleser method in research on psychotherapy does not permit working with speech samples elicited by the standard instructions, if one does not intend to change the psychotherapeutic situation through the investigation itself. Therefore, one must define a summarizing unit, which is satisfactory to the quality of the psychotherapeutic dialogue. In order to describe the situation of a specific psychotherapy sufficiently, we believe that it is necessary to find "natural" summarizing units. We can suggest three

Table 3: Part whole correlations of the different affect scores for selected speech samples with the hour scores.

| | N | HDOt | HDI | AH | Anxiety | Representative for |
|---|---|---|---|---|---|---|
| Samples with Number of Words > 500 | 10 | - | .90*** | .72* | .69* | HDI AH Anxiety |
| First Sample | 17 | - | .70** | .50** | .73*** | HDI AH Anxiety |
| Last Sample | 17 | .48* | .67** | - | - | HDOt HDI |
| 7th Sample | 17 | - | - | - | - | |

approaches for doing so: 1. the single sentence; 2. the individual statement; 3. the individual session. This results in different problems for each level of units which we have tackled, but certainly have not yet totally solved. We were able to show that on all three level of units, findings about affective changes can be made. The observations made from the different levels are based on only one single case study and need to be confirmed by using data from other psychotherapies. It could be demonstrated, for instance, that the analysis of representative sections from a therapeutic session can lead to findings, which are true for the whole psychotherapy. In case this result can be reproduced in other psychotherapies, it would be possible to reduce the amount of scoring considerably. One then could identify the relevant sessions within a long sequence of hours and study those more thoroughly.

Because of the experiences we have gained with the Gottschalk-Gleser method so far, we believe that it is applicable to research on psychotherapy and that it is capable of providing significant information about patient's affects in psychotherapy.

## References

Balck, F.B. Kennzeichen von ängstlichen und aggressiven Affekten in Attektcodierringssequenzen, Hamburg (1977) (unpublished.)

Gottschalk, L.A., Winget, C.N., Gleser, G.C., and Springer, K.J. The measurement of emotional changes during a psychiatric interview: A working model toward quantifying the psychoanalytic concept of affect, in Methods of Research in Psychotherapy. L.A. Gottschalk and A.W. Auerbach, eds. Appleton-Century-Crofts, New York (1966).

Kepecs, J.G. Teaching psychotherapy by use of brief typescripts, (1977) (unpublished).

Schöfer, G. Versuch der Anwendung der Gottschalk-Gleser-Sprachinhalts-analyse auf Psychotherapiematerial. Therapiewoche, 26, 7 (1976a).

Schöfer, G. Erfassung affektiver Veränderungen durch Sprachinhalts-analyse im Psychotherapieverlauf. Biblthca psychiat. No 154, (1976b).

# Introduction to Chapter 49

# The Teaching of Psychotherapy by use of Brief Transcripts

Joseph Kepecs

Introductory Comments by Louis A. Gottschalk

Kepecs provides an ingenious example of the application of the Gottschalk-Gleser method of content analysis of speech to the task of teaching psychotherapy. As anyone knows who has engaged in this worthwhile but uncharted pedagogical enterprise, guidelines are few for helping students to detect the psychodynamic conflicts of the patient during each psychotherapeutic session and teaching students to sort out empirical data from the patient's narrations during the interview to check and substantiate their tentative formulations. Kepecs provides just this kind of method.

Without making much of it, he also provides: 1. an approach to managing and understanding the cumbersome bulk of tape-recorded interviews and the potentially selectively distorted and condensed data generally available from the would-be therapist's process notes by using a 10 minute typescript of the interview; 2. a framework for deriving the psychodynamic focal conflict of the psychotherapeutic session (borrowing liberally from the conceptualizations of Thomas French on arriving at the core thematic conflict of a treatment session); 3. an articulation of the usually automatic cognitive processes

involved in the, otherwise, intuitive formulation by psychotherapists of psychological conflicts expressed in interviews; 4. a rough-and-ready simplification of the Gottschalk-Gleser content analysis scales adaptable to rapid clinical impressionistic applications, such that the complex weighting system is discarded in favor no weighting whatsoever of the relative importance of separate verbal categories (which, essentially, equates the relative contribution of all classes of verbalizations in the process of assessing magnitude of a psychological state, that is, each verbal category carries a weight of plus or minus one); 5. and a potential method for discerning counter-transference distortions of therapists by noting "tracking errors."

The innovative ideas of Kepecs along these lines merit further study and development.

# Teaching Psychotherapy by Use of Brief Typescripts

JOSEPH G. KEPECS, M.D.* | *Madison, Wisc.*

*A typescript of a 10-minute segment of a taped therapeutic interview, coded by using a modification of the Gottschalk scales, quite clearly demonstrates the patient's current focal conflict. Recognition of the current focal conflict is thus taught, and this is used as an organizing principle in supervision of psychotherapy.*

The use of a brief typescript of a part (10 minutes) of a tape recording of a psychotherapeutic interview has definite advantages in supervision and teaching. Brief segments of a tape have been used considerably in psychotherapy research. Mintz and Luborsky[1] conclude that though the whole-session recording has advantages, "The brief segment appears to be a useful research unit for many problems in understanding the process of psychotherapy. Relationships between segment-based and whole session-based descriptions were high enough for most major dimensions of the process to justify taking advantage of the tremendous time saving involved in using segments."

I have found a brief typed sample valuable for the following reasons:

1. It gives focus and precision to the report of an interview. The actual words of patient and therapist are displayed unchanging in space, rather than fleetingly in time. It shows unmistakably exactly what was said, and the relationships between statements can be exactly and carefully observed. Listening without the reference point of the typed words stimulates associations, projects, flights of fancy, and speculation. It is much more subjective and does not lend itself to clarification of the structure of conflicts.

2. An *exact* 10-minute typescript is representative and can give a good idea of what is going on including what the therapist is doing.

A brief section of an interview may be confusing unless there is a way to systematically read it, so as to get at the underlying structure. Levi-Strauss[2] describes "the principles which serve as a basis for any kind of structural analysis: economy of explanation; unity of solution; and ability to reconstruct the whole fragment, as well as further stages from previous ones." With the exception of reconstruction of previous stages, the focal conflict described by Thomas French in *The Integration of Behavior*[3] serves admirably as a conceptual framework for seeking and ordering the underlying structure in these brief typescripts. This is essentially a restatement, with some modi-

*Professor of Psychiatry, University of Wisconsin-Madison, Medical School, 1300 University Avenue, Madison, Wisconsin, 53706.

fications, of dynamic conflict theory. A few quotations will introduce this idea:

> Our first task is to discover the motives or the conflict with which the patient is preoccupied at the time. By this we do not mean the thoughts or motives with which the patient is consciously preoccupied. If the patient were not in conflict, he might stick to one topic; but in a single psychoanalytic session the patient may talk about many topics. Still, the psychoanalyst knows that thoughts that come up, one after another, in free association must be related to one another. His task is to find the center from which the patient's thoughts radiate. This center is usually not conscious but preconscious. We call it the patient's "focal conflict."
>
> Still, searching for the patient's "focal conflict" is an intuitive art which cannot be completely reduced to rules. We do have objective criteria to determine when we have found the patient's "focal conflict." If a particular conflict is focal during a psychoanalytic interview, then we should be able to recognize everything that the patient says or does during the interview as a reaction to this particular conflict.

French describes a disturbing wish or motive, and a reactive motive which repudiates the disturbing wish. This is the focal conflict. The person in conflict is attempting a solution to his conflict.

The focal conflict, an underlying structure, is to be found in almost any 10-minute segment. I have arbitrarily selected the second ten minutes of the hour to be transcribed. But trainees have often chosen other segments because they seemed more interesting, and this does not appear to alter the value of the method. I have modified French's conception by considering as solutions not only hope-oriented adaptive attempts but also various neurotic compromises between the disturbing wish and the reactive motive, namely, symptoms.

The more skill and clinical experience one has, the more easily and accurately can the focal conflict be delineated. I believe developing this skill is a worthwhile part of the learning of a beginning therapist. I have developed a rating system, considerably influenced by the Gottschalk[4] categories, which can be easily used and applied as one reads over the transcript.

I make a few assumptions derived from experience, from psychodynamic theory, especially from French's focal-conflict concept, and am also somewhat influenced by the simplicity of Schafer's[5] action language concepts. The assumptions underlying a focal concept formulation are: A person wants to act or do. He has learned through many experiences that some kinds of actions or potential actions will get him into difficulty with others around him; or, will upset inner balance—homeostasis; or, when external relations have been internalized, will get him into trouble with his conscience (superego and ego ideal). To avoid these difficulties, which are mainly feelings of fear and anxiety, the person will use a variety of solutions some of which are compromises or defenses and others which have varying degrees

of adaptive value. The particular focal conflict is likely to predominate through a particular therapeutic hour, though it may sometimes change within the hour. When it can be identified it serves to orient the therapist and is a guide to interpretations and interventions. With some practice it becomes easily possible to label statements in a transcript. I have tried to describe most possibilities which one is likely to encounter in a 10-minute transcript. The statements are classified as wishes—intentions to do something; reactions to these intentions—generally fear, guilts, and anxieties; and solutions—a variety of defenses, compromises, and adaptations. (Some of the Gottschalk classifications are paraphrased.)

*Classification of the Components of Focal Conflicts*

When it is clear, the sex of the person(s) who are liked, who are feared, who mistreat one, and so forth, should be indicated by the conventional symbols. This often helps clarify the focal conflict. In a male patient, for example, positive feelings toward a female followed by defensive hostility to a male, delineates an Oedipal conflict. When the therapist is referred to, the abbreviation Ther is added to the coding.

The statement to be coded is underlined. Only the patient's words are coded. When one of the constituents of the FC (focal conflict)—most often the reactive motive—is not stated and has to be inferred, it is placed in brackets.

## WISHES

PHR = *Positive Human Relations*

Any statement which refers to self or others supporting, or helping self or others, or wishing to: "He looks out for his mother."♀ "I want to help her."♀

Statements of closeness; loving, congenial relations or desires for them involving self or others: "She loves her child." "I want to be able to be open with him."♂

Concern for others: "He misses her."♀ "I'm worried about him."♂

Praise or approval of others: "She admires him."♂ "I think he's okay."♂

Sexual interest (positive): "I want to go to bed with her."♀ "She's in love with him."♂

Expression: "I want to let all my feelings out." Ther.

HO = *Hostility Out*

Any statements referring to self attacking others ranging all the way from simple angry statements to defiance, to murder: "I hate him."♂ "Damn you!" Ther. Also (what Gottschalk calls covert hostility) any statements

involving anger, criticism, harm or destruction by others to others, including animals, plants, inanimate objects being harmed in some way. Also denial of anger: "She really criticized him."♂ "Not that I'm angry at you." Ther. Also suppressed anger: "I just sizzled inside."

M = *Mastery*

Statements indicating one is in control of one's self and can deal with one's situation. Statements of competence: "I am in control of my life." "I'm able to cope with the situation." "I understand why I did it." Statements about or implying that one is free: "I can do what I want." "I'm able to enjoy myself."

A = *Assertion*

This is related to mastery but having to do with situations where self controls others or refuses to submit to oppression: "I told him to get busy."♂ "I told her to stop trying to run my life."♀

**REACTIONS** *(reactive motive)*

This refers to fears, guilts and anxieties generally involving one's self or existing in others. Usually these feelings will be mentioned as fear, or anxiety, or guilt. Fear of death: "I'm afraid I'll die." Fear of bodily harm: "I'm afraid he'll beat me up."♂ Or involving another person: "She was afraid he was going to hit her."♂ or "I fear cancer." Guilt: "I feel guilty." "I did wrong." Or denial of guilt: "I'm not to blame." Shame: "I was so embarrassed." Fear of separation or loss: "I was afraid (if I got angry) he'd leave me."♂ Fear of own excitement: "I get so excited I don't know what to do." Fear of loss of control: "I'm afraid my anger will break out." Fear of rejection: "I'm afraid she won't want to go out with me."♀ Or fear or anxiety whose cause is not stated. Being "tense," or "uptight," or "upset" if it is clearly anxiety which is meant. Fear of loss of own identity: "If I agree with him♂ I'm afraid I won't know my own feelings."

**SOLUTIONS**

HIN = *Hostility In*

Self threatening to kill self; wanting to, and deserving to die; hating and criticizing one's self; hurting self; feeling in despair; depressed; disappointed in self; unable to live up to one's own standards; denial of hostility to self: "I want to die." "I am no good." "I failed."

MAS = *Masochism*

A variety of statements in which others harm or threaten self; situations injure or mistreat self. Self as martyr. "He always criticizes me."♂ "Things never turn out right for me." "I always have to do the dirty work."

HS = *Helplessness*

Helplessness, confusion, weakness; unable to cope; impotent; withdrawn; sleepy; foggy; can't focus; can't succeed: "I'm so confused I don't know what to do." "I'm too weak to control him."♂ "I'm always in a haze."

*Other defenses are to be specified.* They refer to attempts at solution like: Projection: "It's always his fault."♂ Somatization: "What did you ask me?" "I just got this awful pain." Depersonalization: "My body feels strange to me." Isolation: "I went to bed with him but I didn't feel anything."♂ Withdrawal: "I don't want to be involved with him."♂ Ambivalence: "I just love and hate women."♀ Regression: "I want to go back to school so I don't have to do anything." Repression: "I forgot I had to face my boss."♂ Reaction formation: "I always try very hard to be understanding and accepting."

*Wishes Used Defensively*

DHO = *Defensive Hostility Out*

This is also often found after a PHR statement: "I really like that girl PHR but I'll bet she thinks she's too good for me." Fear of rejection♀. "She's a real bitch." DHO♀

DPHR = *Defensive Positive Human Relations.*

It usually occurs in relationship to an HO (hostility out statement): "My husband is running around with another woman. I could kill him for this HO♂ but if I get angry he'll leave me." Separation Fear. "He really is cute." DPHR♂ "I wish father were nicer to me PHR♂ but he is so mean. MAS♂ I'd rather be with mother." DPHR♀

DM = *Defensive Mastery.*

This is often found after a positive human relations (PHR) statement: "I really like that girl. PHR♀ I'll bet she thinks she's too good for me. Fear of Rejection♀ I can certainly get along without her." DM♀

To decide if wishes are used defensively often involves looking at the entire transcript to determine if a wish is to be considered as primary or defensive. For example, a woman patient may make quite a few hostile statements about men, which are marked HO♂. Then she may say something like: "Men treat me so badly," MAS♂, "I wish they were nicer to me." PHR♂ Here the wish is clearly stated as PHR♂. Then the various HO♂ statements should be reclassified to DHO♂.

ADAC = *Adaptive Activity, Relatively Non-Conflictual Solutions.*

These are instances of maturation, neutralization, insight, self-approval, liberation, hope, humor, stoicism.

Maturation: "I feel more mature and able to handle my family." Neutralization: "I try to think before I act." "Since I can observe them from a distance my family doesn't look so threatening." Liberation: "I freed myself." Insight: "Now I understand why I reacted that way." "I'm trying to figure myself out." Self-approval: "I though what I did was good." "I can do it." Hope: "I know eventually it will be better." Humor: "I had to laugh at myself." Stoicism: "I have to grin and bear it."

## CODING

In seminars or individual supervision the transcript may be coded as it is read. In seminars the section of tape which has been typed is played as members read along. In individual supervision the resident may code the transcript before we meet. If I have a copy before the supervisory hour I will do this too. Or, we may both code it as the resident reads the transcript aloud. When the coding classification is learned, coding may be done quickly, without referring back to the typed classification.

Scoring the transcript is done quite literally phrase by phrase. The phrase to be scored is underlined (shown in italics in the examples below) and coded in the margin. An example follows:

| | |
|---|---|
| *I worry about that,* becoming *too, you know, dependent on you.* | ANX, PHR Ther |
| *I feel like I'm so passive,* such a passive situation. I'm just sitting | HIN |
| here and *I'm accepting everything you say as the truth* and I was | PHR Ther |
| thinking that *I want to, you know, interact with men equally* and not | ADAC♂ |
| always look at them as like a father image or someone who | |
| knows everything. At least *the way I'm seeing it now or sometimes,* | ADAC |
| not all the time because I sit and listen to you and *I think every-* | PHR Ther |
| *thing you say is just right* and that *bothers me* because I'm like that | ANX |
| with most men you know in classes and, um, discussions like | |
| *guys say something I just accept it as being more right than I am,* you | MAS♂ |
| know, not that I'm wrong, I just listen to these guys and they're | |
| so much more aggressive and assertive about the way they feel | |
| that I just don't, you know, extend myself *I can't defend myself,* | HS♂ |
| you know, if I feel differently than a guy about something, I | |
| find, you know, if they ask me how do you feel *I can't say a word,* | HS♂ |
| I just block and, um, *I hate that* I want to get over that. *I've been* | HIN |
| *thinking about going into an assertive training program. I'd really like* | ADAC |
| *to get over that,* I just hate that, I am really aware of that es- | |
| pecially in classes; at work it hasn't been a problem but, you | |
| know, when I'm with a group of men or even one it's—it just | |
| really bothers me that *I always feel that I'm subordinate* and that I | MAS♂ |
| always think—well when I'm by myself I feel, I feel pretty con- | |
| fident and I don't, I feel fine but I, I thought about it and I | |
| realized that when I think about myself in terms of how others | |
| see me especially men I think that *all men see me as really dumb* | MAS♂ |

| | |
|---|---|
| *and spacy. And I just don't like that anymore, I'd like to get over that.* | ADAC |
| I don't know how I attempt to, you know, make myself, that | |
| just seems so hard *I always fall into this really passive role* of just | HS♂ |
| letting men make decisions. | |

## TABULATED CODINGS

| Wish | Reaction | Solution |
|---|---|---|
| | ANX | |
| PHR Ther | | |
| | | HIN |
| PHR Ther | | |
| | | ADAC |
| | | ADAC |
| PHR Ther | | |
| | ANX | |
| | | MAS♂ |
| | | HS♂ |
| | | HS♂ |
| | | HIN |
| | | ADAC |
| | | MAS♂ |
| | | MAS♂ |
| | | ADAC |
| | | HS♂ |

FC *PHR Ther* vs ANX → HIN, ADAC, HS, and MAS♂

The focal conflict here is that this woman has developed a very positive dependent relationship to the therapist. This relationship leads to fear of rejection which she tries to solve by on one hand becoming masochistic and helpless and on the other by showing signs of adaptive activity. (Predominant elements of the FC are italicized.)

A part of a transcript from another patient and another therapist:

| | |
|---|---|
| I took off from all my classes. *I'm really glad I'm, you know* | PHR |
| starting to see, like *I'll be seeing Marge and you know like Bill and* | PHR |
| *Hank* and have *friends again.* It's just, I don't know, it's just | PHR |
| really neat. *The letter from Hank was really nice.* He, um, he said | PHR♂ |
| that he's been thinking about this last summer since last sum- | |
| mer he wanted to take off for a while, *he wanted to know if I wanted* | PHR♂ |
| *to take off with him* and I have to work so I can earn money for | |
| next semester but he's just going to come here for a week. And | |
| Helen will be gone for a couple of weeks and we'll have the | |
| whole place to ourselves and *that'll be the first time I'll ever spend* | PHR♂ |

| | |
|---|---|
| *that long of a time with a guy. I think it will be really nice and um,* I'll | PHR♂ |
| be working more and aside from that I won't have anything to do. It's going to be so much fun. He said that um staying | |
| with me will be great except when we get *in bed I take up ¾* of the bed and *last time I shoved him off the bed* and he said he's not looking forward to that, we'll have to work that out somehow. And I finished my English paper. I did a really weird paper, | DHO (after PHR)♂ |
| *it was another one of those terrible papers,* I just kind of plugged out in one night, and just got it out there. Analyzed two para- | HIN |
| graphs in four pages, *I thought that was ridiculous.* It was a really weird paper, I felt really bad, especially since it was overdue. | HIN |
| And then Helen, last night that was a real putdown. *Last night* | MAS♀ |
| *she really upset me,* and *I don't know what's happening.* Um, I don't know still, you know, understand my feelings towards her and | HS |
| this whole affair but like *I'm really confused* about what happened to her yesterday. She went to, she went to a group yesterday and she went to a counselor and when she went to the counselor, she told him about how she had called her shrink and that, | HS |
| of anyway, last night *she got angry at me again* and, um, slammed. . . | MAS♀ |

## TABULATED CODINGS

| Wish | Reaction | Solution |
|---|---|---|
| PHR | | |
| PHR♂ | | |
| PHR♂ | | |
| PHR♂ | | |
| | | DHO♂ |
| | | HIN |
| | | HIN |
| | | MAS♀ |
| | | HS |
| | | HS |
| | | MAS♀ |

Looking at this scoring shows that wishes for good relations with a man—PHR♂ suddenly changed to defensive hostility toward a male, DHO♂, followed by self punishing—HIN, and helpless HS attitudes, and being punished by a female—MAS♀. The reaction which caused this change is not stated, and has to be inferred: FC = PHR♂ vs [guilt? fear?] → DHO♂, HIN, HS, and MAS♀.

And here is part of a third transcript from still another therapist:

| | |
|---|---|
| But, instead of that *I feel like he's just manipulating her,* that she can't or doesn't want to see it. And when I—there's only a few | HO♂ |

times when I was out there when I said anything at all, and that was when I was asked. That was one of the few times when he was not physically present. And, again I got a defensive apologetic reaction from her, and I . . . so I didn't want to do it, so I thought "*She's putting up with a hell-of-a-lot of shit just day-to-day in* HO
*this thing* so if *I come down hard like I wanted to*, like I started to, HO
then it's like it just seemed like it would make it harder on her.

*T:* So you're feeling bad about adding more fuel to that fire.

*P:* Yea, or like deserting you know, or . . . Bill thinks that I'm jealous of Tom which is probably true.

*T:* Jealous of Tom?

*P:* Yes, for taking up her time. That's Bill's thing.

*T:* Oh, I see, okay, I'm sorry.

*P:* Yea, and I think it's only true as far as he is somebody who just, you know like I just said many times today, that he does not, he is there, you know, *he needs somebody to take up* HO♂
*his time for him so much that he just never goes off* for five minutes by himself, you know, like maybe he goes off to have a beer, with his buddies.

*T:* You seem to be wondering if some of your negative feelings about him are related to that jealousy.

*P:* Yea, I thought about that before and I guess I sort of accepted it, you know, that . . . um . . . well, the first time when he came here last June was right after, and she was coming from New York, he was coming from Montana to see her, and they were meeting here; and they got here on the day after I finished my prelims, *when I was just absolutely wrecked.* MAS
And I had to get ready to go on this summer thing, in four days. And so he came, you know, he sort of moved in and I moved out is what happened. They moved in to where I lived and I went to this rented room anyway, it was just a totally unhinging experience and *I just felt like everything had* MAS
*been taken over.*

*T:* So in other words, did he have your sister completely to himself but they were using your room?

*P:* Yea, right, and it was, I don't know *I was just really in a bad* MAS
*way* I needed some time to rest and be myself and it didn't work at all and . . . then, you know, when I went out there at Christmas too it was the same sort of . . . there was a lot of competition for her attention. Only in both cases there was absolutely no question about where . . . you know, she, I guess she stuck as tight to him as he stuck to her.

*T:* Rather than my initial interpretation of adding fuel to the fire, it seems more like you were quite worried about your angry or jealous feelings breaking up their relationship.

*P:* Yea, that I, yea, I guess I wasn't well focused on that but

| | |
|---|---|
| that was, yea, that bothered me a lot. 'Cause I thought if that were true then *I was just out to destroy that so I could have her back.* | HO |

**Tabulated Codings**

| Wish | Reaction | Solution |
|---|---|---|
| HO♂ | | |
| HO | | |
| HO | | |
| HO♂ | | |
| | | MAS |
| | | MAS |
| | | MAS |
| HO | | |

This man is angry and jealous of another man's interest in his sister. FC = *HO* and HO (covert—another harming another) vs [guilt, incestuous] → *MAS*.

In FC's the most frequent wish is some sort of PHR. HO is only about one fourth as frequent because most HO responses are defensive. Mastery or assertion are infrequent wishes.

There is generally only one FC in the 10-minute samples. Two FC's occur once in every 20 or 25 transcripts.

This method is not particularly useful when the transcript is largely dealing with a dream or its interpretation.

## DISCUSSION

It may be argued that this is an arbitrary method without much reliability. I have found that after working together for a time, residents and I independently usually arrive at the same formulation of the focal conflict. So, consensus is not hard to reach. Validity insofar as it can be established is manifested by consistency of focal conflicts from session to session, and a logical progression of change in focal conflicts as therapy progresses.

Another use of this method is in its enabling both the therapist and supervisor to see some errors objectively. For instance, if there are clear-cut signs of the patient having positive feeling for the therapist which he fails to recognize and code, this is a very challenging demonstration to him of some difficulties that he is having in relationship to the patient.

It could be argued that in many focal conflicts, wish and solution could be reversed. In the first clinical example cited above, the patient could be seen as wishing to assert herself to avoid a masochistic dependency on the therapist. And in some patients a frequent FC like HO vs ANX → MAS could be reversed into its mirror image: MAS vs ANX → DHO. This can

be regarded as an expression of a fundamental human tendency to see the world in terms of polar opposites. Freud[6] describes this primary process characteristic of dreams: "Dreams feel themselves at liberty moreover, to represent any element by its wishful contrary, so that there is no way of deciding at first glance whether any element that admits of a contrary is present in the dream thoughts as a positive or a negative." This characteristic of focal conflicts suggests that though manifest, they do reflect deeper structures. In practice deciding what is wish and what is solution usually presents no great difficulty for context will make this clear. Which part or parts of the FC—wish, reactive motive, or solution, is to be emphasized is a therapeutic decision not dealt with here.

This method has been quite successful and is well liked by residents, some of whom use it as a "self-supervisor." It is an excellent means of teaching both individually and also in seminars.

## SUMMARY

A typescript of a 10-minute segment of a tape recording of a psychotherapy interview (usually the second 10 minutes) has definite advantages for supervision and teaching. It gives focus, precision, and structure and decreases excessive subjectivity on the part of teacher and student. It can easily be coded using a modification of the Gottschalk scales, and by this coding the focal conflict described by French is highlighted. Learning to recognize and organize therapeutic thinking around the focal conflict may be regarded as a cognitive foundation for dynamic psychotherapy, analogous to learning the scales in music.

## REFERENCES

1. Mintz, J., Luborsky, L. Segments vs. Whole Sessions: Which is the Better Unit for Psychotherapy Process Research? *J. Abnorm. Psychol.* 78:180, 1971.
2. Levi-Strauss, Claude. The Structural Study of Myth. In *The Structuralists from Marx to Levi-Strauss,* DeGeorge, Ed. Doubleday Anchor, New York, 1972.
3. French, Thomas. *The Integration of Behavior,* III. University of Chicago Press, Chicago, 1954, pp. 100–101.
4. Gottschalk, L. A. and Gleser, G. C. *The Measurement of Psychological States Through the Content Analysis of Verbal Behavior.* University of California Press, Los Angeles, 1969.
5. Schafer, Roy. Psychoanalysis Without Psychodynamics. *Int. J. Psychoanal.* 56:41–55, 1975.
6. Freud, S. *The Interpretation of Dreams* (1900). In *Standard Edition,* Vol. V, Hogarth Press, London, 1968, p. 318.

# Part VIII

# Psychodynamic and Other Studies

This section includes studies exploring psychodynamic relationships. The first chapter (50) in this group of papers could just as well have been included in Part IV - Psychophysiological and Psychosomatic Studies, and it is entitled "Erection Cycle During Sleep in Relation to Dream Anxiety" (Karacan et al, 1966). This group of investigators was the first to demonstrate, conclusively, that dreams occurring with REM sleep with a high anxiety content, assessed according to the Gottschalk-Gleser Anxiety scale, had no or irregular erections, whereas dreams with low anxiety scores were associated with penile erections. The next chapter (51) in this group, entitled "Affective Reactions in Patient-Therapist Interactions Among more Differentiated than Less Differentiated Patients Early in Therapy" (Witkin et al, 1968) demonstrated that shame anxiety, as measured by the Gottschalk-Gleser content analysis scale, was more likely to be prominent in less differentiated (field dependent) patients and guilt anxiety was more prominent in differentiated (field independent) patients; interesting interactions between the therapist's cognitive style and patient anxiety are suggested in this chapter. Chapter 52,

"Repression, Interference, and Field Dependence as Factors in Dream Forgetting" (Goodenough et al, 1974), explores the relationship of field-dependence and field independence to repression and the recall of dream affect, using the Gottschalk-Gleser content analysis scales. Chapter 53, "The Effects of Stress Films on Dream Affect and on Respiration and Eye-Movement Activity During Rapid-Eye-Movement Sleep" (Goodenough et al, 1975), demonstrates that stress films increased the anxiety in dreams as measured by the Gottschalk-Gleser anxiety scale. In Chapter 54, "Hope and Discomfort as Factors Influencing Treatment Continuance," the authors demonstrate that patients coming to an emergency room who follow treatment recommendations have higher hope scores as measured by the content analysis of their verbal behavior (Perley et al, 1971). Chapter 55, "Free Association Anxiety and Hostility: View from a Junior High School" (Silbergeld et al, 1975), explores the relationship of anxiety and hostility, as assessed by the Gottschalk-Gleser content analysis scales, to social class, ethnic differences, gender, and to interactions with black or white school counselors. The findings from this study, though preliminary, merit comparison with the data from Chapter 4, which explores the effect of different interviewers on affect scores with a sample of German-speaking subjects, and from Part I, B. Children's Studies (specifically, chapters 6, 7, and 8).

# Erection Cycle During Sleep in Relation to Dream Anxiety

I. KARACAN, MD, (Med)DSc; D. R. GOODENOUGH, PhD;
A. SHAPIRO, MD; AND STEVEN STARKER, BA, BROOKLYN, NY

FOLLOWING the work of Aserinsky[1] and Aserinsky and Kleitman,[2] it has been well established that there are periods of rapid, conjugate eye movement (REM periods) occurring at about 90-minute intervals throughout the course of normal sleep in adult human subjects (Ss), and it has been found that most dream reports are obtained after awakenings from these periods.[3] It is also well established that these periods are associated with a low-voltage random electroencephalogram (EEG) record which has been called stage 1 of sleep by Dement and Kleitman.[4] In fact the physiological changes which are associated with REM periods encompass a large cluster of characteristics: increase in respiratory rate and irregularity[1,5-8]; an increase in pulse rate and irregularity[7,8]; a decrease in the number of spontaneous galvanic skin responses[6,9-10]; a greater incidence of isolated wrist activity[11,12]; an increase in the incidence of bruxism (nocturnal grinding of the teeth)[13]; and fine body movements occurring concomitantly with eye movements throughout the REM period.[6,11,14-15] The focus of interest in this paper will be the occurrence of penile erections.[16-17] In a recent study by Fisher,[16] full or partial erections accompanied 95% of all REM periods observed but erections rarely occurred in the absence of REM sleep. The present study was designed to explore further the correlates of erections during REM and nonrapid eye movement (NREM) sleep and the relation to dream anxiety.

There is considerable clinical evidence[18-21] that anxiety may cause temporary impotence during the waking state, and it seemed plausible to hypothesize that the same relationship might exist during sleep. The major hypothesis of the study was that anxiety in the content of a dream experience may prevent or inhibit erection during sleep. Specifically it was hypothesized that less anxious dreams would be reported when Ss are awakened from REM periods with full erection than from REM periods with irregular or no erection.

## Method

The Ss were 16 paid young adult male college or medical students who volunteered to sleep in the laboratory during their normal sleep period. These students were selected for the experiment on the basis of a questionnaire and an intensive interview designed to eliminate prospective Ss who showed evidence of sleep difficulty or any gross psychiatric problems.

Each S slept in the laboratory for six nights, approximately once a week. An attempt was made to awaken the Ss during each REM period and to obtain detailed reports of their preawakening experiences. Fronto-occipital EEG, eye movements, and erections were recorded continuously during sleep. The procedure used for these recordings has been described in detail elsewhere.[22-23] Measurement of erection cycles throughout sleep was accomplished by means of a mercury capillary strain gauge. This transducer is described elsewhere.[24-25] The recording system permitted a measurement of the degree of change in the circumference of the penis during erection. A 3 cm pen deflection was

Submitted for publication Dec 10, 1965.

From the Psychology Laboratory and the Psychiatric Treatment Research Center of the Department of Psychiatry, State University of New York, Downstate Medical Center, Brooklyn, NY. Dr. Karacan is now at the National Institute of Mental Health, Bethesda, Md.

Reprint requests to National Institute of Mental Health, Bethesda, Md 20014 (Dr. Karacan).

made equivalent to a 3 cm increase in circumference in order to measure full erection.[23,25]

Tests on two Ss were run simultaneously in two identical laboratory bedrooms. Each S slept in an air-conditioned, relatively soundproof room, connected electrically and by an intercom system with an adjoining recording laboratory. A bedside plug board was connected with an 8-channel console EEG located in the recording laboratory. The Ss were awakened by a buzzer and responded by picking up a bedside telephone (automatically turning off the stimulus). A tape recorder, also located in the recording laboratory, was used to record all relevant conversation between examiner (E) and S.

On the first two nights, the S was familiarized with the laboratory situation and procedures. Each S was asked to report to the laboratory an hour before he usually went to sleep. During this hour the recording devices were attached and the S was instructed about the study.

The S was then allowed to go to sleep and was awakened 5 to 15 minutes after each REM period began. Immediately after the S gave his spontaneous report, a short inquiry was conducted in an effort to clarify any ambiguity in the report and a mood adjective checklist was presented to permit the S to describe more systematically what his feelings had been prior to awakening. The S then returned to sleep until the next REM period awakening or the final awakening in the morning.

On the first night only EEG and eye-movement recordings were obtained. On the second night erections were also recorded. On nights three through six, the procedures were similar to night two, with one exception. On each of these nights a film was shown to the S before he retired. Two exciting films and two neutral films were used. These films were shown in the hope that it might be possible to manipulate anxiety in the content of the dreams, and thus provide an experimental test of the anxiety/erection inhibition hypothesis. Since no significant differences among film nights were observed, details regarding film comparisons are omitted from the present report.[23]

Two methods were used to assess the emotional content of the dream (REM-awakening report). The mood adjective checklist used in this study was adapted from Nowlis.[26] At each awakening the S was shown a set of mood-descriptive adjectives in randomized order, and he was asked to rate each adjective to correspond with his feeling in the dream. Each word was given a score of from 0 to 3. A 0 score was defined as, "The word does not describe how I felt." Score 1 was "don't know" or "not sure," 2 was "I felt a little like that," and 3—"A lot like that." For scoring purposes 21 of the adjectives were grouped into seven clusters of three adjectives each, with each cluster representing a mood dimension according to the factor analysis of Nowlis.[26] The Ss' ratings on the three adjectives of each cluster were summed in order to obtain a cluster score. The seven dimensions with the three adjectives in each were *aggression* (rebellious, angry, defiant), *anxiety* (clutched up, fearful, jittery), *surgency* (playful, carefree, witty), *social affection* (affectionate, kindly, warmhearted), *depression* (sorry, sad, regretful), *distrust* (skeptical, dubious, suspicious), and *quiet* (still, quiet, placid).

In addition to the mood adjective checklist, the emotional content of the dreams was assessed by scoring transcripts of the dream reports for anxiety, hostility-inward, and hostility-outward, according to procedures developed by Gottschalk.[27] Dream reports of less than 50 words were deemed inadequate for scoring purposes and were discarded for these analyses.

For Gottschalk's anxiety scale, each clause in the dream report was scored for the presence or absence of content considered to be symptomatic of anxiety, including but not limited to subjective reports of feelings of anxiety or fear. All communication by the S which did not describe the content of the dream experience was excluded. In addition, responses by the S to any specific inquiry by E were discarded to eliminate possible bias that might be introduced by E. Only the S's spontaneous report and any additional response to general inquiry by E (eg, "Can you remember any more?") were scored.

The scores for the several clauses in each report were then summed and corrected for word length, following Gottschalk's procedure, in order to obtain a total score.

The hostility-inward and hostility-outward scores were similarly derived.

Wilcoxon's matched-pairs signed-ranks test was used as a test of significance for all comparisons.

## Results

*Erection Pattern During Sleep.*—The data on four nights of sleep for each of the 16 Ss confirmed the findings of Ohlmeyer and Brilmayer[28] and Ohlmeyer et al[29] that during normal sleep, young adult males have cyclically occurring erections. Also confirmed were Fisher's and Shapiro's observations that penile erections most frequently occur in association with stage 1 REM sleep. Of the 237 stage 1 REM periods observed in this study, 80% were accompanied by erection.

A few erections were also observed at other stages of sleep (NREM stages). Characteristics of the REM and NREM erections were as follows:

Erection During REM Sleep: On the average, erections began at approximately the same as the time of onset of the REM period. However, on rare occasions erections began as much as 30 minutes before stage 1 REM sleep and sometimes followed the REM sleep onset by some minutes. Figure 1 shows a record of sleep stages and erection cycles of a typical subject during an eight-hour sleep period.

Each REM period was placed in one of three classes depending on whether ac-

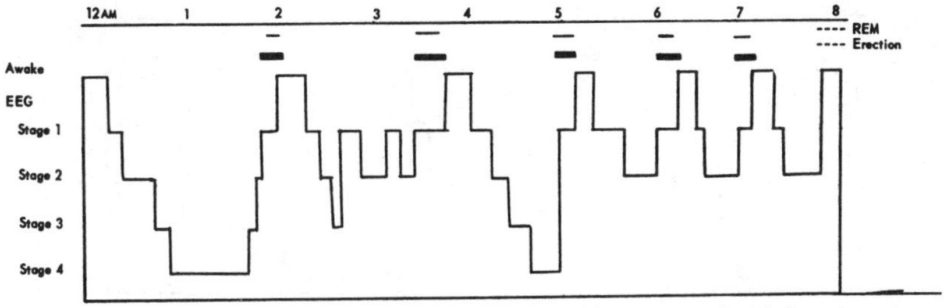


Fig 1.—A typical sleep-REM erection cycle. The subject was awakened five times to obtain REM report.

companied by regular erection, irregular erection, or no erection.

Regular Erection. A regular erection was defined as one which steadily increased to a maximum and continued at the maximum until the time of the experimental awakening. In a total of 237 REM periods observed, 42% or 100 REM periods were accompanied by regular erection. At the awakening, detumescence immediately began and the penile circumference usually returned to the baseline level within a few minutes.

Irregular Erection. An irregular erection was defined as one whose amplitude fluctuated or one in which detumescence occurred before the experimental awakening. This type of erection accompanied 37% or 91 of the 237 REM awakenings.

No Erection. Twenty percent or 46 REM periods were not accompanied by erection.

Erection During NREM Sleep: A total of 19 erections began and ended without any accompanying REM sleep. Three of these erections occurred between the REM periods and no constant pattern could be observed. The remaining 16 were related to REM periods in one of two specific ways.

*Early at Night.* At the time when the first REM period of the night would be expected to occur in a particular subject, there were ten incidents of erection occurring without an accompanying REM period. Figure 2 shows a typical incident of erection occurring when the first REM was expected. In one S on one night the first three erections occurred without accompanying REM periods at times when the first three REM periods would have been expected.

*Late at Night.* After the S was awakened from a REM period late at night and had reported his dream, an erection occasionally occurred in stage 2 or 3 immediately after the S returned to sleep. There were four incidents of this kind. Figure 3 shows one of these (after the fourth REM awakening).

*The Relationship Between Anxiety and Erection During REM Sleep.*—The major hypothesis tested in this study was that anxiety in the dream experience (REM awakening report) may prevent or inhibit erection. To test this hypothesis REM

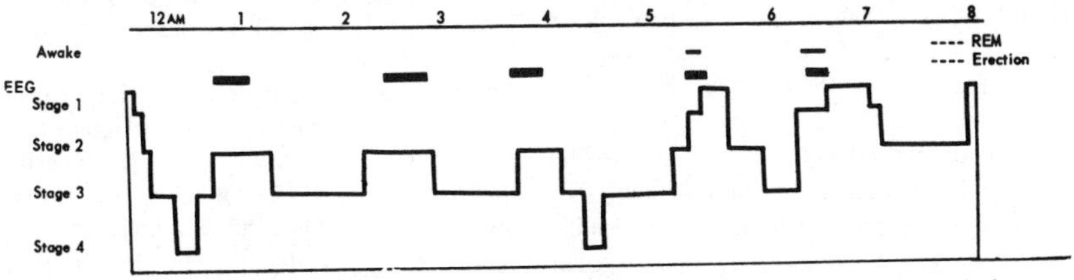


Fig 2.—Delay of stage 1 REM sleep. A typical incidence of three erections occurred during stage 2 sleep cycles when the stage 1 sleep was expected. The first and second REM were accompanied by erections and S was awakened to obtain REM report.

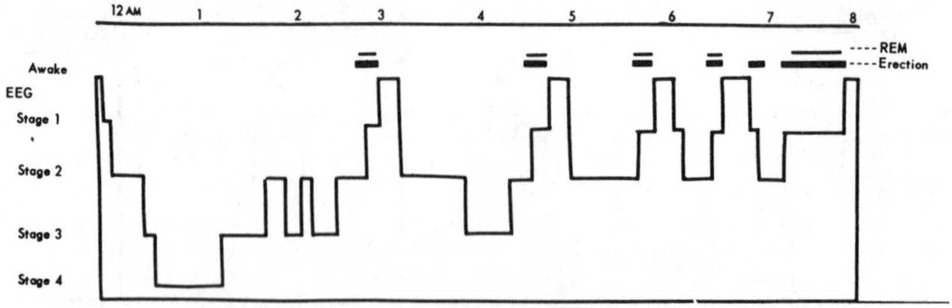


Fig 3.—A typical erection occurring after the fourth awakening while the S was returning to sleep.

periods were classified into two types depending on whether they were accompanied by: (A) regular, or (B) irregular or no erection. The mean of the anxiety scores was then computed for all scorable reports from each type of REM period for each S. The mean of the subject means using Gottschalk's anxiety score was 1.07 for regular erection and 1.29 for the combination of irregular and no erection. This difference was significant, $P < 0.01$. When the anxiety scores obtained for the adjective checklist were compared in the same way, the mean anxiety score for regular erection was 1.6 and for irregular and no erection 1.8. For the adjective list the relationship with erection was in the expected direction but was not significant. Gottschalk's hostility-outward and hostility-inward scores and all other Nowlis mood cluster scores were examined, but no significant differences were found.

With the hope of better understanding these results, the relationships between the Gottschalk scales and the Nowlis anxiety, depression, and anger clusters were examined. For each S the Nowlis anxiety scores for all dream reports were divided into two groups, above the median (high anxiety) and below the median (low anxiety) for that S. The mean Gottschalk scores for low and high groups were then compared for each S. Similar comparisons were made for all combinations of Nowlis and Gottschalk scores. As might be expected, the Gottschalk anxiety scores were significantly higher for high anxiety reports than for low anxiety reports, as determined by the checklist ($P < 0.01$). The Nowlis anger and the Gottschalk hostility-outward scales were also related ($P < 0.01$). The Nowlis depression scale was significantly related ($P < 0.01$) to Gottschalk anxiety, however, rather than to hostility-inward, as we expected. Apparently some Ss when anxious (according to Gottschalk) reported feelings of depression (sad, regretful, sorry) rather than anxiety (jittery, clutched up, fearful).

*Some Additional Correlates of Erections and of Dream Affect.*—REM Period Eye-Movement Activity and Affect: It has been reported [30] that dream reports with more than usual amounts of affect tend to come from REM periods with more eye movements per minute. In order to check on this relationship in our data, eye movements were examined during the last three minutes of each REM period preceding the awakening. These three minutes were divided into three-second segments, and each segment was scored for the presence or absence of eye movements. The percentage of these three-second segments which contained at least one movement was used to characterize the eye-movement activity during the REM period for the statistical analysis.

All REM periods for an S which had fewer than the median number of eye movements for that S were designated as *low-activity* periods, and REM periods above the median for that S were designated as *high-activity* periods. For each REM period the sum of the scores for all affect clusters on the Nowlis checklist (except quiet) was then computed and the mean of these total affect scores obtained for all low-activity and for all high-activity REM periods for

each S. The mean score for total affect for all 16 Ss was 6.8 following low eye-movement activity and 9.3 following high eye-movement activity. This difference was significant ($P < 0.01$), indicating more affect in the dream reports following high eye-movement activity than low eye-movement activity. The only *single* affect showing a significant difference was Aggression, which was higher following REM periods with high eye-movement activity than REM periods with low eye-movement activity ($P < 0.05$). No significant relationships were found when affect was measured by the Gottschalk technique.

REM-Period Eye-Movement Activity and Erection: There was more eye-movement activity with regular erection than with irregular or no erection. Here again the mean eye-movement score was first computed for all REM periods with regular erections and for all periods with irregular or no erections for each S separately before combining the data from all 16 Ss. The mean percent of three-second intervals containing at least one eye movement was 19% with regular erection, and 15% with irregular and no erection. This difference was significant ($P < 0.02$).

Erection and Frequency of Dream Reporting: Ninety-five percent of all awakenings following REM periods with regular erections yielded reports of preawakening experience with some content compared with 85% of all awakenings following irregular or no erection. This difference was significant ($P < 0.01$).

## Comment

As has been reported by Fisher et al [16] and Shapiro,[24] a clear association was observed between erections and REM periods. Erections occurred in association with most of the REM periods observed, and more erections might have been observed if the REM periods had continued without experimental interruption. Under the conditions of the experiment 20% of the REM periods occurred without erections and in the other 37% of the REM periods the erections were irregular.

The major hypothesis of this study was that anxiety dreams would tend to come from REM periods with irregular or no erections. This hypothesis was supported when the Gottschalk content analysis technique was used to measure anxiety, but not when the Nowlis adjective checklist was employed. We have not been able to identify with certainty the basis for the discrepancy between the Gottschalk and Nowlis results. However, the Ss who showed extreme discrepancies gave the impression that they may have been suppressing or denying their feelings when responding to the mood-descriptive adjectives, and this factor might account for the lack of significant relationship between erections and Nowlis anxiety scores.

While anxiety may be one factor responsible for the absence or irregularity of erections, there were some indications in the data that it was not the only factor. There were a number of REM periods without regular erections, with a low rate of eye-movements and yielding no report of dream content. These tended to occur early in the night. It is known that these early REM periods are unique in a number of ways, eg, often interrupted by spindling bursts [31]; higher arousal thresholds.[32] Since these REM periods are similar to NREM sleep in important ways, it is possible that the absence of erection during them may be primarily physiological rather than a psychological inhibition.

A major goal of this study was the examination of incidents in which the REM period and erection coincided. A number of these incidents were observed and classified. However, even when they did not coincide, unexpected indications of the association between REM and erection were found.

Many of the erections without REM occurred at the end of the first sleep cycle of the night. Many of the REM periods without erection also occurred at the end of the first sleep cycle of the night. Other NREM erections occurred after REM period awakenings as the S returned to sleep. REM periods also often occur as the S returns to sleep following REM awakenings, as if a brief interruption does

not always disrupt the basic sleep cycle. At these times then (ie, at the end of the first sleep cycle and after a REM-period awakening) a REM period often occurs without erection or an erection without REM. Although these events are not always concurrent, they do occur at comparable times in the cycle.

An apparent lack of dependence of the erection cycle on sexual experience was also noted. Some Ss spontaneously reported coitus just before coming to the sleep laboratory, but the erection cycle was not noticeably affected. One S had a nocturnal emission during the fourth REM period and then had a regular erection during the fifth (and last) REM period of the night. These observations contribute to an emerging body of evidence [7] that the erection cycle is at least as resistant to change as the REM cycle.

The significantly higher rate of dream reporting from REM with regular erections raises the question of whether erection during NREM sleep might also be a reliable indicator of dreaming, and suggests the possibility that dream reporting might be more closely related to erections than to REM periods.

It is of interest to speculate about the neurophysiological mechanisms which may underlie these relationships. MacLean [33] has shown in the squirrel monkey that erection depends on a number of interrelated centers in the forebrain and diencephalon, some of which, in man, are closely related to centers determining memory, elaboration of thought processes, and emotion. If his observations can be extrapolated to man, the occurrence of erections as such a fundamental part of the sleep cycle and yet partially independent of REM periods, suggests that perhaps the pontine center which Jouvet [34] has found to be the initiator of REM periods, may be partially dependent on forebrain and diencephalonic activity for the elaboration of the full picture of this portion of the sleep cycle.

It remains to be established by further investigations whether penile erection or some other aspect of the physiological pattern associated with REM-period sleep is most intimately related to the occurrence of dreams.

## Summary

This paper presents a study of erection cycles during sleep and the relationship of rapid eye-movement (REM) sleep erection to REM anxiety report. Sixteen young adult male paid volunteers slept in the laboratory during their normal sleep period for six nights, once a week. Electroencephalograms, eye movements, and measurements of penile erection cycles throughout sleep were recorded. Subjects were awakened during each REM-period to obtain detailed reports of their pre-awakening experiences and the dream reports were scored for anxiety. Eighty percent of REM periods were accompanied by erection. A total of 19 erections (three types) began and ended without accompanying REM sleep. Data indicate that those REM awakening reports (dreams) with a high anxiety content had no or irregular erection ($P < 0.01$).

This study was abstracted from a dissertation which was submitted by Dr. Karacan as partial fulfillment of the requirements for the degree of doctor of medical science, May 1965, State University of New York, Downstate Medical Center, Department of Psychiatry, Brooklyn, NY.

This study was supported in part by the National Institutes of Health, Public Health Service grants No. MH-03885, MH-K3-16,619, MH-7336-05, and MH-05518. Dr. A. L. Gottschalk arranged for Carolyn Winget to score the data.

## REFERENCES

1. Aserinsky, E.: *Ocular Motility During Sleep and Its Application to the Study of Rest-Activity Cycles and Dreaming*, unpublished doctoral dissertation, University of Chicago Graduate School, Chicago, 1953.

2. Aserinsky, E., and Kleitman, N.: Regularly Occurring Periods of Eye Motility, and Concomitant Phenomena, During Sleep, *Science* **118**:273, 1953.

3. Dement, W., and Kleitman, N.: The Relation of Eye Movements During Sleep to Dream Activity: An Objective Method for the Study of Dreaming, *J Exp Psychol* **53**:339-346, 1957.

4. Dement, W., and Kleitman, N.: Cyclic Variations in EEG During Sleep and Their Relation to Eye Movements, Body Motility and Dreaming, *Electroenceph Clin Neurophysiol* **9**:673, 1957.

5. Jouvet, M.; Michel, F.; and Mouneir, D.: Analysis electroencephalographique comparee du sommeil physiologique chex le Chat et chex l'Homme, *Rev Neurol* **103**:189, 1960.

6. Kamiya, J.: "Behavioral, Subjective, and Physiological Aspects of Drowsiness and Sleep," in Fiske, D.W., and Maddi, S.R. (eds.): *Functions of Varied Experience*, Homewood, Ill: Dorsey Press, Inc., pp 145-174, 1961.

7. Shapiro, A., et al: Dream Recall and Physiology of Sleep, *J Appl Physiol* **19**:778, 1964.

8. Snyder, F.: The New Biology of Dreaming, *Arch Gen Psychiat* **8**:381, 1963.
9. O'Connell, D.N.; Tursky, B.; and Orne, M.T.: Electrodes for the Recording of Skin Potential: An Evaluation, *Arch Gen Psychiat* **3**:252, 1960.
10. O'Connell, D.N., and Tursky, B.: Special Modification of the Silver-Silver Chloride Sponge Electrode for Skin Recording, *Psychophysiol Newsltr* **8**(2):31, 1962.
11. Wolpert, E.A.: Studies in Psychophysiology of Dreams: II. An Electromyographic Study of Dreaming, *Arch Gen Psychiat* **2**:231, 1960.
12. Roffwarg, H.; Dement, W.; and Fisher, C.: Observations on the Sleep-Dream Pattern in Neonates, Infants, and Children and Adults, *Clin Psychiat Monograph,* 1964.
13. Reding, G.R., et al: Sleep Pattern of Tooth Grinding: Its Relationship to Dreaming, *Science* **145**: 725, 1965.
14. Baldridge, B.J.; Whitman, R.M.; and Kramer, M.: The Concurrence of Fine Muscle Activity and Rapid Eye Movements During Sleep, *Psychosom Med* **27**(No. 1):19-25, 1965.
15. Oswald, I., et al: Melancholia and Barbiturates: A Controlled EEG, Body and Eye-Movement Study of Sleep, *Brit J Psychiat* **109**:66, 1963.
16. Fisher, C.; Gross, J.; and Zuch, J.: Cycle of Penile Erection Synchronous With Dreaming (REM) Sleep: Preliminary Report, *Arch Gen Psychiat* **12**: 29-45, 1965.
17. Karacan, I., et al: Some Psychological and Physiological Correlates of Penile Erection During Sleep, read before the Fifth Annual Meeting of the Association of Psychophysiological Study of Sleep, Washington, DC, March 26-28, 1965.
18. Campbell, M.F.: "Psychologic Factors in Urologic Disorders" and "Impotence," in *Urology,* Philadelphia: W. B. Saunders Co., 1963, vol 3, p 2211.
19. Cooper, A.: *The Sexual Disabilities of Man and Their Treatment,* ed 2, New York: Harper and Row, Publishers, Inc., 1915.
20. Menninger, K.A.: Impotence and Frigidity From the Standpoint of Psychoanalysis, *J Urology* **34**:166, 1935.
21. Wershub, L.P.: *Sexual Impotence in the Male,* Springfield, Ill, Charles C Thomas, Publisher, 1959.
22. Goodenough, D.R., et al: A Comparison of "Dreamers" and "Non-Dreamers," Eye Movements, Electroencephalograms, and the Recall of Dreams, *J Abnorm Soc Psychol* **59**:295-302, 1959.
23. Karacan, I.: *The Effect of Exciting Presleep Events on Dream Reporting and Penile Erections During Sleep,* unpublished doctoral dissertation, Department of Psychiatry, Downstate Medical Center Library, New York University, Brooklyn, NY, May 1965.
24. Shapiro, A.: Personal communication to the authors, 1964.
25. Shapiro, A., and Cohen, H.: The Use of Mercury Capillary Length Gauges for the Measurement of the Volume of Thoracic and Diaphramatic Components of Human Respiration: A Theoretical Analysis and Practical Method, *Trans NY Acad Sci* **27**(series II):634, 1965.
26. Nowlis, V.: Some Dimensions of Mood and Their Interaction, read before the Symposium on Psychobiological Approaches to Social Behavior, Harvard University, Boston, April 19-20, 1963.
27. Gottschalk, L.A., et al: *Manual of Instructions for the Verbal Behavior Method of Measuring Certain Psychological Variables Including Some of the Theoretical Bases,* Cincinnati: Department of Psychiatry, University of Cincinnati, College of Medicine, May 1963.
28. Ohlmeyer, P., and Brilmayer, H.: Periodische Vorgange im Schlaf: II. Mitteling Pflug, *Arch Ges Physiol* **249**:50, 1947.
29. Ohlmeyer, P.; Brilmayer, H.; and Hullstrung, H.: Periodische Vorgange im Schlaf Pflug, *Arch Ges Physiol* **248**:559, 1944.
30. Verdone, P.: Variables Related to the Temporal Reference of Manifest Dream Content, read before the Association for the Psychophysiological Study of Sleep Communication, 1963.
31. Oswald, I.: *Sleeping and Waking, Physiology and Psychology,* New York: Elsevier Publishing Co., 1962, p 142.
32. Goodenough, D.R., et al: Dream Reporting Following Abrupt and Gradual Awakenings From Different Types of Sleep, *J Personality Soc Psychol,* 1965.
33. MacLean, P.D., and Ploog, D.W.: Cerebral Representation of Penile Erection, *J Neurophysiol* **25**:29, 1962.
34. Jouvet, M.: "Telencephalic and Rhombencephalic Sleep in the Cat," in G. E. W. Wolstenholme and M. O'Connor (eds.) *Ciba Foundation Symposium on the Nature of Sleep,* Boston: Little, Brown & Co., 1961, pp 188-205.

# AFFECTIVE REACTIONS AND PATIENT-THERAPIST INTERACTIONS AMONG MORE DIFFERENTIATED AND LESS DIFFERENTIATED PATIENTS EARLY IN THERAPY

HERMAN A. WITKIN, PH.D., HELEN B. LEWIS, PH.D. AND EDMUND WEIL, B.A.[1]

## INTRODUCTION

The findings to be reported here on patients' affective reactions and patients' interactions with their therapists come from a broader study of patient-therapist relations early in therapy. The main focus of the study has been the kind-of-patient variable; the particular personality variable with which we have been concerned is extent of differentiation.

To make clear the relevance of a patient's level of differentiation to his reactions in therapy, a brief account must be given of differentiation as a personal variable. "Psychological differentiation" has served in our studies to conceptualize particular consistencies observed in diverse areas of a person's psychological functioning (30, 31). Degree of differentiation is reflected in perception in extent of field dependence or independence. In a field-dependent style of perceiving, perception is dominated by the overall organization of the field; there is a relative inability to perceive parts of a field as discrete. This global quality is indicative of limited differentiation. Conversely in a field-independent mode of perceiving parts of a field are experienced as discrete from organized background rather than fused with it. This articulated quality is indicative of a relatively differentiated way of functioning. Persons whose field-dependent perception indicates limited differentiation in their experience of the world about them also show limited differentiation in their experience of body and self. They are likely to have a global body concept. In the same way that their perception of a stimulus object is dominated by the field around it, so do they tend to use the prevailing social context for definition of attributes of the self. This lack of a developed sense of separate identity is indicative of limited differentiation. Persons who perceive in field-dependent fashion are also likely to use relatively global defenses as massive repression and primitive denial, indicative of limited differentiation, whereas field-independent perceivers tend to use specialized defenses, as intellectualization and isolation, indicative of developed differentiation. Thus, from the standpoint of level of differentiation, people show self-consistency in their psychological functioning across diverse areas as perception, body concept, sense of separate identity and nature of defenses.

From this description of them we may expect more differentiated and less differentiated patients to differ in identifiable

[1] Psychology Laboratory and Psychiatric Treatment Research Center, Department of Psychiatry, State University of New York Downstate Medical Center, 450 Clarkson Avenue, Brooklyn, New York 11203.

An earlier version of this paper was presented at a symposium on "Some Recent Work on Shame and Guilt" at the American Psychological Association, New York City, September 4, 1966. This work has been supported by Grants M-628 and MH05518 from the National Institutes of Health, U. S. Public Health Service.

ways in their affective reactions during therapy and in their interactions with the therapist. In talking about his experiences, whether "in life" or within the therapy situation itself, a patient's typical feelings under particular circumstances and his characteristic ways of relating to people are revealed. The special feature of therapy that it involves self-revelation to another, who becomes extremely important and may be cast in many roles, is likely to facilitate exposure of the patient's characteristic feelings and object relations and to intensify them.

PATIENTS' AFFECTIVE REACTIONS

At the time this study began, we had specific anticipations about differences in the kinds of affective reactions more differentiated and less differentiated persons might show as patients in therapy. We did not expect them to differ particularly in sheer amount of feeling.[2] We did, however, expect them to differ in proneness to particular kinds of feelings. Specifically, we expected less differentiated patients to be more prone to shame than to guilt,[3] to hostility directed against the self than to hostility directed outward, and to both separation anxiety and diffuse anxiety. Conversely, we expected differentiated patients to react more readily with feelings of guilt than with feelings of shame, with outward-directed hostility than with inward-directed hostility, to be less prone to separation anxiety and to experience anxiety as having a definite source. These expectations were based upon both the known ways of functioning of these two kinds of persons and the phenomenology of the feelings themselves.

[2] This expectation was based in part on the observation that more differentiated and less differentiated persons do not differ in degree of psychological disturbance, although they are different in the kinds of pathology they are likely to develop (29).

[3] "Shame" and "shame anxiety" are used interchangeably here, as are "guilt" and "guilt anxiety."

Considering shame and guilt, first of all, the basis of our predictions for each kind of patient may be briefly stated. A person experiencing shame is acutely and often painfully aware of himself as the object of someone else's disapproval or derision. Shame is particularly connected with being seen, often with being unexpectedly caught, as the saying goes, "with one's pants down." Shame is a reaction in which the opinion of another, real or presumed, is focal, whether the critical "other" is actually present, imagined or represented as an unconscious introject. Persons who are particularly "involved with others" in their on-going functioning, and expecially sensitive to what others feel and think about them, we may speculate, would be easily prone to shame reactions. Relatively undifferentiated persons fall in this category. Numerous experimental studies have shown that undifferentiated persons characteristically use external sources of information for definition of their attitudes, sentiments, feelings and even self-view from moment to moment (see Ref. 30 for a review of these studies). It has been demonstrated, for example, that less differentiated children literally look more at faces of others, particularly when they feel distressed (9). Greater attentiveness to faces, and presumably because of this, better recall of faces, has also been observed in adults who are less differentiated (2, 20). These observations have recently been extended by the finding that less differentiated persons are particularly alert to socially related verbal material (4). Finally, mothers of less differentiated children interact early with them in ways that hamper the child's progress toward separate functioning (3, 30). Involvement with the critical "other" may thus be perpetuated, even when the child is out of the actual mother-child relation, and it may be generalized so that "merging" with others may easily occur. This is one ground on which we expected

less differentiated persons to be prone to shame.

A second ground was that shame has a global quality similar to that which characterizes the global cognitive style of less differentiated persons. Shame is an affect which involves the whole self "at the quick," as Helen Lynd (13) has put it, in an all-consuming feeling of worthlessness and inferiority. The deflation of the whole self can be experienced quite literally, as, for example, in weeping and in feelings of weakness. There is often the wish that one's whole being might disappear, expressed in the impulse to hide, to run away, "to sink through the floor." As Tomkins (26) has observed, shame is "the most reflexive of all affects" in the sense that the phenomenological distinction between the subject and object of shame is lost. Shame seems to be accompanied by diffuse autonomic arousal, as witness, for example, the blushing that often goes with shame. In the ways indicated, shame is a global·kind of experience in the realm of feeling, congruent with the global quality of the experience found in the cognitive realm in a global cognitive style.

Guilt, in contrast to shame, is aroused by violations of one's own moral standards. When it occurs on this basis, guilt does not require an audience; one can feel very guilty about an act to which there has been no witness, real or imagined. When the feeling of guilt is evoked in the context of relations to others, it is the consequence of a real or imagined injury committed by the self against others, in contrast to the arousal of shame through others' real or imagined scorn of the self. Guilt is an affect which involves reference to inner standards, rather than comparisons to standards of others, as in shame, and so depends upon a self which is differentiated.

Guilt, as compared to shame, has a more articulated quality and on this basis again we expected it to be characteristic or differentiated patients whose experience tends to be articulated. Guilt is an experience less likely to involve the whole self. One typically feels guilty about a particular transgression for which there is a specific atonement or expiation that can put an end to the guilt, in contrast to shame from which there seems to be no specific release. Guilt is more ideational[4] and involves less affectively loaded imagery connecting the self and the "other" in a confrontation. Guilt seems less often accompanied by diffuse autonomic arousal. One may feel guilty for failure to do something which one should have done and by implication is able to do. The self may be quite mobilized to make amends to the injured "other," rather than becoming temporarily paralyzed by the scorn of the "other," as in shame.

It is noteworthy that Piers and Singer (21), following the classic Freudian account of the superego, have described guilt as following upon the internalization of authority under the threat of castration. It follows from this concept also that guilt (and castration anxiety as well) would be a more characteristic reaction of differentiated patients. In the Piers-Singer formulation, shame is relatively primitive and guilt is a later development.

Turning to separation anxiety, we may expect that patients with a less developed sense of separate identity would make more references to separation anxiety in verbal accounts of their life experiences and in their actual on-going relation with the therapist.

The prediction of more diffuse anxiety among undifferentiated patients reflected our expectation that the global quality found in their perception would be evident in their feelings as well. Their experience of anxiety is likely to be global in its cognitive content and nonspecific as to its source.

Finally, we need to consider our reasons

[4] As noted, more differentiated persons often use intellectualization as a characteristic defense.

for expecting that hostility, when aroused, will be more likely to be directed against the self in undifferentiated patients and outward in differentiated patients. In the less differentiated person, in whom there is a particularly strong need to be merged with the "other," hostility toward the "other" is dangerous because it may threaten separation. Hostility when aroused, as, for example, by the other telling him he ought to be ashamed, can take only the self as its object. To be hostile to the other with whom one is semimerged is too dangerous, too provocative of separation. Outward projection of hostility is not an easily usable defense. Hostility toward the self in the less differentiated patient is also a more likely reaction because hostility directed against the self is simultaneously directed against the internalized, poorly differentiated representation of the "other one." In this pattern, which has been described for masochistic patients (19, 23), it is mainly the hostility against the self which is experienced or "allowed," resulting in a devalued self-image (27).

In the differentiated patient, we may speculate, hostility can economically be directed outward. In such persons, where separation anxiety is less important than castration anxiety, the object representation is experienced as separate. Outward projection of hostility is a usable defense, as, for example, when hostility is aroused in accompaniment to guilt.

### PATIENT-THERAPIST INTERACTIONS

Along with these differences in their typical affective reactions during theapy, we may also expect more differentiated and less differentiated patients to differ in their characteristic way of relating to the therapist—in other words, in the transference. The structuring of the transference derives in part from the organization of the self. The kinds of differences in organization of the self, and with it in relationships to others, that are implied by a more developed or less developed sense of separate identity should contribute to differences in development of the transference (10, 11). In this connection, it has been observed (5) that less differentiated patients are likely to feel better earlier in therapy than more differentiated patients, although the improvement does not seem to persist. It seems likely that because of their less developed sense of separate identity undifferentiated patients show ready "merging" with the therapist, and it is this which accounts for their early felt improvement.

We may also expect more differentiated and less differentiated patients to differ in their *a priori* expectations of the therapist's role, behavior and attitudes; in their reactions to the therapist's suggestions—whether readily accepting or circumspect; and in their ability to keep separate the transference and the reality aspects of the doctor-patient relationship. As part of their more developed sense of separate identity, differentiated patients may be expected to watch themselves in the midst of their own reactions, that is, to use "distancing" mechanisms (12). Such self-observation would contribute to their ability to give an articulated account of themselves, their problems and their history, regardless of whether dynamically correct or not.

These differences between patients in ways of relating to the therapist should result in specific differences in the interaction process. Two such differences are particularly apparent. Especially in the first sessions of therapy, when the therapist's main task is to obtain some impression of the patient and his problems, it may require a more active inquiry by the therapist if his patient is limitedly differentiated. The outcome will be a large number of therapist interventions and briefer patient utterances, together making for a relatively high frequency of ex-

changes between patient and therapist. It is also possible that the presumed tendency of less differentiated patients to experience shame when telling another about themselves may also affect frequency of exchanges. In some cases, shame may block productivity and so result in brief patient utterances and a greater need for "digging" (or more frequent interventions) by the therapist. On the other hand, when shame results in heightened excitement, it is likely that the patient's utterances will take the form of "spilling" which requires containment; such a reaction to feelings of shame will again make for relatively brief patient utterances and will require more frequent intervention by the therapist in order to contain and direct the patient's verbal flow. Further, the more circumspect approach of differentiated patients to the therapist's suggestions, involving as it does a filtering of what the therapist says through their own more structured system of feelings and frames of reference, and a cautious, qualified response to the therapist's proposals may contribute to typically longer utterances by such patients. This kind of approach, together with their proneness to "distancing" or watching the self, may, in addition, make for longer delays in these patients' rejoinders to the therapist's comments. Thus, we expected a difference between our two kinds of patients both in rate of patient-therapist exhanges per unit time and in the time interval between therapist and patient comments.

#### THERAPIST'S COGNITIVE SYTLE

Pollack and Kiev (22) have shown that psychiatrists who are extremely field-independent in our perceptual tests favor either a directional and instructional or a passive-observational approach to their patients in therapy, whereas relatively more (although not extremely) field-dependent therapists favor personal and mutual relations with their patients. Pollack and Kiev also found field-dependent therapists to be of the "A" type, according to the classification made by Whitehorn and Betz, as summarized by Betz (1), and the relatively field-independent therapists to be of the "B" type. This finding has been confirmed by Shows and Carson (24).

These observations suggested that the extent of the therapists' field dependence may be an important "kind-of-therapist" variable. This variable might particularly affect the frequency of the therapist's interventions and therefore the tempo of patient-therapist interactions. Although our therapists were not selected on the basis of level of differentiation, they were all tested for field dependence after the therapy sessions had been completed.

### SUBJECTS AND PROCEDURE

#### PATIENTS AND THERAPISTS

To select the patients for this study our tests of field dependence and the figure-drawing test (evaluated for articulation of body concept) were included in the initial clinic screening battery given to all patients who came to the Kings County Mental Hygiene Clinic, an outpatient unit. Extensive testing proved necessary both to obtain patients at the extremes of the differentiation dimension and to achieve a reasonable match between patients in the two groups. Two groups of four highly differentiated patients and four relatively undifferentiated patients were formed, matched on a group basis for age, sex, level of schooling and occupation. A more differentiated and less differentiated patient was assigned to individual therapy with each of four therapists (three men and one woman). (Table 1 gives a summary description of each of the eight patients, listed according to patient pairs treated by each therapist.) Controlling for therapist in this way seemed important because of the contribution the kind-of-

TABLE 1
*Description of Patients and Therapists*

| Therapist (No. and Sex) | Patient* | Sex | Age | Education | Occupation | Marital Status | Patient's Reason for Seeking Treatment |
|---|---|---|---|---|---|---|---|
| | | | *yrs* | | | | |
| M1 | D1 | M | 34 | High school graduate | Draftsman | M | Obsessive thoughts re dying |
| M2 | D2 | F | 21 | 2 years college | Housewife | M | Marital difficulty |
| F3 | D3 | M | 20 | Currently 4th year college | Student | S | Not working up to potential in college |
| M4 | D4 | M | 17 | Currently high school senior | Student | S | Suicide attempt (aspirin) |
| M1 | U1 | M | 21 | Currently 1st year college | Clerk | S | Apathy, depression, shy with girls |
| M2 | U2 | F | 21 | Currently 2nd year college | Student | S | Facial tics |
| F3 | U3 | M | 19 | Currently 2nd year college | Student | S | Worry about sex |
| M4 | U4 | M | 35 | High school graduate | Electrical worker | S | Ringing in ears (referred by OTL) |

* First four patients listed are relatively differentiated; last four, relatively undifferentiated.

therapist variable itself may make to the patient-therapist interaction.

The therapists who took part in the study were simply requested to do psychotherapy with the patients in their usual way. They knew nothing of our findings on their patients nor were they told the purpose of the study. It was planned for the therapy to run for 20 sessions, although this number was not achieved in all cases.[5] The patients were informed of the planned duration of the therapy, and they were told that the therapy was part of a research project. All therapy sessions were tape recorded with the patient's knowledge. After the therapy sessions were completed, but before the therapists were informed of their patients' cognitive style and other test results, an interview was conducted with each therapist about his experiences with each of his patients, particularly with respect to the transference. Each therapist was also tested for field dependence on the rod-and-frame test.

[5] One of the therapists originally selected was unable to continue after he had done 10 sessions with his differentiated patient (D4), but before his undifferentiated patient was assigned. Another therapist (M4) took over patient D4 and did 20 sessions with him as well as with his undifferentiated match. The quantitative data on this patient are from the first two sessions with his second therapist.

METHOD OF ASSESSING PATIENTS' AFFECTIVE REACTIONS

To compare the feeling reactions of the two kinds of patients early in therapy, the transcribed therapy records were scored for anxiety and hostility according to the method developed by Dr. Louis Gottschalk and his collaborators (28).[6] This method, devised for assessing feelings in verbal productions, seemed particularly suited to our needs since the categories of feelings about which we had hypotheses are all represented among the Gottschalk categories. In the anxiety area, there are six categories: shame, guilt, separation anxiety and diffuse anxiety (for all of which we had hypotheses), and mutilation anxiety and death anxiety (for which we had no advance hypotheses). In the hostility area, the categories are hostility-in and hostility-out (covert and overt). For both categories of hostility we had advance

[6] We are indebted to Mrs. Carolyn Winget of Dr. Gottschalk's group for scoring our records.

hypotheses. In addition, there is an ambivalent hostility category, which has components of both kinds of hostility. For this category again we had no prediction. In the Gottschalk method, both direct and indirect expressions of feeling are considered, and in scoring verbal phrases for affect, differential weights are assigned according to the intensity of the affect.

Two kinds of measures will be given for each feeling category. The first is Gottschalk's weighted score measure, computed for each feeling category. (See Winget *et al.* [28] for a description of the method of computing this measure.) The second measure, which we devised for this study, is the frequency of spurts of feeling in each category. To compute this measure the transcript of each therapy session was divided into 500-word units. A weighted score was then computed for each unit for each feeling category. Using a weighted score of 1.0 or higher as a cut-off point, the percentage of 500-word units in each session in which this value was exceeded was computed. Data for the two kinds of measures are presented for the first two sessions combined.

### METHODS OF ASSESSING PATIENT-THERAPIST INTERACTIONS

To check the prediction of a higher rate of patient-therapist exchanges among undifferentiated patients, three kinds of measures were computed for each patient: 1) mean number of therapist comments per minute; 2) mean number of words per patient utterance; 3) mean number of seconds per patient utterance. To check the prediction that more differentiated patients would delay longer before responding to the therapist's comment, the interval between each therapist and patient comment was timed from the original tape recording.[7]

[7] We are indebted to Mrs. Lee Davis for her careful work in making these painstaking measurements.

## RESULTS

### PATIENTS' AFFECTIVE REACTIONS

A first finding is that more differentiated and less differentiated patients are not very different in total amount of anxiety in the first two sessions of therapy. Total anxiety scores, based on all six anxiety categories combined, and frequency of spurts in total anxiety scores tend to be greater in less differentiated patients, but the differences are small. (Mean total weighted anxiety scores for more differentiated and less differentiated patients are 2.12 and 2.48, respectively; mean frequencies of spurts are 85.7 and 94.6 per cent. Neither of the differences is significant.) The real difference between the two kinds of patients lies in the distribution of anxiety in the various anxiety categories, rather than in total amount of anxiety.

The most striking difference is in the relative incidence of shame and guilt reactions.[8] As expected, less differentiated patients are more prone to feelings of shame and differentiated patients to feelings of guilt. The data on shame may be found in Table 2, which gives for each patient both his weighted and spurts scores for this feeling category (as well as both kinds of scores for the guilt category). To point up trends in this preliminary study, what we have done in this table and in the other tables in this section is to present a listing of scores for pairs of patients of each therapist. With three of four pairs of patients on the weighted shame measures (scores in columns 1 *vs.* 3 of Table 2), and with all four pairs on the spurts measure (scores in columns 5 *vs.* 7), the score for the undifferentiated member of the pair is higher. Looking at the means, spurts of shame are on the average twice as frequent in undifferentiated as in differentiated pa-

[8] Shame and guilt do not seem very likely to occur together. In only 16.1 per cent of all instances of spurts of shame and guilt do we find them within the same 500-word unit.

TABLE 2

*Comparison of Shame and Guilt Reactions*

| Weighted Scores | | | | | | Percentage of Spurts | | | | | |
|---|---|---|---|---|---|---|---|---|---|---|---|
| Undifferentiated patients | | | Differentiated patients | | | Undifferentiated patients | | | Differentiated patients | | |
| | (Column 1) Shame | (Column 2) Guilt | | (Column 3) Shame | (Column 4) Guilt | | (Column 5) Shame | (Column 6) Guilt | | (Column 7) Shame | (Column 8) Guilt |
| U1 | .89 | .74 | D1 | .82 | 1.00 | U1 | 31.3 | 20.2 | D1 | 23.8 | 38.1 |
| U2 | 1.71 | .82 | D2 | .86 | .60 | U2 | 75.8 | 23.1 | D2 | 25.8 | 17.0 |
| U3 | 1.40 | .90 | D3 | .58 | 1.27 | U3 | 63.1 | 31.4 | D3 | 15.4 | 47.2 |
| U4 | 1.04 | .92 | D4 | 1.28 | 1.37 | U4 | 34.8 | 27.2 | D4 | 33.3 | 55.6 |
| Mean | 1.26 | .84 | Mean | .88 | 1.06 | Mean | 51.2 | 25.5 | Mean | 24.6 | 39.5 |

tients (51.2 *vs.* 24.6 per cent), occurring in the undifferentiated group in about half of all 500-word units. Comparing the two kinds of patients in similar fashion for guilt reactions, we find in Table 2 that the more differentiated patients tend to have higher scores, although the magnitude of the difference between the two groups is not so great as in the shame reactions.

Table 2 has been organized so as to permit also a comparison of relative incidence of shame and guilt reactions within each patient of the two groups. By both the weighted score and spurts measures, we find that every undifferentiated patient was higher on shame than on guilt (columns 1 *vs.* 2 and columns 5 *vs.* 6), whereas three of the four differentiated patients were higher on guilt than on shame (columns 3 *vs.* 4 and columns 7 *vs.* 8). The tendency for undifferentiated patients to show more shame than guilt and for differentiated patients to show more guilt than shame is significant. The $t$ test was significant for both the weighted score measure ($p < .05$) and the percentage of spurts measure ($p < .01$).

In all, the expectation that undifferentiated patients will be more prone to shame anxiety and differentiated patients more prone to guilt anxiety receives support from these data for the early sessions of therapy.

Another category of anxiety in which the two kinds of patients are different is diffuse anxiety. In Gottschalk's rating method, units of the verbal record are scored for diffuse anxiety under any of three conditions: when the anxiety is not adequately characterized to permit its placement in one of the five specific anxiety categories, as shame, guilt, etc.; when the wording does not allow determination of the source of the anxiety; when the anxiety falls into two or more of the specific categories. Anxiety expressed in either of the first two forms is vague as to its nature and/or source; the third form of anxiety involves, in a sense, a "fusion" of feelings and so is nonspecific. On grounds already considered we expected less differentiated patients to show more of these diffuse forms of anxiety. Results for Gottschalk's diffuse anxiety category for our two kinds of patients are in keeping with this expectation. Table 3 shows that in every patient pair, the undifferentiated member of the pair has a higher weighted score and a higher frequency of spurts of diffuse anxiety; in most instances the difference between patient pairs is quite large. Moreover, the differences in means between the two kinds of patients are significant for both the weighted and spurts measures ($p < .05$ in both cases).

The data for the fourth anxiety category for which we had a hypothesis—separation

TABLE 3
*Diffuse Anxiety Reactions*

| Weighted Scores | | | | Percentage of Spurts | | | |
|---|---|---|---|---|---|---|---|
| Undifferentiated patients | | Differentiated patients | | Undifferentiated patients | | Differentiated patients | |
| U1 | 1.52 | D1 | .91 | U1 | 65.2 | D1 | 32.5 |
| U2 | 1.35 | D2 | 1.26 | U2 | 60.8 | D2 | 60.6 |
| U3 | 1.16 | D3 | .74 | U3 | 54.9 | D3 | 27.8 |
| U4 | 2.08 | D4 | .95 | U4 | 85.4 | D4 | 44.4 |
| Mean | 1.53 | Mean | .96 | Mean | 66.6 | Mean | 41.3 |

TABLE 4
*Comparison of Hostility-in and Hostility-Out*

| Weighted Scores | | | | | | Percentage of Spurts | | | | | |
|---|---|---|---|---|---|---|---|---|---|---|---|
| Undifferentiated patients | | | Differentiated patients | | | Undifferentiated patients | | | Differentiated patients | | |
| | (Column 1) Hostility-in | (Column 2) Hostility-out | | (Column 3) Hostility-in | (Column 4) Hostility-out | | (Column 5) Hostility-in | (Column 6) Hostility-out | | (Column 7) Hostility-in | (Column 8) Hostility-out |
| U1 | 1.38 | 1.86 | D1 | 1.22 | .94 | U1 | 64.2 | 61.6 | D1 | 43.1 | 33.8 |
| U2 | 1.70 | 1.63 | D2 | .90 | 1.75 | U2 | 88.4 | 50.0 | D2 | 30.5 | 68.6 |
| U3 | 1.65 | 1.80 | D3 | 1.02 | 1.89 | U3 | 74.9 | 77.4 | D3 | 39.8 | 95.4 |
| U4 | 1.34 | 1.08 | D4 | 1.30 | 2.05 | U4 | 71.4 | 34.2 | D4 | 50.0 | 70.8 |
| Mean | 1.52 | 1.59 | Mean | 1.11 | 1.66 | Mean | 74.7 | 55.8 | Mean | 40.8 | 67.2 |

anxiety—give no indication of differences between the two kinds of patients. Our expectation that undifferentiated patients would show more separation anxiety than differentiated patients is not confirmed. It is possible that this outcome is a result of the generally very low frequency of separation anxiety ratings in our therapy records.[9]

The remaining two anxiety categories, mutilation and death, for which we had no hypotheses, showed no differences between the two kinds of patients, but scores for both these categories were quite rare in our therapy records.

Turning now to feelings of hostility, it was our expectation that in less differentiated patients the self would be more likely to be the object of hostile feelings whereas in differentiated patients hostility would be directed outwards. A comparison of Gottschalk hostility-in and hostility-out scores for our two kinds of patients gives support to this expectation. Table 4 shows the weighted scores and frequency of spurts for the hostility-in category (as well as for the hostility-out category to be considered next). In our four pairs of patients, for both kinds of measures, the values for the undifferentiated patients are higher (columns 1 *vs.* 3, 5 *vs.* 7), indicating a greater amount of hostility directed inward. Spurts of hostility-in occur, on the average, almost twice as frequently in the undifferentiated as in the differentiated group (74.7 *vs.* 40.8 per cent). Examining the corresponding data for the hostility-out category, in Table 4, we find that now the relation is reversed; the tendency is for differentiated patients to score higher (columns 2 *vs.* 4, 6 *vs.* 8), although the overall difference is not so great as that found for hostility-in reactions. In three of the four patient pairs, the score for the

[9] In only two of our eight patients did separation anxiety show some elevation. Both were the male patients of our only woman therapist.

differentiated patient is higher for both the weighted score and spurt measure. Table 4 permits a within-patient comparison of frequency of the two kinds of feelings. When weighted scores are considered, undifferentiated patients do not show a consistent difference between hostility-in and hostility-out scores. For the differentiated patients, hostility-out scores are higher than hostility-in scores in three pairs by quite large amounts; the overall difference, reflected in mean scores, is substantial. When spurt scores are considered, both groups of patients show a tendency in the expected direction: undifferentiated patients tend to have higher hostility-in scores than hostility-out scores and differentiated patients show a reverse trend. A *t* test showed that the tendency for undifferentiated patients to show more hostility-in than hostility-out and for differentiated patient to show more hostility-out than hostility-in is significant in the case of the spurts measure ($p < .05$) although not in the case of the weighted score measure.

When we examine the relation between shame and guilt, on the one hand, and hostility-in and hostility-out, on the other, several interesting observations emerge. Regardless of patient type, a strong tendency is found for *both* shame and guilt to be associated with feelings of hostility. Within this general relation a more specific tendency is noted; again regardless of patient type, shame anxiety is more likely to be associated with feelings of hostility directed toward the self and guilt anxiety to be associated with hostility directed outward. The evidence for this is found in the frequency of coincidence, in 500-word units, of spurts of feelings of shame, guilt, hostility-in and hostility-out.[10] In units where shame spurts occurred there were hostility-in spurts in 62 per cent of the units and hostility-out spurts in only 37 per cent of the units. Conversely, guilt spurts were accompanied by hostility-out spurts in 79 per cent of the units and by hostility-in spurts in 58 per cent of the units.[11, 12]

### PATIENT-THERAPIST INTERACTIONS

Table 5 contains the data needed to check our expectation that early therapy sessions with more differentiated patients would be characterized, first, by a slower rate of exchange and, second, by a longer interval between the time the therapist completed his comment and the time the patient began his. Data are presented for the first two sessions combined.

By all three measures used to assess frequency of exchanges—mean number of

[10] For this analysis the relatively small number of units which contained spurts of both shame and guilt were excluded, since in such instances it is not possible to determine with which of these reactions the accompanying hostility is associated. Also, it must be noted, in some 500-word units, spurts of both kinds of hostility may occur simultaneously with shame or with guilt.

[11] The consistent association between tendency toward shame and tendency toward hostility-in is also evident when results for individual patients are examined. On the whole, persons prone to strong shame reactions are also prone to strong hostility-in reactions, and there is a tendency for the relation to hold over time. No such consistent relation was found in individual patients between tendency toward guilt and tendency toward hostility-out, nor between shame and hostility-out or guilt and hostility-in.

[12] In the Gottschalk method the same phrase may sometimes receive multiple scores. In ordinary language, feelings of shame and feelings of hostility toward the self may at times be given expression in words that are similar; the same is to an extent true of feelings of guilt and feelings of hostility-out. We accordingly considered the possibility that the linkage found between shame and hostility-in may result because both types of scores are based on use of the same information in the records. Similarly, it had to be considered that the association observed between guilt and hostility-out might have a similar basis. Examination of individual scoring units in the therapy records shows that of the 1891 phrases scored in all patient records for guilt and/or hostility-out, 6.9 per cent were scored for both; of 1178 phrases scored for shame and/or hostility-in, 17.1 per cent were scored for both. The extent of overlap is quite small for the guilt-hostility-out combination. It is greater for the shame-hostility-in combination, but hardly sufficient to account for the observed degree of coincidence (62 per cent) of spurts of shame and of hostility-in.

therapist comments per minute, mean number of words per patient comment and mean duration of patient comments in seconds—our first hypothesis is confirmed. In all three instances, the difference between the two groups is large and significant.[13]

The difference in rate of exchange with the two kinds of patients is clearly not a function of a difference in speed of speech. As might be expected, rate of word flow, as measured by number of words spoken per minute, though apparently a highly stable characteristic of a given patient over sessions, is not related to level of differentiation. There is, in fact, some suggestion that rapid speech may have a quite different meaning in the two kinds of patients. In each of our groups there were two patients who had a particularly high rate of word production. The two differentiated "fast-talking" patients had the highest scores of all patients for average duration of their comments (72.6 sec and 56.9 sec per comment), whereas the two undifferentiated "fast-talking" patients had the lowest scores (10.8 sec and 7.4 sec). With this, the records of the fast-talking differentiated patients showed a very low number of therapist interventions and the records of the fast-talking undifferentiated patients a very high number of interventions. These facts, together with impressions gained from a review of the content of the therapy records themselves, suggest that, whereas the rapid speech of the undifferentiated patients reflected a pressured, "spilling over" of not too well organized feelings and ideas, which the therapist sought by his comments to contain and direct, the rapid speech of the differentiated patients was associated with highly organized and extended presentations which they were "pushing" at the therapist.

To assess the interval between therapist's comments and patient's comments, the interval was timed and the percentage frequencies of relatively long patient rejoinders (2 sec or more) and very short patient rejoinders (immediate replies plus actual interruptions of the therapist by the patient) were determined. We see in Table 5 that there was a significantly higher incidence of the first type of delay among differentiated patients and a significantly higher frequency of the second type among undifferentiated patients. Our hypothesis predicting a difference in speed of patient response between the two kinds of patients is thus confirmed.

The contrast between the two patient groups in all the variables that have been considered is evident not only when group means are compared, but also when comparisons are made between the differentiated and undifferentiated patients making up each patient pair. In 18 of the 20 comparisons of patient pairs for the five variables considered, the direction of the

TABLE 5

*Characteristics of Patient-Therapist Interactions*

| Variable | Undifferentiated Patients | Differentiated Patients* |
|---|---|---|
| Number of therapist's comments per minute | 3.5 | 1.4† |
| Mean length of patient comments | | |
| In number of words | 39.1 | 158.2‡ |
| In number of seconds | 12.8 | 50.7‡ |
| Length of delay of patient's comments after therapist's comments | | |
| Percentage of immediate responses + interruptions | 16.5 | 6.8† |
| Percentage of intervals over 2 seconds | 4.8 | 10.5‡ |
| Length of delay of therapist's comment after patient's comment | | |
| Percentage of immediate responses + interruptions | 16.0 | 10.8 |
| Percentage of intervals over 2 seconds | 9.5 | 16.2 |

* Two-tailed tests have been used throughout.
† $p < .01$.
‡ $p < .05$.

[13] There is no difference in length of *therapist* comment with the two kinds of patients.

difference between the two kinds of patients was in accord with our hypothesis.

It is interesting that the observed difference in speed of response to the therapist's comments by our two kinds of patients is matched by a congruent difference in speed of therapist's response. As shown in Table 5, there was a tendency for the therapists, on their part, to delay longer in responding to their differentiated patients than to their undifferentiated patients, although the difference on the therapist's side is less marked than on the patient's side and not statistically significant. This tendency may perhaps reflect the therapist's sense that more differentiated patients may be better able to tolerate silence.

THERAPIST'S COGNITIVE STYLE

On the rod-and-frame test the standard scores of our four therapists were M1, −.89; M2, −.79; F3, +.12; and M4, +.48. (Positive scores indicate more field-dependent perception.) In relation to the general population, two of the therapists (M1 and M2) were quite field-independent (with very similar scores), one (F3) was at the middle of the intermediate range, and one toward the field-dependent end of the intermediate range. Reexamining our data from the standpoint of the therapist's field dependence, we find, first, a tendency for the more field-independent therapists to intervene less. Interventions per minute for each of the four therapists, for their two patients taken together, were 1.8, 1.6, 3.0 and 3.4 for therapists M1, M2, F3 and M4, respectively (Table 6). Since the patient's field dependence has already been shown to be a factor in frequency of patient-therapist interactions, it is of interest to examine the mutual interrelation of the field dependence of each. In undertaking this comparison, we expected that the highest frequency of interaction would occur when both patient and therapist are field-independent and the lowest when both are field-independent. On the premise that extent of patient's field dependence is a more important determinant of frequency of interaction than extent of therapist's field dependence, we also expected more interactions between field-dependent patients and field-independent therapists than between field-independent patients and relatively field-dependent therapists. The data needed to check these expectations are given in Table 6. We see first of all in that table that for every therapist there were considerably more interactions with his undifferentiated than with his differentiated patient, and, as already noted, the frequency of interactions was higher for the relatively field-dependent than for the relatively field-independent therapists. Further, in keeping with our expectation, the combination of relatively field-dependent patient and field-dependent therapist produces a dramatically higher frequency of interactions than the combination of field-independent patient and therapist. Thus, the number of interactions per minute of M4, the most field-dependent therapist, with his field-dependent patient (U4) was 5.1. At the other extreme, for our two field-independent therapists (M1 and M2), with their field-independent patients (D1 and D2, respectively), there were only 1.0 and .8 interactions per minute. In addition, again as expected, the combination of field-dependent patient and field-independent therapist produced more interactions than the reverse combination.

TABLE 6

*Frequency of Interactions as a Function of Extent of Field Dependence of Patient and Therapist*

| Therapists (in Order of Increasing Field Dependence) | Frequency of Interactions per Minute | | |
|---|---|---|---|
| | Field-independent patients | Field-dependent patients | Mean of both patients |
| M1 | 1.0 (D1) | 2.7 (U1) | 1.8 |
| M2 | .8 (D2) | 2.5 (U2) | 1.6 |
| F3 | 2.3 (D3) | 3.7 (U3) | 3.0 |
| M4 | 1.8 (D4) | 5.1 (U4) | 3.4 |

Our two other measures of tempo—mean number of words per patient utterance and mean number of seconds per utterance—show a very similar picture to the one just presented for the frequency of interaction measure, to which they are of course highly related. Thus, it appears that early in therapy the more field-dependent the therapist, the faster the tempo of the session. The same is true of more field-dependent patients, and the interaction effect of therapist's and patient's field dependence seems particularly strong.

When the data on feelings are reexamined from the standpoint of therapist's field dependence, suggestive trends of interest again emerge. In particular, overall patient anxiety tends to be higher with greater therapist field dependence. The Gottschalk total weighted anxiety scores, for their two patients taken together, of therapists M1, M2, F3, and M4 are 2.43, 2.61, 2.90 and 3.03, respectively. The corresponding values for the frequency of spurts measure of total anxiety are 49.8, 57.7, 65.2 and 74.8 per cent. It thus suggested that greater field dependence in the therapist may be associated with more charged feelings in the patient, in addition to a faster tempo of interaction. Of the more specific Gottschalk feeling categories, only "guilt" seems to show any relation to therapist's field dependence, greater therapist field dependence tending to be associated with more patient guilt feelings.

Because of several limitations, the observations just reviewed must be considered as no more than suggestions for further research. One limitation is the small number of therapists in this study. Another is the lack of control for therapist's experience, known to be a factor affecting the quality of therapist's communications (see, for example, Strupp [25]) although the ordering of our therapists and the size of the interval between them on the different variables considered correspond better to their relative standing on the field dependence dimension than to their standing on the years-of-experience dimension.[14]

### DISCUSSION

Patients selected as different in extent of differentiation show predictably different feelings and behavior early in therapy. The finding that a patient's level of differentiation is predictive of his affective reactions and of the tempo of his interaction with the therapist adds another facet to the set of self-consistent psychological characteristics which has been identified through research on the differentiation dimension. Our findings join a growing body of evidence that the patient's personality affects the patient-therapist interaction, particularly evidence from studies of Matarazzo and his collaborators (14, 15, 17). That the differentiation variable may be a generally important one in interview behavior is suggested by the finding that, in interviews conducted by one of us (H. B. L.) with a group of normal young men who were subjects in a longitudinal study we conducted, the tempo of interaction was again faster for the less differentiated subjects than for the more differentiated ones.

Our patients' protocols provide an opportunity to examine the phenomenology of the feelings with which we have been concerned. An excerpt from the first page of the transcript of patient U2, in which she is telling the therapist about her troubles, makes clearly evident the evocation of shame in the context of relations with others. This excerpt in which the patient is ashamed of herself and her tic illustrates two particular features of shame: 1) feelings about others' opinions in concrete imagery of how she looks to others; 2) the experience of being looked at is acutely painful.

[14] For our therapists, years in psychiatry beyond the residency are M1, 5; M2, 19; F3, 6; and M4, 1.

(P) Well I have these nervous habits. I don't know if I'm using the correct term. (T) Well, don't worry about that, just tell me what. (P) Yeah, it's not uh—and this has been going on since I was—since I was a little girl. And I always had some sort of silly little thing that I do. And uhm, you know, it wouldn't be so horrible except for the fact that I hate it (slight laugh). I feel terrible about it. You know, I don't know how it really looks to other people.... When I find somebody looking at me I could die. (T) Could die? (P) Well not literally (slight laugh). That's when I sort of have the feeling that I could crawl through a hole. That's when I do these habits the most.

Another excerpt from this same undifferentiated patient's transcript indicates how the tic symptom, evocative of shame in her, may be set off by simply "looking" at another person who has a tic. The excerpt reminds us of the finding, cited earlier, that less differentiated persons are particularly attentive to faces.

(P) ... in one of my classes one of the—some boy sat up front. He had some sort of ... a facial twitch ... and the girl sitting next to me says, uh mentioned something to the fact that, 'Look at that boy, you know, he's got that funny twitch, you know.' So I looked at him and I got so you know, I felt really uncomfortable; because it reminded me of my own. And that's why I'm going to start up, and—(T) Thought you're going to start up too. (P) Yeah. When I see somebody else with these things it starts me off. Sort of winds me up because I get afraid that I'm going to—(T) Is it kind of contagious? (P) Yeah! And I pick up these—other people's habits too, and I'm so afraid I'm going to do it. I've always—you know, this is how I got my habits in the first place. I copied them through some other child....

There is some evidence connecting differentiation, shame, depression and self-directed hostility with one another in a pattern that may profitably be explored in further research. We have already seen that shame tends to be associated with self-directed hostility, and that less differentiated patients are prone to both these feelings. There is also some evidence that depression is a more common symptom among less differentiated patients than among more differentiated patients (31). Now, to add a further link to the chain, study of our transcripts draws attention to a connection between shame and depression and suggests a dynamic interplay between these feelings.

As one kind of interplay, it is possible that shame reactions are sometimes experienced as depression and/or diffuse anxiety. For example, in her second session patient U2 told the therapist: "Last time (referring to the previous session, which was the very first one), when I first came in, I was, um, and I started talking to you, I was upset, but I didn't know what about. And, um, I sort of felt I was on the verge of tears, but I didn't know why. Therefore I really didn't mention it because I felt ridiculous. There was no reason."

As another example, patient U1 felt "depressed" after leaving one of his sessions. With a little probing by the therapist about this the patient said: "I feel like an idiot sometimes when I think what I told you," illustrating how shameful imagery of himself as an "idiot," coupled with self-directed hostility, may be components of a subjective experience of depression.

In *The Ego and the Id*, Freud (6) contrasted the sense of guilt experienced by the obsessional neurotic with that experienced by the melancholic. He observed that the "object" in obsessional neurosis is "retained," *i.e.*, not introjected, while in melancholia, the distinction between the self and the object has been lost. Jacobson (8) observed that depressives suffer a confusion as to whether they are angry at the self or the object. Fromm-Reichmann (7) also observed that depressives have a weak self, which attaches readily to others and takes on the "coloration" of the environment. The set of associations that has been reviewed—shame is more easily evoked in undifferentiated patients, the association between shame and self-directed

hostility is particularly strong in these patients, and depression is a symptom more common among them than among differentiated patients--suggests that it could be fruitful to investigate this pattern among depressed patients. It would be particularly interesting to study depressed patients varying in extent of differentiation, with a possibility that this approach may provide a basis for distinguishing among patients who arrive at this symptom by different dynamic routes.

The therapists' retrospective accounts of their patients make clear that there was a striking clinical difference between pairs of patients, so that the therapists experienced each member of the pair in a very different way. For example in contrast to the "distancing" of patient D3,[15] patient U3's "clinging" transference was described by his therapist as follows: "I wouldn't call it transference. They (the patient's feelings) just fused." Comparing U3 and D3, she said further:

> ... the similarities were all on the surface. They were both young college boys of about the same age, ... having trouble with their mothers ... had crazy mothers and weak fathers. There was that similarity which is ... all on the surface, because they couldn't have been more different.... (U3) formed this clinging transference—he would come and live with me if I would let him. There was such an attachment, so much clinging wish to be with me.... (U3) aroused more of that motherly feeling.... I felt, you know, you know, fond of him ... the other one (D3) would make me angry by staying away and provoking me in a million ways.

U2's therapist was particularly struck by her need for reassurance and support. He said about her: "She was always saying, is that what you want to know." In contrast, the therapist said about patient D2 that she came and said, "Sit there and shut up and I will tell you what the whole thing is about." The therapist is not only describing his experience of a difference in rate of patient-therapist exchange, but also a difference between dealing with a patient who is prone to shame and self-directed hostility, in contrast with a patient who is expressing self-propelled guilty ideation, in association with hostility directed outward.

The pattern of findings on patient-therapist interaction suggests that the therapist assumed a more active and directive role in dealing with his less differentiated patients. For example, U1's therapist said about him: "I'd have to question him, nudge him, sort of constantly ... it was more work—I was under pressure to talk to him." In contrast, the therapist said of his differentiated patient, D1: "He talked continually during the hour. At some times I don't believe I said a word—I was just sort of bored." Patient D1 brought with him to his first session a long letter which he read to the therapist describing his symptoms. It will be remembered that patient U1, in contrast, suffered from depression, shyness and apathy, feeling states which would tend to require "more work" on the therapist's part. These excerpts from the therapists' comments suggest that the therapists faced a different set of "technical" problems in facilitating the communication of feeling in the two kinds of patients.

The study we performed focused on the kind-of-patient variable. Studies have shown that the behavior of the interviewer may also affect patient-therapist interaction (16, 18). There are suggestions in our own data as well that differences in therapists' level of differentiation may affect the interaction process; and the study by Pollack and Kiev (22), already cited, has also identified differences in therapists' performance as a function of the extent of

[15] This patient provides a particularly good example of the use of a "distancing" mechanism to observe himself during therapy. For example, patient D3 told his therapist, "You know, it's a funny thing.... I considered myself an outsider looking in at a therapeutic session. I really never considered myself involved in this thing.... I spent 50 per cent of the time analyzing [the intake psychiatrist's] methods. You know, of evoking responses from me.

their field dependence. These observations together suggest the usefulness of a study in which therapists selected for extent of differentiation are paired with patients also selected on the basis of level of differentiation.

## REFERENCES


1. Betz, B. J. Experiences in research in psychotherapy with schizophrenic patients. In Strupp, H. H. and Luborsky, L., eds. *Research in Psychotherapy*, vol. 2, pp. 41-60. American Psychological Association, Washington, D. C., 1962.
2. Crutchfield, R. S., Woodworth, D. G. and Albrecht, R. E. Perceptual performance and the effective person. Lackland AFB, Texas, Personnel Lab. Rep. WADC-TN-5860. ASTIA Doc. No. AD 151 039.
3. Dyk, R. B. and Witkin, H. A. Family experiences related to the development of differentiation in children. Child Develop., *30:* 21-55, 1965.
4. Fitzgibbons, D. L., Goldberger, M. and Eagle, M. Field dependence and memory for incidental material. Percept. Motor Skills, *21:* 743–749, 1965.
5. Freedman, N. The processes of symptom modification in psychopharmacological therapy. Paper presented at Dept. of Psychiatry meeting, State University of New York, Downstate Medical Center, Brooklyn, 1962.
6. Freud, S. The ego and the id. In *Collected Works*, vol. 19, Hogarth Press, London, 1961.
7. Fromm-Reichmann, F. In Bullard, D. M., ed. *Psychoanalysis and Psychotherapy*, pp. 221–274. University of Chicago Press, Chicago, 1959.
8. Jacobson, E. The self and the object world: Vicissitudes of their infantile cathexes and their influence on ideational and affective development. In *Psychoanalytic Study of the Child*, vol. 9. International Universities Press, New York, 1954.
9. Konstadt, N. and Forman, E. Field dependence and external directedness. J. Pers. Soc. Psychol., *1:* 490–493, 1965.
10. Lewis, H. B. Over-differentiation and under-differentiation of the self. Psychoanal. Psychoanal. Rev., *45:* 3–24, 1958.
11. Lewis, H. B. Organization of the self as reflected in manifest dreams. Psychoanal. Psychoanal. Rev., *46:* 21–35, 1959.
12. Lewis, H. B. A case of watching as defense against an oral incorporation fantasy. Psychoanal. Rev., *50:* 68–80, 1963.
13. Lynd, H. *On Shame and the Search for Identity*. Harcourt Brace, New York, 1958.
14. Matarazzo, J. D., Hess, H. F. and Saslow, G. Frequency and duration characteristics of speech and silence behavior during interview. J. Clin. Psychol., *18:* 416–426, 1962.
15. Matarazzo, R. G., Matarazzo, J. D., Saslow, G. and Phillips, J. Psychological test and organismic correlates of interview interaction patterns. J. Abnorm. Soc. Psychol., *56:* 329–338, 1958.
16. Matarazzo, J. D., Saslow, G., Wiens, A., Weitman, M. and Allen, B. V. Interviewer head-nodding and interviewee speech durations. Psychother. Theory Res. Pract., *1:* 54-64, 1964.
17. Matarazzo, J. D., Wiens, A. and Saslow, G. Studies of interview speech behavior. In Krasner, L. and Ullmann, L. P., eds. *Research in Behavior Modification: New Developments and Implications*, pp. 179–210. Holt, Rinehart, and Winston, New York, 1965.
18. Matarazzo, J. D., Wiens, A., Saslow, G., Allen, B. V. and Weitman, M. Interviewer mmhmm and interviewee speech duration. Psychother. Theory Res. Pract., *1:* 109–115, 1964.
19. Menaker, E. Masochism: A defense reaction of the ego. Psychoanal. Quart., *22:* 205–220, 1953.
20. Messick, S. and Damarin, F. Cognitive styles and memory for faces. J. Abnorm. Soc. Psychol., *69:* 313–318, 1964.
21. Piers, G. and Singer, M. S. *Shame and Guilt*. Thomas, Springfield, 1953.
22. Pollack, I. W. and Kiev, A. Spatial orientation and psychotherapy: An experimental study of perception. J. Nerv. Ment. Dis., *137:* 93–97, 1963.
23. Reik, T. *Masochism in Modern Man*. Grove Press, New York, 1941.
24. Shows, W. D. and Carson, R. C. The A-B therapist "type" distinction and spatial orientation: Replication and extension. J. Nerv. Ment. Dis., *141:* 456–462, 1965.
25. Strupp, H. H. Psychotherapeutic technique, professional affiliation and experience level. J. Consult. Psychol., *19:* 97–102, 1965.
26. Tomkins, S. *Affect, Imagery, Consciousness*, vol. II. Springer, New York, 1963.
27. Weil, E. The origin and the vicissitudes of the self-image. Psychoanal. J. Psychoanal. Psychol., *6:* 3–19, 1958.
28. Winget, C. M., Gottschalk, L. A. and Gleser, G. A. Manual of instructions for the verbal behavior method of measuring certain psychological variables including some of the theoretical bases. Unpublished manuscript, University of Cincinnati, 1963.
29. Witkin, H. A. Psychological differentiation and forms of pathology. J. Abnorm. Psychol., *70:* 317–336, 1965.
30. Witkin, H. A., Dyk, R. B., Faterson, H. F., Goodenough, D. R. and Karp, S. A. *Psychological Differentiation*. Wiley, New York, 1962.
31. Witkin, H. A., Lewis, H. B. Hertzman, M., Machover, K., Meissner, P. B. and Wapner, S. *Personality through Perception*. Harper, New York, 1954.

# REPRESSION, INTERFERENCE, AND FIELD DEPENDENCE AS FACTORS IN DREAM FORGETTING [1]

DONALD R. GOODENOUGH [2] AND HERMAN A. WITKIN
*Educational Testing Service, Princeton, New Jersey*

HELEN BLOCK LEWIS
*New York, New York*

DAVID KOULACK
*University of Manitoba, Canada*

HARVEY COHEN
*Pennsylvania Hospital, Philadelphia*

A number of hypotheses about the effects of presleep stress on dream recall among field-dependent and field-independent subjects were tested to explore the role of repression and of dream affect in dream recall. The effect of presleep stress was to increase arousal during rapid eye movement sleep and affect in dream reports. The data also suggest that the most affectful dreams are best recalled. Among field-dependent subjects, dream content was reported less frequently on stress than on neutral nights, but no stress effect on dream report frequency was found among field-independent subjects. The results are discussed in terms of repression theory and in terms of a possible alternative explanation that stress-produced anxiety interferes with attentional processes required for dream recall at the moment of awakening.

That we dream far more than we are able to remember the following morning has long been a matter of commonplace knowledge. It was not until the development of the sleep-monitoring method (Aserinsky & Kleitman, 1953), however, that we became aware of how very extensive the phenomenon of dream forgetting actually is. What processes are involved in the loss of so much of the dream life? What is responsible for variations in dream recall from day to day within the same person? Why are some people likely to remember their dreams, as a general personal characteristic, and others to forget them?

These questions have been investigated in three different contexts. The first is the forgetting of dreams under ordinary home circumstances. The second is the inability to report a dream on being awakened in the laboratory, usually from a rapid eye movement (REM) period, when, it may now be assumed, dreaming probably occurs. The third is the inability to recall at some subsequent time a dream that had been reported in an "on-the-spot" awakening during the night.

From the time of the classical writings of Freud in 1900 (Freud, 1953), the primary answer to questions about why particular dreams are not recalled or why some people tend not to remember their dreams has been "repression," that is, the massive after-expulsion of the content of the dream at the moment of awakening. Evidence on the repression issue is mainly the product of studies or observations of dream recall under ordinary home conditions. For example, therapists have noted that dreams are sometimes reported by patients after what appears to be a "working through of the resistance." In more recent investigations comparing people who say they rarely dream (home nonreporters) with people who say they dream often (home reporters), small but significant correlations have frequently but not always been found between personality test measures of repression or denial and classification as nonreporter (e.g., Robbins & Tanck, 1970; Singer & Schonbar, 1961; Tart, 1962).

In addition, it has often been found that home reporters and nonreporters differ in their standing on the dimension of psycho-

[1] This study was partially supported by National Institute of Mental Health grants MH628, MH03885, and MH16,619. The authors are indebted to Frederick Baekeland, Martin Blum, Hanna F. Faterson, and Ismet Karacan for their help in screening the subjects who participated in the study and to Carolyn Winget who conducted the content analyses of dream texts. The authors would like to thank David Cohen, Charles Fisher, Merton Gill, Philip Holzman, Douglas Jackson, and Lester Luborsky for their valuable comments on early drafts of this paper.

[2] Requests for reprints should be sent to Donald R. Goodenough, Division of Psychological Studies, Educational Testing Service, Princeton, New Jersey 08540.

logical differentiation (Witkin, Dyk, Faterson, Goodenough, & Karp, 1962). Frequently, but with exceptions, home nonreporters were found likely to be less differentiated, as reflected in a relatively field-dependent mode of perceiving, whereas reporters were found to be more differentiated, perceiving in relatively field-independent fashion (e.g., Bone, Thomas, & Kinsolving, 1972; Schonbar, 1965; Witkin, 1970). Not only do field-dependent persons tend to be nonreporters, but they are likely to use repression as a predominant defense (Witkin et al., 1962), making it plausible to interpret the relation found between field dependence and home nonreporting in terms of repression.

Evidence on the repression issue from laboratory studies is sparse. Whitman, Kramer, and Baldridge (1963) studied patients in therapy who concurrently were subjects in a laboratory investigation. In a small number of instances a dream was reported either to the laboratory investigator or to the therapist, but not to both. Failure to report the dream to one or the other was attributed to repression. While these instances of selective reporting are dramatic, they are hardly more than anecdotal in nature. Other laboratory studies (e.g., Foulkes & Rechtschaffen, 1964; Larson, 1970) found no relation between frequency of dream reporting after laboratory awakenings and objective personality test measures of repression. Finally, laboratory studies which examined the effects of presleep viewing of stress films on subsequent dream recall may also have some bearing on the repression issue. Cartwright, Bernick, Borowitz, and Kling (1969) found an increase in failure to recall dream content on REM awakenings following the viewing of a sexually exciting film. They attributed these findings to the influence of repression. Foulkes, Pivik, Steadman, Spear, and Symonds (1967) also found more dream recall failures on REM awakenings following presleep stress-film viewing, but Foulkes and Rechtschaffen (1964) and Karacan, Goodenough, Shapiro, and Starker (1966) did not. In sum, the evidence now on hand hardly provides convincing proof for a "repression hypothesis" of dream forgetting.

Turning to the evidence available on other factors influencing dream forgetting, we find a very different picture. A major basis of dream forgetting, now well documented, lies in the operation of the "classical laws" of memory. As one example, the extent of subsequent recall of dreams reported from "on-the-spot" awakening has been shown to be a function of serial position effects, such as primacy, recency, and "length of list" (Baekeland & Lasky, 1968; Meier, Ruff, Ziegler, & Hall, 1968; Trinder & Kramer, 1971). Salience of the dream experience has also been found to affect the ease with which it is later recalled. The longest, most intense, and most affectful dreams of those reported on the spot are likely to be remembered the next morning (Baekeland & Lasky, 1968; Meier et al., 1968; Trinder & Kramer, 1971). Salience may be a factor in immediate, on-the-spot recall failures as well. Congruent with the REM-period characteristics associated with dream reports that are easy to remember at a later time are the characteristics of REM periods from which dream reports are likely to be obtained when the subject is awakened: a large amount of eye movement activity (Goodenough, Lewis, Shapiro, & Sleser, 1965; Hobson, Goldfrank, & Snyder, 1965),[3] low arousal threshold (Goodenough et al., 1965; Snyder, 1960), and rapid and irregular breathing (Hobson et al., 1965; Shapiro, Goodenough, Biederman, & Sleser, 1964; Snyder, 1960). The association of recall with this cluster of characteristics, which have in turn been associated with dream experiences that are intense and affectful (e.g., Goodenough et al., 1965; Hobson et al., 1965), suggests that salience may be as much a factor in immediate recall as it is in postsleep recall.

In summary it seems fair to say that these various studies have produced considerable evidence that the factors responsible for the recall and forgetting of dreams are similar to the factors operating in memory in ordinary waking life, but they have provided little evidence that repression plays a prominent role in dream recall failures.

---

[3] Takeo (1970) found no relationship between eye-movement activity and dream recall, but dream reports obtained from REM periods with great activity tended to be more complicated and distinct.

The absence of convincing laboratory evidence for the repression hypothesis at this moment hardly warrants its rejection, since, as noted, relatively little laboratory research has been done with a specific focus on repression. In part at least the dearth of research on repression is a consequence of the very real difficulties involved in creating and manipulating in a laboratory setting the circumstances under which repression is likely to occur. The manipulation used in the study reported here, in an attempt to achieve this result, was to expose the subject to stress or neutral films immediately prior to sleep. The repression hypothesis led us to predict increased on-the-spot dream recall failure following stress-film viewing. In addition an observation made in the course of an earlier study (Shapiro et al., 1964) led us to hypothesize that this increase would be limited to one particular kind of recall failure which we have designated the "no-content dream" report. Among the many instances of recall failure observed in that study, we were struck by a few in which the subject said he was sure he was dreaming but could not recall any content. In these instances, the subject said the dream was "on the tip of his tongue" as he was awakening but suddenly it was "sucked away." The no-content dream type of dream report is rare in the laboratory. In that study, for example, only three no-content dream reports were obtained in a total of 169 awakenings. In contrast to these rare no-dream reports, what the subject much more commonly reports when unable to recall a dream is that he had been asleep and nothing had been going through his mind ("dreamless sleep" reports).

The no-content dream type of recall failure seems especially interesting in relation to repression, for several reasons. First, its phenomenology is suggestive of the kind of experience that may occur as the forces of repression, activated in the course of awakening, blot out the dream experience. Second, the three no-content dream reports observed came from REM periods with unusually marked breathing irregularity, contrasting with the more regular breathing associated with the far more frequently occurring nothing type of recall failure. Since breathing irregularity is known to be associated with emotion in the waking state and may be related to affective dream content, it seemed reasonable to speculate that no-content dream reports may occur on awakenings from particulary affective REM-period experiences. In fact, it seemed possible that it is the very residue of feeling carried over from the preawakening experience which provides the cue for the subject that "something (a dream) had been going on" during sleep, even though no content remains. It does not follow from repression theory that experiences which are the best candidates for repression are *necessarily* anxiety-provoking at the time they occur (Rapaport, 1950). It may indeed be that a repressible dream gives rise to pleasant rather than unpleasant feelings while it is going on. It seemed plausible to suppose, however, that dreams which are good candidates for repression would more frequently be accompanied by signs of greater affect and greater physiological arousal than the ordinary dream. On the basis of these observations, we hypothesized that the effect of the stressful films on dream recall would show itself specifically in an increase in the no-content dream type of dream loss.

In addition to employing a stressful presleep experience to increase the role of repression, there was a second way in which we sought to bring about this result: that was through the use of subjects prone to employ repression as a characteristic defense. As noted earlier, there is evidence suggesting that repression is particularly characteristic of field-dependent subjects. We hypothesized that field-dependent subjects would show a greater increase in no-content dream reports from the neutral sessions to the stress sessions than field-independent subjects, although these two kinds of subjects would not be particularly different with regard to frequency of no-content dream reports in the neutral sessions.

Another hypothesis relevant to the repression issue was that no-content dream recall failures would come from aroused REM periods. This expectation was based on our earlier tentative observations and does not necessarily come from repression theory as traditionally formulated.

While this study was planned with a focus on repression, its design also made it possible, in several specific ways, to check the role of dream salience on recall. First, if the dreams generated by presleep stress-film viewing are more affectful and intense—in other words, more salient—then on-the-spot dream recall should be greater in stress-film viewing sessions. This prediction about relative frequency of recall in the two types of sleep sessions is opposite in direction to the prediction made from repression theory. Second, we expected that dreamless sleep reports would come from REM periods characterized by low arousal, as has been found in earlier studies, and as might be expected if low arousal is associated with low salience of the original experience. Finally, because the evidence now on hand is so convincing that postsleep loss is related to lack of salience of on-the-spot experiences, we expected to find a similar relation here.

## METHOD

### *Subjects*

In order to make it possible to conduct the study during the day, male night workers (employees of the post office, the transit system, airline terminals, factories, etc.) were paid to serve as subjects. At a screening session the subject was informed in detail about the study. While he was not told the specific content of the films, he was told that he would see exciting and nonexciting films before sleep. The subject was then interviewed and given a battery of screening tests. Bases for selection included the subject's psychological and physical competence to withstand stressful experiences. In addition, subjects were selected as being relatively at one or the other extreme of the psychological-differentiation dimension. To make this determination three tests of field dependence–independence, considered the perceptual indicator of extent of differentiation, were used: the rod-and-frame test, the body-adjustment test and the embedded-figures test. In addition figure drawings were used to assess articulation of body concept, another indicator of differentiation. Using this screening procedure, 28 men were selected, 16 relatively differentiated and 12 relatively undifferentiated. They ranged in age from 19 years to 43 years.

### *Overall Design of the Study*

Each subject had five monitored sleep sessions in the laboratory. The first of these was a training session, used to familiarize him with the laboratory and to instruct him in the various procedures of the study. In the four subsequent sessions, usually scheduled a week apart, the subject was shown a film immediately prior to sleep. In two of these sessions a stress film was used (subincision and birth films) and in the other two a neutral film (travelogues of London and of the Western states), in a counterbalanced order.

Electroencephalogram (EEG), electroculogram and respiration were recorded during film viewing and during sleep. In addition to the usual paper records, the respiratory data were recorded on instrument tape for subsequent computer processing.

In all five sessions an attempt was made to awaken the subject from each Stage-1 REM period for collection of dream reports. Data on affective reactions were obtained through mood-checklist responses given by the subject before and after viewing each film and after each dream report given during REM-period awakenings. In addition, affect in the dream texts was assessed by the technique of Gottschalk, Winget, and Gleser (1969). Following each sleep session the subject was asked to recall the dreams he had reported during on-the-spot awakenings and a detailed inquiry was conducted into his associations to his dreams and into his experience of the film.

### *Procedure*

In the training session an attempt was made to familiarize the subject with his role in the experiment. The procedures were therefore identical with those used in the experimental sessions, except that no film was shown and the subject was encouraged to ask clarifying questions.

The first step taken after the subject's arrival in the morning was to attach the electrodes for eye movement and monopolar frontal and occipital EEG recordings. Mercury-filled capillary strain gauges were also attached in the thoracic and abdominal regions for recording respiration. [The recording techniques have been described in detail elsewhere (Shapiro & Cohen, 1965).]

Just before and just after viewing the film the subject was given the mood checklist, adapted from Nowlis and Nowlis (1956). The list covered seven mood clusters of three adjectives each: hostility, anxiety, quiet, depression, distrust, surgency, and social affection. The films were shown on a screen which the subject was able to view comfortably while propped up in bed. Immediately after the postfilm mood checklist responses were obtained, the subject was allowed to go to sleep.

An attempt was made to awaken the subject from each REM period between 5 and 10 minutes after its onset. Awakening the subject was accomplished by the sound of a loud buzzer. The subject then lifted a wall phone located near his bed, which automatically turned off the buzzer, and gave his report to the experimenter over a telephone intercom system. All conversation between the subject and the experimenter was tape recorded.

The subject was trained to describe in as much detail as possible anything that had been going through his mind before the bell rang without the experimenter saying anything. This procedure was

adopted in an attempt to minimize any possible bias that might be introduced by the experimenter's intervention. For this purpose the subject was instructed in the training session concerning the types of information he should include in reporting his preawakening experience. After the subject's spontaneous report the experimenter was free to ask certain nonleading questions. These questions reminded the subject of any omitted areas he had been trained to cover and encouraged the subject to "tell more." After the subject's report was completed, he responded to the mood checklist according to his mood during the dream. The subject then returned to sleep.

An inquiry was conducted with the subject at his bedside, after the sleep session. The inquiry began by asking him how many times he remembered having been awakened and what report he had given each time. These questions were used to determine spontaneous postsleep recall of on-the-spot reports. Following this, each of the dream experiences was discussed at length. If after all on-the-spot reports the subject remembered had been discussed, the subject still did not remember one or more, he was prompted by a phrase to help his recall. Almost invariably, these prompts did lead to recall.

### *The Films*

The subincision film shows an initiation rite practiced by an aboriginal Australian group, involving an operation on the penis. A number of operation episodes are included. The film is in black and white without a soundtrack and runs for approximately 12 minutes. The birth film is a medical teaching film showing the delivery of a baby. It is in color, has a soundtrack, and runs approximately 6 minutes. The Far West film is an educational travelogue, in color, with a soundtrack, which runs approximately 11 minutes. It describes the geographical, social, and economic characteristics of the Far West. The London film, also a travelogue, is in black and white, was shown without soundtrack and runs for approximately 11 minutes. It describes a number of historic landmarks in London.

### *Data Processing*

The respiratory data on the instrument tapes were converted to digital form for measurement of breath times and breathing irregularity by computer. The computer program was designed to locate the respiratory peak, to measure the time between successive peaks in the record (breath times), and to compute the mean breath time and the root mean of the squared differences between successive breath times (breath time sigma). The latter was used as the measure of breathing irregularity. The respiratory records were analyzed during film viewing and during the three minutes of artifact-free REM sleep closest to the moment of awakening for each REM period. Eye movements were counted for the three minutes of each REM period analyzed for respiration.

The subject's response to each adjective in the mood checklist was scored from 0 (not at all) to 3 (much). These scores were summed for the three adjectives in each mood cluster to form a cluster score with a possible range from 0 to 9 for each cluster. The dream texts obtained at REM-period awakenings were scored for anxiety and hostility according to procedures described by Gottschalk et al. (1969). The judge who conducted these analyses had no knowledge that films and different kinds of subjects had been used, nor did she even know the purpose of the study.

Wilcoxon's matched-pairs signed-ranks test was used for testing significance in correlated samples and Mann-Whitney's $U$ test for independent samples.

## RESULTS

### *The Relationships among Stress, Affect, and Arousal Variables*

Of the results obtained from the present study, only those bearing on the effects of presleep stress on dream recall are dealt with here. The effects of presleep stress on affect and arousal will be described in detail in another report. However, since a precondition for the occurrence of the dream-recall effects we predicted is that the stress films actually increase emotion, before examining the data on dream recall we need to summarize the data showing that the stress films had the intended effect of upsetting the subjects.

First, as measured by changes in the prefilm to postfilm mood checklist responses, stress-film, in contrast to neutral-film viewing significantly increased emotion. Respiratory irregularity, although not breath times, tended to increase during the subincision film, particularly at its operation episodes, suggesting that irregularity may be a transient response to startling events rather than a tonic effect of stress. The effects of the stress films clearly continued beyond the viewing period, as shown by the significantly longer time taken to fall asleep after the stress than after the neutral films. The evidence is clear that these effects persisted into the sleep period itself. Anxiety in reported dreams, as measured by both mood checklist responses and Gottschalk-Winget-Gleser assessments of dream content, was significantly greater in stress than in neutral sessions, particularly among those subjects who showed an affective response during stress film viewing in the waking state. Some evidence was also found

that the stress films increased arousal during REM sleep. Consistent with the findings of Baekeland, Koulack, and Lasky (1968), eye-movement activity tended to be greater during REM periods following the stress films, although this tendency did not reach significance in our data. REM-period respiratory irregularity was also greater on stress nights; this effect was significant for those subjects who showed increased irregularity of breathing during the operation scenes in the subincision film. Finally, figure drawings obtained from the subjects at the end of each sleep session showed significantly increased shading, a commonly recognized sign of anxiety in drawings after stress films (Goldstein & Faterson, 1969). It thus seems clear that the emotion-arousing effect of the stress films persisted not only through the sleep period but into the postsleep period as well.

No significant differences were found between field-dependent and field-independent subjects in any measure of the effect of the stress films on affect or arousal.

*Effect of the Stress Films on Dream Reporting*

For all subjects, regardless of cognitive style, the frequency of no-content dream reports showed a significant change from neutral to stress sessions. No-content dream reports were given in 7% of all neutral-session awakenings, compared with 13% in stress-session awakenings. No significant change was found from neutral to stress sessions for the group as a whole in frequency of either dream reports or dreamless sleep reports.

Examination of the dream recall data for field-dependent and field-independent subjects separately indicates that it was for the former kind of subject only that stress affected dream recall. The data in Table 1 clearly confirm the hypothesis that field-dependent subjects would report dreams less frequently in on-the-spot awakenings under the stress than under the neutral conditions. A significant interaction was found between stress and field dependence in the percentage of REM-period awakenings which led to the report of a dream ($p < .01$). The decrease in dream reporting from neutral to stress sessions was significant for field-dependent subjects ($p < .01$). In contrast, for field-independent subjects there was a slight but insignificant increase in dream reports in the stress sessions.

TABLE 1

DREAM REPORTING AS A FUNCTION OF STRESS AND FIELD DEPENDENCE

| Report type | Subject type | | | |
|---|---|---|---|---|
| | Field dependent | | Field independent | |
| | Neutral nights | Stress nights | Neutral nights | Stress nights |
| Immediate recall | | | | |
| % deam reports | 80** | 65** | 70 | 76 |
| % No-content dream reports | 03* | 12* | 11 | 13 |
| % Dreamless sleep reports | 18 | 23 | 19 | 10 |
| Morning recall | | | | |
| % dream reports | 88 | 73 | 79 | 78 |

* $p < .02$.
** $p < .01$.

Whereas both dreamless sleep and no-content dream types of report failures tended to increase in stress sessions among field-dependent subjects, the increase was significant for no-dream reports only ($p < .02$). Thus our hypothesis that the increase in on-the-spot dream loss for field-dependent subjects would be specific to the no-content dream type of loss is confirmed.

In the data summarized in Table 1, field-dependent subjects were somewhat more likely to report dreams than independent subjects on neutral nights. There was great variability among subjects in dream reporting, however, and the difference between field-dependent and field-independent subjects did not approach significance on either neutral or stress nights. There is evidence from other sources, however, that cognitive style is not related to dream recall on neutral nights under these conditions. Baekeland and Lasky (1968) found no relationship between field dependence and the percentage of dreams reported on abrupt REM-period awakenings, although field-dependent subjects were less likely to recall these once-reported dreams by next morning. The data from one of our earlier studies of 46 subjects (Lewis, Goodenough, Shapiro, & Sleser, 1966) were also analyzed from this point of view. The percentage of abrupt awakenings which led to

dream reports was slightly but not significantly greater for the eight most field-independent subjects (86%) than for the eight most field-dependent subjects (79%).[4]

The pattern emerging from these findings is that field-dependent and field-independent subjects are not very different in tendency to report dreams immediately after abrupt awakenings from REM sleep under ordinary (neutral) conditions. However, in field-dependent subjects, but not in field-independent ones, dream reports are clearly replaced by no-content dream reports as an effect of the stress films.

*Relationship between REM-Period Characteristics and Dream Reporting*

The next question to consider is whether no-content dream reports are the products of emotional dream experiences which have been lost, as we postulated. In the absence of the content of the dream itself, whether or not a given dream was affectful can only be inferred from evidence on arousal during the REM period in which the dream occurred.

Before considering the data on arousal during REM-periods from which no-content dream reports came, it is important to note that in our data the arousal measures taken during REM sleep were related to dream affect in cases where dream reports were obtained. These data are described in detail in another report. In general, breath times tended to be shorter and eye-movement activity greater for REM periods that led to dream reports with high negative affect than for REM periods without affect. For breath time irregularity, the result was somewhat more complex. When all subjects were considered, breathing irregularity was found to be significantly correlated with total affect scores obtained by summing the affect cluster scores over the six mood clusters (excluding quiet). No significant relationship was found with any of the individual cluster scores or with either of the Gottschalk-Winget-Gleser affect scores. However, significant findings were obtained when the subjects were divided into responder and nonresponder groups on the basis of the presence or absence of increased irregularity during the viewing of the operations in the subincision film. Among the waking responders, dream reports with high Gottschalk-Winget-Gleser hostility scores came from REM periods with significantly greater irregularity. In general, then, some evidence was found of relationships between dream affect and each of the arousal measures taken during REM sleep, consistent with previous research. In these relationships no significant differences were found between field-dependent and field-independent subjects.

The evidence that eye-movement activity and breathing during REM sleep are related to affect in reported dreams makes it reasonable to assume that these arousal measures signify affect as well during REM periods in which there are failures of dream reporting. On this assumption REM periods which yielded dream reports and those which did not were compared on each of the arousal measures to examine the relationship between dream affect and dream recall.

In this comparison the no-content dream type of report failure was of particular interest, both because such reports were more frequent in stress sessions and because our previous research suggested the hypothesis that no-content dream reports may come from REM periods characterized by marked breathing irregularity. The large number of no-content dream reports elicited in the present study made it possible to test systematically the hypothesized relation between REM-period arousal and no-content dream reports. The data in Table 2 clearly fail to confirm the hypothesis. In fact, REM periods which led to no-content dream reports showed significantly *more regular* breathing than REM periods from which dreams were obtained. If we consider only those subjects who showed irregular breathing in response to the operation scenes during the subincision film view-

[4] With a gradual awakening method, dream reporting was significantly reduced for field-dependent subjects ($p < .05$). Only 59% of the awakenings by this method led to dream reports among field-dependent subjects. In contrast, no significant effect of the method of awakening was found among field-independent subjects. The data from this study also support the frequent finding that field-dependent subjects tend to be home nonreporters. Only one of the eight field-dependent subjects was a home reporter in contrast to five of the eight field-independent subjects ($p < .05$, one-tailed test).

TABLE 2

DREAM REPORTING AS A FUNCTION OF REM-PERIOD CHARACTERISTICS

| Recall variable 1 | Mean REM characteristic | | | | | |
|---|---|---|---|---|---|---|
| | No. eye movements per minute | *N* of subjects | Breath time (in seconds) | *N* of subjects | Breath time $\sigma$ (secs.) | *N* of subjects |
| Immediate recall | | | | | | |
| Content reported vs. not reported | 11.1 | | 3.53 | | .72 | |
| | 10.0 | 25 | 3.63 | 24 | .63 | 24 |
| Content reported vs. no content | 11.7 | | 3.61 | | .78** | |
| dreams | 11.5 | 18 | 3.65 | 17 | .56** | 17 |
| Content reported vs. dreamless | 9.9* | | 3.49* | | .72 | |
| sleep | 7.6* | 19 | 3.67* | 18 | .80 | 18 |
| Morning recall | | | | | | |
| content reported vs. not reported | 14.3* | | 3.64 | | .74 | |
| | 9.1* | 16 | 3.73 | 14 | .63 | 14 |

* $p < .05$.
** $p < .01$.

ing, the relation between REM-period irregularity and immediate recall is slightly but insignificantly higher.

Since it was among field-dependent subjects that on-the-spot dream recall was significantly reduced by presleep stress, we examined the relationship between dream recall and REM-period breathing irregularity on stress nights for this group of subjects separately. Among these subjects on stress nights the difference between REM periods which did and did not lead to a dream report was particularly pronounced. Under these conditions the mean irregularity score was .76 seconds for REM periods which led to dream reports and .53 seconds for REM periods which did not ($p < .01$). Thus, if anything, the relation between recall failures and regular breathing was clearer under conditions where repression was expected (i.e., stress nights in field-dependent subjects) than it was under neutral conditions or in field-independent subjects.

No significant differences were found between REM periods which led to no-content dream reports and REM periods leading to dream reports in either eye-movement activity or in breath times. Nor was there any evidence from the subjects' verbal reports that no-content dream experiences were unusually affectful. In only 5 of 37 no-content dream awakenings was any feeling reported, and in just two of these instances of remembered feelings was the affect negative in character. There is thus little evidence that when subjects gave such reports they were using residual affect as a cue that they had been dreaming.

The relationship between arousal and dreamless sleep reports is clearer. REM periods which led to dreamless sleep reports were characterized by significantly less eye-movement activity and longer breath times than REM periods which led to dreaming reports. These findings are consistent with the results of earlier studies.

### *Dream Affect and Postsleep Recall*

Among the dream reports obtained at REM-period awakenings, those accompanied by the greatest negative affect were most likely to be subsequently recalled. This tendency reached significance with depression in the mood checklist and for Gottschalk-Winget-Gleser hostility. These data are summarized in Table 3.

TABLE 3

MORNING RECALL AS A FUNCTION OF DREAM AFFECT

| Mood variable | Recalled | Not recalled |
|---|---|---|
| Adjective checklist | | |
| Hostility | .7 | .5 |
| Anxiety | 1.4 | .7 |
| Depression | 1.1* | .6* |
| Gottschalk | | |
| Anxiety | 1.32 | .92 |
| Hostility | 1.35* | 1.06* |

* $p < .05$.

Dreams forgotten in the postsleep period tended to come from REM periods with less eye-movement activity and longer breath times. These data are summarized in Table 2. The relationship with postsleep recall was clearly significant for eye-movement activity, consistent with the findings of Baekeland and Lasky (1968). With regard to REM-period respiratory irregularity, no significant relationship was found with postsleep recall when all subjects were considered. However, when only those subjects who responded with irregular respiration to the subincision operation scenes were considered, a relationship was found. The interaction between the responder and postsleep-recall variables was significant ($p < .05$). As might be expected, responders showed greater REM-period irregularity for dreams that were subsequently recalled (.83 seconds) than for dreams that were not recalled (.66 seconds) ($p < .10$). Nonresponders showed no significant difference between recalled (.51 seconds) and nonrecalled (.54 seconds) dreams.

In keeping with earlier findings, it is entirely clear that among once-recalled dreams, the most salient ones, as judged by the signs considered, are best remembered later on.

*Other Factors Affecting Postsleep Recall*

Our data show, consistent with past findings, that the number of dreams reported in a sleep session is a powerful determinant of the ease with which any of these dreams will be recalled later on. Across all experimental nights, subjects who reported fewer than eight dreams on the spot ($N = 10$) recalled 95% of these dreams in the postsleep period. In contrast, subjects who reported more than 12 dreams on the spot ($N = 9$) subsequently recalled only 58%.

No significant differences in postsleep recall were found as a function of stress or field dependence. However, the wide range in number of dreams reported from night to night and from subject to subject and the striking effect of this variation on postsleep recall made these comparisons inefficient. It is not surprising, therefore, that we were unable to repeat the observation by Baekeland and Lasky (1968) that field-dependent subjects are poorer in morning recall. In their study a fixed number of dreams were collected from each subject during each night, making possible much more effective comparison of morning recall across subjects than was possible in the present study.

## Discussion

The main hypothesis of this study that the stress films would increase the frequency of recall failure among field-dependent subjects but not particularly among field-independent subjects was clearly confirmed. Further, the more specific hypothesis that the increase in recall failures among field-dependent subjects would be limited to the no-content dream type of failure was also confirmed. A similar pattern of results was found in a recent study by Cohen (1972) of the effect of stress upon home dream recall of reporters and nonreporters. Cohen's investigation was based on the preliminary reports of data from the present study and on the hypothesis which guided the collection of those data (Goodenough, 1967; Witkin, 1969; Witkin & Lewis, 1965; 1967). Among nonreporters Cohen found "weak" dreams (no-content dream reports and reports of dream fragments) were given more often under the stress condition (62%) than under the control condition (25%). Among home reporters, in contrast, the frequency of weak dreams was about the same under stress (27%) and neutral (33%) conditions. The results of Cohen's study and the present study become comparable if field-dependent subjects are equated with home nonreporters and field-independent subjects with home reporters.

In addition to the hypotheses about the effects of stress on dream recall, it was also hypothesized that on-the-spot failure of dream recall of the no-content dream type would tend to come from more aroused REM periods. While breathing irregularity, rapid breathing and eye-movement activity were associated with more intense emotion in the content of reported dreams, the expectation that REM periods which led to no-content dream reports would be characterized by greater arousal was not fulfilled.

If repression is in fact responsible for no-content dream reports, our study certainly provided no evidence to support the premise

that dreams which are good candidates for repression tend to be particularly affectual. While we did at the outset consider this premise a plausible one, it is not an essential component of repression theory. It is possible to consider other premises which would make our findings consistent with repression theory. Specifically, the mechanism of repression on which we focused in this study is the elimination of the dream experience from memory at the moment of awakening. Repression has also been conceived to work by preventing entry of charged material into the experienced content of the dream. Dreams that are particularly subject to the action of repression in the second sense (as a mechanism operating upon the dream experience itself) may not be affectual and need not be accompanied by aroused physiology. However, for the dreamer, the cognitive content of these dream experiences may still be linked to their charged latent content. It is possible to imagine that because of this linkage such dreams are subject to the further action of repression (now in the first sense of after-expulsion at awakening) resulting in their total forgetting. In this view, then, dreams which are good candidates for repression need not be particularly affectful or physiologically aroused.

However, another rather simple explanation suggests itself, as an alternative to the repression view with which we undertook this study, to account for the cluster of findings produced on the no-content dream phenomenon. Specifically, it seems possible to account for these findings if we assume that anxiety about the stress films distracts the subject's attention from the dream at the moment of awakening, thereby interfering with recall of the dream experience: that no-content dream reports are the specific products of such interference; and that field-dependent subjects are particularly subject to the affects of interference.

It is a common everyday experience that dreams may quickly "slip away" at awakening unless we give our undivided attention to them. Even a momentary distraction at the time of awakening makes us unable to recall the content of dreams, though we may be left with the sure sense that we had been dreaming. In the tug of war that often goes on between attention to the waning dream experience and attention to the emerging realities of the world outside the dream, the stronger the vector toward that world and the weaker the vector toward the dream, the more likely is the dream to be lost. The demand characteristics of our experimental situation were clearly in the direction of producing dream recall. All the subjects were fully aware—because we told them so directly and because it was evident in many aspects of the conduct of the study—that we were after their dreams. The consequences of this set were often reflected in our subjects' struggle to retrieve their dreams, particularly at times when they had difficulty in recalling any content. It is easy to imagine that the subjects' concern about the stress film could have impaired their concentration on this task, thereby interfering with dream recall.

It is also easy to imagine that no-content dream reports are the particular product of such interfering effects. When a dream experience is remembered on awakening, but then "lost" through interference, there is likely to remain a sense that a dream had taken place, even though the content itself is no longer available. This is precisely the phenomenology of the no-content dream experience. In an ingenious experiment Cohen (personal communication) was recently able to demonstrate that no-content dream reports can, in fact, be produced experimentally through interference. Cohen collected dreams by the home-diary method under two conditions. In one condition the experimental subjects were instructed to telephone the weather information bureau immediately upon awakening, write down the temperature range for the day in their diary, and then write descriptions of their dream experiences. In a control condition, subjects merely lay awake quietly for an equivalent period of time before recording their dreams. Whereas in the experimental condition 43% of all reports were of the no-content dream type, only 18% were of this type in the control condition. In contrast, the frequency of dreamless sleep reports was unaffected by the distracting telephone call. The effect of the telephone call in Cohen's study appears comparable to the effect of the stress film in our study.

The proposal that the no-content dream reports observed in this study on stress nights are the product of the distracting effect of anxiety produced by the stress films leaves open the question of why it is that the increase in no-content dream reports under stress conditions is limited to field-dependent subjects. This finding may be understood in principle in any one of several ways: (*a*) field-dependent persons are made more anxious by stimuli such as the stress films we used; (*b*) the dream experiences of field-dependent persons are less salient, and so more subject to the corrosive effects of interference, or (*c*) field-dependent persons are more affected by interfering factors. There is no evidence to support the first or second of these possibilities, but there is a great deal of evidence in the literature to support the third.

With regard to the first possibility, field-dependent and field-independent subjects did not differ significantly in the effects of the stress films by any indicator of anxiety considered in this study. In no measure of physiology, subjective mood judgment, dream affect, or anxiety indicators in postsleep figure-drawing productions did the stress films have a significantly greater effect on the field-dependent subjects.

With regard to the second possibility, the data are equally clear. In general, field-dependent and field-independent subjects were similar in all indicators of salience of the dream experience: measures of dream affect, measures of intensity, and measures of REM-period arousal.

In contrast, there is substantial evidence that in their cognitive functioning field-dependent persons are particularly subject to the corrosive effects of interference. For example, Gollin and Barron (1954) found that while field-dependent and field-independent subjects were no different in immediate reproduction of a learned list of items, the field-dependent subjects did less well in later recall, when the later recall was preceded by the interpolated learning of similar material, producing retroactive interference effects. These findings make it reasonable to suppose that our field-dependent subjects were particularly subject to the interfering effects of anxiety on dream recall.

While in the present study interference seems attributable to the heightened anxiety generated in the stress sessions, interference may obviously arise from any number of sources. One may expect, therefore, that field-dependent subjects would be poorer dream recallers than field-independent subjects under any conditions where interference has an opportunity to occur. In fact, this appears to be so. As one example, it has been found in studies of the effects of gradual vs. abrupt awakening, conducted under neutral conditions, that among field-dependent subjects gradual awakening impairs recall; in contrast, no effect of the method of awakening was found for field-independent subjects (see Footnote 4). In the hypnopompic state prevailing during gradual awakening, laboratory incorporations frequently occur, suggesting an already emerging awareness of the laboratory situation. This attention to externals may play a distracting role. As a second example, delay in eliciting recall also has an adverse effect on recall in field-dependent persons. Thus, postsleep recall of dreams reported immediately after REM-period awakenings has been found to be significantly worse for field-dependent subjects (Baekeland & Lasky, 1968). In a similar study we did earlier (Witkin et al., 1962) of immediate and long-range recall of the Thematic Apperception Test cards to which the subject had been exposed when taking that test, we found no difference between the two kinds of subjects in immediate recall, but significantly less recall by field-dependent subjects under the long-delay condition. Passage of time may have the observed effect through added opportunity for interfering influences to exert themselves. Thus, anxiety which has the effect of distracting the subject from attention to his dream experience on awakening may be one among many factors which impair recall in field-dependent subjects through interference.

Turning now to our data on postsleep recall of dreams reported immediately after awakenings, they clearly confirm previous findings and support the hypothesis that more salient dreams are better remembered. Dreams not recalled in the postsleep period were pallid in content when compared with re-

called dreams. Moreover, the REM periods which produced the subsequently nonrecalled dream reports were less aroused by all signs examined. To the extent that signs of low arousal are associated with lack of intensity and affect in the dream experience, these findings suggest that not only the forgotten dream reports, but the forgotten dream experiences themselves lacked salience.

In general, our results for dreamless sleep reports given immediately after awakening also confirm previous findings. Such reports came from REM periods with low respiratory rate and low eye-movement frequency, although not more regular breathing. These findings are also consistent with the view that the least salient dream experiences are not recalled immediately after REM-period awakenings.

In overview we may say that in common with many previous investigations, the results of this study suggest that the salience principle may be used to account for a variety of dream recall phenomena. However, this principle does not account for the effect of stress on dream recall which we observed. In view of the apparent increase in dream affect on stress nights, the salience principle would have led us to expect an increase in dream recall. In fact, just the opposite occurred.

Since no-content dream reports are a type of recall failure produced by stress, this outcome suggests such reports need to be explained in some other way than by the salience principle. Either a repression or an interference interpretation of our data on no-content dream reports indeed appears possible. Without knowledge of the content of the lost dreams, it is of course difficult to decide between these alternatives. Unfortunately, the content of the lost dreams was no more available to us than it was to our subjects. In these circumstances it is necessary to persist in the use of repression and interference theory to generate testable hypotheses. Working within the repression framework, our hypothesis that no-content dream reports would come from high-arousal REM periods was clearly disproven. Working within the interference framework, Cohen was able experimentally to vary the frequency of no-dream reports by manipulating the role of interference. In addition, the results of studies on differences in dream recall between field-dependent and field-independent persons seem easily understood on an interference basis.

A combination of salience and interference principles appears capable of accounting for all the phenomena of dream recall observed in this study and a variety of other findings as well. In addition, such an explanation is consistent with the classical literature on recall and forgetting in the waking state.

## REFERENCES


Aserinsky, E., & Kleitman, N. Regularly occurring periods of eye motility and concomitant phenomena during sleep. *Science,* 1953, **118,** 273–274.

Baekeland, F., Koulack, D., & Lasky, R. Effects of a stressful presleep experience on electroencephalograph-recorded sleep. *Psychophysiology,* 1968, **4,** 436–443.

Baekeland, F., & Lasky, R. The morning recall of REM-period reports given earlier in the night. *Journal of Nervous and Mental Disease,* 1968, **147,** 570–579.

Bone, R. N., Thomas, T. A., & Kinsolving, D. L. Relationship of rod-and-frame scores to dream recall. *Psychological Reports,* 1972, **30,** 58.

Cartwright, R. D., Bernick, N., Borowitz, G., & Kling, A. Effect of an erotic movie on the sleep and dreams of young men. *Archives of General Psychiatry,* 1969, **20,** 262–271.

Cohen, D. B. Presleep experience and home dream reporting: An exploratory study. *Journal of Consulting and Clinical Psychology,* 1972, **38,** 122–128.

Foulkes, D., Pivik, T., Steadman, H. S., Spear, P. S., & Symonds, J. D. Dreams of the male child: An EEG study. *Journal of Abnormal Psychology,* 1967, **72,** 457–467.

Foulkes, D., & Rechtschaffen, A. Presleep determinants of dream content: Effects of two films. *Perceptual and Motor Skills,* 1964 (Monograph Supplement 5-V19), 983–1005.

Freud, S. The interpretation of dreams. In J. Strachey (Ed.), *Standard edition of the complete psychological works of Sigmund Freud.* Vol. 4. London, England: Hogarth, 1953.

Goldstein, H. S., & Faterson, H. F. Shading as an index of anxiety in figure drawings. *Journal of Projective Techniques and Personality Assessment,* 1969, **33,** 454–456.

Gollin, E. S., & Barron, A. Response consistency in perception and retention. *Journal of Experimental Psychology,* 1954, **47,** 259–262.

Goodenough, D. R. Some recent studies of dream recall. In H. A. Witkin & H. B. Lewis (Eds.), *Experimental studies of dreaming.* New York: Random House, 1967.

Goodenough, D. R., Lewis, H. B., Shapiro, A., & Sleser, I. Some correlates of dream reporting fol-

lowing laboratory awakenings. *Journal of Nervous and Mental Disease,* 1965, **140**, 365–373.

GOTTSCHALK, L. A., WINGET, C. N., & GLESER, G. C. *Manual of instructions for using the Gottschalk-Gleser content analysis scales: Anxiety, hostility, and social alienation-personal disorganization.* Berkeley and Los Angeles: University of California Press, 1969.

HOBSON, J. A., GOLDFRANK, F., & SNYDER, F. Respiration and mental activity in sleep. *Journal of Psychiatric Research,* 1965, **3**, 79–90.

KARACAN, I., GOODENOUGH, D. R., SHAPIRO, A., & STARKER, S. Erection cycle during sleep in relation to dream anxiety. *Archives of General Psychiatry,* 1966, **15**, 183–189.

LARSON, J. D. Hypnagogic mentation of repressors and sensitizers as influenced by hostile and friendly presleep-conditions. *Journal of Psychophysiology,* 1970, **7**, 327.

LEWIS, H. B., GOODENOUGH, D. R., SHAPIRO, A., & SLESER, I. Individual differences in dream recall. *Journal of Abnormal Psychology,* 1966, **71**, 52–59.

MEIER, C. A., RUFF, H., ZIEGLER, A., & HALL, C. S. Forgetting of dreams in the laboratory. *Perceptual and Motor Skills,* 1968, **26**, 551–557.

NOWLIS, V., & NOWLIS, H. H. The description and analysis of mood. *Annals of the New York Academy of Science,* 1956, **65**, 344–355.

RAPAPORT, D. *Emotions and memory.* New York: International Universities Press, 1950.

ROBBINS, P. R., & TANCK, R. H. The Repression-Sensitization scale, dreams, and dream associations. *Journal of Clinical Psychology,* 1970, **26**, 219–221.

SCHONBAR, R. A. Differential dream recall frequency as a component of "life style." *Journal of Consulting Psychology,* 1965, **29**, 468–474.

SHAPIRO, A., & COHEN, H. The use of mercury capillary length gauges for the measurement of the volume of thoracic and diaphragmatic components of human respiration: A theoretical analysis and a practical method. *Transactions of New York Academy of Science,* 1965, **27**, 634–649.

SHAPIRO, A., GOODENOUGH, D. R., BIEDERMAN, I., & SLESER, I. Dream recall and the physiology of sleep. *Journal of Applied Psychology,* 1964, **19**, 778–783.

SINGER, J. L., & SCHONBAR, R. Correlates of daydreaming: A dimension of self-awareness. *Journal of Consulting Psychology,* 1961, **25**, 1–7.

SNYDER, F. Dream recall, respiratory variability and depth of sleep. Paper presented to the Roundtable on Dream Research at the Annual Meeting of the American Psychiatric Association, Atlantic City, New Jersey, May 1960.

TAKEO, S. Relationships among physiological indices during sleep and characteristics of dreams. *Psychiatria et Neurologia Japonica,* 1970, **72**, 1–18.

TART, C. T. Frequency of dream recall and some personality measures. *Journal of Consulting Psychology,* 1962, **26**, 467–470.

TRINDER, J., & KRAMER, M. Dream recall. *American Journal of Psychiatry,* 1971, **128**, 296–301.

WHITMAN, R. M., KRAMER, M., & BALDRIDGE, B. J. Which dream does the patient tell? *Archives of General Psychiatry,* 1963, **8**, 277–282.

WITKIN, H. A. Presleep experiences and dreams. In J. Fisher & L. Breger (Eds.), *The meaning of dreams: Recent insights from the laboratory. California Mental Health Research Symposium,* 1969, **3**, 1–37.

WITKIN, H. A. Individual differences in dreaming. *International Psychiatric Clinic,* 1970, **7**, 154–164.

WITKIN, H. A., DYK, R. B., FATERSON, H. F., GOODENOUGH, D. R., & KARP, S. A. *Psychological differentiation: Studies of development.* New York: Wiley, 1962.

WITKIN, H. A., & LEWIS, H. B. The relation of experimentally induced presleep experience to dreams: A report on method and preliminary findings. *Journal of the American Psychoanalytic Association,* 1965, **13**, 819–849.

WITKIN, H. A., & LEWIS, H. B. Presleep experiences and dreams. In H. A. Witkin & H. B. Lewis (Eds.), *Experimental studies of dreaming.* New York: Random House, 1967.

# The Effects of Stress Films on Dream Affect and on Respiration and Eye-Movement Activity During Rapid-Eye-Movement Sleep

DONALD R. GOODENOUGH, HERMAN A. WITKIN,
*Educational Testing Service*
DAVID KOULACK,
*University of Manitoba*
AND HARVEY COHEN
*Pennsylvania Hospital*

ABSTRACT

**The effects of stress on the affective content of dreams and on rapid-eye-movement (REM) period eye-movement activity and respiration were studied. The experiment was also designed to examine the similarity between waking and sleeping states in the respiratory correlates of emotion. Sleep records and dream reports were collected following the viewing of stress and neutral films. The stress films significantly increased dream anxiety and also increased REM-period respiratory irregularity among those *S*s who, in the waking state, showed irregular breath patterns in response to stressful film scenes. Some evidence was also found that dream affect is related to REM-period respiratory irregularity among the *S*s who are waking responders. These data are interpreted as supporting the hypothesized congruence between the waking and dream states in the relationship between affect and breathing irregularity.**

**DESCRIPTORS: Sleep, Stress, Dream, Respiration, Emotion.**

This study is concerned with two related issues: (1) the effect of stress on emotion in dreams, and (2) the congruence between waking and dreaming states in the respiratory correlates of emotion.

With regard to the first issue, common experience leaves little doubt that dreams with strong emotional content are likely to occur following stressful daytime experiences. However, studies of the influence of presleep stress on dream affect have not consistently provided support for this everyday impression (Breger, Hunter, & Lane, 1971; Cohen, 1972; Foulkes, Pivik, Steadman, Spear, & Symonds, 1967; Foulkes & Rechtschaffen, 1964; Karacan, 1965; Karacan, Goodenough, Shapiro, & Starker, 1966). The present study was undertaken with the view that a more consistent picture of stress-dream affect relationships might be obtained by using intensely stressful films as presleep stimuli.

With regard to the second issue, there have been several studies of the relationship between respiration during REM sleep and emotion in subsequently reported dreams (Fisher, Byrne, Edwards, & Kahn, 1970; Hauri & Van de Castle, 1970; Hobson, Goldfrank, & Snyder, 1965). The data from these studies suggest that respiratory rate may be higher for emotional than for bland dreams, but little evidence has been found relating irregularity to dream affect. Even in studies where a respiration-emotion relationship has been found in dreaming, it may be argued that this association is mediated in a different way than it is in the waking state. Within a tonic-phasic model of dreaming it has been proposed that a neurophysiological trigger simultaneously activates a number of transient events, including increased respiratory rate and irregularity and eye-movement bursts, as well as an intense dream episode which may be accompanied by affective experience (Aserinsky, 1965; Grosser & Siegal, 1971; Molinari & Foulkes, 1969). In this view no congruence exists between the

This study was partially supported by NIMH Grants MH21989, MH628, MHO3885, and MH16,619. We are indebted to Drs. Frederick Baekeland, Martin Blum, Hanna Faterson, and Ismet Karacan for their help in subject screening, and to Carolyn Winget for content analyses of dream texts.

Address requests for reprints to: Donald R. Goodenough, Division of Psychological Studies, Educational Testing Service, Princeton, NJ 08540.

waking and sleeping states in the nature of the respiration-emotion relationship. Since not all *S*s respond to stress in the same physiological channel in the waking state, the study of individual differences provides one possible approach to the congruence issue. It is possible that *S*s who respond to stress with a particular respiratory change when awake would show a similar psychophysiological relationship during dreams, and that *S*s who do not respond with this change when awake would show no such relationship when asleep. The design of the present study makes it possible to explore this possibility.

It was hypothesized that REM-period eye-movement activity, affect in reported dreams, and REM-period respiration rate and irregularity would be higher on nights following the viewing of stress films than on nights following the viewing of neutral travelogs, particularly among *S*s who showed respiratory responses to stress in the waking state. Finally, it was expected that REM-period respiratory rate and irregularity would be related to affect in reported dreams, particularly among the waking stress responders.

#### Method

Twenty-eight male night workers were paid to participate in the study. These *S*s were selected on the basis of an interview and a battery of screening tests designed to eliminate potential *S*s with medical or serious psychological problems. Sixteen of the *S*s were chosen as extremely field dependent and 12 *S*s as extremely field independent in cognitive style (Witkin, Dyk, Faterson, Goodenough, & Karp, 1962).[1]

Each *S* slept in the laboratory, with EEG and EOG monitoring, for 5 days, during the hours he usually slept at home. The first of these days was used for adaptation and training purposes. The 4 subsequent experimental sessions were scheduled at least a week apart and were used for data collection. The procedures were the same for all sessions except that the *S*s viewed films just before going to bed for the day during each of the 4 experimental sessions. During these 4 sessions 2 stress films (Subincision and Birth) and 2 neutral educational travelogs (London and West) were shown to each *S* in counterbalanced order.

The Subincision film was selected because of considerable evidence in the literature that it has an emotional impact on male subjects and that this impact may be detected physiologically (Lazarus, Speisman, Mordkoff, & Davison, 1962). The film shows a series of operations performed on the penis as part of an initiation rite conducted by aboriginal tribesmen. The Birth film was prepared at the Downstate Medical Center of the State University of New York. It is a teaching film showing delivery of a baby with the use of a vacuum extractor. The London film shows a number of historic landmarks in London and some traditional English pageantry while the West film describes the geography and social and economic characteristics of several western states. Each film runs for approximately 11 min, with the exception of the Birth film which is about 6 min long.

When the *S* arrived in the morning, electrodes were attached for recording of the horizontal vectors of eye movements and for monopolar frontal and occipital EEG. Mercury-filled capillary strain gauges were attached for recording abdominal and thoracic respiratory movements, as described in detail elsewhere (Shapiro & Cohen, 1965). The *S* was then given a mood adjective checklist adapted from Nowlis and Nowlis (1956) to assess baseline affect. Twenty-one adjectives were shown in a series of slides projected in the *S*'s bedroom, and the *S* responded to each by calling out "much," "little," "don't know," or "not-at-all," depending upon how the adjective described his feelings when making the judgment. The film for the session was then shown with the *S* comfortably propped up in bed. Immediately after the film, the mood checklist was given again and the *S* was then allowed to go to sleep.

An attempt was made to awaken the *S*s from each REM period between 5 and 10 min after its onset. A loud buzzer was used as the awakening stimulus which the *S* could turn off by answering the telephone. He then gave his report to *E* over the telephone. *E* was aware of the film condition throughout the run. In order to minimize any possible bias that might be introduced by *E*, the *S* was trained to describe in as much detail as possible what was going through his mind before the bell rang without *E* saying anything. After the *S*'s report he again completed the mood checklist, describing his feelings during the dream, and then returned to sleep. All conversation between *E* and *S* was tape recorded.

#### *Respiratory Records*

Respiratory data from the thoracic and abdominal gauges were recorded continuously on paper during film viewing and during sleep. In addition, film-viewing and REM-sleep periods were recorded on instrument tape for computer measurement of breath characteristics. The data on tape were converted to digital form at a sampling rate of approximately 17/sec. During the conversion process artifacts in the record were identified by eye and eliminated. This was accomplished by inserting, on a separate digital channel, marks defining windows within which one and only one inspiration peak occurred. The computer program was designed to locate the peak within the window and to measure the time between successive peaks in the record (breath times).

The tapes were indexed by inserting file numbers at 30-sec intervals. For the film-watching period, the program computed two statistics describing breathing during each of these 30-sec intervals. The first of these was the mean breath time. The second was the root mean of the squared differences between successive breath times (breath time sigma). The latter was used as the measure of breathing irregularity.

---

[1]The choice of extremes on the field-dependence-independence dimension was made to test a number of hypotheses concerning relationships of cognitive style to dream recall and mode of transformation of film elements in dream content. These issues are described in detail in separate reports. No significant difference was found between field-dependent and field-independent *S*s in any of the analyses reported in this paper with the exception that dream recall was significantly reduced by stress among dependent but not independent *S*s (Goodenough, Witkin, Lewis, Koulack, & Cohen, 1974).

The tape and the file number generator were started before the onset of each film to allow time for checking the adequacy of recording. No attempt was made to synchronize the onset of the film with the start of a file number. As a consequence, the first complete file number within each film could begin anywhere from 0 to 30 sec after the film onset. Variations from record to record due to this factor were assumed to be inconsequential.

All artifact-free file numbers within the films from the third through the eighteenth for the London and Subincision films and from the third through the eleventh for the West and Birth films were analyzed. Estimates obtained by linear interpolation were substituted for file-number statistics that were missing due to artifacts. The film record for each *S* was characterized by the mean of the (16 or 9) file-number statistics.

Respiratory data during REM sleep were analyzed for the 6 complete and artifact-free file numbers closest to the moment of awakening. Separate statistics for each file number were not computed.

#### *Eye-Movement Activity*

Eye movements were counted for the 6 file numbers (3 min) of each REM period analyzed for respiration.

#### *Mood Checklist*

The *S*'s response to each adjective in the mood checklist was scored from 0 (not at all) to 3 (much). These scores were summed for three adjectives in each of seven mood clusters to form cluster scores with a possible range from 0 to 9 for each cluster. The clusters were: hostility, anxiety, surgency, social affection, depression, distrust, quiet.

#### *Content Analyses of Dream Texts*

The dream reports obtained at REM-period awakenings were scored by a blind judge for anxiety, hostility-out, hostility-in, and ambiguous hostility, according to procedures developed by Gottschalk, Winget, and Gleser (1969). The highest score among the three hostility measures was used as an overall hostility measure for each dream report.

#### *Stress vs Neutral Comparisons*

With regard to two formal characteristics, the Subincision film was matched with the London film (black and white, with no sound), and the Birth film was matched with the West film (color and sound). In examining the effects of the stress films during viewing, comparisons were therefore made within each of these stress-neutral pairs. When data from one member of the pair were missing for an *S*, his data from the other member were discarded.

During film viewing the effects of the Subincision film on respiration were also examined by comparing reactions to relatively stressful and relatively nonstressful segments of the film. The recurrent subincision operations were considered particularly stressful segments (Lazarus et al., 1962). To examine the effects of the operations on respiration, the respiratory data were averaged over the first four operations shown in the film. These four events were chosen because they are separated in time by at least a minute, during which preoperation baseline data could be obtained. The 30-sec interval immediately preceding each operation was identified and called the pre-onset (0) interval. The next two intervals were called the operation onset (+30 min and +60 min) intervals, and the next interval was called the post-onset (+90 min) interval. Means were then computed over the four operations for each interval type. Respiration during operation onsets was then compared with pre- plus post-onset intervals.

For REM-period and dream characteristics, the data for both stress sessions were pooled and compared with the pooled data for the neutral sessions.

#### *Statistical Analyses*

Tests of significance include Wilcoxon's matched pairs signed-ranks test for correlated samples and Mann-Whitney's *U*-test for independent samples. One-tailed tests of significance were used throughout since the direction of results is clearly predictable on *a priori* grounds.

## Results

### *Immediate Effects of the Stress Films on Mood and Arousal*

As expected, viewing the presleep stress films had a clear-cut effect on mood as measured by change in pre- to postfilm adjective-checklist responses. In contrast with the London travelog, the Subincision film produced a significant increase in hostility ($p < .05$), anxiety ($p < .01$), depression ($p < .01$), and distrust ($p < .01$). Correspondingly, significant reductions were found in feelings of quietness ($p < .01$) and social affection ($p < .05$). These results are generally consistent with previous findings (e.g., Lazarus et al., 1962).

The Birth film also had significant, but less extensive effects on mood. In contrast with the Western travelog the Birth film produced increased anxiety ($p < .01$) and decreased feelings of quietness ($p < .05$). None of the other mood clusters showed significant pre- to postfilm change.

The impact of the films was also examined by measuring the time taken to fall asleep after completing the postfilm checklist. For this purpose the first sleep spindle observed in the EEG record was used to define sleep onset. After viewing the stress films the *S*s took significantly longer to fall asleep than after viewing the neutral films (10.4 vs 8.1 min; $p < .01$). This finding suggests in still another way that the stress films aroused the *S*s. Whereas no *S* fell asleep while watching the stress films, several did while the neutral films were being shown (5 *S*s during the London film and 5 *S*s during the West film) and had to be awakened for the postfilm checklist.[2]

[2]Cases where *S* fell asleep while watching a neutral film created problems in the analyses of the respiratory variables. When the *S* was clearly awake for at least the first 6 min of the film, the respiratory data were discarded for the section of the record after sleep onset. For this purpose the disappearance of eye-blink artifacts on the EEG and EOG leads was used to determine the point beyond which the data were to be discarded. For *S*s who fell asleep at an earlier point in the film, the respiratory data for that film were discarded entirely.

In summary, it is evident that the stress films had the expected effect of upsetting the *S*s.

### *Respiration During Film Viewing*

The effects of the stress films on mean breath times and breath time variability are summarized in Table 1. As can be seen in that table, neither stress film had a measurable effect on breath times.[3] Respiratory irregularity, on the other hand, was increased during the Subincision film, although not during the Birth film. The thoracic recordings showed significantly greater irregularity for the Subincision film than for the London travelog. The abdominal recording showed a similar, but insignificant difference. The Birth film did not produce an increase in respiratory irregularity in either the thoracic or abdominal channels.

The subincision operations clearly resulted in increased respiratory irregularity. As summarized in Table 2, mean breath time sigmas increased significantly ($p < .05$) during the intervals labeled +30 min and +60 min, which represent the first minute of the four operations analyzed. By the interval labeled +90 min (post-onset) breath-time sigmas had returned to approximately preoperation base levels.

### *Effect of the Stress Films on Sleep Parameters and on Dream Recall*

No significant stress effect was found on the duration of sleep, on the number of REM periods per night, on the number of dreams reported over all *S*s, or on the distribution of dream reports over the course of the night. Three hundred and sixty-six useful REM-period awakenings were conducted from which 264 dream reports were obtained (a 72% recall rate).

### *Effect of the Stress Films on Affective Content in Reported Dreams*

The evidence on affective content in the reported dreams is summarized in Table 3.

TABLE 1
*Mean times for respiratory variables during stress and neutral film viewing*

| Respiratory Variables | Mean Times (sec) | | | | | |
|---|---|---|---|---|---|---|
| | London Film | Subincision Film | N of *S*s | West Film | Birth Film | N of *S*s |
| Breath Time | 3.18 | 3.17 | 20 | 2.91 | 2.97 | 18 |
| Thoracic Breath Time $\sigma$ | 0.43* | 0.55* | 14 | 0.35 | 0.34 | 10 |
| Abdominal Breath Time $\sigma$ | 0.35 | 0.42 | 10 | 0.27 | 0.27 | 9 |

*Significant difference ($p < .05$).

TABLE 2
*The effects on respiration of operation onsets during the subincision film*

| Respiratory Variables | Means for 30 Sec Intervals | | | | N of *S*s |
|---|---|---|---|---|---|
| | Preonset 0 | Operation +30 min | Onsets +60 min | Postonset +90 min | |
| Breath Time | 3.14 | 3.30 | 3.21 | 3.18 | 25 |
| Thoracic Breath Time $\sigma$ | 0.38 | 0.72* | 0.45 | 0.42 | 21 |
| Abdominal Breath Time $\sigma$ | 0.39 | 0.69* | 0.49 | 0.40 | 16 |

*Significant increase ($p < .05$).

TABLE 3
*Stress effects on dream mood*

| Mood Variables | Mean Scores | |
|---|---|---|
| | Neutral Film Night | Stress Film Night |
| Adjective Checklist | | |
| Hostility | 0.9 | 0.8 |
| Anxiety | 0.9 | 1.4 |
| Surgency | 1.6 | 1.8 |
| Social Affection | 2.4* | 1.8* |
| Depression | 0.9 | 1.1 |
| Distrust | 1.4 | 1.8 |
| Quiet | 3.4 | 3.2 |
| Gottschalk | | |
| Anxiety | 1.10* | 1.51* |
| Hostility | 1.33 | 1.49 |

*Significant difference ($p < .05$).

These data suggest, as expected, that the stress films increased dream anxiety. As measured by both mood-checklist responses and Gottschalk-Winget-Gleser assessments of dream content, anxiety was greater in stress than in neutral sessions. The increase in the Gottschalk-Winget-Gleser measure was significant ($p < .05$). In addition, feelings of social affection were significantly lower on stress nights ($p < .05$).

As might be anticipated, the effect of the stress films on dream anxiety was more pronounced among those *S*s (N = 19) who

[3]In detailed analyses of the components of breath time, not reported here, the stress films were found to produce a significant increase in expiration times and a significant reduction in pause times. A detailed account of these respiratory correlates of mood during film viewing will be given in a later report.

During film viewing, variability in peak-to-peak breath times was significantly greater for thoracic than for abdominal recordings. This finding was entirely unexpected and the reasons for it are unclear. It may be that this result is merely a chance occurrence. Whatever the reason, it seemed prudent to examine irregularities separately for thoracic and abdominal recordings.

showed a pre- to poststress film increase in anxiety in their mood-checklist responses—in other words, *S*s who reacted with reports of anxiety during the stress-film experience itself. For these *S*s, the dream mood-checklist score was 0.9 in neutral sessions and 1.7 in stress sessions ($p < .05$); and the Gottschalk-Winget-Gleser anxiety score was 1.04 in neutral and 1.49 in stress sessions ($p < .05$). At least under the conditions of this experiment it seems clear that a stressful event during the day can produce anxiety dreams.

### *The Effects of the Stress Films on REM-Period Eye-Movement Activity and Respiration*

No significant difference was found between stress and neutral sessions in REM-period eye-movement activity, in breath times, or in breathing irregularity when all *S*s and all REM periods were included in the analysis.[4] The mean number of eye movements observed during the 3 min preceding each awakening was 15.2 for the stress sessions and 14.2 for the neutral sessions; the mean breath times were 3.58 sec for stress and 3.59 sec for neutral sessions; and the mean breath time $\sigma$'s were 0.73 sec for stress and 0.69 sec for neutral sessions.

Comparisons between stress and neutral nights were also conducted for subgroups of *S*s who showed and who did not show responses to stress in the waking state. These comparisons produced significant results for breathing irregularity. All *S*s who showed increased irregularity during the first minute of the operation in the Subincision film were designated waking responders (N=16). All other *S*s were designated nonresponders (N = 12). The mean irregularity scores for REM periods following stress and neutral films are shown separately for these two groups of *S*s in Table 4. The interaction between stress and subject type reached significance ($p < .05$). The responders did show significantly more respiratory irregularity for REM periods in stress sessions than for REM periods in neutral sessions ($p < .01$). No such trend was evident among nonresponders. It seems evident from these results that REM-period respiratory irregularity can be increased by presleep stress in some *S*s.

[4]No significant differences were found between REM periods which did and did not lead to a dream report (Goodenough et al., 1974). Periods of both types were included in the analyses of stress effects on REM sleep reported in this section.

TABLE 4

*Mean REM-period respiratory irregularity for waking responders and nonresponders*

| Subject Types | Means: Neutral Night | Means: Stress Night |
|---|---|---|
| Waking Responders | 0.69** | 0.81** |
| Nonresponders | 0.68 | 0.63 |

**Difference between neutral and stress significant ($p<.01$).

The data were also analyzed by classifying the *S*s into responder and nonresponder groups on the basis of the other available measures of waking emotional response to the films. None of these analyses produced significant responder-by-stress interaction effects on REM-period respiratory irregularity. It is also interesting to note that the responder and nonresponder groups did not differ in the effects of the stress films on either REM-period eye-movement activity or breath times.

No evidence was found for congruence between waking and sleeping states in rate response to stress.

### *The Relationship Between REM-Period Eye-Movement Activity and Respiration*

Consistent with the results of Aserinsky (1965) and Spreng, Johnson, and Lubin (1968), it is entirely clear in the data from the present study that respiration rate increases and amplitude decreases during eye-movement bursts. In order to examine this relationship further, all recorded REM periods were sorted into high and low activity groups, depending upon whether the number of eye movements was above or below the median number for the *S*. As might be expected, the mean breath time was significantly less for high-active REM periods (3.52 sec) than for low-active REM periods (3.64 sec) ($p < .01$). The mean breath-time sigmas were not significantly different for high-activity (0.72 sec) and low-activity (0.71 sec) REM periods, however.

### *The Relationship Between REM-Period Characteristics and Affect in Reported Dreams*

In order to explore the hypothesized relationships between dream affect, on the one hand, and eye-movement activity, breath time, and breathing irregularity, on the other hand, REM periods which led to dream reports with high and low affect were compared without regard to the sleep sessions from which they were obtained. These comparisons are shown in Table 5.

TABLE 5

*REM-period characteristics accompanying dreams of high and low affect*

| Mood Variables | | Mean REM Characteristics | | |
|---|---|---|---|---|
| | | Number of Eye Movements per Min | Breath Time (sec) | Breath Time σ (sec) |
| Adjective Checklist | | | | |
| Hostility | present | 16.2* | 3.54* | 0.63 |
| | absent | 10.2* | 3.71* | 0.73 |
| Anxiety | present | 12.3 | 3.60 | 0.69 |
| | absent | 9.1 | 3.66 | 0.84 |
| Depression | present | 10.9 | 3.54* | 0.66 |
| | absent | 10.5 | 3.64* | 0.72 |
| Gottschalk | | | | |
| Anxiety | high | 12.8* | 3.59** | 0.79 |
| | low | 8.9* | 3.71** | 0.76 |
| Hostility | high | 12.8 | 3.60* | 0.73 |
| | low | 11.3 | 3.70* | 0.76 |

*Significant difference ($p < .05$).
**Significant difference ($p < .01$).

For all comparisons eye-movement activity tended to be greater during REM periods which led to high-affect dream reports, as expected. This tendency reached significance for mood-checklist hostility and for Gottschalk-Winget-Gleser anxiety. Breath times also tended to be shorter for high-affect dreams, the relationship achieving significance for most of the negative affect scores. These data generally confirm the findings from previous research.

When all *S*s were included in the analyses, breathing irregularity showed no significant relationship with any of the mood-checklist cluster scores nor with either of the Gottschalk-Winget-Gleser affect scores. Analyses were also conducted for the groups of *S*s who did and did not show breathing irregularity in response to the operations during Subincision film viewing. In general, the relationship between REM-period breathing irregularity and dream affect tended to be higher for the waking responders than for the nonresponders. This tendency reached significance only for the Gottschalk-Winget-Gleser hostility measure, however. For this measure a responder-nonresponder, high-low affect interaction was found ($p<.05$). Among the waking responders dream reports with high hostility scores tended to come from REM periods with greater irregularity than dream reports with low hostility scores ($p<.05$). Among nonresponders there was an insignificant tendency in the opposite direction. Here again, there is some evidence to support the hypothesis that respiratory irregularity is an accompaniment of emotion in both the waking and sleeping states.

## Discussion

The effects of stress upon respiration during the waking state, found in the present study, are entirely consistent with the results of earlier studies. Many previous studies failed to find a significant change in respiration rate during the viewing of stress films (e.g., Koegler & Kline, 1965; Oken, 1967; Zuckerman, 1971), and many have shown that breathing becomes irregular during stress, particularly in response to a shocking or startling event (e.g., Finesinger, 1944; Malmo & Shagass, 1949; Ruckmick, 1936; Woodworth, 1938). The data from the present study tend to confirm these views.

Our data also indicate that the correlates of respiratory rate and respiratory irregularity are dramatically different during REM sleep. We were able to replicate the previous finding that breath times are shorter during REM bursts and, as might be expected from this, mean rates are higher for REM periods with considerable eye-movement activity than for REM periods with little activity. The picture is entirely different for respiratory irregularity. Spreng et al. (1968) have reported that autonomic variability did not differ consistently for 30-sec epochs with high and low incidence of REM bursts. It is therefore not surprising to find no difference in respiratory irregularity between high- and low-activity REM periods, as was indeed the case in our data. These findings suggest that eye-movement activity and breath times may reflect one dimension of difference among REM periods, and breathing irregularity may reflect another, orthogonal dimension. Our data on the association between respiration and emotion suggest that both dimensions are related to emotion, but apparently in different ways.

Considering first the irregularity variable, the relationships with emotion appear to be congruent in the waking and dreaming states. A significant stress effect on REM-period irregularity was found *only* among *S*s who showed increased irregularity in response to stress in the waking state. Similarly, the relationship between irregularity and dream affect

was significant *only* for waking responders. These results seem consistent with the view that, in the case of respiratory irregularity, a common mechanism may mediate the relationships with emotion in the waking and sleeping states.

Considering the dimension tapped by the eye-movement and respiratory-rate variables, we were able to confirm previous findings that emotional dream reports tend to come from REM periods with relatively frequent eye movements and relatively rapid respiration rates. Neither of these variables was significantly affected by the stress films, however. For eye-movement frequency, previous studies of stress effects have not produced consistent results (Baekeland, Koulack, & Lasky, 1968; Foulkes & Rechtschaffen, 1964; Karacan, 1965). Considering that stress was not found to have an effect on respiration rate in the waking state, it is not surprising that it had no effect during REM sleep either. On the other hand, significant stress effects were found on several measures of reported dream affect; and since REM-period eye-movement activity and respiratory rate are clearly related to dream affect, one might expect a similar stress effect on these variables as well. Whatever the reason for the lack of stress effects on eye movements and respiratory rate, the relationship between these variables and affect in reported dreams seems beyond dispute. It is noteworthy that congruent relationships were not observed in the waking state. No division of *S*s into waking responder and nonresponder groups could be found that had any moderating influence on the relationships with dream affect or on REM-period stress effects. In contrast to the picture for respiratory irregularity, our data on respiration rate appear at least consistent with the tonic-phasic model. In this view the phasic period of REM sleep (characterized by REM bursts, more rapid breathing, etc.) may be the time during which hallucinatory, imagery-laden, affectively intense dreaming occurs. Intervals with only the tonic characteristics of REM sleep (e.g., stage 1-EEG, inhibition of tonus in certain muscle groups) may be accompanied by mentation of a more conceptual, prosaic, affectively bland sort, of the kind typical of NREM sleep.

## REFERENCES


Aserinsky, E. Periodic respiratory patterns occurring in conjunction with eye movements during sleep. *Science*, 1965, *150*, 763–766.

Baekeland, F., Koulack, D., & Lasky, R. Effects of a stressful presleep experience on electroencephalograph-recorded sleep. *Psychophysiology*, 1968, *4*, 436–443.

Breger, L., Hunter, I., & Lane, R. W. The effect of stress on dreams. *Psychological Issues*, 1971, *7*(3), 1–213.

Cohen, D. B. Presleep experience and home dream reporting: An exploratory study. *Journal of Consulting & Clinical Psychology*, 1972, *38*, 122–128.

Finesinger, J. E. The effect of pleasant and unpleasant ideas on the respiratory pattern (spirogram) in psychoneurotic patients. *American Journal of Psychiatry*, 1944, *100*, 659–667.

Fisher, C., Byrne, J., Edwards, A., & Kahn, E. A psychophysiological study of nightmares. *Journal of American Psychoanalytical Association*, 1970, *18*, 747–782.

Foulkes, D., Pivik, T., Steadman, H. S., Spear, P. S., & Symonds, J. D. Dreams of the male child: An EEG study. *Journal of Abnormal Psychology*, 1967, *72*, 457–467.

Foulkes, D., & Rechtschaffen, A. Presleep determinants of dream content: Effects of two films. *Perceptual & Motor Skills*, 1964, Monograph Suppl. 5-V19, 983–1005.

Goodenough, D. R., Witkin, H. A., Lewis, H. B., Koulack, D., & Cohen, H. Repression, interference and field independence as factors in dream forgetting. *Journal of Abnormal Psychology*, 1974, *83*, 32–44.

Gottschalk, L. A., Winget, C. N., & Gleser, G. C. *Manual of instructions for using the Gottschalk-Gleser content analysis scales: Anxiety, hostility, and social alienation—personal disorganization.* Berkeley and Los Angeles: University of California Press, 1969.

Grosser, G. S., & Siegal, A. W. Emergence of a tonic-phasic model for sleep and dreaming: Behavioral and physiological observations. *Psychological Bulletin*, 1971, *75*, 60–72.

Hauri, P., & Van de Castle, R. Dream content and physiological arousal. *Psychophysiology*, 1970, *7*, 330–331. (Abstract)

Hobson, J. A., Goldfrank, F., & Snyder, F. Respiration and mental activity in sleep. *Journal of Psychiatric Research*, 1965, *3*, 79–90.

Karacan, I. The effect of exciting presleep events on dream reporting and penile erections during sleep. Unpublished DMSc dissertation, State University of New York, Downstate Medical Center, 1965.

Karacan, I., Goodenough, D. R., Shapiro, A., & Starker, S. Erection cycle during sleep in relation to dream anxiety. *Archives of General Psychiatry*, 1966, *15*, 183–189.

Koegler, R. R., & Kline, L. Y. Psychotherapy research: An approach utilizing autonomic response measurements. *American Journal of Psychotherapy*, 1965, *19*, 268–279.

Lazarus, R. S., Speisman, J. C., Mordkoff, A. M., & Davison, L. A. A laboratory study of psychological stress produced by a motion picture film. *Psychological Monographs*, 1962, *76*(34, Whole No. 553).

Malmo, R. B., & Shagass, C. Physiological studies of

reaction to stress in anxiety and early schizophrenia. *Psychosomatic Medicine*, 1949, *11*, 9–24.
Molinari, S., & Foulkes, D. Tonic and phasic events during sleep: Psychological correlates and implications. *Perceptual & Motor Skills*, Suppl. 1, 1969, *29*, 343–368.
Nowlis, V., & Nowlis, H. H. The description and analysis of mood. *Annals of the New York Academy of Sciences*, 1956, *65*, 344–355.
Oken, D. The psychophysiology and psychoendocrinology of stress and emotion. In M. H. Appley & R. Trumbull (Eds.), *Psychological stress: Issues in research*. New York: Appleton-Century-Crofts, 1967.
Ruckmick, C. A. *The psychology of feeling and emotion*. New York: McGraw-Hill, 1936.
Shapiro, A., & Cohen, H. The use of mercury capillary length gauges for the measurement of the volume of thoracic and diaphragmatic components of human respiration: A theoretical analysis and a practical method. *Transactions of the New York Academy of Sciences*, 1965, *27*, 634–649.
Spreng, L. F., Johnson, L. C., & Lubin, A. Autonomic correlates of eye movement bursts during stage REM sleep. *Psychophysiology*, 1968, *4*, 311–323.
Witkin, H. A., Dyk, R. B., Faterson, H. F., Goodenough, D. R., & Karp, S. A. *Psychological differentiation: Studies of development*. New York: Wiley, 1962.
Woodworth, R. S. *Experimental psychology*. New York: Holt, 1938.
Zuckerman, M. Physiological measures of sexual arousal in the human. *Psychological Bulletin*, 1971, *75*, 297–329.

# Hope and Discomfort as Factors Influencing Treatment Continuance

*By* Janice Perley, Carolyn Winget, and Carlos Placci

MANY AGENCIES, clinics, and hospitals have been increasingly concerned with the high percentage of people who seek help and subsequently discontinue contact during the early stages of diagnostic sessions, intake procedures, or actual treatment. Investigators who have approached the dropout problem by looking at the success of various treatment theories and methods of different schools have been almost unanimous in their findings that no one treatment modality has proven to be more successful than another.[2,12] Recently the emphasis seems to have shifted from studying methods or techniques of treatment, environmental and demographic factors, and personality characteristics to a focus on those attitudes and feelings aroused within the patient and/or doctor early in the treatment relationship which may affect continuance in treatment.[1,4,8]

The purpose of this study was to explore the relationship between feelings of hope and discomfort in the potential psychiatric patient, and how this relationship influences the patient's motivation and capacity to follow recommendations for psychiatric treatment. Hope and discomfort were viewed as polarized motivating forces within the individual. Hope was defined as verbal expressions of optimism regarding a favorable outcome in day-to-day activities as well as in more cosmic, spiritual or imaginary events. Discomfort involved painful affects and psychological distress in the form of anxiety, depression, feelings of inadequacy or inferiority, and self-dissatisfaction. To the extent that these forces exist in different amounts and proportions within the person seeking help, potential patients or clients can be viewed as having varying intensities and qualities of motivation. The present authors hypothesized that motivation to follow through with treatment recommendations would be characterized by high hope and high discomfort, existing in reasonably equal proportions to one another within the individual seeking help.

## Materials and Methods

The subjects studied were drawn from a group of 46 patients seeking psychiatric help in the emergency room of a large general hospital located near the inner core of a midwestern city. The subsample of 27 subjects utilized for this study consisted of all those patients for whom records of treatment recommendations and follow-through were available. Positive follow-through of treatment recommendation was defined as the patient's making formal application for outpatient services and having one or more interviews, or, in cases where the disposition was for inpatient care, the patient signing himself into the hospital for psychiatric treatment.

---

Janice Perley, M.S.W.: *Tufts New England Medical Center, Boston, Mass.* Carolyn Winget, M.A.: *Department of Psychiatry, University of Cincinnati, College of Medicine, Cincinnati, Ohio.* Carlos Placci, M.D.: *Western Psychiatric Institute, Pittsburgh, Pa.*

**Table 1.–Diagnosis for Follow-through and Nonfollow-through Psychiatric Patients**

| Subject Number | Group 1 (Nonfollow-through) | Subject Number | (Follow-through) Group 2 |
|---|---|---|---|
| 1 | Chronic alcoholism<br>Passive-dependent personality | 1 | Chronic alcoholism<br>Hysterical personality |
| 2 | Agitated depression | 2 | Agitated depression |
| 3 | Paranoid reaction | 3 | Paranoid reaction |
| 4 | Hysterical-masochistic character disorder | 4 | Hysterical character disorder |
| 5 | Chronic alcoholism<br>Depressive reaction | 5 | Alcoholism<br>Chronic alcoholism<br>Paranoid reaction |
| 6 | Chronic alcoholism<br>Paranoid-schizophrenic | 6 | Psychotic depressive reaction |
| 7 | Hysterical character disorder | 7 | Hysterical character disorder |
| 8 | Chronic alcoholism<br>Paranoid personality | 8 | Chronic depression<br>Chronic and acute alcoholism |
| 9 | Paranoid reaction<br>Passive-dependent personality | 9 | Paranoid reaction<br>Depressive reaction<br>Passive-dependent personality |
| 10 | Chronic alcoholism<br>Passive-dependent personality | 10 | Depressive reaction<br>Passive-dependent personality |
| 11 | Sociopath<br>Depressive reaction | 11 | Immature personality<br>Chronic alcoholism |
| | | 12 | Agitated depression |
| | | 13 | Chronic and acute depressive reaction |
| | | 14 | Depressive reaction |
| | | 15 | Passive-dependent personality |
| | | 16 | Hysterical personality disorder<br>Chronic alcoholism |

Table 1 shows the diagnoses for the 11 subjects of Group 1 (nonfollow-through) and for the 16 patients in Group 2 (follow-through). Both groups were comparable with regard to race. Group 1 contained eight white subjects and three black subjects. Group 2 consisted of 12 white subjects and four black subjects. Mean age for subjects in Group 1 was 32.1 with a median of 29. In Group 2 the mean age was 38.3, with a median of 35. The two groups were fairly homogeneous with regard to marital status; over 60% of both groups were married. With regard to disposition, 18% of Group 1 and 37% of Group 2 were referred for inpatient psychiatric treatment rather than outpatient treatment. There was a marked sex difference in the two groups: 64% of Group 1 were male, while only 25% of Group 2 were male.

The process of data collection took place several hours per week when each potential psychiatric patient who entered the receiving ward was first seen by a psychiatric resident of the research team. The entire initial evaluation was tape recorded; it included a semi-structured interview used to rate the patient on the Psychiatric Morbidity Scale (PMS), and the collection of a 5-min verbal sample (VS).

The PMS[5] scores were utilized as the index of discomfort for the present study. Briefly, the PMS is rated on the basis of a standardized interview which is designated to elicit major psychiatric symptoms and signs and the degree to which the problems disturb a patient's typical levels of functioning in various areas. The symptom categories are: (1) current psychological symptoms, such as depression, anxiety and fears; (2) current behavioral signs, such as drinking, loss of temper and crying spells; (3) current inner-personal

**Table 2.—Hope and Discomfort Scores for Follow-through and Nonfollow-through Psychiatric Patients**

| Group 1 (Nonfollow-through) N = 11 | | Group 2 (Follow-through) N = 16 | |
|---|---|---|---|
| Hope | Discomfort | Hope | Discomfort |
| −1.48 | 17 | +1.17 | 14 |
| −2.03 | 16 | +2.51 | 24 |
| +0.43 | 25 | +0.80 | 16 |
| −0.63 | 12 | +2.20 | 18 |
| +0.36 | 11 | +0.15 | 13 |
| +0.32 | 8 | −0.80 | 21 |
| +2.57 | 6 | +1.48 | 9 |
| +0.67 | 14 | +0.76 | 12 |
| −1.70 | 14 | −0.98 | 17 |
| −1.46 | 20 | +0.29 | 12 |
| +0.83 | 12 | +1.17 | 16 |
| | | +0.12 | 21 |
| | | +0.21 | 14 |
| | | +0.53 | 14 |
| | | +0.57 | 14 |
| | | −0.46 | 17 |
| $\bar{X}$ = −0.19 | $\bar{X}$ = 14 | $\bar{X}$ = 0.61 | $\bar{X}$ = 16 |
| SD = 1.40 | SD = 5.36 | SD = 0.96 | SD = 3.87 |

Hope: t = 1.76 ($p < .05$ by t test) Discomfort: t = 1.13 not significant

problems and with whom they occurred; and (4) current somatic symptoms. Each of these four symptom categories was rated according to whether it caused mild or marked impairment in vocational, domestic, or psychobiological functioning. Interscorer reliabilities for the PMS range from .66 to .93.

The verbal behavior method[6,7] involves obtaining a 5-min verbal sample in response to standardized instructions that direct the patient to tell about any interesting or dramatic personal life experiences he has had. A variety of content analysis scales have been developed that can be applied to this speech sample to measure various psychological states. The Hope scale, utilized in the present study, has been described elsewhere.[6] It consists of seven possible scoring categories, four of which are positive (+1) and refer to statements of hopefulness, optimism and favorable outcome, and three of which are given a negative weight (−1) and are applicable to statements of hopelessness, loss of support or confidence, and not being the recipient of good fortune or God's favor. Interscorer reliability has not been reported for the use of this scale but has generally been satisfactorily high for other Gottschalk and Gleser scales.[6] The Hope scores of the verbal samples taken during the initial evaluation provide the index of hope used for this study.

## Results

The Hope scores obtained from coding of the verbal samples of the follow-through and nonfollow-through groups of patients are given in Table 2. As hypothesized, the mean Hope score for the follow-through patients, Group 2, was significantly higher ($p > .05$, one-tailed) than that for Group 1, those patients who did not follow recommendations made for treatment. Table 2 also shows the Discomfort (PMS) scores for each patient in the two groups. Although the follow-through group, as hypothesized, had a higher average

Table 3.—Balance According to Standard Z Scores on Hope and Discomfort for Follow-through and Nonfollow-through Psychiatric Patients

| Group 1 (Nonfollow-through) | | | Group 2 (Follow-through) | | |
|---|---|---|---|---|---|
| Discomfort | Hope | Difference | Discomfort | Hope | Difference |
| 0.43 | −1.47 | 1.90 | −0.24 | 0.74 | 0.98 |
| 0.21 | −1.93 | 2.14 | 1.98 | 1.86 | 0.12 |
| 2.20 | 0.13 | 2.07 | 0.21 | 0.43 | 0.22 |
| −0.68 | −0.76 | 0.08 | 0.65 | 1.60 | 0.95 |
| −0.90 | 0.07 | 0.97 | −0.46 | −0.11 | 0.35 |
| −1.57 | 0.03 | 1.60 | 1.31 | −0.90 | 2.21 |
| −2.01 | 1.91 | 3.92 | −1.35 | 1.00 | 2.35 |
| −0.24 | 0.33 | 0.57 | −0.68 | 0.40 | 1.08 |
| −0.24 | −1.65 | 1.41 | 0.43 | −1.05 | 1.48 |
| 1.09 | −1.45 | 2.57 | −0.68 | 0.01 | 0.69 |
| −0.68 | 0.46 | 1.14 | 0.21 | 0.74 | 0.53 |
| | | | 1.31 | −0.13 | 1.44 |
| | | | −0.24 | −0.06 | 0.19 |
| | | | −0.24 | 0.21 | 0.45 |
| | | | −0.24 | 0.24 | 0.48 |
| | | | 0.43 | −0.62 | 1.05 |
| | Total: Balanced = 3 | | | Total: Balanced = 10 | |
| | Unbalanced = 8 | | | Unbalanced = 6 | |

Discomfort score than did the nonfollow-through group, the difference did not reach statistical significance.

The third hypothesis tested stated that patients who follow treatment recommendations are more likely to combine hope and discomfort in reasonably balanced proportions than those patients who do not follow recommendations. Both Hope scores and Discomfort scores were transformed into standardized scores as shown in Table 3.

Balance between Hope and Discomfort was defined as less than one standard deviation difference between the two scores. Group 1, consisting of patients who did not follow through, was found to have three subjects balanced as to Hope and Discomfort and eight subjects judged to have unbalanced scores. In Group 2, ten subjects had balanced scores and six subjects had unbalanced scores. Although the chi square failed to achieve statistical significance ($\chi^2 = 3.24$, 1 d.f.) there was a marked tendency for individuals who followed treatment recommendations to exhibit more balanced proportions of Hope and Discomfort than did those individuals who failed to follow the recommendations for their treatment. Indeed, for the standardized scores the average difference between Discomfort and Hope for Group 1 ($\bar{X} = 1.67$) was significantly different from the average difference for Group 2 ($\bar{X} = .91$, $t = 2.32$, $p < .025$, one-tailed test).

An investigation was also made of the interrelationship between the two variables, hope and discomfort, for both groups. For Group 1, r was equal to −.49, while the r for Group 2 was equal to + .04. Although neither of the correlation coefficients is statistically significant, it is worth noting the differ-

ences. In the nonfollow-through group the correlation is negative and indicates some tendency for the people in this group to have unbalanced Hope and Discomfort scores (low hope and high discomfort or high hope and low discomfort). The correlation for the follow-through group, however, while positive, is very near zero.

## Discussion

The major finding of this study supports the hypothesis that patients who follow treatment recommendations have higher hope, as measured by content analysis of their verbal behavior, than do those who do not follow through on recommended treatment. This is congruent with theories that goal-directed behavior such as seeking psychiatric services is possible only if an individual feels some hope that his distress or discomfort can be relieved in the process.[2,3,10] Our findings tend to confirm those of others[11,14,15] who also found that high hope in the patient was associated with continuance and low hope with discontinuance in treatment. Our findings are not in agreement, however, with those of Van Dyke, who reports that discomfort was a better indicator of follow-through than was hope. Our data did not yield significant differences in Discomfort scores for the two groups, although the follow-through group had a higher mean.

The fact that the present data did not yield a significant positive relationship between discomfort and follow-through may be accounted for in several ways. Since researchers and clinicians alike agree that discomfort is a necessary prerequisite for an individual to subject himself to the painful process of seeking help for personal problems,[2,9,13] an examination of the methodology of this particular research effort may lend some insight into the discrepancy. It is possible that the PMS is not a reliable or true measure of degree of discomfort. It seems more reasonable, however, to look at the character of the present sample. All of the patients were individuals who had come to the emergency room at a large general hospital which administers largely to the indigent and lower classes. It is likely that people who make contact with a helping person in this context represent a different population than those who seek professional help via other channels. One could speculate that coming to an emergency room and being seen by a psychiatric resident represents a last resort for many people who may at that moment be in a state of near panic, in which case Discomfort scores reported here might all have been abnormally high and therefore not able to differentiate among patients. Perhaps measuring the patient's discomfort after he had been seen by the psychiatric resident would have given a clearer picture of the true degree of discomfort experienced in relation to his particular problems.

One must consider the fact that the sample appeared to have a disproportionately large number of subjects who were diagnosed as having a psychotic reaction and/or alcoholism, while in earlier work with the PMS[5] neurotic reactions accounted for 87% of the total sample. It may be, then, that the Discomfort scores in our sample reflect a valid appraisal of the extensity and intensity of the patient's psychological symptoms and impairment but do not reflect the neurotic anxieties, self-dissatisfaction, and willingness to explore

personal problems which make for a good prognosis in those with neurotic reactions.

The second important finding of this study relates to the hypothesis which stated that those patients who follow treatment recommendations are more likely to combine hope and discomfort in reasonably balanced proportions than those patients who discontinue treatment. The finding that the average difference between Hope and Discomfort scores for the dropout group was significantly higher than the average difference on these two factors in the follow-through group offers some support for French's theory that hope and discomfort act as polarized affects which serve complementary roles in the integration of goal-directed behavior (seeking psychiatric treatment). He sees discomfort being experienced as "push" or pressure to seek help and hope being experienced as "pull."[3] There is indeed a strong tendency for hope and discomfort to be more balanced in those patients who are able to sustain motivation enough to follow treatment recommendations. The negative correlation between hope and discomfort in the nonfollow-through group seemed to support further the idea that when hope and discomfort are unbalanced the individual cannot sustain goal-directed behavior but may lapse into a state of nonactive, wish-fulfilling fantasy, or despair.

## Conclusions

Certainly the findings of this study point to the possibility that hope and discomfort are factors which influence treatment continuance. One contribuation of this study is the methodology for the relatively objective measurement of Hope and Discomfort. A more widespread use of measurements such as these could serve to help conceptualize and operationalize better ways of understanding and influencing a patient early in treatment. Positive findings could affect priorities for agency intake procedures which have in the past been more directed toward investigating eligibility than toward assessing and influencing treatment capacity and motivation.

## Acknowledgment

The authors thank Mrs. Bonnie Green, Research Associate, Department of Psychiatry, University of Cincinnati, for her critical reading of this paper.

## References

1. Clemes, S. R., and D'Andrea, V. J.: Patients' anxiety as a function of expectation and degree of initial interview ambiguity. J. Consult. Clin. Psychol. 29:397, 1965.

2. Frank, J.: Persuasion and Healing. New York, Schocken, 1963, p. 71.

3. French, T. M.: The Integration of Behavior. Chicago, University of Chicago Press, 1952, p. 52.

4. Goldstein, A. P.: Therapist and client expectations of personality change in psychotherapy. J. Consult. Clin. Psychol. 7:180, 1960.

5. Gottschalk, L. A., Mayerson, P., and Gottlieb, A.: Prediction and evaluation of outcome in an emergency brief psychotherapy clinic. J. Nerv. Ment. Dis. 144:77, 1967.

6. –, and Gleser, G. C.: The Measurement of Psychological States Through the Content Analysis of Verbal Behavior. Berkeley, University of California Press, 1969, p. 247.

7. –, Winget, C. N., and Gleser, G. C.: A Manual for Using the Gottschalk-Gleser Content Analysis Scales. Berkeley, University

of California Press, 1969.

8. Heine, R. W., and Trosman, H.: Initial expectations for the doctor-patient interaction as a factor in continuance. Psychiatry 23:275, 1960.

9. Lorr, M., Katz, M. J., and Rubinstein, E. A.: The prediction of length of stay in psychotherapy. J. Consult. Clin. Psychol. 22: 321, 1958.

10. Perlman, H: Social Casework. Chicago, University of Chicago Press, 1957, p. 187.

11. Ripple, L.: Factors associated with continuance in casework service. Social Work 2:89, 1957.

12. Strupp, H. S.: Patient-doctor relationships: Psychotherapists in the therapeutic process. *In* Bachrach, A. J. (Ed.): Experimental Foundations of Clinical Psychology. New York, Basic, 1962, p. 576.

13. Taulbee, E. S.: Relationship between certain personality variables and continuation in psychotherapy. J. Consult. Clin. Psychol. 22:83, 1958.

14. Van Dyke, N.: Discomfort and hope: Their relationship to outcome of referral. Smith College Studies in Social Work. 32: 58, 1961.

15. Werble, B.: Motivation, capacity and opportunity in services for adolescent clients: Major findings. Social Work. 4:22, 1959.

# FREE ASSOCIATION ANXIETY AND HOSTILITY: VIEW FROM A JUNIOR HIGH SCHOOL[1]

SAM SILBERGELD[2], RONALD W. MANDERSCHEID, PATRICIA H. O'NEILL

*Mental Health Study Center*

*National Institute of Mental Health, Adelphi, Maryland*

*Summary*.—This study reports component and summary levels of free association anxiety and hostility in junior high school adolescents. Counselor ($n$ = 24) and Noncounselor ($n$ = 19) groups derive from four, brief interpersonal coping classes held at a recently integrated school. These groups consist, respectively, of those referred and those not referred by school guidance personnel. Both groups exhibit higher mean anxiety and hostility levels than do previously studied, normative adult samples. Adolescent development provides one explanation for these differences. Comparison of the two adolescent groups shows that members of the Counselor Groups come from somewhat lower status backgrounds, experience more academic difficulties, and exhibit higher mean anxiety and hostility levels. Three-way analyses of variance discriminate differences due to group, gender, and ethnicity. The concept of role incumbency is useful for explaining the variations observed.

Different age groups portray many faces of anxiety and hostility. In adolescence, the individual confronts independence and loss of security. These pressures engender anxiety and hostility, and require coping. Defiance of authority, truancy, and delinquency reflect failures of coping with self and psychosocial environment (Coelho, Hamburg, & Adams, 1974). Such pressures and failures make the hostile, anxious adolescent a frequent referral to the psychotherapist (Doyal & Friedman, 1974).

Important factors in the development of anxiety, hostility, and inadequate coping include the family and school experiences of the adolescent (Adams & Sarason, 1963; Coelho, *et al.*, 1974). However, pertinent research is generally oriented either toward the family or the school, and often depends exclusively on self-ratings. The validity of such data may be doubtful because of the unwillingness or inability of subjects to report feelings (Chambers, Hopkins, & Hopkins, 1972). To encompass adolescents' family and school experiences, psycholinguistic or verbal content analysis of free association seems appropriate. Such a method is provided by the Free-association Test (Gottschalk & Gleser, 1969), which can reflect preconscious and unconscious thought content. Thus, this test affords a useful means for comparative study of adolescents' anxiety and hostility.

[1]Authors are grateful to: Dorothy P. Simmons for assistance in data analysis and editing; Terri H. Johns for technical assistance; and Charles P. Pautler, Division of Computer Systems, for computer programming.

[2]Requests for reprints should be sent to Sam Silbergeld, Mental Health Study Center, National Institute of Mental Health, 2340 University Boulevard East, Adelphi, Maryland 20783.

The relation of anxiety and hostility to school behavior and cognitive performance (Doyal & Friedman, 1974) attests to the practical importance of investigations in this area. The purpose of the present report is to describe students' test anxiety and hostility at a recently integrated, previously Black, junior high school. This investigation also examines whether several generalizations concerning sources of anxiety and hostility apply to this particular school. Finally, this study provides an empirical clue to tested levels during adolescence as compared to adulthood by contrasting students' results with adult norms. All current data derive from a larger project on the effectiveness of brief interpersonal coping classes and innovative mental health service intervention in the school system.

## METHOD

### *Subjects*

Forty-three junior high school students received innovative mental health service in the form of interpersonal coping classes. Two techniques served to select candidates. Descriptive notices on school bulletin boards alerted students about the classes. Volunteer students were contacted and interviewed. When parents and investigators approved, these students were admitted to the after-school classes designated as CI ($n = 7$) and CII ($n = 12$), or Noncounselor Groups. Shortly after these classes began, two additional classes were formed and designated as CIII ($n = 11$) and CIV ($n = 13$), or Counselor Groups, which met during school hours. These latter groups consisted of students referred by school guidance personnel for a variety of reasons, e.g., absenteeism, behavioral problems, etc.

All students attended a relatively small, urban, junior high school. The school was situated in a stable, lower-income, Black community within a 10-mile radius of a large eastern city. Previously, it had been the only all-Black junior high school in the county. During the two years prior to the present study, the county had to desegregate and implement a plan for racial integration. The initial phase of this plan called for the immediate integration of the all-Black junior high school and an adjacent senior high school. Subsequently, white students came to these schools from nearby predominantly white communities. Collection of the data reported here occurred approximately 3 to 4 mo. after the beginning of the first school year under the county school integration plan.

### *Procedures*

Members of CI-CIV participated in elective interpersonal coping courses, a small class form of mental health service delivery. These brief (15-session) courses were designed to enhance self-esteem and abilities to perceive, interpret, and express communication and feelings. Prior to and following each session, group members completed 5-min. Free-association Test tape recordings that

were later transcribed. An objective scoring protocol (Gottschalk, Winget, & Gleser, 1969) provided guidelines by which each typescript was evaluated for specific types of anxiety (Death, Mutilation, Separation, Guilt, Shame, Diffuse) and hostility (Outward Overt, Outward Covert, Inward, Ambivalent). Scores for the six types of anxiety were combined into a summary measure, Total Anxiety. Summary measures for Total Hostility Outward and Total Inward and Ambivalent Hostility were obtained in a similar manner. For all original and summary variables, scores were corrected for the total number of words in the typescript, and square root transformations calculated.

Since the present investigation focused on anxiety and hostility due to school and family experiences, only presession data were pertinent. For each class member, these scores were averaged across the 15 sessions to control idiosyncratic fluctuations. The resultant by-person means constituted the basic data for statistical analysis.

Simple $t$ tests were employed to contrast the two groups and to compare present results with adult norms. Gottschalk and Gleser (1969) have provided mean scores for samples of adult Psychiatric Outpatients ($n = 50$) and Employed Personnel ($n = 94$). The Psychiatric Outpatient sample included persons with diagnoses of psychological and sociological trait disturbances as well as neuroses. The sample of Employed Personnel consisted of white female and male workers between the ages of 20 and 50 yr.

Three-way analyses of variance were calculated for each anxiety and hostility parameter, with group, gender, and ethnicity as the independent variables. Evaluation of gender and ethnicity was deemed necessary since several studies indicate anxiety and hostility scores vary within these parameters (Gottschalk & Gleser, 1969; Pollack & Valdez, 1973; Semler, *et al.*, 1967).

For the student groups, demographic, family, and grade data were compared by $z$ test for difference of proportions or simple $t$ test. Level of parental education and occupation (Sewell, Haller, & Portes, 1969) and adolescent's career aspiration (Camp, 1968) served as indicators of social status. The effects of social status upon achievement have been well documented (Singell, 1972). Similarly, social status has been found to covary with anxiety and hostility (Semler, *et al.*, 1967). Family and grade data were included as indicators of potential problems at home and in school.

## RESULTS

Table 1 shows that several standard demographic parameters, i.e., gender, ethnicity, and age, do not vary significantly between the Counselor and Noncounselor Groups. Alternately, level of father's and mother's education, and adolescent's career aspiration do show significant differences. In each case, mean levels are higher for members of the Noncounselor Groups. These find-

ings (Table 1) suggest that adolescents in the Noncounselor Groups come from somewhat higher social class backgrounds.

Mean grades indicate uniformly higher levels of achievement by members of the Noncounselor Groups. Specifically, Table 1 shows that these adolescents have mean grades which fluctuate around B. By contrast, for members of the Counselor Groups, mean grades in academic subjects, i.e., English, Social Studies, Science, and Mathematics, are slightly below C, while grades in other subject areas are near C+. These results suggest that members of the Counselor Groups experience more difficulties in the academic setting.

Adolescents in the Counselor Groups are also more likely to experience difficulties at home. Table 1 shows that more than one-half of these students have parents who are not currently married. Consequently, the proportion residing with both parents is small.

TABLE 1

DEMOGRAPHIC, FAMILY, AND GRADE DATA FOR COUNSELOR AND NONCOUNSELOR GROUPS*

| Variable | Counselor | Noncounselor | *p* |
|---|---|---|---|
| Proportion | | | |
| Female | 0.71 | 0.53 | |
| Black | 0.46 | 0.37 | |
| Parents Married | 0.46 | 0.84 | <0.05 |
| Living with Both Parents | 0.46 | 0.84 | <0.05 |
| Mean ± *SEM* | | | |
| Age (years) | 13.71±0.20 | 13.68±0.19 | |
| Grade Level (years) | 7.96±0.19 | 8.47±0.14 | <0.05 |
| Father's Education (years) | 11.50±0.44 | 14.00±0.81 | <0.01 |
| Mother's Education (years) | 11.42±0.26 | 14.11±0.57 | <0.001 |
| Father's Occupation† | 36.48±4.49 | 52.41±5.29 | <0.05 |
| Mother's Occupation† | 43.75±6.03 | 57.18±6.00 | |
| Career Aspiration† | 52.86±6.03 | 71.79±3.72 | <0.05 |
| Mean Grades‡ | | | |
| English | 1.75±0.15 | 2.79±0.18 | <0.001 |
| Social Studies | 1.69±0.13 | 2.74±0.20 | <0.001 |
| Science | 1.58±0.15 | 2.84±0.24 | <0.001 |
| Math/Algebra/Geometry | 1.96±0.23 | 2.95±0.22 | <0.01 |
| Physical Education† | 2.57±0.24 | 3.29±0.17 | <0.05 |
| Home Economics/Shop† | 2.21±0.18 | 2.71±0.18 | |
| Art† | 2.73±0.20 | 3.29±0.18 | |
| Music† | 2.30±0.37 | 3.36±0.20 | <0.05 |

*For the Counselor Groups, $n = 24$, Noncounselor Groups, $n = 19$.
†Occupation is defined in terms of Duncan's Socioeconomic Index (Reiss, *et al.*, 1961) which ranges from 0 through 96. Larger scores indicate greater prestige. For Counselor and Noncounselor Groups, respectively, *n*s are: Father's Occupation, 23 and 17; Mother's Occupation, 12 and 11; Career Aspiration, 22 and 19; Physical Education, 23 and 17; Home Economics/Shop, 19 and 7; Art, 11 and 7; Music, 10 and 11.
‡A = 4, B = 3, C = 2, D = 1, F = 0. This coding scheme permits interpretation in terms of standard Grade Point Average.

Table 2 shows mean Free-association Test scores for Counselor ($n = 24$) and Noncounselor ($n = 19$) Groups, as well as for Psychiatric Outpatients ($n = 50$) and Employed Personnel ($n = 94$). Counselor Groups are significantly higher than Noncounselor Groups on two of 13 Free-association Test variables, i.e., Guilt Anxiety and Hostility Inward. When the two normative samples are compared with each other, six significant differences emerge. Psychiatric Outpatients have significantly higher means on Guilt, Diffuse, and Total Anxiety, Overt and Total Hostility Outward, and Hostility Inward. Employed Personnel are not significantly higher in a single instance.

Counselor Groups score significantly higher than either Psychiatric Outpatients or Employed Personnel on nine variables, i.e., Death, Mutilation, Separation, and Guilt Anxiety, and all of the hostility categories. In addition, Counselor Groups exhibit significantly higher scores than Employed Personnel on Diffuse and Total Anxiety. Shame Anxiety scores reflect no differences among the samples. Gottschalk and Gleser (1969) do not present comparable data for the summary measure, Total Inward and Ambivalent Hostility.

Table 2 shows that levels for Noncounselor Groups are significantly higher than those of Psychiatric Outpatients on eight variables, i.e., Death, Mutilation, Separation, and Guilt Anxiety, Overt, Covert, and Total Hostility Outward, and Ambivalent Hostility. In addition to these eight variables, Noncounselor Groups

TABLE 2

COMPARISON BY FREE-ASSOCIATION TEST OF COUNSELOR AND NONCOUNSELOR GROUPS, PSYCHIATRIC OUTPATIENTS, AND EMPLOYED PERSONNEL

| Variable | Counselor ($n = 24$) $M \pm SEM$ | Noncounselor ($n = 19$) $M \pm SEM$ | Psychiatric Outpatients ($n = 50$) $M \pm SEM$ | Employed Personnel ($n = 94$) $M \pm SEM$ | $p$* |
|---|---|---|---|---|---|
| Death Anxiety | 0.69±0.08 | 0.62±0.10 | 0.26±0.06 | 0.23±0.05 | b,c,d,e |
| Mutilation Anxiety | 0.98±0.08 | 0.91±0.11 | 0.20±0.05 | 0.27±0.06 | b,c,d,e |
| Separation Anxiety | 0.71±0.05 | 0.80±0.08 | 0.38±0.08 | 0.27±0.05 | b,c,d,e |
| Guilt Anxiety | 1.26±0.15 | 0.88±0.10 | 0.42±0.09 | 0.15±0.04 | a,b,c,d,e,f |
| Shame Anxiety | 0.75±0.05 | 0.84±0.07 | 0.65±0.08 | 0.66±0.08 | |
| Diffuse Anxiety | 0.63±0.06 | 0.58±0.08 | 0.57±0.09 | 0.19±0.04 | c,e,f |
| Total Anxiety | 1.95±0.15 | 1.91±0.14 | 1.64±0.10 | 1.35±0.08 | c,e,f |
| Hostility Outward, Overt | 1.44±0.17 | 1.39±0.12 | 0.76±0.08 | 0.47±0.02 | b,c,d,e,f |
| Hostility Outward, Covert | 1.15±0.13 | 0.95±0.08 | 0.68±0.06 | 0.55±0.04 | b,c,d,e |
| Total Hostility Outward | 1.90±0.17 | 1.67±0.11 | 1.06±0.08 | 0.89±0.04 | b,c,d,e,f |
| Inward Hostility | 1.36±0.19 | 0.88±0.09 | 0.80±0.06 | 0.61±0.03 | a,b,c,e f |
| Ambivalent Hostility | 1.13±0.10 | 1.07±0.10 | 0.72±0.07 | 0.69±0.05 | b,c,d,e |
| Total Inward and Ambivalent Hostility | 1.75±0.18 | 1.34±0.12 | | | |

*a,b,c,d e,f $p < 0.05$ for comparison of Counselor and Noncounselor Groups, Counselor Groups and Psychiatric Outpatients, Counselor Groups and Employed Personnel, Noncounselor Groups and Psychiatric Outpatients, Noncounselor Groups and Employed Personnel, and Psychiatric Outpatients and Employed Personnel, respectively.

score significantly higher than Employed Personnel on Diffuse and Total Anxiety, and Hostility Inward.

Table 3 displays main and interaction effects for each of the three-way analyses of variance. With gender and ethnicity controlled, differences emerge between Counselor and Noncounselor Groups on four variables, i.e., Guilt and Total Anxiety, Ambivalent Hostility, and Total Inward and Ambivalent Hostility. In each case, Counselor Groups exhibit higher mean levels.

In Table 3, three Free-association Test variables show main effects on the basis of gender or ethnicity. Females exhibit significantly higher levels of Separation Anxiety than males when group and ethnicity are controlled (see Table 3, Footnote †). Also, whites show significantly higher levels of Shame and Total Anxiety than Blacks when group and gender are controlled.

The group × gender interaction effect on Ambivalent Hostility leaves uncertain the main effect of group on this variable. Inspection of means (see Table 3, Footnote ‡) shows that males from Counselor Groups exhibit the

TABLE 3

MAIN AND INTERACTION EFFECTS OF GROUP, GENDER, AND ETHNICITY ON FREE-ASSOCIATION TEST PARAMETERS FOR ADOLESCENT GROUPS

| Variable | Effects | | | | | |
|---|---|---|---|---|---|---|
| | a | b | c | d | e | f |
| Death Anxiety | | | | | | <0.10 |
| Mutilation Anxiety | | | | | <0.10 | |
| Separation Anxiety | | <0.05 | | | | |
| Guilt Anxiety | <0.05 | | | | | |
| Shame Anxiety | | | <0.05 | | | |
| Diffuse Anxiety | | | | | | |
| Total Anxiety | <0.10 | | <0.10 | | | |
| Hostility Outward, Overt | | | | | | |
| Hostility Outward, Covert | | | | | <0.01 | |
| Total Hostility Outward | | | | | | |
| Hostility Inward | | | | | | |
| Ambivalent Hostility | <0.10 | | | <0.01 | | |
| Total Inward and Ambivalent Hostility | <0.05 | | | | | |

*Note.*—Effects: (a) Group †, (b) Gender †, (c) Ethnicity †, (d) Group by Gender ‡, (e) Group by Ethnicity ‡, and (f) Gender by Ethnicity ‡.

†For each significant difference by Group, Counselor Groups > Noncounselor Groups; by Gender, females > males; and by Ethnicity, whites > Blacks.

‡For each significant interaction effect, means are: Group × Gender (Ambivalent Hostility), 1.36 (male-Counselor), 1.18 (female-Noncounselor), 1.00 (female-Counselor), 0.80 (male-Noncounselor); Group × Ethnicity (Mutilation Anxiety), 1.18 (white-Counselor), 1.03 (Black-Noncounselor), 0.88 (white-Noncounselor), 0.87 (Black-Counselor); Group × Ethnicity (Hostility Outward, Covert), 1.50 (white-Counselor), 1.04 (Black-Noncounselor), 0.87 (Black-Counselor), 0.85 (white-Noncounselor); Gender × Ethnicity (Death Anxiety), 0.68 (white-males), 0.64 (Black-females), 0.57 (Black-males), 0.50 (white-females).

highest levels on this variable, followed by females from Noncounselor Groups, females from Counselor Groups, and males from Noncounselor Groups, respectively.

Group × ethnicity interaction effects occur on Mutilation Anxiety and Hostility Outward, Covert. White members of Counselor Groups have the highest mean levels on both of these variables (see Table 3, Footnote ‡). Blacks from Noncounselor Groups rank second in each case. For Mutilation Anxiety, whites from Noncounselor Groups rank third and Blacks from Counselor Groups, fourth. These latter two positions are reversed for Hostility Outward, Covert.

A gender × ethnicity interaction effect occurs on Death Anxiety. Inspection of means (see Table 3, Footnote ‡) shows that white males rank highest. These are followed by Black females, Black males, and white females, respectively. Three-way interaction effects are not observed.

## Discussion

Across time, stereotypic views of adolescents persist. Contemporary stereotypes include a number of polarities, e.g., victimizer-victim; dangerous-endangered; sexually rampant requiring restraint-sexually inadequate needing encouragement; enviable object to be cut down-repository of adults' unfulfilled ambitions to be built up; redundant family member to be extruded-lost object to be mourned in passing (Anthony, 1969). These polarities exacerbate anxiety and hostility by imposing options necessarily involving conflict. The painful decisions required influence self-definition, the central developmental task of adolescence.

Present results show Free-association Test anxiety and hostility to be higher among the students studied than among normative samples of adults. Whether these differences can be attributed to the dynamics of adolescent development or other factors such as integration or school environment cannot be discerned within the design of the present study. However, pertinent literature serves as a useful guide. Adolescent transition requires a re-evaluation of relationships with the external world, the social world, and one's psychic world (Muuss, 1962). Disposition toward emotional and social difficulties during this period may be substantially greater than during other developmental periods. Environmental (Kiritz & Moos, 1974), societal (Etzioni, 1968), personality (Dembo, 1973), motivational (Lazarus, 1966), and experiential (Erikson, 1959) factors may correlate significantly with levels of stress experienced. Thus, a theoretical perspective focusing on adolescent development seems imperative for understanding the anxiety and hostility of students.

Although the two school groups studied differ significantly in social status and its correlates, e.g., problems at home and school, gender and ethnic composi-

tion do not differentiate the two. These results imply that members of the Counselor Groups may experience more difficulties because of the dynamics of lower class status, rather than because of gender or ethnic membership. Although the samples are small, such findings also suggest that particular gender or ethnic groups are not more likely to exhibit behavioral problems in a newly integrated school.

The analyses of variance permit a more differentiated view of anxiety and hostility in the two student samples. The higher levels of Guilt and Total Anxiety, and Total Inward and Ambivalent Hostility exhibited by members of the Counselor Groups, even when gender and ethnic differences are controlled, suggest that these variables are indicators of school performance. In other words, these students do not successfully meet the expectations of the school either academically, as reflected by course grades, or behaviorally, as reflected by referral to school counselors. This interpretation is congruent with reports implying that Guilt and Ambivalent Hostility are correlates of weak coping ability (Coelho, *et al.*, 1974) and sense of failure (Stierlin, 1974). For Separation Anxiety, gender variations replicate earlier findings (Gottschalk & Gleser, 1969). Ethnic differences in Shame and Total Anxiety could represent effects of integration, since Gottschalk and Gleser (1969) do not note these in normative studies.

Although the gender × ethnicity interaction effect on Death Anxiety is significant at trend level, means are relatively low and differences small (see Table 3, Footnote ‡). By contrast, analysis of means for the group × ethnicity interaction effect on Mutilation Anxiety shows that means are substantially higher and differences larger. In rank order, white members of the Counselor Groups are highest, Black members of the Noncounselor Groups intermediate, and the remaining two categories lowest and essentially equivalent. Social status and the concept of role incumbency (Sarbin & Allen, 1968) may provide an explanation for these differences. Hawkes and Koff (1970) imply that Mutilation Anxiety is higher among lower status students. This effect may be magnified for white members of the Counselor Groups, since they are new to the school setting and are attempting to establish themselves in nonacademically oriented roles. Blacks from the Noncounselor Groups are competing with whites for academically oriented roles in a school environment that at times may be physically threatening. The two remaining groups are likely to feel less threatened since they are role incumbents. A similar rationale can be employed to explain the group × ethnicity interaction on Hostility Outward, Covert.

The group × gender interaction effect on Ambivalent Hostility differentiates males more than females. Males from the Counselor Groups and males from the Noncounselor Groups exhibit, respectively, the highest and lowest levels on this variable. By distinction, females from both groups show inter-

mediate levels and are relatively equivalent. As noted earlier, Ambivalent Hostility correlates with sense of failure (Stierlin, 1974). In contrast to their female counterparts, males from the Counselor Groups may experience this sense of failure more acutely because of the stereotypic attachment of males to the breadwinner role. On the other hand, males from the Noncounselor Groups are meeting role expectations more successfully and are less likely to feel a sense of failure. Since occupational expectations for women are more ambiguous, female students are likely to exhibit somewhat elevated levels of Ambivalent Hostility.

In a junior high school such as the one studied here, educators are working with adolescents possessing high levels of anxiety and hostility. Future analyses of the sources and behavioral correlates of these high levels are required. Like selected other measures of anxiety, e.g., School Anxiety Scale (Phillips, 1969) and Test Anxiety Scale (Spielberger, 1972), the Free-association Test indicates a negative correlation between school grade achievement and anxiety (see Tables 1 and 2). Unlike other measures, the Free-association Test can encompass the family and school experiences of the adolescent and can differentiate among specific forms of anxiety and hostility. For these reasons, this test may be particularly useful in subsequent research on sources and behavioral correlates.

Gottschalk and Gleser (1969) describe numerous validation and reliability studies of the scales of the Free-association Test for different age groups in normative, neurotic, and psychotic populations. Over-all, these investigations show the categories of anxiety and hostility to be useful indicators of underlying psychological states that correlate with a range of cognitive, perceptual, and physiobiochemical criterion measures. Thus, the Free-association Test possesses requisite generalizability and applicability for research on adolescent populations.

In the future, theoretical work should be directed toward the development of an explanatory model that includes the sources, interrelationships among, and behavioral effects of different forms of anxiety and hostility. Recent advances in the analysis of information processing systems via formulations from general systems theory can contribute to this effort. For example, Geyer (1974) has recently presented a comprehensive model for five types of alienation. The present investigators will endeavor in the future to develop a comparable paradigm for anxiety and hostility.

## REFERENCES


ADAMS, E., & SARASON, I. G. Relation between anxiety in children and their parents. *Child Development*, 1963, 34, 237-246.

ANTHONY, J. The reactions of adults to adolescents and their behavior. In G. Caplan & S. Lebovici (Eds.), *Adolescence: psychosocial perspectives.* New York: Basic Books, 1969. Pp. 54-78.

CAMP, W. L. Student aspirations and social status. *Psychology in the Schools*, 1968, 5, 151-154.

CHAMBERS, A. C., HOPKINS, K. D., & HOPKINS, B. R. Anxiety, physiologically and psychologically measured: its effects on mental test performance. *Psychology in the Schools*, 1972, 9, 198-206.

COELHO, G. V., HAMBURG, D. A., & ADAMS, J. E. (Eds.) *Coping and adaptation.* New York: Basic Books, 1974.

DEMBO, R. Critical factors in understanding adolescent aggression. *Social Psychiatry*, 1973, 8, 212-219.

DOYAL, G. T., & FRIEDMAN, R. J. Anxiety in children: some observations for the school psychologist. *Psychology in the Schools*, 1974, 11, 161-164.

ERIKSON, E. H. Identity and the life cycle: selected papers. *Psychological Issues*, 1959, 1, No. 1.

ETZIONI, A. *The active society: a theory of societal and political processes.* New York: Free Press, 1968.

GEYER, F. Alienation and general systems theory. *Sociologia Neerlandica*, 1974, 10, 18-41.

GOTTSCHALK, L. A., & GLESER, G. C. *The measurement of psychological states through the content analysis of verbal behavior.* Berkeley: Univer. of California Press, 1969.

GOTTSCHALK, L. A., WINGET, C. N., & GLESER, G. C. *Manual of instructions for using the Gottschalk-Gleser content analysis scales: anxiety, hostility, and social alienation—personal disorganization.* Berkeley: Univer. of California Press, 1969.

HAWKES, T., & KOFF, R. H. Differences in anxiety of private school and inner city public elementary school children. *Psychology in the Schools*, 1970, 7, 250-259.

KIRITZ, S., & MOOS, R. H. Physiological effects of social environments. *Psychosomatic Medicine*, 1974, 36, 96-114.

LAZARUS, R. S. *Psychological stress and the coping process.* New York: McGraw-Hill, 1966.

MUUSS, R. E. *Theories of adolescence.* New York: Random House, 1962.

PHILLIPS, B. N. An analysis of causes of anxiety among children in school. Final Report, Project No. 2616, U.S.O.E., Cooperative Research Branch, Univer. of Texas, Austin, 1966.

POLLACK, D., & VALDEZ, H. Developmental aspects of sexuality and aggression. *Journal of Genetic Psychology*, 1973, 123, 179-184.

REISS, A. J., JR., with the collaboration of Duncan, O. D., Hatt, P. K., & North C. C. *Occupations and social status.* New York: Free Press of Glencoe, 1961.

SARBIN, T. R., & ALLEN, V. L. Role theory. In G. Lindzey & E. Aronson (Eds.), *The handbook of social psychology.* Vol. 1. (2nd ed.) Reading, Mass.: Addison-Wesley, 1968. Pp. 488-567.

SEMLER, I. J., ERON. L. D., MEYERSON, L. J., & WILLIAMS, J. F. Relationship of aggression in third grade children to certain pupil characteristics. *Psychology in the Schools*, 1967, 4, 85-88.

SEWELL, W. H., HALLER, A. O., & PORTES, A. The educational and early occupational attainment process. *American Sociological Review*, 1969, 34, 82-92.

SINGELL, L. D. Investment in education and ghetto poverty: a note on the dropout decision. *Social Science Quarterly*, 1972, 53, 122.

SPIELBERGER, C. D. (Ed.) *Anxiety: current trends in theory and research.* Vol. II. New York: Academic Press, 1972.

STIERLIN, H. Shame and guilt in family relations. *Archives of General Psychiatry*, 1974, 30, 381-389.

# Part IX

# Psychopolitics

There is only one paper in this section and it is Chapter 56 entitl "Paranoia and the politics of inflammatory rhetoric" (Tolz, 1977). It nicely demonstrates application of these content analysis scales to the analysis of the speeches of political figures.

56

# Paranoia and the Politics of Inflammatory Rhetoric

Robert D. Tolz

Nobody who is aware of current events today can doubt that America's political arena suffers from a severe left-right bipolarization. Mr. Nixon's inaugural pledge to bring the nation together seems to have been lost among the escalating rhetoric between two political camps. Instead of moving towards conciliation, the strongest leaders on both the far right and far left have become famous for a new method of speech known as "inflammatory rhetoric." Calling campus radicals "bums" or referring to police officers as "pigs" creates a great deal of mutual hostility.

Closely associated with hostility is the psychopathological state of paranoia. The paranoid individual is suspicious, overly sensitive, and has delusions of persecution. His perception of others being hostile towards himself is associated with the defense mechanism of projection, in which he is really the one who has the most hostility towards others.

The working hypothesis of this paper is that those who are responsible for inflammatory rhetoric on both the left and right

should show evidence of paranoid behavior and high hostility, while a political figure who does not use inflammatory rhetoric will not manifest any such evidence.

## METHOD

### Procedure

Since it would be extremely difficult to obtain the full cooperation of any political figure in a battery of psychological tests and personal interviews that would be needed to concretely establish any manifestations of paranoid behavior, it is necessary, then, to devise some kind of test that requires the least amount of cooperation from the subject. Fortunately, two such tests do exist and are readily usable for the purposes of this paper. Both involve the content analysis of verbal behavior, exactly what is needed to examine inflammatory rhetoric. We can obtain the speeches of a political figure and then apply these coding procedures.

Walter Weintraub and H. Aronson have devised a system of coding verbal samples in terms of the frequency that a person uses certain adjustive mechanisms in his speech behavior. Weintraub and Aronson have found several such verbal devices that persons with a paranoid "delusional" background use significantly more often than a "normal" control group (see table 1). The most significant category is "explaining," which reflects the paranoid individual's tendency towards rationalization as well as his eagerness to explain his behavior. The paranoid person also is prone to the possession of a "tyrannical, primitive superego" (Weintraub and Aronson, 1965). Following from this great concern with what is good and bad, right and wrong, is a significant tendency to use what Weintraub and Aronson term "evaluators." Paranoids also have a high "negators" score, associated with their oft-used defense mechanisms of negation and denial. Weintraub and Aronson also distinguish a fourth category

which is not applicable to the coding of political speeches, and that is the subject's high probability of making comments about the experimental situation--"direct references" (the normal method of obtaining speech samples is having the subject speak uninterrupted into a tape recorder for ten minutes in a controlled experimental situation). If a politician has paranoid tendencies, then an investigation of his verbal behavior would have to turn up relatively high scores in all three affects--explaining, evaluation, and negation.

There exists another content analysis scale, created by Louis Gottschalk and Goldine Gleser, that measures the amount of hostility present in a verbal sample. What is most important about the Gottschalk-Gleser analysis of verbal hostility is that the concept is broken down into three divisions. The "Hostility Directed Outward Scale" (see table 7) measures "destructive, injurious, critical thoughts and actions directed to others." It is further divided into overt and covert hostility outward. Statements of hostility that emanate from the speaker and are directed towards other people, animals, or situations are coded on the overt portion of the scale, while the speaker's perception of hostility not directly involving himself is coded on the covert portion of the scale. The "Ambivalent Hostility Scale" measures the amount of hostility that the speaker perceives to be directed against himself (see table 8). The "Hostility Directed Inward Scale" determines the amount of self-destructive, self-critical thoughts and actions that the speaker expresses.

Gottschalk and Gleser do not have any statistics to show the degree of correlation between their hostility scales and paranoia. The most they say is that "there is some evidence that the overt scale correlates with the paranoid scale of the MMPI" (Gottschalk and Gleser _Manual_, 1969, p. 63). It seems to me that the Ambivalent

Hostility Scale might also have a bearing on the degree of delusions of persecution that a person has. The Hostility Directed Inward Scale has little to do with this study and will not be used.

Subjects

The only minor difficulty in choosing subjects for the study of speeches involving inflammatory rhetoric was the selection of a suitable control. On the right of the political spectrum the obvious choice is Vice President Spiro Agnew. To counterbalance Agnew on the far left is William Kunstler, well-known attorney for the Chicago Seven trial as well as for many other left activities. Both men have a background of training in law; both have a heavy speaking engagement schedule; both are considered to be eloquent spokesmen for their points of view; both have been accused of resorting to the use of inflammatory rhetoric.

There is no perfect choice for a control. Ideally the proper control personage should have the same qualities mentioned above that Agnew and Kunstler have, but should not be someone who has been accused of using inflammatory rhetoric. In addition the control should have a political ideology pretty much in the middle of the spectrum. The person I have chosen as a control is the Democratic Senator from Maine, Edmund Muskie. He fits the same mold as Agnew and Kunstler--law training, frequent speaker, leader and spokesman. As far as I know, very few people would consider Muskie to frequently resort to the tactic of inflammatory rhetoric. He unfortunately is not right in the center of the political spectrum, but is fairly liberal--of course anyone would be hard put to find an important political figure who was purely middle-of-the-road. I do not believe that Muskie's not being equidistant between Agnew and Kunstler is a critical factor. A secondary reason for choosing Muskie is that at the time of this writing he is the leading figure among those who have been mentioned as possibilities for nomination as the Demo-

cratic presidential candidate in 1972. It is of interest to find out whether a man who may possibly be our next president manifests any evidence of paranoid tendencies or extraordinarily high hostility.

Speeches

Since there is the possibility that the reliability of the scores of the verbal behavior of the three subjects might be unsatisfactory over different occasions and different situations, instead of taking just one sample for each, it was decided that scoring three speeches for each man would give a more reliable portrait.

Speeches for Agnew and Muskie were obtained by request from their offices in the Senate Building. Representative speeches for Kunstler were obtained by contacting Mr. Kunstler's publisher in New York, William Morrow & Co.

It was decided that general subject matter in all speeches chosen should be kept constant; i.e., speeches were chosen only if they contained obviously inflammatory rhetoric or mention of hostility. Agnew's speeches included one in Fort Lauderdale, Florida, where he expressed his displeasure over campus situations at Yale and other universities; an address in Houston, Texas, about the escalation of rhetoric, wherein he admonishes the mass media to cool their rhetoric before he cools his; and a stumping speech in South Dakota in which he calls for the deposing of "radical-liberal" leader George McGovern, defends the President from criticism, labels the Scranton Commission Report as "pablum for the permissivists," and declares that no self-appointed elite shall run the United States. Kunstler's speeches include one at the Greek Theater about an indictment against a group of leftists who had disrupted the courthouse in Seattle in protest against the trial of the Chicago Seven; a speech about the first amendment and political repression associated with the Chicago Seven trial; and a speech broadcast over KPFA radio in Los Angeles in which he makes a plea to "pull the tyrants down."

The purpose of selecting a control in this experiment is to offer a contrast of someone who does not use inflammatory rhetoric; consequently, Muskie's speeches were chosen not on the basis of how hostile or paranoid they seemed to be, but on the basis of the topic of the speech being similar to a topic that Agnew or Kunstler might speak about. Speeches chosen to represent Muskie were an address before the Senate expressing his displeasure with the inclusion of "no-knock" entry and "preventive detention" in the District of Columbia crime bill which he considered to be unconstitutional and a danger of political repression; his televised address on election eve in which he calls for a return to the "politics of trust" instead of the "politics of fear"; and a stumping speech in New Jersey in which he contends that Vice President Agnew's dictionary lacks two words--"plain talk."

Scoring

Both the Weintraub-Aronson scale and the Gottschalk-Gleser scales have clear scoring manuals to facilitate accurate scoring. These were obtained and used liberally.

For the Weintraub-Aronson scale each affect is counted every time it appears and then is expressed in terms of frequency per hundred words. Direct quotations over three sentences in length are neither coded nor added to the total word count. In the Gottschalk-Gleser scales all quotations are coded and included in the word count. The magnitude of an affect in the hostility scales is found by totaling the weights in all categories multiplied by the number of times they appear to provide a total score; then this total is multiplied by a correction factor (100 divided by the number of words in the sample); to this raw score is added one half of the correction factor to obtain a corrected score; then the square root of this figure is used as the final corrected score. A shorthand mathematical formula will summarize:

$$T = \sqrt{\frac{100}{N} \times (f_1w_1 + f_2w_2 \ldots . f_nw_n + 0.5)}$$

where T is the final corrected score, N is the number of words in the sample, f is the number of times a specific category has been coded, and w is the weight of that particular category. In most cases only one category may be coded per clause.

All speeches were re-typed using triple-spacing to ease the coding procedure. Clauses, the unit to be coded in the Gottschalk-Gleser scales, were demarcated, and two copies were made. All speeches were first coded for the Weintraub-Aronson scale, then all were coded for the Gottschalk-Gleser scales. After the initial scoring, the speeches were double and triple checked to insure against errors.

Results

The results of the coding procedures are summarized in tables 3, 4, 5 and 6. Although there are some interesting results with regard to the amount of hostility present in the verbal behavior of the three subjects, my hypothesis that Agnew and Kunstler would show a higher degree of paranoia than Muskie would, was not supported by the evidence gleaned by using the Weintraub-Aronson scale.

Comparing our results for our subjects to results determined by Weintraub and Aronson for delusional patients and normal controls, we see that Vice President Agnew scores below the control group on both explaining and negation, and about half way between the control group and the delusional group. Muskie scores below the controls on explaining and above on both evaluation and negation. Kunstler scores below the controls on both explaining and evaluation, but scores above them on negation. Most importantly, none of the three subjects scores above average on explaining, the affect that most

significantly correlates with delusional paranoid behavior.

By comparing the composite hostility scores of Agnew, Muskie, and Kunstler to percentile scores for nonpsychiatric subjects (table 2) we come up with the percentiles summarized in table 5. Agnew's speeches contain an extraordinarily high amount of hostility outward. His scores on both portions of the scale exceed the 95th percentile. Muskie unexpectedly shows a fairly high degree of hostility outward with a total hostility outward score in the 87th percentile. Kunstler has a medium score on the overt portion of the hostility outward scale, but his exceedingly high score on the covert portion pushes his total score above the 95th percentile along with Agnew's. On the ambivalent hostility scale both Agnew and Kunstler rank in the 72nd percentile, a medium-high score, while Muskie manifests an amazingly low score that places him in only the 7th percentile.

Discussion

As was mentioned earlier, if any of our subjects had any real manifestation of delusional paranoid behavior, they could be expected to show above average scores on all three affects used in the Weintraub-Aronson analysis. Agnew scores above average only on the evaluation category, Muskie on evaluation and negation, and Kunstler on negation only. None of them scored high on explaining, the category that correlates very highly ($p < 0.001$) with delusional paranoid behavior. We must therefore conclude that it is not possible to say, on the basis of the evidence available here, that politicians who use inflammatory rhetoric have clinically paranoid tendencies.

We must somehow account for the finding that both Agnew and Kunstler perceive a large amount of hostility directed from others towards themselves. Also, how is it possible to explain the differences and/or similarities among the three subjects with regard to their own hostility directed outward? I believe that one should not be blinded by attempting to explain these questions solely in terms

of psychological variables. The best way to approach the problem is to talk not in abstracts, but in concrete terms.

Kunstler and Agnew perceive others as being hostile towards themselves not because they are using the defense mechanism of projection, but because others are hostile to them. Muskie's low score reflects the fact that, in reality, he has few enemies. If we restricted ourselves to talking about a clinical explanation of inflammatory rhetoric, then we would not be saying much about the covert portion of the hostility scale, because it ostensibly has little to do with our discussion of clinical paranoia. But it is important to understand the substantial part that the perception of others being hostile to others plays, because from an in-depth reading of Agnew's and Kunstler's speeches, we can see that those people who are the recipients of the hostility are friends (or, in Agnew's case, the President or the system), and those people who project that hostility are enemies. The bulk of Muskie's hostility is related to criticism of situations and "things," not people. As for the differences between Agnew and Kunstler on the overt portion of the hostility directed outward scale, again we must look within the speeches where we find answers that cannot be quantified. Agnew shows more overt hostility than Kunstler not because he is more neurotic or anything like that, but because both men speak to accomplish a common purpose, but use different tactics. Both are attempting to mobilize their "constituencies" to fight "the enemy." Kunstler uses the subtle technique of exposing the system's injustices and paradoxes, expecting to arouse emotions of hostility in others without he himself clearly expressing hostility. Vice President Agnew, on the other hand, takes a much more blunt approach. In addition to trying to expose injustices and paradoxes in the "radical-liberal" movement, he resorts to the tactic of name-calling, perhaps intended to be thought of as his being the conductor of a choir of the silent majority, all singing along in unison. Again the objective seems to

be the mobilization of opinion against the enemy.

This phenomenon can become a circular process. One political leader perceives others to be hostile to him and/or the cause he espouses. There now exists an enemy whose power one must work to diminish. The important thing in the context of our political framework is that "the enemy" is not a paranoid delusion, but truly does exist. "The enemy" then perceives a real threat towards himself and the position he espouses, a threat which must be fought through the mobilization of hostility in others. The amount of hostility can be boosted at each step of the reverberation process, a potentially dangerous situation.

Before concluding I would like to make some remarks about the nature of this report itself. Content analysis of a politician's speeches is at best only a superficial manner of trying to understand a personality. Also, as demonstrated by the impossibility of coding for "direct references" in the Weintraub-Aronson scale, we are working in an area for which these scales were not originally devised. We cannot accurately judge the validity of the scales when used in the context we have used them for in this report. This is an experimental situation which we can do very little to control. There is a difficulty in trying to understand exactly what variables are at work. For instance, it is almost impossible to assess how many speech writers contributed to either Spiro Agnew's or Edmund Muskie's speeches--and what effect they have had thereon. There may be other variables of which we are totally ignorant.

For these reasons we must think in terms not of our results saying something about the personalities of the subjects, but of them saying something about their speeches. It is what is said by the subjects that is really being examined. We need not consider critical such variables as speechwriters if we concern ourselves mainly with the effect of the speeches and not with what the speech says about the speaker.

Summary

The hypothesis was advanced that those politicians on both the left and right of the political spectrum who resorted to "inflammatory rhetoric" would show higher paranoid tendencies than someone in the center who did not use "inflammatory rhetoric." Two content analysis scales--one correlated significantly with delusional paranoid behavior, the other providing scores of relative hostility--were used to code speeches by Spiro Agnew, representing the right, William Kunstler representing the left, and Edmund Muskie acting as the control. The two extremes were found to manifest paranoid "attitudes"--as expressed in their own high outward hostility and their perception of others being hostile towards themselves--not to be confused with a verdict of true clinical, delusional paranoia; for the subjects' scores on the content analysis scale for paranoia itself argued against such a verdict. Paranoid attitudes are to be explained in terms of real things instead of somebody's delusional imagination.

There are questions that this report could not answer, but which could be made the topic of further inquiry. Does the circular reverberation process continue to intensify hostility until a breaking point is reached? or does it reach a saturation point? Is the presence of paranoid attitudes unique to those who use inflammatory rhetoric and vice versa? In talking about the mobilization of political forces, is intensification of hostile emotions a successful tactic? More importantly, is it really necessary considering the possible dangers involved?

Table 1

Verbal Scores of "Delusional" Patients and "Normal" Controls

| Category | Delusional | | | | Control | | | | ρ |
|---|---|---|---|---|---|---|---|---|---|
| | N | Median | Mean | σ | N | Median | Mean | σ | |
| Explaining | 11 | 10.4 | 10.6 | 4.94 | 18 | 6.6 | 5.2 | 2.91 | < .001 |
| Evaluation | 16 | 15.2 | 14.8 | 7.50 | 23 | 6.2 | 7.7 | 6.05 | < .01 |
| Negation | 12 | 16.0 | 17.4 | 8.08 | 19 | 10.1 | 12.0 | 7.50 | < .05 |

(Weintraub and Aronson, 1965)

Table 2

Percentile Scores for Verbal Hostility Scores

in Nonpsychiatric Subject (N=322)

| Percentile Score | Hostility Outward | | | Ambivalent Hostility |
|---|---|---|---|---|
| | Overt | Covert | Total | |
| 95 | 1.45 | 1.52 | 1.95 | 1.45 |
| 90 | 1.21 | 1.30 | 1.67 | 1.20 |
| 80 | 0.96 | 0.97 | 1.35 | 0.86 |
| 70 | 0.83 | 0.83 | 1.17 | 0.67 |
| 60 | 0.70 | 0.68 | 1.04 | 0.58 |
| 50 | 0.62 | 0.58 | 0.91 | 0.49 |
| 40 | 0.54 | 0.49 | 0.78 | 0.40 |
| 30 | 0.46 | 0.42 | 0.63 | 0.35 |
| 20 | 0.38 | 0.35 | 0.51 | 0.30 |
| 10 | 0.30 | 0.28 | 0.40 | 0.25 |
| 5 | 0.25 | 0.24 | 0.30 | 0.22 |
| Mean | 0.69 | 0.70 | 0.96 | 0.61 |
| S.D. | 0.36 | 0.42 | 0.50 | 0.39 |

(Gottschalk and Gleser, 1969, p. 79)

Table 3

Scores of Speeches on Weintraub-Aronson Scale

| Speech | N words | Explaining | Evaluation | Negation |
|---|---|---|---|---|
| $Agnew_1$ | 3539 | 2.0 | 8.5 | 11.0 |
| $Agnew_2$ | 2548 | 1.2 | 6.3 | 7.5 |
| $Agnew_3$ | 3174 | 1.9 | 16.7 | 13.5 |
| $AGNEW_{total}$ | 9263 | 1.7 | 10.7 | 10.9 |
| $Muskie_1$ | 3686 | 3.8 | 13.0 | 15.0 |
| $Muskie_2$ | 1704 | 3.5 | 7.0 | 17.6 |
| $Muskie_3$ | 1321 | 3.0 | 5.3 | 13.6 |
| $MUSKIE_{total}$ | 6711 | 3.6 | 10.0 | 15.3 |
| $Kunstler_1$ | 3430 | 5.8 | 6.1 | 14.6 |
| $Kunstler_2$ | 7322 | 4.0 | 7.3 | 12.9 |
| $Kunstler_3$ | 2331 | 5.6 | 10.3 | 17.2 |
| $KUNSTLER_{total}$ | 13083 | 4.8 | 7.5 | 14.1 |

Table 4

Scores of Speeches on Gottschalk-Gleser Scale

| Speech | N Words | Hostility Outward | | | Ambivalent |
|---|---|---|---|---|---|
| | | Overt | Covert | Total | Hostility |
| $Agnew_1$ | 3591 | 1.50 | 1.62 | 2.20 | 0.68 |
| $Agnew_2$ | 2625 | 1.72 | 2.00 | 2.64 | 1.79 |
| $Agnew_3$ | 3174 | 1.35 | 2.04 | 2.44 | 0.34 |
| $AGNEW_{total}$ | 9390 | 1.51 | 1.87 | 2.40 | 0.71 |
| $Muskie_1$ | 3686 | 1.21 | 0.95 | 1.54 | 0.12 |
| $Muskie_2$ | 1704 | 0.78 | 1.70 | 1.87 | 0.17 |
| $Muskie_3$ | 1321 | 1.05 | 0.89 | 1.36 | 0.51 |
| $MUSKIE_{total}$ | 6711 | 1.07 | 1.17 | 1.59 | 0.23 |
| $Kunstler_1$ | 3430 | 0.75 | 2.38 | 2.49 | 0.64 |
| $Kunstler_2$ | 7322 | 0.82 | 2.07 | 2.22 | 0.70 |
| $Kunstler_3$ | 2700 | 0.95 | 1.81 | 2.04 | 1.15 |
| $KUNSTLER_{total}$ | 13452 | 0.81 | 2.07 | 2.22 | 0.70 |

Table 5

Percentile Hostility for Speaker Scores

| Speaker | Hostility Outward Overt | Covert | Total | Ambivalent Hostility |
|---|---|---|---|---|
| Agnew | 95+ | 95+ | 95+ | 72 |
| Muskie | 84 | 86 | 87 | 7 |
| Kunstler | 68 | 95+ | 95+ | 72 |

TABLE 6

TABULATION OF VERBAL SAMPLES CODED FOR HOSTILITY

1. Agnew on Yale: Correction Factor (C.F.)=0.0278

| Overt | Total Weight | Covert | Total Weight | Ambiv. | Total Weight |
|---|---|---|---|---|---|
| Ic3 x 12 | 36 | IIa3 x 10 | 30 | IIc3 x 4 | 12 |
| Ic2 x 14 | 28 | IIb3 x 2 | 6 | IIa2 x 2 | 4 |
| Ib1 x 16 | 16 | IIc3 x 1 | 3 | | |
| | | IIc2 x 1 | 2 | | |
| | | IId2 x 5 | 10 | | |
| | | IIa1 x 21 | 21 | | |
| | | IIb1 x 11 | 11 | | |
| | | IIc1 x 7 | 7 | | |
| | | IIf1 x 44 | 4 | | |

| | | |
|---|---|---|
| Total........80 | Total.........94 | Total........16 |
| Raw Score..2.22 | Raw Score...2.61 | Raw Score..0.44 |
| Corrected Score (+½C.F.)..2.24 | Corrected Score (+½C.F.)...2.63 | Corrected Score (+½C.F.)..0.46 |
| Square root .......1.50 | Square root ........1.62 | Square root .......0.68 |

Total outward(overt + covert) = 174 x C.F. +½C.F. = 4.85
Square root=2.20

2. Agnew, the escalation of rhetoric: C.F.=0.0381

| Overt | Total Weight | Covert | Total Weight | Ambiv. | Total Weight |
|---|---|---|---|---|---|
| Ib3 x 1 | 3 | IIa3 x 5 | 15 | IIc3 x 28 | 84 |
| Ic3 x 14 | 42 | IIc3 x 18 | 54 | | |
| Ic2 x 9 | 18 | IIc2 x 2 | 4 | | |
| Ib1 x 13 | 13 | IId2 x 2 | 4 | | |
| Ic1 x 1 | 1 | IIa1 x 8 | 8 | | |
| | | IIb1 x 14 | 14 | | |
| | | IIc1 x 3 | 3 | | |
| | | IId1 x 2 | 2 | | |
| | | IIf1 x 1 | 1 | | |
| Total | 77 | | 105 | | 84 |
| Corr. score | 2.95 | | 4.02 | | 3.22 |
| Sq. root | 1.72 | | 2.00 | | 1.79 |

Total outward = 182 x C.F. + ½C.F. = 6.95
Sq. root = 2.64

3. Agnew, in S. Dakota: C.F. = 0.0315

| Overt | Total Weight | Covert | Total Weight | Ambiv. | Total Weight |
|---|---|---|---|---|---|
| Ic3 x 11 | 33 | IIa3 x 2 | 6 | IIc3 x 1 | 3 |
| Ic2 x 5 | 10 | IIb3 x 5 | 15 | | |
| Ib1 x 14 | 14 | IIc3 x 16 | 48 | | |
| | | IIc2 x 2 | 4 | | |
| | | IId2 x 10 | 20 | | |
| | | IIe2 x 3 | 6 | | |
| | | IIa1 x 12 | 12 | | |
| | | IIb1 x 18 | 18 | | |
| | | IIc1 x 1 | 1 | | |

Table 6, cont.

| Overt | Total Weight | Covert | Total Weight | Ambiv. | Total Weight |
|---|---|---|---|---|---|
| | | IId1 x 1 | 1 | | |
| | | IIf1 x 1 | 1 | | |
| Total | 57 | | 132 | | 3 |
| Cor. Score | 1.81 | | 4.17 | | 0.11 |
| Sq. root | 1.35 | | 2.04 | | 0.34 |

Total outward = 189 x C.F. + ½C.F. = 5.95
Sq. root = 2.44

4. Muskie on crime bill: C.F. = 0.272

| Overt | Total Weight | Covert | Total Weight | Ambiv. | Total Weight |
|---|---|---|---|---|---|
| Ic2 x 1 | 2 | IIa3 x 1 | 3 | | |
| Ib1 x 51 | 51 | IIb3 x 2 | 6 | | |
| | | IIc3 x 4 | 12 | | |
| | | IIc2 x 1 | 2 | | |
| | | IId2 x 2 | 4 | | |
| | | IIa1 x 2 | 2 | | |
| | | IIb1 x 2 | 2 | | |
| | | IId1 x 2 | 2 | | |
| Total | 53 | | 33 | | 0 |
| Cor. Score | 1.45 | | 0.91 | | 0.01 |
| Sq. root | 1.21 | | 0.95 | | 0.12 |

Total outward = 86 x C.F. + ½C.F. = 2.36
Sq. root = 1.54

5. Muskie on election eve: C.F. = 0.0587

| Overt | Total Weight | Covert | Total Weight | Ambiv. | Total Weight |
|---|---|---|---|---|---|
| Ic3 x 1 | 3 | IIc3 x 9 | 27 | | |
| Ib1 x 6 | 6 | IIa2 x 1 | 2 | | |
| Ic1 x 1 | 1 | IId2 x 5 | 10 | | |
| | | IIe2 x 2 | 4 | | |
| | | IIa1 x 1 | 1 | | |
| | | IIb1 x 2 | 2 | | |
| | | IIc1 x 2 | 2 | | |
| | | IId1 x 1 | 1 | | |
| Total | 10 | | 49 | | 0 |
| Cor. Score | 0.62 | | 2.91 | | 0.03 |
| Sq. root | 0.78 | | 1.70 | | 0.17 |

Total outward = 59 x C.F. + ½C.F. = 3.49
Sq. root = 1.87

Table 6, cont.

6. Muskie in N.J.: C.F. = 0.0758

| Overt | Total Weight | Covert | Total Weight | Ambiv. | Total Weight |
|---|---|---|---|---|---|
| Ic3 x 11 | 3 | IIb3 x 1 | 3 | IIc3 x 1 | 3 |
| Ic2 x 15 | 10 | IIc3 x 1 | 3 | | |
| Ib1 x 1 | 1 | IIc2 x 1 | 2 | | |
| | | IIb1 x 1 | 1 | | |
| | | IIc1 x 1 | 1 | | |
| Total | 14 | | 10 | | 3 |
| Cor. Score | 1.10 | | 0.80 | | 0.27 |
| Sq. root | 1.05 | | 0.89 | | 0.51 |

Total outward = 24 x C.F. + ½C.F. = 1.85
Sq. root = 1.36

7. Kunstler at the Greek Theater: C.F. = 0.0292

| Overt | Total Weight | Covert | Total Weight | Ambiv. | Total Weight |
|---|---|---|---|---|---|
| Ic3 x 3 | 9 | IIa3 x 22 | 66 | IIa3 x 2 | 6 |
| Ic2 x 2 | 4 | IIb3 x 1 | 3 | IIc3 x 2 | 6 |
| Ib1 x 4 | 4 | IIc3 x 28 | 84 | IIb1 x 1 | 1 |
| Ic1 x 2 | 2 | IId2 x 1 | 2 | | |
| | | IIe2 x 7 | 14 | | |
| | | IIa1 x 13 | 13 | | |
| | | IIb1 x 2 | 2 | | |
| | | IIc1 x 5 | 5 | | |
| | | IId1 x 3 | 3 | | |
| | | IIf1 x 1 | 1 | | |
| Total | 19 | | 193 | | 13 |
| Cor. Score | 0.57 | | 5.65 | | 0.41 |
| Sq. root | 0.75 | | 2.38 | | 0.64 |

Total outward = 212 x C.F. + ½C.F. = 6.21
Sq. root = 2.49

8. Kunstler, the first amendment and political repression: C.F. = 0.0136

| Overt | Total Weight | Covert | Total Weight | Ambiv. | Total Weight |
|---|---|---|---|---|---|
| Ic3 x 6 | 18 | IIa3 x 17 | 51 | IIa3 x 3 | 9 |
| Ic2 x 7 | 14 | IIb3 x 1 | 3 | IIc3 x 3 | 9 |
| Ib1 x 17 | 17 | IIc3 x 67 | 201 | | |
| | | IIc2 x 2 | 4 | | |
| | | IId2 x 1 | 2 | | |
| | | IIe2 x 1 | 2 | | |
| | | IIf2 x 1 | 2 | | |
| | | IIa1 x 10 | 10 | | |
| | | IIb1 x 8 | 8 | | |
| | | IIc1 x 5 | 5 | | |
| | | IId1 x 5 | 5 | | |
| | | IIe1 x 4 | 4 | | |
| Total | 49 | | 297 | | 18 |
| Cor. Score | 0.67 | | 4.05 | | 0.25 |
| Sq. root | 0.82 | | 2.01 | | 0.50 |

Total outward = 346 X C.F. + ½C.F.= 4.71
Sq. root = 2.17

Table 6, cont.

9. Kunstler in L. A.: C.F. = 0,0370

| Overt | Total | Weight | Covert | Total | Weight | Ambiv. | Total | Weight |
|---|---|---|---|---|---|---|---|---|
| Ia3 x | 1 | 3 | IIa3 x | 13 | 39 | IIa3 x | 4 | 12 |
| Ic3 x | 1 | 3 | IIb3 x | 2 | 6 | IIc3 x | 7 | 21 |
| Ic2 x | 4 | 8 | IIc3 x | 5 | 15 | IIa2 x | 1 | 2 |
| Ia1 x | 1 | 1 | IIc2 x | 1 | 2 | | | |
| Ib1 x | 8 | 8 | IId2 x | 4 | 8 | | | |
| Ic1 x | 1 | 1 | IIa1 x | 5 | 5 | | | |
| | | | IIb1 x | 4 | 4 | | | |
| | | | IIc1 x | 5 | 5 | | | |
| | | | IIf1 x | 4 | 4 | | | |
| Total | | 24 | | | 88 | | | 35 |
| Cor. Score | | 0.91 | | | 3.27 | | | 1.31 |
| Sq. root | | 0.95 | | | 1.81 | | | 1.15 |

Total Outward = 112 x C.F. + ½C.F. = 4.16
Sq. root = 2.04

AGNEW OVERALL: C.F. = 0.0106

| Overt | Total | Covert | Total | Ambiv. | Total |
|---|---|---|---|---|---|
| Ib3 | 3 | IIa3 | 51 | IIc3 | 43 |
| Ic3 | 111 | IIb3 | 21 | IIa2 | 4 |
| Ic2 | 56 | IIc3 | 105 | | |
| Ib1 | 43 | IIc2 | 10 | | |
| Ic1 | 1 | IId2 | 34 | | |
| | | IIe2 | 6 | | |
| | | IIa1 | 41 | | |
| | | IIb1 | 42 | | |
| | | IIc1 | 11 | | |
| | | IId1 | 3 | | |
| | | IIf1 | 6 | | |
| Total | 214 | | 330 | | 47 |
| Cor. Score | 2.27 | | 3.48 | | 0.50 |
| Sq. root | 1.51 | | 1.87 | | 0.71 |

Total outward = 544 x C.F. + ½C.F. = 5.77
Sq. root = 2.40

Table 6, cont.

MUSKIE OVERALL: C.F. = 0.0149

| Overt | Total | Covert | Total | Ambiv. | Total |
|---|---|---|---|---|---|
| Ic3 | 6 | IIa3 | 3 | IIc3 | 3 |
| Ic2 | 12 | IIb3 | 9 | | |
| Ib1 | 58 | IIc3 | 42 | | |
| Ic1 | 1 | IIa2 | 2 | | |
| | | IIc2 | 4 | | |
| | | IId2 | 14 | | |
| | | IIe2 | 4 | | |
| | | IIa1 | 3 | | |
| | | IIb1 | 5 | | |
| | | IIc1 | 3 | | |
| | | IId1 | 3 | | |
| Total | 77 | | 92 | | 3 |
| Cor. Score | 1.15 | | 1.38 | | 0.05 |
| Sq. root | 1.07 | | 1.17 | | 0.23 |

Total outward = 169 x C.F. + $\frac{1}{2}$C.F. = 2.53
Sq. root = 1.59

KUNSTLER OVERALL: C.F. = 0.0074

| Overt | Total | Covert | Total | Ambiv. | Total |
|---|---|---|---|---|---|
| Ia3 | 3 | IIa3 | 156 | IIa3 | 27 |
| Ic3 | 30 | IIb3 | 12 | IIc3 | 36 |
| Ic2 | 26 | IIc3 | 300 | IIa2 | 2 |
| Ia1 | 1 | IIc2 | 6 | IIb1 | 1 |
| Ib1 | 29 | IId2 | 12 | | |
| Ic1 | 3 | IIe2 | 16 | | |
| | | IIf2 | 2 | | |
| | | IIa1 | 28 | | |
| | | IIb1 | 14 | | |
| | | IIc1 | 15 | | |
| | | IId1 | 8 | | |
| | | IIe1 | 4 | | |
| | | IIf1 | 5 | | |
| Total | 89 | | 578 | | 66 |
| Cor. Score | 0.66 | | 4.28 | | 0.49 |
| Sq. root | 0.81 | | 2.07 | | 0.70 |

Total outward = 667 x C.F. + $\frac{1}{2}$C.F. = 4.94
Sq. root = 2.22

## TABLE 7

### HOSTILITY DIRECTED OUTWARD SCALE

Destructive, Injurious, Critical Thoughts and Actions Directed to Others

| I. | Overt | II. | Covert |
|---|---|---|---|
| a3* | Self killing, fighting, injuring other individuals or threatening to do so. | a3* | Others (human) killing, fighting, injuring other individuals or threatening to do so. |
| b3 | Self robbing or abandoning other individuals, causing suffering or anguish to others, or threatening to do so. | b3 | Others (human) robbing, abandoning, causing suffering or anguish to other individuals, or threateni ng to do so. |
| c3 | Self adversely criticizing, depreciating, blaming, expressing anger, dislike of other human beings | c3 | Others adversely criticizing, depreciating, blaming, expressing anger, dislike of other human beings |
| a2 | Self killing, injuring or destroying domestic animals, pets, or threatening to do so. | a2 | Others (human) killing, injuring, or destroying domestic animals, pets or threatening to do so. |
| b2 | Self abandoning, robbing, domestic animals, pets, or threatening to do so. | b2 | Others (human) abandoning, robbing, domestic animals, pets or threatening to do so. |
| c2 | Self criticizing or depreciating others in a vague or mild manner. | c2 | Others (human) criticizing or depreciating other individuals in a vague or mild manner. |
| d2 | Self depriving or disappointing other human beings | d2 | Others (human) depriving or disappointing other human beings. |
| | | e2 | Others (human or domestic animals) dying or killed violently in death-dealing situation or threatened with such. |
| | | f2 | Bodies (human or domestic animals) mutilated, depreciated, defiled. |
| a1 | Self killing, injuring, destroying, robbing wildlife, flora, inanimate objects or threatening to do so. | a1 | Wildlife, flora, inanimate objects, injured, broken, robbed, destroyed or threatened with such (with or without mention of agent). |
| b1 | Self adversely criticizing, depreciating, blaming, expressing anger or dislike of subhumans, inanimate objects, places, situations. | b1 | Others (human) adversely criticizing, depreciating, expressing anger or dislike of subhumans, inanimate objects, places, situations. |

*The number serves to give the weight as well as to identify the category. The letter also helps identify the category.

Table 7, cont.

HOSTILITY DIRECTED OUTWARD SCALE (CONT.)

| Overt | | II. Covert |
|---|---|---|
| Self using hostile words, cursing, mention of anger or rage without referent. | c1 | Others angry, cursing without reference to cause or direction of anger; also instruments of destruction not used threateningly. |
| | d1 | Others (human, domestic animals) injured, robbed, dead, abandoned or threatened with such from any source including subhuman and inanimate objects, situations (storms, floods, etc.) |
| | e1 | Subhumans killing, fighting, injuring, robbing, destroying each other or threatening to do so. |
| (Gottschalk and Gleser, 1969) | f1 | Denial of anger, dislike, hatred, cruelty, and intent to harm. |

TABLE 8

AMBIVALENT HOSTILITY SCALE
Destructive, Injurious Critical Thoughts and Actions of Others to Self

a3* Others (human) killing or threatening to kill self.

b3 Others (human) physically injuring, mutilating, disfiguring self or threatening to do so.

c3 Others (human) adversely criticizing, blaming, expressing anger or dislike toward self or threatening to do so.

d3 Others (human) abandoning, robbing self, causing suffering, anguish, or threatening to do so.

a2 Others (human) depriving, disappointing, misunderstanding self or threatening to do so.

b2 Self threatened with death from subhuman or inanimate object, or death-dealing situation.

a1 Others (subhuman, inanimate, or situation), injuring, abandoning, robbing self, causing suffering, anguish.

b1 Denial of blame.

(Gottschalk and Gleser, 1969)

*The number serves to give the weight as well as to identify the category. The letter also helps identify the category.

## BIBLIOGRAPHY

Gottschalk, L.A., Gleser, G.C. The Measurement of Psychological States Through the Content Analysis of Verbal Behavior. University of California Press, Los Angeles (1969).

Gottschalk, L.A., Winget, C.N., Gleser, G.C. Manual of Instructions for Using the Gottschalk-Gleser Content Analysis Scales: Anxiety, Hostility, and Social Alienation-Personal Disorganization. University of California Press, Los Angeles (1969).

Weintraub, W., Aronson, H. The application of verbal behavior analysis to the study of psychological defense mechanisms: III. Speech pattern associated with delusional behavior. Journal of Nervous and Mental Disorders, 141, 172-179 (1965).